Lecture Notes in Computer Science 2138
Edited by G. Goos, J. Hartmanis, and J. van Leeuwen

Springer
*Berlin*
*Heidelberg*
*New York*
*Barcelona*
*Hong Kong*
*London*
*Milan*
*Paris*
*Tokyo*

Rūsiņš Freivalds (Ed.)

# Fundamentals of Computation Theory

13th International Symposium, FCT 2001
Riga, Latvia, August 22-24, 2001
Proceedings

Springer

Series Editors

Gerhard Goos, Karlsruhe University, Germany
Juris Hartmanis, Cornell University, NY, USA
Jan van Leeuwen, Utrecht University, The Netherlands

Volume Editor

Rūsiņš Freivalds
University of Latvia
Raiņa bulvaris 29, LV-1459 Riga, Latvia
E-mail: rusins.freivalds@mii.lu.lv

Cataloging-in-Publication Data applied for

Die Deutsche Bibliothek - CIP-Einheitsaufnahme

Fundamentals of computation theory : 13th international symposium ; proceedings / FCT 2001, Riga, Latvia, August 22 - 24, 2001. Rusins Freivalds (ed.). - Berlin ; Heidelberg ; New York ; Barcelona ; Hong Kong ; London ; Milan ; Paris ; Singapore ; Tokyo : Springer, 2001
(Lecture notes in computer science ; Vol. 2138)
ISBN 3-540-42487-3

CR Subject Classification (1998): F.1, F.2, F.4.1, I.3.5, G.2

ISSN 0302-9743
ISBN 3-540-42487-3 Springer-Verlag Berlin Heidelberg New York



Springer-Verlag Berlin Heidelberg New York
a member of BertelsmannSpringer Science+Business Media GmbH

http://www.springer.de



Typesetting: Camera-ready by author, data conversion by PTP-Berlin, Stefan Sossna
Printed on acid-free paper SPIN 10840143 06/3142 5 4 3 2 1 0

# Preface

The symposia on Fundamentals of Computation Theory are held every two years. Following the tradition established at the first FCT 1977, the conference brings together specialists in theoretical fields of Computer Science from various countries and stimulates mathematical research in theoretical computer science. Topics of interest for the satellite workshop on *Efficient Algorithms* WEA 2001 are: computational complexity, graph and network algorithms, flow and routing algorithms, coloring and partitioning, cuts and connectivity, packing and covering, scheduling algorithms, approximation algorithms, inapproximability results, online problems, randomized algorithms, integer programming, semidefinite programming, algorithmic geometry, polyhedral combinatorics, branch and bound algorithms, cutting plane algorithms, and various applications.

The 13th FCT was held in Riga-Lielupe, August 22-24, 2001 with an additional day (August 25) for the satellite workshop WEA 2001. The previous meetings were held in the following cities:

- Poznan-Kórnik, Poland, 1977
- Wendish-Rietz, Germany, 1979
- Szeged, Hungary, 1981
- Borgholm, Sweden, 1983
- Cottbus, Germany, 1985
- Kazan, Russia, 1987
- Szeged, Hungary, 1989
- Gosen-Berlin, Germany, 1991
- Szeged, Hungary, 1993
- Dresden, Germany, 1995
- Kraków, Poland, 1997
- Iasi, Romania, 1999

This year the number of submitted papers was high. The Program Committee decided to accept 28 submissions as regular papers and 15 submissions as short papers. Additionally, the Program Committee of WEA 2001 accepted 8 papers. This volume contains all the contributed papers. The invited speakers were:

- Jānis Bārzdiņš (Riga, Latvia)
- Gilles Brassard (Montreal, Canada)
- Klaus Jansen (Kiel, Germany)
- Juhani Karhumäki (Turku, Finland)
- Marek Karpinski (Bonn, Germany)
- Boris Plotkin (Jerusalem, Israel)
- Umesh Vazirani (Berkeley, USA)

The invited speakers for WEA 2001 were:

- Foto Afrati (Athens, Greece)
- Andreas Brandstädt (Rostock, Germany)
- Luisa Gargano (Salerno, Italy)
- Stephane Perennes (Sophia-Antipolis, France)

All papers published in the workshop proceedings were selected by the program committee on the basis of referee reports. Each paper was reviewed by at least three referees who judged the papers for originality, quality, and consistency with the topics of the conference. The Program Committee consisted of:

- Andris Ambainis (Berkeley, USA)
- Setsuo Arikawa (Fukuoka, Japan)
- Yuri Breitbart (Bell Labs, USA)
- Cristian Calude (Auckland, New Zealand)
- Bogdan Chlebus (Warsaw, Poland)
- Alexander Dikovsky (Nantes, France)
- Rūsiņš Freivalds (Riga, Latvia), Chair
- Jozef Gruska (Brno, Czech Republic)
- Tero Harju (Turku, Finland)
- Kazuo Iwama (Kyoto, Japan)
- Aleksander Letichevskij (Kiev, Ukraine)
- Andrzej Lingas (Lund, Sweden)
- Christoph Meinel (Trier, Germany)
- Valery Nepomniaschy (Novosibirsk, Russia)
- Jaan Penjam (Tallinn, Estonia)
- Anatol Slissenko (Paris, France)
- Carl Smith (Maryland, USA)
- Esko Ukkonen (Helsinki, Finland)
- Eli Upfal (Brown, USA)
- Mars Valiev (Moscow, Russia)

The Program Committee of the Workshop on *Efficient Algorithms* **WEA 2001** worked in close touch with the Program Committee of *FCT 2001* but made their decisions separately. This Program Committee consisted of:

- Yossi Azar (Tel-Aviv, Israel)
- Evripidis Bampis (Evry, France), Co-chair
- Michael Bender (Stony Brook, USA)
- Thomas Erlebach (Zurich, Switzerland)
- Wenceslas Fernandez De La Vega (Orsay, France)
- Wen-Lian Hsu (Academia Sinica, Taiwan)
- Klaus Jansen (Kiel, Germany), Co-chair
- Elias Koutsoupias (Athens, Greece and Los Angeles, USA)
- Jan Kratochvil (Prague, Czech Republic)
- Seffi Naor (Haifa, Israel)
- Takao Nishizeki (Tohoku, Japan)

- Ingo Schiermeyer (Freiberg, Germany)
- Sergey Sevastianov (Novosibirsk, Russia)
- Martin Skutella (Berlin, Germany)

We would like to thank all the authors who responded to the call for papers, our invited speakers, and the referees.

Furthermore, we thank the members of the Organizing Committee:

- Baiba Apine
- Juris Borzovs, Chair
- Māra Cepīte
- Ārija Deme
- Mārtiņš Dīcis
- Andrejs Dubrovskis
- Rudīte Ekmane
- Anita Ermuša
- Rūsiņš Freivalds
- Marats Golovkins
- Filips Jelisejevs
- Anita Kalniņa
- Maksims Kravcevs
- Ieva Lapiņa
- Ināra Opmane
- Raitis Ozols
- Jānis Plūme
- Juris Smotrovs
- Ārija Sproģe
- Oksana Ščeguļnaja
- Eduards Zvirbulis
- Zaiga Zvirbule

We gratefully acknowledge sponsorship from the Latvian Council of Science, the EU thematic network APPOL *Approximation and On-line Algorithms*, the Institute of Computer Science and Applied Mathematics of the Christian-Albrechts-Universität zu Kiel, and the Department of Computer Science of the University of Evry.

May 2001

Rūsiņš Freivalds
Evripidis Bampis
Klaus Jansen

# Table of Contents

## Invited Papers



## Regular Papers

## Short Papers

## WEA Invited Papers



## WEA Regular Papers

# Towards Axiomatic Basis of Inductive Inference*

Jānis Bārzdiņš[1], Rūsiņš Freivalds[1], and Carl H. Smith[2]

[1] Institute of Mathematics and Computer Science,
University of Latvia, Raiņa bulv. 29, Riga, Latvia***
[2] Department of Computer Science, University of Maryland, U.S.A.†

**Abstract.** The language for the formulation of the interesting statements is, of course, most important. We use first order predicate logic. Our main achievement in this paper is an axiom system which we believe to be more powerful than any other natural general purpose discovery axiom system.
We prove soundness of this axiom system in this paper. Additionally we prove that if we remove some of the requirements used in our axiom system, the system becomes not sound. We characterize the complexity of the quantifier prefix which guaranties provability of a true formula via our system. We prove also that if a true formula contains only monadic predicates, our axiom system is capable to prove this formula in the considered model.

## 1 Introduction

The term "inductive inference" is used for synthesis of general regularities from particular examples. Different formalizations of the inductive inference problems are possible. Since the seminal paper by E.M. Gold [Gold67] the computational learning theory community has been under hypnosis presuming that the main problem in the learning theory is to restore a grammar from samples of language or a program from its sample computations. However scientists in physics and biology have become accustomed to looking for interesting assertions rather than for a universal theory explaining everything. The question arises what language is to be used to formulate these assertions.

One of the most universal languages to formulate such assertions is the first-order predicate logics. Hence along with Gold-style inductive inference it is natural to investigate inference of assertions in predicate logics ("formulas") from local observations of the given model ("elementary facts"). Research in this direction was started already in [OSW91] and [BFS97].

* This project was supported by an International Agreement under NSF Grant 9421640.

*** Research supported by Grant No.01.0354 from the Latvian Council of Science, Contract IST-1999-11234 (QAIP) from the European Commission, and the Swedish Institute, Project ML-2000

† Supported in part by NSF Grant CCR-9732692

R. Freivalds (Ed.): FCT 2001, LNCS 2138, pp. 1–13, 2001.

We can look on the inductive inference from another viewpoint as well, namely, how the inductive inference process is defined. Traditionally, "identification in the limit" is considered [Gold67]. We say that the inductive inference machine (IIM) identifies the given object (for instance, a function) in the limit, if reading from the input more and more input-output examples IIM produces a correct hypothesis (for instance, a correct Gödel number of the target function) and never more changes it (in spite of working on for infinitely long time). Modifications of the "identification in the limit" are considered. For instance at the finite (or, "one-shot") identification the IIM processes the infinitely long sequence of the values of the target function, and at some finite moment the IIM produces only one correct output. Of course, the capability of finite identification is much more limited.

In the paper [BFS96] a new type of inductive inference "learning with confidence" ( or "learning with belief levels") is considered. In some sense this notion is closer to the human inference process. When we produce any hypothesis based on a finite number of observations we are tended estimate some belief level of our hypothesis. This way, we come to a natural inductive inference type "learning first-order predicate logic formulas with belief levels from elementary facts". By "elementary facts" we understand values of the given predicates for specific values of the arguments. This inductive inference type is central in our paper.

We try to axiomatize the possibilities of this inference type. We believe that we have succeeded only thanks to the naturality of this notion. We have no idea how one could axiomatize the possibilities of identifiability in the limit. One of reasons of this difficulty is this identification type's remoteness from the natural human inference.

Why we believe in great importance of the axiomatizability problem? The aim of axiomatization is to find the basic elements of which our practical everyday reasoning is constructed.

Remember the axioms of Euclidean geometry, axioms of first-order predicate logics (in these cases a complete axiomatization was achieved), axioms of Peano arithmetics, Zermelo-Fraenkel axiom system for the set theory. The latter systems are incomplete, and they cannot be made complete (by Gödel incompleteness theorem). However this does not challenge the importance of this axiomatization. For instance, when we speak of Peano axiom system [Peano], then all *natural* assertions in arithmetics can be proved in Peano arithmetics (however not always in a trivial way) but all the counterexamples provided by the proof of the Gödel incompleteness theorem are *highly artificial.*

David Hilbert's system of axioms of the elementary geometry [Hilb1879] has a similar status. Being a more precise version of Euclidean axioms, this system is not a complete system (by a corollary from Gödel incompleteness theorem). Nonetheless Hilbert's system is considered to be the "standard".

A similar status is hold also by Zermelo-Fraenkel axiom system for the set theory [Zer30].

We return to the inductive inference. Until recently, it was investigated only from a pragmatic viewpoint without a deeper search of the mathematical foundations. At first it seems that inductive inference and axiomatization are incompatible notions because axiomatization traditionally is considered as a prerogative of deductive systems. However inductive inference processes (learning from examples) performed by distinct persons show great similarity. This prompts existence of objective regularities in the inductive inference. On the other hand, axiomatization of inductive inference presumes search for objective regularities. It is evident that axioms of inductive inference should differ from axioms of deductive systems, because the latter serve for deducing absolute truth while the former are only hypotheses with higher or less high belief level.

## 2 Learning Formulas with Belief Levels

First of all we go over the necessary logical concepts that will be used. A *model* will be a triple $\langle \Sigma, N, I \rangle$ where $\Sigma$ is a finite set of predicates, called a *signature*, with designated arities, $N$ is the domain of the variables used in the predicates and $I$ is the interpretation of the predicates. Unless otherwise noted, the domain will be the natural numbers, $\mathbb{N}$. For example consider the model $M_0 = \langle \Sigma_0, \mathbb{N}, I_0 \rangle$ where $\Sigma_0$ contains three binary predicates, $P_1$, $P_2$ and $P_3$. The interpretation $I_0$ is given by three formulas: $\hat{P}_1(x, y) : x \leq y$, $\hat{P}_2(x, y) : y = 5x$ and $\hat{P}_3(x, y) : y = x^2$. The *elementary facts* of a model are all of the instantiated predicate symbols of the model with associated truth values. The elementary facts of our example model $M_0$ include $P_1(2, 5) = T$, $P_1(6, 2) = F$, $P_1(4, 5) = T$, $P_2(2, 10) = T$, $P_3(3, 10) = F$. In some of the proofs that follow it will be more convenient to list these elementary facts as $P_1(2, 5)$, $\neg P_1(6, 2)$, $P_1(4, 5)$, $P_2(2, 10)$, $\neg P_3(3, 10)$. A *term* is either a notation for a member of the domain or a variable. The *elementary formulae* of a model $M = \langle \Sigma, N, I \rangle$ include are formulae of the form $P(n_1, \cdots, n_k)$ for $P$ a $k$-ary predicate in $\Sigma$ and each $n_i$ $(1 \leq i \leq k)$ is a term. Next, *formula* of the first-order predicate logics, *validity*, and any other logical notions are defined in the traditional way (see any textbook, e.g. [Kleene52].

Let $M =< \Sigma, , \mathbb{N}, I >$ be a model. By $E_M$ we denote the set of all elementary facts of the model $M$. By $D_M$ we denote the set of all enumerations of elements of $E_M$.

Let some standard axiom system **A** for the first order predicate calculus, (e.g. that from [Kleene52] be fixed. If it is possible to derive a formula $f$ from the elementary facts of some model $M$ via the axiom system, we write $M \vdash f$. Notice that if $E_M$ is, for example, $\{\neg P(0), P(1), \cdots\}$ then $M \vdash \exists x(P(x))$. This follows from the "$P(1) \Rightarrow \exists x(P(x))$" being in **A**.

Now we recall some notions and results from [BFS96] and [BFS97] to be used below.

The main notion from [BFS96] that we need is that of "belief level". A *belief level* is a rational number between 0 and 1, inclusive. A 0 represent a vote of no confidence and 1 indicates absolute certainty.

**Definition 1.** *A* belief formula learning *(abbreviated BFL) machine is an algorithmic device that takes as input an enumeration of the elementary facts of some model and produces as output first order formulae paired with belief levels.*

A BFL produces a sequence of outputs, like an FFL, but unlike the FFL case, the same formula may appear over and over again, with different belief levels. If $L$ is BFL and $D$ is its input data and $f$ is a first order formula, then $B(L, D, f) = (b_1, b_2, \cdots)$ is the sequence of belief levels associated with $f$ that $L$ produces when given $D$ as input, in the order of appearance in the output stream.

**Definition 2.** *We say that a BFL L e-learns formula f from the input data D iff $B(L, D, f)$ monotonically converges to 1. The set of formulas produced this way is denoted by $L(D)$.*

**Definition 3.** *A BFL L is* correct *iff for all models M and all $D \in D_M$, all the formulas in $L(D)$ are true for the model M.*

**Definition 4.** *A correct BFL L is called* absolutely best *if $L'(D) \subseteq L(D)$ holds for arbitrary correct BFL $L'$, for arbitrary model M and arbitrary enumeration of elementary facts $D \in D_M$.*

**Theorem 1.** *(Theorem 24 from [BFS97]) There is no absolutely best BFL.*

**Definition 5.** *A formula f is* e-learnable *iff there is a correct BFL L which e-learns f from every $D \in D_M$ of every model M such that f is true in M.*

**Theorem 2.** *(Theorem 20 from [BFS97]) Let A be an arbitrary Boolean formula with predicate symbols $P_1, \cdots, P_n$, and $x_1, \cdots, x_u, y_1, \cdots, y_v$ be variables of the involved predicates. Then the formula*

$$\forall x_1 \cdots \forall x_u \exists y_1 \cdots \exists y_v A(x_1, \cdots, y_v)$$

*is e-learnable.*

**Theorem 3.** *(Theorem 23 from [BFS97]) If f is a first-order predicate logic formula involving only monadic predicates, then f is e-learnable.*

# 3 Starting Axiomatization: The First Two Axioms for Formula Learning

We start with introducing a new notion

$$A/e$$

where $A$ is a formula and $e$ is a rational number with $0 \leq e \leq 1$. We call the number $e$ the *belief level* of the formula $A$. The intuitive meaning of $A/e$ is that, based on the prior steps of the proof, we have belief level $e$ that the formula $A$ is true. Our new axioms will exploit the notion $A/e$. To formulate the new axioms we need one more notion, namely that of weighting function.

**Definition 6.** *A* weighting function *is a recursive function* $\omega$ *such that*

$$\sum_{n=0}^{\infty} \omega(n) = 1.$$

For example, let $\omega(n) = 1/2^{n+1}$. The idea of the weighting function is that some examples are more relevant than the others. The weighting function will be used to determine the belief level of a universally quantified sentence, based on known examples.

In this section along with the symbol $\vdash$ which denotes the "proves" relation in traditional logic, we use the symbol $\Vdash$ to denote the same relation in extended axiom system that we now present. For example, the first new axiom below says that if something is provable in the standard logic, it is provable with belief level 1 in our new system.

**Axiom 1** *If* $M \vdash A$, *then* $M \Vdash A/1$.

**Axiom 2** *If* $A$ *contains a free variable* $x$, *and* $M \Vdash A(n_1)/e_1, \ldots, M \Vdash A(n_k)/e_k$, *where* $n_i \in \mathbb{N}$ *and* $A(n_i)$ *is obtained from* $A$ *by substituting* $n_i$ *for all occurences of* $x, i = 1, 2, \cdots, k$, *then* $M \Vdash \forall x A(x)/e$, *where* $e = \omega(n_1).e_1 + \ldots + \omega(n_k).e_k$.

**Definition 7.** *We say that a* formula $A$ is e-provable in the model $M$ via the axiom system $\Omega$ *iff for arbitrary enumeration of elementary facts* $D \in D_M$ *and for arbitrary* $\epsilon > 0$ *there is an* $e > 1 - \epsilon$ *such that* $M \Vdash A/e$

It is easy to see that for axiom systems $\Omega$ containing only Axiom 1, Axiom 2 and the axioms Axiom 3' , Axiom 3" or Axiom 3 described below the following theorem holds.

**Theorem 4.** *The class of e-provable formulas does not depend on the particular weighting function.*

The axioms Axiom 1 and Axiom 2 seem to be natural enough. However this system of two axioms is rather weak because the two incorporated mechanisms (the possibilities of the standard logic and the belief levels) are rather disjoint. After usage of Axiom 2 there is no way to apply Axiom 1. We need a mechanism to combine Axioms 1 and 2.

## 4 A Naive Third Axiom

**Axiom 3'** If:
a) $M \vdash\!\!-(A \Rightarrow B)$,
b) $M \Vdash\!\!= A/e$,
then $M \Vdash\!\!= B/e$.

Axiom 3' may be considered to be a good companion for Axioms 1 and 2. However we have

**Theorem 5.** *The system of axioms { Axiom 1, Axiom 2, Axiom 3' } is not sound.*

**Proof.** We prove that there is a model $M$ and a formula $f$ such that $f$ is false in the model $M$ but nonetheless $f$ is e-provable in $M$ via this system of axioms.

Indeed, we consider a model $M$ with one unary predicate $P(x)$ such that $P(1)$ is true and $P(2)$ is false. We consider the formula $\forall x P(x)$ which is false in $M$. Let $\omega(n)$ be the weighting function. Axiom 2 provides us $\forall x P(x)/\omega(1)$.

We construct a formula $Q_k$ being

$$\forall x_1 \forall x_2 \cdots \forall x_k (P(x_1) \vee P(x_2) \vee \cdots P(x_k))$$

A somewhat similar formula being

$$\forall x_1 \forall x_2 \cdots \forall x_k (P(x_1) \vee P(x_2) \vee \cdots P(x_k)) \Rightarrow \forall x P(x)$$

is a tautology in the standard predicate logic. Hence, by Axiom 1, it can be e-proved with belief level 1. Using Axiom 2 $k$ times, we obtain

$$Q_k/1 - (1 - \omega(1))^k.$$

Applying Axiom 3', we get

$$\forall x P(x)/1 - (1 - \omega(1))^k.$$

If $k \to \infty$, then the belief level converges to 1. Hence the false formula $\forall x P(x)$ is e-provable with belief level converging to 1. ⊠

## 5 A Less Naive Third Axiom

Why Axiom 3' caused non-soundness of the axiom system? Where was the essence of the proof of Theorem 5 ? We see that it became possible because we allowed too many quantifiers in the formula $Q_k$.

**Definition 8.** *Let $A$ and $B$ be first order predicate formulas in prenex form. We say that formula $A$* is of no higher quantifier complexity than *$B$ (denoted by $A \preceq_{quant} B$) if the number of quantifiers (no matter, how many quantifier alternations are present) in $A$ is less or equal to the number of quantifiers in $B$.*

For instance, consider formulas

$$A_1 : \forall x \forall y \exists z \exists u (R(17, x, z) \wedge (P(u, 9) \vee S(y))$$

$$A_2 : \exists x \exists v \exists w \exists p ((G(5, w) \wedge H(v, 17, x)) \Rightarrow \neg K(x, p))$$

$$A_3 : \forall g H(g, g, 17)$$

It is easy to see that $A_1 \preceq_{quant} A_2$, $A_2 \preceq_{quant} A_1$,$A_3 \preceq_{quant} A_1$, but $A_1 \neg \preceq_{quant} A_3$.

Please notice that our definition of $\preceq_{quant}$ ignores the names of the bounded variables.

**Axiom 3"** If:
a) $M \vdash (A \Rightarrow B)$,
b) $A \preceq_{quant} B$,
c) $M \Vdash A/e$,
then $M \Vdash B/e$.

However we have

**Theorem 6.** *The system of axioms { Axiom 1, Axiom 2, Axiom 3" } is not sound.*

**Proof.** We consider a model $M$ where the binary predicate $P(x, y)$ means "$y \leq x$". In this model the formula $\exists x \forall y P(x, y)$ is false. We consider the formula $\forall y P(x, y)$ with one free variable $x$. Let $k$ be an arbitrary natural number. Using Axiom 2, we can get the belief level

$$e_k = \omega(1) + \omega(2) + \cdots + \omega(k)$$

for the formula $\forall y P(k, y)$. On the other hand, in the classical logic the formula

$$\forall y P(k, y) \Rightarrow \exists x \forall y P(x, y)$$

is a tautology. Using Axiom 3" with $A = \forall y P(k, y)$ and $B = \exists x \forall y P(x, y)$ we get the belief level $e_k = \omega(1) + \omega(2) + \cdots + \omega(k)$ for the false formula $\exists x \forall y P(x, y)$ not containing $k$. Since $k \to \infty$ implies $e_k \to 1$, we get belief level converging to 1 for a false formula $\exists x \forall y P(x, y)$. ☒

## 6 Final Third Axiom

**Definition 9.** *We say that A* is of no higher constant complexity than *B (denoted by $A \preceq_{const} B$) if there is no constant which is used in A but not used in B.*

For instance, consider formulas

$$A_1 : \forall x \forall y \exists z \exists u (R(17, x, z) \wedge (P(u, 5) \vee S(y))$$

$$A_2 : \exists x \exists v \exists w((G(5,w) \wedge H(v,17,x)) \Rightarrow \neg K(x,x))$$
$$A_3 : \forall g H(g,g,17)$$

It is easy to see that $A_1 \preceq_{const} A_2$, $A_2 \preceq_{const} A_1$,$A_3 \preceq_{const} A_1$, but $A_1 \neg \preceq_{const} A_3$.

**Axiom 3** *If:*
*a)* $M|\!-\!(A \Rightarrow B)$,
*b)* $A \preceq_{quant} B$,
*c)* $A \preceq_{const} B$,
*d)* $M||\!\!=\!A/e$,
*then* $M||\!\!=\!B/e$.

## 7 Soundness of the Axiom System

We will prove in this section that the axiom system $\{Axiom_1, Axiom_2, Axiom_3\}$ is sound. Let us consider only formulas in a prenex form. The quantifierless body of the formula is a Boolean propositional formula made of terms being predicate symbols from the finite signature $\Sigma$ with constants and variable symbols.

Consider, for instance, two formulas

$$A = \forall x \exists y(P(x,7,y) \Rightarrow Q(y,5),$$
$$B = \forall x \exists y(\neg Q(y,5) \vee P(x,7,y).$$

They have the same quantifier prefix (with equal names for the bounded variables) and the quantifierless bodies are equivalent Boolean formulas of the same variables $P(x,7,y)$ and $Q(y,5)$. It is easy to conjecture that $A$ is e-provable in a model $M$ if and only if $B$ is e-provable in $M$. To prove such a conjecture we consider the notion of *reversible equivalence.* We use $A \preceq B$ to denote $A \preceq_{quant} B \wedge A \preceq_{const} B$.

**Definition 10.** *We say that formulas $A$ and $B$ are* reversible equivalent *($A \equiv_r evB$) in the model $M$, if $M|\!-\!(A \Rightarrow B), M|\!-\!(B \Rightarrow A), A \preceq B$ and $B \preceq A$.*

**Definition 11.** *We say that formulas $A$ and $B$ are* equivalent up to names *($A \equiv_{rename} B$) if they differ only in the names of the bounded variables.*

**Definition 12.** *We say that formulas $A$ and $B$ are* generalized reversible equivalent *($A \equiv_{grev} B$) in the model $M$, if there is a formula $C$ such that $A \equiv_{rev} C$, and $C \equiv_{rename} B$ .*

**Lemma 1.** *If $M||\!\!=\!A/e$, and $A \equiv_{grev} B$, then $M||\!\!=\!B/e$.*

**Proof.** $A \equiv_{grev} B$ implies $A \equiv_{rev} C$, $C \equiv_{rename} B$, $M|\!-\!(A \Rightarrow C)$, and $A \preceq B$. Hence $M||\!\!=\!C/e$ by Axiom 3. Finally, the e-proof $M||\!\!=\!B/e$ can be obtained from the e-proof $M||\!\!=\!C/e$ by renaming the variables introduced by usage of Axiom 2. ☒

**Lemma 2.** *For arbitrary formula $B$, there is only a finite number (up to generalized reversible equivalence) of formulas $A$ such that $A \preceq B$.*

**Proof.** For the simplicity sake we consider only formulas in prenex form. Let $S$ be the set of the constants used in $B$. There is only a finite number of different (up to reversible equivalence) Boolean formulas made of terms consisting of predicate symbols from the finite set $\Sigma$, the bounded variables used in $B$ and the constants in $S$. Hence the number of formulas in prenex form is also only finite. The proof in the general case uses the same idea but technically it is more complicate. ☒

**Theorem 7.** *For arbitrary formula $B$ which is false in the model $M$, and for arbitrary weighting function $\omega$, there is a real number $e_0 < 1$ such that e-proofs $M \| \!\! = B/e$ cannot exist for $e > e_0$.*

**Proof.** By induction over the number $k$ of quantifiers used in $B$.

**Basis.** $k = 0$. Obvious.

**k ⇒ k+1** . Assume that Theorem is true for $k$ or less quantifiers used. Assume from the contrary that there is a formula $B$ with $k+1$ quantifiers such that it is false in the model $M$ and $M \| \!\! = B/e$ with arbitrarily high $e > 1$. Consider all possible $A$ such that $A \preceq B$.

-Some of such formulas $A$ are **true**. Then $A \Rightarrow B$ cannot be proved classically in the model $M$. Hence Axiom 3 is not applicable in this case.

-Some of such formulas $A$ have $k$ or less quantifiers, and $A$ is false. Then, by induction assumption, $A/e$ cannot be proved for high enough values of $e$. Hence such an $A$ cannot be used in Axiom 3 to obtain $B/e$ with sufficiently high $e$.

-Some of such formulas $A$ have the same number $k+1$ of quantifiers, and $A$ is false. By Lemma 2 there is only a finite number of distinct (up to generalized reversible equivalence) such formulas $A$. Denote them by $A_1, A_2, \ldots, A_n$. How $M \| \!\! = B/e$ can be proved for arbitrarily high $e < 1$ ? Surely, not by Axiom 1. If the outermost quantifier of $B$ is not $\forall$, the proof cannot be by Axiom 2. If the outermost quantifier of $B$ is $\forall$, $B$ is a formula $\forall x F(x)$ and it is false, consider a particular value $x = a$ such that $F(a)$ is false. $F(a)$ is a formula with $k$ quantifiers and , by induction assumption, it cannot be proved for arbitrarily high values of $e$. Hence the only hope to prove $M \| \!\! = B/e$ with arbitrarily high value of $e$ is by Axiom 3 using $M \vdash A_i \Rightarrow B$ and $M \| \!\! = A_i/e_i$ with arbitrarily high values of $e_i$. Hence for one of $A_1, A_2, \ldots, A_n$ it is needed to prove $A_j/e$ for values of $e$ higher than those described in Axiom 2. However we have no means to do this. ☒

## 8 Usefulness

**Definition 13.** *We say that formula $A$* is e-provable by axiom system *$\Omega$ iff $A$ is e-provable by the axiom system $\Omega$ in every model $M$ such that $A$ is true in $M$.*

This section (and the next one below as well) shows that our axiom system $\{Axiom_1, Axiom_2, Axiom_3\}$ is powerful enough to e-prove the same classes of formulas which are e-learnable by Theorems 2 and 3.

**Theorem 8.** *Let $A$ be an arbitrary Boolean formula with predicate symbols $P_1, \cdots, P_n$, and $x_1, \cdots, x_u, y_1, \cdots, y_v$ be variables of the involved predicates. Then the formula*

$$\forall x_1 \cdots \forall x_u \exists y_1 \cdots \exists y_v A(x_1, \cdots, y_v)$$

*is e-provable by the axiom system $\{Axiom_1, Axiom_2, Axiom_3\}$.*

**Proof.** We prove here only a special case of this theorem when the formula is $\forall x \exists y P(x, y)$ and there is a sequence $\{a_1, a_2, a_3, \cdots\}$ of natural numbers such that $P(1, a_1)$ is true, $P(2, a_2)$ is true, etc. The general case is similar and differs only in more heavy technical notation. The following sequence of proofs is performed via our axiom system.

| | |
|---|---|
| $P(1, a_1)$ | classically |
| $\exists y P(1, y)$ | classically |
| $\exists y P(1, y)$ | Axiom 1 |
| $\forall x \exists y P(x, y)/\omega(1).1$ | Axiom 2 |
| $P(2, a_2)$ | classically |
| $\exists y P(2, y)$ | classically |
| $\exists y P(2, y)$Axiom 1 | |
| $\forall x \exists y P(x, y)/\omega(1).1 + \omega(2).1$ | Axiom 2 |
| $P(3, a_3)$ | classically |
| $\exists y P(3, y)$ | classically |
| $\exists y P(3, y)$ | Axiom 1 |
| $\forall x \exists y P(x, y)/\omega(1) + \omega(2) + \omega(3)$ | Axiom 2 |
| ... | ... |

☒

## 9 Monadic Predicates

**Theorem 9.** *If $f$ is a first-order predicate logic formula involving only monadic predicates, then $f$ is e-provable by the axiom system $\{Axiom_1, Axiom_2, Axiom_3\}$.*

**Proof.** For the simplicity sake we consider only formulas in prenex form. We prove our Theorem by induction. For quantifierless formulas Theorem is obvious. Assume that Theorem is true for $k$ quantifiers and the target formula $f$ contains $k + 1$ quantifiers.

Let $Qx$ be the outermost quantifier of the formula $f$. Suppose that $P_1, \ldots, P_m$ is a complete list of all monadic predicates in $f$ which contain the variable $x$. To simplify the proof, assume that $m = 2$. The generalization to larger values of $m$ is obvious. We define 4 formulae $f_1, f_2, f_3, f_4$ (in general $2^m$ formulae) derived from $f$ substituting, respectively, $P_1(x) = T, P_2(x) = T$ for $f_1$, $P_1(x) = T, P_2(x) = F$ for $f_2$, $P_1(x) = F, P_2(x) = T$ for $f_3$, $P_1(x) = F, P_2(x) = F$ for $f_4$. It is important that $f_1, f_2, f_3, f_4$ have at most $k$ quantifiers. The target formula is equivalent to $Qx((P_1(x)\&P_2(x)\&f_1) \vee (P_1(x)\&\neg P_2(x)\&f_2) \vee (\neg P_1(x)\&P_2(x)\&f_3) \vee (\neg P_1(x)\&\neg P_2(x)\&f_4))$.

We consider the cases $Q = \exists$ and $Q = \forall$ separately.

- Assume that $f$ is $\exists x F(x)$ and it is true for $x = 7$. Then for $x = 7$ only one part out of four

$$\begin{gathered}(P_1(x)\&P_2(x)\&f_1)\vee \\ \vee(P_1(x)\&\neg P_2(x)\&f_2)\vee \\ \vee(\neg P_1(x)\&P_2(x)\&f_3)\vee \\ \vee(\neg P_1(x)\&\neg P_2(x)\&f_4)\end{gathered}$$

can be true. For instance, if $P_1(7)\&\neg P_2(7)$, then for $x = 7$ the second part is true. This implies that $f_2$ is true in the model $M$ for all the values of $x$ (because $f_2$ does not contain $x$). By induction assumption, $M \| \!\!= f_2/e$ for arbitrarily high $e < 1$. Consider Axiom 3 with $A = f_2$ and $B = \forall x F(x)$. We concluded that the requirement a) of the Axiom 3 is satisfied. Notice that $f_2 \preceq \forall x F(x)$ since $f_2$ contains less quantifiers and not a single constant not in $\forall x F(x)$. Hence, the requirement b) also is satisfied.

Since $(f_2 \Rightarrow \exists x F(x))$ is true in the model $M$, and our *classical* proofs of the validity of formulas in models use all the power of Kleene axiom system, it is possible to prove $M \vdash (f_2 \Rightarrow \exists x F(x))$. Hence, by Axiom 3, $M \| \!\!= \exists x F(x)/e$ for arbitrarily high $e < 1$.

-Assume that $f$ is $\forall F(x)$. For every $x$ separately (e.g., for $x = 7$)

$$\begin{gathered}F(7) \equiv [(P_1(7)\&P_2(7)\&f_1)\vee \\ \vee(P_1(7)\&\neg P_2(7)\&f_2)\vee \\ \vee(\neg P_1(7)\&P_2(7)\&f_3)\vee \\ \vee(\neg P_1(7)\&\neg P_2(7)\&f_4)]\end{gathered}$$

In the model $M$ three parts are false but $F(7)$ is true. If, for instance, the part

$$(P_1(7)\&\neg P_2(7)\&f_2)$$

is true, then $f_2$ (not containing $x$) is true, and

$$M \vdash (f_2 \Rightarrow F(7)).$$

Axiom 3 is applicable because a), b) and c) are true. By Axiom 2,

$$\frac{M \| \!\!= F(1)/e, \ldots, M \| \!\!= F(k)/e}{M \| \!\!= \forall x F(x)/e} \tag{9.1}$$

for arbitrarily high $e < 1$. ☒

## 10 Is This Axiom System Complete?

There are at least two natural definitions of completeness of axiom systems for formula learning with belief levels.

**Definition 14.** *We say that axiom system $\Omega$ is* absolutely complete *for formula learning with belief levels iff for every correct BFL L , every model M and every enumeration of elementary facts $D \in D_M$ there holds: if $f \in L(D)$, then $f$ is e-provable by $\Omega$ in the model $M$.*

It is easy to see that there do not exist absolutely complete axiom systems for formula learning with belief levels. We referred in our Section 2 Theorem 24 from [BFS97] asserting that no best correct BFL machine is possible. It is easy to observe that arbitrary axiom system for formula learning with belief levels can be simulated by a BFL machine such that the machine learns all the formulas e-provable via this axiom system. An absolutely complete axiom system would generate a best correct BFL machine which is impossible because of Theorem 24 in [BFS97].

**Definition 15.** *We say that axiom system $\Omega$ is* practically complete *for formula learning with belief levels if every formula which is e-learnable by some BFL , is also e-provable by the axiom system $\Omega$.*

We conjecture that our axiom system $\{Axiom_1, Axiom_2, Axiom_3\}$ is practically complete. Theorems 8 and 9 (compared with Theorems 2 and 3) in a sense support our conjecture.

We conclude with an open problem the solution of which would clarify much (if not everything) for the solution of our conjecture.

**Open Problem.** Let two formulas $f_1$ and $f_2$ be provably equivalent in the classical logic. Let $f_1$ be e-provable in our axiom system with belief level converging to 1. Is the other formula $f_2$ also e-provable in our axiom system with belief level converging to 1?

We used in the proof of our Theorem 5 the fact that provably equivalent formulas can have very much different maximal belief levels. However this leaves open possibility that our Open Problem can have a positive solution.

## References

[BFS96] Jānis Bārzdiņš, Rūsiņš Freivalds and Carl H.Smith. *Learning with confidence.* "Lecture Notes in Computer Science ", Springer, 1996, v.1046, p.207-218.

[BFS97] Jānis Bārzdiņš, Rūsiņš Freivalds and Carl H.Smith. *Learning formulae from elementary facts.* "Lecture Notes in Computer Science ", Springer, 1997, v.1208, p.272-285.

[BFS98] Jānis Bārzdiņš, Rūsiņš Freivalds and Carl H.Smith. *A Logic of Discovery.* "Lecture Notes in Artificial Intelligence ", Springer, 1998, v.1532, p.401-402.

[Fre91] Rūsiņš Freivalds. *Inductive inference of recursive functions: Qualitative theory*. Lecture Notes in Computer Science, 1991, v. 502, p. 77–110.

[Gold67] E. Mark Gold. *Language identification in the limit*. Information and Control, 1967, v. 10, p. 447–474.

[Hilb1879] David Hilbert. *Grundlagen der Geometrie (Festschrift zur Feier der Enthüllung des Gauss-Weber-Denkmals in Göttingen)*, Leipzig, Teubner, 1879.

[Kleene52] Stephen Cole Kleene. *Introduction to Metamathematics*. North-Holland, 1952.

[OSW91] Daniel N. Osherson, Michael Stob, and Scott Weinstein. *A universal inductive inference machine*. Journal of Symbolic Logic, 1991, v. 56, No. 2, p.661–672.

[Peano] Giuseppe Peano. *Selected works of Giuseppe Peano, with a biographical sketch and bibliography by H. C. Kennedy*, London, 1973.

[Zer30] Ernst Zermelo. *Über Grenzzahlen und Mengenbereiche*. Fundamenta Mathematicae, 1930, v. 16, S. 29-47.

# Approximation Algorithms for Fractional Covering and Packing Problems, and Applications

Klaus Jansen[1]

Institut für Informatik und praktische Mathematik,
Christian-Albrechts-Universität zu Kiel, 24 098 Kiel, Germany,
kj@informatik.uni-kiel.de

In this talk we present fast algorithms that find approximate solutions for a general class of problems, which are called fractional packing and covering problems. We describe two main lines of research:

- algorithms by Plotkin, Shmoys and Tardos [7],
- algorithms by Grigoriadis, Khachiyan, Porkolab and Villavicencio [1,2].

and new developments.

Furthermore, we discuss several applications of these techniques: scheduling on unrelated machines [7,4], scheduling of parallel tasks [3], bin packing, strip packing [6], preemptive resource constrained scheduling and fractional graph coloring [5].

## References

1. M.D. Grigoriadis and L.G. Khachiyan, Coordination complexity of parallel price-directive decomposition, *Mathematics of Operations Research* 21 (1996), 321-340.
2. M.D. Grigoriadis, L.G. Khachiyan, L. Porkolab, and J. Villavicencio: Approximate max-min resource sharing for structured concave optimization, *SIAM Journal on Optimization*, to appear.
3. K. Jansen and L. Porkolab, Linear-time approximation schemes for scheduling malleable parallel tasks, *Proceedings of the 10th ACM-SIAM Symposium on Discrete Algorithms* (1999), 490-498.
4. K. Jansen and L. Porkolab, Improved approximation schemes for scheduling unrelated parallel machines, *Proceedings of the 31st ACM Symposium on the Theory of Computing* (1999), 408-417.
5. K. Jansen and L. Porkolab: On resource constrained scheduling: polynomial time approximation schemes, submitted for publication (2001).
6. C. Kenyon, and E. Remila: Approximate strip packing, *37th Annual IEEE Symposium on Foundations of Computer Science*, FOCS 96, 31-36, and *Mathematics of Operations Research*, to appear.
7. S.A. Plotkin, D.B. Shmoys, and E. Tardos: Fast approximation algorithms for fractional packing and covering problems, *Mathematics of Operations Research* 20 (1995), 257-301.

R. Freivalds (Ed.): FCT 2001, LNCS 2138, p. 14, 2001.

# Challenges of Commutation*
## An Advertisement

Juhani Karhumäki[1]

Department of Mathematics and
Turku Centre for Computer Science
University of Turku, 20014 Turku, Finland
karhumak@cs.utu.fi

**Abstract.** We consider a few problems connected to the commutation of languages, in particular finite ones. The goal is to emphasize the challenging nature of such simply formulated problems. In doing so we give a survey of results achieved during the last few years, restate several open problems and illustrate some approaches to attack such problems by two simple constructions.

## 1 Introduction

The commutation equation

$$XY = YX \tag{1.1}$$

is among the most fundamental equations in any algebraic structure. In the case of free monoids, that is to say of words, its solution is well known and folklore: two words commute if and only if they are powers of a common word. In the monoid of languages over a finite alphabet, even if the languages are only finite, the situation changes drastically: it is not likely that a complete solution can be found. This view is supported by the fact that the equation have solutions like, cf. [3],

$$X = a + ab + ba + bb \quad \text{and} \quad Y = X + X^2 + bab + bbb$$

and

$$X = a + aa + aaa + ab + aba + b + ba \quad \text{and} \quad Y = X \setminus \{aa\}.$$

Moreover, from Theorem 3 it follows that the computational complexity of such solutions can be extremely high.

However, if we fix $X$ and ask $Y$ to be the maximal (but not finite) solution of (1) the situation changes essentially. Indeed, it was asked more than 30 years ago by Conway whether such a solution is always rational for a given rational language $X$, cf. [5]. Obviously, such a maximal language, referred to as the *centralizer of* $X$, is unique. Thus we formulate:

* Part of this work was done while the author visited LIAFA at Denis Diderot University. Supported also by the grant 44087 of the Academy of Finland.

R. Freivalds (Ed.): FCT 2001, LNCS 2138, pp. 15–23, 2001.

**Conway's Problem.** Is the centralizer of a rational language rational, as well?

Amazingly this problem is still unanswered, or in fact it is not even known whether the centralizer of a rational $X$ is recursive. The restriction to a finite $X$ does not seem to help to answer these questions. One of the goals of this paper is to summarize the special cases when the Conway's Problem is known to have an affirmative answer.

An interesting case when the solutions of the commutation equation is completely known is that of polynomials (or formal power series) over a field and with noncommuting unknowns. In terms of languages this includes a case of languages viewed as multisets. The characterization proved by Bergman, cf. [1] or [15], is as follows: two polynomials $p,\ q \in K < A >$ commute if and only if there exist a polynomial $r \in K < A >$ and polynomials $h,\ k \in K < b >$ such that

$$p = h(r) \text{ and } q = k(r),$$

where $K < A >$ denotes the polynomials over $K$ with $A$ as the set of unknowns, and $K < b >$ those with the single unknown $b$. This motivates us to state another problem:

**BTC-Problem.** Given a family $\mathcal{F}$ of languages. Does the following hold for all $X,\ Y \in \mathcal{F}$:

$$XY = YX$$

if and only if there exist a set $V$ and sets of indices $I$ and $J$ such that

$$X = \cup_{i \in I} V^i \text{ and } Y = \cup_{j \in J} V^j. \tag{1.2}$$

Intuitively, the above asks when the commutation of languages is characterized by a very similar condition than that for words. As we mentioned the polynomials have such a characterization – this is the source of the abbreviation: Bergman Typy Characterization. *In many cases we require in the BTC-problem only that $X$ is in $\mathcal{F}$ and $Y$ is arbitrary.*

The examples given at the beginning of this section show that the BTC-property does not hold for all finite languages, it even does not hold when $X$ contains only four words. The second goal of this paper is to summarize when the BTC-property is known to hold.

Finally, as the third goal we discuss two simple approaches to attack the above problems.

## 2 Preliminaries and a Basic Lemma

Let $\Sigma$ be a finite alphabet. We denote by $\Sigma^*$ (resp. $\Sigma^+$) the free monoid (resp. free semigroup) generated by $\Sigma$. The identity of $\Sigma^*$ is denoted by 1, and referred to as the empty word. Elements (resp. subsets) of $\Sigma^*$ are called words (resp. languages). We say that a word $u$ is a prefix (resp. suffix) of a word $w$ if we can write $w = ut$ (resp. $w = tu$) for some word $t$. By $u^{-1}w$ (resp. $wu^{-1}$) we denote the left (resp. right) quotient of $w$ by $u$, and these notions are extended to languages in a natural way. For two words $u$ and $v$ the word $u \wedge v$ is their maximal common prefix. The set of all prefixes (resp. suffixes) of a language $X \subseteq \Sigma^*$ is denoted by Pref $X$ (resp. Suf $X$). $\mathrm{Pref}_k(X)$ denotes the set of all prefixes of length $k$ of words in $X$.

Our basic problem is when certain type of languages $X, Y \subseteq \Sigma^*$ satisfy the commutation equation

$$XY = YX.$$

The languages we consider are either finite, rational or of certain types of codes. For a finite set $X$ we denote its cardinality by card $X$. We recall that a *code* $C \subseteq \Sigma^*$ is a set satisfying the implication:

$$x_1 \dots x_n = y_1 \dots y_m \quad \text{with} \quad x_i, \ y_j \in C$$

implies

$$n = m \quad \text{and} \quad x_i = y_i \quad \text{for} \quad i = 1, \ \dots, \ n.$$

Particular cases of codes are those of *prefix codes*, i.e. sets where no word is a proper prefix of another, and *ω-codes*, i.e. sets $C$ satisfying the above implication for $n = m = \infty$. It is well known that the monoid of prefix codes under the operation of the product is free, cf. [13], while the same does not hold for codes or ω-codes.

For a language $X \subseteq \Sigma^*$ we defined its *centralizer* $Z(X)$, or $Z$ in brief, as the maximal set commuting with $X$. Clearly, $Z$ is the union of all languages commuting with $X$, and moreover $Z^2 \subseteq Z$, in other words, $Z$ is a semigroup. Actually, to be precise we can define the centralizer as the maximal monoid or as the maximal semigroup commuting with $X$. Interestingly, these two notions are not related, at least in a trivial way. Indeed, for the $X$ in the first example of Introduction the monoid and the semigroup centralizers are different modulo the empty word, namely $\{a, b\}^*$ and $\{a, b\}^+ \setminus \{b\}$, respectively. In our subsequent considerations the centralizer means the semigroup centralizer. Consequently, it is natural to assume that $X \subseteq \Sigma^+$.

Let $X \subseteq \Sigma^+$ be a language and $Z$ its centralizer. Then clearly $X^n Z = Z X^n$ for all $n \geq 0$, and therefore we obtain simple approximations for the centralizer:

**Lemma 1.** *For any $X \subseteq \Sigma^+$ its centralizer satisfies*

$$X^+ \subseteq Z \subseteq \mathrm{Pref}\ X^* \cap \mathrm{Suf}\ X^*. \tag{2.3}$$

*Moreover, if* card$(X) < \infty$, *then for each $z \in Z$ and $w \in X^\omega$ the word $xw$ is in $X^\omega$.*

The latter sentence follows from the first one by the König's Lemma.

The approximations of $Z$ in (3) deserve a few comments. First they are very easy to deduce. However, to decide whether or not $X^+ \subset Z$ is an open problem, even in the case when $\mathrm{card}(X) < \infty$. On the other hand, to test whether the second inclusion is proper can be done by checking whether or not $X(\mathrm{Pref}\ X^* \cap \mathrm{Suf}\ X^*) = (\mathrm{Pref}\ X^* \cap \mathrm{Suf}\ X^*) \cdot X$ – due to the maximality of $Z$. In the case of rational $X$ this can be tested.

In general, to decide whether two languages commute is computationally difficult. Indeed, we have

**Proposition 1** [7]. Given a context-free language $L$ and a two-element set $X$, it is undecidable whether $L$ and $X$ commute, i.e. $LX = XL$.

The proof is based on Theorem 3.

## 3 A Survey on Conway's Problem

In this section we give a survey when Conway's Problem is known to have an affirmative answer. Despite of being a natural question on computationally very simple languages it is not likely to be an easy problem. This is illustrated by the following surprising open problem.

**Problem 1.** Is the centralizer of a finite set resursive?

It is even more confusing to note that for concrete examples, even for concrete rational languages, the centralizer can normally be found quite easily, cf. Section 5. Still we only know that the centralizer is in co-Re – and hence Problem 1 is equivalent to a question whether the centralizer is recursively enumerable, cf. [11].

As positive results we have:

**Theorem 1.** *Conway's Problem is known to have an affirmative answer in the following cases:*

*(i)* *$X$ is a rational prefix code, cf. [14];*
*(ii)* $\mathrm{card}(X) \leq 2$, *cf. [3];*
*(iii)* $\mathrm{card}(X) = 3$, *cf. [11];*
*(iv)* *$X$ is a finite code which is elementary, synchronizing or contains a word of length* 1, *cf. [3];*
*(v)* *$X$ is a rational $\omega$-code, cf. [8].*

The proofs of these results use quite different techniques. Historically the oldest result is that of (i). Its proof is nothing but a combinatorial analysis of words, but not at all trivial. It is a challenge to find a simple proof for this nice result. Actually, even in the case of biprefix sets a simple proof is not obvious. Note also that, although the monoid of prefix sets is free and thus the tools used in the word case are available, the difficultiness remains since the problem asks the commutation of $X$ with arbitrary sets.

Problems (ii) and (iv) are solved by using Lemma 1 and so-called graph lemma on combinatorics on words. These proofs are not difficult, and in fact we give in Section 5 even a simpler solution to (ii).

Problem (iii) is solved by a complicated analysis of certain language equations of very restricted types. Finally, to solve Problem (v) again a new method is used, namely unambiguous formal power series, and hence results of Bergman and Cohn are employed, cf. [1] and [4].

It is also worth mentioning that in most cases when the answer to Conway's Problem is known, the centralizer is very simple rational language: in cases (i), (ii), (iv) and (v) it coincides with $X^+$ (unless in case (ii) it is even simpler, namely $t^+$ for some word $t$).

As natural open problems we state:

**Problem 2.** Does Conway's Problem have an affirmative answer for all finite sets $X$?

**Problem 3.** Does Conway's Problem have an affirmative answer for all codes $X$?

In Problem 3, even the case when card $X = 4$ is open.

## 4 A Survey on the BTC-Problem

This section is devoted to the BTC-problem, that is to say to search for families of languages for which the commutation of languages can be described by a word type condition (3) of Section 1. Note that in all these cases the assumption is that only $X$ is from some family, and not that both $X$ and $Y$ are from the same family. Results are parallel to those – with one exception – presented in Theorem 1.

**Theorem 2.** *The BTC-property holds in the following cases:*

*(i)* $X$ *is a prefix set, cf. [14];*
*(ii)* card $X \leq 2$, *cf. [3];*
*(iii)* card $X = 3$ *and* $X$ *is a code, cf. [11];*
*(iv)* $X$ *is a code which is elementary, synchronizing or contains a word of length* 1, *cf. [3];*
*(v)* $X$ *is an* $\omega$*-code, cf. [8].*

In cases (i), (ii), (iv) and (v) the proofs are based on the fact that the centralizer of $X$ is $X^+$ and the observation of [15] that for codes this fact implies the validity of the BTC-property. Consequently, only in case (iii) we have a slightly different result than the corresponding one in Theorem 1: here we need the assumption that $X$ is also a code. The proof is not very easy.

As in the previous section we have some natural open questions:

**Problem 4.** Does the BTC-property hold for all finite codes?

**Problem 5.** Does the BTC-property hold in the case when card $X = 3$?

It follows from the example in Introduction that the bound for card $X$ in Problem 5 would be optimal. Actually, we conjecture that the answer to Problem 5 is positive, however, to prove it seems to require complicated combinatorial considerations.

## 5 Two Technical Approaches

In this section we introduce two methods to attack our commutation problems.

Let $X \subseteq \Sigma^+$ be finite with card $\Sigma \geq 2$. We say that a word $w \in \mathrm{Pref}\, X^+$ is *branching* if $w\, \mathrm{pref}_1 X \subseteq \mathrm{Pref}\, X^+$ and that $w$ is *critical* if it is branching and not in $X^+$. We denote these sets by $B$ and $C$, respectively. Obviously every word in $X^+$ is branching. Moreover we have:

**Lemma 2.** *Let $X \subseteq \Sigma^+$ be finite. Then the centralizer $Z$ of $X$ is $X^+$ if and only if $C = \emptyset$.*

*Proof.* Since the centralizer is a semigroup, for any element $z$ in $Z$ and any $x$ in $X$, the word $zx$ is in the centralizer, and hence by Lemma 1, in Pref $X^+$. Consequently, any element of the centralizer is a branching point. So the result follows from the definition of critical points. □

Lemma 2 provides a very simple proof for the case (ii) in Theorems 1 and 2:

**Theorem 3.** *Let $X \subseteq \Sigma^+$ with* card $X = 2$. *Then the centralizer of $X$ is $X^+$ or $t^+$, where $t$ (if exists) is the minimal word such that $X \subseteq t^*$, and any set commuting with $X$ is either of the form $\bigcup_{i\in I} X^i$ for some $I \subseteq \mathbf{N}$, or of the form $\bigcup_{i\in I} t^i$ for some $I \subseteq \mathbf{N}$, respectively.*

*Proof.* If there exists a word $t$ such that $X \subseteq t^*$ the result is a simple combinatorial application of Lemma 1. In the other case we know that $X = \{x,\ y\}$ satisfies the condition $xy \neq yx$, cf. [2]. Consequently, the set

$$X' = (xy \wedge yx)^{-1}\ X(xy \wedge yx)$$

is *marked*, i.e. the words start with different letters. Further, for any $X \subseteq a\Sigma^*$ and any $Y$

$$XY = YX \text{ if and only if } a^{-1}Xaa^{-1}Ya = a^{-1}Yaa^{-1}Xa,$$

implying that

$$Z(a^{-1}Xa) = a^{-1}Z(X)a.$$

It follows that

$$Z(X') = (xy \wedge yx)^{-1} Z(X)(xy \wedge yx).$$

But $X'$ is marked so that, by Lemma 2, $Z(X') = X'^{+}$. Therefore also $Z(X) = X^{+}$.

Now the BTC property follows from an observation in [14], cf. also [3]. □

We believe that this approach can be extended to give a simpler proof for the nice results of [14], that is case (i) in Theorems 2 and 3, and for all three-element sets. However, this seems to lead, especially in the latter case, to complicated considerations.

As the second approach we introduce a method to define the centralizer as the *maximal fixed point* of a mapping, cf. [6] and [10].

Let $X \subseteq \Sigma^+$ be an arbitrary language. We define recursively

$$X_0 = \mathrm{Pref}\ X^+ \cap \mathrm{Suf}\ X^+$$

and

$$X_{i+1} = X_i \setminus (X^{-1}(XX_i \triangle X_i X) \cup (XX_i \triangle X_i X)X^{-1}), \quad \text{for } i \geq 0,$$

where $\triangle$ denotes the *symmetric difference* of languages. Finally, we set

$$Z_0 = \bigcap_{i \geq 0} X_i.$$

Then it is not difficult to show that

(i) $X_{i+1} \subseteq X_i$ for all $i \geq 0$,
(ii) $X_i \supseteq Z$ for all $i \geq 0$,
(iii) $XZ_0 = Z_0 X$.

Consequently, we obtain

**Theorem 4.** *The language $Z_0$ is the centralizer of $X$, that is $Z_0 = Z(X)$.*

Note that, by construction, $Z_0$ is the maximal fixed point of the mapping

$$\varphi : Y \longmapsto Y \setminus (X^{-1}(YX \triangle XY) + (YX \triangle XY)X^{-1}).$$

Unfortunately, however, this approach might give the centralizer only as the limit, and therefore does not allow a solution to Conway's Problem, although all $X_i$'s are rational whenever $X$ is so.

On the other hand, in practice this method seems to be a way to compute the centralizer of a rational language. Experiments show that it typically converges in a finite number of steps to the centralizer, which, moreover, is of one of the following forms:

(i) $X^+$;
(ii) $S = \{w \in \Sigma^+ | wX \subseteq XX^+ \text{ and } Xw \subseteq XX^+\}$;
(iii) $Z_0 = \bigcap_{i \geq 0} X_i$, but different from $X^+$ and $S$.

In all experiments the centralizer has turned out to be rather easily definable rational language.

## 6 Conclusions

We have discussed two problems connected to the commutation of languages, and in particular to that of finite languages. Our goal was to point out that there are very challenging and simply formulated problems on this field.

The following two general observations can be seen as partial explanations of the difficultiness of these problems. First the *commutation requirement*, that is the fact that a word $z$ is in the centralizer only if two specified local operations $x\cdot$ and $\cdot y^{-1}$ together lead to another element of $Z$, resembles a computational step in *tag systems* of Post, cf. [12]. Second, the requirement is that, for all $x$ in $X$, there must exist an $y \in X$ such the $xzy^{-1}$ is again in $Z$. In other words, we have a problem of $\forall\exists$-type, and such problems are in many cases known to be difficult.

Despite of the above we would guess that the answer to Conway's Problem is affirmative – at least for finite $X$. Consequently, this problem would be a splended example of problems, which define something "simple", but to prove this seems to be very difficult. Of course, there exist similar "jewels" in the theory of rational languages. For example, the nonconstructive rationality of an equality set of two prefix morphisms is such an example, cf. [16]. Another example is Higman's theorem stating that for any language its upwards closure under the partial ordering of "being a scattered factor" is rational, cf. [9] or [2].

**Acknowledgement.** The author is grateful to M. Hirvensalo and I. Petre for useful comments.

## References

1. G. Bergman, Centralizers in free associative algebras, Trans. Amer. Math. Soc. 137, 327–344, 1969.
2. C. Choffrut and J. Karhumäki, Combinatorics of Words, In: G. Rozenberg and A. Salomaa (eds), Handbook of Formal Languages, vol. 1, 329–438, Springer, 1997.
3. C. Choffrut, J. Karhumäki and N. Ollinger, The commutation of finite sets: a challenging problem, Theoret. Comput. Sci., to appear.
4. P. M. Cohn, Centralizateurs dans les corps libre, In: J. Berstel (ed.), Séries Formelles 45–54, Paris, 1978.
5. J. H. Conway, Regular Algebra and Finite Machines, Chapman Hall, 1971.
6. K. Culik II and J. Karhumäki, manuscript, in preparation.
7. T. Harju, O. Ibarra, J. Karhumäki and A. Salomaa, Decision problems concerning semilinearity, morphisms and commutation of languages, Proceedings of ICALP01, to appear.
8. T. Harju and I. Petre, On commutation and primitive roots of codes, manuscript.
9. G. Higman, Ordering with divisibility in abstract algebras, Proc. London Math. Soc. 3, 326–336, 1952.
10. M. Hirvensalo, personal commutation.
11. J. Karhumäki and I. Petre, Conway's problem for three word sets, Theoret. Comput. Sci., to appear; preliminary version in LNCS 1853, 536–546.

12. M. Minsky, Computation: Finite and Infinite Machines, Prentice Hall, 1967.
13. D. Perrin, Codes conjugués, Inform. and Control 20, 221–231, 1972.
14. B. Ratoandramanana, Codes et motifs, RAIRO Theoret. Inform. 23, 425–444, 1989.
15. Ch. Reutenauer, Centralizers of Noncommutative Series and Polynomials, In: M. Lothaire, Algebraic Combinatorics on Words, Chapter 9, Cambridge University Press, to appear.
16. K. Ruohonen, Reversible machines and Post's correspondence problem for biprefix morphisms, J. Inform. Process. Cybernet. EIK 21, 579–595, 1985.

# Approximating Bounded Degree Instances of NP-Hard Problems

Marek Karpinski*

University of Bonn

**Abstract.** We present some of the recent results on computational complexity of approximating bounded degree combinatorial optimization problems. In particular, we present the best up to now known explicit nonapproximability bounds on the very small degree optimization problems which are of particular importance on the intermediate stages of proving approximation hardness of some other generic optimization problems.

## 1 Introduction

An interesting approximation hardness phenomenon of combinatorial optimization was discovered in [PY91] and [ALMSS92], to the effect that the bounded degree instances of several optimization problems are hard to approximate to within an arbitrary constant. This fact seemed to be a bit puzzling at the time as bounded degree instances of many optimization problems were known to have trivial approximation algorithms dramatically improving performances of the best known approximation algorithms on general instances. An interesting artifact on their *complementary*, i. e. dense, instances was also the existence of polynomial time approximation schemes (PTASs) for them [AKK95], [KZ97], see [K01] for a survey. We discuss here explicit approximation lower bounds for bounded degree instances with a very small bounds on degrees like 3 or 4, and also the best known approximation algorithms on that instances. These instances have turned out to be particularly important at the intermediate reduction stages for proving hardness of approximation of some other important optimization problems, like Set Cover, some restricted versions of Traveling Salesman Problem, and the problem of Sorting by Reversals motivated recently by molecular biology, cf. [F98], [PY91], [PY93], [BK99], [FK99], [E99], [EK00]. We mention here some interesting new results on asymptotic relations between hardness of approximation and bounds on a degree of instances [H00], [T01]. These results do not yield though explicit lower approximation bounds for small degree instances needed in applications mentioned before.

* Supported in part by DFG grants, DIMACS, and IST grant 14036 (RAND-APX), and by the Max-Planck Research Prize. Research partially done while visiting Department of Computer Science, Yale University. Email: marek@cs.uni-bonn.de.

R. Freivalds (Ed.): FCT 2001, LNCS 2138, pp. 24–34, 2001.

We survey in this paper the best known up to now explicit approximation lower bounds for the small degree (number of variable occurrences) optimization problems, like the problems of maximization or minimization of the satisfiability of systems of linear equations mod 2, MAX-CUT, MAX- and MIN-BISECTION, MAX-2SAT, MAXIMUM INDEPENDENT SET, and MINIMUM NODE COVER [BK99], [BK01b]. We move on, and apply these results to get explicit lower approximation bounds for the problem of Sorting by Reversals [BK99], and the Traveling Salesman Problem with distances one and two [EK00]. Finally, we mention recent improvement on approximation ratios of algorithms for small degree MAX-CUT and MAX-BISECTION problems based on local enhancing methods for semidefinite programming [FKL00a], [FKL00b], [KKL00].

## 2 Bounded Degree Maximization Problems

We are going to define basic optimization problems of this section.

- MAX-E$k$-LIN2: Given a set of equations mod 2 with exactly $k$ variables per equation, construct an assignment maximizing the number of equations satisfied.
- $b$-OCC-MAX-E$k$-LIN2: Given a set of equations mod 2 with exactly $k$ variables per equation and the number of occurrences of each variable bounded by $b$, construct an assignment maximizing the number of equations satisfied.
- $b$-OCC-MAX-HYBRID-LIN2: Given a set of equations mod 2 with exactly two or three variables per equation, and the number of occurrences of each variable bounded by $b$, construct an assignment maximizing the number of equations satisfied.
- $b$-OCC-MAX-2SAT: Given a conjunctive normal form formula with two variables per clause, construct an assignment maximizing the number of clauses satisfied.
- $d$-MAX-CUT: Given an undirected graph of degree bounded by $d$, partition its vertices into two groups so as to maximize the number of edges with exactly one endpoint in each group.
- $d$-MIS: Given an undirected graph of degree bounded by $d$, construct a maximum cardinality subset of vertices such that no two vertices of it are adjacent.

We are going to display now approximation preserving reductions which reduce from the MAX-E2-LIN2 and the MAX-E3-LIN2 problems. The method of reductions depends on a new *wheel-amplifier* construction of Berman and Karpinski [BK99] designed specially for bounded degree problems. This kind of amplifier has turned out to be more efficient than the standard expander amplifiers (cf. e.g., Arora and Lund [AL97]) for small degree, and number of occurrences, optimization problems.

We start with the following known inapproximability results of Håstad [H97].

**Theorem 1.** *([H97])* For any $0 < \epsilon < \frac{1}{2}$, it is NP-hard to decide whether an instance of MAX-E2-LIN2 with 16n equations has its optimum value above $(12 - \epsilon)n$ or below $(11 + \epsilon)$.

**Theorem 2.** *([H97])* For any $0 < \epsilon < \frac{1}{2}$, it is NP-hard to decide whether an instance of MAX-E3-LIN2 with $2n$ equations has its optimum value above $(2-\epsilon)n$ or below $(1+\epsilon)n$.

In Berman and Karpinski [BK99] the following polynomial time *randomized approximation preserving* reductions were constructed:

- $f_1$ : MAX-E2-LIN2 $\rightarrow$ 3-OCC-MAX-E2-LIN2,
- $f_2$ : MAX-E2-LIN2 $\rightarrow$ 3-MAX-CUT,
- $f_3$ : MAX-E3-LIN2 $\rightarrow$ 3-OCC-MAX-HYBRID-LIN2,

The constructions for $f_1$, and $f_2$ use variants of *wheel-amplifier* methods, whereas a construction for $f_3$ uses certain 3-hypergraph extension of it. The following *optimizing* properties of $f_1, f_2$, and $f_3$ were proven in [BK99].

**Theorem 3.** *([BK99])* For any $0 < \epsilon < \frac{1}{2}$, it is NP-hard to decide whether an instance of $f_1$(MAX-E2-LIN2) $\in$ 3-OCC-MAX-E2-LIN2 with 336 edges has its optimum value above $(332-\epsilon)n$ or below $(331+\epsilon)n$.

A similar result can be proven for $f_2$, and the 3-MAX-CUT-problem.

**Theorem 4.** *([BK99])* For any $0 < \epsilon < \frac{1}{2}$, it is NP-hard to decide whether an instance of $f_2$(MAX-E2-LIN2) $\in$ 3-MAX-CUT with 336 edges has its optimum value above $(332-\epsilon)n$ or below $(331+\epsilon)n$.

For $f_3$ and MAX-HYBRID-LIN2 we have

**Theorem 5.** *([BK99])* For any $0 < \epsilon < \frac{1}{2}$, it is NP-hard to decide whethr an instance of $f_3$(MAX-E3-LIN2) $\in$ 3-OCC-MAX-HYBRID-LIN2 with $60n$ equations with exactly two variables and $2n$ equations with exactly three variables has its optimum value above $(62-\epsilon)n$ or below $(61+\epsilon)n$.

Theorem 4 can be also used to derive the following bound for 3-OCC-MAX-2SAT.

**Theorem 6.** *([BK99])* For any $0 < \epsilon < \frac{1}{2}$, it is NP-hard to decide whether an instance of 3-OCC-MAX-2SAT, with $2016n$ clauses has its optimum above $(2012-\epsilon)n$ or below $(2011+\epsilon)n$.

The 3-OCC-MAX-HYBRID-LIN2 problem and Theorem 5 can be used to derive lower bounds for 4-MIS problem, and using some more subtle construction, even for 3-MIS problem.

**Theorem 7.** *([BK99])* For any $0 < \epsilon < \frac{1}{2}$, it is NP-hard to decide whether an instance of 4-MIS with $152n$ nodes has its optimum value above $(74-\epsilon)n$ or below $(73+\epsilon)n$, and whether an instance of 3-MIS with $284n$ nodes has its optimum value above $(140-\epsilon)n$ or below $(139+\epsilon)n$.

The results above imply the following explicit nonapproximability results.

**Corollary 1.** For every $\epsilon > 0$, it is NP-hard to approximate:

(1) *3-OCC-MAX-E2-LIN2 and 3-MAX-CUT to within a factor* $332/331 - \epsilon$,
(2) *3-OCC-MAX-HYBRID-LIN2 to within a factor* $62/61 - \epsilon$,
(3) *3-OCC-MAX-2SAT to within a factor* $2012/2011 - \epsilon$,
(4) *4-MIS to within a factor* $74/73 - \epsilon$*, and 3-MIS to within a factor* $140/139 - \epsilon$.

The best to our current knowledge gaps between upper and lower approximation bounds are summarized in Table 1. The upper approximation bounds are from [GW94], [BF94], [BF95], [FG95], [FKL00a].The technical results of this section will be used also later on in our paper.

**Table 1.** Bounded Degree Maximization Problems

| Problem | Approx. Upper | Approx. Lower |
|---|---|---|
| 3-OCC-MAX-E2-LIN2 | 1.0858 | 1.0030 |
| 3-OCC-MAX-HYBRID-LIN2 | 2 | 1.0163 |
| 3-MAX-CUT | 1.0858 | 1.0030 |
| 3-OCC-MAX-2SAT | 1.0741 | 1.0005 |
| 3-MIS | 1.2 | 1.0071 |
| 4-MIS | 1.4 | 1.0136 |

## 3 Bounded Degree Minimization Problems

We are going to introduce now the following minimization problems.

- d-Node Cover: Given an undirected graph of degree bounded by $d$, construct a minimum cardinality subset of vertices such that each edge of a graph has hat least one of its endpoints in it.
- MIN-E$k$-LIN2: Given a set of equations mod 2 with exactly $k$ variables per equation, construct an assignment minimizing the number of equations satisfied.
- $b$-OCC-MIN-E$k$-LIN2: Given a set of equations mod 2 with exactly $k$ variables per equation and the number of occurrences of each variable exactly equal to $b$, construct an assignment minimizing the number of equations satisfied.
- MIN-BISECTION: Given an undirected graph, partition the vertices into two equal halves so as to minimize the number of edges with exactly one endpoint in each half.

– *d*-MIN-BISECTION: Given a *d*-regular graph, partition the vertices into two equal halves so as to minimize the number of edges with exactly one endpoint in each half.

We will specialize now techniques of Section 2 to obtain lower approximation bounds on bounded degree minimization problems.

We start with a direct application of Theorem 7 towards d-Node Cover problem. For a given undirected graph $G = (V, E)$, and a *maximum independent* set $I$ of $G$, $V \backslash I$ is a *minimum node cover* of $G$. We take now an instance of 4-MIS with $152n$ nodes. It is NP-hard, for any $0 < \epsilon < \frac{1}{2}$, to decide whether 4-Node Cover has its optimum value above $(152 - 73 - \epsilon)n = (79 - \epsilon)n$ or below $(152 - 74 + \epsilon)n = (78 + \epsilon)n$. Similarly for 3-Node Cover. Thus we have

**Theorem 8.** For any $0 < \epsilon < \frac{1}{2}$, it is NP-hard to decide whether an instance of 4-Node Cover with $152n$ nodes has its optimum value above $(79 - \epsilon)n$ or below $(78 + \epsilon)n$, and whether an instance of 3-Node Cover with $284n$ has its optimum value above $(145 - \epsilon)n$ or below $(144 + \epsilon)n$.

Theorem 8 gives the following approximation lower bounds for 4-Node Cover and 3-Node Cover problems.

**Corollary 2.** For every $\epsilon > 0$, it is NP-hard to approximate

1. *3-Node Cover to within a factor* $145/144 - \epsilon$,
2. *4-Node Cover to within a factor* $79/78 - \epsilon$.

We turn now to the bounded occurrence minimum satisfiability of linear equations.

We need the following recent result of Dinur, Kindler, Raz and Safra [DKRS00] (see also [DKS98], [KST97]).

**Theorem 9.** *([DKRS00])* MIN-LIN2 is NP-hard to approximate to within a factor $n^{c/loglogn}$ for some constant c.

MIN-LIN2 is equivalent to the well known Nearest Codeword problem (cf. [ABSS93]). Only very recently the first sublinear approximation ratio $O(n/logn)$ algorithm was designed by Berman and Karpinski [BK01b].

We introduce now a notion of an $(r, t)$-approximation algorithm. For two functions $r$ and $t$, we call an approximation algorithm $A$ for an optimization problem $P$, an $(r(n), t(n))$-approximation algorithm if $A$ approximates $P$ within an approximation ratio $r(n)$ and $A$ works in $O(t(n))$ time for $n$ a size of an instance.

Berman and Karpinski [BK01b] proved the following result on the $(r, t)$-approximations of the 3-OCC-MIN-E3-LIN2 problem.

**Theorem 10.** *([BK01b])* There exists a constant $c$ such that if there exists an $(r(n), t(n))$-approximation algorithm for 3-OCC-MIN-E3-LIN2, then there exists an $(r(cn), t(cn))$-approximation algorithm for MIN-LIN2.

Theorem 9 entails now

**Theorem 11.** The problem 3-OCC-E3-LIN2 is NP-hard to approximate to within a factor $n^{c/loglogn}$ for some constant $c$.

The 3-OCC-MIN-E3-LIN2 problem is equivalent to the exactly-3 bounded occurrence 3-ary Nearest Codeword problem (c.f. [KST97]), and therefore we have

**Corollary 3.** The 3-ary Nearest Codeword problem with the number of occurrences of each variable exactly equal to 3 is NP-hard to approximate to within a factor $n^{c/loglogn}$ for some constant $c$.

We apply a similar technique for the problem of MIN-BISECTION. Here our result will be only relative to the approximation hardness of MIN-BISECTION, the status of which is wide open, and we know currently of no proof technique which excludes existence of a PTAS for that problem.

Somewhat surprisingly in that context, Berman and Karpinski [BK01b] proved the following result on approximation hardness of bounded degree version of MIN-BISECTION.

**Theorem 12.** *([BK01b])* If there exists an $(r(n), t(n))$-approximation algorithm for 3-MIN-BISECTION, then there exists an $(r(n^3), t(n^3))$- approximation algorithm for MIN-BISECTION.

The best currently known approximation algorithm for the MIN-BISECTION is $O(log^2 n)$ due to Feige and Krauthgamer [FK00]. Any asymptotic improvement on approximation ratio $r$ for 3-regular graphs, say $r = o(log^2 n)$, will entail, by Theorem 11, an improvement on an approximation ratio for the general MIN-BISECTION.

A similar technique can be also used to prove approximation hardness result for the general planar MIN-BISECTION of the planar MIN-BISECTION problem on 3-regular graphs.

## 4 Some Application

We are going to apply our previous results for some other generic optimization problems. The first problem is one of the most important problems in analysis of genome rearrangements, and it is being recently also motivated by other algorithmic problems of computational molecular biology.

- MIN-SBR (Sorting by Reversals): Given a permutation, construct a minimum length sequence of reversals (see for definitions [BP96]) which transforms it to the identity permutation.

We refer also to some other variants of Sorting by Reversals problems studied in [C99], called MSBR and Tree SBR (see the definitions there).

The proof technique used in [BK99] to prove explicit approximation lower bound of Theorem 7 for 4-MIS can be adapted to prove for the first time the inapproximability of MIN-SBR, and, in fact, also giving an explicit approximation lower bound for that problem.

**Theorem 13.** *([BK99])* For every $\epsilon > 0$, it is NP-hard to approximate MIN-SBR within a factor $1237/1236 - \epsilon$.

Caprara [C99] has used the above result to prove inapproximability of the both beforementioned problems, MSBR, and Tree SBR, and to compute the first explicit approximation lower bounds for those problems.

We turn now to another application of the results of Section 2. We denote by (1,2)-TSP the Traveling Salesman Problem with distances one and two, and its asymmetric version by (1,2)-ATSP (cf. [PY93], [V92]).

Engebretsen and Karpinski [EK00] has used recently the result on 3-OCC-MAX-HYBRID-LIN2 of Theorem 5 to prove the following explicit inapproximability result for (1,2)-ATSP problem.

**Theorem 14.** *([EK00])* For every $\epsilon > 0$, it is NP-hard to approximate (1,2)-ATSP within a factor $321/320 - \epsilon$.

The construction used by Engebretsen and Karpinski [EK00] could be also adapted to yield an explicit result for (1,2)-TSP.

**Theorem 15.** *([EK00])* For every $\epsilon > 0$, it is NP-hard to approximate (1,2)-TSP within a factor $743/742 - \epsilon$.

## 5 New Upper Approximation Bounds

The intricacy of proving the first explicit approximation lower bounds for small degree optimization problems, and the resulting huge gaps between upper and lower approximation bounds has stimulated research on improving approximation ratios for those problems as well as for some other generic problems.

The first gap for 3-MAX-CUT (and 3-OCC-MAX-E2-LIN2) was improved recently by Feige, Karpinski and Langberg [FKL00a], see Table 1. The technique of [FKL00a] is based on a new local enhancing method for semidefinite programs.

**Theorem 16.** *([FKL00a])* There exists a polynomial time algorithm approximating 3-MAX-CUT within a factor 1.0858.

We note that the best approximation ratio currently known for MAX-CUT problem on general graphs is 1.1383 ([GW94]), and the best known approximation lower bound is 1.0624 [H97]. We note also that for the semidefinite relaxation of MAX-CUT used in [GW94], the integrality gap is at least 1.1312, even for 2-regular graphs. Thus the bound of Theorem 16 beats the integrality bound even for 2-regular graphs.

We turn now to the special case of regular bounded degree graphs, and will investigate approximation algorithms for the MAX-CUT and MAX-BISECTION (partitioning of a graph into two halves so as to maximize a number of the edges between them).

R$d$-MAX-CUT and R$d$-MAX-BISECTION are the MAX-CUT and MAX-BISECTION problems, respectively, restricted to $d$-regular graphs.

Feige, Karpinski and Langberg [FKL00a], [FKL00b] were able to improve the best known approximation ratios for both bounded degree problems, R$d$-MAX-CUT, and R$d$-MAX-BISECTION. The best known approximation ratio for MAX-BISECTION on general graphs is 1.4266 [HZ00].

**Theorem 17.** *([FKL00a], [FKL00b])* There are polynomial time algorithms that approximate R3-MAX-CUT and R3-MAX-BISECTION problems within factor 1.0823 and 1.1991, respectively.

Using an additional local adhancement method, Karpinski, Kowaluk and Lingas [KKL00], have further improved approximation ratios of the low degree R$d$-MAX-BISECTION problems.

**Theorem 18.** *([KKL00])* There exists a polynomial time algorithm approximating R3-MAX-BISECTION within a factor 1.1806.

Interestingly, the first improvements on approximation ratios of MAX-BISECTION on low degree planar graphs undertaken in [KKL00] has lead to design of the first PTASs for the general planar MAX-BISECTION as well as for other geometrically defined classes of graphs (see [JKLS01]).

On the lower bounds side, we note that the techniques of [BK99] yield also the best up to now explicit approximation lower bounds for R3-MAX-CUT, and R3-MAX-BISECTION problems equal to the lower approximation bound for 3-MAX-CUT problem of Section 2.

## 6 Summary of Approximation Results on Bounded Degree Minimization Problems

We present here (Table 2) the results of Section 3 and 4 on bounded degree minimization problems and the best to our knowledge gaps between upper and lower approximation bounds on those problems. The upper approximation bounds are from [BF94], [BF95], [BK01b], [FK00], [BHK01], [V92], [PY93].

## 7 Open Problems and Further Research

An obvious open problem is to improve on both the lower and upper approximation bounds of bounded degree optimization problems, especially on those with the very small degree bounds. The essential improvements on the explicit lower bounds for these problems might be of paramount difficulty though, but same time they are also of great interest. Any such improvement would have immediate effects on the explicit lower bounds for other optimization problems, as

**Table 2.** Bounded Degree and Weight Minimization Problems

| Problem | Approx. Upper | Approx. Lower |
|---|---|---|
| 3-Node Cover | 1.1666 | 1.0069 |
| 4-Node Cover | 1.2857 | 1.0128 |
| 3-OCC-MIN-E3-LIN2 | $O$(n/logn) | $n^{\Omega(1)/\log\log n}$ |
| 3-MIN-BISECTION | $O(\log^2 n)$ | Equal to MIN-BISECTION |
| MIN-SBR | 1.375 | 1.0008 |
| (1,2)-TSP | 1.1667 | 1.0013 |
| (1,2)-ATSP | 1.4167 | 1.0031 |

indicated in this paper. Perhaps somewhat easier undertaking would be improving on upper approximation bounds. Here essential improvements were already achieved on the problems like a small degree MAX-CUT, and MAX-BISECTION mentioned in Section 5. How about improvements on other bounded degree optimization problems?

## References

[ABSS93] S. Arora, L. Babai, J. Stern and Z. Sweedyk, *The Hardness of Approximate Optima in Lattice, Codes, and Systems of Linear Equations*, Proc. of 34th IEEE FOCS, 1993, 724-733.

[AKK95] S. Arora, D. Karger, and M. Karpinski, *Polynomial Time Approximation Schemes for Dense Instances of NP-Hard Problems*, Proc. 27th ACM STOC (1995), pp. 284-293; the full version appeared in J. Comput. System Sciences 58 (1999), pp. 193-210.

[AL97] S. Arora and C. Lund, *Hardness of Approximations*, in *Approximation Algorithms for NP-Hard Problems* (D. Hochbaum, ed.), PWS Publ. Co. (1997), pp. 399-446.

[ALMSS92] S. Arora, C. Lund, R. Motwani, M. Sudan and M. Szegedy, *Proof Verification and Hardness of Approximation Problems*, Proc. 33rd IEEE FOCS (1992), pp. 14-20.

[BF94] P. Berman and M. Fürer, *Approximating Maximum Independent Set in Bounded Degree Graphs*, Proc. 5th ACM-SIAM SODA (1994), pp. 365-371.

[BF95] P. Berman and T. Fujito, *Approximating independent sets in degree 3 graphs*, Proc. 4th Workshop on Algorithms and Data Structures, LNCS Vol. 955, Springer-Verlag, 1995, pp. 449-460.

[BHK01] P. Berman, S. Hannenhalli and Karpinski, *1.375-Approximation Algorithm for Sorting by Reversals*, Manuscript, 2001.

[BK99] P. Berman and M. Karpinski, *On Some Tighter Inapproximability Results*, Proc. 26th ICALP (1999), LNCS 1644, Springer, 1999, pp. 200-209.

[BK01a] P. Berman and M. Karpinski, *Approximating Minimum Unsatisfiability of Linear Equations*, ECCC Technical Report TR01-025 (2001).

[BK01b] P. Berman and M. Karpinski, *Approximation Hardness of Bounded Degree MIN-CSP and MIN-BISECTION*, ECCC Technical Report TR01-026 (2001).

[BP96] V. Bafna and P. Pevzner, *Genome Rearrangements and Sorting by Reversals*, SIAM J. on Computing 25 (1996), pp. 272-289.

[C99] A. Caprara *Formulations and Hardness of Multiple Sorting by Reversals*, Proc. ACM RECOMB'99, pp. 84-93.

[DKS98] I. Dinur, G. Kindler and S. Safra, *Approximating CVP to Within Almost Polynomial Factors is NP-hard*, Proc. of 39th IEEE FOCS, 1998, 99-109.

[DKRS00] I. Dinur, G. Kindler, R. Raz and S. Safra, *An Improved Lower Bound for Approximating CVP*, 2000, submitted.

[E99] L. Engebretsen, *An Explicit Lower Bound for TSP with Distances One and Two*, Proc. 16th STACS (1999), LNCS 1563 (1999), Springer, 1999, pp. 371-382.

[EK00] L. Engebretsen and M. Karpinski, *Approximation Hardness of TSP with Bounded Metrics*, ECCC Technical Report TR00-089 (2000), to appear in Proc. 28th ICALP (2001).

[F98] U. Feige, *A Threshold of ln n for Approximation Set Cover*, J. of ACM **45** (1998), pp. 634-652.

[FG95] U. Feige and M. Goemans, *Approximating the Value of Two Prover Proof Systems with Applications to MAX-2SAT and MAX-DICUT*, Proc. 3rd Israel Symp. on Theory of Computing and Systems, 1995, pp. 182-189.

[FK00] U. Feige and R. Krauthgamer, *A Polylogarithmic Approximation of the Minimum Bisection*, Proc. 41st IEEE FOCS (2000), pp. 105 - 115.

[FKL00a] U. Feige, M. Karpinski, and M. Langberg, *Improved Approximation of MAX-CUT on Graphs of Bounded Degree*, ECCC Technical Report TR00-021 (2000), submitted to J. of Algorithms.

[FKL00b] U. Feige, M. Karpinski, and M. Langberg, *A Note on Approximation MAX-BISECTION on Regular Graphs*, ECCC Technical Report TR00-043 (2000), to appear in Information Processing Letters.

[FK99] W. Fernandez de la Vega and M. Karpinski, *On Approximation Hardness of Dense TSP and Other Path Problems*, Information Processing Letters 70 (1999), pp. 53-55.

[GW94] M. Goemans and D. Williamson, *.878-approximation Algorithms for MAX-CUT and MAX2SAT*, Proc. 26th ACM STOC (1994), pp. 422-431.

[H97] J. Håstad, *Some Optimal Inapproximability Results*, Proc. 29th ACM STOC (1997), pp. 1-10.

[H00] J. Håstad, *On Bounded Occurrence Constraint Satisfaction*, Information Processing Letters 74 (2000), pp. 1-6.

[HZ00] E. Halperin and U. Zwick, *Improved Approximation Algorithms for Maximum Graph Bisection Problems*, Manuscript, 2000.

[JKLS01] K. Jansen, M. Karpinski, A. Lingas, and E. Seidel, *Polynomial Time Approximation Schemes for MAX-BISECTION on Planar and Geometric Graphs*, Proc. 18th STACS (2001), LNCS 2010, Springer, 2001, pp. 365-375.

[K01] M. Karpinski, *Polynomial Time Approximation Schemes for Some Dense Instances of NP-Hard Optimization Problems*, Algorithmica **30** (2001), pp. 386-397.

[KKL00] M. Karpinski, M. Kowaluk, and A. Lingas, *Approximation Algorithms for MAX-BISECTION on Low Degree Regular Graphs and Planar Graphs*, ECCC Technical Report TR00-051 (2000).

[KZ97] M. Karpinski and A. Zelikovsky, *Approximating Dense Cases of Covering Problems*, ECCC Technical Report TR 97-004, 1997, also in Proc. DIMACS Workshop on Network Design: Connectivity and Facilities Location, Princeton, 1997, DIMACS Series in Discrete Mathematics and Theoretical Computer Science 40 (1998), pp. 169-178.

[KST97] S. Khanna, M. Sudan and L. Trevisan, *Constraint Satisfaction: the approximability of minimization problems*, Proc. of 12th IEEE Computational Complexity, 1997, 282-296.

[PY91] C. Papadimitriou and M. Yannakakis, *Optimization, Approximation and Complexity Classes*, J. Comput. System Sciences 43 (1991), pp. 425-440.

[PY93] C. H. Papadimitriou and M. Yannakakis, *The Traveling Salesman Problem with Distances One and Two*, Math. of Oper. Res. 18 (1993), pp. 1-11.

[T01] L.Trevisan, *Non-approximability Results for Optimization Problems on Bounded Degree Instances*, to appear in Proc. 33rd ACM STOC (2001).

[V92] S. Virhwanathan, *An Approximation Algorithm for the Asymetric Travelling Salesman Problem with Distances One and Two*, Information Processing Letters 44 (1992), pp. 297-302.

# Universal Algebra and Computer Science

Boris Plotkin[1] and Tanya Plotkin[2]

[1] Institute of Mathematics, The Hebrew University,
Jerusalem 91904, Israel
borisov@math.huji.ac.il
[2] Department of Mathematics and Computer Science
Bar-Ilan University, 52-900 Ramat-Gan, Israel
plot@macs.biu.ac.il

**Abstract.** This paper considers interrelations between universal algebra, algebraic logic, geometry and computer science. The key idea of the paper is to show that problems, coming from computer science, require introducing of highly non-trivial mathematical structures. On the other hand, algebraic models in computer science give deeper understanding of problems essence.
This general idea is illustrated on the example of knowledge bases. Theorems concerning the knowledge base equivalence problem are formulated.

## 1 Introduction

Universal algebra had been started from the clear desire to illuminate the common core of various classical algebraic structures, that is to distinguish the common features of groups, semigroups, rings, and others. The development of universal algebra gave rise also to its own new problems, which have been inspired by the ties with logic and category theory.

At the meantime the progress of universal algebra is determined, to great extent, by its computer science ties. In particular, computer science applications motivate the use of operations with arbitrary arity and a special attention is paid on multysorted algebras. Computer science also extends the application area of algebraic logic.

Algebraic models in computer science are intended to give better explanation of the essence of the problems. This general rule works in the database theory, in knowledge theory and also in the theory of computations.

On the other hand, computer science stimulates the appearance of new ideas, problems and constructions in universal algebra. This exchange essentially enriches algebra and category theory (see for example [1], [2], [3], [4], [5], [6], [8], [9]).

It should be underlined specially that the interrelations between algebra and computer science assume heavy use of advanced algebraic structures, which are far from simple algebraic notions.

These general statements we will illustrate on the example of knowledge bases. We will formulate two theorems concerning the knowledge bases equivalence problem. These theorems produce an algorithm for processing of such an

R. Freivalds (Ed.): FCT 2001, LNCS 2138, pp. 35–44, 2001.

equivalence. They can be used in practice ignoring all algebraic difficulties of their proofs [7], [8].

In the next section we give all necessary preliminary notions.

## 2 Knowledge

We consider elementary knowledge, i.e., knowledge represented in the First Order Logic (FOL).

We assume that there are three components of knowledge:

1) The *description* of the knowledge.

It is the syntactical part of the knowledge, written out in the language of the given logic. The description reflects, what we want to know. In knowledge bases (KB) it is a query.

2) The *subject* of the knowledge which is an object in the given field of application, that is, an object for which we determine knowledge.

3) *Content* of the knowledge (its semantics). This is a reply in KBs.

The first two components are relatively independent, while the third one is uniquely determined by the previous two.

The following example explains this approach. Let $R$ be a field of real numbers. Consider it as a *subject* of knowledge. Knowledge is *described* by a system of equations $T$ of $n$ variables with real coefficients. *Content* of knowledge is the locus in the space $R^n$ given by the system of equations $T$.

We will consider also a situation when the system $T$ contains not only equalities, but arbitrary formulas of FOL. In other words, we describe knowledge in some logical language and interpret its content as a geometrical image. This is the starting point for further considerations.

## 3 Algebra

In the subsequent three sections we give background on algebra, logic and geometry.

Fix a variety of algebras $\Theta$, reflecting knowledge type. It is given by a system of operations $\Omega$ and a system of identities controlling operations action. For example, we have a variety of all boolean algebras or a variety of automata.

An important fact is that every variety contains free algebras. Elements of a free algebra $W = W(X)$ for a set $X$ are terms (or $\Theta$-terms, or $\Theta$-words). They are built from the elements of the set $X$ with the help of operations of the system $\Omega$ and the rules of the variety $\Theta$. The main property of these $W$ can be expressed by formula

$$\begin{array}{ccc} X & \xrightarrow{id} & W \\ & {}_{\nu}\searrow & \downarrow \mu \\ & & G \end{array}$$

*id* - embedding of $X$ in $W = W(X)$

$\nu$ - calculates the value of variables in an arbitrary algebra $G \in \Theta$

$\mu$ - calculates the value of terms in $G$

$\mu$ is a homomorphism of algebras, extending the mapping $\mu$. It is fully determined by *id* and $\nu$.

Along with algebras we consider also *models.* A system of symbols of relations $\Phi$ is fixed. The symbols are realized in the algebras $G$ from $\Theta$. In the model $(G, \Phi, f)$ the function $f$ realizes every symbol $\varphi \in \Phi$ in the given algebra $G$. If a symbol $\varphi$ is a symbol of $n$-ary relation, then $f(\varphi)$ is a subset in the space $G^n$. Further we will regard such functions $f$ as *instances* of a KB.

In the sequel the models $(G, \Phi, f)$ represent subject of knowledge.

In order to compare KBs we need a notion of *multimodel* $(G, \Phi, F)$, where $F$ is a set of admissible realizations $f$. We write $KB = KB(G, \Phi, F)$.

A reply to a query to a KB is a subset in some $G^n$, $G \in \Theta$. Cartesian powers $G^n$ we consider as affine spaces of points. Elements of $G^n$ are points $a = (a_1, \ldots, a_n)$, $a_i \in G$. Thus a reply to a query accepts a geometrical meaning and therefore the geometrical approach starts.

Another presentation of an affine space $G^n$, more suitable in our case, is the set $Hom(W(X), G)$ of all homomorphisms $\mu : W(X) \to G$ for the set $X = \{x_1, \ldots, x_n\}$.

A bijection

$$\alpha_X : Hom(W(X), G) \to G^n$$

is determined by the rule $\alpha_X(\mu) = (\mu(x_1), \ldots, \mu(x_n))$. This rule allows to consider the set $Hom(W(X), G)$ as an affine space. Now the points are homomorphisms $\mu : W(X) \to G$.

## 4 Logic

We have to deal not with a pure logic but with logic in a given variety $\Theta$. Fix a variety $\Theta$, a set of symbols of relations $\Phi$, and a finite set of variables $X$. Consider a set of symbols of logical operations

$$L_X = L = \{\vee, \wedge, \neg, \exists x, x \in X\}$$

We describe knowledge with the help of a set (algebra) of formulas, denoted by $L\Phi W(X)$, $X$ is finite. The set $L\Phi W(X)$ consists of atomic formulas of the form

$$w \equiv w', \text{ and } \varphi(w_1, \ldots, w_n), \ \varphi \in \Phi, \quad w, w', w_1, \ldots, w_n \in W(X).$$

and arbitrary formulas which are built from atomic ones using operations from the signature $L$.

Along with algebra of formulas, we consider another algebra in the same signature $L$, denoted by $Bool(W(X), G)$. It consists of all subsets of the affine space $Hom(W(X), G)$. Boolean operations $\vee, \wedge, \neg$ are defined in the usual way. Let us define quantifiers. For $A \subset Hom(W(X), G)$ we set

$$\mu \in \exists x A \quad \Leftrightarrow \quad \exists \nu \in A : \mu(y) = \nu(y) \ \ \forall y \neq x.$$

This definition exactly reflects the geometrical meaning of the existential quantifier.

In order to obtain content of knowledge by its description, let us define the notion of the value of a formula. Denote by $Val(u)$, $u \in L\Phi W$ the value of a formula for a model $(G, \Phi, f)$. Here $Val(u)$ is a subset of an affine space $Hom(W(X), G)$. Define the value of atomic formulas:

$$1) \quad \mu : W \to G \in Val(w \equiv w') \quad \Leftrightarrow \quad w^{\mu} = w'^{\mu} \quad in \;\; G.$$

$$2) \quad \mu \in Val(\varphi(w_1, \ldots, w_n)) \quad \Leftrightarrow \quad (w_1^{\mu}, \ldots, w_n^{\mu}) \in f(\varphi).$$

Values of arbitrary formulas are defined by induction, using the rules:

$$Val(u_1 \vee u_2) = Val(u_1) \cup Val(u_2),$$

$$Val(u_1 \wedge u_2) = Val(u_1) \cap Val(u_2),$$

$$Val(\exists x u) = \exists x Val(u).$$

Here, for example, $u_1 \vee u_2$ is a formal description of knowledge, while $Val(u_1) \cup Val(u_2)$ is its content.

It follows from the definitions above, that the value of the formula $\varphi(x_1, \ldots, x_n)$ on the model $(G, \Phi, f)$ determines the instance $f$ of the model, namely

$$\alpha_X Val_f(\varphi((x_1, \ldots, x_n)) = f(\varphi).$$

Consider a correspondence between the description of the knowledge and its content. Let $T$ be a set of formulas of $L\Phi W$, determining description of knowledge. Let us define content of knowledge $T^f$ for the subject of knowledge (model) $(G, \Phi, f)$ by the rule

$$T^f = \bigcap_{u \in T} Val(u).$$

From the *geometrical point of view* the knowledge content $T^f$ is an *algebraic variety of points* in the affine space $Hom(W, G)$, or locus. In the next section we will consider geometrical nature of such content of knowledge.

## 5 Geometry

According to the approach above, one can look at knowledge content as at geometric object, namely, an algebraic variety in the corresponding affine space. Algebraic variety turns to be a geometrical object if we consider it in the frames of some special category. Denote by $K_{\Phi\Theta}(f)$ a category of algebraic varieties for the given model $(G, \Phi, f)$. Objects of this category are pairs $(X, A)$, where $A$ is an algebraic variety in the space $Hom(W, G)$. Morphisms $(X, A) \to (Y, B)$ are given by homomorphisms of algebras $s : W(Y) \to W(X)$. To every $s$ it corresponds a map of affine spaces

$$\tilde{s} : Hom(W(X), G) \to Hom(W(Y), G)$$

defined by the rule: for the point $\nu : W(X) \to G$ we set $\tilde{s}(\nu) = \nu s : W(Y) \to H$. In order to define morphisms we take those $s$ for which $\tilde{s}(\nu) \in B$ for every point $\nu \in A$. These $s$ are considered as morphisms in the category $K_{\Phi\Theta}(f)$. Such morphisms give connections between algebraic varieties. In particular, for every object $(X, A)$ morphisms $(X, A) \to (X, A)$ are tied with the movement inside given $A$.

This is the *first* occurrence of geometry in $A$. Another dynamics in $A$ relates to the group of automorphisms of the model $Aut(f)$, also acting in $A$ and giving the *second* occurrence of geometry. The *third* one is appeared as the system of all subvarieties in the given algebraic variety.

## 6 Category of Knowledge

Category of knowledge is defined for the model $(G, \Phi, f)$ and is denoted by $Know_{\Phi\Theta}(f)$. Its objects (knowledge) are denoted by $(X, T, A)$. In addition to the content of knowledge $A$ we fix its description $T$. Morphisms

$$s : (X, T_1, A) \to (Y, T_2, B)$$

are given like in the category $K_{\Phi\Theta}(f)$. It is proven that they connect not only content of knowledge but also its description.

## 7 Algebraic Logic

Construction of algebraic model of knowledge base requires replacement of the pure logic by algebraic logic.

Every logical calculus assumes that there are some definite sets of formulas of the calculus, axioms of logic and rules of inference. This is the base to define the syntactic equivalence of formulas, well correlated with their semantical equivalence. The transition from logic to algebraic logic is grounded on treating logical formulas up to such equivalence which gives compressed formulas.

This transition leads to various special algebraic structures. Boolean algebras, associated with the propositional turns to be the free boolean algebra. Similarly, Heyting algebras, associated with intuitionistic propositional calculus turn to be the free Heyting algebras. However, for FOL the corresponding algebraic structures are not free.

The construction of logical calculus usually assumes some fixed infinite set of variables. Let us denote it by $X^0$. It looks better to substitute this universal $X^0$ by the system of all its finite subsets $X$. This leads us to multisorted logic and multisorted algebraic logic. Every formula here has its sort $X$. In particular, we come to multisorted Halmos algebras, defined further. This gives some new view of the algebraization of FOL. Besides, let us note that the logic here is related to a fixed variety of algebras $\Theta$ (compare [5]). We need all this for universal algebraic geometry and applications in knowledge science.

We fix here some variety of algebras $\Theta$. This assumes a signature $\Omega = \Omega(\Theta)$ and a system of identities $Id(\Theta)$.

Further we define Halmos categories for the given $\Theta$.

First we define existential quantifiers for a given Boolean algebra $B$. These are the mappings $\exists : B \to B$ with conditions

1. $\exists 0 = 0$
2. $a < \exists a,\ a(\exists a) = a$
3. $\exists(a \wedge \exists b) = \exists a \wedge \exists b,\ \ 0, a, b \in B$

Quantifiers $\forall : B \to B$ are defined dually:

1. $\forall 1 = 1$
2. $a > \forall a$
3. $\forall(a \wedge \forall B) = \forall a \wedge \forall b$

Let now $B$ be a Boolean algebra and $X$ a set. We say that $B$ is a quantorian $X$-algebra if for every $x \in X$ we have a quantifier $\exists x : B \to B$ and for every two $x, y \in X$ it holds the equality $\exists x \exists y = \exists y \exists x$.

One may consider also *quantifier $X$-algebras $B$ with equalities* over $W(X)$. In such algebras to each pair of elements $w, w' \in W(X)$ of it corresponds an element $w \equiv w' \in B$ satisfying the conditions

1) $w \equiv w$ is the unit in $B$

2) $(w_1 \equiv w_1' \wedge \ldots \wedge w_n \equiv w_n') < (w_1 \ldots w_n \omega \equiv w_1' \ldots w_n' \omega)$ where $\omega$ is an operation in $\Omega$.

Now for the given variety $\Theta$ we consider the category $\Theta^0$ of all free in $\Theta$ algebras $W = W(X)$, where $X$ is an arbitrary finite set. Morphisms here are homomorphisms in $\Theta$. The category $\Theta^0$ plays an important role in equational geometry.

The same role in the geometry in FOL plays the category $\mathrm{Hal}_{\Phi\Theta}$ of formulas in FOL. This category $\mathrm{Hal}_{\Phi\Theta}$ are connected with the category $\Theta^0$. An arbitrary Halmos category $H$ for every finite $X$ fixes some quantorian $X$-algebra with equalities $H(X)$. These are objects in $H$.

The morphisms in $H$ are connected with morphisms in $\Theta^0$. For every $s : W(X) \to W(Y)$in $\Theta^0$ we have a morphism

$$s_* = s : H(X) \to H(Y).$$

These are all morphisms in $H$.

We assume that

1) The transitions $W(X) \to H(X)$ and $s \to s_*$ constitute a (covariant) functor $\Theta^0 \to H$.

2) Every $s_* : H(X) \to H(Y)$ is a Boolean homomorphism.

3) The coordination with the quantifiers is the following:

3.1) $s_1 \exists x a = s_2 \exists x a,\ \ a \in H(X)$ if $s_1 y = s_2 y$ for every $y \in X, y \neq x$.

3.2) $s \exists x a = \exists (sx)(sa)$ if $sx = y \in Y$ and $y = sx$ does not lie in the support of $sx', x' \in X, x' \neq x$.

4) The following conditions describe coordination with equalities

4.1) $s_*(w \equiv w') = (sw \equiv sw')$ for $s$: $W(X) \to W(Y)$, $w, w' \in W(X)$.

4.2) $s^x_w a \wedge (w \equiv w') < s^x_{w'} a$ for an arbitrary $a \in H(X)$, $x \in X$, $w, w' \in W(X)$, and $s^x_w: W(X) \to W(X)$ is defined by the rule: $s^x_w(x) = w, sy = y, y \in X,\ y \neq x$.

So, the definition of Halmos category is given.

Suppose now that all finite $X$ are subsets of some infinite universum $X^0$. In this case the Halmos category can be considered as a multisorted Halmos algebra.

Multisorted Halmos algebra is an algebra of the form

$$H = (H(X), X \subset X^0)$$

where every $H(X)$ is an object of the category $H$ with its algebraic structure and morphisms of the category are considered to be algebraic operations on the algebra $H$.

Multisorted Halmos algebras determine a variety which is denoted by $Hal_\Theta$.

The principal examples of Halmos algebras and categories have the form $Hal_\Theta(\Phi)$ and $Hal_\Theta(G)$, where $\Phi$ is a set of symbols of relations and $G$ is an algebra in the variety $\Theta$. The algebra $Hal_\Theta(\Phi)$ is the algebra of compressed formulas. The algebra $Hal_\Theta(G)$ is defined by

$$\mathrm{Hal}_\Theta(G)(X) = Bool(W(X), G)$$

and for every $s : W(X) \to W(Y)$ in $\Theta^0$ we have

$$s = s_* : Bool(W(X), G) \to Bool(W(Y), G),$$

in $Hal_\Theta(G)$.

For every model $(G.\Phi, f)$ there is a homomorphism of Halmos algebras

$$\mathrm{Val}_f : \mathrm{Hal}_\Theta(\Phi) \to \mathrm{Hal}_\Theta(G).$$

This homomorphism computes values of the formulas.

## 8 Knowledge Bases

We do not give here a formal definition of a knowledge base as a mathematical structure. Instead, we provide a kind of descriptive definition that uses the main ingredients of the formal one.

Knowledge base is defined for a fixed multimodel $(G, \Phi, F)$, $G \in \Theta$. The variety of algebras $\Theta$ is fixed. As a logical ground of knowledge bases we take the Halmos algebra $Hal_\Theta(\Phi)$.

Take $T \subset Hal_\Theta(\Phi)(X)$ and $A \subset Hal_\Theta(G)(X)$. For $f \in F$ we set

$$T^f = A = \bigcap_{u \in T} Val_f(u)$$

$$A^f = T = \{u | A \subset Val_f(u)\}$$

The set $T$ is considered as knowledge description. This is a query to knowledge base.

The set $A = T^f$ is a content of knowledge, i.e., the reply to a query. By definition, a reply to a query is an algebraic set and it is an object of the category $K_{\Phi\Theta}(f)$.

The set $T = A^f$ is a filter of the boolean algebra $Hal_\Theta(\Phi)(X)$. The factor algebra by this filter is an invariant of the algebraic set $A$.

## 9 Isomorphism and Equivalence of Knowledge Bases

Let two multimodels $(G_1, \Phi_1, F_1)$ and $(G_2, \Phi_2, F_2)$ be given. Denote the corresponding knowledge bases by $KB_1$ and $KB_2$. In order to compare them, let us define the notion of isomorphism of knowledge bases.

**Definition 1**
*Knowledge bases $KB_1$ and $KB_2$ are isomorphic, if $\Phi_1 = \Phi_2 = \Phi$ and*

1. *There is a bijection $\alpha : F_1 \to F_2$,*
2. *For all $f \in F_1$ there is an isomorphism of categories*
$$\gamma_f : K_{\Phi\Theta}(f) \to K_{\Phi\Theta}(f^\alpha)$$
*i.e., $\gamma_f$ is a bijection on the objects, preserving all links,*
3. *For all $T$ it holds*
$$\gamma_f(T^f) = T^{f^\alpha}, \quad f \in F_1.$$

The notion of equivalence is much weaker. First, $\Phi_1 = \Phi_2$ is not required, and, second, knowledge bases meet only two conditions.

**Definition 2**
*Knowledge bases $KB_1$ and $KB_2$ are equivalent, if*

1. *There is a bijection $\alpha : F_1 \to F_2$,*
2. *For all $f \in F_1$ there is an isomorphism of categories*
$$\gamma_f : K_{\Phi_1\Theta}(f) \to K_{\Phi_2\Theta}(f^\alpha).$$

It is proven that such a definition of equivalence exactly reflects the idea of informational equivalence of knowledge bases.

## 10 Main Results

**Definition 3**
*Multimodels $(G_1, \Phi, F_1)$ and $(G_2, \Phi, F_2)$ are isomorphic if there is a bijection $\alpha : F_1 \to F_2$ such that the models $(G_1, \Phi, f)$ and $(G_2, \Phi, f^\alpha)$ are isomorphic.*

**Theorem 1**
*Knowledge bases $KB_1$ and $KB_2$ with the finite $G_1$, $G_2$ are isomorphic if and only if the corresponding multimodels are isomorphic.*

**Definition 4**
*Models $(G_1, \Phi_1, f_1)$ and $(G_2, \Phi_2, f_2)$ are automorphic equivalent if*

1. *Algebras $G_1$ and $G_2$ are isomorphic,*
2. *Groups of automorphisms $Aut(f_1)$ and $Aut(f_2)$ are conjugated by some isomorphism $\delta : G_2 \to G_1$, i.e., $Aut(f_2) = \delta^{-1} Aut(f_1)\delta$.*

**Definition 5**
*Multimodels $(G_1, \Phi_1, F_1)$ and $(G_2, \Phi_2, F_2)$ are automorphic equivalent if there is a bijection $\alpha : F_1 \to F_2$ for which the models $(G_1, \Phi_1, f)$ and $(G_2, \Phi_2, f^\alpha)$ are automorphic equivalent for all $f \in F_1$.*

**Theorem 2**
*Knowledge bases $KB_1$ and $KB_2$ with finite $G_1$, $G_2$ are equivalent if and only if the multimodels $(G_1, \Phi_1, F_1)$ and $(G_2, \Phi_2, F_2)$ are automorphic equivalent.*

These two theorems allow to build an algorithm of verification of knowledge bases isomorphism and equivalence.

Proofs of these results are based on a special Galois-Krasner theory which is built for this particular situation.

*Example*
There are a lot of automorphic equivalent but not isomorphic boolean models, that certifies that isomorphism is much more strict condition for informational equivalence. For example, let an arbitrary boolean algebra $B$ be given. Consider a ternary symbol of relation $\varphi$ which is realised on $B$ in two ways: for $a, b, c \in B$

$$(a, b, c) \in f_1(\varphi) \quad \Leftrightarrow \quad a \vee b = c,$$

$$(a, b, c) \in f_2(\varphi) \quad \Leftrightarrow \quad a \wedge b = c.$$

Denote the corresponding models $(B, \varphi, f_1)$ and $(B, \varphi, f_2)$. They are not isomorphic. Indeed, let these models be isomorphic with the isomorphism $\delta$. Then, from $a \vee b = c$ it follows, from the one hand, $\delta(a) \vee \delta(b) = \delta(c)$, but from the other hand $\delta(c) = \delta(a) \wedge \delta(b)$. Contradiction.

However $Aut(f_1) = Aut(B) = Aut(f_2)$. Groups $Aut(f_1)$ and $Aut(f_2)$ are conjugated by an identical automorphism of the algebra $B$. This means that these models are automorphic equivalent and the corresponding knowledge bases are informationally equivalent.

## References

1. Birkhoff, G., Bartee, T.C.: Modern Applied Algebra, McGraw Hill, (1974)
2. Category Theory and Computer Programming, Lecture Notes in Computer Science, Vol.240. Springer-Verlag (1986)
3. Georgescu, J.: A categorical approach to knowledge-based systems. In: Comput. Artificial Int. (1) Springer-Verlag (1984) 105–113
4. MacLane, S.: Categories for the Working Mathematician. Springer (1971)
5. Plotkin, B.I.: Universal Algebra, Algebraic Logic, and Databases. Kluwer Acad. Publ. (1994)
6. Plotkin, B.I.: Algebra, categories, and databases. In: Handbook of algebra, Vol. 2. Elsevier (2000) 81–148

7. Plotkin, B.I., Plotkin, T.: Geometrical Aspect of Databases and Knowledgebases. Algebra Universalis (2001) to appear
8. Plotkin, T. Relational databases equivalence problem In: Advances of databases and information systems. Springer (1996) 391–404
9. Scott, P.J.: Some aspects of categories in computer science. In: Handbook of algebra, Vol. 2. Elsevier (2000) 5–77

# Quantum Algorithms

Umesh Vazirani

University of California
Berkeley, CA 94720
vazirani@cs.berkeley.edu

Quantum computers are the only model of computing to credibly violate the modified Church-Turing thesis, which states that any reasonable model of computation can be simulated by a probabilistic Turing Machine with at most polynomial factor simulation overhead. This is dramatically demonstrated by Shor's polynomial time algorithms for factorization and discrete logarithms [12]. Shor's algorithm, as well as the earlier algorithm due to Simon [11] can both be cast into the general framework of the hidden subgroup problem (see for example [9]). Two recent papers [10,8] study how well this this framework extends to solving the hidden subgroup problem for non-abelian groups (which includes the graph isomorphism problem).

Indeed, there are very few superpolynomial speedups by quantum algorithms that do not fit into the framework of the hidden subgroup problem. One example is the recursive fourier sampling problem [1], which provided early evidence about the power of quantum algorithms. Very recently, van Dam and Hallgren give a polynomial time quantum algorithm for solving the shifted Legendre symbol problem [3]; the algorithm does not appear to fit into the HSP framework.

There is another class of quantum algorithms that have their roots in Grover's search algorithm, which gives a quadratic speedup over brute force search. There is a matching lowerbound [2], thus showing that it will be hard to find polynomial time quantum algorithms for NP-complete problems.

Finally, last year an intruiging new paradigm for the design of quantum algorithms by adiabatic evolution was introduced [5]. Encouraging results from numerical simulations of this algorithm on small instances of NP-complete problems appeared in the March issue of Science [6]. Very recently, a few analytic results about this new paradigm have been obtained [4] — first, adiabatic quantum computing is truly quantum, since it gives a quadratic speedup for general search. Secondly, there is a simple class of combinatorial optimization problems on which adiabatic quantum algorithms require exponential time.

## References

1. Bernstein E and Vazirani U, 1993, Quantum complexity theory, *SIAM Journal of Computation* **26** 5 pp 1411–1473 October, 1997.
2. Bennett, C. H., Bernstein, E., Brassard, G. and Vazirani, U., "Strengths and weaknesses of quantum computation," SIAM J. Computing, 26, pp. 1510-1523 (1997).
3. van Dam, W., Hallgren, H., "Efficient Quantum Algorithms for Shifted Quadratic Character Problems", quant-ph/0011067.

R. Freivalds (Ed.): FCT 2001, LNCS 2138, pp. 45–46, 2001.

4. van Dam, W., Mosca, M., Vazirani, U., "How Powerful is Adiabatic Quantum Computing?" manuscript, 2001.
5. E. Farhi, J. Goldstone, S. Gutmann, and M. Sipser, "Quantum Computation by Adiabatic Evolution", quant-ph report no. 0001106 (2000)
6. E. Farhi, J. Goldstone, S. Gutmann, J. Lapan, A. Lundgren, and D. Preda, "A Quantum Adiabatic Evolution Algorithm Applied to Random Instances of an NP-Complete Problem", *Science,* Vol. 292, April, pp. 472–476 (2001)
7. Grover, L., "Quantum mechanics helps in searching for a needle in a haystack,' ' Phys. Rev. Letters, 78, pp. 325-328 (1997).
8. Grigni, M., Schulman, S., Vazirani, M., Vazirani, U., "Quantum Mechanical Algorithms for the Nonabelian Hidden Subgroup Problem", In *Proceedings of the Thirty-third Annual ACM Symposium on the Theory of Computing,* Crete, Greece, 2001.
9. L. Hales and S. Hallgren. Quantum Fourier Sampling Simplified. In *Proceedings of the Thirty-first Annual ACM Symposium on the Theory of Computing,* pages 330-338, Atlanta, Georgia, 1-4 May 1999.
10. Hallgren, S., Russell, A., Ta-Shma, A., "Normal subgroup reconstruction and quantum computation using group representations", In *Proceedings of the 32nd Annual ACM Symposium on Theory of Computing,* 627–635, 2000.
11. D. Simon. "On the power of quantum computation." In *Proc. 35th Symposium on Foundations of Computer Science (FOCS), 1994.*
12. Shor P W, Polynomial-time algorithms for prime factorization and discrete logarithms on a quantum computer, *SIAM J. Comp.*, **26**, No. 5, pp 1484–1509, October 1997.

# A Discrete Approximation and Communication Complexity Approach to the Superposition Problem

Farid Ablayev* and Svetlana Ablayeva

[1] Dept. of Theoretical Cybernetics, Kazan State University,
[2] Department of Differential Equations, Kazan State University,
420008 Kazan, Russia

**Abstract.** The superposition (or composition) problem is a problem of representation of a function $f$ by a superposition of "simpler" (in a different meanings) set $\Omega$ of functions. In terms of circuits theory this means a possibility of computing $f$ by a finite circuit with 1 fan-out gates $\Omega$ of functions.
Using a discrete approximation and communication approach to this problem we present an *explicit* continuous function $f$ from Deny class, that can not be represented by a superposition of a lower degree functions of the same class on the first level of the superposition and arbitrary Lipshitz functions on the rest levels. The construction of the function $f$ is based on particular Pointer function $g$ (which belongs to the uniform $AC^0$) with linear one-way communication complexity.

## 1 Introduction

In complexity theory the superposition approach provides a new proof of the separating of monotone $NC^1$ from monotone $P$ [KaRaWi]. In classic mathematic the problem of representation of functions by functions of "simpler" (in some sense) quality has a long history and is based on the following problem. It is known that a common equation $a_1x^n + a_2x^{n-1} + \cdots + a_nx + a_{n+1} = 0$ for $n \leq 4$ can be solved over radicals. In terms of the superposition problem this means that the roots of the equation can be represented by a superposition of arithmetic operations and one variable function of the form $\sqrt[n]{a}$ $(n = 2,\ 3)$ of coefficients of the equation. Galois and Abel proved that a common equation of the 5-th order can not be solved in radicals (can not be represented as a superposition of this special form). Hilbert [Hi], formulated the 13-th problem the problem of *representing a solution of a common equation of the 7-th order as a superposition of functions of two variables.* The importance of the 13-th Hilbert problem is that it demonstrates one of the points of growth of function theory: it motivated an investigation of different aspects of the superposition problem.

* The research Supported partially Russia Fund for Basic Research under the grant 99-01-00163 and Fund "Russia Universities" under the grant 04.01.52

R. Freivalds (Ed.): FCT 2001, LNCS 2138, pp. 47–58, 2001.

Arnold [Ar] and Kolmogorov [Ko] proved that *arbitrary continuous function* $f(x_1, \ldots, x_k)$ *on* $[0,1]^k$ *can be represented as a superposition of continuous functions of one variable and sum operation:*

$$f(x_1, \ldots, x_k) = \sum_{i=1}^{2k+1} f_i \left( \sum_{j=1}^{k} h_{ij}(x_j) \right) \tag{1.1}$$

Note that the functions $h_{ij}$ are chosen independently from $f$ and as it is proved in [Lo], the functions $h_{ij}$ belong to Hölder class.

Vitushkin made an essential advance in the investigation of the superposition problem. Let $\mathcal{F}_p^k$ denote the class of all continuous functions of $k$ variables which has restricted continuous partial derivatives up to the $p$-th order. Vitushkin (see a survey [Vi]) proved the following theorem

**Theorem 1.** *There exists a function from* $\mathcal{F}_p^k$ *which can not be represented by a superposition of functions from* $\mathcal{F}_q^t$ *if* $\frac{k}{p} > \frac{t}{q}$.

Later Kolmogorov gave a proof of Theorem 1 that was based on comparing complexity characteristics (entropy of discrete approximation of functional spaces) of classes $\mathcal{F}_p^k$ and $\mathcal{F}_q^t$. Kolmogorov's proof shows that the classic superposition problem has a complexity background. The notion of entropy of functional spaces that was introduced by Kolmogorov was a result of the influence of Shannon's ideas. *Note that Kolmogorov's and Vitushkin's proofs show only the existence of the functions of Theorem 1 and do not present an example of a function from* $\mathcal{F}_p^k$ *that can not be represented by a superposition of functions from* $\mathcal{F}_q^t$. See the survey [Vi] and [Lo] for more information on the subject.

Further advance in presenting "constructive" continuous function which is not presented by certain superposition of simpler functions ("hard continuous function") was made in the paper [Ma]. It was proved that a function $f_G \in \mathcal{F}_p^k$ that is defined by a most hard (in terms of general circuits complexity) boolean function $G$ can not be represented by a superposition of functions from $\mathcal{F}_q^t$ if $\frac{k}{p} > \frac{t}{q}$. Remind that almost all boolean functions are hard, but an explicit example of hard boolean function is not known, yet.

In this paper we generalize results of [Ab] where first example of *explicit* "hard continuous function" has been presented. We use a discrete approximation of continuous functions and the communication complexity technique for the investigation of the superposition problem. Using certain Pointer boolean function $g$ from the uniform $AC^0$ with the linear one-way communication complexity we define an explicit continuous function that can not be represented by a superposition of a lower degree functions of the same class on the first level of the superposition and arbitrary Lipschitz functions on the rest levels.

The proof method of this result based on the following. Having continuous function $f$ we suppose that it is presented by a superposition $S$ of some kind of continuous functions. We consider their proper discrete approximations $df$ and $DS$ and compare the communication complexity $C_{df}$ and $C_{DS}$ of $df$ and $DS$

respectively. By showing $C_{DS} < C_{df}$ we prove that $f$ can not be presented by the superposition $S$.

The theoretical model for the investigation of communication complexity of computation was introduced by Yao [Yao]. We refer to books [Hr,KuNi] for more information on the subject.

## 2 The Function $f_{\omega,g}$

We define explicit continuous function $f_{\omega,g}$ of $k$ arguments on the cube $[0,1]^k$by explicit boolean function $g$ (more precisely sequence $g = \{g_n\}$ of explicit boolean functions). Informally speaking our construction of $f_{\omega,g}$ can be described as follows. We partition cube $[0,1]^k$to the infinite number of cubes (to $2^{kn}$ cubes for each $n > n_0$). We encode each of $2^{kn}$ cubes by binary sequences of the length $kn$. Boolean function $f_{\omega,g}$ over $kn$ arguments determines the behavior of $f_{\omega,g}$ in each of $2^{kn}$ cubes.

Now tern to the formal definition of $f_{\omega,g}$. We consider $n = 2^j - 1,\ j \geq 1$ throughout the paper in order not use ceiling and floor brackets. Let $I_n = [\frac{1}{n+1}, \frac{2}{n+1}]$ be a closed interval, $I_n^k = \underbrace{I_n \times \cdots \times I_n}_{k}$, and $I^k = \bigcup_{n\geq 1} I_n^k$. Let $\Sigma = \{0,1\}$. We consider the following mapping $a : \Sigma^* \to [0,1]$. For a word $v = \sigma_1 \ldots \sigma_n$ we define

$$a(v) = \frac{1}{n+1}\left(1 + \sum_{i=1}^{n} \sigma_i 2^{-i} + \frac{1}{2^{n+1}}\right).$$

Denote $A_n = \{a(v) : v \in \Sigma^n\}$. For a number $a(v) \in A_n$ denote

$$I_n(a(v)) = \left[a(v) - \frac{1}{(n+1)2^{n+1}},\ a(v) + \frac{1}{(n+1)2^{n+1}}\right].$$

a closed interval of real numbers of size $\delta(n) = \frac{1}{(n+1)2^n}$. From the definitions of $A_n$ and $I_n(a(v))$ it holds that:

1. For $a(v),\ a(v') \in A_n$ and $a(v) \neq a(v')$ segments $I_n(a(v))$, and $I_n(a(v'))$ can intersect only by boundary.
2. $\bigcup_{a(v)\in A_n} I_n(a(v)) = I_n$

Let us define the function $\Psi_{n,a(v)}(x)$ on the segment $I_n(a(v)),\ a(v) \in A_n$ as follows

$$\Psi_{n,a(v)}(x) = \begin{cases} 1 + \frac{2}{\delta(n)}(x - a(v)), & a(v) - \frac{\delta(n)}{2} \leq x \leq a(v) \\ 1 - \frac{2}{\delta(n)}(x - a(v)), & a(v) \leq x \leq a(v) + \frac{\delta(n)}{2} \\ 0, & \text{else} \end{cases} \tag{2.2}$$

From the definition it follows that the function $\Psi_{n,a(v)}(x)$ reaches the maximum value 1 in the center of the segment $I_n(a(v)),\ a(v) \in A_n$ and value 0 in the border points of this segment.

For a sequence $v = (v_1,\dots,v_k)$, where $v_i \in \Sigma^n$, $1 \le i \le k$, denote $I_n^k(b(v)) = I_n(a(v_1)) \times \cdots \times I_n(a(v_k))$ a $k$-dimension cube of size $\delta(n)$, where $b(v) = (a(v_1),\dots,a(v_k))$.

Consider the following continuous function $\Psi_{n,b(v)}(x)$ inside each cube $I_n^k(b(v))$, $v = (v_1,\dots,v_k) \in S_n$, $b(v) = (a(v_1),\dots,a(v_k))$.

$$\Psi_{n,b(v)}(x) = \prod_{i=1}^{k} \Psi_{n,a(v_i)}(x_i),$$

Function $\Psi_{n,b(v)}(x)$ has following important properties: it reaches the maximum value 1 in the center of the cube $I_n^k(b(v))$; for all border points $x$ of cube $I_n^k(b(v))$ it holds that $\Psi_{n,b(v)}(x) = 0$.

Let $g = \{g_n(v)\}$, where

$$g_n : \underbrace{\Sigma^n \times \cdots \times \Sigma^n}_{k} \to \{0,1\}$$

be the sequence of the following Pointer boolean functions. For a sequence $v = (v_1,\dots,v_k)$, where $v_i \in \Sigma^n$, $1 \le i \le k$, we will consider the following partition $pat(n,k)$: each word $v_i$ of the sequence $v$ is divided into two parts: the beginning $u_i$ and the end $w_i$ of length $l(n,k) = n - d(n,k)$ and $d(n,k) = \lceil (\log kn)/k \rceil$ respectively. We will write $v = (u,w)$ and call $u = (u_1,\dots,u_k)$ the first part of the input sequence $v$ and $w = (w_1,\dots,w_k)$ the second part of the input sequence $v$.

*Function $g_n(u,w) = 1$ iff $(ord(w_1 \dots w_k) + 1)$-th bit in the word $u_1 \dots u_k$ is one ($ord(\bar\sigma)$ denotes the integer whose binary representation is $\bar\sigma$. The numeration of bits in the words starts from 1). We will use both notation $g_n(v)$ and $g_n(u,w)$ for the boolean function $g_n$.*

The function $g_n$ can be formally described by the following formula:

$$g_n(u,w) = \bigvee_{\substack{\sigma \\ 0 \le ord(\sigma) \le |u|-1}} \bigwedge_{i=1}^{kd(n,k)} y_i^{\sigma_i} \wedge x_{ord(\sigma)},$$

where $y_j$ ($x_j$) is the j-th symbol of the sequence $w$ ($u$) in the common numeration of its elements. Clear that $g$ is in the uniform class $\Sigma_2$ ($AC^0$).

Let $\omega(\delta)$ be a continuous function such that $\lim_{\delta \to 0} \omega(\delta) = 0$. Define a continuous function $f_{\omega,g}$ on cube $[0,1]^k$ as follows:

$$f_{\omega,g}(x) = \sum_{\substack{n=2^j-1, \\ j \ge k}} \sum_{v \in \Sigma^n} (2g_n(v) - 1)\omega(\delta(n))\Psi_{n,b(v)}(x), \tag{2.3}$$

## 3 The Result

Remind definitions from functions theory. Denote $C$ to be a class of continuous functions of $k \ge 1$ variables which are defined on closed cube $[0,1]^k$. It is known that functions from $C$ are uniformly continuous. Following functions theory for each $f(x_1, \ldots, x_k) \in C$ define *modulus of continuous* $\omega_f(\delta)$. That is, $\omega_f(\delta)$ is a least upper bound of $|f(x) - f(x')|$, for all $x, x' \in [0,1]^k$ such that $|x - x'| = \max_{1 \le i \le k} |x_i - x'_i| \le \delta$.

We use the following standard definitions. Denote

$$\mathcal{H}_\omega = \{f \in C : \omega_f(\delta) \le M\omega(\delta), \text{ for some } M > 0\},$$

Denote $\widehat{\mathcal{H}}_\omega$ an essential subset of $\mathcal{H}_\omega$. That is,

$$\widehat{\mathcal{H}}_\omega = \{f \in C : M_1\omega(\delta) \le \omega_f(\delta) \le M_2\omega(\delta),$$

for some $M_1, M_2 > 0$. The following classes are known as Hölder classes in functions theory:

$$\mathcal{H}_\gamma = \{f \in C : \omega_f(\delta) \le M\delta^\gamma, \text{ for } M > 0\} \quad (\gamma \in (0,1])).$$

The following properties are known as classic properties:

1. $\mathcal{H}_{\gamma'} \subset \mathcal{H}_\gamma$ if $\gamma < \gamma'$.

2. Well known class $\mathcal{F} \subset C$ of continuous functions which have continuous derivatives is a proper subclass of $\mathcal{H}_1$. The class $\mathcal{H}_1$ is known also as Lipschitz class.

3. Class $\mathcal{H}_\gamma$ — is a class of constant functions if $\gamma > 1$.

More general class of functions

$$\mathcal{D} = \left\{ f \in C : \lim_{\delta \to 0} \omega_f(\delta) \log \frac{1}{\delta} = 0 \right\}$$

is known as Deny class. Deny class contains Hölder classes properly.

Let $p > 1$, $a = 1/(e^{p+1})$, and

$$\omega_p(\delta) = \begin{cases} 1/(\ln 1/\delta)^p & \text{if } 0 < x \le a \\ 1/(\ln 1/a)^p & \text{if } x > a, \end{cases}$$

Class $\mathcal{H}_{\omega_p}$ is a subclass of Deny class $\mathcal{D}$.

Let $\Omega$ be some set of functions. We define the superposition of functions of $\Omega$ as a function computable by a leveled circuit with a constant number of 1 fan-out gates from the set $\Omega$.

**Theorem 2.** *Function $f_{\omega_p,g}(x)$ over $k \ge 4$ variables belongs to the class $\widehat{\mathcal{H}^k_{\omega_p}}$ and is not represented by a following superposition of functions:*

1. *Superposition contains on the first level functions of $t$, $t < k$, variables from the class $\widehat{\mathcal{H}^t_{\omega_p}}$.*
2. *Superposition contains arbitrary continuous functions from $\mathcal{H}_1$ on the remaining levels of superposition.*

Below we present more general theorem 3. Theorem 2 is a corollary of it. Let $\mathbf{A}^t$, $\mathbf{B}^s$ be some classes of continuous functions of $t$ and $s$ variables. Define $\mathcal{S}p^k[\mathbf{A}^t, \mathbf{B}^s]$ class of continuous functions of $k$ variables that can be represented by a superposition of the following form

$$F\left(h_1(x_1^1, \ldots, x_t^1), \ldots, h_s(x_1^s, \ldots, x_t^s)\right),$$

where $F(y_1, \ldots, y_s)$ is a function from class $\mathbf{B}^s$, and $\{h_i(x_1, \ldots, x_t) : 1 \leq i \leq s\} \subseteq \mathbf{A}^t$.

From the definition it holds that for modules of continuous $\omega_1(\delta)$, $\omega_2(\delta)$ it holds that the function $\omega(\delta) = \omega_2(\omega_1(\delta))$ is a modules of continuous and $\mathcal{S}p^k[\mathcal{H}_{\omega_1}^t, \mathcal{H}_{\omega_2}^s] \subseteq \mathcal{H}_\omega^k$.

**Theorem 3.** *Let $\omega_1(\delta)$ be an increasing function such that $\frac{\omega_1(\delta)}{\delta}$ does not increase when $\delta$ increase and*

$$\log \frac{1}{\omega_1(\delta)} = o\left(\left(\log \frac{1}{\delta}\right)^{1-t/k}\right). \tag{3.4}$$

*Then for $s \geq 1$, $M > 0, \gamma \in (0,1]$, $\omega_2(\delta) = M\delta^\gamma$, $\omega(\delta) = \omega_2(\omega_1(\delta))$ function $f_{\omega,g}(x)$ belongs to $\mathcal{H}_\omega^k \backslash \mathcal{S}p^k[\widehat{\mathcal{H}}_{\omega_1}^t, \mathcal{H}_{\omega_2}^s]$.*

The proof of general theorem 3 we present in the next section.

**Proof of theorem 2.** First. Function $\omega_p(\delta)$ satisfy the conditions for the $\omega_1$ of theorem 3 for arbitrary constant $c > 0$ and especially for $c = 1 - \frac{t}{k}$, $t < k$. Next. Superposition of arbitrary functions from the class $\mathcal{H}_1$ is again a function from $\mathcal{H}_1$. From theorem 3 results the statement of theorem 2. □

## 4 The Proof

The proof of the fact that $f_{\omega,g} \in \widehat{\mathcal{H}}_\omega^k$ results from the following property.

*Property 1.* For the function $f_{\omega,g}$ it holds that

1. In each cube $I_n^k(b(v)) \in I^k$ function $f_{\omega,g}$ gets its maximum (minimum) value $\omega(\delta(n))$ $(-\omega(\delta(n)))$ in the center and value zero in the border of the border of the cube $I_n^k(b(v))$.
2. If in addition function $\omega(\delta)$ is such that $\frac{\omega(\delta)}{\delta}$ does not increase when $\delta$ increase then for modules of continuous $\omega_f$ of the function $f_{\omega,g}$ it holds that
   a) $\omega(\delta(n)) \leq \omega_f(\delta(n)) \leq 2k\omega(\delta(n))$.
   b) for arbitrary $\delta$ $\omega_f(\delta) \leq 2k\omega(\delta)$.

**Proof.** The proof use standard technique from functions theory. It will be presented in a complete paper. □

The proof of the second part of the theorem 3 use communication complexity arguments and is based on computing communication complexity of discrete approximations of the function $f_{\omega,g}$.

Let $f$ be an arbitrary continuous function defined on the cube $[0,1]^k$. Denote

$\alpha(n) = \min\{f(x) : x \in I_n^k = [\frac{1}{n}, \frac{2}{n}]^k\}$, and $\beta(n) = \max\{f(x) : x \in I_n^k = [\frac{1}{n}, \frac{2}{n}]^k\}$.

**Definition 1.** *Let $f(x_1, \ldots, x_k)$ be a continuous function on the cube $[0,1]^k$. Call a discrete function $df : \underbrace{\Sigma^n \times \cdots \times \Sigma^n}_{k} \to [\alpha(n), \beta(n)]$ an $\varepsilon(n)$-approximation of the function $f(x_1, \ldots, x_k)$, if for arbitrary $v = (v_1, \ldots, v_k) \in \Sigma^n \times \cdots \times \Sigma^n$ it holds that*

$$|f(b(v)) - df(v)| \le \varepsilon(n).$$

We will use the standard one-way communication computation for computing the boolean function $g_n \in g$. That is, two processors $P_u$ and $P_w$ obtain inputs in accordance with the partition $pat(n,k)$of input $v$. The first part $u = (u_1, \ldots, u_k)$ of the input sequence $v$ is known to $P_u$ and the second part $w = (w_1, \ldots, w_k)$ of $v$ is known to $P_w$.

The communication computation of a boolean function $g_n$ is performed in accordance with a one-way protocol $\psi$ as follows. $P_u$ sends message $m$ (binary word) to $P_w$. Processor $P_w$ computes and outputs the value $g_n(u,w)$. The communication complexity $C_\psi$ of the communication protocol $\psi$ for the partition $pat(n,k)$of an inputs $v = (v_1, \ldots, v_k)$ is the length $|m|$ of the message $m$.

The communication complexity $C_{g_n}(pat(n,k))$ of a boolean function $g_n$ is $\min\{C_\psi : \psi \text{ computes } g_n\}$.

**Lemma 1.** *For the boolean function $g_n \in g$ it holds that*

$$C_{g_n}(pat(n,k)) \ge k(n-1) - \log kn.$$

**Proof.** With the function $g_n(u,w)$ we associate a $2^{kl(n,k)} \times 2^{kd(n,k)}$ communication matrix $CM_{g_n}$ whose $(u,w)$ entry is $g_n(u,w)$.

Using the fact that $C_{g_n}(pat(n,k)) = \lceil \log nrow(CM_{g_n}) \rceil$, where $nrow(CM_{g_n})$ is the number of distinct rows of communication matrix $CM_{g_n}$ (see [Yao]) and the fact that for the $g_n$ it holds that $nrow(CM_{g_n}) = 2^{kl(n,k)} \ge \frac{2^{k(n-1)}}{kn}$ we obtain the statement of the lemma. □

We will use the same one-way communication computation for computing a discrete function $df(v)$. Let $pat(n,k)$be a partition of input $v$, $v = (u,w)$. Let $P_u$ and $P_w$ be processors which receive inputs according to $pat(n,k)$. Let $\phi(pat(n,k))$ be a one-way communication protocol, which compute $df(u,w)$. The communication complexity $C_\phi$ of the $\phi(pat(n,k))$ is the total number of bits transmitted among processors $P_u$ and $P_w$. et The communication complexity $C_{df}(pat(n,k))$ of a discrete function $df$ we define as follows

$$C_{df}(pat(n,k)) = \min\{C_\phi : \phi(pat(n,k)) \text{ compute } df(v)\}.$$

**Definition 2.** *Define a communication complexity $C_f(pat(n,k), \varepsilon(n))$ of an $\varepsilon(n)$-approximation of the function $f$ as follows:*
$C_f(pat(n,k), \varepsilon(n)) = \min\{C_{df}(pat(n,k)) : df(v)$ — $\varepsilon(n)$*-approximation of* $f\}$.

**Lemma 2.** *For $\varepsilon(n) < \omega(\delta(n))$, for arbitrary $\varepsilon(n)$-approximation $df$ of the function $f_{\omega,g}$ it holds that*

$$C_{g_n}(pat(n,k)) \leq C_f(pat(n,k), \varepsilon(n)).$$

**Proof.** Suppose that

$$C_{g_n}(pat(n,k)) > C_f(pat(n,k), \varepsilon(n)). \tag{4.5}$$

This means that there exists an $\varepsilon(n)$-approximation $df$ of the function $f(x_1, \ldots, x_k)$ such that for $2^{kl(n,k)} \times 2^{kd(n,k)}$ communication matrices $CM_{g_n}$ and $CM_{df}$ of functions $g_n$ and $df$ it holds that

$$nrow(CM_{g_n}) > nrow(CM_{df}).$$

From the last inequality it follows that there exist two inputs $u$ and $u'$ such that two rows $row_{g_n}(u)$ and $row_{g_n}(u')$ are different but two rows $row_{df}(u)$ and $row_{df}(u')$ are equal. This means that there exists an input sequence $w$ for which it holds that

$$g_n(u,w) \neq g_n(u',w), \tag{4.6}$$
$$df(u,w) = df(u',w). \tag{4.7}$$

Let $g_n(u,w) = 1$, $g_n(u',w) = 0$. Let us denote $v = (u,w)$, $v' = (u',w)$.Then form the definition of the $f_{\omega,g}$ we have:

$$f_{\omega,g}(b(v)) = \omega(\delta(n)), \tag{4.8}$$
$$f_{\omega,g}(b(v')) = -\omega(\delta(n)). \tag{4.9}$$

From the definition of the $\varepsilon(n)$-approximation of the $f_{\omega,g}$ and the property (1) it holds that

$$|f_{\omega,g}(b(v)) - df(v)| \leq \varepsilon(n) < \omega(\delta(n)), \tag{4.10}$$
$$|f_{\omega,g}(b(v')) - df(v')| \leq \varepsilon(n) < \omega(\delta(n)). \tag{4.11}$$

From our conjunction that $df(v) = df(v')$, from (4.8), (4.9), (4.10), and (4.11) we have that

$$2\omega(\delta(n)) = |f_{\omega,g}(b(v)) - f_{\omega,g}(b(v'))| \leq$$
$$\leq |f_{\omega,g}(b(v)) - df(v)| + |f_{\omega,g}(b(v')) - df(v')| < 2\omega(\delta(n)).$$

The contradiction proofs that $df(v) \neq df(v')$. □

Let $dh_i : \underbrace{\Sigma^n \times \cdots \times \Sigma^n}_{t} \to \mathcal{Z}$, $1 \leq i \leq t$ , be a discrete functions and $DF$ : $\underbrace{\Sigma^n \times \cdots \times \Sigma^n}_{k} \to \mathcal{Z}$, here $\mathcal{Z}$ denote the set of real numbers, be a following discrete function:

$$DF = F(dh_1(v_1^1, \ldots, v_t^1), \ldots, dh_s(v_1^s, \ldots, v_t^s)),$$

where function $F(y_1, \ldots, y_s)$ is an arbitrary continuous function.

**Lemma 3.** *For a discrete function $DF(v_1, \ldots, v_k)$it holds that*

$$C_{DF}(pat(n,k)) \leq \sum_{i=1}^{s} C_{dh_i}(pat(n,k))$$

**Proof** Communication protocol $\phi^*(pat(n,k))$ for the function $DF$ consists of processors $P_u^*$ and $P_w^*$. Given an input $u, w$ $\phi^*(pat(n,k))$ simulate in parallel protocols $\phi_1(pat(n,k))$, $\phi_2(pat(n,k))$,..., $\phi_s(pat(n,k))$ which computes $dh_1$, $dh_2, \ldots, dh_s$, respectively. The processor $P_w^*$ on received a message from $P_u^*$ and the input $w$ computes outputs $y_1$,... ,$y_s$ of protocols $\phi_1(pat(n,k))$, $\phi_2(pat(n,k))$, ... $\phi_s(pat(n,k))$ and then computes and outputs a value $F(y)$, $y = (y_1, \ldots, y_s)$. □

**Lemma 4.** *Let functions $\omega_1, \omega_2$ satisfy conditions of the theorem 3 and let $\omega(\delta) = \omega_2(\omega_1(\delta))$. Let the function $f_{\omega,g}(x_1, \ldots, x_k)$ can be represented as a superposition of the form*

$$F\left(h_1(x_1^1, \ldots, x_t^1), \ldots, h_s(x_1^s, \ldots, x_t^s)\right),$$

*where $F \in \mathcal{H}_{\omega_2}^s$ and $\{h_i(x_1, \ldots, x_t) : 1 \leq i \leq s\} \subset \widehat{\mathcal{H}}_{\omega_1}^t$.*
*Then there exists an $\varepsilon'(n) < \omega(\delta(n))$, such that*

$$C_{f_{\omega,g}}(pat(n,k), \varepsilon'(n)) = o(n).$$

**Proof.** We will denote $f$ our function $f_{\omega,g}$ in the proof of the theorem.
Let $\varepsilon = \omega_1(\delta(n)) / \log \frac{1}{\omega_1(\delta(n))}$. Consider arbitrary function $h \in \{h_1, \ldots, h_s\}$. Let $\alpha(n) = \min\{h(x) : x \in I_n^t = [\frac{1}{n}, \frac{2}{n}]^t\}$, and $\beta(n) = \max\{h(x) : x \in I_n^t = [\frac{1}{n}, \frac{2}{n}]^t\}$. Let

$$\mathcal{R}_{\varepsilon(n)} = A \cup \{\beta(n)\},$$

where

$$A = \left\{\alpha_i : \alpha_i = \alpha(n) + \varepsilon(n)i,\ i \in \{0, 1, \ldots, \lfloor \tfrac{\beta(n)-\alpha(n)}{\varepsilon(n)} \rfloor\right\}.$$

Due to selection of the value $\varepsilon(n)$, from the condition (3.4) of the theorem 3, and from the equality $\delta(n) = \frac{1}{(n+1)2^n}$ we have that:

$$|\mathcal{R}_{\varepsilon(n)}| = 2^{o(n^{1-t/k})} \tag{4.12}$$

Or $|\mathcal{R}_{\varepsilon(n)}| < 2^{nt}$. This means that there exists an $\varepsilon(n)$-approximator $dh$ of continuous function $h$,

$$dh : \underbrace{\Sigma^n \times \cdots \times \Sigma^n}_{t} \to \mathcal{R}_{\varepsilon(n)}.$$

For the prove of the statement of the lemma we show that the discrete function

$$DF(v_1, \ldots, v_k) = F(dh_1(v_1^1, \ldots, v_t^1), \ldots, dh_s(v_1^s, \ldots, v_t^s))$$

is the $\varepsilon'(n)$-approximation of the function $f$ and

$$C_{DF}(pat(n,k)) = o(n). \tag{4.13}$$

Let $v = (v_1, \ldots, v_k) \in \Sigma^n \times \cdots \times \Sigma^n$. First we prove that for some $\varepsilon'(n) < \omega(\delta)$ it holds that

$$|f(b(v)) - DF(v_1, \ldots, v_k)| \le \varepsilon'(n). \tag{4.14}$$

Denote $x = (x_1, \ldots, x_k) = b(v) = (a(v_1), \ldots, a(v_k))$. Due to the fact that for each $i \in \{1, 2, \ldots, s\}$ function $dh_i$ is $\varepsilon(n)$-approximation of the continuous function $h_i$ it holds that

$$|h_i(x_1^i, \ldots, x_t^i) - dh_i(v_1^i, \ldots, v_t^i)| \le \varepsilon(n).$$

As function $\omega(\delta)$ decreases when $\delta$ decreases then we have

$$|F\left(h_1(x_1^1, \ldots, x_t^1), \ldots, h_s(x_1^s, \ldots, x_t^s)\right) -$$

$$F(dh_1(v_1^1, \ldots, v_t^1), \ldots, dh_s(v_1^s, \ldots, v_t^s))| \le$$

$$\le \omega_F(\varepsilon(n)) \le \frac{M_1}{\left(\log \frac{1}{\omega_1(\delta(n))}\right)^{\gamma}} \left(\omega_1\left(\delta(n)\right)\right)^{\gamma} = \varepsilon'(n).$$

From some $n_0$ for $n > n_0$ it holds that

$$\varepsilon'(n) < \omega(\delta(n)).$$

Last inequality proves (4.14).

Consider now an arbitrary discrete function $dh$ from $\{dh_1, \ldots, dh_s\}$.

It is sufficient to prove that

$$C_{dh}(pat(n,k)) = o(n) \tag{4.15}$$

Then using lemma 3 the (4.13) results.

With the function $dh$ we associate a $2^{tl(n,k)} \times 2^{td(n,k)}$ communication matrix $CM_{dh}(n)$ whose $(u, w)$ entry is $dh(u, w)$.

$$C_{dh}(pat(n,k), \varepsilon(n)) = \lceil \log nrow(CM_{dh}(n)) \rceil. \quad (4.16)$$

Clearly we have that

$$nrow(CM_{dh}(n)) \leq \min \left\{ 2^{tl(n,k)}, |\mathcal{R}_{\varepsilon(n)}|^{2^{td(n,k)}} \right\}$$

or

$$nrow(CM_{dh}(n)) \leq |\mathcal{R}_{\varepsilon(n)}|^{2^{td(n,k)}}. \quad (4.17)$$

From the definition of the partition $pat(n, k)$ we have that $d(n, k) = \lceil \frac{\log nk}{k} \rceil$. Using (4.17), (4.12) for the equality (4.16) we obtain inequality (4.15). □

Finally combining statements of lemmas 4, 2, and 1 we obtain the proof of the theorem 3.

## 5 Concluding Remarks

The communication technique in this paper gives a clear information explanation of the statements of theorems 2 and 3. That is, functions $h$ from the class $\widehat{\mathcal{H}}^t_{\omega_1}$ which satisfies the condition (3.4) of the theorem 3 can be approximated by discrete functions $dh$ with small communication complexity $o(n)$ (see (4.15)). Such discrete functions $dh$ on the first level of superposition "can mix" some different inputs during transformation and no functions on the remaining levels can reconstruct this information.

We conclude with open problems. Whether using discrete approximation together with communication technique is possible to present an explicit function

(i) from $\mathcal{H}^k_1$ which could not be presented by a superposition of functions from $\mathcal{H}^t_1$ if $t < k$;

(ii) from $\mathcal{F}^k_p$ which could not be represented by a superposition of functions from $\mathcal{F}^t_q$, if $\frac{k}{p} > \frac{t}{q}$?

**Acknowledgment.** We are grateful to Marek Karpinski for helpful discussions on the subject of the paper.

## References

[Ab] F. Ablayev, Communication method of the analyses of superposition of continuous functions, *in Proceedings of the international conference "Algebra and Analyses part II. Kazan,* 1994, 5-7 (in Russian). See also F. Ablayev, Communication complexity of probabilistic computations and some its applications, Thesis of doctor of science dissertation, Moscow State University, 1995, (in Russian).

[Ar] V. Arnold, On functions of Three Variables, *Dokladi Akademii Nauk*, 114, 4, (1957), 679-681.

[Hi] D. Hilbert, Mathematische Probleme, *Nachr. Akad. Wiss.* Gottingen (1900) 253-297; Gesammelete Abhandlungen, Bd. 3 (1935), 290-329.

[Hr] J. Hromkovic, Communication Complexity and Parallel Computing, *EATCS Series, Springer-Verlag,* (1997).

[KaRaWi] M. Karchmer, R. Raz, and A. Wigderson, Super-logarithmic Depth Lower Bounds Via the Direct Sum in Communication Complexity, *Computational Complexity*, 5, (1995), 191-204.

[Ko] A. Kolmogorov, On Representation of Continuous Functions of Several Variables by a superposition of Continuous Functions of one Variable and Sum Operation. *Dokladi Akademii Nauk*, 114, 5, (1957), 953-956.

[KuNi] E. Kushilevitz and N. Nisan, Communication complexity, *Cambridge University Press*, (1997).

[Lo] G. Lorenz, Metric Entropy, Widths and Superpositions Functions, *Amer. Math. Monthly* 69, 6, (1962), 469-485.

[Ma] S. Marchenkov, On One Method of Analysis of superpositions of Continuous Functions, *Problemi Kibernetici*, 37, (1980), 5-17.

[Vi] A. Vitushkin, On Representation of Functions by Means of Superpositions and Related Topics, *L'Enseignement mathematique*, 23, fasc.3-4, (1977), 255-320.

[Yao] A. C. Yao, Some Complexity Questions Related to Distributive Computing, *in Proc. of the 11th Annual ACM Symposium on the Theory of Computing,* (1979), 209-213.

# On Computational Power of Quantum Branching Programs

Farid Ablayev*, Aida Gainutdinova**, and Marek Karpinski***

[1] Dept. of Theoretical Cybernetics of Kazan State University
420008 Kazan, Russia,
{ablayev,aida}@ksu.ru
[2] Dept. of Computer Science, University of Bonn, 53117 Bonn.
marek@cs.uni-bonn.de

**Abstract.** In this paper we introduce a model of a Quantum Branching Program (QBP) and study its computational power. We define several natural restrictions of a general QBP model, such as a read-once and a read-$k$-times QBP, noting that *obliviousness* is inherent in a quantum nature of such programs.
In particular we show that any Boolean function can be computed deterministically (*exactly*) by a read-once QBP in width $O(2^n)$, contrary to the analogous situation for quantum finite automata. Further we display certain symmetric Boolean function which is computable by a read-once QBP with $O(\log n)$ width, which requires a width $\Omega(n)$ on any deterministic read-once BP and (classical) randomized read-once BP with permanent transitions in each levels.
We present a general lower bound for the width of read-once QBPs, showing that the upper bound for the considered symmetric function is almost tight.

## 1 Introduction

Richard Feynman observed in 1982 ([7]) that certain quantum mechanical effects cannot be simulated effectively on a classical computer. This observation led to the general idea that perhaps computation in general could be more efficient in some cases if it uses quantum effects. During the last decade the area of research and developing of such algorithms that use different theoretical quantum computational models became an intensively growing area. Shor's quantum algorithm for factoring [10] that runs in polynomial time is well known.

As it is mentioned in [4] quantum computers may have two parts: a quantum part and a classical part with communications between these two parts. In that

* Supported by Russia Fund for Basic Research 99-01-00163 and Fund "Russia Universities" 04.01.52. Research partially done while visiting Dept. of Computer Science, University of Bonn.

** Supported by Russia Fund for Basic Research 99-01-00163 and Fund "Russia Universities" 04.01.52.

*** Supported in part by DFG grants, DIMACS, and IST grant 14036 (RAND-APX).

R. Freivalds (Ed.): FCT 2001, LNCS 2138, pp. 59–70, 2001.

case, the quantum part will be considerably more expensive than the classical part. Therefore, it will be useful to make the quantum part as simple as possible. This motivates the study of restricted models of quantum computations.

During the last decade different restricted quantum computational models have been investigated. In particular quantum finite automata has been introduced and first investigated by Kondacs and Watrous [9], see [6] for more information on the subject. It has been shown that one-way quantum finite automata with bounded error cannot accept arbitrary regular languages [9]. But Ambainis and Freivalds [4] presented certain regular language which can be presented by quantum finite automata with bounded error much (exponentially) *cheaper* than by the classical randomized finite automates.

In the paper we introduce a model of quantum branching programs. A branching program is a very convenient model for implementing different restricted variants of the computational model. Leveled oblivious permutation BPs are well known in complexity theory, their computational power is strong enough (deterministic leveled oblivious permutation constant width BPs have the same power as $\log n$ depth circuits [5]). Next, from our point of view branching programs are very natural model for comparing computational power of quantum models with the deterministic ones.

Note that from quantum point of view deterministic leveled oblivious permutation BPs model of BPs are a particular case of quantum BPs.

In the paper we investigate the properties of the important restricted computational variant — quantum read-once BP. We first show that read-once exact quantum BPs (noting that *obliviousness* is inherently in a quantum nature of such programs) can compute arbitrary Boolean function. Next we display certain symmetric Boolean function which is computable by read-once QBP with $O(\log n)$ width, which requires width $\Omega(n)$ on any deterministic read-once BP and (classical) randomized read-once BP with permanent transitions in each levels. We present a general lower bound for the width of read-once QBPs, showing that the upper bound for the considered symmetric function is almost tight.

## 2 Preliminaries and Definitions

Consider a $d$-dimensional Hilbert complex space $\mathcal{H}^d$ with a norm $||.||$. That is, for $z \in \mathcal{H}^d$, $z = \{z_1, \dots, z_d\}$, $||z|| = \sqrt{\sum_{i=1}^{d} |z_i|^2}$. Denote $\mathbb{C}^d$ a sphere of radius 1 of the space $\mathcal{H}^d$, $\mathbb{C}^d = \{z : ||z|| = 1\}$.

Recall some basic notations from quantum mechanics. A pure quantum state (or superposition) of a quantum system QS with $d$ stable states $\{1, \dots, d\}$ ($d$-state QS) can be expressed by associating an amplitude $z_i$ (complex number) to each state $i$ of QS. Quantum mechanics uses for this the following notations. Consider quantum *basis states* $\{|1\rangle, \dots, |d\rangle\}$ where $\{|i\rangle\}$ is the set of $d$-dimensional orthogonal basis vectors of $\mathbb{C}^d$ where $|i\rangle$ denotes the unit vector with value 1 at $i$ and 0 elsewhere. A pure quantum state or *configuration* of QS can be specified as

$$|\psi\rangle = \sum_{i=1}^{d} z_i|i\rangle$$

or just $|\psi\rangle = (z_1, \ldots, z_d)$ where $|\psi\rangle \in \mathbb{C}^d$. The specific notation $|\psi\rangle$ is so called Dirac notation for expressing column-vector $(z_1, \ldots, z_d)$. Element $z_i$ of $|\psi\rangle$ is called amplitude of the basis state $|i\rangle$ of QS, and $|z_i|^2$ is the probability of finding QS in the state $i$ when QS is measured.

Time evolution of configurations of QS in discrete steps is reversible and conveniently expressed using Heisenberg's matrix mechanics. That is, if in a current step a configuration of QS is $|\psi\rangle$ then in the next step a configuration of QS would be $|\psi'\rangle$ where $|\psi'\rangle = U|\psi\rangle$ and $U$ is $d \times d$ unitary matrix.

Now we formally define a *quantum transformation* as follows. Let $X = \{x_1, \ldots, x_n\}$ be a set of Boolean variables. Define quantum transformation ($d$-dimensional quantum transformation) on $|\psi\rangle \in \mathbb{C}^d$ as a triple $\langle j, U(0), U(1)\rangle$ where $j$ is the index of variable $x_j \in X$ and $U(0), U(1)$ are reversible transformations of $\mathbb{C}^d$ presented by unitary $d \times d$ matrices. Quantum transformation $\langle j, U(0), U(1)\rangle$ of $|\psi\rangle$ acts as follows: $U|\psi\rangle = |\psi'\rangle$. If $x_j = 1$ then $U = U(1)$ else $U = U(0)$.

## 2.1 Definition of a QBP

A Quantum Branching Program of width $d$ and of length $l$ ($(d,l)$-QBP) based on QS is defined by a

$$P = \langle T, |\psi_0\rangle, F\rangle$$

where $T$ is a sequence (of the length $l$) of $d$-dimensional quantum transformations of $d$-state QS:

$$T = (\langle j_i, U_i(0), U_i(1)\rangle)_{i=1}^{l},$$

$|\psi(0)\rangle$ is the initial configuration of $P$. $F \subseteq \{1, \ldots, d\}$ is the set of accepting states. We define a computation on $P$ for an input $\sigma = \sigma_1, \ldots, \sigma_n \in \{0,1\}^n$ as follows:

1. A computation of $P$ starts from the superposition $|\psi_0\rangle$. On the $i$-th step, $1 \leq i \leq l$, of computation $P$ transforms superposition $|\psi\rangle$ to a superposition $|\psi'\rangle = U_i(\sigma_{j_i})|\psi\rangle$.
2. After the $l$-th (last) step of quantum transformation $P$ measures its configuration $|\psi_\sigma\rangle$ where $|\psi_\sigma\rangle = U_l(\sigma_{i_l})U_{l-1}(\sigma_{i_{l-1}})\ldots U_1(\sigma_{i_1})|\psi_0\rangle$ . Measurement is presented by a diagonal zero-one projection matrix $M$ where $M_{ii} = 1$ if $i \in F$ and $M_{ii} = 0$ if $i \notin F$. The probability $p_{accept}(\sigma)$ of $P$ accepting input $\sigma$ is defined by

$$p_{accept}(\sigma) = ||M|\psi_\sigma\rangle||^2.$$

Denote by $k$QBP a QBP with the restriction that each variable $x \in \{x_1, \ldots, x_n\}$ occurs in the sequence $T$ of quantum transformations of $P$ at most $k$ times.

### 2.2 Function Presentation

- A QBP $P$ is said to compute (compute with an unbounded error) a Boolean function $f_n : \{0,1\}^n \to \{0,1\}$ if for all $\sigma \in f^{-1}(1)$ the probability of $P$ accepting $\sigma$ is greater than $1/2$ and for all $\sigma \in f^{-1}(0)$ the probability of $P$ accepting $\sigma$ is at most $1/2$.
- A QBP $P$ computes $f_n$ with bounded error if there exists an $\varepsilon > 0$ such that for all $\sigma \in f^{-1}(1)$ the probability of $P$ accepting $\sigma$ is at least $1/2 + \varepsilon$ and for all $\sigma \in f^{-1}(0)$ the probability of $P$ accepting $\sigma$ is at most $1/2 - \varepsilon$. We call $\varepsilon$ the margin and say that $P$ $(1/2 + \varepsilon)$-computes $f_n$.
- We say that a QBP $P$ exactly computes $f_n$ if $P$ computes $f_n$ with the margin $1/2$ (with zero error).

## 3 Computational Properties

First we show that bounded error read-once QBPs are powerful enough to compute arbitrary Boolean function. In contrast, we notice that one-way quantum finite automata when accepting with bounded error can only accept a proper subset of regular languages [9]. See also [6] for the last results on complexity properties of quantum finite automata.

*Property 1.* For arbitrary Boolean function $f_n$, there exists $(2^n, n)$-1QBP that exact computes $f_n$.

**Proof:** The proof is evident. For example, the following $(2^n, n) - 1QBP\ P$ is a $QBP$ satisfied the proposition. All possible configurations of $P$ are trivial. That is, a configuration $|\psi\rangle$ of $P$ contains exactly one 1 and all the rest components of $|\psi\rangle$ are 0. An initial configuration of $P$ is $|\psi_0\rangle = (1, 0, \dots, 0)$. $P$ reads input variables in order $x_1, x_2, \dots, x_n$ .

In each step $i, 1 \le i \le n$ , $P$ reads input $\sigma_i$ and transforms its current configuration $|\psi\rangle$ as follows. If $\sigma_i = 0$ then $|\psi\rangle$ does not changed. If $\sigma_i = 1$, then the 1 of the configuration $|\psi\rangle$ is "moved" to $2^{n-i}$ positions to the right in the next configuration $|\psi'\rangle$.

For an input sequence $\sigma = \sigma_1, \dots .\sigma_n$ denote $l_\sigma$ the number of position of 1 in the final (after reading $\sigma$) configuration of $P$. Clearly we have that $l_\sigma \ne l_{\sigma'}$ iff $\sigma \ne \sigma'$.

Now determine the set of accepting states $F$ of $P$ as follows: if $f(\sigma) = 1$, then $q_{l_\sigma} \in F$. If $f(\sigma) = 0$, then $q_{l_\sigma} \notin F$. □

Let the class **EP**-QBP$_{const}$ be the class of all Boolean functions exactly computed by constant width and polynomial length (in the number of function variables).

*Property 2.* For the complexity class $\mathbf{NC^1}$ it is holds that

$$\mathbf{NC^1} \subseteq \mathbf{EP}\text{-}QBP_{const}.$$

**Proof:** Proof is evident since known result of Barrington [5]. Having width 5 permutation deterministic branching program $P$ which computes Boolean function $f_n$ it is easy to construct a $(const, poly)$-QBP $P'$ which exact computes $f_n$. □

Consider the following symmetric Boolean function $f_{n,p_n}$: For an input $\sigma = \sigma_1, \ldots, \sigma_n \in \{0,1\}^n$ we have $f_{n,p_n}(\sigma) = 1$ iff a number of ones in $\sigma$ is divisible by $p_n$, where $p_n$ is a prime and $p_n \leq n/2$.

**Theorem 1.** *The function $f_{n,p_n}$ can be presented by a read-once $(O(\log p_n), n)$-1QBP with one-sided error $\varepsilon \geq 0$.*

The proof of this theorem will be presented in the section below. We have clearly that any deterministic OBDD for $f_{n,p_n}$ needs $\Omega(p_n)$ width.

Note that $f_{n,p_n}$ is based on regular language $L_p$ considered in [4]. For a prime $p$ language $L_p$ over a single letter alphabet defined as follows. $L_p = \{u : |u| \text{ is divisible by } p\}$. In [4] it is proved that for any $\varepsilon > 0$, there is a QFA with $O(\log p)$ states recognizing $L_p$ with probability $1 - \varepsilon$.

We clearly have that any finite deterministic automaton for $L_p$ needs at least $p$ states. In [4] it was shown that constant bounded error finite probabilistic automata also need at least $p$ number of states to recognize $L_p$. The proof of this lower bound use the Markov chain technique (finite probabilistic automata over single letter alphabet is exactly a Markov chain). But for probabilistic OBDDs it is not the case (probabilistic transitions on the different levels of OBDD can be different). Therefore we can not use directly the proof method of [4] for general probabilistic OBDD case. But in a particular (known enough) case when the transitions (for 0 and 1) in each level are the same we can use Markov chain technique for proving linear (in $p_n$) width for presentation $f_{n,p_n}$ in such probabilistic OBDDs.

### 3.1 Proof of the Theorem 1

We construct a QBP $P$ accepting inputs $\sigma \in f^{-1}_{n,p_n}(1)$ with probability 1 and rejecting inputs $\sigma \in f^{-1}_{n,p_n}(0)$ with probability at least 1/8. Consider $(2,n)$-1QBP $P^k$ for $k \in \{1, \ldots, p_n - 1\}$. Quantum program $P^k = \langle T^k, |\psi_0^k\rangle, F^k\rangle$ based on 2-state quantum system. Here $T^k = (\langle i, U^k(0), U^k(1)\rangle)_{i=1}^n$ where

$$U^k(0) = \begin{pmatrix} 1 & 0 \\ 0 & 1 \end{pmatrix}, U^k(1) = \begin{pmatrix} \cos(2\pi k/p_n) & -\sin(2\pi k/p_n) \\ \sin(2\pi k/p_n) & \cos(2\pi k/p_n) \end{pmatrix}, |\psi_0^k\rangle = \begin{pmatrix} 1 \\ 0 \end{pmatrix}, F^k = \{1\}.$$

Denote by $l(\sigma)$ a number of 1-s in the sequence $\sigma$, $l(\sigma) = \sum_{i=1}^n \sigma_i$.

**Lemma 1 ([4]).** *After reading an input $\sigma = \sigma_1, \ldots, \sigma_n$ the superposition of $P^k$ is*

$$|\psi\rangle = \cos\left(\frac{2\pi\, l(\sigma) k}{p_n}\right)|1\rangle + \sin\left(\frac{2\pi\, l(\sigma) k}{p_n}\right)|2\rangle.$$

**Proof:** The proof is omitted. It is similar to that of in [4]. □

If the number of ones in an input $\sigma$ is divisible by $p_n$ then $2\pi\, l(\sigma)k/p_n$ is a multiple of $2\pi$, $\cos\Big(2\pi\, l(\sigma)k/p_n\Big) = 1$, $\sin\Big(2\pi\, l(\sigma)k/p_n\Big) = 0$ . Therefore all $QBP$ $P^k$ accept inputs $\sigma \in f^{-1}_{n,p_n}(1)$ with probability 1.

Following [4] call $P^k$ "good" for input $\sigma \in f^{-1}_{n,p_n}(0)$ if $P^k$ reject $\sigma$ with probability at least 1/2.

**Lemma 2.** *For any $\sigma \in f^{-1}_{n,p_n}(0)$, at least $(p_n - 1)/2$ of all $P^k$ are "good".*

**Proof:** According to the Lemma 1 after reading an input $\sigma = \sigma_1, \ldots, \sigma_n$ the superposition of $P^k$ is

$$|\psi\rangle = \cos\left(\frac{2\pi\, l(\sigma)k}{p_n}\right)|1\rangle + \sin\left(\frac{2\pi\, l(\sigma)k}{p_n}\right)|2\rangle.$$

Therefore, the probability of accepting the input $\sigma \in f^{-1}_{n,p_n}(0)$ is $\cos^2\Big(2\pi\, l(\sigma)k/p_n\Big)$. $\cos^2\Big(2\pi\, l(\sigma)k/p_n\Big) \leq 1/2$ iff $\Big|\cos\Big(2\pi\, l(\sigma)k/p_n\Big)\Big| \leq 1/\sqrt{2}$. This happens if and only if $\Big(2\pi\, l(\sigma)k/p_n\Big)$ is in $[\pi/4 + 2\pi j, 3\pi/4 + 2\pi j]$ or in $[5\pi/4+2\pi j, 7\pi/4+2\pi j]$ for some $j \in N$. $\Big(2\pi\, l(\sigma)k/p_n\Big) \in [\pi/4+2\pi j, 3\pi/4+2\pi j]$ iff $\Big(2\pi\,(l(\sigma)k \bmod p_n)/p_n\Big) \in [\pi/4, 3\pi/4]$. $p_n$ is prime, $l(\sigma)$ is relatively prime with $p_n$. Therefore, $l(\sigma) \bmod p_n$, $2l(\sigma) \bmod p_n, \ldots,$ $(p_n - 1)l(\sigma) \bmod p_n$ is $1, 2, \ldots, p_n - 1$ in different order. Consequently, it is enough to find the power of a set $I = \{i_1, \ldots, i_l\} \subset \{1, \ldots, p_n - 1\}$ such that $2\pi\, i_j\,/p_n \in [\pi/4, 3\pi/4]$ or $2\pi\, i_j\,/p_n \in [5\pi/4, 7\pi/4]$. A straightforward counting show that $|I| \geq (p_n - 1)/2$. □

Following [4] call a set of quantum programs $S = \{P^{i_1}, \ldots, P^{i_t}\}$ "good" for $\sigma \in f^{-1}_{n,p_n}(0)$ if at least 1/4 of all its elements are "good" for this $\sigma$.

**Lemma 3.** *There is a set $S$ of 1QBPs with $|S| = t = \lceil 8 \ln p_n \rceil$ which is "good" for all inputs $\sigma \in f^{-1}_{n,p_n}(0)$.*

**Proof:** The proof is omitted. It is similar to that of in [4]. □

We construct a 1QBP $P$ accepting inputs $\sigma \in f^{-1}_{n,p_n}(1)$ with probability 1 and rejecting inputs $\sigma \in f^{-1}_{n,p_n}(0)$ with probability at least 1/8 as follows. The 1QBP $P$ consists of "good" 1QBPs $\{P^{i_1}, \ldots, P^{i_t}\}$, which work in parallel. In the starting superposition of $P$ all these programs represented with equal amplitudes.

Inputs $\sigma \in f^{-1}_{n,p_n}(1)$ are always accepted with probability 1 because all $P^k$s accept them. For any input $\sigma \in f^{-1}_{n,p_n}(0)$, at least 1/4 of all $P^k \in S$ reject it with probability at least 1/2 and the total probability of rejecting any $\sigma \in f^{-1}_{n,p_n}(0)$ is at least 1/8.

Using the technique of the paper [4] it is possible to increase the probability of correct answer to $(1 - \epsilon)$ for an arbitrary $\epsilon \geq 0$. In this case the width of 1QBP will be $O(\log p_n)$. □

# 4 Lower Bounds

Below we present a general lower bound on the width of 1QBP and compare it with the width of deterministic OBDD presenting the same Boolean function.

**Theorem 2.** *Let $\varepsilon \in (0, 1/2)$. Let $f_n$ be a Boolean function $(1/2 + \varepsilon)$-computed (computed with margin $\varepsilon$) by 1QBP Q. Then it is holds that*

$$width(Q) = \Omega\left(\frac{\log width(P)}{\log\log width(P)}\right)$$

*where P is a deterministic OBDD of minimal width computing $f_n$.*

Next theorem presents more precise lower bound for a particular margin $\varepsilon$ of computation. This lower bound show that the result of the Theorem 1 is tight enough

**Theorem 3.** *Let $\varepsilon \in (3/8, 1/2)$. Let $f_n$ be a Boolean function $(1/2+\varepsilon)$-computed (computed with margin $\varepsilon$) by 1QBP Q. Then it is holds that*

$$width(Q) = \Omega\left(\frac{\log width(P)}{2\log(1 + 1/\tau)}\right)$$

*where P is a deterministic OBDD of minimal width computing $f_n$ and* $\tau = \sqrt{1 + 2\varepsilon - 4\sqrt{1/2 - \varepsilon}}$.

Proofs of theorems are presented in the section below.

## 4.1 Proofs of Theorems 2 and 3

Proofs of theorems 2, 3 use the same idea. We construct a deterministic OBDD $P$ that presents the same function $f_n$ and

$$width(P) \le \left(1 + \frac{2}{\theta}\right)^{2\,width(Q)}. \tag{4.1}$$

Proofs of theorems 2, 3 differ only in estimating parameter $\theta > 0$ depending on $\varepsilon$.

**A Deterministic OBDD-Presentation of a 1QBP.** Let $d = width(Q)$. Let $\pi = \{i_1, i_2, \ldots, i_n\}$ be an ordering of variables testing of $Q$. From now we consider that input sequences $\sigma \in \{0,1\}^n$ are ordered in the order $\pi$ determined by $Q$. We define a deterministic OBDD $LQ$ based on $Q$ as follows. $LQ$ use the ordering $\pi$ of variables testing and presented by the following labeled complete binary tree.

- The initial node of $LQ$ is marked by intial configuration $|\psi_0\rangle$ of $Q$. Two outgoing vertices of the initial node are marked by $x_{i_1} = 1$ and $x_{i_1} = 0$.
- Two nodes of $LQ$ on the level 1 are marked by configurations $|\psi_1(0)\rangle$ and $|\psi_1(1)\rangle$ of $Q$ where $|\psi_1(\sigma_1)\rangle$ is the configuration after the first step of computation after reading $x_{i_1} = \sigma_1$ for $\sigma_1 \in \{0,1\}$.
  Vertex $x_{i_1} = \sigma_1$ leads from the node $|\psi_0\rangle$ to the node $|\psi_1(\sigma_1)\rangle$ iff $|\psi_1(\sigma_1)\rangle = U_1(\sigma_1)|\psi_0\rangle$.
- Consider a level $j$ of $LQ$. $2^j$ nodes of $LQ$ of the level $j$ are marked by configurations $\{|\psi_j(\sigma_1\ldots\sigma_j)\rangle \in \Psi : \sigma_1\ldots\sigma_j \in \{0,1\}^j\}$ where $|\psi_j(\sigma_1\ldots\sigma_j)\rangle$ is a configuration of $Q$ after reading the first part $\sigma_1\ldots\sigma_j$ of input $\sigma \in \{0,1\}^n$.
  Vertex (market by $x_{i_{j+1}} = \sigma_{j+1}$) from the node $|\psi_j(\sigma_1\ldots\sigma_j)\rangle$ leads to the node $|\psi_{j+1}(\sigma_1\ldots\sigma_j\sigma_{j+1})\rangle$ iff $|\psi_{j+1}(\sigma_1\ldots\sigma_j\sigma_{j+1})\rangle = U_{j+1}(\sigma_{j+1})|\psi_j(\sigma_1\ldots\sigma_j)\rangle$.
- Consider the last level $n$ of $LQ$. We mark $2^n$ nodes of $LQ$ on the level $n$ by configurations $|\psi_n(\sigma_1\ldots\sigma_n)\rangle \in \Psi : (\sigma_1\ldots\sigma_n) \in \{0,1\}^n$ and in addition we mark them by 0 and 1 as follows. We mark node $|\psi_n(\sigma_1\ldots\sigma_n)\rangle$ by 1 if for configuration $|\psi_n(\sigma_1\ldots\sigma_n)\rangle$ it is holds that $p_{accept}(\sigma_1\ldots\sigma_n) \geq 1/2+\varepsilon$. We mark node $|\psi_n(\sigma_1\ldots\sigma_n)\rangle$ by 0 if for configuration $|\psi_n(\sigma_1\ldots\sigma_n)\rangle$ it is holds that $p_{accept}(\sigma_1\ldots\sigma_n) \leq 1/2-\varepsilon$.

*Property 3.* A deterministic OBDD $LQ$ presents the same Boolean function $f_n$ as $Q$.

**Proof:** Evident and follows from the construction of $LQ$. □

**A metric Automaton Characterization of $LQ$.** We view on OBDD $LQ$ with the ordering $\pi$ of variables testing as a following metric time-variant automaton that reads its input sequences $\sigma \in \{0,1\}^n$ in the order $\pi$:

$$LQ = \langle \{0,1\}, \Psi, \{\delta_j\}_{j=1}^n, |\psi_0\rangle, \mathcal{F}_\varepsilon \rangle$$

where $\{0,1\}$ is the input alphabet, $\Psi = \{|\psi\rangle\}$ is a set of states (set of all possible configurations of $Q$ during its computations on inputs from $\{0,1\}^n$). That is, $\Psi = \cup_{j=0}^n \Psi_j$ where $\Psi_j$ is the set of states of $LQ$ on the level $j$. Automaton transition function $\delta_j : \Psi_{j-1} \times \{0,1\} \to \Psi_j$ determines transitions on the step $j$, $1 \leq j \leq n$, ($\delta_j$ is defined in according of transitions of $LQ$ on the level $j-1$). Finally $|\psi_0\rangle$ is the initial state and $\mathcal{F}_\varepsilon = \{|\psi\rangle \in \Psi_n : ||M|\psi\rangle||^2 \geq 1/2+\varepsilon\}$ is the accepting set of states of $LQ$.

For $j \in \{1,\ldots,n\}$ denote $\Delta_j : \Psi_{j-1} \times \{0,1\}^{n-j+1} \to \Psi_n$ automaton transitive closer of the sequence $\delta_j,\ldots,\delta_n$ of transition functions. That is,

$$\Delta_j(|\psi\rangle, \sigma_j\ldots\sigma_n) = \delta_n(\ldots(\delta_j(|\psi\rangle,\sigma_j),\ldots,\sigma_n).$$

**Lemma 4.** *Let $f_n$ be a Boolean function $(1/2+\varepsilon)$-computed by LQ. Let $\theta > 0$ and for arbitrary $|\psi\rangle \in \mathcal{F}_\varepsilon$ and arbitrary $|\psi\rangle' \in \Psi_n \backslash \mathcal{F}_\varepsilon$ it holds that*

$$|| \, |\psi\rangle - |\psi'\rangle \, || \geq \theta.$$

*Then, there exists a deterministic OBDD B which computes $f_n$ and*

$$width(B) \leq \left(1 + \frac{2}{\theta}\right)^{2d}.$$

**Proof:** Recall known notions of metric spaces we need in the proof (see for example [3]). A Hilbert space $\mathcal{H}_d$ is a metric space with a metric defined by the norm $|| \cdot ||$. Points $\mu, \mu'$ from $\mathcal{H}_d$ are connected through $\theta$-chain if there exists a finite set of points $\mu_1, \mu_2, \ldots, \mu_m$ from $\mathcal{H}_d$ such that $\mu_1 = \mu, \mu_m = \mu'$ and $||\mu_i - \mu_{i+1}|| \leq \theta$ for $i \in \{1, \ldots, m-1\}$. For $\mathcal{H}_d$ its subset $C$ is called $\theta$-component if arbitrary two points $\mu, \mu' \in C$ are connected through $\theta$-chain. It is known [3] that if $\mathcal{D}$ is a finite diameter subset of a subspace of $\mathcal{H}_d$ (diameter of $\mathcal{D}$ is defined as $\sup_{\mu,\mu' \in \mathcal{D}}\{||\mu - \mu'||\}$ then for $\theta > 0$ $\mathcal{D}$ is partitioned to a finite number $t$ of its $\theta$-components. Set $\Psi$ of states of $LQ$ belongs to sphere of radius 1 which has center $(0, 0, \ldots, 0)$ in $\mathcal{H}_d$ because for all $|\psi\rangle \in \Psi$ it holds that $|| \, |\psi\rangle \, || = 1$. For each $j \in \{0, \ldots, n\}$ Denote by $[\Psi_j] = \{C_1, \ldots, C_{t_j}\}$ the set of $\theta$-components of $\Psi_j \subset \mathcal{H}_d$.

From the condition of the lemma it follows that subset $\mathcal{F}_\varepsilon$ of $\Psi_n$ is a union of some $\theta$-components of $\Psi_n$. Transition functions $\delta_j$, $1 \leq j \leq n$, preserves the distance. That is, for arbitrary $|\psi\rangle$ and $|\xi\rangle$ from $\Psi_j$ and arbitrary $\gamma \in \{0, 1\}$ it holds that

$$|| \, |\psi\rangle - |\xi\rangle \, || = ||\delta_j(|\psi\rangle, \gamma) - \delta_j(|\xi\rangle, \gamma)||. \tag{4.2}$$

From (4.2) it holds that for $C \in [\Psi_j]$ and for $\gamma \in \{0, 1\}$ there exists $C' \in [\Psi_{j+1}]$ such that $\delta_j(C, \gamma) = C'$. Here $\delta_j(C, \gamma)$ is defined as $\delta_j(C, \gamma) = \cup_{|\psi\rangle \in C} \delta_j(|\psi\rangle, \gamma)$.

Now we describe deterministic OBDD $B$ in terms of time-variant finite automaton that computes $f_n$.

$$B = \langle \{0, 1\}, \, [\Psi], \, \{\delta_j\}_{j=1}^n, \, C_0, \, F \rangle$$

where $[\Psi] = \cup_{j=0}^n [\Psi_j]$ is a set of states of $B$ (remind that $[\Psi_j]$ is a set of states on the step $j$ of computation of $B$);
$\delta_j : [\Psi_{j-1}] \times \{0, 1\} \to [\Psi_j]$ is a transition function of $B$ on the step $j$;
an initial state $C_0 = \{|\psi_0\rangle\}$ is a one-element $\theta$-component of $\Psi_0$; finite set $F$ of $B$ defined as follows $F = \{C_i \in [\Psi_n] : C_i \subseteq \mathcal{F}_\varepsilon\}$.

From the construction of $B$ we have that OBDD $B$ and $LQ$ compute the same function $f_n$. The width $width(B)$ of $B$ is $t = \max\{t_0, \ldots, t_n\}$.

Let $t = t_j$ We estimate the number $t$ of $\theta$-components (number of states of $B$) of $\Psi_j$ as follows. For each $\theta$-component $C$ select one point $|\psi\rangle \in C$. If we draw a sphere of the radius $\theta/2$ with the center $|\psi\rangle \in C$ then all such spheres do not intersect pairwise. All the $t$ these spheres are in large sphere of radius $1 + \theta/2$

which has center $(0, 0, \ldots, 0)$. The volume of a sphere of a radius $r$ in $\mathcal{H}_d$ is $cr^{2d}$ where the constant $c$ depends on the metric of $\mathcal{H}_d$. Note that for estimating the volume of the sphere we should take in account that $\mathcal{H}_d$ is $d$-dimensional *complex* space and each complex point is a 2-dimensional point. So it holds that

$$width(B) \leq \frac{c\,(1+\theta/2)^{2d}}{c\,(\theta/2)^{2d}} = \left(1+\frac{2}{\theta}\right)^{2d}.$$

□

Below we present a technical lemma that estimates the number of components of $\Psi$ for different $\varepsilon$.

**Lemma 5.** *Let an LQ $(1/2+\varepsilon)$-computes function $f_n$. Then for arbitrary $|\psi\rangle \in \mathcal{F}_\varepsilon$ and arbitrary $|\psi'\rangle \notin \mathcal{F}_\varepsilon$ it holds that*

1. $\| |\psi\rangle - |\psi'\rangle \| \geq \theta_1 = \varepsilon/\sqrt{d}$ *and*
2. $\| |\psi\rangle - |\psi'\rangle \| \geq \theta_2 = \sqrt{1+2\varepsilon-4\sqrt{1/2-\varepsilon}}$.

**Proof:** For the simplification we denote a configuration $|\psi\rangle = z_1|1\rangle + \cdots + z_d|d\rangle$ just by $\psi = (z_1, \ldots, z_d)$. Let $\psi = (z_1, \ldots, z_d)$ and $\psi' = (z'_1, \ldots z'_d)$. Consider a norm $||.||_1$ defined as $||\psi||_1 = \sum_{i=1}^{d} |z_i|$.

**1.** From the definition of $LQ$ it holds that

$$2\varepsilon \leq \sum_{s_i\in F} (|z_i|^2 - |z'_i|^2) = \sum_{s_i\in F} (|z_i| - |z'_i|)(|z_i| + |z'_i|) \leq$$

$$\leq 2\sum_{s_i\in F} (|z_i| - |z'_i|) \leq 2\sum_{s_i\in F} |z_i - z'_i| \leq 2||\psi - \psi'||_1$$

Using an inequality

$$a_1b_1 + a_2b_2 + \ldots + a_db_d \leq \sqrt{a_1^2 + a_2^2 + \ldots + a_d^2}\sqrt{b_1^2 + b_2^2 + \ldots + b_d^2}, \qquad (4.3)$$

for $b_1 = b_2 = \ldots = b_d = 1$ we get that $||\psi||_1 \leq \sqrt{d}||\psi||$. Therefore,

$$2\varepsilon \leq 2||\psi - \psi'||_1 \leq 2\sqrt{d}||\psi - \psi'||$$

Finally, we have

$$||\psi - \psi'|| \geq \varepsilon/\sqrt{d}.$$

**2.** Consider now the next variant of a lower bound for $||\psi - \psi'||$.

$$||\psi - \psi'|| = \sqrt{\sum_{i=1}^{d} |z_i - z'_i|^2} \geq \sqrt{\sum_{i=1}^{d} (|z_i| - |z'_i|)^2} =$$

$$= \sqrt{\sum_{i=1}^{d} |z_i|^2 + \sum_{i=1}^{d} |z'_i|^2 - 2\sum_{i=1}^{d} |z_i||z'_i|} \geq$$

$$\geq \sqrt{\sum_{s_i\in F} |z_i|^2 + \sum_{s_i\notin F} |z'_i|^2 - 2\sum_{s_i\in F} |z_i||z'_i| - 2\sum_{s_i\notin F} |z_i||z'_i|}.$$

From the definition of $LQ$ we have that $\sum_{s_i\in F}|z_i|^2 \geq 1/2+\varepsilon$, $\sum_{s_i\notin F}|z_i'|^2 \geq 1/2+\varepsilon$. Now from the above we get that

$$||\psi - \psi'|| \geq \sqrt{1/2+\varepsilon+1/2+\varepsilon-2\sum_{s_i\in F}|z_i||z_i'| - 2\sum_{s_i\notin F}|z_i||z_i'|}.$$

Using inequality (4.3) we get from the above that

$$||\psi - \psi'|| \geq \sqrt{1+2\varepsilon-2\sqrt{\sum_{s_i\in F}|z_i|^2}\sqrt{\sum_{s_i\in F}|z_i'|^2}-2\sqrt{\sum_{s_i\notin F}|z_i|^2}\sqrt{\sum_{s_i\notin F}|z_i'|^2}}.$$

Using the property $\sum_{s_i\notin F}|z_i|^2 \leq 1/2-\varepsilon$, $\sum_{s_i\in F}|z_i'|^2 \leq 1/2-\varepsilon$, $\sum_{s_i}|z_i|^2 \leq 1$, and $\sum_{s_i}|z_i'|^2 \leq 1$, we finally get that

$$||\psi - \psi'|| \geq \sqrt{1+2\varepsilon-4\sqrt{1/2-\varepsilon}} = \theta_2.$$

□

Note that the lower bound above for $||\psi - \psi'||$ is nontrivial (positive) if $\varepsilon \in (\alpha, 1/2)$ where $\alpha$ is about 3/8. For $\varepsilon \in (0,\alpha]$ it holds that $1+2\varepsilon-4\sqrt{1/2-\varepsilon} \leq 0$. In this case the lower bound $||\psi-\psi'|| \geq \varepsilon/\sqrt{d}$ is more precise.

Now we turn to formal estimation of the lower bounds of Theorems 2 and 3.

**Proof of Theorem 2:** From Lemma 4 and Lemma 5 it follows that

$$t \leq \left(1+\frac{2\sqrt{d}}{\varepsilon}\right)^{2d}$$

or $\log t = O(d\log d)$. From that we get that

$$d = \Omega\left(\frac{\log t}{\log\log t}\right).$$

**Proof of Theorem 3:** From lemma 4 and lemma 5 it follows that

$$t \leq \left(1+\frac{2}{\theta_2}\right)^{2d}$$

or $2d \geq \log t/\log(1+2/\theta_2)$. From this we have that

$$d \geq \frac{\log t}{2\log(1+1/\theta_2)}.$$

## References


1. F. Ablayev and M. Karpinski, On the power of randomized branching programs, *Electronic Colloquium in Computational Complexity*, ECCC TR98-004, (1998), available at `http://www.eccc.uni-trier.de/eccc/` , also appeared in Proc. 28th ICALP (1996), LNCS Vol. 1099, Springer, 1996, 348-356.
2. F. Ablayev and M. Karpinski, A Lower Bound for Integer Multiplication on Randomized Read-Once Branching Programs, ECCC TR98-011 (1998), available at `http://www.eccc.uni-trier.de/eccc/`.
3. P. Alexandrov, Introduction to set theory and general topology, Berlin, 1984.
4. A. Ambainis and R. Freivalds, 1-way quantum finite automata: strengths, weaknesses and generalization, In *Proceeding of the 39th IEEE Conference on Foundation of Computer Science*, 1998, 332-342. See also quant-ph/9802062 v3.
5. D. Barrington, Bounded-width Polynomial-Size Branching Programs Recognize Exactly Those Languages in $NC^1$, *Journal of Comp. and System Sci.* 38, (1989), 150-164.
6. A.Brodsky and N.Pippenger. Characterization of 1-way quantum finite automata. *quant-ph/9903014*, available at `http://xxx.lanl.gov/archive/quant-ph`. See also its Russian mirror: `http://xxx.itep.ru`.
7. R. Feynman, Simulation Physics with Computers, *International Journal of Theoretical Physics*, (1982), 21, 467.
8. R. Freivalds, Quantum finite automata, *Manuscript 2000*, personal communication.
9. A.Kondacs and J.Watrous. On the power of quantum finite state automata. In *proceedings of the 38th Annual Symposium on Foundations of Computer Science*, 1997, 66-75.
10. P. Shor, Polynomial-time algorithms for prime factorization and discrete logarithms on a quantum computer, *SIAM J. on Computing*, 26(5), (1997), 1484-1509.

# Efficient Computation of Singular Moduli with Application in Cryptography

Harald Baier*

Darmstadt University of Technology, Department of Computer Science,
Alexanderstr. 10, D-64283 Darmstadt, Germany,
**hbaier@cdc.informatik.tu-darmstadt.de**

**Abstract.** We present an implementation that turns out to be most efficient in practice to compute singular moduli within a fixed floating point precision. First, we show how to efficiently determine the Fourier coefficients of the modular function $j$ and related functions $\gamma_2$, $\mathfrak{f}_2$, and $\eta$. Comparing several alternative methods for computing singular moduli, we show that in practice the computation via the $\eta$-function turns out to be the most efficient one. An important application with respect to cryptography is that we can speed up the generation of cryptographically strong elliptic curves using the Complex Multiplication Approach.

**Keywords:** class group, complex multiplication, cryptography, elliptic curve, Fourier series, modular function, ring class polynomial, singular modulus

## 1 Introduction

Modular functions are studied for a long time by the number theory community. The most famous modular function is the $j$-function, which is holomorphic on the upper half plane $\mathfrak{h}$ and which has a single pole at infinity. However, given an element $\tau \in \mathfrak{h}$ the computation of the value $j(\tau)$ is in general a challenging task. In this paper we show how to efficiently compute $j(\tau)$ in practice within a given floating point precision $F$. To be more precise, we compute a complex number $j_\tau$ such that $|j_\tau - j(\tau)| < 10^{-F}$, and we equate $j(\tau)$ and $j_\tau$.

We compare several alternative methods to compute $j(\tau)$ using the cube root $\gamma_2$ of $j$, the Weber function $\mathfrak{f}_2$, and Dedekind's $\eta$-function, respectively. To be able to compare the running times of alternative approaches for computing $j(\tau)$ we first have to determine the Fourier series of these four functions. For the determination of the Fourier coefficients of $j$ and $\gamma_2$ we make use of efficient algorithms due to Mahler [Mah76]. Furthermore, in the case of $\mathfrak{f}_2$ and $\eta$ we develop efficient formulae in Sect. 3.

Efficient computation of $j(\tau)$, $\gamma_2(\tau)$, and $\mathfrak{f}_2(\tau)$ has an important application in cryptography: The generation of cryptographically strong elliptic curves

* supported by FairPay, a project funded by the German Department of Trade and Industry

R. Freivalds (Ed.): FCT 2001, LNCS 2138, pp. 71–82, 2001.

via Complex Multiplication (CM) ([AM93], [LZ94], [BB00]). The general CM-method requires the computation of a ring class polynomial $R$, which is in general the most time consuming step of the CM-method. Hence speeding up the computation of $R$ yields a significant speed up of the CM-method. In Sect. 2 we present the relation between efficient computation of $R$ and fast computation of singular moduli $j(\tau)$. Thus our approach of efficiently computing singular moduli yields a significant speed up of generating elliptic curves using the CM-method. Furthermore, our most efficient approach of computing singular moduli has the advantage that no precomputation or no storage of any coefficients is needed.

We tested our algorithms on two platforms: First a SUN UltraSPARC-IIi running Solaris 2.6 at 333 MHz and having 512 MByte main memory. Second a Pentium III running Linux 2.2.14 at 850 MHz and having 128 MByte main memory. All algorithms are implemented in C++ using the library LiDIA 2.0 ([LiDIA]) with libI as underlying multiprecision package and the GNU compiler 2.95.2 using the optimization flag O2. Sample tests indicate that running times on the Pentium are about a quarter of the timings on the SUN.

The paper is organized as follows: We first review the connection between modular functions and the CM-method in Sect. 2. Furthermore, we define the functions mentioned above. Then Sect. 3 presents efficient algorithms to compute the Fourier series of these functions. Finally, in Sect. 4 we compare different methods to compute singular moduli.

## 2 The Ring Class Polynomial and Singular Moduli

Let us review some basic facts on class groups and ring class polynomials. Ring class polynomials play a crucial role in generating elliptic curves for cryptographic purposes using the CM-method. A ring class polynomial $R$ only depends on an imaginary quadratic discriminant $\Delta$, that is we have $\Delta < 0$, $\Delta \equiv 0, 1 \bmod 4$. Each imaginary quadratic discriminant $\Delta$ uniquely determines a set $C(\Delta) = \{(a,b,c) \in \mathbb{Z}^3 : c = \frac{b^2-\Delta}{4a}, \gcd(a,b,c) = 1, |b| \leq a \leq c, b > 0 \text{ if } |b| = a \text{ or } a = c\}$. $C(\Delta)$ is called the *class group* of discriminant $\Delta$. The class group is a finite set whose cardinality $h(\Delta)$ is the *class number*. Furthermore we set $h_p(\Delta) = \#\{(a,b,c) \in C(\Delta) : b \geq 0\}$. An element $Q$ of the class group is called a *reduced representative*.

With each reduced representative $Q = (a,b,c)$ of the class group $C(\Delta)$ we associate an imaginary quadratic number $\tau_Q$ : We set $\tau_Q = \frac{-b+i\sqrt{|\Delta|}}{2a}$ with the imaginary unit $i$. Obviously we have $\tau_Q \in \mathfrak{h}$ for all $Q \in C(\Delta)$.

We next define the Dedekind $\eta$-function, the Weber function $\mathfrak{f}_2$, the function $\gamma_2$, and finally the modular function $j$. For $\tau \in \mathfrak{h}$ we set $q = e^{2\pi i\tau}$. Then we have

$$\eta(\tau) = q^{\frac{1}{24}} \cdot \prod_{n=1}^{\infty}(1-q^n)\,, \tag{2.1}$$

$$\mathfrak{f}_2(\tau) = \sqrt{2}q^{\frac{1}{24}} \prod_{n=1}^{\infty}(1+q^n)\,, \tag{2.2}$$

$$\gamma_2(\tau) = \frac{\mathfrak{f}_2(\tau)^{24} + 16}{\mathfrak{f}_2(\tau)^8} , \tag{2.3}$$

$$j(\tau) = \gamma_2(\tau)^3 . \tag{2.4}$$

We fix the discriminant $\Delta$ and set $K = \mathbb{Q}(\sqrt{\Delta})$. The First Main Theorem of Complex Multiplication ([Cox89], Theorem 11.1) states that all values $j(\tau_Q)$ are conjugated over $K$ and hence have the same minimal polynomial over $K$ : The ring class polynomial $R$. Thus we can write $R = \prod_{Q \in C(\Delta)}(X - j(\tau_Q))$. It turns out that $R$ is an irreducible polynomial in $\mathbb{Z}[X]$. The values $j(\tau_Q)$ are called *singular moduli*. Hence efficient computation of the singular moduli yields a fast algorithm to compute $R$. In Sect. 3.1 we will estimate the range of the coefficients of $R$; this leads to a formula for the floating point precision $F$ to compute $R$ in practice.

## 3 Efficient Computation of Fourier Series

In this section we discuss algorithms to compute the Fourier series of the functions $j$, $\gamma_2$, $\eta$, and $\mathfrak{f}_2$, respectively. These series will be used in Sect. 4.

### 3.1 The Fourier Coefficients of the $j$-Function

We determine the Fourier series of the modular function $j$. As mentioned above the $j$-function is defined on the upper half plane $\mathfrak{h}$. As $j$ is holomorphic on $\mathfrak{h}$ and invariant under the action of $\mathrm{SL}(2,\mathbb{Z})$ it is periodic with period 1. Thus there is a unique Fourier series with $j(\tau) = \sum_{n=-\infty}^{\infty} c_n \cdot q^n$. Furthermore, as $j$ has a single pole at infinity we have $c_n = 0$ for $n \le -2$ ([Cox89], Theorem 11.8, p.225).

To compute the coefficients $c_n$ we make use of recursive formulae due to K. Mahler. Setting 0 for an empty sum we have for all $n \in \mathbb{N}$ ([Mah76], p.91, equations 46):

$$c_{4n} = c_{2n+1} + \frac{c_n^2 - c_n}{2} + \sum_{k=1}^{n-1} c_k c_{2n-k} , \tag{3.5}$$

$$\begin{aligned} c_{4n+1} = {} & c_{2n+3} - c_2 c_{2n} + \frac{c_{n+1}^2 - c_{n+1}}{2} + \frac{c_{2n}^2 + c_{2n}}{2} \\ & + \sum_{k=1}^{n} c_k c_{2n-k+2} - \sum_{k=1}^{2n-1} (-1)^{k-1} c_k c_{4n-k} + \sum_{k=1}^{n-1} c_k c_{4n-4k} , \end{aligned} \tag{3.6}$$

$$c_{4n+2} = c_{2n+2} + \sum_{k=1}^{n} c_k c_{2n-k+1} , \tag{3.7}$$

$$\begin{aligned} c_{4n+3} = {} & c_{2n+4} - c_2 c_{2n+1} - \frac{c_{2n+1}^2 - c_{2n+1}}{2} \\ & + \sum_{k=1}^{n+1} c_k c_{2n-k+3} - \sum_{k=1}^{2n} (-1)^{k-1} c_k c_{4n-k+2} + \sum_{k=1}^{n} c_k c_{4n-4k+2} . \end{aligned} \tag{3.8}$$

However, to make use of the formulae (3.5) - (3.8), we have to know the coefficients $c_{-1}$, $c_0$, $c_1$, $c_2$, $c_3$, and $c_5$ : Obviously, for $n = 1$ the equations depend on $c_1, \ldots c_3$. However, (3.6) yields $c_5 = c_5$ in this case, and we have to know $c_5$ before using Mahler's equations.

Thus we first determine these coefficients by evaluating the representation of $j$ by the normalized Eisenstein series $E_4$ and $E_6$ of weight 4 and 6, respectively: $j(\tau) = 1728 \cdot \frac{E_4(\tau)^3}{E_4(\tau)^3 - E_6(\tau)^2}$. For a definition of the Eisenstein series we refer to [Kob93]. The Fourier coefficients of the Eisenstein series can easily be computed. We refer to [Bai01] for details. Finally making use of Mahler's equations (3.5) - (3.8) we compute the values of $c_n$ up to $n = 50000$ and store them in a file of size 38.7 MByte. The running time on the Pentium III was 9.87 hours. We have $c_{-1} = 1$, $c_0 = 744$, $c_1 = 196884$, $c_2 = 21493760$, $c_3 = 864299970$, $c_4 = 20245856256$, and $c_5 = 333202640600$.

We are now able to estimate the range of the coefficients of the ring class polynomial $R$ for a discriminant $\Delta$. As in Sect. 2 set $q = e^{2\pi i \tau_Q}$ with $Q = (a, b, c)$. We first remark that for $(a, b, c)$ and $(a, -b, c)$ the respective values of $q$ are conjugate complex numbers. Hence if $(a, b, c)$ and $(a, -b, c)$ are both in $C(\Delta)$ the Fourier series of $j$ shows that we have $j(\tau_{(a,-b,c)}) = \overline{j(\tau_{(a,b,c)})}$. Thus computing $j(\tau_{(a,b,c)})$ yields $j(\tau_{(a,-b,c)})$ for free in this case. We can therefore restrict to reduced representatives $(a, b, c)$ with $b \geq 0$. Furthermore, we have $|q| = e^{-\frac{\pi\sqrt{|\Delta|}}{a}}$. Hence, for fixed $\Delta$, $|q|$ only depends on $a$, and using the Fourier series of $j$ we get $|j(\tau_Q)| \approx |\frac{1}{q}| = e^{\frac{\pi\sqrt{|\Delta|}}{a}}$. Thus the constant term of $R$ is up to sign of order of magnitude $e^{\pi\sqrt{|\Delta|}\sum_{(a,b,c)\in C(\Delta)}\frac{1}{a}}$. In most cases the constant term of $R$ is up to sign the biggest coefficient. Hence the floating point precision

$$F = 5 + \frac{h(\Delta)}{4} + \frac{\pi\sqrt{|\Delta|}}{\log 10} \cdot \sum_{(a,b,c)\in C(\Delta)} \frac{1}{a} \qquad (3.9)$$

as proposed in [LZ94] is in practice sufficient to compute $R$. The correction term $5 + \frac{h(\Delta)}{4}$ takes into account both the approximation $|j(\tau_Q)| \approx |\frac{1}{q}|$ and the fact that the constant term of $R$ may not be up to sign the biggest coefficient. We computed dozens of polynomials $R$, and we are not aware of any counterexample where $F$ does not yield a right result.

We remark that there is another efficient method to compute the Fourier coefficients of $j$ due to M. Kaneko ([Kan]), who extends work of D. Zagier. We refer to his paper for details.

### 3.2 Computing the Fourier Coefficients of $\gamma_2$

For $\tau \in \mathfrak{h}$ one can easily derive the formula $\gamma_2(\tau) = q^{-\frac{1}{3}} \cdot \sum_{n=0}^{\infty} g_n q^n$. As in the case of the modular function $j$, we present recursive formulae due to Mahler to compute the Fourier coefficients $g_n$.

However, Mahler takes a slightly different representation: He multiplies the term $q^{-\frac{1}{3}}$ into the sum and writes $\gamma_2(\tau) = q^{-\frac{1}{3}} + \sum_{n=0}^{\infty} b_{3n+2} q^{\frac{3n+2}{3}}$. Hence we have $g_0 = 1$ and $g_n = b_{3n-1}$ for $n \geq 1$. If we set 0 for an empty sum we have for all $n \in \mathbb{N}_0$ ([Mah76], p.115, equations 79):

$$b_{12n+2} = b_{6n+2} + \sum_{k=0}^{n-1} b_{3k+2} b_{6n-3k-1} \,, \tag{3.10}$$

$$\begin{aligned} b_{12n+5} = {} & b_{6n+5} - b_2 b_{6n+2} + \frac{b_{3n+2}^2 - b_{3n+2}}{2} + \frac{b_{6n+2}^2 + b_{6n+2}}{2} \\ & + \sum_{k=0}^{n-1} b_{3k+2} b_{6n-3k+2} - \sum_{k=0}^{2n-1} (-1)^{k-1} b_{3k+2} b_{12n-3k+2} \\ & + \sum_{k=0}^{n-1} b_{3k+2} b_{12n-12k-4} \,, \end{aligned} \tag{3.11}$$

$$b_{12n+8} = b_{6n+5} + \sum_{k=0}^{n-1} b_{3k+2} b_{6n-3k+2} + \frac{b_{3n+2}^2 - b_{3n+2}}{2} \,, \tag{3.12}$$

$$\begin{aligned} b_{12n+11} = {} & b_{6n+8} - b_2 b_{6n+5} - \frac{b_{6n+5}^2 - b_{6n+5}}{2} + \sum_{k=0}^{n} b_{3k+2} b_{6n-3k+5} \\ & - \sum_{k=0}^{2n} (-1)^{k-1} b_{3k+2} b_{12n-3k+8} + \sum_{k=0}^{n} b_{3k+2} b_{12n-12k+2} \,. \end{aligned} \tag{3.13}$$

Evaluating these equations for $n = 0$ we have $b_2 = b_2$, $b_5 = b_5$, $b_8 = b_5 + (b_2^2 - b_2)/2$ and $b_{11} = b_8 - b_2 b_5 - (b_5^2 - b_5)/2 + b_2 b_5 + b_2 b_8 + b_2^2$. Hence $b_2$ and $b_5$ uniquely determine all coefficients $b_n$. The defining equation of the $g_n$ yields $j(\tau) = \gamma_2^3(\tau) = q^{-1} \cdot (1 + 3g_1 q + 3(g_1^2 + g_2)q^2 + O(q^3))$. Thus comparing with the Fourier series of the $j$-function we get $g_1 = c_0/3$ and $g_2 = c_1/3 - g_1^2$, hence $g_1 = 248$ and $g_2 = 4124$. Using $g_n = b_{3n-1}$ for $n \geq 1$, we computed the coefficients $g_n$ up to $n = 50000$. The memory to store these coefficients is 22.3 MByte. The computation took us 5.23 hours on the Pentium III.

## 3.3 Computing the Fourier Coefficients of the $\eta$-Function

We next determine formulae to compute the Fourier coefficients of the $\eta$-function. We first make use of a result due to Euler, which states

$$\eta(\tau) = q^{\frac{1}{24}} \sum_{n \in \mathbb{Z}} (-1)^n q^{\frac{3n^2+n}{2}} \,. \tag{3.14}$$

Multiplying $q^{\frac{1}{24}}$ into the sum and using some properties of the Jacobi symbol $\left(\frac{\cdot}{\cdot}\right)$, we get $\eta(\tau) = \sum_{n \in \mathbb{Z}} (-1)^n q^{\frac{(6n+1)^2}{24}} = \sum_{n=1}^{\infty} \left(\frac{12}{n}\right) q^{\frac{n^2}{24}}$.

Equation (3.14) shows that we can define a sequence $(e_n)_{n \in \mathbb{N}_0}$ by $\eta(\tau) = q^{\frac{1}{24}} \sum_{n=0}^{\infty} e_n q^n$. We prove the following result:

**Proposition 1.** *Let $e_n$ be as defined above. Then we have for all $n \in \mathbb{N}_0$*

$$e_n = \begin{cases} 0, & if \quad 24n+1 \text{ is not a square in } \mathbb{Z}, \\ \left(\frac{12}{\sqrt{24n+1}}\right), & if \quad 24n+1 \text{ is a square in } \mathbb{Z}. \end{cases}$$

**Proof:** The representation of the $\eta$-function by the Jacobi symbol and the definition of the $e_n$ yield $\sum_{m=1}^{\infty}\left(\frac{12}{m}\right) q^{\frac{m^2}{24}} = \sum_{n=0}^{\infty} e_n q^{\frac{24n+1}{24}}$. Comparing the coefficients, we get $e_n = \left(\frac{12}{\sqrt{24n+1}}\right)$, if $m^2 = 24n+1$, and $e_n = 0$ otherwise. □

Proposition 1 shows that we have $e_n \in \{-1, 0, 1\}$. Furthermore, as the exponents in (3.14) grow quadratically coefficients $e_n \neq 0$ are rather sparse. Making use of proposition 1 we computed $e_n$ up to $n = 5000000$, which took us 16.3 seconds on the Pentium III. The memory to store these coefficients is 9.54 MByte.

### 3.4 Computing the Fourier Coefficients of the Weber Function $\mathfrak{f}_2$

The main task in computing the coefficients of the Fourier series of $\mathfrak{f}_2$ is to determine the representation of the infinite product in (2.2) by a power series in $q$. Obviously this product can uniquely be written as a Fourier series $\sum_{n=0}^{\infty} f_n q^n$. Making use of the equations (2.1) and (2.2) one easily sees $\mathfrak{f}_2(\tau) = \sqrt{2} \cdot \frac{\eta(2\tau)}{\eta(\tau)}$. In Sect. 3.3 we derived the formula $\eta(\tau) = q^{\frac{1}{24}} \sum_{n=0}^{\infty} e_n q^n$. As the $\eta$-function does not vanish on $\mathfrak{h}$ we use the Fourier series of $\mathfrak{f}_2$ and $\eta$ to get

$$\sum_{n=0}^{\infty} e_n q^{2n} = \sum_{n=0}^{\infty} f_n q^n \cdot \sum_{n=0}^{\infty} e_n q^n = \sum_{n=0}^{\infty} \left( \sum_{k=0}^{n} f_k e_{n-k} \right) \cdot q^n. \tag{3.15}$$

Hence, making use of $e_0 = f_0 = 1$, equation (3.15) yields for $n \in \mathbb{N}$

$$f_n = \begin{cases} -\sum_{k=0}^{n-1} f_k e_{n-k}, & if \quad 2 \nmid n, \\ e_{\frac{n}{2}} - \sum_{k=0}^{n-1} f_k e_{n-k}, & if \quad 2 \mid n. \end{cases}$$

This yields an algorithm for computing the coefficients $f_n$. According to our experience this is the most efficient way in practice to compute the Fourier coefficients of $\mathfrak{f}_2$. As in the case of the $j$- and the $\gamma_2$-function we determined all coefficients $f_n$ up to $n = 50000$, which took us 22 minutes on the Pentium III. The necessary amount of storage is 5.48 MByte.

## 4 Efficient Computation of Singular Moduli

This section deals with comparing alternative methods to compute singular moduli. First let an imaginary quadratic discriminant $\Delta$ and a reduced representative $Q \in C(\Delta)$ be given. Furthermore, fix a floating point precision $F$. We show that in practice the computation of $j(\tau_Q)$ within precision $F$ using an efficient representation of the $\eta$-function is by far the most efficient alternative. Furthermore, we present running times for all alternatives we make use of. We conclude that the computation of a ring class polynomial of degree 200, which may be explored for cryptographic purposes, takes about 5 minutes on the SUN.

The formulae and relations of Sect. 2 make the following proceeding plausible: As the functions $j$, $\gamma_2$, and $\mathfrak{f}_2$ can be expressed in terms of Dedekind's $\eta$-function, we first compare three different approaches to determine the value $\eta(\tau_Q)$. Next we explore alternatives of computing $\mathfrak{f}_2(\tau_Q)$ by its product formula (2.2), its Fourier series from Sect. 3.4, and finally by the term $\mathfrak{f}_2(\tau_Q) = \sqrt{2}\frac{\eta(2\tau_Q)}{\eta(\tau_Q)}$; in the last expression we make use of our results on the $\eta$-function. Similarly we deal with $\gamma_2$ and $j$.

## 4.1 Efficient Computation of the $\eta$-Function

Section 3.3 yields three different methods for computing $\eta(\tau)$ : Making use of the product formula $q^{\frac{1}{24}} \cdot \prod_{n=1}^{\infty}(1-q^n)$, evaluating the Fourier series $q^{\frac{1}{24}} \sum_{n=0}^{\infty} e_n q^n$, or using the Euler sum (3.14). These tasks are performed by our algorithms `computeEtaViaProduct`, `computeEtaViaFourierSeries`, and `computeEtaViaEulerSum`, respectively. In this section we show that using `computeEtaViaEulerSum` turns out to be in practice the most efficient way for computing $\eta(\tau)$ for a given floating point precision $F$.

Input of all three algorithms is a complex number $\tau$ in the upper half plane $\mathfrak{h}$ and a floating point precision $F$ that we use in our computations. Each algorithm returns the value $\eta(\tau)$ within the precision $F$. Both the first and second algorithm are straightforward. Hence we only explain our algorithm `computeEtaViaEulerSum`$(\tau, F)$. We have

$$q^{\frac{1}{24}} \sum_{n\in\mathbb{Z}} (-1)^n q^{\frac{3n^2+n}{2}} = q^{\frac{1}{24}} \left(1 + \sum_{n=1}^{\infty} (-1)^n \left(q^{\frac{3n^2-n}{2}} + q^{\frac{3n^2+n}{2}}\right)\right).$$

We split the sum in two partial sums and set $N_-(n_-) = \frac{3n_-^2 - n_-}{2}$ respectively $N_+(n_+) = \frac{3n_+^2 + n_+}{2}$. Hence $N_-$ respectively $N_+$ are the exponents of each partial sum. The difference of two exponents is $N_-(n_- + 1) - N_-(n_-) = 3n_- + 1$ and $N_+(n_+ + 1) - N_+(n_+) = 3n_+ + 2$, respectively. Depending on whether the current value of $N_-$ respectively $N_+$ is the minimum of $\{N_-, N_+\}$ we compute the appropriate power of $q$ and adapt the value of $N_-$ respectively $N_+$. It is easy to see that we always have $N_- \neq N_+$.

Running times on the SUN of our three algorithms for all reduced representatives of discriminant $\Delta = -21311$ are plotted in the appendix. $\Delta$ is the maximal discriminant of class number 200. Further timings for discriminants of class numbers up to 500 can be found in [Bai01]. The results indicate that `computeEtaViaEulerSum`$(\tau_Q, F)$ is the most efficient of our algorithms to compute $\eta(\tau_Q)$ for a high precision $F$, i.e. $F \geq 2000$. We remark that the runtime benefit of `computeEtaViaEulerSum` becomes more definitely for growing $a$, hence with growing $q$, which is the important case for computing ring class polynomials. However, we tested our algorithms for low precisions and got similar results.

**computeEtaViaEulerSum**($\tau, F$)
**Input:** A complex number $\tau \in \mathfrak{h}$.
A natural number $F$ serving as floating point precision.
**Output:** The value $\eta(\tau)$ within the floating point precision $F$.

```
n₋ ← 2; n₊ ← 2;
N₋ ← 5; N₊ ← 7; // to store the exponents of q in the partial sums
l ← 2; // to store the previous used exponent of q
q ← e^(2πiτ); q_n ← q^2; // q_n stores the values q^n
η ← 1 − q − q_n; // η stores the current approximation of η(τ)/q^(1/24)
while true do
  s ← 1; // s stores the sign
  if N₋ < N₊ then
    q_n ← q_n · q^(N₋−l);
    if 2 ∤ n₋ then
      s ← −1;
    end if
    l ← N₋;
    N₋ ← N₋ + 3n₋ + 1; n₋ ← n₋ + 1;
  else
    q_n ← q_n · q^(N₊−l);
    if 2 ∤ n₊ then
      s ← −1;
    end if
    l ← N₊;
    N₊ ← N₊ + 3n₊ + 2; n₊ ← n₊ + 1;
  end if
  η ← η + s · q_n;
  if |q_n| < 10^(−F) then
    return( q^(1/24) · η );
  end if
end while
```

### 4.2 Efficient Computation of the Weber Function $\mathfrak{f}_2$

We now turn to the Weber function $\mathfrak{f}_2$. Our three approaches to compute $\mathfrak{f}_2(\tau_Q)$ are already mentioned in the beginning of Sect. 4 and are similar to the case of the previous section. The task of determining the value $\mathfrak{f}_2(\tau_Q)$ is performed by our three algorithms `computeF2ViaProduct`, `computeF2ViaFourierSeries`, and `computeF2ViaEta`. We will see that using `computeF2ViaEta` is in practice the most efficient approach.

Input of all three algorithms is the same as in the case of the $\eta$-function. Each algorithm returns the value $\mathfrak{f}_2(\tau)$ within the precision $F$. The algorithms `computeF2ViaProduct` and `computeF2ViaFourierSeries` are straightforward. However, `computeF2ViaEta` makes use of the equation $\mathfrak{f}_2(\tau_Q) = \sqrt{2}\frac{\eta(2\tau_Q)}{\eta(\tau_Q)}$. Then the main observation is that we can compute numerator and denominator of this expression simultaneously; this is an obvious consequence of $q(2\tau) = q^2$. Hence we get our algorithm `computeF2ViaEta`$(\tau, F)$ from `computeEtaViaEulerSum`$(\tau, F)$ if we change the following lines ($\eta_2$ stores the current approximation of $\eta(2\tau)/q^{\frac{1}{12}}$):

| computeEtaViaEulerSum | computeF2ViaEta |
|---|---|
| $\eta \leftarrow 1 - q - q_n;$ | $\eta \leftarrow 1 - q - q_n; \quad \eta_2 \leftarrow 1 - q^2 - q_n^2;$ |
| $\eta \leftarrow \eta + s \cdot q_n;$ | $\eta \leftarrow \eta + s \cdot q_n; \quad \eta_2 \leftarrow \eta_2 + s \cdot q_n^2$ |
| return( $q^{\frac{1}{24}} \cdot \eta$ ); | return( $\sqrt{2} q^{\frac{1}{24}} \cdot \frac{\eta_2}{\eta}$ ); |

Obviously `computeF2ViaEta` returns the value $\mathfrak{f}_2(\tau)$ within the precision $F$. We compare the running times of all three algorithms for the reduced representatives of $C(-21311)$ in the appendix. Further practical results are listed in [Bai01]. As in the previous section `computeF2ViaEta` seems to be the most efficient of our algorithms to compute $\mathfrak{f}_2(\tau_Q)$ for high precision $F$, i.e. $F \geq 2000$. However, according to our experiments the same holds for low precisions.

### 4.3 Efficient Computation of the Functions $\gamma_2$ and $j$

Next we turn to the computation of the functions $\gamma_2$ and $j$. The result of the previous two sections is that we have to compare the running time of the computation of $\gamma_2$ by its Fourier series of Sect. 3.2 to the computation via the defining equation (2.3) using the algorithm `computeF2ViaEta`. This yields our algorithms `computeGamma2ViaFourierSeries`$(\tau, F)$ and `computeGamma2ViaEta`$(\tau, F)$, respectively. The input of the algorithms is the same as in the previous sections; both algorithms return the value $\gamma_2(\tau)$ within the precision $F$. Furthermore, their implementation is straightforward. Practical results for $C(-21311)$ are plotted in the appendix. It turns out that `computeGamma2ViaEta` is more efficient in practice.

Finally we regard the computation of singular moduli. As in the case of the function $\gamma_2$ we take two approaches into account: First we use algorithm `computeJViaFourierSeries`$(\tau, F)$, which implements the computation of $j(\tau)$ by its Fourier series of Sect. 3.1. Second we make use of the definition (2.4) and algorithm `computeGamma2ViaEta`$(\tau, F)$; this approach yields our algorithm `computeJViaEta`$(\tau, F)$. The input of both algorithms is as above. The running times for the class group of discriminant $\Delta = -21311$ can be found in the appendix. Further practical results are listed in Table 1. Obviously `computeJViaEta` is more efficient in practice. We remark that `computeJViaEta` does not need any precomputation and storage of coefficients. Furthermore, it only requires a small amount of main memory.

We conclude that the computation of the ring class polynomial of $\Delta = -21311$ using our efficient algorithm `computeJViaEta` takes about 5 minutes on the SUN; hence the generation of elliptic curves suitable for use in cryptography and having an endomorphism ring of class number 200 is feasible even when using ring class polynomials. This is in contrast to the opinion in the cryptographic community that using singular moduli does not yield an algorithm for generating elliptic curves having complex multiplication by an order of class

**Table 1.** Total running times on the SUN of the two alternatives to compute all $h_p(\Delta)$ values $j(\tau_{(a,b,c)})$ for $(a,b,c) \in C(\Delta)$, $b \geq 0$. $t_\eta$ denotes the running time of `computeJViaEta`, $t_f$ the running time of `computeJViaFourierSeries`.

| $\Delta$ | $h(\Delta)$ | $h_p(\Delta)$ | $F$ | $t_\eta$ in $s$ | $t_f$ in $s$ | $t_\eta/t_f$ |
|---|---|---|---|---|---|---|
| -21311 | 200 | 101 | 2234 | 290.10 | 486.86 | 0.59585918 |
| -30551 | 250 | 126 | 2837 | 594.02 | 1068.57 | 0.55590181 |
| -34271 | 300 | 151 | 3288 | 935.46 | 1765.62 | 0.52981955 |
| -47759 | 350 | 176 | 3982 | 1808.78 | 3663.97 | 0.49366671 |
| -67031 | 400 | 201 | 4809 | 2907.84 | 6235.32 | 0.46634976 |
| -75599 | 450 | 226 | 5331 | 3792.89 | 8371.53 | 0.45307011 |
| -96599 | 500 | 251 | 6104 | 5623.53 | 12827.73 | 0.43838855 |

number 200 and having reasonable practical running times. This becomes more evident when realizing that our SUN platform is far from being high-end.

## References


[AM93] A.O.L. Atkin and F. Morain. Elliptic curves and primality proving. *Mathematics of Computation*, 61:29–67, 1993.

[Bai01] H. Baier. Efficient Computation of Fourier Series and Singular Moduli with Application in Cryptography. Technical Report, Darmstadt University of Technology, 2001.

[BB00] H. Baier and J. Buchmann. Efficient Construction of Cryptographically Strong Elliptic Curves. In *Progress in Cryptology - INDOCRYPT2000*, LNCS 1977, pages 191–202, Berlin, 2000. Springer-Verlag.

[BSI00] Geeignete Kryptoalgorithmen gemäß §17(2) SigV, April 2000. Bundesamt für Sicherheit in der Informationstechnik.

[Cox89] D. Cox. Primes of the form $x^2 + ny^2$. John Wiley & Sons, 1989.

[Kan] M. Kaneko. Traces of singular moduli and the Fourier coefficients of the elliptic modular function $j(\tau)$. private communicated.

[Kob93] N. Koblitz. Introduction to Elliptic Curves and Modular Forms. Springer-Verlag, 1993.

[LiDIA] LiDIA. A library for computational number theory. Darmstadt University of Technology.
URL: http://www.informatik.tu-darmstadt.de/TI/LiDIA/Welcome.html.

[LZ94] G.-J. Lay and H.G. Zimmer. Constructing elliptic curves with given group order over large finite fields. In *Proceedings of ANTS I*, LNCS 877, pages 250–263, 1994.

[Mah76] K. Mahler. On a class of non-linear functional equations connected with modular functions. *Journal of the Australian Mathematical Society*, 22, Series A:65–120, 1976.

# A Running Times

We present running times on the SUN for all our algorithms of Sect. 4 to compute the values $\eta(\tau_Q)$, $\mathfrak{f}_2(\tau_Q)$, $\gamma_2(\tau_Q)$, and $j(\tau_Q)$ for all reduced representatives $Q = (a, b, c)$ of $C(-21311)$ with $b \geq 0$. We choose $\Delta = -21311$ as $\Delta$ is the maximal imaginary quadratic field discriminant of class number 200. Namely, for cryptographic purposes the German Information Security Agency [BSI00] recommends to use imaginary quadratic field discriminants of class number $\geq 200$.

As explained in Sect. 3.1 the running time to compute the value for a reduced representative $(a, b, c)$ mainly depends on $a$. Hence we plot the running time as a function of $a$. We use the floating point precision $F = 2234$, which comes from formula (3.9).

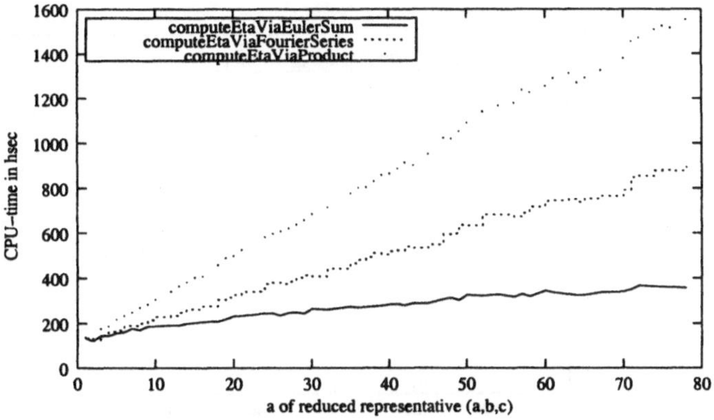


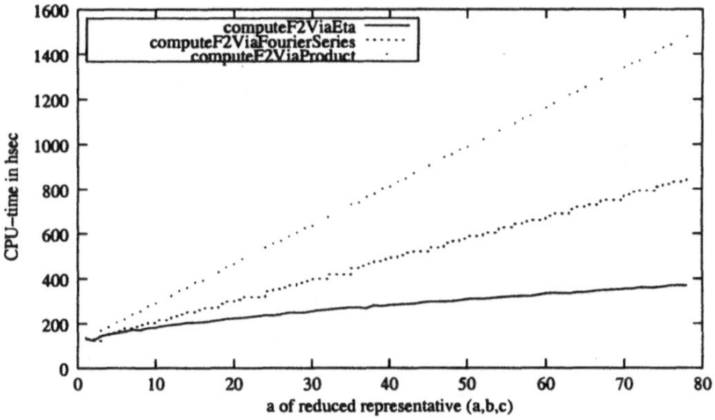

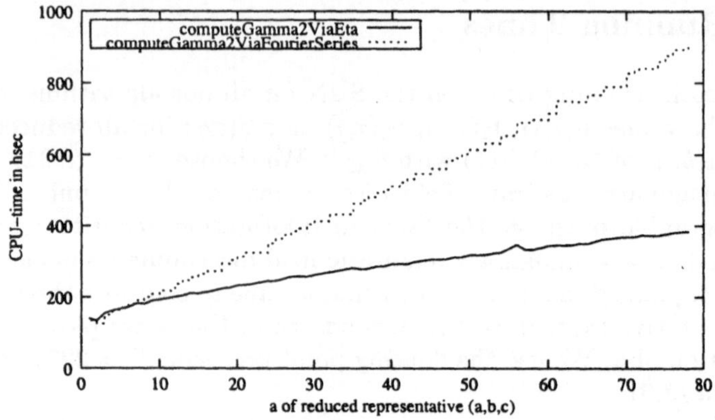
computeGamma2ViaEta
computeGamma2ViaFourierSeries
CPU–time in hsec
a of reduced representative (a,b,c)
0
200
400
600
800
1000
10
20
30
40
50
60
70
80

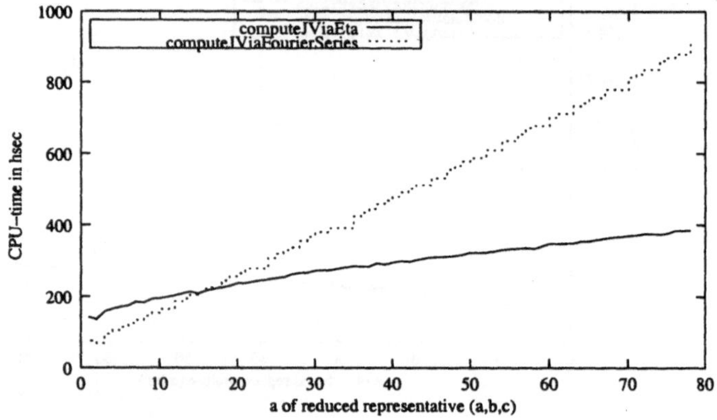
computeJViaEta
computeJViaFourierSeries
CPU–time in hsec
a of reduced representative (a,b,c)
0
200
400
600
800
1000
10
20
30
40
50
60
70
80

# Ambainis-Freivalds' Algorithm for Measure-Once Automata

Aija Bērziņa[1] and Richard Bonner[2]

[1] Institute of Math and Computer Science University of Latvia,
Raiņa bulvāris 29,LV-1459, Riga, Latvia ***
A.Berzina@itsystems.lv
[2] Department of Mathematics and Physics,
Malardalen University, Wasteras, Sweeden †
richard.bonner@mdh.se

**Abstract.** An algorithm given by Ambainis and Freivalds [1] constructs a quantum finite automaton (QFA) with $O(\log p)$ states recognizing the language $L_p = \{a^i |\ i \text{ is divisible by } p\}$ with probability $1 - \varepsilon$ , for any $\varepsilon > 0$ and arbitrary prime $p$. In [4] we gave examples showing that the algorithm is applicable also to quantum automata of very limited size. However, the Ambainis-Freivalds algoritm is tailored to constructing a *measure-many* QFA (defined by Kondacs and Watrous [2]), which cannot be implemented on existing quantum computers. In this paper we modify the algorithm to construct a *measure-once* QFA of Moore and Crutchfield [3] and give examples of parameters for this automaton. We show for the language $L_p$ that a measure-once QFA can be twice as space efficient as measure-many QFA's.

## 1 Introduction

For a background on quantum finite automata (QFA) and quantum computation in general, see Gruska's monograph [5]. Roughly, two models of quantum automata are current, the measure-once model due to Moore and Crutchfield [2] and the measure-many model due to Kondacs and Watrous [2]. Essentially, the former differs from the latter in that the quantum measurement is done once only at the end of the processing of an input string. Though the limitation to a single measurement limits the processing power of the automaton, it also saves computing space - an essential practical advantage, considering that the quantum computers of today have no larger than a few bits register. In this spirit, the present paper investigates the space efficiency of QFA's recognizing the languages $L_p = \{a^i |\ i \text{ is divisible by } p\}$ where $p$ is a prime integer. Our point of departure is an algorithm given by Ambainis and Freivalds [1] to construct

*** Research supported by Grant No. 01.0354 from the Latvian Council of Science, Contract IST-1999-11234 (QAIP) from the European Commission, and the Swedish Institute, Project ML-2000

† Supported by the ML-2000 project sponsored by the Sweedish Institute

R. Freivalds (Ed.): FCT 2001, LNCS 2138, pp. 83–93, 2001.

a measure-many quantum finite automata with $O(\log p)$ states recognizing the language $L_p$ with probability $1-\varepsilon$, for any $\varepsilon > 0$. In [4] we showed by examples that the algorithm is applicable to quantum automata of very limited size, though in general not small enough to be implemented on existing quantum computers. In this paper we modify the algorithm to construct a *measure-once* QFA of Moore and Crutchfield [3] recognizing $L_p$ and give examples of parameters for this automaton. We show in particular that the language $L_p$ can be recognized twice as space-efficiently by a measure-once QFA than by measure-many QFA's.

## 2 Measure-Once One-Way QFA

A measure-once 1-way QFA [2] is a tuple $U = (Q, \Sigma, \delta, q_0, F)$ where $Q$ is a set of states of finite cardinality $n$ with a singled out starting state $q_0 \in Q$ and a subset $F \subset Q$ of accepting states, $\Sigma$ is finite input alphabet with left end-marker symbol ¢ and right end-marker symbol \$ and $\delta = \delta(q, \sigma, q')$ is a unitary transition function

$$\delta : Q \times \Sigma \times Q \to \mathbb{C}$$

representing the probability density amplitude that flows from state $q$ to state $q'$ upon reading a symbol $\sigma$; the unitarity of $\delta$ is understood as the unitarity of the $n \times n$ matrix $T_\sigma$ defined by $\delta(q, \sigma, q')_{q,q' \in Q}$ for every $\sigma \in \Sigma$. An input string $x = x_1 x_2 \ldots x_m \in \Sigma^m$ is read left to right; we assume all input ends with the end-marker \$, the last symbol read before the computation terminates. At the end of a computation, the automaton measures its configuration and outputs a probability of acceptance of the input string. The computation and measurement are done as follows. The matrices $T_\sigma$ act on $n$-dimentional complex unit vectors $|\Psi\rangle \in \mathbb{C}^Q$, the *configurations* of $U$. In the orthonormal basis $\{|q\rangle\}_{q \in Q}$ corresponding to the states $q \in Q$ of $U$,one writes $|\Psi\rangle = \sum_{q \in Q} \alpha_q \cdot |q\rangle$, $\sum_{q \in Q} |\alpha_q|^2 = 1$, saying that $|\Psi\rangle$ is a linear superposition of (pure) states $q \in Q$. The coefficient $\alpha_q$ is interpreted as the probability density amplitude of $U$ being in state $q$. Then, if $U$ is in configuration $|\Psi\rangle$ and reads symbol $\sigma$, it moves into a new configuration

$$T_\sigma |\Psi\rangle = \sum_{q,q' \in Q} \alpha_q \cdot \delta(q, \sigma, q') \cdot |q'\rangle ,$$

and hence, after starting in the state $q_0$ and reading a string $x = x_1 x_2 \ldots x_m$, its configuration becomes $|\Psi_x\rangle = T_{x_m} T_{x_{m-1}} \ldots T_{x_1} |q_0\rangle$ . The measurement is then performed by a diagonal zero-one projection matrix $P$ with $P_{qq} = 1$ if and only if $q \in F$; the probability of accepting the string $x$ is defined as

$$p_M(x) = \langle \Psi_x | P | \Psi_x \rangle = \| P |\Psi_x\rangle \|^2 .$$

## 3 The Ambainis-Freivalds Algorithm for Measure-Once Automata

Let $p$ be a prime integer and consider the language $L_p$ consisting of all words in a single letter $a$ of length divisible by $p$.

**Theorem 1.1** *For any $\varepsilon > 0$, there is a QFA with $O(\log p)$ states recognizing $L_p$ with probability 1-$\varepsilon$.*

**Theorem 1.2** *Any deterministic 1-way finite automaton recognizing $L_p$ has at least $p$ states.* Generally, 1-way probabilistic finite automata can recognize some languages with the number of states being close to the logarithm of the number of states needed by a deterministic automaton; see [2] and [3]. However, this is not the case with $L_p$.

**Theorem 1.3** *Any 1-way probabilistic finite automaton recognizing $L_p$ with probability $\frac{1}{2} + \varepsilon$, for a fixed $\varepsilon > 0$, has at least $p$ states.*

**Corollary 1.1** *There is a language $L_p$ such that the number of states needed by a probabilistic automaton is exponential in the number of states needed by a 1-way QFA.* Complete proofs of the theorems are given in [1]. In this paper we only relate the algorithm by which the automaton in Theorem 1.1 can be constructed and which was used to find examples given bellow. First, we construct an automaton accepting all words in $L_p$ with probability 1 and accepting all words not in $L_p$ with probability at most 7/8.

Let $U_k$, for $k \in \{1,..,p-1\}$ be a quantum automaton with a set of states $Q = \{q_0, q_{acc}\}$, a starting state $|q_0\rangle$, $F = \{q_{acc}\}$. The transition function is defined as follows. Reading $a$ maps $|q_0\rangle$ to $\cos\varphi|q_0\rangle + i\sin\varphi|q_{acc}\rangle$ and $|q_{acc}\rangle$ to $i\sin\varphi|q_0\rangle + \cos\varphi|q_{acc}\rangle$ where $\varphi = \frac{2\pi jk}{p}$. The superposition of $U_k$ after reading $a^j$ is $\cos(\frac{2\pi jk}{p})|q_0\rangle + \sin(\frac{2\pi jk}{p})|q_{acc}\rangle$. Therefore, the probability of $U_k$ accepting $a^i$ is $\cos^2(\frac{2\pi jk}{p})$. If $j$ is divisible by $p$, then $\frac{2\pi jk}{p}$ is a multiple of $2\pi$, $\cos^2(\frac{2\pi jk}{p}) = 1$ and, therefore, all automata $U_k$ accept words in $L_p$ with probability 1. For any word $a^j$ not in $L_p$, at least $\frac{p-1}{2}$ of all $U_k$ reject $a^j$ with probability at least $\frac{1}{2}$. We call such $U_k$ "good".

Next, we consider sequences of $\lceil 8\ln p\rceil$ $k$'s. A sequence is good for $a^j$ if at least $\frac{1}{4}$ of all its elements are good for $a^j$. There is a sequence, which is good for all $j \in \{1,..,p-1\}$. This sequence is good for $a^j$ not in $L_p$ with $j > p$ as well because any $U_k$ returns to the starting state after $a^p$ and, hence, works in the same way on $a^j$ and $a^{j mod p}$.

Now, we use a good sequence $k_1, ..., k_{\lceil 8\ln p\rceil}$ to construct a quantum automaton recognizing $L_p$. The automaton consists of $U_{k1}$, $U_{k2}$ , ... ,$U_{k\lceil 8\ln p\rceil}$ and a distinguished starting state. Upon reading the left endmarker ¢, it passes from the starting state to a superposition where $|q_0\rangle$ of all $U_{kl}$ have equal amplitudes. Words in $L_p$ are always accepted because all $U_k$ accept them. Words not in $L_p$ are rejected with probability at least $\frac{1}{8}$. Finally, we sketch how to increase the probability of correct answer to $1-\varepsilon$ for an arbitrary $\varepsilon > 0$. We do it by increasing the probability of correct answer for each $U_k$. Namely, we consider an automaton $U'_k$ with $2^d$ states where $d$ is a constant depending on the required probability $1-\varepsilon$. The states are labeled by strings of $0'$s and $1'$s of length $d$ : $q_{0\ldots00}$ , $q_{0\ldots.01}$ and so on. The starting state is the state $q_{0\ldots00}$ corresponding to the all - 0 string. The transition function is defined by

$$\delta(q_{x_1\ldots x_d}, a, q_{y_1\ldots y_d}) = \prod_{j=1}^{d} \delta(q_{x_1}, a, q_{y_1}).$$

The only accepting state is $q_{0\ldots00}$. The amplitude of $|q_0\rangle \otimes \ldots \otimes |q_0\rangle = q_{0\ldots00}$ in this superposition is $\cos^d(\frac{2\pi jk}{p})$. If $j$ is a multiple of $p$, then this is 1, meaning that words in $L_p$ are always accepted. For $a^j$ not in $L_p$, we call $U'_k$ $\delta$ - good if it rejects $a^j$ with probability at least $1-\delta$. For a suitable constant $d$, at least $1-\delta$ of all $U'_k$ are good. Taking $\delta = \frac{\varepsilon}{3}$ and choosing $d$ so that it satisfies the previous condition completes the proof.

The idea of the proof may be visualised geometrically as follows. We mark amplitudes of $|q_0\rangle$ on one axis and amplitudes of $|q_1\rangle$ on another. The automaton starts in superposition $|q_0\rangle$ (see Fig. 1, $a^0$). As the letter $a$ is read, the vector is

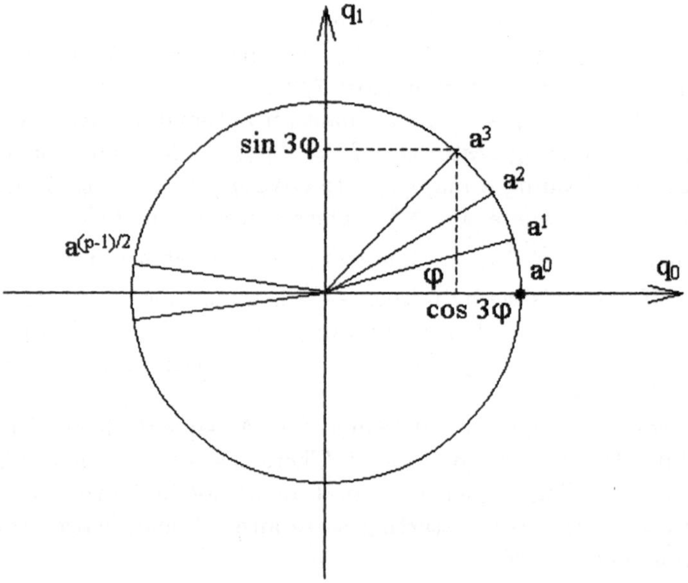


**Fig. 1.**

rotated by angle $\varphi$, where $\varphi = \frac{2\pi k}{p}$. After rotation the end of vector is located at point $a^1$. Reading next letter a new rotation is performed and $a^2$ is reached and so on. It is easy to see that the vector returns to starting state after reading $p$ $a$'s, hence, the automaton works in the same way on $a^j$ and $a^{j mod p}$ and we can consider $j \in \{0,..,p-1\}$. The amplitudes of $|q_0\rangle$ and $|q_1\rangle$ after reading $a^j$ equals to vector projections onto the axes $q_0$ and $q_1$ respectively (Fig. 1, dotted line). Every input word is accepted with probability $\cos^2(j\varphi)$. It equals to 1, if $j$ is a multiple of $p$, and is less than 1 otherwise. So in the abstract $L_p$ can be recognized even with one $U_k$, however, in fact $\varphi$ approaches 0 as $p$ grows and for more and more $j$'s the number $\cos^2(j\varphi)$ is close to 1.

The main idea of the algorithm is thus to take several $k_1, k_2, .., k_n$ countervailing bad cases of one another. In the instance shown in Fig. 2 $k_1 = 1, k_2 = 2$ and $p = 5$. We can see that the input word $a^1$ will be accepted by $U_2$ with large probability ($a^1$ in brackets) and will be accepted by $U_1$ with small probability ($a^1$ without brackets). And vice versa with $a^3$ - $U_1$ will accept it with large probability, but $U_2$ with small. Using the two automata at a time, they mutually correct "bad" probabilities and performs better than each of them individually.

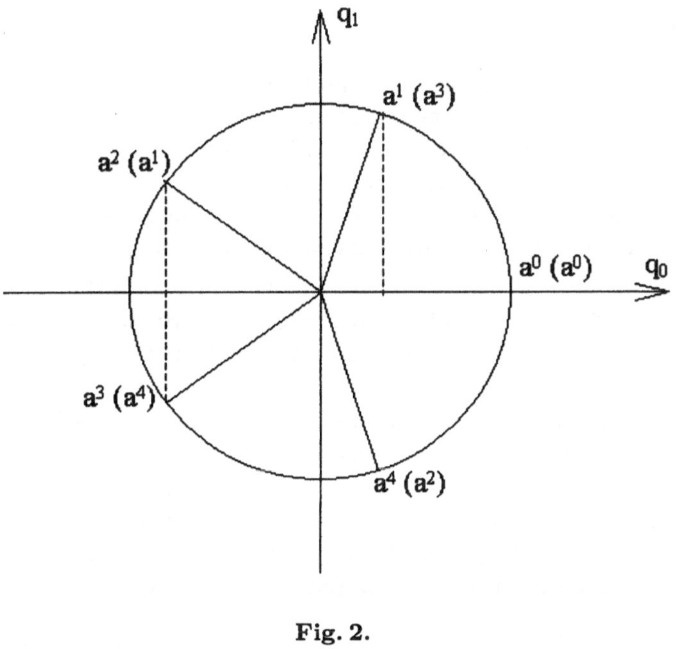


**Fig. 2.**

## 4 Examples of Parameters

Assuming the largest quantum computer built has seven bits of memory, none of our examples may have more than $2^7 = 128$ states. To implement each $U_k$ two states are needed - one accepting and one simple working state. Additionally one starting state is necessary common for all $U_k$'s. So, if we arbitrary choose a sequence of $\lceil 8lnp \rceil U_k$ as described before, then $\lceil 8lnp \rceil < 128/2 = 64$ and it follows that $p$ can not be greater than 2971.

However, we can choose shorter sequences of $U_k$ and still obtain good results. We denote by $\psi = \frac{2\pi}{p}$ the smallest angle by which the rotation can be performed after reading an input symbol /a/ and take it for unit angle.

| | | | |
|---|---|---|---|
| 1 | 2 | ... | p −1 |
| 2 | 4 | ... | 2*(p − 1) mod p |
| ... | .... | .... | .... |
| p −1 | 2*(p − 1) mod p | ... | (p − 1)² mod p |

**Fig. 3.**

Let us examine tables of products modulo $p$, i.e. tables containing numbers $(i * j) \, mod \, p$, where $i$ is a number of row and $j$ is a number of column. The $k^{th}$ row of the table corresponds to automaton $U_k$ and the $j^{th}$ column of the $k^{th}$ row shows, by how many units the vector is turned away from the starting state after $j$ input symbols are read. I.e. the $2^{-nd}$ row describes automaton which superposition vector rotates by angle $2\psi = 2\frac{2\pi}{p}$ (by 2 units) after reading every input symbol /a/, and the $3^{-rd}$ column in this row shows that after reading 3 symbols /a/ the vector is rotated by angle $3*2\psi = 6\frac{2\pi}{p}$ (6 units). For any language $L_p$ (for any $p$) we aim to find a combination of automata $U_{k1}, U_{k2}, ..., U_{kn}$ such that:

1. a number of automata in combination is as small as possible;
2. a probability of giving correct answer is as big as possible.

So we search for a sequence of rows $r_1, r_2, .., r_n$ in table such that the greatest sum $\sum_{i=1}{}^{n} \cos^2(\psi * r_{ij})$ - the probability of accepting a word not in $L_p$ - is as small as possible ($r_{ij}$ is the $j^{th}$ element of the $i^{th}$ row, $j \in \{1, \dots, p-1\}$).

To ease the search the table can be reduced as follows.

1. As $(p - i) \cdot (p - j) = p^2 - ip - jp + ij \equiv ij (\text{mod } p)$ the table is symmetrical for center, and this means that rows $i$ and $(p - i)$ are mirror displaying each other.
   Additionally, $i(p - j) \equiv ip - ij \equiv -ij (\text{mod } p)$ so $a_j = p - a_{p-j}$.

| | | | | |
|---|---|---|---|---|
| $a_1$ | $a_2$ | ... | $a_{p-2}$ | $a_{p-1}$ |
| $a_{p-1}$ | $a_{p-2}$ | ... | $a_2$ | $a_1$ |

**Fig. 4.**

2. Since operation of multiplication is commutative, the table is also symmetrical with respect to main diagonal and $1^{st}$ assertion is also right for columns.
3. It is possible to notice in figures given above that $U_k$ accepts input words $a_j$ and $a_{p-j}$ with equal probabilities. Indeed, $\cos^2(\frac{2\pi k(p-j)}{p}) = \cos^2(-\frac{2\pi kj}{p}) = \cos^2(\frac{2\pi kj}{p})$. Thus we can replace all the numbers greater than $\frac{p-1}{2}$ by numbers $p-j$.
4. It follows form statements 1 and 2 that the $i^{th}$ and the $(p-i)^{th}$ rows will be identical after replacement, and the same can be said about the columns. For example, for $p = 11$ the table looks as shown in Fig. 5.

| | | | | | | | | | |
|---|---|---|---|---|---|---|---|---|---|
| 1 | 2 | 3 | 4 | 5 | 6 | 7 | 8 | 9 | 10 |
| 2 | 4 | 6 | 8 | 10 | 1 | 3 | 5 | 7 | 9 |
| 3 | 6 | 9 | 1 | 4 | 7 | 10 | 2 | 5 | 8 |
| 4 | 8 | 1 | 5 | 9 | 2 | 6 | 10 | 3 | 7 |
| 5 | 10 | 4 | 9 | 3 | 8 | 2 | 7 | 1 | 6 |
| 6 | 1 | 7 | 2 | 8 | 3 | 9 | 4 | 10 | 5 |
| 7 | 3 | 10 | 6 | 2 | 9 | 5 | 1 | 8 | 4 |
| 8 | 5 | 2 | 10 | 7 | 4 | 1 | 9 | 6 | 3 |
| 9 | 7 | 5 | 3 | 1 | 10 | 8 | 6 | 4 | 2 |
| 10 | 9 | 8 | 7 | 6 | 5 | 4 | 3 | 2 | 1 |

→

| | | | | | | | | | |
|---|---|---|---|---|---|---|---|---|---|
| 1 | 2 | 3 | 4 | 5 | 5 | 4 | 3 | 2 | 1 |
| 2 | 4 | 5 | 3 | 1 | 1 | 3 | 5 | 4 | 2 |
| 3 | 5 | 2 | 1 | 4 | 4 | 1 | 2 | 5 | 3 |
| 4 | 3 | 1 | 5 | 2 | 2 | 5 | 1 | 3 | 4 |
| 5 | 1 | 4 | 2 | 3 | 3 | 2 | 4 | 1 | 5 |
| 5 | 1 | 4 | 2 | 3 | 3 | 2 | 4 | 1 | 5 |
| 4 | 3 | 1 | 5 | 2 | 2 | 5 | 1 | 3 | 4 |
| 3 | 5 | 2 | 1 | 4 | 4 | 1 | 2 | 5 | 3 |
| 2 | 4 | 5 | 3 | 1 | 1 | 3 | 5 | 4 | 2 |
| 1 | 2 | 3 | 4 | 5 | 5 | 4 | 3 | 2 | 1 |

**Fig. 5.**

So it is enough to consider the part of the table with row and column numbers ranging from 1 to $\frac{p-1}{2}$. We tint cells in the matrix, containing numbers $r_{ij}$ that

| | | | | |
|---|---|---|---|---|
| 1 | 2 | 3 | 4 | 5 |
| 2 | 4 | 5 | 3 | 1 |
| 3 | 5 | 2 | 1 | 4 |
| 4 | 3 | 1 | 5 | 2 |
| 5 | 1 | 4 | 2 | 3 |

**Fig. 6.**

we consider "bad", i.e. having $|\cos(r_{ij}\psi)|$ greater than some fixed constant $\delta$, and search for combinations of rows, containing no columns with number of tinted cells greater than $\frac{1}{2}$ of number of rows. This guarantees that a sufficient number of $U_k$'s gives the right answer with good probability after any number of letters read.

It is very important to choose right constant $\delta$. If it is too big, amount of check variants increases unnecessary, if the constant is too small - it becomes impossible to find any combination meeting the initial demands. In addition, small $\delta$ does not guarantee that the combination found will be successful, and it is possible that taking greater $\delta$ allows finding a better combination.

Take, for example, $p = 23$ and $\delta = 0.9$. Taking $k_1 = 1$, $k_2 = 2$, $k_3 = 6$ and $k_4 = 10$, the words not in $L_p$ are accepted with probability at most 0.62579395. If $\delta = 0.8$, this combination turn impossible, because $1^{st}$ column contains 3 "bad" cells. We construct a new automaton from 4 $U_k$'s, by adding a common starting state to them. And since words not in $L_p$ are accepted with probability greater than 1/2, even if $p$ is as small as 23, we add another new state to our automaton, so as word is rejected with some probability without reading any letters. Thus the automaton accepts words not in $L_p$ with probability less than 1/2, but words in $L_p$ - with probability greater than $\frac{1}{2}$. So altogether we need $4 * 2 + 1 + 1 = 10$ states. The greatest $p$ for which $L_p$ can be recognized with deterministic or probabilistic automaton having at most 10 states is 7. However a QFA can be constructed for much greater p's.

| | | | | | | | | | | |
|---|---|---|---|---|---|---|---|---|---|---|
| 1 | 2 | 3 | 4 | 5 | 6 | 7 | 8 | 9 | 10 | 11 |
| 2 | 4 | 6 | 8 | 10 | 11 | 9 | 7 | 5 | 3 | 1 |
| 6 | 11 | 5 | 1 | 7 | 10 | 4 | 2 | 8 | 9 | 3 |
| 10 | 3 | 7 | 6 | 4 | 9 | 1 | 11 | 2 | 8 | 5 |

| | | | | | | | | | | |
|---|---|---|---|---|---|---|---|---|---|---|
| 1 | 2 | 3 | 4 | 5 | 6 | 7 | 8 | 9 | 10 | 11 |
| 2 | 4 | 6 | 8 | 10 | 11 | 9 | 7 | 5 | 3 | 1 |
| 6 | 11 | 5 | 1 | 7 | 10 | 4 | 2 | 8 | 9 | 3 |
| 10 | 3 | 7 | 6 | 4 | 9 | 1 | 11 | 2 | 8 | 5 |

**Fig. 7.**

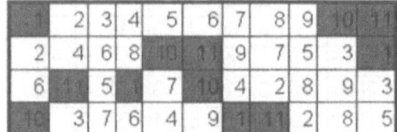

For every prime $p$ we search for a combination of 4 automata $U_{k1}$, $U_{k2}$, $U_{k3}$, $U_{k4}$, represented by their numbers $k_1$, $k_2$, $k_3$ and $k_4$ such that the greatest sum $\sum_{i=1}^{4} \cos^2(\psi * k_i * j)$ $(j \in \{1, ..., \frac{p-1}{2}\})$ is as small as possible. The values were calculated by computer. Results are shown in Fig. 8. In the first column of table the values of $p$ are given, the next 4 columns contain values chosen for $k_1, k_2, k_3$ and $k_4$, and the last - probability of getting a correct answer from the new automaton. So every row of the table means: "If prime $p$ is given, then to recognize language $L_p$ 4 automata $U_k$ should be taken. The first automaton rotates by $k_1$ units after reading every input symbol, the second - by $k_2$ units, etc. The automaton constructed in such way recognizes language $L_p$ with probability given in last column."

Example, if $p = 23$, then the automaton composed from $U_1, U_2, U_6$ and $U_{10}$, will accept words in $L_{23}$ with probability 0.687103025 and will reject words not in $L_{23}$ with probability at least 0.687103025. We can notice that as $p$ grows, as probability of correct answer decreases. Enlarging a number of $U_k'$s can increase it. The table shown in Fig. 9 is analogical to that in Fig. 8, though now six $U_k$' are combined. We can see that the probability of the correct answer is greater that in case of 4 k's, but the amount of states needed is increased and we need 6*2+2 = 14 states instead of 10. To show better the relationship between number of states and the probability, we use following characteristic. If n rows are chosen

| p | $k_1$ | $k_2$ | $k_3$ | $k_4$ | Probability |
|---|---|---|---|---|---|
| 23 | 1 | 2 | 6 | 10 | 0.687103025 |
| 41 | 1 | 3 | 8 | 18 | 0.65570911 |
| 47 | 3 | 4 | 16 | 21 | 0.653772575 |
| 53 | 2 | 18 | 22 | 23 | 0.648914555 |
| 61 | 3 | 7 | 22 | 30 | 0.640072135 |
| 67 | 2 | 8 | 9 | 31 | 0.639009085 |
| 71 | 8 | 10 | 33 | 34 | 0.63593091 |
| 73 | 3 | 7 | 8 | 30 | 0.633975595 |
| 79 | 26 | 34 | 36 | 39 | 0.628642435 |
| 101 | 4 | 6 | 17 | 49 | 0.620153905 |
| 239 | 119 | 117 | 100 | 65 | 0.586297676 |
| 541 | 270 | 11 | 29 | 122 | 0.56089205 |
| 1223 | 611 | 8 | 69 | 188 | 0.54200882 |

**Fig. 8.**

from the table and we select an arbitrary column in these rows, then the rows corresponding to numbers in column, contain all the same combinations as initial rows.

| p | $k_1$ | $k_2$ | $k_3$ | $k_4$ | $k_5$ | $k_6$ | Probability |
|---|---|---|---|---|---|---|---|
| 41 | 1 | 2 | 6 | 9 | 13 | 18 | 0.69159491 |
| 47 | 1 | 6 | 8 | 10 | 13 | 22 | 0.68688036 |
| 79 | 1 | 23 | 27 | 31 | 36 | 38 | 0.6716339 |
| 239 | 3 | 116 | 104 | 39 | 105 | 82 | 0.63069038 |

**Fig. 9.**

Example, $p = 23$, we choose rows 1,2,6 and 10. Then we select any column, let's say $7^{th}$. The column contains numbers 1,4,7 and 9. Now, if we take $1^{st}, 4^{th}, 7^{th}$ and $9^{th}$ row, that the columns contain the same combinations as rows 1,2,6 and 10 (Fig. 10).

Thus we can get $\frac{p-1}{2}$ different automata, which have the same probability of correct answer but have different "worst" words. It is possible to construct a new automaton as combination of two such automata. The new automaton is two times bigger, but has better probability.

Example. p = 1223. We use for combination the example given above, and after that make the combination from result of the first. Thus we make an automaton with 18 states from two automata having 10 states each, and then an automaton having 34 states from two automata with 18 states. Automata con-

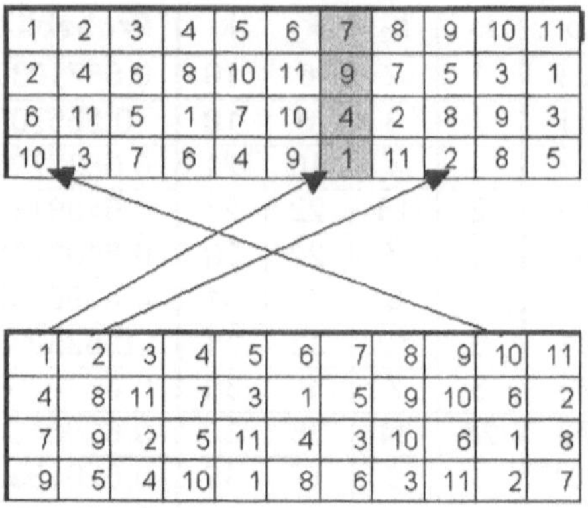


**Fig. 10.**

structed in such way are far from being optimal, but this method is easy to use and it gives certain improvement of probability. Overall these examples show,

| | | | | | | | | | | | | | | | | |
|---|---|---|---|---|---|---|---|---|---|---|---|---|---|---|---|---|
| 8 | 69 | 188 | 611 | | | | | | | | | | | | | 0.54200882 |
| 8 | 69 | 188 | 253 | 266 | 379 | 553 | 611 | | | | | | | | | 0.59806329 |
| 8 | 30 | 61 | 69 | 159 | 188 | 253 | 266 | 273 | 379 | 471 | 480 | 497 | 504 | 553 | 611 | 0.65173586 |

**Fig. 11.**

that, by increasing number of states, it is possible to construct a quantum automaton giving the correct answer with large probability. On the other hand, if we acquiesce in a smaller probability, we can reduce the size of automaton notably. And finally, all the examples show that quantum automata can be very space-efficient. The automaton in last example has 34 states, and it recognizes $L_{1223}$ with probability 0.65173586. At the same time, any deterministic or probabilistic automaton recognizing this language has at least 1223 states.

We can see also that the $measure - once$ quantum finite automata is about 2 times more space efficient than corresponding $measure - many$ automaton because of its simple construction. Indeed, every $U_k$ for $measure - once$ has 2 states while for $measure - many$ automata 4 states are needed.

## References

1. A. Ambainis, R.Freivalds, 1-way quantum finite automata: strengths, weaknesses and generalizations. *LANL e-print quant-ph/980262 v3.*
2. A. Kondacs, J. Watrous, On the power of quantum finite state automata. *Proceedings of the 38th IEEE Conference on Foundations of Computer Science,* 66-75, 1997.

3. C. Moore, J. Crutchfield. Quantum automata and quantum grammars. Santa-Fe Institute Working Paper 97-07-062, 1997. Also quant-ph/9707031.
4. A. Berzina, R. Bonner and R. Freivalds. Parameters in Ambainis-Freivalds Algorithm. *Proc. Int. Workshop on Quantum Computation and Learning, Sundbyholm, May 2000.*
5. J. Gruska. Quantum Computing, McGraw Hill (1999)

# Are There Essentially Incomplete Knowledge Representation Systems?

Jānis Cīrulis

University of Latvia,
Riga LV-1586, Latvia
jc@fmf.lu.lv

**Abstract.** A mathematical model of a knowledge representation system (KR-system) is proposed. Its prototype is the concept of an information system in the sense of Z. Pawlak; however, the model is, in fact, a substantial extension of the latter. In our model, attributes may form an arbitrary category, where morphisms represent built-in functional dependencies, and uncertainty of knowledge is treated in terms of category theory via monads. Several notions of simulation are also considered for such KR-systems. In this general setting, the semiphilosophical problem mentioned in the title, still open, is given a precise meaning.

**Keywords:** complete information, fuzzification, knowledge representation system, simulation, uncertainty

## 1 Introduction

**1.** Z. Pawlak introduced his notion of information system in late 70'ies [13]. Various versions of this notion has been given other names; probably, the best known terms are 'attribute system' and 'knowledge representation system' (see [12,2]). We choose here the traditional term and adopt the later one for our general systems in the subsequent section.

A *deterministic information system* is a system of the form $(Ob, At, Val, f)$, where

- $Ob$ is a non-empty set of *objects*,
- $At$ is a set of their *attributes*,
- $Val$ is a family $(Val_a, a \in At)$ of sets: each $Val_a$ is considered as the set of *values of* $a$,
- $f$ is a function $Ob \times At \to \bigcup(Val_a\colon a \in At)$ such that $f(o,a) \in Val_a$; it is called the *information function.*

Supposing that the information function here might be of type

$$Ob \times At \to \bigcup(P_0(Val_a)\colon a \in At)$$

and satisfy the condition $f(o,a) \subset P_0(Val_a)$, where $P_0(X)$ stands for the set of nonempty subsets of $X$, we come to a wider class of information systems

R. Freivalds (Ed.): FCT 2001, LNCS 2138, pp. 94–105, 2001.

which contains also nondeterministic ones. Formally, any deterministic information system can be regarded as a *complete* system of this kind with each $f(o,a)$ a singletone. With this in mind, we shall further discuss only these general systems.

**2.** Now a question can be posed as to whether there exist essentially indeterministic information systems. The easy answer is negative; however, it makes sense to state the problem more formally and to examine some details of its solution.

Let $\boldsymbol{S} := (Ob, At, Val, f)$ and $\boldsymbol{S}' := (Ob', At', Val', f')$ be two information systems. Intuitively, $\boldsymbol{S}'$ contains more information than $\boldsymbol{S}$ if the objects of $\boldsymbol{S}$ can be modelled by those of $\boldsymbol{S}'$ in the following sense: there are

- a mapping $m\colon Ob \to P_0(Ob')$ representing each object from $Ob$ as a (fusion of a) collection of objects of $\boldsymbol{S}'$.
- a function $I\colon At \to At'$ which codes each attribute of $\boldsymbol{S}$ by an attribute of $\boldsymbol{S}'$,
- a family $\lambda$ of functions $\lambda_a\colon Val'_{I(a)} \to Val_a$ which interprets in $\boldsymbol{S}$ values of these codes in $\boldsymbol{S}'$,

such that, for all $o \in Ob$ and $a \in At$

$$f(o,a) = \{\lambda_a(v')\colon v' \in f'(o', I(a)) \text{ for some } o' \in m(o)\} \ . \tag{1.1}$$

In particular, if $At \subset At'$, $Val'_a \subset Val_a$, and $I$ and $\lambda_a$ are all the identity mappings, then (1.1) amounts to

$$f(o,a) = \bigcup(f'(o',a)\colon o' \in m(o)) \ .$$

We could consider a more general concept of modelling, where $I$ interprets $At$ into $P_0(At')$ and each $\lambda_a$ is a function of type $\prod(Val'_b\colon b \in I(a)) \to Val_a$. Alternatively, the subsets of attributes we are interested in could be included in $At$ as additional elements ("complex attributes"); in doing so, some structure on $At$ should be introduced. This is the way we proceed in the next section, but these refinements are not relevant to the present discussion.

Our problem can now be stated as follows:

> are there information systems that cannot be modelled by a deterministic one?

As we noted above, the answer is negative. Indeed, let $\boldsymbol{S} = (Ob, At, Val, f)$ be an information system. Put $Ob'$ to be the set of all maps $\varphi\colon At \to \bigcup(Val_a\colon a \in At)$ such that $\varphi(a) \in V_a$ for all $a \in At$, and define the function $f'$ on $Ob' \times At$ by $f(\varphi, a) := \varphi(a)$. Then $\boldsymbol{S}' := (Ob', At, Val, f')$ is a deterministic information system. Given an object $o \in Ob$, denote by $m(o)$ the subset $\{\varphi \in Ob'\colon \varphi(a) \in f(a,o) \text{ for all } a \in At\}$. If $I$ and all $\lambda_a$ are the identity selfmaps on $At$ and $Val_a$ respectively, then the triple $(I, \lambda, m)$ shows that $\boldsymbol{S}$ is modelled by $\boldsymbol{S}'$.

**3.** Our aim in this paper is to call attention to this "determinability" problem in a maximally general setting, in which case it could have a negative answer as well. Towards this end, we propose a rather general concept of an information system (renamed below a knowledge representation, or KR-system), which is described in terms of category theory. Consider $At$ as a discrete category, $Val$ as an $At$-shaped diagram in the category of sets $\mathbb{S}$, and $Ob$ as an object of $\mathbb{S}$. For each $a \in At$, the function $f$ induces a family $f^*$ of mappings $f_a\colon Ob \to P_0(V_a)$ by $f_a(o) := f(o,a)$. Then $(At, Val, Ob, f^*)$ is an extremely simple example of an extended knowledge representation system. The basic definition (Def. 1) is motivated even by likewise rearranged deterministic information systems.

Aside from this introduction, the paper consists of three sections. In Sect. 2, we introduce the concepts of a (deterministic) KR-system over an arbitrary category $\mathsf{C}$ and a simulation for these systems, and show that KR-systems form a category if simulations are taken for morphisms. We also discuss here the intuitive meaning of our abstract definitions. KR-systems admitting uncertainty, or fuzzy (in a wide sense of the term) systems are considered in Sect. 3. Formally, they are deterministic KR-systems over the Kleisli category of $\mathsf{C}$ w.r.t. some monad, and uncertainty becomes apparent only when they are reinterpreted relatively to $\mathsf{C}$ itself. At last, Sect. 4 contains a precise statement of the mentioned problem and some related preliminary results.

In this introductory paper we primarily tried to elaborate the very concepts of a (model of) knowledge representation system and simulation. The presented results, all without proofs, are mainly technical or illustrative. The reader is supposed to be familiar with the basic notions of category theory, such as a functor, a natural transformation, a (co)limit of a functor, a monad, and is referred to [6,11,15] for further information on these matters.

## 2 Knowledge Representation Systems

**1.** Let $\mathsf{C}$ be some category.

**Definition 1.** *By an* knowledge representation system, *or just* KR-system *(relatively to* $\mathsf{C}$*) we mean a quadruple* $\boldsymbol{S} := (\mathsf{A}, V, S, \Pi)$, *where*

- $\mathsf{A}$ *is a small category (with the object set* $|\mathsf{A}|$*),*
- $V$ *is a contravariant functor from* $\mathsf{A}$ *to* $\mathsf{C}$ *that respects colimits (i.e. take them into limits in* $V(\mathsf{A})$*),*
- $S$ *is a* $\mathsf{C}$*-object, and*
- $\Pi$ *is a cone* $(\pi_a\colon S \to V(a)), a \in |A|)$ *in* $\mathsf{C}$ *to the base* $V$.

Let us shortly discuss the intuitive meaning of this formal scheme.

Intuitively, the objects of $\mathsf{A}$ are *attributes* which the system $\boldsymbol{S}$ "recognises", and $V$ assigns to every attribute $a$ a $\mathsf{C}$-object $V_a := V(a)$ interpreted as the stock of *possible values of* $a$. An arrow from $a$ to $b$ in $\mathsf{A}$ indicates that $a$ depends on $b$ (see below). If $b \in A$ is the colimit of some diagram $D$ in $\mathsf{A}$, then we may think of the attribute $b$ as a complex attribute "consisting" of the nodes of $D$

as interconnected components. It is, then, natural to regard that the value of $b$ is completely determined by the values of these components. This is why $V$ was required to respect colimits of A.

As usual, attributes in A are thought of as attributes of certain objects or (to avoid misunderstanding of the term 'object' in the present context) entities. Following the tradition of Pawlak's information systems, the object $S$ should be considered as the object of these entities. We prefer a somewhat different interpretation; namely, we call $S$ the object of *knowledge states*, each state being considered as representing a more or less complete description of an entity. Accordingly, each value, attached to the corresponding attribute, is then thought of as a restricted piece of knowledge admitting a direct access "by name". To put this another way, the possible queries to a KR-system are supposed to be of the kind "What is the value of this attribute?".

In this paper we do not discuss relations between a KR-system and the world of entities. In particular, the question whether the chosen system of attributes is sufficient to separate entities does not concern us here; we avoid entities from the following discussions at all (the only exception is at the beginning of the final section).

The projection $\pi_a$ provides the potential value of $a$ (the answer to the query) in a given state of the system. Since $\Pi$ is a cone, if $\alpha$ is an arrow from $a$ to $b$, then values of $a$ can be calculated from those of $b$ in virtue of the corresponding C-morphism $\overleftarrow{\alpha} := V(\alpha)\colon V_b \to V_a$.

What about the possibility to get to know values of several attributes simultaneously? Let us call a set $A$ of attributes *compatible* if there is an attribute $b$ and a set of coordinated arrows to $b$ from each $a \in A$: then the values of all $a$'s can be consistently calculated from the values of $b$. More precisely, if $\Delta_A$ is the embedding functor of the full subcategory of A spanned on $A$ into A, then $A$ is compatible if and only if there is a cone from $\Delta_A$ to $b$ (some authors call such cones *cocones*). We postulate that the query "What are the values of attributes in $A$?" does not make sense for the given KR-system if the set $A$ is not compatible in the system. Thus the category of attributes should to be rich enough.

We call the attribute category A *(finitely) saturated* if every (finite) compatible set of attributes is presented by a complex attribute, i.e. if every functor $\Delta_A$ with $A$ (finite and) compatible has the colimit. In particular, then A has an initial element.

**2.** This informal semantics becomes very suggestive in the case when C is the category of sets. However, the described interpretation of A-arrows then actually brings about the restriction that each morphism set $\mathsf{A}(X, Y)$ should contain at most one arrow (see (2.2) below), i.e. that A should be merely a preordered set.

Suppose that $\boldsymbol{S} := (\mathsf{A}, V, S, \Pi)$ is a KR-system relatively to $\mathbb{S}$. A *(full) description* is defined to be a function $d$ on $|\mathsf{A}|$ that assigns an element of $V_a$ to every attribute $a$ so that

$$d(a) = \overleftarrow{\alpha}(d(b)) \tag{2.2}$$

for every arrow $\alpha\colon a \to b$. We can associate with any state $s \in S$ the description $d_s$ defined by $d_s(a) := \pi_a(s)$; thus, the cone $P$ might be replaced by the family $(d_s\colon s \in S)$. Conversely, any family $(d_t\colon t \in S')$ of descriptions gives rise to a KR-system $(\mathsf{A}, V, S', \Pi')$, where $\pi'_a(t) = d_t(a)$.

Now let $K := \{(a,u)\colon a \in |\mathsf{A}|, u \in V_a\}$ be the set of all pieces of knowledge directly available in $\boldsymbol{S}$ (see above). We say that a piece $(a,u)$ is *less informative* than $(b,v)$ (in symbols, $(a,u) \le (b,v)$), if there is an arrow $\alpha\colon a \to b$ in $\mathsf{A}$ with $u = \overleftarrow{\alpha}(v)$. The relation $\le$ is a preorder on $K$; for the sake of the simplicity we, however, assume in this informal discussion that it is an order. We are going to show that, under certain natural conditions, the poset $K$ can be endowed with a kind of entailment relation in the sense of [3]; the details, however, will be omitted.

Some authors call a poset a *domain* if it is finitely bounded complete, i.e. if every finite subset of it bounded from above has the least upper bound. The empty subset is not excluded; so a domain has the bottom $\bot$. Now, if $\mathsf{A}$ is finitely saturated, then the poset $K$ is a domain. We assume that it is the case.

Let as define the *forcing* relation $\Vdash$ on $S \times K$ is by

$$s \Vdash (a,u) :\equiv \pi_s(a) = u \ .$$

A simple axiom checking shows that then the pair $(S, \Vdash)$ is a *possible world space* for $K$ in the sense of [3]. Hence, the relation $\models$ naturally defined by

$$(b,v) \models (a,u) \text{ iff } \forall s (s \Vdash (b,v) \Rightarrow s \Vdash (a,u))$$

is an entailment on $K$ (see [3, Proposition 3]).

If $\mathsf{A}$ is even saturated, then the domain $K$ is bounded complete, hence, a meet semilattice, and can be equipped with the knowledge revision operation along the lines of Sect. 6 in [3].

**3.** Next we describe the concept of simulation for our abstract KR-systems.

**Definition 2.** *Let $\boldsymbol{S} := (\mathsf{A}, V, S, \Pi)$ and $\boldsymbol{S}' := (\mathsf{A}', V', S'\Pi')$ be two KR systems. A* simulation *of $\boldsymbol{S}$ into $\boldsymbol{S}'$ is a triple $\boldsymbol{m} := (I, \lambda, \mathsf{m})$, where*

- *$I$ is a functor $\mathsf{A} \to \mathsf{A}'$ that preserves existing colimits,*
- *$\lambda$ is a contravariant natural transformation $V'I \to V$, viewed as a family of $\mathsf{C}$-morphisms*

  $$(\lambda_a\colon V'_{I(a)} \to V_a,\ a \in |\mathsf{A}|)$$

  *such that every arrow $\alpha\colon a \to b$ from $\mathsf{A}$ yields the identity*

  $$V(\alpha)\,\lambda_b = \lambda_a\, V'(I(\alpha)) \ , \tag{2.3}$$

- *$\mathsf{m}$ is $\mathsf{C}$-morphism $S \to S'$ such that*

  $$\pi_a = \lambda_a\, \pi'_{I(a)}\, \mathsf{m} \tag{2.4}$$

  *for all $a \in A$.*

We say the $\boldsymbol{S}'$ *simulates* $\boldsymbol{S}$ if there is a simulation of $\boldsymbol{S}$ into $\boldsymbol{S}'$, and that the systems are *equivalent* if each of them simulates the other. Of course, equivalent systems need not be isomorphic.

**Proposition 1.** *KR-systems and their simulations make up a category, the composition of simulations being defined componentwise.*

We denote this category by $\mathsf{KR(C)}$, or just $\mathsf{KR}$ if misunderstanding is not likely. Given a subcategory $\mathcal{K}$ of $\mathsf{KR}$, we call a KR-system $\boldsymbol{S}$ from $\mathcal{K}$

- *reduced* in $\mathcal{K}$ if the cone $\Pi$ is separating: any two parallel $\mathcal{K}$-morphisms $\varphi$ and $\psi$ to $S$ coincide whenever $\pi_a\varphi = \pi_a\psi$ for all $a \in |\mathsf{A}|$,
- *universal* in $\mathcal{K}$ if every KR-system from $\mathcal{K}$ is simulated by it.

Note that a universal system in this sense may be not universal in the sense of category theory: it need not be a terminal object of $\mathcal{K}$. One reason for this is that a terminal KS-system is always reduced. However, all universal systems are equivalent.

**4.** We are now going to isolate certain interesting subcategories of $\mathsf{KR}$ in which the definitions of a KR-system and simulation can be considerably simplified. (Some special categories of Pawlak's information systems are studied in [14].)

A *frame* over $\mathsf{C}$ is defined to be a pair $(\mathsf{A}, V)$ satisfying the two first axioms of a KR-system. In particular, the pair consisting of the first two components of a KR-system $\boldsymbol{S}$ is said to be the *frame of* $\boldsymbol{S}$. Clearly, every frame is the frame of an appropriate KR-system.

We denote by $\mathsf{KR}[\mathsf{A}, V]$ the full subcategory of $\mathsf{KR}$ consisting of all KR-systems having a fixed frame $(\mathsf{A}, V)$, and of those simulations in which $I$ is the identity functor and $\lambda$ is the identity transformation. Then (2.3) holds trivially. We may regard the objects of $\mathsf{KR}[\mathsf{A}, V]$ to be just pairs $(S, \Pi)$ satisfying the last two axioms of a KR-system, and morphisms to be just $\mathsf{C}$-morphisms $\mathsf{m}$ satisfying the correspondingly reduced version of (2.4), i.e. the condition $\pi_a = \pi'_a\,\mathsf{m}$. The following simple category-theoretic observation is useful.

**Proposition 2.** *The following statements are equivalent for a KR-system* $\boldsymbol{S} := (S, \Pi)$ *from* $\mathsf{KR}[\mathsf{A}, V]$*:*

(a) $\boldsymbol{S}$ *is terminal,*
(b) $\boldsymbol{S}$ *is universal and reduced,*
(c) $S$ *is a limit of the functor* $V$*, and* $\Pi$ *is the corresponding limiting cone.*

Therefore, if the category $\mathsf{C}$ is small-complete, then each $\mathsf{KR}[\mathsf{A}, V]$ has a terminal system. For example, if $\mathsf{C} = \mathcal{S}$ and $(d_s\colon s \in S)$ is a family of all descriptions (relatively to $(\mathsf{A}, V)$), then the KR-system $(S, \Pi)$, where each $\pi_a$ is defined by $\pi_a(s) := d_s(a)$, is terminal.

## 3 Uncertainty in KR-Systems

**1.** KR-systems, as they were defined in the preceding section, seem to be determined: every state completely determines values of all attributes. We shall show in this section that KR-systems with uncertainty nevertheless fall under the same formal scheme.

To this end, we fix some monad $\mathbb{F} := (F, \eta, \mu)$ over $\mathsf{C}$. The functor $F$ is interpreted as fuzzification (in a wide sense of the term). Thus, if $\mathsf{C}$ is the category of sets, the object $F(X)$ consists of "fuzzy subsets" of $X$ interpreted as available "vague pieces of information" about, or "vague specifications" of, elements of $X$, while the function $F(\varphi)$, where $\varphi$ itself maps a set $X$ into $Y$, transforms a vague specification of, say, an element $x \in X$ into the corresponding vague specification of $\varphi(x) \in Y$. The function $\eta_X := \eta(X)$: $X \to F(X)$ associates with each element of $X$ a "crisp specification" of this element; so such a specification is a particular case of vague ones. At last, the function $\mu_X := \mu(X)$: $F(F(X)) \to F(X)$ provides completeness of $F(X)$ in the sense that a "vaguely specified vague specification" over $X$ always is a vague specification over the same $X$.

A useful derived notion related to monads is that of an extension map. Given a $\mathsf{C}$-morphism $\varphi$: $X \to F(Y)$, its *extension* $\varphi^\sharp$: $F(X) \to F(Y)$ is defined to be the composition $\mu_Y F(\varphi)$. Conversely, $F(\varphi) = (\eta_Y \varphi)^\sharp$ and $\mu_X = (\varepsilon_{F(X)})^\sharp$, where $\varepsilon_Y$ stands for the identity morphism of $Y$. One may view a $\mathsf{C}$-morphism $\varphi$: $X \to F(Y)$ as an $X$-indexed family of specifications over $Y$, and a vague specification over $X$ as a specification over this family. Then $\varphi^\sharp$ converts such a vague specified member of the family into a specification over $Y$. Thus the extension map $\sharp$ is a counterpart of $\mu$; in fact, the monad could be replaced by the triple $(F, \eta, \sharp)$, where $F$ is now treated merely as an object map.

This interpretation of monads is detailed, and an appropriate general mathematical theory of fuzzy sets is developed, in [8]. In particular, it is shown in Sect. 1 of [8] that crisp, probabilistic, possibilistic and Zadeh's fuzzy set theories, as well as some other models of uncertainty, all come under this pattern. The main result of [9] is that so does the theory of Goguen's $L$-fuzzy sets. These ideas come back to [1]; a brief account of them is given in the review [7]. See, however, Sect. 7.2 of [5] for some criticism on, and modification of, this approach.

Following [8, Def. 4.4], we call the monad $\mathbb{F}$ *consistent* if the functor $F$ is faithful or, equivalently, if all the morphisms $\eta_X$ are monomorphisms. A monad is interesting as a tool for fuzzification only if it is consistent (in $\mathcal{S}$, if $\mathbb{F}$ is inconsistent, then no object $F(X)$ contains more than one element). Accordingly, in what follows we assume that $\mathbb{F}$ is consistent.

A morphism from $X$ to $F(Y)$ in $\mathsf{C}$ may be interpreted also as a fuzzy relation between $X$ and $Y$. Any morphism $\chi$: $X \to Y$ gives rise to such a relation $\chi^\flat := \eta_Y \varphi$. We recall that the Kleisli category of $\mathbb{F}$ is the category $\mathsf{C}_\mathbb{F}$ with the same object class as $\mathsf{C}$ and morphism classes $\mathsf{C}_\mathbb{F}(X, Y) := \mathsf{C}(X, F(Y))$. Composition is given in $\mathsf{C}_\mathbb{F}$ by $\psi \circ \varphi := \psi^\sharp \varphi$ . Clearly, $\mathsf{C}_\mathbb{F}$ reduces to $\mathsf{C}$ if $\mathbb{F}$ is the trivial monad. There is a simple functor $\flat$: $\mathsf{C} \to \mathsf{C}_\mathbb{F}$ defined by

$$\flat(X) := X, \quad \flat(\chi) := \chi^\flat \ . \tag{3.5}$$

It follows from [6, Theorem V.6.2] that the functor preserves colimits, for it has the left adjoint $\sharp\colon \mathsf{C}_{\mathbb{F}} \to \mathsf{C}$ which takes any $\mathsf{C}_{\mathbb{F}}$-object $X$ into $F(X)$ and each $\mathsf{C}_{\mathbb{F}}$-morphism $\varphi$ into $\varphi^{\sharp}$ ([6, Theorem VI.5.1]).

**2.** Now we turn to the category $\mathsf{KR}(\mathsf{C}_{\mathbb{F}})$. Its objects, KR-systems over $\mathsf{C}_{\mathbb{F}}$, will be reinterpreted as generalised KR-systems over $\mathsf{C}$. This means, first of all, that we still shall regard $V_a$ rather than $F(V_a)$ to be the stock of values for $a$. While a KR-system in the previous sense (i.e. an object of $\mathsf{KR}(\mathsf{C})$) can be regarded as as a system with complete information, there are two different ways in which uncertainty may appear in such a generalised system $\boldsymbol{S} := (\mathsf{A}, V, S, \Pi)$. First, each $\pi_a$, being a $\mathsf{C}$-morphism $S \to F(V_a)$, now provides vague information about the values of the attribute $a$; this might mean that knowledge states in $S$, generally, do not contain full information about entities (another possible explanation is discussed in the next section). Second, values of $a$ need not be completely determined any more by those of $b$ when there is an arrow from $a$ to $b$: instead of crisp functional dependencies between attributes fuzzy dependencies now may appear.

For all that, this vagueness is apparent in some cases, as every $\mathsf{KR}(\mathsf{C})$-system $\boldsymbol{T} := (\mathsf{A}, U, S, P)$ can be identified with the $\mathsf{KR}(\mathsf{C}_{\mathbb{F}})$-system $\boldsymbol{T}^{\flat} := (\mathsf{A}, \flat U, S, P^{\flat})$, where $\flat U$ is the composition of $U$ with the functor $\flat$ defined in (3.5), and $P^{\flat}$ is the cone $(\rho^{\flat}\colon S \to \flat U(\alpha))$ (see Theorem 1 below). Recall that $\flat$ preserves colimits; hence, so does $\flat U$ as well, and $\boldsymbol{T}^{\flat}$ is indeed a KR-system.

**Definition 3.** *A* $\mathsf{KR}(\mathsf{C}_{\mathbb{F}})$*-system* $\boldsymbol{S}$ *is said to be* (information) complete *if it can be presented as* $\boldsymbol{T}^{\flat}$ *for some* $\boldsymbol{T}$ *from* $\mathsf{KR}(\mathsf{C})$*, and* incomplete *if otherwise.*

**3.** We now give an example of an extended KR-system which was studied in other connection in [18].

Let $P_0$ be the (weak) powerset endofunctor of $\mathbb{S}$ defined as follows: If $M$ is a set, then $P_0(M)$ stands for the set of non-empty subsets of $M$, and if $f$ is a function $M \to N$, then $P_0(f)$ stands for the mapping $P_0(M) \to P_0(N)$ defined by

$$P_0(f)(X) := \{f(x)\colon x \in X\} \ .$$

In fact, this endofunctor induces a monad $\boldsymbol{P}^* := (P_0, \eta, \mu)$, where $\eta_M$ takes every element $x$ of $M$ into the singleton $\{x\}$, and $\mu_M$ takes a non-empty set $U$ of non-empty subsets of $M$ into the union of $U$.

Let $X$ and $Y$ be nonempty sets, and let $X^*$ and $Y^*$ be the set of all words (finite strings) over $X$, resp. $Y$. We first consider $X^*$ and $Y^*$ as posets, where $p \leq q$ means that the word $p$ is an initial segment of $q$. Hence, $X^*$ may be viewed as a category in the usual fashion. This gives rise to a functor $V\colon X^* \to \mathbb{S}$, the set $Y^{(p)}$ of all words from $Y^*$ of the same length as $p$ being assigned to a word $p$, and the mapping $ini^q_p\colon Y^{(q)} \to Y^{(p)}$ such that $ini^q_p(b)$ is an initial segment of $b$, to an arrow $p \to q$.

A *sequential ND-operator over* $[X, Y]$ (see [16, Def. II.4.3]) is defined to be a mapping $\varphi\colon X^* \to P_0(Y^*)$ subject to the axioms

- $(\forall q \in X^*)\, \varphi(q) \subset Y^{(q)}$,
- $(\forall p \in X^*)(\forall a \in \varphi(p))(\forall q \in X^*)\, (p \le q \Rightarrow (\exists b \in Y^*)\, (a \le b \,\&\, b \in \varphi(q)))$,
- $(\forall q \in X^*)(\forall b \in \varphi(q))(\forall a \in Y^*)\, (a \le b \Rightarrow (\exists p \in X^*)\, (p \le q \,\&\, a \in \varphi(p)))$.

According to Theorem II.4.1 in [16], every such an operator characterises behaviour of an appropriate initial non-deterministic automaton (and conversely). Let $(\varphi_s, s \in S)$ be a family of sequential ND-operators, and assume that, for each $q \in X^*$, the function $\pi_q\colon S \to P_0(Y^q)$ is defined by $\pi_q(s) := \varphi_s(q)$. The family $\Pi$ of all such functions is a cone from $S$ to the functor $P_0 V$ in the category of sets. Now, the system $(X^*, V, S, \Pi)$ is a knowledge representation system with respect to the monad $P_0$. It can be shown that this notion is equipollent with that of non-deterministic automaton with a fixed subset of initial states. Note that its attribute system $X^*$ is finitely saturated (in fact, even saturated).

**4.** The notion of simulation has also extended in $\mathsf{KR}(\mathsf{C}_\mathbb{F})$. Indeed, related back to $\mathsf{C}$, a simulation of $\boldsymbol{S}$ into $\boldsymbol{S}'$ consists of a functor $I\colon \mathsf{A} \to \mathsf{A}'$, a natural $\mathsf{C}$-transformation $\lambda\colon V'I \to FV$, and a $\mathsf{C}$-morphism $\mathsf{m}\colon S \to F(S')$. Then the identities (2.3) and (2.4) characterising simulations take the form

$$(V(\alpha))^\sharp\, \lambda_b = \lambda_a{}^\sharp\, V'(I(\alpha)) \quad \text{and} \quad \pi_a = \lambda_a{}^\sharp\, \pi'_{I(a)}{}^\sharp\, \mathsf{m} \ ,$$

respectively. We are now going to pick out some simulations of a special type.

Let $\boldsymbol{S} := (\mathsf{A}, V, S, \Pi)$ and $\boldsymbol{S}' := (\mathsf{A}', V', S', \Pi')$ be two KR-systems from $\mathsf{KR}(\mathsf{C}_\mathbb{F})$. Suppose we are given a triple $\boldsymbol{n} := (I, \varkappa, \mathsf{n})$, where $I$ is a functor $\mathsf{A} \to \mathsf{A}'$, $\varkappa$ is a contravariant natural transformation $V'I \to V$ and $\mathsf{n}$ is a $\mathsf{C}$-morphism $S \to S'$. Suppose, furthermore, that $\lambda = \varkappa^\flat$ (i.e. $\lambda_a = \varkappa_a^\flat$ for all $a \in |\mathsf{A}|$) and $\mathsf{m} = \mathsf{n}^\flat$. Then $\lambda$ is a contravariant natural $\mathsf{C}$-transformation $V'I \to FV$ and $\mathsf{m}$ is a $\mathsf{C}$-morphism $S \to F(S)$. We denote the derived triple $(I, \lambda, \mathsf{m})$ by $\boldsymbol{n}^\flat$. Note that due to consistency of $\mathbb{F}$, the triple $\boldsymbol{n}$ is uniquely determined by $\boldsymbol{n}^\flat$.

**Definition 4.** *The simulation* $\boldsymbol{m} := (I, \lambda, \mathsf{m})$ *is said to be* strict *if it can be presented as* $\boldsymbol{n}^\flat$ *for some triple* $\boldsymbol{n}$.

It follows that $\boldsymbol{S}$ is simulated by $\boldsymbol{S}'$ iff $\boldsymbol{S}$ is strictly simulated by the system $\boldsymbol{S}'^\sharp := (\mathsf{A}', V', F(S'), \Pi'^\sharp)$, where $\Pi'^\sharp$ stands for the family $(\pi'_a{}^\sharp, a \in \mathsf{A}')$.

The following technical lemma gives a useful independent characteristic of strict simulations. We note that the consistency of $\mathbb{F}$ is essential for the 'if' direction in it.

**Lemma 1.** $\boldsymbol{n}^\flat$ *is a simulation of* $\boldsymbol{S}$ *into* $\boldsymbol{S}'$ *if and only if*

$$V(\alpha)\, \varkappa_b = F(\varkappa_a)\, V'(I(\alpha)) \quad \textit{and} \quad \pi_a = F(\varkappa_a)\, \pi'_{I(a)}\, \mathsf{n} \ . \tag{3.6}$$

For example, every $\mathsf{KR}(\mathsf{C})$-simulation induces a strict $\mathsf{KR}(\mathsf{C}_\mathbb{F})$-simulation. Suppose that $\boldsymbol{T} := (\mathsf{A}, U, S, P)$ and $\boldsymbol{T}' := (\mathsf{A}', U', S', P')$ are KR-systems from $\mathsf{KR}(\mathsf{C})$ and that $\boldsymbol{n} := (I, \varkappa, \mathsf{n})$ is a simulation of $\boldsymbol{T}$ into $\boldsymbol{T}'$. Then it follows from the lemma that the triple $\boldsymbol{n}^\flat$ is a strict simulation of $\boldsymbol{T}^\flat$ into $\boldsymbol{T}'^\flat$. Every strict simulation between complete KR-systems arises this way.

Observe that strict simulations constitute a subcategory of $\mathsf{KR}(\mathsf{C}_\mathbb{F})$ with the same object class. Let us denote it by $\mathsf{KR_s}(\mathsf{C}_\mathbb{F})$.

**5.** We sum up a part of the above discussion as follows.

**Theorem 1.** (a) *Complete KR-systems and their strict simulations make up a subcategory* $\mathsf{KR_c(C_{\mathbb{F}})}$ *of* $\mathsf{KR_s(C_{\mathbb{F}})}$.
(b) *The transformations* $\boldsymbol{T} \mapsto \boldsymbol{T}^\flat, \boldsymbol{n} \mapsto \boldsymbol{n}^\flat$ *yield a faithful functor* $\mathsf{KR(C)} \to \mathsf{KR_s(C_{\mathbb{F}})}$. *In fact, it is an isomorphism of* $\mathsf{KR(C)}$ *onto* $\mathsf{KR_c(C_{\mathbb{F}})}$.

To underline the described reinterpretation of the category $\mathcal{KR}(\mathsf{C_{\mathbb{F}}})$ as the category of fuzzy KR-systems relatively to $\mathsf{C}$, we rename it into $\mathsf{KR^{\mathbb{F}}(C)}$. Moreover, the category $\mathsf{C}$ will be supposed to be fixed in the rest of the paper, and we usually shall omit the reference to it in notation of this kind at all.

We retain the previous definitions of a reduced, universal and terminal system and a frame. Needless to say, all the observations made at the end of the preceding section hold true in $\mathsf{KR^{\mathbb{F}}}$. As to the available pieces of knowledge (when $\mathsf{C} = \mathcal{S}$), there are good reasons to consider now the wider set

$$K^{\mathbb{F}} := \{(a, \sigma) \colon a \in |\mathsf{A}|, \sigma \in F(V_a)\}$$

rather than $K$. In the light of the short discussion on $K$ in Sect. 2.2 , investigating the structure of $K^{\mathbb{F}}$ seems to be of interest.

## 4 Is an Incomplete KR-System Substantially Incomplete?

**1.** In general, there is a suggestive analogy between KR-systems, on the one hand, and quantum systems on the other: observables of a quantum system are replaced by the attributes in a KR-system, and the probabilistic distributions on the value set of an observable is a kind of vague specifications on the set. Such an analogy between automata and quantum systems has been noticed as early as in [10]; see also [4,17,18].

The famous hidden variables problem in quantum mechanics arises from attempts to interpret quantum systems classically. The indeterminateness of such a system could be explained this way: its states are thought of as probability distributions on some hypothetical set of sharp, or deterministic, states, each of which completely determines values of all observables. The essence of the problem, then, is to show that it is always possible to find additional parameters (the hidden variables) which could operationally describe these deterministic states and, hence, help to restore classical physics. It is known that the hidden variable problem in quantum mechanics is solved negatively. See, e.g., [17] for more information.

One could try to explain incompleteness of a particular KR-system after the same fashion. Our experience with Pawlak's information systems in Sect. 1 shows that it may well be that an entire class of KR-systems admits a uniform way to introduce "hidden variables". On the other hand, experience of quantum mechanics holds us back from being too optimistic in this respect. Moreover, we should take into account the possibility that a KR-system with uncertainty (traditionally called incomplete) is, in fact, complete in the sense that each of its states provides maximally full information about the corresponding entity: they could be the entities themselves which actually have uncertain values of their attributes.

**2.** We now move from this informal discussion to more precise formulations.

Let $\mathcal{K}$ be some subcategory of $\mathsf{KR}^{\mathbb{F}}$. When speaking on simulation of a $\mathcal{K}$-system, we shall always have in mind its $\mathcal{K}$-simulation (i.e., by another $\mathcal{K}$-system, and via a simulation from $\mathcal{K}$).

**Definition 5.** *A KR-system from $\mathcal{K}$ is said to be* weakly complete *in $\mathcal{K}$ if it is simulated by a complete system. We say that $\mathcal{K}$* has enough complete systems, *or is* uncertainty-free *if every KR-system in $\mathcal{K}$ is weakly complete.*

For example, the category of Pawlak's information systems has enough complete systems. Now we can state our principal question as follows.

*Problem 1.* Has the category $\mathsf{KR}^{\mathbb{F}}$ enough complete systems?

If it is not the case, then two other problems arise:

*Problem 2.* Characterise the uncertainty-free subcategories of $\mathsf{KR}^{\mathbb{F}}$.

*Problem 3.* Find interesting examples of subcategories of $\mathsf{KR}^{\mathbb{F}}$ that have not enough complete systems.

The following observation on categories with universal systems is helpful when $\mathsf{C}$ is small complete.

**Proposition 3.** *If the category $\mathcal{K}$ has universal systems at all, then it is uncertainty-free if and only if it has a complete one.*

A bit more can be said about the category of KR-systems generated by a frame.

Let $(\mathsf{A}, V)$ be some frame relatively to $\mathsf{C}_{\mathbb{F}}$. We assume that there is also a frame $(\mathsf{A}, U)$ relatively to $\mathsf{C}$ such that $V = \flat U$. Obviously, this condition is necessary and sufficient in order that $\mathsf{KR}^{\mathbb{F}}[\mathsf{A}, V]$ could have complete KR-systems. Note that a system $\boldsymbol{S}$ is universal in $\mathsf{KR}^{\mathbb{F}}[\mathsf{A}, V]$ iff $\boldsymbol{S}^{\sharp}$ is (see the paragraph just after Def. 4 for this latter notation).

**Theorem 2.** *The following holds for the category $\mathsf{KR}^{\mathbb{F}}[\mathsf{A}, V]$:*

(a) *if $\mathsf{KR}^{\mathbb{F}}[\mathsf{A}, V]$ has enough complete systems, then it has an universal system if and only if so does $\mathsf{KR}[\mathsf{A}, U]$,*
(b) *if $\boldsymbol{S}$ and $\boldsymbol{T}$ are universal systems in $\mathsf{KR}^{\mathbb{F}}[\mathsf{A}, V]$ and $\mathsf{KR}[\mathsf{A}, V]$ respectively, then $\mathsf{KR}^{\mathbb{F}}[\mathsf{A}, V]$ has enough complete systems if and only if $\boldsymbol{S}$ is equivalent to $\boldsymbol{T}^{\flat}$.*

## References

1. Arbib, M., Manes, E.: Fuzzy machines in category. Bull. Austral. Math. Soc. **13** (1975), 169–210.
2. Archangelsky, D.A., Taitslin, M.A.: A logic for information systems. Stud. Log. **58** (1997), 3–16.
3. Cīrulis, J.: An algebraic approach to knowledge representation. MFCS'99, LNCS **1672** (1999), 299–309.
4. Finkelstein, D., Finkelstein, S.R.: Computational Complementarity. Internat. J. Theoret. Phys. **22** (1983), 753–779.
5. Goodman, I.R., Nguyen, H.T.: Uncertainty models for knowledge based systems. North-Holland, Amsterdam e.a., 1985.
6. Mac Lane, S.: Categories for the Working Mathematician. Springer-Verlag, N.Y. e.a., 1971.
7. Manes, E.G.: Review of "Fuzzy Sets and Systems: Theory and Applications", by D. Dubois and H. Prade, Acad. Press, 1980. Bull. Amer. Math. Soc. **7** (1982), 603–612.
8. Manes, E.G.: A class of fuzzy theories. Math. Anal. Appl. **85** (1982), 409–451.
9. Madner, J.: Standard monads. Arch. Math. (Brno) **23** (1987), 77–88.
10. Moore, E,F.: Gedanken-experiments on sequential machines. In: Shannon, C.E., McCharty, J. (eds): Automata Studies, Princeton Univ. Press, 1956, 129–156.
11. van Oosten, J.: Basic Category Theory. BRICS Lecture Series LS-95-1, Univ. of Aarhus, 1995.
12. Orłovska, E., Pawlak, Z.: Representation of nondeterministic information. Theoret. Comput. Sci. **29** (1984), 27–39.
13. Pawlak, Z.: Information systems — theoretical foundations. Inform. Systems **6** (1981), 205–218.
14. Pomykała, J.A., de Haas, E.: A note on categories of information systems. Demonstr. Math. **37**, (1991) 663–671.
15. Poigné, A.: Basic category theory. In: Handbook of Logic in Computer Science, Vol. 1. Clarendon Press, Oxford, 1992, 416–640.
16. Starke, P.H.: Abstrakte Automaten. WEB Deutscher Verl. Wissensch., Berlin, 1969.
17. Svozil, K.: Quantum Logic. Springer-Verlag Singapore Pte. Ltd., 1998.
18. Tsirulis, Ya.P.: Variations on the theme of quantum logic (in Russian). In: Algebra i Diskretnaya Matematika, Latv. State Univ., Riga, 1984, 146–158.

# Best Increments for the Average Case of Shellsort

Marcin Ciura

Department of Computer Science, Silesian Institute of Technology,
Akademicka 16, PL–44–100 Gliwice, Poland

**Abstract.** This paper presents the results of using sequential analysis to find increment sequences that minimize the average running time of Shellsort, for array sizes up to several thousand elements. The obtained sequences outperform by about 3% the best ones known so far, and there is a plausible evidence that they are the optimal ones.

## 1 Shellsort

A well implemented Shellsort is among the fastest general algorithms for sorting arrays of several dozen elements, and even for huge arrays it is not prohibitively slow. Moreover, it is an *adaptive* method that runs faster on "nearly sorted" arrays that often occur in practice. Published by D. L. Shell in 1959 [11], it is one of the earliest sorts discovered, it can be easily understood and implemented, yet its analysis is difficult and still incomplete.

Shellsort for $N$ elements $X[0,\ldots,N-1]$ is based on a predetermined sequence of integer *increments* $0 < h_0,\ldots,h_{t-1} < N$, where $h_0 = 1$. In general, the increment sequences can change with $N$, but customarily initial elements of some infinite sequence are used for simplicity.

The algorithm performs $t$ *passes* over the array: one pass for each increment from $h_{t-1}$ down to $h_0$. The pass number $t-k$ sorts by straight insertion all the subarrays that consist of elements $h_k$ apart: $X[0,h_k,\ldots]$,$X[1,h_k+1,\ldots],\ldots,$ $X[h_k-1,2h_k-1,\ldots]$. This way each pass involves sorting subarrays that are either small or nearly in order, and straight insertion sort performs well in these circumstances.

The number of operations made by the algorithm depends on the increment sequence, and indeed many sequences have been proposed and used. References [7,10] contain broad surveys of previous research on Shellsort. Theoretical analysis of its running time is, however, confined to worst case. The average running time was susceptible to analysis only in cases that do not cover the sequences used in practice [2,5,14]. Also, sequences of increments that minimize the average running time of Shellsort were not known so far.

## 2 Sequential Analysis

Sequential analysis is a method of verifying statistical hypotheses developed by Abraham Wald in the 1940s [13]. Whereas classical statistical criteria fix the

R. Freivalds (Ed.): FCT 2001, LNCS 2138, pp. 106–117, 2001.

size of the random sample before it is drawn, in sequential analysis its size is determined dynamically by analyzing a sequentially obtained series of data.

Sequential analysis has been employed in fields, where sampling is costly, for example drug investigation and destructive qualification testing of goods. We use it to determine in reasonable time the best increments for the average case of Shellsort. For example, suppose that we are interested in minimizing $C$, the number of comparisons made by a five-increment Shellsort when sorting 128 elements. A good fairy tells us that there are only a few dozen sequences, for whose the average number of comparisons $EC$ is less than 1005, and the distribution of $C$ for all of them, being inherently discrete, can be approximated by the normal distribution with a standard deviation $SC \approx 34$. After all, $EC < 1005$ surely causes $SC$ to be $\leq \sigma_{\max} = 40$.

Using this information, we can construct a sequential test that acts like a low-band filter and allows to shorten the time of computations by a factor of thousands. We are willing to accept a good sequence when its $EC < \theta_0 = 1005$ and reject a bad one when, say, $EC > \theta_1 = 1015$. We consent to accidental rejecting a good sequence with probability $\alpha = 0.01$ and accidental accepting a bad one with probability $\beta = 0.01$. With each sequence probed, we are running Shellsort on randomly generated permutations and summing $c_i$, the number of comparisons made in the $i$th trial. We prolong the test as long as

$$a_k = \frac{\sigma_{\max}^2}{\theta_1 - \theta_0} \ln \frac{\beta}{1-\alpha} + k\frac{\theta_0 + \theta_1}{2} \leq \sum_{i=1}^{k} c_i \leq \frac{\sigma_{\max}^2}{\theta_1 - \theta_0} \ln \frac{1-\beta}{\alpha} + k\frac{\theta_0 + \theta_1}{2} = r_k .$$

If the sum is less than $a_k$, the sequence is accepted; if it is greater than $r_k$, the sequence is rejected; if it is between $a_k$ and $r_k$, $k$ gets incremented, $a_k$ and $r_k$ are adjusted, and another trial is made.

The sequences that passed the test have biased estimate of the average number of comparisons, so it has to be evaluated again on some number of independent permutations, but the vast majority of sequences (those with large $EC$) is rejected in the test after just a few trials. Fig. 1 shows the mean and standard deviation of the number of comparisons made by Shellsort using 790 sequences that passed the test described above, evaluated subsequently in 10000 trials.

To make the sequential test fast, it is essential to choose $\theta_0$ near the actual minimal $EC$. To estimate $EC$ and $SC$ of the best sequences in default of a fairy, we can use a random sample of sequences that begin with increments known to be good (more on good increments below).

If our assumptions are true, we should have missed no more than 1% of sequences with $EC < 1005$. In fact, the distribution of the number of comparisons is not normal, but skewed (see Fig. 2 for a typical example). In an attempt to compensate this asymmetry, the chosen value of $\sigma_{\max}$ is greater than the actual standard deviations. Moreover, by the Central Limit Theorem, the sum of $c_i$'s obtained in independent trials tends to the normal distribution.

This reasoning can seem fallacious, as it involves knowing in advance, what we are looking for [1], but in fact it is not. If there exists a sequence with $EC < \theta_0$ and $SC > \sigma$, the probability that it was accidentally rejected is less than 1/2

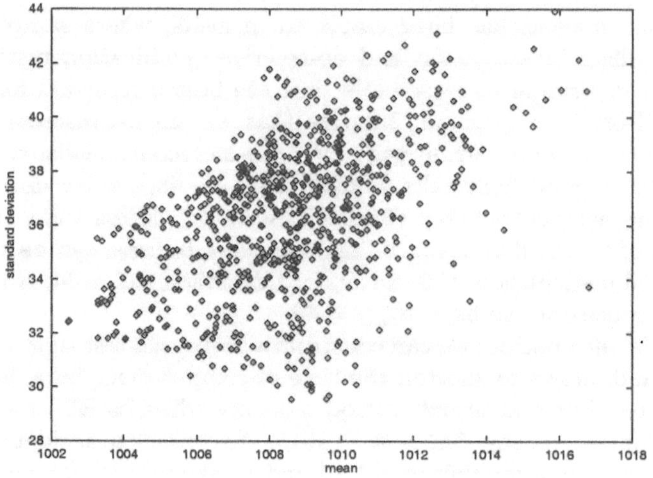


**Fig. 1.** Mean and standard deviation of the number of comparisons in Shellsort. Five-increment sequences for sorting 128 elements that passed the sequential test are shown

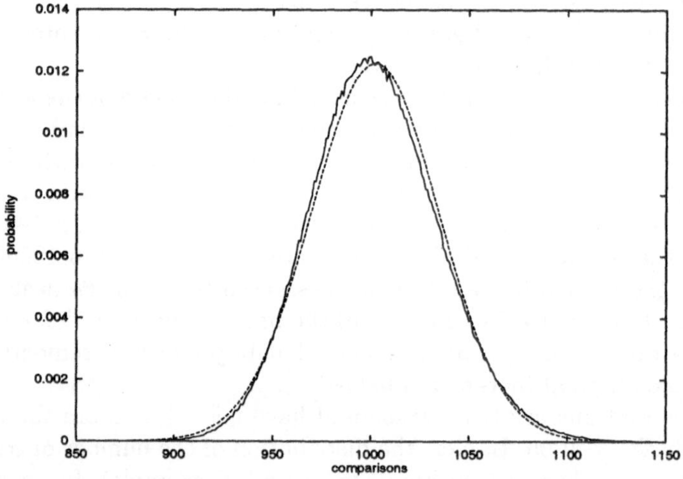


**Fig. 2.** Distribution of the number of comparisons in Shellsort using the sequence (1, 4, 9, 24, 85) for sorting 128 elements (*solid line*), and the normal distribution with the same mean and standard devistion (*dashed line*)

in the symmetrical distribution model, and still less than one for any skewed distribution. Therefore, when the search is independently run several times, the sequence should pass the test at least once. It never happened in author's search: the standard deviation of the best sequences was always similar.

## 3 The Dominant Operation in Shellsort

Almost all studies of Shellsort treat its running time as proportional to the number of element moves. It is probably because the number of moves can be expressed in terms of the number of permutation inversions, and there are known techniques for inversion counting. These techniques give satisfactory answers for algorithms like insertion sort, where the ratio of the number of comparisons to the number of moves approaches 1 quickly.

In Shellsort, the picture is different. Figures 3 and 4 show the average number of computer cycles per move and per comparison for $10 \leq N \leq 10^8$. They concern Knuth's implementation of Shellsort for his mythical computer MIX and several increment sequences: Hibbard's $(1, 3, 7, 15, \ldots)$ [3], Knuth's $(1, 4, 13, 40, \ldots \mid 2h_k < N)$ [7], Tokuda's $(h_k = \lceil (9(\frac{9}{4})^k - 4)/5 \rceil \mid \frac{9}{4}h_k < N)$ [12], Sedgewick's $(1, 5, 19, 41, \ldots)$ [9], Incerpi-Sedgewick $(1, 3, 7, 21, \ldots)$ [4], and $(1, 4, 10, 23, 57, 132, 301, 701)$ (up to $N = 4000$) [see below]. Knuth's discussion assumes that the running time can be approximated as $9\times$number of moves, while Figures 3 and 4 show that for each sequence the number of key comparisons is a better measure of the running time than the number of moves. The asymptotic ratio of 9 cycles per move is not too precise for $N \leq 10^8$, and, if some hypothetical sequence makes $\Theta(N \log N)$ moves, it is never attained. Analogous plots for other computer architectures would lead to the same conclusion.

Treating moves as the dominant operation leads to mistaken conclusions about the optimal sequences. Table 1 leads us to believe that the move-optimal sequence is Pratt's one $(1, 2, 3, 4, 6, 8, 9, 12, \ldots) = \{2^p 3^q\}$ [8], with $\Theta(\log^2 N)$ passes. However, the best practical sequences known so far are approximately geometrical, so they make $\Theta(\log N)$ passes. Also, a recent result [6] is that if there is a sequence that yields Shellsort's average running time $\Theta(N \log N)$, it has to make precisely $\Theta(\log N)$ passes.

Compare-optimal sequences seem to make $\Theta(\log N)$ passes. It is illustrated in Tables 1 and 2 that show the best sequences of various length for sorting 128 elements, obtained in the above described way with respect to the average number of moves and comparisons. In Table 1, there are no empirical sequences with more than 12 increments, since finding them would take too much time, but hopefully the point is clear. In Table 2, the difference between the last two lines is within possible error; sequences with more than six increments do not improve the results.

In fact, concentrating on the number of moves, we can obtain sequences that are good for practical purposes, but we have to guess an appropriate number of passes for a given $N$, lest they be too 'stretched' or too 'squeezed.' When

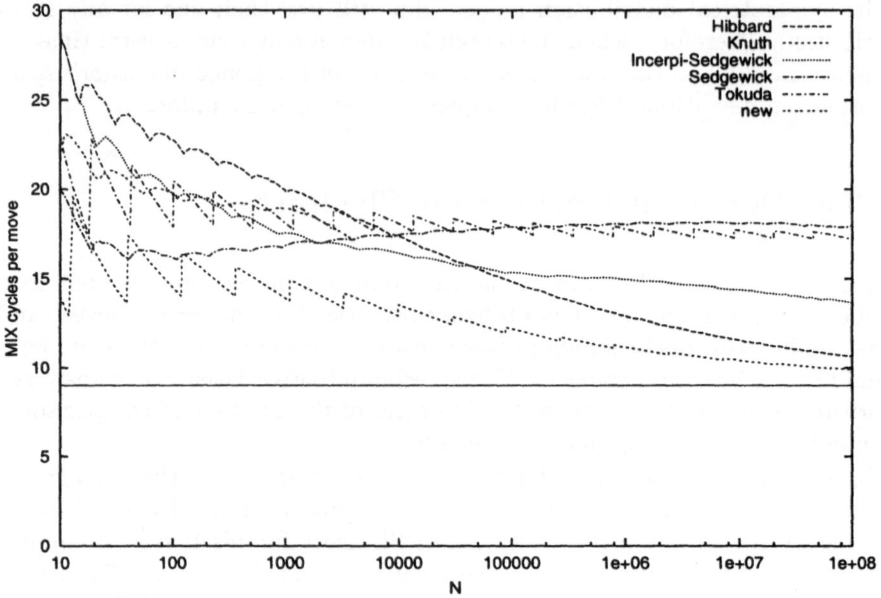


**Fig. 3.** Average MIX computer time per move in Shellsort using various sequences of increments

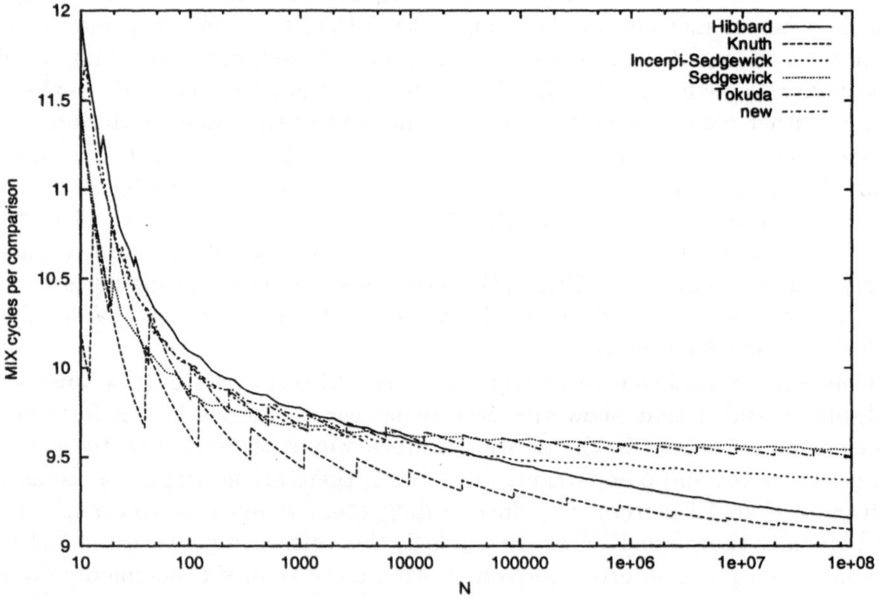


**Fig. 4.** Average MIX computer time per comparison in Shellsort using various sequences of increments

**Table 1.** Move-optimal sequences for sorting 128 elements

| Increments | Moves | Comparisons | MIX time |
|---|---|---|---|
| 1 | 4064.0 | 4186.8 | 37847 |
| 1 8 | 1280.2 | 1506.2 | 13958 |
| 1 4 17 | 762.80 | 1090.69 | 10422.4 |
| 1 4 9 24 | 588.25 | 1018.74 | 9956.9 |
| 1 3 7 15 35 | 506.56 | 1032.39 | 10256.0 |
| 1 3 7 12 20 51 | 458.18 | 1071.99 | 10761.8 |
| 1 3 4 10 15 28 47 | 427.43 | 1151.14 | 11625.6 |
| 1 2 5 7 13 22 33 56 | 405.20 | 1220.71 | 12393.3 |
| 1 3 4 6 11 18 26 35 56 | 389.36 | 1308.48 | 13323.4 |
| 1 2 3 5 8 12 18 27 41 75 | 375.70 | 1390.80 | 14301.2 |
| 1 2 3 5 8 12 18 27 38 59 84 | 365.83 | 1440.45 | 14717.1 |
| 1 2 3 4 6 11 14 18 27 37 62 86 | 357.63 | 1545.17 | 15793.3 |
| ................................ | | | |
| 1 2 3 4 6 8 9 12 16 18 ... 96 108 | 338.08 | 2209.59 | 22700.4 |

**Table 2.** Compare-optimal sequences for sorting 128 elements

| Increments | Comparisons | Moves | MIX time |
|---|---|---|---|
| 1 | 4186.8 | 4064.0 | 37847 |
| 1 9 | 1504.6 | 1280.7 | 13945 |
| 1 4 17 | 1090.69 | 762.80 | 10422.4 |
| 1 4 9 38 | 1009.75 | 598.90 | 9895.0 |
| 1 4 9 24 85 | 1002.22 | 538.06 | 9919.9 |
| 1 4 9 24 85 126 | 1002.25 | 535.71 | 9933.2 |

working with comparisons, at least choosing the number of passes too high does no harm.

## 4 Further Enhancements to the Method

The investigations were begun for small $N$ and a broad range of sequences with $2 \leq h_1 \leq 10$ and $1 < h_k/h_{k-1} < 4$ for $k > 1$. It turns out that the best sequences had $h_1 \in \{4, 5\}$ and $h_k/h_{k-1} \in (2, 3)$, for $k > 0$; except perhaps the last increments, where a larger value of $h_k/h_{k-1}$ is sometimes better. Also, having $h_{k+1} \bmod h_k = 0$ is always a hindrance.

The smallest increments are stable among the best sequences with a maximal $t$ for various $N$. Indeed, for $N$ greater than a few dozen, the best sequences are $(1, 4, 9, \ldots)$, $(1, 4, 10, \ldots)$, $(1, 4, 13, \ldots)$, $(1, 5, 11, \ldots)$. A few other beginnings are also not bad, yet consistently worse than these four. The increment $h_3$ crystallizes when $N \approx 100$, and the top sequences are $(1, 4, 9, 24, \ldots)$, $(1, 4, 9, 29, \ldots)$, $(1, 4, 10, 21, \ldots)$, $(1, 4, 10, 23, \ldots)$, and $(1, 4, 10, 27, \ldots)$.

As $N$ grows, the feasible values of the remaining increments show up, too: given $(h_0, \ldots, h_{k-1})$, there is always a small set of good values for $h_k$. Figures 5 and 6 show the average number of comparisons made by sequences beginning with $(1, 4, 10, 23)$ and $(1, 4, 10, 21)$ when sorting 300 and 1000 elements as a function of $h_4$.

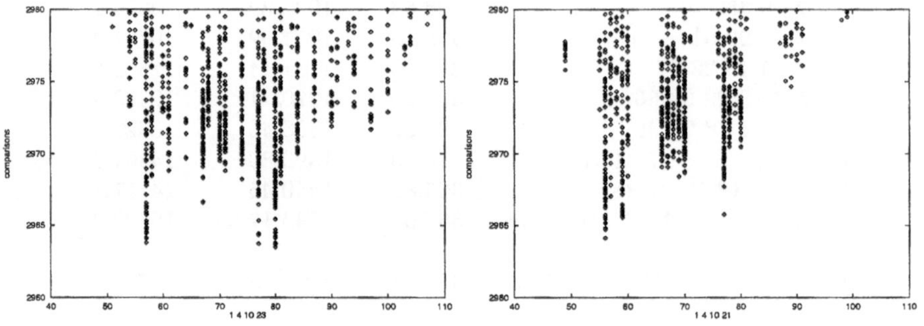


**Fig. 5.** Performance of Shellsort that uses the sequences $(1, 4, 10, 23, h_4, h_5)$ and $(1, 4, 10, 21, h_4, h_5)$ for $N = 300$ depending on $h_4$

Thus, we can speed the search up, considering only the sequences beginning with these increments, and imposing more strict conditions on the remaining increments. The author would like to stress that he took a conservative approach and checked a much wider fan of sequences. It was seeing some patterns consistently losing for several $N$'s that encouraged him not to consider them for a greater number of elements.

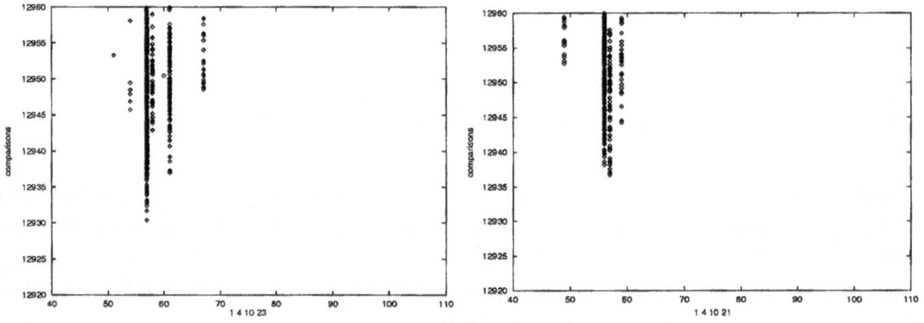


**Fig. 6.** Performance of Shellsort that uses the sequences $(1, 4, 10, 23, h_4, h_5, h_6)$ and $(1, 4, 10, 21, h_4, h_5, h_6)$ for $N = 1000$ depending on $h_4$

## 5 The Results

The size of this paper limits the author to present only a digest of his numerical results. Table 3 shows the best sequences of length 6–8 for sorting 1000 elements, and, for some increments, the best sequences beginning with them. The omitted sequences differ only with the biggest increments from those shown. However, there is a chance that some sequences that should be on these lists were accidentally rejected in the sequential test.

**Table 3.** The best 6-, 7-, and 8-pass sequences for sorting 1000 elements

| Increments | Comparisons |
|---|---|
| 1 4 13 32 85 290 | $13059.0 \pm 195.9$ |
| 1 4 13 32 85 284 | $13060.4 \pm 196.3$ |
| 1 5 11 30 81 278 | $13061.5 \pm 198.2$ |
| 1 5 11 30 81 277 | $13063.1 \pm 201.2$ |
| 1 4 10 23 57 156 409 | $12930.4 \pm 157.5$ |
| 1 4 10 23 57 155 398 | $12931.7 \pm 157.5$ |
| 1 4 10 23 57 156 401 | $12932.4 \pm 157.6$ |
| (21 seq. omitted) | |
| 1 4 10 21 57 143 390 | $12936.8 \pm 157.9$ |
| (14 seq. omitted) | |
| 1 4 10 21 56 125 400 | $12938.5 \pm 157.0$ |
| (22 seq. omitted) | |
| 1 4 9 24 58 153 396 | $12940.3 \pm 158.9$ |
| 1 4 10 23 57 156 409 995 | $12928.9 \pm 158.1$ |
| 1 4 10 23 57 156 409 996 | $12929.0 \pm 157.2$ |
| 1 4 10 23 57 155 393 984 | $12929.1 \pm 156.9$ |
| (98 seq. omitted) | |
| 1 4 10 21 56 135 376 961 | $12931.9 \pm 155.8$ |
| (18 seq. omitted) | |
| 1 4 10 21 57 143 382 977 | $12932.1 \pm 156.2$ |
| (735 seq. omitted) | |
| 1 4 10 23 61 154 411 999 | $12936.6 \pm 159.9$ |
| (366 seq. omitted) | |
| 1 4 10 23 58 135 388 979 | $12937.9 \pm 155.5$ |
| (278 seq. omitted) | |
| 1 4 9 24 58 153 403 991 | $12938.6 \pm 158.1$ |

As the greatest increments play a minor role in the overall performance of a sequence, the author abandoned the idea of finding truly optimal sequences up to the greatest increment for greater $N$, and concentrated instead on finding the feasible values of the middle increments.

To this end, 6-increment beginnings perform best for $N = 1000, 2000, 4000$ were selected. For each of them, all the sequences with $h_6 \in (2h_5, 3h_5)$ and

$h_7 \in (2h_6, 3h_6)$ were generated. For each of the 8-increment beginnings obtained, 100 random endings $h_8 \in (2h_7, 3h_7)$, $h_9 \in (2h_8, \min(3h_8, 8000))$ were drawn. The sequential test was then run for each 10-increment sequence for $N = 8000$. The percentage of $(h_8, h_9)$ endings that passed the test was recorded for each $(h_0, \ldots, h_7)$. The top 8-increment beginnings were re-examined in 10000 independent tests.

**Table 4.** The best 8-increment beginnings of 10-pass sequences for sorting 8000 elements

| Increments | Ratio passed |
|---|---|
| 1 4 10 23 57 132 301 758 | 0.6798 |
| 1 4 10 23 57 132 301 701 | 0.6756 |
| 1 4 10 21 56 125 288 717 | 0.6607 |
| 1 4 10 23 57 132 301 721 | 0.6573 |
| 1 4 10 23 57 132 301 710 | 0.6553 |
| 1 4 9 24 58 129 311 739 | 0.6470 |
| 1 4 10 23 57 132 313 726 | 0.6401 |
| 1 4 10 21 56 125 288 661 | 0.6335 |
| 1 4 10 23 57 122 288 697 | 0.6335 |

From limited experience with yet larger array sizes, the author conjectures that the sequence beginning with $1, 4, 10, 23, 57, 132, 301, 701$ shall turn up optimal for greater $N$.

## 6 Why Are Some Sequences Better than Others

It seems that some sequences are better than others on the average not only due to a good global ratio $h_{k+1}/h_k$, but also because they cause less redundant comparisons, that is comparisons between elements that have already been directly or indirectly compared, which depends on local interactions between passes. Tables 5 and 6 show the average number of comparisons $C_i$ and redundant comparisons $R_i$ in each pass for two increment sequences.

Some heuristic rules on good sequences can be deduced from the observation that the subarrays sorted in each pass are quite well ordered and the elements move just a few $h$ on the average in each $h$-sorting, as exemplified in Fig. 7.

Let's consider $h_{k+1}$ expressed as a linear combination with integer coefficients of $h_{k-1}$ and $h_k$. Patterns like these on Figures 5 and 6 can be forecasted to some extent using the following rule: if there is a solution of the Diophantine equation $h_{k+1} = ah_k + bh_{k-1}$ with a small value of $|b|$, say $\leq 5$, then this $h_{k+1}$ is certainly not a good choice. The value of $b$ in analogous expressions with small multiples of $h_{k+1}$ on the left side is nearly as much important.

The distribution of the distance travelled in a given pass is similar for all the elements far enough from the ends of the table. The order of two elements that are $h_{k+1}$ apart after $h_{k+1}$-sorting is known. In subsequent pass both elements move

**Table 5.** Average number of comparisons and redundant comparisons for Shellsort using the sequence (1, 4, 10, 23, 57, 132, 301, 701, 1750), for $N = 40, 400, 4000$

| $h_k$ | $C_i$ | $R_i$ |
|---|---|---|
| 23 | 17 | 0 |
| 10 | 41.3 ± 2.6 | 0 |
| 4 | 62.4 ± 5.5 | 3.3 ± 2.3 |
| 1 | 90.8 ± 10.5 | 25.0 ± 7.6 |
| $\Sigma$ | 211.5 ± 12.1 | 28.3 ± 8.7 |

| $h_k$ | $C_i$ | $R_i$ |
|---|---|---|
| 301 | 99 | 0 |
| 132 | 334 ± 6 | 0 |
| 57 | 543 ± 14 | 0 |
| 23 | 720 ± 27 | 2.6 ± 2.3 |
| 10 | 792 ± 38 | 41 ± 14 |
| 4 | 809 ± 33 | 158 ± 24 |
| 1 | 976 ± 41 | 354 ± 33 |
| $\Sigma$ | 4274 ± 73 | 557 ± 51 |

| $h_k$ | $C_i$ | $R_i$ |
|---|---|---|
| 1750 | 2570 ± 10 | 0 |
| 701 | 5200 ± 40 | 0 |
| 301 | 6740 ± 70 | 0 |
| 132 | 7720 ± 110 | 7 ± 4 |
| 57 | 8410 ± 180 | 90 ± 20 |
| 23 | 9020 ± 190 | 370 ± 50 |
| 10 | 8570 ± 130 | 840 ± 60 |
| 4 | 8310 ± 100 | 1880 ± 90 |
| 1 | 9830 ± 140 | 3700 ± 120 |
| $\Sigma$ | 66370 ± 430 | 6890 ± 220 |

**Table 6.** Average number of comparisons and redundant comparisons for Shellsort using Knuth's sequence (1, 4, 13, 40, 121, 364, 1093), for $N = 40, 400, 4000$

| $h_k$ | $C_i$ | $R_i$ |
|---|---|---|
| 13 | 36.4 ± 1.9 | 0 |
| 4 | 74.0 ± 7.1 | 0.02 ± 0.2 |
| 1 | 98.4 ± 13.0 | 22.7 ± 9.2 |
| $\Sigma$ | 208.8 ± 15.5 | 22.7 ± 9.2 |

| $h_k$ | $C_i$ | $R_i$ |
|---|---|---|
| 121 | 401 ± 7 | 0 |
| 40 | 713 ± 21 | 0 |
| 13 | 984 ± 51 | 53 ± 16 |
| 4 | 1223 ± 116 | 164 ± 54 |
| 1 | 1092 ± 47 | 376 ± 44 |
| $\Sigma$ | 4413 ± 153 | 593 ± 81 |

| $h_k$ | $C_i$ | $R_i$ |
|---|---|---|
| 1093 | 4480 ± 30 | 0 |
| 364 | 7430 ± 50 | 0 |
| 121 | 9850 ± 170 | 560 ± 40 |
| 40 | 11930 ± 310 | 1470 ± 120 |
| 13 | 14860 ± 930 | 2160 ± 280 |
| 4 | 15050 ± 770 | 3530 ± 460 |
| 1 | 11020 ± 40 | 4100 ± 100 |
| $\Sigma$ | 74620 ± 1800 | 11510 ± 780 |

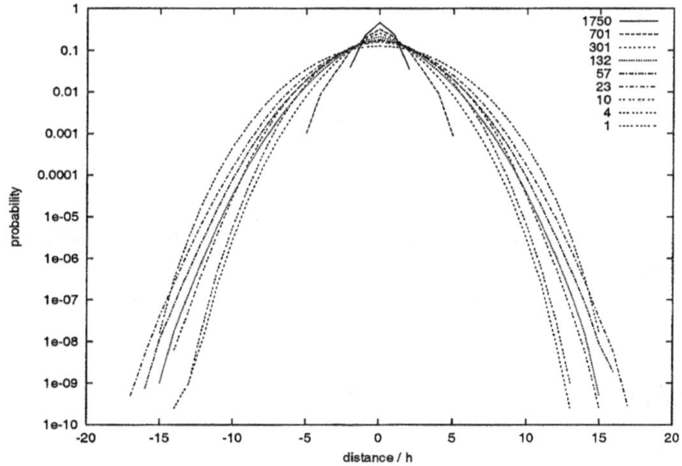


**Fig. 7.** Distance travelled by elements in subsequent passes of Shellsort using the sequence (1, 4, 10, 23, 57, 132, 301, 701, 1750) for sorting 4000 elements

a few $h_k$ to the left or to the right, and then their distance is $d = h_{k+1} + ah_k$. If $d$ turns out to be a multiple of $h_{k-1}$, then they are redundantly compared again in subsequent $h_{k-1}$-sorting.

Unfortunately, the interdependence between the quality of a sequence and the solutions of equations $h_{k+1} = a_0 h_k + \ldots + a_l h_{k-l}$ becomes more and more obscure as $l$ grows. However, there is some evidence that in good sequences the norm of the shortest vector-solution $(a_0, \ldots, a_l)$ for fixed $l$ asymptotically grows as we move on to greater increments. It seems to exclude the possibility that the optimal uniform sequence can be defined by a linear recurrence with constant coefficients or by interleaving such sequences. See Fig. 8 for a plot of average number of comparisons made by Shellsort using various increment sequences. Both Knuth's and Hibbard's sequences are relatively bad, because they are defined by simple linear recurrences. The Sedgewick's sequence that consists of two interleaved sequences defined by linear recurrences, also becomes to deteriorate for $N > 10^6$.

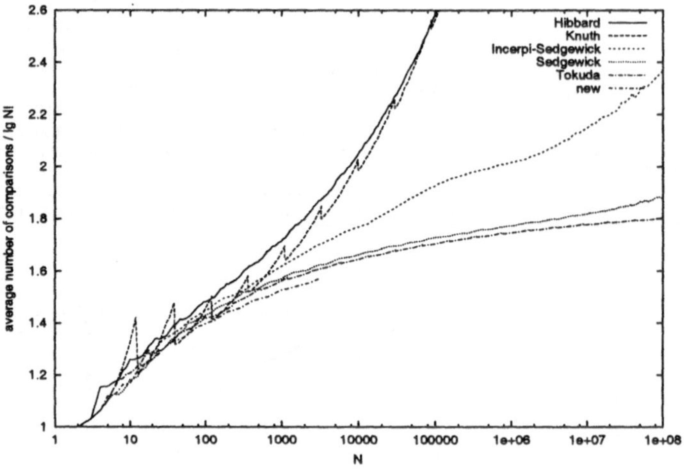


**Fig. 8.** Average number of comparisons divided by $\lg N!$ for Shellsort using selected increment sequences

## 7 Summary

Using sequential analysis, the search for optimal increment sequences for Shellsort was accelerated enough to find them for arrays up to several thousand elements. The obtained results show that comparisons rather than moves should be considered the dominant operation in Shellsort. It was also possible to state some heuristic rules about good sequences of increments.

However, the sequences obtained so far are too short to draw a reliable conclusion whether an appropriate sequence of increments can make Shellsort a $\Theta(N \log N)$ sorting method on the average. Some hypotheses may be possible when the sequences are prolonged to sort arrays of about $10^5$ elements.

## References


1. Ἀριστοτέλης: *Ἀναλυτικὰ πρότερα*, $64^{\text{b}}28$–$65^{\text{a}}37$; *Σοφιστικοὶ ἔλεγχοι*, $181^{\text{a}}15$. In: *Aristotelis Opera. Vol. 1: Aristoteles græce*, Academia Regia Borussica, Berolini, 1831.
2. Ghoshdastidar, D., Roy, M. K.: A study on the evaluation of Shell's sorting technique. *Computer Journal* **18** (1975), 234–235.
3. Hibbard, T. N.: An empirical study of minimal storage sorting. *Communications of the ACM* **6** (1963), 206–213.
4. Incerpi, J., Sedgewick, R.: Improved upper bounds on Shellsort. *Journal of Computer and System Sciences* **31** (1985), 210–224.
5. Janson, S., Knuth, D. E.: Shellsort with three increments. *Random Structures and Algorithms* **10** (1997), 125–142.
6. Jiang, T., Li, M., Vitányi, P.: The average-case complexity of Shellsort. *Lecture Notes in Computer Science* **1644** (1999), 453–462.
7. Knuth, D. E.: *The Art of Computer Programming. Vol. 3: Sorting and Searching.* Addison-Wesley, Reading, MA, 1998.
8. Pratt, V. R.: *Shellsort and Sorting Networks.* Garland, New York, 1979, PhD thesis, Stanford University, Department of Computer Science, 1971.
9. Sedgewick, R: A new upper bound for Shellsort. *Journal of Algorithms* **7** (1986), 159–173.
10. Sedgewick, R.: Analysis of Shellsort and related algorithms. *Lecture Notes in Computer Science* **1136** (1996), 1–11.
11. Shell, D. L.: A high-speed sorting procedure. *Communications of the ACM* **2** (1959), 30–32.
12. Tokuda, N: An improved Shellsort. *IFIP Transactions* **A-12** (1992), 449–457.
13. Wald, A.: *Sequential Analysis.* J. Wiley & Sons, New York, 1947.
14. Yao, A. C.: An analysis of $(h, k, 1)$-Shellsort. *Journal of Algorithms* **1** (1980), 14–50.

# Approximating Minimum Cocolourings

Fedor V. Fomin*[1], Dieter Kratsch[2], and Jean-Christophe Novelli[3]

[1] Faculty of Mathematics and Mechanics, St. Petersburg State University, Bibliotechnaya sq. 2, St. Petersburg, 198904, Russia.
fomin@gamma.math.spbu.ru

[2] Laboratoire d'Informatique Théorique et Appliquée, Université de Metz, 57045 Metz Cedex 01, France.
kratsch@lita.sciences.univ-metz.fr

[3] LIFL, Université Lille 1, 59655 Villeneuve d'Ascq Cedex, France.
novelli@lifl.fr

**Abstract.** A cocolouring of a graph $G$ is a partition of the vertex set of $G$ such that each set of the partition is either a clique or an independent set in $G$. Some special cases of the minimum cocolouring problem are of particular interest.
We provide polynomial-time algorithms to approximate a mimimum cocolouring on graphs, partially ordered sets and sequences. In particular, we obtain an efficient algorithm to approximate within a factor of 1.71 a minimum partition of a partially ordered set into chains and antichains, and a minimum partition of a sequence into increasing and decreasing subsequences.

## 1 Introduction

A cocolouring of a graph $G$ is a partition of the vertices such that each set of the partition is either a clique or an independent set in $G$. The cochromatic number of $G$ is the smallest cardinality of a cocolouring of $G$. The cochromatic number was originally studied in [18]. Subsequent papers addressed various topics including the structure of critical graphs, bounds on the cochromatic numbers of graphs with certain properties (e.g., fixed number of vertices, bounded clique size, fixed genus) and algorithms for special graph classes (e.g., chordal graphs and cographs) [1,4,6,7,8,11,12,20].

In this paper, besides cocolouring of graphs in general we study cocolourings of permutation graphs, comparability graphs and cocomparability graphs. The cocolouring problem on permutation graphs is equivalent to the cocolouring problem on repetition-free sequences of integers (one may assume a permutation

* The work of the first author was done while he was at the Centro de Modelamiento Matemático, Universidad de Chile and UMR 2071-CNRS, supported by FONDAP and while he was a visiting postdoc at DIMATIA-ITI partially supported by GAČR 201/99/0242 and by the Ministry of Education of the Czech Republic as project LN00A056. Also this work was supported by Netherlands Organization for Scientific Research (NWO grant 047.008.006.)

R. Freivalds (Ed.): FCT 2001, LNCS 2138, pp. 118–125, 2001.

of the first $n$ integers) which has the following motivation: if one has to sort such a sequence, it is desirable to have a partition into a small number of sets of already sorted elements, i.e., subsequences which are either increasing or decreasing. Now the minimum number of monotone subsequences partitioning the original sequence is exactly the cochromatic number of the permutation graph corresponding to the sequence. This problem was studied in [2,21].

Wagner showed that the problem "Given a sequence and an integer $k$, decide whether the sequence can be partitioned into at most $k$ monotone (increasing or decreasing) subsequences" is NP-complete [21]. In our paper we provide a first constant-factor approximation algorithm for cocolouring sequences. More precisely our algorithm approximates a minimum cocolouring of a sequence within a factor of 1.71.

In fact we derive our 1.71-approximation algorithm for the minimum cocolouring problem on comparability (or cocomparability) graphs. This problem is equivalent to the cocolouring problem on partially ordered sets, i.e. the problem to partition a partially ordered set $P$ into a minimum number of subsets each being a chain or an antichain of $P$. Since every permutation graph is a comparability graph, our algorithm can also be used to approximate within a factor of 1.71 a minimum cocolouring of a permutation graph, and a minimum partition of a sequence of integers into increasing and decreasing subsequences.

We also present a greedy algorithm to approximate a minimum cocolouring of perfect graphs within a factor of $\log n$. Finally we show the following hardness result for the minimum cocolouring problem on graphs in general: for every $\epsilon > 0$, no polynomial-time algorithm approximates a minimum cocolouring within a factor of $n^{1/2-\epsilon}$, unless NP $\not\subseteq$ ZPP.

## 2 Definitions

We denote by $G = (V, E)$ a finite undirected and simple graph with $n$ vertices and $m$ edges. For every $W \subseteq V$, the subgraph of $G = (V, E)$ induced by $W$ is denoted by $G[W]$. For simplicity we denote the graph $G[V \setminus A]$ by $G - A$.

A *clique* $C$ of a graph $G = (V, E)$ is a subset of $V$ such that all the vertices of $C$ are pairwise adjacent. A subset of vertices $I \subseteq V$ is *independent* if no two of its elements are adjacent. We denote by $\omega(G)$ the maximum number of vertices in a clique of $G$ and by $\alpha(G)$ the maximum number of vertices in an independent set of $G$.

An *$r$-colouring* of a graph $G = (V, E)$ is a partition $\{I_1, I_2, \dots, I_r\}$ of $V$ such that for each $1 \leq j \leq r$, $I_j$ is an independent set. The *chromatic number* $\chi(G)$ is the minimum size of such a partition and $\kappa(G) = \chi(\overline{G})$ is the minimum size of a partition $\{C_1, C_2, \dots, C_s\}$ of the vertices of $G$ into cliques. Analogously, a *cocolouring* of $G$ is a partition $\{I_1, I_2, \dots, I_r, C_1, C_2, \dots, C_s\}$ of $V$ such that each $I_j$, $1 \leq j \leq r$, is an independent set and each $C_j$, $1 \leq j \leq s$, is a clique. The smallest cardinality of a cocolouring of $G$ is the *cochromatic number* $z(G)$. Therefore, $z(G) \leq \min\{\chi(G), \kappa(G)\}$.

A graph $G = (V, E)$ is *perfect* if $\chi(G[W]) = \omega(G[W])$ for every $W \subseteq V$. Perfect graphs and classes of perfect graphs play an important role in graph theory and algorithmic graph theory. The following well-known classes of perfect graphs will be studied in the sequel: comparability, cocomparability and permutation graphs. For all information on these graph classes and their properties not given in our paper we refer to [3,13].

Let $\mathcal{F} = \{F_1, F_2, \dots, F_s\}$ and $\mathcal{F}' = \{F'_1, F'_2, \dots, F'_t\}$ be two set families of subsets of a ground set $U$. We denote by $\bigcup \mathcal{F}$ the set $\bigcup_{i=1}^{s} F_i$. We denote by $\mathcal{F}_1 \circ \mathcal{F}_2$ the set family $\{F_1, F_2, \dots, F_s, F'_1, F'_2, \dots, F'_t\}$.

## 3 Partially Ordered Sets and Comparability Graphs

Let $P = (V(P), \prec)$ be a finite partially ordered set, i.e. $\prec$ is a reflexive, antisymmetric and transitive relation on the finite ground set $V(P)$. Two elements $a, b$ of $P$ are comparable if $a \prec b$ or $b \prec a$. Now a subset $C \subseteq V(P)$ is a *chain* of $P$ if every two elements of $P$ are comparable, and a subset $A \subseteq V(P)$ is an *antichain* of $P$ if no two elements of $A$ are comparable.

An orientation $H = (V, D)$ of an undirected graph $G = (V, E)$ assigns one of the two possible directions to each edge $e \in E$. The orientation is *transitive* if $(a, b) \in D$ and $(b, c) \in D$ implies $(a, c) \in D$. A graph $G = (V, E)$ is a *comparability graph* if there is a transitive orientation $H = (V, D)$ of $G$. A graph is a *cocomparability graph* if its complement is a comparability graph.

Consider the following well-known relation between partially ordered sets and comparability graphs. Let $P = (V(P), \prec)$ be a partially ordered set. We define an undirected graph with vertex set $V(P)$ and an edge between $a$ and $b$ iff $a$ and $b$ are comparable. Then this graph is a comparability graph, its cliques correspond to chains in $P$ and its independent sets correspond to antichains in $P$. On the other hand, suppose $G = (V, E)$ is a comparability graph, and let $H$ be a transitive orientation of graph $G$. Since $H$ is an acyclic and transitive directed graph it induces a partially ordered set with ground set $V$ where $u \prec w$ $(u \neq w)$ iff there is a directed path from $u$ to $w$ in $H$. Now every chain in the partially ordered set corresponds to a directed path in $H$ which corresponds to a clique in $G$ due to transitivity. Furthermore every antichain in the partially ordered set corresponds to an independent set in $G$. Thus the well known Dilworth theorem saying that the maximum cardinality of an antichain in $P$ is equal to the minimum number of chains in a chain partition of $V(P)$ implies that comparability (and cocomparability) graphs are perfect.

More important for our paper, a cocolouring of a comparability (or cocomparability) graph $G$ corresponds to a partition of a partially ordered set into chains and antichains. Now we study cocolourings of comparability graphs.

A *maximum $k$-colouring* $\mathcal{I}_k$ is a family of $k$ independent subsets of a graph $G$ covering a maximum number of vertices. Let $\alpha_k(G)$ denote the size of the maximum $k$-colouring, i.e. the number of vertices in a maximum $k$-chromatic subgraph of $G$. A *maximum $h$-covering* $\mathcal{C}_h$ is a family of $h$ cliques of $G$ covering a maximum number of vertices. We denote by $\kappa_h(G)$ the maximum size of an $h$-covering of $G$, i.e. the number of vertices in a maximum subgraph of $G$ partitionable into $h$ cliques.

Our approximation algorithm is based on the following results by Frank [10] which can be seen as algorithmic proofs of Greene and Kleitman's [14,15] generalizations of Dilworth's theorem.

**Theorem 1** **([10]).** *There is an $O(nm)$ time algorithm which computes for any given comparability graph $G = (V, E)$ simultaneously*

**(a)** *for all integers $k$ with $1 \leq k \leq \chi(G)$ a maximum $k$-colouring $\mathcal{I}_k$, and*
**(b)** *for all integers $h$ with $1 \leq h \leq \kappa(G)$ a maximum $h$-covering $\mathcal{C}_h$.*

*The essential part of the algorithm is a minimum-cost flow algorithm on a network associated to $G$ (via a partially ordered set $P$ having comparability graph $G$).*

We shall also need the procedure SQRTPartition which is based on a result by Erdős et al. [7] (see also Brandstädt et al. [2]).

SQRTPartition
Input: perfect graph $G = (V, E)$ with $n < \frac{k(k+1)}{2}$ vertices, $k \geq 2$.
Output: cocolouring $\mathcal{Z}$ of $G$

- $\mathcal{Z} := \emptyset$; $U := V$;
- **while** $U \neq \emptyset$ **do**
  **begin**
  - **if** $\chi(G[U]) < k + 1$ **then** compute a $k$-colouring $\mathcal{I} = \{I_1, I_2, \ldots, I_k\}$ of $G[U]$; $\mathcal{Z} := \mathcal{Z} \circ \mathcal{I}$
    **else** choose a clique $C$ of size at least $k + 1$ and add $C$ to $\mathcal{Z}$;
  - $U := U - \bigcup \mathcal{Z}$; $k := k - 1$.

  **end**

**Lemma 1** **([7]).** *For every perfect graph $G = (V, E)$ with $n < \frac{k(k+1)}{2}$, $k \geq 2$, procedure* SQRTPartition *outputs a cocolouring of size at most $k$. Thus $z(G) \leq \lfloor \sqrt{2n + 1/4} - 1/2 \rfloor$ for every perfect graph.*

*Proof.* For the sake of completeness we provide the simple proof by induction on $k$. For $k = 2$ the theorem is true. Suppose that theorem is true for $k \geq 2$.

Let $G$ be a perfect graph with $n < \frac{(k+1)(k+2)}{2}$ vertices. If $\chi(G) < k + 2$ then the procedure outputs a cocolouring of size at most $k + 1$.

If $\chi(G) \geq k + 2$ then the procedure chooses a clique $C$ of $G$ such that $|C| \geq k + 2$ which exists by the perfectness of $G$. The procedure removes all vertices of $C$ from $G$, thus the number of remaining vertices in $G - C$ is less than $\frac{k(k+1)}{2}$. By induction hypothesis $G - C$ has a cocolouring of size at most $k$ and thus the theorem is true for $k + 1$. □

**Lemma 2.** *Procedure* SQRTPARTITION *has polynomial running time on perfect graphs and its running time on comparability graphs is* $O(\sqrt{n}m)$.

*Proof.* The running time of SQRTPARTITION depends on the best known running time of an algorithm to solve the problems minimum colouring and maximum clique on our special classes of graphs.

The best known running time is polynomial on perfect graphs [16] and linear on comparability graphs [13]. □

Now we are in the position to describe our algorithm to approximate a minimum cocolouring on comparability graphs.

APPROX COCOLOURING

INPUT: comparability graph $G = (V, E)$

OUTPUT: cocolouring $\mathcal{Z}$ of $G$

- Compute a $k$-colouring $\mathcal{I}_k = \{I_1, I_2, \dots, I_k\}$ and an $h$-covering $\mathcal{C}_h = \{C_1, C_2, \dots, C_h\}$ of $G$ such that the sum $k + l$ is minimum subject to the condition $\alpha_k(G) + \kappa_h(G) \geq n$;
- $\mathcal{Z}' := \{I_1, I_2, \dots, I_k, C_1 \setminus \bigcup \mathcal{I}_k, C_2 \setminus \bigcup \mathcal{I}_k, \dots, C_h \setminus \bigcup \mathcal{I}_k\}$;
- Compute a cocoluring $\mathcal{Z}''$ of the graph $G - \bigcup \mathcal{Z}'$ by calling SQRT-PARTITION;
- $\mathcal{Z} := \mathcal{Z}' \circ \mathcal{Z}''$.

**Theorem 2.** *The* $O(nm)$ *time algorithm* APPROX COCOLOURING *approximates a minimum cocolouring of a comparability graph within a factor of 1.71.*

*Proof.* Let $\mathcal{I}_k = \{I_1, I_2, \dots, I_k\}$ and $\mathcal{C}_h = \{C_1, C_2, \dots, C_h\}$ be the sets produced at the first step of the algorithm. Then by the choice of $k$ and $l$ as well as $\mathcal{I}_k$ and $\mathcal{C}_h$ we have that $k + h \leq z(G)$.

The number of vertices in $\mathcal{Z}'$ is at least

$$|\bigcup \mathcal{I}_k| + |\bigcup \mathcal{C}_h| - |(\bigcup \mathcal{I}_k) \cap (\bigcup \mathcal{C}_h)| \geq n - kh$$

since $\mathcal{I}_k$ is a family of independent sets and $\mathcal{C}_h$ is a family of cliques, implying $|\bigcup(\mathcal{I}_k) \cap (\bigcup \mathcal{C}_h)| \leq kh$.

Therefore, the graph $G - \bigcup \mathcal{Z}'$ has at most $kh$ vertices and by Lemma 1 procedure SQRTPARTITION computes a cocolouring of $G - \bigcup \mathcal{Z}'$ having size at most $\sqrt{2kh}$. Consequently, APPROX COCOLOURING computes a cocolouring $\mathcal{Z}$ of $G$ of size at most

$$k + h + \sqrt{2kh} \leq (k + h)(1 + \frac{1}{\sqrt{2}}) \leq (1 + \frac{1}{\sqrt{2}})z(G) \leq 1.71 \cdot z(G).$$

The time bound follows from Theorem 1 and Lemma 2. □

**Corollary 1.** *The algorithm* APPROX COCOLOURING *can also be used to approximate within a factor of* 1.71

**(a)** *a minimum cocolouring of a partially ordered set,*
**(b)** *a minimum partition of a (repetition-free) sequence (of integers) into increasing and decreasing subsequences,*
**(c)** *a minimum cocolouring of a permutation graph, and*
**(d)** *a minimum cocolouring of a cocomparability graph.*

## 4 Perfect Graphs

We consider the following greedy algorithm for minimum cocolouring on graphs

GREEDY COCOLOURING
INPUT: graph $G = (V, E)$
OUTPUT: cocolouring $\mathcal{Z}$ of $G$

- $\mathcal{Z} := \emptyset$;
- $U := V$;
- **while** $U \neq \emptyset$ **do**
  **begin**
  - Compute a maximum independent set $I_U$ and a maximum clique $C_U$ of $G[U]$;
  - Choose $X$ to be $I_U$ or $C_U$ such that $|X| = \max(|I_U|, |C_U|)$ and add $X$ to $\mathcal{Z}$;
  - $U := U - X$.

  **end**

**Theorem 3.** *The* GREEDY COCOLOURING *algorithm approximates a minimum cocolouring of a perfect graph within a factor of* $\ln n$.

*Proof.* To obtain the approximation ratio of the algorithm let us consider a hypergraph $\mathcal{H} = (V, E_H)$, where the vertex set of $\mathcal{H}$ is the vertex set $V$ of the input graph $G$ and $E_H$ is the set of all independent sets and cliques in $G$, i.e. every hyperedge of $\mathcal{H}$ is either an independent set or a clique in $G$.

Any minimum cocolouring on $G$ is equivalent to a minimum set cover of $\mathcal{H}$ and vice versa. Moreover GREEDY COCOLOURING can be seen as the greedy algorithm for the minimum set cover problem on input $\mathcal{H}$ (the only difference is that GREEDY COCOLOURING won't inspect all hyperedges of $\mathcal{H}$). It is well known [5,17,19] that the greedy algorithm for the minimum set cover problem is an $\ln n$-approximation algorithm. □

By a well-known result of Grötschel et al. [16] a maximum independent set and a maximmum clique can be computed by a polynomial-time algorithm on perfect graphs.

**Corollary 2.** *The* GREEDY COCOLOURING *algorithm is a polynomial-time algorithm to approximate a minimum cocolouring within a factor of* $\ln n$ *on each graph class* $\mathcal{G}$ *for which there are polynomial-time algorithms to compute a maximum clique and a maximum independent set. In particular this is the case for perfect graphs.*

## 5 Hardness of Approximation

The following lemma allows us to obtain a first hardness result concerning the approximation of minimum cocolouring.

**Lemma 3.** *[11]* $\chi(G) = z(nG)$*, where* $nG$ *is the disjoint union of* $n$ *copies of* $G$.

We shall rely on a well-known result on the hardness of approximating the chromatic number of a graph.

**Theorem 4.** *[9] It is hard to approximate the chromatic number to within* $n^{1-\epsilon}$ *for any* $\epsilon > 0$*, assuming* NP $\not\subseteq$ ZPP. *(Here, ZPP denotes the class of languages decidable by a random expected polynomial-time algorithm that makes no errors.)*

Combining Lemma 3 with Theorem 4 we obtain the following

**Theorem 5.** *It is hard to approximate the cochromatic number to within* $n^{1/2-\epsilon}$ *for any* $\epsilon > 0$*, assuming* NP $\not\subseteq$ ZPP.

*Proof.* Let $G$ be any input to the problem minimum colouring. Then $G' = nG$ is our input to the problem minimum cocolouring. By Lemma 3, we have $\chi(G) = z(nG)$. Since the number of vertices of $G'$ is the square of the number of vertices of $G$, by Theorem 4 we obtain the theorem. □

## 6 Concluding Remarks

We leave many questions unanswered, a few of them are:

1. The problem of finding a minimum partition of a sequence into monotone subsequences is NP-hard. We provide a 1.71-approximation algorithm for this problem. A natural question is if there exists a PTAS for this problem?
2. We have proved that GREEDY COCOLOURING is a $\ln n$-approximation algorithm for perfect graphs. Are there nontrivial classes of perfect graphs for which GREEDY COCOLOURING approximates the cochromatic number within a constant factor?
3. What is the computational complexity of computing a maximum $k$-colouring and a maximum $h$-covering for perfect graphs? A polynomial time algorithm computing these parameters for perfect graphs will imply that our 1.71-approximation algorithm for a minimum cocolouring on comparability graphs is also a polynomial time algorithm on perfect graphs.

## References


1. N. Alon, M. Krivelevich, and B. Sudakov, *Subgraphs with a large cochromatic number*, J. Graph Theory, 25 (1997), pp. 295–297.
2. A. Brandstädt and D. Kratsch, *On partitions of permutations into increasing and decreasing subsequences*, Elektron. Informationsverarb. Kybernet., 22 (1986), pp. 263–273.
3. A. Brandstädt, V. B. Le, and J. P. Spinrad, *Graph classes: a survey*, SIAM Monographs on Discrete Mathematics and Applications, Society for Industrial and Applied Mathematics, Philadelphia, 1999.
4. I. Broere and M. Burger, *Critically cochromatic graphs*, J. Graph Theory, 13 (1989), pp. 23–28.
5. J. Cheriyan and R. Ravi, *Approximation algorithms for network problems*, 1998, manuscript.
6. P. Erdős and J. Gimbel, *Some problems and results in cochromatic theory*, in Quo vadis, graph theory?, North-Holland, Amsterdam, 1993, pp. 261–264.
7. P. Erdős, J. Gimbel, and D. Kratsch, *Some extremal results in cochromatic and dichromatic theory*, J. Graph Theory, 15 (1991), pp. 579–585.
8. P. Erdős, J. Gimbel, and H. J. Straight, *Chromatic number versus cochromatic number in graphs with bounded clique number*, European J. Combin., 11 (1990), pp. 235–240.
9. U. Feige and J. Kilian, *Zero knowledge and the chromatic number*, J. Comput. System Sci., 57 (1998), pp. 187–199. Complexity 96—The Eleventh Annual IEEE Conference on Computational Complexity (Philadelphia, PA).
10. A. Frank, *On chain and antichain families of a partially ordered set*, J. Combin. Theory Ser. B, 29 (1980), pp. 176–184.
11. J. Gimbel, D. Kratsch, and L. Stewart, *On cocolourings and cochromatic numbers of graphs*, Discrete Appl. Math., 48 (1994), pp. 111–127.
12. J. Gimbel and H. J. Straight, *Some topics in cochromatic theory*, Graphs Combin., 3 (1987), pp. 255–265.
13. M. C. Golumbic, *Algorithmic Graph Theory and Perfect Graphs*, Academic Press, New York, 1980.
14. C. Greene, *Some partitions associated with a partially ordered set*, J. Combinatorial Theory Ser. A, 20 (1976), pp. 69–79.
15. C. Greene and D. J. Kleitman, *The structure of Sperner k-families*, J. Combinatorial Theory Ser. A, 20 (1976), pp. 41–68.
16. M. Grötschel, L. Lovász, and A. Schrijver, *Geometric algorithms and combinatorial optimization*, Springer-Verlag, Berlin, 1988.
17. D. S. Johnson, *Approximation algorithms for combinatorial problems*, J. Comput. System Sci., 9 (1974), pp. 256–278. Fifth Annual ACM Symposium on the Theory of Computing (Austin, Tex., 1973).
18. L. M. Lesniak-Foster and H. J. Straight, *The cochromatic number of a graph*, Ars Combin., 3 (1977), pp. 39–45.
19. L. Lovász, *On the ratio of optimal integral and fractional covers*, Discrete Math., 13 (1975), pp. 383–390.
20. H. J. Straight, *Note on the cochromatic number of several surfaces*, J. Graph Theory, 4 (1980), pp. 115–117.
21. K. Wagner, *Monotonic coverings of finite sets*, Elektron. Informationsverarb. Kybernet., 20 (1984), pp. 633–639.

# Curved Edge Routing

Kārlis Freivalds

University of Latvia
Institute of Mathematics and Computer Science
Raina blvd. 29, LV-1459, Riga, Latvia
karlisf@mii.lu.lv
Fax: +371 7820153

**Abstract.** We consider the problem of drawing a graph where edges are represented by smooth curves between the associated nodes. Previously curved edges were drawn as splines defined by carefully calculated control points. We present a completely different approach where finding an edge is reduced to solving a differential equation. This approach allows to represent the graph drawing aesthetics directly, even the most complex ones denoting the dependencies among the paths.

**Keywords.** Graph drawing, edge placement, curved edges.

## 1 Introduction

Edge placement is one of the fundamental problems in graph drawing [2]. There are two traditional strategies for edge placement: edges are placed together with nodes, or nodes are laid out first and then edges are routed. Placing edges together with nodes allows to create drawings with proven quality [4,9]. However, if a more complex line style than a straight-line segment is used, it gets very hard to describe the edge influence on the node placement. The independent edge placement [6,13] has the advantage of exploiting complex edge routing using general-purpose node layout algorithms. This is also the only strategy in interactive graph layout where the user specifies the node positions.

In this paper we follow the second strategy and assume that nodes are already positioned by the user or some layout algorithm and we have to route the edges.

There are several graphical representations of a graph [1,2]. Nodes are basically represented by two-dimensional symbols, most commonly by upright rectangular boxes or circles. In this paper we will use only rectangular boxes. We also assume that nodes do not overlap, so there is some space for edge routing.

The visual appearance of the drawing is mostly influenced by the edge representation. Well-known edge drawing standards are orthogonal, straight-line, polyline and curved [1,2]. Here we focus on curved edges, where the edge is represented by a smooth curve between the associated nodes.

The common approach for curved edge routing is finding a piecewise linear path which does not cross node boxes and then smoothing it using a spline. Such approach is natural in drawing layered graphs. In layered drawings edges are

R. Freivalds (Ed.): FCT 2001, LNCS 2138, pp. 126–137, 2001.

replaced with polyline paths having bendpoints on every level. This construction provides a useful framework for smoothing the polyline paths with splines.

Such approach is used in the graph drawing program dot [8] where virtual node boxes are used to describe the free space in the hierarchical drawing where the path can go. At first the calculated polyline path is smoothed with a spline. Then if the spline goes outside the virtual node boxes, control points are adjusted or the spline is subdivided. In VCG [14] Bezier spline is fitted using adaptive subdivision, adjusting control points if the bounding triangle of a Bezier spline segment intersects a node or a path.

Dobkin [6] describes a more general method applicable to any graph. Again the polyline path is calculated first. Then a smooth spline is fitted, which does not intersect any obstacle. This method produces nice drawings, but only for each path separately. Crossings of several paths are not taken into account.

Obtaining a smooth path among obstacles is a well-studied problem in robot motion planning. Finding a shortest constrained curvature path of a robot in the workspace with obstacles is explored in [3]. It is shown that such path can be constructed from straight-line segments and circle arcs with a constant radius corresponding to the maximal allowed curvature.

Latombe [10] suggests a potential field method for path planning. He simulates the movement of a particle in the electrostatic field when the particle is attracted to the target and repelled from the obstacles. This seems very interesting approach, but it deals with such physical properties as speed and acceleration and application of this method to graph drawing does not seem to be straightforward.

Sethian [15] develops a general theory called level set methods and shows how to apply it to produce a shortest path of a robot within the environment of constraints. He reduces the problem to a differential equation and applies the fast marching method to solve it. We have found another application of this theory. Using Sethian's approach it is easy to find curves according to specific rules. In our case the rules are constructed in a special way to reflect the aesthetics of graph drawing and allows finding the path directly, avoiding usage of splines.

The rest of the paper is organized as follows. In Section 2 we define the aesthetic edge routing problem by choosing a cost function and then finding the edge drawing according to this cost function. Section 3 gives details how to construct the cost function to represent the curved edge drawing aesthetics. Section 4 presents an algorithm to route a path according to the given cost function. In Section 5 we give the analysis of the results and sketch the possible improvements.

## 2 Problem Definition

At first we have to find out how the well-routed edges should look like. There are a number of commonly accepted aesthetics criteria for graph drawing [6,2, 9]. We consider the following for curved edge drawings:

(1) edges are short,
(2) edges are well separated from node boxes and other edges,
(3) edges do not turn sharply,
(4) edge crossing number is small,
(5) edges cross in wide angles.

An intuitive way how to represent these aesthetics is to assign some cost $h(x,y)$ to every point $(x,y)$ on the plane expressing how good it is for the edge to go through this point. Then the edge is searched as a path between its node boxes that has the smallest total cost. For now we can assume that the path is joining the node centers $(x_0, y_0)$ and $(x_1, y_1)$. Formally each individual path can be expressed as a curve $L$ with fixed endpoints $(x_0, y_0)$ and $(x_1, y_1)$ which minimizes the integral

$$\int_L h(x,y)dL. \tag{2.1}$$

This definition corresponds only to one path, but the aesthetics criteria express also relations between several edges. To overcome this limitation we construct the paths one by one but incorporating the previously routed paths into the cost function.

At the beginning we have only nodes, so the cost function is calculated for them. When a new path is routed the cost function is updated to reflect the current configuration. Since we are adding paths one by one the drawing is dependent on the order in which they are added. To reduce the sensitivity to the order, paths are routed iteratively e.g. after initial routing they are rerouted several times by taking one path at a time, deleting it and routing it again. This method is summarized in the algorithm *routeEdges*.

```
algorithm routeEdges
  Build the initial cost function corresponding to nodes
  for each path P
    Route P
    Update the cost function with P
  endfor
  for iter = 1 to MAX_ITER
    for each path P
      Delete P from the cost function
      Route P
      Update the cost function with P
    endfor
  endfor
end
```

Two parts of the algorithm need to be explained: how to build the cost function, and how to find the path corresponding to the defined cost function. These problems are discussed in the following sections.

# 3 Finding the Cost Function

Let us look how to construct the cost function $h(x,y)$ to incorporate the above mentioned aesthetics. We express $h(x,y)$ as a weighted sum of functions, where each function expresses the influence of one drawing element (node or path). We add also some constant $c_1$, which expresses the cost of the length of the path. The general form of the function is

$$h(x,y) = c_1 + c_2 \sum_i b_i(x,y) + c_3 \sum_i p_i(x,y), \tag{3.2}$$

where $b_i$ are the functions for nodes and $p_i$ are the functions for paths. For nodes we want the function to be infinite inside the nodes to prohibit the paths from crossing them, and decreasing with the distance from nodes to keep the paths some distance apart from them. For paths we want the function to be of some finite magnitude near the path and decreasing with the distance from the path. Constants $c_2$ and $c_3$ are weighting factors for the influence of the nodes and paths respectively. We found that setting $c_1 = 1$, $c_2 = 1.5$ and $c_3 = 5$ is adequate.

Denoting the distance from a point $(x,y)$ to the drawing element by $d(x,y)$ our choice for the function for nodes was

$$b(x,y) = \begin{cases} \frac{1}{d(x,y)} & \text{if } (x,y) \text{ is outside the node} \\ \infty & \text{if } (x,y) \text{ is inside the node} \end{cases} \tag{3.3}$$

In practice the value of $b_i$ inside the node is set to a large enough constant for paths not to cross the node. This simplifies the algorithm and allows us to route the paths between the node centers.

For paths two kinds of functions were considered:

$$p(x,y) = \max(1 - \frac{d(x,y)}{\sigma}, 0), \tag{3.4}$$

$$p(x,y) = e^{-\frac{d(x,y)^2}{\sigma^2}}, \tag{3.5}$$

where $\sigma$ controls the desirable separation between paths. In the Fig. 1 we can see the drawings of a graph using different cost functions for the paths. Both functions give good results, but the second one overall seemed to be a little better, so further we will work with it. For the further discussion we must choose a good representation of the cost function. We chose the simplest approach to represent the cost function by sampling values on the orthogonal grid. Other choices are also possible, for example triangular meshes, but that seemed to be more complex.

Let us look how to calculate the cost function on the grid quickly. We have to notice that the functions $b_i$ and $p_i$ have some influence only in a small neighborhood near the corresponding object. In other points we can set the function to zero without affecting the resulting drawing too much. We need to find all the points where the function is large enough.

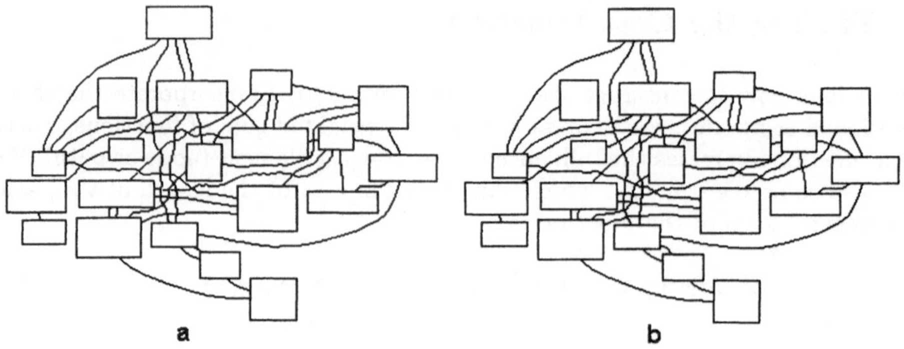


**Fig. 1.** Drawings of a graph using linear cost function for paths ($a$), and exponential one ($b$)

For node boxes this is easy since all such points are contained in a rectangle around the node. Size of this rectangle can be easily calculated from the definition of $b_i$.

For paths the situation is more complex, because the path is approximated with many short line segments and determination of the distance for the point to the path requires testing all the path segments. We use the property that our functions are monotonically decreasing with the distance from the object.

The algorithm*cost_function_for_path* calculates the function by starting at the path and expanding the zone if the function is greater than some threshold. For this purpose a priority queue ordered by the function $p$ value is used. For each point in the queue the nearest path segment is kept and the function is calculated depending only from this one segment. The queue is initialized with the midpoints of all the segments. In the loop of the algorithm we get the point with the highest function value from the queue and calculate the function for its neighbors. If the function is larger than the given threshold for them, we put them into the queue. Since the priority queue can be implemented that one operation takes $O(\log n)$ time [5], it can be easily seen that this algorithm finds the correct function in time $O(n \log n)$, where $n$ is the number of the affected points.

```
algorithm cost_function_for_path
  for each segment S of the path
    M = midpoint of S
    d = distance from M to S
    Calculate the function value h depending on the distance d
    Put <M,S,h> into the priority queue
  endfor
  while the queue is not empty
    Get <M,S,h> with the largest h value from the queue
    if h < threshold then terminate
    for each of the four neighbour points N of M
```

```
      if the function has not been calculated for N then
         d = distance from N to S
         Calculate the function value h1 depending on d
         Put < N, S, h1 > into the priority queue
      endif
    endfor
  endwhile
end
```

# 4 Finding the Path

For the given cost function our task is to find the path between two given node centers. The simplest approach would be to search for the shortest path in the grid neighbor graph. But this does not give acceptable solution because of the orthogonal structure of the graph. We need a continuous, direction independent solution approximated on the grid.

We use a method essentially the same as the Dijkstra's shortest path searching [5,11]. At first the distance map is calculated for all points and then the path is determined by tracing backwards from the destination point. But there are differences in the distance map calculation and back tracing. In the Fig. 2 we can see the cost function and the distance map of the cost function shown in Fig. 5. The starting point was chosen in the middle of the map.

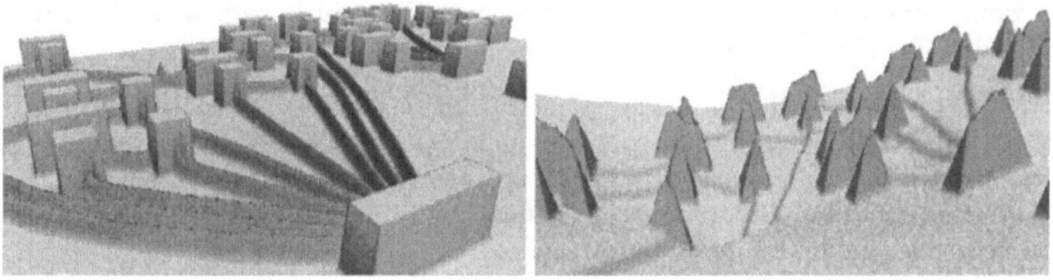

**Fig. 2.** The cost function (*left*) and the corresponding distance map (*right*) plotted in three dimensions

## 4.1 Calculation of the Distance Map

The distance map is a function $f(x, y)$ which denotes the distance from the starting point $(x_0, y_0)$ in the environment of varying costs. It is easy to imagine the distance map as a pit-like function in three dimensions, where the height of the pit surface is the value of the distance map at the given point. It is very interesting that this pit is the same as develops when the sand of non-uniform structure run out from the box with a little hole at the bottom. If the sand can hold at the maximum slope $h(x, y)$ then it is exactly our distance map. Moreover this construction has a prototype in the mining industry when an open pit must satisfy the given slope requirements [12]. The distance map $f(x,y)$ satisfies the following equation

$$\|\nabla f\| = h(x,y). \tag{4.6}$$

This means that the slope of $f$ is our cost function $h$. After adding the starting condition and writing the gradient explicitly the problem can be stated as follows:

$$\begin{cases} \left(\frac{\partial f}{\partial x}\right)^2 + \left(\frac{\partial f}{\partial y}\right)^2 &= h(x,y)^2 \\ f(x_0,y_0) &= 0 \end{cases}. \tag{4.7}$$

This equation can be solved with numerical methods by approximating derivatives with differences. For example the central differences can be used:

$$\begin{aligned} D_x &= \frac{f(x+1,y)-f(x-1,y)}{2}, \\ D_y &= \frac{f(x,y+1)-f(x,y-1)}{2}, \end{aligned} \tag{4.8}$$

and the problem is transformed to

$$\begin{cases} D_x^2 + D_y^2 = h(x,y)^2 \\ f(x_0,y_0) = 0 \end{cases}. \tag{4.9}$$

The solution can be obtained by iterative solving the equation at each grid point. But this is very slow because many iterations are needed.

Sethian [15] proposes a faster method. He observes that the solution can be constructed by propagating the front like in Dijkstra's shortest path algorithm. He uses one-side differences instead of central ones selecting the direction, which the front came from. As a result one pass over the grid is sufficient. According to Sethian the algorithm works as follows:

```
algorithm distanceMap
  for all (x,y) f(x,y) = ∞
  f(x0,y0) = 0
  Put (x0,y0) into the priority queue
  while the queue is not empty
    Get and remove the point (x,y) with the smallest f value
    from the queue
    if (x,y) = (x1,y1) then terminate
    for each of the four neighbour points (u,v) of (x,y)
      if f(u,v) = ∞ then
         compute value of f(u,v) by selecting the largest solution
         z of the quadratic equation:
           (max(z − min(f(u − 1,v), f(u + 1,v)), 0))^2+
           (max(z − min(f(u,v − 1), f(u,v + 1)), 0))^2 = h(u,v)^2
         Put (u,v) into the priority queue.
      endif
    endfor
  endwhile
end
```

The algorithm terminates when the priority queue is empty or the destination point is reached. In [15] Sethian proves the correctness of the algorithm as well as the time complexity of $O(n \log n)$, where $n$ is the number of affected grid points.

## 4.2 Back Tracing

Now when we have the distance map calculated we can search for the path. The simplest way is to trace back from the current point to its lowest neighbor, starting at the other endpoint of the path. This approach does not find the best path because of the two dominant directions imposed by the grid.

Another way is to walk in the direction of the gradient with a fixed step. This approach is rather complicated because a sub-cell accuracy is needed.

We have implemented a different approach (algorithm *findPath*) similar to the error diffusion paradigm in computer graphics [7]. We walk gridpoint by gridpoint like in the first approach, but correcting the direction pointed by the gradient. At the current gridpoint we calculate the gradient, normalize it and walk to the neighboring gridpoint, which is the closest to the gradient. Then the error is calculated by subtracting the gradient vector from the direction moved. This error is added to the gradient for the next point.

```
algorithm findPath
  error = 0
  P = (x1, y1)
  while P ≠ (x0, y0)
    add P to the path
    calculate the gradient G at the point P
    G = G / |G|
    G = G + error
    V = P + G
    P = the closest gridpoint to V
    error = V − P
  endwhile
end
```

The walk always terminates in the starting point because from its construction $f(x, y)$ contains only one minima at the starting point. This method gives us the exact curve approximated on the grid as a chain of gridpoints. In the Fig. 3 we can see the paths generated by the lowest neighbor walk and the algorithm findPath using unity cost function. It can be seen that the latter produces a perfectly straight line on the grid. Fig. 4 shows the path corresponding to a realistic cost function.

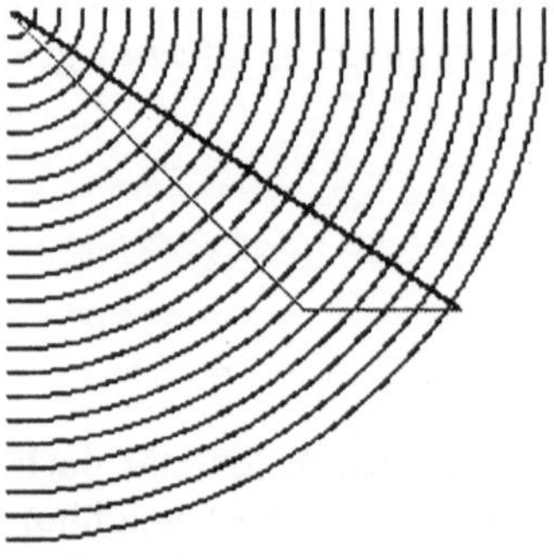

**Fig. 3.** Paths generated by the lowest neighbor walk (*thin*) and the algorithm findPath (*thick*) using the unity cost function

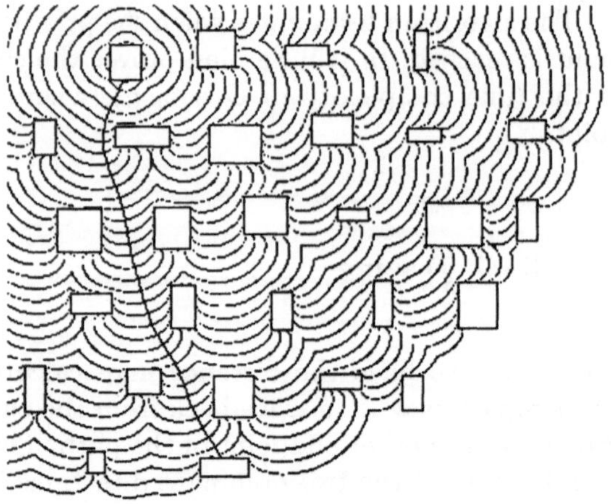

**Fig. 4.** A distance map and a path corresponding to it

To reduce the memory required for the path representation the path is approximated by a polyline. A simple algorithm is used where the sequence of gridpoints is approximated by a line segment if all points approximately fall on a common line. This algorithm has a quadratic worst-case complexity but in practice it is very fast in comparison with other parts of the program.

## 5 Implementation and Results

We have implemented the curved path router as a separate program, which takes graph description as an input and routes all the paths. The input must contain node positions and sizes and the edge connectivity information.

In Fig. 5 to Fig. 8 we can see some drawings produced by the proposed edge placement algorithm. The drawings of the edges appear natural, easily perceptible for the user. The drawing conforms to all the mentioned aesthetics. The relations between several paths are represented correctly, edge separation is good and edges cross in wide angles, what is hard to achieve with previously known approaches [6,8,14].

The desired behavior is easily customizable by adjusting the weights for nodes or paths, or changing the cost function to incorporate new aesthetics.

Sometimes when the node is large the paths coming from node center leads to uneven distribution of the edges along the node border. To remedy this we could alternatively modify the distance map calculation by starting at all the border of the start node and ending when the border of the destination node is reached.

Our implementation of the proposed edge routing approach is not fast. For example it took 12 seconds to route the edges of the graph shown in the Fig. 5 on a Pentium III 800 MHz computer. The most expensive part is the distance

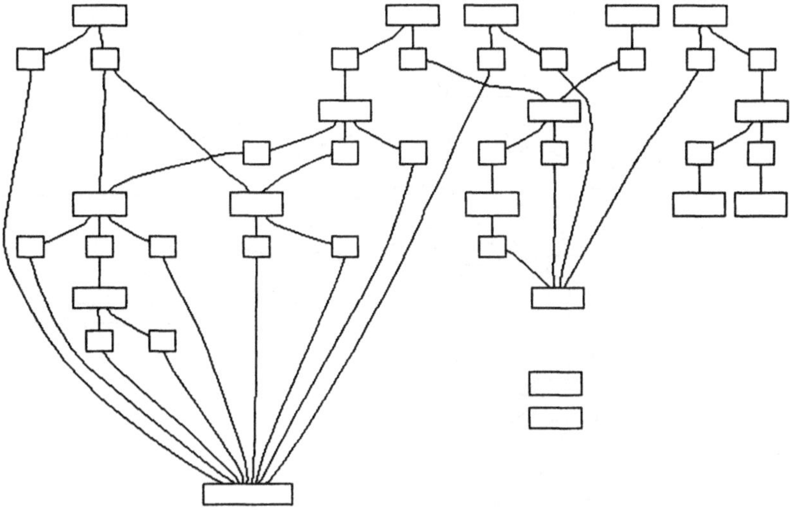

**Fig. 5.**

map calculation. We have observed that its time complexity of routing one edge is approximately $O(L^2 \log L)$, where $L$ is the length of the path in grid units.

The speed of the program was not the goal of this research, so there is much room for optimizations. The grid step has the greatest impact on the running time, so it is crucial to choose the right value to compromise the quality with the running time. We chose the grid size equal to the pixel size on the screen for the best visual quality. However we believe that more sophisticated choices dependant from the characteristics of the graph are possible.

Another improvement could be propagating the front only in the most promising directions. However our first experiments using goal directed search [11] failed, because in Sethian's approach the propagation must be carried out in a strict distance ordering.

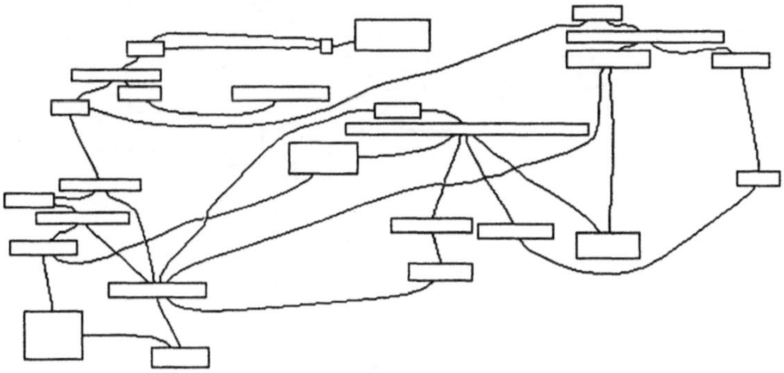

**Fig. 6.**

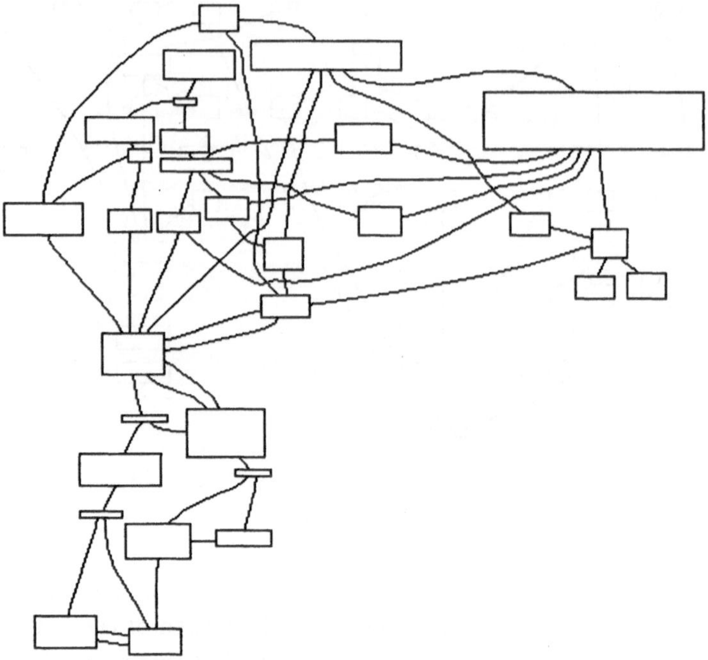

**Fig. 7.**

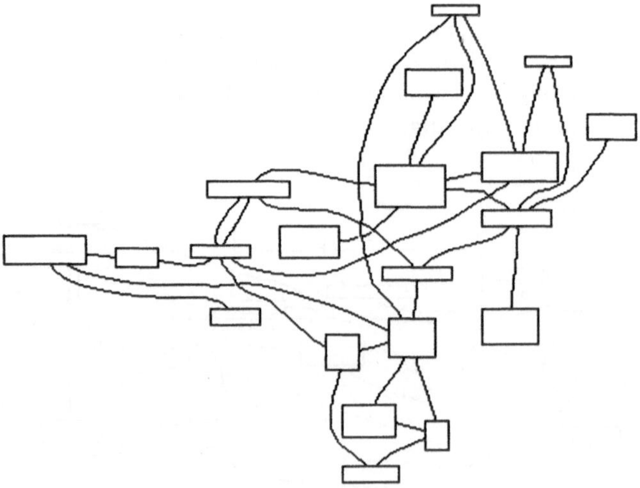

**Fig. 8.**

The number of iterations also plays a significant role. In the most cases 3 to 5 iterations are sufficient, so in our experiments we always make 5 iterations. Some adaptive criteria could do better. The initial ordering of the paths is also important. May be it would be worth routing the shortest paths first. Thus we might reduce the iteration count and also the crossing number could be smaller.

## References

1. G. Di Battista, P. Eades, R. Tamassia, I. G. Tollis. Algorithms for drawing graphs: an annotated bibliography, *Computational Geometry: Theory and Applications*, vol. 4, no. 5, 1994, pp. 235-282.
2. G. Di Battista, P. Eades, R. Tamassia, I. G. Tollis. Graph Drawing. Prentice Hall, 1999.
3. A. Bicchi, G. Casalino, C. Santilli. Planning Shortest Bounded-Curvature Paths for a Class of Nonholonomic Vehicles among Obstacles. *Proc. IEEE Int. Conf. on Robotics and Automation*, pp.1349-1354, 1995.
4. C. C. Cheng, C. A. Duncan, M. T. Goodrich, S. G. Koburov. Drawing Planar Graphs with Circular Arcs. Symp. on Graph Drawing GD'99, *Lecture Notes in Computer Science*, vol.1731 , pp.117-126, 1999.
5. T. H. Cormen, C. E. Leiserson, R. L. Rivest, Introduction to Algorithms. MIT Press. Cambridge, Massachusetts. xvii, 1990.
6. D.P. Dobkin, E.R. Gansner, E. Koutsofios, Stephen C. North. Implementing a General-Purpose Edge Router. Symp. on Graph Drawing GD'97, *Lecture Notes in Computer Science*, vol.1353 , pp.262-271, 1998.
7. J. D. Foley, A. vanDam, S. K. Feiner, J. F. Huges, Computer Graphics: principles and practice, Addison-Wesley, 1993.
8. E. R. Gansner, E. Koutsofios, Stephen C. North, Kiem-Phong Vo. A Technique for Drawing Directed Graphs. TSE 19(3), pp.214-230 (1993)
9. M. T. Goodrich, C. G. Wagner. A Framework for Drawing Planar Graphs with Curves and Polylines. Symp. on Graph Drawing GD'98, *Lecture Notes in Computer Science*, vol.1547 , pp.153-166, 1998.
10. J.C. Latombe. Robot Motion Planning. Kluwer Academic Publishers, Boston, 1991.
11. T. Lengauer. Combinatorial Algorithms for Integrated Circuit Layout. John Wiley & Sons, 1990.
12. H. Lerchs, I. G. Grossmann. Optimum Design of Open-Pit Mines. Transactions, C.I.M., Volume LXVIII, 1965, pp.17-24.
13. K. Miriyala, S. W. Hornick, R. Tamassia. An Incremental Approach to Aesthetic Graph Layout, *Proc. International Workshop on Computer-Aided Software Engineering*, 1993.
14. G. Sander. Graph Layout through the VCG Tool. Technical Report A03-94, Universität des Saarlandes, FB 14 Informatik, 1994.
15. J.A. Sethian. Level Set Methods. Cambridge University Press, 1996.

# Time/Space Efficient Compressed Pattern Matching

Leszek Gasieniec[1] and Igor Potapov[2]

[1] Department of Computer Science, University of Liverpool, Liverpool L69 7ZF, UK, leszek@csc.liv.ac.uk.

[2] Department of Computer Science, University of Liverpool, Liverpool L69 7ZF, UK, igor@csc.liv.ac.uk.

**Abstract.** An exact pattern matching problem is to find all occurrences of a pattern $p$ in a text $t$. We say that the pattern matching algorithm is *optimal* if its running time is linear in the sizes of $t$ and $p$, i.e. $O(t+p)$. Perhaps one of the most interesting settings of the pattern matching problem is when one has to design an efficient algorithm with a help of *small* extra space. In this paper we explore this setting to the extreme. We use an additional assumption that the text $t$ is available only in a compressed form, represented by a *straight-line program*. The compression methods based on efficient construction of straight-line programs are as competitive as the compression standards, including Lempel-Ziv's compression scheme and recently intensively studied compression via *block sorting*, due to Burrows and Wheeler. Our main result consists in solving compressed string matching problem in optimal linear time when only a constant size of extra space is available. We also discuss an efficient implementation of a version our algorithm showing that the new concept may have also interesting real applications.

## 1 Introduction

The importance of data compression methods and their use on everyday basis have been steadily growing over the past few decades. Especially the last ten years - due to unprecedented popularity of the Internet and the World Wide Web - bring enormous (still exponential) increase of electronic data available. This phenomenon creates a new challenge in the fields of text algorithms and data compression – a need for new tools that allow to store data in a succinct form that preserves fast and easy access. The *string/pattern matching* problem, where one is interested in finding one/all appearances of a *pattern* $p$ in the *text* $t$ (usually much larger), is a key problem in efficient text searching. The running time of a string matching algorithm is very often expressed in terms of a number of comparisons between the pattern and the text symbols. We say that the running time of a string matching is optimal if it's linear in the sizes of the text and the pattern. A number of optimal $O(t+p)$-time[1] string matching algorithms has

[1] We allow names of strings to be used in the context of asymptotic notation, e.g. $O(w)$ stands for functions that are linear in the length of string $w$, however if $w$ stands alone we use a standard notation $|w|$ to denote its length.

R. Freivalds (Ed.): FCT 2001, LNCS 2138, pp. 138–149, 2001.

been introduced both in the theoretical as well as in a practical setting, [5]. Many aspects of efficient textual search has been investigated, but perhaps one of the most interesting settings is when one has to design an efficient algorithm with a help of no (or very small) extra space. Galil and Seiferas observed in [8] that the string matching problem can be solved in linear time while using only additional memory of a constant size. Later work in this field was focused on determining an exact complexity of constant space string matching. The running time of a constant space string matching was first estimated by Crochemore and Perrin [4]. Their searching procedure performs at most $2|t|$ comparisons for linearly ordered alphabets. An alternative algorithm designed for general alphabets with complexity $(2+\varepsilon)|t|$ was later presented by Gasieniec, Plandowski and Rytter in [9]. The first small space algorithm which beats the bound of $2|t|$ comparisons was presented by Breslauer in [3]. He designed a variant of Crochemore and Perrin algorithm that uses at most $(\frac{3}{2}+\varepsilon)|t|$ comparisons while preserving constant additional space. In [10] Gąsieniec *et. al.* presented very simple constant space string matching algorithm with searching stage performing at most $2n$ comparisons and more complicated one requiring at most $(1+\varepsilon)|t|$ comparisons. In this paper we explore constant space string matching to the extreme. We use an additional assumption that the text $t$ is available only in compressed form. Under this assumption we deliver constant space string matching algorithm that works in time $O(t)$. We didn't intend to study an exact constant of our linear solution. Our intention was rather to show that such a linear algorithm exists.

The problem of searching in compressed files has been studied recently quite intensively. The focus was on the searching time and most of the algorithms used at least linear additional space. Several efficient solutions were designed for LZ/LZW-compressed files, see e.g. [1,6,11]. There was some interest in compressed pattern matching for straight-line programs too, however first solutions required linear memory in the size of a compressed file too, see e.g. [16]. Only recently more space competitive algorithm that uses only linear (in the size of a dictionary) extra space was presented in [20]. In contrast, our algorithm requires only constant extra space and it is independent on the size of dictionary. Also very recently Amir *et al.* in [2] stated problem of the compressed pattern matching in small extra space. They propose time/space efficient pattern matching algorithm that works for run-length encoding. Their algorithm (designed for 2d-pattern matching) works in linear time and requires only linear space in the size of a compressed pattern. Their result is possible due to the fact that run-length coding is extremely simple, but unfortunately it doesn't give such a good compression as the other methods do. Another interesting aspect of the compressed search has been recently studied by Ferragina and Manzini, see [7]. They have delivered a novel data structure for indexing and searching with a space occupancy being a (linear) function of the entropy of the underlying data sets.

The rest of the paper is organised as follows. In section 2 we recall some basic string definitions as well as we expose more details on data compression via straight-line programs. In section 3 we show how the actual text search is performed. We first show how to traverse straight-line programs and then how to combine that with an on-line efficient search. In section 4 we discuss an implementation of our algorithm as well as the results of several experiments. We conclude (section 5) with several remarks on the subject.

## 2 Preliminaries

We start with some formal definitions. Let $s =< s[1], s[2], .., s[m] >$ be a string over an alphabet $\Sigma$ with $|\Sigma| \geq 2$. We shall frequently denote $s$ by $s[1, .., m]$. An initial segment $s[1, .., i]$, for $i = 1, \ldots, m$, is called a prefix of string $s$, and final segment $s[j, .., m]$ is called a suffix of $s$. A *period* of $s$ is a positive integer $q$ such that for any $i$, $1 \leq i \leq m - q$, $s[i] = s[i + q]$. The shortest period of string $s$ is called *the period* of $s$ and we will denote it by $per(s)$. String $s$ is called *primitive* iff $per(s) = m$. String $s$ is called *periodic* if $per(s) \leq \frac{m}{2}$; otherwise it is called *non-periodic.* Assume that string $s$ is non-periodic, but it has a periodic prefix $\pi$ with the period $q$. A pair $(a, b)$ that breaks period $q$ is a left most pair of positions in $s$, s.t. $b - a = q$ and $s[a] \neq s[b]$.

**Example 1** String *abracadabra* has two periods: 7 and 10, and $per(abracadabra) = 7$. On the other hand, strings *igor* and *leszek* are primitive and their periods are 4 and 6, respectively.

Given two strings built over alphabet $\Sigma$: pattern $p = p[1, ..., m]$ and text $t = t[1, ..., n]$. We say that pattern $p$ occurs at position $i$ in text $t$ if $p[j] = p[i + j - 1]$, for all $j = 1, .., m$. A *string matching* problem is to find all occurrences of pattern $p$ in text $t$.

**Definition.** A *straight-line program* (SLP) $R$ is a sequence of assignment statements:

$$X_1 := expr_1;\ X_2 := expr_2;\ \cdots;\ X_u := expr_u;$$

where $X_i$ are variables and $expr_i$ are expressions of the form: $expr_i$ is a symbol of a given alphabet $\Sigma$, or $expr_i = X_{j_1} \cdot X_{j_2} \cdot \ldots \cdot X_{j_k}$, for some $1 < l \leq k$, $j_l < i$, where $X \cdot Y$ denotes the concatenation of $X$ and $Y$.

In other words SLP is a simple context-free grammar with a set of productions of the form: $X_i \rightarrow X_{j_1} \ldots X_{j_k}$, for some $1 < l \leq k$, $j_l < i$. As in context-free grammars each SLP has a *starting nonterminal* that stands for a whole string generated by the SLP.

**Example 2** SLP for Fibonacci words:
$F(n) \rightarrow F(n-1) \cdot F(n-2)$
$F(n-1) \rightarrow F(n-2) \cdot F(n-3)$
...
$F(3) \rightarrow F(2) \cdot F(1)$, $F(1) = a$, $F(2) = b$

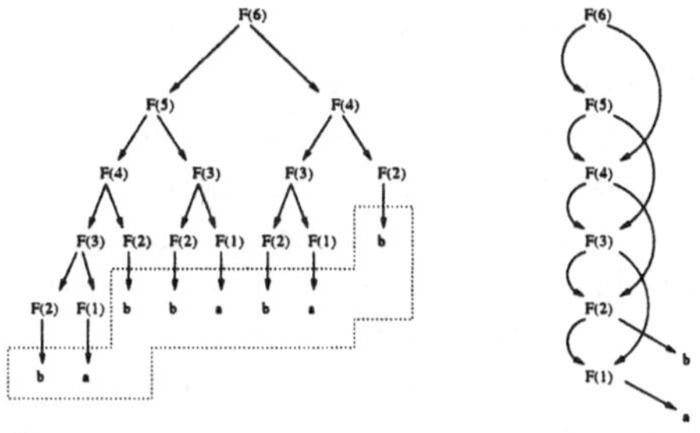


**Fig. 1.** SLP for 6th Fibonacci word. F(6) is a starting nonterminal.

## 2.1 Compression via Straight-Line Programs

There are several compression methods based on construction of simple deterministic grammars, e.g. see [12]. The crucial idea used here is to find the smallest possible set of productions, a *dictionary*, that generates a source string.

In this paper we adopt a *recursive pairing* [14] scheme that generates relatively small set of productions. Assume that initially a source (to be compressed) string $s \in A^*$, where $A$ is a source alphabet, and dictionary $\mathcal{D}$ is empty. At any stage of the compression process alphabet $A$ is extended to $\mathcal{A}$ and it is used to encode a current version $\mathcal{S}$ of the source string. We start each stage by finding the most frequent pair of neighbouring symbols $(a, b)$ in $\mathcal{S}$. We replace each occurrence of $(a, b)$ by a new symbol $\alpha$, we store production $\alpha \rightarrow (a, b)$ in dictionary $\mathcal{D}$, and we extend alphabet $\mathcal{A} = \mathcal{A} \cup \{\alpha\}$. We repeat this process as long as it makes sense, e.g. when it still leads to a better compression. When this process is finished both dictionary $\mathcal{D}$ and alphabet $\mathcal{A}$ are encoded (using e.g. arithmetic coding) to minimize the size of the compressed source string. The compressed representation of an input string is formed by a triplet $(\mathcal{D}, \mathcal{A}, \mathcal{S})$, where $\mathcal{D}$ is the dictionary (i.e. set of SLP productions), A is the extended alphabet and $\mathcal{S}$ is a compressed string built over extended alphabet $\mathcal{A}$. Note that cardinality of dictionary $\mathcal{D}$ is not greater than cardinality of extended alphabet $\mathcal{A}$.

**Example 3.** A compression of $abbababbabbababbababbabbababbabba \in \{a, b\}^*$.

| string $\mathcal{S}$ | new production | alphabet $\mathcal{A}$ |
|---|---|---|
| $abbababbabbababbababbabbababbabba$ | | $\mathcal{A} = A = \{a, b\}$ |
| $AbAAbAbAAbAAbAbAAbAba$ | $A \rightarrow ab$ | $\mathcal{A} = \{a, b, A\}$ |
| $BABBABABBABBa$ | $B \rightarrow Ab$ | $\mathcal{A} = \{a, b, A, B\}$ |
| $CBCCBCBBa$ | $C \rightarrow BA$ | $\mathcal{A} = \{a, b, A, B, C\}$ |
| $DCDDBa$ | $D \rightarrow CB$ | $\mathcal{A} = \{a, b, A, B, C, D\}$ |

A compressed representation of string $abbababbabbababbababbabbababbabba$ is a triplet $(\mathcal{D}, \mathcal{A}, \mathcal{S})$, where dictionary $\mathcal{D} = \{A \rightarrow ab, B \rightarrow Ab, C \rightarrow BA, D \rightarrow CB\}$, extended alphabet $\mathcal{A} = \{a, b\} \cup \{A, B, C, D\}$, and compressed string $\mathcal{S} = DCDDBa$.

Another compression method based on generation of SLPs has been recently introduced by Nevill-Manning and Witten, see [18]. Their algorithm traverses a source string from left to right introducing a new production as soon as a frequency of some pair passes a certain threshold. The advantage of the new approach is better compression ratio and faster compression time, though the final size of the dictionary is unpredictable. While in the recursive pairing method we could stop creation of new productions at any time, e.g. when we were happy with the achieved compression ratio or when further processing doesn't lead to a better compression. Similar control in Nevill-Manning and Witten's algorithm must be more complicated or perhaps even impossible.

## 3 Space Efficient Compressed Text Searching

As the input our searching algorithm gets a dictionary (sequence of productions), compressed version of text $t$, and pattern $p$. As the output the algorithm reports all occurrences of pattern $p$ in text $t$. Our solution is a combination of space efficient traversing of *directed acyclic graphs* (*dags*) and time efficient constant space string matching. We start with a short reminder of Schorr-Waite algorithm [19] and then we show how to use it in the context of time/space efficient searching in SLPs.

### 3.1 Schorr-Waite Algorithm

A Schorr-Waite algorithm [19] was primarily used to traverse directed graphs in the presence of small extra memory (one bit per node of the graph). However for some certain classes of graphs like trees and directed acyclic graphs (dags) the traversal can be performed in place, i.e. with a help of a constant size extra memory (i.e. few additional registers). The concept of their algorithm is very simple and it is based on reversing directions of edges in the graph. We give here a simple illustration of Schorr-Waite algorithm on the example of directed binary trees, see Figure 2.

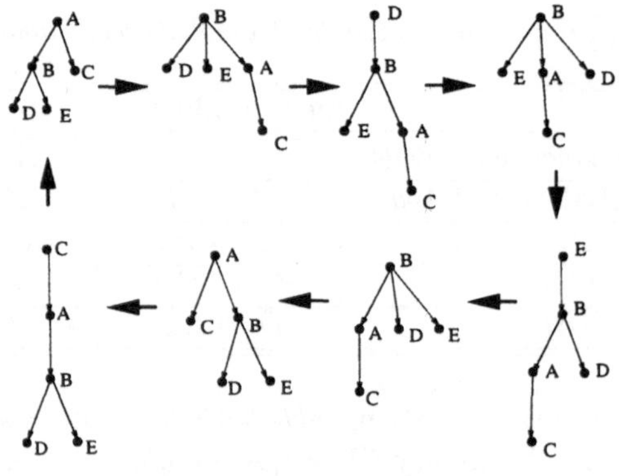

**Fig. 2.** Full round of Schorr-Waite algorithm

### 3.2 Traversing SLPs

A straight-line program (SLP) can be represented as a *dag* $G$, where all nodes of out-degree $> 0$ stand for nonterminals (new symbols of extended alphabet $\mathcal{A}$) and all nodes of out-degree 0 stand for terminals (symbols in original alphabet $A$). All productions are determined by nonterminal nodes and their outgoing edges. An SLP can be also expressed as a (usually much larger) rooted tree $T$ with the root labeled by SLP *starting* nonterminal, see figure 1. A string generated by the SLP can be formed by traversing rooted tree $T$ in infix order and reporting content of consecutive leaves in $T$.

The idea of Schorr-Waite traversing strategy is based on manipulation of pointers (dags edges). However in case of an SLP each pointer is represented as an element of some production, thus simple manipulation on pointers has to be replaced by more complicated manipulation on SLP productions. In what follows we show how such manipulation can be performed efficiently.

**Definition.** An SLP configuration is a tuple $K = (\bar{S}, p)$, where $\bar{S} = (s1, \ldots, s_k)$ is a set of productions and $p = (X, b)$ is an ordered pair of SLP symbols, where symbol $X$ stands for current SLP starting nonterminal.

**Definition.** An initial SLP configuration is a tuple $K_0 = (\bar{S_0}, p_0)$, where $\bar{S_0}$ is an SLP that generate a source string and $p_0$ is an ordered pair formed by the leftmost nonterminal symbol in the starting SLP production and a special symbol #.

**Definition.** Let $K = (\bar{S}, p)$ and $K' = (\bar{S'}, p')$ be two SLP configurations. Then configuration $K'$ is reachable from configuration $K$, we write $K \Rightarrow K'$, iff one of the two conditions holds:

- $p = (X_i, b)$ and there is production $s_i$ in configuration $K$ of the form $X_i \rightarrow A_1 \ldots A_k$, then $K'$ is obtained from $K$ by changing production $s'_i$ to $X_i \rightarrow A_2 \ldots X_{k-1}, b$ and $p'$ to $(A_1, X_i)$,
- $p = (A, B)$ and there is no production in configuration $K$ of the form $A \rightarrow A_1 \ldots A_k$, then $\bar{S} = \bar{S'}$ and $p' = (B, A)$.

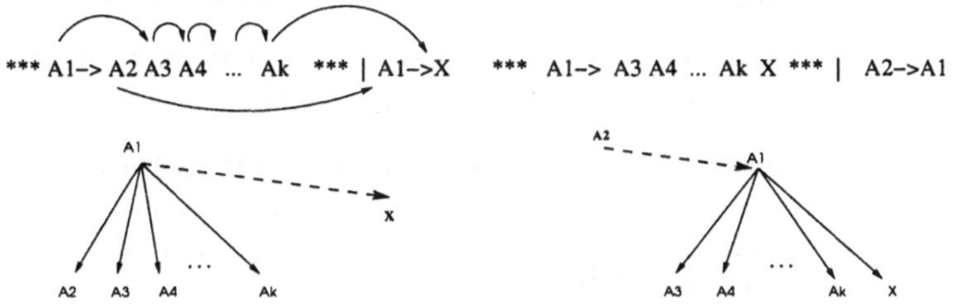


**Fig. 3.** Traversing by changing configurations

**Example 4.** Sequence of configurations in Figure 2.
$(A \to BC, B \to DE|A\#) \Rightarrow (A \to C\#, B \to DE|BA) \Rightarrow$
$(A \to C\#, B \to EA|DB) \Rightarrow (A \to C\#, B \to EA|BD) \Rightarrow$
$(A \to C\#, B \to AD|EB) \Rightarrow (A \to C\#, B \to AD|BE) \Rightarrow$
$(A \to C\#, B \to DE|AB) \Rightarrow (A \to \#B, B \to DE|CA) \Rightarrow$
$(A \to \#B, B \to DE|AC) \Rightarrow (A \to BC, B \to DE|\#A) \Rightarrow$
$(A \to BC, B \to DE|A\#)$
The following lemma holds.

**Lemma 1.** *For any SLP that generates string of length $n$ and each production is of size $k$ there exists a unique sequence of configurations $K_0, K_1, \ldots, K_r$, s.t.*

- $K_0 \Rightarrow K_1 \Rightarrow \ldots \Rightarrow K_r \Rightarrow K_0$, *where $K_0$ is initial configuration, where*
- $r = (\frac{k+1}{k-1} + 2) \cdot n - \frac{k+1}{k-1}$.

**Corollary 1.** *The number of reachable configurations $r \leq 5 \cdot n - 3$, for any $k \geq 2$.*

The algorithm traversing SLPs via configurations is as follows:

```
Procedure SLP-traverse
K = K_0; {set initial configuration}
repeat
      if ( A is a non-terminal symbol ) then
            replace in current configuration K production
            s_i = A -> A_1 ... A_k by A -> A_2 ... X_{k-1}B
            and pair p' = (A, B) by (A_1, A);
      else {A is a leaf of the tree}
            report nonterminal A and replace in configuration
            pointer (A, B) by (B, A);
until ((top of K) = # )
```

Since the length of a sequence of reachable configurations $K_0 \Rightarrow K_1 \Rightarrow \ldots \Rightarrow K_r \Rightarrow K_0$ is at most $5n - 3$, each production can be accessed in time $O(1)$ (all productions are of the same size $k$ and they are stored in alphabetic order), and a number of modifications associated with a change of a configuration is also $O(1)$, the total running time of SLP-traverse is linear, i.e. $O(n)$.

**Theorem 1.** *We can traverse SLP-compressed text $t$ reporting consecutive symbols in $t$ with a help of constant extra space in time $O(t)$.*

Recall that compression by *recursive pairing* results in factorization of source string $t$ into substrings $t_1, t_2, .., t_l$, s.t. $t = t_1 t_2 .. t_l$ where each $t_i$, for $i = 1, .., l$ is encoded by some SLP. Since each $t_i$ can be traversed in time $O(t_i)$, the total traversing time is bounded by $\sum_{i=1}^{l} O(t_i) = O(t)$.

We have just shown that we can traverse consecutive symbols of a compressed string in linear time. In the next section we will show how this traversal can be combined with a constant space string matching.

### 3.3 Constant Space String Matching

We start with a short reminder of Knuth-Morris-Pratt (KMP) algorithm. The KMP algorithm inspects text symbols from left to right updating information about the longest currently recognised prefix of the pattern. If the next text symbol is the same as the next pattern symbol, the text symbol is consumed and currently recognised pattern prefix is extended. Otherwise (a mismatch occurred) the appropriate shift (of the pattern) is made and the size of recognised pattern prefix is decreased respectively with a help of a *failure function*, see e.g. [13].

In our setting KMP algorithm has a straightforward implementation assuming that we can use $O(p)$ space to store the values of the failure function. However the task here is to design an algorithm that uses only a constant extra space. The main idea is to mimic the performance of KMP algorithm by efficient algorithmic implementation of the failure function. A similar concept of a use of approximate failure function was proposed earlier by Gąsieniec *et al.* in [10].

The computation of a shift requires a use of a constant space string matching algorithm. We use here *sequential sampling* algorithm [10]. However the sequential sampling requires a preprocessing when one has to find the longest periodic prefix of the pattern including a pair (of symbols) that breaks this period (if any). Since our algorithm have no preprocessing at all, the computation of the longest periodic prefix has to be done on-the-fly.

The concept of our algorithm is as follows. The algorithm works in stages. Each stage corresponds to an attempt to recognition of a pattern prefix $\pi_k$ of size $2^k$, for $k = 1, .., \log m$. We will use the following invariant. We enter some stage when a successful recognition of prefix $\pi_k$ is completed. We also assume that in the beginning of any stage we know what is the longest periodic prefix of $\pi_k$, what is its period, and what is the leftmost pair of symbols that break this period.

Any stage starts with a naive comparison of consecutive symbols in $\pi_{k+1}$ (following an occurrence of $\pi_k$) with corresponding symbols in text $t$. If all symbols in $\pi_{k+1}$ are compared with a success, we enter the next stage with a larger prefix to be found. Otherwise the mismatch $\mu$ (between the text and prefix symbols) is found and we do the appropriate shift updating information about current $\pi_k$.

In what follows we assume that pattern $p$ is non-periodic to make the presentation clearer. However the algorithm can be easily implemented for periodic patterns applying standard trick of looking for a sequence of consecutive occurrences of its longest non-periodic prefix, see e.g. [10].

(1) **Procedure** SM;
(2) $\pi_k \leftarrow \pi_0$; $i \leftarrow 1$;
(3) **if** $\pi_{k+1} = t[i, .., i + |\pi_{k+1}| - 1]$ **then**
(4)     **if** $\pi_{k+1} = p[1, .., m]$ **then**
(5)         **report** occurrence of $p$ at $i$; $i \leftarrow i + \frac{|p|}{2}$; $\pi_k \leftarrow \pi_0$; GOTO (3)
(6)         **else** $\pi_k \leftarrow \pi_{k+1}$; Process($\pi_k$); GOTO (3);
(7)     **else** { mismatch $\mu$ has been found}

(8) **if** $\pi_k$ is non-periodic **then**
(9) $i \leftarrow i + \frac{|\pi_k|}{2}$; $\pi_k \leftarrow \pi_0$; GOTO (3)
(10) **else** { prefix $\pi_k$ has a short period $q$ }
(11) **if** mismatch breaks periodicity $q$ **then**
(12) $i \leftarrow i + |\pi_k| - q$; $\pi_k \leftarrow \pi_0$; GOTO (3)
(13) **else** $i \leftarrow i + q$ GOTO (3)

Procedure Process($\pi_k$) computes the longest periodic prefix of $\pi_k$, its period $q$, and a pair of symbols that breaks this period (if any) under inductive assumption that the same information is available for prefix $\pi_{k-1}$ (condition required to enter a new stage). There are two cases. If prefix $\pi_{k-1}$ is non-periodic we search for all occurrences of $\pi_{k-1}$ in $\pi_k$, using e.g. sequential sampling, [10]. A constant number of occurrences of $\pi_{k-1}$ ($\pi_{k-1}$ is non-periodic) determine a constant number of candidates for the longest periodic prefix of $\pi_k$. We check all the candidates naively in time $O(\pi_k)$. If prefix $\pi_{k-1}$ is periodic with a period $r$ we extend this period as far as we can in $\pi_k$, i.e. until the breaking pair of symbol is found or the end of $\pi_k$ is reached. Since operation is done in time $O(\pi_k)$, the running time of procedure Process($\pi_k$) is also bounded by $O(\pi_k)$.

**Theorem 2.** *There is a constant space SLP-compressed pattern matching that works in time $O(t)$.*

*Proof.* We prove here that algorithm SM works in time $O(t)$. We use amortisation argument, i.e. we show that the time $c$ spent (number of symbol comparisons) in each stage, is eventually amortized by a shift of size $\Omega(c)$. And then since the total sum of shifts is bounded by the length of the text $t$ the running time of the algorithm is bounded by $O(t)$. In each stage the cost of algorithm SM can be estimated by analysis of one of several cases. During a stage that we enter with prefix $\pi_k$ already recognised we use an invariant that the time spent (so far) to process prefix $\pi_k$ is $O(\pi_k)$. The following holds

1. If prefix $\pi_{k+1}$ is recognized successfully and $\pi_{k+1} = p$ (line 5), we report the occurrence of pattern $p$ and we do the shift of size $\frac{|p|}{2}$. The work determined by earlier processing of $\pi_k$ and naive test of symbols in $\pi_{k+1}$ is bounded by $O(\pi_{k+1}) = O(p)$. The shift is of size $\Omega(p)$, thus the amortisation argument is fine, see Figure 4a.
2. If prefix $\pi_{k+1}$ is recognized successfully and $\pi_{k+1} \neq p$, we go to the next stage with $\pi_k \leftarrow \pi_{k+1}$. The total cost of processing is $O(\pi_{k+1})$, which is fine with our invariant, see Figure 4b. Through the remaining cases, we work under assumption that prefix $\pi_{k+1}$ has not been recognised, i.e. a mismatch $\mu$ has been found.
3. If prefix $\pi_k$ is non-periodic; the processing of $\pi_k$ and a naive check of symbols of $\pi_{k+1}$ is bounded by $O(\pi_k)$. Since we do a shift of size $\Omega(\pi_k)$ the amortisation argument is fine, see Figure 4c.
4. If prefix $\pi_k$ is periodic with the period $q$, but mismatch $\mu$ breaks this period; the processing of $\pi_k$ and a naive check of symbols of $\pi_{k+1}$ is bounded by $O(\pi_k)$. Since we do a shift of size $|\pi_k| - q = \Omega(\pi_k)$ the amortisation argument is fine, see Figure 4d.

5. If prefix $\pi_k$ is periodic and mismatch $\mu$ continues periodicity $q$, we do a shift of size $q$ that amortises cost of lost first $q$ symbols in $\pi_k$ and we stay with a long recognised prefix in the same stage. Thus the amortisation argument is fine in this case too, see Figure 4e.

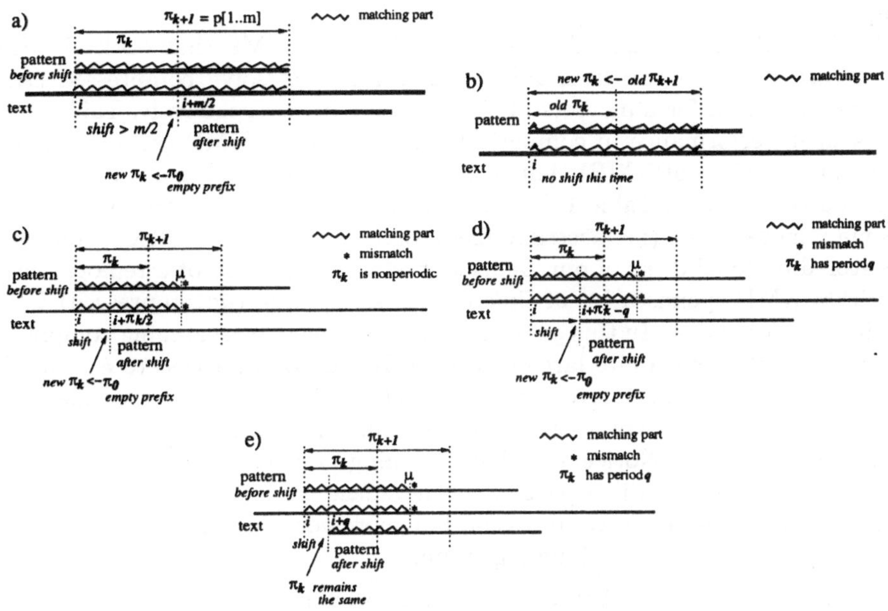

**Fig. 4.** Five cases: a,b,c,d,e (starting from the top)

# 4 Experimental Work

In this section we discuss efficient implementation of KMP algorithm in SLP-compressed texts. We have made several experiments with SLP extended alphabets of bounded size. In particular we were interested in alphabet sizes 256 and 1024, see Tables 1 and 2. We have used three test files: *dna.human* of the *Biomedical Corpus*, and two arbitrary files of the *Large Canterbery Corpus*: *Bible.txt* and *kjv.gutenberg*.

**Table 1.** Compression efficiency

| | original text | PE-256 | PE-1024 | Gzip |
|---|---|---|---|---|
| dna.human | 3170608 | 1178871 | 1047300 | 968094 |
| Bible.txt | 4047392 | 2042252 | 1539550 | 1176856 |
| kjv.gutenberg | 4846137 | 2343010 | 1781395 | 1416051 |

Our simple implementation of *recursive pairing* compression algorithm (with alphabets of size 256 and 1024) is almost as good as compression done by UNIX *gzip* command (based on Lempel-Ziv method [15], [21]) for file *dna.human*, and slightly worse for files *Bible.txt* and *kjv.gutenberg*. Note that *recursive pairing* method deals usually with much larger alphabets that lead to more efficient compression.

We have also implemented a version of algorithm KMP that works for SLP-compressed texts. Algorithms *PE-256* and *PE-1024* solve compressed string matching problem for alphabets of size 256 and 1024 respectively. Table 2 witnesses their performance in comparison with algorithm KMP (running time of PE-*/running time of KMP) that works with uncompressed files. We used the same source files as in Table 1. You can see here a difference between searching files via remote access (i.e. access to files stored in our global UNIX system) and files stored on local disks of our *Linux* workstations. In case of a remote access, algorithm KMP spends a lot of time on accessing large (uncompressed) UNIX files from a global disk. In this case a speed-up achieved by searching compressed (much smaller) files is quite large (4 times). In case of an access to a local disk the speed-up is less impressive however searching time in compressed file is still 2 times faster then a use of a straightforward implementation of algorithm KMP in uncompressed files. Notice also that searching in compressed files with larger alphabet is slower. This is a part of a time/space trade-off, i.e. use of a larger alphabet leads to a better compression but more complex SLPs, that are to be traversed by the string matching algorithm.

**Table 2.** Searching speed-up

| | Remote access | | Local Hard-Drive | |
|---|---|---|---|---|
| | PE-256 | PE-1024 | PE-256 | PE-1024 |
| dna.human | 21.49% | 24.29% | 50.16% | 56.66% |
| Bible.txt | 14.21% | 18.93% | 44.28% | 54.27% |
| kjv.gutenberg | 14.01% | 18.35% | 43.75% | 53.75% |

## 5 Conclusion

We have introduced first optimal linear time constant space compressed string matching algorithm that works for SLP-compressed files. The choice of straight-line programs (SLPs) as a compression method is due to their compression efficiency and suitability for a compressed search. We performed also a number of experiments showing that KMP algorithm performed in compressed environment and constant extra memory is superior to KMP algorithm run on uncompressed text. Our algorithm has also very straightforward application in other settings of a string matching problem. For example, if we allow to use $O(p)$ extra memory we can easily implement $O(tp)$-time standard algorithm solving approximate pattern matching with edit distance. We believe that this could be very useful in many applications dealing with huge biological data, and where the space constraints are critical [17].

## References


1. A. Amir, G. Benson, and M. Farach, Let sleeping files lie: Pattern matching in Z-compressed files, *Proc. of 5th Annual ACM-SIAM Symposium on Discrete Algorithms*, January 1994.
2. A. Amir, G.M. Landau, and D. Sokol, Inplace Run-Length 2d Compressed Search, In Proceedings of 11th Annual ACM-SIAM Symposium on Discrete Algorithms, SODA'2000, San Francisco, pp. 817–818.
3. D. Breslauer. Saving comparisons in the Crochemore-Perrin string matching algorithm. *Theoretical Computer Science*, 158(1–2):177–192, May 1996.
4. M. Crochemore and D. Perrin. Two-way string-matching. *Journal of the ACM*, 38(3):651–675, July 1991.
5. M. Crochemore, W. Rytter, Text algorithms, Oxford University Press, 1994.
6. M. Farach and M. Thorup, String Matching in Lempel-Ziv Compressed Strings, *Proc. 27th ACM Symposium on Theory of Computing*, pp. 703–713, 1994.
7. P. Ferragina and G. Manzini, Opportunistic Data Structures with Applications. *Proc. 41st IEEE Symposium on Foundations of Computer Science*, (FOCS'00). Redondo Beach (CA), 2000, pp. 390–398.
8. Z. Galil and J. Seiferas. Time-space-optimal string matching. *Journal of Computer and System Sciences*, 26(3):280–294, June 1983.
9. L. Gąsieniec, W. Plandowski, and W. Rytter. The zooming method: a recursive approach to time-space efficient string-matching. *Theoretical Computer Science*, 147(1-2):19–30, August 1995
10. L. Gąsieniec, W. Plandowski, and W. Rytter. Constant-space string matching with smaller number of comparisons: Sequential sampling. In Proc. of *6th Combinatorial Pattern Matching*, LNCS 937 , pages 78–89, Espoo, Finland, July 5–7, 1995.,
11. L. Gąsieniec and W. Rytter. Almost optimal fully compressed pattern matching. In Proceedings of *Data Compression Conference* (DCC'99), Snowbird, March 1999.
12. J.C. Kieffer, A Survey of Advances in Hierarchical Data Compression, Technical Report, Department of Electrical & Computer Engineering, University of Minnesota, 2000.
13. D. Knuth, J. Morris, and V. Pratt, Fast pattern matching in strings, *SIAM J. on Computing*, 6 (1977), pp. 323–360.
14. N.J. Larsson, Structures of String Matching and Data Compression. Ph.D. Dissertation, Dept. of Computer Science, Lund University, Sweden, 1999.
15. A. Lempel and J. Ziv On the complexity of finite sequences, *IEEE Transactions on Information Theory*, pp. 22:75–81, 1976.
16. M. Miyazaki, A. Shinohara, and M. Takeda, An Improved Pattern Matching for Strings in Terms of Straight-Line Programs, *Journal of Discrete Algorithms*, Vol. 1(1), pp. 187–204, 2000.
17. L. Mouchard, Presentation at *London Algorithms Workshop*, LAW'2000, King's College London.
18. C. Nevill-Manning and I. Witten, Identifying Hierarchical Structure in Sequences: A Linear-Time Algorithm, *Journal of Artificial Intelligence*, Vol. 7, pp. 67–82, 1997.
19. H. Schorr and W.M. Waite, An Efficient Machine-Independent Procedure for Garbage Collection in Various List Structure, In *CACM* 8(10), August 1967.
20. Y. Shibata, T. Kida, S. Fukamachi, M. Takeda, A. Shinohara, T. Shinohara, Speeding up pattern matching by text compression, In Proceedings of *4th Italian Conference on Algorithms and Complexity*, CIAC 2000, March 1-3, 2000 Rome, Italy.
21. J. Ziv and A. Lempel, A universal algorithm for sequential data compression, *IEEE Transactions on Information Theory*, pp. IT-23(3):337–343, 1977.

# Modelling Change with the Aid of Knowledge and Time

Bernhard Heinemann

Fachbereich Informatik, FernUniversität Hagen,
PO Box 940, D–58084 Hagen, Germany
bernhard.heinemann@fernuni-hagen.de

**Abstract.** This paper is about a formalism describing the change of a given set in the course of time. Starting at the Halpern–Moses semantics of evolving knowledge in distributed systems and restricting attention to synchronous ones, then the knowledge state of an agent having a part in the system represents a paradigm for such a changing set, and also a guide to our modelling attempt. We develop an appropiate language of change and axiomatize the set of theorems of a corresponding logic. Afterwards, we are concerned with the basic properties of the resulting system: semantic completeness, decidability, and complexity. It turns out that simplicity of the facts is reflected as simplicity of the system, in a sense.

## 1 Introduction

*Temporal logic* has turned out to be one of the long–lasting and most prominent logics in computer science. The main reason for this is that temporal logic provides a basic and flexible formalism for modelling and reasoning about concurrency. Both linear time and branching time systems have actually proved their usefulness concerning these tasks in many respects. Let the textbooks of Manna and Pnueli, [17] and [18], witness this in place of the waste literature on that subject. The flexibility of linear time temporal logic, for instance, can be justified in its 'readiness for synergy'. In fact, this logic acts effectively in combination with different approaches to modelling non–sequential scenarios. Let us mention two corresponding examples, which are rather remote from each other: the integration of partial orders, cf [1], and the point of view of reasoning about knowledge, cf [10].

Especially the second field deserves attention presently since it is closely related to the topic of this paper. Halpern and Moses have reasonably shown how the notion of knowledge may help to attack certain problems arising in connection with distributed systems, in their award–winning article cited above (Gödel Prize 1997). For our purposes it is sufficient to have a quick glance at this notion, which is done in the following.

A certain kind of *knowledge* can be ascribed to each processor in a distributed system, or, more generally, to every agent $A$ involved in a multi–agent system. This knowledge coincides, by definition, with the set of formulas being valid in

R. Freivalds (Ed.): FCT 2001, LNCS 2138, pp. 150–161, 2001.

every state of the system the agent considers *possible.* The relation of possiblity between states, $R_A$, occurring here throws the bridge to knowledge as a term of philosophy, investigated by Hintikka in [16]. In connection with distributed systems, however, possibility specializes in an equivalence relation meaning *indistinguishability of states* to the agent. Thus every equivalence class represents some *knowledge state* of $A$ about the system. There is a corresponding *logic of knowledge,* which may be identified with the multi–modal system $S5_m$ in case of $m$ agents; see [6]. Now, combining $S5_m$ and linear time temporal logic yields in particular a language which is expressive enough to treat interesting aspects of the *development of knowledge* formally. For example, the notions of *synchronous systems, perfect recall,* and *no learning,* have been studied to a certain extent in the literature; see [11] and [5], e.g. Subsequently we confine ourselves to such 'synchronous systems', where the agents have access to a common clock. Then, roughly speaking, 'perfect recall' means a *successive shrinking* of the agent's knowledge state, while 'no learning' means *increasing* of this set *in the course of time.*

One would expect that, concerning the agent $A$, phases of learning, i.e., decrease of the knowledge state (corresponding with 'perfect recall'), and phases of forgetting, i.e., growth of the knowledge state (corresponding with 'no learning'), generally alternate. It is exactly this alternating behaviour of a given set which we are going to model in the present paper. With this aim in view we have to alter linear time temporal logic appropriately. Moreover, we have to take into account the way of how the temporal and knowledge connectives of the combined languages interact with respect to the just indicated semantics. All that will be mirrored in the new language and the formal system to be defined in the technical part.

There is a further aspect worth to be mentioned here. Disregarding the knowledge context we obtain a logical framework modelling qualitatively the *temporal change of sets.* This might be of interest to people working on (spatio–)temporal databases or corresponding reasoning formalisms, for instance. In fact, enlargements of the present system can provide the theoretical basis for such tasks. For now we content ourselves with these hints. We believe that enough reasons have been given showing that the topic of the paper may be of interest to a wider audience from different computer science communities.

Logics of changing sets and knowledge states, respectively, emerge from modal logics of *topology.* The paper [4] is the fundamental one for that. As to the class of *trees* studied from a topological and a modal point of view at the same time we refer to the paper [8]. Relevant to the current situation we move to a *temporal* setting. The papers [13] and [14] can be viewed as predecessors of the present one, in a sense. Dealing satisfactorily with linearity, i.e., the linear structure of sets with respect to time, makes up the improvement compared with [13], and considering full linear time temporal logic instead of only its *nexttime*–fragment goes beyond [14].

We divide the paper into three parts. First, we treat *shrinking* sets. We introduce the syntax and semantics of a corresponding language, axiomatize the set of 'theorems of shrinking', sketch briefly how semantic completeness of this axiomatization can be proved, and discuss effectiveness properties. It turns out that the issues of this part already give hints to what can be expected in case of increasing sets, and for the whole system as well. So, our exposition is somewhat more detailed here. Afterwards, in the second part, we proceed in a similar way with respect to *growing*. Finally, we glue together both parts suitably.

We assume acquaintance of the reader with basic modal and temporal logic. All that we need is contained in the standard textbooks; cf [3], [7], and [9], for example.

The paper is intended to provide some fundamentals concerning certain 'knowledge–sensitive' computations. So, neither additional references to applications are given deliberately nor even case studies, apart from this introduction. Moreover, numerous details are omitted due to the lack of space; this especially goes for proofs.

## 2 Temporal Logic of Decreasing Sets

As has been set out in the introduction we want to formalize, in a sense, the change of the knowledge state of some agent in the course of time. In the present section we assume that this set *shrinks* gradually. While shrinking will be expressed by the usual connectives *nexttime, henceforth* and *until* of propositional linear time temporal logic ($\bigcirc, \Box, \mathcal{U}$), the *knowledge operator* $K$ associated with the agent quantifies over the set at any time.

In order to define the set $\mathrm{WFF_d}$ of well–formed formulas of the logical language we let $\mathrm{PV} = \{p, q, r, \ldots\}$ be an enumerable set of *propositional variables;* the index 'd' indicates 'decreasing'. Designating formulas by lower case Greek letters the set $\mathrm{WFF_d}$ is determined by the following recursive conditions then:

$$\alpha \;:\equiv\; p \mid \neg\alpha \mid \alpha \wedge \beta \mid \boxtimes_{\mathrm{d}}\alpha \mid \Box_{\mathrm{d}}\alpha \mid \alpha\,\mathcal{U}_{\mathrm{d}}\beta \mid K\alpha.$$

Concerning *duals* of the one–place operators, we let

$$\bigcirc_{\mathrm{d}}\alpha :\equiv \neg \boxtimes_{\mathrm{d}} \neg\alpha, \quad \Diamond_{\mathrm{d}}\alpha :\equiv \neg\Box_{\mathrm{d}}\neg\alpha, \quad L\alpha :\equiv \neg K \neg\alpha.$$

Moreover, the boolean connectives $\vee$ and $\rightarrow$ are treated as abbreviations. Note that we regard as basic the 'universal' version of *nexttime*, because we will have only *partial* functionality of the associated accessibility relation.

Next we define the semantics of our language for the 'shrinking'–case. As we would like to treat the decrease of a given set $X$, certain subsets of $X$ have to be included in the formal model. Consequently, we take $X$ and the system of those subsets, $\mathcal{O}$, as basic ingredients of the domains where formulas are evaluated. However, the set $\mathcal{O}$ carries a time structure which is made explicit by the following definition. — Subsequently, let $\mathcal{P}(S)$ denote the powerset of $S$, for an arbitrary set $S$.

**Definition 1.** *1. Let $X \neq \emptyset$ be a set and $\mathcal{O}$ a set of subsets of $X$. Furthermore, suppose that $(I, \leq)$ is an initial segment of $(\mathbb{N}, \leq)$, and there exists an order-reversing surjective mapping from $I$ onto $\mathcal{O}$:*

$$d : (I, \leq) \longrightarrow (\mathcal{O}, \subseteq).$$

*Then $\mathcal{S} := (X, I \xrightarrow{d} \mathcal{O})$ is called a* sequence of decreasing sets.

*2. Let $\mathcal{S} = (X, I \xrightarrow{d} \mathcal{O})$ be a sequence of decreasing sets and $V : \mathrm{PV} \longrightarrow \mathcal{P}(X)$ a mapping. Then $V$ is called a* valuation, *and $\mathcal{M} := (X, I \xrightarrow{d} \mathcal{O}, V)$ is called a* temporal model of decreasing sets, *or briefly a* model *(based on $\mathcal{S}$).*

Notice that 'the future includes the present', as it is common in computer science.

We are going to evaluate formulas in models at *situations* of the underlying sequence of decreasing sets, $(X, I \xrightarrow{d} \mathcal{O})$. Such situations are simply pairs $x, U_i$ satisfying $x \in U_i = d(i) \in \mathcal{O}$, where $i \in I$; these pairs are designated without brackets.

**Definition 2.** *Let be given a model $\mathcal{M} = (X, I \xrightarrow{d} \mathcal{O}, V)$ and a situation $x, U_i$ of the sequence of decreasing sets which $\mathcal{M}$ is based on. Then we define*

$$
\begin{array}{ll}
x, U_i \models_{\mathcal{M}} p & \textit{iff } x \in V(p) \\
x, U_i \models_{\mathcal{M}} \neg\alpha & \textit{iff } x, U_i \not\models_{\mathcal{M}} \alpha \\
x, U_i \models_{\mathcal{M}} \alpha \wedge \beta & \textit{iff } x, U_i \models_{\mathcal{M}} \alpha \textit{ and } x, U_i \models_{\mathcal{M}} \beta \\
x, U_i \models_{\mathcal{M}} K\alpha & \textit{iff } \forall y \in U_i : y, U_i \models_{\mathcal{M}} \alpha \\
x, U_i \models_{\mathcal{M}} \boxtimes_{\mathrm{d}}\alpha & \textit{iff } j+1 \in I \textit{ and } x \in U_{j+1} \textit{ imply } x, U_{j+1} \models_{\mathcal{M}} \alpha \\
x, U_i \models_{\mathcal{M}} \Box_{\mathrm{d}}\alpha & \textit{iff } \forall j \geq i : (j \in I \textit{ and } x \in U_j \textit{ imply } x, U_j \models_{\mathcal{M}} \alpha) \\
x, U_i \models_{\mathcal{M}} \alpha\,\mathcal{U}_{\mathrm{d}}\beta & \textit{iff } \exists j \geq i : \begin{cases} j \in I \textit{ and } x \in U_j \textit{ and } x, U_j \models_{\mathcal{M}} \beta \\ \textit{and } \forall j \geq k \geq i : x, U_k \models_{\mathcal{M}} \alpha, \end{cases}
\end{array}
$$

*for all $p \in \mathrm{PV}$ and $\alpha, \beta \in \mathrm{WFF_d}$.*

In case $x, U_i \models_{\mathcal{M}} \alpha$ is satisfied we say that $\alpha$ *holds in $\mathcal{M}$ at the situation $x, U_i$;* moreover, the formula $\alpha \in \mathrm{WFF_d}$ is said to be *valid in $\mathcal{M}$*, iff it holds in $\mathcal{M}$ at every situation.

Now we present a list of schemata aimed at providing a *sound* and *complete* axiomatization of all the formulas which are valid in every temporal model of decreasing sets. The schemata are divided into three groups, called *axioms of sets, time,* and *decrease,* respectively.

- *Axioms of sets:*

| | |
|---|---|
| $(S1)$ | All instances of propositional tautologies |
| $(S2)$ | $K(\alpha \to \beta) \to (K\alpha \to K\beta)$ |
| $(S3)$ | $K\alpha \to \alpha$ |
| $(S4)$ | $K\alpha \to KK\alpha$ |
| $(S5)$ | $L\alpha \to KL\alpha$ |

– *Axioms of time:*

$$\begin{array}{ll}(T\,0) & (p \rightarrow \boxtimes_{\mathrm{d}} p) \wedge (\neg p \rightarrow \boxtimes_{\mathrm{d}} \neg p)\\ (T1) & \boxtimes_{\mathrm{d}}(\alpha \rightarrow \beta) \rightarrow (\boxtimes_{\mathrm{d}}\alpha \rightarrow \boxtimes_{\mathrm{d}}\beta)\\ (T\,2) & \bigcirc_{\mathrm{d}}\alpha \rightarrow \boxtimes_{\mathrm{d}}\alpha\\ (T\,3) & \Box_{\mathrm{d}}(\alpha \rightarrow \beta) \rightarrow (\Box_{\mathrm{d}}\alpha \rightarrow \Box_{\mathrm{d}}\beta)\\ (T\,4) & \Box_{\mathrm{d}}\alpha \rightarrow \alpha \wedge \boxtimes_{\mathrm{d}}\Box_{\mathrm{d}}\alpha\\ (T\,5) & \Box_{\mathrm{d}}(\alpha \rightarrow \boxtimes_{\mathrm{d}}\alpha) \rightarrow (\alpha \rightarrow \Box_{\mathrm{d}}\alpha)\\ (T\,6) & \alpha\,\mathcal{U}_{\mathrm{d}}\beta \rightarrow \Diamond_{\mathrm{d}}\beta\\ (T\,7) & \alpha\,\mathcal{U}_{\mathrm{d}}\beta \leftrightarrow \beta \vee (\alpha \wedge \bigcirc_{\mathrm{d}}(\alpha\,\mathcal{U}_{\mathrm{d}}\beta))\end{array}$$

– *Axioms of decrease:*

$$\begin{array}{ll}(D\,1) & K \boxtimes_{\mathrm{d}} \alpha \rightarrow \boxtimes_{\mathrm{d}} K\alpha\\ (D\,2) & \boxtimes_{\mathrm{d}} K\alpha \rightarrow K \boxtimes_{\mathrm{d}} \alpha \vee \boxtimes_{\mathrm{d}}\beta\end{array}$$

The schemata of the $S$–group make the operator $K$ an S5–modality. This means to the accessibility relation $R$ of a usual Kripke frame $(W, R)$ validating $(S\,3)$, $(S\,4)$ and $(S\,5)$, to be an equivalence. In addition, $(S\,1)$ – $(S\,5)$ determine the logic of knowledge of a single 'ideal' agent; see [6]. Presently these axioms enable us to realize sets as equivalence classes.

Axiom $(T\,0)$ of the second group is due to the fact that the semantics of propositional variables is defined independently of the set component of a situation; in particular, all $p \in \mathrm{PV}$ are true and false respectively, regardless of time. Moreover, the modality $\boxtimes_{\mathrm{d}}$ represents a partial function because of the schema $(T\,2)$; i.e., this axiom is valid in a Kripke frame $(W, R)$, iff the accessibility relation $R$ is *partially functional.* In our language of sets these axioms provide for the linear structure of sequences of decreasing sets on the level of *points.* The schemata $(T\,4)$ and $(T\,5)$ are intended to express that the accessibility relation corresponding with $\Box_{\mathrm{d}}$ is the reflexive and transitive closure of the accessibility relation corresponding with $\boxtimes_{\mathrm{d}}$. Finally, $(T\,6)$ and $(T\,7)$ describe the relevant properties of the *until*–operator; its 'fixed–point character', in particular, is captured by the last axiom of this group.

The third group of axioms is the decisive one. The schemata of this group formalize the interaction of the unary operators (the 'modal' connectives) involved in the system. $(D\,1)$ is the real 'axiom of shrinking' and is typical of the various systems of topological reasoning; see [4]. Finally, $(D\,2)$ is responsible for the linear structure of sequences of decreasing sets on the level of *sets.*

Adding the following usual rules yields a logical system designated **D**; this letter should remind one of 'decrease', too:

$$(1)\ \frac{\alpha \rightarrow \beta, \alpha}{\beta} \qquad (2)\ \frac{\alpha}{\boxtimes_{\mathrm{d}}\alpha} \qquad (3)\ \frac{\alpha}{\Box_{\mathrm{d}}\alpha} \qquad (4)\ \frac{\alpha}{K\alpha}$$

Our first result states the soundness of the just defined system. The proof is easy by reverting to the above definitions.

**Proposition 1.** *Let $\alpha \in \mathrm{WFF}_{\mathrm{d}}$ be an* **D***–derivable formula. Then $\alpha$ is valid in every temporal model of decreasing sets.*

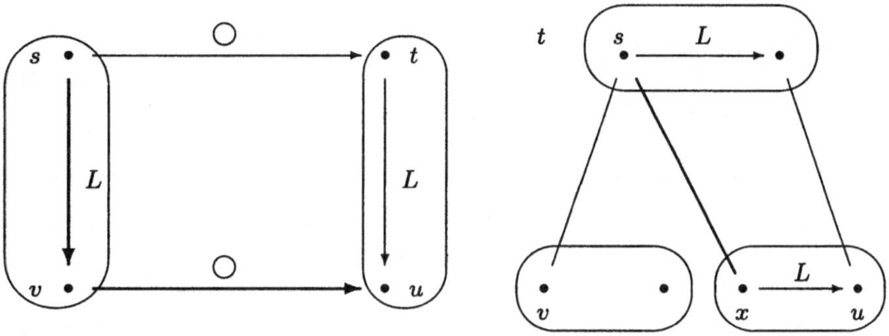


**Fig. 1.** *Diagram properties*

Semantic completeness is much more complicated to prove. One starts off with a canonical model construction. Let

$$\stackrel{\bigcirc}{\longrightarrow}, \quad \stackrel{\diamond}{\longrightarrow} \text{ and } \stackrel{L}{\longrightarrow}$$

denote the accessibility relations belonging to the one–place connectives ⊠, □ and $K$, respectively, of the canonical model. (Notice that we have omitted the index 'd', and we do so for the rest of this section.) The above axioms provide for some good behaviour of these relations. In fact, we get the following important *diagram properties:*

(1) For all points $s, t, u$ of the canonical model such that $s \stackrel{\bigcirc}{\longrightarrow} t \stackrel{L}{\longrightarrow} u$ there exists a point $v$ such that $s \stackrel{L}{\longrightarrow} v \stackrel{\bigcirc}{\longrightarrow} u$.

This is valid because of $(D\,1)$.

(2) For all $s, t, u, v$ such that $s \stackrel{L}{\longrightarrow} t \stackrel{\bigcirc}{\longrightarrow} u$ and $s \stackrel{\bigcirc}{\longrightarrow} v$ there exists a point $x$ such that $s \stackrel{\bigcirc}{\longrightarrow} x \stackrel{L}{\longrightarrow} u$.

For this, $(D\,2)$ is responsible; see Figure 1.

It is crucial for our purposes that properties (1) and (2) are transmitted to a special filtration of the canonical model: the one having filtration set Moss and Parikh's filtration set $\Gamma$ (see [4], p. 92) built on Goldblatt's filtration set (see [9], p. 92), and the minimal filtrations $\stackrel{\bigcirc}{\longmapsto}$ and $\stackrel{L}{\longmapsto}$ of $\stackrel{\bigcirc}{\longrightarrow}$ and $\stackrel{L}{\longrightarrow}$, respectively. (We need not consider $\stackrel{\diamond}{\longrightarrow}$ at the moment.) In fact, marking elements of the filtration with a bar we get

**Proposition 2.** *1. The relation* $\stackrel{L}{\longmapsto}$ *is an equivalence relation.*

*2. Suppose that we have* $\bar{s} \stackrel{\bigcirc}{\longmapsto} \bar{t} \stackrel{L}{\longmapsto} \bar{u}$. *Then there exists a point* $v$ *such that* $\bar{s} \stackrel{L}{\longmapsto} \bar{v} \stackrel{\bigcirc}{\longmapsto} \bar{u}$.

3. *Assume that* $\bar{s} \overset{\bigcirc}{\longmapsto} \bar{v}$ *and* $\bar{s} \overset{L}{\longmapsto} \bar{t} \overset{\bigcirc}{\longmapsto} \bar{u}$ *is valid for elements* $\bar{s}$, $\bar{t}$, $\bar{u}$, $\bar{v}$ *of the filtration. Furthermore, let* $\boxtimes\beta \in s$ *for some formula* $\boxtimes\beta \in \Gamma$. *Then there exists a point* $\bar{x}$ *such that* $\bar{s} \overset{\bigcirc}{\longmapsto} \bar{x} \overset{L}{\longmapsto} \bar{u}$.

Beyond usual linear time temporal logic one has to be able to select a suitable successor of the whole $\overset{L}{\longmapsto}$–equivalence class of a point $\bar{s}$ under consideration, at least as far as the realization of $\boxtimes$–formulas contained in $\Gamma$ is concerned. That this faithfully is possible can be guaranteed by (3) of Proposition 2.

Now, after some preprocessing peculiar to the new system the unwinding procedure known from linear time temporal logic ([9], p. 96) is applicable, yielding a certain intermediate Kripke model $\mathcal{M}'$. With the aid of this model we can construct the desired temporal model $\mathcal{M}$ of decreasing sets. The domain of $\mathcal{M}$ is a suitable *space of partial functions* having domain contained in $\mathbb{N}$ and range contained in $\mathcal{M}'$; furthermore, a function $f$ belongs to the $i$–th subset iff $f(i)$ exists, for all $i \in \mathbb{N}$. We can then prove an appropriate *truth lemma,* using the *diagram properties* essentially. This implies the first of our main results.

**Theorem 1.** *Let the formula* $\alpha \in \mathrm{WFF}$ *be valid in every temporal model of decreasing sets. Then* $\alpha$ *is* **D**–*derivable.*

The completeness proof roughly sketched above does not obviously yield the finite model property of our logical system. We have to proceed differently in order to achieve this result. First we introduce some prerequisite notions. To this end, let $\mathcal{I} := (I, \leq)$ be an initial segment of $(\mathbb{N}, \leq)$.

1. A subset $\emptyset \neq I' \subseteq I$ is called a *segment* of $\mathcal{I}$, iff there is no $i \in I \setminus I'$ strictly between any two elements of $I'$.
2. A partition of $I$ into segments is called a *segmentation* of $\mathcal{I}$.

Let be given a formula $\alpha$ and a model $\mathcal{M} = (X, I \overset{d}{\longrightarrow} \mathcal{O}, V)$. We will have to consider segmentations of $\mathcal{I} = (I, \leq)$ such that the truth value of $\alpha$ remains unaltered on every segment, in the following sense.

**Definition 3.** *Let* $\alpha \in \mathrm{WFF}$ *be a formula and* $\mathcal{M} = (X, I \overset{d}{\longrightarrow} \mathcal{O}, V)$ *a model. Furthermore, let* $\Lambda$ *be an indexing set and* $\mathcal{P} := \{\mathcal{I}_\lambda \mid \lambda \in \Lambda\}$ *a segmentation of* $\mathcal{I} = (I, \leq)$. *Then* $\alpha$ *is called* stable *on* $\mathcal{P}$, *iff for all* $\lambda \in \Lambda$ *and* $x \in X$ *we have*

$$\forall i \in \mathcal{I}_\lambda : (x \in U_i \Longrightarrow x, U_i \models \alpha), \ \text{or} \ \forall i \in \mathcal{I}_\lambda : (x \in U_i \Longrightarrow x, U_i \models \neg\alpha).$$

Actually, one can always get a finite segmentation of $\mathcal{I}$ on which $\alpha$ is stable.

**Proposition 3.** *Let* $\mathcal{M} = (X, I \overset{d}{\longrightarrow} \mathcal{O}, V)$, $\mathcal{I}$ *and* $\alpha$ *be as above. Then there exists a finite segmentation* $\mathcal{P}_\alpha := \{\mathcal{I}_1, \ldots, \mathcal{I}_n\}$ *of* $\mathcal{I}$ *such that* $\alpha$ *is stable on* $\mathcal{P}_\alpha$. *Moreover,* $\mathcal{P}_\alpha$ *can be chosen such that it refines* $\mathcal{P}_\beta$ *for every subformula* $\beta$ *of* $\alpha$, *and the number of segments is polynomial in the length of* $\alpha$.

$\mathcal{P}_\alpha$ can be constructed inductively, starting with the trivial segmentation $\{\{\mathcal{I}\}\}$ in case of a propositional variable (due to axiom $(T\,0)$).

According to the first statement in Proposition 3 the question whether a given formula $\alpha$ is satisfiable can be reduced to models of 'finite depth'. By a standard procedure of the logic of set spaces this question can then be whittled down to models which are of 'finite width' additionally; cf [8], 3.35, e.g. This eventually yields the finite model property, which implies decidability.

But we get even more, due to the second statement in Proposition 3: counting segments carefully along the tree structure of $\alpha$ and utilizing the S5–properties of $K$ (among other things) we obtain that the **D**–satisfiability problem is NP–complete. In view of [19], Theorem 4.1, i.e., already because of the presence of the $\bigcirc$– and the $\Box$–operator, this result is somewhat surprising at first glance. However, axioms $(T\,0)$ and $(D\,2)$ are responsible for breaking down the complexity.

**Theorem 2.** *The set of formulas $\alpha \in$ WFF being valid in every model, is co–NP complete.*

## 3 Temporal Logic of Increasing Sets

In this section we model the successive growth of some given non–empty set $X$. Our proceeding here is very similar to that in Section 2; so, we may be brief currently and point up the differences only.

Concerning the syntax we merely alter the index 'd' and let it be an 'i', indicating increasing. Semantically the same structures are considered as before, but we look upward the chain of subsets of $X$ now, i.e., take $(\mathcal{O}, \supseteq)$ instead of $(\mathcal{O}, \subseteq)$ in Definition 1. Correspondingly, frames are called *sequences of increasing sets.* As to the validity relation between situations and formulas with respect to models, $\models_{\mathcal{M}}$, nothing is changed; see Definition 2. Notice that the requirements '$x \in U_{j+1}$' and '$x \in U_j$' in the clauses concerning $\boxtimes_{\mathrm{i}}$, $\Box_{\mathrm{i}}$ and $\mathcal{U}_{\mathrm{i}}$, respectively, become redundant now and can be left out therefore.

More interesting things happen to the axiom schemata. One expects that the third group is concerned. In fact, while the axioms of sets and time remain unaltered we have the following

- *Axiom of increase:*

$$(I\,1) \quad \boxtimes_{\mathrm{i}} K\alpha \rightarrow K \boxtimes_{\mathrm{i}} \alpha$$

Interestingly enough, a further axiom of increase is missing, in contrast to the case of shrinking. The reason for this is that $(I\,1)$ is stronger than $(D\,1)$, in a sense. Here is an explanation: The *diagram property* corresponding with the schema $(I\,1)$ reads

(3) for all points $s, t, u$ of the canonical model such that $s \stackrel{L}{\longrightarrow} t \stackrel{\bigcirc}{\longrightarrow} u$ there exists a point $v$ such that $s \stackrel{\bigcirc}{\longrightarrow} v \stackrel{L}{\longrightarrow} u$.

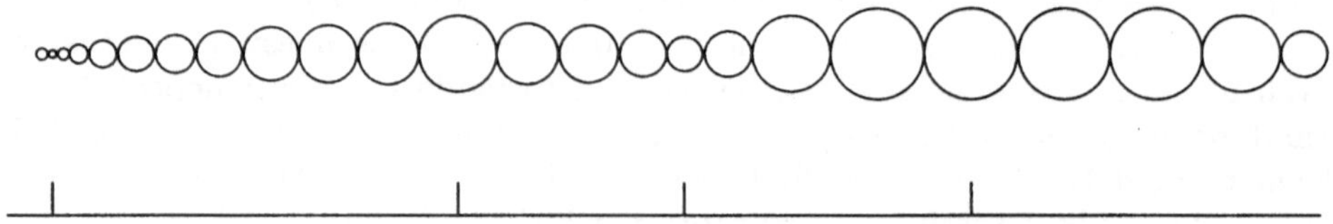

**Fig. 2.** Phases of a changing set

Now, it is not hard to prove that this together with partial functionality of the relation $\xrightarrow{O}$ implies linearity of the time structure of the $\xrightarrow{L}$–equivalence classes. Moreover, property (3) is also passed to the filtration considered in Section 2, which serves its purposes again thus.

Let the system indicated above be designated **I**. Taking into account the described modifications one gets:

**Theorem 3.** *The system* **I** *is sound and complete with respect to models of increasing sets. Furthermore, the set of* **I***–derivable formulas* $\alpha \in \mathrm{WFF_i}$ *is co–*NP *complete.*

The segmentation techniques sketched in the previous section apply correspondingly, yielding the effectiveness issues of Theorem 3. The complexity result is somewhat surprising anew, in view of [12], 4.7. Note that we are confronted once again with a situation similar to that of the preceding section: axiom $(T\,0)$ works together with a 'linearity axiom for sets', which equals $(I\,1)$ this time. But, since $(I\,1)$ is also an axiom of the usual logic of knowledge in synchronous systems with no learning, see Theorem 3.8 in [11], $(T\,0)$ is 'dominant' in the present case. (In fact, in the proof of the result 4.7 in [12] it is used that Axiom $(T\,0)$ does *not* hold for the common logic of knowledge.)

Completeness and decidability of a system similar to the present one has been obtained in [15].

## 4 Combining the Systems D and I

The final system is a combination of the systems **D** and **I** in the following sense: Building the set of well–formed formulas, each of the preceding rules is allowed. Concerning the semantics, the set $\mathcal{O}$ of subsets of the domain is structured by phases of growing and shrinking respectively; see Figure 2. This is made precise through the next definition.

**Definition 4.** *1. Let* $X$ *be a non–empty set,* $I$ *an initial segment of* $\mathbb{N}$ *and* $d : I \longrightarrow \mathcal{P}(X)$ *a mapping. Furthermore, let* $I'$ *be a segment of* $I$*. Then* $d$ *is called* increasing on $I'$, *iff* $i \leq j \iff d(i) \subseteq d(j)$ *for all* $i, j \in I'$*, and* decreasing on $I'$, *iff* $i \leq j \iff d(i) \supseteq d(j)$ *for all* $i, j \in I'$*.*

2. *Let $X$, $I$ and $d$ be as above. Moreover, let $\mathcal{I} := (I_k^{c_k})_{k \in J}$ be a segmentation of $I$, where $J$ is a suitable initial segment of $\mathbb{N}$, and $c_k \in \{\mathrm{d}, \mathrm{i}\}$ for all $k \in J$. Then $d$ is called* faithful on $\mathcal{I}$, *iff $d$ is increasing on $I_k^{c_k}$ in case $c_k = \mathrm{i}$, and $d$ is decreasing on $I_k^{c_k}$ in case $c_k = \mathrm{d}$, for all $k \in J$.*

We then regard as relevant only sequences of sets $\mathcal{S} = (X, I \xrightarrow{d} \mathcal{O})$ which are partitioned by a segmentation $\mathcal{I}$ in a way such that $d$ is faithful on $\mathcal{I}$. Let us call such structures *proper*. The evaluation of formulas in models based on proper sequences of sets respects the phases of $\mathcal{I}$, and follows Definition 2 otherwise.

Let us explain this more detailedly. So, let be given a model

$$\mathcal{M} = (X, I \xrightarrow{d} \mathcal{O}, V)$$

based on a proper sequence of sets. Let $\mathcal{I} = (I_k^{c_k})_{k \in J}$ be the corresponding segmentation of $I$, i.e., the segmentation where $d$ is faithful on. Finally, let $x, U_i$ be a situation of $\mathcal{S}$. Then there exists a unique $k \in J$ such that $i \in I_k^{c_k}$. We write $I_{k(i)}^{c_{k(i)}}$ for the latter set. Quantification is defined with respect to this phase then. For example:

$$x, U_i \models_{\mathcal{M}} \Box_{\mathrm{d}} \alpha : \Longleftrightarrow \forall j \geq i : \left( j \in I_{k(i)}^{c_{k(i)}} \wedge c_{k(i)} = \mathrm{d} \wedge x \in U_j \Longrightarrow x, U_j \models_{\mathcal{M}} \alpha \right)$$

In case of $\boxtimes_{\mathrm{c}}$ it has to be required that $i+1$ is contained in some 'c–phase', in the premise of the implication on the right–hand side ($\mathrm{c} \in \{\mathrm{d}, \mathrm{i}\}$).

Apart from the schemata of Section 2 and Section 3 there is a single axiom of change expressing the transition from a shrinking phase to a growing one, and vice versa.

- *Axiom of change:*

$$(C1) \quad K \boxtimes_{\mathrm{d}} \alpha \vee K \boxtimes_{\mathrm{i}} \beta$$

The corresponding system, **C**, is thus determined by the schemata $(S1)$ – $(S5)$, $(T1)$ – $(T7)$, $(D1)$, $(D2)$, $(I1)$ and $(C1)$, and the rules given in Section 2.

Let us discuss the axiom of change. Its effect on the canonical model is described in the following proposition.

**Proposition 4.** *Let $[s]$ be an $\xrightarrow{L}$ –equivalence class of the canonical model. Then there do not exist $u, t \in [s]$ and points $t', u'$ such that $t \xrightarrow{\bigcirc_{\mathrm{d}}} t'$ and $u \xrightarrow{\bigcirc_{\mathrm{i}}} u'$.*

Consequently, the desired behaviour can be guaranteed on the canonical model: every equivalence class as a whole can exclusively be extended with respect to growing or shrinking, if it can be extended at all.

Fortunately the behaviour of the equivalence classes is transmitted to the filtration, at least in the meaning of Proposition 2(3), i.e., as far as $\boxtimes_{\mathrm{c}}$–formulas contained in the filtration set are concerned ($\mathrm{c} \in \{\mathrm{d}, \mathrm{i}\}$). The reason for this is that we have taken the minimal filtration of $\xrightarrow{\bigcirc_{\mathrm{d}}}$ and $\xrightarrow{\bigcirc_{\mathrm{i}}}$ respectively. This suffices for our purposes. For, the unwinding procedure mentioned in Section 2 leads to a proper sequence of sets then. In this way we get semantic completeness of the system **C**.

The previous decidability and complexity assertions remain valid in case of the combined system as well. In fact, segmentation of a given model is carried out with respect to the separate phases here so that only the last one is crucial to the finite model property. This property follows as above, and hence decidability, too.

As to complexity, it must only be guaranteed additionally that the number of phases is polynomial in the length of the formula under consideration. But this is clear since that number coincides with the degree of alternately nesting d– and i–operators in the formula.

We can state the main result of this paper now.

**Theorem 4.** *1. The system* **C** *is sound and complete with respect to proper sequences of sets.*
*2. The set of* **C***–theorems is co–*NP *complete.*

## 5 Concluding Remarks

We have presented a formalism originating from the logic of knowledge of an agent involved in a synchronous system. The underlying language can describe the change of the knowledge state of the agent 'from his own point of view'. Moreover, the language can be viewed as a core language expressing in general the change of a given set in the course of time.

Our results include completeness of the given axiomatization, decidability of the logic, and the determination of the complexity of the set of theorems. It turned out that the latter set is 'only' complete in co–NP. This result can be interpreted as *simplicity* of the logic. In fact, due to our special axioms neither the temporal component of the system contributes to the complexity nor the interplay between knowledge and time, so that the knowledge component has a determining influence on this alone (cf [6], Section 3.5).

In view of the second possible field of application of our system remarked above it is desirable to extend the formalism in order to get to grips with points inside the given set explicitly (among other things). Maybe *hybrid logic,* see [2], is a good candidate for this. Hybrid subset space logics will be a subject of future research.

Another topic worth to be investigated is the purely *modal* treatment of changing sets. Interestingly enough, a complete axiomatization of structures of the type $(X, \mathcal{O})$, where $X$ is a non–empty set and $\mathcal{O}$ forms a *chain* of subsets of $X$ with respect to inclusion, is still missing in the framework of the modal logic of topology.

## References


1. Girish Bhat and Doron Peled. Adding Partial Orders to Linear Temporal Logic. *Fundamenta Informaticae*, 36:1–21, 1998.
2. Patrick Blackburn. Representation, Reasoning, and Relational Structures: a Hybrid Logic Manifesto. *Logic Journal of th IGPL*, 8:339–365, 2000.
3. Patrick Blackburn, Maarten de Rijke, and Yde Venema. Modal Logic. Forthcoming (preprint web–available).
4. Andrew Dabrowski, Lawrence S. Moss, and Rohit Parikh. Topological Reasoning and The Logic of Knowledge. *Annals of Pure and Applied Logic*, 78:73–110, 1996.
5. Clare Dixon and Michael Fisher. Clausal Resolution for Logics of Time and Knowledge with Synchrony and Perfect Recall. In *International Conference on Temporal Logic 2000*, pages 43–52, Leipzig, October 2000. University of Leipzig.
6. Ronald Fagin, Joseph Y. Halpern, Yoram Moses, and Moshe Y. Vardi. *Reasoning about Knowledge.* MIT Press, Cambridge (Mass.), 1995.
7. Dov M. Gabbay, Ian Hodkinson, and Mark Reynolds. *Temporal Logic: Mathematical Foundations and Computational Aspects*, volume 28 of *Oxford Logic Guides.* Clarendon Press, Oxford, 1994.
8. Konstantinos Georgatos. Knowledge on Treelike Spaces. *Studia Logica*, 59:271–301, 1997.
9. Robert Goldblatt. *Logics of Time and Computation*, volume 7 of *CSLI Lecture Notes.* Center for the Study of Language and Information, Stanford, second edition, 1992.
10. Joseph Y. Halpern and Yoram Moses. Knowledge and Common Knowledge in a Distributed Environment. *Journal of the ACM*, 37:549–587, 1990.
11. Joseph Y. Halpern, Ron van der Meyden, and Moshe Y. Vardi. Complete Axiomatizations for Reasoning about Knowledge and Time. Preprint (web–available), 1997.
12. Joseph Y. Halpern and Moshe Y. Vardi. The Complexity of Reasoning about Knowledge and Time. I. Lower Bounds. *Journal of Computer and System Sciences*, 38:195–237, 1989.
13. Bernhard Heinemann. Temporal Aspects of the Modal Logic of Subset Spaces. *Theoretical Computer Science*, 224(1–2):135–155, 1999.
14. Bernhard Heinemann. Extending Topological Nexttime Logic. In S. D. Goodwin and A. Trudel, editors, *Temporal Representation and Reasoning, 7th International Workshop, TIME-00*, pages 87–94, Los Alamitos, Ca., 2000. IEEE Computer Society Press.
15. Bernhard Heinemann. Generalizing the Modal and Temporal Logic of Linear Time. In T. Rus, editor, *Algebraic Methodology and Software Technology, 8th International Conference, AMAST 2000*, volume 1816 of *Lecture Notes in Computer Science*, pages 41–56. Springer, 2000.
16. Jaakko Hintikka. *Knowledge and Belief.* Cornell University Press, Ithaca, N.Y., 1977. 5th Printing.
17. Zohar Manna and Amir Pnueli. *The Temporal Logic of Reactive and Concurrent Systems.* Springer, New York, 1991.
18. Zohar Manna and Amir Pnueli. *Temporal Verification of Reactive Systems.* Springer, New York, 1995.
19. A. Prasad Sistla and Edmund M. Clarke. The Complexity of Propositional Linear Temporal Logics. *Journal of the ACM*, 32:733–749, 1985.

# If P ≠ NP then Some Strongly Noninvertible Functions Are Invertible

Lane A. Hemaspaandra[1]*, Kari Pasanen[2], and Jörg Rothe[3]**

[1] Department of Computer Science, University of Rochester, Rochester, NY 14627, USA.
lane@cs.rochester.edu

[2] Nokia Networks and University of Jyväskylä
P.O. Box 12, FIN-40101 Jyväskylä, Finland.
kari.pasanen@nokia.com.

[3] Heinrich-Heine-Universität Düsseldorf, Abteilung für Informatik, 40225 Düsseldorf, Germany.
rothe@cs.uni-duesseldorf.de

**Abstract.** Rabi, Rivest, and Sherman alter the standard notion of noninvertibility to a new notion they call strong noninvertibility, and show—via explicit cryptographic protocols for secret-key agreement ([RS93,RS97] attribute this to Rivest and Sherman) and digital signatures [RS93,RS97]—that strongly noninvertible functions would be very useful components in protocol design. Their definition of strong noninvertibility has a small twist ("respecting the argument given") that is needed to ensure cryptographic usefulness. In this paper, we show that this small twist has a large, unexpected consequence: Unless P = NP, some strongly noninvertible functions are invertible.

**Keywords:** Computational and Structural Complexity.

## 1 Introduction

Rabi, Rivest, and Sherman developed novel cryptographic protocols that require one-way functions with algebraic properties such as associativity (see [RS93, RS97] and the attributions and references therein, esp. [She86,KRS88]). Motivated by these protocols, they initiated the study of two-argument (2-ary, for short) one-way functions in worst-case cryptography. To preclude certain types of attacks, their protocols require one-way functions that are not invertible in polynomial time even when the adversary is given not just the function's output

* Supported in part by grants NSF-CCR-9322513 and NSF-INT-9815095/DAAD-315-PPP-gü-ab. Work done in part while visiting Julius-Maximilians-Universität Würzburg.

** Corresponding author. Supported in part by grant NSF-INT-9815095/DAAD-315-PPP-gü-ab and a Heisenberg Fellowship of the Deutsche Forschungsgemeinschaft. Work done in part while visiting the University of Rochester.

R. Freivalds (Ed.): FCT 2001, LNCS 2138, pp. 162–171, 2001.

but also one of the function's inputs. Calling this property of one-way functions "strong noninvertibility" (or "strongness," for short), they left as an open problem whether there is any evidence—e.g., any plausible complexity-theoretic hypothesis—ensuring the existence of one-way functions with all the properties the protocols require, namely ensuring the existence of total, commutative, associative one-way functions that are strongly noninvertible. This problem was recently solved by Hemaspaandra and Rothe [HR99] who show that if P $\neq$ NP then such one-way functions do exist.

Unfortunately, Hemaspaandra and Rothe [HR99] write: "Rabi and Sherman [RS97] also introduce the notion of *strong* one-way functions—2-ary one-way functions that are hard to invert even if one of their arguments is given. Strongness implies one-way-ness." The latter sentence could be very generously read as meaning "strong, one-way functions" when it speaks of "strongness," especially since strongness alone, by definition, does not even require honesty, and without honesty the sentence quoted above would be provably, trivially, false. However, a more natural reading is that [HR99] is assuming that strongly noninvertible functions are always noninvertible. The main result of the present paper is that if P $\neq$ NP then this is untrue. So, even when one has proven a function to be strongly noninvertible, one must not merely claim that noninvertibility automatically holds (as it may not), but rather one must prove the noninvertibility.[1]

In the present paper, we study appropriately honest, polynomial-time computable 2-ary functions. We prove that if P $\neq$ NP then there exist strongly noninvertible such functions that are invertible (see Section 2 for precise definitions). This is a rather surprising result that at first might seem paradoxical. To paint a full picture of what happens if P $\neq$ NP, we also show the (nonsurprising) result that if P $\neq$ NP then there exist appropriately honest, polynomial-time computable 2-ary functions that are noninvertible, yet not strongly noninvertible.

So, why is the surprising, paradoxical-seeming result (that if P $\neq$ NP then some strongly noninvertible functions are invertible) even possible? Let us informally explain. Let $\sigma$ be a 2-ary function. We say $\sigma$ is noninvertible if there is no polynomial-time inverter that, given an image element $z$ of $\sigma$, outputs some preimage of $z$. We say $\sigma$ is strongly noninvertible if even when, in addition to any image element $z$ of $\sigma$, one argument of $\sigma$ is given such that there exists another string with which this argument is mapped to $z$, computing one such other argument is not a polynomial-time task. So, why does strongness alone not outright imply noninvertibility? One might be tempted to think that from some given

[1] Since in [HR99] only strong noninvertibility is explicitly proven, one might worry that the functions constructed in its proofs may be invertible. Fortunately, the constructions in the proofs in [HR99] do easily support and implicitly give noninvertibility as well; thus, all the claims of [HR99] remain correct. Most crucially, on page 654 of [HR99], inverting the output $\langle x, x \rangle$ in polynomial time would give strings containing one witness for membership of $x$ in the given set in NP $-$ P (if there are any such witnesses), which is impossible.

polynomial-time inverter $g$ witnessing the invertibility of $\sigma$ one could construct polynomial-time inverters $g_1$ and $g_2$ such that $g_i$ inverts $\sigma$ in polynomial time even when the $i$th argument is given (see Definition 2 for the formal details). This approach does not work. In particular, it is not clear how to define $g_1$ when given an output $z$ of $\sigma$ and a first argument $a$ that together with a corresponding second argument is mapped to $z$, yet $a$ is not the first component of $g(z)$. (In fact, our main theorem implies that *no* approach can in general accomplish the desired transformation from $g$ to $g_1$, unless $\mathrm{P} = \mathrm{NP}$.)

But then, why don't we use a different notion of strongness that automatically implies noninvertibility? The answer is that the definitional subtlety that opens the door to the unexpected behavior is absolutely essential to the cryptographic protocols for which Rabi, Rivest, and Sherman created the notion in the first place. For example, suppose one were tempted to redefine "strongly noninvertible" with the following quite different notion: $\sigma$ is "strongly noninvertible" if, given any image element $z$ of $\sigma$ and any one argument of $\sigma$ such that there exists another string with which this argument is mapped to $z$, computing *any preimage of* $z$ (as opposed to "any other argument respecting the argument given") is not a polynomial-time task. The problem with this redefinition is that it completely loses the core of why strongness precludes direct attacks against the protocols of Rabi, Rivest, and Sherman (it is difficult to explain why without giving here in full their protocols, and this isn't a formal claim as their arguments themselves are not formal proofs of security, so suffice it to say that their intuitive argument is crucially drawing on the fact that the definition of strong noninvertibility includes the "respecting the argument given" feature, and this dependence will be immediately clear to anyone who reads their protocols). We will call the just-defined notion "overstrongness," as it seems to be overrestrictive in terms of motivation—and we will prove that if $\mathrm{P} \neq \mathrm{NP}$ then overstrongness indeed is a properly more restrictive notion than strongness.

## 2 Definitions

Fix the binary alphabet $\Sigma = \{0,1\}$. Let $\epsilon$ denote the empty string. Let $\langle\cdot,\cdot\rangle : \Sigma^* \times \Sigma^* \to \Sigma^*$ be some standard pairing function, that is, some total, polynomial-time computable bijection that has polynomial-time computable inverses and is nondecreasing in each argument when the other argument is fixed. Let FP denote the set of all polynomial-time computable total functions. The standard definition of one-way-ness used here is essentially due to Grollmann and Selman except that they require one-way functions to be one-to-one ([GS88], see also [Ko85,Ber77] and the surveys [Sel92,BHHR99]); as in the papers [RS97, HR99,Hom00], their notion is tailored below to the case of 2-ary functions. Any general notions not explicitly defined can be found in standard complexity texts [BC93,Pap94,BDG95].

**Definition 1.** [GS88,RS97,HR99] *Let* $\rho : \Sigma^* \times \Sigma^* \to \Sigma^*$ *be any (possibly nontotal, possibly many-to-one) 2-ary function.*

1. *We say* $\rho$ *is* honest *if and only if there exists a polynomial* $q$ *such that:*

$$(\forall z \in \text{image}(\rho))\,(\exists (a,b) \in \text{domain}(\rho))\,[|a| + |b| \leq q(|z|) \wedge \rho(a,b) = z].$$

2. *We say* $\rho$ *is* (polynomial-time) noninvertible *if and only if the following does not hold:*

$$(\exists g \in \text{FP})\,(\forall z \in \text{image}(\rho))\,[\rho(g(z)) = z].$$

3. *We say* $\rho$ *is* one-way *if and only if it is honest, polynomial-time computable, and noninvertible.*

We now define strong noninvertibility (or strongness), which is a stand-alone property (i.e., with one-way-ness not necessarily required) of 2-ary functions. If one wants to discuss strongness in a nontrivial way, one needs some type of honesty that is suitable for strongness. To this end, we introduce below, in addition to honesty as defined above, the notion of s-honesty.[2]

**Definition 2.** (see, essentially, [RS97,HR99]) *Let* $\sigma : \Sigma^* \times \Sigma^* \to \Sigma^*$ *be any (possibly nontotal, possibly many-to-one) 2-ary function.*

1. *We say* $\sigma$ *is* s-honest *if and only if there exists a polynomial* $q$ *such that both* (a) *and* (b) *hold:*
   **(a)** $(\forall z, a : (\exists b)\,[\sigma(a,b) = z])\,(\exists b')\,[|b'| \leq q(|z| + |a|) \wedge \sigma(a,b') = z]$.
   **(b)** $(\forall z, b : (\exists a)\,[\sigma(a,b) = z])\,(\exists a')\,[|a'| \leq q(|z| + |b|) \wedge \sigma(a',b) = z]$.
2. *We say* $\sigma$ *is* (polynomial-time) invertible with respect to the first argument *if and only if*

$$(\exists g_1 \in \text{FP})\,(\forall z \in \text{image}(\sigma))\,(\forall a,b : (a,b) \in \text{domain}(\sigma) \wedge \sigma(a,b) = z)$$
$$[\sigma(a, g_1(\langle a, z\rangle)) = z].$$

3. *We say* $\sigma$ *is* (polynomial-time) invertible with respect to the second argument *if and only if*

$$(\exists g_2 \in \text{FP})\,(\forall z \in \text{image}(\sigma))\,(\forall a,b : (a,b) \in \text{domain}(\sigma) \wedge \sigma(a,b) = z)$$
$$[\sigma(g_2(\langle b, z\rangle), b) = z].$$

4. *We say* $\sigma$ *is* strongly noninvertible *if and only if* $\sigma$ *is neither invertible with respect to the first argument nor invertible with respect to the second argument.*
5. *We say* $\sigma$ *is* strongly one-way *if and only if it is s-honest, polynomial-time computable, and strongly noninvertible.*

---

[2] The strongly noninvertible functions in [HR99] clearly are all s-honest, notwithstanding that s-honesty is not explicitly discussed in [HR99] (or [RS97,RS93]).

It is easy to see that there are honest, polynomial-time computable 2-ary functions that are not s-honest,[3] and that there are s-honest, polynomial-time computable 2-ary functions that are not honest.[4]

For completeness, we also give a formal definition of the notion of overstrongness mentioned in the last paragraph of the introduction. Note that overstrongness implies both noninvertibility and strong noninvertibility.

**Definition 3.** *Let $\sigma : \Sigma^* \times \Sigma^* \to \Sigma^*$ be any (possibly nontotal, possibly many-to-one) 2-ary function. We say $\sigma$ is* overstrong *if and only if for no $f \in \mathrm{FP}$ with $f : \{1,2\} \times \Sigma^* \times \Sigma^* \to \Sigma^* \times \Sigma^*$ does it hold that for each $i \in \{1,2\}$ and for all strings $z, a \in \Sigma^*$:*

$$((\exists b \in \Sigma^*)[(\sigma(a,b) = z \wedge i = 1) \vee (\sigma(b,a) = z \wedge i = 2)]) \\ \Longrightarrow \ \sigma(f(i,z,a)) = z.$$

## 3 On Inverting Strongly Noninvertible Functions

It is well-known (see, e.g., [Sel92,BDG95]) that 1-ary one-way functions exist if and only if $\mathrm{P} \neq \mathrm{NP}$; as mentioned in [HR99,RS97], the standard method to prove this result can also be used to prove the analogous result for 2-ary one-way functions.

**Theorem 1.** (see [HR99,RS97]) $\mathrm{P} \neq \mathrm{NP}$ *if and only if total 2-ary one-way functions exist.*

Now we show the main, and most surprising, result of this paper: If $\mathrm{P} \neq \mathrm{NP}$ then one can invert some functions that are strongly noninvertible.

**Theorem 2.** *If* $\mathrm{P} \neq \mathrm{NP}$ *then there exists a total, honest 2-ary function that is a strongly one-way function but not a one-way function.*

**Proof.** Assuming $\mathrm{P} \neq \mathrm{NP}$, by Theorem 1 there exists a total 2-ary one-way function $\rho$. Define a function $\sigma : \Sigma^* \times \Sigma^* \to \Sigma^*$ as follows:

$$\sigma(a,b) = \begin{cases} 0\rho(x,y) & \text{if } (\exists x,y,z \in \Sigma^*)\, [a = 1\langle x,y\rangle \wedge b = 0z] \\ 0\rho(y,z) & \text{if } (\exists x,y,z \in \Sigma^*)\, [a = 0x \wedge b = 1\langle y,z\rangle] \\ 1xy & \text{if } (\exists x,y \in \Sigma^*) \\ & \quad [(a = 0x \wedge b = 0y) \vee (a = 1x \wedge b = 1y)] \\ ab & \text{if } a = \epsilon \vee b = \epsilon. \end{cases}$$

[3] For example, consider the function $\rho : \Sigma^* \times \Sigma^* \to \Sigma^*$ defined by $\rho(a,b) = 1^{\lceil \log\log(\max(|b|,2))\rceil}$ if $a = 0$, and $\rho(a,b) = ab$ if $a \neq 0$. This function is honest (as proven by $\rho(\epsilon,x) = x$) but is not s-honest, since for any given polynomial $q$ there are strings $b \in \Sigma^*$ and $z = 1^{\lceil \log\log(\max(|b|,2))\rceil}$ with $\rho(0,b) = z$, but the smallest $b' \in \Sigma^*$ with $\rho(0,b') = z$ satisfies $|b'| > q(|z| + |0|) = q(\lceil \log\log(\max(|b|,2))\rceil + 1)$.

[4] For example, consider the function $\sigma : \Sigma^* \times \Sigma^* \to \Sigma^*$ that is defined by $\sigma(a,b) = 1^{\lceil \log\log(\max(|a|,2))\rceil}$ if $|a| = |b|$, and that is undefined otherwise. This function is s-honest but not honest.

It is a matter of routine to check that $\sigma$ is polynomial-time computable, total, honest, and s-honest (regardless of whether or not $\rho$, which is honest, is s-honest).

If one could invert $\sigma$ with respect to one of its arguments then one could invert $\rho$, contradicting that $\rho$ is a one-way function. In particular, supposing $\sigma$ is invertible with respect to the first argument via inverter $g_1 \in \mathrm{FP}$, we can use $g_1$ to define a function $g \in \mathrm{FP}$ that inverts $\rho$. To see this, note that given any $w \in \mathrm{image}(\rho)$ with $w \neq \epsilon$, $g_1(\langle 0, 0w\rangle)$ must yield a string of the form $b = 1\langle y, z\rangle$ with $\rho(y, z) = w$. Thus, $\sigma$ is not invertible with respect to the first argument. An analogous argument shows that $\sigma$ is not invertible with respect to the second argument. Thus, $\sigma$ is strongly noninvertible. However, $\sigma$ is invertible, since every string $z \in \mathrm{image}(\sigma)$ has an inverse of the form $(\epsilon, z)$; so, the FP function mapping any given string $z$ to $(\epsilon, z)$ is an inverter for $\sigma$. Hence, $\sigma$ is not a one-way function. ∎

The converse of Theorem 2 immediately holds, as do the converses of Proposition 1, Corollary 1, and Theorems 3, 4, and 5. However, although all these results in fact are equivalences, we will focus on only the interesting implication direction.

For completeness, we mention in passing that, assuming P $\neq$ NP, one can construct functions that—unlike the function constructed in the proof of Theorem 2—are strongly one-way *and* one-way. An example of such a function is the following modification $\hat{\sigma}$ of the function $\sigma$ constructed in the proof of Theorem 2. As in that proof, let $\rho$ be a total 2-ary one-way function, and define function $\hat{\sigma} : \Sigma^* \times \Sigma^* \to \Sigma^*$ by

$$\hat{\sigma}(a,b) = \begin{cases} 0\rho(x,y) & \text{if } (\exists x,y,z \in \Sigma^*)\,[a = 1\langle x,y\rangle \wedge b = 0z] \\ 0\rho(y,z) & \text{if } (\exists x,y,z \in \Sigma^*)\,[a = 0x \wedge b = 1\langle y,z\rangle] \\ 1ab & \text{otherwise.} \end{cases}$$

Note that $\hat{\sigma}$ even is overstrong; hence, $\hat{\sigma}$ is both noninvertible and strongly noninvertible. That is:

**Proposition 1.** *If* P $\neq$ NP *then there exists a total, honest, s-honest, 2-ary overstrong function. (It follows that if* P $\neq$ NP *then there exists a total 2-ary function that is one-way and strongly one-way.)*

Corollary 1 below shows that if P $\neq$ NP then there is an s-honest 2-ary one-way function that is not strongly one-way. First, we establish a result that is slightly stronger: For a function to be not strongly noninvertible, it is enough that it is invertible with respect to at least one of its arguments. The function $\sigma$ to be constructed in the proof of Theorem 3 below even is invertible with respect to each of its arguments.

**Theorem 3.** *If* P $\neq$ NP *then there exists a total, s-honest 2-ary one-way function $\sigma$ such that $\sigma$ is invertible with respect to its first argument and $\sigma$ is invertible with respect to its second argument.*

**Proof.** It is well-known ([Sel92, Prop. 1], in light of the many-to-one analog of his comment [Sel92, p. 209] about totality) that under the assumption $\mathrm{P} \neq \mathrm{NP}$ there exists a total 1-ary one-way function $\rho : \Sigma^* \to \Sigma^*$. Define a function $\sigma : \Sigma^* \times \Sigma^* \to \Sigma^*$ as follows:

$$\sigma(a, b) = \begin{cases} 1\rho(a) & \text{if } a = b \\ 0ab & \text{if } a \neq b. \end{cases}$$

Note that $\sigma$ is polynomial-time computable, total, s-honest, and honest. If $\sigma$ were invertible in polynomial time then $\rho$ would be too; so, $\sigma$ is a one-way function. However, $\sigma$ is invertible with respect to each of its arguments. For an inverter with respect to the first argument, consider the function $g_1 : \Sigma^* \to \Sigma^*$ defined by

$$g_1(x) = \begin{cases} b \text{ if } (\exists a, b, z \in \Sigma^*)\,[x = \langle a, 0z\rangle \wedge z = ab] \\ a \text{ if } (\exists a, z \in \Sigma^*)\,[x = \langle a, 1z\rangle] \\ \epsilon \text{ otherwise.} \end{cases}$$

Clearly, $g_1 \in \mathrm{FP}$. Note that for every $y \in \mathrm{image}(\sigma)$ and for every $a \in \Sigma^*$ for which there exists some $b \in \Sigma^*$ with $\sigma(a, b) = y$, it holds that $\sigma(a, g_1(\langle a, y\rangle)) = y$, completing the proof that $\sigma$ is invertible with respect to the first argument. To see that $\sigma$ also is invertible with respect to the second argument, an analogous construction (with the roles of the first and the second argument interchanged) works to give an inverter $g_2$ for a fixed second argument. ∎

**Corollary 1.** *If* $\mathrm{P} \neq \mathrm{NP}$ *then there exists a total, s-honest 2-ary one-way function that is not strongly one-way.*

One might wonder whether functions that are not strongly noninvertible (which means they are invertible with respect to at least one of their arguments) outright must be invertible with respect to both of their arguments. The following result states that this is not the case, unless $\mathrm{P} = \mathrm{NP}$.

**Theorem 4.** *If* $\mathrm{P} \neq \mathrm{NP}$ *then there exists a total, s-honest 2-ary one-way function that is invertible with respect to one of its arguments (thus, it is not strongly one-way), yet that is not invertible with respect to its other argument.*

**Proof.** Assuming $\mathrm{P} \neq \mathrm{NP}$, by Theorem 1 there exists a total 2-ary one-way function, call it $\rho$. Since our pairing function is onto and one-to-one, and its inverses are efficiently computable, the functions—$\pi_1$ and $\pi_2$—mapping from each string in $\Sigma^*$ to that string's first and second components when interpreted as a pair are well-defined, total, polynomial-time functions; for all $b \in \Sigma^*$, $b = \langle \pi_1(b), \pi_2(b)\rangle$. Define a function $\sigma : \Sigma^* \times \Sigma^* \to \Sigma^*$ as follows:

$$\sigma(a, b) = \rho(\pi_1(b), \pi_2(b))$$

It is clear that $\sigma$ is honest (via $\rho$'s honesty) and s-honest. Let $a_0$ be any fixed string, and define $g_2(w) = a_0$ for all strings $w$. Clearly, $g_2 \in \mathrm{FP}$. The definition of $\sigma$ implies that for each $z = \rho(x, y) \in \mathrm{image}(\sigma)$ and for each $b \in \Sigma^*$ such that

$\sigma(a, b) = z$ for some $a \in \Sigma^*$, it also holds that $\sigma(a_0, b) = z$. Thus, $\sigma$ is invertible with respect to the second argument via $g_2$. However, if $\sigma$ were also invertible with respect to the first argument via some function $g_1 \in \mathrm{FP}$, then $g_1$ could be used to invert $\rho$, which would contradict the noninvertibility of $\rho$. Hence, $\sigma$ is invertible with respect to its first, yet not with respect to its second argument. Analogously, we can define a function that is invertible with respect to its second argument, yet not with respect to its first argument. ∎

Finally, let us turn to the notion of overstrongness (see Definition 3) mentioned in the last paragraph of the introduction. As noted there, this notion is not less restrictive than either noninvertibility or strong noninvertibility, and so if a given polynomial-time computable, honest, s-honest function is overstrong then it certainly is both one-way and strongly one-way. Even though overstrongness is not well-motivated by the cryptographic protocols of Rabi, Rivest, and Sherman [RS97], for the purpose of showing that the notions do not collapse, we will prove that the converse does not hold, unless P = NP.

**Theorem 5.** *If* P ≠ NP *then there exists a total, honest, s-honest 2-ary function that is noninvertible and strongly noninvertible but that is not overstrong.*

**Proof.** Assume P ≠ NP. It is known (see [Sel92]) that this assumption implies that total 1-ary one-way functions exist. Let $\widehat{\rho}$ be one such function, and let $\widehat{\rho}$ be such that it additionally satisfies $(\exists r \geq 2)\,(\forall x \in \Sigma^*)\,[|\widehat{\rho}(x)| = |x|^r + r]$. Henceforth, $r$ will denote this value $r$. That this condition can be required follows easily from the standard "accepting-paths-based" proofs that P ≠ NP implies the existence of total 1-ary one-way functions.

Define a total function $\rho : \Sigma^* \to \Sigma^*$ as follows:

$$\rho(a) = \begin{cases} 1\widehat{\rho}(x) & \text{if } (\exists x \in \Sigma^*)\,[a = 1x] \\ a & \text{if } (\exists x \in \Sigma^*)\,[a = 0x] \\ \epsilon & \text{if } a = \epsilon. \end{cases}$$

Note that $\rho$ is a 1-ary, total one-way function satisfying that for each $i \geq 0$, $\rho(0^i) = 0^i$. Now define the total function $\sigma : \Sigma^* \times \Sigma^* \to \Sigma^*$ as follows:

$$\sigma(a, b) = \begin{cases} 1\langle \rho(x), 0^{|y|}\rangle & \text{if } (\exists x, y \in \Sigma^*)\,[|x| = |y| \wedge a = 0\langle x, y\rangle = b] \\ 1\langle \rho(x), 0^{|y|}\rangle & \text{if } (\exists x, y \in \Sigma^*) \\ & \quad [|x| = |y| \wedge a = 1\langle x, 0y\rangle \wedge b = 1\langle x, 1\widehat{\rho}(y)\rangle] \\ 1\langle \rho(x), 0^{|y|}\rangle & \text{if } (\exists x, y \in \Sigma^*) \\ & \quad [|x| = |y| \wedge a = 1\langle x, 1\widehat{\rho}(y)\rangle \wedge b = 1\langle x, 0y\rangle] \\ 0\langle a, b\rangle & \text{otherwise.} \end{cases}$$

Clearly, $\sigma$ is polynomial-time computable, honest, s-honest, and commutative. If $\sigma$ were invertible, $\rho$ would be too. Thus, $\sigma$ is a one-way function.

Note that $\sigma$ is strongly noninvertible, for if it could be inverted with respect to either argument then $\widehat{\rho}$ could be inverted too. Suppose, for example, $\sigma$ were invertible with respect to the first argument via inverter $g_1 \in \mathrm{FP}$. Then $\widehat{\rho}$ could be inverted as follows. Given any $z \in \Sigma^*$, if there is no $k \in \mathbb{N}$ with $k^r + r =$

$|z|$, there is no inverse of $z$ under $\widehat{\rho}$; so, in that case we may output anything. Otherwise (i.e., there is a $k \in \mathbb{N}$ with $k^r + r = |z|$), run $g_1$ on input $\langle a, w \rangle$, where $a = 1\langle 0^k, 1z \rangle$ and $w = 1\langle 0^k, 0^k \rangle$. By the definition of $\sigma$, if $z \in \text{image}(\widehat{\rho})$, the result of $g_1(\langle a, w \rangle)$ must be of the form $1\langle 0^k, 0\hat{z} \rangle$ for some preimage $\hat{z}$ of $z$ under $\widehat{\rho}$, and we can verify this by running $\widehat{\rho}$ on input $\hat{z}$ and checking whether or not $\widehat{\rho}(\hat{z}) = z$. A similar argument shows that $\sigma$ is not invertible with respect to the second argument. Hence, $\sigma$ is strongly one-way.

Finally, we claim that $\sigma$ is not overstrong. Here is what an inverter $f$ does when given $i = 1$,[5] an alleged first argument $a \in \Sigma^*$ of $\sigma$, and an alleged output $z \in \Sigma^*$ of $\sigma$:

$$f(1, a, z) = \begin{cases} (x, y) & \text{if } (\exists x, y \in \Sigma^*)\, [z = 0\langle x, y \rangle] \\ (a, a) & \text{if } (\exists x, y \in \Sigma^*)\, (\exists m \in \mathbb{N}) \\ & \quad [a = 0x \wedge z = 1\langle y, 0^m \rangle] \\ (0\langle w, w \rangle, 0\langle w, w \rangle) & \text{if } (\exists w, x, y \in \Sigma^*)\, (\exists m \in \mathbb{N}) \\ & \quad [a = 1\langle w, 0x \rangle \wedge z = 1\langle y, 0^m \rangle] \\ (0\langle w, w \rangle, 0\langle w, w \rangle) & \text{if } (\exists w, x, y \in \Sigma^*)\, (\exists m \in \mathbb{N}) \\ & \quad [a = 1\langle w, 1x \rangle \wedge z = 1\langle y, 0^m \rangle] \\ (\epsilon, \epsilon) & \text{otherwise.} \end{cases}$$

Note that $f \in \mathrm{FP}$. Whenever there exists some string $b \in \Sigma^*$ for which $\sigma(a, b) = z$, it holds that $\sigma(f(1, a, z)) = z$. (If there is no such $b$, it does not matter what $f(1, a, z)$ outputs.) Hence $\sigma$ is not overstrong. ∎

**Acknowledgments.** We thank Osamu Watanabe for mentioning to us the notions, different from those used here though slightly reminiscent, from average-case theory, of claw-free collections, collision-free pseudorandom generators, and collision-free hash functions. We thank Chris Homan for suggesting overstrongness.

## References

[BC93] D. Bovet and P. Crescenzi. *Introduction to the Theory of Complexity*. Prentice Hall, 1993.

[BDG95] J. Balcázar, J. Díaz, and J. Gabarró. *Structural Complexity I*. EATCS Texts in Theoretical Computer Science. Springer-Verlag, second edition, 1995.

[Ber77] L. Berman. *Polynomial Reducibilities and Complete Sets*. PhD thesis, Cornell University, Ithaca, NY, 1977.

[BHHR99] A. Beygelzimer, L. Hemaspaandra, C. Homan, and J. Rothe. One-way functions in worst-case cryptography: Algebraic and security properties are on the house. *SIGACT News*, 30(4):25–40, December 1999.

[GS88] J. Grollmann and A. Selman. Complexity measures for public-key cryptosystems. *SIAM Journal on Computing*, 17(2):309–335, 1988.

[5] Since $\sigma$ is commutative, this implicitly also shows how to handle the case $i = 2$.

[Hom00] C. Homan. Low ambiguity in strong, total, associative, one-way functions. Technical Report TR-734, University of Rochester, Department of Computer Science, Rochester, NY, August 2000.

[HR99] L. Hemaspaandra and J. Rothe. Creating strong, total, commutative, associative one-way functions from any one-way function in complexity theory. *Journal of Computer and System Sciences*, 58(3):648–659, 1999.

[Ko85] K. Ko. On some natural complete operators. *Theoretical Computer Science*, 37(1):1–30, 1985.

[KRS88] B. Kaliski Jr., R. Rivest, and A. Sherman. Is the data encryption standard a group? (Results of cycling experiments on DES). *Journal of Cryptology*, 1(1):3–36, 1988.

[Pap94] C. Papadimitriou. *Computational Complexity*. Addison-Wesley, 1994.

[RS93] M. Rabi and A. Sherman. Associative one-way functions: A new paradigm for secret-key agreement and digital signatures. Technical Report CS-TR-3183/UMIACS-TR-93-124, Department of Computer Science, University of Maryland, College Park, Maryland, 1993.

[RS97] M. Rabi and A. Sherman. An observation on associative one-way functions in complexity theory. *Information Processing Letters*, 64(2):239–244, 1997.

[Sel92] A. Selman. A survey of one-way functions in complexity theory. *Mathematical Systems Theory*, 25(3):203–221, 1992.

[She86] A. Sherman. *Cryptology and VLSI (a Two-Part Dissertation)*. PhD thesis, MIT, Cambridge, MA, 1986. Available as Technical Report MIT/LCS/TR-381.

# Prediction-Preserving Reducibility with Membership Queries on Formal Languages*

Kouichi Hirata[1] and Hiroshi Sakamoto[2]

[1] Department of Artificial Intelligence, Kyushu Institute of Technology
Kawazu 680-4, Iizuka 820-8502, Japan
Tel: +81-948-29-7622, Fax: +81-948-29-7601
hirata@ai.kyutech.ac.jp

[2] Department of Informatics, Kyushu University
Hakozaki 6-10-1, Fukuoka 812-8581, Japan
Tel: +81-92-642-2693, Fax: +81-92-642-2698
hiroshi@i.kyushu-u.ac.jp

**Abstract.** This paper presents the *prediction-preserving reducibility with membership queries* (*pwm-reducibility*) on formal languages, in particular, simple CFGs and finite unions of regular pattern languages. For the former, we mainly show that DNF formulas are pwm-reducible to CFGs that is sequential or that contains at most one nonterminal. For the latter, we show that both bounded finite unions of *regular* pattern languages and unbounded finite unions of *substring* pattern languages are pwm-reducible to DFAs.

**Keywords**: prediction-preserving reduction with membership queries, prediction with membership queries, context-free grammars, pattern languages, grammatical inference, learning theory.

## 1 Introduction

The task of predicting the classification of a new example is frequently discussed from the viewpoints of both *passive* and *active* settings. In a passive setting, the examples are all chosen independently according to a fixed but unknown probability distribution, and the learner has no control over selection of examples [12, 18]. In an active setting, on the other hand, the learner is allowed to ask about particular examples, that is, the learner makes *membership queries*, before the new example to predict is given to the learner [3,6].

Concerned with language learning, we can design a polynomial-time algorithm to predict deterministic finite automata (DFAs) in an active setting [3], while predicting DFAs is as hard as computing certain apparently hard cryptographic predicates in a passive setting [12]. Furthermore, predicting nondeterministic finite automata (NFAs) and context-free grammars (CFGs) is also hard

* This work is partially supported by Japan Society for the Promotion of Science, Grant-in-Aid for Scientific Research (B) nos. 11558040, 13558029 and 13558036, and Grant-in-Aid for Encouragement of Young Scientists no. 12780233.

R. Freivalds (Ed.): FCT 2001, LNCS 2138, pp. 172–183, 2001.

under the same cryptographic assumptions in an active setting [6]. Here, the *cryptographic assumptions* denote the intractability of inverting RSA encryption, recognizing quadratic residues and factoring Blum integers.

Pitt and Warmuth [18] have been formalized the model of a prediction and a reduction between two prediction problems that preserves polynomial-time predictability called the *prediction-preserving reduction* in a passive setting. Angluin and Kharitonov [6] have extended to the prediction and the reduction in an active setting. The reduction is called the *prediction-preserving reduction with membership queries* or a *pwm-reduction* for short.

The prediction is an weaker learning model than PAC-learning or query learning models [5,6,18]; If a class is polynomial-time learnable with equivalence (and membership) queries, then it is polynomial-time PAC-learnable (with membership queries), and if a class is polynomial-time PAC-learnable (with membership queries), then it is polynomial-time predictable (with membership queries).

Except the above general results, the detailed results of the pwm-reducibility on formal languages, for example, the restricted CFGs or another languages such as pattern languages, have few found elsewhere. Furthermore, many researchers have been interested in the pwm-reducibility on Boolean concepts but not on formal languages [6,12,18]. Hence, in this paper, we pay our attention to the pwm-reducibility on simple CFGs and finite unions of regular pattern languages.

For the former classes, we introduce several simple CFGs as follows: the *linear grammars* ($\mathcal{L}_{\text{linear}}$), the *right-linear grammars* ($\mathcal{L}_{\text{right-linear}}$), and the *left-linear grammars* ($\mathcal{L}_{\text{left-linear}}$) as usual; the *k-bounded CFGs* [4] ($\mathcal{L}_{k\text{-bounded-CFG}}$) each of which right-hand side of productions contains at most $k$ nonterminals; the *sequential CFGs* [7,24] ($\mathcal{L}_{\text{sqCFG}}$) that the set of nonterminals has a partial order $\leq$ such that $T \to vUw$ iff $T \leq U$ for nonterminals $T$ and $U$; the *properly sequential* or *loop-free CFGs* ($\mathcal{L}_{\text{psqCFG}}$) that is sequential but disallowing to occur the same nonterminal in both left- and right-hand sides for each production; the *k-CFGs* ($\mathcal{L}_{k\text{-CFG}}$) that contains at most $k$ nonterminals; the *parenthesis grammars* [16] ($\mathcal{L}_{\text{paren}}$) that each production is of the form $T \to [w]$.

On the other hand, a *pattern* [2] is a string consisting of constant symbols and variables, a *regular* pattern [25] is a pattern in which each variable occurs at most once, and a *substring* pattern [26] is a regular pattern of the form $xwy$ for a constant string $w$ and variables $x$ and $y$. The *language of a pattern* is the set of constant strings obtained by substituting nonempty constant strings for variables in the pattern. Then, for the latter classes, we deal with the *bounded finite union* of regular pattern languages by some constant $m$ ($\mathcal{L}_{\cup_m \text{RP}}$) and the *unbounded finite union* of regular or substring pattern languages ($\mathcal{L}_{\cup\text{RP}}$ or $\mathcal{L}_{\cup\text{subP}}$).

We denote that $\mathcal{L}_1$ is pwm-reducible to $\mathcal{L}_2$ by $\mathcal{L}_1 \trianglelefteq_{\text{pwm}} \mathcal{L}_2$, and that $\mathcal{L}_1 \trianglelefteq_{\text{pwm}} \mathcal{L}_2$ and $\mathcal{L}_2 \trianglelefteq_{\text{pwm}} \mathcal{L}_1$ by $\mathcal{L}_1 \cong_{\text{pwm}} \mathcal{L}_2$. Then, this paper presents the results described as Fig. 1. Hence, we can conclude the following polynomial-time predictability with membership queries.

| |
|---|
| $\mathcal{L}_{\text{NFA}} \cong_{\text{pwm}} \mathcal{L}_{\text{right-linear}}, \mathcal{L}_{\text{left-linear}}$ |
| $\mathcal{L}_{\text{NFA}} \trianglelefteq_{\text{pwm}} \mathcal{L}_{\text{linear}}, \mathcal{L}_{k\text{-bounded-CFG}}$ |
| $\mathcal{L}_{\text{DNF}} \trianglelefteq_{\text{pwm}} \mathcal{L}_{\text{sqCFG}}, \mathcal{L}_{\text{psqCFG}}, \mathcal{L}_{k\text{-CFG}}$ |
| $\mathcal{L}_{\cup\text{DFA}} \trianglelefteq_{\text{pwm}} \mathcal{L}_{\text{paren}}$ |
| $\mathcal{L}_{\cup_m\text{RP}}, \mathcal{L}_{\cup\text{subP}} \trianglelefteq_{\text{pwm}} \mathcal{L}_{\text{DFA}}$ |

**Fig. 1.** The pwm-reducibility

1. $\mathcal{L}_{\text{linear}}$, $\mathcal{L}_{\text{right-linear}}$, $\mathcal{L}_{\text{left-linear}}$, $\mathcal{L}_{k\text{-bounded-CFG}}$ $(k \geq 1)$ and $\mathcal{L}_{\text{paren}}$ are not polynomial-time predictable with membership queries under the cryptographic assumptions.
2. If $\mathcal{L}_{\text{sqCFG}}$, $\mathcal{L}_{\text{psqCFG}}$ and $\mathcal{L}_{k\text{-CFG}}$ $(k \geq 1)$ are polynomial-time predictable with membership queries, then so are DNF formulas.
3. $\mathcal{L}_{\cup_m\text{RP}}$ $(m \geq 0)$ and $\mathcal{L}_{\cup\text{subP}}$ are polynomial-time predictable with membership queries.

Concerned with the statement 2, this paper corrects and extends some results obtained by the paper [23]. Furthermore, concerned with the statement 3, we can show that $\mathcal{L}_{\text{DNF}} \trianglelefteq_{\text{pwm}} \mathcal{L}_{\cup\text{RP}}$, so if $\mathcal{L}_{\cup\text{RP}}$ is polynomial-time predictable with membership queries, then so are DNF formulas [22].

## 2 Preliminaries

Let $\Sigma$ and $N$ be two non-empty finite sets of symbols such that $\Sigma \cap N = \emptyset$. A *production* $A \rightarrow \alpha$ *on* $\Sigma$ *and* $N$ is an association from a nonterminal $A \in N$ to a string $\alpha \in (N \cup \Sigma)^*$. A *context-free grammar* (*CFG*, for short) is a 4-tuple $(N, \Sigma, P, S)$, where $S \in N$ is the distinguished *start symbol* and $P$ is a finite set of productions on $\Sigma$ and $N$. Symbols in $N$ are said to be *nonterminals*, while symbols in $\Sigma$ *terminals*. Then, we deal with the following subclasses of CFGs.

- A *linear grammar* is a CFG $G = (N, \Sigma, P, S)$ such that each production in $P$ is of the forms $T \rightarrow wUv$ or $T \rightarrow w$ for $T, U \in N$ and $w, v \in \Sigma^*$. In particular, a *right-linear* (*resp.*, *left-linear*) *grammar* if it is a linear grammar such that each production is of the forms either $T \rightarrow wU$ (*resp.*, $T \rightarrow Uw$) or $T \rightarrow w$ for $T, U \in N$ and $w \in \Sigma^*$.
- A CFG $G = (N, \Sigma, P, S)$ is called *k-bounded* [4] if the right-hand side of each production in $P$ has at most $k$ nonterminals.
- A CFG $G = (N, \Sigma, P, S)$ is called *sequential* [7,24] if the nonterminals in $N$ are labeled $S = T_1, \ldots, T_n$ such that, for each production $T_i \rightarrow w$, $w \in (\Sigma \cup \{T_j \mid i \leq j \leq n\})^*$. In particular, a sequential CFG satisfying that $w \in (\Sigma \cup \{T_j \mid i < j \leq n\})^*$ for each production $T_i \rightarrow w$ is called *properly sequential* or *loop-free*.
- A CFG $G = (N, \Sigma, P, S)$ is called *a k-CFG* if $|N| \leq k$.
- A *parenthesis grammar* [16] is a CFG $G = (N, \Sigma \cup \{[, ]\}, P, S)$ such that each production in $P$ is of the form $T \rightarrow [w]$ for $T \in N$ and $w \in (N \cup \Sigma)^*$.

Let $G$ be a CFG $(N, \Sigma, S, P)$ and $\alpha$ and $\beta$ be strings in $(\Sigma \cup N)^*$. We denote $\alpha \Rightarrow_G \beta$ if there exist $\alpha_1, \alpha_2 \in (\Sigma \cup N)^*$ such that $\alpha = \alpha_1 X \alpha_2$, $\beta = \alpha_1 \gamma \alpha_2$ and $X \to \gamma \in P$. We extend the relation $\Rightarrow_G$ to the reflexive and transitive closure $\Rightarrow_G^*$. For a nonterminal $A \in N$, the *language* $L_G(A)$ *of* $A$ is the set $\{w \in \Sigma^* \mid A \Rightarrow_G^* w\}$. The *language* $L(G)$ *of* $G$ just refers to $L_G(S)$.

Next, we introduce the notions of *patterns* [2]. Let $X$ be a countable set of *variables* such that $\Sigma \cap X = \emptyset$. A *pattern* is an element of $(\Sigma \cup X)^+$. A pattern $\pi$ is called *regular* [25] if each variables in $\pi$ occurs at most once. In particular, a regular pattern of the form $xwy$ is called a *substring* pattern [26] if $x, y \in X$ and $w \in \Sigma^+$.

A *substitution* is a homomorphism from patterns to patterns that maps each symbol $a \in \Sigma$ to itself. A substitution that maps some variables to an empty string $\varepsilon$ is called an $\varepsilon$-*substitution*. In this paper, we do not deal with $\varepsilon$-substitutions. By $\pi\theta$, we denote the image of a pattern by a substitution $\theta$. For a pattern $\pi$, the *pattern language* $L(\pi)$ is the set $\{w \in \Sigma^+ \mid w = \pi\theta \text{ for some substitution } \theta\}$.

## 3 Prediction with Membership Queries

In this section, we introduce definitions and theorems for prediction and prediction-preserving reduction with membership queries due to Angluin and Kharitonov [6].

Let $U$ denote $\Sigma^*$. If $w$ is a string, $|w|$ denotes its length. For each $n > 0$, $U^{[n]} = \{w \in U \mid |w| \leq n\}$. A *representation of concepts* $\mathcal{L}$ is any subset of $U \times U$. We interpret an element $\langle u, w \rangle$ of $U \times U$ as consisting a *concept representation* $u$ and an *example* $w$. The example $w$ is a member of a concept $u$ if $\langle u, w \rangle \in \mathcal{L}$. Define the *concept represented by* $u$ as $\kappa_{\mathcal{L}}(u) = \{w \mid \langle u, w \rangle \in \mathcal{L}\}$. The *set of concepts represented by* $\mathcal{L}$ is $\{\kappa_{\mathcal{L}}(u) \mid u \in U\}$.

To represent CFGs, we define the class $\mathcal{L}_{\mathrm{CFG}}$ as the set of pairs $\langle u, w \rangle$ such that $u$ encodes a CFG $G$ and $w \in L(G)$. Also we define the classes $\mathcal{L}_{\mathrm{linear}}$, $\mathcal{L}_{\mathrm{right\text{-}linear}}$, $\mathcal{L}_{\mathrm{left\text{-}linear}}$, $\mathcal{L}_{k\text{-}\mathrm{bounded\text{-}CFG}}$, $\mathcal{L}_{\mathrm{seqCFG}}$, $\mathcal{L}_{\mathrm{psqCFG}}$, $\mathcal{L}_{k\text{-}\mathrm{CFG}}$, and $\mathcal{L}_{\mathrm{paren}}$, corresponding to linear grammars, right-linear grammars, left-linear grammars, $k$-bounded CFGs, sequential CFGs, properly sequential CFGs, $k$-CFGs, and parenthesis grammars, respectively, as similar.

To represent finite unions of regular pattern languages, we define the class $\mathcal{L}_{\cup_m \mathrm{RP}}$ as the set of pairs $\langle u, w \rangle$ such that $u$ encodes $m$ and a finite set $\pi_1, \cdots, \pi_m$ of $m$ regular patterns and $w$ is in the concept represented by $c$ iff $w \in L(\pi_i)$ for at least one $\pi_i$. Similarly, we define the class $\mathcal{L}_{\cup \mathrm{RP}}$ (*resp.*, $\mathcal{L}_{\cup \mathrm{subP}}$) as the set of pairs $\langle u, w \rangle$ such that $u$ encodes a finite set $\pi_1, \cdots, \pi_r$ of regular (*resp.*, substring) patterns and $w$ is in the concept represented by $c$ iff $w \in L(\pi_i)$ for at least one $\pi_i$. Note that $\mathcal{L}_{\cup_m \mathrm{RP}}$ denotes the *bounded* finite unions, whereas $\mathcal{L}_{\cup \mathrm{RP}}$ and $\mathcal{L}_{\cup \mathrm{subP}}$ denote the *unbounded* finite unions.

Additionally, we introduce the following classes. The class $\mathcal{L}_{\mathrm{DFA}}$ (*resp.*, $\mathcal{L}_{\mathrm{NFA}}$) denotes the set of pairs $\langle u, w \rangle$ such that $u$ encodes a DFA (*resp.*, NFA) $M$ and $M$ accepts $w$. The class $\mathcal{L}_{\cup \mathrm{DFA}}$ of finite union of DFAs denotes the set of pairs $\langle u, w \rangle$

such that $u$ encodes a finite set $M_1, \cdots, M_r$ of DFAs and $w$ is in the concept represented by $c$ iff at least one $M_i$ accepts $w$. The class $\mathcal{L}_{\text{DNF}}$ denotes the set of pairs $\langle u, w \rangle$ such that $u$ encodes a positive integer $n$ and a DNF formula $d$ over $n$ Boolean variables $x_1, \cdots, x_n$ such that $|w| = n$ ($w = w_1 \cdots w_n$) and the assignment $x_i = w_i$ $(1 \leq i \leq n)$ satisfies $d$.

Angluin and Kharitonov [6] have generalized the definitions of Pitt and Warmuth of prediction algorithm [18] to allow membership queries as follows.

**Definition 1 (Angluin & Kharitonov [6]).** A *prediction with membership queries algorithm*, or *pwm-algorithm*, is a possibly randomized algorithm $A$ that takes as input $n$ (a bound on the size of examples), $s$ (a bound on the size of the target concept representations), and $\epsilon$ (an accuracy bound). It may make three different kinds of oracle calls, the responses to which are determined by the unknown target concept $c_*$ and the unknown distribution $D$ on $U^{[n]}$.

1. A *membership query* [3,6] takes a string $w \in U$ as input and returns 1 if $w \in c_*$; and 0 otherwise.
2. A *request for a random classified example* takes as no input and returns a pair $\langle w, b \rangle$, where $w$ is a string chosen independently according to $D$ and $b = 1$ if $x \in c_*$ and $b = 0$ otherwise.
3. A *request for an element to predict* takes no input and returns a string $w$ chosen independently according to $D$.

$A$ may make any number of membership queries or requests for random classified examples, whereas $A$ must eventually make one and only one request for an element to predict and then eventually halt with an output 0 or 1 without making any further oracle calls. The output is interpreted as $A$'s guess of how the target concept classifies the element returned by the request for an element to predict. *$A$ runs in polynomial time* if its running time (counting one step per oracle call) is bounded by a polynomial in $n$, $s$ and $1/\epsilon$.

**Definition 2 (Angluin & Kharitonov [6]).** Let $\mathcal{L}$ be a representation of concepts and $c_*$ be the unknown target concept in $\mathcal{L}$. We say that $A$ *successfully predicts* $\mathcal{L}$ if, for each positive integer $n$ and $s$, for each positive rational $\epsilon$, for each concept representation $u \in U^{[n]}$, for each probability distribution $D$ on $U^{[n]}$, when $A$ is run with input $n$, $s$ and $\epsilon$, and oracles determined by $c_* = \kappa_{\mathcal{L}}(u)$ and $D$, $A$ asks membership queries that are in $U$ and the probability in at most $\epsilon$ that the output of $A$ is not equal to the correct classification of $w$ by $\kappa_{\mathcal{L}}(u)$, where $w$ is the string returned by the (unique) request for an element of predict.

**Definition 3 (Angluin & Kharitonov [6]).** A representation $\mathcal{L}$ of concepts is *polynomial-time predictable with membership queries* if there exists a pwm-algorithm $A$ that runs in polynomial time and successfully predicts $\mathcal{L}$.

It is well known the following statements:

1. *$\mathcal{L}_{\text{DFA}}$ is polynomial-time predictable with membership queries* [3].

2. $\mathcal{L}_{\mathrm{UDFA}}$, $\mathcal{L}_{\mathrm{NFA}}$ *and* $\mathcal{L}_{\mathrm{CFG}}$ *are not polynomial-time predictable with membership queries under the cryptographic assumptions* [6].
3. $\mathcal{L}_{\mathrm{DNF}}$ *is either polynomial-time predictable or not polynomial-time predictable with membership queries, if there exist one-way functions that cannot be inverted by polynomial-sized circuits* [6].

**Definition 4 (Angluin & Kharitonov [6]).** Let $\mathcal{L}_i$ be a representation of concepts over domain $U_i$ ($i = 1, 2$). We say that *predicting* $\mathcal{L}_1$ *reduces to predicting* $\mathcal{L}_2$ *with membership queries* (*pwm-reduces*, for short), denoted by $L_1 \trianglelefteq_{\mathrm{pwm}} \mathcal{L}_2$, if there exist an *instance mapping* $f : \mathbf{N} \times \mathbf{N} \times U_1 \to U_2$, a *concept mapping* $g : \mathbf{N} \times \mathbf{N} \times \mathcal{L}_1 \to \mathcal{L}_2$, and a *query mapping* $h : \mathbf{N} \times \mathbf{N} \times U_2 \to U_1 \cup \{\top, \bot\}$ satisfying the following conditions.

1. For each $x \in U_1^{[n]}$ and $u \in \mathcal{L}_1^{[s]}$, $x \in \kappa_{\mathcal{L}_1}(u)$ iff $f(n, s, x) \in \kappa_{\mathcal{L}_2}(g(n, s, u))$.
2. $f$ is computable in time bounded by a polynomial in $n$, $s$ and $|x|$.
3. The size of $g(n, s, u)$ is bounded by a polynomial in $n$, $s$ and $|u|$.
4. For each $x' \in U_2$ and $u \in \mathcal{L}_1^{[s]}$, if $h(n, s, x') = \top$ then $x' \in \kappa_{\mathcal{L}_2}(g(n, s, u))$; if $h(n, s, x') = \bot$ then $x' \notin \kappa_{\mathcal{L}_2}(g(n, s, u))$; if $h(n, s, x') = x \in U_1$, then it holds that $x' \in \kappa_{\mathcal{L}_2}(g(n, s, u))$ iff $x \in \kappa_{\mathcal{L}_1}(u)$.
5. $h$ is computable in time bounded by a polynomial in $n$, $s$ and $|x'|$.

Furthermore, we denote that $\mathcal{L}_1 \trianglelefteq_{\mathrm{pwm}} \mathcal{L}_2$ and $\mathcal{L}_2 \trianglelefteq_{\mathrm{pwm}} \mathcal{L}_1$ by $\mathcal{L}_1 \cong_{\mathrm{pwm}} \mathcal{L}_2$.

The following theorem is useful for showing the predictability or the hardness of predictability of the representations of concepts.

**Theorem 1 (Angluin & Kharitonov [6]).** *Let* $\mathcal{L}_1$ *and* $\mathcal{L}_2$ *be representations of concepts and suppose that* $\mathcal{L}_1 \trianglelefteq_{\mathrm{pwm}} \mathcal{L}_2$.

1. *If* $\mathcal{L}_2$ *is polynomial-time predictable with membership queries, then so is* $\mathcal{L}_1$.
2. *If* $\mathcal{L}_1$ *is not polynomial-time predictable with membership queries, then neither is* $\mathcal{L}_2$.

## 4 Prediction-Preserving Reducibility with Membership Queries

In this section, we fix $f$, $g$ and $h$ to an instance mapping, a concept mapping, and a query mapping. Furthermore, the parameters $n$ and $s$ denote the bounds of examples and representations, respectively. For simplicity, we assume that the length of examples for Boolean concepts is always fixed to the upper bound $n$.

### 4.1 Simple CFGs

First of all, by using the transformation from a DFA to a right-linear grammar (*cf.* [8,9]), it holds that $\mathcal{L}_{\mathrm{DFA}} \trianglelefteq_{\mathrm{pwm}} \mathcal{L}_{\text{right-linear}}$, because the size of the right-linear grammar is bounded by a polynomial in the size of a DFA. Note that the converse direction $\mathcal{L}_{\text{right-linear}} \trianglelefteq_{\text{pwm}} \mathcal{L}_{\text{DFA}}$ does not follows from the transformation from a right-linear grammar to a DFA, because the size of the DFA is not bounded by a polynomial in the size of a right-linear grammar in general.

Furthermore, we point out that $\mathcal{L}_{\text{DNF}} \trianglelefteq_{\text{pwm}} \mathcal{L}_{\cup\text{DFA}}$, while $\mathcal{L}_{\text{DNF}} \trianglelefteq \mathcal{L}_{\text{DFA}}$ [18]. Here, the $\trianglelefteq$ means the prediction-preserving reduction without membership queries introduced by Pitt and Warmuth [18], that is, there exist $f$ and $g$ satisfying the requirement from 1 to 3 in Definition 4. Note that we cannot apply the same proof of $\mathcal{L}_{\text{DNF}} \trianglelefteq \mathcal{L}_{\text{DFA}}$ to proving $\mathcal{L}_{\text{DNF}} \trianglelefteq_{\text{pwm}} \mathcal{L}_{\text{DFA}}$; In this case, we cannot construct $h$ correctly.

On the other hand, by regarding the equivalent transformation between an NFA and a right-linear grammar [8,9] as a concept mapping $g$, we observe that $\mathcal{L}_{\text{NFA}} \cong_{\text{pwm}} \mathcal{L}_{\text{right-linear}}$. Furthermore, for a CFG $G = (N, \Sigma, P, S)$, let $G^R$ be a CFG $(N, \Sigma, P', S)$ such that $T \to w^R \in P'$ for each $T \to w \in P$. Here, $R$ denotes the reversal of a word. Then, for a right-linear (*resp.*, left-linear) grammar $G$, construct the following $f$, $g$ and $h$:

$$\begin{aligned} f(n, s, e) &= e^R, \\ g(n, s, G) &= G^R, \\ h(n, s, e') &= e'^R. \end{aligned}$$

It is obvious that $\mathcal{L}_{\text{right-linear}} \trianglelefteq_{\text{pwm}} \mathcal{L}_{\text{left-linear}}$ (*resp.*, $\mathcal{L}_{\text{left-linear}} \trianglelefteq_{\text{pwm}} \mathcal{L}_{\text{right-linear}}$), so it holds that $\mathcal{L}_{\text{right-linear}} \cong_{\text{pwm}} \mathcal{L}_{\text{left-linear}}$. Similarly, we also observe that $\mathcal{L}_{\text{NFA}} \trianglelefteq_{\text{pwm}} \mathcal{L}_{\text{linear}}$ and $\mathcal{L}_{\text{NFA}} \trianglelefteq_{\text{pwm}} \mathcal{L}_{k\text{-bounded-CFG}}$ for each $k \geq 1$. Summary:

**Theorem 2.** *$\mathcal{L}_{\text{NFA}} \cong_{\text{pwm}} \mathcal{L}$ for $\mathcal{L} \in \{\mathcal{L}_{\text{right-linear}}, \mathcal{L}_{\text{left-linear}}\}$. Also, $\mathcal{L}_{\text{NFA}} \trianglelefteq_{\text{pwm}} \mathcal{L}_{\text{linear}}$ and $\mathcal{L}_{\text{NFA}} \trianglelefteq_{\text{pwm}} \mathcal{L}_{k\text{-bounded-CFG}}$ for each $k \geq 1$.*

**Theorem 3.** *$\mathcal{L}_{\text{DNF}} \trianglelefteq_{\text{pwm}} \mathcal{L}$ for $\mathcal{L} \in \{\mathcal{L}_{\text{psqCFG}}, \mathcal{L}_{\text{sqCFG}}\}$.*

*Proof.* Let $d$ be a DNF formula $t_1 \vee \cdots \vee t_m$ over $n$ Boolean variables $x_1, \ldots, x_n$. First, we define $w_i^j$ $(1 \leq i \leq n, 1 \leq j \leq m)$ as follows:

$$w_i^j = \begin{cases} 1 & \text{if } t_j \text{ contains } x_i, \\ 0 & \text{if } t_j \text{ contains } \overline{x_i}, \\ T & \text{otherwise.} \end{cases}$$

Then, construct $f$, $g$ and $h$ as follows:

$$\begin{aligned} f(n, s, e) &= e, \\ g(n, s, d) &= (\{S, T\}, \{0, 1\}, S, \{S \to w_1^1 \cdots w_n^1 \mid \cdots \mid w_1^m \cdots w_n^m,\ T \to 0 \mid 1\}), \\ h(n, s, e') &= e'. \end{aligned}$$

Note that $g(n, s, d)$ is a properly sequential CFG. It is obvious that the above $f$, $g$ and $h$ satisfy the conditions of Definition 4. □

**Theorem 4.** *For each $k \geq 1$, $\mathcal{L}_{\text{DNF}} \trianglelefteq_{\text{pwm}} \mathcal{L}_{k\text{-CFG}}$.*

*Proof.* Theorem 3 implies that $\mathcal{L}_{\text{DNF}} \trianglelefteq_{\text{pwm}} \mathcal{L}_{k\text{-CFG}}$ for each $k \geq 2$, so it is sufficient to show that $\mathcal{L}_{\text{DNF}} \trianglelefteq_{\text{pwm}} \mathcal{L}_{1\text{-CFG}}$. Let $d = t_1 \vee \cdots \vee t_m$ be a DNF formula over $n$ Boolean variables $x_1, \ldots, x_n$. First, define $w_i^j$ $(1 \leq i \leq n, 1 \leq j \leq m)$ as follows:

$$w_i^j = \begin{cases} 1 & \text{if } t_j \text{ contains } x_i, \\ 0 & \text{if } t_j \text{ contains } \overline{x_i}, \\ S & \text{otherwise.} \end{cases}$$

Then, construct $f$, $g$ and $h$ as follows:

$$\begin{aligned} f(n,s,e) &= e, \\ g(n,s,d) &= (\{S\}, \{0,1\}, S, \\ &\qquad \{S \to 0 \mid 1 \mid w_1^1 \cdots w_n^1 \mid \cdots \mid w_1^m \cdots w_n^m \mid \underbrace{S \cdots S}_{n+1} \mid \cdots \mid \underbrace{S \cdots S}_{2n}\}), \end{aligned}$$

$$h(n,s,e') = \begin{cases} e' & \text{if } |e'| = n, \\ \bot & \text{if } 1 < |e'| < n, \\ \top & \text{if } |e'| = 1 \text{ or } |e'| > n. \end{cases}$$

For each $e \in \{0,1\}^n$, it holds that $e$ satisfies $d$ iff $S \Rightarrow^*_{g(n,s,d)} f(n,s,e)$. Furthermore, for each $e' \in \{0,1\}^*$, if $h(n,s,e') = \bot$, then $S \not\Rightarrow^*_{g(n,s,d)} e'$, because $g(n,s,d)$ generates no strings of length more than 1 and less than $n$; If $h(n,s,e') = e'$, then it holds that $S \Rightarrow^*_{g(n,s,d)} e'$ iff $h(n,s,e')$ satisfies $d$.

Finally, consider the case that $h(n,s,e') = \top$. It is sufficient to show that, for each $k \geq 1$, it holds that $S \Rightarrow^*_{g(n,s,d)} \underbrace{S \cdots S}_{kn+m}$ for each $m$ $(1 \leq m \leq n)$. If $k = 1$, then, by the definition, it holds that $S \Rightarrow^*_{g(n,s,d)} \underbrace{S \cdots S}_{n+m}$ for each $m$ $(1 \leq m \leq n)$. Suppose that, for some $k \geq 1$, $S \Rightarrow^*_{g(n,s,d)} \underbrace{S \cdots S}_{kn+m}$ for each $m$ $(1 \leq m \leq n)$. Then, it holds that $S \Rightarrow^*_{g(n,s,d)} \underbrace{S \cdots S}_{kn+(m-1)}\ S \Rightarrow_{g(n,s,d)} \underbrace{S \cdots S}_{kn+(m-1)}\ \underbrace{S \cdots S}_{n+1} = \underbrace{S \cdots S}_{(k+1)n+m}$ for each $m$ $(1 \leq m \leq n)$. Hence, $g(n,s,d)$ generates all strings of length more than $n$, so if $h(n,s,e') = \top$, then $S \Rightarrow^*_{g(n,s,d)} e'$. □

**Theorem 5.** $\mathcal{L}_{\cup\text{DFA}} \trianglelefteq_{\text{pwm}} \mathcal{L}_{\text{paren}}$.

*Proof.* Let $M_1, \ldots, M_r$ be DFAs with the same alphabet $\Sigma$ ($[, ] \notin \Sigma$) and with mutually distinct states. For each $M_i = (Q_i, \Sigma, \delta_i, q_0^i, F_i)$ $(1 \leq i \leq r)$, construct a parenthesis grammar $G_i(n,s,M_i) = (Q_i, \Sigma \cup \{[,]\}, P_i, q_0^i)$ such that $q \to [a\delta_i(q,a)] \in P_i$ for each $q \in Q_i$ and $a \in \Sigma$; $q \to [\varepsilon]$ for each $q \in F_i$, where $\varepsilon$ is an empty string. By using $G_i(n,s,M_i)$, let $P_{M_1,\ldots,M_r}$ be the following set of productions for $S \notin (\cup_{1 \leq i \leq r} Q_i) \cup \Sigma \cup \{[,]\}$:

$$P_{M_1,\ldots,M_r} = \{S \to [q_0^1] \mid \cdots \mid [q_0^r]\} \cup (\cup_{1 \leq i \leq r} P_i).$$

Then, construct $f$, $g$ and $h$ as follows:

$$f(n,s,e_1e_2\cdots e_l) = [[e_1[e_2[\cdots[e_l[\varepsilon]]\cdots]]]] \text{ for } e_i \in \Sigma,$$
$$g(n,s,\{M_1,\ldots,M_r\}) = (\{S\}\cup(\cup_{1\le i\le r}Q_i), \Sigma\cup\{[,]\}, S, P_{M_1,\ldots,M_r}),$$
$$h(n,s,e') = \begin{cases} e_1\cdots e_l \text{ if } e' = [[e_1[e_2[\cdots[e_l[\varepsilon]]\cdots]]]] \text{ and } e_i\in\Sigma, \\ \bot \quad \text{otherwise.}\end{cases}$$

Note that $L(g(n,s,\{M_1,\ldots,M_r\})) \subseteq \{[[e_1[e_2[\cdots[e_m[\varepsilon]]\cdots]]]] \mid m\ge 1, e_i \in \Sigma\}$, so if $h(n,s,e') = \bot$, then $S \not\Rightarrow^*_{g(n,s,\{M_1,\ldots,M_r\})} e'$. Also it is obvious that $S \Rightarrow^*_{g(n,s,\{M_1,\ldots,M_r\})} [[e_1[e_2[\cdots[e_l[\varepsilon]]\cdots]]]]$ iff $e_1e_2\cdots e_l \in L(M_i)$ for some $i$ ($1\le i\le r$). Hence, it holds that $\mathcal{L}_{\cup\mathrm{DFA}} \trianglelefteq_{\mathrm{pwm}} \mathcal{L}_{\mathrm{paren}}$. □

Sakakibara [19] has shown that $\mathcal{L}_{\mathrm{paren}}$ is polynomial-time learnable with membership and equivalence queries if the structural information is available. Furthermore, Sakamoto [21] has shown that $\mathcal{L}_{\mathrm{paren}}$ is polynomial-time learnable with membership queries and *characteristic examples*. The above theorem claims that the structural information or the characteristic examples are essential for efficient learning of $\mathcal{L}_{\mathrm{paren}}$.

### 4.2 Finite Unions of Regular Pattern Languages

Since each regular pattern language is regular [25], we can construct a DFA $M_\pi$ such that $L(M_\pi) = L(\pi)$ for each regular pattern $\pi$ as follows: Suppose that $\pi$ is a regular pattern of the form $\pi = x_0\alpha_1x_1\alpha_2\cdots x_{n-1}\alpha_nx_n$, where $x_i \in X$ and $\alpha_i = a^i_1a^i_2\cdots a^i_{m_i} \in \Sigma^+$. Then, the *corresponding DFA for* $\pi$ is the DFA $M_\pi = (\Sigma, Q, \delta, q_0, F)$ such that:

1. $Q = \{q_0, p^1_1,\ldots,p^1_{m_1}, q_1, p^2_1,\ldots,p^2_{m_2}, q_2,\ldots,q_{n-1},p^n_1,\ldots,p^n_{m_n},q_n\}$ and $F = \{q_n\}$,
2. $\delta(q_i,a) = p^{i+1}_1$ and $\delta(q_n,a) = q_n$ for each $a\in\Sigma$ and $0\le i\le n-1$,
3. $\delta(p^i_j,a^i_j) = p^i_{j+1}$ and $\delta(p^i_{m_i},a^i_{m_i}) = q_i$ for each $1\le i\le n$ and $1\le j\le m_i-1$,
4. $\delta(p^i_j,a) = p^i_1$ for each $a\in\Sigma$ such that $a\ne a^i_j$.

It is obvious that $|M_\pi|$ is bounded by a polynomial in $|\pi|$.

By using the corresponding DFAs, we can easily shown that $\mathcal{L}_{\mathrm{RP}} \trianglelefteq_{\mathrm{pwm}} \mathcal{L}_{\mathrm{DFA}}$ by constructing the following $f$, $g$ and $h$ for each regular pattern $\pi$:

$$f(n,s,e) = e,$$
$$g(n,s,\pi) = M_\pi,$$
$$h(n,s,e') = e'.$$

Then, $\mathcal{L}_{\mathrm{RP}}$ is polynomial-time predictable with membership queries, which is implied by the result of Matsumoto and Shinohara [15] that $\mathcal{L}_{\mathrm{RP}}$ is polynomial-time learnable with equivalence and membership queries. Furthermore, the following theorem holds:

**Theorem 6.** *For each* $m\ge 0$, $\mathcal{L}_{\cup_m\mathrm{RP}} \trianglelefteq_{\mathrm{pwm}} \mathcal{L}_{\mathrm{DFA}}$.

*Proof.* Let $\pi_1,\ldots,\pi_m$ be $m$ regular patterns. Also let $M_{\pi_i} = (Q_i,\Sigma,\delta_i,q^i_0,F_i)$ be the corresponding DFA of $\pi_i$. First, construct a DFA $M_{\pi_1,\ldots,\pi_m} = (Q_1\times\cdots\times Q_m, \Sigma, \delta, (q^1_0,\ldots,q^m_0), F_1\times\cdots\times F_m)$ such that $\delta((q_1,\ldots,q_m),a) = (p_1,\ldots,p_m)$ iff $\delta_i(q_i,a) = p_i$ for each $i$ ($1\le i\le m$). Then, construct $f$, $g$ and $h$ as follows:

$$f(n, s, e) = e,$$
$$g(n, s, \{\pi_1, \dots, \pi_m\}) = M_{\pi_1, \dots, \pi_m},$$
$$h(n, s, e') = e'.$$

Recall that the size of $g(n, s, \{\pi_1, \dots, \pi_m\})$ is bounded by a polynomial in $s$, that is, $O(s^m)$. It is obvious that $L(\pi_1) \cup \cdots \cup L(\pi_m) = L(M_{\pi_1, \dots, \pi_m})$, which implies that $\mathcal{L}_{\cup_m \mathrm{RP}} \trianglelefteq_{\mathrm{pwm}} \mathcal{L}_{\mathrm{DFA}}$. □

For the unbounded finite unions of regular pattern languages, the following theorem holds from our previous result.

**Theorem 7 (Sakamoto *et al.* [22]).** $\mathcal{L}_{\mathrm{DNF}} \trianglelefteq_{\mathrm{pwm}} \mathcal{L}_{\cup \mathrm{RP}}$.

The idea of the proof of Theorem 7 in [22] is similar as one of Theorem 4: First, for each term $t_j$ $(1 \leq j \leq m)$ in a DNF formula $d = t_1 \vee \cdots \vee t_m$ over $x_1, \dots, x_n$, construct a regular pattern $\pi_j = \pi_1^j \cdots \pi_n^j$ as follows:

$$\pi_i^j = \begin{cases} 1 & \text{if } t_j \text{ contains } x_i, \\ 0 & \text{if } t_j \text{ contains } \overline{x_i}, \\ x_i^j & \text{otherwise.} \end{cases}$$

Furthermore, let $\pi$ be a regular pattern $x_1 \cdots x_n x_{n+1}$. Then, we can construct $f$ and $h$ as same as Theorem 4 and $g$ as $g(n, s, d) = \{\pi_1, \dots, \pi_m, \pi\}$. Note that $L(\pi) = \Sigma^* - \Sigma^{[n]}$, because of disallowing $\varepsilon$-substitutions.

For the unbounded finite unions of substring pattern languages, we obtain the following theorem.

**Theorem 8.** $\mathcal{L}_{\cup \mathrm{subP}} \trianglelefteq_{\mathrm{pwm}} \mathcal{L}_{\mathrm{DFA}}$.

*Proof.* Let $\pi_1, \dots, \pi_r$ be substring patterns such that $\pi_i = x_i w_i y_i$. For a set $\{w_1, \dots, w_r\}$ of constant strings, consider the following modification of a *pattern matching machine* (*pmm*) $M_{w_1, \dots, w_r}$ [1]. The goto function is defined as same as a pmm. For the state $j$ transitioned from the right-most constant of $w_i$ by the goto function, the failure function maps $j$ to $j$ itself; otherwise, the failure function is defined as same as a pmm. The output function is not necessary.

Since this modified pmm is also a DFA, construct $f$, $g$ and $h$ as follows:

$$f(n, s, e) = e,$$
$$g(n, s, \{\pi_1, \dots, \pi_r\}) = M_{w_1, \dots, w_r},$$
$$h(n, s, e') = e'.$$

Note that the size of $g(n, s, \{\pi_1, \dots, \pi_r\})$ is $O(|w_1| + \cdots + |w_r|)$ [1]. Furthermore, it is obvious that $L(g(n, s, \{\pi_1, \dots, \pi_r\})) = L(\pi_1) \cup \cdots \cup L(\pi_r)$, which implies that $\mathcal{L}_{\cup \mathrm{subP}} \trianglelefteq_{\mathrm{pwm}} \mathcal{L}_{\mathrm{DFA}}$. □

Shinohara and Arimura [26] have discussed the inferability of $\mathcal{L}_{\cup_m \mathrm{RP}}$, $\mathcal{L}_{\cup \mathrm{RP}}$ and $\mathcal{L}_{\cup \mathrm{subP}}$ in the framework of inductive inference. They have shown that $\mathcal{L}_{\cup_m \mathrm{RP}}$ and $\mathcal{L}_{\cup \mathrm{subP}}$ are inferable from positive data in the limit, whereas $\mathcal{L}_{\cup \mathrm{RP}}$ is not. In contrast, by Theorem 6, 7 and 8, $\mathcal{L}_{\cup_m \mathrm{RP}}$ and $\mathcal{L}_{\cup \mathrm{subP}}$ are polynomial-time predictable with membership queries, whereas $\mathcal{L}_{\cup \mathrm{RP}}$ is not if neither are DNF formulas.

## 5 Conclusion

In this paper, we have presented the results of pwm-reducibility on formal languages described as Fig. 1 in Section 1.

The results in Section 4.1 tell us that the efficient predictability of CFGs may be necessary to assume some deterministic application for productions. Ishizaka [10] showed that the *simple deterministic grammars* are polynomial-time learnable with *extended* equivalence and membership queries. The extended equivalence query can check whether or not the hypothesis is generated by simple deterministic grammars. It remains open whether or not simple deterministic grammars are polynomial-time predictable with membership queries.

Angluin [4] showed that $\mathcal{L}_{k\text{-bounded-CFG}}$ is polynomial-time predictable with *nonterminal* membership queries, and Sakakibara [20] extended Angluin's result to *extended simple formal systems*. In our previous work, we extended the pwm-reduction to prediction-preserving reduction with nonterminal membership queries partially [22]. It is important to investigate the properties of it in more detail.

In Section 4.2, we only deal with the finite unions of *regular* pattern languages. Many researchers such as [2,11,13,14,15,17,26] have developed the learnability/predictability of non-regular pattern languages. In particular, the learnability of the languages of *k-variable patterns* [2,11] that contain at most $k$ variables, *kμ-patterns* [15] each of which variable occurs at most $k$ times, and *erasing patterns* [17,26] that allow $\varepsilon$-substitutions have been widely studied in the various learning frameworks. It is a future work to investigate the pwm-reducibility of them or their finite unions.

**Acknowledgment.** The authors would like to thank Hiroki Arimura in Kyushu University for the idea of the proof of Theorem 8 and also valuable comments.

## References

1. A. V. Aho, M. J. Corasick, *Efficient string matching: An aid to bibliographic search*, Comm. ACM **18**(6) (1975), 333–340.
2. D. Angluin, *Finding patterns common to a set of strings*, J. Comput. System Sci. **21**(1) (1980) 46–62.
3. D. Angluin, *Learning regular sets from queries and counterexamples*, Inform. Comput. **75**(2) (1987) 87–106.
4. D. Angluin, *Learning k-bounded context-free grammars*, Technical Report YALEU/DCS/RR-557, Yale University, 1987.
5. D. Angluin, *Queries and concept learning*, Mach. Learn. **2**(4) (1988) 319–342.
6. D. Angluin, M. Kharitonov, *When won't membership queries help?*, J. Comput. System Sci. **50**(2) (1995) 336–355.
7. A. Ginsburg, *The mathematical theory of context free languages* (McGraw-Hill, 1966).
8. M. A. Harrison, *Introduction to formal language theory* (Addison-Wesley, 1978).

9. J. E. Hopcroft, J. D. Ullman, *Introduction to automata theory, languages and computation* (Addison-Wesley, 1979).
10. H. Ishizaka, *Polynomial time learnability of simple deterministic languages*, Mach. Learn. **5**(2) (1990) 151–164.
11. M. Kearns, L. Pitt, *A polynomial-time algorithm for learning k-variable pattern languages from examples*, in: Proc. 2nd Ann. Conf. on Computational Learning Theory (ACM, 1989) 57–71.
12. M. Kearns, L. Valiant, *Cryptographic limitations on learning Boolean formulae and finite automata*, J. ACM **41**(1) (1994) 67–95.
13. A. Marron, *Identification of pattern languages from examples and queries*, Inform. Comput. **74**(2) (1987) 91–112.
14. A. Marron, *Learning pattern languages from a single initial example and from queries*, in: Proc. 1st Ann. Workshop on Computational Learning Theory (ACM, 1988) 345–358.
15. S. Matsumoto, A. Shinohara, *Learning pattern languages using queries*, in: Proc. 3rd Euro. Conf. on Computational Learning Theory, LNAI **1208** (Springer, 1997) 185–197.
16. R. McNaughton, *Parenthesis grammars*, J. ACM **14**(3) (1967) 490–500.
17. J. Nessel, S. Lange, *Learning erasing pattern languages with queries*, in: Proc. 11th Internat. Conf. on Algorithmic Learning Theory, LNAI **1968** (Springer, 2000) 86–100.
18. L. Pitt, M. K. Warmuth, *Prediction-preserving reduction*, J. Comput. System Sci. **41**(3) (1990) 430–467.
19. Y. Sakakibara, *Learning context-free grammars from structural data in polynomial time*, Theor. Comput. Sci. **76**(2-3) (1990) 223–242.
20. Y. Sakakibara, *On learning Smullyan's elementary formal systems: Towards an efficient learning method for context-sensitive languages*, Adv. Soft. Sci. Tech. **2** (1990) 79–101.
21. H. Sakamoto, *Language learning from membership queries and characteristic examples*, in: Proc. 6th Internat. Workshop on Algorithmic Learning Theory, LNAI **997** (Springer, 1995) 55–65.
22. H. Sakamoto, K. Hirata, H. Arimura, *Learning elementary formal systems with queries*, Technical Report DOI-TR-179, Department of Informatics, Kyushu University, 2000. Also available at `http://www.i.kyushu-u.ac.jp/doi-tr.html`.
23. N. Sugimoto, T. Toyoshima, S. Shimozono, K. Hirata, *Constructive learning of context-free languages with a subpansive tree*, in: Proc. 5th Internat. Colloq. on Grammatical Inference, LNAI **1891** (Springer, 2000) 270–283.
24. E. Shamir, *On sequential languages and two classes of regular events*, Zeit. Phone., Sprach. und Kommun. **18** (1965) 61–69.
25. T. Shinohara, *Polynomial time inference of extended regular pattern languages*, in: Proc. RIMS Symposia on Software Science and Engineering, LNCS **147** (Springer, 1982) 115–127.
26. T. Shinohara, H. Arimura, *Inductive inference of unbounded unions of pattern languages from positive data*, Theor. Comput. Sci. **241** (2000) 191–209.

# Dense Families and Key Functions of Database Relation Instances

Jouni Järvinen

Turku Centre for Computer Science (TUCS)
Lemminkäisenkatu 14 A, FIN-20520 Turku, Finland
jjarvine@cs.utu.fi

**Abstract.** In this paper dense families of database relations are introduced. We characterize dependencies and keys of relation instances in terms of dense families. Key functions are also introduced. They are isotone Boolean functions, which minimal true vectors are the characteristic vectors of the keys. We show that each dense family determines an isotone Boolean function which is the dual of the key function. We also show how to determine for a given relation $r$ an $r$-dense family which size is at most $m^2/2-m/2+1$, where $m$ is the number of tuples in $r$.

**Keywords:** Armstrong system; Dense family; Functional dependency; Key; Key function; Matrix representation.

## 1 Introduction

We begin with recalling some notions and results concerning relational databases, which can be found in [5], for example. A *relation schema* $R(A)$ consists of a relation *name* $R$ and a set of *attributes* $A = \{a_1, \ldots, a_n\}$. The *domain* of an attribute $a \in A$ is denoted by $\mathrm{dom}(a)$. It is also assumed that the attributes in $A$ have some certain fixed order.

A *relation* $r$ of the relation schema $R(A)$ is a set of $n$-tuples $r = \{t_1, \ldots, t_m\}$. Each $n$-tuple $t \in r$ is an ordered list of values $t = (v_1, \ldots, v_n)$, where every value $v_i$, $1 \le i \le n$, is a member of $\mathrm{dom}(a_i)$.

Let $R(A)$ be a relational schema and let $r$ be a relation of the schema $R(A)$. We denote by $t[a]$ the value of attribute $a \in A$ in a tuple $t \in r$. If $B = \{b_1, \ldots, b_k\}$ is a subset of $A$ ordered by the order induced by the order of $A$, then $t[B]$ denotes the ordered list of values $(t[b_1], \ldots, t[b_k])$.

The concept of functional dependency between sets of attributes was introduced by Armstrong [1]. For any subsets $B$ and $C$ of $A$, a *functional dependency*, denoted by $B \to C$, is defined by the following condition:

$$B \to C \text{ if and only if } (\forall t_1, t_2 \in r)\ t_1[B] = t_2[B] \Rightarrow t_1[C] = t_2[C].$$

This means that the values of the $B$ component of tuples uniquely determine the values of the $C$ component. We denote by $F_r$ the set of all functional dependencies that hold in a relation $r$.

R. Freivalds (Ed.): FCT 2001, LNCS 2138, pp. 184–192, 2001.

For a relation $r$ of a schema $R(A)$, a set of attributes $B \subseteq A$ is a *superkey* of $r$ if $B \to A \in F_r$. A *key* is a superkey with the property that removal of any attribute from $C$ will cause $C$ not to be a superkey any more. By definition, each tuple of a relation must be distinct. Thus, the values of a key can be used to identify tuples. Note that a relation may have several keys.

*Example 1.* Let us consider the relation schema $R(A)$, where the attribute set is $A = \{\text{SSN}, \text{LNAME}, \text{FNAME}, \text{DEPT}, \text{AGE}\}$. In Figure 1 is given a relation $r$ of this schema.

| SSN | LNAME | FNAME | DEPT | AGE |
|---|---|---|---|---|
| 422-11-2320 | Benson | Barbara | Mathematics | Young |
| 533-69-1238 | Ashly | Dick | Computer Science | Old |
| 489-22-1100 | Benson | Mary | Mathematics | Middle-aged |
| 305-61-2345 | Davidson | Dick | Computer Science | Old |

**Fig. 1.** Relation $r$

It is obvious that {SSN} is a key of $r$ since two persons cannot have the same value for SSN. Note that {LNAME, FNAME} is also a key of $r$.

In practice, functional dependencies and keys are viewed as properties of a *schema*; they should hold in every relation of that schema. Furthermore, keys and dependencies are usually specified by database designers. But as in the previous example, relations may have additional keys which designers are not necessarily aware of. Here we study dependencies and keys of a given relation *instance*. Especially, we consider the *problem of checking the possible existence of unknown keys*. This can be viewed as a data mining problem since our goal is to find new properties of data instances. Note that the problem of deciding whether there exists a key of cardinality at most $k$ is NP-complete (see e.g. [8]). Moreover, the worst-case number of keys is $\binom{n}{\lfloor n/2 \rfloor} = O(2^n n^{-1/2})$, where $n$ is the number of attributes (see e.g. [4], where further references can be found).

In this paper we introduce the notion of dense families. An $r$-dense family is a collection of subsets of $A$, which by applying certain condition induces the set $F_r$. We characterize dependencies and keys in terms of dense families, and show that generating all keys of a relation instance $r$ can be reduced to generating all minimal transversals of a simple hypergraph $\min\{X^{\mathsf{C}} \mid X \in \mathcal{S}, X \neq A\}$, where $\mathcal{S}$ is any $r$-dense family.

The author introduced in [7] matrices of preimage relations and here we present a similar matrix representation for database relations. We show that the family consisting of the entries of the matrix of a database relation $r$ forms an $r$-dense family which size is at most $m^2/2 - m/2 + 1$, where $m$ is the number of tuples in $r$.

We introduce key functions which are isotone Boolean functions such that their minimal true vectors are the characteristic vectors of the keys. Note that key functions are somewhat similar to the discernibility functions of information systems defined in [9]. We show that each $r$-dense family determines an isotone Boolean function which is the dual of the key function. This implies that the problem of checking whether there exists an unknown key can be reduced to problem of deciding whether two isotone Boolean functions are mutually dual. Furthermore, the problem of enumerating the set of all keys of a relation instance can be reduced to the problem of finding the dual of an isotone Boolean function.

Note that in [6] Fredman and Khachiyan showed that for a pair of isotone Boolean functions $f$ and $g$ given by their minimal true vectors $\min T(f)$ and $\min T(g)$, respectively, we can test in time $k^{o(\log k)}$, whether $f$ and $g$ are mutually dual, where $k = |\min T(f)| + |\min T(g)|$. The above result implies also that for an isotone Boolean function $f$ given by its minimal true vectors and for a subset $G \subset \min T(f^d)$, a new vector $v \in \min T(f^d) - G$ can be computed in time $nk^{o(\log k)}$, where $k = |\min T(f)| + |G|$ (see e.g. [2] for further details). This means also that for any isotone Boolean function $f$ given by its minimal true vectors, $f^d$ can be computed in time $nk^{o(\log k)}$, where $k = |\min T(f)| + |\min T(f^d)|$.

Our paper is structured as follows. In the next section we give some fundamental properties of Armstrong systems. In particular, we show that each family of subsets of $A$ induces an Armstrong system. Based on this observation we introduce dense families of a relation. In Section 3 we study matrix representations of relation instances. The final section is devoted to key functions.

We also note that some proofs are safely left as exercises for the reader.

## 2 Armstrong Systems and Dense Families

Let $r$ be a relation of a schema $R(A)$. In the following we denote $F_r$ simply by $F$, that is, $F$ is the set of all functional dependencies that hold in $r$. It is well-known (see [5], for example) that the following conditions hold for all $B, C, D \subseteq A$:

(A1) if $B \supseteq C$, then $B \to C \in F$;
(A2) if $B \to C \in F$, then $(B \cup D) \to (C \cup D) \in F$;
(A3) if $B \to C \in F$ and $C \to D \in F$, then $B \to D \in F$.

Conditions (A1)–(A3) are called *Armstrong axioms*.

Let $A$ be a set and let $F$ be a set of pairs $B \to C$, where $B, C \subseteq A$. We say that the pair $(A, F)$ is an *Armstrong system*, if $A$ is finite and $F$ satisfies conditions (A1)–(A3). Next we present some simple properties of Armstrong systems.

Let $(A, F)$ be an Armstrong system. We denote by $B^+$ the union of all sets, which are dependent on $B$, that is,

$$B^+ = \bigcup \{C \subseteq A \mid B \to C \in F\}.$$

It follows easily from Armstrong axioms that $B^+$ is the greatest set dependent on $B$. It is also easy to verify that for all $B, C \subseteq A$:

(C1) $B \subseteq B^+$;
(C2) $B \subseteq C$ implies $B^+ \subseteq C^+$;
(C3) $(B^+)^+ = B^+$.

Conditions (C1)–(C3) mean that the map $\wp(A) \to \wp(A), B \mapsto B^+$, is a *closure operator*. Here $\wp(A)$ denotes the *power set* of $A$, that is, the set of all subsets of $A$. Furthermore, the family

$$\mathcal{L}_F = \{B^+ \mid B \subseteq A\}$$

is a *closure system*. This means that $\mathcal{L}_F$ is closed under arbitrary intersections, that is, $\bigcap \mathcal{H} \in \mathcal{L}_F$ for all $\mathcal{H} \subseteq \mathcal{L}_F$. Note that $X^+ = X$ for all $X \in \mathcal{L}_F$. It is also obvious that

$$B \to C \in F \iff C^+ \subseteq B^+.$$

Let $\mathcal{S} \subseteq \wp(A)$ be a family of subsets of a $A$. We define a set $F_{\mathcal{S}}$ of pairs of subsets of $A$ by the following condition:

$$F_{\mathcal{S}} = \{B \to C \mid (\forall X \in \mathcal{S})\ B \subseteq X \Rightarrow C \subseteq X\}.$$

**Proposition 1.** *If $\mathcal{S}$ is a family of subsets of a finite set $A$, then the pair $(A, F_{\mathcal{S}})$ is an Armstrong system.*

In the previous proposition we showed that each collection of subsets of a finite set induces an Armstrong system. Next we introduce dense families of a database relation.

**Definition 1.** Let $R(A)$ be a relation schema and let $r$ be a relation of that schema. We say that a family $\mathcal{S} \subseteq \wp(A)$ of attribute sets is *$r$-dense* (or *dense in $r$*) if $F_r = F_{\mathcal{S}}$.

The problem is how to find dense families. Our next proposition guarantees the existence of at least one dense family. Recall that each Armstrong system $(A, F)$ determines a closure system $\mathcal{L}_F$. In the sequel we denote the closure system $\mathcal{L}_{(F_r)}$ simply by $\mathcal{L}_r$.

**Proposition 2.** *The family $\mathcal{L}_r$ is $r$-dense.*

Next we present some fundamental properties of dense families.

**Proposition 3.** *If $\mathcal{S}$ is $r$-dense, then the following conditions hold for all $B, C \subseteq A$.*

(a) $\mathcal{S} \subseteq \mathcal{L}_r$.
(b) $B^+ = \bigcap\{X \in \mathcal{S} \mid B \subseteq X\}$.
(c) $B \to C \in F_r$ *if and only if* $(\forall X \in \mathcal{S})\ B \subseteq X \Rightarrow C \subseteq X$.

*Remark 1.* Note that by Propositions 2 and 3(a), $\mathcal{L}_r$ is the greatest $r$-dense family. Furthermore, Proposition 3(b) implies that each $r$-dense family generates the family $\mathcal{L}_r$.

We end this section by studying keys of a relation by means of dense families. Recall that a set of attributes $B \subseteq A$ is a *superkey* of $r$ if $B \to A \in F_r$, and a *key* is a minimal superkey.

For any $B \subseteq A$, we denote by $B^{\mathsf{C}}$ the *complement* of $B$ with respect to the set $A$, that is, $B^{\mathsf{C}} = \{a \in A \mid a \notin B\}$. Let $\mathcal{S}$ be $r$-dense. It is clear that the following conditions are equivalent for all $X \in \mathcal{S}$ and $B \subseteq A$:

(K1) $B$ is a superkey of $r$;
(K2) $B \to A \in F_r$;
(K3) $B \subseteq X \Rightarrow X = A$;
(K4) $X \neq A \Rightarrow B \nsubseteq X$;
(K5) $X \neq A \Rightarrow B \cap X^{\mathsf{C}} \neq \emptyset$.

Note that the equivalence of (K2) and (K3) follows from Proposition 3(c). Since (K1) and (K5) are equivalent, we can give our characterization of keys and superkeys in terms of dense families.

**Theorem 1.** *Let $R(A)$ be a relation schema and let $r$ be a relation of that schema. If $\mathcal{S}$ is $r$-dense, then the following conditions hold.*

(a) *$B$ is a superkey of $r$ if and only if it contains an element from each set in $\{X^{\mathsf{C}} \mid X \in \mathcal{S}, X \neq A\}$.*
(b) *$B$ is a key of $r$ if and only if it is minimal with respect to the property of containing an element from each set in $\{X^{\mathsf{C}} \mid X \in \mathcal{S}, X \neq A\}$.*

*Remark 2.* Note that an element $a \in A$ belongs to *all* keys if $X^{\mathsf{C}} = \{a\}$ for some $X \in \mathcal{S}$, where $\mathcal{S}$ is an $r$-dense family.

A family $\mathcal{H}$ is of subsets of $A$ is a *simple hypergraph* on $A$, if $X \subseteq Y$ implies $X = Y$ for all $X, Y \in \mathcal{H}$. A *transversal* $B$ of a simple hypergraph $\mathcal{H}$ is a subset intersecting all the sets of $\mathcal{H}$, that is, $B \cap X \neq \emptyset$ for all $X \in \mathcal{H}$. Transversals are also called *hitting sets*. By Theorem 1(b) it is now clear that a set $B$ is a key of $r$ iff $B$ is a minimal transversal of the hypergraph $\min\{X^{\mathsf{C}} \mid X \in \mathcal{S}, X \neq A\}$, where $\mathcal{S}$ is any $r$-dense family.

The following algorithm, which can be found in [3], computes all minimal transversals of a hypergraph $\mathcal{H}$ in time $O((\prod_{X \in \mathcal{H}} |X|)^2)$.

**Algorithm** Minimal Transversals.
*Input.* A simple hypergraph $\mathcal{H}$ on $A$.
*Output.* The family $\mathcal{T}$ of minimal transversals of $\mathcal{H}$.

$\mathcal{T} \leftarrow \{\emptyset\}$;
**for** each $X \in \mathcal{H}$ **do**
  $\mathcal{T} \leftarrow \{Y \cup \{x\} \mid Y \in \mathcal{T} \text{ and } x \in X\}$;
  $\mathcal{T} \leftarrow \{Y \in \mathcal{T} \mid (\forall Z \in \mathcal{T})\ Z \nsubseteq Y\}$.

In Section 4 we will present an another method for enumerating the keys.

## 3 Matrix Representation

In this section we study certain matrices defined by database relations. We show that the set consisting of the entries of the matrix of a database relation $r$ forms an $r$-dense family.

**Definition 2.** Let $R(A)$ be a relation schema and let $r = \{t_1, \ldots, t_m\}$ be a relation of that schema. The *matrix of the relation* $r$, denoted by $M(r) = (c_{ij})_{m \times m}$, is defined by

$$c_{ij} = \{a \in A \mid t_i[a] = t_j[a]\}.$$

The above definition means that the entry $c_{ij}$ is the set of all attributes $a$ such that the tuples $t_i$ and $t_j$ have the same $a$-value.

Now our following proposition holds.

**Proposition 4.** *If $R(A)$ is a relation schema, $r$ is a relation of that schema, and $M(r) = (c_{ij})_{m \times m}$ is the matrix of $r$, then the family*

$$\{c_{ij} \mid 1 \leq i, j \leq m\}$$

*is $r$-dense.*

*Proof.* Assume that $r = \{t_1, \ldots, t_m\}$. Let us denote $\mathcal{S} = \{c_{ij} \mid 1 \leq i, j \leq m\}$. We show that $F_r = F_{\mathcal{S}}$.

Suppose that $B \to C \in F_r$. This means that for all tuples $t_i, t_j \in r$, $t_i[B] = t_j[B]$ implies $t_i[C] = t_j[C]$. Let $c_{ij} \in \mathcal{S}$ and assume that $B \subseteq c_{ij}$. This means that $t_i[B] = t_j[B]$, and so $t_i[C] = t_j[C]$ by the assumption $B \to C \in F_r$. Hence, $C \subseteq c_{ij}$ and we obtain $B \to C \in F_{\mathcal{S}}$.

On the other hand, let $B \to C \in F_{\mathcal{S}}$. Assume that $t_i[B] = t_j[B]$ for some $1 \leq i, j \leq m$. This means that $B \subseteq c_{ij}$. But $B \to C \in F_{\mathcal{S}}$ implies $C \subseteq c_{ij}$. Hence, also $t_i[C] = t_j[C]$ must hold and thus $B \to C \in F_r$. □

It is easy to see that the $r$-dense family consisting of the entries of $M(r)$ has at most $m^2/2 - m/2 + 1$ elements.

*Example 2.* Let us consider the relation $r$ presented in Fig. 1. We denote the attributes SSN, LNAME, FNAME, DEPT, and AGE simply by the numbers 1, 2, 3, 4, and 5, respectively. Moreover, we denote the subsets of $A$ which differ from $\emptyset$ and $A$ simply by sequences of numbers. For example, $\{1, 2, 3\}$ is written as 123.

The matrix $M(r)$ is the following:

$$\begin{pmatrix} A & \emptyset & 24 & \emptyset \\ \emptyset & A & \emptyset & 345 \\ 24 & \emptyset & A & \emptyset \\ \emptyset & 345 & \emptyset & A \end{pmatrix}$$

By Proposition 4 the family $\mathcal{S} = \{\emptyset, 24, 345, A\}$ consisting of the entries of $M(r)$ is $r$-dense. For example, the dependency $23 \to A$ holds, since 23 and $A$ are included in the same sets of $\mathcal{S}$.

It is also easy to form the set $\mathcal{L}_r = \{\emptyset, 4, 24, 345, A\}$. This is the closure system generated by the family $\mathcal{S}$.

Let us denote $\mathcal{F} = \{X^{\mathtt{C}} \mid X \in \mathcal{S}, X \neq A\} = \{A, 135, 12\}$. Obviously, 1, 23, and 25 are the minimal sets with respect to inclusion which contain an element from each set in family $\mathcal{F}$. This means by Theorem 1(b) that {SSN} and {LNAME, FNAME} are keys of $r$, as we already mentioned. But we have found also a new key of $r$, namely {LNAME, AGE}.

## 4 Key Functions

In this section we consider key functions. First we recall some basic notions concerning Boolean functions (see e.g. [2], where further references can be found). A *Boolean function* is a map $f\colon \{0,1\}^n \to \{0,1\}$. An element $v \in \{0,1\}^n$ is called a *Boolean vector*. If $f(v) = 1$ (resp. $f(v) = 0$), then $v$ is called a *true* (resp. *false*) *vector* of $f$. The set of all true (resp. false) vectors of $f$ is denoted by $T(f)$ (resp. $F(f)$).

Let $A = \{a_1, \ldots, a_n\}$ and $B \subseteq A$. The *characteristic vector* $\chi(B)$ of $B$ is a vector $(v_1, \ldots, v_n)$ such that $v_i = 1$ if $a_i \in B$ and $v_i = 0$ if $a_i \notin B$.

**Definition 3.** Let $R(A)$ be a relation schema, where $A = \{a_1, \ldots, a_n\}$, and let $r$ be a relation of that schema. The *key function* of $r$ is a Boolean function $f_r\colon \{0,1\}^n \to \{0,1\}$ such that for all $B \subseteq A$,

$$\chi(B) \in T(f_r) \iff B \text{ is a superkey of } r.$$

Next we present some properties of key functions. Let $u = (u_1, \ldots, u_n)$ and $v = (v_1, \ldots, v_n)$. We set $u \leq v$ if and only if $u_i \leq v_i$ for all $1 \leq i \leq n$. A Boolean function $f$ is *isotone* if $u \leq v$ always implies $f(u) \leq f(v)$.

Let $f\colon \{0,1\}^n \to \{0,1\}$ be an isotone Boolean function. A true vector $v$ of $f$ is *minimal* if there is no true vector $v'$ of $f$ such that $v' < v$. We denote by $\min T(f)$ the set of all minimal true vectors. A *maximal* false vector and the set $\max F(f)$ are defined analogously.

Now the following obvious proposition holds.

**Proposition 5.** *Let $R(A)$ be a relation schema, where $A = \{a_1, \ldots, a_n\}$, and let $r$ be a relation of that schema. The key function $f_r\colon \{0,1\}^n \to \{0,1\}$ of $r$ is an isotone Boolean function such that* $\min T(f_r) = \{\chi(B) \mid B \textit{ is a key of } r\}$.

If $f$ is an isotone Boolean function it is known that there is one-to-one correspondence between prime implicants and minimal true vectors. For example, an isotone Boolean function $f\colon \{0,1\}^3 \to \{0,1\}, f = 12 \vee 23 \vee 31$, where 12 stands for $x_1 \wedge x_2$ and so on, has prime implicants 12, 23 and 31, which correspond to minimal true vectors 110, 011, 101, respectively.

By Proposition 5, the minimal true vectors of a key function are exactly the characteristic vectors of keys. The problem is how to find the key function. It turns out that each dense family defines an isotone Boolean function, which is the dual of the key function.

The *dual* of a Boolean function $f$, denoted by $f^d$, is defined by $f^d(x) = \overline{f}(\overline{x})$, where $\overline{f}$ and $\overline{x}$ denote the complements of $f$ and $x$, respectively. It is known that $(f^d)^d = f$ and that the DNF expression of $f^d$ is obtained from that of $f$ by exchanging $\vee$ and $\wedge$ as well as constants 0 and 1, and then expanding the resulting formula. For example the dual of $f = 3 \vee 14 \vee 24$ is $f^d = 3 \wedge (1 \vee 4) \wedge (2 \vee 4) = 34 \vee 123$. It is well-known and obvious that for any isotone Boolean function $f$,

$$\min T(f) = \{\overline{v} \mid v \in \max F(f^d)\}.$$

Let $R(A)$ be a relation schema, where $A = \{a_1, \ldots, a_n\}$, and let $r$ be a relation of that schema. For any $r$-dense family of subsets $\mathcal{S}$ of $r$, we define an isotone function $g_\mathcal{S}\colon \{0,1\}^n \to \{0,1\}$ by setting

$$\min(g_\mathcal{S}) = \min\{\chi(X^\mathsf{C}) \mid X \in \mathcal{S}, X \neq A\}. \tag{4.1}$$

Our next proposition shows that $g_\mathcal{S}$ is the dual of the key function.

**Proposition 6.** *Let $R(A)$ be a relation schema and let $r$ be a relation of that schema. For all $r$-dense families $\mathcal{S}$,*

$$f_r = (g_\mathcal{S})^d.$$

*Proof.* Let $A = \{a_1, \ldots, a_n\}$. We will show that for all $v \in \{0,1\}^n$,

$$v \in T(f_r) \iff \overline{v} \in F(g_\mathcal{S}),$$

which means that $f_r = (g_\mathcal{S})^d$.

Suppose that $\chi(B) \in T(f_r)$ and assume that $\overline{\chi(B)} \notin F(g_\mathcal{S})$. This means that $\overline{\chi(B)} \in T(g_\mathcal{S})$. Then by the definition of $g_\mathcal{S}$, there exists an $X \in \mathcal{S}$ such that $X \neq A$ and $\chi(X^\mathsf{C}) \leq \overline{\chi(B)} = \chi(B^\mathsf{C})$. This is equivalent to $X^\mathsf{C} \subseteq B^\mathsf{C}$ and $B \subseteq X$. Since conditions (K1) and (K4) are equivalent, this means that $B \to A \notin F_r$. Thus, $B$ is not a superkey of $r$ and $\chi(B) \notin T(f_r)$, a contradiction! Hence, $\overline{\chi(B)} \in F(g_\mathcal{S})$.

On the other hand, suppose that $\chi(B) \in F(f_r)$. Because $\chi(B)$ is a false vector of $f_r$, $B \to A \notin F_r$, and hence there exists an $X \in \mathcal{S}$ such that $X \neq A$ and $B \subseteq X$. This implies that $X^\mathsf{C} \subseteq B^\mathsf{C}$ and $\chi(X^\mathsf{C}) \leq \chi(B^\mathsf{C}) = \overline{\chi(B)}$. Because

$$\min(g_\mathcal{S}) = \min\{\chi(X^\mathsf{C}) \mid X \in \mathcal{S}, X \neq A\},$$

we obtain $\overline{\chi(B)} \in T(g_\mathcal{S})$. □

*Example 3.* Let us continue Example 2. As we already mentioned, the family $\mathcal{S} = \{\emptyset, 24, 345, A\}$ consisting of the entries of $M(r)$ is $r$-dense. By the definition of $g_\mathcal{S}$,

$$\min T(g_\mathcal{S}) = \min\{\chi(X^\mathsf{C}) \mid X \in \mathcal{S}, X \neq A\} = \{10101, 11000\}.$$

The Boolean function $g_\mathcal{S}\colon \{0,1\}^5 \to \{0,1\}$ has a DNF expression $135 \vee 12$, where 12 stands for $x_1 \wedge x_2$, and so on. This implies that

$$f_r = (g_\mathcal{S})^d = (1 \vee 3 \vee 5) \wedge (1 \vee 2) = 1 \vee 23 \vee 25.$$

Hence, the key function $f_r$ has minimal true vectors 10000 and 01100, and 01001. These vectors are the characteristic vectors of {SSN}, {LNAME, FNAME}, and {LNAME, AGE}, respectively, and thus these sets are the keys of $r$.

**Conclusions.** We studied dense families of relation instances and characterized dependencies and keys in terms of dense families. We studied certain matrices of database relations and showed that the family consisting of the entries of this kind of matrix is dense. We also showed how the problem of checking the possible existence of unknown keys can be reduced to the problem of deciding whether two isotone Boolean functions are mutually dual.

A set of functional dependencies $E$ is a *cover* of a relation $r$, if the set of functional dependencies which can be inferred from $E$ by applying Armstrong axioms (AS1)–(AS3) equals $F_r$. Obviously, we can use dense families to solving the problem of determining a cover of a relation instance. Namely, the set $\mathcal{L}_r$ can be generated by any $r$-dense family by using the operation intersection. We can also compute for any $X \in \mathcal{L}_r$ the set key($X$) of all keys of the relation $r'$, where $r'$ is the relation $r$ restricted to the schema $R(X)$. Furthermore, if $\mathcal{L}_r = \{X_1, \dots, X_p\}$, then apparently the set

$$E = \{B_1 \to X_1 \mid B_1 \in \text{key}(X_1)\} \cup \dots \cup \{B_p \to X_p \mid B_p \in \text{key}(X_p)\}$$

is a cover of $r$.

## References

1. W. W. Armstrong, Dependency structure of data base relationships, in: *Information Processing* **74** (North-Holland, Amsterdam, 1974) 580–583.
2. J. C. Bioch, T. Ibaraki, Complexity of identification and dualization of positive Boolean functions, *Information and Computation* **123** (1995) 50–63.
3. C. Berge, *Hypergraphs. Combinatorics of Finite Sets* (North-Holland, Amsterdam, 1989).
4. J. Demetrovics, G. O. H. Katona, D. Miklos, O. Seleznjev, B. Thalheim, Asymptotic properties of keys and functional dependencies in random databases, *Theoretical Computer Science* **190** (1998) 151–166.
5. R. Elmasri, S. B. Navathe, *Fundamentals of Database Systems, 3rd ed.* (Addison–Wesley, Reading, Massachusetts, 2000).
6. M. Fredman, L. Khachiyan, On the complexity of dualization of monotone disjunctive normal forms, *Journal of Algorithms* **21** (1996) 618–628.
7. J. Järvinen, Preimage relations and their matrices, in: L. Polkowski, A. Skowron, eds., *Rough Sets and Current Trends in Computing*, Lecture Notes in Artificial Intelligence **1424** (Springer, Berlin, 1998) 139–146.
8. W. Lipski, Jr., Two NP-complete problems related to information retrieval, in: M. Karpiński, ed., *Proceedings of the 1977 International Conference on Fundamentals of Computation Theory*, Lecture Notes in Computer Science **56** (Springer, Berlin, 1977) 452–458.
9. A. Skowron, C. Rauszer, The discernibility matrices and functions in information systems, in: R. Słowinski, ed., *Intelligent Decision Support. Handbook of Applications and Advances of the Rough Set Theory*, (Kluwer, Dordrecht, 1991) 331–362.

# On the Complexity of Decidable Cases of Commutation Problem for Languages
## (Extended Abstract)

Juhani Karhumäki[1] *, Wojciech Plandowski[2] **, and Wojciech Rytter[2,3] ***

[1] Department of Mathematics and and Turku Centre for Computer Science, Turku, 20014 Finland. karhumak@cs.utu.fi
[2] Instytut Informatyki, Uniwersytet Warszawski, Banacha 2, 02–097 Warszawa, Poland. wojtekpl@mimuw.edu.pl
[3] Department of Computer Science, University of Liverpool, Great Britain. rytter@mimuw.edu.pl

**Abstract.** We investigate the complexity of basic decidable cases of the *commutation problem for languages*: testing the equality $XY = YX$ for two languages $X$, $Y$, given different types of representations of $X$, $Y$. We concentrate on (the most interesting) case when $Y$ is an explicitly given finite language. This is motivated by a renewed interest and recent progress, see [12,1], in an old open problem posed by Conway [2]. We show that the complexity of the commutation problem varies from co-$NEXPTIME$-complete, through $P\text{-}SPACE$ complete and co-$NP$ complete, to deterministic polynomial time. Classical types of description are considered: nondeterministic automata with and without cycles, regular expressions and grammars. Interestingly, in most cases the complexity status does not change if instead of explicitly given finite $Y$ we consider general $Y$ of the same type as that of $X$. For the case of commutation of two finite sets we provide polynomial time algorithms whose time complexity beats that of a naive algorithm. For deterministic automata the situation is more complicated since the complexity of concatenation of deterministic automaton language $X$ with a finite set $Y$ is asymmetric: while the minimal *dfa*'s for $XY$ would be polynomial in terms of *dfa*'s for $X$ and $Y$, that for $YX$ can be exponential.

## 1 Introduction

Research on word equations during the past few deacades has revealed several amazing results, most notably the Makanin's algorithm and its extensions [15,4, 16]. The situation changes completely when equations on languages (or even on finite languages) are considered. Very little, or in fact almost nothing, is known about their solutions [11]. The exception being the case when such restricted

* Supported by Academy of Finland under grant 44087.
** Supported in part by KBN grant 8T11C03915.
*** Supported in part by KBN grant 8T11C03915.

R. Freivalds (Ed.): FCT 2001, LNCS 2138, pp. 193–203, 2001.

equations with two operations - union and concatenation - are considered where certain fixed point results become applicable. An example is the method to compute the rational expression for a given finite automaton, see [13] for a general survey. Such a theory, however, does not have a counterpart in word equations.

The equation corresponding to the *commutation problem* is: $XY = YX$. Even this deceiptively simple equation proposes several natural and combinatorially intersting problems. Recently there was a renewed interest in commutation problem due to the partial solution to the problem posed about 30 years ago by Conway [2]:

Assume $X$ is the maximal solution to $XY = YX$ for a given finite set $Y$. Is the language $X$ regular ?

An affirmative answer has been given in [12] for $|Y| \leq 3$, but the case $|Y| > 3$ is still unresolved. It seems that further study of commuting with finite sets is needed. In this paper we study the following **commutation problem for languages**:

**Instance:** Given descriptions of two formal languages $X$ and $Y$,
**Question:** What is the complexity of testing the equality $X \cdot Y = Y \cdot X$ ?

We can change the way we formulate a problem instance by changing the type of description: deterministic and nondenterministic finite automata (*nfa*'s, in short) with and without cycles, context-free grammars (*cfg*'s, in short) and regular expressions. Even the exact complexity of the case of an explicitely given finite $X$ is nontrivial. The set $Y$ is in most cases an explicitely given finite language, unless it is specified explicitly otherwise. Then the size of $Y$ is to be understood as the total length of its memeber words. Also a secondary size is considered: the cardinality of $Y$.

We assume that throughout the whole paper $\Sigma$ is a set of single symbols. Our next proposition is a special case of a theorem in [17].

**Proposition 1.** *Assume* $X \cap \Sigma^m \neq \emptyset$, $\epsilon \notin X$ *and* $X\Sigma = \Sigma X$. *Then* $\Sigma^m \subseteq X$.

*Proof.* Let $Z = \Sigma^m \cap X$. We show by induction the following statement for each $k \leq m$:

$$\forall (y \in \Sigma^k)\ \exists (x \in Z)\ y \text{ is a prefix of } x.$$

This is clearly true for $k = 1$. Then, since $\Sigma Z \subseteq Z\Sigma$ we have that all words of size $k+1$, as they are prefixes of $\Sigma Z$ by inductive assumption, should be prefixes of words in $Z$.

Denote:

$$L^{\leq n} = L^1 \cup L^2 \cup L^3 \ldots \cup L^n$$

As immediate consequence of the proposition we have the following useful facts.

**Lemma 1.**
*1. Assume* $L = \Sigma^*$ *or* $L = \Sigma^* - \{u\}$ *for some word* $u$. *Then* $L\Sigma = \Sigma L \Leftrightarrow L = \Sigma^*$.
**2.** *Assume* $\forall (1 \leq k \leq m)\ L \cap \Sigma^k \neq \emptyset$, $\epsilon \notin L$ *and* $L \subseteq \Sigma^{\leq n}$. *Then* $L\Sigma = \Sigma L \Leftrightarrow L = \Sigma^{\leq n}$.

## 2 Regular Expressions and Nondeterministic Automata

Regular languages can be represented by regular expressions or *nfa*'s. Unfortunately the representations are not polynomially equivalent. For each regular expression $R$ there is an polynomial size (with respect to the size of $R$) *nfa* that accepts the language represented by $R$ and such an *nfa* can be constructed in polynomial time [9,8,10]. The opposite is not true: there is an *nfa* accepting a regular language $L$ such that the smallest regular expression for $L$ is of size exponential wrt. the size of the *nfa* [5]. Nevertheless, independently of the representation we prove that the commutation problem for a regular language and a finite language is *P-SPACE* complete. As a consequence we have that the commutation problem for two regular languages is also *P-SPACE* complete.

**Theorem 1.** *Let $X$ be a regular language given by a regular expression. Then the commutation problem for $X$ and $Y = \Sigma$ is P-SPACE hard.*

*Proof.* Let $M$ be any deterministic Turing machine working in polynomial space. We assume that $M$ stops on every input. Let $p_M(n)$ be the size of maximal space used by $M$ during the computation for a word of size $n$. Clearly, $p_M(n) \leq cn^k$ for some constants $c$ and $k$. Let $w$ be any word over $\{a, b\}$. A history of a computation of $M$ on the word $w$ is a word $history(w)$ which is of the form $\#w_0\#w_1\#\ldots\#w_m\#$ where $|w_i| = c|w|^k + 1$ and $w_i$ is a configuration of $M$ at step $i$ of the computation of $M$ on the word $w$. Then $w_0 = q_0wB^j$ where $q_0$ is the starting state of $M$ and $B$ is a blank symbol of the tape of $M$ and $j = cn^k - 1$. Moreover we assume that after configuration $w_m$ the machine $M$ stops.

Let $\Sigma = \{a, b, B\} \cup Q$ where $Q$ is the set of states of $M$. Now we construct a regular expression $R$ of polynomial size on $|w|$ such that $R = \Sigma^*$ if $w$ is not accepted by $M$ and $R = \Sigma^* - \{history(w)\}$ if $w$ is accepted by $M$. Then the result is a consequence of Lemma 1.
The expression $R = R_1 \cup R_2 \cup R_3 \cup R_4$. $R_1$ describes words which are not of the form $\#u_0\#u_1\#\ldots\#u_k\#$ where $u_i$ are of length $c|w|^k + 1$ and they contain exactly one state of $M$. $R_2$ describes words which are not of the form $\Sigma^*qxu\#u'q'\Sigma^*$ where $q$, $q' \in Q$, $x \in \{a, b\}$, $M$ being in state $q$ changes the state to $q'$ if $x$ is the symbol under the head of $M$, $||xu\#u'| - cn^k| = 1$ and the exact length of $xu\#u'$ depends on whether $M$ moves head to the left or right. $R_3$ describes the words which are not of the form $\#uau'\#wa$ where $|u| = |w|$ and the symbol $a$ is not close to a state $q$ in $uau'$. $R_4$ describes the words which do not contain $w_0$ as a prefix or do not contain an accepting configuration as a suffix.

**Corollary 1.** *Let $X$, $Y$ be regular languages given by nfa's or regular expressions. Then the commutation problem for $X$ and $Y$ is P-SPACE complete.*

*Proof.* By Theorem 1 it is enough to prove that the problem is in *P-SPACE* when $X$ and $Y$ are given by two *nfa*'s. Since $X$ and $Y$ are regular, the languages $XY$ and $YX$ are regular, too. Moreover they representation as two *nfa*'s can be computed in polynomial time. Now it is enough to solve the equivalence problem for two *nfa*'s in *P-SPACE*. The latter problem is *P-SPACE* complete, see [6].

As a straightforward consequence of Theorem 1 and Corollary 1 we have.

**Theorem 2.** *Let $X$ be a regular language given by an nfa or a regular expression, and let $Y$ be a finite language given explicitely or by acyclic nfa. Then the commutation problem for $X$ and $Y$ is $P$-$SPACE$ complete.*

**Theorem 3.** *Let $X$ be a finite language given by an acyclic nfa, and let $Y = \Sigma$. Then the commutation problem for $X$ and $Y$ is co-$NP$ hard.*

*Proof.* The problem is in co-NP because all words in $XY$ and $YX$ are of polynomial length so to prove that $XY \neq YX$ it is enough to guess a word which distinguishes these two languages and check that it belongs to one of the languages and does not to the other.

The proof of co-NP hardness is analogous to the proof of Theorem 1. We want to prove that checking $XY \neq YX$ is NP-hard. We take a nondeterministic Turing machine $M$ which works in polynomial time. We assume that $M$ stops for every input and every nondeterministic choice. For a given word $w$ define a set $HISTORY(w)$ being the set of all possible histories of computation of $M$ on the word $w$. All words in $HISTORY(w)$ are of polynomial size wrt to $|w|$. Choose $c$ and $k$ such that

$$\forall w \forall u \in HISTORY(w) |u| \leq c|w|^k.$$

Now from technical reasons we define

$$HISTORY'(w) = \{uB^j : u \in HISTORY(w), j = c|w|^k - |u|\}.$$

All words in $HISTORY'(w)$ are of the same length $c|w|^k$ which depends only on $|w|$. Denote by $Accept(w)$ the subset of $HISTORY'(w)$ containing all accepting histories for $w$. Given a word $w$ denote $m = c|w|^k$. Now we construct a regular language $R$ such that $R = \Sigma^m$ if $HISTORY(w)$ does not contain an accepting history for $w$ and $R = \Sigma^m - Accept(w)$ if $HISTORY(w)$ contains an accepting history for $w$. The result is a consequence of Lemma 1.
The expression $R = R_1 \cup R_2 \cup R_3 \cup R_4$. $R_1$ describes words which are not of the form $\#u_0\#u_1\#\ldots\#u_k\#B^j$ where $u_i$ are of proper length and they contain exactly one state of $M$. $R_2$ describes words of length $m$ which are not of the form $\Sigma^* qxu\#u'q'\Sigma^*$ where $q$, $q' \in Q$, $x \in \{a, b\}$, $M$ being in state $q$ changes the state to $q'$ if $x$ is the symbol under the head of $M$, $||xu\#u'| - cn^k| = 1$ and the exact length of $xu\#u'$ depends on whether $M$ moves head to the left or right. $R_3$ describes the words of length $m$ which are not of the form $\#uau'\#wa$ where $|u| = |w|$ and the symbol $a$ is not close to a state $q$ in $uau'$. $R_4$ describes the words of length $m$ which do not contain $w$ as a prefix or do not contain an accepting configuration as the last configuration of the word.

**Corollary 2.** *Let $X$ be a finite language given by an acyclic nfa and $Y$ be a finite language given explicitely or by an acyclic nfa. Then the commutation problem for $X$ and $Y$ is co-$NP$-complete.*

*Proof.* We may assume that $Y$ is given by an acyclic nfa. First we guess $w$ in $X$ and $v$ in $Y$ such that $wv$ is not in $YX$ or $vw$ is not in $XY$. $w$ and $v$ are of polynomial size. Checking that a guess is correct can be done in polynomial time since the languages $XY$ and $YX$ are regular.

Observe here that if we replace acyclic *nfa*'s by a star-free regular expressions then the complexities of considered problems are the same.

## 3 Context-Free Grammars

Context-free languages (*cfl*'s, in short) are much more complicated than regular sets, in particular the commutation of an infinite *cfl* and a finite set is even undecidable [7].

**Proposition 2.** *Let $X$ be a cfl given by a cfg and $Y$ be a two element set. Then the commutation problem for $X$ and $Y$ is undecidable.*

Obviously the problem is decidable if $X$ is a finite *cfl*. However a *cfg* can generate doubly exponential number of different words, even if we assume that $L(G)$ is finite. However the lengths of words are only singly exponential.

**Lemma 2.** *Assume a cfg $G$, of size $m$, generates a finite language. Then the length of each word in $L(G)$ is bounded by a singly exponential function with respect to $G$.*

Denote by co-$NEXPTIME$ the class of problems whose complements are solvable in nondeterministic singly exponential time. Observe that the direct determinization of a problem in this class requires doubly exponential deterministic time.

We use pushdown automata (*pda*'s, in short) instead of context-free grammars (*cfg*'s, in short). A *pda* with linear number of states can use its stack to count exponential numbers.

**Lemma 3.** [Exponential counting.]
**1.** *There is a pda with $O(n)$ states which accepts the language*
$$L_{eq} = \{a^i \# b^i \ : \ 1 \le i \le 2^n\}$$
**2.** *Assume $\# \notin \Sigma$, then there is a polynomial time pda accepting the finite language*
$$\{x \in (\Sigma \cup \#)^* \ : \ |x| \le 2^{cn},\ x \text{ contains a subword } y \in \#\Sigma^*\# \text{ such that } |y| \ne 2^n\}$$

*Proof.* Using its stack $A$ can store a counter represented in binary, with the least significant digit at the top of the stack. The height of the stack is $n$, except intermediate steps. The stack of such height can store all numbers n the range $1 \le i \le 2^n$. We can add and subtract one from the counter by changing the stack appropriately. For example to add one, we go down the stack to find the first zero. We change this zero to one and replace erased ones by zeros. We remember in the state how deeply we entered into the stack and we can restore it. Hence the finite control of the *pda* keeps the position of a binary digit to be changed, and the stack stores the whole numbers.

**Lemma 4.** *For each pda $A$ with $n$ states, which at each step places on the stack a constant-size string, there is a polynomial-size cfg generating $L(A)$*

**Theorem 4.** *Assume we are given a cfg $G$ generating a finite set. The problem of testing $L\Sigma = \Sigma L$ is co-$NEXPTIME$-hard.*

*Proof.*
We show that there is a short grammar generating all sequences of exponential size which are invalid histories of accepting computation of a Turing machine working in nondeterministic exponential time. We can use the ideas from Lemma 3 to construct a *pda* $A$ accepting all strings of size at most $2^{cn}$ except valid accepting histories. Assume the accepting history is a string of the form $\#w_1\#w_2\#w_3\ldots\#w_t$, where $t = 2^n$ and $|w_i| = 2^n$, $w_i \in \Sigma^*$, and $\# \notin \Sigma$.

The *pda* can use the stack for counting. It guesses which of consecutive codes $w_i$, $w_{i+1}$ of configurations (of not necessarily the same size, but bounded by an exponential function) do not correspond to a valid move of the Turing machine. Assume $w_i$ and $w_{i+1}$ differ at position $j$. $A$ puts the number $j$ in binary on the stack (still keeping below the representation of $i$) and records the mismatch symbol. Then it skips nondeterministically at most $2^n$ symbols of $w_i$ and finds the $j$-th position in $w_{i+1}$ using the stack. Then it skips at most $2^n$ positions in $w_{i+1}$. It does not check if the number of skipped positions in $w_i$ and $w_{i+1}$ is the same, but keeps track of the exponential bound of skipped position.
Nondeterministically $A$ also acceptes the language from the second point of Theorem 3 for the constant $c = 3$.

Eventually the *pda* accepts all strings of length at most $2^{cn}$, if there is no valid history of computation in $2^n$ time of the Turing machine. If there is a valid computation then $A$ acceptes some string of length at most $2^{cn}$, and at the same time it does not accept some string of a same length. We can use Lemma 1. Due to Lemma 4 $A$ can be transformed into an equiavelent *cfg* of a polynomial size.

**Corollary 3.** *Let a finite language $L$ be given by a context-free grammar $G$ and let $Y$ be a finite language given explicitely or by an acyclic* nfa *or by a context-free grammar $G'$. Then the commutation problem for $L$ and $Y$ is co-$NEXPTIME$-complete.*

*Proof.* It is enough to prove that the problem is in co-$NEXPTIME$ so it is enough to prove that the problem $LY \neq YL$ is in $NEXPTIME$. We may assume that $Y$ is given by a cfg. First we guess words $w$ in $L$ and $v$ in $Y$ such that $wv$ is not in $YL$ or $vw$ is not in $LY$. By Lemma 2 the word $wv$ is of length at most exponential wrt the sizes of $G$ and $G'$ and $YL$ is context-free so checking whether $wv$ is in $YL$ can be done in exponential time. Similarly we can check whether $vw$ is in $LY$.

## 4 Deterministic Finite Automata

For deterministic finite automata the complexity status of the commutation problem is open. This is caused by the assymetry of the complexity of concatenating a *dfa* language by a finite set from the left and from the right.

We have partial results, which suggest that the problem would be $PSPACE$-complete. Let us consider the problem of the complexity of a language of the form $L' = L(A) \cdot Y$, where $Y$ is a finite language, measured in the number of states of a minimal *dfa* accepting $L'$. Observe that if we take $L(A) = \Sigma^*$ and $Y = 1 \cdot \Sigma^k$ then $A$ can have only one state, the automaton for $Y$ has $O(k)$ states but the smallest *dfa* for $L'$ needs an exponential number of states. This happens because the total size of $Y$ is exponential wrt. $k$. The situation is much different when the total size of $Y$ is part of the input size. In this case $L'$ is accepted by a *dfa* of a polynomial size. However for the language $Y \cdot L(A)$ the situations is dramatically different. Our next theorem can be found in [18]. We present a proof which is more suitable for our considerations.

**Theorem 5.**
**1.** *Assume $A$ is a deterministic automaton and $Y$ is a finite language. Then we can construct in polynomial time a deterministic automaton accepting $L(A) \cdot Y$, which has a polynomial number of states.*
**2.** *There are dfa's $A$ and finite languages $Y$, where the size of $A$ and $Y$ together is $n$, such that the number of states of any minimal dfa accepting $Y \cdot L(A)$ is exponential.*

*Proof.*
**1. Polynomial-size *dfa* for $L(A) \cdot Y$**
Let $q_0$ be an initial state of $A$ and $ACC_A$ be the set of its accepting states. We construct the automaton $A'$ which for an input string $x$ remembers (in its finite control) the pair $(q, z)$, where:

$z$ is a longest suffix of $x$ which is a prefix of a word in $Y$;
$q = \delta_A(q_0, y)$, where $y$ is a prefix of $x$ such that $x = yz$.

The automaton $A'$ acceptes iff $q \in ACC_A$ and $z \in Y$. We omit the details.
**2. Exponential-size *dfa* for $Y \cdot L(A)$**
Consider the language

$$L_{\neq}(n) \;=\; \{1^n\$u\#v \;:\; u, v \in \{a,b\}^n,\ (\exists 1 \le i \le n)\ u_i \neq v_i\}$$

It is easy to see that a *dfa* for $L_{\neq}(n)$ needs an exponential number of states, on the other hand we can write

$$L_{\neq}(n) \;=\; 1^n \cdot (L_1 \cup L_2 \cup L_3 \ldots \cup L_n)$$

where each $L_i$ is accepted by a linear size *dfa*, $L_i$ is "in charge" of testing inequality on the $i$-the position. Define the languages:

$$L \;=\; 1 \cdot L_1 \cup 1^2 \cdot L_2 \cup 1^3 \cdot L_3 \ldots 1^n \cdot L_n,$$
$$\text{and } Y \;=\; 1 \cup 1^2 \cup 1^3 \ldots 1^n \cup L^n$$

The language $L$ is a accepted by a linear size *dfa* (combination of *dfa*'s for $L_i$'s). The corresponding automaton simply reads the number of leading ones, before the symbol "\$". Then depending on this number switches to simulate the corresponding *dfa* for $L_i$. Then

$$(Y \cdot L) \cap (1^n\$ \cdot \Sigma^*) \;=\; L_{\neq}(n).$$

Hence any *dfa* for $Y \cdot L$ should have exponential number of states. Otherwise $L_{\neq}(n)$ would have a small *dfa*, as a product of the *dfa* for $Y \cdot L$ and linear size *dfa* for $1^n\$ \cdot \Sigma^*$.

**Theorem 6.**
*Let $A$ be a dfa.*
**1.** *If $Y$ is an explicitly given finite language then we can test the inclusion $Y \cdot L(A) \subseteq L(A) \cdot Y$ in deterministic polynomial time.*
**2.** *If $Q$ is a finite prefix set that is given explicitely then we can test the equality $Q \cdot L(A) = L(A) \cdot Q$ in deterministic polynomial time.*

*Proof.* Due to Theorem 5 we can construct a deterministic automaton $A'$ for $L(A) \cdot Y$ with polynomial number of states. Let $A''$ be the complement of $A'$. We also construct a *nfa* $C$ for $Y \cdot L(A)$ with polynomial number of states. Then it is enough to check $L(C) \cap L(A'') = \emptyset$. This can be done by combining $C$ and $A''$ into a single *nfa* $D$ with polynomial number of states (as a product of automata). Hence we can test $L(C) \cap L(A'') = \emptyset$ by checking if $L(D) = \emptyset$. This problem is reducible to a path problem in a graph.
The second point follows from the fact that $Q \cdot L(A)$ is a language accepted by a polynomial size *dfa*.

Observe that the complexity of all previously considered problems is determined by the complexity of the problem $\Sigma L = L\Sigma$. For instance if $X$, $Y$ were regular then the commutation problem for $X$ and $Y$ is PSPACE-complete. Thus it is of the same complexity as the commutation problem in which $X$ is regular and $Y = \Sigma$. Similar situatoin is with other our problems considered in previous chapters. By point (2) of Theorem 6 the problem if $\Sigma L = L\Sigma$ for a regular $L$ given by a dfa can be solved in polynomial time. This suggests that the commutation problem for languages given by dfas is in P.

We have however strong arguments that it is not the case. In the following we will try to convince the reader that it is unlikely that equality $Y \cdot L(A) = L(A) \cdot Y$, for finite $Y$, and a *dfa* $A$, can be tested in polynomial deterministic time.

**Theorem 7.** *Let $A$ and $B$ be dfa's and $Y$ an explicitly given finite language. Testing the inclusion $L(B) \subseteq Y \cdot L(A)$ is PSPACE-complete.*

*Proof.* Let $M$ be a deterministic Turing machine $M$ working in space $m$ for the input string $w$ of size $n$. We construct a *dfa* accepting non-valid computations of $M$ for $w$ similarly as we constructed a *dfa* for the language $L_{\neq}(m)$.

We define a sequence of languages $L_1$, $L_2, \ldots L_n$ which together "test" that two consecutive configurations of $M$ are invalid. This can be done in a similar way as for the language $L_{\neq}(n)$. We omit the details. Eventually we construct the language $L$ such that

$1^n\$\Sigma^* \subseteq Y \cdot L$ iff there is no valid accepting computation of $M$.
The language $1^n\$\Sigma^*$ can be accepted by a *dfa* with $n + 2$ states.

## 5 Finite Languages

Let $X$ be an explicitely given finite language. Denote by $|X|$ the number of words in $X$ and by $||X||$ the total size of all words in $X$.

**Lemma 5.**

1. *Let $X$ be a finite set of words over a non-unary alphabet $\Sigma$ then* $|X| \leq \frac{||X||}{\log_{|\Sigma|}||X||}$.
2. *Let $X$ and $Y$ are two finite languages over a finite alphabet $\Sigma$ and let $|X| = n$ and $|Y| = m$. Then $||XY|| \leq m||X|| + n||Y||$.*

*Proof.* (1) Fix the number $N$ and consider a set of words $X$ such that

1. $||X|| \leq N$,
2. the cardinality of $X$ is largest possible,
3. among all sets $Y$ having properties 1 and 2 the number $||X||$ is smallest possible.

Consider a trie $T$ for $X$. The trie has $|X|$ distinguished nodes and each path from the root of $T$ to distinguished vertex of $T$ is labelled by a word in $X$. Clearly each leaf of $T$ is distinguished.

*Claim.* 1. $T$ is a balanced tree.
2. Any son of a vertex with less than $|\Sigma|$ sons in $T$ is a leaf.
3. Each vertex in $T$ is distinguished.

*Proof. (of the claim)*
(1) Suppose that the difference between depths of two leaves of $T$ is at least 2. Then we remove the deeper one and put it as a son of the other one. In this way the cardinality of the obtained set is the same as the cardinality of $X$ and its size is strictly smaller than $||X||$. A contradiction.

(2) Suppose there is a vertex $v$ in $T$ having less than $\Sigma$ sons which is not a leaf. Then we remove a leaf whose ancestor is $v$ and put it as a son of $v$. Again the set represented by a new trie has the same number of elements as $X$ and is of smaller size. A contradiction.

(3) Since each leaf is distinguished, we may assume that an internal vertex $v$ of $T$ is not distinguished. Then we take any path from $v$ to a leaf, remove $v$ and move all other vertices of the path one level up. New trie corresponds to a set of the same cardinality as $X$ and smaller size. A contradiction.

By the claim we may assume that $T$ is a full $|\Sigma|$-ary tree of $|X|$ nodes. Such a tree has at least $|X|/2$ leaves and is of height at least $\log_{|\Sigma|}|X|$. Hence,

$$\frac{|X|}{2}\log_{|\Sigma|}|X| \leq ||X||.$$

This completes the proof of point (1).
*Proof of point* (2):

$$||XY|| \leq \Sigma_{x\in X, y\in Y}|xy| \leq \Sigma_{x\in X}\Sigma_{y\in Y}(|x| + |y|) \leq \Sigma_{x\in X}(m|x| + \Sigma_{y\in Y}|y|)$$
$$\leq \Sigma_{x\in X}(m|x| + ||Y||) \leq m||X|| + n||Y||$$

**Theorem 8.** *Let $X$ and $Y$ be explicitly finite languages over a constant size alphabet. Then the commutation problem for $X$ and $Y$ can be solved in $O(|X| \cdot ||Y|| + |Y| \cdot ||X||)$ time. In particular if the total size of the languages is $n$ then the problem can be solved in $O(\frac{n^2}{\log n})$ time.*

*Proof.* First we construct a trie for the language $XY$. Then for each word in $YX$ we check whether it is in $XY$. Next we construct a trie for the language $YX$ and for each word in $XY$ we check whether it is in $YX$.
The estimation $O(\frac{n^2}{\log n})$ is a consequence of Lemma 1.

When most of the words in $X, Y$ are long words then a better measure of the input size is a pair $(k, n)$, where $n$ is the total length of all words in $X \cup Y$ and $k$ is the number of words. Usually $k << n$.

**Theorem 9.** *Let $X$ and $Y$ be finite explicitly given languages of total size $n$ and cardinality at most $k$. Then the commutation problem for $X$ and $Y$ can be solved in $O((k^2 + n) \log n)$ time.*

*Proof.* Denote $W = X \cup Y$. We use the concept of the *dictionary of basic factors*, denoted $DBF(W)$, for the set $W$ of words, see [3]. The subwords of words in $W$ whose lengths are powers of two, are called basic factors. The dictionary $DBF(W)$ assigns to each subword $w$ an integer $name(w) \in [1, \ldots, n]$ such that each basic factor $w$ is uniquely identified by the pair $(length(w), name(w))$.
The following fact has been shown in [3].

*Claim.* $DBF(W)$ can be constructed in time $O(n \log n)$.

For words whose length is not necessarily a power of two define

$$code(w) = (length(w), name(w'), name''(w)),$$

where $w'$, $w'$ are respectively the largest prefix and the largest suffix of $w$ whose length is a power of two.
For a set $X$ of words denote: $code(X) = \{code(x) \ : \ x \in X\}$.
We replace the sets $X$ and $Y$ by $X' = code(X)$, $Y' = code(Y)$. for two codes $x'$, $y'$ of words $x$, $y$ denote by $x' \otimes y' = z'$, where $z'$ is the code of $xy$.

*Claim.* Given a dictionary $DBF(X \cup Y)$, for any two $x', y' \in code(X \cup Y)$ we compute $x' \otimes y'$ in $O(\log n)$ time.

It is easy to see that:

$$X' \otimes Y' = Y' \otimes X' \ \Leftrightarrow \ XY = YX$$

Now the algorithm is very simple. We compute $X' \otimes Y'$ and $Y' \otimes X'$ and test equality of two sets consisting of triples of short integers. We can do it by sorting these sets lexicographically and testing equality of sorted lists.

## 6 Related Questions

We end with posing some open problems. What is the complexity of commutation problem for $X$ and $Y$ if

*1.* $X$ and $Y$ are regular languages given by *dfa*'s?
*2.* $X$ is given by a deterministic *dfa* and $Y$ is finite?
*3.* $X$ is finite and given by a deterministic *dfa* and $Y$ is finite?
*4.* $X$ is given by a *dpda* and $Y$ is finite?
*5.* $X$ is finite and given by a *dpda* and $Y$ is finite?
*6.* $X$ is regular and $Y = \Sigma$ where size of $\Sigma$

is a constant ($|Y| \leq k$ for a given $k$)?

## References


1. C. Choffrut, J. Karhumaki, N. Ollinger, *The commutation of finite sets: a challenging problem*, TUCS Technical Report 303, http://www.tucs.fi/, 1999.
2. J. H. Conway, *Regular algebra and finite machines*, Chapman Hall, 1971.
3. M. Crochemore, W. Rytter, *Text algorithms*, Oxford University Press, 1994
4. V. Diekert, Makanin's algorithm, in *Lothaire II*, to appear.
5. A. Ehrenfeucht, P. Zeiger, Complexity measures for expressions, *J. Comput. System Sci.* 12, 134-146, 1976.
6. M.R. Garey, D.S. Johnson, *Computers and Intractability: A guide to the theory of NP-completeness*, San Francisco: H.Freeman, 1978.
7. T. Harju, O. Ibarra, J. Karhumäki, A. Salomaa, *Decision questions concerning semilinearity, morphisms and commutation of languages*, TUCS Technical Report 376, http://www.tucs.fi/, 2000.
8. C. Hagenach, A. Muscholl, *Computing $\varepsilon$-free NFA from regular expressions in $O(n \log^2 n)$ time*, LNCS 1450, 277-285, 1998.
9. J. Hromkovic, S. Seibert, T. Wilke, *Translating regular expressions into small $\varepsilon$-free nondeterministic finite automata*, LNCS 1200, 55-66, 1997.
10. J. Hopcroft, J. Ullman, *Introduction to Automata Theory, Languages, and Computation*, Addison-Wesley, 1979.
11. J. Karhumäki, *Combinatorial and computational problems on finite sets of words*, Proc. MCU 2001, LNCS, to appear.
12. J. Karhumäki, I. Petre, *On the centralizer of a finite set*, Proc. ICALP 2000, LNCS 1853, 536-514, 2000.
13. E. Leiss, *Language equations*, Springer-Verlag, 1998.
14. M. Lothaire, *Combinatorics on words*, Addison-Wesley, 1983.
15. G.S. Makanin, The problem of solvability of equations in a free semigroup, *Mat. Sb.* 103(2), 147-236, in russian; english translation in: *Math. USSR Sbornik*, 32, 129-198, 1977.
16. W. Plandowski, Satisfiability of word equations with constants is in PSPACE, Proc. FOCS 1999, 1999.
17. B. Ratoandramanana, Codes et motifs, *RAIRO Theor. Informat.* 23, 425-444, 1989.
18. S. Yu, Regular languages, in G. Rozengerg, A. Salomaa (eds.), *Handbook of Formal Languages*, Springer, 41-110, 1997.

# Cones, Semi-AFPs, and AFPs of Algebraic Power Series

Werner Kuich

Technische Universität Wien
Wiedner Hauptstraße 8–10, A–1040 Wien
kuich@tuwien.ac.at

**Abstract.** A complete characterization of cones, semi-AFPs and AFPs (abstract families of power series) of algebraic power series in terms of algebraic systems is given.

## 1 Introduction

Berstel [1] states on page 267 that "up to now, no characterization of the family of context-free grammars generating the languages of a cone is known". In this paper this problem is solved not only for (principal, full) cones but also for (principal, full) semi-AFPs and AFPs.

In several papers, the author has characterized cones of algebraic power series (Kuich [5,6]) and abstract families of algebraic power series (Kuich, Karner [4]) in terms of algebraic systems. In Kuich, Salomaa [8], Theorem 13.24, cones of algebraic power series are characterized in terms of pushdown automata.

In this paper, we give a complete characterization of cones, semi-AFPs and AFPs of algebraic power series in terms of algebraic systems. The paper contains this and another two sections. In Section 2, we show that each principal full cone (resp. principal cone) of algebraic power series has a full cone generator (resp. cone generator) that is the first component of the unique solution of an algebraic system in a certain normal form, called cone form. This leads to a characterization of principal (full) cones by the first components of the least solutions of certain algebraic systems given in matrix form. An easy extension of this result yields a characterization of (full) cones. In Section 3, these characterizations are used to characterize (principal, full) semi-AFPs and AFPs.

The reader is assumed to have a basic knowledge of formal power series. All notions and notations used in this paper are from Kuich, Salomaa [8] or Kuich [7].

## 2 Cones of Algebraic Power Series

In this paper, $\Sigma_\infty$ denotes a fixed infinite alphabet. All finite alphabets $\Sigma$, possibly provided with indices, are subalphabets of $\Sigma_\infty$. In the following constructions

R. Freivalds (Ed.): FCT 2001, LNCS 2138, pp. 204–216, 2001.

we sometimes assume without loss of generality that $\Sigma_\infty$ contains "special symbols" ¢, \$ or # not belonging to any of the finite alphabets $\Sigma$ discussed in the same construction.

A multiplicative morphism $\mu : \Sigma^* \to (A^{\mathrm{rat}}\langle\langle \Sigma'^* \rangle\rangle)^{Q\times Q}$ is called *rational representation.* It is called *regulated* iff there exists a $k \geq 1$ such that, for all $w \in \Sigma^*$ with $|w| \geq k$, $(\mu(w), \varepsilon) = 0$. A *rational transducer* (*with input alphabet* $\Sigma$ *and output alphabet* $\Sigma'$) $\mathfrak{T} = (Q, \mu, S, P)$ is given by

(i) a finite set $Q$ of *states*,
(ii) a *rational representation* $\mu : \Sigma^* \to (A^{\mathrm{rat}}\langle\langle \Sigma'^* \rangle\rangle)^{Q\times Q}$,
(iii) $S \in (A^{\mathrm{rat}}\langle\langle \Sigma'^* \rangle\rangle)^{1\times Q}$, called *initial state vector*,
(iv) $P \in (A^{\mathrm{rat}}\langle\langle \Sigma'^* \rangle\rangle)^{Q\times 1}$, called *final state vector.*

The mapping $||\mathfrak{T}|| : A\langle\langle \Sigma^* \rangle\rangle \to A\langle\langle \Sigma'^* \rangle\rangle$ *realized* by a rational transducer $\mathfrak{T} = (Q, \mu, S, P)$ is defined by

$$||\mathfrak{T}||(r) = \sum_{q_1,q_2\in Q} \sum_{w\in\Sigma^*} S_{q_1}(r,w)\mu(w)_{q_1,q_2}P_{q_2}, \quad r \in A\langle\langle \Sigma^* \rangle\rangle .$$

The rational transducer $\mathfrak{T}$ is called *regulated* iff $\mu$ is a regulated rational representation. A mapping $\tau : A\langle\langle \Sigma^* \rangle\rangle \to A\langle\langle \Sigma'^* \rangle\rangle$ is called a *rational transduction* (resp. *regulated rational transduction*) iff there exists a rational transducer (resp. regulated rational transducer) $\mathfrak{T}$ such that $\tau(r) = ||\mathfrak{T}||(r)$ for all $r \in A\langle\langle \Sigma^* \rangle\rangle$. Our rational transductions are a straightforward generalization of the rational transductions of Berstel [1], Proposition III.7.3 to power series.

Here and in the sequel, $A$ always denotes a *commutative* semiring. If we deal with rational representations or rational transducers that are not regulated, $A$ will be additionally *continuous.* This makes sure that all infinite sums that occur in connection with representations and rational transducers are well-defined.

Our basic semiring will now be $A\langle\langle \Sigma_\infty^* \rangle\rangle$. The subsemiring of $A\langle\langle \Sigma_\infty^* \rangle\rangle$ containing all power series whose supports are contained in some $\Sigma^*$ is denoted by $A\{\{\Sigma_\infty^*\}\}$, i. e.,

$$A\{\{\Sigma_\infty^*\}\} = \{r \in A\langle\langle \Sigma_\infty^* \rangle\rangle \mid \text{there exists a finite alphabet } \Sigma \subset \Sigma_\infty \text{ such that } \mathrm{supp}(r) \subseteq \Sigma^*\}.$$

For $\Sigma \subset \Sigma_\infty$, $A\langle\langle \Sigma^* \rangle\rangle$ is isomorphic to a subsemiring of $A\{\{\Sigma_\infty^*\}\}$. Hence, we may assume that $A\langle\langle \Sigma^* \rangle\rangle \subset A\{\{\Sigma_\infty^*\}\}$. Furthermore, we define two subsemirings of $A\{\{\Sigma_\infty^*\}\}$, namely, the semiring of algebraic power series by

$$A^{\mathrm{alg}}\{\{\Sigma_\infty^*\}\} = \{r \in A\{\{\Sigma_\infty^*\}\} \mid \text{there exists a finite alphabet } \Sigma \subset \Sigma_\infty \text{ such that } r \in A^{\mathrm{alg}}\langle\langle \Sigma^* \rangle\rangle\},$$

and the semiring of rational power series by

$$A^{\mathrm{rat}}\{\{\Sigma_\infty^*\}\} = \{r \in A\{\{\Sigma_\infty^*\}\} \mid \text{there exists a finite alphabet } \Sigma \subset \Sigma_\infty \text{ such that } r \in A^{\mathrm{rat}}\langle\langle \Sigma^* \rangle\rangle\}.$$

Let $\mathfrak{T} = (Q, \mu, S, P)$ be a rational transducer with input alphabet $\Sigma$. The extended mapping $||\mathfrak{T}|| : A\{\{\Sigma_\infty^*\}\} \to A\{\{\Sigma_\infty^*\}\}$ is then defined by

$$||\mathfrak{T}||(r) = \sum_{q_1,q_2 \in Q} \sum_{w \in \Sigma^*} S_{q_1}(r, w)\mu(w)_{q_1,q_2} P_{q_2}, \quad r \in A\{\{\Sigma_\infty^*\}\}.$$

Here the rational representation $\mu$ is extended to $\mu : \Sigma_\infty^* \to (A^{\mathrm{rat}}\{\{\Sigma_\infty^*\}\})^{Q\times Q}$ by $\mu(w) = 0$ if $w \notin \Sigma^*$. Hence $\mathfrak{T}$ translates only words $w$ of $\Sigma^*$ and maps words not in $\Sigma^*$ to 0. Again, a mapping $\tau : A\{\{\Sigma_\infty^*\}\} \to A\{\{\Sigma_\infty^*\}\}$ is called a *(regulated) rational transduction* iff there exists a (regulated) rational transducer $\mathfrak{T}$ such that $\tau(r) = ||\mathfrak{T}||(r)$ for all $r \in A\{\{\Sigma_\infty^*\}\}$.

Each nonempty subset $\mathfrak{L}$ of $A\{\{\Sigma_\infty^*\}\}$ is called *family of power series.* In the sequel, $\mathfrak{L}$ will denote a family of power series. A family of power series closed under rational transductions (resp. regulated rational transductions) is called a *full cone* (resp. *cone*). Define

$$\hat{\mathfrak{M}}(\mathfrak{L}) = \{\tau(r) \mid r \in \mathfrak{L} \text{ and } \tau \text{ is a rational transduction}\}$$

and

$$\mathfrak{M}(\mathfrak{L}) = \{\tau(r) \mid r \in \mathfrak{L} \text{ and } \tau \text{ is a regulated rational transduction}\}.$$

Since rational transductions and regulated rational transductions are closed under functional composition (Kuich [7], Theorem 7.9), $\mathfrak{L}$ is a full cone iff $\mathfrak{L} = \hat{\mathfrak{M}}(\mathfrak{L})$ and $\mathfrak{L}$ is a cone iff $\mathfrak{L} = \mathfrak{M}(\mathfrak{L})$. A cone $\mathfrak{L}$ is called *principal full* (resp. *principal*) iff there exists a power series $r \in A\{\{\Sigma_\infty^*\}\}$ such that $\mathfrak{L} = \hat{\mathfrak{M}}(r)$ (resp. $\mathfrak{L} = \mathfrak{M}(r)$). The power series $r$ is then a *full cone generator* of the full cone $\mathfrak{L}$ (resp. *cone generator* of the cone $\mathfrak{L}$). (See Berstel [1]; and Ginsburg [2], where cones are called trios.) Again, if we deal with full cones our semiring $A$ will be *commutative* and *continuous.*

We now want to characterize full cones and cones of algebraic power series by algebraic systems in cone form. Here an algebraic system is in *cone form* iff it is of the form

$$y_i = \sum_{\pi \in Z} a_{i\pi} x_{i\pi} \pi, \quad 1 \le i \le n,$$

where $a_{i\pi} \in A$, $a_{iy_i} = 1$, $x_{i\pi} \in \Sigma$, $\pi \in Z$, $Z = Y^3 \cup Y^2 \cup Y \cup \{\varepsilon\}$, $1 \le i \le n$, $Y = \{y_i \mid 1 \le i \le n\}$, and $\{x_{i\pi} \mid \pi \in Z - \{y_i\},\ 1 \le i \le n\} \cap \{x_{iy_i} \mid 1 \le i \le n\} = \emptyset$.

In a series of theorems and lemmas we will prove that with respect to the generation of principal cones the cone form is a normal form.

**Theorem 1.** *A mapping $\tau : A\langle\langle\Sigma^*\rangle\rangle \to A\langle\langle\Sigma'^*\rangle\rangle$ is a rational transduction (resp. regulated rational transduction) iff there exists an $r_0 \in A^{\mathrm{rat}}\langle\langle\Sigma'^*\rangle\rangle$, a rational representation (resp. regulated rational representation) $\mu : \Sigma^* \to (A\langle\langle\Sigma'^*\rangle\rangle)^{Q\times Q}$ and $i, t \in Q$, $i \ne t$, such that, for all $r \in A\langle\langle\Sigma^*\rangle\rangle$,*

$$\tau(r) = (r, \varepsilon)r_0 + \sum_{w \in \Sigma^+} (r, w)\mu(w)_{i,t}.$$

*Proof.* Use the construction in the proof of Theorem 9.4 of Kuich, Salomaa [8]. It works for both, regulated rational transductions (with commutative semiring $A$) and rational transductions (with commutative continuous semiring $A$). The proof of Theorem 9.4 of Kuich, Salomaa [8] is valid in both cases. □

We often will use the following corollary of Theorem 1 without further mention.

**Corollary 21** *Let $\tau : A\{\{\Sigma_\infty^*\}\} \to A\{\{\Sigma_\infty^*\}\}$ be a rational transduction (resp. regulated rational transduction). Then there exists a rational representation $\mu : \Sigma_\infty^* \to (A^{\mathrm{rat}}\{\{\Sigma_\infty^*\}\})^{Q\times Q}$ and $i, t \in Q$, $i \neq t$, such that, for each $r \in A\{\{\Sigma_\infty^*\}\}$ with $(r, \varepsilon) = 0$,*

$$\tau(r) = \sum_{w\in\Sigma^*} (r, w)\mu(w)_{i,t} = \mu(r)_{i,t}\,.$$

**Lemma 22** *Each principal full cone (resp. principal cone) has a quasiregular full cone generator (resp. cone generator).*

*Proof.* By Theorem 11.31 of Kuich, Salomaa [8]. □

**Lemma 23** *Let $h : \Sigma^* \to (\Sigma \cup ¢)^*$ be the morphism defined by $h(x) = x¢$ for all $x \in \Sigma$. Then, for $r \in A\langle\langle\Sigma^*\rangle\rangle$, $\hat{\mathfrak{M}}(r) = \hat{\mathfrak{M}}(h(r))$ and $\mathfrak{M}(r) = \mathfrak{M}(h(r))$.*

*Proof.* By Lemma 13.18 of Kuich, Salomaa [8]. □

**Lemma 24** *Let $h : \Sigma^* \to (\Sigma \cup ¢)^*$ be the morphism defined by $h(x) = x¢$ for all $x \in \Sigma^*$. Then, for all $r \in A\langle\langle\Sigma^*\rangle\rangle$ with $(r, \varepsilon) = 0$, there exists a strict algebraic system $y_i = q_i$, $1 \leq i \leq n+1$, where $\mathrm{supp}(q_i) \subseteq \Sigma\{y_{n+1}\} \cup \Sigma\{y_{n+1}\}Y \cup \Sigma\{y_{n+1}\}Y^2$, $1 \leq i \leq n$, and $q_{n+1} = ¢$, such that $h(r)$ is the $y_1$-component of its unique solution.*

*Proof.* By Theorem 14.33 of Kuich, Salomaa [8], $r$ is the first component of the unique solution of an algebraic system $y_i = p_i$, $1 \leq i \leq n$, in Greibach normal form with $\mathrm{supp}(p_i) \subseteq \Sigma \cup \Sigma Y \cup \Sigma Y^2$:

$$\begin{aligned} y_i = {} & \textstyle\sum_{x\in\Sigma}(p_i, x)x + \sum_{1\leq j\leq n}\sum_{x\in\Sigma}(p_i, xy_j)xy_j + \\ & \textstyle\sum_{1\leq j,k\leq n}\sum_{x\in\Sigma}(p_i, xy_jy_k)xy_jy_k, \quad 1 \leq i \leq n\,. \end{aligned}$$

Assume that $\sigma$ is the unique solution of $y_i = p_i$, $1 \leq i \leq n$. We claim that $h(\sigma)$ is the unique solution of the algebraic system

$$\begin{aligned} y_i = {} & \textstyle\sum_{x\in\Sigma}(p_i, x)h(x) + \sum_{1\leq j\leq n}\sum_{x\in\Sigma}(p_i, xy_j)h(x)y_j + \\ & \textstyle\sum_{1\leq j,k\leq n}\sum_{x\in\Sigma}(p_i, xy_jy_k)h(x)y_jy_k, \quad 1 \leq i \leq n\,. \end{aligned}$$

The claim is shown by substituting $h(\sigma)$ into this algebraic system:

$$\begin{aligned} & \textstyle\sum_{x\in\Sigma}(p_i, x)h(x) + \sum_{1\leq j\leq n}\sum_{x\in\Sigma}(p_i, xy_j)h(x)h(\sigma_j) + \\ & \textstyle\sum_{1\leq j,k\leq n}\sum_{x\in\Sigma}(p_i, xy_jy_k)h(x)h(\sigma_j)h(\sigma_k) = \\ & h(p_i(\sigma_1, \ldots, \sigma_n)) = h(\sigma_i), \quad 1 \leq i \leq n\,. \end{aligned}$$

By Lemma 14.25 of Kuich, Salomaa [8], $(h(r), h(\sigma_2), \ldots, h(\sigma_n), ¢)$ is the unique solution of the algebraic system with variables in $\{y_1, \ldots, y_n, y_{n+1}\}$

$$\begin{aligned} y_i &= \textstyle\sum_{x\in\Sigma}(p_i, x)xy_{n+1} + \sum_{1\le j\le n}\sum_{x\in\Sigma}(p_i, xy_j)xy_{n+1}y_j + \\ &\quad \textstyle\sum_{1\le j,k\le n}\sum_{x\in\Sigma}(p_i, xy_jy_k)xy_{n+1}y_jy_k, \quad 1 \le i \le n, \\ y_{n+1} &= ¢ . \end{aligned}$$

**Lemma 25** *Let $h : \Sigma^* \to (\Sigma \cup ¢)^*$ be the morphism defined by $h(x) = x¢$ for all $x \in \Sigma^*$. Then, for all $r \in A\langle\langle\Sigma^*\rangle\rangle$ with $(r, \varepsilon) = 0$, there exists a strict algebraic system*

$$y_i = \sum_{\pi\in Z} a_{i\pi}x_{i\pi}\pi, \quad 1 \le i \le n,$$

*where $a_{i\pi} \in A$, $a_{iy_i} = 0$, $x_{i\pi} \in \Sigma$, $\pi \in Z$, $Z = \{\varepsilon\} \cup Y \cup Y^2 \cup Y^3$, $1 \le i \le n$, such that $h(r)$ is the first component of its unique solution.*

*Proof.* By Lemma 5, $h(r)$ is the first component of the unique solution of a strict algebraic system $y_i = p_i$, $1 \le i \le t$, where $\mathrm{supp}(p_i) \subseteq ¢ \cup \Sigma(Y - y_i) \cup \Sigma Y^2 \cup \Sigma Y^3$:

$$\begin{aligned} y_i = (p_i, ¢)¢ &+ \textstyle\sum_{1\le j\le t}\sum_{x\in\Sigma}(p_i, xy_j)xy_j + \\ &\textstyle\sum_{1\le j,k\le t}\sum_{x\in\Sigma}(p_i, xy_jy_k)xy_jy_k + \\ &\textstyle\sum_{1\le j,k,m\le t}\sum_{x\in\Sigma}(p_i, xy_jy_ky_m)xy_jy_ky_m, \quad 1 \le i \le t. \end{aligned}$$

Consider now the strict algebraic system with variables in $\{y_i^x \mid x \in \Sigma,\ 1 \le i \le t\}$

$$\begin{aligned} y_i^x = (p_i, ¢)¢ &+ \textstyle\sum_{1\le j\le t}\sum_{x\in\Sigma}(p_i, xy_j)xy_j^x + \\ &\textstyle\sum_{1\le j,k\le t}\sum_{x\in\Sigma}(p_i, xy_jy_k)xy_j^xy_k^x + \\ &\textstyle\sum_{1\le j,k,m\le t}\sum_{x\in\Sigma}(p_i, xy_jy_ky_m)xy_j^xy_k^xy_m^x, \quad 1 \le i \le t,\ x \in \Sigma. \end{aligned}$$

We claim that the $y_i^x$-component, $x \in \Sigma$, $1 \le i \le t$, of the unique solution is given by $\sigma_i$. This claim is easily shown by substituting this unique solution into the equations of the above algebraic system.

Since $(p_i, xy_i) = 0$ for $x \in \Sigma$, $1 \le i \le t$, our lemma is proven. □

**Lemma 26** *Let $\tau : A\langle\langle\Sigma^*\rangle\rangle \to A\langle\langle\Sigma \cup \$)^*\rangle\rangle$ be the substitution defined by $\tau(x) = \$^*x$, $x \in \Sigma$. Then, for all $r \in A\langle\langle\Sigma^*\rangle\rangle$, $\hat{\mathfrak{M}}(r) = \hat{\mathfrak{M}}(\tau(r))$ and $\mathfrak{M}(r) = \mathfrak{M}(\tau(r))$.*

*Proof.* Clearly, for $r \in A\langle\langle\Sigma^*\rangle\rangle$, $\tau(r) \in \mathfrak{M}(r)$. Hence, $\mathfrak{M}(\tau(r)) \subseteq \mathfrak{M}(r)$ and $\hat{\mathfrak{M}}(\tau(r)) \subseteq \hat{\mathfrak{M}}(r)$. Conversely, define the substitution $\tau' : A\langle\langle(\Sigma\cup\$)^*\rangle\rangle \to A\langle\langle\Sigma^*\rangle\rangle$ by $\tau'(x) = x$, $x \in \Sigma$, $\tau'(\$) = 0$. Then $\tau'(\tau(r)) = r$ for all $r \in A\langle\langle\Sigma^*\rangle\rangle$. Hence, $\mathfrak{M}(r) \subseteq \mathfrak{M}(\tau(r))$ and $\hat{\mathfrak{M}}(r) \subseteq \hat{\mathfrak{M}}(\tau(r))$. □

**Lemma 27** *Let $\sigma$ be the unique solution of an algebraic system $y_i = p_i$, $1 \le i \le n$, where $\mathrm{supp}(p_i) \subseteq \Sigma Y^*$. Let $\tau : A\langle\langle\Sigma^*\rangle\rangle \to A\langle\langle(\Sigma \cup \$)^*\rangle\rangle$ be the substitution defined by $\tau(x) = \$^*x$, $x \in \Sigma$. Assume that $\sigma'$ is the unique solution of the algebraic system $y_i = p_i + \$y_i$, $1 \le i \le n$. Then $\sigma' = \tau(\sigma)$.*

*Proof.* (i) We prove that $\tau(\sigma)$ is the unique solution of the system $y_i = \$^* p_i$, $1 \le i \le n$:

$$\begin{aligned} &\$^* p_i(\tau(\sigma_1), \ldots, \tau(\sigma_n)) = \\ &\textstyle\sum_{x \in \Sigma} \sum_{\alpha \in Y^*} (p_i, x\alpha) \$^* x\alpha(\tau(\sigma_1), \ldots, \tau(\sigma_n)) = \\ &\textstyle\sum_{x \in \Sigma} \sum_{\alpha \in Y^*} (p_i, x\alpha) \tau(x\alpha(\sigma_1, \ldots, \sigma_n)) = \\ &\tau(p_i(\sigma_1, \ldots, \sigma_n)) = \tau(\sigma_i), \quad 1 \le i \le n. \end{aligned}$$

(ii) Consider the linear system

$$y_i = \$ y_i + p_i(\sigma'_1, \ldots, \sigma'_n), \quad 1 \le i \le n.$$

By Theorem 4.17 of Kuich, Salomaa [8], its unique solution is given by

$$(\$^* p_1(\sigma'_1, \ldots, \sigma'_n), \ldots, \$^* p_n(\sigma'_1, \ldots, \sigma'_n)).$$

But $(\sigma'_1, \ldots, \sigma'_n)$ is also a solution. Hence, $\sigma'_i = \$^* p_i(\sigma'_1, \ldots, \sigma'_n)$, $1 \le i \le n$.

(iii) Since the system $y_i = \$^* p_i$, $1 \le i \le n$, has a unique solution, we infer that $\sigma' = \tau(\sigma)$. □

**Theorem 2.** *Each principal full cone (resp. principal cone) in $A^{\mathrm{alg}}\{\{\Sigma_\infty^*\}\}$ has a full cone generator (resp. cone generator) that is the first component of the unique solution of an algebraic system in cone form.*

*Proof.* By Lemmas 3–6, each principal full cone (resp. principal cone) has a full cone generator (resp. cone generator) that is the first component of the unique solution of a strict algebraic system

$$y_i = \sum_{\pi \in Z} a_{i\pi} x_{i\pi} \pi, \quad 1 \le i \le n,$$

where $a_{i\pi} \in A$, $a_{iy_i} = 0$, $x_{i\pi} \in \Sigma$, $\pi \in Z$, $Z = \{\varepsilon\} \cup Y \cup Y^2 \cup Y^3$, $1 \le i \le n$. By Lemma 8 we can add to the $i$-th equation of this algebraic system the term $\$ y_i$, $1 \le i \le n$, and get a first component of the unique solution of the new system that is again a full cone generator (resp. cone generator) of the considered principal full cone (resp. principal cone).

Our theorem is proved by the observation that the new algebraic system is in cone form. □

**Corollary 28** *Let $\mathfrak{L} \subseteq A^{\mathrm{alg}}\{\{\Sigma_\infty^*\}\}$. Then $\mathfrak{L}$ is a principal full cone (resp. principal cone) iff it has a full cone generator (resp. cone generator) that is the first component of the unique solution of an algebraic system in cone form.*

Let $\mathfrak{S}$ be an algebraic system $y_i = p_i$, $1 \le i \le n$, in cone form, i.e.,

$$\begin{aligned} p_i = (p_i, x_i)x_i &+ \textstyle\sum_{1 \le j \le n} (p_i, x_{ij} y_j) x_{ij} y_j + \\ &\textstyle\sum_{1 \le j,k \le n} (p_i, x_{ijk} y_j y_k) x_{ijk} y_j y_k + \\ &\textstyle\sum_{1 \le j,k,m \le n} (p_i, x_{ijkm} y_j y_k y_m) x_{ijkm} y_j y_k y_m, \qquad 1 \le i \le n, \end{aligned} \tag{$*$}$$

where $x_i, x_{ij}, x_{ijk}, x_{ijkm} \in \Sigma$, $(p_i, x_{ii} y_i) = 1$, $1 \le i, j, k, m \le n$, and $(\{x_i \mid 1 \le i \le n\} \cup \{x_{ij} \mid 1 \le i, j \le n,\ j \ne i\} \cup \{x_{ijk} \mid 1 \le i, j, k \le n\} \cup \{x_{ijkm} \mid$

$1 \le i, j, k, m \le n\}) \cap \{x_{ii} \mid 1 \le i \le n\} = \emptyset$. Then, by definition, $\hat{\mathfrak{M}}(\mathfrak{S})$ is the collection of all the following algebraic systems written in matrix form:

$$\begin{aligned} Y_i = (p_i, x_i) \otimes \mu(x_i) + \textstyle\sum_{1\le j\le n}(p_i, x_{ij}y_j) \otimes \mu(x_{ij})Y_j + \\ \textstyle\sum_{1\le j,k\le n}(p_i, x_{ijk}y_jy_k) \otimes \mu(x_{ijk})Y_jY_k + \\ \textstyle\sum_{1\le j,k,m\le n}(p_i, x_{ijkm}) \otimes \mu(x_{ijkm})Y_jY_kY_m, \qquad 1 \le i \le n\,. \end{aligned} \tag{$**$}$$

Here $Y_i = (y^i_{jk})_{1\le j,k\le t}$, $1 \le i \le n$, is a $t \times t$-matrix of variables and $\mu$ is a rational representation defined by $\mu : \Sigma \to (A\langle \Sigma' \cup \varepsilon\rangle)^{t\times t}$, $t \ge 1$. Moreover, $\otimes$ denotes the Kronecker product (see Kuich, Salomaa [8]). Furthermore, $\mathfrak{M}(\mathfrak{S})$ is the collection of all algebraic systems defined above where the matrices $\mu(x_i), \mu(x_{ij}), \mu(x_{ijk}), \mu(x_{ijkm})$ satisfy the following additional condition:

> There exists an $s \ge 1$ such that each product of $s$ of these matrices is quasiregular. (Hence, if the matrix $M$ is such a product then $(M, \varepsilon) = 0$.)

The $y^1_{1t}$-component of the least solution of the algebraic system defined above is called the *principal* component of this least solution. We are now ready to characterize principal full cones (resp. principal cones) in $A^{\mathrm{alg}}\{\{\Sigma^*_\infty\}\}$ by the principal components of the least solutions of the algebraic systems in $\hat{\mathfrak{M}}(\mathfrak{S})$ (resp. $\mathfrak{M}(\mathfrak{S})$).

**Theorem 3.** *Let $r$ be the first component of the unique solution of an algebraic system $\mathfrak{S}$ in cone form. Then the principal full cone $\hat{\mathfrak{M}}(r)$ (resp. principal cone $\mathfrak{M}(r)$) coincides with the collection of all principal components of least solutions of the algebraic systems in $\hat{\mathfrak{M}}(\mathfrak{S})$ (resp. $\mathfrak{M}(\mathfrak{S})$).*

*Proof.* Let $\mathfrak{S}$ be given by the equations $(*)$. Define the algebraic principal cone type (see Kuich, Salomaa [8], page 281) $(\{y_1, \ldots, y_n\}, \Sigma, T, y_1)$ by

$$\begin{aligned} T_{y_i\pi,\pi} &= (p_i, x_i)x_i, \\ T_{y_i\pi,y_j\pi} &= (p_i, x_{ij}y_j)x_{ij}, \\ T_{y_i\pi,y_jy_k\pi} &= (p_i, x_{ijk}y_jy_k)x_{ijk}, \\ T_{y_i\pi,y_jy_ky_m\pi} &= (p_i, x_{ijkm}y_jy_ky_m)x_{ijkm}, \end{aligned}$$

$1 \le i, j, k, m \le n$, $\pi \in \{y_1, \ldots, y_n\}^*$. Then, by Theorem 10.7 of Kuich, Salomaa [8], the unique solution of $\mathfrak{S}$ is given by $((T^*)_{y_i,\varepsilon})_{1\le i\le n}$. Hence, $r = (T^*)_{y_1,\varepsilon}$.

Consider now the algebraic system $(**)$, where $\mu$ is a regulated rational representation. Since $((T^*)_{y_i,\varepsilon})_{1\le i\le n}$ is the unique solution of $(*)$, substitution of $\mu(T^*)_{y_i,\varepsilon}$ for $Y_i$, $1 \le i \le n$ shows that $(\mu(T^*)_{y_i,\varepsilon})_{1\le i\le n}$ is a solution of $(**)$. By Theorem 10.7 of Kuich, Salomaa [8], it is the unique solution of $(**)$.

We first prove the case of the principal cone. Assume that $s \in \mathfrak{M}(\mathfrak{S})$. Then, by Corollary 2, there exists a regulated rational representation $\mu' : \Sigma^* \to (A^{\mathrm{rat}}\langle\langle \Sigma'^* \rangle\rangle)^{t'\times t'}$, $t' \ge 2$, such that $s = \mu'(r)_{1,t'}$. Hence, $s = \mu'((T^*)_{y_1,\varepsilon})_{1,t'}$. Observe that $T$ is a loop type (see Kuich, Salomaa [8], page 226). Hence, by Theorem 11.46 of Kuich, Salomaa [8], there exists a regulated rational representation $\mu$ defined by $\mu : \Sigma \to (A\langle \Sigma' \cup \varepsilon\rangle)^{t\times t}$, $t \ge t'$, such that $((\mu'(T)^*)_{y_1,\varepsilon})_{1,t'} = ((\mu(T)^*)_{y_1,\varepsilon})_{1,t'}$. Since $t' \ge 2$, renaming yields $s = ((\mu(T)^*)_{y_1,\varepsilon})_{1,t}$ and $s$ is the principal solution of an algebraic system in $\mathfrak{M}(\mathfrak{S})$.

We now show the converse. Let $s$ be the principal component of the unique solution of (**). Then $s = (\mu(T^*)_{y_1,\varepsilon})_{1,t} = \mu(r)_{1,t}$, $t \geq 1$, and $s \in \mathfrak{M}(r)$.

We now consider the case of the principal full cone. Given a rational representation $\mu'' : \Sigma^* \to (A^{\mathrm{rat}}\langle\langle \Sigma'^* \rangle\rangle)^{t' \times t'}$, $t' \geq 1$, let $\mu'$ be the regulated rational representation $\mu' : \Sigma^* \to (A^{\mathrm{rat}}\langle\langle (\Sigma' \cup \{z\})^* \rangle\rangle)^{t' \times t'}$ defined by $\mu'(x) = (\mu''(x), \varepsilon)z + \sum_{w \in \Sigma'^+} (\mu''(x), w)w$, $x \in \Sigma$, where $z \in \Sigma_\infty - \Sigma'$. Let $h : (\Sigma' \cup \{z\})^* \to \Sigma'^*$ be the morphism defined by $h(x) = x$, $x \in \Sigma'$, and $h(z) = \varepsilon$. Then, for each $r \in A\langle\langle \Sigma^* \rangle\rangle$, we obtain $\mu''(r) = h(\mu'(r))$.

Assume now that $s \in \hat{\mathfrak{M}}(\mathfrak{S})$. Then there exists a regulated rational representation $\mu' : \Sigma^* \to (A^{\mathrm{rat}}\langle\langle (\Sigma' \cup \{z\})^* \rangle\rangle)^{t' \times t'}$ such that $s = h(\mu'(r)_{1,t'}) = h(\mu'((T^*)_{y_1,\varepsilon})_{1,t'})$. As above there exists now a regulated rational representation $\mu$ defined by $\mu : \Sigma \to (A\langle(\Sigma' \cup \{z\}) \cup \varepsilon\rangle)^{t \times t}$ such that $s = h((\mu(T)^*)_{y_1,\varepsilon})_{1,t}$.

By Theorems 7.10 and 7.4 of Kuich [7], $(h((\mu(T)^*)_{y_i,\varepsilon}))_{1 \leq i \leq n}$ is the least solution of (**). Hence, $s$ is the principal solution of an algebraic system in $\hat{\mathfrak{M}}(\mathfrak{S})$. Conversely, let $s$ be the principal component of the least solution of (**). Then by Theorems 7.10 and 7.4 of Kuich [7], $s = (\mu(T^*)_{y_1,\varepsilon})_{1,t} = \mu(r)_{1,t}$. Hence, $s \in \hat{\mathfrak{M}}(r)$. □

**Corollary 29** $\mathfrak{L} \subseteq A^{\mathrm{alg}}\{\{\Sigma_\infty^*\}\}$ *is a principal full cone (resp. principal cone) iff* $\mathfrak{L}$ *coincides with the collection of all principal components of least solutions of the algebraic systems in* $\hat{\mathfrak{M}}(\mathfrak{S})$ *(resp.* $\mathfrak{M}(\mathfrak{S})$*) for some algebraic system* $\mathfrak{S}$ *in cone form.*

For $A = \mathbb{B}$ this is a characterization of principal full cones and principal cones by context-free grammars.

*Example 1.* The *restricted one counter languages* form a principal full cone that is generated by the Łukasiewicz language (see Greibach [3], Berstel [1]). These restricted one counter languages are generalized by Kuich, Salomaa [8] to power series. Again these *restricted one counter power series* form a principal full cone and again it is generated by the solution of the algebraic system $y = x_1yy + x_2$. Clearly, this principal full cone is also generated by the solution of the algebraic system $y = x_1yy + xy + x_2$ in cone form. Hence, a power series is a restricted one counter power series iff it is the $y_{1t}$-component of the least solution of an algebraic system $Y = M_1YY + MY + M_2$. Here $Y$ is a $t \times t$-matrix of variables $y_{jk}$, $1 \leq j, k \leq t$ and $M, M_1, M_2 \in (A\langle \Sigma \cup \varepsilon \rangle)^{t \times t}$, $t \geq 1$. □

We now characterize full cones and cones of algebraic power series by algebraic systems in cone form.

**Theorem 4.** $\mathfrak{L} \subseteq A^{\mathrm{alg}}\{\{\Sigma_\infty^*\}\}$ *is a full cone (resp. cone) iff there exist algebraic systems* $\mathfrak{S}_i$, $i \in I$, *in cone form such that* $\mathfrak{L}$ *coincides with the collection of all principal components of least solutions of systems in* $\hat{\mathfrak{M}}(\mathfrak{S}_i)$ *(resp.* $\mathfrak{M}(\mathfrak{S}_i)$*),* $i \in I$.

*Proof.* We first consider the case of the full cone. Let $\mathfrak{L} = \hat{\mathfrak{M}}(\mathfrak{L}')$. Then $\mathfrak{L} = \bigcup_{r \in \mathfrak{L}'} \hat{\mathfrak{M}}(r)$. Hence, our theorem is proved by Corollary 12.

The proof for the case of the cone is analogous. □

## 3 Semi-AFPs and AFPs

Let $\mathfrak{L}$ be a family of power series. Then $\hat{\mathfrak{S}}(\mathfrak{L})$ (resp. $\mathfrak{S}(\mathfrak{L})$) is the smallest submonoid of $\langle A\{\{\Sigma_\infty^*\}\}, +, 0\rangle$ that is closed under rational transductions (resp. regulated rational transductions) and contains $\mathfrak{L}$. The notation $\hat{\mathfrak{F}}(\mathfrak{L})$ (resp. $\mathfrak{F}(\mathfrak{L})$) is used for the smallest rationally closed subsemiring of $A\{\{\Sigma_\infty^*\}\}$ that is closed under rational transductions (resp. regulated rational transductions) and contains $\mathfrak{L}$.

A family $\mathfrak{L}$ of power series is called a *full semi-AFP* or a *full AFP* (resp. *semi-AFP* or *AFP*) iff $\mathfrak{L} = \hat{\mathfrak{S}}(\mathfrak{L})$ or $\mathfrak{L} = \hat{\mathfrak{F}}(\mathfrak{L})$ (resp. $\mathfrak{L} = \mathfrak{S}(\mathfrak{L})$ or $\mathfrak{L} = \mathfrak{F}(\mathfrak{L})$). Here AFP stands for *"abstract family of power series"*.

If there exists an $\mathfrak{L}'$ such that $\mathfrak{L} = \hat{\mathfrak{M}}(\mathfrak{L}')$, $\mathfrak{L} = \hat{\mathfrak{S}}(\mathfrak{L}')$ or $\mathfrak{L} = \hat{\mathfrak{F}}(\mathfrak{L}')$ (resp. $\mathfrak{L} = \mathfrak{M}(\mathfrak{L}')$, $\mathfrak{L} = \mathfrak{S}(\mathfrak{L}')$ or $\mathfrak{L} = \mathfrak{F}(\mathfrak{L}')$) then $\mathfrak{L}'$ is called *full cone, full semi-AFP* or *full AFP generating family* (resp. *cone, semi-AFP* or *AFP generating family*). If $\mathfrak{L}$ is a (full) cone, a (full) semi-AFP or a (full) AFP then $\mathfrak{L}$ is always a generating family.

If $\mathfrak{L}'$ contains only one power series $r \in A\{\{\Sigma_\infty^*\}\}$ then $\mathfrak{L}$ is called *principal full semi-AFP* or *principal full AFP* (resp. *principal semi-AFP* or *principal AFP*). In this case $r$ is termed *full semi-AFP* or *full AFP generator* (resp. *semi-AFP* or *AFP generator*). In this case we write $\mathfrak{L} = \hat{\mathfrak{S}}(r)$ or $\mathfrak{L} = \hat{\mathfrak{F}}(r)$ (resp. $\mathfrak{L} = \mathfrak{S}(r)$ or $\mathfrak{L} = \mathfrak{F}(r)$). For $A = \mathbb{B}$, our operators $\hat{\mathfrak{S}}$, $\hat{\mathfrak{F}}$, $\mathfrak{S}$ and $\mathfrak{F}$ coincide with the operators $\hat{\mathcal{S}}$, $\hat{\mathcal{F}}$, $\mathcal{S}$ and $\mathcal{F}$ of Ginsburg [2], respectively.

We first consider full semi-AFPs and semi-AFPs. The next lemma is proved analoglously to Theorems 11.31 and 11.35 of Kuich, Salomaa [8] by help of Lemma 7.

**Lemma 31** *If $\mathfrak{L}'$ is a full semi-AFP (resp. semi-AFP) generating family of the full semi-AFP (resp. semi-AFP) $\mathfrak{L}$, then*

$$\mathfrak{L}'' = \{ \sum_{1 \le k \le m} \$^* ¢ r_k \mid r_k \in \mathfrak{L}',\ 1 \le k \le m,\ m \ge 1\}$$

*is a full cone (resp. cone) generating family of $\mathfrak{L}$.*

We now will characterize full semi-AFPs and semi-AFPs of algebraic power series by algebraic systems of a certain form.

Let $\mathfrak{S}_j$, $j \in J$, be algebraic systems in the cone form with equations $y_i^j = p_i^j$, $1 \le i \le n_j$. An algebraic system is called *semi-AFP system* iff its equations are

$$y_0 = ¢ y_1^{j_1} + \cdots + ¢ y_1^{j_m} + \$ y_0, \quad y_i^{j_k} = p_i^{j_k}, \qquad 1 \le i \le n_{j_k},$$

for some $j_1, \ldots, j_m \in J$, $m \ge 1$, and is denoted by $[\mathfrak{S}_{j_1}, \ldots, \mathfrak{S}_{j_m}]$. Let $r_j$ be the first component of the unique solution of $\mathfrak{S}_j$, $j \in J$. Then the $y_0$-component of the unique solution of the semi-AFP system $[\mathfrak{S}_{j_1}, \ldots, \mathfrak{S}_{j_m}]$ is given by $\sum_{1 \le k \le m} \$^* ¢ r_{j_k}$, $j_1, \ldots, j_m \in J$, $m \ge 1$. Observe that a semi-AFP system $[\mathfrak{S}_{j_1}, \ldots, \mathfrak{S}_{j_m}]$ is in the cone form. Hence, the collections $\hat{\mathfrak{M}}([\mathfrak{S}_{j_1}, \ldots, \mathfrak{S}_{j_m}])$

(resp. $\mathfrak{M}([\mathfrak{S}_{j_1}, \ldots, \mathfrak{S}_{j_m}])$) are defined. The equation $y_0 = ¢y_1^{j_1} + \cdots + ¢y_m^{j_m} + \$y_0$ gives rise to a matrix equation

$$Y_0 = \mu(¢)Y_1^{j_1} + \cdots + \mu(¢)Y_1^{j_m} + \mu(\$)Y_0\,,$$

where $Y_0 = (y_{jk}^0)_{1 \le j,k \le t}$ is a $t \times t$-matrix of variables and $\mu$ is a rational (resp. regulated rational) representation defined by $\mu : \Sigma \to (A\langle \Sigma' \cup \varepsilon \rangle)^{t \times t}$. By definition, the $y_{1t}^0$-component of the least solution of an algebraic system in $\hat{\mathfrak{M}}([\mathfrak{S}_{j_1}, \ldots, \mathfrak{S}_{j_m}])$ (resp. $\mathfrak{M}([\mathfrak{S}_{j_1}, \ldots, \mathfrak{S}_{j_m}])$) is called the *principal component* of this least solution.

**Theorem 5.** *Let $\mathfrak{S}_j$, $j \in J$, be algebraic systems in the cone form. Let $r_j$, $j \in J$, be the first component of the unique solution of $\mathfrak{S}_j$. Then the full semi-AFP $\hat{\mathfrak{S}}(\{r_j \mid j \in J\})$ (resp. semi-AFP $\mathfrak{S}(\{r_j \mid j \in J\})$) coincides with the collection of all principal components of the least solutions of the algebraic systems in $\hat{\mathfrak{M}}([\mathfrak{S}_{j_1}, \ldots, \mathfrak{S}_{j_m}])$ (resp. $\mathfrak{M}([\mathfrak{S}_{j_1}, \ldots, \mathfrak{S}_{j_m}])$) for all $j_1, \ldots, j_m \in J$, $m \ge 1$.*

*Proof.* We only proof the case of the semi-AFP. The proof for full semi-AFPs is analogous.

Lemma 14 implies

$$\mathfrak{S}(\{r_j \mid j \in J\}) = \mathfrak{M}(\{\sum_{1 \le k \le m} \$^* ¢ r_{j_k} \mid j_1, \ldots, j_m \in J,\ m \ge 1\})\,.$$

Since $\sum_{1 \le k \le m} \$^* ¢ r_{j_k}$ is the $y_0$-component of the unique solution of the semi-AFP system $[\mathfrak{S}_{j_1}, \ldots, \mathfrak{S}_{j_m}]$, $j_1, \ldots, j_m \in J$, $m \ge 1$, the collection of all principal components of the least solutions of the algebraic systems in $\mathfrak{M}([\mathfrak{S}_{j_1}, \ldots, \mathfrak{S}_{j_m}])$ coincides, by Theorem 11, with $\mathfrak{M}(\{\sum_{1 \le k \le m} \$^* ¢ r_{j_k} \mid j_1, \ldots, j_m \in J,\ m \ge 1\})$. The equality

$$\mathfrak{M}(\{\sum_{1 \le k \le m} \$^* ¢ r_{j_k} \mid j_1, \ldots, j_m \in J,\ m \ge 1\}) = \bigcup_{j_1, \ldots, j_m \in J,\ m \ge 1} \mathfrak{M}(\{\sum_{1 \le k \le m} \$^* ¢ r_{j_k}\})$$

proves our theorem. □

**Corollary 32** *$\mathfrak{L} \subseteq A^{\mathrm{alg}}\{\{\Sigma_\infty^*\}\}$ is a full semi-AFP (resp. semi-AFP) iff $\mathfrak{L}$ coincides with the collection of all principal components of the least solutions of the algebraic systems in $\hat{\mathfrak{M}}([\mathfrak{S}_{j_1}, \ldots, \mathfrak{S}_{j_m}])$ (resp. $\mathfrak{M}([\mathfrak{S}_{j_1}, \ldots, \mathfrak{S}_{j_m}])$), $j_1, \ldots, j_m \in J$, $m \ge 1$, for some algebraic systems $\mathfrak{S}_j$, $j \in J$, in the cone form.*

Since every principal full cone (resp. principal cone) is a full semi-AFP (resp. semi-AFP), the characterization of principal (full) cones in Section 2 is valid also for principal (full) semi-AFPs (see Kuich, Salomaa [8], Theorem 11.26, and Berstel [1], Example V.4.2).

We now consider full AFPs and AFPs. The next lemma is proved analoglously to Theorem 11.31 and Corollary 11.41 of Kuich, Salomaa [8] by help of Lemma 7.

**Lemma 33** *If $\mathfrak{L}'$ is a full AFP (resp. AFP) generating family of the full AFP (resp. AFP) $\mathfrak{L}$, then*

$$\mathfrak{L}'' = \{(\sum_{1\leq k\leq m} \$^*¢r_k)^*\$^*\# \mid r_k \in \mathfrak{L}',\ 1 \leq k \leq m,\ m \geq 1\}$$

*is a full cone (resp. cone) generating family of $\mathfrak{L}$.*

We now will characterize full AFPs and AFPs of algebraic power series by algebraic systems of a certain form.

Let $\mathfrak{S}_j$, $j \in J$, be algebraic systems in the cone form with equations $y_i^j = p_i^j$, $1 \leq i \leq n_j$. An algebraic system is called *AFP system* iff its equations are

$$y_0 = ¢y_1^{j_1}y_0 + \cdots + ¢y_1^{j_m}y_0 + \$y_0 + \#, \quad y_i^{j_k} = p_i^{j_k}, \qquad 1 \leq i \leq n_{j_k},$$

for some $j_1, \ldots, j_m \in J$, $m \geq 1$. This AFP system is denoted by $[\![\mathfrak{S}_{j_1}, \ldots, \mathfrak{S}_{j_m}]\!]$. Let $r_j$ be the first component of the unique solution of $\mathfrak{S}_j$, $j \in J$. Then the $y_0$-component of the unique solution of the AFP system $[\![\mathfrak{S}_{j_1}, \ldots, \mathfrak{S}_{j_m}]\!]$ is given by $(\sum_{1\leq k\leq m} \$^*¢r_{j_k})^*\$^*\#$, $j_1, \ldots, j_m \in J$, $m \geq 1$. Observe that an AFP system $[\![\mathfrak{S}_{j_1}, \ldots, \mathfrak{S}_{j_m}]\!]$ is in the cone form. Hence, the collections $\hat{\mathfrak{M}}([\![\mathfrak{S}_{j_1}, \ldots, \mathfrak{S}_{j_m}]\!])$ (resp. $\mathfrak{M}([\![\mathfrak{S}_{j_1}, \ldots, \mathfrak{S}_{j_m}]\!])$) are defined. The equation $y_0 = ¢y_1^{j_1}y_0 + \cdots + ¢y_m^{j_m}y_0 + \$y_0 + \#$ gives rise to a matrix equation

$$Y_0 = \mu(¢)Y_1^{j_1}Y_0 + \cdots + \mu(¢)Y_1^{j_m}Y_0 + \mu(\$)Y_0 + \mu(\#),$$

where $Y_0 = (y_{jk}^0)_{1\leq j,k\leq t}$ is a $t \times t$-matrix of variables and $\mu$ is a rational (resp. regulated rational) representation defined by $\mu : \Sigma \to (A\langle \Sigma' \cup \varepsilon \rangle)^{t\times t}$. By definition, the $y_{1t}^0$-component of the least solution of an algebraic system in $\hat{\mathfrak{M}}([\![\mathfrak{S}_{j_1}, \ldots, \mathfrak{S}_{j_m}]\!])$ (resp. $\mathfrak{M}([\![\mathfrak{S}_{j_1}, \ldots, \mathfrak{S}_{j_m}]\!])$) is called the *principal component* of this least solution.

**Theorem 6.** *Let $\mathfrak{S}_j$, $j \in J$, be algebraic systems in the cone form. Let $r_j$, $j \in J$, be the first component of the unique solution of $\mathfrak{S}_j$. Then the full AFP $\hat{\mathfrak{F}}(\{r_j \mid j \in J\})$ (resp. AFP $\mathfrak{F}(\{r_j \mid j \in J\})$) coincides with the collection of all principal components of the least solutions of the algebraic systems in $\hat{\mathfrak{M}}([\![\mathfrak{S}_{j_1}, \ldots, \mathfrak{S}_{j_m}]\!])$ (resp. $\mathfrak{M}([\![\mathfrak{S}_{j_1}, \ldots, \mathfrak{S}_{j_m}]\!])$) for all $j_1, \ldots, j_m \in J$, $m \geq 1$.*

*Proof.* Similar to the proof of Theorem 15; but use now Lemma 17. □

**Corollary 34** *$\mathfrak{L} \subseteq A^{\mathrm{alg}}\{\{\Sigma_\infty^*\}\}$ is a full AFP (resp. AFP) iff $\mathfrak{L}$ coincides with the collection of all principal components of the least solutions of the algebraic systems in $\hat{\mathfrak{M}}([\![\mathfrak{S}_{j_1}, \ldots, \mathfrak{S}_{j_m}]\!])$ (resp. $\mathfrak{M}([\![\mathfrak{S}_{j_1}, \ldots, \mathfrak{S}_{j_m}]\!])$), $j_1, \ldots, j_m \in J$, $m \geq 1$, for some algebraic systems $\mathfrak{S}_j$, $j \in J$, in the cone form.*

The last case to be considered is the case of principal full AFPs and principal AFPs. The next lemma is proved analogously to Theorem 11.42 of Kuich, Salomaa [8] by help of Lemma 7.

**Lemma 35** *If $r \in A\{\{\Sigma_\infty^*\}\}$ is a full AFP (resp. AFP) generator of the principal full AFP (resp. principal AFP) $\mathfrak{L}$ then $(\$^*¢r)^*\$^*\#$ is a full cone (resp. cone) generator of $\mathfrak{L}$.*

We will now characterize principal (full) AFPs of algebraic power series by algebraic systems of a certain form. Let $\mathfrak{S}$ be an algebraic system in the cone form with equations $y_i = p_i$, $1 \leq i \leq n$. An algebraic system is called *principal AFP-system (with basis $\mathfrak{S}$)* iff its equations are of the form

$$y_0 = ¢y_1y_0 + \$y_0 + \#, \qquad y_i = p_i, \quad 1 \leq i \leq n\,.$$

This principal AFP-system is denoted by $[\![\mathfrak{S}]\!]$. Observe that a principal AFP-system is a special case of an AFP-system. Hence, the next two results are corollaries of Theorem 18.

**Corollary 36** *Let $\mathfrak{S}$ be an algebraic system in the cone form. Let $r$ be the first component of the unique solution of $\mathfrak{S}$. Then the principal full AFP $\hat{\mathfrak{F}}(r)$ (resp. principal AFP $\mathfrak{F}(r)$) coincides with the collection of all principal components of the least solutions of the algebraic systems in $\hat{\mathfrak{M}}([\![\mathfrak{S}]\!])$ (resp. $\mathfrak{M}([\![\mathfrak{S}]\!])$).*

**Corollary 37** *$\mathfrak{L} \subseteq A^{\mathrm{alg}}\{\{\Sigma_\infty^*\}\}$ is a principal full AFP (resp. principal AFP) iff $\mathfrak{L}$ coincides with the collection of all principal components of the least solutions of the algebraic systems in $\hat{\mathfrak{M}}([\![\mathfrak{S}]\!])$ (resp. $\mathfrak{M}([\![\mathfrak{S}]\!])$) for some algebraic system $\mathfrak{S}$ in cone form.*

*Example 2.* The *one counter languages* form a principal full AFL that is generated by the Lukasiewicz language (see Greibach [3], Berstel [1]). These one counter languages are generalized by Kuich, Salomaa [8] to power series. These *one counter power series* form a principal full AFP that is again generated by the solution of the algebraic system $y = x_1yy + x_2$. Clearly, this principal full AFP is also generated by the solution of the algebraic system $y = x_1yy + xy + x_2$. Hence, a power series is a one counter power series iff it is the $z_{1t}$-component of the least solution of an algebraic system

$$\begin{aligned} Z &= M_3YZ + M_4Z + M_5\,, \\ Y &= M_1YY + MY + M_2\,. \end{aligned}$$

Here $Z, Y$ are $t \times t$-matrices of variables $z_{jk}, y_{jk}$, $1 \leq j, k \leq t$, respectively, and $M, M_1, M_2, M_3, M_4, M_5 \in (A\langle\Sigma \cup \varepsilon\rangle)^{t\times t}$, $t \geq 1$. □

## References

1. Berstel, J.: Transductions and Context-Free Languages. Teubner, 1979.
2. Ginsburg, S.: Algebraic and Automata-Theoretic Properties of Formal Languages. North-Holland, 1975.
3. Greibach, S.: An infinite hierarchy of context-free languages. J. Assoc. Comput. Mach. 16(1969) 91–106.

4. Karner, G., Kuich, W.: On certain closure operators defined by families of semiring morphisms. J. Algebra 217(1999) 1–20.
5. Kuich, W.: An algebraic characterization of some principal regulated rational cones. J. Comput. Systems Sci. 25(1982) 377–401.
6. Kuich, W.: Matrix systems and principal cones of algebraic power series. Theoret. Comput. Sci. 57(1988) 147–152.
7. Kuich, W.: Semirings and formal power series: Their relevance to formal languages and automata theory. In: Handbook of Formal Languages (Eds.: G. Rozenberg and A. Salomaa), Springer, 1997, Vol. 1, Chapter 9, 609–677.
8. Kuich, W., Salomaa, A.: Semirings, Automata, Languages. EATCS Monographs on Theoretical Computer Science, Vol. 5. Springer, 1986.
9. Nivat, M.: Transductions des langages de Chomsky. Ann. Inst. Fourier 18(1968) 339–455.

# New Small Universal Circular Post Machines

Manfred Kudlek[1] and Yurii Rogozhin[2]

[1] Fachbereich Informatik, Universität Hamburg,
Vogt-Kölln-Straße 20, D-22527 Hamburg, Germany
kudlek@informatik.uni-hamburg.de

[2] Institute of Mathematics and Computer Science, Academy of Sciences of Moldova,
Str. Academiei 5, MD-2028 Chişinău, Republica Moldova
rogozhin@math.md

**Abstract.** We consider a new kind of machines with a circular tape and moving in one direction only, so-called Circular Post machines. Using 2-tag systems we construct some new small universal machines of this kind.

## 1 Introduction

In 1956 Shannon [19] introduced the problem of constructing very small universal (deterministic) Turing machines. The underlying model of Turing machines is defined by instructions in form of quintuples $(\mathbf{p}, x, y, m, \mathbf{q})$ with the meaning that the machine is in state $\mathbf{p}$, reads symbol $x \in \Sigma$, overwrites it by $y$, moves by $m \in \{-1, 0, 1\}$, and goes into state $\mathbf{q}$. Another equivalent model is defined by quadruples $(\mathbf{p}, x, \alpha, \mathbf{q})$ where $\alpha \in \Sigma \cup \{-1, 0, 1\}$. This model is also equivalent to so called *Post* machines [12]. Whereas the quintuple model allows to construct equivalent machines with 2 states this is impossible for the quadruple model [1].

Let $\mathbf{UTM}(m, n)$ be a class of universal Turing machine with $m$ states and $n$ symbols. It was known that there exist universal Turing machines in the following classes: **UTM(22,2)**, **UTM(10,3)**, **UTM(7,4)**, **UTM(5,5)**, **UTM(4,6)**, **UTM(3,10)**, **UTM(2,18)** [17,18] and the classes **UTM(2,2)** [5], **UTM(2,3)**, and **UTM(3,2)** [13] are empty. Recently it was shown that there exist universal Turing machines in the classes **UTM(19,2)** [3] and **UTM(3,9)** [7], improving the previous results **UTM(22,2)** and **UTM(3,10)**. The last results reduce the number of classes $\mathbf{UTM}(m, n)$ with an unsettled emptiness problem (i.e if $\mathbf{UTM}(m, n)$ is empty) from 49 to 45.

We introduce (deterministic) Circular Post machines (**CPM**). These are similar to those presented in [2], with the difference that the head can move only in one direction on the circular tape. It is also possible to erase a cell or to insert a new one. We consider 5 variants of such machines, distinguished by the way a new cell is inserted. In [6] it has been shown that all variants are equivalent to each other, and also to Turing machines. We also show that for all variants there exist equivalent Circular Post machines with 2 symbols, as well as with 2 states.

To construct small universal Circular Post machines we use a method first presented in [10] (see also [16,17]). This method uses tag systems [9] which

R. Freivalds (Ed.): FCT 2001, LNCS 2138, pp. 217–226, 2001.

are special cases of monogenic Post Normal systems [15], namely of the form $s_i vu \to u\alpha_i$ with $v \in \Sigma^{k-1}$ and $k > 1$ a constant. In [10] it is also shown that 2-tag systems (i.e. $k = 2$) suffice to simulate all Turing machines, with halting only when encountering the special symbol $s_H$.

Since Circular Post machines are also monogenic Post Normal systems we expect to get a more natural simulation of tag systems and perhaps smaller universal machines.

Circular Post machines may be useful for studying the formal models of biocomputing where the DNA molecules are present in the form of a circular sequence [14].

In a previous article [6] it was shown that such machines can simulate all Turing machines, and some small universal circular Post machines have been constructed, namely in the classes **UPM0(7, 7)**, **UPM0(8, 6)**, **UPM0(11, 5)**, and **UPM0(13, 4)**. In this article we present some new results on circular Post machines, and more universal machines, namely **UPM0(4, 18)**, **UPM0(5, 11)**, **UPM0(6, 8)**, **UPM0(9, 5)** (improvement of **UPM0(11, 5)**), **UPM0(12, 4)** (improvement of **UPM0(13, 4)**), and **UPM0(18, 3)**. Here **UPMi(m, n)** denotes the class of universal circular Post machines of variant $i$ with $m$ states and $n$ symbols.

## 2 Definitions

Here we introduce some variants of circular Post machines.

**Definition 1.** *A Circular Post machine is a quintuple* $(\Sigma, Q, \mathbf{q}_0, \mathbf{q}_f, P)$ *with a finite alphabet* $\Sigma$ *where* 0 *is a the blank, a finite set of states* $Q$*, an initial state* $\mathbf{q}_0 \in Q$*, a terminal state* $\mathbf{q}_f \in Q$*, and a finite set of instructions of the forms*

$\mathbf{p}x \to \mathbf{q}$ *(erasing of the symbol read)*

$\mathbf{p}x \to y\mathbf{q}$ *(overwriting and moving to the right)*

$\mathbf{p}0 \to y\mathbf{q}0$ *(overwriting and creation of a blank)*

*The storage of such a machine is a circular tape, the read and write head moving only in one direction (to the right), and with the possibility to cut off a cell or to create and insert a new cell with a blank.*

This version is called variant 0 (**CPM0**). Note that by erasing symbols the circular tape might become empty. This can be interpreted that the machine, still in some state, stops. However, in the universal machines constructed later, this case will not occur.

In this article it will assumed that all machines are deterministic.

There are variants equivalent to such machines [6].

Variant **CPM1** : The instructions are of the form

$\mathbf{p}x \to \mathbf{q}$ $\quad\quad$ $\mathbf{p}x \to y\mathbf{q}$ $\quad\quad$ $\mathbf{p}x \to x\mathbf{q}0$ (0 blank)

Variant **CPM2** : The instructions are of the form
$\mathbf{p}x \rightarrow \mathbf{q}$ $\mathbf{p}x \rightarrow y\mathbf{q}$ $\mathbf{p}x \rightarrow y\mathbf{q}0$ (0 blank)
Variant **CPM3** : The instructions are of the form
$\mathbf{p}x \rightarrow \mathbf{q}$ $\mathbf{p}x \rightarrow y\mathbf{q}$ $\mathbf{p}x \rightarrow yz\mathbf{q}$.
Variant **CPM4** : The instructions are of the form
$\mathbf{p}x \rightarrow \mathbf{q}$ $\mathbf{p}x \rightarrow y\mathbf{q}$ $\mathbf{p}x \rightarrow yx\mathbf{q}$.

□

## 3 Basic Results

Here we present some new basic results on circular Post machines. The first results show that there are no universal circular Post machines with either only one state or one symbol, respectively.

**Theorem 1. CPM's** *with one symbol* 0 *simulate finite automata only.*

*Proof.* Since there is only one symbol the instructions are of the form $\mathbf{p}0 \rightarrow \mathbf{q}$, $\mathbf{p}0 \rightarrow \mathbf{q}0$, or $\mathbf{p}0 \rightarrow \mathbf{q}00$. These are essentially productions of Right Regular (Büchi) systems [21], and therefore generating only regular sets.

□

**Theorem 2. CPM's** *with one state have decidable word, emptiness, and finiteness problems.*

*Proof.* Since there is only one state, such a **CPM** can also be interpreted as an **EON** system (context-free normal system) with productions of the form $x \rightarrow \lambda$, $x \rightarrow y$, or $x \rightarrow yz$. Moreover, these systems are deterministic since there is only one productions for one symbol. For languages generated by such systems the following inclusions hold [4] :

**DON** ⊆ **EDON** ⊆ **EDTOL** , **ON** ⊆ **EON** ⊆ **ETOL**.

Therefore, the problems mentioned above, are decidable.

□

In the previous theorem **ON** denotes the class of languages generated by *context-free Post Normal systems*, i.e. rewriting systems with productions of the form $au \rightarrow u\alpha$. Such systems are called *deterministic*, denoted by **DON**, if for each symbol $a$ there is at most one production. The letter **E** denotes the fact that the generated language consists only of words from a subalphabet of terminal symbols. Finally, **EDTOL** and **ETOL** denote the classes of (deterministic) context-free *Lindenmayer* systems with tables and subalphabet of terminal symbols [20].

**Lemma 1.** *Each Circular Post machine can be simulated by another one with the circular tape always of length* $\geq 2$.

*Proof.* Encode any $w \in \Sigma^*$ by $AAw$ with $A \notin \Sigma$, and add the instructions $\mathbf{p}A \to A\mathbf{p}$.

□

In [6] was shown

**Proposition 1.** *For any* **CPMi** $(i = 2, 3, 4)$ *there exists an equivalent* **CPMi** *with 2 states (excluding the halting state).*

□

Here we prove it also for $i = 0, 1$.

**Theorem 3.** *For any* **CPMi** $(i = 0, 1)$ *there exists a simulating* **CPMi** *with 2 states.*

*Proof.* By Lemma 1 it suffices to consider **CPMi**'s with the tape always of length $\geq 2$. Only the third form of instruction has to be considered.

Simulation of $\mathbf{p}0 \to y\mathbf{q}0$.

Length 2 :

$$\mathbf{1}\tbinom{0}{p}s \to \tbinom{\bar0}{p}\mathbf{2}s \to \mathbf{2}\tbinom{\bar0}{p}\tilde s \to \tbinom{\bar0}{p}\mathbf{2}\tilde s \to \mathbf{1}\tbinom{\bar0}{p}\tbinom{\tilde s}{0} \to \tbinom{\bar0}{p-1}\mathbf{2}\tbinom{\tilde s}{0} \to \mathbf{1}\tbinom{\bar0}{p-1}\tbinom{\tilde s}{1} \to \cdots \to$$
$$\mathbf{1}\tbinom{\bar0}{0}\tbinom{\tilde s}{p} \to A\mathbf{2}\tbinom{\bar0}{0}\tbinom{\tilde s}{p} \to A\hat0\mathbf{1}\tbinom{\tilde s}{p} \to \tbinom{\hat s}{p}\mathbf{2}A\hat0 \to \tbinom{\hat s}{p}\tbinom{A}{0}\mathbf{1}\hat0 \to \mathbf{1}\tbinom{\hat s}{p}\tbinom{A}{0}\hat0 \to$$
$$\tbinom{\hat s}{p-1}\mathbf{2}\tbinom{A}{0}\hat0 \to \tbinom{\hat s}{p-1}\tbinom{A}{1}\mathbf{1}\hat0 \to \cdots \to \mathbf{1}\tbinom{\hat s}{0}\tbinom{A}{p}\hat0 \to s\mathbf{1}\tbinom{A}{p}\hat0 \to s\tbinom{\dot y}{q}\mathbf{2}\hat0 \to$$
$$\mathbf{1}s\tbinom{\dot y}{q}\tbinom{0}{0} \to s\mathbf{1}\tbinom{\dot y}{q}\tbinom{0}{0} \to s\tbinom{\dot y}{q-1}\mathbf{2}\tbinom{0}{0} \to s\tbinom{\dot y}{q-1}\tbinom{0}{1}\mathbf{1} \to$$
$$\mathbf{1}\tbinom{\dot y}{q-1}\tbinom{0}{0} \to \cdots \to \mathbf{1}s\tbinom{\dot y}{0}\tbinom{0}{q} \to s\mathbf{1}\tbinom{\dot y}{0}\tbinom{0}{q} \to sy\mathbf{1}\tbinom{0}{q}$$

Length 3 :

$$\mathbf{1}\tbinom{0}{p}st \to \tbinom{\bar0}{p}\mathbf{2}st \to \tbinom{\bar0}{p}\tilde s\mathbf{2}t \to \mathbf{2}\tbinom{\bar0}{p}\tilde s\tilde t \to \tbinom{\bar0}{p}\mathbf{2}\tilde s\tilde t \to \tbinom{\bar0}{p}\tbinom{\tilde s}{0}\mathbf{1}\tilde t \to \mathbf{1}\tbinom{\bar0}{p}\tbinom{\tilde s}{0}\tilde t \to$$
$$\tbinom{\bar0}{p-1}\mathbf{2}\tbinom{\tilde s}{0}\tilde t \to \tbinom{\bar0}{p-1}\tbinom{\tilde s}{1}\mathbf{1}\tilde t \to \mathbf{1}\tbinom{\bar0}{p-1}\tbinom{\tilde s}{1}\tilde t \to \cdots \to \mathbf{1}\tbinom{\bar0}{0}\tbinom{\tilde s}{p}\tilde t \to A\mathbf{2}\tbinom{\bar0}{0}\tbinom{\tilde s}{p}\tilde t \to$$
$$A\hat0\mathbf{1}\tbinom{\tilde s}{p}\tilde t \to A\hat0\tbinom{\hat s}{p}\mathbf{2}\tilde t \to \mathbf{1}A\hat0\tbinom{\hat s}{p}\tbinom{\tilde t}{0} \to A\mathbf{1}\hat0\tbinom{\hat s}{p}\tbinom{\tilde t}{0} \to A\hat0\mathbf{1}\tbinom{\hat s}{p}\tbinom{\tilde t}{0} \to$$
$$A\hat0\tbinom{\hat s}{p-1}\mathbf{2}\tbinom{\tilde t}{0} \to \mathbf{1}A\hat0\tbinom{\hat s}{p-1}\tbinom{\tilde t}{1} \to \cdots \to \mathbf{1}A\hat0\tbinom{\hat s}{0}\tbinom{\tilde t}{p} \to A\mathbf{1}\hat0\tbinom{\hat s}{0}\tbinom{\tilde t}{p} \to$$
$$A\hat0\mathbf{1}\tbinom{\hat s}{0}\tbinom{\tilde t}{p} \to A\hat0s\mathbf{1}\tbinom{\tilde t}{p} \to \mathbf{2}A\hat0s\tbinom{\hat t}{p} \to \tbinom{A}{0}\mathbf{1}\hat0s\tbinom{\hat t}{p} \to \tbinom{A}{0}\hat0\mathbf{1}s\tbinom{\hat t}{p} \to$$
$$\tbinom{A}{0}\hat0s\mathbf{1}\tbinom{\hat t}{p} \to \mathbf{1}\tbinom{\hat t}{p}\tbinom{A}{0}\hat0s \to \tbinom{\hat t}{p-1}\mathbf{2}\tbinom{A}{0}\hat0s \to \tbinom{\hat t}{p-1}\tbinom{A}{1}\mathbf{1}\hat0s \to \cdots \to$$
$$\mathbf{1}\tbinom{\hat t}{p-1}\tbinom{A}{1}\hat0s \to \cdots \to \mathbf{1}\tbinom{\hat t}{0}\tbinom{A}{p}\hat0s \to t\mathbf{1}\tbinom{A}{p}\hat0s \to t\tbinom{\dot y}{q}\mathbf{2}\hat0s \to$$
$$t\tbinom{\dot y}{q}\tbinom{0}{0}\mathbf{1}s \to \cdots \to \mathbf{1}\tbinom{\dot y}{q}\tbinom{0}{0}st \to \tbinom{\dot y}{q-1}\mathbf{2}\tbinom{0}{0}st \to \tbinom{\dot y}{q-1}\tbinom{0}{1}\mathbf{1}st \to \cdots \to$$
$$\mathbf{1}\tbinom{\dot y}{q-1}\tbinom{0}{1}st \to \cdots \to \mathbf{1}\tbinom{\dot y}{0}\tbinom{0}{q}st \to y\mathbf{1}\tbinom{0}{q}st$$

Length $> 3$ : as for length 3.

Instructions used

| | |
|---|---|
| $\mathbf{1}s \to s\mathbf{1}$ | $\mathbf{2}s \to \tilde{s}\mathbf{2}$ |
| $\mathbf{1}\tilde{s} \to \tilde{s}\mathbf{1}$ | $\mathbf{2}\tilde{s} \to \binom{\tilde{s}}{0}\mathbf{1}$ |
| $\mathbf{1}A \to A\mathbf{1}$ | $\mathbf{2}A \to \binom{A}{0}\mathbf{1}$ |
| $\mathbf{1}\hat{0} \to \hat{0}\mathbf{1}$ | $\mathbf{2}\hat{0} \to \binom{0}{0}\mathbf{1}$ |
| $\mathbf{1}\binom{0}{p} \to \binom{\bar{0}}{p}\mathbf{2}$ | $\mathbf{2}\binom{0}{q} \to \binom{0}{q+1}\mathbf{1}$ $0 \le q < n$ |
| $\mathbf{1}\binom{\bar{0}}{p} \to \binom{\bar{0}}{p-1}\mathbf{2}$ | $\mathbf{2}\binom{\bar{0}}{p} \to \binom{\breve{0}}{p}\mathbf{2}$ |
| $\mathbf{1}\binom{\tilde{s}}{p} \to \binom{\hat{s}}{p}\mathbf{2}$ | $\mathbf{2}\binom{\tilde{s}}{q} \to \binom{\tilde{s}}{q+1}\mathbf{1}$ |
| $\mathbf{1}\binom{\bar{0}}{0} \to A\mathbf{2}\binom{\bar{0}}{0}$ | $\mathbf{2}\binom{\bar{0}}{0} \to \bar{0}\mathbf{1}$ |
| $\mathbf{1}\hat{0} \to \hat{0}\mathbf{1}$ | $\mathbf{2}\hat{0} \to \binom{0}{0}\mathbf{1}$ |
| $\mathbf{1}\binom{\hat{s}}{p} \to \binom{\hat{s}}{p-1}\mathbf{2}$ | |
| $\mathbf{1}\binom{A}{p} \to \binom{\dot{y}}{q}\mathbf{2}$ | $\mathbf{2}\binom{A}{q} \to \binom{A}{q-1}\mathbf{1}$ |
| $\mathbf{1}\binom{\hat{s}}{0} \to s\mathbf{1}$ | |
| $\mathbf{1}\binom{\dot{y}}{q} \to \binom{\dot{y}}{q-1}$ | |
| $\mathbf{1}\binom{\dot{y}}{0} \to y\mathbf{1}$ | |

Simulation of $\mathbf{p}x \to y\mathbf{q}0$.

Replace $\binom{0}{r}$ by $\binom{x}{r}$, $\binom{\bar{0}}{r}$ by $\binom{\bar{x}}{r}$, $A$ by $X$, $\binom{A}{r}$ by $\binom{X}{r}$, as well as $\mathbf{1}\binom{\bar{0}}{0} \to A\mathbf{2}\binom{\bar{0}}{0}$ by $\mathbf{1}\binom{\bar{x}}{0} \to X\mathbf{2}\binom{\bar{0}}{0}$, and $\mathbf{1}\binom{A}{p} \to \binom{\dot{y}}{q}\mathbf{2}$ by $\mathbf{1}\binom{X}{p} \to \binom{\dot{y}}{q}\mathbf{2}$ in the previous part.

□

For completeness we also mention [6] :

**Proposition 2.** *To every* **CPMi** *($i = 0, 1, 2, 3, 4$) there exists an equivalent* **CPMi** *with 2 symbols.*

□

## 4 Universal Circular Post Machines

Here we present a number of new universal circular Post machines of variant 0. In the tables $y\mathbf{q}$ stands for $\mathbf{p}x \to y\mathbf{q}$, $y$ for $\mathbf{p}x \to y\mathbf{p}$, $\mathbf{q}$ for $\mathbf{p}x \to \mathbf{q}$, $y\mathbf{q}x$ for $\mathbf{p}x \to y\mathbf{q}x$, and **H** for the unique halting state.

**UPM0(4, 18)**

| | I | c | e | b | a | g | d | h | f | x | y | p | r | s | t | u | z | q |
|---|---|---|---|---|---|---|---|---|---|---|---|---|---|---|---|---|---|---|
| **1** | **2** | **3** | | b | a | g | d | | | | p**4**y | p | r | s | t | u | q | q |
| **2** | I | c | e | h**1** | f | x**1** | **H** | h | f | x | r**4**y | p | r | s | t | u | d | q |
| **3** | **3** | **4** | | b | a | g | d**1** | b | a | g | e | I | c | a | b | g | | |
| **4** | p | r | y | t | s | u | z | h | f | x | y | p | r | f**1** | h**2** | d**2** | g**3** | d**3** |

$N_1 = 1$, $N_{k+1} = N_k + m_k \quad (1 \leq k < n)$, $N_{n+1} = N_n + m_n - 1$
blank : $y$
Encoding of symbol $s_i$ : $I^{N_i}c$
Encoding of $\alpha_i$ : $a^{N_{i1}}b \cdots ba^{N_{im(i)}}g$, of $\alpha_n$ : $a^{N_{n1}}b \cdots a^{N_{nm(n)}}$
Separators : $e$, $d$

The initial configuration is

$$eba^{N_{11}}b \cdots ba^{N_{1m(1)}}g \cdots ga^{N_{n1}}b \cdots ba^{N_{nm(n)}}d\mathbf{1}I^{N_r}cI^{N_s}c \cdots cI^{N_w}c\,.$$

In the first stage $I^{N_r}$ is read, altogether $N_r$ $b$'s and $g$'s are changed into $h$'s and $x$'s, respectively, the $a$'s in between into $f$'s, and $I^{N_r}cI^{N_s}c$ is erased, giving $ehf^{N_{11}}h \cdots hf^{N_{1m(1)}}x \cdots xa^{N_{r1}}b \cdots ba^{N_{rm(r)}}g \cdots ba^{N_{nm(n)}}d\mathbf{4}I^{N_t}c \cdots cI^{N_w}c$.

In the second stage, starting with **4**, $I^{N_t}c \cdots cI^{N_w}c$ becomes $p^{N_t}r \cdots rp^{N_w}r$, $e$ is changed into $y$, $d$ into $z$, $a^{N_{r1}}b \cdots ba^{N_{rm(r)}}g$ into $s^{N_{r1}}t \cdots ts^{N_{rm(r)}}u$ and copied as $p^{N_{r1}}r \cdots rp^{N_{rm(r)}}r$ at the end of $p^{N_t}r \cdots rp^{N_w}r$.

In the third stage, starting with **4**, both parts of the tape are restored, and a new cycle may start.

The machine stops if in the first stage **2** encounters $d$.

□

**UPM0(5, 11)**

| | I | c | e | b | a | g | d | h | f | x | y |
|---|---|---|---|---|---|---|---|---|---|---|---|
| **1** | **2** | **3** | | b | a | g | d**2** | c | I | | c**3**y |
| **2** | I | c | e | h**3** | f | x**3** | | h | f | | h**4**y |
| **3** | **3** | **4** | | b | a | g | d**1** | b | a | g | e |
| **4** | f | h | y | h**1** | f**5** | g**3** | **H** | h | f | x | y |
| **5** | | | | b | a | g | d | h | f | | f**4**y |

$N_1 = 1$, $N_{k+1} = N_k + m_k \quad (1 \leq k \leq n)$
blank : $y$
Encoding of symbol $s_i$ : $I^{N_i}c$
Encoding of $\alpha_i$ : $a^{N_{i1}}b \cdots ba^{N_{im(i)}}g$
Separators : $e$, $d$

The initial configuration is

$$eba^{N_{11}}b \cdots ba^{N_{1m(1)}}g \cdots ga^{N_{n1}}b \cdots ba^{N_{nm(n)}}gd\mathbf{1}I^{N_r}cI^{N_s}c \cdots cI^{N_w}c\,.$$

In the first stage $I^{N_r}$ is read, altogether $N_r$ $b$'s and $g$'s are changed into $h$'s and $x$'s, respectively, the $a$'s in between into $f$'s, and $I^{N_r}cI^{N_s}c$ is erased, giving $ehf^{N_{11}}h \cdots hf^{N_{1m(1)}}x \cdots xa^{N_{r1}}b \cdots ba^{N_{rm(r)}}g \cdots ba^{N_{nm(n)}}d\mathbf{4}I^{N_t}c \cdots cI^{N_w}c$.

In the second stage, starting with **4**, $I^{N_t}c \cdots cI^{N_w}c$ becomes $f^{N_t}h \cdots hf^{N_w}h$, $e$ is changed into $y$, $a^{N_{r1}}b \cdots ba^{N_{rm(r)}}g$ into $f^{N_{r1}}h \cdots hf^{N_{rm(r)}}g$ and copied as $f^{N_{r1}}h \cdots hf^{N_{rm(r)}}h$ at the end of $f^{N_t}h \cdots hf^{N_w}h$.

In the third stage, starting with **3**, both parts of the tape are restored, and a new cycle may start.

The machine stops if in the first stage **4** encounters $d$.

□

**UPM0(6, 8)**

| | I | c | e | b | a | d | h | f |
|---|---|---|---|---|---|---|---|---|
| **1** | **2** | **3** | c**3**e | b**3** | a**6** | | c | I |
| **2** | I | c | e | h**3** | f | | h | f |
| **3** | **3** | **4** | e | b | a | d**1** | b | a |
| **4** | f | h | e | h**1** | f**5** | **H** | h | f |
| **5** | | | f**4**e | b | a | d | h | f |
| **6** | | | h**4**e | b | a | d | h | f |

$N_1 = 1,\ N_{k+1} = N_k + m_k + 1 \qquad (1 \le k \le n)$
blank : $e$
Encoding of symbol $s_i$ : $I^{N_i}c$
Encoding of $\alpha_i$ : $a^{N_{i1}}b \cdots ba^{N_{im(i)}}bb$
Separators : $e$, $d$

The initial configuration is

$$eba^{N_{11}}b \cdots ba^{N_{1m(1)}}bb \cdots bba^{N_{n1}}b \cdots ba^{N_{nm(n)}}bbd\mathbf{1}I^{N_r}cI^{N_s}c \cdots cI^{N_w}c\ .$$

In the first stage $I^{N_r}$ is read, $N_r$ $b$'s are changed into $h$s, the $a$s in between into $f$'s, and $I^{N_r}cI^{N_s}c$ is erased, giving
$ehf^{N_{11}}h \cdots hf^{N_{1m(1)}}hh \cdots hha^{N_{r1}}b \cdots ba^{N_{rm(r)}}g \cdots ba^{N_{nm(n)}}d\mathbf{4}I^{N_t}c \cdots cI^{N_w}c.$

In the second stage, starting with **4**, $I^{N_t}c \cdots cI^{N_w}c$ becomes $f^{N_t}h \cdots hf^{N_w}h$, the part $a^{N_{r1}}b \cdots ba^{N_{rm(r)}}bb$ is changed into $f^{N_{r1}}h \cdots hf^{N_{rm(r)}}hb$ and copied as $f^{N_{r1}}h \cdots hf^{N_{rm(r)}}h$ at the end of $f^{N_t}h \cdots hf^{N_w}h$.

In the third stage, starting with **3**, both parts of the tape are restored, and a new cycle may start.

The machine stops if in the first stage **4** encounters $d$.

□

**UPM0(9, 5)**

| | I | c | a | b | d |
|---|---|---|---|---|---|
| **1** | **2** | **4** | a**7** | b**4** | |
| **2** | I | c | I | c**3** | d |
| **3** | | c**1** | a | b | |
| **4** | **4** | **5** | a**8** | **H** | |
| **5** | I | c | I**6** | c**1** | d |
| **6** | I | c | a | b | I**5**d |
| **7** | I | c | a | b | c**5**d |
| **8** | I | c | a | b | c**9**d |
| **9** | a | b | a | b**3** | d |

$N_1 = 1,\ N_{k+1} = N_k + 2m_k - 1 \qquad (1 \le k \le n)$
blank : $d$
Encoding of symbol $s_i$ : $I^{N_i}c$
Encoding of $\alpha_i$ : $a^{N_{i1}}bb \cdots bba^{N_{im(i)}}b$
Separators : $d$, $bbc$

The initial configuration is

$$dba^{N_{11}}bb \cdots bba^{N_{1m(1)}}b \cdots ba^{N_{n1}}bb \cdots bba^{N_{nm(n)}}bbbc\mathbf{1}I^{N_r}cI^{N_s}c \cdots cI^{N_w}c\ .$$

In the first stage $I^{N_r}$ is read, $N_r$ $b$'s are changed into $c$'s, the $a$'s in between into $I$'s, and $I^{N_r}cI^{N_s}c$ is erased, giving
$dcI^{N_{11}}cc \cdots ccI^{N_{1m(1)}}c \cdots ca^{N_{r1}}bb \cdots bba^{N_{rm(r)}}b \cdots bba^{N_{nm(n)}}bbbc\mathbf{5}I^{N_t}c \cdots cI^{N_w}c.$

In the second stage, starting with **5**, the part $a^{N_{r1}}bb\cdots bba^{N_{rm(r)}}b$ becomes $I^{N_{r1}}cc\cdots ccI^{N_{rm(r)}}c$, and is copied behind $I^{N_t}c\cdots I^{N_w}c$ as $I^{N_{r1}}c\cdots cI^{N_{rm(r)}}c$.

In the third stage, starting with **9**, the instruction part of the tape is restored, and a new cycle may start.

The machine stops if in the first stage **5** encounters $bbb$.

□

**UPM0(12, 4)**

| | I | c | a | b |
|---|---|---|---|---|
| **1** | **2** | **5** | | |
| **2** | I | c | a**3** | b**1** |
| **3** | b | a**4** | a | b |
| **4** | I | c | | b**2** |
| **5** | **5** | **6** | | |
| **6** | I | c | a**7** | b**A** |
| **7** | b**8** | a**9** | a | b |
| **8** | I | c | I**6**a | b |
| **9** | I**0** | c**A** | a**B** | **H** |
| **0** | I | c | c**6**a | b |
| **A** | I | c | c**9**a | b**6** |
| **B** | | c**4** | c | I |

$N_1 = 1,\ N_{k+1} = N_k + m_k + 1 \qquad (1 \le k \le n)$
blank : $a$
Encoding of symbol $s_i$ : $I^{N_i}c$
Encoding of $\alpha_i$ : $I^{N_{i1}}c\cdots cI^{N_{im(i)}}cc$
Separators : $a$, $bcb$

The initial configuration is

$$acI^{N_{11}}c\cdots cI^{N_{1m(1)}}cc\cdots ccI^{N_{n1}}c\cdots cI^{N_{nm(n)}}ccbcb\mathbf{1}I^{N_r}cI^{N_s}c\cdots cI^{N_w}c\ .$$

In the first stage $I^{N_r}$ is read, $N_r$ $c$'s are changed into $a$'s, the $I$'s in between into $b$'s, and $I^{N_r}cI^{N_s}c$ is erased, giving
$aab^{N_{11}}a\cdots ab^{N_{1m(1)}}aa\cdots aaI^{N_{r1}}c\cdots cI^{N_{rm(r)}}cc\cdots ca^{N_{nm(n)}}ccbcb\mathbf{5}I^{N_t}c\cdots cI^{N_w}c$.

In the second stage, starting with **6**, the part $I^{N_{r1}}c\cdots ca^{N_{rm(r)}}cc$ becomes $a^{N_{r1}}b\cdots ba^{N_{rm(r)}}ac$, and is copied behind $I^{N_t}c\cdots I^{N_w}c$ as $I^{N_{r1}}c\cdots cI^{N_{rm(r)}}c$.

In the third stage, starting with **9**, the instruction part of the tape is restored, and a new cycle may start.

The machine stops if in the first stage **7** encounters $bcb$.

□

**UPM0(18, 3)**

| | I | c | a |
|---|---|---|---|
| **1** | **2** | **7** | |
| **2** | I | c | a**3** |
| **3** | **H** | c**4** | I |
| **4** | I**6** | c**5** | I |
| **5** | I**1** | c | a |
| **6** | I**C** | c**3** | I**D** |
| **7** | **7** | **8** | a**K** |
| **8** | I | c | a**9** |
| **9** | | c**6** | I**0** |
| **0** | I**A** | c | a |
| **A** | I | c | I**8**a |
| **B** | I**E** | c | a |
| **C** | I | c**9** | |
| **D** | | c**B** | a**F** |
| **E** | I | c | c**8**a |
| **F** | I**G** | c | a |
| **G** | I | c | c**7**a |
| **K** | a | c | a**5** |

$N_1 = 1,\ N_{k+1} = N_k + m_k \qquad (1 \le k \le n)$
blank : $a$
Encoding of symbol $s_i$ : $I^{N_i}c$
Encoding of $\alpha_i$ : $I^{N_{i1}}cac\cdots cacI^{N_{im(i)}}caac$
Separators : $a$, $cc$

The initial configuration is

$$acaca^{N_{11}}cac\cdots caca^{N_{1m(1)}}caac\cdots caaca^{N_{n1}}cac\cdots caca^{N_{nm(n)}}caacccI\mathbf{1}I^{N_r}cI^{N_s}c \cdots cI^{N_w}c\ .$$

In the first stage $I^{N_r}$ is read, altogether $N_r$ $cac$'s and $caac$'s are changed into $cIc$'s and $cIIc$'s, respectively, the $I$'s in between into $a$'s, and $I^{N_r}cI^{N_s}c$ is erased, giving
$acIcI^{N_{11}}cIc\cdots cIcI^{N_{1m(1)}}cIIc\cdots cIIca^{N_{r1}}cac\cdots caca^{N_{rm(r)}}caac\cdots I^{N_{n1}}b \cdots cac^{N_{nm(n)}}caacccI\mathbf{8}I^{N_t}c\cdots cI^{N_w}c.$

In the second stage, starting with **8**, the part $a^{N_{r1}}cac\cdots caca^{N_{rm(r)}}caac$ is changed into $I^{N_{r1}}cIc\cdots cIcI^{N_{rm(r)}}cIac$, and copied to the end of $I^{N_t}c\cdots I^{N_w}c$ as $I^{N_{r1}}c\cdots cI^{N_{rm(r)}}c$.

In the third stage, starting with **7**, the instruction part of the tape is restored, and a new cycle may start.

The machine stops if in the second stage **9** encounters $ccI$.

□

**Acknowledgement.** The authors acknowledge the very helpful contribution of *INTAS project* 97-1259 for enhancing their cooperation, giving the best conditions for producing the present result.

## References


1. Anderaa, S., Fischer, P. : The Solvability of the Halting Problem for 2-state Post Machines. JACM **14** no. 4 (1967) 677–682.
2. Arbib, M. A. : Theories of Abstract Automata. Prentice Hall, Englewood Cliffs, 1969.
3. Baiocchi, C. : Three Small Universal Turing Machines. LNCS **2055** (2001), Accepted for MCU'2001, to appear.
4. Kudlek, M. : Context Free Normal Systems. Proceedings MFCS'79, LNCS **74** (1979) 346–353.
5. Kudlek, M. : Small deterministic Turing machines. TCS **168-2** (1996) 241–255.
6. Kudlek, M., Rogozhin, Yu. : Small Universal Circular Post Machines. Computer Science Journal of Moldova, **9**, no. 10 (2001), Accepted for MCU'2001, to appear.
7. Kudlek, M., Rogozhin, Yu. : A New Small Universal Turing Machine, submitted (2001).
8. Margenstern, M. : Frontier between decidability and undecidability: a survey. TCS **231-2** (2000) 217–251.
9. Minsky, M. L. : Recursive Unsolvability of Posts Problem of "tag" and Other Topics in the Theory of Turing Machines. Annals of Math. **74** (1961) 437–454.
10. Minsky, M. L. : Size and Structure of universal Turing Machines Using Tag Systems. In *Recursive Function Theory, Symposia in Pure Mathematics, AMS* **5** (1962) 229–238.
11. Minsky, M. L. : Computation: Finite and Infinite Machines. Prentice Hall International, London, 1972.
12. Nelson, R. J. : Introduction to Automata. John Wiley & Sons, New York, 1968.
13. Pavlotskaya, L. : Sufficient conditions for halting problem decidability of Turing machines. Avtomaty i mashiny (Problemi kibernetiki), Moskva, Nauka **33** (1978) 91–118 (in Russian).
14. Păun, G., Rozenberg, G., Salomaa, A. : DNA Computing: New Computing Paradigms. Springer, 1998.
15. Post, E. : Formal Reduction of the General Combinatorial Decision Problem. Amer. Journ. Math. **65** (1943) 197–215.
16. Robinson, R. M. : Minsky's Small Universal Turing Machine. Intern. Journ. of Math. **2** no. 5 (1991) 551–562.
17. Rogozhin, Yu. V. : Small Universal Turing Machines. TCS **168-2** (1996) 215–240.
18. Rogozhin, Yu. : A Universal Turing Machine with 22 States and 2 Symbols. Romanian Journal of Information Science and Technology **1** no. 3 (1998) 259–265.
19. Shannon, C. E. : A Universal Turing Machine with Two Internal States. In *Automata Studies*, Ann. Math. Stud. **34**, Princeton Uni. Press (1956) 157–165.
20. Rozenberg, G., Salomaa, A. : The Mathematical Theory of L Systems. Academic Press, New York, 1980.
21. Salomaa, A. : Theory of Automata. Pergamon Press, Oxford, 1969.

# Divisibility Monoids: Presentation, Word Problem, and Rational Languages

Dietrich Kuske

Department of Mathematics and Computer Science
University of Leicester
LEICESTER
LE1 7RH, UK
D.Kuske@mcs.le.ac.uk

**Abstract.** We present three results on divisibility monoids. These divisibility monoids were introduced in [11] as an algebraic generalization of Mazurkiewicz trace monoids. (1) We give a decidable class of presentations that gives rise precisely to all divisibility monoids. (2) We show that any divisibility monoid is an automatic monoid [5]. This implies that its word problem is solvable in quadratic time. (3) We investigate when a divisibility monoid satisfies Kleene's Theorem. It turns out that this is the case iff the divisibility monoid is a rational monoid [25] iff it is width-bounded. The two latter results rest on a normal form for the elements of a divisibility monoid that generalizes the Foata normal form known from the theory of Mazurkiewicz traces.

## 1 Introduction

Different mathematical structures have been proposed to model the behavior of concurrent systems, among them process algebras, sets of partially ordered sets, Petri nets etc. One particular approach in this line of research is that introduced by Mazurkiewicz [21], now known as trace monoids. Since Mazurkiewicz's observation that trace monoids can be used to model the behavior of 1-safe Petri nets, much research has dealt with the topic, see [9] for a collection of surveys. Despite their success, certain limitations of trace monoids have been observed. Therefore, several generalizations were considered. One of these generalizations are divisibility monoids [12].[1] In this paper, we describe the relation to other classes of monoids known in theoretical computer science, namely to automatic [17], rational [25] and Kleene monoids. As corollaries, we obtain a quadratic lower bound for the complexity of the word problem and a characterization of those divisibility monoids that satisfy Kleene's theorem.

Mazurkiewicz traces model the sequential behavior of a parallel system in which the order of two independent actions is regarded as irrelevant. One considers pairs $(\Sigma, I)$ where $\Sigma$ is the set of actions, and $I$ is a symmetric and

[1] Similar monoids have been considered in [7,6] where they are related to braid and other groups traditionally of interest in mathematics.

R. Freivalds (Ed.): FCT 2001, LNCS 2138, pp. 227–239, 2001.

irreflexive binary relation on $\Sigma$ describing the independence of two actions. The trace monoid or free partially commutative monoid $\mathbb{M}(\Sigma, I)$ is then defined as the quotient $\Sigma^\star/\!\sim$ where $\sim$ is the congruence on the free monoid $\Sigma^\star$ generated by all equations $ab \sim ba$ with $(a,b) \in I$. Thus, originally, trace monoids are defined by a decidable class of presentations. An algebraic characterization of trace monoids was given only later by Duboc [13]. Divisibility monoids are a lattice theoretically easy generalization of these algebraic conditions. Our first result (Theorem 1) describes a decidable class of presentations that give rise precisely to all divisibility monoids. Since the canonical presentations for trace monoids belong to this class, our result can be seen as an extension of Duboc's characterization to the realm of divisibility monoids.

For trace monoids, the word problem can be solved in linear time [8]. From our presentation result, an exponential algorithm for the word problem in divisibility monoids follows immediately. But we show that one can do much better: The work on automatic groups [15] has been generalized to the realm of semigroups. Intuitively, a semigroup is automatic if it admits a presentation such that the equality can be decided by an automaton and such that the multiplication by generators can be performed by an automaton [17,5]. In particular, Campbell et al. [5] showed that the word problem for any automatic semigroup is solvable in quadratic time. Theorem 2 shows that any divisibility monoid is an automatic semigroup. Hence, we can infer from the result of Campbell et al. that the word problem for any divisibility monoid can be solved in quadratic time. We do not know whether this result can be improved, but we have serious doubts that a linear time algorithm exists. Kleene [18] showed that in a free finitely generated monoid the recognizable languages are precisely the rational ones. It is known that in general this is false, but Kleene's result was generalized in several directions, e.g. to formal power series by Schützenberger [26], to infinite words by Büchi [4], and to rational monoids by Sakarovitch [25]. In all these cases, the notions of recognizability and of rationality were shown to coincide. This is not the case in trace monoids any more. Even worse, in any trace monoid (which is not a free monoid), there exist rational languages that are not recognizable. But a precise description of the recognizable languages in trace monoids using c-rational expressions could be given by Ochmański [22]. A further generalization of Kleene's and Ochmański's results to concurrency monoids was given in [10]. The proofs by Ochmański as well as by Droste heavily used the internal structure of the elements of the corresponding monoid. The original motivation for the consideration of divisibility monoids in [12] was the search for an algebraic version of these proofs. We succeeded showing that in a divisibility monoid with finitely many residuum functions, the recognizable languages coincide with the (m)c-rational ones (cf. [12] for precise definitions of these terms). Thus, two main directions of generalization of Kleene's Theorem in monoids are represented by Sakarovitch's rational monoids and by trace monoids. Since the only trace monoids that satisfy Kleene's Theorem are free monoids, these two directions are "orthogonal", i.e. the intersection of the classes of monoids in consideration is the set of free monoids. In [12] we already remarked that there are divisibility monoids that satisfy Kleene's Theorem and are not free. Thus, our further extension of Ochmański's result to divisibility monoids [12] is not "orthogonal" any more. In this paper, we describe the class of divisibility monoids that satisfy Kleene's Theorem. Essentially, Theorem 3 says that a divisibility monoid satisfies Kleene's Theorem if and only if it is rational if and only if it is width-bounded. Thus, in the context of divisibility monoids, the classes of Kleene monoids and rational monoids coincide which is not the case in general [23], and we give an internal characterization of these monoids.

Our proofs that any divisibility monoid is automatic as well as the proof that any divisibility monoid satisfying Kleene's Theorem is rational, use a normal form for the elements of a divisibility monoid. This normal form generalizes the Foata normal form from trace theory. It is studied in Section 3. Furthermore, we rely on the results by Campbell et al. from [5] on automatic semigroups, by Sakarovitch from [25] on rational monoids, on basic properties of distributive lattices that can be found in [2] and on Ramsey's Theorem [24].

## 2 Basic Definitions

### 2.1 Order and Monoid Theoretic Definitions

Let $(P, \leq)$ be a partially ordered set and $y \in P$. By $\downarrow y$, we denote the *principal ideal* generated by $y$, i.e. the set $\{x \in P \mid x \leq y\}$. For $x, y \in P$, we write $x \longrightarrow\!\!\!< y$ if $x < y$ and there is no element properly between $x$ and $y$. A set $A \subseteq P$ is an *antichain* if any two distinct elements of $A$ are incomparable. The *width* of a partially ordered set $(P, \leq)$ is the supremum over all natural numbers $n$ such that there exists an antichain $A \subseteq P$ with $n = |A|$. The width of $P$ is denoted by $w(P, \leq)$. If the width of $(P, \leq)$ is finite, any antichain in $P$ has at most $w(P, \leq)$ elements. If the width is infinite, $(P, \leq)$ contains finite antichains of arbitrary size. In particular, the width of a finite partially ordered set is always finite. A *chain* is a set $C \subseteq P$ whose elements are mutually comparable. For $x \in P$, the *height* $h(x)$ in the poset $(P, \leq)$ is the maximal size of a chain all of whose elements are properly below $x$. The *length* of the poset $(P, \leq)$ is the maximal height of its elements.

A *lattice* is a partially ordered set $(P, \leq)$ where any two elements $x, y \in P$ admit a supremum $x \vee y$ and an infimum $x \wedge y$, i.e. a least upper and a largest lower bound. The lattice $(P, \leq)$ is *distributive* if for any $x, y, z \in P$ we have $x \vee (y \wedge z) = (x \vee y) \wedge (x \vee z)$. For many results concerning lattices see [2]. In particular, any two maximal chains in a finite distributive lattice have the same size.

A triple $(M, \cdot, 1)$ is a *monoid* if $M$ is a set, $\cdot : M \times M \to M$ is an associative operation and $1 \in M$ is the *unit element* satisfying $1 \cdot x = x \cdot 1 = x$ for any $x \in M$. Let $(M, \cdot, 1)$ be a monoid and $X \subseteq M$. Then, by $\langle X \rangle$ we denote the submonoid of $M$ generated by $X$, i.e. the intersection of all submonoids of $M$ that contain $X$. If $\langle X \rangle = M$, $X$ is a *set of generators of* $M$. The monoid $M$ is *finitely generated* if it has a finite set of generators. Let $X$ be a set. Then $X^\star$

denotes the set of all words over $X$. With the usual concatenation of words and the empty word as unit element, this becomes a *free monoid generated by* $X$.

A subset $L$ of a monoid $M$ is *rational* if it can be constructed from the finite subsets of $M$ by the operations concatenation $\cdot$, union $\cup$ and iteration $\langle . \rangle$ (also known as Kleene-star). A set $L \subseteq M$ is *recognizable* iff there exists a finite monoid $(S, \cdot, 1)$ and a homomorphism $\eta : M \to S$ such that $L = \eta^{-1}\eta(L)$. Recognizable sets are sometimes called recognizable *languages.* In general, the sets of recognizable and of rational subsets of a monoid are different and even incomparable. If the notions of recognizability and rationality coincide in a monoid $M$, then the monoid $M$ is said to be a *Kleene monoid.* Kleene showed that this holds in free finitely generated monoids:

**Kleene's Theorem [18].** *Let $X$ be a finite set. Then a set $L \subseteq X^\star$ is rational iff it is recognizable.*

Let $X$ be a set and $\beta : X^\star \to X^\star$ a function which is not necessarily an homomorphism. Let furthermore $M$ be a monoid. The function $\beta$ is a *normal form function for $M$* if it is idempotent, the kernel $\ker(\beta) = \{(v, w) \in X^\star \times X^\star \mid \beta(v) = \beta(w)\}$ is a monoid congruence, and $X^\star/\ker(\beta) \cong M$. A monoid $M$ is *rational* [25] if there exist a finite alphabet $X$ and a normal form function $\beta : X^\star \to X^\star$ for $M$ such that $\{(v, \beta(v)) \mid v \in X^\star\}$ is a rational subset of the monoid $X^\star \times X^\star$.

In [25,23], the authors are particularly interested in closure properties of the class of rational monoids. Sakarovitch [25, Theorem 4.1] also shows that any rational monoid is a Kleene monoid (there are Kleene monoids which are not rational, see [23] for an example).

### 2.2 Divisibility Monoids

Let $M = (M, \cdot, 1)$ be a monoid. We call $M$ *cancellative* if $x \cdot y \cdot z = x \cdot y' \cdot z$ implies $y = y'$ for any $x, y, y', z \in M$. This in particular ensures that $M$ does not contain a zero element (i.e. an element $z$ such that $z \cdot x = x \cdot z = z$ for any $x \in M$). For $x, z \in M$, *$x$ is a left divisor of $z$* (denoted $x \leq z$) if there is $y \in M$ such that $x \cdot y = z$. In general, the relation $\leq$ is not antisymmetric, but reflexive and transitive, i.e., a preorder.

**Lemma 1.** *Let $(M, \cdot, 1)$ be a cancellative monoid and $a \in M$. Then the mapping $a : (M, \leq) \to (a \cdot M, \leq)$ defined by $a(x) := a \cdot x$ is a preorder isomorphism.*

Let $\Sigma := (M \setminus \{1\}) \setminus (M \setminus \{1\})^2$. The set $\Sigma$ consists of those elements of $M$ that do not have a proper divisor, its elements are called *irreducible.* Note that $\Sigma$ is contained in any set generating $M$.

**Definition 1.** *A monoid $(M, \cdot, 1)$ is called a* left divisibility monoid *provided the following hold*

1. *$M$ is cancellative and its irreducible elements form a finite set of generators of $M$,*

*2.* $x \wedge y$ *exists for any* $x, y \in M$*, and*
*3.* $(\downarrow x, \leq)$ *is a finite distributive lattice for any* $x \in M$.

*A left divisibility monoid is* width-bounded *if there exists a natural number* $n \in \mathbb{N}$ *such that* $w(\downarrow x, \leq) \leq n$ *for any* $x \in M$*, i.e. if the widths of the distributive lattices* $\downarrow x$ *are uniformly bounded.*

Note that by the third axiom the prefix relation in a left divisibility monoid is a partial order relation. Since, by Lemma 1, $y \leq z$ implies $x \cdot y \leq x \cdot z$, a left divisibility monoid is a left ordered monoid. Ordered monoids where the order relation is the intersection of the prefix and the suffix relation were investigated e.g. in [2] under the name "divisibility monoid". Despite that we require more than just the fact that $(M, \cdot, \leq)$ be a left ordered monoid, this might explain why we call the monoids defined above "left divisibility monoid". Since Birkhoff's divisibility monoids will not appear in our investigations any more, we will simply speak of "divisibility monoids" as an abbreviation for "left divisibility monoid". "Divisibility semigroups" are investigated in several papers by Bosbach, e.g. [3]. Despite the similarity of the name, we baptized our monoids independently and there seems to be no intimate relation between Bosbach's divisibility semigroups and our divisibility monoids.

Let $(M, \cdot, 1)$ be a divisibility monoid and let $x, y \in M$ with $x \cdot y = 1$. Then $1 \leq x \leq 1$ implies $x = 1$ since by the third axiom $\leq$ is a partial order. Hence we have $y = x \cdot y = 1$, i.e. there are no proper divisors of the unit element.

By the second requirement on divisibility monoids, the partial order $(M, \leq)$ can be seen as the set of compacts of a Scott-domain. This in particular ensures that any set $A \subseteq M$ that is bounded above in $(M, \leq)$ has a supremum in this partial order. Since, in addition, any element of $M$ dominates a finite[2] distributive lattice, $(M, \leq)$ is even the set of compacts of a dI-domain (cf. [1, 27]). Thus, we have in particular $(x \vee y) \wedge z = (x \wedge z) \vee (y \wedge z)$ whenever the left hand side is defined.

*Example 1.* Using standard results from trace theory [21,9], it is easily seen that any (finitely generated) trace monoid is a divisibility monoid. Now let $\Sigma = \{a, b, c, d\}$ be an alphabet. Let $\sim^1$ be the least congruence on the free monoid $\Sigma^\star$ that identifies the words *ab* and *cd*. In a trace monoid, the equality $ab = cd$ implies $\{a, b\} = \{c, d\}$ for any generators $a, b, c, d$. Hence the quotient monoid $\Sigma^\star/{\sim^1}$ is not a trace monoid. But, as we will see later, it is a divisibility monoid. Similarly, let $\sim^2$ identify *aa* and *bb*. Again, $\Sigma^\star/{\sim^2}$ is no trace but a divisibility monoid. Finally, identifying *aa* and *bc* again results in a divisibility monoid as Theorem 1 below shows.

Since a divisibility monoid $(M, \cdot, 1)$ is generated by the set $\Sigma$ of its irreducible elements, there is a natural epimorphism nat : $\Sigma^\star \to M$. Let $|x|$ denote the length of the lattice $\downarrow x$ which equals the size of any maximal chain deduced by

[2] We just remark that the requirement (in the definition of a divisibility monoid) on the lattices $\downarrow x$ to be finite is not really necessary since it already follows from the other stipulations [12].

1. It is easily checked that $x \multimap y$ iff there exists $a \in \Sigma$ with $x \cdot \mathrm{nat}(a) = y$ for any $x, y \in M$. Hence the maximal chains in $\downarrow x$ correspond to the words $w \in \Sigma^\star$ with $\mathrm{nat}(w) = x$. This implies that any two such words have the same length which equals $|x|$.

Since nat is an epimorphism, there is a congruence $\sim$ on the free monoid $\Sigma^\star$ such that $\Sigma^\star/\!\sim$ is isomorphic to the divisibility monoid $(M, \cdot)$. Hence, we can reformulate the stipulations in Definition 1 into requirements on the congruence $\sim$. E.g. the property of $M$ to be cancellative would be reformulated to "for any words $u, v, w \in \Sigma^\star$ with $uv \sim uw$ or $vu \sim wu$, we get $v \sim w$". Although such a reformulation might look more effective than the original definition, it is not finite since it makes statements on words of arbitrary length. We now show that there is a decidable class of finite representations that gives rise precisely to divisibility monoids.

In [12, Lemma 3.4], we showed that the congruence $\sim$ is generated by equations of the from $ab \sim cd$ for $a, b, c, d \in \Sigma$. So let $\Sigma$ be a finite set and let $\sim$ be a congruence on the free monoid $\Sigma^\star$ that is generated by all equivalences $ab \sim cd$ for $a, b, c, d \in \Sigma$. We aim at a characterization of the fact that $M = \Sigma^\star/\!\sim$ is a divisibility monoid. In this monoid, the elements from $\Sigma$ (more precisely, the equivalence classes $[a]$ for $a \in \Sigma$) are the irreducible elements since $\sim$ is length preserving. Hence $M$ is finitely generated by its irreducible elements. To ensure that $M$ is cancellative, we need at least that the following holds for any elements $a, b, c, b', c' \in \Sigma$:

$$abc \sim ab'c' \text{ or } bca \sim b'c'a \text{ implies } bc \sim b'c'. \tag{2.1}$$

Note that (2.1) requires the cancellation for words of length 3, only. In the same spirit, we now weaken the second requirement concerning the existence of infima: Suppose $b \neq c$, but $ab \sim a'b'$ and $ac \sim a'c'$ for some $a, b, c, a', b', c' \in \Sigma$. Then one can infer from (2.1) that $ab \not\sim ac$. Since $\sim$ is length preserving, $[a]$ and $[a']$ are maximal lower bounds of $[ab]$ and $[ac]$. Since by the second axiom of divisibility monoids infima of any two elements exist, we obtain $a = a'$. Thus, the following requirement is a weakening of the above mentioned second axiom to words of length 2:

$$ab \sim a'b', ac \sim a'c' \text{ and } b \neq c \text{ imply } a = a' \tag{2.2}$$

for any letters $a, b, c, a', b', c' \in \Sigma$. The third axiom on divisibility monoids is restricted verbatim to words of length 3:

$$(\downarrow([abc]), \leq) \text{ is a distributive lattice} \tag{2.3}$$

for any letters $a, b, c \in \Sigma$. The following theorem states that the three properties we identified are sufficient to characterize all divisibility monoids:

**Theorem 1.** *Let $\Sigma$ be a finite set and $E$ a set of equations of the form $ab \sim cd$ with $a, b, c, d \in \Sigma$. Let $\sim$ be the least congruence on $\Sigma^\star$ containing $E$. Then $\Sigma^\star/\!\sim$ is a divisibility monoid if and only if (2.1), (2.2) and (2.3) hold for any $a, b, c, a', b', c' \in \Sigma$. Conversely, each divisibility monoid arises this way.*

We indicated that indeed any divisibility monoid arises this way. For the first statement let $R = \{ab \to cd \mid (ab, cd) \in E\}$ be the (symmetric) semi Thue system associated with the set of equations $E$. Any two $R$-equivalent words can be transformed into each other by at most one application of a rule from $R$ at the first position (this statement is proved using deep results from the theory of semimodular and of distributive lattices [2]). From this property of $R$, one can then infer that $\Sigma^\star/\!\sim$ is a divisibility monoid (cf. [19, Chapter 8] or [20]).

Note that for a finite set of equations $E$ of the form $ab \sim cd$, it can be checked effectively whether the three properties (2.1), (2.2) and (2.3) are satisfied by the least congruence containing $E$. Hence Theorem 1 describes a decidable class of finite presentations that give rise to the class of all divisibility monoids. Christian Pech of Dresden using the GAP4-system [16] computed that there are 219 divisibility monoids with 4 generators and 8371 divisibility monoids with 5 generators as opposed to only 10 resp. 34 trace monoids.

## 3 A Foata Normal Form

Throughout this section, let $(M, \cdot, 1)$ be a fixed divisibility monoid and let $\Sigma$ denote the set of its irreducible elements. In this section, we will define a Foata normal form for elements of $M$ that generalizes the known Foata normal forms from the theory of Mazurkiewicz traces. These Foata normal forms are the basis for our proofs in the following sections that any divisibility monoid is automatic and that a width-bounded divisibility monoid is rational. We define the set of *cliques* $\mathcal{C}\ell$ to consist of all nonempty subsets of $\Sigma$ that are bounded above, i.e., $\mathcal{C}\ell = \{A \subseteq \Sigma \mid \emptyset \neq A \text{ and } \sup(A) \text{ exists}\}$

Next we define the set $\mathrm{FNF} \subseteq \mathcal{C}\ell^\star$ of Foata normal forms as

$$\{A_1 A_2 \ldots A_n \in \mathcal{C}\ell^\star \mid \forall t \in A_{i+1} \forall B \in \mathcal{C}\ell : \sup B \neq (\sup A_i) \cdot t \text{ for } 1 \leq i < n\}.$$

Since the condition that constitutes membership in FNF is local, FNF is a rational language in the free monoid $\mathcal{C}\ell^\star$. Let $\alpha' : \mathcal{C}\ell \to M$ denote the mapping that associates with any clique $A \in \mathcal{C}\ell$ its supremum $\sup A$ in $M$. This mapping extends uniquely to a monoid homomorphism $\alpha$ from $\mathcal{C}\ell^\star$ to $M$. Then $\alpha(A_1 A_2 \ldots A_n) = (\sup A_1) \cdot (\sup A_2) \cdots (\sup A_n)$. This mapping is not injective, but surjective since $\alpha(\{a_1\}\{a_2\} \ldots \{a_n\}) = a_1 \cdot a_2 \cdots a_n$ for any $a_i \in \Sigma$ and $\Sigma$ generates $M$. The set FNF is particularly useful since it provides normal forms for the elements of $M$, i.e. since the restriction of $\alpha$ to FNF is a bijection:

**Lemma 2.** *The mapping* $\alpha \restriction \mathrm{FNF} : \mathrm{FNF} \to M$ *is bijective.*

*Proof.* To show injectivity, one proves for any $A_1 A_2 \ldots A_n \in \mathrm{FNF}$ that $A_1$ is the set of irreducible elements $a \in \Sigma$ that divide $\alpha(A_1 A_2 \ldots A_n)$ and continues by induction.

To show surjectivity, one builds the Foata Normal Form of $x$ inductively by setting $x_1 = x$, $A_i = \{a \in \Sigma \mid a \leq x_i\}$, and $\alpha(A_i) \cdot x_{i+1} = x_i$. □

Thus, for any $x \in M$, the set $\alpha^{-1}(x) \cap \text{FNF}$ is a singleton. We denote the unique preimage of $x$ in FNF by $\text{fnf}(x)$ and call it the *Foata Normal Form* of $x$.

Now let $\beta : \mathcal{C}\ell^\star \to \mathcal{C}\ell^\star$ be defined by $\beta = \text{fnf} \circ \alpha$, i.e. $\beta(W)$ is the Foata normal form of the element $\alpha(W)$ for any word $W$ over the alphabet $\mathcal{C}\ell$. This function is idempotent. Since fnf is injective, we obtain $\ker(\alpha) = \ker(\beta)$. Since $\alpha$ is a monoid homomorphism, $\ker(\beta)$ is a congruence. Finally $\mathcal{C}\ell^\star / \ker(\beta) = \mathcal{C}\ell^\star / \ker(\alpha) \cong M$ holds since $\alpha$ is surjective. Thus, we obtain

**Lemma 3.** *The function* $\text{fnf} \circ \alpha : \mathcal{C}\ell^\star \to \mathcal{C}\ell^\star$ *is a normal form function for the divisibility monoid* $M$.

Next we show that the Foata Normal Form of $\text{nat}(w)$ can be computed from the word $w \in \Sigma^\star$ by an automaton. In general, this automaton has infinitely many states, but for width-bounded divisibility monoids its accessible part will be shown to be finite.

An *automaton over the monoid* $S$ is a tuple $\mathcal{A} = (Q, S, E, I, F)$ where

1. $Q$ is a set of *states*,
2. $E \subseteq Q \times S \times Q$ is a set of *transitions*, and
3. $I, F \subseteq Q$ are the sets of *initial and final states*, respectively.

The automaton $\mathcal{A}$ is *finite* if $E$ is. A *computation* in $\mathcal{A}$ is a finite sequence of transitions:

$$p_0 \stackrel{a_1}{\to} p_1 \stackrel{a_2}{\to} p_2 \cdots \stackrel{a_n}{\to} p_n.$$

It is *successful* if $p_0 \in I$ and $p_n \in F$. The *label* of the computation is the element $a_1 \cdot a_2 \cdots a_n$ of the monoid $S$. For a computation with first state $p_0$, last state $p_n$ and label $a$, we will usually write $p_0 \stackrel{a}{\to} p_n$ without mentioning the intermediate states. The *behavior of* $\mathcal{A}$ is the subset $|\mathcal{A}|$ of $S$ consisting of labels of successful computations in $\mathcal{A}$.

**Lemma 4.** *There exists an automaton* $\mathcal{A}_M$ *with state set* $M \times (\mathcal{C}\ell \cup \{\varepsilon\})$ *over the monoid* $\Sigma^\star \times \mathcal{C}\ell^\star$ *that has a computation* $(1, \varepsilon) \stackrel{(w, B_1 B_2 \dots B_m)}{\longrightarrow} (z, C)$ *iff*

$B_m = C$, $\text{fnf}(\text{nat}(w) \cdot z) = B_1 B_2 \dots B_m$, *and* $|\text{fnf} \circ \text{nat}(w)| = m$.

*for any* $w \in \Sigma^\star$, $B_i \in \mathcal{C}\ell$ *for* $1 \leq i \leq m$, $z \in M$ *and* $C \in \mathcal{C}\ell_\varepsilon = \mathcal{C}\ell \cup \{\varepsilon\}$.

*Proof.* For $(x, A), (z, C) \in M \times \mathcal{C}\ell_\varepsilon$ and $(a, B) \in \Sigma \times \mathcal{C}\ell_\varepsilon$, there is a transition $(x, A) \stackrel{(a,B)}{\to} (z, C)$ iff

**1.** $a \leq x$, $B = \varepsilon$, $a \cdot z = x$, and $C = A$, or
**2.** $a \not\leq x$, $B = C \neq \varepsilon$, $AB \in \text{FNF}$, and $a \cdot z = x \cdot (\sup B)$. □

We can think of $(1, \varepsilon) \stackrel{(w, B_1 B_2 \dots B_m)}{\longrightarrow} (z, C)$ as denoting the fact that, on input of the word $w \in \Sigma^\star$, the automaton outputs $B_1 B_2 \dots B_m$ and reaches the state $(z, C)$. Thus, by the lemma above, the automaton stores the last letter of its output $B_m$ from $\mathcal{C}\ell$ in the second component $C$ of the state reached. Furthermore, it outputs the Foata normal form of some element $\text{nat}(w) \cdot z$ of $M$ that is an extension of the input. The "difference" between the input $\text{nat}(w)$ and the output $\alpha(B_1B_2\dots B_m)$ (seen as elements of $M$) equals $z$ and is stored in the first component of the reached state. The last property mentioned in the lemma above ensures that the Foata normal forms of $\mathrm{nat}(w)$ and of $\mathrm{nat}(w)\cdot z$ have the same length $m$. Intuitively, the difference between the input $\mathrm{nat}(w)$ and the output $\alpha(B_1B_2\dots B_m)$ is not too "large".

Note that the automaton outputs only elements of FNF. Even more, if $z = 1$ the automaton outputs the Foata normal form of the input. Let $(1,\varepsilon)$ be the only initial state and let the set of final states be $\{1\}\times \mathcal{C}\ell_\varepsilon$. Then the behavior of the automaton $\mathcal{A}_M$ is (the graph of) the function $\mathrm{fnf}\circ\mathrm{nat} : \Sigma^\star \to \mathcal{C}\ell^\star$.

## 4 Divisibility Monoids Are Automatic – The Word Problem

Since the equations that define a divisibility monoid are length preserving, the word problem for any divisibility monoid is decidable. In this section, we show that it can be solved in quadratic time.

For an alphabet $\Sigma$, let $\Sigma_\varepsilon = \Sigma\dot\cup\{\varepsilon\}$ and $\Sigma_2 = \Sigma_\varepsilon\times\Sigma_\varepsilon\setminus\{(\varepsilon,\varepsilon)\}$. Let furthermore $v = s_1s_2\dots s_m$ and $w = t_1t_2\dots t_n$ be words over $\Sigma$ with $s_i, t_j\in\Sigma$. We define

$$(v,w)^\diamond = \begin{cases}(s_1,t_1)(s_2,t_2)\dots(s_n,t_n)(\varepsilon,t_{n+1})(\varepsilon,t_{n+2})\dots(\varepsilon,t_m) & \text{if } n<m\\ (s_1,t_1)(s_2,t_2)\dots(s_n,t_n) & \text{if } n=m\\ (s_1,t_1)(s_2,t_2)\dots(s_m,t_m)(s_{m+1},\varepsilon)(s_{m+2},\varepsilon)\dots(s_n,\varepsilon) & \text{if } n>m\end{cases}$$

Then $(v,w)^\diamond$ is an element of the free monoid $\Sigma_2^\star$. Now let $M$ be a monoid, $\Sigma$ a finite set, $L\subseteq\Sigma^\star$ a recognizable language in the free monoid $\Sigma^\star$ and $\eta:\Sigma^\star\to M$ a homomorphism. Then $(\Sigma, L,\eta)$ is an *automatic structure for M* [5] if $\eta(L) = M$ and if the sets

$$L_= = \{(v,w)^\diamond \mid v,w\in L \text{ and } \eta(v)=\eta(w)\} \text{ and}$$
$$L_a = \{(v,w)^\diamond \mid v,w\in L \text{ and } \eta(va)=\eta(w)\}$$

are rational subsets of $\Sigma_2^\star$ for any $a\in\Sigma$. The monoid $M$ is an *automatic monoid* if it admits an automatic structure.

We will show that any divisibility monoid is automatic. More precisely, let $M$ be a divisibility monoid. For $A\in\mathcal{C}\ell$, choose a word $w_A\in\Sigma^\star$ with $\mathrm{nat}(w_A) = \alpha(A)$. Then the mapping $\mathcal{C}\ell\to\Sigma^\star : A\mapsto w_A$ admits a unique extension to a monoid homomorphism $\psi:\mathcal{C}\ell^\star\to\Sigma^\star$. Let $L=\psi(\mathrm{FNF})$ denote all words over $\Sigma$ of the form $\psi(A_1)\psi(A_2)\dots\psi(A_n)$ for some cliques $A_i$ such that $A_1A_2\dots A_n$ is a Foata normal form. We are going to prove that the triple $(\Sigma, L, \mathrm{nat})$ is an automatic structure for the divisibility monoid $M$:

Note that $\alpha = \mathrm{nat}\circ\psi$. Since, by Lemma 2, the mapping $\alpha\restriction\mathrm{FNF}$ is surjective, we obtain $M = \alpha(\mathrm{FNF}) = \mathrm{nat}\circ\psi(\mathrm{FNF}) = \mathrm{nat}(L)$.

Next, we show that $L_=$ is rational. Recall that $\mathrm{FNF}\subseteq\mathcal{C}\ell^\star$ is rational. Hence its image $L$ with respect to the homomorphism $\psi$ is rational, too. This implies immediately that the set $\{(v,v)^\diamond \mid v \in L\}$ is rational in $\Sigma_2^\star$. Now let $v,w \in L$ with $\mathrm{nat}(v) = \mathrm{nat}(w)$. Then $v = \psi \circ \mathrm{fnf} \circ \mathrm{nat}(v) = \psi \circ \mathrm{fnf} \circ \mathrm{nat}(w) = w$. Hence we showed $L_= = \{(v,v)^\diamond \mid v \in L\}$ which is rational in $\Sigma_2^\star$.

It remains to show that for $a \in \Sigma$ the set $L_a$ is rational in $\Sigma_2^\star$. Note that $L_a = \{(v, \psi(\mathrm{fnf} \circ \mathrm{nat}(va))) \mid v \in L\}$. To show that this set is rational, we have to construct an automaton that outputs $\psi(\mathrm{fnf} \circ \mathrm{nat}(va))$ on input of $v$ for $v \in L$. Since this can indeed be achieved (cf. [20]), we obtain

**Theorem 2.** *Let $M$ be a divisibility monoid. Then $M$ is an automatic monoid.*

Using that the word problem for automatic monoids can be solved in quadratic time [5], we obtain immediately

**Corollary 1.** *Let $M$ be a divisibility monoid. Then the word problem for $M$ can be solved in quadratic time.*

## 5 When Does Kleene's Theorem Hold?

As mentioned in the introduction, Kleene's Theorem holds in a divisibility monoid $M$ iff it is width-bounded iff it is rational. To obtain this result, we first sketch the proof that any width-bounded divisibility monoid is rational. The crucial step in the proof is expressed by the following lemma

**Lemma 5.** *Let $(M,\cdot,1)$ be a width-bounded divisibility monoid and $n \in \mathbb{N}$ such that $w(\downarrow x, \leq) \leq n$ for any $x \in M$. Let $x,z \in M$ with $|\mathrm{fnf}(xz)| = |\mathrm{fnf}(x)|$. Then $|z| < 2(n+1)|\Sigma|$.*

Using Lemma 4, we obtain that the automaton $\mathcal{A}_M$ has only finitely many reachable states for $M$ width-bounded, i.e., the reachable part $\mathcal{A}$ of the automaton $\mathcal{A}_M$ is a finite automaton. Note that the behavior of $\mathcal{A}$ and that of $\mathcal{A}_M$ coincide. Thus, by [14], the behavior $|\mathcal{A}| = |\mathcal{A}_M| = \{(w, \mathrm{fnf} \circ \mathrm{nat}(w)) \mid w \in \Sigma^\star\}$ is a rational set in the monoid $\Sigma^\star \times \mathfrak{Cl}^\star$.

We consider again the homomorphism $\psi : \mathfrak{Cl}^\star \to \Sigma^\star$ that we constructed in the previous section. Since $\psi$ is a homomorphism, the set $\{(W, \psi(W)) \mid W \in \mathfrak{Cl}^\star\}$ is rational in $\mathfrak{Cl}^\star \times \Sigma^\star$. Furthermore, $\mathrm{nat} \circ \psi = \alpha$ and therefore $\mathrm{fnf} \circ \alpha = \mathrm{fnf} \circ \mathrm{nat} \circ \psi$. Hence the function $\mathrm{fnf} \circ \alpha$ is the product of two rational functions $\mathrm{fnf} \circ \mathrm{nat}$ and $\psi$. This implies by [14] that the set $\{(W, \mathrm{fnf} \circ \alpha(W)) \mid W \in \mathfrak{Cl}^\star\}$ is rational since $\Sigma^\star$ is a free monoid. Recall that by Lemma 3, the function $\mathrm{fnf} \circ \alpha$ is a normal form function for the divisibility monoid $M$. Hence we showed that a width-bounded divisibility monoid indeed admits a rational normal form function, i.e. is a rational monoid:

**Proposition 1.** *Any width-bounded divisibility monoid is rational.*

By [25, Theorem 4.1], this proposition implies that any width-bounded divisibility monoid is a Kleene monoid. The remainder of this section is devoted to the inverse implication: Let $M$ be a divisibility monoid that is not width-bounded, i.e., for any $n \in \mathbb{N}$, there is $z \in M$ such that the width of the distributive lattice $\downarrow z$ is at least $n$. This implies, that for any $k \in \mathbb{N}$, there exists $z \in M$, such that the lattice $(\{1,2,3,\ldots,k\}^2, \leq)$ (with the coordinatewise order) can be embedded into the lattice $\downarrow z$. Let $f$ be such embedding. If the divisibility monoid $M$ has finitely many residuum functions (see below), we can apply Ramsey's Theorem [24] twice and obtain $1 \leq i < i' \leq n$, $1 \leq j < j' \leq n$, and $x, y \in M$ such that $f(i,j) \cdot x = f(i,j')$, $f(i',j) \cdot x = f(i',j')$, $f(i,j) \cdot y = f(i',j)$, and $f(i,j') \cdot y = f(i',j')$. By cancellation, this implies $x \cdot y = y \cdot x$. Furthermore $x \parallel y$ since $f$ is a lattice embedding and $M$ is cancellative. This was the proof of the following lemma that we state after defining residuum functions: Let $M$ be a divisibility monoid and $x, y \in M$. We say that $x$ and $y$ are *complementary* (denoted $x \parallel y$) if $x \wedge y = 1$ and the set $\{x, y\}$ is bounded above. Hence, two nonidentity elements of $M$ are complementary if they are complements in one of the lattices $\downarrow z$ with $z \in M$. Since bounded elements have a supremum, there exists $y' \in M$ with $x \cdot y' = x \vee y$. This element $y'$ is uniquely determined by $x$ and $y$ since $M$ is cancellative. We call it the *residuum of $y$ after $x$* and denote it by $r_x(y)$. Thus, $r_x$ is a partial function from $M$ to $M$ whose domain is the set of elements that are complements of $x$. Let $\mathbb{R}_M$ denote the set of all partial functions $r_x$ for some $x \in M$. The divisibility monoid $M$ is said to have *finitely many residuum functions* if $\mathbb{R}_M$ is finite.[3]

**Lemma 6.** *Let $(M, \cdot, 1)$ be a divisibility monoid with finitely many residuum functions that is not width-bounded. Then there exist $x, y \in M \setminus \{1\}$ such that $x \parallel y$ and $x \cdot y = y \cdot x$.*

Now we can characterize the divisibility monoids that satisfy Kleene's Theorem.

**Theorem 3.** *Let $(M, \cdot, 1)$ be a divisibility monoid. Then the following assertions are equivalent*
*1. $M$ is width-bounded,*
*2. $M$ is a rational monoid and has finitely many residuum functions, and*
*3. $M$ is a Kleene monoid and has finitely many residuum functions.*

*Proof.* A width-bounded divisibility monoid is rational by Proposition 1. Now let $s_i, t_i \in M$ for $1 \leq i \leq n$ such that $x = s_1 \cdot s_2 \cdots s_n$ and $y = t_1 \cdot t_2 \cdots t_n$ are complementary. Then the elements $s_1 \cdot s_2 \cdots s_k \vee t_1 \cdot t_2 \cdots t_{n-k}$ for $1 \leq k < n$ form an antichain that is bounded above by $z = x \vee y$. Hence the lattice $\downarrow z$ has width at least $n-1$. Now let $M$ be width-bounded such that the lattices $\downarrow z$ have width at most $n-2$. Then, as we just saw, at most one of two complementary elements of $M$ has length at least $n$. Let $M_n$ denote the finite set of elements of $M$ of length at most $n$. For $x \in M \setminus M_n$, the domain of $r_x$ is therefore contained in $M_n$ and, since $r_x$ is length-preserving, so is its image. Hence there are only finitely many residuum functions $r_x$ for $x \in M \setminus M_n$. Since $M_n$ is finite, $M$ therefore has only finitely many residuum functions.

[3] It is not known whether this class is a proper subclass of all divisibility monoids.

Any rational monoid is a Kleene monoid by [25, Theorem 4.1]. For the remaining implication assume by contradiction $M$ not to be width-bounded. Then, by Lemma 6, there are $x, y \in M \setminus \{1\}$ such that $x \cdot y = y \cdot x$ and $x \parallel y$. Hence the mapping $(0,1) \mapsto x$ and $(1,0) \mapsto y$ can be extended to a monoid embedding from $(\mathbb{N} \times \mathbb{N}, +)$ into $M$. The image of $\{(n,n) \mid n \in \mathbb{N}\}$ in $M$ under this embedding is a rational set which is not recognizable. Thus, $M$ is not a Kleene-monoid. □

## 6 Open Questions

There are several open questions that call for a treatment: Is the lower bound for the complexity of the word problem given in Corollary 1 optimal? We did not consider the nonuniform word problem, i.e. the complexity of an algorithm that takes as input a presentation as described in Theorem 1 and two words and outputs whether these two words denote the same monoid element. Furthermore, we still do not know whether there exist divisibility monoids with infinitely many residuum functions.

## References

1. G. Berry. Stable models of typed λ-calculi. In *5th ICALP*, Lecture Notes in Comp. Science vol. 62, pages 72–89. Springer, 1978.
2. G. Birkhoff. *Lattice Theory.* Colloquium Publications vol. 25. American Mathematical Society, Providence, 1973.
3. B. Bosbach. Representable divisibility semigroups. *Proc. Edinb. Math. Soc., II. Ser.*, 34(1):45–64, 1991.
4. J.R. Büchi. On a decision method in restricted second order arithmetics. In E. Nagel et al., editor, *Proc. Intern. Congress on Logic, Methodology and Philosophy of Science*, pages 1–11. Stanford University Press, Stanford, 1960.
5. C. M. Campbell, E. F. Robertson, N. Ruškuc, and R. M. Thomas. Automatic semigroups. *Theoretical Computer Science*, 250:365–391, 2001.
6. R. Corran. *On monoids related to braid groups.* PhD thesis, University of Sydney, 2000.
7. P. Dehornoy and L. Paris. Gaussian groups and Garside groups, two generalizations of Artin groups. *Proc. London Math. Soc.*, 79:569–604, 1999.
8. V. Diekert. *Combinatorics on Traces.* Lecture Notes in Comp. Science vol. 454. Springer, 1990.
9. V. Diekert and G. Rozenberg. *The Book of Traces.* World Scientific Publ. Co., 1995.
10. M. Droste. Recognizable languages in concurrency monoids. *Theoretical Comp. Science*, 150:77–109, 1995.
11. M. Droste and D. Kuske. On recognizable languages in divisibility monoids. In G. Ciobanu and Gh. Paun, editors, *FCT99*, Lecture Notes in Comp. Science vol. 1684, pages 246–257. Springer, 1999.
12. M. Droste and D. Kuske. Recognizable languages in divisibility monoids. *Mathematical Structures in Computer Science*, 2000. To appear.
13. C. Duboc. Commutations dans les monoïdes libres: un cadre théorique pour l'étude du parallelisme. Thèse, Faculté des Sciences de l'Université de Rouen, 1986.

14. C.C. Elgot and G. Mezei. On relations defined by generalized finite automata. *IBM J. Res. Develop.*, 9:47–65, 1965.
15. D.B.A. Epstein, J.W. Cannon, D.F. Holt, S.V.F. Levy, M.S. Paterson, and W.P. Thurston. *Word Processing In Groups.* Jones and Bartlett Publishers, Boston, 1992.
16. The GAP Group, Aachen, St Andrews. *GAP – Groups, Algorithms, and Programming, Version 4.2*, 1999. (http://www-gap.dcs.st-and.ac.uk/~gap).
17. J.F.P. Hudson. Regular rewrite systems and automatic structures. In J. Almeida, G.M.S. Gomes, and P.V. Silva, editors, *Semigroups, Automata and Languages*, pages 145–152, Singapure, 1996. World Scientific.
18. S.C. Kleene. Representation of events in nerve nets and finite automata. In C.E. Shannon and J. McCarthy, editors, *Automata Studies*, Annals of Mathematics Studies vol. 34, pages 3–40. Princeton University Press, 1956.
19. D. Kuske. Contributions to a Trace Theory beyond Mazurkiewicz Traces. Technical report, TU Dresden, 1999.
20. D. Kuske. On rational and on left divisibility monoids. Technical Report MATH-AL-3-1999, TU Dresden, 1999.
21. A. Mazurkiewicz. Concurrent program schemes and their interpretation. Technical report, DAIMI Report PB-78, Aarhus University, 1977.
22. E. Ochmański. Regular behaviour of concurrent systems. *Bull. Europ. Assoc. for Theor. Comp. Science*, 27:56–67, 1985.
23. M. Peletier and J. Sakarovitch. Easy multiplications. II. Extensions of rational semigroups. *Information and Computation*, 88:18–59, 1990.
24. F.P. Ramsey. On a problem of formal logic. *Proc. London Math. Soc.*, 30:264–286, 1930.
25. J. Sakarovitch. Easy multiplications. I. The realm of Kleene's Theorem. *Information and Computation*, 74:173–197, 1987.
26. M.P. Schützenberger. On the definition of a family of automata. *Inf. Control*, 4:245–270, 1961.
27. G. Winskel. Event structures. In W. Brauer, W. Reisig, and G. Rozenberg, editors, *Petri nets: Applications and Relationships to Other Models of Concurrency*, Lecture Notes in Comp. Science vol. 255, pages 325–392. Springer, 1987.

# Concurrency in Timed Automata*

Ruggero Lanotte, Andrea Maggiolo-Schettini, and Simone Tini

Dipartimento di Informatica, Università di Pisa,
Corso Italia 40, 56125 Pisa, Italy

**Abstract.** We introduce Concurrent Timed Automata (*CTAs*) where automata running in parallel are synchronized. We consider the subclasses of *CTAs* obtained by admitting, or not, diagonal clock constraints and constant updates, and by letting, or not, sequential automata to update the same clocks. We prove that such subclasses recognize the same languages but differ from the point of view of succinctness.

## 1 Introduction

Since their introduction by Alur and Dill [1], Timed Automata (*TAs*) have been one of the most studied models for real-time systems. *TAs* extend classic $\omega$-Automata by introducing variables measuring time, called *clocks*: Transitions are guarded by *clock constraints*, which compare the value of a clock with some constant, and perform *reset updates*, which reset a clock to the initial value 0.

Later, both *diagonal clock constraints*, which compare the values of two clocks, and *constant updates*, which set the value of a clock to some constant, have been added to *TAs*. These new features do not increase the class of languages accepted by *TAs* (see [5,6]). In fact, for each *TA* of size $n$ and with $d$ diagonal clock constraints there is an equivalent *TA* of size $n \times 2^d$ without diagonal clock constraints (see [2] for the proof). Moreover, for each *TA* of size $n$ there is an equivalent *TA* of size polynomial w.r.to $n$ and with only reset updates.

Extensions of *TAs* to deal with parallelism have been proposed by Bornot and Sifakis [3,4] and by Lanotte et al. [8]. In the model of [3,4], an action from the environment is sensed either by all automata running in parallel, if the action is a "communication action", or by one single automaton, otherwise. In the model of [8], the environment performs more than one action at the same instant, and each of the automata running in parallel can sense its own subset of actions.

In the present paper we propose a variant of *TAs* with parallelism, called Concurrent Timed Automata (*CTAs*), where automata running in parallel are perfectly synchronized, in the sense that they can compute only by sensing, at each instant, the same action from the environment. *CTAs* can be translated into equivalent Alur and Dill's *TAs* by using the cartesian product. *CTAs* without clocks correspond to Drusinsky and Harel's Concurrent Automata [7]. Such Concurrent Automata can be mapped to $\omega$-Automata, and the exponential lower bound of this mapping has been proved in [7]. From this result, the exponential lower bound of mapping *CTAs* to Alur and Dill's *TAs* follows.

* Research partially supported by MURST Progetto Cofinanziato TOSCA.

R. Freivalds (Ed.): FCT 2001, LNCS 2138, pp. 240–251, 2001.

Our model is included in those of [3,4] and of [8]. We show that notwisthanding its simplicity, our model is suitable to investigate the rôle that some features, which may or may not be offered by the model, play in the parallel setting.

First of all we analyze the power of diagonal clock constraints. We show that mapping *CTAs* with diagonal clock constraints to *CTAs* without diagonal clock constraints is always possible, and we prove both the exponential lower and upper bounds of such a mapping. Note that the upper bound in the sequential case is polynomial w.r.to the number of states and transitions and exponential only w.r.to the number of diagonal clock constraints (see [2]).

Then, we analyze the power of constant updates. We show that mapping *CTAs* with constant updates to *CTAs* with only reset updates is always possible, and we prove both the exponential lower and upper bounds of such a mapping. Note that the upper bound in the sequential case is polynomial.

Finally, we consider *CTAs* with *private clocks*, i.e. the subset of *CTAs* where the value of a clock can be updated by only one sequential automaton (the *owner* of the clock), and can be read by all sequential automata running in parallel. We prove the exponential lower and upper bounds of mapping *CTAs* without diagonal clock constraints and with constant updates to *CTAs* with private clocks and with the same sets of clock constraints and updates. We prove also the polynomial upper bound of mapping the other subclasses of *CTAs* (i.e. *CTAs* with diagonal clock constraints and *CTAs* without diagonal clock constraints and with only reset updates) to the corresponding subclasses with private clocks.

We view our results as a starting step towards the study of parallelism in *TAs*. We intend to study in the future the rôle of the nondeterministic updates, introduced in [5,6], in the parallel setting. We intend also comparing communication through clocks, which is used both in our model and in that of [3,4], with explicit communication (automata view the current state of other automata and the time elapsed since their activation), which is used in the model of [8].

## 2 Concurrent Timed Automata

**Timed words**

Given a *time domain* $\mathcal{T}$, a *timed sequence* over $\mathcal{T}$ is an infinite non decreasing sequence $(t_i)_{i\geq 1}$ such that, for each $t \in \mathcal{T}$, there is some $t_i > t$.

Given a finite alphabet of *actions* $\Sigma$, a *timed word* $\omega = (a_i, t_i)_{i\geq 1}$ over $\Sigma$ and $\mathcal{T}$ is an infinite sequence such that $(a_i)_{i\geq 1}$ is a sequence of actions, denoted also $untimed(\omega)$, and $(t_i)_{i\geq 1}$ is a timed sequence over $\mathcal{T}$.

**Clock valuations and clock constraints**

We assume a set $\mathcal{X}$ of variables, called *clocks*. A *clock valuation* over $\mathcal{X}$ is a mapping $v : \mathcal{X} \to \mathcal{T}$ assigning time values to clocks. For a clock valuation $v$ and a time value $t$, $v + t$ denotes the clock valuation such that $(v + t)(x) = v(x) + t$.

Given a subset of clocks $X \subseteq \mathcal{X}$, the most general set of *clock constraints* over $X$, denoted $\mathcal{C}(X)$, is defined by the following grammar, where $\phi$ ranges over $\mathcal{C}(X)$, $x, y \in X$, $q \in \mathcal{T}$ and $\# \in \{<, \leq, =, \neq, >, \geq\}$.

$$\phi ::= x \# q \mid x - y \# q \mid \phi \wedge \phi \mid \neg\phi \mid \phi \vee \phi \mid true$$

Constraints of the form $x - y \# q$ are called *diagonal clock constraints*. The subset of *diagonal free clock constraints*, denoted $\mathcal{C}_{df}(X)$, excludes such constraints. We write $v \models \phi$ when *the clock valuation* $v$ *satisfies the clock constraint* $\phi$. Formally, $v \models x \# q$ iff $v(x) \# q$, $v \models x - y \# q$ iff $v(x) - v(y) \# q$, $v \models \phi_1 \wedge \phi_2$ iff $v \models \phi_1$ and $v \models \phi_2$, $v \models \neg\phi$ iff $v \not\models \phi$, $v \models \phi_1 \vee \phi_2$ iff $v \models \phi_1$ or $v \models \phi_2$, and $v \models true$.

**Updates**

*Updates* modify values of clocks. Formally, an update $up$ over a set of clocks $X$ is a finite collection $(up^i)_{1 \leq i \leq k}$, where $up^i$ is a *simple update* of the form $x_i := q_i$, with $x_i \in X$ and $q_i \in \mathcal{T}$, and $x_i = x_j$ implies $q_i = q_j$, for every $1 \leq i < j \leq k$. The update $up$ maps a given clock valuation $v$ to the valuation $up(v)$ such that:

$$up(v)(x) = \begin{cases} q_i & \text{if } x = x_i \text{ and } up^i \text{ is the simple update } x_i := q_i \\ v(x) & \text{if } x \notin \{x_1, \ldots, x_k\} \end{cases}$$

For a set $X \subseteq \mathcal{X}$, let $\mathcal{U}(X)$ denote the set of updates over $X$, and let $\mathcal{U}_0(X)$ denote the set of *reset updates*, i.e. updates with simple updates of the form $x_i := 0$.

**The formalism**

A *Concurrent Timed Automaton* is a tuple $\mathcal{A} = (\Sigma, X, A_1, \ldots, A_m, R)$, where:

- $\Sigma$ is a finite alphabet of actions.
- $X$ is a finite subset of clocks in $\mathcal{X}$.
- $A_i = (S_i, s_i^0, \delta_i)$ is a *sequential automaton*, with *states* $S_i = \{s_i^0, \ldots, s_i^{|S_i|}\}$, *initial state* $s_i^0$ and set of *transitions* $\delta_i \subseteq S_i \times [\mathcal{C}(X) \times \Sigma \times \mathcal{U}(X)] \times S_i$.
- $R \subseteq \bigcup_{1 \leq i \leq m} S_i$ is the set of *repeated states*.

A *configuration* of $\mathcal{A}$ is a collection of states $c = (s_1^{h_1}, \ldots, s_m^{h_m}) \in S_1 \times \ldots \times S_m$. The *initial configuration* $c_0$ is the collection of the initial states $(s_1^0, \ldots, s_m^0)$. There is a *step* from a configuration $c = (s_1^{h_1}, \ldots, s_m^{h_m})$ to a configuration $c' = (s_1^{k_1}, \ldots, s_m^{k_m})$ through action $a$, written $c \stackrel{a}{\Longrightarrow} c'$, if there are transitions $s_i^{h_i} \stackrel{\phi_i, a, up_i}{\longrightarrow} s_i^{k_i}$, $1 \leq i \leq m$ (all automata read $a$), and $(up_1, \ldots, up_m)$ is an update.

A *path* $P$ in $\mathcal{A}$ is an infinite sequence of steps $c_0 \stackrel{a_1}{\Longrightarrow} c_1 \stackrel{a_2}{\Longrightarrow} c_2 \ldots$. It is *accepting* if it passes infinitely often through configurations containing some state in $R$.

A *run* $r$ of $\mathcal{A}$ through the path $P$ is a sequence $\langle c_0, v_0 \rangle \stackrel{a_1, t_1}{\Longrightarrow} \langle c_1, v_1 \rangle \stackrel{a_2, t_2}{\Longrightarrow} \langle c_2, v_2 \rangle \ldots$, where $(t_i)_{i \geq 1}$ is a time sequence, and, if $c_i$ is the configuration $(s_1^{h_{i,1}}, \ldots, s_m^{h_{i,m}})$ and the step $c_i \stackrel{a_{i+1}}{\Longrightarrow} c_{i+1}$ of $P$ is formed by the set of transitions $s_j^{h_{i,j}} \stackrel{\phi_j^{i+1}, a_{i+1}, up_j^{i+1}}{\longrightarrow} s_j^{h_{i+1,j}}$, with $1 \leq j \leq m$, then it holds that:

- $v_0(x) = 0$ for every $x \in X$
- $v_i + (t_{i+1} - t_i) \models \phi_j^{i+1}$ for each $1 \leq j \leq m$
- $v_{i+1} = (up_1^{i+1}, \ldots, up_m^{i+1})(v_i + (t_{i+1} - t_i))$.

The *label* of the run $r$ is the timed word $\omega = (a_1, t_1), (a_2, t_2) \ldots$. If the path $P$ is accepting then the timed word $\omega$ is *accepted* by $\mathcal{A}$. The set of all timed words accepted by $\mathcal{A}$ is denoted by $\mathcal{L}(\mathcal{A})$, and is the (*timed*) *language* accepted by $\mathcal{A}$. We denote with $untimed(\mathcal{L}(\mathcal{A}))$ the set $\{untimed(\omega) \mid \omega \in \mathcal{L}(A)\}$.

**The subclasses**

Given sets $\mathcal{C} \subseteq \mathcal{C}(X)$ and $\mathcal{U} \subseteq \mathcal{U}(X)$, the class $CTA(\mathcal{C},\mathcal{U})$ contains the *CTAs* whose transitions are guarded by constraints in $\mathcal{C}$ and perform updates in $\mathcal{U}$.

The subclass of $CTA(\mathcal{C},\mathcal{U})$ with *private clocks*, denoted $CTA_{pr}(\mathcal{C},\mathcal{U})$, contains the *CTAs* $\mathcal{A} = (\Sigma, X, A_1, \ldots, A_m, R)$ in $CTA(\mathcal{C},\mathcal{U})$ where there is a partition $X_1, \ldots, X_m$ of $X$ s.t., if an update $x := q$ is in $A_i$, then $x \in X_i$. $A_i$ is called the *owner* of the clocks in $X_i$ and is the unique automaton that updates them.

The subclass of *sequential* $CTA(\mathcal{C},\mathcal{U})$, denoted $STA(\mathcal{C},\mathcal{U})$, contains the *CTAs* in $CTA(\mathcal{C},\mathcal{U})$ having only one sequential component. Alur and Dill's model corresponds to $STA(\mathcal{C}_{df}(X),\mathcal{U}_0(X))$. Note that $STA(\mathcal{C},\mathcal{U})$ and $STA_{pr}(\mathcal{C},\mathcal{U})$ coincide.

We shall consider the classes of Fig.1. We shall prove that they do not differ from the point of view of expressiveness, but do differ from that of succinctness.

Given two classes of *CTAs* $\mathcal{C}$ and $\mathcal{C}'$, we write:

- $\mathcal{C} \sim \mathcal{C}'$ iff for each element $\mathcal{A} \in \mathcal{C}$ there is an equivalent (i.e. accepting the same language) element $\mathcal{A}' \in \mathcal{C}'$ that is polynomial w.r.to $\mathcal{A}$, and conversely;
- $\mathcal{C} \xrightarrow{u} \mathcal{C}'$ iff for each element $\mathcal{A} \in \mathcal{C}$ there is an equivalent element $\mathcal{A}' \in \mathcal{C}'$ that is at most exponential w.r.to $\mathcal{A}$;
- $\mathcal{C} \xrightarrow{l} \mathcal{C}'$ iff there is a family of languages $(L_m)_{m\geq 0}$ accepted by a family $(\mathcal{A}_m)_{m\geq 0} \in \mathcal{C}$, with $\mathcal{A}_m$ polynomial w.r.to $m$, and every family $(\mathcal{B}_m)_{m\geq 0} \in \mathcal{C}'$ accepting $(L_m)_{m\geq 0}$ is such that $\mathcal{B}_m$ is at least exponential w.r.to $m$;
- $\mathcal{C} \longrightarrow \mathcal{C}'$ iff $\mathcal{C} \xrightarrow{l} \mathcal{C}'$ and $\mathcal{C} \xrightarrow{u} \mathcal{C}'$, and $\mathcal{C} \longleftrightarrow \mathcal{C}'$ iff $\mathcal{C} \longrightarrow \mathcal{C}'$ and $\mathcal{C}' \longrightarrow \mathcal{C}$.

**Theorem 1.** *All relations of Fig.1 hold.*

In Sect. 3 we prove that $\mathcal{C} \sim \mathcal{C}'$ for each pair of classes $\mathcal{C}$, $\mathcal{C}'$ such that $\mathcal{C} \sim \mathcal{C}'$ is in Fig.1. In Sect. 4 (resp. Sect. 5) we prove that $\mathcal{C} \xrightarrow{u} \mathcal{C}'$ (resp. $\mathcal{C} \xrightarrow{l} \mathcal{C}'$) for each pair of classes $\mathcal{C}$, $\mathcal{C}'$ such that either $\mathcal{C} \longrightarrow \mathcal{C}'$ or $\mathcal{C} \longleftrightarrow \mathcal{C}'$ is in Fig.1.

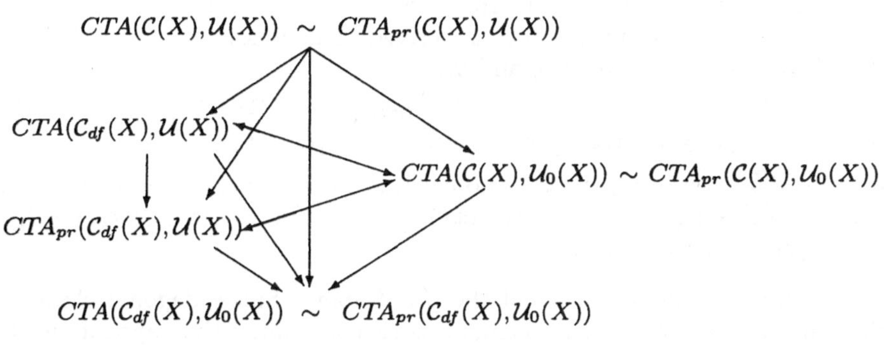


**Fig. 1.** Relations of succinctness

## 3 Polynomial Reductions

Here we prove that all relations $\sim$ in Fig.1 hold. Without loss of generality, we assume that clock constraints $x \# q$ and $x - y \# q$ are such that $\# \in \{\geq, <\}$.

**Proposition 1.** $CTA(\mathcal{C}(X), \mathcal{U}_0(X)) \sim CTA_{pr}(\mathcal{C}(X), \mathcal{U}_0(X))$.

*Proof.* Since $CTA(\mathcal{C}(X), \mathcal{U}_0(X)) \supseteq CTA_{pr}(\mathcal{C}(X), \mathcal{U}_0(X))$, it suffices to prove that, for each $\mathcal{A} = (\Sigma, X, A_1, \ldots, A_m, R) \in CTA(\mathcal{C}(X), \mathcal{U}_0(X))$, there is some $\mathcal{A}' \in CTA_{pr}(\mathcal{C}(X), \mathcal{U}_0(X))$ polynomial w.r.t. $\mathcal{A}$ such that $\mathcal{L}(\mathcal{A}) = \mathcal{L}(\mathcal{A}')$.
We obtain $\mathcal{A}' = (\Sigma, \bigcup_{x \in X}\{x_1, \ldots, x_m\}, A'_1, \ldots, A'_m, R)$ as follows:

1. each clock $x$ is replaced by $x_1, \ldots, x_m$, owned by $A'_1, \ldots, A'_m$, respectively;
2. each reset $x := 0$ in $A_i$ is replaced by $x_i := 0$ in $A'_i$;
3. each constraint $x \geq q$ (resp.: $x < q$, $x - y \geq q$, $x - y < q$) is replaced by $\bigwedge_{i \in [1,m]} x_i \geq q$ (resp.: $\bigvee_{i \in [1,m]} x_i < q$, $\bigwedge_{i \in [1,m]} \bigvee_{j \in [1,m]} x_i - y_j \geq q$, $\bigvee_{i \in [1,m]} \bigwedge_{j \in [1,m]} x_i - y_j < q$).

Intuitively, $x$ is reset in $\mathcal{A}$ iff some $x_i \in \{x_1, \ldots, x_m\}$ is reset in $\mathcal{A}'$. Therefore, $x \geq q$ (resp. $x < q$) iff the clock $x_h \in \{x_1, \ldots, x_m\}$ that has been most recently reset satisfies $x_h \geq q$ (resp. $x_h < q$), i.e. $\bigwedge_{i \in [1,m]} x_i \geq q$ (resp. $\bigvee_{i \in [1,m]} x_i < q$). Moreover, if $y_k \in \{y_1, \ldots, y_m\}$ is the clock replacing $y$ that has been most recently updated, $x - y \geq q$ (resp. $x - y < q$) iff $x_h - y_k \geq q$ (resp. $x_h - y_k < q$), i.e. $\bigwedge_{i \in [1,m]} \bigvee_{j \in [1,m]} x_i - y_j \geq q$, (resp. $\bigvee_{i \in [1,m]} \bigwedge_{j \in [1,m]} x_i - y_j < q$).
We note that $\mathcal{A}'$ is polynomial in size w.r.t. $\mathcal{A}$. We prove that $\mathcal{L}(\mathcal{A}') \subseteq \mathcal{L}(\mathcal{A})$. The other inclusion can be proved analogously.
Assume a timed word $\omega' = (a_1, t_1)(a_2, t_2) \ldots \in \mathcal{L}(\mathcal{A}')$. There is a run $r' = \langle c_0, v'_0 \rangle \stackrel{a_1, t_1}{\Longrightarrow} \langle c_1, v'_1 \rangle \stackrel{a_2, t_2}{\Longrightarrow} \ldots$ such that $c_0 \stackrel{a_1}{\Longrightarrow} c_1 \stackrel{a_2}{\Longrightarrow} \ldots$ is an accepting path. Let $v_0 = v'_0$. To prove that $\omega' \in \mathcal{L}(\mathcal{A})$, we prove that there is a run $r = \langle c_0, v_0 \rangle \stackrel{a_1, t_1}{\Longrightarrow} \langle c_1, v_1 \rangle \stackrel{a_2, t_2}{\Longrightarrow} \ldots$ such that $v_i(x) = min\{v'_i(x_1), \ldots, v'_i(x_m)\}$.
It suffices to prove that $\langle c_i, v'_i \rangle \stackrel{a_{i+1}, t_{i+1}}{\Longrightarrow} \langle c_{i+1}, v'_{i+1} \rangle$ implies $\langle c_i, v_i \rangle \stackrel{a_{i+1}, t_{i+1}}{\Longrightarrow} \langle c_{i+1}, v_{i+1} \rangle$. This follows from two facts:
1) If $v'_i + t_{i+1} - t_i \models \phi'$ for an arbitrary constraint $\phi'$, then $v_i + t_{i+1} - t_i \models \phi$, with $\phi$ the constraint from which $\phi'$ is derived. This follows from the definition of $\phi'$ and the relation between $v'_i$ and $v_i$.
2) If $\langle c_i, v'_i \rangle \stackrel{a_{i+1}, t_{i+1}}{\Longrightarrow} \langle c_{i+1}, v'_{i+1} \rangle$ resets $x_h$, then $\langle c_i, v_i \rangle \stackrel{a_{i+1}, t_{i+1}}{\Longrightarrow} \langle c_{i+1}, v_{i+1} \rangle$ resets $x$, and $0 = v_{i+1}(x) = min\{v'_{i+1}(x_1), \ldots, 0, \ldots, v'_{i+1}(x_m)\}$.
If $\langle c_i, v'_i \rangle \stackrel{a_{i+1}, t_{i+1}}{\Longrightarrow} \langle c_{i+1}, v'_{i+1} \rangle$ resets no clock in $\{x_1, \ldots, x_m\}$, then it holds that $v_{i+1}(x) = v_i(x) + t_{i+1} - t_i = min\{v'_i(x_1) + t_{i+1} - t_i, \ldots, v'_i(x_m) + t_{i+1} - t_i\} = min\{v'_{i+1}(x_1), \ldots, v'_{i+1}(x_m)\}$. □

Let us consider the $CTA$ $\mathcal{A}'$ of the proof above. Since diagonal clock constraints are derived only from diagonal clock constraints that appear in $\mathcal{A}$, if $\mathcal{A} \in CTA(\mathcal{C}_{df}(X), \mathcal{U}_0(X))$ then $\mathcal{A}' \in CTA_{pr}(\mathcal{C}_{df}(X), \mathcal{U}_0(X))$. Therefore, we infer the following result.

**Proposition 2.** $CTA(\mathcal{C}_{df}(X), \mathcal{U}_0(X)) \sim CTA_{pr}(\mathcal{C}_{df}(X), \mathcal{U}_0(X))$.

We consider now *CTA*s with diagonal constraints and constant updates.

**Proposition 3.** $CTA(\mathcal{C}(X),\mathcal{U}(X)) \sim CTA_{pr}(\mathcal{C}(X),\mathcal{U}(X))$.

*Proof.* Since $CTA(\mathcal{C}(X),\mathcal{U}(X)) \supseteq CTA_{pr}(\mathcal{C}(X),\mathcal{U}(X))$, it suffices to prove that, for each $\mathcal{A} = (\Sigma,\{x^1,\ldots,x^n\},A_1,\ldots,A_m,R) \in CTA(\mathcal{C}(X),\mathcal{U}(X))$, there is some $\mathcal{A}' \in CTA_{pr}(\mathcal{C}(X),\mathcal{U}(X))$ polynomial w.r.t. $\mathcal{A}$ such that $\mathcal{L}(\mathcal{A}) = \mathcal{L}(\mathcal{A}')$.

The proof is done in two steps. In the first step we construct the *CTA* $\mathcal{A}'' = (\Sigma, X'', A''_1,\ldots,A''_m,A''_{m+1},\ldots,A''_{m+n},R) \in CTA(\mathcal{C}(X),\mathcal{U}(X))$ such that:

- $X'' = X \cup \bigcup_{k\in[1,m]} \bigcup_{j\in[1,n]}\{s^j_k,t^j_k\} \cup \bigcup_{j\in[1,n]}\{y^j,z^j\}$.
- Each component $A''_k$, with $k \in [1,m]$, is obtained by adding to each transition $t$ in $A_k$, and for each clock $x^j$, either $\{s^j_k := 0, t^j_k := 1\}$, if $x^j$ is updated in $t$, or $\{s^j_k := 0, t^j_k := 0\}$, otherwise. Note that $t^j_k - s^j_k = 1$ if $A''_k$ updates $x^j$, whereas $t^j_k - s^j_k = 0$ otherwise.
- Each component $A''_{m+j}$, with $j \in [1,n]$, keeps track of the component that has most recently updated $x^j$. More precisely, $A''_{m+j}$ sets clocks $y^j$ and $z^j$ so that, for each $1 \le k \le m$, $z^j - y^j = k-1$ iff the most recent update on $x^j$ has been done by the component $A''_k$. We define $A''_{m+j}$ as follows:
  - $A''_{m+j}$ has states $is_1, will_1,\ldots,is_m,will_m$, with $is_1$ initial. State $is_k$ is entered iff $A''_k$ is the component that has most recently updated $x^j$ and $A''_{m+j}$ predicts that $x^j$ is not updated in the current step. State $will_k$ is entered iff $A''_{m+j}$ predicts that $A''_k$ is updating $x^j$ in the current step.
  - For each action $a$ there are transitions
    1. $\langle is_h, \wedge_{i\in[1,m]}(t^j_i - s^j_i = 0), a, \{\}, is_h\rangle$
    2. $\langle is_h, \wedge_{i\in[1,m]}(t^j_i - s^j_i = 0), a, \{z^j := k-1, y^j := 0\}, will_k\rangle$
    3. $\langle will_k, t^j_k - s^j_k = 1, a, \{\}, is_k\rangle$
    4. $\langle will_k, t^j_k - s^j_k = 1, a, \{z^j := h-1, y^j := 0\}, will_h\rangle$.

    The first checks that the prediction that $x^j$ was not updated in the past step is correct ($\wedge_{i\in[1,m]}(t^j_i - s^j_i = 0)$), and predicts that $x^j$ is not updated in the current step ($is_h$ is entered). The second checks that $x^j$ was not updated in the past step and predicts that $x^j$ is updated in the current step by $A''_k$ ($will_k$ is entered). The third checks that $x^j$ was updated by $A''_k$ in the past step ($t^j_k - s^j_k = 1$) and predicts that $x^j$ is not updated in the current step. The last checks that $x^j$ was updated by $A''_k$ in the past step and predicts that $x^j$ is updated by $A''_h$ in the current step.

In the second step we replace each clock $x^j$ by $x^j_1,\ldots,x^j_m$, with $x^j_i$ owned by $A''_i$. We replace each update $x^j := q$ in $A''_i$ with $x^j_i := q$. We add $n$ components that ensure that if in a step two different clocks $x^j_h$, $x^j_k$ replacing $x^j$ are updated, then they have the same value. We derive $\mathcal{A}' = (\Sigma, X', A'_1,\ldots,A'_{m+2n},R)$ as follows:

- $X' = (X'' \setminus X) \cup \bigcup_{j\in[1,n]} \bigcup_{i\in[1,m]}\{x^j_i\}$
- for each $i \in [1,m]$, $A'_i$ is obtained from $A''_i$ by replacing each update $x^j := q$ with $x^j_i := q$, and by modifying constraints of transitions as follows:

  - $x^j \geq q$ becomes $\bigwedge_{h\in[1,m]}(z^j - y^j = h-1 \Rightarrow x^j_h \geq q)$
  - $x^j < q$ becomes $\bigwedge_{h\in[1,m]}(z^j - y^j = h-1 \Rightarrow x^j_h < q)$
  - $x^j - x^i \geq q$ becomes $\bigwedge_{h\in[1,m]}(z^j - y^j = h-1 \Rightarrow \bigwedge_{k\in[1,m]}(z^i - y^i = k-1 \Rightarrow x^j_h - x^i_k \geq q))$
  - $x^j - x^i < q$ becomes $\bigwedge_{h\in[1,m]}(z^j - y^j = h-1 \Rightarrow \bigwedge_{k\in[1,m]}(z^i - y^i = k-1 \Rightarrow x^j_h - x^i_k < q))$.
- for each $1 \leq j \leq n$, $A'_{m+j} = A''_{m+j}$
- for each $1 \leq j \leq n$, $A'_{m+n+j}$ checks that if in the previous step two different clocks $x^j_h$ and $x^j_k$ were both updated, then they have the same value. It has a state $s$ and transitions $\langle s, \wedge_{h\in[1,m]k\in[1,m]}((t^j_h - s^j_h = 1) \wedge (t^j_k - s^j_k = 0)) \Rightarrow x^j_h - x^j_k = 1, a, \{\}, s\rangle$.

$\mathcal{A}''$ (resp. $\mathcal{A}'$) is polynomial w.r.t. $\mathcal{A}'$ (resp. $\mathcal{A}$) and $\mathcal{L}(\mathcal{A}'') = \mathcal{L}(\mathcal{A}') = \mathcal{L}(\mathcal{A})$. □

# 4 Exponential Upper Bounds

Here we prove that $CTA(\mathcal{C}(X),\mathcal{U}(X)) \stackrel{u}{\longrightarrow} CTA(\mathcal{C}_{df}(X),\mathcal{U}_0(X))$, from which it follows that all arrows in Fig.1 represent exponential upper bounds.

**Proposition 4.** *$CTA(\mathcal{C}(X),\mathcal{U}(X)) \stackrel{u}{\longrightarrow} CTA(\mathcal{C}_{df}(X),\mathcal{U}_0(X))$.*

*Proof.* Given any $CTA$ $\mathcal{A} \in CTA(\mathcal{C}(X),\mathcal{U}(X))$, we obtain an equivalent automaton $\mathcal{S} \in STA(\mathcal{C}(X),\mathcal{U}(X))$, exponential w.r.to $\mathcal{A}$, by cartesian product. Following [2], we transform $\mathcal{S}$ into an equivalent $\mathcal{S}' \in STA(\mathcal{C}_{df}(X),\mathcal{U}(X))$, with $|\mathcal{S}'| = |\mathcal{S}| \times 2^d$, where $|\mathcal{S}'|$ and $|\mathcal{S}|$ are the size of $\mathcal{S}'$ and $\mathcal{S}$, and $d$ is the number of diagonal constraints in $\mathcal{S}$. So, $\mathcal{S}'$ is exponential w.r.to $\mathcal{A}$. As pointed out in [5], $\mathcal{S}'$ can be transformed into an equivalent $\mathcal{S}'' \in STA(\mathcal{C}_{df}(X),\mathcal{U}_0(X))$, polynomial w.r.to $\mathcal{S}'$. So, $\mathcal{S}''$ is equivalent to $\mathcal{A}$ and exponential w.r.to $\mathcal{A}$. □

**Corollary 1.** *If $\mathcal{C} \longrightarrow \mathcal{C}'$ or $\mathcal{C} \longleftrightarrow \mathcal{C}'$ is in Fig.1, then $\mathcal{C} \stackrel{u}{\longrightarrow} \mathcal{C}'$.*

# 5 Exponential Lower Bounds

In this section we prove that all arrows in Fig.1 represent exponential lower bounds. The result follows from $CTA_{pr}(\mathcal{C}(X),\mathcal{U}_0(X)) \stackrel{l}{\longrightarrow} CTA(\mathcal{C}_{df}(X),\mathcal{U}(X))$, $CTA_{pr}(\mathcal{C}_{df}(X),\mathcal{U}(X)) \stackrel{l}{\longrightarrow} CTA(\mathcal{C}(X),\mathcal{U}_0(X))$ and $CTA(\mathcal{C}_{df}(X),\mathcal{U}(X)) \stackrel{l}{\longrightarrow} CTA_{pr}(\mathcal{C}_{df}(X),\mathcal{U}(X))$, which are proved below.

**Simulation of diagonal constraints**

We show that $CTA_{pr}(\mathcal{C}(X),\mathcal{U}_0(X)) \stackrel{l}{\longrightarrow} CTA(\mathcal{C}_{df}(X),\mathcal{U}(X))$, i.e. simulating diagonal constraints implies, in general, an exponential growth of the $CTA$.

Let $(\mathcal{A}_m)_{m\geq 0} = ((\{a,b\}, \bigcup_{0\leq i\leq m}\{x_i,y_i\}, A_0, \ldots, A_m, \{q'_0\}))_{m\geq 0}$ be the family in $CTA_{pr}(\mathcal{C}(X),\mathcal{U}_0(X))$ with $A_0$ and $A_k$, $k \geq 1$, represented in Fig.2. The family $(\mathcal{A}_m)_{m\geq 0}$ accepts the family $(L_m)_{m\geq 0}$ of timed languages over $\{a,b\}$ such that:

– $untimed(L_m) = (b^* a^{2^{m+1}})^\omega$
– every timed sequence underlying a timed word in $L_m$ is strictly increasing.

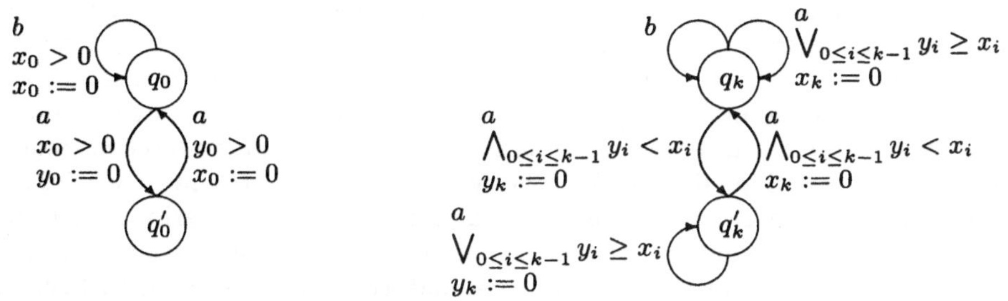


**Fig. 2.** Automata $A_0$ and $A_k$, $k \ge 1$ ($q_0$ and $q_k$ are the initial states)

The idea is that $A_0, \dots, A_m$ are able to count $2^{m+1}$ occurrences of the action $a$. More precisely, $A_0, \dots, A_m$ implement a counter modulo $2^{m+1}$.
Let $b_0, \dots, b_m$ be coefficients in $\{0,1\}$. When $\sum_{0\le k\le m} 2^k \times b_k$ occurrences of $a$ have been counted, the component $A_k$ is either in state $q_k$, if $b_k = 0$, or in state $q'_k$, if $b_k = 1$. So, every $2^{m+1} = 1 + \sum_{0\le k\le m} 2^k$ occurrences of $a$, $A_0, \dots, A_m$ are in state $q_0, \dots, q_m$, respectively, and occurrences of $b$ can be read.
Whenever $a$ is read, $A_k$ changes its state iff $A_0, \dots, A_{k-1}$ are in state $q'_0, \dots, q'_{k-1}$. This corresponds to the fact that $b_k$ switches from 0 to 1, or conversely, every $1 + \sum_{0\le i\le k-1} 2^i$ occurrences of $a$. The component $A_k$ infers that $A_0, \dots, A_{k-1}$ are in state $q'_0, \dots, q'_{k-1}$, respectively, by the fact that $y_0 < x_0 \wedge \dots \wedge y_{k-1} < x_{k-1}$. This is correct, since clock $y_i$ (resp. $x_i$) is reset every time $q'_i$ (resp. $q_i$) is entered.
This example shows that a sequential component can use diagonal clock constraints to communicate its actual state to other components.

**Proposition 5.** $CTA_{pr}(\mathcal{C}(X),\mathcal{U}_0(X)) \stackrel{l}{\longrightarrow} CTA(\mathcal{C}_{df}(X),\mathcal{U}(X))$.

*Proof.* Let $(L_m)_{m\ge 0}$ be the family of languages accepted by the family $(\mathcal{A}_m)_{m\ge 0}$ in $CTA_{pr}(\mathcal{C}(X),\mathcal{U}_0(X))$ considered above. Since $\mathcal{A}_m$ is polynomial w.r.to $m$, it suffices to prove that every family $(\mathcal{B}_m)_{m\ge 0}$ in $CTA(\mathcal{C}_{df}(X),\mathcal{U}(X))$ accepting $(L_m)_{m\ge 0}$ is such that $\mathcal{B}_m$ is at least exponential w.r.to $m$.
Assume any family $(\mathcal{B}_m)_{m\ge 0}$ in $CTA(\mathcal{C}_{df}(X),\mathcal{U}(X))$ accepting $(L_m)_{m\ge 0}$. Since $\mathcal{B}_m$ can count $2^{m+1}$ occurrences of $a$, it has at least $2^{m+1}$ configurations. If such occurrences of $a$ are counted by a single sequential component of $\mathcal{B}_m$, then such a component has at least $2^{m+1}$ states. So, it suffices to prove that the occurrences of $a$ cannot be counted by $n > 1$ components in $\mathcal{B}_m$, through any cooperation.
Assume, by contradiction, that such components $B_1, \dots, B_n$ exist. In this case, there must be some $B_i$ that can check whether another $B_j$, with $j \ne i$, is in some state $q_j$ or not. The condition "$B_j$ is in state $q_j$" must correspond to some non diagonal clock constraint, since the components of $\mathcal{B}_m$ can communicate only through clocks. So, let $\phi_j$ be the diagonal free constraint representing "$B_j$ is in

state $q_j$". Let us rewrite $\phi_j$ as $\phi_{j,1} \vee \ldots \vee \phi_{j,h}$, with each $\phi_{j,i}$ a conjunction of atomic constraints $x\#q$. First of all we note that no constraint $x_{j,i} = q_{j,i}$ can appear in $\phi_{j,i}$, since conditions "$B_j$ is in state $q_j$" and "$B_j$ is not in state $q_j$" must hold for intervals and not for discrete instants. Moreover, we can prove that some constraint $x_{j,i} < q_{j,i}$, or $x_{j,i} \leq q_{j,i}$, appears in $\phi_{j,i}$ for each $1 \leq i \leq h$. In fact, in the contrary case, some step must be performed to set the clocks, so to maintain $\phi_{j,i}$ (and, therefore, $\phi_j$) false when $q_j$ is not active (otherwise the growing of clocks will make $\phi_j$ true when $q_j$ is not active). Since such a step can be performed only when receiving $a$ or $b$, the input rate results to be constrained. This is a contradiction, since in $L_m$ the input rate is free (more precisely, the interval of time between two subsequent actions can be arbitrarily large). So, we have proved that some constraint $x_{j,i} < q_{j,i}$, or $x_{j,i} \leq q_{j,i}$, appears in $\phi_{j,i}$ for each $1 \leq i \leq h$. Now, whenever $q_j$ is enabled and $\phi_j$ is going to become false (i.e., every $\phi_{j,i}$ is going to become false), a step must be performed to set the clocks, thus maintaining $\phi_j$ true. Once again, such a step can be performed only when receiving $a$ or $b$, the input rate results to be constrained, and this is a contradiction, since in $L_m$ the rate of the input is free. □

**Simulation of constant updates**

Here we show that $CTA_{pr}(\mathcal{C}_{df}(X),\mathcal{U}(X)) \stackrel{l}{\longrightarrow} CTA(\mathcal{C}(X),\mathcal{U}_0(X))$, i.e. simulating constant updates implies, in general, an exponential growth of the $CTA$.

Let $(\mathcal{A}_m)_{m\geq 0} = ((\{a,b\}, \bigcup_{0\leq i\leq m}\{x_i,z_i\}, A_0,\ldots,A_m,\{q_0\}))_{m\geq 0}$ be the family in $CTA_{pr}(\mathcal{C}_{df}(X),\mathcal{U}(X))$ with $A_0$ and $A_k$, $k \geq 1$, represented in Fig.3. The family $(\mathcal{A}_m)_{m\geq 0}$ accepts the family $(L_m)_{m\geq 0}$ of timed languages over $\{a,b\}$, where $L_m$ contains the timed words $(a,t_0),(b,t'_0),(a,t_1),(b,t'_1)\ldots$ such that:

- $t_0 > 5$ and, for each $i \geq 0$, $t_{i+1} < t_i + 5$
- for each $0 \leq i \leq 2^{m+1} - 1$, $t'_{i+(2^{m+1}\times n)} - t_{i+(2^{m+1}\times n)}$ is in a set $T_i$. More precisely, if $i = \sum_{0\leq k\leq m} 2^k \times b_k$, with $b_0,\ldots,b_m \in \{0,1\}$, then, for each $0 \leq k \leq m$, either $1 - 1/2^k \in T_i$, if $b_k = 0$, or $1 - 1/2^{k+m} \in T_i$, if $b_k = 1$.

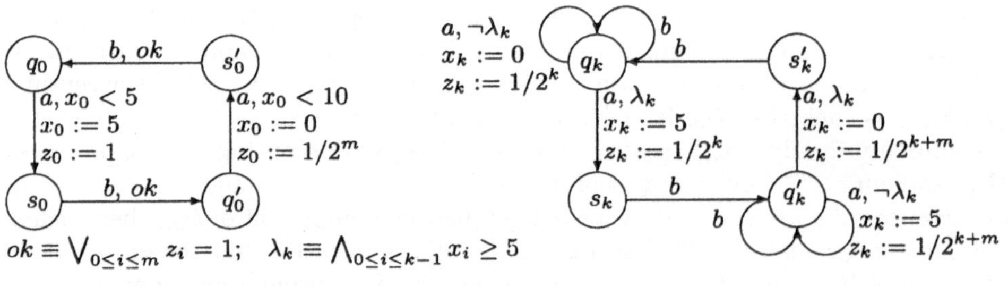


**Fig. 3.** Automata $A_0$ and $A_k$, $k \geq 1$ ($q_0$ and $q_k$ are the initial states)

The idea is that $A_0,\ldots,A_m$ are able to count $2^{m+1}$ occurrences of the action $a$. More precisely, $A_0,\ldots,A_m$ implement a counter modulo $2^{m+1}$.

Let $b_0, \ldots, b_m$ be coefficients in $\{0,1\}$. When $i = \sum_{0 \leq k \leq m} 2^k \times b_k$ occurrences of $a$ have been counted, the component $A_k$ is either in a state in $\{q_k, s'_k\}$, if $b_k = 0$, or in a state in $\{q'_k, s_k\}$, if $b_k = 1$. So, when the subsequent occurrence of $a$ is read, the clock $z_k$ takes either $1/2^k$, if $b_k = 0$, or $1/2^{k+m}$, if $b_k = 1$. This implies that the time elapsed between the $a$ and the next occurrence of $b$ is in the set $T_i$, which contains either $1 - 1/2^k$, if $b_k = 0$, or $1 - 1/2^{k+m}$, if $b_k = 1$.
Note that the sets $T_0, \ldots, T_{2^{m+1}-1}$ are pairwise different.
Whenever $a$ is read, $A_k$ changes its state iff $A_0, \ldots, A_{k-1}$ are in state $q'_0, \ldots, q'_{k-1}$, respectively. This corresponds to the fact that $b_k$ switches from 0 to 1, or conversely, every $1 + \sum_{0 \leq i \leq k-1} 2^i$ occurrences of $a$. The component $A_k$ infers that $A_0, \ldots, A_{k-1}$ are in state $q'_0, \ldots, q'_{k-1}$ by the fact that $x_0 \geq 5 \wedge \ldots \wedge x_{k-1} \geq 5$. This is correct, since clock $x_i$ is set to 5 (resp. 0) every time $q_i$ (resp. $q'_i$) is left, and two subsequent occurrences of $a$ are separated by less that 5 units of time.

This example shows that a sequential component can use constant updates to communicate its actual state to other components.

**Proposition 6.** $CTA_{pr}(\mathcal{C}_{df}(X), \mathcal{U}(X)) \xrightarrow{l} CTA(\mathcal{C}(X), \mathcal{U}_0(X))$.

*Proof.* Let $(L_m)_{m \geq 0}$ be the family of languages accepted by the family $(\mathcal{A}_m)_{m \geq 0}$ in $CTA_{pr}(\mathcal{C}_{df}(X), \mathcal{U}(X))$ considered above. Since $\mathcal{A}_m$ is polynomial w.r.to $m$, it suffices to prove that every family $(\mathcal{B}_m)_{m \geq 0}$ in $CTA(\mathcal{C}(X), \mathcal{U}_0(X))$ accepting $(L_m)_{m \geq 0}$ is such that $\mathcal{B}_m$ is at least exponential w.r.to $m$.
Assume an arbitrary $\mathcal{B}_m$ in $CTA(\mathcal{C}(X), \mathcal{U}_0(X))$ accepting $L_m$. It must have at least $2^{m+1}$ configurations, $c_0, \ldots, c_{2^{m+1}-1}$, such that, whenever $c_i$ is activated, an occurrence of $b$ must be read after a time chosen in $T_i$. First of all we observe that, whenever $c_i$ is activated, to check whether a time in $T_i$ is elapsed we can observe only clocks that are reset (and not arbitrarily set, since constant updates are not allowed) when $c_i$ is activated. We mean that we cannot observe clocks that are reset before. The reason is that the step leading to $c_i$ is caused by an occurrence of $a$ that arrives nondeterministically in the interval $[t, t+5)$, where $t$ is the arrival time of the previous occurrence of $a$. As a consequence, from every state in $c_i$ at least $|T_i|$ transitions depart, each representing waiting for a time in $T_i$. This implies that no state in $c_i$ can be in any configuration $c_j$, with $j \neq i$. It follows that at least $2^{m+1}$ states are in $\mathcal{B}_m$, which implies the thesis. □

**Simulation of private clocks**

Here we show that $CTA(\mathcal{C}_{df}(X), \mathcal{U}(X)) \xrightarrow{l} CTA_{pr}(\mathcal{C}_{df}(X), \mathcal{U}(X))$, i.e. simulating non private clocks implies an exponential growth of the $CTA$ with diagonal free clock constraints and constant updates.

Let $(\mathcal{A}_m)_{m \geq 1} = ((\{a\}, \{x\}, A_1, \ldots, A_m, \{q_0\}))_{m \geq 1}$ be the family in $CTA(\mathcal{C}_{df}(X), \mathcal{U}(X))$ such that $A_k$, $k \geq 1$, is represented in Fig.4.
The family $(\mathcal{A}_m)_{m \geq 1}$ accepts the family $(L_m)_{m \geq 1}$ of timed languages over $\{a\}$ containing the timed words $(a, t_1)^*(a, t_2)^* \ldots (a, t_n)^* \ldots$ such that:

- $t_1 = 2m + 1$ and $t_2 - t_1 \in \{2m + 1 - 1, 2m + 1 - 2, \ldots, 2m + 1 - m\}$;
- $t_i - t_{i-1} \in T_i$ implies $t_{i+1} - t_i \in (T_i \setminus \{2m + 1 - k\}) \cup \{2m + 1 - (k + m)\}$ or $t_{i+1} - t_i \in (T_i \setminus \{2m + 1 - (k + m)\}) \cup \{2m + 1 - k\}$, for some $1 \leq k \leq m$.

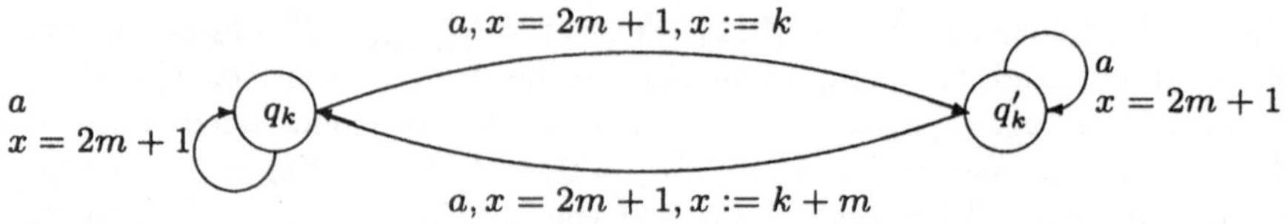


**Fig. 4.** The automaton $A_k$, $k \geq 1$ ($q_k$ is the initial state)

At instant $t_1 = 2m+1$, there is a finite sequence of $n \geq 0$ steps from configuration $(q_1, \ldots, q_m)$ to itself. Moreover, there is a step where an automaton $A_k$, for some $1 \leq k \leq m$, leaves state $q_k$, enters state $q'_k$ and sets the clock $x$ to value $k$, and where automata $A_1, \ldots, A_{k-1}, A_{k+1}, \ldots, A_m$ perform the transitions leaving and entering states $q_1, \ldots, q_{k-1}, q_{k+1}, \ldots, q_m$, respectively. Now, the next step is performed at instant $t_2 = t_1 + (2m + 1 - k)$. Since $k$ can be arbitrarily chosen in $\{1, \ldots, m\}$, it holds that $t_2 - t_1 \in \{2m + 1 - 1, 2m + 1 - 2 \ldots, 2m + 1 - m\}$.

Now, assume that at time $t_{i-1}$ $A_k$ leaves $q_k$ (resp. $q'_k$), enters $q'_k$ (resp. $q_k$) and sets $x$ to $k$ (resp. $k + m$), and that $A_1, \ldots, A_{k-1}, A_{k+1}, \ldots, A_m$ do not change state. The time $t_i - t_{i-1}$ that elapses until the next step is performed is $2m+1-k$ (resp. $2m + 1 - (k + m)$). Moreover, the time that elapses between $t_i$ and $t_{i+1}$ cannot be $2m + 1 - k$ (resp. $2m + 1 - (k + m)$), and can be $2m + 1 - (k + m)$ (resp. $2m + 1 - k$). In fact, the transition from $q'_k$ to $q_k$ (resp. from $q_k$ to $q'_k$) can be performed at time $t_i$, and that from $q_k$ to $q'_k$ (resp. from $q'_k$ to $q_k$) cannot.

**Proposition 7.** $CTA(\mathcal{C}_{df}(X), \mathcal{U}(X)) \stackrel{l}{\longrightarrow} CTA_{pr}(\mathcal{C}_{df}(X), \mathcal{U}(X))$.

*Proof.* Let $(L_m)_{m \geq 1}$ be the family of languages accepted by the family $(\mathcal{A}_m)_{m \geq 1}$ in $CTA(\mathcal{C}_{df}(X), \mathcal{U}(X))$ considered above. Since $\mathcal{A}_m$ is polynomial w.r.to $m$, it suffices to prove that every family $(\mathcal{B}_m)_{m \geq 1}$ in $CTA_{pr}(\mathcal{C}_{df}(X), \mathcal{U}(X))$ accepting $(L_m)_{m \geq 1}$ is such that $\mathcal{B}_m$ is at least exponential w.r.to $m$.
Assume, by contradiction, that a family $(\mathcal{B}_m)_{m \geq 1}$ in $CTA_{pr}(\mathcal{C}_{df}(X), \mathcal{U}(X))$ accepting $(L_m)_{m \geq 1}$ exists which is not exponential w.r.to $m$.
Since $\mathcal{B}_m$ accepts words $(a, t_1)^*(a, t_2)^* \ldots (a, t_n)^* \ldots$, where $t_{i+1} - t_i$ can be in one of $2^m$ different sets, $\mathcal{B}_m$ has at least $2^m$ different configurations simulating configurations $c_1, \ldots, c_{2^m}$ of $\mathcal{A}_m$. Therefore, $\mathcal{B}_m$ cannot have only one sequential component. So, let us assume that it has $n$ sequential components, $B_1, \ldots, B_n$.
Let us call $T_{i+1}$ the set of possible values of $t_{i+1} - t_i$.
Since $T_2 = \{2m+1-1, 2m+1-2, \ldots 2m+1-m\}$ and, for each $i \geq 2$, $T_{i+1}$ is either $(T_i \setminus \{2m+1-k\}) \cup \{2m+1-(k+m)\}$ or $(T_i \setminus \{2m+1-(k+m)\}) \cup \{2m+1-k\}$ for some $1 \leq k \leq m$, it holds that from each configuration $c_i$ it is possible to reach $m$ configurations in $\{c_1, \ldots, c_{2^m}\}$ through a step. Let $c_{i,1}, \ldots, c_{i,m}$ be the configurations such that $c_{i,j}$ is reached from $c_i$ when $A_j$ changes state and assigns $\tau_j \in \{j, j + m\}$ to $x$, and $A_1, \ldots, A_{j-1}, A_{j+1}, \ldots A_m$ do not change state.
Assume that $c_i$ is the $u^{th}$ configuration entered, i.e. time elapsed between entering $c_i$ and exiting $c_i$ is in set $T_u$.
Let $s_1, \ldots, s_n$ be the states in the sequential components $B_1, \ldots, B_n$, respectively, such that $c_i = (s_1, \ldots, s_n)$. There is a total function $f : \{1, \ldots, m\} \rightarrow$

$\{1,\ldots,n\}$ such that, given any $1 \leq h \leq m$, there are: 1) a state $s_{f(h)}$ with $f(h) \in \{1,\ldots,n\}$, 2) a transition from state $s_{f(h)}$ to a state $s'_{f(h)}$ assigning a value $\gamma_h$ to some clock $x_{f(h)}$ of $B_{f(h)}$, 3) a transition either from $s'_{f(h)}$ or from a state that is entered whenever $s'_{f(h)}$ is, guarded by a clock constraint $x_{f(h)} = q_{f(h)}$, where such a guard checks that the amount of time $2m+1-\tau_h$ is elapsed. The transition from $s'_{f(h)}$ is needed because there must be a step leaving $c_{i,h}$ $2m+1-\tau_h$ instants after $c_{i,h}$ is entered.
Now, given $h_1 \neq h_2$, in general it holds that $f(h_1) \neq f(h_2)$, otherwise there is a state in $\mathcal{B}_m$ for each configuration of $\mathcal{A}_m$, thus contradicting that $\mathcal{B}_m$ is not exponential w.r.to $m$. So, let us assume that $f(h_1) \neq f(h_2)$. There is a step from $(s_1,\ldots,s_n)$ to a configuration where both $s'_{f(h_1)}$ and $s'_{f(h_2)}$ are active. In such a configuration, both a transition guarded by the clock constraint $x_{f(h_1)} = q_{f(h_1)}$, and a transition guarded by the clock constraint $x_{f(h_2)} = q_{f(h_2)}$ can be performed. This implies that an occurrence of $a$ can be read in this configuration $2m+1-\tau_{f(h_1)}$ or $2m+1-\tau_{f(h_2)}$ units of time after it is entered. This implies that $T_{u+1} \setminus T_u$ has two elements, thus contradicting that $\mathcal{B}_m$ accepts $L_m$. □

From Propositions 5, 6 and 7 it follows that all arrows in Fig.1 represent exponential lower bounds.

**Corollary 2.** *If $C \longrightarrow C'$ or $C \longleftrightarrow C'$ is in Fig.1, then $C \stackrel{l}{\longrightarrow} C'$.*

## References

1. R. Alur and D.L. Dill: *A theory of timed automata.* Theoretical Computer Science **126**, 183–235, 1994.
2. B. Bérard, V. Diekert, P. Gastin, and A. Petit: *Characterization of the power of silent transitions in timed automata.* Fundamenta Informaticae **36**, 145–182, 1998.
3. S. Bornot and J. Sifakis: *Relating time progress and deadlines in hybrid systems.* In Proc. of HART '97, Springer LNCS 1201, 266–300, 1997.
4. S. Bornot and J. Sifakis: *On the composition of hybrid systems.* In Proc. of HSCC '98, Springer LNCS 1386, 69–83, 1998.
5. P. Bouyer, C. Dufourd, E. Fleury, and A. Petit: *Are timed automata updatable?* In Proc. of CAV 2000, Springer LNCS 1855, 464-479, 2000.
6. P. Bouyer, C. Dufourd, E. Fleury, and A. Petit: *Expressiveness of updatable timed automata.* In Proc. of MFCS 2000, Springer LNCS 1893, 232–242, 2000.
7. D. Drusinsky and D. Harel: *On the power of bounded concurrency I: finite automata.* Journal of the ACM **41**, 217–539, 1994.
8. R. Lanotte, A. Maggiolo-Schettini, and A. Peron: *Timed Cooperating Automata.* Fundamenta Informaticae **43**, 153–173, 2000.

# How Powerful Are Infinite Time Machines?

Grégory Lafitte

Ecole Normale Supérieure de Lyon, Laboratoire de l'Informatique du Parallélisme, 46 allée d'Italie, 69364 Lyon Cedex 07, France
glafitte@ens-lyon.fr

**Abstract.** We study the power of finite machines with *infinite time* to complete their task. To do this, we define a variant to Wojciechowski automata, investigate their recognition power, and compare them to infinite time Turing machines. Furthermore, using this infinite time, we analyse the ordinals *comprehensible* by such machines and discover that one can in fact go beyond the recursive realm. We conjecture that this is somehow already the case with Wojciechowski automata.

## Introduction

Finite automata on infinite sequences have been introduced by Büchi in [5] to prove the decidability of the monadic second order theory of $\langle \omega, < \rangle$. Büchi automata differ from finite automata on finite sequences only by its condition of acceptance of a word. A word is *accepted* by a Büchi automata if and only if the set of states, through which the automata goes an infinite number of times during an *execution* (there may be several executions if the automata is nondeterministic), contains at least a final state.

Independently, Muller introduced in [11] deterministic automata on infinite words such that a word is *accepted* if and only if the set of states, through which the automata goes an infinite number of times during an *execution* (there may be several executions if the automata is nondeterministic), belongs to a table given with the automata.

McNaughton proved in [10] that (deterministic) Muller automata and nondeterministic Büchi automata accept the same infinite sequences and that those infinite sequences can be described by $\omega$-regular expressions of the form $\bigcup_{i=0}^{n} \alpha_i \cdot \beta_i^{\omega}$ where $\alpha_i$ and $\beta_i$ are regular expressions of finite words and such that none of the $\beta_i$'s contain the $\emptyset$ symbol.

Then Büchi introduced in [6] finite automata that are able to describe transfinite sets of sequences. Using those automata, he proved the decidability of the monadic second order theory of $\langle \alpha, < \rangle$, where $\alpha$ is a countable ordinal. It featured special transitions for limit ordinal stages such that the state reached at that limit stage $\xi$ depends only on previously reached states $\{s \in S \mid \forall \beta < \xi \, \exists \gamma > \beta \, \varphi(\gamma) = s\}$. He modified again the definition to use them to prove the decidability of the monadic second order theory of $\langle \omega_1, < \rangle$.

Choueka generalized in [7] Büchi's ideas to get automata on transfinite sequences of *length* less than $\omega^n$ for a given $n < \omega$. The difference with Büchi's

R. Freivalds (Ed.): FCT 2001, LNCS 2138, pp. 252–263, 2001.

approach is in the behaviour at limit stages : for a limit ordinal $\xi = \beta + \omega^n$ ($n < \omega$ and $\beta = 0$ or $\beta \geq \omega^n$), $s$ belongs to $\varphi(\xi)$ if and only if there is an infinite number of $k < \omega$ satisfying $\varphi(\beta + \omega^{n-1} \cdot k) = s$. Note that $\varphi$ is only defined for $n < \omega$ and that $\varphi(\xi)$ depends only on $(\varphi(\alpha))_{\alpha<\xi}$. These automata recognize (as the Büchi automata) words that can be described by regular expressions similar to Büchi's $\omega$-regular expressions.

Wojciechowski then introduced in [15] automata on arbitrary transfinite sequences, similar to Büchi's, and corresponding regular expressions (in [16]), describing words recognized by these automata, with a $\sharp$ operator[1] that is the transfinite analogue of the $\omega$ operator. If we work only on words used by Choueka automata, Wojciechowski and Choueka automata are equivalent. Wojciechowski automata are thus the automata that we will use for our base study.

Following those definitions, several studies of Bedon, Carton and Perrin [4,1, 2,3,12] have focused on generalization of classical finite automata theorems and characterizations to infinite and transfinite words. In fact, it is Perrin and Pin's [13] that brought some years ago the study of finite automata on infinite words to the author's attention and stirred his interest in the field.

$\omega$ is only the first infinite ordinal, hence automata on arbitrary transfinite sequences constitute a *natural* generalization of automata on infinite words, read $\omega$-indexed words. Studying the behaviour of automata on ordinals is also liable to lead us to the right concepts for automata at large, including automata on $\omega$-words. Moreover, these automata have potential applications in semantics and in decidability problems, e.g. Büchi's results. Muller had also introduced his automata on infinite words in order to study the behaviour of asynchronous circuits. Physicists have already investigated tasks involving infinitely many steps, called supertasks, the first of which is done, for example, in a half second, the next in a quarter second, and so on, so that the entire job is completed in a finite amount of time. More useful supertasks, perhaps, have been proposed to determine the truth of an existential number-theoretic question. Physicists have been surprisingly able to construct general relativistic models in which the supertasks can apparently be carried out. But our interest resides in not so much finding what is physically possible to compute in a supertask so much as what is *mathematically* possible.

In order to study the power of infinite time, we define a natural extension to Wojciechowski automata, called $\mathcal{W}^2$-automata. $\mathcal{W}^2$-automata work on a two-way $\omega$-tape and have pebbles that appear only after an infinite amount of steps after their usage. The two-way tape lets us study the recognition power of our automata on common objects as finite sequences on a finite alphabet, read finite inputs, or $\omega$-sequences on a finite alphabet, read reals for input. This lets us compare the power of recognition of our automata to that of common abstract state machines, e.g. pushdown automata, counter machines, Turing machines... A first surprising result about those automata is the power obtained by infinite time combined with the eventual pebbles. By using the non-bounded property of in-

[1] $a^{\#}$ is either the empty word or the letter $a$ repeated a finite number, an infinite number or a transfinite number of times.

finite time, we manage to use potentially an infinite amount of pebbles and bridge directly the gap between (finite time) Turing computability and regular languages.

Still another model of supertasks is infinite time Turing machines. Jeffrey Kidder defined infinite time Turing machines in 1989, and he and Joel Hamkins worked out the early theory at Berkeley. With a fresh look in 1996, a few of the formerly puzzling questions were answered, and a more advanced theory developed and appeared in [8]. Some still more puzzling questions were answered later on in 2000 by Philip Welch in [14] to arrive now at a more mature theory.

We begin by recalling in section 1 the definitions of Büchi and Wojciechowski automata and by giving some simple examples of them. Next in section 2, we define $\mathcal{W}^2$-automata and investigate their power compared to pushdown automata. We also prove a "pumping lemma" (lemma 3) for Wojciechowski automata in order to differentiate their power to $\mathcal{W}^2$-automata's. Our analysis of the power of $\mathcal{W}^2$-automata leads in section 3 to the comparison with infinite time Turing machines (theorem 3 and 4). We highlight, in section 4, the ordinal oriented aspects of our study. We show in theorem 10 that the ordinals *comprehensible* by $\mathcal{W}^2$-automata go much farther than what is usually thought and conjecture about ordinals comprehensible by regular Wojciechowski automata.

# 1 Infinite Words and Finite Automata

## 1.1 Büchi and Wojciechowski Automata

**Definition 1.** *A* Büchi automaton *is a quintuplet* $\mathcal{A} = (Q, \Sigma, \delta, Z, F)$ *where* $(Q, \Sigma, \delta)$ *is a finite automaton, and* $Z$ *and* $F$ *are subsets of* $Q$ *called respectively set of initial states and set of final states.*

A finite path of $\mathcal{A}$ is *successful* if its origin is in $Z$ and its end is in $F$. An infinite path is *successful* if its origin is in $Z$ and it goes infinitely often through states of $F$. The set of finite (respectively infinite) words *recognized* by $\mathcal{A}$ is the set of labels of successful finite (respectively infinite) paths of $\mathcal{A}$. A set of words $M$ is *recognizable* if there is an automata $\mathcal{A}$ that recognizes precisely the words of $M$.

The set of words described by $\{a, b\}^\star a^\omega$ is not recognizable by a deterministic Büchi automaton. However it is recognizable by a nondeterministic Büchi automaton. Nondeterministic Büchi automaton are thus more powerful than deterministic ones. Muller automata give a more satisfying definition from that point of view.

Let us now consider words $u$ of a finite alphabet $\Sigma$ as $\alpha$-sequences ($\alpha$ is an ordinal) on $\Sigma$. We now define *continuous* $\alpha$-sequences in order to define Wojciechowski automata.

**Definition 2.** *An* $\alpha$*-sequence* $\varphi$ *on* $Q$ *is* continuous *if for any successor ordinal* $\beta$, $\varphi(\beta) \in Q$ *and if for any limit ordinal* $\beta$,

$$\varphi(\beta) = \{q \in Q \mid \{\gamma < \beta \mid \varphi(\gamma) = q\} \textit{ is cofinal to } \beta\}$$

**Remark 1.** *A continuous $\alpha$-sequence is completely determined by its values at successor ordinals $\{\varphi(\beta) \mid \beta \in Succ, \beta < \alpha\}$.*

**Definition 3.** *A* Wojciechowski automaton, *or* $\mathcal{W}$-automaton, *is a quintuplet $\mathcal{A} = (Q, \Sigma, \delta, i, F)$ with $\Sigma$ a finite alphabet, $Q$ the finite set of its states, $\delta \subseteq \wp(Q) \times \Sigma \times Q$ the transition relation, $i \in Q$ the initial state, and $F \subseteq \wp(Q)$ the finite set of its final states.*

From now on, by *state* we mean an element of $\wp(Q) = P(Q) \cup Q$.

**Definition 4.** *A* run *with label $u \in \Sigma^\alpha$, $\alpha \in Ord$, of an $\mathcal{W}$-automaton $\mathcal{A} = (Q, \Sigma, \delta, i, F)$ is a continuous $(\alpha + 1)$-sequence $\varphi$ such that $\varphi(0) = i$ and for all $\beta < \alpha$,*

$$(\varphi(\beta), u(\beta), \varphi(\beta + 1)) \in \delta$$

*A run is* successful *if $\varphi(\alpha) \in F$.*

A word $u \in \Sigma^\#$ is *recognized* by $\mathcal{A}$ if and only if there is a successful run of $\mathcal{A}$ with label $u$. A set of words $M$ is *recognizable* by $\mathcal{A}$ if this automaton recognizes only the words belonging to $M$.

One can easily build (see [9]) $\mathcal{W}$-automata recognizing respectively $a^\omega$, $a^\#$, $a^{\omega^2}$, $\{a^\alpha \mid \alpha \in Succ\}$, $\{a^\alpha \mid \alpha \in Lim\}$ and $a^\#$.

Here is an example[2] of an automaton recognizing $a^\alpha$ for $\alpha < \omega_1$ but not recognizing $a^{\omega_1}$.

*Example* 1.1

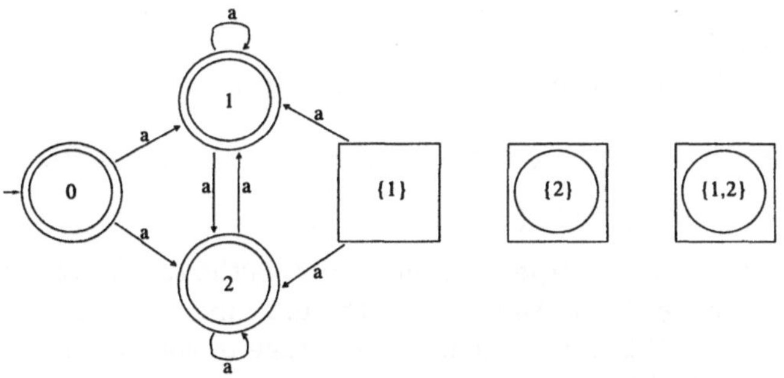


**Fig. 1.** A $\mathcal{W}$-automaton recognizing[3] $a^\alpha$ for $\alpha < \omega_1$

[2] A *square* state is a state belonging to $P(Q)$. A final state is with an inner (smaller) circle.

[3] Why? See [9]. This example prompts questions about recognizable ordinals: for what ordinal $\alpha$, is there an $\mathcal{W}$-automaton recognizing the singleton $a^\alpha$? for what ordinal $\alpha$, is there an $\mathcal{W}$-automaton recognizing a word of "length" $\alpha$? For some time, it was commonly thought that we would not go further than $\epsilon_0$ (not to talk about $\omega_1^{ck}$). We come back to those questions at the end of the paper.

## 2 Infinite Time Finite Automata on Reals

### 2.1 Infinite Time Behaviour

We propose the following variant of Wojciechowski automata. It will hopefully turn out to help us in understanding Wojciechowski automata and infinite time machines at large.

A 2-way Wojciechowski automaton, or $\mathcal{W}^2$-automaton is a $\mathcal{W}$-automaton on a 2-way countable tape. The special behaviour of the automaton compared to normal Wojciechowski behaviour is at limit stages. At a limit stage, the head of the tape is plucked from wherever it might have been racing towards, and placed on top of the first cell.

If we have a finite input, there are several ways of delimiting the input. We can have special end markers $\vdash$ and $\dashv$ that indicate the boundaries of the input. We will opt for a letter $\flat$ representing "blank" cells (we are working with "infinite time"... surely, we cannot restrict ourselves to a finite accessible part of the tape).

An $\mathcal{W}^2$-automaton also has its tape changed at limit stages in the following way : if at a previous successor stage the head of the tape stayed (stopped) on a cell for at least one stage, this cell has now the value $\natural$ if it didn't before and is erased to $\flat$ if it already contained the value $\natural$ (the value of the cell is toggled between $\natural$ and $\flat$).

**Definition 5.** *A* $\mathcal{W}^2$-automaton *is a quintuplet* $\mathcal{A} = (Q, \Sigma, \delta, i, F)$ *with:* $\Sigma$ *a finite alphabet,* $Q$ *the finite set of its states,* $\delta \subseteq \wp(Q) \times \Sigma \cup \{\flat, \natural\} \times Q \times \{\leftarrow, \downarrow, \rightarrow\}$ *the transition relation,* $i \in Q$ *the initial state, and* $F \subseteq \wp(Q)$ *the finite set of its final states.*

*A* run *with label* $\sigma \in (\Sigma \cup \{\flat, \natural\})^{\omega\alpha}$ *(*$\sigma$ *is a function of the form* $\alpha \to (\omega \to (\Sigma \cup \{\flat, \natural\}))$*),* $\alpha \in Ord$*, of an* $\mathcal{W}^2$*-automaton* $\mathcal{A} = (Q, \Sigma, \delta, i, F)$ *is a continuous* $(\alpha + 1)$*-sequence* $(\varphi_q, \varphi_{pos})$ *on* $\wp(Q) \times \mathbb{N}$ *such that* $\varphi_q(0) = i$*,* $\varphi_{pos}(0) = 0$ *and* $\sigma(0) \in \Sigma^\omega$ *is the original content of the tape and for any ordinal* $\beta < \alpha$*,*

$$(\varphi_q(\beta), \sigma(\beta)(\varphi_{pos}(\beta)), \varphi_q(\beta + 1), \rho(\varphi_{pos}(\beta + 1) - \varphi_{pos}(\beta))) \in \delta \tag{2.1}$$

*where* $\rho(1) =\rightarrow$*,* $\rho(0) =\downarrow$ *and* $\rho(-1) =\leftarrow$*,*

$\sigma$ is the evolution of the tape's content : $\sigma(\beta)$ is the tape's content at stage $\beta$. $\varphi_q$ and $\varphi_{pos}$ give respectively the state of the machine and position of its tape's head at every stage. (2.1) says that from one stage to the next one, the machine obeys its transition relation $\delta$.

*and if* $\beta$ *is a successor ordinal,* $\sigma(\beta) = \sigma(\beta - 1)$*, otherwise (*$\beta$ *is a limit ordinal),* $\forall n \in \omega$*,*

$$\sigma(\beta)(n) = \begin{cases} \tau(\sigma(\beta_-)(n)) & \text{if } \exists \beta_- \leq \gamma < \beta \text{ such that } \varphi_{pos}(\gamma + 1) = \varphi_{pos}(\gamma) = n, \\ \sigma(\beta_-)(n) & \text{otherwise,} \end{cases}$$

*and* $\varphi_{pos}(\beta) = 0$*, where* $\beta_-$ *is the greatest limit ordinal* $< \beta$ *and for all* $a \in \Sigma \cup \{\flat, \natural\}$*,* $\tau(a) = \natural$ *if* $a \neq \natural$*,* $\flat$ *otherwise.*

$\sigma$ only changes at limit ordinal stages, where the tape's head goes back to the origin and the cells where the head stopped before this limit stage (and after the previous limit stage) alternate between $\natural$ and $\flat$ : if the value belonged to $\Sigma \cup \{\flat\}$, it is now $\natural$; if it was $\natural$, it is now $\flat$. If we are at an hyper-limit (limit of limits) ordinal stage, the value of the cell is the converging value if there is one, $\natural$ otherwise.

A run is *successful* if $\varphi_q(\alpha) \in F$. A word $u \in \Sigma^\omega$ is *recognized* by $\mathcal{A}$ if and only if there is a successful run of $\mathcal{A}$ with $u$ as the original tape content. A set of words $M$ is *recognizable* by $\mathcal{A}$ if this automaton recognizes only the words belonging to $M$.

The reader is invited to guess what language the following $\mathcal{W}^2$-automaton recognizes.

*Example* 2.2

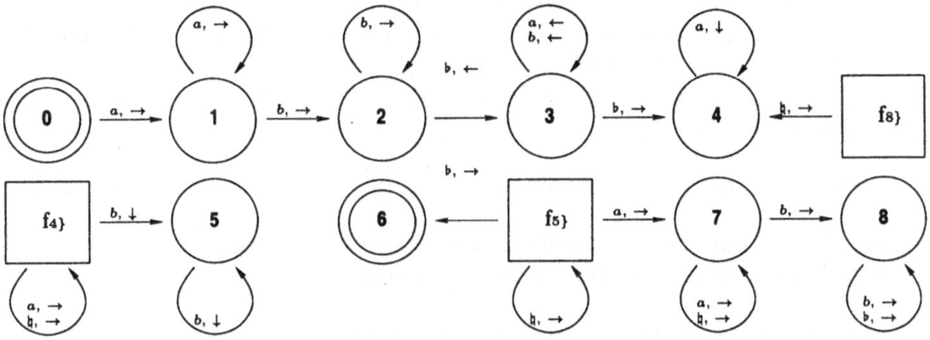


**Fig. 2.** A $\mathcal{W}^2$-automaton recognizing ... (see proposition 1)

We will work with an alphabet of only two letters, say $\{0, 1\}$ or $\{a, b\}$, beyond the other technical letters as $\flat$ and $\natural$.

In order to justify our definition of $\mathcal{W}^2$-automata, we prove[4] the following simple lemmae.

**Lemma 1.** *Every 2-way finite automaton can be transformed in a never stopping 2-way finite automaton with the same language of recognized words.*

**Lemma 2.** *The following two variants of $\mathcal{W}^2$-automata recognize the same languages (of finite or infinite words) than $\mathcal{W}^2$-automata :*

- *put to $\natural$, at limit stages, only those cells where the head has stopped previously infinitely often;*

[4] For the proof, see [9]. Due to space limitations, this is applicable whenever the proof is omitted.

– *replace*[5] *the "change the stopped cells at limit" behaviour by having pebbles who are used in the same way than in traditional pebble automata with the difference that the pebbles are actually placed only at limit stages on the requested cells, i.e. where the automaton previously asked to place them. So, the pebbles become only "visible" then.*

**Proposition 1.** $L_{eq} = \{a^n b^n \mid n \in \mathbb{N}\}$ *is recognizable by* $\mathcal{W}^2$*-automata.*

*Proof.* We describe the behaviour of the required automata :

1. first, we need to verify that the tape is composed by $a$'s followed by $b$'s;
2. we repeat the following two points at either the state following the previous point or at the limit state $\{q_\ddagger\}$ :
   a) check that there are still $b$'s at the end of the tape,
   b) starting from the first cell, we look for the first $a$ on the tape (after the potential $\natural$'s) and loop (stopping there) on a special state $q_\dagger$,
   c) from the $\{q_\dagger\}$ state, we look for the first $b$ (after the potential $\natural$ and $a$'s) and loop (stopping there) on a special state $q_\ddagger$,
3. if there are no more $b$'s at the end of the tape and only *natural*'s on the tape, we enter the "accept" state.

The described automata clearly recognizes only the words belonging to $L_{eq}$.

The reader should have recognized the behaviour of the automaton of example 2.2 and thus guessed the language recognized.

**Theorem 2.** *Algebraic languages* $\subseteq$ *languages recognized by* $\mathcal{W}^2$*-automata.*

**Proposition 2.** *The languages* $L_{pal} = \{s \in \{a,b\}^\star \mid s = s^R\}$, $L_{eq^{1/3}} = \{a^n b^n a^n \mid n \in \mathbb{N}\}$, $L_{eq^{n,m}} = \{a^n b^m a^n b^m \mid n, m \in \mathbb{N}\}$, $L_{weq} = \{ss \mid s \in \{a,b\}^\star\}$ *are recognized by* $\mathcal{W}^2$*-automata even if some are not algebraic.*

Proposition 2 shows that $\mathcal{W}^2$-automata recognize strictly more than algebraic languages using the infinite time at its disposal. We will see in the next section where the limit is.

Do $\mathcal{W}^2$-automata gain something compared to $\mathcal{W}$-automata? To see this, we prove the following "pumping lemma" for $\mathcal{W}$-automata.

[5] The transition relation now has two more fields $(\times\{\circ,\bullet\} \times \{yes, no\})$ : the first one looks for the presence ($\bullet$) or absence ($\circ$) of a pebble on the cell and the second commands the dropping of the (not yet visible) pebble. A *run* with label $\sigma$ and pebbles labels $\sigma_{pebbles} \in \{\circ,\bullet\}^{\omega\alpha}$, $\sigma_{drop} \in \{yes, no\}^{\omega\alpha}$ is then now a continuous $(\alpha+1)$-sequence $(\varphi_q, \varphi_{pos})$ such that $\sigma_{pebbles}(0)(n) = \circ$ for all $n$ and for any ordinal $\beta < \alpha$, $(\varphi_q(\beta), \sigma(\beta)(\varphi_{pos}(\beta)), \varphi_q(\beta+1), \rho(\varphi_{pos}(\beta+1) - \varphi_{pos}(\beta)), \sigma_{pebbles}(\beta)(\varphi_{pos}(\beta)), \sigma_{drop}(\beta)(\varphi_{pos}(\beta))) \in \delta$ Now, only the pebble *monitor* ($\sigma_{pebbles}$) changes; the tape's content does not change anymore. At limit stages, $\sigma_{pebbles}$ reflects the pebbles (virtually) dropped ($\sigma_{drops}$) at earlier successor stages .

**Lemma 3.** *Let $\mathcal{A} = (Q_A, \Sigma, \delta_A, i_A, F_A)$ be an $\mathcal{W}$-automaton. For each reachable state $q \in P(Q_A)$ (there is a run $\varphi$ of $\mathcal{A}$ going through $q$), there is a state $q' \in Q_A$ such that $q' \in q$ and a* sub-run *out of $\varphi$ going from $q'$ to itself without going through a state of $P(Q_A)$ ($\exists \eta, \eta' \in Ord\ \varphi(\eta) = \varphi(\eta') = q'$ et $\forall \eta < \xi < \eta'\ \varphi(\xi) \notin P(Q_A)$).*

**Corollary 1.** *$\mathcal{W}^2$-automata are strictly more powerful (recognition-wise) than $\mathcal{W}$-automata.*

*Proof.* The argument is exactly the usual one, proving that $L_{eq}$ is not regular, with our pumping lemma 3 instead of the usual finite automata pumping lemma.

## 3 Compared to Infinite Time Turing Machines...

### 3.1 Infinite Time Turing Machines

Hamkins and Lewis [8] defined infinite time Turing machines. They simply extend the Turing machine concept into transfinite ordinal time.

**Definition 6.** *An* infinite time Turing machine *is a Turing machine with three separate tapes, one for input, one for scratch work, and one for output. The scratch and output tape are filled with zeros at the beginning of any computation. At non-limit stages, it behaves like a normal Turing machine according to its transition relation. At limit stages, the head is plucked from wherever it might have been racing towards, and placed on top of the first cell. Moreover, it is placed in a special distinguished* limit state. *For a given cell of the tape, at a limit stage it takes the value of the lim sup of the cell's values before the limit.*

Hamkins and Lewis studied the theory of such infinite time machines and obtained a nice theory. The power of these machines lies between $\Pi^1_1$ and $\Delta^1_2$. The finite time Turing machine halting problem becomes decidable. They generalize the classical s-m-n and recursion theorems and study the basic features of the structure of infinite time degrees.

### 3.2 Where Is the Limit?

**Theorem 3.** *$\mathcal{W}^2$-automata recognize any (finite time) decidable language.*

$\mathcal{W}^2$ thus really have more recognition power than finite automata or even pushdown automata.

**Corollary 2.** *All the languages in theorem 2 and proposition 2 are recognizable by $\mathcal{W}^2$-automata.*

We now know that sets recognizable (which is the same thing as writable sets from scratch) with finite time Turing machines are recognizable by $\mathcal{W}^2$-automata. The $\mathcal{W}^2$-automata used so far are with a $\mathbb{N}$-tape. Having a $\mathbb{Z}$-tape bridges the gap to infinite time Turing machines. Of course, $\mathcal{W}^2_{\mathbb{N}}$-automata have the same power of recognition as $\mathcal{W}^2_{\mathbb{Z}}$-automata. It suffices to encode the *right* part of the $\mathbb{Z}$-tape on even positions of the $\mathbb{N}$-tape and folding the *left* part on the odd positions.

**Theorem 4.** *$\mathcal{W}^2$-automata recognize any infinite time decidable language.*

*Proof.* Having a $\mathbb{Z}$-tape, we can encode the two counters at the *left* of the origin (*first cell*) of the tape and use the right part of the tape as an $\mathbb{N}$-tape for the one-tape Turing simulation.

Using Wojciechowski-type limit states, we can easily simulate the one-limit-state behaviour of infinite time Turing machines. In the simulation of the Turing machine by the two-counter automaton, when the transition says to change from 0 to 1 or vice versa we need to go through a special state $q_{lim\ sup}$ to ensure that if it changes infinitely often, we will able to notice it and simulate a value of 1 (the lim sup of 0 and 1).

**Remark 5.** *The simulation of the "one-limit-state behaviour" in the proof of theorem 4 takes at most $\omega^2$ steps. By doing a crude job, we can make it take* exactly *$\omega^2$ steps.*

**Theorem 6.** *$\mathcal{W}^2$-automata recognizable languages are infinite time decidable.*

*Proof.* The only difficulty is in simulating the Wojciechowski-type limit states.

We take some place on the work tape to put flags, initialized to 0, for each state of the simulated automaton. When we simulate the automaton and are in state $q_{now}$, we put the flag corresponding to $q_{now}$ to 1 and put to zero the other flags corresponding to states $q \neq q_{now}$. Hence, at a limit stage our infinite Turing machine will be in its limit state and by looking at the flags on the scratch tape, we will be able to see what are the states through which our machine has gone infinitely often (whose flags have toggled infinitely and so are now equal to the lim sup 1) and thus what Wojciechowski-type limit state we should simulate.

## 4 Machine Comprehensible Ordinals

We have already seen in the examples of section 1 that we can construct $\mathcal{W}$-automata to recognize only the word $a^\alpha$ for certain ordinals $\alpha$ like $\omega$ and $\omega^2$. For certain ordinals $\lambda$ like $\omega_1$, we can construct $\mathcal{W}$-automata recognizing all $a^\alpha$ for $\alpha < \lambda$ but not $a^\lambda$.

For machines with a countable tape, we can code countable ordinals on the tape by the encoding of its well ordering $\in$ in a real : a well order $R$ is encoded in $r \in \mathbb{R}$ ($r$ is a sequence of 0 and 1's) by

$$\textit{for all } n, m \in \mathbb{N}, \quad n\,R\,m \textit{ if and only if } r_{\langle n,m\rangle} = 1$$

where $\langle .,. \rangle$ is a canonical pairing function. Hamkins and Lewis have shown that many ordinals are writable (in the above way) from scratch (blank input tape) by infinite Turing machines.

**Theorem 7.** *Infinite time Turing machines can write the ordinal $\alpha$ for any $\alpha < \lambda_{inf}$ where $\lambda_{inf}$ is a recursively inaccessible countable ordinal. Hence, the writable ordinals cover easily the recursive ordinals[6], $\omega_1^{ck}$ and much more.*

[6] A countable ordinal is *recursive* if encodable, as described above, by a Turing computable real. $\omega_1^{ck}$ (ck is for Church-Kleene) denotes the smallest non recursive ordinal.

*Proof.* See [8].

**Corollary 3.** *$\mathcal{W}^2$-automata can recognize the ordinal $\alpha$ for any $\alpha < \lambda_{inf}$, hence all the recursive ordinals, $\omega_1^{ck}$ and much more.*

*Proof.* By theorem 4.

**Definition 7.** *An ordinal $\alpha$ is* clockable *by a class of machines $C$ if there is $r_0 \in C_{dom}$*[7] *and a machine belonging to $C$ that halts in the "accept" state on input $r_0$ in $\alpha$ many steps.*

*An ordinal $\alpha$ is* all-til clockable *by a class of machines $C$ if $\alpha$ is not clockable and there is a machine $M$ belonging to $C$ such that for all $\beta < \alpha$, there is $r_\beta \in C_{dom}$ such that $M$ halts in the "accept" state on input $r_\beta$ in $\beta$ many steps.*

For $\mathcal{W}$-automata, recognizable and clockable ordinals are the same because of the one-way nature of the tape's head. As we saw at the beginning of this section, $\omega$ and $\omega^2$ are clockable by $\mathcal{W}$-automata and $\omega_1$ is all-til clockable by $\mathcal{W}$-automata.

**Theorem 8.** *Recursive ordinals, $\omega_1^{ck} + \omega$ and many ordinals less than an* unreachable *ordinal $\gamma_{inf}$ are clockable by infinite time Turing machines with many gaps in between. In fact, no admissible ordinal is clockable.*

*Proof.* See [8].

**Corollary 4.** *For every clockable (by infinite time Turing machines) ordinal $\alpha < \gamma_{inf}$, there is a countable ordinal $\beta \geq \alpha$ such that $\beta$ is clockable by $\mathcal{W}^2$-automata.*

Welch [14] has shown the following theorem.

**Theorem 9.** *$\gamma_{inf}$ is in fact $\lambda_{inf}$ and so is recursively inaccessible.*

**Corollary 5.** *$\gamma_{\mathcal{W}^2}$, the supremum of clockable ordinals by $\mathcal{W}^2$-automata, is equal to $\lambda_{inf}$, the supremum of writable ordinals by infinite time Turing machines, and is recursively*[5] *inaccessible.*

*Proof.* Use corollary 4 and Welch's theorem 9.

**Lemma 4.** *Every ordinal up to $\omega^\omega$ is clockable by $\mathcal{W}^2$-automata.*

*Proof.* If $\alpha$ is clockable by $\mathcal{W}^2$-automata, then so are $\alpha + 1$ and $\alpha + \omega$.

We can go much farther for ordinals clockable by $\mathcal{W}^2$-automata :

---

[7] $C_{dom}$ is the set of inputs accepted by machines of class $C$. Of course, for $C = \mathcal{W}^2$-automata, $C_{dom} = \mathbb{R}$; and $\mathcal{W}{-}automata_{dom}$ is transfinite sequences on $\Sigma$.

**Theorem 10.** *Recursive ordinals*[8] *are clockable by* $\mathcal{W}^2$*-automata.*

**Theorem 11.** *The ordinal* $\omega_1^{ck} + \omega^2$ *is clockable by* $\mathcal{W}^2$*-automata.*

See [9] for the proofs of theorems 10 and 11.

**Theorem 12.** *If an ordinal* $\alpha$ *is clockable by infinite time Turing machines,* $\omega\alpha$ *is clockable by* $\mathcal{W}^2$*-automata.*

*Proof.* Remark 5 tells us that for a task that will take $\omega$ steps (one limit stage behaviour) on an infinite time Turing machine, we can crudely simulate it in $\omega^2$ steps with an $\mathcal{W}^2$-automaton.

All-til clockable ordinals are more of a mystery than clockable ordinals. Recognizable ordinals are not comparable inclusion-wise with all-til clockable ordinals, even if both families of ordinals contain the clockable ones. No admissible ordinal is clockable (see [8]) even if some are writable (or recognizable). Even $\omega_1$ is an all-til clockable ordinal by $\mathcal{W}$-automata!

The picture for comprehensible ordinals by infinite time machines is the following.

$$\begin{array}{ccc} & & \textit{recognizable ordinals} \\ & \nearrow & \\ \textit{clockable ordinals} & & \nmid \\ & \searrow & \\ & & \textit{all} - \textit{til clockable ordinals} \end{array}$$

Using theorem 10, one can construct an $\mathcal{W}^2$-automaton proving that $\omega_1^{ck}$ is all-til clockable by such automata. All-til clockability is clearly an intriguing property showing the extent of the power of the underlying machines. There is some reasons to think that many ordinals are even all-til clockable by $\mathcal{W}$-automata.

We conjecture the following.

**Enthusiastic Conjecture.** *Many*[9] proper[10] all-til clockable ordinals by $\mathcal{W}^2$-automata are all-til clockable by $\mathcal{W}$-automata.

## Concluding Remarks

The remarkable property of $\mathcal{W}^2$ is that by adding very few *power* (or *features*), compared to $\mathcal{W}$-automata on a two-way tape, we obtain directly Turing power. Moreover, when using the pebble variant (see lemma 2) of definition 5, to be able to get (finite time) Turing recognizability power, we only need to use very few pebbles and more surprisingly, infinitely rarely.

In section 4, we see that there are many more (and greater) ordinals *comprehensible* by finite state machines than usually thought. We conjecture that this is also the case with original $\mathcal{W}$-automata.

[8] See the note for theorem 7.

[9] At least some other than $\omega_1$.

[10] Non-clockable but still all-til clockable.

Less raving questions are the following :

Is $\omega_1^{ck}$ all-til clockable by $\mathcal{W}$-automata? Is there some all-til clockable (by $\mathcal{W}$-automata) admissible ordinal?

**Acknowledgements.** I would like to thank Jacques Mazoyer for his remarks on this paper, his suggestions and his boundless enthusiasm. I am especially indebted to Jean-Eric Pin who started me off on this topic years ago.

## References

1. N. Bedon, *Finite automata and ordinals*, Theoretical Computer Science **156** (1996), 119–144.
2. ———, *Automata, semigroups and recognizability of words on ordinals*, International Journal of Algebra and Computation **8** (1998), 1–21.
3. ———, *Langages reconnaissables de mots indexés par des ordinaux*, Ph.D. thesis, Université de Marne-la-Vallée, 1998.
4. N. Bedon and O. Carton, *An Eilenberg theorem for words on countable ordinals*, Latin'98: Theoretical Informatics (Cláudio L. Lucchesi and Arnaldo V. Moura, eds.), Lect. Notes in Comput. Sci., vol. 1380, Springer-Verlag, 1998, pp. 53–64.
5. J. R. Büchi, *On a decision method in the restricted second-order arithmetic*, Logic, Methodology, and Philosophy of Science: Proc. **1960** Intern. Congr., Stanford University Press, 1962, pp. 1–11.
6. ———, *Decision methods in the theory of ordinals*, Bulletin of the American Mathematical Society **71** (1965), 767–770.
7. Y. Choueka, *Finite automata, definable sets and regular expressions over $\omega^n$-tapes*, Journal of Computer and System Sciences **17** (1978), 81–97.
8. J. D. Hamkins and A. Lewis, *Infinite time Turing machines*, Journal of Symbolic Logic **65** (2000), no. 2, 567–604.
9. G. Lafitte, *How powerful are infinite time machine?*, RR 2001-16, LIP, Ecole Normale Supérieure de Lyon, March 2001, ftp://ftp.ens-lyon.fr/pub/LIP/Rapports /RR/RR2001/.
10. R. McNaughton, *Testing and generating infinite sequences by a finite automaton*, Information and Control **9** (1966), 521–530.
11. D. E. Müller, *Infinite sequences and finite machines*, Proceedings of the Fourth Annual Symposium on Switching Circuit Theory and Logical Design (Chicago, Illinois), IEEE, October 1963, pp. 3–16.
12. D. Perrin, *Recent results on automata and infinite words*, Mathematical foundations of computer science (Berlin) (M. P. Chytil and V. Koubek, eds.), Lecture Notes in Computer Science, vol. 176, Springer-Verlag, 1984, pp. 134–148.
13. D. Perrin and J.-E. Pin, *Mots infinis*, to appear, 1997.
14. P. Welch, *The length of infinite time Turing machine computations*, Bulletin of the London Mathematical Society **32** (2000), no. 2, 129–136.
15. J. Wojciechowski, *Classes of transfinite sequences accepted by finite automata*, Annales Societatis Mathematicæ Polonæ, Fundamenta Informaticæ **VII** (1984), no. 2, 191–223.
16. ———, *Finite automata on transfinite sequences and regular expressions*, Annales Societatis Mathematicæ Polonæ, Fundamenta Informaticæ **VIII** (1985), no. 3-4, 379–396.

# Equivalence Problem of Composite Class Diagrams

Ģirts Linde

University of Latvia,
Raiņa bulvāris 29, LV-1459, Riga, Latvia
**glinde@acm.org**

**Abstract.** Multiplicity constraints in a UML composite class diagram may be inconsistent. An algorithm is given for eliminating all such inconsistencies. Using this algorithm an algorithm is constructed which for two given composite class diagrams solves the equivalence problem. These algorithms can be embedded in CASE tools for automated detection of multiplicity inconsistencies.

## 1 Introduction

As object modeling gains popularity, starting from the pioneering work [1], a need emerges for methods of handling and evaluating models. Object models are used in various stages of system development - from requirements definition to system design. One problem is to validate the model as it gets transformed and refined in the lifecycle of system development. Research is already being done on this topic [2,3,4,5]. A more general problem is to compare several alternative object models of the same "real world".

The ultimate goal of our current research is to formalize this "intuitive" equivalence for object models represented with UML class diagrams. Consider the class diagrams modeling directed graphs shown on Figure 1.

Formally, we have here 3 totally different class diagrams. Each of them describes different instance diagrams. But intuitively we know that all these 3 diagrams describe the same "real world" - directed graphs.

Formalization of this "intuitive" equivalence is based on composite classes and before we can proceed, certain problems have to be solved. The equivalence of composite classes is one of the problems, and it gives immediate applicable results. The results of the research on the equivalence of composites are presented in this paper.

## 2 Composites in UML Class Diagrams

Composition is a form of aggregation with strong ownership and coincident lifetime of part with the whole, as described in [6,7]. The parts of a composition may include classes and associations. The meaning of an association in a composition is that any tuple of objects connected by a single link must all belong to the

R. Freivalds (Ed.): FCT 2001, LNCS 2138, pp. 264–274, 2001.

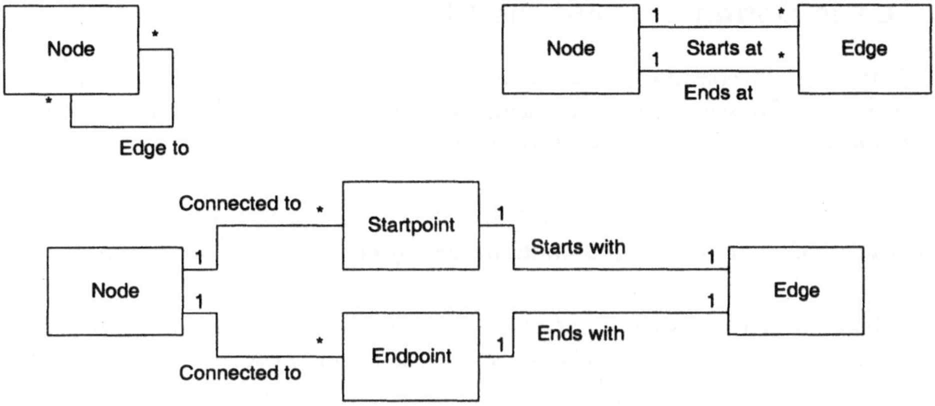


**Fig. 1.** Three class diagrams of a directed graph

same container object. One of the ways of showing composition is by graphical nesting of the symbols of the elements for the parts within the symbol of the element for the whole. A nested class element may have a multiplicity within its composite element. The multiplicity is shown in the upper right corner of the symbol for the part. An example of a composite class "Cat" and its instance are shown in Figure 2.

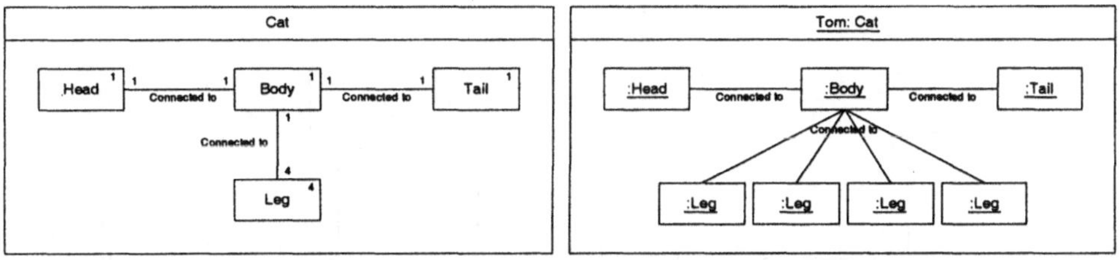


**Fig. 2.** A composite class and its instance

In this paper we consider only a simplified class diagram (only binary associations and only four most popular multiplicity intervals: 1..1, 0..1, 1..*, 0..*) that represents the contents of one composite class. Such diagram we will call a composite class diagram.

Actually, any class diagram can be regarded as the content of the composite class "World" where every class has multiplicity 0..* if no other multiplicity is specified.

## 3 Basic Definitions and the Main Theorem

**Definition 1.** A composite class diagram *(CCD) is a class diagram consisting of classes and binary associations, where every class has a multiplicity and only four multiplicities for classes and associations are allowed: 1..1, 0..1, 1..*, 0..*,*

**Definition 2.** *Two CCDs are* identical *if they are equal as labeled graphs (where graph labels are the names and multiplicities of classes and associations).*

**Definition 3.** An instance *of a CCD $X$ is an instance diagram that satisfies all the multiplicity constraints of classes and associations of $X$.*

**Definition 4.** *Two instance diagrams are* identical *if they are equal as labeled graphs (where graph labels are the class names of objects and association names of links).*

**Definition 5.** *Two CCDs $X$ and $Y$ are* equivalent *if their corresponding sets of instances are identical (i.e. for every instance i of $X$ there exists an instance i′ of $Y$ such that i and i' are identical, and for every instance i of $Y$ there exists an instance i′ of $X$ such that i and i' are identical).*

As it turns out, the equivalence problem is not trivial. Figure 3 shows three composite class diagrams that look quite different, but it can be proved that they describe the same set of instance diagrams, so they are equivalent by our definition.

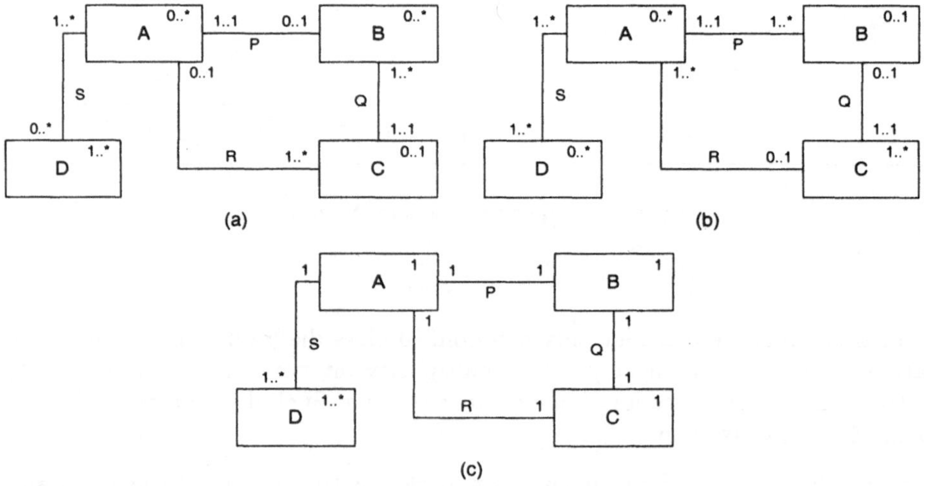


**Fig. 3.** Equivalent composites

The diagram (c) in Figure 3 has the strongest multiplicities and (incidentally) it is the most precise of all possible composite class diagrams that describe the same set of instance diagrams. We will introduce a special term – a canonical composite class diagram – to denote diagrams with this property.

The main result of this paper is the following Theorem.

**Theorem 1.** *The equivalence problem of CCDs is algorithmically decidable.*

## 4 Reduction Rules

The algorithm for solving the equivalence problem of CCDs is based on the reduction of inconsistent multiplicities within those CCDs. Before we present the reduction rules, we will introduce notation for working with multiplicities of classes and associations.

Consider the following fragment of a CCD - two classes $A$ and $B$, connected with an association $R$ (Figure 4).

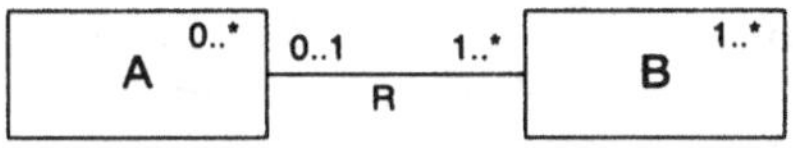


**Fig. 4.** A fragment of a composite class diagram

The fact, that the association $R$ connects the classes $A$ and $B$, we will denote as $< A - R - B >$. Multiplicities of the classes and the association ends we will denote as $card(A)$, $card(B)$, $card(R.A)$ and $card(R.B)$, respectively.

Now we will introduce *the multiplicity reduction rules* for elimination of multiplicity inconsistencies in CCDs. There are 6 multiplicity reduction rules.

**Rule 1.** If a CCD contains a cycle of associations (Figure 5) $< A_1 - R_1 - A_2 - R_2 - ... - A_n >$, where $A_1 = A_n$ and for every $i = 1..n-1 : card(R_i.A_i) = 0..1 or 1..1$ and $card(R_i.A_{i+1}) = 1..1 or 1..*$, then for every $i = 1..n-1$ we replace the multiplicities of $R_i.A_i$ and $R_i.A_{i+1}$ with 1..1.

**Rule 2.** If a CCD contains a fragment $< A - R - B >$, where $card(A) = 0..1 or 1..1$ and $card(R.A) = 1..1$ and $card(R.B) = 0..1 or 1..1$ and $card(B) = a..*$ $(a = 0 or 1)$, then we replace the multiplicity of the class $B$ with $a..1$ (further in the text we will use the assignment symbol ":=" for denotation of a replacement – in this case it would be $card(B) := a..1$).

**Rule 3.** If a CCD contains a fragment $< A - R - B >$, where $card(A) = 1..1 or 1..*$ and $card(R.B) = 1..1 or 1..*$ and $card(B) = 0..a (a = 1 or *)$, then $card(B) := 1..a$.

**Rule 4.** If a CCD contains a fragment $< A - R - B >$, where $card(B) = 0..1 or 1..1$ and $card(R.B) = a..*$ $(a = 0..1)$, then $card(R.B) := a..1$.

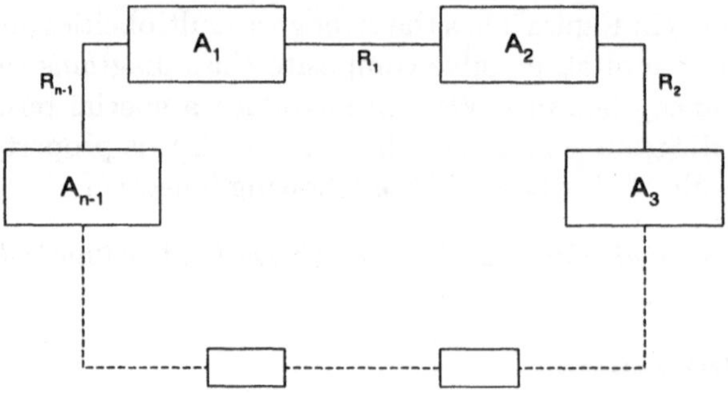


**Fig. 5.** A cycle of associations

**Rule 5.** If a CCD contains a fragment $< A - R - B >$, where $card(A) = 1..1$ and $card(R.A) = 1..1$ and $card(B) = 1..1or1..*$ and $card(R.B) = 0..a(a = 1or*)$, then $card(R.B) = 1..a$.

**Rule 6.** If a CCD contains a fragment $< A{-}R{-}B >$ and a chain of associations $< C_1 - R_1 - C_2 - R_2 - ... - C_n >$ (Figure 6), where $C_1 = A$ and $C_n = B$ and $card(A) = 0..1$ and $card(R.A) = 1..1$ and
for every $i = 1..n - 1 : card(R_i.C_{i+1}) = 1..1or1..*$ and
$card(R.B) = 0..a(a = 1or*)$,
then $card(R.B) := 1..a$.

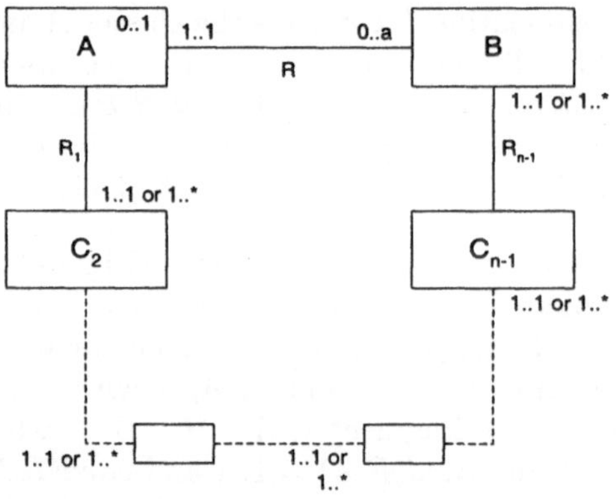


**Fig. 6.** Conditions for the reduction rule 6

It is easy to prove the following Lemma.

**Lemma 1.** *The multiplicity reduction rules retain the equivalence of CCDs.*

**Definition 6.** *A CCD is* canonical *if it is not possible to apply any of the multiplicity reduction rules to it.*

**Definition 7.** *The* canonical form *of a CCD X is a canonical CCD, that is obtained from X using the multiplicity reduction rules.*

From Lemma 1 follows that two CCDs are equivalent iff their canonial forms are equivalent. So Theorem 1 will be proved if we will prove Theorem 2.

**Theorem 2.** *Two canonical CCDs are equivalent iff they are identical.*

The proof will be presented in the last section. In the following sections we will introduce some Lemmas needed for the proof.

## 5 Properties of CCDs

In this section some easily provable properties of CCDs are formulated.

**Lemma 2.** *For every CCD X there exists an instance containing exactly one object from every class and one link from every association of X.*

**Lemma 3.** *If a CCD X contains a fragment $< A - R - B >$, where $card(R.A) = card(R.B) = 1..1$, then every instance of X contains an equal number of objects of classes A and B.*

**Lemma 4.** *If a CCD X contains a fragment $< A - R - B >$, where $card(R.A) = 0..1 or 1..1$ and $card(R.B) = 1..1 or 1..*$, then for every instance d of X holds the inequality $a \leq b$, where a – the number of objects of the class A in d, and b – the number of objects of the class B in d.*

**Lemma 5.** *If a CCD X contains a fragment $< A - R - B >$, where $card(R.A) = 0..* or 1..*$ or $card(R.B) = 0..1 or 0..*$, then for every two integers a and b that satisfy the inequality $a > b \geq 1$, there exists an instance of X, in which the number of objects of class A equals a and the number of objects of class B equals b.*

**Lemma 6.** *Let CCD X contain a fragment $< A-R-B >$. Let d be an instance of X. Let d′ be another instance diagram, obtained from d by changing only the links of the association R. If the resulting configuration of R links in d′ satisfies the multiplicity constraints of the association R, then d′ is an instance of X.*

## 6 Properties of Canonical CCDs

In this section some properties of *canonical* CCDs are formulated.

**Lemma 7.** *For every canonical CCD there exists an instance containing exactly 1 object from every class with multiplicity 1..1 or 1..* and no objects from classes with multiplicity 0..1 or 0..*.*

**Lemma 8.** *For every canonical CCD there exists an instance containing exactly 1 object from every class with multiplicity 0..1 or 1..1 and 2 objects from every class with multiplicity 1..* or 0..*.*

**Lemma 9.** *If a canonical CCD X contains a fragment* $< A - R - B >$*, where* $card(A) = 0..1$ *and* $card(R.A) = 1..1$ *and* $card(R.B) = 0..1 or 0..*$*, then there exists an instance of X, containing exactly 1 object of the class A and no objects of the class B.*

**Lemma 10.** *If a canonical CCD X contains a fragment* $< A - R - B >$*, where* $card(R.B) = 0..* or 1..*$*, then* $card(B) = 0..* or 1..*$.

**Lemma 11.** *If a canonical CCD X contains a fragment* $< A - R - B >$*, where* $card(A) = 1..1$ *and* $card(R.A) = 1..1$ *and* $card(R.B) = 0..1 or 0..*$*, then* $card(B) = 0..1 or 0..*$.

**Lemma 12.** *If a canonical CCD X contains a fragment* $< A - R - B >$*, where* $card(R.A) = 0..1 or 1..1$ *and* $card(R.B) = 1..1 or 1..*$ *and* $card(B) = 1..* or 0..*$*, then there exists an instance of X, containing exactly 1 object of the class A and 2 objects of the class B.*

Proof of these Lemmas is based on Lemmas 3, 4 and 5.

## 7 Proof of Theorem 2

It is obvious that two identical CCDs are equivalent. So, we need to prove that two canonical CCDs that are not identical are not equivalent - i.e., there exists an instance diagram that satisfies one of the CCDs but not the other one.

If two CCDs are not identical, then there can be 3 cases: one CCD contains a class or an association that is not present in the other CCD, multiplicities of some class differ, or multiplicities of some association end differ. Let's examine each of these cases.

*Case 1.* One CCD $X$ contains a class or an association $A$ that is not present in the other CCD $Y$.

From Lemma 2 there exists an instance $d$ of $X$ that contains one object or link of $A$. Obviously this instance $d$ doesn't satisfy the CCD $Y$. So $X$ and $Y$ are not equivalent.

*Case 2.* Multiplicities of some class $A$ differ. There are two subcases:

1. In one CCD ($X$) $card(A) = 0..1 or 0..*$, but in the other CCD ($Y$) $card(A) = 1..1 or 1..*$. Then from Lemma 7 follows that there exists an instance $d$ of CCD $X$ that contains no objects of $A$. This instance $d$ doesn't satisfy the CCD $Y$. So $X$ and $Y$ are not equivalent.
2. In one CCD ($X$) $card(A) = 0..* or 1..*$, but in the other CCD ($Y$) $card(A) = 0..1 or 1..1$. Then from Lemma 8 follows that there exists an instance $d$ of CCD $X$ that contains 2 objects of $A$. This instance $d$ doesn't satisfy the CCD $Y$. So $X$ and $Y$ are not equivalent.

So, if multiplicities of some class $A$ differ, then CCDs are not equivalent.

*Case 3.* Multiplicities of some association end differ.

First we define an enumeration $N$ for the four used multiplicities as follows: 1: 0..*, 2: 0..1, 3: 1..*, 4: 1..1.

Consider two canonical CCDs $X$ and $Y$ that both contain a fragment $< A-R-B >$, and in the enumeration $N$ $card(R.B)$ in $X$ comes before $card(R.B)$ in $Y$. To prove that these CCDs are not equivalent, we will find an instance of $X$ that doesn't satisfy $card(R.B)$ in $Y$. A set of instances of $X$ that contains such an instance we will call *a set of representative instances* for the association end $R.B$. We will prove that such a set exists for all possible multiplicities of $A$, $R.A$, $R.B$ and $B$.

To help to find sets of representative instances we define *a set of representative fragments* of instance diagrams for every multiplicity of $R.B$ (according to the enumeration $N$) containing one or two instance diagram fragments. Figure 7 shows all the eight sets of representative fragments. For each of the multiplicities of $R.B$ there are two or three subcases, depending on the multiplicities of $A$ and $R.A$. For example, let R.B have the multiplicity 1: 0..*. If $card(A) = 0..* or 1..*$ then the corresponding set of representative fragments is 1.$a$, consisting of just one fragment 1.$a$.1. But if $card(A) = 0..1 or 1..1$ and $card(R.A) = 0..1$ then the corresponding set of representative fragments is 1.$b$, consisting of two fragments - 1.$b$.1 and 1.$b$.2.

It is easy to see that, if in the enumeration $N$ multiplicity $a$ comes before multiplicity $b$, then its set of representative fragments contains a fragment, that doesn't satisfy $b$. For example, the fragment 1.b.1 doesn't satisfy multiplicity 2: 0..1, the fragment 1.b.2 doesn't satisfy multiplicity 3: 1..*, and both of them don't satisfy multiplicity 4: 1..1.

**Definition 8.** The set of representative instances *of CCD $X$ for a given association end $R.B$ is a set of instances of $X$, where for every representative fragment of $card(R.B)$ there is one instance that contains it.*

For each of the ten representative fragments (Figure 7) we will prove that there exists an instance of the canonical CCD $X$ that contains exactly the number of objects of the two involved classes that we need for the fragment. Then

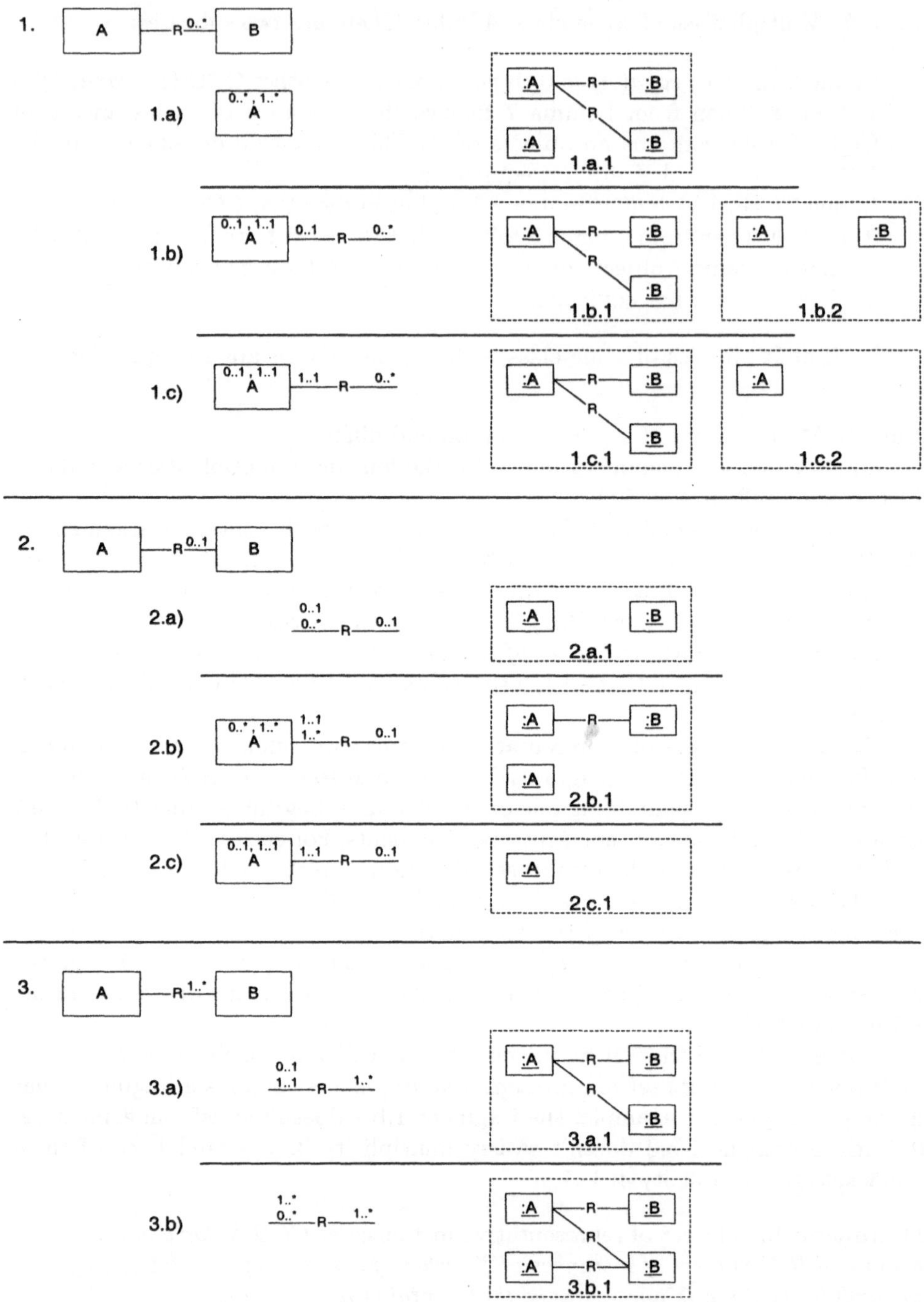


**Fig. 7.** Representative fragments for multiplicities of an association end

according to Lemma 6 we can reorganize links to get the instance containing the fragment.

*Fragment 1.a.1.* According to Lemma 10 $card(B) = 0..*or1..*$. Then according to Lemma 8 there is an instance containing 2 objects from the class $A$ and 2 objects from the class $B$.

*Fragment 1.b.1.* According to Lemma 10 $card(B) = 0..*or1..*$. Then according to Lemma 8 there is an instance containing 1 object from the class $A$ and 2 objects from the class $B$.

*Fragment 1.b.2.* According to Lemma 2 there is an instance containing exactly 1 object from every class.

*Fragment 1.c.1.* According to Lemma 10 $card(B) = 0..*or1..*$. Then according to Lemma 8 there is an instance containing 1 object from the class $A$ and 2 objects from the class $B$.

*Fragment 1.c.2.* If $card(A) = 1..1$, then according to Lemma 11 $card(B) = 0..1or0..*$. Then according to Lemma 7 there is an instance containing 1 object from the class $A$ and no objects of the class $B$.

If $card(A) = 0..1$, then according to Lemma 9 there is an instance containing 1 object from the class $A$ and no objects of the class $B$.

*Fragment 2.a.1.* According to Lemma 2 there is an instance containing exactly 1 object from every class.

*Fragment 2.b.1.* According to Lemma 12 there is an instance containing 2 objects from the class $A$ and 1 object from the class $B$.

*Fragment 2.c.1.* If $card(A) = 1..1$, then according to Lemma 11 $card(B) = 0..1or0..*$. Then according to Lemma 7 there is an instance containing 1 object from the class $A$ and no objects of the class $B$.

If $card(A) = 0..1$, then according to Lemma 9 there is an instance containing 1 object from the class $A$ and no objects of the class $B$.

*Fragment 3.a.1.* According to Lemma 10 $card(B) = 0..*or1..*$. Then according to Lemma 12 there is an instance containing 1 object from the class $A$ and 2 objects from the class $B$.

*Fragment 3.b.1.* According to Lemma 10 $card(A) = 0..*or1..*$ and $card(B) = 0..*or1..*$. Then according to Lemma 8 there is an instance containing 2 objects from the class $A$ and 2 objects from the class $B$.

So, if multiplicities of some association end $R.B$ differ, then CCDs are not equivalent.

This concludes the proof of Theorem 2.

## 8 Conclusion

In the paper a reduction algorithm is presented that for a given composite class diagram produces the corresponding canonical composite class diagram. It uses a set of rules to eliminate the multiplicity inconsistencies in the diagram.

We prove that two composite class diagrams are equivalent if and only if they can be reduced to the same canonical composite class diagram.

These presented algorithms can be used in CASE diagramming tools to detect multiplicity inconsistencies in class diagrams.

Besides that we are planning to use these results in solving the "intuitive" equivalence problem for class diagrams. One way of defining the "intuitive" equivalence of class diagrams is via composite classes: two class diagrams we call "intuitively" equivalent, if, by replacing some classes with composite classes, they can be transformed into class diagrams that are strictly equivalent.

## References

1. J.Rumbaugh, M.Blaha, W.Premerlani, F.Eddy W.Lorsen. Object-oriented modeling and design. Englewood Cliffs, NJ: Prentice Hall 1991.
2. A.S.Evans, R.B.France, K.C.Lano, B.Rumpe. The UML as a Formal Modelling Notation. UML'98. LNCS, Vol. 1618, Springer, 1999
3. K.Lano, J.Bicarregui. Semantics and Transformations for UML Models. UML'98. LNCS, Vol. 1618, Springer, 1999
4. A.S.Evans. Reasoning with UML class diagrams. WIFT'98. IEEE CS Press, 1998
5. K.C.Lano, A.S.Evans. Rigorous Development in UML. FASE'99, ETAPS'99. LNCS, Vol. 1577, Springer, 1999
6. Object Management Group. OMG Unified Modeling Language Specification, version 1.3. http://www.rational.org/uml. June 1999.
7. J.Rumbaugh, G.Booch, I.Jacobson. The Unified Modeling Language Reference Manual. Addison-Wesley, 1999.

# Differential Approximation Results for the Traveling Salesman Problem with Distances 1 and 2
## (Extended Abstract)

Jérôme Monnot, Vangelis T. Paschos, and Sophie Toulouse

LAMSADE, Université Paris-Dauphine,
Place du Maréchal De Lattre de Tassigny, 75775 Paris Cedex 16, France,
{monnot,paschos,toulouse}@lamsade.dauphine.fr

**Abstract.** We prove that both minimum and maximum traveling salesman problems on complete graphs with edge-distances 1 and 2 are approximable within 3/4. Based upon this result, we improve the standard approximation ratio known for maximum traveling salesman with distances 1 and 2 from 3/4 to 7/8. Finally, we prove that, for any $\epsilon > 0$, it is **NP**-hard to approximate both problems within better than $5379/5380 + \epsilon$.

## 1 Introduction

Given a complete graph on $n$ vertices, denoted by $K_n$, with edge distances either 1 or 2 the minimum traveling salesman problem (min_TSP12) consists in minimizing the cost of a Hamiltonian cycle, the cost of such a cycle being the sum of the distances on its edges (in other words, in finding a Hamiltonian cycle containing a maximum number of 1-edges). The maximum traveling salesman problem (max_TSP) consists in maximizing the cost of a Hamiltonian cycle (in other words, in finding a Hamiltonian cycle containing a maximum number of 2-edges). A generalization of TSP12, denoted by TSP$ab$, is the one where the edge-distances are either $a$, or $b$, $a < b$. Both min_ and max_TSP12, and TSP$ab$ are **NP**-hard.

Given an instance $I$ of an **NP** optimization (**NPO**) problem $\Pi$ and a polynomial time approximation algorithm A feasibly solving $\Pi$, we will denote by $\omega(I)$, $\lambda_{\mathtt{A}}(I)$ and $\beta(I)$ the values of the worst solution of $I$, of the approximated one (provided by A when running on $I$), and the optimal one for $I$, respectively. Commonly ([9]), the quality of an approximation algorithm for an **NP**-hard minimization (resp., maximization) problem $\Pi$ is expressed by the ratio (called standard in what follows) $\rho_{\mathtt{A}}(I) = \lambda(I)/\beta(I)$, and the quantity $\rho_{\mathtt{A}} = \inf\{r : \rho_{\mathtt{A}}(I) < r, I \text{ instance of } \Pi\}$ (resp., $\rho_{\mathtt{A}} = \sup\{r : \rho_{\mathtt{A}}(I) > r, I \text{ instance of } \Pi\}$) constitutes the approximation ratio of A for $\Pi$. Another approximation-quality criterion used by many well-known researchers ([2,1,3,4,14,15]) is what in [7,

R. Freivalds (Ed.): FCT 2001, LNCS 2138, pp. 275–286, 2001.

6] we call *differential-approximation ratio*. It measures how the value of an approximate solution is placed in the interval between $\omega(I)$ and $\beta(I)$. More formally, the differential-approximation ratio of an algorithm A is defined as $\delta_{\mathtt{A}}(I) = |\omega(I)-\lambda(I)|/|\omega(I)-\beta(I)|$. The quantity $\delta_{\mathtt{A}} = \sup\{r : \delta_{\mathtt{A}}(I) > r, I \text{ instance of } \Pi\}$ is the differential approximation ratio of A for $\Pi$. Another type of ratio, very close to the differential one, has been defined and used in [5]. There, instead of $\omega(I)$, the authors used a value $z_R$, called *reference-value*, smaller than $\omega(I)$. The ratio introduced in [5] is defined as $d_{\mathtt{A}}(I) = |\beta(I) - \lambda_{\mathtt{A}}(I)|/|\beta(I) - z_R|$. The quantity $|\beta(I) - \lambda_{\mathtt{A}}(I)|$ is called deviation of A, while $|\beta(I) - z_R|$ is called absolute deviation. For reasons of economy, we will call $d_{\mathtt{A}}(I)$ *deviation ratio*. For a given problem, setting $z_R = \omega(I)$, $d_{\mathtt{A}}(I) = 1 - \delta_{\mathtt{A}}(I)$ and both ratios have, as it has already mentioned above, a natural interpretation as the estimation of the relative position of the approximate value in the interval worst solution-value – optimal value. In [2], the term "trivial solution" is used to denote the solution realizing the worst among the feasible solution-values of an instance. Moreover, all the examples in [2] carry over **NP**-hard problems for which worst solution can be trivially computed. This is for example the case of maximum independent set where, given a graph, the worst solution is the empty set, or of minimum vertex cover, where the worst solution is the vertex-set of the input-graph, or even of the minimum graph-coloring where one can trivially color the vertices of the input-graph using a distinct color per vertex. On the contrary, for TSP things are very different. Let us take for example min_TSP. Here, given a graph $K_n$, the worst solution for $K_n$ is a maximum total-distance Hamiltonian cycle, i.e., the optimal solution of max_TSP in $K_n$. The computation of such a solution is very far from being trivial since max_TSP is **NP**-hard. Obviously, the same holds when one considers max_TSP and tries to compute a worst solution for its instance, as well as for optimum satisfiability, for minimum maximal independent set and for many other well-known **NP**-hard problems. In order to remove ambiguities about the concept of the worst-value solution of an instance $I$ of an **NPO** problem $\Pi$, we will defined it as the optimal solution $\text{opt}(\Pi')$ of an **NPO** problem $\Pi'$ having the same set of instances and feasibility constraints as $\Pi$ verifying

$$\text{opt}(\Pi') = \begin{cases} \max & \text{opt}(\Pi) = \min \\ \min & \text{opt}(\Pi) = \max \end{cases}$$

In general, no apparent links exist between standard and differential approximations in the case of minimization problems, in the sense that there is no evident transfer of a positive, or negative, result from the one framework to the other. Hence a "good" differential-approximation result signifies nothing for the behavior of the approximation algorithm studied when dealing with the standard framework and vice-versa. When dealing with maximization problems, we show in [11] that the approximation of a maximization **NPO** problem $\Pi$ within differential-approximation ratio $\delta$, implies its approximation within standard-approximation ratio $\delta$.

The best known standard-approximation ratio known for min_TSP12 is 7/6 (presented in [12]), while the best known standard inapproximability bound is

$5381/5380 - \epsilon$, for any $\epsilon > 0$ ([8]). On the other hand,the best known standard-ratio max_TSP is 3/4 ([13]). To our knowledge, no better result is known in standard approximation for max_TSP12. Furthermore, no special study of TSP$ab$ has been performed until now (a trivial standard-approximation ratio or $b/a$ of $a/b$ is in any case very easily deduced for min_ or max_TSP$ab$).

Here we show that min_ and max_TSP12 and min_ and max_TSP$ab$ are all equi-approximable within 3/4 for the differential approximation. We also prove that all these problems are inapproximable within better (more than) $3475/3476 + \epsilon$, for any $\epsilon > 0$. Finally, we improve the *standard*-approximation ratio of max_TSP12 from 3/4 ([13]) to 7/8.

In what follows, we will denote by $V = \{v_1, \dots, v_n\}$ the vertex-set of $K_n$, by $E$ its edge-set and, for $v_iv_j \in E$, we denote by $d(v_i, v_j)$ the distance of the edge $v_iv_j \in E$; we consider that the distance-vector is symmetric and integer. Given a feasible TSP-solution $T(K_n)$ of $K_n$ (both min_ and max_TSP have the same set of feasible solutions), we denote by $d(T(K_n))$ its (objective) value. Given a graph $G$, we denote by $V(G)$ its vertex-set. Finally, given any set $C$ of edges, we denote by $d(C)$ the total distance of $C$, i.e., the quantity $\sum_{v_iv_j \in C} d(i,j)$.

## 2 Differential-Approximation Preserving Reductions for TSP12

**Theorem 1.** *min_TSP12, max_TSP12, min_TSPab and max_TSPab are all equi-approximable for the differential approximation.*

*Proof (sketch).* In order to prove the theorem we will prove the following stronger quoted proposition.

> *Consider any instance $I = (K_n, \mathbf{d})$ (where $\mathbf{d}$ denotes the edge-distance vector of $K_n$). Then, any legal transformation $\mathbf{d} \mapsto \gamma.\mathbf{d} + \eta.\mathbf{1}$ of $\mathbf{d}$ ($\gamma, \eta \in \mathbb{Q}$) produces differentially equi-approximable TSP-problems.*

Suppose that TSP can be approximately solved within differential-approximation ratio $\delta$ and remark that both the initial and the transformed instance have the same set of feasible solutions. By the transformation considered, the value $d(T(K_n))$ of any tour $T(K_n)$ is affinely transformed into $\gamma d(T(K_n)) + \eta n$. Since differential-approximation ratio is stable under affine transformation, the equi-approximability of the original and of the transformed problem is immediately deduced, concluding so the proof of the quoted proposition.

In order to prove that min_TSP12 and max_TSP12 are equi-approximable it suffices to apply the proposition above with $\gamma = -1$ and $\eta = 3$. On the other hand, in order to prove that min_ or max_TSP12 reduces to min_ or max_TSP$ab$, we apply the quoted proposition with $\gamma = 1/(b-a)$ and $\eta = (b-2a)/(b-a)$, while for the converse reduction we apply the quoted proposition with $\gamma = b - a$ and $\eta = 2a - b$. Since the reductions presented are transitive and composable, the equi-approximability of the pairs (min_TSP12, max_TSP12) and (TSP12, TSP$ab$) proves the theorem.

## 3 Approximating Min_TSP12

Let us first recall that, given a graph $G$, a 2-matching is a set $M$ of edges of $G$ such that if $V(M)$ is the set of the endpoints of $M$, the vertices of the graph $(V(M), M)$ have degree at most 2; in other words, the graph $(V(M), M)$ is a collection of cycles and simple paths. A 2-matching is optimal if it is the largest over all the 2-matchings of $G$. It is called perfect if any vertex of the graph $(V(M), M)$ has degree equal to 2, i.e., if it constitutes a partition of $V(M)$ into cycles. Remark that determining a maximum 2-matching in a graph $G$ is equivalent to determining a minimum total-distance vertex-partition into cycles into $G \cup \bar{G}$ (the complement of $G$), where the edges of $G$ are considered of distance 1 and the ones of $\bar{G}$ of distance 2.

As it is shown in [10], *an optimal triangle-free 2-matching can be computed in polynomial time.* As it is mentioned just above, this becomes to compute a triangle-free minimum-distance collection of cycles in a complete graph $K_n$ with edge-distances 1 and 2. Let us denote by $M$ such a collection. Starting from $M$, we will progressively patch its cycles in order to finally obtain a unique Hamiltonian cycle in $K_n$.

In what follows, for reasons of paper length's constraints, lemmata 4 and 5 are presented without their proofs which can be found in [11].

### 3.1 Preprocessing $M$

**Definition 1.** *Let $C_1$ and $C_2$ be two vertex-disjoint cycles. Then:*

- *a* 2-exchange *is any exchange of two edges $v_1u_1 \in C_1$, $v_2u_2 \in C_2$ by the edges $v_1v_2$ and $u_1u_2$;*
- *a* 2-patching *of $C_1$ and $C_2$ is any cycle $C$ resulting from a 2-exchange on $C_1$ and $C_2$, i.e., $C = (C_1 \cup C_2) \setminus \{v_1u_1, v_2u_2\} \cup \{v_1v_2, u_1u_2\}$, for any pair $(v_1u_1, v_2u_2) \in C_1 \times C_2$.*

A matching minimal with respect to the 2-exchange operation will be called *2-minimal.*

**Definition 2.** *A 2-matching $M = (C_1, C_2, \ldots, C_{|M|})$ is 2-minimal if it verifies, $\forall (C_i, C_j) \in M \times M$, $C_i \neq C_j$, $\forall v_1u_1 \in C_i$, $\forall v_2u_2 \in C_j$, $d(v_1, v_2) + d(u_1, u_2) > d(u_1v_1) + d(u_2v_2)$.*

In other words, a 2-matching $M$ is 2-minimal if any 2-patching of its cycles produces a 2-matching of total distance strictly greater than the one of $M$. Obviously, *starting from a 2-matching $M$ transformation of $M$ into a 2-minimal one can be performed in polynomial time.* Moreover, suppose that there exist two distinct cycles $C$ and $C'$ of $M$, both containing 2-edges and denote by $uv \in C$ and $u'v' \in C'$ two such edges. Then, $d(uu') + d(vv') \geqslant 4$, while $d(uv) + d(u'v') = 4$, a contradiction. So, the following proposition holds.

**Proposition 1.** *In any 2-minimal 2-matching, at most one of its cycles contains 2-edges.*

*Remark 1.* If the size of a 2-minimal triangle-free 2-matching $M$ is 1, then, since a Hamiltonian tour is a particular case of triangle-free 2-matching, $M$ is an optimal min_TSP12-solution. Hence, in what follows we will suppose 2-matchings of size at least 2.

Assume now a 2-minimal triangle-free 2-matching $M = (C_1, \dots, C_p, C_0)$, verifying remark 1, where by $C_0$ is denoted the unique cycle of $M'$ (if any) containing 2-edges. Construct a graph $H = V_H, E_H)$ where $V_H = \{w_1, \dots, w_p\}$ and contains a vertex per cycle of $M'$ and, for $i \neq j$, $w_i w_j \in E_H$ iff $\exists (u, v) \in C_i \times C_j$ such that $d(u, v) = 1$. Consider a maximum matching $M_H$, $|M_H| = q$, of $H$. With any edge $w_{i^s} w_{j^s}$ of $M_H$ we associate the pair $(C_{i^s}, C_{j^s})$ of the corresponding cycles of $M$. So, $M$ can be described (up to renaming its cycles) as

$$M = \bigcup_{s=1}^{q} \{C_1^s, C_2^s\} \bigcup_{t=1}^{r=p-2q} \{C_t\} \bigcup \{C_0\} \tag{3.1}$$

where for $s = 1, \dots, q$, $\exists e^s \in V(C_1^s) \times V(C_2^s)$ such that $d(e^s) = 1$.

Consider $M$ as expressed in expression (3.1), denote by $V_s$ the set of the four vertices of $C_1^s$ and $C_2^s$ adjacent to the endpoints of $e^s$, and construct the bipartite graph $B = (V_B^1 \cup V_B^2, E_B)$ where $V_B^1 = \{w_1, \dots, w_r\}$ (i.e., we associate a vertex with a cycle $C_t$, $t = 1, \dots, r$), $V_B^2 = \{w^1 1, \dots, w^q\}$ (i.e., we associate a vertex with a pair $(C_1^s, C_2^s)$, $s = 1, \dots q$) and, $\forall (t, s)$, $w_t w^s \in E_B$ iff $\exists u \in C_t$, $\exists v \in V_s$ such that $d(u, v) = 1$. Compute a maximum matching $M_B$, $|M_B| = q'$ in $B$. With any edge $w_t w^s \in M_B$ we associate the triple $(C_1^s, C_2^s, C_t)$. So, $M$ can be described (up to renaming its cycles) as

$$M = \bigcup_{s=1}^{q'} \{C_1^s, C_2^s, C_3^s\} \bigcup_{s=q'+1}^{q} \{C_1^s, C_2^s\} \bigcup_{t=1}^{r'=r-q'} \{C_t\} \bigcup \{C_0\} \tag{3.2}$$

where for $s = 1, \dots, q'$, $\exists f^s \in V_s \times V(C_3^s)$ such that $d(f^s) = 1$. In what follows we will reason with respect to $M$ as it has been expressed in expression (3.2).

## 3.2 Computation and Evaluation of the Approximate Solution and a Lower Bound for the Optimal Tour

In the sequel, call s.d.e.p. a set of vertex-disjoint elementary paths, denote by PREPROCESS the algorithm of the achievement of $M$ (expression (3.2)) following from the discussion of section 3.1 and consider the following algorithm.

```
BEGIN (*TSP12*)
      compute a 2-minimal triangle-free 2-matching M in K_n;
      M ← PREPROCESS(M);
      D ← ∅;
(1)   FOR s ← 1 TO q' DO
          let g_1^s be the edge of C_1^s adjacent to both e^s and f^s;
          choose in C_2^s an edge g_2^s adjacent to e^s;
```

```
        choose in C_3^s an edge g_3^s adjacent to f^s;
        D ← D ∪ C_1^s ∪ C_2^s ∪ C_3^s \ {g_1^s, g_2^s, g_3^s} ∪ {e^s, f^s};
    OD
(2) FOR s ← q' + 1 TO q DO
        choose in C_1^s an edge g_1^s adjacent to e^s;
        choose in C_2^s an edge g_2^s adjacent to e^s;
        D ← D ∪ C_1^s ∪ C_2^s \ {g_1^s, g_2^s} ∪ {e^s};
    OD
(3) FOR t ← 1 TO r' DO
        choose any edge g_t in C_t;
        D ← D ∪ C_t \ {g_t};
    OD
(4) IF there exists in C_0 an 1-edge e
       THEN choose an edge g_0 of C_0 adjacent to e;
       ELSE choose any edge g_0 of C_0;
       D ← D ∪ C_0 \ {g_0};
    FI
(5) complete D in order to obtain a Hamiltonian tour T(K_n);
    OUTPUT T(K_n);
END (*TSP12*)
```

Both achievement of a 2-minimal triangle free 2-matching and the PREPROCESS of it, can be performed in polynomial time. Moreover, steps (1) to (4) are also executed in polynomial time. Finally, step 5) can be performed by arbitrarily ordering (mod$|D|$) the chains of the s.d.e.p. $D$ and then, for $i = 1, \dots, |D|$, adding in $D$ the edge linking the "last" vertex of chain $i$ to the "first" vertex of chain $i+1$. Consequently, the whole algorithm TSP12 is polynomial.

**Lemma 1.** *$d(T(K_n)) \leqslant d(M) + q + r'$.*

*Proof.* During steps (1) to (4) of algorithm TSP12, set $D$ remains a s.d.e.p. At the end of step (4), $D$ contains $M$ minus the $3q' + 2(q - q') + r' = q' + 2q + r'$ 1-edges of the set $\cup_{s=1}^{q'} \{g_1^s, g_2^s, g_3^s\} \cup_{s=q'+1}^{q} \{g_1^s, g_2^s\} \cup_{s=1}^{r'} \{g_t\}$ minus (if $C_0 \neq \emptyset$) one 2-edge of $C_0$ plus the $2q' + (q - q') = q' + q$ 1-edges of the set $cup_{s=1}^{q'}\{e_1^s, f_2^s\}cup_{s=q'+1}^{q}\{e^s\}$. So $D$ is a s.d.e.p. of size $n - (q + r') - \mathbf{1}_{C_0 \neq \emptyset}$ and of total distance $d(M) - (q + r') - 2.\mathbf{1}_{C_0 \neq \emptyset}$. Completion of $D$ in order to obtain a tour in $K_n$, can be done by adding $q + r' + \mathbf{1}_{C_0 \neq \emptyset}$ new edges. Each of these new edges can be, at worst, of distance 2. We so have $d(T(K_n)) \leqslant d(M) - (q + r' + 2.\mathbf{1}_{C_0 \neq \emptyset}) + 2(q + r' + \mathbf{1}_{C_0 \neq \emptyset}) = d(M) + q = r'$, q.e.d.

On the other hand, the optimal tour being a particular triangle-free 2-matching, the following lemma holds immediately.

**Lemma 2.** *$\beta(K_n) \geqslant d(M)$.*

### 3.3 Evaluation of the Worst-Value Solution

In what follows in this section we will bring to the fore a s.d.e.p., all of its edges being of distance 2 (called 2-s.d.e.p.). Given such a s.d.e.p. $W$, one can proceed as in step (5) of algorithm TSP12 (section 3.2), in order to construct a Hamiltonian tour $T_w$ whose total distance is a lower bound for $\omega(K_n)$.

Denote by $E2$ the set of 2-edges of cycle $C_0$. If $q = 0$, i.e., $M_H = \emptyset$, and if $C_0 = E2$, then the tour computed by TSP12 is optimal.

**Lemma 3.** $((q = 0) \wedge (C_0 = E2)) \Rightarrow \delta_{\mathtt{TSP12}}(K_n) = 1$.

*Proof.* Let $k = |V(C_0)| = d(M) - n$ and set $V(C_0) = \{a_1, \ldots, a_k\}$. By the fact that $M$ is 2-minimal, all the edges of $K_n$ incident to these vertices have distance 2. On the other hand, between two distinct cycles in the set $\{C_1, \ldots, C_{p=r'}\}$ of $M$, there exist only edges of distance 2. Consider the family

$$\mathcal{F} = \{\{a_1\}, \ldots, \{a_k\}, V(C_1), \ldots V(C_p)\}.$$

By the remarks just above, any edge linking vertices of two distinct sets of $\mathcal{F}$ is a 2-edge. Any feasible tour of $K_n$ (a posteriori an optimal one) integrates the $k + p$ sets of $\mathcal{F}$ by using at least $k + p$ 2-edges pairwise linking these sets. Hence, any tour uses at least $k + p$ 2-edges, so does tour $T(K_n)$ computed by algorithm TSP12, q.e.d.

So, we suppose in the sequel that $q = 0 \Rightarrow C_0 \neq C_2$. We will now prove the existence of a 2-s.d.e.p. $W$ of size $d(M) + 4(q + r') - n$, where $M$ is as expressed by expression (3.2).

**Proposition 2.** *Between two cycles $C_a$ and $C_b$ of $M$ of size at least $k$, there always exists a path, alternating vertices of $C_a$ and $C_b$, containing at least $k$ 2-edges.*

*Proof.* Let $\{a_1, \ldots, a_{k+1}\}$ and $\{b_1, \ldots, b_{k+1}\}$ be $k + 1$ successive vertices of two distinct cycles $C_a$ and $C_b$ of size at least $k$ (eventually $a_1 = a_{k+1}$ if $|V(C_a)| = k$ and $b_1 = b_{k+1}$ if $|V(C_b)| = k$). We will show that there exists a path, alternating vertices of $C_a$ and $C_b$, of size $2k - 1$ and of distance at least $3k - 1$. Consider paths $C = \cup_{i=1}^{k} \{a_i b_i\} \cup_{i=1}^{k-1} \{a_{i+1} b_i\}$ and $D = \cup_{i=2}^{k+1} \{a_i b_i\} \cup_{i=1}^{k-1} \{a_i b_{i+1}\}$. By the 2-minimality of M we get: $\forall i = 1, \ldots, k$

$$\max\{d(a_i, b_i), d(a_{i+1}, b_{i+1})\} = 2 \Rightarrow d(a_i, b_i) + d(a_{i+1}, b_{i+1}) \geqslant 3$$

and $\forall i = 1, \ldots, k - 1$

$$\max\{d(a_i, b_{i+1}), d(a_{i+1}, b_i)\} = 2 \Rightarrow d(a_i, b_{i+1}) + d(a_{i+1}, b_i) \geqslant 3$$

Summing the terms of the expression above member-by-member, one obtains:

$$\sum_{i=1}^{k} (d(a_i, b_i) + d(a_{i+1}, b_{i+1})) + \sum_{i=1}^{k-1} (d(a_{i+1}, b_i) + d(a_i, b_{i+1})) \geqslant 6k - 3$$

$$\Longleftrightarrow d(C) + d(D) \geqslant 6k - 3 \;\Rightarrow\; \max\{d(C), d(D)\} \geqslant \left\lceil \frac{6k - 3}{2} \right\rceil = 3k - 1.$$

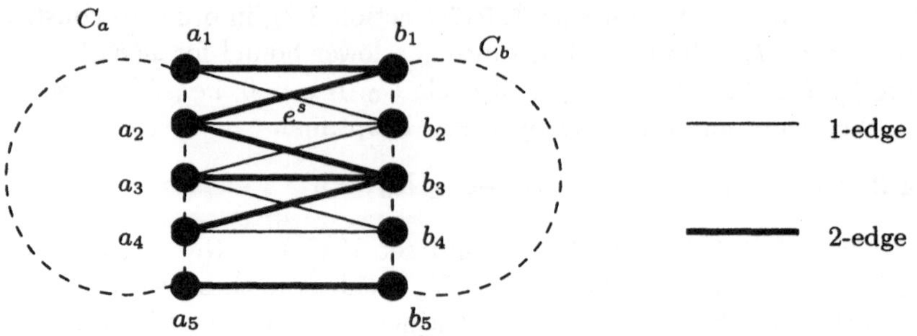


**Fig. 1.** An example of claim 1.

Application of proposition 2 in any pair $(C_1^s, C_2^s)$ of M results to the following.

**Claim 1.** *$\forall s = 1, \ldots, q$, there exists a 2-s.d.e.p. $W^s$ of size 4, alternating vertices of cycles $C_1^s$ and $C_2^s$, containing a vertex of $V_s$ whose degree with respect to $W^s$ is 1.*

In figure 1, we show an application of claim 1. We assume $e^s = a_2b_2$; then $\{a_1, b_1\} \subset V_s$. The 2-s.d.e.p. $W^s$ claimed is $\{b_1a_2, (a_3b_3, a_4b_4), a_5b_5\}$ and the degree of $b_1$ with respect to $W^s$ is 1.

Consider now the s.d.e.p. $W_t^s = W^s \cup W'^s_t$, where $W^s$ as in claim 1 and $W'^s_t$ is any path of size 4 alternating vertices of $C_3^s$ and of $C_t$, $s = 1, \ldots, q'$, $t = 1, \ldots, r'$. By the optimality of $M_H$, any edge linking vertices of $C_3^s$ to vertices of $C_t$ is a 2-edge. Consequently, $W_t^s$ is a 2-s.d.e.p. and the following claim holds.

**Claim 2.** *$\forall s = 1, \ldots, q'$, $\forall t = 1, \ldots, r'$, there exists a 2-s.d.e.p. $W_t^s$ of size 8, alternating vertices of the cycles $C_1^s$ and $C_2^s$, and of the cycles $C_3^s$ and $C_t$.*

For $s = q' + 1, \ldots, q$, $t = 1, \ldots r'$, consider the triple $(C_1^s, C_2^s, C_t)$. Let $e^s = e_1^s e_2^s$, $V_s = \{u_1^s, v_1^s, u_2^s, v_2^s\}$ and consider any four vertices $a_t$, $b_t$, $c_t$ and $d_t$ of $C_t$. By the optimality of $M_B$, any vertex of $C_t$ is linked to any vertex of $V^s$ exclusively by 2-edges. Moreover, the 2-minimality of $M$ implies that at least one of $u_1^s e_2^s$ and $e_1^s u_2^s$ is of distance 2. If we suppose $d(u_1^s, e_2^s) = 2$ (figure 2), then the path $\{e_2^s, u_1^s, a_t, v_1^s, b_t, u_2^s, c_t, v_2^s, d_t\}$ is a 2-s.e.d.p. In all, the following claim holds.

**Claim 3.** *$\forall s = q' + 1, \ldots, q$, $\forall t = 1, \ldots, r'$, there exists a 2-s.d.e.p. $W_t^s$ of size 8, alternating vertices of the cycles $C_1^s$, $C_2^s$ and $C_t$.*

Let $r' \geqslant 2$ and consider the (residual) cycles $C_t$, $t = 1, \ldots, r'$. All edges between these cycles are of distance 2. If we denote by $a_t$, $b_t$, $c_t$ and $d_t$ four vertices of $C_t$, the path

$$\{a_1, \ldots, a_t, \ldots, a_{r'}, b_1, \ldots, b_t, \ldots, b_{r'}, c_1, \ldots, c_t, \ldots, c_{r'}, d_1, \ldots, d_t, \ldots, d_{r'}\}$$

is a 2-s.d.e.p. of size $4r' - 1$ and the following claim holds.

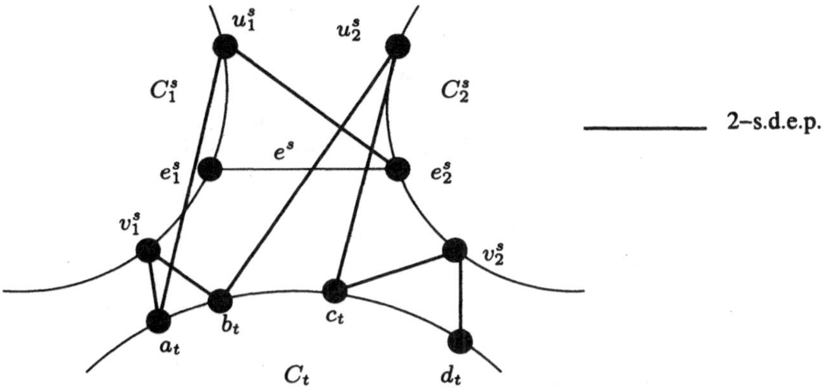


**Fig. 2.** The 2-s.d.e.p. $W_t^s$ of claim 3.

**Claim 4.** *If* $r' \geqslant 2$, *then there exists a 2-s.d.e.p.* $W^{r'}$ *of size* $4r' - 1$ *alternating vertices of cycles* $C_t$, $t = 1, \ldots, r'$.

**Lemma 4.** $((q \geqslant 1) \vee ((C_0 \neq C_2) \wedge (r \neq 1))) \Rightarrow \delta_{\text{TSP12}}(K_n) \geqslant 3/4$.

Lemma 4 is proved in [11]. There, we use claims 1, 2, 3 and 4 in order to bring to the fore a 2-s.d.e.p. $W$ of total distance $4(q+r') - \mathbf{1}_{q=0} + d(M) - n + \mathbf{1}_{C_0 \neq E2} \geqslant d(M) - n + 4(q+r')$, the completion of which produces a Hamiltonian tour of distance $d(M) +' (q+r')$ at least.

**Lemma 5.** $((q = 0) \wedge (r = 1) \wedge (C_0 \neq C_2)) \Rightarrow \delta_{\text{TSP12}}(K_n) \geqslant 3/4$.

In all, combining lemmata 1, 2, 3 and 5, the following theorem can be immediately proved.

**Theorem 2.** *min_TSP12 is approximable within differential-approximation ratio 3/4.*

Theorems 1 and 2 induce the following corollary.

**Corollary 1.** *min_ and max_TSP12 as well as min_ and max_TSPab are approximable within differential-approximation ratio 3/4.*

Consider two cliques and number their vertices by $\{1, \ldots, 4\}$ and by $\{5, 6, \ldots, n+8\}$, respectively. Edges of both cliques have all distance 1. Cross-edges $ij$, $i = 1, 3$, $j = 5, \ldots, n+8$, are all of distance 2, while every other cross-edge is of distance 1. Unraveling of TSP12 will produce: $T = \{1, 2, 3, 4, 5, 6, \ldots, n+7, n+8, 1\}$ (cycle-patching on edges $(1,4)$ and $(5, n+8)$), while $T_w = \{1, 5, 2, 6, 3, 7, 4, 8, 9 \ldots, n+7, n+8, 1\}$ (using 2-edges $(1,5)$, $(6,3)$, $(3,7)$ and $(n+8, 1)$) and $T^* = \{1, 2, n+8, n+7, \ldots, 5, 4, 3, 1\}$ (using 1-edges $(4,5)$ and $(2, n+8)$). In figure 3, $T^*$ and $T_w$ are shown for $n = 2$ ($T = \{1, \ldots, 10, 1\}$). Consequently, $\delta_{\text{TSP12}}(K_{n+8}) = 3/4$ and the following proposition holds.

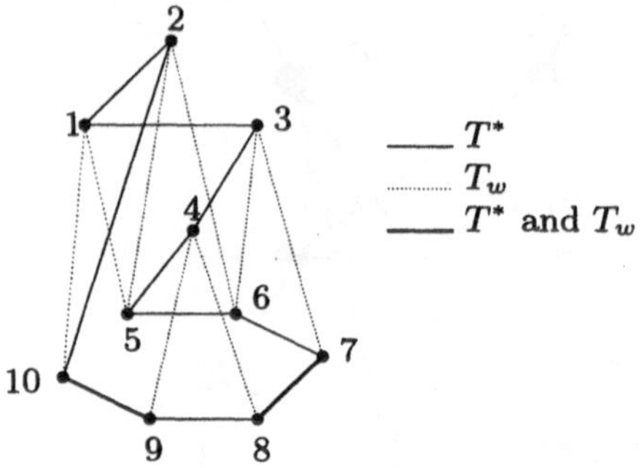


**Fig. 3.** Tightness of the TSP12 approximation ratio.

**Proposition 3.** *Ratio 3/4 is tight for TSP12*

Let us note that the differential approximation ratio of the 7/6-algorithm of [12], when running on $K_{n+8}$, is also 3/4. The authors of [12] bring also to the fore a family of worst-case instances for their algorithm: one has $k$ cycles of length four arranged around a cycle of length $2k$. We have performed a limited comparative study between their algorithm and ours one, for $k = 3, 4, 5, 6$ (on 24 graphs). The average differential and standard approximation ratios for the two algorithms are presented in table 1. Using corollary 1 and the facts that $\omega(K_n) \leqslant bn$ and $\beta(K_n) \geqslant an$, the following holds.

**Table 1.** A limited comparison between TSP12 and the algorithm of [12] on some worst-case instances of the latter.

| | $k$ | TSP12 | The algorithm of [12] |
|---|---|---|---|
| Differential ratio | 3 | 0.931100364 | 0.846702091 |
| | 4 | 0.9000002 | 0.833333 |
| | 5 | 0.920289696 | 0.833333 |
| | 6 | 0.9222222 | 0.833333 |
| Standard ratio | 3 | 0.923350955 | 0.87013 |
| | 4 | 0.9094018 | 0.857143 |
| | 5 | 0.92646313 | 0.857143 |
| | 6 | 0.928178 | 0.857143 |

**Proposition 4.** *min_TSPab is approximable within $\rho \leqslant (1 + (b - a/4a)$ in the standard framework. This ratio tends to $\infty$ when $b = o(a)$.*

Revisit min_TSP12. Using $n \leqslant \beta(K_n) \leqslant \omega(K_n) \leqslant 2n$, one can see that approximation of min_TSP12 within $\delta = 1 - \epsilon$ implies its approximation within $\rho = 2 - (1 - \epsilon) = 1 + \epsilon$, $0 \leqslant \epsilon \leqslant 1$. Using the result of [8] and theorem 1, one gets the following differential-inapproximability result.

**Theorem 3.** *min_ and max_TSPab and min_ and max_TSP12 are inapproximable within differential-ratio greater than, or equal to,* $5379/5380 + \epsilon$, $\forall\epsilon > 0$, *unless* ***P=NP***.

## 4 An Improvement of the Standard Ratio for the Maximum Traveling Salesman with Distances 1 and 2

Combining expressions $\delta_{\max\_TSP12} \geqslant 3/4$, $\omega_{\max}(K_n) \geqslant an$ and $\beta_{\max}(K_n) \leqslant bn$, one deduces $\rho_{\max\_TSP12} \geqslant (3/4) + (a/4b)$. Setting $a = 1$ and $b = 2$, the following theorem immediately holds.

**Theorem 4.** *max_TSP12 is polynomially approximable within standard-approximation ratio bounded below by 7/8.*

The algorithm of [12] in $\bar{K}_n$ solves max_TSP on $K_n$ within standard-approximation ratio bounded below by 2/3.

Note that standard-approximation ratio 7/8 can be obtained by the following direct method.

```
BEGIN /max_TSP12/
      find a triangle-free 2-matching M = {C1, C2, ...};
      FOR all Ci DO delete a minimum-distance edge from Ci OD
      let MT the collection of the paths obtained;
      properly link the paths of MT to get a Hamiltonian cycle T;
      OUTPUT T;
END. /max_TSP12/
```

Let $p$ be the number of cycles of $M$ where 2-edges have been removed during the FOR-loop of algorithm max_TSP12. Then, $\lambda_{\max\_TSP12}(K_n) \geqslant d(M) - p$, $\beta(K_n) \leqslant d(M)$ and, since $M$ is triangle-free, $d(M) \geqslant 8p$. Consequently, $\lambda_{\max\_TSP12}(K_n)/\beta_{\max}(K_n) \geqslant 7/8$.

## References

1. A. Aiello, E. Burattini, M. Furnari, A. Massarotti, and F. Ventriglia. Computational complexity: the problem of approximation. In C. M. S. J. Bolyai, editor, *Algebra, combinatorics, and logic in computer science*, volume I, pages 51–62, New York, 1986. North-Holland.
2. G. Ausiello, A. D'Atri, and M. Protasi. Structure preserving reductions among convex optimization problems. *J. Comput. System Sci.*, 21:136–153, 1980.
3. G. Ausiello, A. Marchetti-Spaccamela, and M. Protasi. Towards a unified approach for the classification of NP-complete optimization problems. *Theoret. Comput. Sci.*, 12:83–96, 1980.

4. M. Bellare and P. Rogaway. The complexity of approximating a nonlinear program. *Math. Programming*, 69:429–441, 1995.
5. G. Cornuejols, M. L. Fisher, and G. L. Nemhauser. Location of bank accounts to optimize float: an analytic study of exact and approximate algorithms. *Management Science*, 23(8):789–810, 1977.
6. M. Demange, P. Grisoni, and V. T. Paschos. Differential approximation algorithms for some combinatorial optimization problems. *Theoret. Comput. Sci.*, 209:107–122, 1998.
7. M. Demange and V. T. Paschos. On an approximation measure founded on the links between optimization and polynomial approximation theory. *Theoret. Comput. Sci.*, 158:117–141, 1996.
8. L. Engebretsen. An explicit lower bound for TSP with distances one and two. In *Proc. STACS'99*, volume 1563 of *LNCS*, pages 373–382. Springer, 1999.
9. M. R. Garey and D. S. Johnson. *Computers and intractability. A guide to the theory of NP-completeness.* W. H. Freeman, San Francisco, 1979.
10. D. B. Hartvigsen. *Extensions of matching theory.* PhD thesis, Carnegie-Mellon University, 1984.
11. J. Monnot, V. T. Paschos, and S. Toulouse. Differential approximation results for the traveling salesman problem. Cahier du LAMSADE 172, LAMSADE, Université Paris-Dauphine, 2000.
12. C. H. Papadimitriou and M. Yannakakis. The traveling salesman problem with distances one and two. *Math. Oper. Res.*, 18:1–11, 1993.
13. A. I. Serdyukov. An algorithm with an estimate for the traveling salesman problem of the maximum. *Upravlyaemye Sistemy*, 25:80–86, 1984.
14. S. A. Vavasis. Approximation algorithms for indefinite quadratic programming. *Math. Programming*, 57:279–311, 1992.
15. E. Zemel. Measuring the quality of approximate solutions to zero-one programming problems. *Math. Oper. Res.*, 6:319–332, 1981.

# On the Category of Event Structures with Dense Time*

Nataly S. Moskaljova and Irina B. Virbitskaite

Institute of Informatics Systems
Siberian Division of the Russian Academy of Sciences
6, Acad. Lavrentiev av., 630090, Novosibirsk, Russia
fax: (+7)83822323494, virb@iis.nsk.su

**Abstract.** The intention of the paper is first to show the applicability of the general categorical framework of open maps to the setting of true concurrent models with dense time. In particular, we define a category of timed event structures and an accompanying path (sub)category of timed words. Then we use the framework of open maps to obtain an abstract notion of bisimulation which is established to be equivalent to the standard notion of timed bisimulation. Using the fact, we finally show decidability of timed bisimulation in the setting of finite timed structures.

**Keywords:** category theory, timed event structures, timed bisimulation

## 1 Introduction

As a response to the numerous models for concurrency proposed in the literature Winskel and Nielsen have used category theory as an attempt to understand the relationship between models like event structures, Petri nets, trace languages and asynchronous transition systems [22]. Further, to provide a convincing way to adjoining abstract equivalences to a category of models, Joyal, Nielsen, and Winskel proposed the notion of span of open maps [10] that is an abstract generalization of Park and Milner's bisimulation. Furthermore, in [18] open maps have been used to define different notions of bisimulation for a range of models, but none of these have modelled real-time.

Recently, the demand for correctness analysis of real time systems, i.e. systems whose descriptions involve a quantitative notion of time, increases rapidly. Timed extensions of interleaving models have been investigated thoroughly in the last ten years. Various recipes on how to incorporate time in transition systems — the most prominent interleaving model — are, for example, described in [1,17]. Timed bisimulation was shown decidable for finite timed transition systems by Čerāns in [5], and since then more efficient algorithms have been discovered in [13,20].

* This work is partially supported by the Russian Fund of Basic Research (Grant N 00-01-00898).

R. Freivalds (Ed.): FCT 2001, LNCS 2138, pp. 287–298, 2001.

On the other hand, the incorporation of quantitative information into non-interleaving abstract models has received scant attention: a few extensions are known of causal trees [6], pomsets [4], configurations [15], sets of posets [11], net processes [14], and event structures [12,16].

The contribution of the paper is first to show the applicability of the general categorical framework of open maps to the setting of true concurrent models with dense time. Here we define a category of timed event structures, where the morphisms are to be thought of as simulations, and an accompanying path (sub)category of timed words, which, following [10], provides us with notions of open maps and bisimulation. Furthermore, we show within the framework of open maps that timed bisimulation is decidable for finite timed event structures.

There have been several motivations for this work. One has been given by the papers [19,21,22] which have proposed and investigated categorical characterizations of event structure models. A next origin of this study has been a number of papers (see [5,13,20] among others), which have extensively studied time-sensitive equivalence notions for interleaving models. However, to our best knowledge, the literature of timed true concurrent models has hitherto lacked such the equivalences. In this regard, the papers [2,16] is a welcome exception, where the decidability question of timed testing has been treated in the framework of event structures with time notions. Finally, another motivation has been given by the paper [9], which provides an alternative proof of decidability of bisimulation for finite timed transition systems in terms of open maps, and illustrates the use of open maps in presenting timed bisimularity.

The rest of the paper is organized as follows. The basic notions concerning timed event structures are introduced in the next section. A category of timed event structures and an accompanying path (sub)category of timed words, are defined in section 3. A notion of $TW$-open morphisms and its alternative characterization are provided in section 4. In section 5, basing on spans of $TW$-open maps, the resulting notion of bisimulation is studied, and shown to coincide with the standard notion of timed bisimulation. Section 6 is devoted to decidability of timed bisimulation in our framework. Section 7 contains conclusion and future work.

## 2 Timed Event Structures

In this section, we introduce some basic notions and notations concerning timed event structures.

We first recall a notion of an event structure [21]. The main idea behind event structures is to view distributed computations as action occurrences, called events, together with a notion of causality dependency between events (which reasonably characterized via a partial order). Moreover, in order to model non-determinism, there is a notion of conflicting (mutually incompatible) events. A labelling function records which action an event corresponds to.

Let *Act* be a finite set of actions. A *(labelled) event structure* over *Act* is 4-tuple $S = (E, \leq, \#, l)$, where $E$ is a countable set of events; $\leq \subseteq E \times E$ is a partial order (the *causality relation*), satisfying the *principle of finite causes*: $\forall e \in E \circ \{e' \in E \mid e' \leq e\}$ is finite; $\# \subseteq E \times E$ is a symmetric and irreflexive relation (the *conflict relation*), satisfying the *principle of conflict heredity*: $\forall e, e', e'' \in E \circ e \# e' \leq e'' \Rightarrow e \# e''$; $l : E \longrightarrow Act$ is a labelling function.

Let $C \subseteq E$. Then $C$ is *left-closed* iff $\forall e, e' \in E \circ e \in C \wedge e' \leq e \Rightarrow e' \in C$; $C$ is *conflict-free* iff $\forall e, e' \in C \circ \neg(e \# e')$; $C$ is a *configuration of $S$* iff $C$ is left-closed and conflict-free. Let $\mathcal{C}(S)$ denote the set of all finite configurations of $S$. For $C \in \mathcal{C}(S)$, we define $En(C) = \{e \in E \mid C \cup \{e\} \in \mathcal{C}(S)\}$.

Next we present a model of timed event structures which are a timed extension of event structures by associating their events with two timing constraints that indicate earliest and latest event occurrence times both with regard to global clock. Events once ready — i.e., all their causal predecessors have occurred and their timing constraints are respected — are forced to occur, provided they are not disabled by others events. A state of a timed event structure is a set of its event occurred, equipped with a set of clocks corresponding to the events and recording a global time moment at which events occur. A timed event structure progresses through a sequence of states by occurring events at a certain time moment. An event occurrence takes no time. Let $\mathbf{N}$ be the set of natural numbers, $\mathbf{R}_0^+$ the set of nonnegative real numbers.

**Definition 1** *A* timed (labelled) event structure *over Act is a tuple* $TS = (S, Eft, Lft)$, *where*

- $S$ *is a (labelled) event structure over Act;*
- $Eft, Lft : E \to \mathbf{R}_0^+$ *are functions of the* earliest *and* latest occurrence times *of events, satisfying* $Eft(e) \leq Lft(e)$ *for all* $e \in E$.

In a graphic representation of a timed event structure, the corresponding action labels and time intervals are drawn near to events. If no confusion arises, we will often use action labels rather event identities to denote events. The <-relations are depicted by arcs (omitting those derivable by the transitivity), and conflicts are also drawn (omitting those derivable by the conflict heredity). Following these conventions, a trivial example of a labelled timed event structure is shown in Fig. 1.

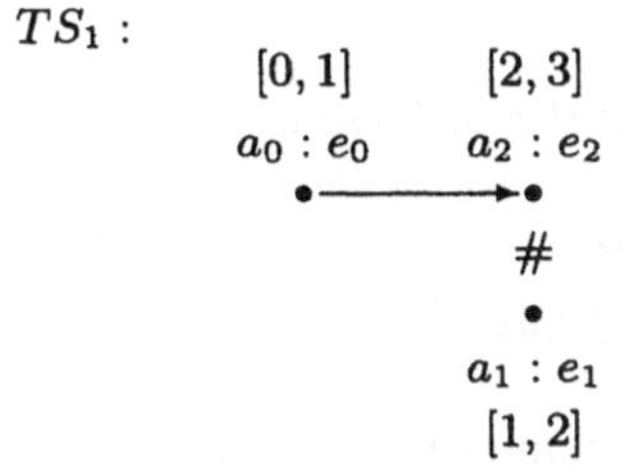


**Fig. 1.**

Let $\Gamma(TS) = [E \to \mathbf{R}_0^+]$ be the set of *time assignments* for events from $E$. Given $\nu \in \Gamma(TS)$, we let $\Delta(\nu) = \max\{\nu(e) \mid e \in E\}$. A *state* of $TS$ is a pair $(C, \nu)$, where $C \in \mathcal{C}(S)$ and $\nu \in \Gamma(TS)$. The *initial state* of $TS$ is a pair $(C_S, \nu_{TS}) = (\emptyset, 0)$.

In a state $(C, \nu)$, the occurrence of an event $e$ after passing a time $d \in \mathbf{R}_0^+$ *leads to* the state $(C', \nu')$ (denoted $(C, \nu) \overset{(e,d)}{\longrightarrow} (C', \nu')$), if $C' = C \cup \{e\}$, $\nu' \mid_{E \setminus \{e\}} = \nu$, $\nu'(e) = \Delta(\nu) + d$ and $Eft(e) \leq \nu'(e) \leq \min\{Lft(e') \mid e' \in En(C)\}$. We shall write $(C, \nu) \overset{(a,d)}{\longrightarrow} (C', \nu')$, if $(C, \nu) \overset{(e,d)}{\longrightarrow} (C', \nu')$ and $l(e) = a$. A state $(C, \nu)$ is *reachable* iff either $(C, \nu) = (C_S, \nu_{TS})$ or there exists a reachable state $(C', \nu')$ such that $(C', \nu') \overset{(e,d)}{\longrightarrow} (C, \nu)$ for some $e \in E$ and $d \in \mathbf{R}_0^+$. Let $RS(TS)$ denote the set of all reachable states of $TS$.

A *timed word* $w$ of an alphabet *Act* over $\mathbf{R}_0^+$ is a finite sequence of pairs: $w = (a_1, d_1)(a_2, d_2) \ldots (a_n, d_n)$, where $a_i \in Act$ and $d_i \in \mathbf{R}_0^+$ for all $1 \leq i \leq n$. Given a timed word $w = (a_1, d_1)(a_2, d_2) \ldots (a_n, d_n)$, a *run* $r$ of $w$ is a finite sequence of the form: $r = (\emptyset, 0) \overset{(a_1,d_1)}{\longrightarrow} (C_1, \nu_1) \overset{(a_2,d_2)}{\longrightarrow} (C_2, \nu_2) \ldots (C_{n-1}, \nu_{n-1}) \overset{(a_n,d_n)}{\longrightarrow} (C_n, \nu_n)$. As an illustration, we construct the set of the timed words corresponding to the runs of the timed event structure $TS_1$ (see Fig. 1): $\{(a_0, d_0) \mid 0 \leq d_0 \leq 1\} \cup \{(a_1, d_1) \mid d_1 = 1\} \cup \{(a_0, d_0)(a_1, d_1) \mid 0 \leq d_0 \leq 1,\ 1 \leq d_0 + d_1 \leq 2\} \cup \{(a_1, d_1)(a_0, d_0) \mid d_1 = 1,\ d_0 = 0\} \cup \{(a_0, d_0)(a_2, d_2) \mid 0 \leq d_0 \leq 1,\ d_0 + d_2 = 2\}$.

## 3 A Category of Timed Event Structures

In this section, we define a category of timed event structures and an accompanying path (sub)category of timed words.

The morphisms of our model category will be simulation morphisms following the approach of [10]. This leads to the following definition of a morphism that is a function, mapping events of the simulated system to simulating events of the other, satisfying some requirements.

**Definition 2** *A* morphism *between timed event structures* $TS = (S = (E, \leq, \#, l), Eft, Lft)$ *and* $TS' = (S' = (E', \leq', \#', l'), Eft', Lft')$, $\mu : TS \to TS'$, *is a function* $\mu : E \to E'$ *such that:*

- $l' \circ \mu = l$;
- $C \in \mathcal{C}(S) \Rightarrow \mu\, C \in \mathcal{C}(S')$ *and the following constraints hold:*
  - $\forall e, e' \in C \circ \mu(e) = \mu(e') \Rightarrow e = e'$;
  - $\forall e \in C \circ Eft'(\mu(e)) \leq Eft(e)$;
  - $\min\{Lft(e) \mid e \in En(C)\} \leq \min\{Lft'(e) \mid e \in En(\mu\, C)\}$.

Here we assume that the minimal value of the empty set is equal to $-\infty$.

As an illustration, consider a morphism from the timed event structure $TS_2$ in Fig. 2 to the timed event structure $TS_1$ in Fig. 1 mapping events $e_i'$ to $e_i$ $(0 \leq i \leq 2)$. It is easy to check that the constraints in Definition 2 are satisfied.

Let us consider a simulation property of a morphism defined prior to that.

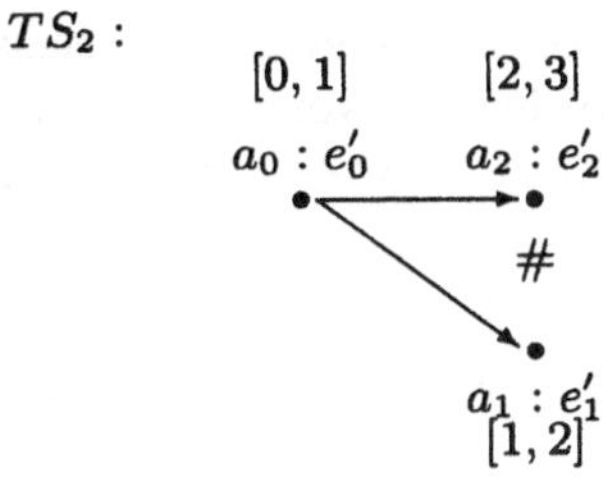


**Fig. 2.**

**Theorem 1** *Given a morphism $\mu : TS \to TS'$ and a timed word $(a_1, d_1) \ldots (a_n, d_n)$. If $(C_S, \nu_{TS}) = (C_0, \nu_0) \stackrel{(a_1,d_1)}{\longrightarrow} (C_1, \nu_1) \ldots (C_{n-1}, \nu_{n-1}) \stackrel{(a_n,d_n)}{\longrightarrow} (C_n, \nu_n)$ is a run in $TS$, then $(C_{S'}, \nu_{TS'}) = (\mu\ C_0, \nu'_0) \stackrel{(a_1,d_1)}{\longrightarrow} (\mu\ C_1, \nu'_1) \ldots (\mu\ C_{n-1}, \nu'_{n-1}) \stackrel{(a_n,d_n)}{\longrightarrow} (\mu\ C_n, \nu'_n)$ is a run in $TS'$.*

**Proof Sketch.** We will prove this theorem by induction on $n$.

As base case, we have the empty run with just one initial state. The result is obvious. For the induction step, assume $(C_S, \nu_{TS}) = (C_0, \nu_0) \stackrel{(a_1,d_1)}{\rightarrow} (C_1, \nu_1) \ldots (C_{n-1}, \nu_{n-1}) \stackrel{(a_n,d_n)}{\rightarrow} (C_n, \nu_n)$ in $TS$, and $(C_{S'}, \nu_{TS'}) = (\mu\ C_0, \nu'_0) \stackrel{(a_1,d_1)}{\longrightarrow} (\mu\ C_1, \nu'_1) \ldots \stackrel{(a_{n-1},d_{n-1})}{\rightarrow} (\mu\ C_{n-1}, \nu'_{n-1})$ in $TS'$. According to the definition of the relation $\stackrel{(a_n,d_n)}{\rightarrow}$, there exists $e_n \in E_S$ such that $l(e_n) = a_n$, $C_n = C_{n-1} \cup \{e_n\}$, $\nu_n\ |_{E \setminus \{e_n\}} = \nu_{n-1}$, $\nu_n(e_n) = \Delta(\nu_{n-1}) + d_n$, and $Eft(e_n) \leq \nu_n(e_n) \leq \min\{Lft(e) \mid e \in En(C_{n-1})\}$. Since $\mu$ is a morphism, then $\mu\ C_{n-1}, \mu\ C_n \in \mathcal{C}(S')$. We now check that $(\mu\ C_n \setminus \mu\ C_{n-1}) = \{\mu(e_n)\}$. Suppose a contrary, i.e., $\mu(e_n) \in \mu\ C_{n-1}$. Then there is an event $e' \in C_{n-1}$ such that $\mu(e') = \mu(e_n)$. From the definition of a morphism we get $e' = e_n$, but it is impossible because $e_n \notin C_{n-1}$. Hence $(\mu\ C_n \setminus \mu\ C_{n-1}) = \{\mu(e_n)\}$. Again, from the definition of a morphism we have $l'(\mu(e_n)) = l(e_n) = a_n$, $Eft'(\mu(e_n)) \leq Eft(e_n) \leq \Delta(\nu_{n-1}) + d_n = \Delta(\nu'_{n-1}) + d_n \leq \min\{Lft(e) \mid e \in En(C_{n-1})\} \leq \min\{Lft'(e) \mid e \in En(\mu\ C_{n-1})\}$. Thus, $(\mu\ C_{n-1}, \nu'_{n-1}) \stackrel{(a_n,d_n)}{\rightarrow} (\mu\ C_n, \nu'_n)$ with $\nu'_n\ |_{E' \setminus \{\mu(e_n)\}} = \nu'_{n-1}$, and $\nu'_n(\mu(e_n)) = \Delta(\nu'_{n-1}) + d_n$, by the definition of the relation $\stackrel{(a_n,d_n)}{\rightarrow}$. □

Hence, in the formal sense of Theorem 1 we have shown that the morphisms from Definition 2 do represent a notion of simulation. So, define a category of timed event structures as follows.

**Definition 3** *Timed event structures (labelled over Act) with morphisms between them form a category of timed event structures $\mathcal{CTS}_{Act}$, in which the composition of two morphisms $\mu_1 : TS_0 \longrightarrow TS_1$ and $\mu_2 : TS_1 \longrightarrow TS_2$ is $(\mu_2 \circ \mu_1) : TS_0 \longrightarrow TS_2$, and the identity morphism is the identity function.*

**Proposition 1** *$\mathcal{CTS}_{Act}$ is a category.*

Following the standards of timed event structures and the paper [10], we would like to choose timed words with word extension so as to form a subcategory of $\mathcal{CTS}_{Act}$. For each timed word $w$, we shall construct a timed event structure as follows.

**Definition 4** *Given a timed word $w = (a_1, d_1)(a_2, d_2) \ldots (a_n, d_n)$, we define a timed event structure $TS_w = (E, \leq, \#, l, Eft, Lft)$ as follows: $E = \{1, 2, \cdots, n\}$; $\leq = \{(i, j) \in E \times E \mid 1 \leq i \leq j \leq n\}$; $\sharp = \emptyset$; $l(i) = a_i$ $(i = 1, 2 \cdots n)$; $Eft(i) = Lft(i) = d_1 + \ldots + d_i$.*

The purpose of the construction is to represent the category of timed words with extension inside $\mathcal{CTS}_{Act}$, and to identify runs of $w$ in $TS$ with morphisms from $TS_w$ to $TS$, as expressed formally in the following two results.

**Proposition 2** *The construction of the timed event structure $TS_w$ from a timed word $w$ extends to a full and faithful functor from the category of timed words (as objects) and word extensions (as morphisms) into $\mathcal{CTS}_{Act}$.*

**Theorem 2** *Given a timed event structure $TS$ and a timed word $w = (a_1, d_1) \ldots (a_n, d_n)$. For all run of $w$ in $TS$, $(C_S, \nu_{TS}) = (C_0, \nu_0) \stackrel{(a_1,d_1)}{\longrightarrow} (C_1, \nu_1) \ldots (C_{n-1}, \nu_{n-1}) \stackrel{(a_n,d_n)}{\longrightarrow} (C_n, \nu_n)$ such that $C_i \setminus C_{i-1} = \{e_i\}$ $(0 < i \leq n)$, we can associate a morphism $\mu : TS_w \to TS$ such that $\mu(i) = e_i$. Furthermore, this association is a bijection between the runs of $w$ in $TS$ and morphisms $\mu : TS_w \to TS$.*

**Proof Sketch.** From the definition of a run and the construction of $TS_w$ it follows that $\mu$ as defined is indeed a morphism.

Next, assume $\mu : TS_w \to TS$ to be a morphism. We associate with $\mu$ the run $r$ of $w$ as follows: $r = (C_S, \nu_{TS}) = (C_0, \nu_0) \stackrel{(a_1,d_1)}{\longrightarrow} (C_1, \nu_1) \ldots (C_{n-1}, \nu_{n-1}) \stackrel{(a_n,d_n)}{\longrightarrow} (C_n, \nu_n)$, where $C_i = \mu\ \{1, \ldots, i\}$. According to the definition of a morphism, $r$ is indeed a run of $w$ in $TS$. It is easy to check that the correspondence given above is one to one. □

## 4 *TW*-Open Morphisms

Given our categories of timed event structures and timed words, we can apply the general framework from [10], defining a notion of $TW$-open maps.

**Definition 5** *A morphism $\mu : TS \to TS'$ in $\mathcal{CTS}_{Act}$ is $TW$-open iff for all timed words $w$ and $w'$, and morphisms such that the following diagram commutes:*

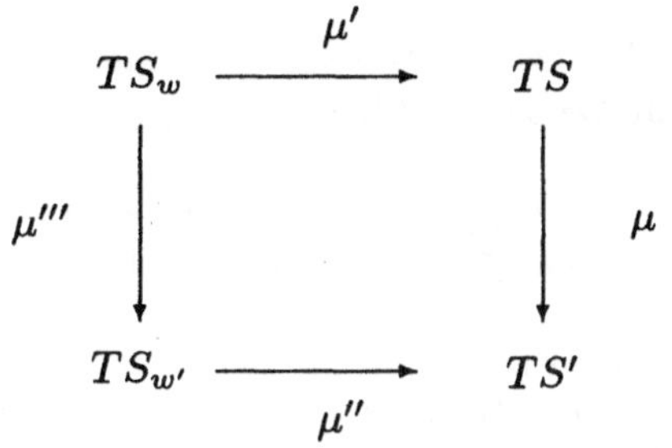


*there exists a morphism* $\widetilde{\mu} : TS_{w'} \to TS$ *such that in the diagram*

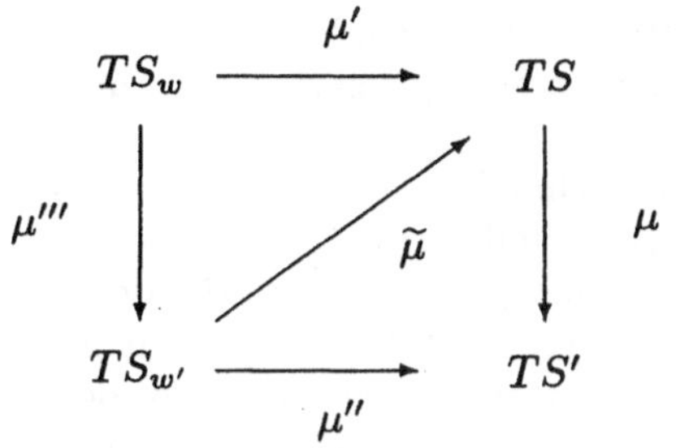


*the two triangles commute.*

Our next aim is to characterize $TW$-openness of morphisms.

**Theorem 3** *Let* $(C_1, \nu_1)$ *and* $(\mu\ C_1, \nu_1')$ *be reachable by* $w$ *in* $TS$ *and* $TS'$, *respectively. A morphism* $\mu : TS \to TS'$ *is* $TW$*-open iff whenever* $(\mu\ C_1, \nu_1') \stackrel{(a,d)}{\longrightarrow} (C_2', \nu_2')$ *in* $TS'$ *then* $(C_1, \nu_1) \stackrel{(a,d)}{\longrightarrow} (C_2, \nu_2)$ *in* $TS$ *and* $\mu\ C_2 = C_2'$.

**Proof Sketch.** It follows similar lines as other standard proofs of the characterization the $TW$-openness of a morphism (see e.g., [9]), using the definition of a morphism and Theorem 2. □

We do not require for the category $\mathcal{CTS}_{Act}$ to have pullbacks. The following weak result suffices.

**Theorem 4** *Given two* $TW$*-open morphisms* $\mu_1 : TS_1 \to TS$ *and* $\mu_2 : TS_2 \to TS$. *There exists a timed event structure* $TS_x$ *and* $TW$*-open morphisms* $\mu_1' : TS_x \to TS_1$, $\mu_2' : TS_x \to TS_2$ *such that the diagram commutes:*

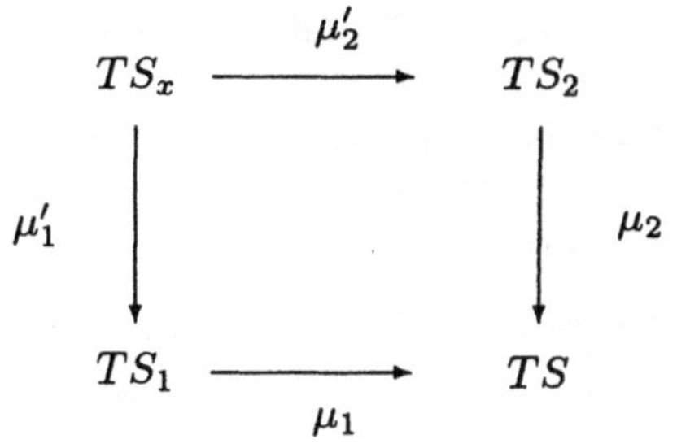


**Proof Sketch.** As a first step we construct a structure $TS_x = (S_x, Eft_x, Lft_x)$ as follows:

- $S_x = +\,(S_{C_1\times C_2} \mid C_i \in \mathcal{C}(S_i), \exists C \in \mathcal{C}(S) \diamond C$ is maximal configuration in $S$, $C = \mu_i\ C_i\ (i = 1,2))$ with $S_{C_1\times C_2} = (E_{C_1\times C_2}, \leq_{C_1\times C_2}, \#_{C_1\times C_2}, l_{C_1\times C_2})$, where
  - $E_{C_1\times C_2} = \{(e_1, e_2) \in C_1 \times C_2 \mid \exists e \in C \diamond e = \mu_i(e_i)\ (i = 1,2)\}$;
  - $(e_1, e_2) \leq_{C_1\times C_2} (e_1', e_2') \Leftrightarrow e_i \leq_i e_i'$ for some $i \in \{1,2\}$;
  - $\#_{C_1\times C_2} = \emptyset$;
  - $l_{C_1\times C_2}((e_1, e_2)) = l_i(e_i)$ for some $i \in \{1,2\}$;
- $Eft_x(e_1, e_2) = \max\{Eft_1(e_1), Eft_2(e_2)\}$;
- $Lft_x(e_1, e_2) = \min\{Lft_1(e_1), Lft_2(e_2)\}$.

Notice that the algebraic operation + is usually 'interpreted' by indicating that all events in one component are in the #-relation with all events in the others (see [7] for more explanation).

It is straightforward to show that $TS_x$ is a timed event structure.

Next, define maps $\mu_1'$ and $\mu_2'$ as follows: $\mu_i'(e_1, e_2) = e_i\ (i = 1,2)$. It is easy to check that $\mu_1'$ and $\mu_2'$ are indeed morphisms. From the definition of a morphism and the construction of $TS_x$, it immediately follows that $\mu_1 \circ \mu_1' = \mu_2 \circ \mu_2'$.

Finally, we check $TW$-openness of $\mu_1'$ (checking $TW$-openness of $\mu_2'$ is similar). Assume $(C_{S_x}, \nu_{TS_x}) \overset{(a_1,d_1)}{\to} \dots \overset{(a_n,d_n)}{\to} (C_x, \nu_x)$ in $TS_x$, and $(\mu_1'\ C_{S_x}, \nu_{TS_1}) \overset{(a_1,d_1)}{\to} \dots \overset{(a_n,d_n)}{\to} (\mu_1'\ C_x, \nu_1) \overset{(a,d)}{\to} (C_1', \nu_1')$ in $TS_1$. According to Theorem 1, we get $(\mu_1 \circ \mu_1'\ C_{S_x}, \nu_{TS}) \overset{(a_1,d_1)}{\to} \dots \overset{(a_n,d_n)}{\to} (\mu_1 \circ \mu_1'\ C_x, \nu) \overset{(a,d)}{\to} (\mu_1\ C_1', \nu')$ in $TS$. Again, by Theorem 1 it holds $(\mu_2'\ C_{S_x}, \nu_{TS_2}) \overset{(a_1,d_1)}{\to} \dots \overset{(a_n,d_n)}{\to} (\mu_2'\ C_x, \nu_2)$ in $TS_2$. Using the fact that the diagram above is commutative, we have $\mu_1 \circ \mu_1' = \mu_2 \circ \mu_2'$. Since $\mu_2$ is a $TW$-open morphism, then $(\mu_2'\ C_x, \nu_2) \overset{(a,d)}{\to} (C_2', \nu_2')$ in $TS_2$, and $\mu_2\ C_2' = \mu_1\ C_1'$, by Theorem 3. Suppose $\{e_1'\} = (C_1' \setminus \mu_1'\ C_x)$, and $\{e_2'\} = (C_2' \setminus \mu_2'\ C_x)$. Then from the construction of $TS_x$, it follows $(C_x, \nu_x) \overset{(a,d)}{\to} ((C_x \cup \{(e_1', e_2')\}), \nu_x')$. By the definition of a morphism, we obtain $\mu_1'\ (C_x \cup \{(e_1', e_2')\}) = C_1'$. Hence $\mu_1'$ is a $TW$-open morphism, by Theorem 3. □

## 5 Timed Bisimulation

In this section, we first introduce a notion of $TW$-bisimulation, using the concept of $TW$-open maps. Then the standard notion of timed bisimulation is defined in terms of states of timed event structures. Finally, the coincidence of the bisimularity notions is shown.

As was reported in [10], the open map approach provides a general concept of bisimularity for any categorical model of computation. The definition is given in terms of spans of $TW$-open maps.

**Definition 6** *Timed event structures $TS_1$ and $TS_2$ are $TW$-bisimilar iff there exists a span $TS_1 \overset{\mu}{\longleftarrow} TS \overset{\mu'}{\longrightarrow} TS_2$ with vertex $TS$ of $TW$-open morphisms.*

Notice that it follows from [10] and Theorem 4 that $TW$-bisimulation is exactly the equivalence generated by $TW$-open maps.

Next, the notion of timed bisimulation is defined in terms of reachable states of timed event structures as follows.

**Definition 7** *Two timed event structures $TS_1$ and $TS_2$ are timed bisimilar iff there exists a relation $\mathcal{B} \subseteq RS(TS_1) \times RS(TS_2)$, satisfying the following conditions: $((C_{S_1}, \nu_{TS_1}), (C_{S_2}, \nu_{TS_2})) \in \mathcal{B}$ and for all $((C_1, \nu_1), (C_2, \nu_2)) \in \mathcal{B}$ it holds:*

*(a) if $(C_1, \nu_1) \xrightarrow{(a,d)} (C_1', \nu_1')$ in $TS_1$, then $(C_2, \nu_2) \xrightarrow{(a,d)} (C_2', \nu_2')$ in $TS_2$ and $((C_1', \nu_1'), (C_2', \nu_2')) \in \mathcal{B}$ for some $(C_2', \nu_2') \in RS(TS_2)$;*
*(b) if $(C_2, \nu_2) \xrightarrow{(a,d)} (C_2', \nu_2')$ in $TS_2$, then $(C_1, \nu_1) \xrightarrow{(a,d)} (C_1', \nu_1')$ in $TS_1$ and $((C_1', \nu_1'), (C_2', \nu_2')) \in \mathcal{B}$ for some $(C_1', \nu_1') \in RS(TS_1)$.*

Finally, the coincidence of the bisimularity notions is established.

**Theorem 5** *Timed event structures $TS_1$ and $TS_2$ are $TW$-bisimilar iff they are timed bisimilar.*

**Proof Sketch.**
($\Rightarrow$) Let $TS_1 \xleftarrow{\mu_1} TS \xrightarrow{\mu_2} TS_2$ be a span of $TW$-open maps. Define a relation $\mathcal{B}$ as follows: $\mathcal{B} = \{((C_1, \nu_1), (C_2, \nu_2)) \mid (C_i, \nu_i) \in RS(TS_i),\ \exists (C, \nu) \in RS(TS) \circ \mu_i\, C = C_i,\ \nu_i \circ \mu_i = \nu\ (i = 1, 2)\}$. Using Theorem 3, it is a routine to show that $\mathcal{B}$ is a timed bisimulation.
($\Leftarrow$) Assume $TS_1$ and $TS_2$ to be timed bisimilar with a relation $\mathcal{B}$ as defined in Definition 7. We construct a span of $TW$-open maps with a vertex $TS = (S, \leq, \#, l, Eft, Lft)$ defined as follows:

- $S = + (S_{C_1 \times C_2} \mid \exists ((C_1, \nu_1), (C_2, \nu_2)) \in \mathcal{B} \circ C_i$ is a maximal configuration in $S_i$, $i = 1, 2)$ with
  - $E_{C_1 \times C_2} = \{(e_1, e_2) \in C_1 \times C_2 \mid \exists C_i',\ C_i'' \subseteq C_i \circ ((C_1', \nu_1'), (C_2', \nu_2')), ((C_1'', \nu_1''), (C_2'', \nu_2'')) \in \mathcal{B},\ (C_i', \nu_i') \xrightarrow{(e_i, d)} (C_i'', \nu_i''),\ i = 1, 2,\ l_1(e_1) = l_2(e_2)\}$;
  - $(e_1, e_2) \leq_{C_1 \times C_2} (e_1', e_2') \Leftrightarrow e_i \leq_i e_i'$ for some $i \in \{1, 2\}$;
  - $\#_{C_1 \times C_2} = \emptyset$;
  - $l_{C_1 \times C_2}((e_1, e_2)) = l_1(e_1) = l_2(e_2)$;
- $Eft(e_1, e_2) = \max\{Eft_1(e_1),\ Eft_2(e_2)\}$;
- $Lft(e_1, e_2) = \min\{Lft_1(e_1),\ Lft_2(e_2)\}$.

It is straightforward to show that $TS$ is a timed event structure.
Next, define maps $\mu_i : TS \to TS_i$ as follows: $\mu_i((e_1, e_2)) = e_i$ $(i = 1, 2)$. By the construction of $TS$ we obtain that $\mu_1$ and $\mu_2$ are indeed morphisms. We shall check $TW$-openness of $\mu_1$ ($TW$-openness of $\mu_2$ is proved in a similar way). Assume $(C_S, \nu_{TS}) \xrightarrow{(a_1,d_1)} \ldots \xrightarrow{(a_n,d_n)} (C, \nu)$ in $TS$. According to Theorem 1, we get: $(\mu_1\ C_S, \nu_{TS_1}) \xrightarrow{(a_1,d_1)} \ldots \xrightarrow{(a_n,d_n)} (\mu_1\ C, \nu_1)$ in $TS_1$, and $(\mu_2\, C_S, \nu_{TS_2}) \xrightarrow{(a_1,d_1)} \ldots \xrightarrow{(a_n,d_n)} (\mu_2\, C, \nu_2)$ in $TS_2$. Suppose $(\mu_1\, C, \nu_1) \xrightarrow{(a,d)} (C_1', \nu_1')$ in $TS_1$. By the definition of timed bisimulation, we have: $((\mu_1\, C, \nu_1), (\mu_2\, C, \nu_2)) \in \mathcal{B}$, $(\mu_2\ C, \nu_2) \xrightarrow{(a,d)} (C_2', \nu_2')$, and $((C_1', \nu_1'), (C_2', \nu_2')) \in \mathcal{B}$, for some $(C_2', \nu_2') \in$

$RS(TS_2)$. Let $\{e_1\} = (C'_1 \setminus \mu_1\ C)$, and $\{e_2\} = (C'_2 \setminus \mu_2\ C)$. From the construction of $TS$, it follows that $(e_1, e_2) \in E_S$ and $C' = C \cup \{(e_1, e_2)\}$ is a configuration in $S$. Again, from the construction of $TS$ we get $(C, \nu) \stackrel{(a,d)}{\rightarrow} (C', \nu')$ in $TS$, and $\mu_1\ C' = C'_1$. Thus, $\mu_1$ is a $TW$-open morphism, by Theorem 3. □

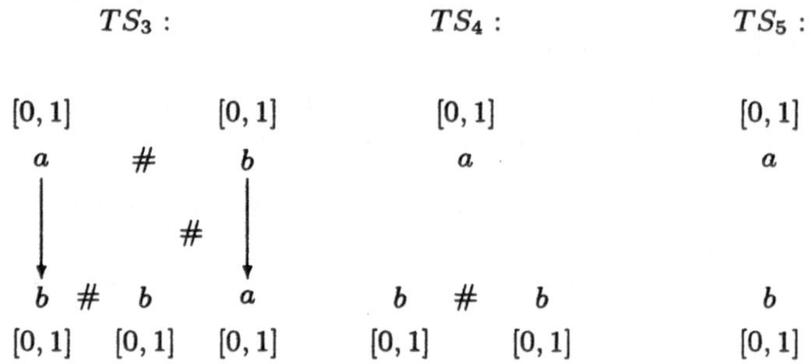


**Fig. 3.**

The timed event structures $TS_1$ and $TS_2$, shown in Fig. 1 and 2 respectively, are not bisimilar. Next, consider the timed event structures in Figure 4. It is easy to see that there are morphisms from $TS_3$ to $TS_4$ and to $TS_5$, and these morphisms are $TW$-open. Hence we have a span of $TW$-open maps between $TS_4$ and $TS_5$. Timed bisimularity between $TS_4$ and $TS_5$ follows from Theorem 5.

## 6 Decidability

In this section, we consider decidability questions for $TW$-openness of a morphism and for timed bisimulation in the setting finite timed event structures. i.e. structures with finite set of events and for which all constants referred to in the earliest and latest occurrence times of events are natural valued. The subclass of timed event structures is denoted by $\mathcal{TS}_{\mathbf{N}}$.

As for many existing results for timed models, including results concerning verification of real-time systems, our decision procedure relies heavily on the idea behind regions (equivalence classes of states) of [1], which essentially provides a finite description of the state-space of timed event structures.

Given a timed event structure $TS$ and $\nu, \nu' \in \Gamma(TS)$, we let $\nu \simeq \nu'$ iff (i) for each $e \in E$ it holds: $\lfloor \nu(e) \rfloor = \lfloor \nu'(e) \rfloor$, and (ii) for each $e, e' \in E$ it holds: $\wr \nu(e) \wr \leq \wr \nu(e') \wr \Leftrightarrow \wr \nu'(e) \wr \leq \wr \nu'(e') \wr$, and $\wr \nu(e) \wr = 0 \Leftrightarrow \wr \nu'(e) \wr = 0$. Here, for $d \in \mathbf{R}_0^+$, $\wr d \wr$ and $\lfloor d \rfloor$ denote its fractional and smallest integer parts, respectively. For $\nu \in \Gamma(TS)$, let $[\nu]$ denote the *region* to which it belongs. Given $TS \in \mathcal{TS}_{\mathbf{N}}$, an *extended state* of $TS$ is defined as a pair $(C, [\nu])$ with $(C, \nu) \in RS(TS)$. We consider $(C_S, [\overline{0}])$ as the *initial region* of $TS$.

**Proposition 3** *Let $TS \in \mathcal{TS}_{\mathbf{N}}$.*

*(a) Given an event e and a region* $[\nu]$,
$Eft(e) \leq \nu(e) \leq Lft(e) \;\Rightarrow\; \forall \nu_1 \in [\nu] \circ Eft(e) \leq \nu_1(e) \leq Lft(e)$.
*(b) Given extended states* $(C,[\nu]),(C',[\nu'])$,
$(C,\nu) \xrightarrow{(a,d)} (C',\nu') \Rightarrow \forall \nu_1 \in [\nu] \circ (C,\nu_1) \xrightarrow{(a,d')} (C',\nu'_1)$ *for some* $\nu'_1 \in [\nu']$ *and* $d' \in \mathbf{R}_0^+$.

For extended states $(C,[\nu]),(C',[\nu'])$, we shall write $(C,[\nu]) \xrightarrow{(a,d)} (C',[\nu'])$, if $(C,\nu) \xrightarrow{(a,d)} (C',\nu')$. An extended state $(C,[\nu])$ is called *reachable by a timed word w*, if $(C,\nu)$ is reachable by a timed word $w$.

We can now give a characterization of $TW$-open maps in terms of extended states.

**Theorem 6** *Let* $TS_1, TS_2 \in \mathcal{TS}_{\mathbf{N}}$, *and* $(C_1,[\nu_1])$, $(\mu\, C_1,[\nu'_1])$ *be extended states reachable by w in* $TS_1$ *and* $TS_2$, *respectively. A morphism* $\mu : TS_1 \to TS_2$ *is TW-open iff whenever* $(\mu\, C_1,[\nu'_1]) \xrightarrow{(a,d)} (C'_2,[\nu'_2])$ *in* $TS_2$, *then* $(C_1,[\nu_1]) \xrightarrow{(a,d)} (C_2,[\nu_2])$ *in* $TS_1$ *and* $\mu\, C_2 = C'_2$.

**Proof Sketch.** It follows from Theorem 3 and Proposition 3. □

Notice, that the theorem above implies decidability of $TW$-openness of a morphism between $TS$ and $TS'$ from $\mathcal{TS}_{\mathbf{N}}$.

**Theorem 7** *Let* $TS_1, TS_2 \in \mathcal{TS}_{\mathbf{N}}$. *If there exists a span of TW-open maps* $TS_1 \xleftarrow{\mu_1} TS \xrightarrow{\mu_2} TS_2$ *then there exists* $TS' \in \mathcal{TS}_{\mathbf{N}}$ *of size bounded by the size of* $TS_1$ *and* $TS_2$ *and with TW-open morphisms* $TS_1 \xleftarrow{\mu'_1} TS' \xrightarrow{\mu'_2} TS_2$.

**Proof Sketch.** Since $TS_1 \xleftarrow{\mu_1} TS \xrightarrow{\mu_2} TS_2$ is a span of $TW$-open maps, then $TS_1$ and $TS_2$ are $TW$-bisimilar, by Theorem 5. This means that there exists a timed bisimulation $\mathcal{B}$ between states of $TS_1$ and $TS_2$. Using $\mathcal{B}$ we construct $TS'$ as in the converse part of the proof of Theorem 5. From the construction it follows that $TS' \in \mathcal{TS}_{\mathbf{N}}$. The number of extended states in $TS'$ is bounded by $\mid E \mid! \cdot 2^{2|E|} \cdot (c+1)^{|E|}$, where $\mid E \mid = \mid E_1 \mid * \mid E_2 \mid$ ($\mid E_i \mid$ is the number of events in $TS_i$ $(i = 1,2)$), and $c$ is the greatest constant appearing in the timing constraints in $TS_1$ and $TS_2$. □

**Corollary 1** *Timed bisimulation is decidable for* $TS, TS' \in \mathcal{TS}_{\mathbf{N}}$.

## 7 Conclusion

In this paper, we tried to develop a categorical framework of open maps for timed event structures to take into account processes' timing behaviour in addition to their degrees of relative concurrency and nondeterminism, and then to apply the framework to characterize and, also, to decide timed bisimulation.

In a future work, we will extend the results obtained to other behavioural equivalences of timed systems (e.g., timed variants of pomset based equivalences). Some investigation on the existence of coreflection between timed true concurrent models (timed net processes and timed event structures) are now under way and we plan to report on this work elsewhere.

## References


1. R. Alur, D. Dill. The theory of timed automata. *Theoretical Computer Science* **126** (1994) 183–235.
2. Andreeva M.V., Bozhenkova E.B., Virbitskaite I.B. Analysis of timed concurrent models based on testing equivalence. *Fundamenta Informaticae* **43(1-4)**(2000) 1–20.
3. C. Baier, J.-P. Katoen, D. Latella. Metric semantics for true concurrent real time. Proc. *25th Int. Colloquium, ICALP'98*, Aalborg, Denmark, 1998, 568–579.
4. R.T. Casley, R.F. Crew, J. Meseguer, V.R. Pratt. Temporal structures. *Mathematical Structures in Computer Science* **1**(2) (1991) 179–213.
5. K. Čerāns. Decidability of bisimulation equivalences for parallel timer processes. *Lecture Notes in Computer Science* **663** (1993) 302–315.
6. C. Fidge. A constraint-oriented real-time process calculus. *Formal Description Techniques V, IFIP Transactions* C-**10** (1993) 363–378.
7. R. Glabbeek, U. Goltz. Equivalence notions for concurrent systems and refinement of actions. *Lecture Notes in Computer Science* **379** (1989) 237 – 248.
8. M. Hennessy, R. Milner. Algebraic laws for nondeterminism and concurrency. *Journal of ACM* **32** (1985) 137–162.
9. T. Hune, M. Nielsen. Timed bisimulation and open maps. *Lecture Notes in Computer Science* **1450** (1998) 378–387.
10. A. Joyal, M. Nielsen, G. Winskel. Bisimulation from open maps. *Information and Computation* **127(2)** (1996) 164–185.
11. W. Janssen, M. Poel, Q. Wu, J. Zwiers. Layering of real-time distributed processes. *Lecture Notes in Computer Science* **863** (1994) 393–417.
12. J.-P. Katoen, R. Langerak, D. Latella, E. Brinksma. On specifying real-time systems in a causality-based setting. *Lecture Notes in Computer Science* **1135** (1996) 385–404.
13. F. Laroussinie, K.G. Larsen, C. Weise. From timed automata to logic and back. *Lecture Notes in Computer Science* **969** (1995) 529–539.
14. Lilius, J. Efficient state space search for time Petri nets. Proc. MFCS'98 Workshop on Concurrency, August 1998, Brno (Czech Republic), FIMU Report Series, FIMU RS-98-06 (1998) 123–130.
15. A. Maggiolo-Schettini, J. Winkowski. Towards an algebra for timed behaviours. *Theoretical Computer Science* **103** (1992) 335–363.
16. D. Murphy. Time and duration in noninterleaving concurrency. *Fundamenta Informaticae* **19** (1993) 403–416.
17. X. Nicolin, J. Sifakis. An overview and synthesis on timed process algebras. *Lecture Notes in Computer Science* **600** (1992) 526–548.
18. M. Nielsen, A. Cheng. Observing behaviour categorically. *Lecture Notes in Computer Science* **1026** (1996) 263–278.
19. M. Nielsen, G. Winskel. Petri nets and bisimulation. *Theoretical Computer Science* **153** (1996).
20. C. Weise, D. Lenzkes. Efficient scaling-invariant checking of timed bisimulation. *Lecture Notes in Computer Science* **1200** (1997) 176–188.
21. Winskel G. An introduction to event structures. *Lecture Notes in Computer Science* **354** (1988) 364–397.
22. G. Winskel, M. Nielsen. Models for concurrency. In *Handbook of Logic in Computer Science* **4** (1995).

# Closure of Polynomial Time Partial Information Classes under Polynomial Time Reductions

Arfst Nickelsen and Till Tantau

Technische Universität Berlin
Fakultät für Elektrotechnik und Informatik
10623 Berlin, Germany
{nicke, tantau}@cs.tu-berlin.de

**Abstract.** Polynomial time partial information classes are extensions of the class P of languages decidable in polynomial time. A partial information algorithm for a language $A$ computes, for fixed $n \in \mathbb{N}$, on input of words $x_1, \dots, x_n$ a set $P$ of bitstrings, called a pool, such that $\chi_A(x_1, \dots, x_n) \in P$, where $P$ is chosen from a family $\mathcal{D}$ of pools. A language $A$ is in P[$\mathcal{D}$], if there is a polynomial time partial information algorithm which for all inputs $(x_1, \dots, x_n)$ outputs a pool $P \in \mathcal{D}$ with $\chi_A(x_1, \dots, x_n) \in P$. Many extensions of P studied in the literature, including approximable languages, cheatability, p-selectivity and frequency computations, form a class P[$\mathcal{D}$] for an appropriate family $\mathcal{D}$.
We characterise those families $\mathcal{D}$ for which P[$\mathcal{D}$] is closed under certain polynomial time reductions, namely bounded truth-table, truth-table, and Turing reductions. We also treat positive reductions. A class P[$\mathcal{D}$] is presented which strictly contains the class P-sel of p-selective languages and is closed under positive truth-table reductions.

**Keywords:** structural complexity, partial information, polynomial time reductions, verboseness, p-selectivity, positive reductions.

If a language $A$ is not decidable in polynomial time one may ask whether it nevertheless exhibits some polynomial time behaviour. If there is no polynomial time algorithm that answers the question "$x \in A$?" for all inputs $x$, there may still exist a *partial information algorithm.* For a tuple of input words $(x_1, \dots, x_n)$ such an algorithm outputs some partial information on membership of these words with respect to $A$. More precisely it narrows the range of possibilities for values of $\chi_A(x_1, \dots, x_n)$, where $\chi_A$ is the characteristic function for $A$. Many types of partial information have been studied, including verboseness, approximability, (strong) membership comparability, cheatability, frequency computations, easily countable languages, multiselectivity, sortability. For detailed definitions and discussions of these notions see for example [2,1,6,15,8,14,13].

To get a more unified picture, [5] introduced the recursion theoretic notion of $\mathcal{D}$-*verboseness*, where the type of partial information is specified by a family $\mathcal{D}$ of sets of bitstrings. The class of *polynomially* $\mathcal{D}$-verbose languages, whose formal

R. Freivalds (Ed.): FCT 2001, LNCS 2138, pp. 299–310, 2001.

definition given below, is denoted $P[\mathcal{D}]$. Basic properties of these polynomial time $\mathcal{D}$-verboseness classes are presented in [19].

Reduction closures of partial information classes have been the focus of much interest, mostly due to the fact that the polynomial time Turing reduction closure of P-sel, the class of p-selective sets, is exactly P/poly. Hence, a language is Turing reducible to a p-selective language iff the language has polynomial size circuits. It is also known that P-sel is closed under positive truth-table reductions, but not under 1-tt reductions. Reductions to p-selective sets have been studied in detail in [12]. Opposed to selectivity, *cheatability* behaves quite differently: The class of $n$-cheatable languages is known [3] to be closed under Turing reductions. For other notions like strongly membership comparable sets [17] only little was previously known concerning their closure properties.

Another important motivation to look at reductions to partial information classes is that one can prove results of the following type: if $P[\mathcal{D}]$ contains, for certain families $\mathcal{D}$, languages which are NP-hard for certain polynomial time reductions, then P = NP. One of the best results [7,8] in this respect is that if $P[3\text{-SIZE}_2]$ contains a language which is NP-hard for $n^{1-\epsilon}$-tt reductions, then P = NP.

We fully characterise the partial information classes $P[\mathcal{D}]$ which are closed under 2-tt reductions, bounded truth-table reductions and under Turing reductions. It turns out that *exactly* the classes of $n$-cheatable languages are closed under any of these reductions. We also treat positive truth-table reductions and present a class $P[\mathcal{D}]$ strictly containing P-sel which is closed under positive truth-table reductions.

This paper is organised as follows. First we give some definitions and basic facts concerning partial information classes. In *Section 2* we briefly discuss closure under many-one and 1-tt reductions and give a simple combinatorial characterisation of the classes $P[\mathcal{D}]$ closed under these reductions. In *Section 3* we show the main theorem which characterises the classes $P[\mathcal{D}]$ that are closed under different truth-table and Turing reductions. In *Section 4* we examine positive truth-table reductions. Here again, we reduce the question of whether a class $P[\mathcal{D}]$ is closed under positive $k$-tt reductions to finite combinatorics.

# 1 Preliminaries

*Notations.* Languages are subsets of $\Sigma^* = \{0,1\}^*$. The *join* of two languages $A$ and $B$ is $A \oplus B := \{0x \mid x \in A\} \cup \{1x \mid x \in B\}$. Let $\mathbb{B} := \{0,1\}$. For a language $A$ the *characteristic function* $\chi_A \colon \Sigma^* \to \mathbb{B}$ is defined by $\chi_A(x) = 1$ iff $x \in A$. We extend $\chi_A$ to tuples of words by $\chi_A(x_1, \dots, x_n) := \chi_A(x_1) \cdots \chi_A(x_n)$. In the following, elements of $\Sigma^*$ for which membership in languages is of interest are called words, elements of $\mathbb{B}^*$ which are considered as possible values of characteristic functions are called bitstrings. For a bitstring $b$ the number of 1's in $b$ is denoted $\#_1(b)$, $b[i]$ is the $i$-th bit of $b$, and $b[i_1, \dots, i_k] := b[i_1] \cdots b[i_k]$. We extend this to sets of bitstrings by setting $P[i_1, \dots, i_k] := \{b[i_1, \dots, i_k] \mid b \in P\}$.

*Partial information classes.* In order to define partial information classes, we first need the notion of pools and families.

**Definition 1 ($n$-Pools, $n$-Families).** *Let $n \geq 1$. A subset $P \subseteq \mathbb{B}^n$ is called an* $n$-pool. *A set $\mathcal{D} = \{P_1, \ldots, P_r\}$ of $n$-pools is called an* $n$-family *if*

1. *$\mathcal{D}$ covers $\mathbb{B}^n$, that is $\bigcup_{i=1}^r P_i = \mathbb{B}^n$, and*
2. *$\mathcal{D}$ is closed under subsets, that is $P \in \mathcal{D}$ and $Q \subseteq P$ implies $Q \in \mathcal{D}$.*

**Definition 2 (Polynomially $\mathcal{D}$-Verbose).** *For a given $n$-family $\mathcal{D}$ a language $A$ is in* the partial information class $\mathrm{P}[\mathcal{D}]$ *(respectively $\P_{\text{dist}}[\mathcal{D}]$) iff there is a polynomially time-bounded deterministic Turing machine that on input of $n$ words (respectively distinct words) $x_1, \ldots, x_n$ outputs a pool $Q \in \mathcal{D}$ such that $\chi_A(x_1, \ldots, x_n) \in Q$. The languages in $\mathrm{P}[\mathcal{D}]$ are called* polynomially $\mathcal{D}$-verbose.

We present some definitions that make it easier to deal with polynomial $\mathcal{D}$-verboseness and then state some known facts which will be applied in the following. For more details on polynomial $\mathcal{D}$-verboseness see [19].

**Definition 3 (Operations on Bitstrings).**

1. *Let $S_n$ be the group of permutations of $\{1, \ldots, n\}$. For $\sigma \in S_n$ and $b \in \mathbb{B}^n$ we define $\sigma(b) := b[\sigma(1)] \cdots b[\sigma(n)]$.*
2. *For $i \in \{1, \ldots, n\}$ and $c \in \mathbb{B}$ define* projections *$\pi_i^c \colon \mathbb{B}^n \to \mathbb{B}^n$ by $\pi_i^c(b) := b[1] \cdots b[i-1]\, c\, b[i+1] \cdots b[n]$.*
3. *For $i, j \in \{1, \ldots, n\}$ define a* replacement operation *$\rho_{i,j} \colon \mathbb{B}^n \to \mathbb{B}^n$ by $\rho_{i,j}(b) := b'$ where $b'[k] := b[k]$ for $k \neq j$ and $b'[j] := b[i]$.*

*We extend these operations from bitstrings to pools by $\omega(P) := \{\omega(b) \mid b \in P\}$. An $n$-family $\mathcal{D}$ is said to be* closed under permutations, projections and replacements *if for all permutations, projections and replacements $\omega$ and all $P \in \mathcal{D}$ we have $\omega(P) \in \mathcal{D}$.*

**Definition 4 (Normal Form).** *An $n$-family is* in normal form *if it is closed under permutations, projections and replacements.*

**Fact 1 (Normal Form).** *For every $n$-family $\mathcal{D}$ there is a unique $n$-family $\mathcal{D}'$ in normal form with* $\mathrm{P}[\mathcal{D}] = \mathrm{P}[\mathcal{D}']$.

**Fact 2 (Class Inclusion Reduces to Family Inclusion).** *For all $n$-families $\mathcal{D}$ and $\mathcal{E}$ in normal form we have $\mathrm{P}[\mathcal{D}] \subseteq \mathrm{P}[\mathcal{E}]$ iff $\mathcal{D} \subseteq \mathcal{E}$.*

**Fact 3 (Change of Tuple Length).** *Let $\mathcal{D}$ be an $m$-family and $m < n$. Define the following $n$-family $\lceil \mathcal{D} \rceil_n := \{P \subseteq \mathbb{B}^n \mid \forall i_1 < \cdots < i_m \colon P[i_1, \ldots, i_m] \in \mathcal{D}\}$. Then $\mathrm{P}[\mathcal{D}] = \mathrm{P}\big[\lceil \mathcal{D} \rceil_n\big]$. Furthermore, if $\mathcal{D}$ is in normal form so is $\lceil \mathcal{D} \rceil_n$.*

**Fact 4 (Intersection).** *For all $n$-families $\mathcal{D}$ and $\mathcal{E}$ in normal form we have* $\mathrm{P}[\mathcal{D}] \cap \mathrm{P}[\mathcal{E}] = \mathrm{P}[\mathcal{D} \cap \mathcal{E}]$.

**Definition 5 (Generated $n$-Family).** *For $n$-pools $D_1, \dots, D_r$ the minimal $n$-family $\mathcal{D}$ in normal form for which $\{D_1, \dots, D_r\} \subseteq \mathcal{D}$ is denoted by $\langle D_1, \dots, D_r\rangle$. It is the closure of $\{D_1, \dots, D_r\}$ under subsets, permutations, projections and replacements. We say that $D_1, \dots, D_r$* generate *$\langle D_1, \dots, D_r\rangle$.*

Some $n$-families are of special interest as their partial information classes have been studied extensively in the literature. We write these special families in capital letters with the tuple length attached as index.

**Definition 6 (Special Families).**

1. *Let* $\text{SEL}_n := \langle\{0^{n-i}1^i \mid 0 \le i \le n\}\rangle$.
2. *For* $1 \le k \le 2^n$ *let* $k\text{-SIZE}_n := \{P \subseteq \mathbb{B}^n \mid |P| \le k\}$.
3. *For* $1 \le k \le n+1$ *let* $k\text{-CARD}_n := \{P \subseteq \mathbb{B}^n \mid |\{\#_1(b) \mid b \in P\}| \le k\}$.
4. *Let* $\text{BOTTOM}_n := \langle\{b \mid \#_1(b) \le 1\}\rangle$ *and* $\text{TOP}_n := \langle\{b \mid \#_1(b) \ge n-1\}\rangle$.

The class $\text{P}[\text{SEL}_2]$ is exactly the class P-sel of *p-selective languages*, that is languages $A$ which have a polynomial time selector function. Such a selector gets two words $u$ and $v$ as input and selects one of them. Provided $u \in A$ or $v \in A$, the selected word must also lie in $A$. The class of p-selective languages has been extensively studied, starting with [20].

**Fact 5 (SEL).** $\text{P-sel} = \text{P}[\text{SEL}_2] = \text{P}[\text{SEL}_n]$ *for* $n \ge 2$.

Languages in $\text{P}[(2^n-1)\text{-SIZE}_n]$ are called *$n$-approximable, $n$-membership comparable, non-$n$-p-superterse* or *$n$-p-verbose.* The languages in $\text{P}[n\text{-SIZE}_n]$ are sometimes called *$n$-cheatable* in the literature, but especially in the older literature this term is also used for the languages in $\text{P}[2^n\text{-SIZE}_{2^n}]$. The following important fact is implicitly proven in [4]:

**Fact 6 (SIZE).** $\text{P}[k\text{-SIZE}_k] = \text{P}[k\text{-SIZE}_n]$ *for* $n \ge k$.

Languages in $\text{P}[n\text{-CARD}_n]$ are called *easily countable* [15]. The languages in $\text{P}[\text{TOP}_n]$ and $\text{P}[\text{BOTTOM}_n]$ have no special names in the literature, but they will come up in different places in the following proofs.

*Reductions.* In this paper all reductions under consideration will be polynomial time truth-table or Turing reductions defined in the standard way, see [18] for detailed definitions. We write $\le_{\text{m}}^{\text{P}}$ for many-one reductions, $\le_{k\text{-tt}}^{\text{P}}$ for truth-table reductions with $k$ queries, $\le_{\text{btt}}^{\text{P}}$ for truth-table reductions with a constant number of queries, $\le_{\text{tt}}^{\text{P}}$ for truth-table reductions with a polynomial number of queries, and $\le_{\text{T}}^{\text{P}}$ for Turing reductions. We write $\le_{k\text{-ptt}}^{\text{P}}$ for positive truth-table reductions with $k$ queries. In a positive reduction for each input word the boolean function that evaluates the answers to the queries is a monotone function. We write $\le_{\text{ptt}}^{\text{P}}$ for positive truth-table reductions with a polynomial number of queries.

## 2 Many-One and 1-tt Reductions

We review what is known [19] about closure under polynomial time many-one and 1-tt reductions for classes $\mathrm{P}[\mathcal{D}]$ and $\P_{\text{dist}}[\mathcal{D}]$.

**Theorem 1 (Many-One Reductions).** *Let $\mathcal{D}$ be an $n$-family. Then $\mathrm{P}[\mathcal{D}]$ is closed under $\leq^{\mathrm{p}}_{\mathrm{m}}$-reductions. But $\P_{\text{dist}}[\mathcal{D}]$ is not closed under $\leq^{\mathrm{p}}_{\mathrm{m}}$-reductions, unless $\P_{\text{dist}}[\mathcal{D}] = \mathrm{P}[\mathcal{D}']$ for some $n$-family $\mathcal{D}'$.*

Not all $\mathrm{P}[\mathcal{D}]$ are closed under 1-tt reductions. To characterize the families $\mathcal{D}$ for which this closure property holds, a new type of operation on bitstrings and pools is needed:

**Definition 7 (Bitflip).** *For $n \geq 1$ and $i \in \{1, \dots, n\}$ define the* bitflip operation $\mathrm{flip}_i \colon \mathbb{B}^n \to \mathbb{B}^n$ *by* $\mathrm{flip}_i(b) := b[1] \cdots b[i-1]\big(1 - b[i]\big)b[i+1] \cdots b[n]$. *This operation is extended to pools and families of pools in the obvious way. An $n$-family $\mathcal{D}$ is called* closed under bitflip *if* $\mathrm{flip}_i(\mathcal{D}) = \mathcal{D}$ *for all* $1 \leq i \leq n$.

**Theorem 2 (1-tt Reductions).** *For all $n$-families $\mathcal{D}$ in normal form, $\mathrm{P}[\mathcal{D}]$ is closed under $\leq^{\mathrm{p}}_{1\text{-tt}}$-reductions iff $\mathcal{D}$ is closed under bitflip.*

If an $n$-family $\mathcal{D}$ is closed under bitflip then $\mathrm{P}[\mathcal{D}]$ is also closed under complement. The converse does not hold as the family $\mathcal{D} = \mathrm{SEL}_2$ shows.

## 3 From 2-tt to Turing Reductions

As we know from [20,16] the closure of P-sel under polynomial time Turing reductions equals P/poly. But all $\mathrm{P}[\mathcal{D}]$ are proper subclasses of P/poly. Therefore we have:

**Fact 7.** *For $\mathrm{SEL}_n \subseteq \mathcal{D} \neq 2\text{-}^n\mathrm{SIZE}_n$ the class $\mathrm{P}[\mathcal{D}]$ is not closed under polynomial time Turing reductions.*

In [8, Theorem 2.9] Beigel, Kummer and Stephan construct languages $A$ and $B$ such that $A \leq^{\mathrm{p}}_{\mathrm{tt}} B \in \P_{\text{dist}}[\mathrm{TOP}_3]$ and $A \notin \mathrm{P}\big[(2^n - 1)\text{-}\mathrm{SIZE}_n\big]$ for all $n$. In terms of closure under reductions this yields:

**Fact 8.** *Let $\mathcal{D} \neq 2^n\text{-}\mathrm{SIZE}_n$ be in normal form. If $\mathrm{TOP}_n \subseteq \mathcal{D}$ or $\mathrm{BOTTOM}_n \subseteq \mathcal{D}$, then $\mathrm{P}[\mathcal{D}]$ is not closed under $\leq^{\mathrm{p}}_{\mathrm{tt}}$-reductions.*

On the other hand Amir, Beigel and Gasarch [3,1] and Goldsmith, Joseph and Young [11,10] showed that cheatability classes are closed under polynomial time Turing reductions.

**Fact 9.** *For all $n \geq 1$ the classes $\mathrm{P}[n\text{-}\mathrm{SIZE}_n]$ are closed under $\leq^{\mathrm{p}}_{\mathrm{T}}$-reductions.*

In the following we show that this cannot be extended to other classes and even that the cheatability classes are the only nontrivial classes in our context which are closed under 2-tt reductions.

To deal with $k$-tt reductions, we introduce for each language $A$ a language $A_{k\text{-tt}}$ which is many-one complete for the $k$-tt reduction closure of $A$.

**Definition 8.** *For a language $A$ and $k \geq 1$ define*

$$A_{k\text{-tt}} := \{ \langle x_1, \dots, x_k, \phi \rangle \mid \phi \colon \mathbb{B}^k \to \mathbb{B},\ \phi(\chi_A(x_1, \dots, x_k)) = 1 \}.$$

This definition is inspired by the study of btt-cylinders [22,9,8]. A language is a $k$-tt cylinder iff $A_{k\text{-tt}} \leq^{\mathrm{p}}_{\mathrm{m}} A$.

**Lemma 1.** *For all languages $A$ and $B$ we have $B \leq^{\mathrm{p}}_{k\text{-tt}} A$ iff $B \leq^{\mathrm{p}}_{\mathrm{m}} A_{k\text{-tt}}$.*

*Proof.* Suppose $B \leq^{\mathrm{p}}_{k\text{-tt}} A$ via $M$. If on input $x$ the machine $M$ computes queries $q_1, \dots, q_k$ and a boolean function $\phi_x$ such that $\phi_x(\chi_A(q_1, \dots, q_k)) = \chi_B(x)$, then $x \in B$ iff $\langle q_1, \dots, q_k, \phi_x \rangle \in A_{k\text{-tt}}$. Thus $B \leq^{\mathrm{p}}_{\mathrm{m}} A_{k\text{-tt}}$.

Suppose $B \leq^{\mathrm{p}}_{\mathrm{m}} A_{k\text{-tt}}$ via $M$. If on input $x$ the reduction machine $M$ computes $\langle q_1, \dots, q_k, \phi_x \rangle$, then asking the oracle $A$ with queries $q_1, \dots, q_k$ and evaluating the answers with $\phi_x$ constitutes the $k$-tt reduction to $A$. □

As an immediate corollary we obtain that a language class $\mathcal{C}$ closed under polynomial time many-one reductions is also closed under $k$-tt reductions, iff for every $A \in \mathcal{C}$ we also have $A_{k\text{-tt}} \in \mathcal{C}$.

In order to prove the main results of this section we first show a rather basic fact on bounded truth-table reductions. Although this fact should be well known, we could not find it in the literature. It states that polynomial time $k$-tt reductions can be replaced by sequences of 2-tt reductions.

**Lemma 2.** *Let $A$ and $B$ be languages with $A \leq^{\mathrm{p}}_{k\text{-tt}} B$. Then there exist intermediate languages $C_1, \dots, C_r$ such that $A \leq^{\mathrm{p}}_{2\text{-tt}} C_1 \leq^{\mathrm{p}}_{2\text{-tt}} \cdots \leq^{\mathrm{p}}_{2\text{-tt}} C_r \leq^{\mathrm{p}}_{2\text{-tt}} B$.*

*Proof.* Let $\mathbb{B}^k = \{b_1, \dots, b_{2^k}\}$ where the $b_i$ are in lexicographic order. The chain of 2-tt reductions from $A$ to $B$ will consist of the following two subchains

$$\begin{aligned} A &\leq^{\mathrm{p}}_{2\text{-tt}} D_{b_1} \leq^{\mathrm{p}}_{2\text{-tt}} D_{b_2} \leq^{\mathrm{p}}_{2\text{-tt}} \cdots \leq^{\mathrm{p}}_{2\text{-tt}} D_{b_{2^k}} \\ &\leq^{\mathrm{p}}_{2\text{-tt}} H_k \leq^{\mathrm{p}}_{2\text{-tt}} H_{k-1} \leq^{\mathrm{p}}_{2\text{-tt}} \cdots \leq^{\mathrm{p}}_{2\text{-tt}} H_1 \leq^{\mathrm{p}}_{2\text{-tt}} B. \end{aligned}$$

The languages $H_i$ for $i \in \{1, \dots, k\}$ are defined as follows:

$$H_i := \{ \langle x_1, \dots, x_i, b \rangle \mid \chi_B(x_1, \dots, x_i) = b \in \mathbb{B}^i \}.$$

Clearly, $H_1 \leq^{\mathrm{p}}_{1\text{-tt}} B$ and $H_{i+1} \leq^{\mathrm{p}}_{2\text{-tt}} H_i$. Thus, the second part of the chain from $A$ to $B$ is correct.

The first part consists of the following languages $D_b$ with $b \in \mathbb{B}^k$:

$$D_b := \Big( B_{k\text{-tt}} \cap \{ \langle x_1, \dots, x_k, \phi \rangle \mid \chi_B(x_1, \dots, x_k) \geq_{\text{lex}} b \} \Big) \oplus H_k.$$

Note that $D_{b_1} = B_{k\text{-tt}} \oplus H_k$ and hence by Lemma 1 we have $A \leq^{\mathrm{p}}_{1\text{-tt}} D_{b_1}$. Note furthermore that we also have $D_{b_{2^k}} \leq^{\mathrm{p}}_{1\text{-tt}} H_k$.

To show $D_{b_i} \leq^{\mathrm{p}}_{2\text{-tt}} D_{b_{i+1}}$, let $x$ be an input word. If $x = 1y$ then we must decide whether $y \in H_k$ which can trivially be done by passing on $1y$ as a query to $D_{b_{i+1}}$. If $x = 0\langle x_1, \dots, x_k, \phi \rangle$ we ask two queries: we ask $q_1 := 0\langle x_1, \dots, x_k, \phi \rangle$ and $q_2 := 1\langle x_1, \dots, x_k, b_i \rangle$. If the answer to the second query is "yes" we know $\chi_b(x_1, \dots, x_k) = b_i$ and output $\phi(b_i)$, ignoring the answer to the first query. If the answer to the second query is "no" we output the answer to the first query which is, indeed, correct. □

**Corollary 1.** *A language class $C$ is closed under $\le^{\mathrm{P}}_{\mathrm{btt}}$-reductions iff $C$ is closed under $\le^{\mathrm{P}}_{\mathrm{2\text{-}tt}}$-reductions.*

For the formulation of our Main Theorem 4, we need the following definition:

**Definition 9 ($k$-Cone).** *For $n, k \ge 1$ and an $n$-family $\mathcal{D}$ in normal form an $nk$-pool $P$ is a* $k$-cone for $\mathcal{D}$ *if for all tuples $(\phi_1, \ldots, \phi_n)$ of functions $\phi_i \colon \mathbb{B}^k \to \mathbb{B}$, the set of bitstrings*

$$\{\phi_1(b[1, \ldots, k])\, \phi_2(b[k+1, \ldots, 2k]) \cdots \phi_n(b[(n-1)k+1, \ldots, nk]) \mid b \in P\}$$

*is a pool of $\mathcal{D}$. The $nk$-family of all $k$-cones for $\mathcal{D}$ is denoted by* $k\text{-cones}(\mathcal{D})$.

**Theorem 3.** *For an $n$-family $\mathcal{D}$ in normal form and $k \ge 1$, $\mathrm{P}[\mathcal{D}]$ is closed under polynomial time $k$-tt reductions iff $\lceil \mathcal{D} \rceil_{nk} \subseteq k\text{-cones}(\mathcal{D})$.*

*Proof.* Suppose $\lceil \mathcal{D} \rceil_{nk} \subseteq k\text{-cones}(\mathcal{D})$. Then every pool $D \in \lceil \mathcal{D} \rceil_{nk}$ is a $k$-cone for $\mathcal{D}$. To prove that $\mathrm{P}[\mathcal{D}]$ is closed under $\le^{\mathrm{P}}_{k\text{-tt}}$-reductions, by Lemma 1 and Theorem 1 it suffices to show that for every $A \in \mathrm{P}[\mathcal{D}]$ we have $A_{k\text{-tt}} \in \mathrm{P}[\mathcal{D}]$.

Let $A \in \mathrm{P}\big[\lceil \mathcal{D} \rceil_{nk}\big]$ via $M$. Then $A_{k\text{-tt}} \in \mathrm{P}[\mathcal{D}]$ is witnessed by the following algorithm. On input $x_1, \ldots, x_n$ test whether the $x_i$ are in syntactically correct form, that is test whether $x_i = \langle y^i_1, \ldots, y^i_k, \phi_i \rangle$ for some $y^i_j$ and $\phi_i$. If not, replace $x_i$ by an $x'_i$ of correct syntax. If we have found a pool $D$ for this input of correct syntax, we find a pool for the original input by projecting $D$ in the $i$-th component to 0, using that $\mathcal{D}$ is closed under projections. So suppose the $x_i$ are all of the form $x_i = \langle y^i_1, \ldots, y^i_k, \phi_i \rangle$. Let $M$ compute a pool $D' \in \lceil \mathcal{D} \rceil_{nk}$ for $y^1_1, \ldots, y^1_k, y^2_1, \ldots, y^2_k, \ldots, y^n_1, \ldots, y^n_k$. Because $D'$ is a $k$-cone for $\mathcal{D}$, the pool

$$D := \{\phi_1(b^1_1, \ldots, b^1_k)\phi_2(b^2_1, \ldots, b^2_k) \cdots \phi_n(b^n_1, \ldots, b^n_k) \mid b^1_1 \cdots b^n_k \in D'\}$$

is a pool in $\mathcal{D}$ and by definition of $A_{k\text{-tt}}$ we have $\chi_{A_{k\text{-tt}}}(x_1, \ldots, x_n) \in D$.

For the opposite direction, suppose that $\mathrm{P}[\mathcal{D}]$ is closed under $\le^{\mathrm{P}}_{k\text{-tt}}$-reductions. We will show $\lceil \mathcal{D} \rceil_{nk} \subseteq k\text{-cones}(\mathcal{D})$ by showing $\mathrm{P}\big[\lceil \mathcal{D} \rceil_{nk}\big] \subseteq \mathrm{P}\big[k\text{-cones}(\mathcal{D})\big]$ and using Fact 2. Consider a language $A \in \mathrm{P}\big[\lceil \mathcal{D} \rceil_{nk}\big]$. We will exhibit an algorithm $M_A$ which witnesses $A \in \mathrm{P}\big[k\text{-cones}(\mathcal{D})\big]$. Because $A \in \mathrm{P}\big[\lceil \mathcal{D} \rceil_{nk}\big]$, we have $A \in \mathrm{P}[\mathcal{D}]$; and because $\mathrm{P}[\mathcal{D}]$ is closed under $k$-tt reductions by Lemma 1 there is a machine $M$ which witnesses $A_{k\text{-tt}} \in \mathrm{P}[\mathcal{D}]$.

In order to keep the rest of the proof more readable, we introduce some ad-hoc definitions and abbreviations:

$$\begin{aligned}
\Phi &:= \{(\phi_1, \ldots, \phi_n) \mid \phi_i \colon \mathbb{B}^k \to \mathbb{B} \text{ for } 1 \le i \le n\}, \\
\phi &:= (\phi_1, \ldots, \phi_n), \\
x &:= (x^1_1, \ldots, x^1_k, x^2_1, \ldots, x^2_k, \ldots, x^n_1, \ldots, x^n_k), \\
b &:= b^1_1 \cdots b^1_k\, b^2_1 \cdots b^2_k \,\cdots\, b^n_1 \cdots b^n_k.
\end{aligned}$$

Furthermore, for every input tuple $x \in (\Sigma^*)^{nk}$ and every $\phi \in \Phi$ we write

$$x \circ \phi := \big(\langle x^1_1, \ldots, x^1_k, \phi_1 \rangle, \langle x^2_1, \ldots, x^2_k, \phi_2 \rangle, \ldots, \langle x^n_1, \ldots, x^n_k, \phi_n \rangle\big).$$

For a bitstring $b \in \mathbb{B}^{nk}$, a pool $D \subseteq \mathbb{B}^{nk}$ and some $\phi \in \Phi$ we write

$$\phi(b) := \phi_1(b_1^1 \cdots b_k^1) \cdots \phi_n(b_1^n \cdots b_k^n),$$
$$\phi(D) := \{\phi(b) \mid b \in D\}.$$

Finally, for a pool $D \subseteq \mathbb{B}^n$ and $\phi \in \Phi$ we write $\phi^{-1}(D) := \{b \mid \phi(b) \in D\}$. We describe how algorithm $M_A$ on input $x$ computes a pool $D_x$ for $x$:

For all $\phi \in \Phi$:
 Compute $M(x \circ \phi) =: D_\phi \in \mathcal{D}$. (We then know $\chi_{A_{k\text{-tt}}}(x \circ \phi) \in D_\phi$.)
 Then compute $\phi^{-1}(D_\phi)$. (It holds $\chi_A(x) \in \phi^{-1}(D_\phi)$.)
Now compute

$$D_x := \bigcap_{\phi \in \Phi} \phi^{-1}(D_\phi).$$

Then $\chi_A(x) \in D_x$, and $D_x \in k\text{-cones}(\mathcal{D})$ as $\phi(D_x) \subseteq D_\phi \in \mathcal{D}$ for all $\phi \in \Phi$. □

**Lemma 3.** *Let $\mathcal{D}$ be an $n$-family in normal form. If* $\mathrm{P}[\mathcal{D}]$ *is closed under polynomial time $n$-tt reductions, then $\mathcal{D} = m\text{-SIZE}_n$ for some $m \in \mathbb{N}$.*

*Proof.* Suppose $\mathrm{P}[\mathcal{D}]$ is closed under $n$-tt reductions, where $n$ is a fixed constant. Let $m$ be minimal with $\mathcal{D} \subseteq m\text{-SIZE}_n$. Let $D = \{b_1, \dots, b_m\} \in \mathcal{D}$ be a pool of maximal size. We have to show that for every pool $E \subseteq \mathbb{B}^n$ with $|E| = m$ already $E \in \mathcal{D}$. Suppose $E = \{e_1, \dots, e_m\}$. By Fact 3 for change of tuple-length we know that the pool $D' := \{(b_i)^n \mid b_i \in D\}$, where each bitstring consists of $n$ copies of an original bitstring from $D$, is in $\lceil \mathcal{D} \rceil_{n^2}$. Now define boolean functions $\phi_1, \dots, \phi_n$ such that $\phi_i(b_j) = e_j[i]$. Then the image of $D'$ under $(\phi_1, \dots, \phi_n)$ is $E$. Because $D'$ is an $n$-cone for $\mathcal{D}$, it follows that $E \in \mathcal{D}$. □

**Lemma 4.** *Let $\mathcal{D}$ be an $n$-family in normal form with $\mathrm{SEL}_n \subseteq \mathcal{D}$ such that* $\mathrm{P}[\mathcal{D}]$ *is closed under polynomial time $2^n$-tt reductions. Then $\mathcal{D} = 2^n\text{-SIZE}_n$.*

*Proof.* Because $\mathrm{P}[\mathcal{D}]$ is closed under $2^n$-tt reductions, by Theorem 3 we know that $\lceil \mathcal{D} \rceil_{n2^n} \subseteq 2^n\text{-cones}(\mathcal{D})$. It suffices to exhibit a pool $D \in \lceil \mathcal{D} \rceil_{n2^n}$ and $2^n$-ary boolean functions $\phi_1, \dots, \phi_n$ such that the image of $D$ under $(\phi_1, \dots, \phi_n)$ is $\mathbb{B}^n$. Note that because $\lceil \mathrm{SEL}_n \rceil_{n2^n} = \mathrm{SEL}_{n2^n}$ by Fact 5, we have $\mathrm{SEL}_{n2^n} \subseteq \lceil \mathcal{D} \rceil_{n2^n}$. We choose $D \subseteq \mathbb{B}^{n2^n}$ as a pool of size $2^n$:

$$D := \{b_1, \dots, b_{2^n}\} \text{ with } b_i := (0^{2^n - i} 1^i)^n.$$

This means that each bitstring $b_i$ consists of the concatenation of $n$ copies of a bitstring of length $2^n$. Because the bitstrings in $D$ form an ascending chain (see Definition 6) $D \in \mathrm{SEL}_{n2^n} \subseteq \lceil \mathcal{D} \rceil_{n2^n}$. Let $\mathbb{B}^n = \{c_1, \dots, c_{2^n}\}$. Now define boolean functions $\phi_j$ such that $\phi_j(0^{2^n - i} 1^i) = c_i[j]$. For those $b$ which are not of the form $0^{2^n - i} 1^i$ choose some arbitrary value for $\phi_j(b)$. The choice of $\phi_j$ ensures

$$(\phi_1, \dots, \phi_n)(b_i) = \phi_1(0^{2^n - i} 1^i) \cdots \phi_n(0^{2^n - i} 1^i) = c_i[1] \cdots c_i[n] = c_i.$$

This yields $(\phi_1, \dots, \phi_n)(D) = \mathbb{B}^n$. □

We sum up the preceding results in the following theorem which characterises the classes closed under 2-tt reductions as well as under Turing reductions:

**Theorem 4 (Main Theorem).** *For $n$-families $\mathcal{D}$ in normal form with $\mathcal{D} \neq 2^n\text{-SIZE}_n$ the following are equivalent:*

1. $\mathcal{D} = m\text{-SIZE}_n$ *for some* $m \leq n$.
2. $\mathrm{P}[\mathcal{D}]$ *is closed under polynomial time 2-tt reductions.*
3. $\mathrm{P}[\mathcal{D}]$ *is closed under polynomial time Turing reductions.*

*Proof.* The class $\mathrm{P}[m\text{-SIZE}_n]$ with $m \leq n$ is equal to $\mathrm{P}[m\text{-SIZE}_m]$ by Fact 6. The class $\mathrm{P}[m\text{-SIZE}_m]$ is closed under polynomial time Turing reductions by Fact 9. A class closed under Turing reductions is also closed under 2-tt reductions.

If for an $n$-family $\mathcal{D}$ in normal form $\mathrm{P}[\mathcal{D}]$ is closed under 2-tt reductions, then by Corollary 1 it is also closed under polynomial time $n$-tt and $2^n$-tt reductions. By Lemma 3, $\mathcal{D} = m\text{-SIZE}_n$ for some $m$. By assumption $m \neq 2^n$. If $m > n$ we would have $\text{SEL}_n \subseteq \mathcal{D}$, which is impossible by Lemma 4. Therefore $\mathcal{D} = m\text{-SIZE}_n$ for some $m \leq n$. □

## 4 Positive Reductions

A motivation to investigate positive reductions is the fact that NP is closed under polynomial time positive Turing reductions. In general, when dealing with classes which are not (known to be) closed under 1-tt reductions it suggests itself to look for closure under some kind of positive reduction. Regarding reductions to languages in partial information classes it can happen that a reduction type, although more powerful than some other in general, looses its extra power when the oracle is taken from $\mathrm{P}[\mathcal{D}]$ for certain $\mathcal{D}$. For example it can be shown that querying an arbitrary number of queries to a language $B \in \mathrm{P}[k\text{-SIZE}_k]$ can always be replaced by putting only $k-1$ of these queries to oracle $B$. Regarding positive reductions, Selman [21] showed that a polynomial time positive truth-table reduction to a p-selective language can always be replaced by a many-one reduction. It follows that P-sel $= \mathrm{P}[\text{SEL}_2]$ is closed under ptt-reductions. We extend this result to $\text{SEL}_2 \cup 2\text{-SIZE}_2$, a family in normal form strictly above $\text{SEL}_2$. The partial information class $\mathrm{P}[\text{SEL}_2 \cup 2\text{-SIZE}_2]$ is exactly the class of languages $L$, for which $L$ and its complement $\overline{L}$ are strictly 2-membership comparable, see [17].

**Theorem 5.** *If $A \leq^{\mathrm{p}}_{\mathrm{ptt}} B$ and $B \in \mathrm{P}[\text{SEL}_2 \cup 2\text{-SIZE}_2]$ then $A \leq^{\mathrm{p}}_{\mathrm{m}} B$.*

*Proof.* First, note that $\text{SEL}_2 \cup 2\text{-SIZE}_2 = \text{SEL}_2 \cup \{01, 10\}$. In the following we will call this latter pool the xor-pool.

Let $A \leq^{\mathrm{p}}_{\mathrm{ptt}} B$ via a reduction $R$ and let $B \in \mathrm{P}[\text{SEL}_2 \cup 2\text{-SIZE}_2]$ via a machine $M$. To show $A \leq^{\mathrm{p}}_{\mathrm{m}} B$, upon input $x$ we must compute a query $q$ such that $\chi_A(x) = \chi_B(q)$. Let $q_1, \ldots, q_k$ be the polynomially many queries produced by $R$ upon input $x$ and let $\phi$ be the monotone evaluation function used by $R$. Note that for once $k$ depends on the length of the input $x$.

We define a graph $G = (V, E)$ with coloured edges as follows. The vertices $V = \{q_1, \ldots, q_k\}$ are exactly the queries $q_i$. For each pair $(q_i, q_j)$ with $q_i <_{\text{lex}} q_j$

the machine $M$ outputs (possibly a subset of) one of the three pools $\{00, 01, 11\}$, $\{00, 10, 11\}$ and the xor-pool $\{01, 10\}$. In the first case there is a black directed edge from $q_i$ to $q_j$, in the second case there is a black directed edge from $q_j$ to $q_i$. If the xor-pool is output, $q_i$ and $q_j$ are connected by an undirected red edge.

This graph has the following two properties: First, if $q_i \in B$ then for every black edge going from $q_i$ to a vertex $q_j$ we also have $q_j \in B$. Second, if $q_i$ and $q_j$ are connected by a red edge, then $q_i \in B$ iff $q_j \notin B$.

We compute a single query $q = q_i$ such that knowing $\chi_B(q)$ yields $\chi_B(q_j)$ for all other vertices. To do so, we apply the following pruning algorithm to the graph:

Search for a red edge $(q_i, q_j)$ plus another node $q_\ell$ which is connected to both $q_i$ and $q_j$ by black edges. If both black edges go from $q_\ell$ to $q_i$ and $q_j$ we *know* $\chi_B(q_\ell) = 0$, for being connected by a red edge exactly one of the two words $q_i$ and $q_j$ must be in $B$. Thus we can remove $q_\ell$ from the graph. Likewise, if both edges go from $q_i$ and $q_j$ to $q_\ell$ we know $\chi_B(q_\ell) = 1$ and we can also remove $q_\ell$. Now, if the first black edge goes from $q_i$ to $q_\ell$ and the second from $q_\ell$ to $q_j$, the graph property yields $\chi_B(q_i) = 1$ and $\chi_B(q_j) = 0$. Conversely, if the black edges go the other way round, we know $\chi_B(q_i) = 0$ and $\chi_B(q_j) = 1$. In either case we can remove both $q_i$ and $q_j$.

For the remaining graph $G' = (E', V')$ there are two possible situations: either the graph no longer contains a red edge or it contains a red spanning tree.

If the graph contains no red edge, it is a tournament; that is for all vertices in the graph the machine $R$ behaves like a selector. Using this selector we can compute a pool from $\text{SEL}_{|E'|}$ for the characteristic string of the vertices in the graph. To compute the special query $q$, we proceed as follows: for each bitstring $b \in P$, in order of increasing number of 1's, compute $\phi(b)$. If $\phi(b) = 0$ (or $\phi(b) = 1$) for all $b$, we do not have to query the oracle at all. Otherwise there is exactly one bitstring such that $\phi(b) = 0$, but $\phi(b') = 1$ for the next bitstring. We take the word at the position where a 0 in $b$ changes into a 1 in $b'$ as our query $q$.

If the graph has a red spanning tree, knowing the characteristic value of any vertex in the graph immediately yields the characteristic values of all other vertices. Hence, we can compute two bitstrings $b_0$ and $b_1$ such that $\chi_B(q_1, \ldots, q_k) \in \{b_0, b_1\}$. Compute $\phi(b_0)$ and $\phi(b_1)$. If these are equal, we do not need to query $B$ at all. If they are different, there must exists a position $i$ such that $b_0[i] = \phi(b_0)$ and $b_1[i] = \phi(b_1)$ and we can ask $q := q_i$. □

**Corollary 2.** *Let $\mathcal{D}$ be a family with $\text{P}[\mathcal{D}] \subseteq \text{P}[\text{SEL}_2 \cup 2\text{-SIZE}_2]$. Then $\text{P}[\mathcal{D}]$ is closed under polynomial time positive truth-table reductions.*

*Proof.* If $A \leq^{\text{p}}_{\text{ptt}} B \in \text{P}[\mathcal{D}]$, then $A \leq^{\text{p}}_{\text{m}} B$ by Theorem 5. But $\text{P}[\mathcal{D}]$ is closed under many-one reductions by Theorem 1. Therefore $A \in \text{P}[\mathcal{D}]$. □

We now exhibit some families $\mathcal{D}$ for which $\text{P}[\mathcal{D}]$ is not even closed under 2-ptt reductions. To do this, we proceed similarly as in the previous section where we showed that certain $\text{P}[\mathcal{D}]$ are not closed under $k$-tt reductions. For every $A$ we introduce a typical language $A_{k\text{-ptt}}$ which is $k$-ptt reducible to $A$. We then define positive $k$-cones and with these we characterize the families $\text{P}[\mathcal{D}]$ closed under

$k$-ptt reductions. Finally we present some special families that do not comply with this characterization.

**Definition 10.** *For a language $A$ and $k \geq 1$ define*

$$A_{k\text{-ptt}} := \{\, \langle x_1, \ldots, x_k, \phi \rangle \mid \phi\colon \mathbb{B}^k \to \mathbb{B} \textit{ is monotone}, \phi(\chi_A(x_1, \ldots, x_k)) = 1 \,\}.$$

The following lemma is the analogue of Lemma 1 for positive reductions. A proof is almost identical to the proof of that lemma and is therefore omitted.

**Lemma 5.** *For all languages $A$ and $B$ we have $B \leq^{\mathrm{P}}_{k\text{-ptt}} A$ iff $B \leq^{\mathrm{P}}_{\mathrm{m}} A_{k\text{-ptt}}$.*

**Definition 11 (Positive $k$-Cone).** *For $k \geq 1$ and an $n$-family $\mathcal{D}$ in normal form, an $nk$-pool $P$ is a* positive $k$-cone *for $\mathcal{D}$ if for all tuples $(\phi_1, \ldots, \phi_n)$ of $k$-ary monotone boolean functions $\phi_i$ the set of bitstrings*

$$\{\phi_1(b[1, \ldots, k])\, \phi_2(b[k+1, \ldots, 2k]) \cdots \phi_n(b[(n-1)k+1, \ldots, nk]) \mid b \in P\}$$

*is a pool of $\mathcal{D}$. By $k$-pcones$(\mathcal{D})$ we denote the $nk$-family of all positive $k$-cones for $\mathcal{D}$.*

**Theorem 6.** *Let $\mathcal{D}$ be an $n$-family. Then $\mathrm{P}[\mathcal{D}]$ is closed under $\leq^{\mathrm{P}}_{k\text{-ptt}}$-reduction iff $\lceil \mathcal{D} \rceil_{nk} \subseteq k$-pcones$(\mathcal{D})$.*

The omitted proof is essentially the same as for Theorem 3 for $k$-tt reductions.

**Theorem 7.** *Let $\mathcal{D}$ be a 2-family with* $\mathrm{BOTTOM}_2 \subseteq \mathcal{D}$. *If $\mathrm{P}[\mathcal{D}]$ is closed under 2-ptt reductions, then $\mathcal{D} = 4\text{-}\mathrm{SIZE}_2$.*

*Proof.* The pool $\{00, 01, 10\}$ is in $\mathcal{D}$ and therefore with the definition from Fact 3 for change of tuple-length, it is easy to check that $D = \{0000, 0010, 0100, 1001\}$ is in $\lceil \mathcal{D} \rceil_4$. Choose $\phi_1 = \phi_2$ as the 2-ary boolean or-function. Then we have $(\phi_1, \phi_2)(D) = \{00, 01, 10, 11\} = \mathbb{B}^2$. Because $\mathcal{D}$ is closed under 2-ptt reductions $(\phi_1, \phi_2)(D)$ has to be in $\mathcal{D}$. It follows that $\mathcal{D} = 4\text{-}\mathrm{SIZE}_2$. □

If a class $\mathcal{C}$ is closed under 2-ptt reductions then co-$\mathcal{C}$ also is closed under 2-ptt reductions. Therefore Theorem 7 also holds if $\mathrm{TOP}_2 \subseteq \mathcal{D}$.

We have now characterised the families $\mathcal{D}$ for tuple-length $n = 2$ for which $\mathrm{P}[\mathcal{D}]$ is closed under positive truth-table reductions:

**Theorem 8.** *For 2-families $\mathcal{D}$ in normal form with $\mathcal{D} \neq 4\text{-}\mathrm{SIZE}_2$ the following are equivalent:*

1. *$\mathrm{P}[\mathcal{D}]$ is closed under polynomial time ptt reductions.*
2. *$\mathrm{P}[\mathcal{D}]$ is closed under polynomial time 2-ptt reductions.*
3. *$\mathcal{D} \subseteq \mathrm{SEL}_2 \cup 2\text{-}\mathrm{SIZE}_2$.*
4. *$\mathrm{BOTTOM}_2 \not\subseteq \mathcal{D}$ and $\mathrm{TOP}_2 \not\subseteq \mathcal{D}$.*

While in the previous section on general $k$-tt and Turing reductions a complete picture was presented, in the case of positive reductions there remains work to be done. The above result should be extended to general tuple-lengths $n$ and to positive Turing reductions.

## References


1. A. Amir, R. Beigel, and W. Gasarch. Some connections between bounded query classes and non-uniform complexity. In *Proc. 5th Structure in Complexity Theory*, 1990.
2. A. Amir and W. Gasarch. Polynomial terse sets. *Inf. and Computation*, 77, 1988.
3. R. Beigel. *Query-Limited Reducibilities.* PhD thesis, Stanford University, 1987.
4. R. Beigel. Bounded queries to SAT and the boolean hierarchy. *Theoretical Comput. Sci.*, 84(2), 1991.
5. R. Beigel, W. Gasarch, and E. Kinber. Frequency computation and bounded queries. In *Proc. 10th Structure in Complexity Theory*, 1995.
6. R. Beigel, M. Kummer, and F. Stephan. Quantifying the amount of verboseness. In *Proc. Logical Found. of Comput. Sci.*, volume 620 of *LNCS*. Springer, 1992.
7. R. Beigel, M. Kummer, and F. Stephan. Approximable sets. In *Proc. 9th Structure in Complexity Theory*, 1994.
8. R. Beigel, M. Kummer, and F. Stephan. Approximable sets. *Inf. and Computation*, 120(2), 1995.
9. L. Berman and J. Hartmanis. On isomorphisms and density of NP and other complete sets. *SIAM J. Comput.*, 6(2):305–322, 1977.
10. J. Goldsmith, D. Joseph, and P. Young. Using self-reducibilities to characterize polynomial time. *Inf. and Computation*, 104(2):288–308, 1993.
11. J. Goldsmith, D. A. Joseph, and P. Young. Using self-reducibilities to characterize polynomial time. Technical Report CS-TR-88-749, University of Wisconsin, Madison, 1988.
12. L. Hemaspaandra, A. Hoene, and M. Ogihara. Reducibility classes of p-selective sets. *Theoretical Comput. Sci.*, 155:447–457, 1996.
13. L. A. Hemaspaandra, Z. Jiang, J. Rothe, and O. Watanabe. Polynomial-time multi-selectivity. *J. of Universal Comput. Sci.*, 3(3), 1997.
14. M. Hinrichs and G. Wechsung. Time bounded frequency computations. In *Proc. 12th Conf. on Computational Complexity*, 1997.
15. A. Hoene and A. Nickelsen. Counting, selecting, and sorting by query-bounded machines. In *Proc. STACS 93*, volume 665 of *LNCS*. Springer, 1993.
16. K.-I. Ko. On self-reducibility and weak p-selectivity. *J. Comput. Syst. Sci.*, 26:209–221, 1983.
17. J. Köbler. On the structure of low sets. In *Proc. 10th Structure in Complexity Theory*, pages 246–261. IEEE Computer Society Press, 1995.
18. R. E. Ladner, N. A. Lynch, and A. L. Selman. A comparison of polynomial time reducibilities. *Theoretical Comput. Sci.*, 1(2):103–123, Dec. 1975.
19. A. Nickelsen. On polynomially $\mathcal{D}$-verbose sets. In *Proc. STACS 97*, volume 1200 of *LNCS*, pages 307–318. Springer, 1997.
20. A. Selman. P-selective sets, tally languages and the behaviour of polynomial time reducibilities on NP. *Math. Systems Theory*, 13:55–65, 1979.
21. A. L. Selman. Reductions on NP and p-selective sets. *Theoretical Comput. Sci.*, 19:287–304, 1982.
22. P. Young. On semi-cylinders, splinters, and bounded-truth-table reducibility. *Trans. of the AMS*, 115:329–339, 1965.

# Monte-Carlo Polynomial versus Linear Time - The Truth-Table Case

Robert Rettinger and Rutger Verbeek

FernUniversität Hagen, Dep. of computer science, Theoretische Informatik II, D-58084 Hagen, Germany
{Robert.Rettinger, Rutger.Verbeek}@fernuni-hagen.de
Fax: +49-2331-987-339

**Abstract.** We show that under some truth-table oracle B there are almost exponential gaps in the (infinite often) hierarchy of bounded-error probabilistic time, in particular $BPP_{tt}^{B} = ZPTIME_{tt}^{B}(n)$. This proves a main theorem in [5], which is extended to the theoretical limit.

## 1 Introduction

Separation and hierarchy theorems are among the earliest and most basic results in structural complexity theory. Without dense hierarchies it makes not much sense to look for lower bounds. After discovering good separation results for nondeterministic complexities, the topic seemed to be finished up to some small open problems (e.g. the logarithmic gap in the deterministic time hierarchy).

The situation changed when probabilistic algorithms gained in importance. The problem of separating complexity classes of probabilistic machines with small error probability (Monte-Carlo machines) came to our attention, when we unsuccessfully tried to derive separations for Monte-Carlo space classes from the existence of very slowly increasing Monte-Carlo space constructable bounds [8], [9] (cf. also [4]). Then Fortnow and Sipser [5] claimed the existence of an oracle, under which Monte-Carlo polynomial time collapses to linear time. This had been the first example of a relativized collapse of a natural complexity hierarchy. As known since several years this proof is not complete (cf. Berg and Håstad [3] and [6] and a lot of e-mail discussions between L. Fortnow and the second author since September 1989). For an overview of the problem cf. also Hemaspaandra [7].

There is a small number of other oracle constructions, which yield hierarchy gaps under oracles. All of them are related to nondeterministic time: Rackoff and Seiferas [11] show that the small gaps in the time hierarchy (i.e. the requirement, that $t(n+1) \in o(T(n))$, cf. [12]) cannot be closed using relativizable techniques and Allender, Beigel, Hertrampf and Homer [1] present an oracle, under which there are almost exponential gaps in the almost-everywhere hierarchy.

In this paper we present a rigorous proof for the result claimed by Fortnow and Sipser for truth-table oracle machines, that is we give the complete

R. Freivalds (Ed.): FCT 2001, LNCS 2138, pp. 311–322, 2001.

construction for an oracle $B$, under which $ZPTIME^B_{tt}(n) = BPP^B_{tt}$. Furthermore we extend the gap to the theoretical limit, which is given by relativizable separation techniques (see [1]). In particular there exist oracles $C$ so that

$$ZPTIME^C_{tt}(n) = BPTIME^C_{tt}(f), \text{ if } \forall k, i \in \mathbb{N}. f^{(k)} \in O(2^{\sqrt[i]{n}}).$$

We will divide the proof of this result into two parts. In a first part (Sections 2.1 - 2.4) we attack the main combinatorical problems in our proof of the relativized collapse. Here we consider a special coloring problem of graphs. Based on these results we will give a proof of a relativized collapse in Section 3. In Section 4 we will add some conclusions and discuss open problems connected with the presented results.

Our main result can also be proven for general (not only truth-table) oracle machines and for some other complexity classes [10], but the proof is even more involved than in this case. Earlier doubts in the completeness of the proof caused us

- to restrict this paper to the truth-table case and
- to include a detailed proof rather than a broad discussion of the general case.

We assume that the reader is familiar with the fundamental notions of standard Turing machine models and asymptotic analysis (cf. [2]). So we won't give detailed exposition of the definitions but rather a short setting of the notations we will use throughout. We will give some mathematical notations next. Machine related notations, especially definitions of Monte-Carlo, Las-Vegas machines and truth-table oracles, will be given in Section 3.

Let $\Sigma := \{0, 1\}$. By $\Sigma^*$ we denote the free monoid over $\Sigma$. For words $w \in \Sigma^*$ we denote the length of $w$ by $|w|$. The set of natural numbers is denoted by $\mathbb{N}$. log will denote the logarithm to base 2 throughout this paper.

Let two sets $M$ and $M'$ be given. The cardinality of $M$ is denoted by $\sharp M$, the set of subsets of $M$ is denoted by $2^M$. We will denote partial (total) mappings by $A :\subseteq M \to M'$ ($A : M \to M'$). In the latter case we write also $A \in (M')^M$. Given a subset $N \subseteq M$ and a relation $A \subseteq M \times M'$ we define $A(N)$ by $A(N) = \{m \in M' \mid \exists n \in N.(n, m) \in A\}$.

Given partial mappings $A, B, C :\subseteq M \to M'$ we denote the domain of $A$ by $dom(A)$ and the restriction of $A$ to a subset $N$ of $M$ by $A|_N$. Furthermore we extend the inclusion, union and difference of sets to mappings by

$$A \subseteq B :\Leftrightarrow dom(A) \subseteq dom(B) \wedge B|_{dom(A)} = A,$$
$$A \cup B = C :\Leftrightarrow dom(C) = dom(A) \cup dom(B) \wedge A \subseteq C \wedge B \subseteq C \text{ and}$$
$$[A \setminus B] = C :\Leftrightarrow dom(C) = dom(A) \setminus dom(B) \wedge C \subseteq A.$$

## 2 Graph Colorings

### 2.1 A Special Kind of Graph

We will use rather frequently directed graphs together with 'evaluation' mappings, which will always fulfill common restrictions. To simplify matters, we will thus denote these graphs and mappings by $G = (V, E)$ and $\sigma$, respectively, where we will assume the following restrictions on $G$ and $\sigma$ throughout this paper.

The set $V$ of vertices will always be assumed to be determined by

**(G1)** $V = \{(i, x, u) | i \in \mathbb{N}, x \in \{0,1\}^*, u \in \{0,1\}^*, |x| \geq 2^{100+2^{2^i}}$ and $|u| = 3 \cdot |x|\}$.

Furthermore we will assume that the set $E \subseteq V \times V$ of edges fulfills

**(G2)** $\forall (i, x, u), (i, x, v) \in V.\quad E(i, x, u) = E(i, x, v)$ and
**(G3)** $\forall (i, x, u), (j, y, v) \in V.\quad (j, y, v) \in E(i, x, u) \Rightarrow |y| \leq |x|^{2^{i+1}}$.

Condition (G2) above forces edges of $G$ to depend on pairs $(i, x)$ rather than on triples $(i, x, u)$. Let $\sigma$ be a mapping $\sigma :\subseteq V \times \{0, 1, ?\}^V \to \{0, 1, e\}$ so that for all $(i, x, u)$, $(i, x, u')$ in $V$ and all $c, c' \in \{0, 1, ?\}^V$ condition (G4) hold

**(G4)** if $c(j, y, v) = c'(j, y, v)$ for all $(j, y, v) \in E(i, x, u) = E(i, x, u')$ then $\sigma((i, x, u), c) = \sigma((i, x, u), c') = \sigma((i, x, u'), c)$.

In particular, also $\sigma$ does only depend on pairs $(i, x)$ (rather than on triples $(i, x, u)$). $\sigma$ will be interpreted as a kind of 'evaluation' mapping: Given the values of all neighbors (determined by some $c$) of a pair $(i, x)$, $\sigma$ evaluates to 'accepting' ($\sigma((i, x, u), c) = 1$) or 'rejecting' ($\sigma((i, x, u), c) = 0$) or 'error' ($\sigma((i, x, u), c) = e$). It is not hard to guess that $\sigma$ will be given by the oracle-machines later on.

Given $(G, \sigma)$ we say that $c \in \{0, 1, ?\}^V$ is a coloring of $(i, x, u) \in V$ in $(G, \sigma)$, iff either

$$\sigma((i, x, u), c) \neq 0,\ |\{(i, x, u') \in V | c(i, x, u') = 1\}| > \tfrac{1}{2} 2^{3 \cdot |x|} \text{ and } \{(i, x, u') \in V | c(i, x, u') = 0\} = \emptyset$$

or

$$\sigma((i, x, u), c) \neq 1,\ |\{(i, x, u') \in V | c(i, x, u') = 0\}| > \tfrac{1}{2} 2^{3 \cdot |x|} \text{ and } \{(i, x, u') \in V | c(i, x, u') = 1\} = \emptyset.$$

We call $c \in \{0, 1, ?\}^V$ a coloring of $(G, \sigma)$ iff for all $i \in \mathbb{N}$ either there exist $(i, y, v) \in V$ fulfilling $\sigma((i, y, v), c) = e$ or $c$ is a coloring of almost all $(i, x, u) \in V$ in $(G, \sigma)$, i.e. there exist $n_i \in \mathbb{N}$ so that $c$ is a coloring for all $(i, x, u)$ with $|x| \geq n_i$.

## 2.2 A Simple Game

In this section we will assume that for all $(i, x, u) \in V$ there exist small neighborhoods $C$ of $(i, x, u)$ in $G$ totally determining $\sigma$. We will call this small set of vertices 'set of critical strings' (of $(i, x)$ in $G$). We will prove that in this case (that is, sets of critical strings exist), there always exists a coloring of $(G, \sigma)$. (This is a central step towards a relativized collapse because, as we will see later on, suitable truth-table oracles can be easily defined by colorings.) Although the assumption of the existence of critical sets is to strong to prove a relativized collapse of the polynomial time hierarchy, it will serve as a base for and motivation of the more complex definitions and methods in the next sections. Notice that our proof of a relativized collapse in Section 3 does not depend on any results given in this Section 2.2!

To simplify matters let $B_n$ for $n \in \mathbb{N}$ denote the set of all mappings $c \in \{0,1,?\}^V$ so that $c$ is a coloring of $(j,y,v) \in V$ for all $j < n$. Given $(G,\sigma)$ and a triple $(i,x,u) \in V$ let us call a set $C \subseteq E(i,x,u)$ critical for $(i,x,u)$, iff $\sigma((i,x,u),c) = \sigma((i,x,u),c')$ for all $c,c' \in B_i$ with $c|_C = c'|_C$. (We will call a mapping $C : V \to 2^V$ a critical mapping in $(G,V)$ iff $C(i,x,u)$ is a critical set of $(i,x,u)$ for all $(i,x,u) \in V$.)

**Lemma 1.** *Let $(G,\sigma)$, $G = (V,E)$ be given so that for each $(i,x,u) \in V$ there exists a critical set $C_{(i,x,u)}$ of size at most $2^{(log(|x|))^{2^{i+1}}}$. Then there exist colorings of $(G,\sigma)$.*

*Proof.* As we have already mentioned $\sigma((i,x,u),c)$ does not depend on $u$. Thus we can choose $C_{(i,x,u)}$ so that $C_{(i,x,u)} = C_{(i,x,u')}$ for all $(i,x,u),(i,x,u') \in V$. We will construct a sequence $c_0 \subseteq c_1 \subseteq \ldots$ of mappings $c_i :\subseteq V \to \{0,1,?\}$ so that $c = \bigcup_{i\in\mathbb{N}} c_i$ is a coloring of $(G,\sigma)$. For given $c :\subseteq V \to \{0,1,?\}$ and $n \in \mathbb{N}$ let $B_n(c) := \{c' \in B_n \mid c' \supseteq c\}$. Let $c_0$ be determined by

$$\begin{aligned} c_0(i,x,u) = ? &\text{ iff } (i,x,u) \in dom(c_0) \\ &\text{ iff there exist } (j,y,v) \in V \text{ so that } |y| \le 2\cdot|x| \text{ and} \\ &\quad (i,x,u) \in C_{(j,y,v)} \end{aligned}$$

for all $(i,x,u) \in V$. Given $c_n$ let $c_{n+1}$ be determined by

$$dom(c_{n+1}) = \{(i,x,u) \in V \mid |x| < n+1\} \cup dom(c_n)$$

and

$$c_{n+1}(j,y,v) = \begin{cases} 1 & : \quad \exists b \in B_j(c_n).\sigma((j,y,v),b) = 1 \\ 0 & : \quad \text{otherwise} \end{cases}$$

for all $(j,y,v) \in dom(c_{n+1}) \setminus dom(c_n)$.

Let $c = \bigcup_{i\in\mathbb{N}} c_i$. We will now prove $c \in B_n(c_i)$ for all $n,i \in \mathbb{N}$ (and thus prove the lemma). As $c' \in B_0(c_i)$ for all $i \in \mathbb{N}$ and all $c' \in \{0,1,?\}^V$ with $c' \supseteq c_i$ we have $c \in B_0(c_i)$. Assuming $c \notin B_{n+1}(c_i)$ but $c \in B_n(c_i)$ for some $n,i \in \mathbb{N}$, there have to exist a triple $(n,x,u) \in V$ so that $c$ is not a coloring of $(n,x,u)$ in $(G,\sigma)$. In the definition of $c_{|x|+1}$ above we fix either $c_{|x|+1}(n,x,v) = 1$ for all $(n,x,v) \in V \setminus dom(c_{|x|})$ or $c_{|x|+1}(n,x,v) = 0$ for all $(n,x,v) \in V \setminus dom(c_{|x|})$. As $(n,x,v) \in V \setminus dom(c_{|x|}) \Leftrightarrow (n,x,v) \in V \setminus dom(c_0)$ we have $c_{|x|+1}(n,x,v) = ?$ for all vertices $(n,x,v) \in dom(c_{|x|})$. Moreover there are at most

$$\begin{aligned} \sharp\{(n,x,v) \in dom(c_0)\} &\le \log^{(3)}(2|x|)\cdot 2|x| \cdot 2^{2|x|} \cdot 2^{(\log(2|x|))^{2^{\log^{(3)}(2|x|)}}} \\ &\le 2^{3log(|x|)} \cdot 2^{2|x|} \cdot 2^{(log(2|x|))^{loglog(2|x|)}} \qquad (2.1) \\ &< \tfrac{1}{2}2^{\frac{1}{2}|x|} \cdot 2^{2|x|} \cdot 2^{\frac{1}{2}|x|} = \tfrac{1}{2}2^{3|x|} \end{aligned}$$

vertices fixed in $c_{|x|}$ ( $|x| \ge 2^{100}$ by definition!), where $\log^{(3)}$ denotes log log log. Thus we may distinguish the following cases:

**Case 1** $\sharp\{(n,x,v) \in V \mid c(n,x,v) = 1\} > \frac{1}{2}2^{3\cdot|x|}$ and $\{(n,x,v) \in V \mid c(n,x,v) = 0\} = \emptyset$.

Then by construction there exist $b \in B_n(c_{|x|})$ so that $\sigma((n,x,u),b) = 1$. As $C_{(n,x,u)} \subseteq dom(c_{|x|})$ and $c \in B_n(c_{|x|})$ we have $\sigma((n,x,u),b) = \sigma((n,x,u),c) = 1$. (Notice: $C_{(n,x,u)}$ is a critical set of $(n,x,u)$!) That means, $c$ is a coloring of $(n,x,u)$ in contradiction to the assumption.

**Case 2** $\sharp\{(n,x,v) \in V \mid c(n,x,v) = 0\} > \frac{1}{2}2^{3\cdot|x|}$ and $\{(n,x,v) \in V \mid c(n,x,v) = 1\} = \emptyset$.

In this case we have $\sigma((n,x,u),b) \neq 1$ for all $b \in B_n(c_{|x|})$. Thus (as $C_{(n,x,u)} \subseteq dom(c_{|x|})$ and $c \in B_n(c_{|x|})$) we have $\sigma((n,x,u),c) \neq 1$. Again $c$ is a coloring of $(n,x,u)$ in contradiction to our assumption.

□

### 2.3 Coloring with Exceptions

As we have already mentioned, the conditions introduced in the previous section are too strong to prove a relativized collapse; Even for truth-table machines we cannot guarantee the existence of critical mappings. In this section we will therefore generalize the ideas of the proof of Lemma 1, especially the concept of critical mappings $C$.

Let $(G,\sigma)$, $G = (V,E)$ be given so that (G1)-(G4) are fulfilled. Until otherwise stated let $C$ denote a mapping $C :\subseteq V \to 2^V$ so that

**(C1)** $C(i,x,u) \subseteq E(i,x,u)$,
**(C2)** $C(i,x,u) = C(i,x,v)$ and
**(C3)** $\sharp C(i,x,u) \leq 2^{(log(|x|))^{2i+1}}$

for all $(i,x,u),(i,x,v) \in V$. Notice that we have not restricted $C$ to determine $\sigma$ as we have done in the definition of critical mappings. We will add a similar condition in (C4) later on. Similar to the proof of Lemma 1 let $c_0^C$ denote the mapping $c_0^C :\subseteq V \to \{0,1,?\}$ such that

$$\begin{aligned} c_0^C(i,x,u) =? &\text{ iff } (i,x,u) \in dom(c_0^C) \\ &\text{ iff there exist } (j,y,v) \in V \text{ so that } |y| \leq 2\cdot|x| \text{ and } \\ &\quad (i,x,u) \in C(j,y,v) \end{aligned}$$

for all $(i,x,u) \in V$. In the proof of Lemma 1, any $(i,x,u) \in C_{(j,y,v)}$ belongs to $dom(c_n)$ as long as $|y| < n$ and furthermore, for any such $(j,y,v)$, there exist $b \in B_j(c_n)$ so that $b$ is a coloring of $(j,y,v)$. These are the only features of $c_n$ we have used to prove that $c$ is indeed a coloring (beside the fact that $c = \bigcup_{n\in\mathbb{N}} c_n$ is total). Let us therefore generalize $B_n$ first. This time we will take into account that, given an index $i \in \mathbb{N}$, a coloring $c$ of $(G,\sigma)$ have to be a coloring of almost all $(i,x,u) \in V$ only and might be not a coloring of any $(i,x,u)$ if there exist $y$ and $v$ so that $\sigma((i,y,v),c) = e$. Let $l \in (\mathbb{N} \cup \{\infty\})^{\mathbb{N}}$, $n \in \mathbb{N}$ and $b :\subseteq V \to \{0,1,?\}$ be given. By $B_n^C(b,l)$ we denote the set of all $b' \in \{0,1,?\}^V$, $b' \supseteq c_0^C$ so that

**(B1)** $b' \supseteq b$, $[b' \setminus c_0^C](V) \subseteq \{0,1\}$,
**(B2)** if $l(i) \in \mathbb{N}$ then $b'$ is a coloring of all $(i,x,u) \in V$ with $|x| > l(i)$ and
**(B3)** if $l(i) = \infty$ then there exist $(i,x,u) \in V$ so that $\sigma((i,x,u),b') = e$,

for all $i < n$. Now we will generalize the set $\{c_n \mid n \in \mathbb{N}\}$: Given $l$ as above let $A^C(l)$ denote the set of all $b :\subseteq V \to \{0,1,?\}$, $b \supseteq c_0^C$ so that

**(A1)** for all $(i,x,u) \in dom(b) \setminus dom(c_0^C)$
  **(A1.1)** $b(i,x,u) \neq ?$,
  **(A1.2)** $(j,y,v) \in dom(b)$ for all $(j,y,v) \in C(i,x,u)$ and
  **(A1.3)** if $l(i) \in \mathbb{N}$ and $l(i) < |x|$ then there exist colorings $c \in B_i^C(b,l)$ of $(i,x,u)$ in $(G,\sigma)$,
**(A2)** there exist $m \in \mathbb{N}$ such that $(i,x,u) \in dom(c_0^C)$ for all $(i,x,u) \in dom(b)$ with $|x| > m$ and
**(A3)** for all $i \in \mathbb{N}$ with $l(i) = \infty$ there exist $(i,x,u) \in V$ and $b' \in \{0,1,?\}^V$, $b' \supseteq b$ so that $\sigma((i,x,u),b') = e$ and $(j,y,v) \in dom(b)$ for all $(j,y,v) \in E(i,x,u)$.

Notice that for $b \in A^C(l)$ and $i \in \mathbb{N}$ with $l(i) = \infty$ there exists $(i,x,u) \in V$ so that $\sigma((i,x,u),b') = e$ for all $b' \in \{0,1,?\}^V$ with $b' \supseteq b$. The following results can be easily verified.

**Lemma 2.** *Let $l_0$ be given by $l_0(i) = 0$ for all $i \in \mathbb{N}$. Then $c_0^C \in A^C(l_0)$.*

**Lemma 3.** *Let $n,m \in \mathbb{N}$, $l \in (\mathbb{N} \cup \{\infty\})^{\mathbb{N}}$, $b \in A^C(l)$ and $c \in B_n^C(b,l)$ be given so that $(i,x,u) \in dom(c_0^C)$ or $|x| \leq m$ for all $(i,x,u) \in dom(b)$. Then $b' \in A^C(l')$ where*

$$b'(i,x,u) = \begin{cases} c(i,x,u) & : \ |x| \leq m \\ c_0^C(i,x,u) & : \ \textit{otherwise} \end{cases}$$

*for all $(i,x,u) \in V$ and*

$$l'(i) = \begin{cases} l(i) & : \ i < n \\ m & : \ \textit{otherwise} \end{cases}$$

*for all $i \in \mathbb{N}$.*

Now we are prepared to give the definition of weakly critical mappings: We call $C : V \to 2^V$ a weakly critical mapping of $i \in \mathbb{N}$ in $(G,\sigma)$ iff (C1),(C2) and (C3) above are fulfilled and the following condition (C4) hold

**(C4)** for all $(i,x,u) \in V$, all $l \in (\mathbb{N} \cup \{\infty\})^{\mathbb{N}}$ with $l(i) \neq \infty$ and all $b \in A^C(l)$ either there exist $c \in B_i^C(b,l)$ and $(j,y,v) \in V$ with $j \leq i$, $l(j) \neq \infty$ and $\sigma((j,y,v),c) = e$ or $\sigma((i,x,u),c') = \sigma((i,x,u),c'') \neq e$ for all $c',c'' \in B_i^C(b,l)$ with $c'|_{C(i,x,u)} = c''|_{C(i,x,u)}$.

We call $C$ a weakly critical mapping in $(G,\sigma)$ iff $C$ is weakly critical for all $i \in \mathbb{N}$ in $(G,\sigma)$.

**Lemma 4.** *If there exist weakly critical mappings in $(G,\sigma)$ then there also exist colorings of $(G,\sigma)$.*

Before we prove Lemma 4 we will state a result which will be proven in the next section (see Lemma 6).

**Lemma 5.** *Let $i \in \mathbb{N}$, $C$ be a weakly critical mapping of all $j < i$ in $(G, \sigma)$ and $l \in (\mathbb{N} \cup \{\infty\})^{\mathbb{N}}$ be given. Then for all $b \in A^C(l)$ so that $B_i^C(b, l) = \emptyset$ there exist $j < i$, $(j, x, u) \in V$ and $c \in B_j^C(b, l)$ so that $l(j) \in \mathbb{N}$ and $\sigma((j, x, u), c) = e$.*

*Proof.* (of Lemma 4) Let $C$ be a weakly critical mapping in $(G, \sigma)$. We will determine sequences $c_0 \subseteq c_1 \subseteq \ldots$ and $l_0, l_1, \ldots$ with $l_n \in (\mathbb{N} \cup \{\infty\})^{\mathbb{N}}$ and $c_n \in A^C(l_n)$ so that for all $n \in \mathbb{N}$

**(i)** $l_m(n) = l_{n+1}(n)$ for all $m > n$,
**(ii)** $(j, x, u) \in dom(c_n)$ for all $(j, x, u) \in V$ with $|x| < n$ and
**(iii)** $\sigma((j, x, u), b) \neq e$ for all $(j, x, u) \in V$ and all $b \in B_j^C(c_n, l_n)$ with $j < n$ and $l_n(j) \in \mathbb{N}$.

It is easy to verify that $c = \bigcup_{n \in \mathbb{N}} c_n$ is a coloring of $(G, \sigma)$, once we have determined $(c_n)_{n \in \mathbb{N}}$ so that (i) and (ii) hold. Now let $c_0$ and $l_0$ be determined by $c_0 = c_0^C$ and $l_0(i) = 0$ for all $i \in \mathbb{N}$. Given $n \in \mathbb{N}$ and $c_n$, $l_n$, so that conditions (i)-(iii) above are fulfilled, there exist $b \in B_n^C(c_n, l_n)$: If there exist $(n, x, u) \in V$ and $d \in B_n^C(c_n, l_n)$ so that $\sigma((n, x, u), d) = e$ then take $b = d$. Otherwise there exist such $b \in B_n^C(c_n, l_n)$ according to Lemma 5. In both cases we can find suitable $l_{n+1}$ and $c_{n+1} \in A^C(l_{n+1})$ by the construction given in Lemma 3 (in the first case we additionally have to fix $l_{n+1}(n) = \infty$!).

□

## 2.4 Combining Colorings

Until now, we have not mentioned how to restrict $\sigma$ so that (weakly) critical mappings exist. To prove the existence of such mappings in Section 3, we have to tackle a variation of the following problem: Given two colorings $c'$, $c''$ of $(G, \sigma)$ and two subsets $V'$, $V''$ of $V$. Does there exist a coloring $c$ of $(G, \sigma)$ so that $c|_{V'} = c'|_{V'}$ and $c|_{V''} = c''|_{V''}$? In this section we will give a sufficient condition for the restricted case $c, c', c'' \in B_n^C(b, l)$ (for given $n$, $b$, $l$ and $C$).

First we will introduce a restricted kind of 'transitive closure' in $G$. Let $C :\subseteq V \to 2^V$ be given so that conditions (C1) - (C3) of Section 2.3 are fulfilled. Furthermore let $V'$ be a subset of $V$ and $n \in \mathbb{N}$ be given. By $T_n^{C,G}(V')$ we denote the smallest subset $V''$ of $V$ so that

**(T1)** $V' \subseteq V''$ and
**(T2)** $C(i, x, u) \subseteq V''$ for all $(i, x, u) \in V'' \setminus dom(c_0^C)$ with $i < n$.

We can bound the number of vertices in $T_n^{C,G}(V')$ for finite $V'$ according to

$$\sharp T_n^{D,G}(\{(i, x, u)\}) \leq 2^{(log(|x|))^{2^n+2}} \tag{2.2}$$

We state the following lemma only because of technical reasons. In the sequel we will need only Corollary 1.

**Lemma 6.** *Let $i \in \mathbb{N}$, $C$ be a weakly critical mapping of all $j < i$ in $(G, \sigma)$, $l \in (\mathbb{N} \cup \{\infty\})^{\mathbb{N}}$ and $b \in A^C(l)$ be given. Furthermore let $V', V'' \subseteq V$ so that there exist $b', b'' \supseteq b$ with $b', b'' \in A^C(l)$, $dom(b') \supseteq V'$, $dom(b'') \supseteq V''$ and $b'|_{T_i^{C,G}(V') \cap T_i^{C,G}(V'')} = b''|_{T_i^{C,G}(V') \cap T_i^{C,G}(V'')}$. Then at least one of the following statements holds*

**(i)** *there exist $j < i$, $(j, x, u) \in V$ and $c \in B_j^C(b, l)$ so that $l(j) \in \mathbb{N}$ and $\sigma((j, x, u), c) = e$ or*
**(ii)** *there exist $c \in B_i^C(b, l)$ so that $c|_{V'} = b'|_{V'}$ and $c|_{V''} = b''|_{V''}$.*

*Proof.* Let $C$, $l$, $b, b', b''$, $V', V''$ and $i$ be given as above. W.l.o.g. we will assume that $dom(b) \subseteq V'$. Furthermore let us assume that statement (i) is false, i.e. $\sigma((j, x, u), c) \neq e$ for all $j < i$ with $l(j) \in \mathbb{N}$, all $(j, x, u) \in V$ and all $c \in B_j^C(b, l)$. Then we have a situation similar to the proof of Lemma 1 in Section 2.2: $\sigma((j, y, v), c') = \sigma((j, y, v), c'')$ for all $j < i$ with $l(j) \in \mathbb{N}$ and all $c', c'' \in B_j^C(b, l)$ with $c'|_{C(j,y,v)} = c''|_{C(j,y,v)}$. Starting with $c_0 = b$ we determine $c_{n+1}$ by $dom(c_{n+1}) = \{(j, y, v) \in V \mid |y| < n + 1\} \cup dom(c_n)$. Furthermore given $(j, y, v) \in dom(c_{n+1}) \setminus dom(c_n)$ let $c_{n+1}(j, y, v) = b'(j, y, v) \quad (= b''(j, y, v))$ if $(j, y, v) \in T_i^{C,G}(V') \quad (\in T_i^{C,G}(V''))$. If $(j, y, v) \notin T_i^{C,G}(V') \cup T_i^{C,G}(V'')$ then let $c_{n+1}(j, y, v) = 1$ iff there exist $d \in B_j^C(c_n, l)$ so that $\sigma((j, y, v), d) = 1$ and $c_{n+1}(j, y, v) = 0$ otherwise. Let $c = \bigcup_{i \in \mathbb{N}} c_i$. As $c|_{V'} = b'|_{V'}$ and $c|_{V''} = b''|_{V''}$ by definition, we have only to prove $c \in B_j^C(c_n, l)$ for all $n \in \mathbb{N}$ and $j \leq i$. This can be verified by arguments which are almost identical to the arguments of Lemma 1. Beside the cases we have distinguished there, we have here also to consider a third case $(j, y, v) \in T_i^{C,G}(V') \cup T_i^{C,G}(V'')$.

□

Notice that Lemma 5 is indeed a special case of Lemma 6 where $V' = V'' = \emptyset$. Furthermore we get the

**Corollary 1.** *Let $i$, $C$, $l$ and $b$ be given as in Lemma 6 so that additionally $l(j) = \infty$ for all $(j, x, u) \in V$ and all $c \in B_j^C(b, l)$ with $j < i$ and $\sigma((j, x, u), c) = e$. Furthermore let $m \in \mathbb{N}$, $V', V'' \subseteq V$ and $c', c'' \in B_i^C(b, l)$ be given so that $c'|_{T_i^{C,G}(V') \cap T_i^{C,G}(V'')} = c''|_{T_i^{C,G}(V') \cap T_i^{C,G}(V'')}$ and $|y| < m$ for all $(j, y, v) \in V' \cup V''$.*

*Then there exist $c \in B_i^C(b, l)$ so that $c|_{V'} = c'|_{V'}$ and $c|_{V''} = c''|_{V''}$.*

## 3 A Relativized Collapse

In this section we will use the results of the last sections to prove a relativized collapse of the polynomial time hierarchy of Monte-Carlo truth-table (oracle) machines. Before we state this result formally, we will give some basic notations concerning machines and furthermore we will state a connection between oracles and colorings.

We use the standard model of probabilistic multitape Turing machines with a finite number of tapes (see [2]). Given such a probabilistic machine $M$ we denote the time complexity and language of $M$ by $t_M$ and $L_M$ respectively. Furthermore we will assume that outputs of $M$ on its computation paths belong to $\{0,1,?\}$. Let $\pi_M^0(x)$, $\pi_M^1(x)$, ..., $\pi_M^{m_M(x)-1}(x)$ denote both the different computation paths of $M$ on input $x \in \Sigma^*$ and their outputs. Given a predicate $Q$ on computation paths let $P_{M,x}[Q]$ denote the set $P_{M,x}[Q] = \{0 \le p < m_M(x) | Q(\pi_M^p(x))\}$. For example we have $x \in L_M \Leftrightarrow \sharp P_{M,x}[\pi_M^p(x) = 1] > \frac{1}{2} m_M(x)$.

We say that $M$ respects the Monte-Carlo property on $x$ ($M \in MCM(x)$ for short) iff either $\sharp P_{M,x}[\pi_M^p(x) = 1] > \frac{2}{3} m_M(x)$ or $\sharp P_{M,x}[\pi_M^p(x) = 0] > \frac{2}{3} m_M(x)$. $M$ is called a Monte-Carlo machine ($M \in MCM$) iff $M \in MCM(x)$ for all $x \in \Sigma^*$. A probabilistic machine is called Las-Vegas machine, iff for all $x$ either $\sharp P_{M,x}[\pi_M^p(x) = 1] > \frac{1}{2} m_M(x)$ and $\sharp P_{M,x}[\pi_M^p(x) = 0] = 0$ or $\sharp P_{M,x}[\pi_M^p(x) = 0] > \frac{1}{2} m_M(x)$ and $\sharp P_{M,x}[\pi_M^p(x) = 1] = 0$.

Probabilistic Turing machines can be relativized in a canonical way. Here we will assume that an oracle may also answer ?, that is an oracle is a mapping $A : \Sigma^* \to \{0,1,?\}$ rather than a subset $A \subseteq \Sigma^*$.

Given an oracle $A$ we adopt the above definitions and denote the relativized versions by $t_M^A$, $L_M^A$, $m_M(x,A)$, $\pi_M^p(x,A)$, $MCM(x,A)$ and $MCM(A)$. Furthermore we also adopt $P_{M,x}[Q]$ and denote its relativized version by $P_{M,x}^A[Q]$. Given a computation path $\pi$ of an oracle machine let $q(\pi)$ denote the set of oracle questions asked during the computation of $\pi$. We call a probabilistic oracle machine $M$ a truth-table machine iff for all $x \in \Sigma^*$ and all oracles $A, B : \Sigma^* \to \{0,1,?\}$ we have $m_M(x,A) = m_M(x,B)$ and $q(\pi_M^p(x,A)) = q(\pi_M^p(x,B))$ for all $0 \le p < m_M(x,A)$. In the case of truth-table machines we will omit the oracle $A$ iff it is clear. We denote the time complexity classes determined by Monte-Carlo and Las-Vegas truth-table machines with oracle $A$ by $BPTIME_{tt}^A()$ and $ZPTIME_{tt}^A()$ respectively. Monte-Carlo polynomial time is also denoted by $BPP_{tt}^A$.

Let $\langle\cdot,\cdot,\cdot\rangle : \mathbb{N} \times \Sigma^* \times \Sigma^* \to \Sigma^*$ be determined by $\langle i,x,u\rangle = 0^i 10^{|x|} 1xu$ for all $i \in \mathbb{N}$ and $x, u \in \Sigma^*$. Furthermore let $V$ be determined as in Section 2.1 and $A_0$ be a mapping $A_0 :\subseteq \Sigma^* \to \{0,1,?\}$ so that $dom(A_0) = \{\langle i,x,u\rangle \mid (i,x,u) \in V\}$. Once we have fixed such an $A_0$ (in the sequel we will assume so) we have a one to one correspondence between $c \in \{0,1,?\}^V$ and oracles $A : \Sigma^* \to \{0,1,?\}$ with $A \supseteq A_0$: given $c \in \{0,1,?\}^V$ let $A_c \supseteq A_0$ be determined by $A(\langle i,x,u\rangle) = c(i,x,u)$ for all $(i,x,u) \in V$. Given a computation path $\pi$ we will denote by $\boldsymbol{q}(\pi)$ the set $\{(i,x,u) \in V | \langle i,x,u\rangle \in q(\pi)\}$ and by $\boldsymbol{q}(M,x)$ the set $\bigcup_{0 \le p < m_M(x)} \boldsymbol{q}(\pi_M^p(x))$ (for given truth-table machine $M$ and input $x$).

Now we are prepared to prove the main lemma.

**Lemma 7.** *There exist $\varepsilon > 0$ and $A : \Sigma^* \to \{0,1,?\}$ so that*

$$BPTIME_{tt}^A(n^{1+\varepsilon}) = ZPTIME_{tt}^A(n).$$

*Proof.* Let $0 < \varepsilon < 1$ and an enumeration $M_0$, $M_1$, ... of (clocked) probabilistic truth-table machines be given so that $t_{M_i}^A(x) < |x|^2$ for all $i \in \mathbb{N}$, $x \in \Sigma^*$ and all oracles $A : \Sigma^* \to \{0,1,?\}$. Furthermore we will assume that for all $A : \Sigma^* \to \{0,1,?\}$ and all $L \in BPTIME_{tt}^A(n^{1+\varepsilon})$ there exist $n_L \in \mathbb{N}$ such that

$M_{n_L} \in MCM(A)$ and $x \in L \Leftrightarrow x \in L^A_{M_{n_L}}$ for almost all $x \in \Sigma^*$. The existence of such an enumeration can be easily verified by standard techniques.

In the sequel we will determine $(G, \sigma)$, $G = (V, E)$ so that

$$E(j, y, v) \supseteq \{(i, x, u) | \langle i, x, u \rangle \in q(M_j, x)\} \tag{3.3}$$

and

$$\sigma((j, y, v), c) = \begin{cases} 1 & : \quad M_j \in MCM(y, A_c) \wedge y \in L^{A_c}_{M_j} \\ 0 & : \quad M_j \in MCM(y, A_c) \wedge y \notin L^{A_c}_{M_j} \\ e & : \quad \text{otherwise} \end{cases} \tag{3.4}$$

for all $(j, y, v) \in V$ and $c \in \{0, 1, ?\}^V$. Notice that $\sigma$ is uniquely determined by $E$ and (3.4) above. Thus we will give only a construction of $G = (V, E)$ and denote the corresponding $\sigma$ according to (3.4) by $\sigma_G$.

The following claim can be easily verified.

*Claim.* Let $(G, \sigma)$ be given so that (3.3) and (3.4) are fulfilled and there exists a coloring $c$ of $(G, \sigma)$. Then $BPTIME^{A_c}_{tt}(n^{1+\varepsilon}) = ZPTIME^{A_c}_{tt}(n)$.

Thus we have to construct $(G, \sigma)$ so that weakly critical mappings exist. Next we will determine a sequence $E_0 \subseteq E_1 \subseteq ...$ and furthermore a sequence $C_0 \subseteq C_1 \subseteq ...$, $C_i :\subseteq V \to 2^V$ for all $i \in \mathbb{N}$, so that $C = \bigcup_{n \in \mathbb{N}} C_n$ is a weakly critical mapping in $(G, \sigma_G)$, $G = (V, E)$ where $E = \bigcup_{n \in \mathbb{N}} E_n$. Furthermore we will determine $C_n$ so that $dom(C_n) = \{(i, x, u) \in V | i < n\}$.

Let $E_0(j, y, v) = q(M_j, y)$ for all $(j, y, v) \in V$ and $C_0$ be determined by $dom(C_0) = \emptyset$. Notice that we have $|x| < |y|^2$ for all $(i, x, u), (j, y, v) \in V$ with $(i, x, u) \in E_0(j, y, v)$. Given $n \in \mathbb{N}$, $E_n$ and $C_n$ we will first determine $C_{n+1}$: Let $(n, x, u) \in V$ be given and $M = M_n$. Furthermore let $V(p) = T^{C_n, G_n}_n(q(\pi^p_M(x))$ for $0 \leq p < m_M(x)$. Then determine $C_{n+1}(n, x, u)$ by $C_{n+1}(n, x, u) = \{(j, y, v) \in V \mid \sharp P_{M,x}[(j, y, v) \in V(p)] > (4 \cdot \max_{0 \leq p < m_M(x)} \sharp V(p))^{-1} \cdot m_M(x)\}$. Now let

$$E_{n+1}(j, y, v) = \begin{cases} E_n(j, y, v) & : \quad j \neq n \\ E_n(j, y, v) \cup C_{n+1}(j, y, v) & : \quad \text{otherwise} \end{cases}$$

for all $(j, y, v) \in V$.

To complete this proof we have to verify that $C = \bigcup_{n \in \mathbb{N}} C_n$ is a weakly critical mapping in $(G, \sigma_G)$, $G = (V, E)$ where $E = \bigcup_{n \in \mathbb{N}} E_n$.

*Claim.* Let $G$, $\sigma_G$ and $C$ be given as above. Then $G$ fulfills conditions (G1)-(G4) of Section 2.1 and $C$ is a weakly critical mapping in $(G, \sigma_G)$. Thus there exist colorings $c$ of $(G, \sigma_G)$.

*Proof.* It can be easily verified that (G1)-(G4) and (C1),(C2),(C3) hold for $(G, \sigma_G)$ and $C$ respectively. To prove (C4) let $i \in \mathbb{N}$, $l \in (\mathbb{N} \cup \{\infty\})^{\mathbb{N}}$ and $b \in A^C(l)$ be given so that for all $(j, y, v) \in V$ with $j \leq i$ and $l(j) \neq \infty$ and for all $c \in B^C_i(b, l)$ we have $\sigma_G((j, y, v), c) \neq e$. Furthermore let us assume that there exist $(i, x, u) \in V$ and $c', c'' \in B^C_i(b, l)$ so that $\sigma_G((i, x, u), c') = 0$, $\sigma_G((i, x, u), c'') = 1$ and $c'|_{C(i,x,u)} = c''|_{C(i,x,u)}$. We will now prove the existence of $c \in B^C_i(b, l)$ so that $\sigma((i, x, u), c) = e$ and thus verify (C4).

Given $p$ with $0 \leq p < m_{M_i}(x)$ let $V(p)$ be determined by

$$V(p) = T_i^{C_i,G_i}(q(\pi^p_{M_i}(x)).$$

Furthermore given $d \in \{0,1,?\}^V$ let $P^d_=$ denote the set $P^d_= = P_{M_i,x}[d|_{V(p)} = c'|_{V(p)}]$ and $P^d_{\neq} = \{0,...,m_{M_i}(x)-1\} \setminus P^d_=$. Let $||d,c'||$ be determined by $||d,c'|| = \sharp P^d_{\neq}$. Now let $d \in B_i^C(b,l)$ be given so that $d|_{C(i,x,u)} = c'|_{C(i,x,u)}$, $\sigma((i,x,u),d) = 1$ and $||d,c'||$ is minimal among these mappings. Because of $\sigma((i,x,u),d) = 1$, $\sigma((i,x,u),c') = 0$ and by Corollary 1 there exist $\hat{p} \in P^d_{\neq}$ and $c \in B_i^C(b,l)$ so that $c|_{V'} = c'|_{V'}$ and $c|_{V''} = d|_{V''}$ where $V' = V(\hat{p}) \cup \bigcup\{V(p)|p \in P^d_=\}$ and $V'' = \bigcup\{V(p)|p \in P^d_{\neq} \wedge V(p) \cap V(\hat{p}) \subseteq C(i,x,u)\}$. Obviously we have $||c,c'|| < ||d,c'||$ and $c|_{C(i,x,u)} = c'|_{C(i,x,u)}$. Furthermore we have

$$\sharp P_{M_i,x}[d|_{V(p)} \neq c|_{V(p)}\}] \leq \frac{1}{4\sharp V(\hat{p})}\sharp V(\hat{p}) \cdot m_{M_i}(x) = \frac{1}{4} \cdot m_{M_i}(x)$$

and thus $\sharp P_{M_i,x}[\pi^p_{M_i}(x,A_c) = 1] \geq \frac{2}{3} \cdot m_{M_i}(x) - \frac{1}{4} \cdot m_{M_i}(x) > \frac{1}{3} \cdot m_{M_i}(x)$ so that $\sigma((i,x,u),c) = e$ by minimality of $||d,c'||$.

□

## 4 Conclusions and Open Problems

In this section we will first give a few conclusions of Lemma 7; for further discussion see [5]. By standard padding arguments we get the main theorem:

**Theorem 1.** *There exist oracles A such that*

$$BPP^A_{tt} = ZPTIME^A_{tt}(n).$$

Notice that our proof of Lemma 7 and thus of $A$ is not constructive because the construction of $c_{n+1}$ in Lemma 4 is not. To solve this problem we will first assume $l_{n+1} \neq \infty$ (see prove of Lemma 4) until we recognize that our guess is wrong. A carefull analysis of the construction shows that for all $(i,x,u) \in V$ we can find a step so that $A$ need not be altered later on. Thus the oracle $A$ can be chosen to be recursively.

Furthermore by a carefull analysis of equation (2.1) (Section 2.2) and the proof of Lemma 7 we can weaken the time bound of the machines $(M_i)_{i \in \mathbb{N}}$ in the proof of Lemma 7 so that $t_{M_i} \in O(f)$ for all $i$ and a function $f$ with $\forall k, i \in \mathbb{N}. f^{(k)} \in O(2^{\sqrt[i]{n}})$. Together we can extend Theorem 1 to the following theorem.

**Theorem 2.** *Let $f$ be a function such that $\forall k, i \in \mathbb{N}. f^{(k)} \in O(2^{\sqrt[i]{n}})$. Then there exists a decidable oracle $B$ so that*

$$BPTIME^B_{tt}(f) = ZPTIME^B_{tt}(n).$$

Obviously Theorem 1 is not true for all oracles: even under random oracles $BPP^C \neq BPTIME^C(n)$. The same is true under any oracle $C$ with $P^C = NP^C$.

For general (Monte-Carlo) oracle machines and a few other semantic models it is also possible to define appropriate graph coloring problems. But in these cases graphs and (weakly) critical mappings depend on colorings and vice versa. An interesting open problem is to find simpler proofs of such relativized collapses.

The central problem remains to prove or disprove the unrelativized existence of polynomial time hierarchies for Monte-Carlo machines (and several other so called semantic machine classes). However, the results given in this paper and in [10] indicate that the separation of the time hierarchy classes will be a non-trivial task. Notice that even strong relations to other problems are not known.

**Acknowledgments.** The authors would like to thank Marek Karpinski for helpfull discussions on the problem of BPTIME-hierarchies and the proof of the main theorem in [5].

## References

1. Allender, Beigel, Hertrampf, Homer, *Almost-everywhere Complexity Hierarchies for Nondeterministic Time*, TCS 115(1993), pp. 225-241.
2. Balcazar, Diaz, Gabarro, *Structural Complexity 2*, Springer 1990.
3. Berg, Håstad, *On the BPP Hierarchy Problem*, Technical Report TRITA-NA-9702, Royal Inst. of Technology, Stockholm 1997.
4. Freivalds, *Probabilistic two-way Machines*, Proc. MFCS, LNCS 118, Springer 1981, pp. 33-45.
5. Fortnow, Sipser, *Probabilistic Computation and Linear Time*, ACM Symposium on Theory of Computing (STOC), 1989, pp. 148-156.
6. Fortnow, Sipser, *Retraction of Probabilistic Computation and Linear Time*, ACM Symposium on Theory of Computing (STOC), 1997, p. 750.
7. Hemaspaandra, *Complexity Theory Column 11*, SIGACT News 26,4 (1995), pp. 5-15.
8. Karpinski, Verbeek, *On the Monte Carlo Space Constructible Functions and Separation Results for Probabilistic Complexity Classes*, Information and Computation 75 (1987), pp. 178-189.
9. Karpinski, Verbeek, *Randomness, Provability and the Separation of Monte Carlo Time and Space*, Computation Theory and Logic, LNCS 270 (1987), pp. 189-207.
10. Rettinger, *Orakelabhängige Zeithierarchiesätze*, PhD thesis, FernUniversität Hagen, 1999.
11. Rackoff, Seiferas, *Limitations on Separating Nondeterministic Complexity Classes*, SIAM Journal on Computing 10 (1981), pp. 742-745.
12. Seiferas, Fischer, Meyer, *Separating Nondeterministic Time Complexity Classes*, JACM 25, pp. 146-167.

# Relating Automata-Theoretic Hierarchies to Complexity-Theoretic Hierarchies*

V.L. Selivanov

A.P. Ershov Institute of Informatics Systems
Siberian Division of Russian Academy of Sciences
vseliv@nspu.ru

**Abstract.** We show that some natural refinements of the Straubing and Brzozowski hierarchies correspond (via the so called leaf-languages) step by step to similar refinements of the polynomial-time hierarchy. This extends a result of H.-J. Burtschik and H. Vollmer on relationship between the Straubing and the polynomial hierarchies. In particular, this applies to the boolean hierarchy and the plus–hierarchy.

## 1 Introduction

In complexity theory, the so called leaf-language approach to defining complexity classes became recently rather popular. Let us recall some relevant definitions. Consider a polynomial-time nondeterministic Turing machine $M$ working on an input word $x$ over some alphabet $X$ and printing a letter from another alphabet $A$ after finishing any computation path. These values are the leaves of the binary tree defined by the nondeterministic choices of $M$ on input $x$. An ordering of the tuples in the program of $M$ determines a left-to-right ordering of all the leaves. In this way, $M$ may be considered as a deterministic transducer computing a total function $M : X^* \to A^*$ from the set of words $X^*$ over $X$ to the set of words over $A$. Now, relate to any language $L \subseteq A^*$ (called in this situation a leaf language) the language $M^{-1}(L) \subseteq X^*$. Denote by $Leaf(L)$ the set of languages $M^{-1}(L)$, for all machines $M$ specified above. For a set of languages $\mathcal{C}$, let $Leaf(\mathcal{C})$ be the union of $Leaf(L)$, for all $L \in \mathcal{C}$.

It turns out that many inportant complexity classes have natural and useful descriptions in terms of leaf languages (see e.g. [BCS92, V93, HL+93). In particular, a close relationship between some classes of regular leaf languages and complexity classes within $PSPACE$ was established in [HL+93]. In [BV98], a close relationship between the Straubing hierarchy $\{\mathcal{S}_n\}$ and the polynomial hieararchy $\{\Sigma_n^p\}$ was established: $Leaf(\mathcal{S}_n) = \Sigma_n^p$, for any $n > 0$.

In this paper, we consider the possibility of extending the last result to some refinements of the above–mentioned hierarchies (in the context of complexity theory, these refinements were introduced and studied in [Se93, Se94, Se95, Se99]).

* Supported by the Alexander von Humboldt Foundation, by the German Research Foundation (DFG) and by the Russian Foundation for Basic Research Grant 00-01-00810.

R. Freivalds (Ed.): FCT 2001, LNCS 2138, pp. 323–334, 2001.

Our interest in results of this kind is motivated by the hope that such relationships between automata–theoretic and complexity–theoretic notions may lead to nontrivial applications of one theory to the other. For an example of this see Section 7 below.

Note that for the important particular case of the boolean hiearachy over $NP$ a result similar to ours was earlier established in [SW98, Theorem 6.3], and we actually use the idea of proof of that theorem. We make also an essential use of a result from [PW97] cited in Section 3.

In Section 2 we give the exact definitions of our hierarchies, in Section 3 we consider some relevant notions from language theory, in Sections 4—6 we present our main results, and further we give some examples and discussions.

## 2 Hierarchies

In different areas of mathematics, people consider a lot of hierarchies which are typically used to classify some objects according to their complexity. Here we define and discuss some hierarchies relevant to the topic of this paper.

We already mentioned the polynomial hierarchy $\{\Sigma_n^p\}$ which is one of the most popular objects of complexity theory. Note that classes (or levels) of the polynomial hierarchy are classes of languages over some finite alphabet $X$. In the context of complexity theory, the cardinality of $X$ is not important (provided that it is at least 2), so it is often assumed that $X$ is just the binary alphabet $\{0,1\}$. For detailed definition and properties of the polynomial hierarchy and other relevant notions see any standard textbook on complexity theory, say [BDG88, BDG90]. Sometimes it is convenient to use more compact notation for the polynomial hierarchy, namely $PH$; hence $PH = \{\Sigma_n^p\}$.

Let us define now two hierarchies which are rather popular in automata theory. A word $u = u_0 \ldots u_n \in A^+$ ($A^+$ denotes the set of finite nonempty words over an alphabet $A$, while $A^*$—the set of all finite words over $A$, including the empty word $\varepsilon$) may be considered as a first–order structure $\mathbf{u} = (\{0,\ldots,n\};<, Q_a,\ldots)$, where $<$ has its usual meaning and $Q_a (a \in A)$ are unary predicates on $\{0,\ldots,n\}$ defined by $Q_a(i) \leftrightarrow u_i = a$. By Theorem of McNaughton and Papert [MP71], the so called star–free regular languages are exactly the sets of words $u$, for which $\mathbf{u}$ satisfies a first–order sentence of signature $\sigma_A = \{<, Q_a,\}_{a\in A}$.

For any $n > 0$, let $\mathcal{S}_n$ denote the class of languages defined by $\Sigma_n$–sentences of signature $\sigma$ (i.e., sentences in prenex normal form starting with the existential quantifier and having $n-1$ quantifier alternations); the sequence $SH = \{\mathcal{S}_n\}$ is known as the Straubing (or Straubing–Thérien) hierarchy. In cases when it is important to specify the alphabet, we denote the $n$-th level as $A^+\mathcal{L}_n$, and the whole hierarchy as $A^+SH$. There is also a *-version of the Straubing hierarchy which will be denoted as $A^*SH = \{A^*\mathcal{S}_n\}$; the relationship between both versions is very easy: $A^*\mathcal{S}_n = A^+\mathcal{S}_n \cup A^+\mathcal{S}_n^\varepsilon$ (for any class $\mathcal{X}$ of subsets of $A^+$ we denote $\mathcal{X}^\varepsilon = \{X \cup \{\varepsilon\} | X \in \mathcal{X}\}$).

The Brzozowski hierarchy is defined in the same way, only in place of $\sigma_A$ one takes the signature $\sigma'_A = \sigma_A \cup \{\bot, \top, s\}$, where $\bot$ and $\top$ are constant symbols and $s$ is a unary function symbol ($\bot, \top$ are assumed to denote the least and the greatest element respectively, while $s$ denotes the successor function). Brzozowski hierarchy will be denoted by $BH = \{\mathcal{B}_n\}$, with the corresponding variations in case when we need to mention the alphabet explicitely.

Note that in automata theory people usually define the Straubing and Brzozowski hierarchies by means of regular expressions; the equivalence of those definitions to definitions used here is known from [T82, PP86]. For more information on logical aspects of automata–theoretic hierarchies see also [Se01].

Next we would like to define some refinements of the introduced hierarchies. In order to do this in a uniform way, we need a technical notion of a base. Let $(B; \cup, \cap, \bar{}, 0, 1)$ be a boolean algebra (b.a.). Without loss of generality, one may think that $B$ is a class of subsets of some set. By *a base in* $B$ we mean any sequence $L = \{L_n\}_{n<\omega}$ of sublattices of $(B; \cup, \cap, 0, 1)$, satisfying the inclusions $L_n \cup co(L_n) \subseteq L_{n+1}$ (here $co(L_n)$ denotes the dual set $\{\bar{x} | x \in L_n\}$ for $L_n$). Note that levels of the hierarchies introduced above (as well as of many other popular hierarchies) are bases (take in place of $L_n$ respectively $\Sigma^p_{n+1}$, $\mathcal{S}_{n+1}$ and $\mathcal{B}_{n+1}$).

With any base $L = \{L_n\}_{n<\omega}$ one can associate a sequence of new subsets of $B$ as follows. Let $T$ be the set of terms of the signature $(\cup, \cap, \bar{}, 0, 1)$ with variables $v^n_k (k, n < \omega)$. We call $v^n_k (k < \omega)$ *variables of type* $n$, and elements of $T$—*typed boolean terms*. Relate to any term $t \in T$ the set $t(L)$ of all its values when variables of type $n$ range over $L_n$. We call the sequence $\{t(L)\}_t$ *the typed boolean hierarchy over* $L$.

Let us state some easy properties of the introduced classes.

**Lemma 1.**
*(i) Typed boolean hierarchy is a refinement of* $L$*, i.e. any class* $L_n$ *is among the classes* $t(L), t \in T$.
*(ii) If* $L$ *is a base in* $B$*,* $L'$ *is a base in* $B'$ *and* $f : B \to B'$ *is a homomorphism of boolean algebras such that* $f(L_n) \subseteq L'_n$ *for all* $n < \omega$*, then* $f(t(L)) \subseteq t(L')$ *for any* $t \in T$.

**Proof.**
(i) Let $t = v^n_0$, then $t(L) = L_n$.
(ii) We have to deduce $f(a) \in t(L')$ from $a \in t(L)$. Let $t = t(x_0, \ldots, x_k)$, where $x_0, \ldots, x_k$ are some typed variables. By definition of $t(L)$, $a = t(a_0, \ldots, a_k)$ for some $a_0, \ldots, a_k \in B$ such that $a_j \in L_n$ whenever $x_j$ is of type $n$. By a property of homomorphisms, $f(a) = t(f(a_0), \ldots, f(a_k))$. From $f(L_n) \subseteq L'_n$ it follows that $f(a_j) \in L'_n$ whenever $x_j$ is of type $n$. Hence, $f(a) \in t(L')$. This completes the proof.

Now we prove a more subtle property useful for some considerations below. Let $L$ be a base in a b.a. $B$, and let $B' = B \times \{0, 1\}$ be the cartesian product of $B$ and of the 2-element b.a. $\{0, 1\}$. Hence, $B' = \{(b, c) | b \in B, c \leq 1\}$ and the boolean operations in $B'$ are componentwise. We will state a close relationship between the typed boolean hierarchies over $L$ and over the base $L'$ in $B'$ defined by $L'_n = L_n \times \{0, 1\}$.

Let $B^c = B \times \{c\}$, then $B' = B^0 \cup B^1$ and $B^c$ may be considered as a b.a. isomorpic to $B$ (isomorphism is given of course by the function $b \mapsto (b, c)$; note that symbols $\cap, \cup$ have the same interpretations in $B^c$ as they have in $B'$, while the symbol $\bar{}$ has slightly different interpretations in $B^0$ and $B^1$). Let $L^c$ be the base in $B^c$ induced by $L$ under this isomorphism, i.e. $L_n^c = L_n \times \{c\}$. Then $L'_n = L_n^0 \cup L_n^1$.

We call a boolean term $t(x_0, \dots, x_k)$ *nontrivial*, if the function induced by this term on $\{0,1\}$ is not constant, i.e. for any $c \leq 1$ there are $c_j \leq 1$ satisfying $t(c_0, \dots, c_k) = c$. As is well known, a term is nontrivial iff it is not equivalent to the constant boolean terms $0, 1$ in the theory of boolean algebras.

**Lemma 2.**
*(i) For any $t \in T$ and $c \leq 1$, $t(L^c) = t(L) \times \{c\}$.*
*(ii) For any nontrivial $t \in T$, $t(L') = t(L^0) \cup t(L^1)$.*

**Proof.**
(i) follows from Lemma 1.
(ii) Let $t = t(x_0, \dots, x_k)$ for some typed variables $x_j$, and let $a \in t(L'), a = (b, c) \in B'$. Then $a = t((b_0, c_0), \dots, (b_k, c_k))$ for some $(b_j, c_j) \in B'$ such that $(b_j, c_j) \in L'_n$ whenever $x_j$ is of type $n$. We have $a = (t(b_0, \dots, b_k), t(c_0, \dots, c_k))$, and $b_j \in L_n$ whenever $x_j$ is of type $n$. Hence, $b \in t(L)$ and $a \in t(L) \times \{c\} = t(L^c)$.

It remains to check the inclusion $t(L) \times \{c\} \subseteq t(L')$. By nontriviality of $t$, $c = t(c_0, \dots, c_k)$ for some $c_j \leq 1$. Let $a = (b, c) \in t(L) \times \{c\}$, then $b = t(b_0, \dots, b_k)$ for some $b_0, \dots, b_k \in B$ such that $b_j \in L_n$ whenever $x_j$ is of type $n$. We have $a = t((b_0, c_0), \dots, (b_k, c_k))$ and $(b_j, c_j) \in L'_n$ whenever $x_j$ is of type $n$. Hence, $a \in t(L')$ completing the proof.

Taking in place of $L$ the base $PH = \{\Sigma_{n+1}^p\}_n$, we get the typed Boolean hierarchy $\{t(PH)\}$ over $PH$ introduced and studied in [Se94, Se94a, Se95, Se99]. In particular, the following fact was established.

**Lemma 3.** *All classes of the typed boolean hierarchy over $PH$ are closed downwards under the polynomial $m$-reducibility and contain polynomially $m$-complete sets.*

Taking in place of $L$ the base $SH$ (the base $BH$), we get the typed boolean hierarchy $\{t(SH)\}$ (resp., $\{t(BH)\}$) over $SH$ (resp., over $BH$). A study of these hierarchies, as well as of fine hierarchies over $SH$ and $BH$ defined below was initiated in [SS00]. If we want to specify the alphabet explicitly we again use notation like $t(A^+SH)$.

The three examples of the typed Boolean hierarchy introduced above will be the main objects of this paper. Let us state some easy facts on the typed boolean hierarchies over $SH$ and $BH$. The foolowing assertion follows from Lemma 1.

**Lemma 4.**
*(i) For any $n > 0$ and any alphabet $A$, $A^+\mathcal{S}_n \subseteq A^*\mathcal{S}_n$ and $A^+\mathcal{S}_n \subseteq A^+\mathcal{B}_n$.*
*(ii) For any $t \in T$ and any alphabet $A$, $t(A^+SH) \subseteq t(A^*SH)$ and $t(A^+SH) \subseteq t(A^+BH)$.*

Now we establish a relationship between the *- and +-versions of the typed boolean hierarchy over $SH$ which informally means the equivalence of the both versions for the purposes of this paper.

**Lemma 5.**
*(i) For any nontrivial* $t \in T$ *and any alphabet* $A$, $t(A^*SH) = t(A^+SH) \cup t(A^+SH)^\varepsilon$.
*(ii) For any* $t \in T$ *and any alphabet* $A$, $Leaf(t(A^*SH)) = Leaf(t(A^+SH))$.

**Proof.**
(i) Let $B = P(A^+)$ and $L = A^+SH$. Then b.a. $P(A^*)$ is naturally isomorphic to the b.a. $B' = B \times \{0,1\}$ (the isomorphism $h : B \times \{0,1\} \to P(A^*)$ is defined by $h(L,0) = L$ and $h(L,1) = L \cup \{\varepsilon\}$). Using notation introduced before Lemma 2, we have $h(L'_n) = A^*\mathcal{S}_n$. Now the assertion follows from Lemma 2.
(ii) If $t$ is equivalent (in the theory of boolean algebras) to 0, then $t(A^*SH) = \{\emptyset\} = t(A^+SH)$, and the equation follows. If $t$ is equivalent to 1, then $t(A^*SH) = \{A^*\}$ and $t(A^+SH) = \{A^+\}$. But $Leaf(A^*) = X^* = Leaf(A^+)$, because the leaf word is always nonempty. Finally, let $t$ be nontrivial. Then the equation follows from (i), because $Leaf(t(A^+SH)^\varepsilon) = Leaf(t(A^+SH))$, again by the nonemptyness of the leaf word. This completes the proof of the lemma.

We will consider also another hierarchy called the *fine hierarchy* over $L$. It was introduced by the author in the context of recursion theory and then considered also in several other contexts. Let us briefly recall the definition of the fine hierarchy over $L$. Its classes (or levels) $S_\alpha$ are numbered by ordinals $\alpha < \varepsilon_0$, where $\varepsilon_0 = sup\{\omega, \omega^\omega, \omega^{\omega^\omega}, \ldots\}$ (for more information about the well–known ordinal $\varepsilon_0$ and the ordinal arithmetic see e.g. [KM67]).

We define the classes $S^n_\alpha$, where $n$ is an auxiliary parameter, by induction on $\alpha$ as follows (simplifying notation we write in this definition $ab$ in place of $a \cap b$):

$S^n_0 = 0$; $S^n_{\omega^\gamma} = S^{n+1}_\gamma$ for $\gamma > 0$;
$S^n_{\alpha+1} = \{u_0x_0 \cup u_1x_1 | u_i \in L_n, x_0 \in S^n_\alpha, x_1 \in co(S^n_\alpha), u_0u_1x_0 = u_0u_1x_1\}$;
$S^n_{\delta+\omega^\gamma} = \{u_0x_0 \cup u_1x_1 \cup \bar{u}_0\bar{u}_1y | u_i \in L_n, x_0 \in S^n_\alpha, x_1 \in co(S^n_\alpha), y \in S^n_\delta, u_0u_1x_0 = u_0u_1x_1\}$ for $\delta = \omega^\gamma \cdot \delta' > 0, \gamma > 0$.

To see that this definition is correct note that every nonzero ordinal $\alpha < \varepsilon_0$ is uniquely representable in the form $\alpha = \omega^{\gamma_0} + \cdots + \omega^{\gamma_k}$ for a finite sequence $\gamma_0 \geq \cdots \geq \gamma_k$ of ordinals $< \alpha$. Applying the definition we subsequently get $S^n_{\omega^{\gamma_0}}, S^n_{\omega^{\gamma_0}+\omega^{\gamma_1}}, \ldots, S^n_\alpha$. Finally, let $S_\alpha = S^0_\alpha$.

For information on the properties of the fine hierarchy see e.g. [Se95].

## 3 Families of Languages

By a *+-class of languages* [PW97] we mean a correspondence $\mathcal{C}$ which associates with each finite alphabeth $A$ a set $A^+\mathcal{C} \subseteq P(A^+)$, where $P(A^+)$ is the set of all subsets of $A^+$. In this paper we need classes of languages with some minimal closure properties as specified in the following

**Definition.** By a *+-family of languages* we mean a +-class $\mathcal{C} = \{A^+\mathcal{C}\}_A$ such that

(1) for every semigroup morphism $\phi : A^+ \to B^+$, $L \in B^+\mathcal{C}$ implies $\phi^{-1}(L) \in A^+\mathcal{C}$;

(2) if $L \in A^+\mathcal{C}$ and $a \in A$, then $a^{-1}L = \{v \in A^+ | av \in L\}$ and $La^{-1} = \{v \in A^+ | va \in L\}$ are in $A^+\mathcal{C}$.

This notion is obtained from the notion of a positive +-variety introduced in [PW97] by omitting the condition that any $A^+\mathcal{C}$ is closed under finite union and intersection. The notion of a *-family of languages is obtained from the above definition by using * in place of + and monoid morphism in place of the semigroup morphism (as again in [PW97] for the notion of a positive *-variety).

The following evident fact will be of some use in the next section.

**Lemma 6.** *Let $\mathcal{C}$ be a *-family of languages and $A, B$ be any alphabets of the same cardinality. Then $Leaf(A^*\mathcal{C}) = Leaf(B^*\mathcal{C})$.*

**Proof.** By symmetry, it suffices to check the inclusion in one direction, say $Leaf(A^*\mathcal{C}) \subseteq Leaf(B^*\mathcal{C})$. Let $K \in Leaf(A^*\mathcal{C})$, then $K = M^{-1}(L)$ for an $L \in A^*\mathcal{C}$ and a suitable machine $M$. Let $\phi : A \to B$ be a one-one correspondence between $A$ and $B$, and $\phi_1 : B^* \to A^*$ be the monoid morphism induced by $\phi^{-1}$. Then $L_1 = \phi_1^{-1}(L) \in B^*\mathcal{C}$ and $K = M_1^{-1}(L_1)$, where $M_1$ is a machine behaving just as $M$ with the only difference that it prints $\phi(a)$ whenever $M$ prints $a$. Hence, $K \in Leaf(B^*\mathcal{C})$ completing the proof.

From results in [PW97] we easily deduce the following facts about classes of hierarchies introduced in Section 2.

**Lemma 7.**
- *(i) For any $n > 0$, $\{A^+\mathcal{S}_n\}_A$ and $\{A^+\mathcal{B}_n\}_A$ are positive +-varieties, while $\{A^*\mathcal{S}_n\}_A$ is a positive *-variety.*
- *(ii) For any typed Boolean term $t$, $\{t(A^+SH)\}_A$ and $\{t(A^+BH)\}_A$ are +-families of languages while $\{t(A^*SH)\}_A$ is a *-family of languages.*
- *(iii) For any $\alpha < \varepsilon$, $\{S_\alpha(A^+SH)\}_A$ and $\{S_\alpha(A^+BH)\}_A$ are +-families of languages while $\{S_\alpha(A^+SH)\}_A$ is a *-family of languages.*

**Proof.**
- (i) s proved in [PW97] and plays a principal role for our paper.
- (ii) Let $\phi : A^+ \to B^+$ be a semigroup morphism and let $L \in t(B^+\mathcal{S})$. By (i), the preimage map $\phi^{-1}$ satisfies conditions of Lemma 2.(ii). Hence, $\phi^{-1}(L) \in t(A^+\mathcal{S})$. Property (2) from definition of the family of languages, as well as the remaining assertions from (ii) and the assertion (iii), are checked in the same way.

## 4 Typed Boolean Hierarchy over *SH*

In this section we relate some hierarchies introduced in Section 2 via the leaf language approach. First we consider languages from classes of the typed boolean hierarchy over $SH$ as leaf languages.

**Theorem 1.** *For any typed boolean term $t$, $\cup_A Leaf(t(A^*SH)) = t(PH) = \cup_A Leaf(t(A^+SH))$.*

**Proof.** By Lemma 5, it suffices to prove the equality $\cup_A Leaf(t(A^*SH)) = t(PH)$. First let us note that the result from [BV98] cited in the Introduction is exactly formulated as the equality $\cup_A Leaf(A^*\mathcal{S}_n) = \Sigma_n^p$, for any $n > 0$.

Now let us check the inclusion $\cup_A Leaf(t(A^*SH)) \subseteq t(PH)$. Let $K \in Leaf(t(A^*SH))$, then $K = M^{-1}(L)$ for some polynomially bounded nondeterministic Turing machine $M$ and some $L \in t(A^*SH)$. The map $M^{-1} : P(A^*) \to P(X^*)$ is a homomorphism of boolean algebas satisfying (by the Theorem of Burtschick and Vollmer) the inclusions $M^{-1}(A^*\mathcal{S}_n) \subseteq \Sigma_n^p$. By Lemma 1.(ii), $K = M^{-1}(L) \in t(PH)$, as desired.

For the converse inclusion, choose any $K$ in $t(PH)$ and let $t = t(x_0, \dots, x_k)$, where $x_j$ are typed variables. Then $K = t(K_0, \dots, K_k)$ for some $K_0, \dots, K_k \subseteq X^*$ such that $K_j \in \Sigma_{n+1}^p$ whenever $x_j$ is of type $n$. By the Theorem of Burtschik and Vollmer, there exist alphabets $A_0, \dots, A_k$ and languages $L_j \subseteq A_j^*$ such that $K_j \in Leaf(L_j)$ and $L_j \in \mathcal{S}_{n+1}$ whenever $x_j$ is of type $n$. By Lemma 3.2, the alphabets $A_0, \dots, A_k$ may be without loss of generality assumed pairwise disjoint. Let $A = A_0 \cup \dots \cup A_k$. Now it suffices to show that $K \in Leaf(t(A^*SH))$.

Let $M_0, \dots, M_k$ be nondeterministic polynomyal time Turing machines satisfying $K_j = M_j^{-1}(L_j)$. Consider the nondeterministic polynomial time Turing machine $M$ which behaves as follows: on input $x \in X^*$, it branches nondeterministically into $k+1$ computation paths, and on the j-th (from left to right) path just mimicks completely the behavior of the machine $M_j$. Note that the leaf string $M(x)$ will be the concatenation of the leaf strings $M_j(x)$, i.e. $M(x) = M_0(x) \cdots M_k(x)$.

For any $j \leq k$, let $\phi_j : A^* \to A_j^*$ be the morphism erasing all letters not in $A_j$. Then, by Lemma 3.3, $\phi_j^{-1}(L_j) \in \mathcal{L}_{n+1}$ whenever $x_j$ is of type $n$. Hence, the language $P = t(\phi_0^{-1}(L_0), \dots, \phi_k^{-1}(L_k))$ is in $t(A^*SH)$. Hence, it suffices to check that $K = M^{-1}(P) = t(M^{-1}(\phi_0^{-1}(L_0)), \dots, M^{-1}(\phi_k^{-1}(L_k))$. But $\phi_j(M(x)) = M_j(x)$, hence $M^{-1}(\phi_j^{-1}(L_j)) = M_j^{-1}(L_j)$ and the desired equality follows immediately from the equality $K = t(K_0, \dots, K_k) = t(M_0^{-1}(L_0), \dots, M_k^{-1}(L_k))$. This concludes the proof of the theorem.

In [BV98] the result was proved in a more exact form than it was formulated above. They proved also that for any $n > 0$ there is an alphabet $A$ and a language $L \in A^+\mathcal{S}_n$ such that $Leaf(L) = \Sigma_n^p$. This is also generalizable to the typed boolean hierarchy.

**Theorem 2.** *For any $t \in T$ there exist an alphabet $A$ and a language $L \in t(A^+SH)$ such that $Leaf(L) = t(PH)$.*

**Proof.** By Lemma 3, there exists a language $K \subseteq X^*$ polynomially $m$-complete in $t(PH)$. By Theorem 4.1, there exist an alphabet $A$ and a language $L \in t(A^+SH)$ such that $K \in Leaf(L) \subseteq t(PH)$. It is well–known [BCS92] that the class $Leaf(L)$ is closed downwards under the polynomial $m$-reducibility. Hence, $t(PH) \subseteq Leaf(L)$ completing the proof.

## 5 Typed Boolean Hieararchy over $BH$

The next result is an evident analog of Theorem 1 for the Brzozowski hierarchy.

**Theorem 3.** *For any* $t \in T$, $t(PH) = \cup_A Leaf(t(A^+BH))$.

The relationships between automata–theoretic hierarchies and the complexity–theoretic ones established in Theorems 1 and 3 look dependent on the alphabet. It seems that for the Straubing case the dependence is really essential (though we have yet no formal proof of this). Our next result shows that for the Brzozowski case one can get an alphabet–independent version of Theorem 3.

**Theorem 4.** *For any* $t \in T$ *and any alphabet* $A$ *having at least two symbols,* $Leaf(t(A^+BH)) = t(PH)$.

The idea of proof is evident: to code symbols of a bigger alphabet by sequences of symbols of a smaller alphabet using the presence of the successor function in the signature $\sigma'_A$ from Section 2. In the next few lemmas we collect observations needed for realization of this idea. For technical convenience, we will assume in these lemmas that the alphabet $A$ is a finite subset of $\omega$.

Define a function $f : \omega \to \{0,1\}^+$ by $f(n) = 01\ldots10$, where the sequence of 1's is of length $n+1$. With any alphabet $A \subseteq \omega$ we associate a semigroup morphism $f = f_A : A^+ \to \{0,1\}^+$ induced by the restriction of $f$ to $A$. E.g., for $A = \{0,1,2\}$ and $w = 0212$ we get $f(w) = 01001110011001110$. In general, if $w = a_0 \cdots a_k$ for $a_j \in A$ then $f(w)$ is the superposition $f(a_0) \cdots f(a_k)$. For $i \leq k$, let $i'$ denote the position of the first letter of $f(a_j)$ (this letter is of course 0) in the word $f(w)$. As usual, the length of a word $v$ is denoted by $|v|$, and for $i \leq |v|$ the $i$-th letter in $v$ is denoted by $v_i$. The following assertion is evident.

**Lemma 8.**
*(i) For all* $i,j \leq |w|$, $i < j$ *iff* $i' < j'$.
*(ii) For any* $l \leq |f(w)|$, $l \in \{i' | i \leq |w|\}$ *iff* $(f(w))_l = 0$ *and* $(f(w))_{l+1} = 1$.

Let $\sigma_A = \{<, Q_a\}_{a\in A}$ and $\sigma' = \sigma'_{\{0,1\}} = \{<, Q_0, Q_1, \bot, \top, s\}$ be the signatures discussed in Section 2. Relate to any formula $\phi$ of $\sigma_A$ a formula $\phi'$ of $\sigma'$ by the following induction:

if $\phi$ is $x = y$ or $x < y$ then $\phi'$ is $\phi$;
if $\phi$ is $Q_a(x)$ then $\phi'$ is $Q_0(x) \wedge Q_1(s(x)) \wedge \cdots \wedge Q_1(s^{a+1}(x)) \wedge Q_0(s^{a+2}(x))$;
if $\phi$ is $\phi_1 \wedge \phi_2$ then $\phi'$ is $\phi'_1 \wedge \phi'_2$;
if $\phi$ is $\neg\phi_1$ then $\phi'$ is $\neg\phi'_1$;
if $\phi$ is $\forall x \phi_1$ then $\phi'$ is $\forall x(Q_0(x) \wedge Q_1(s(x)) \to \phi'_1)$.

The other connectives $\vee, \to, \exists$ are expressed through $\wedge, \neg, \forall$ in the usual way. Below we discuss structures of the form $\mathbf{w}$ related to words $w$ as specified in Section 2. When we want to stress the signature in which we consider the structure, we use notation like $(\mathbf{w}; \sigma_A)$. For $i_0, \ldots, i_k \leq |w|$, $(\mathbf{w}; \sigma_A, i_0, \ldots, i_k)$ denotes the usual enrichment of the structure $(\mathbf{w}; \sigma_A)$ by constants $i_j$. From Lemma 8 we easily get

**Lemma 9.**
*(i) Let* $\phi = \phi(x_0, \ldots, x_k)$ *be a formula of signature* $\sigma_A$, $w \in A^+$ *and* $i_0, \ldots, i_k \leq |w|$. *Then we have* $(\mathbf{w}; \sigma_a, i_0, \ldots, i_k) \models \phi(x_0, \ldots, x_k)$ *iff* $(\mathbf{f(w)}; \sigma', i'_0, \ldots, i'_k) \models \phi'(x_0, \ldots, x_k)$.

*(ii)* *For any* $w \in A^+$ *and any sentence* $\phi$ *of* $\sigma_A$*, we have* $(\mathbf{w};\sigma_A) \models \phi$ *iff* $(\mathbf{f}(\mathbf{w});\sigma') \models \phi'$.

Let $\Phi$ be the set of all sentences of signature $\sigma_A$. For $\phi, \psi \in \Phi$, let $L_\phi = \{w \in A^+ | \mathbf{w} \models \phi\}$ and let $\phi \equiv \psi$ iff $L_\phi = L_\psi$. Let $B$ be the quotient of the structure $(\Phi; \wedge, \vee, \neg, true, false)$ under the congruence relation $\equiv$. As is well–known, $B$ is a boolean algebra; abusing (and simplifying) notation, we denote elements of $B$ as corresponding sentences. For $n < \omega$, let $L_n$ be the subset of $B$ corresponding to the set of $\Sigma_{n+1}$-sentences; then $L = \{L_n\}$ is a base in $B$. When we want to stress the alphabet, we denote this base by $L_A$.

The construction from preceding paragraph applies also to sentences of $\sigma'_A$ in place of $\sigma_A$ (as well as to sentences of any other signature). We denote the corresponding base as $L' = L'_A$. The next lemma follows from Lemma 1.

**Lemma 10.** *Let* $t \in T$ *and* $A$ *be any alphabet,* $A \subseteq \omega$.

*(i)* $L \in t(A^+SH)$ *iff* $L = L_\phi$ *for some* $\phi \in t(L_A)$*, and similarly for* $A^+BH$ *and for the base* $L'_A$.
*(ii)* *If* $\phi \in t(L_A)$ *then* $\phi' \in t(L'_{\{0,1\}})$.

Now we are able to give a proof of the theorem.

**Proof of Theorem 4.** The inclusion $Leaf(t(A^+BH)) \subseteq t(PH)$ was already noticed above. For the converse, it clearly suffices to check that $t(PH) \subseteq Leaf(t(\{0,1\}^+BH))$. By Theorem 1 and Lemma 6, it suffices to check the inclusion $Leaf(t(A^+SH)) \subseteq Leaf(t(\{0,1\}^+BH))$, for any alphabet $A \subseteq \omega$. So assume that $K \in Leaf(t(A^+SH))$. Then $K = M^{-1}(L)$ for a suitable machine $M$ and for some $L \in t(A^+SH)$. By Lemma 10, $L = L_\phi$ for some $\phi \in t(L_A)$. Again by Lemma 5.5, $\phi' \in t(L'_{\{0,1\}})$ and $L_{\phi'} \in t(\{0,1\}^+BH)$. Hence, it remains to check that $M^{-1}(L_\phi) \in Leaf(L_{\phi'})$. In other words, it remains to find a suitable machine $M_1$ satisfying $M^{-1}(L_\phi) = M^{-1}(L_{\phi'})$.

Let $M_1$ on the input $x$ behaves exactly as $M$ on input $x$, with the only exception that at the end of any computation path, whenever $M$ prints $a \in A$, the machine $M_1$ "prints" the word $f(a) \in \{0,1\}^+$ (more exactly, $M_1$ branches nondeterministically to $|f(a)|$ paths and on these paths prints subsequently bits of the word $f(a)$). In this way we get $M_1(x) = f(M(x))$. By Lemma 9, $M(x) \models \phi$ iff $M_1(x) \models \phi'$. In other words, $x \in M^{-1}(L_\phi)$ iff $x \in M_1^{-1}(L_{\phi'})$, for any $x \in X^*$. Hence, $M^{-1}(L_\phi) = M^{-1}(L_{\phi'})$ completing the proof of the theorem.

As in Section 4, we automatically get

**Corollary 1.** *For any* $t \in T$ *there exists a language* $L \in t((\{0,1\}^*BH))$ *satisfying* $Leaf(L) = t(PH)$.

## 6 Fine Hierarchy

In two preceeding sections we have described the situation with the typed boolean hierarchy rather comprehensively. Here we discuss similar questions for the fine hierarchy. The general question is to understand the relationships between classes $Leaf(S_\alpha(A^+SH))$, $Leaf(S_\alpha(A^+BH))$ and $S_\alpha(PH)$, for any $\alpha < \varepsilon_0$. We give some partial information relevant to this question.

The proof of the next fact is strightforward.

**Proposition 1.** *For any $\alpha < \varepsilon_0$ and any alphabet $A$, $Leaf(S_\alpha(A^+SH)) \subseteq Leaf(S_\alpha(A^+BH)) \subseteq S_\alpha(PH)$.*

Unfortunately, till now we were unable to prove the remaining inclusion $S_\alpha(PH) \subseteq Leaf(\cup_A A^+S_\alpha(SH))$. The problem is that the fine hierarchy is defined in terms of values of boolean terms, values of whose variables satisfy some constraints (see Section 2). It is not clear how to preserve those constraints under transfer to another hierarchy.

The next result, which is reminscent of Theorem 4 and which is proved in the same way, shows that for the Brzozowski case we again may "reduce" alphabets.

**Proposition 2.** *For any $\alpha < \varepsilon_0$ and any alphabet $A$, $Leaf(S_\alpha(A^+SH)) \subseteq Leaf(S_\alpha(\{0,1\}^+BH))$.*

## 7 Examples and Discussion

The typed boolean hierarchy and the fine hierarchy are rather abstract and rich structures. In this section we formulate and discuss some interesting particular cases.

Let again $B = (B; \cup, \cap, \bar{}, 0, 1)$ be a b.a. Define an operation of addition of classes $X, Y \subseteq B$ by the equali

ty $X + Y = \{x \Delta y | x \in X, y \in Y\}$, where $x \Delta y$ is the symmetric difference of $x$ and $y$. This operation is induced by the operation of addition modulo 2, hence it is associative and commutative and we may a fortiori freely use expressions like $X_0 + \cdots + X_n$.

Let $L$ be a sublattice of $(B; \cup, \cap, 0, 1)$. For any $k > 0$, let $D_k = L + \cdots + L$ ($k$ summonds in the righthand side). In [KSW86] it was shown that the sequence $\{D_k(L)\}$ coincides with the well–known boolean (or difference) hierarchy over $L$.

Taking now $NP$ in place of $L$, one gets the boolean hiearachy over $NP$, a rather popular object in complexity theory introduced in [WW85]. More generally, one could consider the boolean hierarchy $\{D_k(\Sigma_n^p)\}$ over the $n$-th level of the polynomial hierarchy. It is natural to ask: is there a natural description of these classes in terms of leaf languages? To answer the question, one have only to note that for any base $L$ in $B$ the boolean hierarchy over any class $L_n$ is a fragment of the typed boolean hierarchy (as well as of the fine hierarchy), see [Se94]. E.g., we could consider the boolean hierarchy over any class $\mathcal{B}_n = \{0,1\}^+\mathcal{B}_n$ of the Brzozowski hierarchy and immediately get

**Corollary 2.** *For all $n, k > 0$, $Leaf(D_k(\mathcal{B}_n)) = D_k(\Sigma_n^p)$.*

For the case of the boolean hierarchy over $NP$ and the boolean hierarchy over $\mathcal{S}_1$ the corresponding result was earlier obtained in [SW98].

Another interesting example is the plus–hierarchy introduced implicitly in [Se94, Se95] and explicitely in [Se94a, Se99]. The levels of the plus–hierarchy over any base $L$ are obtained when one applies the operation $+$ introduced above to the levels $L_n$, for all $n < \omega$. Any finite nonempty string $\sigma = (n_0, \ldots, n_k)$ of natural numbers satisfying $n_0 \geq \cdots \geq n_k$ defines the level $P_\sigma(L) = L_{n_0} + \cdots + L_{n_k}$ of the plus–hierarchy over $L$. One easily checks that in this way we get actually all the levels of the plus–hierarchy, that the finite sequences specified above are ordered lexicographically with the order type $\omega^\omega$, and that $P_\sigma \cup co(P_\sigma) \subseteq P_\tau$ whenever $\sigma < \tau$.

The plus–hierarchy is again a fragment of the typed boolean hierarchy, so we get e.g.

**Corollary 3.** *For any sequence $\sigma$ as above, $Leaf(P_\sigma(\{0,1\}^+BH)) = P_\sigma(PH)$.*

What is the aim of proving results of this type? In our opinion, the existence of nontrivial connections between automata–theoretic and complexity–theoretic hierarchies is interesting in its own right and is somewhat unexpected. Maybe, some time results of this type may be even of use. E.g., assume for a moment that the Brzozowski hierarchy collapses. By the Theorem of Burtschik and Vollmer, the polynomial hierarchy would then collapse too. This is of course unlikely, hence the Brzozowski hierarchy should not collapse. And this is actually a proven fact of the automata theory [BK78]. From [Ka85] we know that the boolean hierarchy over any $\Sigma_n^p$ does not collapse, provided that $PH$ does not collapse. Hence, the boolean hierarchy over any level of $BH$ also should not collapse. And this was indeed proved in [Sh98,SS00], though the proofs are rather involved.

Actually, we can even deduce results of this type from some known facts of complexity theory. As an example consider the following generalization of results from [Sh98, SS00].

**Corollary 4.** *The plus–hierarchy over $\{0,1\}^+BH$ does not collapse.*

**Proof.** Suppose the contrary. Then, by relativization of Corollary 3, the relativization (with any oracle) of the plus–hierarchy over $PH$ would collapse. By [Se94, Se94a, Se99], the relativization of $PH$ (with any oracle) would collapse too, contradicting to a well–known result of complexity theory.

**Acknowledgements.** This work was started at RWTH Aachen in spring of 1999 and finished 2 years later at the University of Würzburg. I am grateful to Wolfgang Thomas and Klaus Wagner for hospitality and for making those visits possible. I thank also both of them, as well as Heribert Vollmer, for helpfull discussions.

## References

[BDG88] J. L. Balcázar, J. Díaz and J. Gabarró. *Structural Complexity I*, volume 11 of *EATCS Monographs on Theoretical Computer Science*. Springer-Verlag, 1988.

[BDG90] J. L. Balcázar, J. Díaz and J. Gabarró. *Structural Complexity II*, volume 11 of *EATCS Monographs on Theoretical Computer Science*. Springer-Verlag, 1990.

[BCS92] D. P. Bovet, P. Crescenzi and R. Silvestri. A uniform approach to define complexity classes. *Theoret. Comp. Sci*, 104 (1992), 263—283.

[BK78] J. A. Brzozowski and R Knast. The dot-depth hierarchy of star–free languages is infinite. *J. Comp. Systems Sci.*, 16 (1978), 37—55.

[BV98] H.-J. Burtschick and H. Vollmer. Lindström Quatifiers and Leaf Language Definability. *Int. J. of Foundations of Computer Science*, 9 (1998), 277—294.

[HL+93] U. Hertrampf, C. Lautemann, T. Schwentick, H. Vollmer and K. W. Wagner. On the power of polynomial time bit-reductions, *Proc. 8th Structure in Complexity Theory*, 1993, 200—207.

[KM67] K. Kuratowski and A. Mostowski. *Set Theory*. North Holland, 1967.

[KSW86] J. Köbler, U. Shöning and K.W. Wagner: The difference and truth-table hierarchies for NP. Dep. of Informatics, Koblenz. Preprint 7 (1986).

[MP71] R. McNaughton and S. Papert. *Counter–free automata*. MIT Press, Cambridge, Massachusets, 1971.

[PP86] D. Perrin and J.-E. Pin. First order logic and star–free sets. *J. Comp. and Syst. Sci.*, 32 (1986), 393—406.

[PW97] J.-E. Pin and P. Weil. Polynomial closure and unambiguous product. *Theory of Computing Systems*, 30 (1997), 383—422.

[Se94] V. L. Selivanov. Two refinements of the polynomial hierarchy. In: Proc. of Symposium on Theor. Aspects of Computer Science STACS–94, *Lecture Notes in Computer Science*, v. 775. Springer: Berlin 1994, p. 439—448.

[Se94] V. L. Selivanov. Refining the polynomial hierarchy, Preprint No 9, the University of Heidelberg, Chair of Mathematical Logic, 1994, 20 p.

[Se95] V. L. Selivanov. Fine hierarchies and Boolean terms. *Journal of Symbolic Logic*, 60 (1995), p. 289—317.

[Se99] V. L. Selivanov. Refining the polynomial hierarchy. *Algebra and Logic*, 38 (1999), 456—475 (Russian, there is an English translation).

[Se01] V. L. Selivanov. A logical approach to decidability of hierarchies of regular star-free languages. In: Proc. of 18-th Int. Symposium on Theor. Aspects of Computer Science STACS-2001 in Dresden, Germany, *Lecture Notes in Computer Science*, v. 2010. Berlin: Springer, 2001, 539–550.

[SS00] V. L. Selivanov and A. G. Shukin. On hierarchies of regular star-free languages (in Russian). Preprint 69 of A.P. Ershov Institute of Informatics Systems, 2000, 28 p.

[Sh98] A. G. Shukin. Difference hierarchies of regular languages. *Comp. Systems*, Novosibirsk, 161 (1998), 141—155 (in Russian).

[SW98] H. Schmitz and K. W Wagner. The Boolean hierarchy over level 1/2 of the Sraubing–Therien hierarchy, Technical Report 201, Inst. für Informatik, Univ. Würzburg (available at http://www.informatik.uni-wuerzburg.de).

[T82] W. Thomas. Classifying regular events in symbolic logic. *J. Comp. and Syst. Sci.*,25 (1982), 360—376.

[V93] N. K. Vereshchagin. Relativizable and non-relativizable theorems in the polynomial theory of algorithms. *Izvestiya Rossiiskoi Akademii Nauk*, 57 (1993), 51—90 (in Russian).

[WW85] G. Wechsung and K. Wagner. On the Boolean closure of NP. In: *Proceedings of the 1985 Int. Conf. on Fundamentals of Computation theory*, v.199 of *Lecture Notes in Computer Science*, p.485—493. Springer–Verlag, 1985.

# Polynomial Time Algorithms for Finding Unordered Tree Patterns with Internal Variables

Takayoshi Shoudai[1], Tomoyuki Uchida[2], and Tetsuhiro Miyahara[2]

[1] Department of Informatics, Kyushu University, Kasuga 816-8580, Japan
shoudai@i.kyushu-u.ac.jp
[2] Faculty of Information Sciences,
Hiroshima City University, Hiroshima 731-3194, Japan
{uchida@cs,miyahara@its}.hiroshima-cu.ac.jp

**Abstract.** Many documents such as Web documents or XML files have tree structures. A term tree is an unordered tree pattern consisting of internal variables and tree structures. In order to extract meaningful and hidden knowledge from such tree structured documents, we consider a minimal language (MINL) problem for term trees. The MINL problem for term trees is to find a term tree $t$ such that the language generated by $t$ is minimal among languages, generated by term trees, which contain all given tree structured data. Firstly, we show that the MINL problem for regular term trees is computable in polynomial time if the number of edge labels is infinite. Next, we show that the MINL problems with optimizing the size of an output term tree are NP-complete. Finally, in order to show that our polynomial time algorithm for the MINL problem can be applied to data mining from real-world Web documents, we show that regular term tree languages are polynomial time inductively inferable from positive data if the number of edge labels is infinite.

## 1 Introduction

Many documents such as Web documents or XML files have tree structures. In order to extract meaningful and hidden knowledge from such documents, we need tree structured patterns which can explain them. As tree structured patterns, a tree pattern [1,3,4], a type of objects [9] and a tree-expression pattern [12] were proposed. In [5,11], we presented the concept of term trees as a graph pattern suited for representing unordered tree structured data. A term tree is an unordered tree pattern which consists of internal variables and tree structures. A term tree is different from the other representations proposed in [1,3,4,9,12] in that a term tree has internal structured variables which can be substituted by arbitrary trees. A term tree $t$ is said to be regular if the labels of all variables are different. In [7], we proved that the matching problem for an extended regular term tree and a standard tree is NP-complete. However, in [6], we showed that the matching problem for a regular term tree whose variables consist of two vertices is computable in polynomial time. Then in this paper, we consider only such a regular term tree. Since a variable can be replaced by any tree, overgeneralized

R. Freivalds (Ed.): FCT 2001, LNCS 2138, pp. 335–346, 2001.

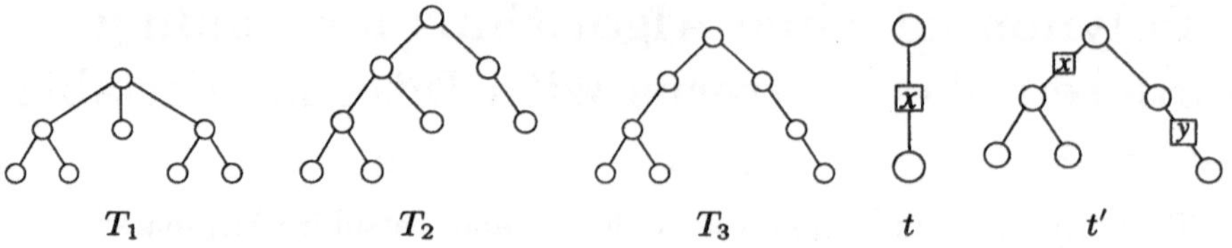


**Fig. 1.** A term tree $t$ and a term tree $t'$ as an overgeneralized term tree and one of the least generalized term trees explaining $T_1$, $T_2$ and $T_3$, respectively. A variable is represented by a box with lines to its elements. The label of a box is the variable label of the variable.

patterns explaining all given data are meaningless. Then the purpose of this work is to find one of the least generalized term trees explaining tree structured data. In Fig. 1, we give examples of term trees $t$ and $t'$ which can explain all trees $T_1$, $T_2$ and $T_3$. The term tree $t$ is an overgeneralized term tree which is meaningless. But the term tree $t'$ is one of the least generalized term trees.

The concept represented by a term tree, which is called a term tree language, is the set of all trees obtained by replacing all variables by arbitrary trees. The minimal language (MINL) problem is the problem of finding a term tree whose term tree language is minimal among term tree languages containing all given trees. In [5,11], for a special type of regular term trees, which are called a regular term caterpillar, we showed that the MINL problem for regular term caterpillars is computable in polynomial time. In this paper, we show that the MINL problem for regular term trees is computable in polynomial time if the number of edge labels is infinite. Moreover, we consider the following two problems. Firstly, MINL with Variable-size Minimization is the problem of finding a term tree $t$ such that the term tree language of $t$ is minimal and the number of variables in $t$ is minimum. Secondly, MINL with Tree-size Maximization is the problem of finding a term tree $t$ such that the term tree language of $t$ is minimal and the number of vertices in $t$ is maximum. Then we prove that the both two problems are NP-complete. These results show the hardness of finding the optimum regular term tree representing all given data.

In order to show that our polynomial time algorithm for the MINL problem can be applied to data mining from real-world Web documents, we show that regular term tree languages are polynomial time inductively inferable from positive data if the number of edge labels is infinite. In [8], we proposed a tag tree pattern which is a special type of a regular term tree and is suited for expressing structures of XML documents, and presented an algorithm for generating all maximally frequent tag tree patterns. The results of this paper give a theoretical foundation of the result in [8].

This paper is organized as follows. In Section 2, we give the notion of a term tree as a tree structured pattern. Also we formally define the MINL problem for regular term trees. In Section 3, we give a polynomial time algorithm solving the MINL problem for regular term trees if the number of edge labels is infinite. And we show the hardness of finding the optimal term tree which explaining all given data in Section 4. We show that regular term tree languages are polynomial time inductively inferable from positive data in Section 5.

## 2 Preliminaries – Term Trees as Tree Structured Patterns

Let $T = (V_T, E_T)$ be a rooted unordered tree (or simply a tree) with a set $V_T$ of vertices, a set $E_T$ of edges, and an edge labeling. A *variable* in $T$ is a list $[u, u']$ of two distinct vertices $u$ and $u'$ in $V_T$. A label of a variable is called a *variable label.* $\Lambda$ and $X$ denote a set of edge labels and a set of variable labels, respectively, where $\Lambda \cap X = \phi$. For a set $S$, the number of elements in $S$ is denoted by $|S|$.

**Definition 1.** A triplet $g = (V_g, E_g, H_g)$ is called a *rooted term tree* (or simply a *term tree*) if $H_g$ is a finite set of variables such that for any $[u, u'] \in H_g$, $[u', u]$ is not in $H_g$, and the graph $(V_g, E_g \cup E'_g)$ is a tree where $E'_g = \{\{u, v\} \mid [u, v] \in H_g\}$. A term tree $g$ is called *regular* if all variables in $H_g$ have mutually distinct variable labels in $X$. In particular, a term tree with no variable is called a *ground term tree* and considered to be a standard tree. $\mathcal{RTT}$ and $\mathcal{GTT}$ denote the set of all regular term trees and the set of all ground term trees, respectively.

For a term tree $f$ and its vertices $v_1$ and $v_i$, a *path* from $v_1$ to $v_i$ is a sequence $v_1, v_2, \ldots, v_i$ of distinct vertices of $f$ such that for $1 \leq j < i$, there exists an edge or a variable which consists of $v_j$ and $v_{j+1}$. If there is an edge or a variable which consists of $v$ and $v'$ such that $v$ lies on the path from the root of $f$ to $v'$, then $v$ is said to be the *parent* of $v'$ and $v'$ is a *child* of $v$. Without loss of generality, we assume that $v'$ is a child of $v$ if $[v, v']$ is a variable in $f$.

Let $f = (V_f, E_f, H_f)$ and $g = (V_g, E_g, H_g)$ be regular term trees. We say that $f$ and $g$ are *isomorphic*, denoted by $f \equiv g$, if there is a bijection $\varphi$ from $V_f$ to $V_g$ such that (i) the root of $f$ is mapped to the root of $g$ by $\varphi$, (ii) $\{u, v\} \in E_f$ if and only if $\{\varphi(u), \varphi(v)\} \in E_g$ and the two edges have the same edge label, and (iii) $[u, v] \in H_f$ if and only if $[\varphi(u), \varphi(v)] \in H_g$. Two isomorphic regular term trees are considered to be identical.

Let $f$ and $g$ be term trees with at least two vertices. Let $\sigma = [u, u']$ be a list consisting of the root $u$ of $g$ and another vertex $u'$ in $g$. The form $x := [g, \sigma]$ is called a *binding* for $x$. A new term tree $f\{x := [g, \sigma]\}$ is obtained by applying the binding $x := [g, \sigma]$ to $f$ in the following way: Let $e_1 = [v_1, v'_1], \ldots, e_m = [v_m, v'_m]$ be the variables in $f$ with the variable label $x$. Let $g_1, \ldots, g_m$ be $m$ copies of $g$ and $u_i, u'_i$ the vertices of $g_i$ corresponding to $u, u'$ of $g$, respectively. For each variable $e_i = [v_i, v'_i]$, we attach $g_i$ to $f$ by removing the variable $e_i$ from $H_f$ and by identifying the vertices $v_i, v'_i$ with the vertices $u_i, u'_i$ of $g_i$. We define the root of the resulting term tree as the root of $f$. A *substitution* $\theta$ is a finite collection of bindings $\{x_1 := [g_1, \sigma_1], \cdots, x_n := [g_n, \sigma_n]\}$, where $x_i$'s are mutually distinct variable labels in $X$. The term tree $f\theta$, called the *instance* of $f$ by $\theta$, is obtained by applying the all bindings $x_i := [g_i, \sigma_i]$ on $f$ simultaneously. For term trees $f$ and $g$, if there exists a substitution $\theta$ such that $f \equiv g\theta$, we write $f \preceq g$. Especially we write $f \prec g$ if $f \preceq g$ and $g \not\preceq f$. In Fig. 2 we give examples of a regular term tree, a substitution and an instance.

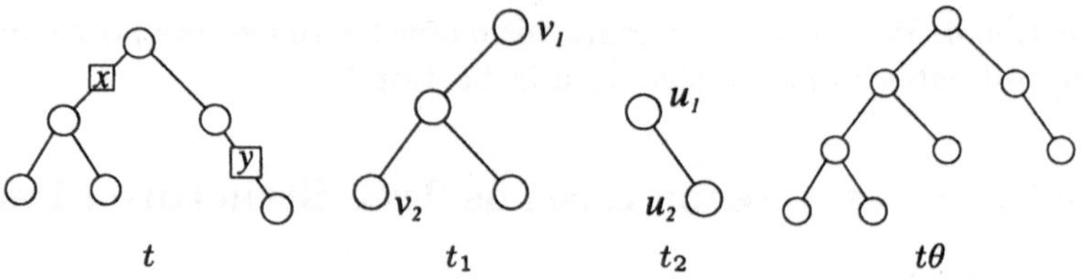


**Fig. 2.** Ground term trees $t_1$ and $t_2$, and an instance $t\theta$ which is obtained by applying a substitution $\theta = \{x := [t_1, [v_1, v_2]], y := [t_2, [u_1, u_2]]\}$ to the regular term tree $t$. A variable is represented by a box with lines to its elements. The label of a box is the variable label of the variable.

For a (regular) term tree $g$, the *(regular) term tree language* $L(g)$ of $g$ is defined as $L(g) = \{h \in \mathcal{GTT} \mid h \equiv g\theta \text{ for a substitution } \theta\}$. The class $\mathcal{RTTL}$ of all regular term tree languages is defined as $\mathcal{RTTL} = \{L(g) \mid g \in \mathcal{RTT}\}$. Let $S$ be a nonempty finite subset of $\mathcal{GTT}$ and $r$ be a regular term tree. A regular term tree language $L(r)$ is *minimal for* $(S,\mathcal{RTT})$ if (i) $S \subseteq L(r)$ and (ii) $L(s) \subsetneq L(r)$ implies $S \not\subseteq L(s)$ for any $s \in \mathcal{RTT}$.

**Minimal Language (MINL) Problem for $\mathcal{RTT}$**
**Instance**: A nonempty finite subset $S$ of $\mathcal{GTT}$.
**Question**: Find a regular term tree $r$ such that $L(r)$ is minimal for $(S,\mathcal{RTT})$.

## 3 Polynomial Time Algorithm for Finding Minimal Regular Term Languages

Since solving the minimal language problem for $\mathcal{RTT}$ is essential to the learnability of regular term tree languages, we give the following theorem.

**Theorem 1.** *The minimal language problem for $\mathcal{RTT}$ with infinite edge labels is computable in polynomial time.*

*Proof.* We show that the procedure *MINL*($S$) (Fig. 3) works correctly for finding a regular term tree $r$ such that the language $L(r)$ is minimal for $(S, \mathcal{RTT})$. Let $f = (V_f, E_f, H_f)$ and $g = (V_g, E_g, H_g)$ be term trees. We write $h \approx g$ if there exists a bijection $\xi : V_h \to V_g$ such that for $u, v \in V_h$, $\{u, v\} \in E_h$ or $[u, v] \in H_h$ if and only if $\{\xi(u), \xi(v)\} \in E_g$ or $[\xi(u), \xi(v)] \in H_g$. For $\mathcal{RTT}$ with infinite edge labels, the following two claims hold:

*Claim 1.* For any $g, h \in \mathcal{RTT}$ with $h \approx g$, $h \preceq g$ if and only if $L(h) \subseteq L(g)$.

*Proof of Claim 1.* If $h \preceq g$, we have $L(h) \subseteq L(g)$ straightforwardly. Then we show that $h \preceq g$ if $L(h) \subseteq L(g)$. Since $h \approx g$, there exists a bijection $\xi$ such that for $u, v \in V_h$, $\{u, v\} \in E_h$ or $[u, v] \in H_h$ if and only if $\{\xi(u), \xi(v)\} \in E_g$ or $[\xi(u), \xi(v)] \in H_g$. If there does not exist a bijection $\xi$ such that $[\xi(u), \xi(v)]$ is in $H_g$ for all $[u, v] \in H_h$, the ground term tree which is obtained by replacing all

```
Procedure MINL(S);
Input:  a nonempty finite set S of ground term trees.
Output: a regular term tree g such that the language L(g) is minimal for (S, RTT).
begin
  g := Basic-Tree(S);
  foreach variable [u, v] ∈ H_g do
    foreach edge label c which appears in S do begin
      let g' be a term tree which is obtained from g
        by replacing variable [u, v] with an edge labeled with c;
      if S ⊆ L(g') then begin g := g'; break end
    end
end;
```

```
Procedure Basic-Tree(S);
begin // Each variable is assumed to be labeled with a distinct variable label.
  d := 0; g := ({r}, ∅, ∅);
  g := breadth-expansion(r, g, S);
  max-depth :=the maximum depth of the trees in S;
  d := d + 1;
  while d ≤ max-depth − 1 do begin
    v :=a vertex at depth d which is not yet visited;
    g :=breadth-expansion(v, g, S);
    while there exists a sibling of v which is not yet visited do begin
      Let v' be a sibling of v which is not yet visited;
      g :=breadth-expansion(v', g, S)
    end;
    d := d + 1
  end;
  return g
end;
```

```
Procedure breadth-expansion(v, g, S);
begin
  g' :=depth-expansion(v, g, S);
  while g ≠ g' do begin
    g := g';
    g' :=depth-expansion(v, g, S)
  end;
  return g
end;
```

```
Procedure depth-expansion(v, g, S);
begin
  Let g be (V_g, ∅, H_g);
  Let v' be a new vertex and
  [v, v'] a new variable;
  g' := (V_g ∪ {v'}, ∅, H_g ∪ {[v, v']});
  while S ⊆ L(g') do begin
    g := g'; v := v';
    Let v' be a new vertex and
    [v, v'] a new variable;
    g' := (V_g ∪ {v'}, ∅, H_g ∪ {[v, v']})
  end;
  return g
end;
```

**Fig. 3.** *MINL*($S$): An algorithm for finding a regular term tree $r$ such that the language $L(r)$ is minimal for $(S, \mathcal{RTT})$.

variables in $h$ with an edge label which does not appear in $g$ is not in $L(g)$. Then $[\xi(u), \xi(v)] \in H_g$ for all $[u, v] \in H_h$. Therefore $h \preceq g$. (*End of Proof of Claim 1*)

By Claim 1 we can replace the inclusion relation $\subseteq$ on $\mathcal{RTTL}$ with the relation $\preceq$ on $\mathcal{RTT}$.

*Claim 2.* Let $g = (V_g, E_g, H_g)$ be an output regular term tree by the procedure *MINL*, given a nonempty finite set $S$ of ground term trees. If there exists a regular term tree $h$ with $S \subseteq L(h) \subseteq L(g)$, then $h \approx g$.

*Proof of Claim 2.* Let $g'$ be the regular term tree which is obtained by *Basic-Tree*($S$). Then $L(h) \subseteq L(g) \subseteq L(g')$ and $g \approx g'$. Let $h'$ be the regular term tree which is obtained by replacing all edges in $h$ with variables. Then $h \approx h'$ and $L(h) \subseteq L(h')$. Let $\theta$ be a substitution which realizes $h \equiv g'\theta$ and $\theta'$ a substitution which obtained by replacing all edges appearing in $\theta$ with variables. Then $h' \equiv g'\theta'$. Since $S \subseteq L(h) \subseteq L(h')$, $S \subseteq L(g'\theta')$. Since *Basic-Tree*($S$) generates a regular term tree whose language is minimal for $(S, \{g \in \mathcal{RTT} \mid g \text{ has no edge}\})$, $g'\theta' \equiv g'$. Therefore $h' \equiv g'$, then $h \approx g$. (*End of Proof of Claim 2*)

Suppose that there exists a regular term tree $h = (V_h, E_h, H_h)$ such that $S \subseteq L(h) \subsetneq L(g)$. From the above two claims, we obtain $h \prec g$ and $h \approx g$. There exist a variable $[u, v] \in H_g$ labeled with $x$ and an edge label $a$ such that $h \preceq g\{x := [T_a, [u', v']]\}$ where $T_a$ is a tree consisting of an edge $\{u', v'\}$ labeled with $a$. We denote by $f$ the regular term tree which is obtained in the procedure *MINL* before trying to replace the variable $[u, v]$ with an edge labeled with $a$. Then we have that $S \not\subseteq L(f\{x := [T_a, [u', v']]\})$ and there exists a substitution $\theta$ with $g \equiv f\theta$. From $h \preceq g\{x := [T_a, [u', v']]\} \equiv f\theta\{x := [T_a, [u', v']]\} \equiv f\{x := [T_a, [u', v']]\}\theta$, we have $h \preceq f\{x := [T_a, [u', v']]\}$. Thus $S \subseteq L(h) \subseteq L(f\{x := [T_a, [u', v']]\})$. This contradicts $S \not\subseteq L(f\{x := [T_a, [u', v']]\})$.

In [6], we gave an algorithm for deciding whether or not a given ground term tree $T$ is a member of $L(g)$ for a given regular term tree $g$. The algorithm runs in $O(n^2 N^{3.5})$ time where $n$ and $N$ are the number of vertices in $g$ and $T$ respectively. Let $N_{max}$ and $N_{min}$ be the maximum and minimum numbers of vertices of ground term trees in $S$ respectively. Since the final regular term tree $g$ is no larger than the smallest ground term tree in $S$, the algorithm *MINL*($S$) checks at most $O(N_{min})$ time whether or not $S \subseteq L(g)$. Therefore the algorithm runs in $O(N_{min}^3 N_{max}^{3.5} |S|)$ time. □

## 4 Hardness Results of Finding Regular Term Trees of Minimal Language

In Section 3, we have given a polynomial time algorithm for finding *a* regular term tree of minimal language from a given sample. In this section, we discuss MINL problems with optimizing the size of an output regular term tree.

**MINL with Variable-size Minimization**
**Instance**: A nonempty finite subset $S$ of $\mathcal{GTT}$ and a positive integer $K$.

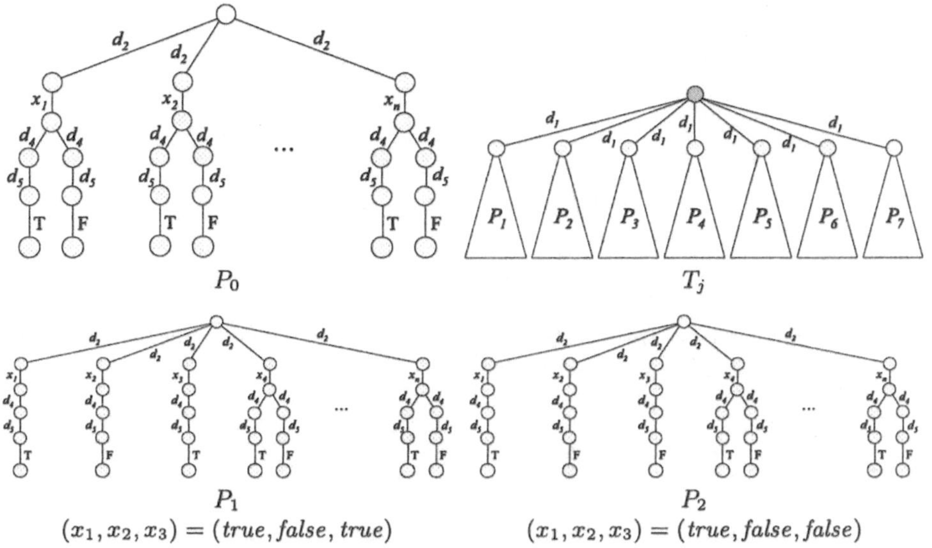


**Fig. 4.** $T_j$ for a clause $c_j = \{x_1, \bar{x_2}, x_3\}$. $P_i$ ($1 \leq i \leq 7$) is constructed systematically by removing appropriate 3 branches labeled with T or F from $P_0$. We describe only $P_1$ and $P_2$ in this figure.

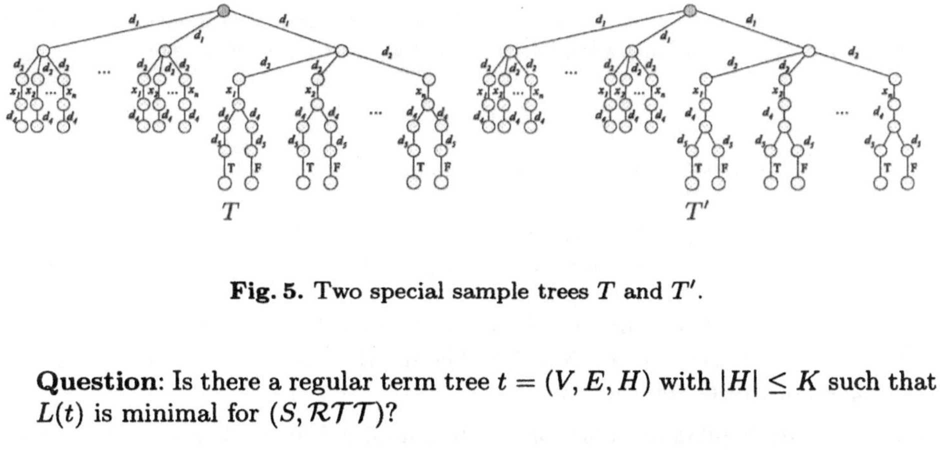


**Fig. 5.** Two special sample trees $T$ and $T'$.

**Question**: Is there a regular term tree $t = (V, E, H)$ with $|H| \leq K$ such that $L(t)$ is minimal for $(S, \mathcal{RTT})$?

**Theorem 2. MINL with Variable-size Minimization** *is NP-complete.*

*Proof.* Membership in NP is obvious. We transform 3-SAT to this problem. Let $U = \{x_1, \ldots, x_n\}$ be a set of variables and $C = \{c_1, \ldots, c_m\}$ be a collection of clauses over $U$ such that each clause $c_j$ ($1 \leq j \leq m$) has $|c_j| = 3$. We use symbols $\mathtt{T}, \mathtt{F}, d_1, d_2, d_4, d_5, x_1, \ldots, x_n$ as edge labels.

We construct trees $T_1, \ldots, T_m$ from $c_1, \ldots, c_m$. Let $P_0$ be the tree which is described in Fig. 4. For a clause $c_j$, which contains $x_{j_1}, x_{j_2}, x_{j_3}$ as positive or negative literals, we have the 7 truth assignments to $x_{j_1}, x_{j_2}, x_{j_3}$ which satisfy the clause $c_j$. For the $i$th truth assignment $(x_{j_1}, x_{j_2}, x_{j_3}) = (b_{i1}, b_{i2}, b_{i3})$ ($i =$

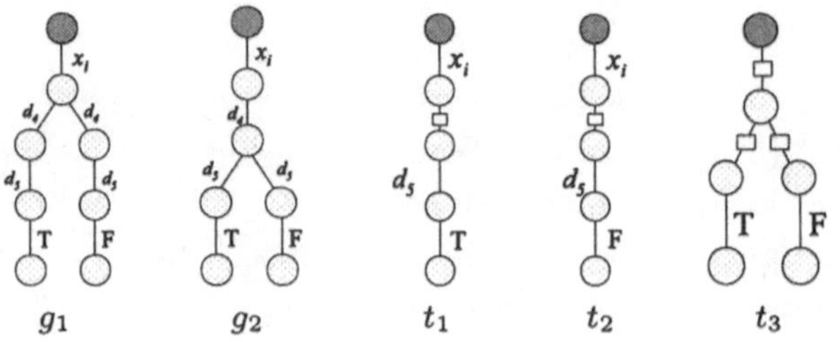


**Fig. 6.** The regular term trees $t_1, t_2, t_3$ which generate minimal languages for $\{g_1, g_2\}$ where both $g_1$ and $g_2$ have the same edge label $x_i$.

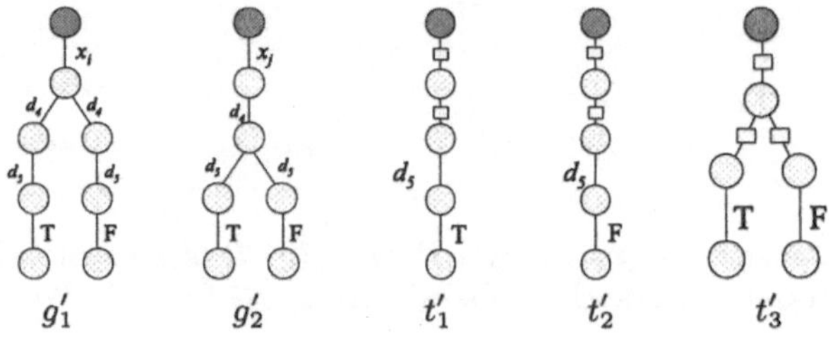


**Fig. 7.** The regular term trees $t_1', t_2', t_3'$ which generate minimal languages for $\{g_1', g_2'\}$ where $g_1$ and $g_2$ have distinct edge labels $x_i$ and $x_j$ $(i \neq j)$, respectively.

$1, 2, \ldots, 7)$, we construct $P_i$ by removing the branches which are labeled with $\bar{b_{i1}}, \bar{b_{i2}}, \bar{b_{i3}}$ from the subtrees corresponding to $x_{j_1}, x_{j_2}, x_{j_3}$ of $P_0$, respectively. For example, for a clause $\{x_1, \bar{x_2}, x_3\}$ the tree $P_1$ in Fig. 4 shows an assignment $x_1 = true, x_2 = false, x_3 = true$ and the tree $P_2$ shows $x_1 = true, x_2 = false, x_3 = false$. We also construct two special trees $T$ and $T'$ (Fig. 5). $T$ and $T'$ have 7 subtrees like $T_j$. Only one subtree of them is distinct. Let $S = \{T_1, \ldots, T_m, T, T'\}$ be a sample set. Lastly we set $K = 7n$. The depth of a vertex $v$ is the length of the unique path from the root to $v$.

*Fact 1.* For any regular term tree $g$ which is minimal for $(S, \mathcal{RTT})$, (i) the root of $g$ has just 7 children which connect to the root by edges labeled with $d_1$, (ii) each vertex of depth 1 of $g$ has just $n$ children which connect to the parent by edges labeled with $d_2$, and (iii) each vertex of depth 2 of $g$ has just one child.

This fact means that any regular term tree $g$ which is minimal for $(S, \mathcal{RTT})$ has at least $7n$ variables each of which locates at each subtree rooted at a vertex of depth 3.

*Fact 2.* Let $g_1$ and $g_2$ be trees described in Fig. 6. There are only three regular term trees which are minimal for $(\{g_1, g_2\}, \mathcal{RTT})$. The three regular term trees are described in Fig. 6.

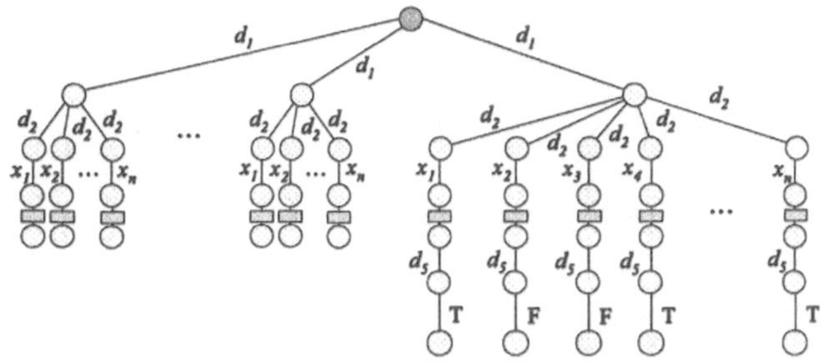


**Fig. 8.** The output regular term tree when there is a truth assignment which satisfies $C$ (Theorem 2).

*Fact 3.* Let $g'_1$ and $g'_2$ be trees described in Fig. 7. There are only three regular term trees which are minimal for $(\{g'_1, g'_2\}, \mathcal{RTT})$. The three regular term trees are described in Fig. 7.

From the above facts, if 3-SAT has a truth assignment which satisfies all clauses in $C$, there is a regular term tree $t = (V, E, H)$ with $|H| = 7n$ such that $L(t)$ is minimal for $(S, \mathcal{RTT})$ (Fig. 8). Conversely, if there is a regular term tree $t = (V, E, H)$ with $|H| = 7n$ such that $L(t)$ is minimal for $(S, \mathcal{RTT})$, the regular term tree is isomorphic to the one which is described in Fig. 8 by ignoring edge labels T and F. For $1 \leq i \leq n$, we assign *true* to $x_i$ if the nearest edge label from $x_i$ of type T,F is T, otherwise we assign *false* to $x_i$. Then this truth assignment satisfies $C$. □

Next we show that it is hard to compute the regular term tree of maximum tree-size which is minimal for $(S, \mathcal{RTT})$ for a given sample set $S$.

**MINL with Tree-size Maximization**
**Instance**: A nonempty finite subset $S$ of $\mathcal{GTT}$ and a positive integer $K$.
**Question**: Is there a regular term tree $t = (V, E, H)$ with $|V| \geq K$ such that $L(t)$ is minimal for $(S, \mathcal{RTT})$?

**Theorem 3. MINL with Tree-size Maximization** *is NP-complete.*

*Proof.* (Sketch) Membership in NP is obvious. We transform 3-SAT to this problem in a similar way to Theorem 2. We use only *blank* as an edge label. Each variable $x_i$ $(1 \leq i \leq n)$ transforms a tree of the form shown in Fig. 9. It is easy to see that the number of vertices of a regular term tree which matches the trees corresponding to $x_i$ and $x_j$ $(i \neq j)$ is at most $5(n+1)$.

We construct trees $T_1, \ldots, T_m$ from $c_1, \ldots, c_m$ in a similar way to Theorem 2 but we use subtrees $P_1, \ldots$ ($P_1$ is shown in Fig. 10) instead of $P_1, \ldots$ in Fig. 4. Moreover we construct one special tree $T$ (Fig. 10). Let $S = \{T_1, \ldots, T_m, T\}$ be a sample set of $\mathcal{GTT}$. Lastly we set $K = 35n^2 + 92n + 8$. Then, we can compute a regular term tree $t = (V, E, H)$ with $|H| = K$ such that $L(t)$ is minimal for $(S, \mathcal{RTT})$ (Fig. 11) if and only if 3-SAT has a truth assignment which satisfies all clauses in $C$. □

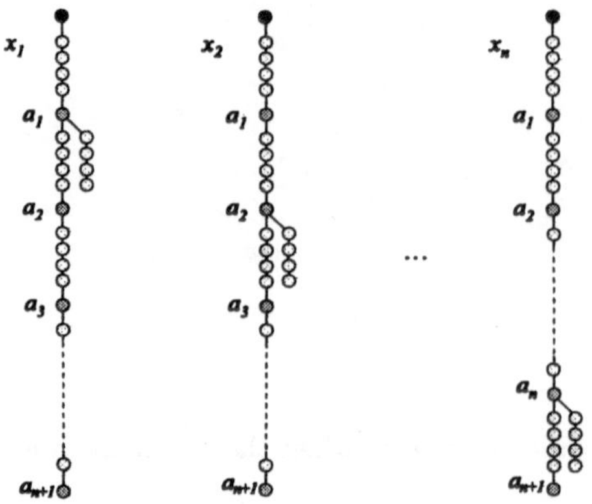


**Fig. 9.** Subtrees corresponding to $x_1, \ldots, x_n$.

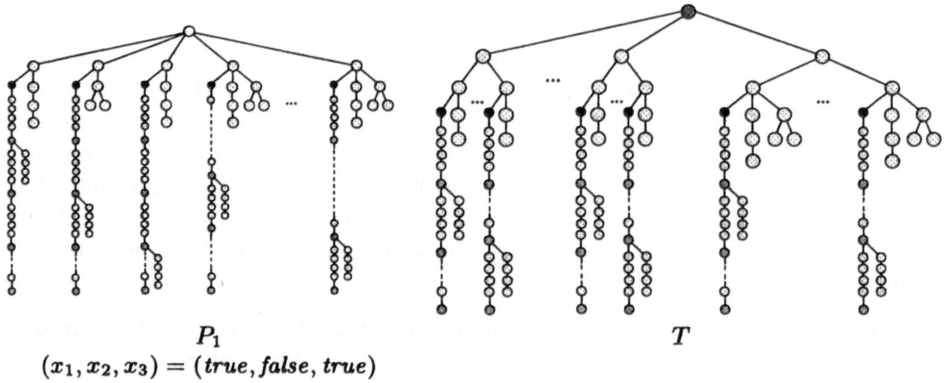


**Fig. 10.** A subtree $P_1$ corresponding to a truth assignment and a special sample tree $T$.

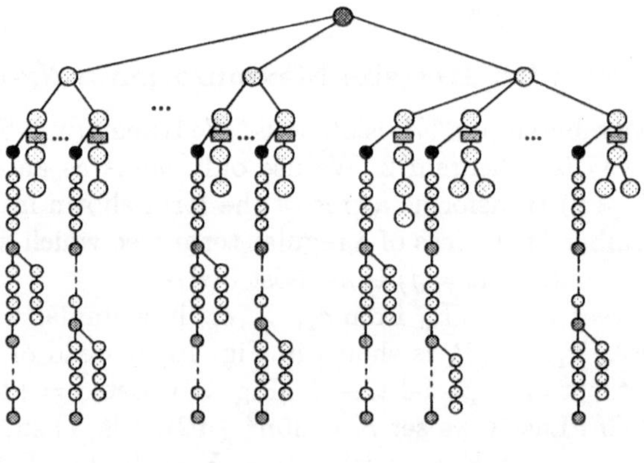

**Fig. 11.** The output regular term tree when there is a truth assignment which satisfies $C$ (Theorem 3).

# 5 Polynomial Time Inductive Inference of Regular Term Tree Languages from Positive Data

In this section, a *language* is a subset of $\mathcal{GTT}$. An *indexed family of recursive languages* (or simply a *class*) is a family of languages $\mathcal{C} = \{L_1, L_2, \ldots\}$ such that there is an effective procedure to decide whether $w \in L_i$ or not, given a tree $w$ and an index $i$. In our setting, an index is a term tree, and the language $L_i$ with an index $i$ is the term tree language $L(i)$ of a term tree $i$. A class $\mathcal{C}$ is said to *have finite thickness*, if for any nonempty finite set $T \subseteq \mathcal{GTT}$, the cardinality of $\{L \in \mathcal{C} \mid T \subseteq L\}$ is finite.

An *inductive inference machine* (IIM, for short) is an effective procedure which requests inputs from time to time and produces indices as hypotheses from time to time. A *positive presentation* $\sigma$ of a nonempty language $L$ is an infinite sequence $w_1, w_2, \cdots$ of trees in $\mathcal{GTT}$ such that $\{w_1, w_2, \cdots\} = L$. We denote by $\sigma[n]$ the $\sigma$'s initial segment of length $n \geq 0$. For an IIM and a finite sequence $\sigma[n] = w_1, w_2, \cdots, w_n$, we denote by $M(\sigma[n])$ the last hypothesis produced by $M$ which is successively presented $w_1, w_2, \cdots, w_n$ on its input requests. An IIM is said to *converge to an index* $r$ for a positive presentation $\sigma$, if there is an $n \geq 1$ such that for any $m \geq n$, $M(\sigma[m])$ is $r$. Let $\mathcal{C}$ be a class and $M$ be an IIM for $\mathcal{C}$. An IIM $M$ is said to *infer a class* $\mathcal{C}$ *in the limit from positive data*, if for any $L \in \mathcal{C}$ and any positive presentation $\sigma$ of $L$, $M$ converges to an index $r$ for $\sigma$ such that $L = L_r$. A class $\mathcal{C}$ is said to be *inferable in the limit from positive data*, if there is an IIM which infers $\mathcal{C}$ in the limit from positive data.

A class $\mathcal{C}$ is said to be *polynomial time inductively inferable from positive data* if there exists an IIM for $\mathcal{C}$ which outputs hypotheses in polynomial time with respect to the length of the input data read so far, and infers $\mathcal{C}$ in the limit from positive data.

**Theorem 4 ([2],[10]).** *Let $\mathcal{C}$ be a class. If $\mathcal{C}$ has finite thickness, and the membership problem and the minimal language problem for $\mathcal{C}$ are computable in polynomial time, then $\mathcal{C}$ is polynomial time inductively inferable from positive data.*

The membership problem for $\mathcal{RTTL}$ is, given a ground term tree $g$ and a regular term tree $t$, the problem of deciding whether or not $g \in L(t)$. We gave a polynomial time algorithm for the membership problem for $\mathcal{RTTL}$ [6]. Since the class $\mathcal{RTTL}$ has finite thickness [5], from Theorem 1,4, we have Theorem 5.

**Theorem 5.** *The class $\mathcal{RTTL}$ with infinite edge labels is polynomial time inductively inferable from positive data.*

# 6 Conclusions

The minimal language problem is a kernel problem in learning methods such as inductive inference. We have given a polynomial time algorithm for solving the minimal language problem for regular term trees. From the viewpoint of computational complexity, we have shown that it is hard to solve the minimal language problems with optimizing the size of an output regular term tree. By using our polynomial time algorithm, we have shown the regular term tree language with infinite edge labels is polynomial time inductively inferable from positive data.

We can give membership and MINL algorithms to the following two classes of regular term trees with no edge label: $\mathcal{RTTL}_1 = \{L(g) \mid g \in \mathcal{RTT}$ and the number of children of every vertex in $g$ is not $2\}$ and $\mathcal{RTTL}_2 = \{L(g) \mid g \in \mathcal{RTT}$ and (i) for every pair of vertices in $t$ whose degrees are more than 2, there exists a vertex of degree 2 on the path between them, and (ii) there is no vertex of degree 3 in $t$ such that the distance between any leaf and the vertex is at least $2\}$. Therefore the classes are polynomial time inductively inferable from positive data. But it is an open question whether or not the class of all regular term tree languages with no edge label is polynomial time inductively inferable from positive data.

## References


1. T. R. Amoth, P. Cull, and P. Tadepalli. Exact learning of unordered tree patterns from queries. *Proc. COLT-99, ACM Press*, pages 323–332, 1999.
2. D. Angluin. Finding patterns common to a set of strings. *Journal of Computer and System Science*, 21:46–62, 1980.
3. H. Arimura, T. Shinohara, and S. Otsuki. Polynomial time algorithm for finding finite unions of tree pattern languages. *Proc. NIL-91, Springer-Verlag, LNAI 659*, pages 118–131, 1993.
4. S. Goldman and S. Kwek. On learning unions of pattern languages and tree patterns. *Proc. ALT-99, Springer-Verlag, LNAI 1720*, 1720:347–363, 1999.
5. S. Matsumoto, Y. Hayashi, and T. Shoudai. Polynomial time inductive inference of regular term tree languages from positive data. *Proc. ALT-97, Springer-Verlag, LNAI 1316*, pages 212–227, 1997.
6. T. Miyahara, T. Shoudai, T. Uchida, T. Kuboyama, K. Takahashi, and H. Ueda. Discovering new knowledge from graph data using inductive logic programming. *Proc. ILP-99, Springer-Verlag, LNAI 1634*, pages 222–233, 1999.
7. T. Miyahara, T. Shoudai, T. Uchida, K. Takahashi, and H. Ueda. Polynomial time matching algorithms for tree-like structured patterns in knowledge discovery. *Proc. PAKDD-2000, Springer-Verlag, LNAI 1805*, pages 5–16, 2000.
8. T. Miyahara, T. Shoudai, T. Uchida, K. Takahashi, and H. Ueda. Discovery of frequent tree structured patterns in semistructured web documents. *Proc. PAKDD-2001, Springer-Verlag, LNAI 2035*, pages 47–52, 2001.
9. S. Nestorov, S. Abiteboul, and R. Motwani. Extracting schema from semistructured data. *Proceedings of ACM SIGMOD International Conference on Management of Data*, pages 295–306, 1998.
10. T. Shinohara. Polynomial time inference of extended regular pattern languages. In *Springer-Verlag, LNCS 147*, pages 115–127, 1982.
11. T. Shoudai, T. Miyahara, T. Uchida, and S. Matsumoto. Inductive inference of regular term tree languages and its application to knowledge discovery. *Information Modelling and Knowledge Bases XI, IOS Press*, pages 85–102, 2000.
12. K. Wang and H. Liu. Discovering structural association of semistructured data. *IEEE Trans. Knowledge and Data Engineering*, 12:353–371, 2000.

# Piecewise and Local Threshold Testability of DFA

A.N. Trahtman

Bar-Ilan University, Dep. of Math. and CS,
52900, Ramat Gan, Israel
trakht@macs.biu.ac.il

**Abstract.** The necessary and sufficient conditions for an automaton to be locally threshold testable are found. We introduce the polynomial time algorithm to verify local threshold testability of the automaton of time complexity $O(n^5)$ and an algorithm of order $O(n^3)$ for the local threshold testability problem for syntactic semigroup of the automaton. We modify necessary and sufficient conditions for piecewise testability problem for deterministic finite automaton and improve the Stern algorithm to verify piecewise testability for the automaton. The time complexity of the algorithm is reduced from $O(n^5)$ to $O(n^2)$. An algorithm to verify piecewise testability for syntactic semigroup of the automaton of order $O(n^2)$ is presented as well.
The algorithms have been implemented as a $C/C^{++}$ package.
**Keywords:** automaton, locally threshold testable, piecewise testable, locally testable, transition graph, syntactic semigroup, algorithm

## Introduction

The concept of local testability was introduced by McNaughton and Papert [11] and by Brzozowski and Simon [5]. Local testability can be considered as a special case of local $l$-threshold testability for $l = 1$.

Locally testable automata have a wide spectrum of applications. Regular languages and picture languages can be described by help of a strictly locally testable languages [4], [9]. Local automata (a kind of locally testable automata) are heavily used to construct transducers and coding schemes adapted to constrained channels [1]. Locally testable languages are used in the study of DNA and informational macromolecules in biology [8].

Kim, McNaughton and McCloskey [10] have found necessary and sufficient conditions of local testability and a polynomial time algorithm for local testability problem based on these conditions. The realization of the algorithm is described by Caron [6]. A polynomial time algorithm for local testability problem for semigroups was presented in [17].

The locally threshold testable languages were introduced by Beauquier and Pin [2]. These languages generalize the concept of locally testable language and have been studied extensively in recent years. An important reason to study locally threshold testable languages is the possibility of being used in pattern

R. Freivalds (Ed.): FCT 2001, LNCS 2138, pp. 347–358, 2001.

recognition [13]. Stochastic locally threshold testable languages, also known as $n-grams$ are used in pattern recognition, particular in speech recognition, both in acoustic-phonetics decoding as in language modeling [19].

For the state transition graph $\Gamma$ of an automaton, we consider some subgraphs of the cartesian product $\Gamma \times \Gamma$ and $\Gamma \times \Gamma \times \Gamma$. In this way, necessary and sufficient conditions for a deterministic finite automaton to be locally threshold testable are found. It gives a positive answer on Caron's question [7]. We present here $O(n^5)$ time algorithm to verify local threshold testability of the automaton based on this characterization. By $n$ is denoted here the sum of the nodes and edges of the graph of the automaton ($n$ can be also considered as the product of the number of states by the size of the alphabet).

The local threshold testability problem for semigroup is, given a semigroup, to decide, if the semigroup is locally threshold testable or not. We present a polynomial time algorithm for this problem of order $O(n^3)$. By $n$ is denoted here the size of the semigroup.

A language is piecewise testable iff its syntactic monoid is $J$-trivial [15].

Stern [14] modified these necessary and sufficient conditions and described a polynomial time algorithm to verify piecewise testability of deterministic finite automaton of order $O(n^5)$. The algorithm was implemented by Caron [6]. Our aim is to reduce the last estimation.

We modify necessary and sufficient conditions [15], [14] for the piecewise testability problem and describe an algorithm to verify piecewise testability of deterministic finite automaton and of his syntactic semigroup of order $O(n^2)$.

Necessary and sufficient conditions of local testability [10] are considered in this paper in terms of reachability in the graph $\Gamma \times \Gamma$. New version of $O(n^2)$ time algorithm to verify local testability based on this approach will be presented too.

The considered algorithms have been implemented as a part of $C/C^{++}$ package TESTAS (testability of automata and semigroups).

## Notation and Definitions

Let $\Sigma$ be an alphabet and let $\Sigma^+$ denote the free semigroup on $\Sigma$. If $w \in \Sigma^+$, let $|w|$ denote the length of $w$. Let $k$ be a positive integer. Let $i_k(w)$ [$t_k(w)$] denote the prefix [suffix] of $w$ of length $k$ or $w$ if $|w| < k$. Let $F_{k,j}(w)$ denote the set of factors of $w$ of length $k$ with at least $j$ occurrences. A language $L$ [a semigroup $S$] is called **l-threshold k-testable** if there is an alphabet $\Sigma$ [and a surjective morphism $\phi : \Sigma^+ \to S$] such that for all $u$, $v \in \Sigma^+$, if $i_{k-1}(u) = i_{k-1}(v)$, $t_{k-1}(u) = t_{k-1}(v)$ and $F_{k,j}(u) = F_{k,j}(v)$ for all $j \leq l$, then either both $u$ and $v$ are in $L$ or neither is in $L$ [$u\phi = v\phi$].

An automaton is **$l$-threshold $k$-testable** if the automaton accepts a $l$-threshold $k$-testable language [the syntactic semigroup of the automaton is **$l$-threshold $k$-testable**].

A language $L$ [a semigroup, an automaton] is **locally threshold testable** if it is $l$-threshold $k$-testable for some $k$ and $l$.

Piecewise testable languages are the finite boolean combinations of the languages of the form $A^*a_1A^*a_2A^*...A^*a_kA^*$ where $k \geq 0$, $a_i$ is a letter from the alphabet $A$ and $A^*$ is a free monoid over $A$.

$|\Gamma|$ denotes the number of nodes of the graph $\Gamma$.

$\Gamma^i$ denotes the direct product of $i$ copies of the graph $\Gamma$.

The edge $\mathbf{p}_1, ..., \mathbf{p}_n \rightarrow \mathbf{q}_1, ..., \mathbf{q}_n$ in $\Gamma^i$ is labeled by $\sigma$ iff for each $i$ the edge $\mathbf{p}_i \rightarrow \mathbf{q}_i$ in $\Gamma$ is labeled by $\sigma$.

A maximal strongly connected component of the graph will be denoted for brevity as **SCC**, a finite deterministic automaton will be denoted as **DFA**. Arbitrary **DFA** is not necessary complete. A node from an $SCC$ will be called for brevity as an **SCC − node**. **SCC − node** can be defined as a node that has a right unit in transition semigroup of the automaton.

The graph with trivial SCC is called **acyclic**.

If an edge $\mathbf{p} \rightarrow \mathbf{q}$ is labeled by $\sigma$ then let us denote the node $\mathbf{q}$ as $\mathbf{p}\sigma$.

We shall write $\mathbf{p} \succeq \mathbf{q}$ if the node $\mathbf{q}$ is reachable from the node $\mathbf{p}$ or $\mathbf{p} = \mathbf{q}$.

In the case $\mathbf{p} \succeq \mathbf{q}$ and $\mathbf{q} \succeq \mathbf{p}$ we write $\mathbf{p} \sim \mathbf{q}$ (that is $\mathbf{p}$ and $\mathbf{q}$ belong to one $SCC$ or $\mathbf{p} = \mathbf{q}$).

The **stabilizer** $\Sigma(\mathbf{q})$ of the node $\mathbf{q}$ from $\Gamma$ is the subset of letters $\sigma \in \Sigma$ such that any edge from $\mathbf{q}$ labeled by $\sigma$ is a loop $\mathbf{q} \rightarrow \mathbf{q}$.

Let $\Gamma(\Sigma_i)$ be the directed graph with all nodes from the graph $\Gamma$ and edges from $\Gamma$ with labels only from the subset $\Sigma_i$ of the alphabet $\Sigma$.

So, $\Gamma(\Sigma(\mathbf{q}))$ is a directed graph with nodes from the graph $\Gamma$ and edges from $\Gamma$ that are labeled by letters from stabilizer of $\mathbf{q}$.

A semigroup without non-trivial subgroups is called **aperiodic** [2].

Let $\rho$ be a binary relation on semigroup $S$ such that for $a, b \in S$ $a\rho b$ iff for some idempotent $e \in S$ $ae = a$, $be = b$. Let $\lambda$ be a binary relation on $S$ such that for $a, b \in S$ $a\lambda b$ iff for some idempotent $e \in S$ $ea = a$, $eb = b$.

The unary operation $x^\omega$ assigns to every element $x$ of a finite semigroup $S$ the unique idempotent in the subsemigroup generated by $x$.

# 1 The Necessary and Sufficient Conditions of Local Threshold Testability

Let us formulate the result of Beauquier and Pin [2] in the following form:

**Theorem 11** *[2] A language $L$ is locally threshold testable if and only if the syntactic semigroup $S$ of $L$ is aperiodic and for any two idempotents $e$, $f$ and elements $a$, $u$, $b$ of $S$ we have*

$$eafuebf = ebfueaf \tag{1.1}$$

**Lemma 12** *Let the node $(\mathbf{p}, \mathbf{q})$ be an SCC-node of $\Gamma^2$ of a locally threshold testable DFA with state transition graph $\Gamma$ and suppose that $\mathbf{p} \sim \mathbf{q}$.*

*Then $\mathbf{p} = \mathbf{q}$.*

Proof. The transition semigroup $S$ of the automaton is finite and aperiodic [12]. Let us consider the node $(\mathbf{p},\mathbf{q})$ from $SCC$ $X$ of $\Gamma^2$. Then for some element $e \in S$ we have $\mathbf{q}e = \mathbf{q}$ and $\mathbf{p}e = \mathbf{p}$. In view of $\mathbf{q}e^i = \mathbf{q}$, $\mathbf{p}e^i = \mathbf{p}$ and finiteness of $S$ we can assume $e$ is an idempotent. In the $SCC$ $X$ for some $a$, $b$ from $S$ we have $\mathbf{p}a = \mathbf{q}$ and $\mathbf{q}b = \mathbf{p}$. Hence, $\mathbf{p}eae = \mathbf{q}$, $\mathbf{q}ebe = \mathbf{p}$. So $\mathbf{p}eaebe = \mathbf{p} = \mathbf{p}(eaebe)^i$ for any integer $i$. There exists a natural number $n$ such that in the aperiodic semigroup $S$ we have $(eae)^n = (eae)^{n+1}$. From theorem 11 it follows that for the idempotent $e$, $eaeebe = ebeeae$. We have $\mathbf{p} = \mathbf{p}eaebe = \mathbf{p}(eaeebe)^n = \mathbf{p}(eae)^n(ebe)^n = \mathbf{p}(eae)^{n+1}(ebe)^n = \mathbf{p}(eae)^n(ebe)^n eae = \mathbf{p}eae = \mathbf{q}$. So $\mathbf{p} = \mathbf{q}$.

**Theorem 13** *For DFA* $\mathbf{A}$ *with state transition graph* $\Gamma$ *the following three conditions are equivalent:*

*1)*$\mathbf{A}$ *is locally threshold testable.*

*2)If the nodes* $(\mathbf{p},\mathbf{q}_1,\mathbf{r}_1)$ *and* $(\mathbf{q},\mathbf{r},\mathbf{t}_1,\mathbf{t})$ *are SCC-nodes of* $\Gamma^3$ *and* $\Gamma^4$*, correspondingly, and*

$(\mathbf{q},\mathbf{r}) \succeq (\mathbf{q}_1,\mathbf{r}_1)$, $(\mathbf{p},\mathbf{q}_1) \succeq (\mathbf{r},\mathbf{t})$, $(\mathbf{p},\mathbf{r}_1) \succeq (\mathbf{q},\mathbf{t}_1)$ *holds in* $\Gamma^2$

*then* $\mathbf{t} = \mathbf{t}_1$.

*3)If the node* $(\mathbf{w},\mathbf{v})$ *is an SCC-node of the graph* $\Gamma^2$ *and* $\mathbf{w} \sim \mathbf{v}$ *then* $\mathbf{w} = \mathbf{v}$.

*If the nodes* $(\mathbf{p},\mathbf{q}_1,\mathbf{r}_1)$*,* $(\mathbf{q},\mathbf{r},\mathbf{t})$*,* $(\mathbf{q},\mathbf{r},\mathbf{t}_1)$ *are SCC-nodes of the graph* $\Gamma^3$ *and*

$(\mathbf{q},\mathbf{r}) \succeq (\mathbf{q}_1,\mathbf{r}_1)$, $(\mathbf{p},\mathbf{q}_1) \succeq (\mathbf{r},\mathbf{t})$, $(\mathbf{p},\mathbf{r}_1) \succeq (\mathbf{q},\mathbf{t}_1)$ *hold in* $\Gamma^2$*,*

*then* $\mathbf{t} \sim \mathbf{t}_1$.

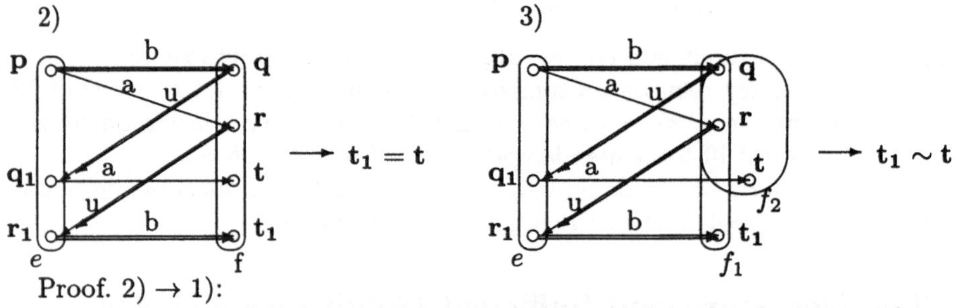


Proof. 2) → 1):

Let us consider the nodes $\mathbf{z}ebfueaf$ and $\mathbf{z}eafuebf$ where $\mathbf{z}$ is an arbitrary node of $\Gamma$, $a$, $u$, $b$ are arbitrary elements from transition semigroup $S$ of the automaton and $e$, $f$ are arbitrary idempotents from $S$. Let us denote

$\mathbf{z}e = \mathbf{p}$, $\mathbf{z}ebf = \mathbf{q}$, $\mathbf{z}eaf = \mathbf{r}$, $\mathbf{z}eafue = \mathbf{r}_1$, $\mathbf{z}ebfue = \mathbf{q}_1$, $\mathbf{z}ebfueaf = \mathbf{t}$, $\mathbf{z}eafuebf = \mathbf{t}_1$.

By condition 2), we have $\mathbf{t} = \mathbf{t}_1$, whence $\mathbf{z}ebfueaf = \mathbf{z}eafuebf$. Thus, the condition $eafuebf = ebfueaf$ (1.1) holds for the transition semigroup $S$. By theorem 11, the automaton is locally threshold testable.

1) → 3):

If the node $(\mathbf{w},\mathbf{v})$ belongs to some $SCC$ of the graph $\Gamma^2$ and $\mathbf{w} \sim \mathbf{v}$ then by lemma 12 local threshold testability implies $\mathbf{w} = \mathbf{v}$.

The condition $eafuebf = ebfueaf$ ((1.1), theorem 11) holds for the transition semigroup $S$ of the automaton. Let us consider nodes $\mathbf{p},\mathbf{q},\mathbf{r},\mathbf{t},\mathbf{q}_1,\mathbf{r}_1,\mathbf{t}_1$ satisfying the condition 3). Suppose

$(\mathbf{p}, \mathbf{q}_1, \mathbf{r}_1)e = (\mathbf{p}, \mathbf{q}_1, \mathbf{r}_1)$, $(\mathbf{q}, \mathbf{r}, \mathbf{t})f_2 = (\mathbf{q}, \mathbf{r}, \mathbf{t})$, $(\mathbf{q}, \mathbf{r}, \mathbf{t}_1)f_1 = (\mathbf{q}, \mathbf{r}, \mathbf{t}_1)$
for some idempotents $e, f_1, f_2 \in S$, and

$$(\mathbf{p}, \mathbf{q}_1)a = (\mathbf{r}, \mathbf{t}),\ (\mathbf{p}, \mathbf{r}_1)b = (\mathbf{q}, \mathbf{t}_1),\ (\mathbf{q}, \mathbf{r})u = (\mathbf{q}_1, \mathbf{r}_1)$$

for some elements $a, b, u \in S$. Then $\mathbf{p}eaf_2 = \mathbf{p}eaf_1$ and $\mathbf{p}ebf_2 = \mathbf{p}ebf_1$.

We have $\mathbf{t}_1 f_2 = \mathbf{p}eaf_1uebf_1f_2$. By theorem 11, $\mathbf{p}ebf_jueaf_j = \mathbf{p}eaf_juebf_j$ for $j = 1, 2$. So we have $\mathbf{t}_1f_2 = \mathbf{p}eaf_1uebf_1f_2 = \mathbf{p}ebf_1ueaf_1f_2$. In view of $\mathbf{p}ebf_2 = \mathbf{p}ebf_1$ and $f_i = f_if_i$ we have $\mathbf{t}_1f_2 = \mathbf{p}ebf_2f_2ueaf_1f_2$. By theorem 11, $\mathbf{t}_1f_2 = \mathbf{p}e(bf_2)f_2ue(af_1)f_2 = \mathbf{p}e(af_1)f_2ue(bf_2)f_2$. Now in view of $\mathbf{p}eaf_2 = \mathbf{p}eaf_1$ let us exclude $f_1$ and obtain $\mathbf{t}_1f_2 = \mathbf{p}eaf_2uebf_2 = \mathbf{t}$. So $\mathbf{t}_1f_2 = \mathbf{t}$. Analogously, $\mathbf{t}f_1 = \mathbf{t}_1$.

Hence, $\mathbf{t}_1 \sim \mathbf{t}$. Thus 3) is a consequence of 1).

3) $\rightarrow$ 2):

Suppose that $(\mathbf{p}, \mathbf{q}_1, \mathbf{r}_1)e = (\mathbf{p}, \mathbf{q}_1, \mathbf{r}_1)$, $(\mathbf{q}, \mathbf{r}, \mathbf{t}, \mathbf{t}_1)f = (\mathbf{q}, \mathbf{r}, \mathbf{t}, \mathbf{t}_1)$, for some idempotents $e$, $f$ from transition semigroup $S$ of the automaton and

$$(\mathbf{p}, \mathbf{q}_1)a = (\mathbf{r}, \mathbf{t}),\ (\mathbf{p}, \mathbf{r}_1)b = (\mathbf{q}, \mathbf{t}_1),\ (\mathbf{q}, \mathbf{r})u = (\mathbf{q}_1, \mathbf{r}_1)$$

for some elements $a$, $u$, $b \in S$. Therefore

$$(\mathbf{p}, \mathbf{q}_1)eaf = (\mathbf{p}, \mathbf{q}_1)af = (\mathbf{r}, \mathbf{t})$$
$$(\mathbf{p}, \mathbf{r}_1)ebf = (\mathbf{p}, \mathbf{r}_1)bf = (\mathbf{q}, \mathbf{t}_1)$$
$$(\mathbf{q}, \mathbf{r})u = (\mathbf{q}, \mathbf{r})fue = (\mathbf{q}_1, \mathbf{r}_1)$$

for idempotents $e$, $f$ and elements $a$, $u$, $b \in S$.

For $f = f_1 = f_2$ from 3) we have $\mathbf{t} \sim \mathbf{t}_1$. Notice that $(\mathbf{t}_1, \mathbf{t})f = (\mathbf{t}_1, \mathbf{t})$. The node $(\mathbf{t}_1, \mathbf{t})$ belongs to some $SCC$ of the graph $\Gamma^2$ and $\mathbf{t} \sim \mathbf{t}_1$, whence by lemma 12, $\mathbf{t} = \mathbf{t}_1$.

**Lemma 14** *Let the nodes $(\mathbf{q}, \mathbf{r}, \mathbf{t}_1)$ and $(\mathbf{q}, \mathbf{r}, \mathbf{t}_2)$ be SCC-nodes of the graph $\Gamma^3$ of a locally threshold testable DFA with state transition graph $\Gamma$. Suppose that $(\mathbf{p}, \mathbf{r}_1) \succeq (\mathbf{q}, \mathbf{t}_1)$, $(\mathbf{p}, \mathbf{r}_1) \succeq (\mathbf{q}, \mathbf{t}_2)$ in the graph $\Gamma^2$ and $\mathbf{p} \succeq \mathbf{r} \succeq \mathbf{r}_1$.*

*Then $\mathbf{t}_1 \sim \mathbf{t}_2$.*

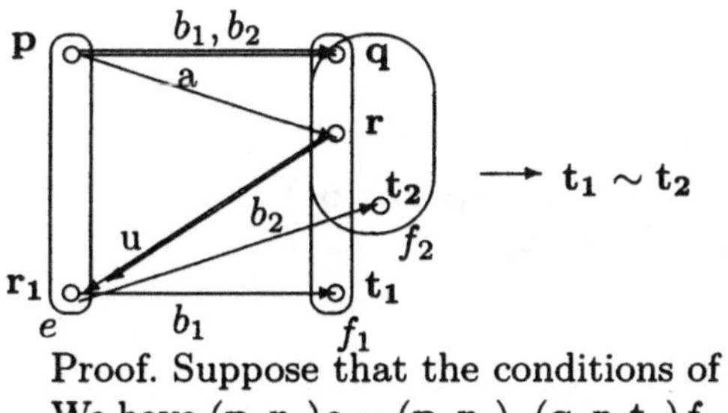


Proof. Suppose that the conditions of the lemma hold but $\mathbf{t}_1 \not\sim \mathbf{t}_2$.

We have $(\mathbf{p}, \mathbf{r}_1)e = (\mathbf{p}, \mathbf{r}_1)$, $(\mathbf{q}, \mathbf{r}, \mathbf{t}_1)f_1 = (\mathbf{q}, \mathbf{r}, \mathbf{t}_1)$, $(\mathbf{q}, \mathbf{r}, \mathbf{t}_2)f_2 = (\mathbf{q}, \mathbf{r}, \mathbf{t}_2)$, for some idempotents $e$, $f_2$, $f_2$ from the transition semigroup $S$ of the automaton and

$$(\mathbf{p}, \mathbf{r}_1)b_1 = (\mathbf{q}, \mathbf{t}_1),\ (\mathbf{p}, \mathbf{r}_1)b_2 = (\mathbf{q}, \mathbf{t}_2),\ \mathbf{p}a = \mathbf{r},\ \mathbf{r}u = \mathbf{r}_1$$

for some elements $a$, $u$, $b_1$, $b_2 \in S$.

If $\mathbf{t}_1f_2 \sim \mathbf{t}_2$ and $\mathbf{t}_2f_1 \sim \mathbf{t}_1$ then $\mathbf{t}_2 \sim \mathbf{t}_1$ in spite of our assumption. Therefore let us assume for instance that $\mathbf{t}_1 \not\sim \mathbf{t}_2f_1$. (And so $\mathbf{t}_1 \neq \mathbf{t}_2f_1$). This gives us an opportunity to consider $\mathbf{t}_2f_1$ instead of $\mathbf{t}_2$. So let us denote $\mathbf{t}_2 = \mathbf{t}_2f_1$, $f = f_1 = f_2$. Then $\mathbf{t}_2f = \mathbf{t}_2$, $\mathbf{t}_1f = \mathbf{t}_1$ and $\mathbf{t}_1 \not\sim \mathbf{t}_2$. Now

$$\mathbf{p}eaf = \mathbf{p}af = \mathbf{r}$$
$$(\mathbf{p},\mathbf{r}_1)eb_1f = (\mathbf{p},\mathbf{r}_1)b_1f = (\mathbf{q},\mathbf{t}_1)$$
$$(\mathbf{p},\mathbf{r}_1)eb_2f = (\mathbf{p},\mathbf{r}_1)b_2f = (\mathbf{q},\mathbf{t}_2)$$
$$\mathbf{r}u = \mathbf{r}ue = \mathbf{r}_1$$

Let us denote $\mathbf{q}_1 = \mathbf{q}ue$ and $\mathbf{t} = \mathbf{q}_1af_1$. Then
$(\mathbf{p},\mathbf{q}_1,\mathbf{r}_1)e = (\mathbf{p},\mathbf{q}_1,\mathbf{r}_1)$, $(\mathbf{q},\mathbf{r})ue = (\mathbf{q}_1,\mathbf{r}_1)$, $(\mathbf{q},\mathbf{r},\mathbf{t},\mathbf{t}_i)f = (\mathbf{q},\mathbf{r},\mathbf{t},\mathbf{t}_i)$

So the node $(\mathbf{p},\mathbf{q}_1,\mathbf{r}_1)$ is an $SCC$-node of the graph $\Gamma^3$, the nodes $(\mathbf{p},\mathbf{q},\mathbf{r},\mathbf{t}_i)$ are $SCC$-nodes of the graph $\Gamma^4$ for $i = 1,2$ and we have $(\mathbf{q},\mathbf{r}) \succeq (\mathbf{q}_1,\mathbf{r}_1)$, $(\mathbf{p},\mathbf{q}_1) \succeq (\mathbf{r},\mathbf{t})$ and $(\mathbf{p},\mathbf{r}_1) \succeq (\mathbf{q},\mathbf{t}_i)$ for $i = 1,2$.

Therefore, by theorem 13, (2), we have $\mathbf{t}_1 = \mathbf{t}$ and $\mathbf{t}_2 = \mathbf{t}$. Hence, $\mathbf{t}_1 \sim \mathbf{t}_2$, contradiction.

**Définition 15** *For any four nodes $\mathbf{p},\mathbf{q},\mathbf{r},\mathbf{r}_1$ of the graph $\Gamma$ of a DFA such that $\mathbf{p} \succeq \mathbf{r} \succeq \mathbf{r}_1$, $\mathbf{p} \succeq \mathbf{q}$ and the nodes $(\mathbf{p},\mathbf{r}_1)$, $(\mathbf{q},\mathbf{r})$ are SCC- nodes, let $T_{SCC}(\mathbf{p},\mathbf{q},\mathbf{r},\mathbf{r}_1)$ be the SCC of $\Gamma$ containing the set*

$$T(\mathbf{p},\mathbf{q},\mathbf{r},\mathbf{r}_1) := \{t \mid (\mathbf{p},\mathbf{r}_1) \succeq (\mathbf{q},\mathbf{t}) \text{ and } (\mathbf{q},\mathbf{r},\mathbf{t}) \text{ is an SCC-node}\}$$

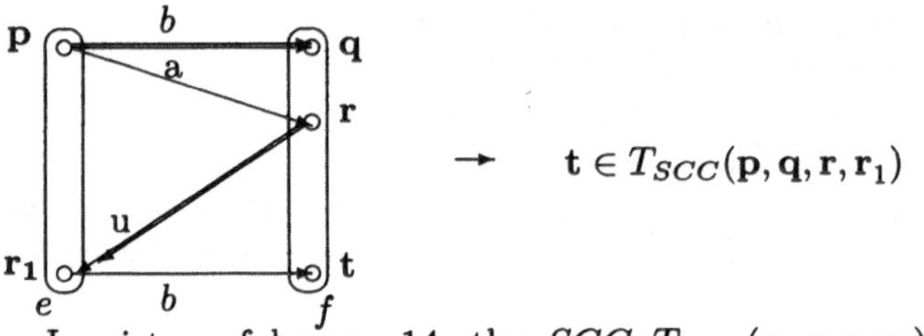


In virtue of lemma 14, the $SCC$ $T_{SCC}(\mathbf{p},\mathbf{q},\mathbf{r},\mathbf{r}_1)$ of a locally threshold testable $DFA$ is well defined (but empty if the set $T(\mathbf{p},\mathbf{q},\mathbf{r},\mathbf{r}_1)$ is empty). Lemma 14 and theorem 13 (3) imply the following theorem

**Theorem 16** *A DFA* **A** *with state transition graph $\Gamma$ is locally threshold testable iff*

*1)for every SCC-node $(\mathbf{p},\mathbf{q})$ of $\Gamma^2$ $\mathbf{p} \sim \mathbf{q}$ implies $\mathbf{p} = \mathbf{q}$*

*and*

*2)for every five nodes $\mathbf{p},\mathbf{q},\mathbf{r},\mathbf{q}_1,\mathbf{r}_1$ of the graph $\Gamma$ such that*

- *the non-empty SCC $T_{SCC}(\mathbf{p},\mathbf{q},\mathbf{r},\mathbf{r}_1)$ and $T_{SCC}(\mathbf{p},\mathbf{r},\mathbf{q},\mathbf{q}_1)$ exist,*
- *the node $(\mathbf{p},\mathbf{q}_1,\mathbf{r}_1)$ is an SCC-node of the graph $\Gamma^3$,*
- *$(\mathbf{q},\mathbf{r}) \succeq (\mathbf{q}_1,\mathbf{r}_1)$ in $\Gamma^2$,*

*holds $T_{SCC}(\mathbf{p},\mathbf{q},\mathbf{r},\mathbf{r}_1) = T_{SCC}(\mathbf{p},\mathbf{r},\mathbf{q},\mathbf{q}_1)$.*

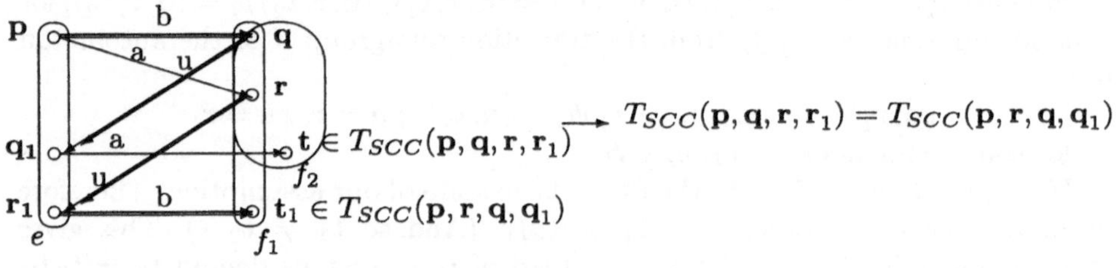


Let us go to the semigroup case.

**Lemma 17** *Elements $s, t$ from semigroup $S$ belong to subsemigroup $eSf$ where $e$ and $f$ are idempotents if and only if $s\rho t$ and $s\lambda t$.*

The proof follows from the definitions of $\rho$ and $\lambda$.

**Theorem 18** *A language $L$ is locally threshold testable if and only if the syntactic semigroup $S$ of $L$ is aperiodic and for any three elements $s$, $u$, $t$ of $S$ such that $s\rho t$ and $s\lambda t$ we have*

$$sut = tus \tag{1.2}$$

The proof follows from theorem 11 and lemma 17.

# 2 An Algorithm to Verify Local Threshold Testability of DFA

A linear depth-first search algorithm finding all $SCC$ (see [16]) will be used.

By $n$ will be denoted the sum of the nodes and edges of the graph.

## 2.1 To Check the Reachability on an Oriented Graph

For a given node $\mathbf{q_0}$, we consider depth-first search from the node. First only $\mathbf{q_0}$ will be marked. Every edge is crossed two times. Given a node, the considered path includes first the ingoing edges and then the outgoing edges. After crossing an edge in the positive direction from the marked node $\mathbf{q}$ to the node $\mathbf{r}$ we mark $\mathbf{r}$ too. The process is linear in the number of edges (see [10] for details).

The set of marked nodes forms a set of nodes that are reachable from $\mathbf{q_0}$. The procedure may be repeated for any node of the graph $G$.

The time of the algorithm for all pairs of nodes is $O(n^2)$.

## 2.2 To Verify Local Threshold Testability of DFA

Let us find all $SCC$ of the graphs $\Gamma$, $\Gamma^2$ and $\Gamma^3$ and mark all $SCC$-nodes ($O(n^3)$ time complexity).

Let us recognize the reachability on the graph $\Gamma$ and $\Gamma^2$ and form the table of reachability for all pairs of $\Gamma$ and $\Gamma^2$. The time required for this step is $O(n^4)$.

Let us check the conditions of lemma 12. For every $SCC$-node $(\mathbf{p}, \mathbf{q})$ $(\mathbf{p} \neq \mathbf{q})$ from $\Gamma^2$ let us check the condition $\mathbf{p} \sim \mathbf{q}$. A negative answer for any considered node $(\mathbf{p}, \mathbf{q})$ implies the validity of the condition. In opposite case the automaton is not locally threshold testable. The time of the step is $O(n^2)$.

For every four nodes $\mathbf{p}, \mathbf{q}, \mathbf{r}, \mathbf{r_1}$ of the graph $\Gamma$, let us check the following conditions (see 15): $\mathbf{p} \succeq \mathbf{r} \succeq \mathbf{r_1}$ and $\mathbf{p} \succeq \mathbf{q}$. In a positive case, let us form $SCC$ $T_{SCC}(\mathbf{p}, \mathbf{q}, \mathbf{r}, \mathbf{r_1})$ of all nodes $\mathbf{t} \in \Gamma$ such that $(\mathbf{p}, \mathbf{r_1}) \succeq (\mathbf{q}, \mathbf{t})$ and $(\mathbf{q}, \mathbf{r}, \mathbf{t})$ with $(\mathbf{p}, \mathbf{r_1})$ are $SCC$-nodes. In case that $SCC$ $T_{SCC}$ is not well defined the automaton is not threshold testable. The time required for this step is $O(n^5)$.

For every five nodes $\mathbf{p}, \mathbf{q}, \mathbf{r}, \mathbf{q_1}, \mathbf{r_1}$ from $\Gamma$ we check now the second condition of theorem 16. If non-empty components $T_{SCC}(\mathbf{p}, \mathbf{q}, \mathbf{r}, \mathbf{r_1})$ and $T_{SCC}(\mathbf{p}, \mathbf{r}, \mathbf{q}, \mathbf{q_1})$

exist, the node $(\mathbf{p}, \mathbf{q}_1, \mathbf{r}_1)$ is an $SCC$-node of the graph $\Gamma^3$ and $(\mathbf{q}, \mathbf{r}) \succeq (\mathbf{q}_1, \mathbf{r}_1)$ in $\Gamma^2$, let us verify the equality $T_{SCC}(\mathbf{p}, \mathbf{q}, \mathbf{r}, \mathbf{r}_1) = T_{SCC}(\mathbf{p}, \mathbf{r}, \mathbf{q}, \mathbf{q}_1)$. If the answer is negative then the automaton is not threshold testable. A positive answer for all considered cases implies the validity of the condition of the theorem. The time required for this step is $O(n^5)$.

The whole time of the algorithm to check the local threshold testability is $O(n^5)$.

## 3 Verifying Local Threshold Testability of Finite Semigroup

The algorithm is based on the theorem 18.

Let $s_i$ be an element of the semigroup $S$, $n = |S|$.

- For any $s \in S$ let us find $s^\omega$ and check the aperiodity. The semigroup $S$ is not locally threshold testable for non-aperiodic $S$.
- Let us form a binary square table $L$ $[R]$ of the size $n$ in the following way: For any $i, j \leq n$ suppose $L_{i,j} = 1$ $[R_{i,j} = 1]$ if there exists an idempotent $e \in S$ such that $es_i = s_i$ and $es_j = s_j$ $[\ s_ie = s_i$ and $s_je = s_j\ ]$. In opposite case $L_{i,j}[R_{i,j}] = 0$.
  The step has order $O(n^3)$.
- Let us find the intersection $\rho \cap \lambda$ and form a binary square table $LR$: $LR_{i,j} = L_{i,j}R_{i,j}$.
- For any triple $s_i, s_j, s_k \in S$ where $s_i(\rho \cap \lambda)s_j$, let us check the condition $s_is_ks_j = s_js_ks_i$. The validity of the condition for any triple of elements implies local threshold testability of $S$. In opposite case $S$ is not locally threshold testable.
  The step has order $O(n^3)$.

The algorithm to verify local threshold testability of the semigroup $S$ has order $O(n^3)$.

## 4 An Algorithm to Verify Local Testability of DFA

We present now necessary and sufficient conditions of local testability of Kim, McNaughton and McCloskey ([10]) in the following form:

**Theorem 41** *([10]) A DFA with state transition graph $\Gamma$ and transition semigroup $S$ is locally testable iff the following two conditions hold:*

*1)For any SCC-node $(\mathbf{p}, \mathbf{q})$ from $\Gamma^2$ such that $\mathbf{p} \sim \mathbf{q}$ we have $\mathbf{p} = \mathbf{q}$.*

*2)For any SCC-node $(\mathbf{p}, \mathbf{q})$ from $\Gamma^2$ such that $\mathbf{p} \succ \mathbf{q}$ and arbitrary element $s$ from $S$ we have $\mathbf{p}s \succeq \mathbf{q}$ is valid iff $\mathbf{q}s \succeq \mathbf{q}$.*

The theorem implies

**Corollary 42** *A DFA with state transition graph $\Gamma$ over alphabet $\Sigma$ is locally testable iff the following two conditions hold:*

*1)For any SCC-node $(\mathbf{p}, \mathbf{q})$ from $\Gamma^2$ such that $\mathbf{p} \sim \mathbf{q}$ we have $\mathbf{p} = \mathbf{q}$.*

*2)For any node $(\mathbf{r}, \mathbf{s})$ and any SCC-node $(\mathbf{p}, \mathbf{q})$ from $\Gamma^2$ such that $(\mathbf{p}, \mathbf{q}) \succeq (\mathbf{r}, \mathbf{s})$, $\mathbf{p} \succeq \mathbf{q}$, $\mathbf{s} \succeq \mathbf{q}$ and for arbitrary $\sigma$ from $\Sigma$ we have $\mathbf{r}\sigma \succeq \mathbf{s}$ is valid iff $\mathbf{s}\sigma \succeq \mathbf{s}$.*

In [10], a polynomial time algorithm for local testability problem was considered. Now we present another simplified version of such algorithm with the same time complexity.

Let us form a table of reachability on the graph $\Gamma$ ($O(n^2)$ time complexity).

Let us find $\Gamma^2$ and all $SCC$-nodes of $\Gamma^2$.

For every $SCC$-node $(\mathbf{p}, \mathbf{q})$ $(\mathbf{p} \neq \mathbf{q})$ from $\Gamma^2$ let us check the condition $\mathbf{p} \sim \mathbf{q}$. ($O(n^2)$ time complexity). If the condition holds then the automaton is not locally testable (42).

Then we add to the graph new node $(\mathbf{0}, \mathbf{0})$ with edges from this node to every $SCC$-node $(\mathbf{p}, \mathbf{q})$ from $\Gamma^2$ such that $\mathbf{p} \succeq \mathbf{q}$. Let us consider first-depth search from the node $(\mathbf{0}, \mathbf{0})$.

We do not visit edges $(\mathbf{r}, \mathbf{s}) \to (\mathbf{r}, \mathbf{s})\sigma$ from the graph $\Gamma^2$ such that $\mathbf{s}\sigma \not\succeq \mathbf{s}$ and $\mathbf{r}\sigma \not\succeq \mathbf{s}$. In the case that from the two conditions $\mathbf{s}\sigma \succeq \mathbf{s}$ and $\mathbf{r}\sigma \succeq \mathbf{s}$ only one is valid the algorithm stops and the automaton is not locally testable.

In the case of absence of such cases on the path the automaton is locally testable. ($O(n^2)$ time complexity).

The whole time of the algorithm to check the local testability is $O(n^2)$.

## 5 Piecewise Testability

The following result is due to Simon:

**Theorem 51** *[15] Let $L$ be a regular language over the alphabet $\Sigma$ and let $\Gamma$ be the minimal automaton accepting $L$. The language $L$ is piecewise testable if and only if the following conditions hold*

*(i) $\Gamma$ is a directed acyclic graph;*

*(ii) for any subset $\Sigma_i$ from alphabet $\Sigma$ each connected component of the graph $\Gamma(\Sigma_i)$ has a unique maximal state.*

**Lemma 52** *Let the state transition graph $\Gamma$ of some DFA be acyclic. Suppose that for some subset $\Sigma_i$ of the alphabet $\Sigma$ the graph $\Gamma(\Sigma_i)$ has two distinct connected maximal nodes.*

*Then for some node $\mathbf{p}$ from $\Gamma$ the graph $\Gamma(\Sigma(\mathbf{p}))$ has also two distinct connected maximal nodes where the node $\mathbf{p}$ is one of these maximal nodes.*

Proof. Suppose that the states $\mathbf{q}$ and $\mathbf{p}$ are distinct maximal nodes in some connected component $X$ of the graph $\Gamma(\Sigma_i)$. The graph $\Gamma$ of a piecewise testable deterministic finite automaton has only trivial $SCC$ (theorem 51), whence $\mathbf{p} \not\succ \mathbf{q}$

or $\mathbf{q} \not\succ \mathbf{p}$. Suppose that $\mathbf{q} \not\succ \mathbf{p}$ and let us consider the graph $\Gamma(\Sigma(\mathbf{p}))$. $\Gamma(\Sigma_i) \subset \Gamma(\Sigma(\mathbf{p}))$, whence the node $\mathbf{p}$ is a maximal node of the graph $\Gamma(\Sigma(\mathbf{p}))$. The states $\mathbf{q}$ and $\mathbf{p}$ are connected in the graph $\Gamma(\Sigma(\mathbf{p}))$ too. The node $\mathbf{q}$ or some successor of $\mathbf{q}$ is a maximal node in the same component of $\Gamma(\Sigma(\mathbf{p}))$ and this maximal node is not equal to $\mathbf{p}$ because $\mathbf{q} \not\succ \mathbf{p}$.

Last lemma gives us opportunity to present necessary and sufficient conditions for piecewise testability in the following form:

**Theorem 53** *Let $L$ be a regular language over the alphabet $\Sigma$ and let $\Gamma$ be a minimal automaton accepting $L$. The language $L$ is piecewise testable if and only if the following conditions hold*

*(i) $\Gamma$ is a directed acyclic graph;*

*(ii) for any node $\mathbf{p}$ the maximal connected component $C$ of the graph $\Gamma(\Sigma(\mathbf{p}))$ such that $\mathbf{p} \in C$ has a unique maximal state.*

Let us formulate the Simon's result in the following form:

**Theorem 54** . *Finite semigroup $S$ is piecewise testable iff $S$ is aperiodic and for any two elements $x$, $y \in S$ holds*

$$(xy)^{\omega}x = y(xy)^{\omega} = (xy)^{\omega}$$

## 6 An Algorithm to Verify Piecewise Testability for Automata

- Check that the graph $\Gamma$ is acyclic. If not then the automaton is not piecewise testable and the procedure stops.
- For any state $\mathbf{p}$, let us compute
  - the stabilizer $\Sigma(\mathbf{p})$.
  - the graph $\Gamma(\Sigma(\mathbf{p}))$.
    The node $\mathbf{p}$ is a maximal node of some SCC of the graph $\Gamma(\Sigma(\mathbf{p}))$ and our aim is to find some more maximal nodes of the component or to prove their absence.
  - non-oriented copy $N$ of the graph $\Gamma(\Sigma(\mathbf{p}))$ and maximal connected component $C$ of $N$ that contains $\mathbf{p}$. A linear depth-first search algorithm is used for to find $C$.
  - for any node $\mathbf{r}$ ($\mathbf{r} \neq \mathbf{p}$) from $C$ let us do the following:
    If $\mathbf{r}$ has no outgoing edges in the graph $\Gamma(\Sigma(\mathbf{p}))$ or all its outgoing edges are loops then the automaton is not piecewise testable and the procedure stops.

**Theorem 61** *Let $L$ be a regular language over the alphabet $\Sigma$ and let $\Gamma$ be a minimal automaton accepting $L$. The considered algorithm to verify the piecewise testability of the language $L$ has order $O(n^2)$ where $n$ is the sum of nodes and edges of the graph $\Gamma$.*

Proof. The number of graphs $\Gamma(\Sigma(\mathbf{p}))$ we consider is not greater than the number of nodes of the graph $\Gamma$. The process of finding of the graph $\Gamma(\Sigma(\mathbf{p}))$ is linear in the number of nodes of the graph $\Gamma$.

Depth-first search algorithm is linear in $n$ too.

The process of excluding loops in the graph $\Gamma(\Sigma(\mathbf{p}))$ is linear in the number of nodes of $\Gamma(\Sigma(\mathbf{p}))$.

The finding of node without outgoing edges is linear in the number of nodes.

## 7 An algorithm to Verify Piecewise Testability for Semigroups

The algorithm is based on the theorem 54.

- For any $x \in S$ let us find $x^\omega$ equal to $x^i$ such that $x^i = x^{i+1}$. If $x^\omega$ is not found then the semigroup $S$ is not piecewise testable.
  For given element $x$, the step is linear in the size of semigroup.
- For any pair $x, y \in S$, let us check the condition $(xy)^\omega x = y(xy)^\omega = (xy)^\omega$. The validity of the condition for any pair of elements implies piecewise testability of $S$. In opposite case $S$ is not piecewise testable.

The algorithm under consideration has order $O(n^2)$ where $n = |S|$.

## References

1. M.-P. Beal, J. Senellart, On the bound of the synchronization delay of local automata, *Theoret. Comput. Sci.* 205, **1-2**(1998), 297-306.
2. D. Beauquier, J.E. Pin, Factors of words, *Lect. Notes in Comp. Sci.* Springer, Berlin, **372**(1989), 63-79.
3. D. Beauquier, J.E. Pin, Languages and scanners, *Theoret. Comp. Sci.* 1, **84**(1991), 3-21.
4. J.-C. Birget, Strict local testability of the finite control of two-way automata and of regular picture description languages, *J. of Alg. Comp.* 1, **2**(1991), 161-175.
5. J.A. Brzozowski, I. Simon, Characterizations of locally testable events, *Discrete Math.* 4, (1973), 243- 271.
6. P. Caron, LANGAGE: A Maple package for automaton characterization of regular languages, Springer, *Lect. Notes in Comp. Sci.* **1436**(1998), 46-55.
7. P. Caron, Families of locally testable languages, *Theoret. Comput. Sci.*, **242**(2000), 361-376.
8. T. Head, Formal languages theory and DNA: an analysis of the generative capacity of specific recombinant behaviors, *Bull. Math. Biol.* **49**(1987), 4, 739-757.
9. F. Hinz, Classes of picture languages that cannot be distinguished in the chain code concept and deletion of redundant retreats, *Springer, Lect. Notes in Comp. Sci.* **349**(1990), 132-143.
10. S. Kim, R. McNaughton, R. McCloskey, A polynomial time algorithm for the local testability problem of deterministic finite automata, *IEEE Trans. Comput.* **40**(1991) N10, 1087-1093.
11. R. McNaughton, S, Papert, *Counter-free automata* M.I.T. Press. Mass., 1971.

12. J. Pin, Finite semigroups and recognizable languages. An introduction, Semigroups and formal languages, *Math. and Ph. Sci.* **1466**(1995), 1-32.
13. J. Ruiz, S. Espana, P. Garcia, Locally threshold testable languages in strict sense: Application to the inference problem. Springer, *Lect. Notes in Comp. Sci* **1433**(1998), 150-161.
14. J. Stern, Complexity of some problems from the theory of automata. Inf. and Control, 66(1985), 163-176.
15. I. Simon, Piecewise testable events, Springer, *Lect. Notes in Comp. Sci.*, **33**(1975), 214-222.
16. R.E. Tarjan, Depth first search and linear graph algorithms, *SIAM J. Comput.* **1**(1972), 146-160. *J. of Comp. System Sci.* **25**(1982), 360-376.
17. A.N. Trahtman, A polynomial time algorithm for local testability and its level. *Int. J. of Algebra and Comp.* v. 9, **1**(1998), 31-39.
18. A.N. Trahtman, A precise estimation of the order of local testability of a deterministic finite automaton, Springer, *Lect. Notes in Comp. Sci.* **1436**(1998), 198-212.
19. E. Vidal, F. Casacuberta, P. Garcia, Grammatical inference and automatic speech recognition. In *speech recognition and coding* Springer, 1995, 175-191.

# Compositional Homomorphisms of Relational Structures
## (Modeled as Multialgebras)

Michał Walicki*, Adis Hodzic[1], and Sigurd Meldal[2]

[1] University of Bergen, Dept. of Informatics, P.Box 7800, 5020 Bergen, Norway,
{michal,adis}@ii.uib.no

[2] CalPoly, Dept. of CS, 1 Grand Ave., San Luis Obispo, CA 93407, USA,
smeldal@phoenix.calpoly.edu

**Abstract.** The paper attempts a systematic study of homomorphisms of relational structures. Such structures are modeled as multialgebras (i.e., relation is represented as a set-valued function). The first, main, result is that, under reasonable restrictions on the form of the definition of homomorphism, there are exactly nine compositional homomorphisms of multialgebras. Then the comparison of the obtained categories with respect to the existence of finite limits and co-limits reveals two of them to be finitely complete and co-complete. Without claiming that compositionality and categorical properties are the only possible criteria for selecting a definition of homomorphism, we nevertheless suggest that, for many purposes, these criteria actually *might* be acceptable. For such cases, the paper gives an overview of the available alternatives and a clear indication of their advantages and disadvantages.

## 1 Background and Motivation

In the study of universal algebra, the central place occupies the pair of "dual" notions of congruence and homomorphism: every congruence on an algebra induces a homomorphism into a quotient and every homomorphism induces a congruence on the source algebra. Categorical approach attempts to express *all* (internal) properties of algebras in (external) terms of homomorphisms. When passing to relational structures or power set structures, however, the close correspondence of these internal and external aspects seems to get lost.

The most common, and natural, generalisation of the definition of homomorphism to relational structures says:

**Definition 1.1** *A set function $\phi : \underline{A} \to \underline{B}$,[1] where both sets are equipped with respective relations $R^A \subseteq \underline{A}^n$ and $R^B \subseteq \underline{B}^n$, is a (weak) homomorphism iff*

$$\langle x_1 ... x_n \rangle \in R^A \;\Rightarrow \langle \phi(x_1) ... \phi(x_n) \rangle \in R^B$$

* The first author gratefully acknowledges the financial support from the Norwegian Research Council.

[1] Underlying sets will be used to indicate the "bare, unstructured sets" as opposed to power sets or other sets with structure. For the moment, one may ignorte this notational convention.

R. Freivalds (Ed.): FCT 2001, LNCS 2138, pp. 359–371, 2001.

With this definition *any* equivalence on $\underline{A}$ gives rise to a weak homomorphism and, conversely, a weak homomorphism induces, in general, only an equivalence relation on $\underline{A}$. Hence this homomorphism does not capture the notion of congruence and this is just one example of an internal property of relational structures that cannot be accounted for by relational homomorphisms (in various variants). Probably for this reason, the early literature on homomorphisms of relations is extremely meagre [22,26] and most work on relations concerns the study of relation algebras, various relational operators and their axiomatizations. Although in recent years several authors begun studying relational structures and their homomorphisms in various contexts, a general treatement of relational homomorphisms is still missing. This growing interest is reflected in numerous suggestions on how the definition of such a homomorphism could be specialized to obtain a more useful notion. This issue is our main objective.

In a more concise, relational notation, definition 1.1 is written as $R^A; \phi \subseteq \phi; R^B$. This somehow presupposes that $R$ is a binary relation, since composition $\_;\_$ has a standard definition only for binary relations. There seems to be no generally accepted definition of composition of relations of arbitrary arities. In the following we will compose arbitrary relations (within the structures), like $R$ above, with binary relations (obtained from homomorphisms between the structures), according to the following definition.

**Definition 1.2** *The composition of relations $R^A \subseteq \underline{A}^{n+1}$, resp. $R^B \subseteq \underline{B}^{n+1}$, with a binary relation $\phi \subseteq \underline{A} \times \underline{B}$ as a relation on $\underline{A}^n \times \underline{B}$, is given by:*

$$\langle a_1 ... a_n, b\rangle \in R^A; \phi \Leftrightarrow \exists a \in \underline{A} : \langle a_1 ... a_n, a\rangle \in R^A \ \wedge \ \langle a, b\rangle \in \phi$$
$$\langle a_1 ... a_n, b\rangle \in \phi; R^B \Leftrightarrow \exists b_1 ... b_n \in \underline{B} : \langle b_1 ... b_n, b\rangle \in R^B \ \wedge \ \langle a_i, b_i\rangle \in \phi$$

This definition is certainly not the only possible one – [28,8] contain more general suggestions. The reason for this choice is our intension to treat relations in an algebraic way. It allows us to view relations as set-valued functions and turns relational structures into algebraic ones (*algebras of complexes* from [15,16]). In particular, it admits composition of relations of arbitrary arities analogous to composition of functions.

Now, table 1 presents a sample of proposed definitions of relational homomorphisms gathered from [22,9,7,20,25,3,23,24]. It uses binary relations but with the above definition 1.2 it may be used for relations $R$ of arbitrary arity. The names are by no means standard and taken from the articles introducing the respective definitions.

This paper is an attempt to bring at least some order into this situation which we experience as rather unsatisfactory. Given the combinatorial possibilities of defining homomorphisms of relational structures, a complete classification seems hardly possible. Even the very issue of the "criteria of usefulness", depending on the intended applications, may be debatable. We hope that a more algebraic perspective may bring at least some clarification. Instead of listing and defending new definitions, we have chosen the compositionality of homomorphisms and the elementary properties of the resulting categories as the basis for comparison.

**Table 1.** Some definitions of relational homomorphisms

| homomorphism $\phi$ | | relational def. | logical def. $\forall x, y:$ |
|---|---|---|---|
| 1. | weak | $\phi^-; R^A; \phi \subseteq R^B$ | $R^A(x,y) \Rightarrow R^B(\phi(x), \phi(y))$ |
| 2. | loose | $R^A; \phi \subseteq \phi; R^B$ | 1. |
| 3. | full | $\phi^-; R^A; \phi = \phi^-; \phi; R^B; \phi^-; \phi$ | $\exists x', y' : R^A(x', y') \Leftrightarrow R^B(\phi(x), \phi(y))$ |
| 4. | 'strong' | $\phi^-; R^A; \phi \supseteq \phi^-; \phi; R^B; \phi^-; \phi$ | $\exists x', y' : R^A(x', y') \Leftarrow R^B(\phi(x), \phi(y))$ |
| 5. | outdegree | $R^A; \phi = \phi; R^B; \phi^-; \phi$ | $\exists x' : R^A(x', y) \Leftrightarrow R^B(\phi(x), \phi(y))$ |
| 6. | indegree | $\phi^-; R^A = \phi^-; \phi; R^B; \phi^-$ | $\exists y' : R^A(x, y') \Leftrightarrow R^B(\phi(x), \phi(y))$ |
| 7. | 'very strong' | $\phi; \phi^-; R^A; \phi \supseteq \phi; R^B$ | $\exists x', y' : R^A(x', y') \Leftarrow R^B(\phi(x), y)$ |
| 8. | regular | 5. & 6. | 5. & 6. |
| 9. | closed | $R^A; \phi \supseteq \phi; R^B$ | $\exists y' : R^A(x, y') \Leftarrow R^B(\phi(x), y)$ |
| 10. | strong | $R^A = \phi; R^B; \phi^-$ | $R^A(x,y) \Leftrightarrow R^B(\phi(x), \phi(y))$ |
| 11. | tight | $R^A; \phi = \phi; R^B$ | 2. & 9. |

– primed symbol $z'$ denotes some element such that $\phi(z') = \phi(z)$ (in 7 and 9 a $y' : \phi(y') = y$)
– for $\phi \subseteq \underline{A} \times \underline{B}$, $\phi^-$ denotes the inverse $\langle b, a\rangle \in \phi^- \Leftrightarrow \langle a, b\rangle \in \phi$

Section 2 introduces mulitalgebras as a possible way of representing relations and motivates this choice. Section 3 addresses the question of composition of homomorphisms: 3.1 gives a characterization of homomorphisms which are closed under composition – in fact, most of the suggested defintions, like most of those in table 1, do *not* enjoy this property which we believe is crucial. The proof, included here, is a significant improvement of the original proof of this result from [29]. Subsection 3.2 characterizes the equivalences associated with various compositional homomorphisms. Section 4 summarizes the results on (finite) completeness and co-completeness of the obtained categories.

Except for the statement of the compositionality theorem, the results concerning the three "inner" categories were published earlier in [29,30]. This paper is the first complete overview with the results for the remaining six categories from [11].

**Preliminary definitions and notation** A *relational signature* $\Sigma$ is a pair $\langle \mathcal{S}, \mathcal{R}\rangle$ where $\mathcal{S}$ is a set (of sort symbols) and $\mathcal{R}$ is a set of relation symbols with given arities (also called *type* of relation), written $[R_i : s_1 \times ... \times s_n] \in \mathcal{R}$. Similarly, *an algebraic signature* is a pair $\langle \mathcal{S}, \mathcal{F}\rangle$ where $\mathcal{F}$ is a set of function symbols with associated sorts and arities, written $[f : s_1 \times ... \times s_n \rightarrow s] \in \mathcal{F}$. A *relational structure* over a signature $\Sigma = \langle \mathcal{S}, \mathcal{R}\rangle$ is a pair $A = \langle |A|, \mathcal{R}^A\rangle$, where $|A|$ is an $\mathcal{S}$-sorted set called the *carrier* and $\mathcal{R}^A$ is a set of relations, such that for each $[R_i : s_1 \times ... \times s_n] \in \mathcal{R}$ there is $R_i^A \subseteq |A|_{s_1} \times ... \times |A|_{s_n}$. An *algebra* over a signature $\Sigma = \langle \mathcal{S}, \mathcal{F}\rangle$ is again a pair $A = \langle |A|, \mathcal{F}^A\rangle$, where $|A|$ is an $\mathcal{S}$-sorted set called the *carrier*, and $\mathcal{F}^A$ is a set of functions, with a function $f^A : |A|_{s_1} \times ... \times |A|_{s_n} \rightarrow |A|_s$ for each $[f : s_1 \times ... \times s_n \rightarrow s] \in \mathcal{F}$.

In order to reduce the complexity of notation, we shall limit ourselves to single sorted structures and algebras ($\mathcal{S}$ has only one element) claiming that the results carry over to a multi-sorted case.

We will study algebras over carriers being power sets. For such a structure $A$ with $|A| = \wp(\underline{A})$, the set $\underline{A}$ will be called the *underlying set*. Given a function

$f : \underline{A} \to \underline{B}$, we will often use additive pointwise extension without making it explicit in the notation – for any $X \subset \underline{A}$, we write $f(X)$ meaning $\bigcup_{x \in X} f(x)$. Also, we do not make explicit the distinction between elements and one-element sets – if $A = \wp(\underline{A})$ and $a \in \underline{A}$, we write $a \in A$ meaning $\{a\} \in A$. Homomorphisms of multialgebras map underlying sets to underlying sets, just as the homomorphisms of relational structures do.

Composition is written in diagrammatic order $f;g$ for $g(f(\_))$. For a binary relation/function $\phi$, $\phi^-$ denotes its inverse $= \{\langle y, x\rangle : \langle x, y\rangle \in \phi\}$.

## 2 Multialgebras

Our interest in relational structures originates from earlier studies of multialgebras [4,5,10,13,17,21,27,30,32] which provide means for modeling nondeterminism in the context of algebraic specification of abstract data types [13,17,18, 19,31,32,33]. Multilagebras can be viewed as relational structures with a specific composition of relations of arbitrary arities. According to definition 1.2, relations are viewed as set-valued functions where the last, $n$-th argument corresponds to an element of the result set obtained by applying the function to the first $n-1$ arguments. This view appears in [26], was elaborated in [15,16], then in [27] and re-emerged in recent years in the algebraic approaches to nondeterminism. It is based on the simple observation that any (set-valued) operation $f : A_1 \times ... \times A_n \to \wp(A)$ determines a relation $R_f \subseteq A_1 \times ... \times A_n \times A$ and vice versa, via the isomorphism:

$$A_1 \times ... \times A_n \to \wp(A) \;\simeq\; \wp(A_1 \times ... \times A_n \times A) \qquad (2.1)$$

Based on this fact, [15,14] introduced the concept of *algebra of complexes* which we call *multialgebras* – with one proviso: the carrier of a multialgebra is a power set but Boolean operations are not part of the multialgebraic signature. This seemingly negligible differece turns out to have significant consequences, since signatures determine homomorphisms.

**Definition 2.1** *Given a signature $\Sigma = \langle S, \mathcal{F}\rangle$, a $\Sigma$-multialgebra $M$ is given by:*

- *a carrier $|M| = \{|M|_s\}_{s \in S}$, where for each $s \in S$, $|M|_s = \wp(\underline{M}_s)$ of some underlying set $\underline{M}_s$, with the obvious embedding $\underline{M}_s \hookrightarrow \wp(\underline{M}_s)$;*
- *a function $f^M : \underline{M}_{s_1} \times ... \times \underline{M}_{s_n} \to \wp(\underline{M}_s)$ for each $f : s_1 \times ... \times s_n \to s \in \mathcal{F}$, with composition defined through additive extension to sets, i.e. $f^M(X_1, ..., X_n) = \bigcup_{x_i \in X_i} f^M(x_1, ..., x_n)$.*

Multialgebras are "partial" in the sense that operations may return empty set of values. By the pointwise extension of operations, they are strict in all arguments. Notice also that we allow empty carriers, i.e. $\wp(\emptyset) = \{\emptyset\}$ is a possible carrier of a multialgebra.

One consequence of modeling relations by set-valued functions is that possible requirement on the definitions of homomorphisms to be invariant under permutation of variables becomes little (if at all) relevant. Such a requirement is not satisfied, for instance, by homomorphisms 5., 6., 7., 9. and 11. in the table 1 so, using this criterion, one would claim that these definitions are not "appropriate". Functions, on the other hand, do have ordered arguments and, above all, distinguish one relational argument as the result. Thus, the definitions of homomorphisms are indeed invariant under permutation of the argument variables, but there seems to be no reason to require such an invariance under permutation of (some) argument variable(s) with the result.

Although multialgebras introduce some structure not present within the corresponding relational structures, the isomorphism (2.1) allows one to convert any multialgebra to the corresponding relational structure and vice versa. Morover, any definition of a homomorphism of multialgebras can be transfered to the relational structures and vice versa, although this may require forgetting/introducing the distinction between the argument and result variables. We now turn to multialgebraic homomorphisms but, for convenience, we will mostly use relational notation.

# 3 Compositionality of Multialgebraic Homomorphisms

Theorem 3.5, which is the main result of this section, gives an exhaustive characterization of compositional definitions. We begin by giving a counter-example for compositionality of one of the homomorphisms from table 1.

Full homomorphisms were considered in [22,20] as *the* homomorphisms between relations. In a more special form, they also appear in the study of partial algebras [6]. In the context of partial algebras, it is known that these homomorphisms do not compose. But it is not clear if all the authors were aware of this fact in the general setting.

**Example 3.1** *Let $A, B, C$ be structures with one relation $R$ – a) presents a many-sorted counter-example and b) the single-sorted case.*

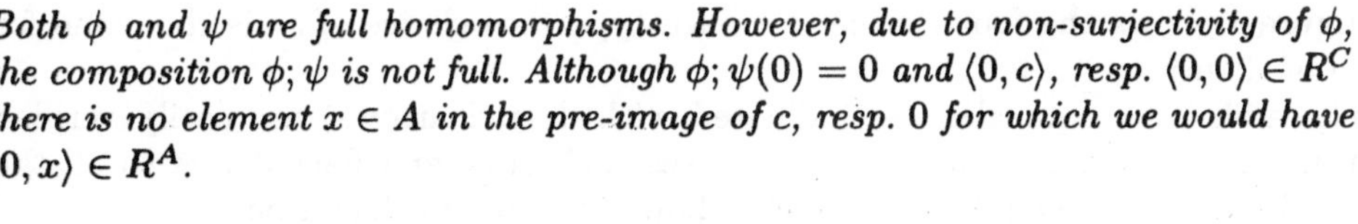

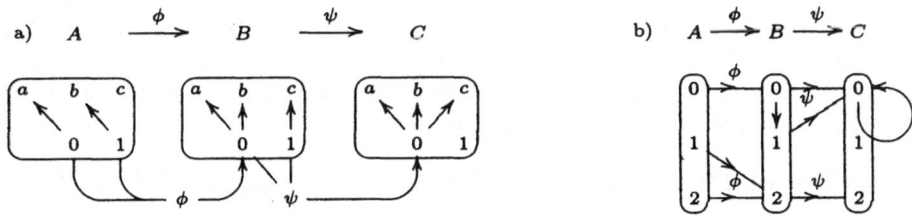


*Both $\phi$ and $\psi$ are full homomorphisms. However, due to non-surjectivity of $\phi$, the composition $\phi;\psi$ is not full. Although $\phi;\psi(0) = 0$ and $\langle 0, c\rangle$, resp. $\langle 0, 0\rangle \in R^C$ there is no element $x \in A$ in the pre-image of $c$, resp. 0 for which we would have $\langle 0, x\rangle \in R^A$.*

## 3.1 Compositional Homomorphisms

We assume a fixed relational signature, with $R$ ranging over all relation symbols, and consider definitions of homomorphisms $\phi : A \to B$ of the form

$$\Delta[\phi] \quad \Leftrightarrow \quad l_1[\phi]; R^A; r_1[\phi] \quad \bowtie \quad l_2[\phi]; R^B; r_2[\phi] \tag{3.2}$$

where $l[\_]$'s and $r[\_]$'s are relational expressions (using only relational composition and inverse and parameterized by _), and $\bowtie$ is one of the set-relations $\{=, \subseteq, \supseteq\}$.

**Definition 3.2** *A definition is* compositional *iff for all* $\phi : A \to B$, $\psi : B \to C$, *we have* $\Delta[\phi]$ & $\Delta[\psi] \Rightarrow \Delta[\phi;\psi]$, *i.e.:*

$$l_1[\phi]; R^A; r_1[\phi] \bowtie l_2[\phi]; R^B; r_2[\phi] \quad \&$$
$$l_1[\psi]; R^B; r_1[\psi] \bowtie l_2[\psi]; R^C; r_2[\psi]$$
$$\Rightarrow l_1[\phi;\psi]; R^A; r_1[\phi;\psi] \quad \bowtie \quad l_2[\phi;\psi]; R^C; r_2[\phi;\psi]$$

The number of syntactic expressions of the kind $l[\phi]$ is infinite, however, since homomorphisms are functions we have the simple fact:

**Fact 3.3** *a)* $\phi^-;\phi;\phi^- = \phi^-$ *b)* $\phi;\phi^-;\phi = \phi$ *c)* $\phi^-;\phi = id_{\phi[\underline{A}]}$

Thus the length of each of the expression $l[\phi]$, resp. $r[\phi]$ (measured by the number of occurring $\phi$'s or $\phi^-$'s) can be limited to 2.

On the other hand, both sides of a definition from (3.2) must yield relational expressions of the same type, i.e., of one of the four types $A \times A$, $A \times B$, ..., which will be abbreviated as $AA, AB, \ldots$

For each choice of $\bowtie$, this leaves us with four possibilities for each type. For instance, for $AB$ we have the following four possibilities:

$\top_{AB} : \phi;\phi^-;R^A;\phi \bowtie \phi;R^B;\phi^-;\phi$ $\quad$ $\bot_{AB} : R^A;\phi \bowtie \phi;R^B$

$E_{AB} : \phi;\phi^-;R^A;\phi \bowtie \phi;R^B$ $\quad$ $W_{AB} : R^A;\phi \bowtie \phi;R^B;\phi^-;\phi$

The symbols denoting the respective possibilities are chosen for the following reason. Relational composition preserves each of the relations $\bowtie$, i.e., given a particular choice of $\bowtie$ and any relations $C, D$ (of appropriate type), we have: $R_1 \bowtie R_2 \Rightarrow C;R_1 \bowtie C;R_2$ and $R_1 \bowtie R_2 \Rightarrow R_1;D \bowtie R_2;D$. Starting with $\bot_{AB}$ and pre-composing (on the "*E*ast") both sides of $\bowtie$ with $\phi;\phi^-;(\_)$, we obtain $E_{AB}$; post-composing (on the "*W*est") both sides of $\bowtie$ with $(\_);\phi^-;\phi$, we obtain $W_{AB}$. Dual compositions lead from there to $\top_{AB}$. Thus we have that $\bot_{AB} \Rightarrow E_{AB}, W_{AB} \Rightarrow \top_{AB}$ and the corresponding lattices are obtained for the other three types starting, respectively, with

$$\bot_{AA} : R^A \bowtie \phi;R^B;\phi^- \qquad \bot_{BB} : \phi^-;R^A;\phi \bowtie R^B \qquad \bot_{BA} : \phi^-;R^A \bowtie R^B;\phi^-$$

Figure 1 shows the four lattices for each type (the choice of $\bowtie$ is the same for all of them).

The additional equivalences (indicated with dotted arrows) are easily verified using the fact that composition preserves each of $\bowtie$ and Fact 3.3. Also all the top definitions are equivalent which follows by simple calculation.

These observations simplify the picture a bit, leading, for each choice of $\bowtie$, to the order of 9 possible definitions shown in figure 2.

Furthermore, choosing $\subseteq$ for $\bowtie$, the above ordering collapses.

**Proposition 3.4** *All definitions (of the form (3.2)) involving* $\subseteq$ *are equivalent.*

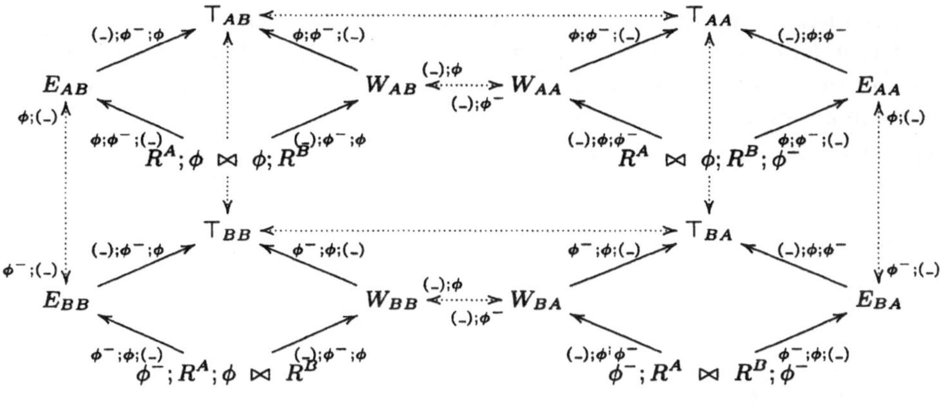

**Fig. 1.** Lattices for each relation type for each choice of $\bowtie$).

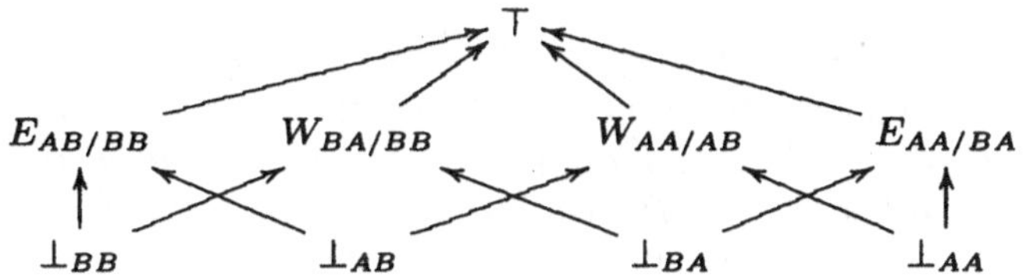

**Fig. 2.** Possible definitions (for a given choice of $\bowtie$).

We are thus left with one definition involving $\subseteq$ and 18 other definitions obtained from two instances (with $=$, resp. $\supseteq$ for $\bowtie$) of the orderings in figure 2. The following, main theorem shows that only the bottom elements of these orderings yield compositional definitions.

**Theorem 3.5** *[30] A definition is compositional iff it is equivalent to one of the following forms:*

1) $R^A;\phi \bowtie \phi;R^B$ 2) $\phi^-;R^A;\phi \rhd R^B$ 3) $\phi^-;R^A \rhd R^B;\phi^-$ 4) $R^A \rhd \phi;R^B;\phi^-$

*where* $\bowtie\, \in \{=,\subseteq,\supseteq\}$ *and* $\rhd \in \{=,\supseteq\}$.

PROOF: For the "if" part, one easily checks that 1)–4) do yield compositional definitions. In fact, this part of the theorem holds for *any* transitive set-relation $\bowtie$. For instance, for 3) we verify:

$$\begin{array}{rl} & \phi^-;R^A \bowtie R^B;\phi^- \quad \& \quad \psi^-;R^B \bowtie R^C;\psi^- \\ \Rightarrow & \psi^-;\phi^-;R^A \bowtie \psi^-;R^B;\phi^- \;\&\; \psi^-;R^B;\phi^- \bowtie R^C;\psi^-;\phi^- \\ & \Rightarrow (\phi;\psi)^-;R^A \bowtie R^C;(\phi;\psi)^- \end{array}$$

The "only if" part is shown providing counter-examples for the remaining possibilities. Although there are 10 cases left, they are easily shown by the following

three counter-examples. In all cases, the given homomorphisms $\phi, \psi$ satisfy the respective definition with $=$ for $\rhd$ (hence, also for $\supseteq$), while their composition does not satisfy the respective definition with $\supseteq$ for $\rhd$. Thus we obtain immediately counter-examples for both $\rhd \in \{=, \supseteq\}$.
Vertical arrows represent the relation $(R)$ in respective multialgebras; the dotted arrows illustrate the images under the respective homomorphisms:

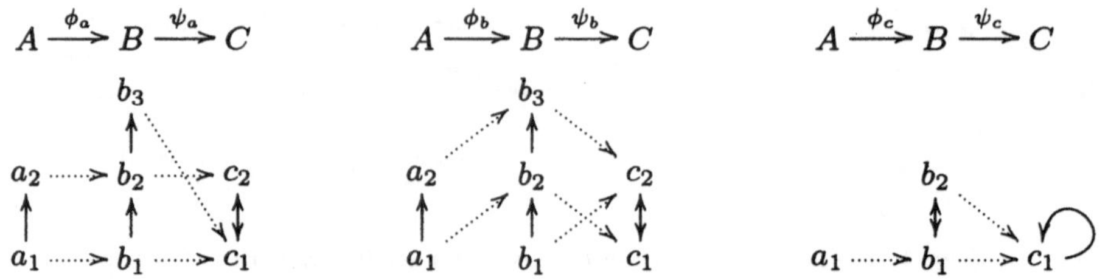

a) b) c)

**a)** for $W_{BB} : \phi^-;R^A;\phi \ \rhd\ R^B;\phi^-;\phi$. We have: $\phi_a^-;R^A;\phi_a = R^B;\phi_a^-;\phi_a$ and $\psi_a^-;R^B;\psi_a = R^C;\psi_a^-;\psi_a$. However, for the composition $\rho_a = \phi_a;\psi_a$, we have $\langle c_2, c_1\rangle \in R^C;\rho_a^-;\rho_a$ but $\langle c_2, c_1\rangle \notin \rho_a^-;R^A;\rho_a$, i.e., $\rho_a^-;R^A;\rho_a \not\supseteq R^C;\rho_a^-;\rho_a$.
**b)** for $E_{BB} : \phi^-;R^A;\phi \rhd \phi^-;\phi;R^B$ is quite analogous. $\phi_b^-;R^A;\phi_b = R^B;\phi_b^-;\phi_b$ and $\psi_b^-;R^B;\psi_b = R^C;\psi_b^-;\psi_b$, but $\rho_b^-;R^A;\rho_b \not\supseteq \rho_b^-;\rho_b;R^C$ with $\langle c_2, c_1\rangle$ as a witness to this negation.
Both these examples can also be used as counter-examples for compositionality of $\top$, represented by $\top_{BB}$. For instance, in the first case, we have $R^B;\phi_a^-;\phi_a = \phi_a^-;\phi_a;R^B;\phi_a^-;\phi_a$ and the corresponding equality holds for $\psi_a$ and $R^C$ – so exactly the same argument yields a counter-example also for this case.
**c)** for both $W_{AA/AB}$ and $E_{AA/BA}$ (this is essentially example 3.1.b). Both $\phi_c$ and $\psi_c$ are obviously $W_{AB}$: $R^A;\phi_c = \phi_c;R^B;\phi_c^-;\phi_c$ and $R^B;\psi_c = \psi_c;R^C;\psi_c^-;\psi_c$. However, their composition yields: $\emptyset = R^A;\rho_c \not\supseteq \rho_c;R^C;\rho_c^-;\rho_c = \langle c_1, c_1\rangle$.
This gives also counter-example for $E_{BA} : \phi_c^-;R^A \rhd \phi_c^-;\phi_c;R^B;\phi_c^-$. □

This leaves us with 9 basic compositional definitions (more can be obtained by their conjunctions (see [11]). Inspecting the table 1, we can see that 1. and 2. define actually the same notion, and the only other compositional definitions are 9., 10. and 11.

Notice that, although we have used a rather special definition of relational composition, all counter-examples involve only binary relations. Thus, even if one defined composition of relations differently, as long as it subsumes the standard composition of binary relations, the theorem gives the maximal number of compositional definitions of homomorphisms.

On the other hand, one might probably come up with other forms of defining homomorphisms that are not covered by our theorem. [2] However, the majority

[2] E.g., using complementation in addition to composition and inverse, or else using relations instead of functions as homomorphisms. We have to leave such generalizations to future research.

(if not all) of commonly used forms do conform to this format. Occasionally, some authors consider certain modifications of the definitions from table 1. For instance, full outdegree and indegree homomorphisms (3,5,6) with the extra surjectivity requirement do compose. This restriction merely enforces the equality $\phi^{-};\phi = id_B$, and leads to a special case of cases 2), 1) and 3) from the Theorem 3.5, respectively.

### 3.2 Congruences on Multialgebras

Congruences of relational and power structures were studied, for instance, in [1, 2,3,4,5]. As observed before, any equivalence gives rise to a (weak) homomorphism. However, the more specific definitions from theorem 3.5 may lead to more specific relations. We consider first equational definitions from the theorem, and characterize these kernels which turn out to be not merely equivalences but congruences of a sort. To proceed further we need a notion of a quotient:

**Definition 3.6** *Given a structure* $A = \langle \underline{A}, R_1^A, R_2^A ... \rangle$ *and an equivalence* $\sim \subseteq \underline{A} \times \underline{A}$*, a quotient* $A/_{\sim} = Q$ *is given by* $\underline{Q} = \{[x] : x \in \underline{A}\}$ *and* $R_i^Q = \phi^{-}; R_i^A; \phi$*, where* $[x] = \{y \in \underline{A} : x \sim y\}$*, and* $\phi : \underline{A} \to \underline{Q}$ *is defined by* $\phi(x) = [x]$.

Obviously, $\sim$ is the kernel of $\phi$, i.e., $x \sim y$ iff $\phi(x) = \phi(y)$, and $\sim = \phi; \phi^{-}$.

**Proposition 3.7** *Let* $\sim$ *be an equivalence on* $A$ *and* $Q, \phi$ *be as in def. 3.6.*

| | if $\sim$ satisfies | then |
|---|---|---|
| 2) | | $\phi^{-}; R^A; \phi = R^Q$ |
| 1) | $\sim; R^A; \sim = R^A; \sim$ | $R^A; \phi = \phi; R^Q$ |
| 3) | $\sim; R^A; \sim = \sim; R^A$ | $\phi^{-}; R^A = R^Q; \phi^{-}$ |
| 4) | $\sim; R^A; \sim = R^A$ | $R^A = \phi; R^Q; \phi^{-}$ |

In 1), 3) and 4) the relation $\sim$ is not just an arbitrary equivalence but has a flavour of a congruence:

1) can be stated as: $\forall \overline{a}, b : (\exists b' \sim b, \overline{a}' \sim \overline{a} : R^A(\overline{a}', b')) \Leftrightarrow (\exists b' \sim b : R^A(\overline{a}, b'))$, which gives: $\forall \overline{a}, b, \overline{a}' : R^A(\overline{a}, b) \wedge \overline{a} \sim \overline{a}' \Rightarrow \exists b' \sim b : R^A(\overline{a}', b')$;
3) yields a dual condition: $\forall \overline{a}, b, b' : R^A(\overline{a}, b) \wedge b' \sim b \Rightarrow \exists \overline{a}' \sim \overline{a} : R^A(\overline{a}', b')$;
4) is strongest: $\forall \overline{a}, b, \overline{a}', b' : R^A(\overline{a}, b) \wedge \overline{a}' \sim \overline{a} \wedge b' \sim b \Rightarrow R^A(\overline{a}', b')$.[3]

For any (at least weak) homomorphism we have the converse of 3.7:

**Proposition 3.8** *Given a homomorphism* $\phi : A \to B$*, let* $\sim$ *be the kernel of* $\phi$

| | if $\phi : A \to B$ satisfies | then $\sim$ is an equivalence and |
|---|---|---|
| 1) | $R^A; \phi = \phi; R^B$ | $\sim; R^A; \sim = R^A; \sim$ |
| 3) | $\phi^{-}; R^A = R^B; \phi^{-}$ | $\sim; R^A; \sim = \sim; R^A$ |
| 4) | $R^A = \phi; R^B; \phi^{-}$ | $\sim; R^A; \sim = R^A$ |

[3] Following a suggestion from an anonymous referee, one might want to compare this case to the notion of bisimulation of process.

There is no line for condition 2) since $\phi^-; R^A; \phi = R^B$ obviously implies that $\sim$ is an equivalence but, in fact, this follows for any mapping $\phi$.

This is not the strongest formulation of this fact. For $\sim$ being an equivalence it suffices, of course, that $\phi$ is a weak homomorphism. Furthermore, for instance 1) implies $R^A; \phi = \phi; R^B; \phi^-; \phi$ which is sufficient to establish the respective property of $\sim$. In general, since $\sim$ is induced only from the image of $A$ under $\phi$, restricting the homomorphisms' definitions on the $R^B$-side to this image (i.e. by $\phi^-; \phi$) will yield the same properties of $\sim$.

Similar results do not follow for the "closed" versions, i.e., for the homomorphisms defined by $\supseteq$ in place of $=$. We can uniformly replace $=$ by $\supseteq$ in proposition 3.8, but then the statements in the right column are trivial for any mapping $\phi$. If the target algebra is total then the kernel may retain the flavour of congruence. But, in general, "closed" homomorphisms induce only equivalence.

## 4 Categories of Multialgebras

Theorem 3.5 gave three possibilities for $\bowtie$. The category substituting for $\bowtie$ the relation $\subseteq$ is called "weak", those with $=$ are "tight", and those with $\supseteq$ "closed". (These names are, to some extent, motivated by the tradition within partial algebras and multialgebras.) In lack of better names, we then call the categories of kind 1) "inner" (since $\phi^-, \phi$ occur "inside", closest to $\bowtie$), of kind 2) "left", of kind 3) "outer" and of kind 4) "right". For a given signature $\Sigma$, we thus have 9 categories, with homomorphisms $\phi : A \to B$ given by the respective compositional definition:

| | inner | left | outer | right |
|---|---|---|---|---|
| closed | $\mathsf{MAlg}_{IC}(\Sigma)$ : $R^A; \phi \supseteq \phi; R^B$ | $\mathsf{MAlg}_{LC}(\Sigma)$ : $\phi^-; R^A; \phi \supseteq R^B$ | $\mathsf{MAlg}_{OC}(\Sigma)$ : $\phi^-; R^A \supseteq R^B; \phi^-$ | $\mathsf{MAlg}_{RC}(\Sigma)$ : $R^A \supseteq \phi; R^B; \phi^-$ |
| tight | $\mathsf{MAlg}_{IT}(\Sigma)$ : $R^A; \phi = \phi; R^B$ | $\mathsf{MAlg}_{LT}(\Sigma)$ : $\phi^-; R^A; \phi = R^B$ | $\mathsf{MAlg}_{OT}(\Sigma)$ : $\phi^-; R^A = R^B; \phi^-$ | $\mathsf{MAlg}_{RT}(\Sigma)$ : $R^A = \phi; R^B; \phi^-$ |
| weak | $\mathsf{MAlg}_W(\Sigma) : R^A; \phi \subseteq \phi; R^B$ | | | |

Table 2 summarizes finite (co-)completeness of the respective categories: '+' means the existence of the respective (co-)limit for arbitrary $\Sigma$; '−' indicates that there exists a counter-example: a signature $\Sigma$ and $\Sigma$-multilagebras for which the respective (co-)limit does not exist.

With a few exceptions, the positive results are obtained by constructions similar to (though never the same as) those in the standard category of algebras. The proofs for the inner (and weak) categories can be found in [29], and for the remaining ones in [11].

It has perhaps been a prevailing opinion among mathematicians interested in the question that weak homomorphisms of relational structures provide the most useful notion. They were certainly the most commonly used ones. The above results do, if nothing else, justify and demonstrate this opinion: the category $\mathsf{MAlg}_W(\Sigma)$ possesses many desirable properties not possessed by the other categories. There is, however, an exception to this claim, namely, the category

**Table 2.** Finite limits and co-limits in the categories of multialgebras

| | initial obj. | co-products | co-equalizers | terminal obj. | products | equalizers |
|---|---|---|---|---|---|---|
| $\mathsf{MAlg}_W(\Sigma)$ | + | + | + | + | + | + |
| $\mathsf{MAlg}_{IC}(\Sigma)$ | − | − | − | + | − | − |
| $\mathsf{MAlg}_{IT}(\Sigma)$ | − | − | + | − | − | − |
| $\mathsf{MAlg}_{LC}(\Sigma)$ | − | − | + | + | − | − |
| $\mathsf{MAlg}_{LT}(\Sigma)$ | − | − | + | − | − | − |
| $\mathsf{MAlg}_{OC}(\Sigma)$ | + | + | − | + | − | + |
| $\mathsf{MAlg}_{OT}(\Sigma)$ | + | + | + | (+) | ? | + |
| $\mathsf{MAlg}_{RC}(\Sigma)$ | + | + | + | + | + | + |
| $\mathsf{MAlg}_{RT}(\Sigma)$ | + | − | − | − | − | + |

$\mathsf{MAlg}_{RC}(\Sigma)$ which, too, is finitely complete and co-complete. A possible exception is also the category $\mathsf{MAlg}_{OT}(\Sigma)$. We are almost certain that terminal objects, marked with (+), exist and can be obtained by an interesting kind of term-model construction which has been shown to work in special cases. Also products, marked with '?', remain still under investigation.[4] If the conjecture about completeness of $\mathsf{MAlg}_{OT}(\Sigma)$ turns out to be true, this might be the most interesting of all the investiagted categories. This can be further strengthened by observing that $\phi^-; R^A = R^B; \phi^-$ implies $R^A; \phi \subseteq \phi; R^B$, so that properties of the most common, weak homomorphisms are actually implied by outer-tightness.

## 5 Conclusions

We started by considering the relational structures but the suggested definition of composition of relations of arbitrary arities turned such structures into algebras – namely, multialgebras. These provide a convenient way for algebraic study of relational structures, as well as for modeling phenomena like partiality and nondeterminism within a unified framework.

We have given, in theorem 3.5, a general characterization of compositional homorphisms of multilagebras. The characterization applies equally to relational structures. Thus, from the manifold of alternative proposed definitions of such homomorphisms, we identified 9 which allow a categorical approach. We have also described the equivalence relations which emerge as kernels of the corresponding (compositional) homomorphisms and which have various flavours of congruences.

We have then studied in detail the obtained categories with respect to the existence of (finite) limits and co-limits. The categories with weak and right-closed homomorphisms, $\mathsf{MAlg}_W(\Sigma)$, $\mathsf{MAlg}_{RC}(\Sigma)$, possess all constructions. The former has been widely used and is probably the most accepted standard. It remains to be seen whether the structural properties of the latter category demonstrated here will offer grounds for comparable applications. We conjecture that also the

[4] Hopefully, the details and proofs of these constructions will be completed by the time of the conference. We suggest the interested reader to contact the first author.

category $\mathsf{MAlg}_{OT}(\Sigma)$ is finitely (co-)complete and may be, in fact, highly interesting, but its terminal objects and products need further investigation.

The remaining categories have much poorer structural properties. Thus, accepting compositionality and the categorical properties we have studied as the criteria for the evaluation of the homomorphisms, our results leave quite limited choice. These criteria may, of course, be debatable and we by no means claim their universal validity. However, even if one does not want to base one's choice exclusively on these criteria, the results of this paper, in particular, the characterization of compositional definitions, can provide a useful tool preventing one from looking for new, idiosyncratic notions serving only very peculiar purposes.

We have studied only the categories of *all* multialgebras over a given signature. The really interesting question might be whether the properties of (co-)completeness can be lifted to axiomatic classes. The problem with answering such a question is that one would first have to decide on the logical language in which one writes the axioms. This question is far from settled and faces different proposals from different authors working on multialgebras. Still, even though we have not considered axiomatic classes, our results can serve, at least, the negative purpose. We have studied axiomatic classes over *empty* sets of axioms – hence, at least the negative results, the demonstrated non-existence of some constructions, will remain valid when lifted to axiomatic classes specified in arbitrary languages.

## References


[1] Bandler, W. and Kohout, L. J. On new types of homomorphisms and congruences for partial algebras and n-ary relations. *Int. J. General Systems 12*, 149–157. (1986).

[2] Bandler, W. and Kohout, L. J. On the general theory of relational morphisms. *Int. J. General Systems 13*, 47–66. (1986).

[3] Boyd, J. P. Relational homomorphisms. *Social Networks 14*, 163–186. (1992).

[4] Brink, C. Power structures. *Algebra Universalis 30*, 177–216. (1993).

[5] Brink, C., Jacobs, D., Netle, K., and Sekran, R. Generalized quotient algebras and power algebras. (1997), [unpublished].

[6] Burmeister, P. *A Model Theoretic Oriented Approach to Partial Algebras.* Akademie-Verlag, Berlin. (1986).

[7] Cohn, P. M. *Universal Algebra.* D. Reidel Publishing Company. (1981), [series "Mathematics and Its Applications", vol. 6].

[8] Glenn, P. Identification of certain structures as split opfibrations over $\delta^{op}$. (1997), [to appear in Journal of Pure and Applied Algebra].

[9] Gratzer, G. *Universal Algebra.* Springer. (1968).

[10] Hansoul, G. A subdirect decomposition theorem for multialgebras. *Algebra Universalis 16.* (1983).

[11] Hodzic, A. Categories of multialgebras. Technical report, M.Sc. Thesis at University of Bergen, Dept. of Informatics. (2001), [forthcoming].

[12] Hussmann, H. *Nondeterministic algebraic specifications.* Ph. D. thesis, Fak. f. Mathematik und Informatik, Universitat Passau. (1990).

[13] Hussmann, H. *Nondeterminism in Algebraic Specifications and Algebraic Programs.* Birkhäuser. (1993), [revised version of [12]].

[14] JÓNSSON, B. Varieties of relation algebras. *Algebra Universalis 15*, 273–298. (1982).

[15] JÓNSSON, B. AND TARSKI, A. Boolean algebras with operators i. *American J. Mathematics 73*, 891–939. (1951).

[16] JÓNSSON, B. AND TARSKI, A. Boolean algebras with operators ii. *American J. Mathematics 74*, 127–162. (1952).

[17] KAPUR, D. *Towards a Theory of Abstract Data Types.* Ph. D. thesis, Laboratory for CS, MIT. (1980).

[18] KONIKOWSKA, B. AND BIAŁASIK, M. Reasoning with nondeterministic specifications. *Acta Informatica 36*, 5, 375–403. (1999).

[19] KRIAUČIUKAS, V. AND WALICKI, M. *Reasoning and rewriting with set-relations II: the non-ground case.* LNCS vol. 1130, Springer. (1996).

[20] ŁOŚ, J. Homomorphisms of relations. (1985), [manuscript, Warszawa].

[21] MADARÁSZ, R. Remarks on power structures. *Algebra Universalis 34*, 2, 179–184. (1995).

[22] MOSTOWSKI, A. *Mathematical Logic.* Warszawa-Wrocław. (1948), [in Polish].

[23] NIPKOW, T. Non-deterministic data types: models and implementations. *Acta Informatica 22*, 629–661. (1986).

[24] NIPKOW, T. *Observing non-deterministic data types.* LNCS vol. 332, Springer. (1987).

[25] PATTISON, P. The analysis of semigroups of multirelational systems. *J. Mathematical Psychology 25*, 87–117. (1982).

[26] PICKERT, G. Bemerkungen zum homomorphie-begriff. *Mathematische Zeitschrift 53.* (1950).

[27] PICKETT, H. Homomorphisms and subalgebras of multialgebras. *Pacific J. of Mathematics 21*, 327–342. (1967).

[28] TOPENTCHAROV, V. V. Composition générale des relations. *Algebra Universalis 30*, 119–139. (1993).

[29] WALICKI, M. AND BIAŁSIK, M. Relations, multialgebras and homomorphisms. Technical Report 838, Institute of Computer Science, Polish Academy of Sciences. (1997).

[30] WALICKI, M. AND BIAŁSIK, M. (some) categories of relational structures. *Recent Trends in ADT, LNCS 1376.* (1997).

[31] WALICKI, M. AND MELDAL, S. A complete calculus for the multialgebraic and functional semantics of nondeterminism. *ACM ToPLaS 17*, 2. (1995).

[32] WALICKI, M. AND MELDAL, S. *Multialgebras, power algebras and complete calculi of identities and inclusions.* LNCS vol. 906, Springer. (1995).

[33] WALICKI, M. AND MELDAL, S. Algebraic approaches to nondeterminism – an overview. *ACM Computing Surveys 29*, 1 (March). (1997).

# Representation of Autonomous Automata

Jānis Buls[1], Vaira Buža[2], and Roberts Glaudiņš[3]

[1] University of Latvia, 19, Rainis boulevard, Rīga, LV-1586, Latvia buls@fmf.lu.lv
[2] Cēsis District Council Regional Shool-board, 5, Bērzaines Street, Cēsis, LV-4100 Latvia vairab@cesis.lanet.lv
[3] Agrobusiness College Jēkabpils, 1, Pasta Street, Jēkabpils, LV-5201 Latvia robertsg@lanet.lv

**Abstract.** An autonomous automaton is a finite automaton with output in which the input alphabet has cardinality one when special reduced. We define the transition from automata to semigroups via a representation *successful* if given two incomparable automata (neither simulate the other), the semigroups representing the automata are distinct. We show that representation by the transition semigroup is not successful. We then consider a representation of automata by semigroups of partial transformations. We show that in general transition from automata to semigroups by this representation is not successful either. In fact, the only successful transition presented is the transiton to this semigroup of partial transformations together with its generating set, and in this case success occurs only with autonomous automata.

## 1 Introduction

Let $V = \langle Q, A, B, \circ, * \rangle$ be a finite automaton with output, where $Q, A, B$ are finite, nonempty sets; $Q \times A \xrightarrow{\circ} Q$ is a function and $Q \times A \xrightarrow{*} B$ is a surjecive function. The sets $Q, A, B$ are called the set of *states*, the *input alphabet* and the *output alphabet*, respectively. The mapping $\circ$ is called the *transition function* of the automaton $V$ and $*$ is called the *output function* of $V$.

Let $Q = \{q_1, q_2, \ldots, q_k\}$, $A = \{a_1, a_2, \ldots, a_m\}$, $B = \{b_1, b_2, \ldots, b_n\}$. In [1] Balode and Buls considered the following representation of $V$ by partial transformations on $Q$. For $(a_i, b_j) \in A \times B$ define

$$\gamma(a_i, b_j) = \begin{pmatrix} q_1 & q_2 & \cdots & q_k \\ q_{ij}^1 & q_{ij}^2 & \cdots & q_{ij}^k \end{pmatrix},$$

where for every $s$

$$q_{ij}^s = \begin{cases} q_s \circ a_i, & \text{if } q_s * a_i = b_j, \\ \text{undefined}, & \text{otherwise.} \end{cases}$$

Let $P(V)$ denote the semigroup generated by $\gamma(A \times B)$. That is, $P(V) = \langle \mathrm{Im}\gamma \rangle$. The semigroup $P(V)$ is called an *autonomaton semigroup*.

Simulation was first discussed by Hartmanis [2] forty years ago. This concept describes the possibility on abstract level in which one machine could be replaced

R. Freivalds (Ed.): FCT 2001, LNCS 2138, pp. 372–375, 2001.

by other in applications. If we like to treet the automata by semigroups as it done till now and develop the theory not only as selfsufficient discipline the connections between simulation and semigroups should be considered from every point of view too. Thus we say that a transition from automata to semigroups through some representation is *successful* if it adequatly characterizes simulation. In this note we demonstrate that the transition from autonomous automata to automaton semigroups can only be deemed to be successful if we consider not only the automaton semigroup but its generating set of partial transformations as well. That is, the representation which maps an automaton $V$ with output to the pair $(\mathrm{Im}\gamma, P(V))$ yields a successful transition in the case of autonomous automata but the transition to the representation of $V$ by $P(V)$ is not successful even in the autonomous case.

## 2 Successful Transitions

If $C$ and $'C$ are alphabets, any mapping $C \xrightarrow{h} 'C$ can be extended in the usual way to a mapping, also denoted $h$, from $C^*$ to $'C^*$. Thus if $V = \langle Q, A, B, \circ, *\rangle$ we may extend the mappings $\circ$ and $*$ to $Q \times A^*$ by defining

$$q \circ \epsilon = q, \qquad q \circ (ux) = (q \circ u) \circ x$$
$$q * \epsilon = \epsilon, \quad q * (ux) = (q * u)((q \circ u) * x),$$

for all $q \in Q$, $(u, x) \in A^* \times A$, and where $\epsilon$ is the empty word. Henceforth, we shall omit parantheses if there is no danger of confusion. So, for example, we will write $q \circ u * x$ instead of $(q \circ u) * x$.

**Definition 1.** *Let $V = \langle Q, A, B\rangle$, $'V = \langle 'Q, 'A, 'B\rangle$ be automata. We say that $V$* simulates *$'V$ by*

$$'Q \xrightarrow{h_1} Q, \quad 'A \xrightarrow{h_2} A, \quad B \xrightarrow{h_3} 'B$$

*if the diagram*

$$\begin{array}{ccc} 'Q \times 'A^* & \xrightarrow{*} & 'B^* \\ h\downarrow & \downarrow h_2 & \uparrow h_3 \\ Q \times A^* & \xrightarrow{*} & B^* \end{array}$$

*commutes. That is, if*

$$'q * 'u = h_3(h_1('q) * h_2('u)) \qquad \text{for all} \quad ('q, 'u) \in 'Q \times 'A^*.$$

We write $V \geq 'V(h_1, h_2, h_3)$ if $V$ simulates $'V$ by $h_1, h_2, h_3$. We say $V$ *simulates* $'V$ if there exist maps such that $V \geq 'V(h_1, h_2, h_3)$. We write $V \geq 'V$ if $V$ simulates $'V$.

The two automata $V$ and $'V$ are *incomparable* if $V \not\geq 'V$ and $'V \not\geq V$. If, on the other hand, $V \geq 'V$ and $'V \geq V$ then we say that $V$ *mutually simulates* $'V$ and we write $V \bowtie 'V$.

Let $V = \langle Q, A, B\rangle$ and $'V = \langle 'Q, A, 'B\rangle$, and let $q \in Q$, $'q \in 'Q$. The states $q$ and $'q$ are called *distinguishable* if there exists a $u \in A^*$ such that $q * u \neq 'q * u$.

Otherwise, these states are said to be *indistinguishable*. If every state in $Q$ is distinguishable from every other state in $Q$ then the automaton is called *a reduced automaton*.

The automaton $V$ *distinguishes the letters* $a_1, a_2$ if there exists a state $q \in Q$ and a word $u \in A^*$ such that $q * a_1 u \neq q * a_2 u$. A reduced automaton that distingushes every pair of letters in its output alphabet is called *a special reduced automaton*. By [3], for every automaton $V$ there exists up to isomorphism a unique special reduced automaton $'V$ such that $V \bowtie {'V}$. Because of this we may restrict our attention to special reduced automata.

We say that a representation of finite automata with output is *successful* if incomparable special reduced automata have nonisomorphic representations.

The focus of our investigations will be so-called *autonomous* automata which provide the counterexamples that we need to demonstrate that our representation of finite automata by automata semigroups cannot be deemed successful.

**Definition 2.** *An automaton* $V = \langle Q, A, B \rangle$ *is called autonomous if*

$$\forall q \in Q \, \forall a \in A \, \forall x \in A \, (q \circ a = q \circ x \wedge q * a = q * x).$$

Thus the input alphabet $A$ of a special reduced atonomous automaton has precisely one letter.

### 2.1 Representation by *T(Q)*

Let $T(Q)$ denote the semigroup of all transformations on the set $Q$. For each $a_i \in A$ define $\alpha(a_i) \in T(Q)$ by

$$\alpha(a_i) = \begin{pmatrix} q_1 \, q_2 \cdots q_k \\ q_1' \, q_2' \cdots q_k' \end{pmatrix}, \quad \text{where} \quad \forall s \, (q_s' = q_s \circ a_i).$$

We say $\langle \mathrm{Im}\alpha \rangle$ is the automaton $V$ *transition semigroup.*

**Proposition 1.** *There exist special reduced incomparable autonomous automata with the same transition semigroup.*

Consequently, the transition semigroup representation of finite automata with output cannot be regarded as successful.

### 2.2 Representation by Similar Partitions

Define $\mathrm{Dom}\, V = \{ \mathrm{Dom}\sigma \mid \sigma \in \mathrm{Im}\gamma \}$, where $\mathrm{Dom}\sigma$ is the domain of the partial transformation $\sigma$. The following result is easy to establish.

**Proposition 2.** *If* $V$ *is autonomous then* $\mathrm{Dom}\, V$ *is a partition of* $Q$.

Two equivalence relations, $S$ and $'S$ on $Q$ and $'Q$, respectively, are said to be *similar* if there is a bijection $Q \xrightarrow{f} {'Q}$ such that $S(q,z) \Leftrightarrow {'S}(f(q), f(z))$, for all $q, z \in Q$. Likewise, two partitions are *similar* if they induce similar equivalence relations.

The following proposition is easily verified.

**Proposition 3.** *Let $V$ and $'V$ be isomorphic special reduced autonomous automata. If $\gamma$ and $'\gamma$ are the representations of $V$ and $'V$, respectively, by partial transformations on $Q$, then* $\mathrm{Dom}\,V$ *and* $\mathrm{Dom}'V$ *are similar.*

However, we also have the following.

**Proposition 4.** *There exist incomparable special reduced autonomous automata $V$ and $'V$ with* $\mathrm{Dom}\,V = \mathrm{Dom}\,'V$.

## 3 Similar Sets of Partial Transformations

**Definition 3.** *Sets $T \subseteq PT(Q)$ and $'T \subseteq PT('Q)$ are called* similar *if there exist bijections*

$$Q \xrightarrow{f} 'Q, \quad T \xrightarrow{\psi} 'T$$

*such that a diagram*

$$\begin{array}{ccc} Q & \xrightarrow{\sigma} & Q \\ f\downarrow & & \downarrow f \\ 'Q & \xrightarrow{\psi(\sigma)} & 'Q \end{array}$$

*is commutative for all $\sigma \in T$.*

So, this means that
(i) $q\sigma$ is defined iff $qf\psi(\sigma)$ is defined (we write $qf\psi(\sigma)$ instead of $(\psi(\sigma))(f(q)))$;
(ii) if $q\sigma$ and $qf\psi(\sigma)$ is defined then $q\sigma f = qf\psi(\sigma)$.

**Theorem 1.** *Let $A \times B \xrightarrow{\gamma} PT(Q)$ and $'A \times 'B \xrightarrow{'\gamma} PT('Q)$ be representations of special reduced autonomous automata $V$ and $'V$ respectively. Then $V$ and $'V$ are isomorphic iff* $\mathrm{Im}\gamma$ *and* $\mathrm{Im}'\gamma$ *are similar.*

**Theorem 2.** *Let $V = \langle Q, A, B\rangle$ and $'V = \langle 'Q, 'A, 'B\rangle$ are special reduced autonomous automata with one and the same automaton semigroup. If for every $\sigma \in \mathrm{Im}\gamma$ with $|\mathrm{Dom}\sigma| = 1$ there is a $'\sigma \in \mathrm{Im}'\gamma$ such that $\sigma = '\sigma$ then $V$ and $'V$ are isomorphic.*

We conclude by stating that the condition on the members of $\mathrm{Im}\gamma$ of domain size one is crucial.

**Proposition 5.** *There exist incomparable special reduced autonomous automata with one and the same automaton semigroup.*

## References

1. Balode, I., Buls, J.: Automaton Representation of a Semigroup. Proceedings of the Latvian Academy of Scieces. Section **B**, Vol. **50**, No.**1(582)** (1996), 1-3.
2. Hartmanis J.: On the State Assignment Problem for Sequential Machines I. IRE Transactions on Electronic Computers. Vol. EC-**10**, No.**2**(June) (1961), 157-165.
3. Buls, J.: Modelirovanie avtomatov Mili. Latv.univ., Riga (dep. v Latv. NIINTI 30.05.88, No121-La88), (1988) (Russian)

# Quantum Reversibility and a New Model of Quantum Automaton

Massimo Pica Ciamarra*

Dipartimento di Scienze Fisiche, Università di Napoli "Federico II" and INFM, Via Cintia, 80126 Napoli, Italy
picaciam@na.infn.it

**Abstract.** Since a quantum computational system is a generalization of a classical computational system, its computational power should be greater or equal than that of the classical system. In spite of that the computational power of 1-way quantum finite automata has been shown to be smaller than that of their classical counterpart. I argue that this paradox lies on the ground that the currently accepted definition of quantum automaton neglects the concept of quantum reversibility. In this article I review the role that reversibility plays into quantum computing and I propose a new model of 1-way quantum finite automata whose computational power is at least equal to that of classical automata.

## 1 The Current Model of 1-Way Quantum Finite Automaton

1-way quantum finite automata has been defined by Kondacs and Watrous [4]. A quantum finite automaton $\mathcal{Q}$ is a 6-tuple

$$\mathcal{Q} = (H,\ |s_0\rangle,\ H_{\text{acc}},\ P_{\text{acc}},\ A,\ U_{\text{A}})$$

where $H$ is the internal states Hilbert space, $|s_0\rangle \in H$ with $\left||s_0\rangle\right|^2 = 1$ is the initial state vector, $H_{\text{acc}} \subseteq H$ is the accepting space, $P_{\text{acc}}$ is an operator that projects into $H_{\text{acc}}$, $A$ is the input alphabet (composed of classical symbols). For each symbol $a \in A$ there is a unitary transition matrix $U_a$ acting on $H$: $U_{\text{A}}$ is the set of these matrices.

Using the shorthand $U_w = U_{w_1} U_{w_2} \dots U_{w_k}$ the language accepted by $\mathcal{Q}$ is the function $f^{\mathcal{Q}}(w) = |P_{\text{acc}} U_w |s_0\rangle|^2$ from words $w = w_1 w_2 \dots w_k \in A^*$ to probabilities in $[0, 1]$.

The input alphabet consists of classical elements, whereas the internal states are represented by quantum symbols (by vectors of a Hilbert space): this automaton is not fully quantum. Moreover, it is neither reversible. In fact from the

* This work is for the most part based on my degree thesis. I particularly tank my supervisor, Prof. Giuseppe Trautteur, and my co-supervisor, Prof. Vincenzo R. Marigliano, both at the Dipartimento di Scienze Fisiche dell'Università di Napoli "Federico II".

R. Freivalds (Ed.): FCT 2001, LNCS 2138, pp. 376–379, 2001.

final state $U_w|s_0\rangle$ one cannot retrace the computation as $w$ is unknown. To retrace the computation one will need some information that is not encoded in the final state, i.e., the operator $U_w$. As to the computational power of this model of quantum automaton, first A. Kondacs and J. Watrous [4] have showed that there is a regular language it cannot accept. Then, A. Brodosky and N. Pippenger [2] have demonstrated that it cannot recognize a whole class of regular languages. Its computational power is then smaller than that of 1-way classical finite automata.

## 2 Quantum Reversibility

To perform a quantum computation we apply to the quantum system that codifies the information we want to process some unitary operators. Quantum computing is a reversible process because unitary operators are invertible.

It is well known that every classical irreversible computation can be transformed into a classical reversible one introducing *source* and *garbage*, and that the *garbage* can be recycled so that it grows linearly with the input size [1,3]. We don't know if it is possible to achieve this result in the quantum framework, but certainly it cannot be achieved with the same trick used in the classical case. In fact to recycle the garbage using the classical trick a copy operation is needed, but in the quantum framework a copy operation is not always allowed because of the no-cloning theorem. So, in general, a quantum computation produces some *garbage* that cannot be recycled.

In quantum computing we are not interested in computing backward, and typically we cannot compute backward because we lost reversibility performing the final measurement. So, is there any good reason to store the *garbage*? Classically, if we compute with a reversible system but we don't want to compute backward, we can erase the *garbage* and use it as new source, improving the consumption of space. Quantum mechanically this is not allowed. In the general case, in fact, the *garbage* is entangled with the computational system and we cannot erase it without messing the computation.

To summarize, the unitary evolution imposed by quantum mechanics implies that quantum transition functions and quantum gates must be reversible. Entanglement forbids the construction of an irreversible quantum system for information processing based on these reversible building blocks.

## 3 A New Model of 1-Way Quantum Finite Automaton

To construct a quantum automaton that is fully quantum and strictly reversible we can generalize to the quantum case a classical model of reversible automaton. Does a model of 1-way classical reversible finite automaton exist? It turns out that if we apply Bennett procedure [1] to transform an irreversible Turing machine that moves only to the right and that doesn't write on its tape (i.e. a 1-way classical finite automaton) into a reversible one, we end up with a 2-tape reversible Turing machine that moves only to the right and that writes on its

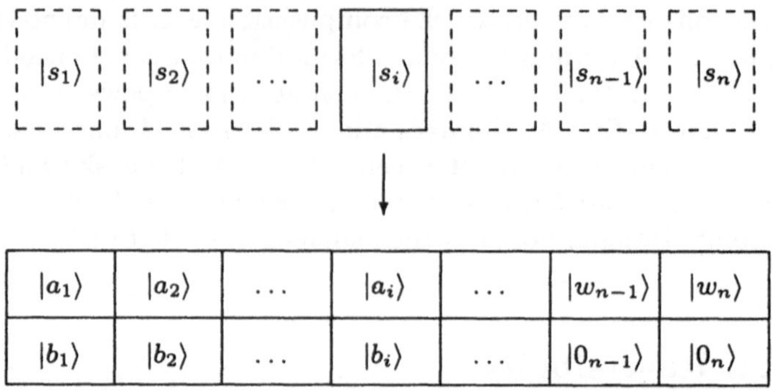


**Fig. 1.** Quantum finite automaton. It is supposed that the internal state and the states of the cells factorize.

tapes[1]. I call this system "1-way reversible finite automaton", and here below I generalize it to the quantum case.

A quantum finite automaton $\mathcal{Q}$ is a 9-tuple:

$$Q = (H_{\text{in}},\ |s_0\rangle,\ H_{\text{acc}},\ P_{\text{acc}},\ I,\ SG,\ \mathcal{I},\ \mathcal{SG},\ U)$$

where $H_{\text{in}}$ is the Hilbert space of internal states, $|s_0\rangle \in H_{\text{in}}$ with $\left||s_0\rangle\right|^2 = 1$ is the initial internal state, $H_{\text{acc}} \subseteq H_{\text{in}}$ is the accepting space, $P_{\text{acc}}$ is an operator that projects into $H_{\text{acc}}$, $I$ and $SG$ are two Hilbert spaces, $\mathcal{I}$ and $\mathcal{SG}$ are two quantum tapes whose cells are quantum systems described respectively by vectors of $I$ and $SG$. $U$ is the (time independent) unitary evolution operator, $U : H_{\text{in}} \otimes I \otimes SG \to H_{\text{in}} \otimes I \otimes SG$.

The input alphabet is composed by an orthonormal basis of $I$. The dimension of $I$ depends on the automaton we are constructing. The dimension of $SG$ is related to the way the unitary evolution operator $U$ acts.

The state of the $k^{th}$ cell of $\mathcal{I}$ is described by a vector belonging to the space $I_k = I$, while the state of the $k^{th}$ 'cell' of $\mathcal{SG}$ is described by a vector belonging to $SG_k = SG$. If the input string is $|w\rangle = |w_1\rangle|w_2\rangle \dots |w_n\rangle$, with $|w_k\rangle \in I_k$, then the tape $\mathcal{SG}$ contains $|0_1\rangle|0_2\rangle \dots |0_n\rangle$, with $|0_k\rangle \in SG_k$. This situation recurs in all models of reversible computation: the value of the *source* must be set appropriately at the beginning of the computation.

In order to understand how this automaton works it turns useful to define:

$$\widetilde{U}_i = \mathbb{I}_1 \otimes \mathbb{I}_2 \otimes \dots \otimes \mathbb{I}_{i-1} \otimes \mathbb{I}_{i+1} \otimes \dots \otimes \mathbb{I}_n \otimes U_i \ ,$$

where $\mathbb{I}_k$ is the identity of $I_k \otimes SG_k$ and $U_i$ the unitary operator $U$ when applied to $H_{\text{in}} \otimes I_i \otimes SG_i$. Moreover we define

$$|0\rangle^n = |0_1\rangle \otimes |0_2\rangle \otimes \dots \otimes |0_n\rangle \ ,$$

[1] It is not useful to add a $3rd$ tape as Bennett [1] did because, as pointed out in the previous section, in the quantum framework we cannot use it to recycle the garbage.

with $|0_k\rangle \in SG_k$. Using this notation $|w\rangle = |w_1\rangle|w_2\rangle \dots |w_n\rangle$ is accepted with probability

$$P(|w\rangle) = \left|P_{\text{acc}}\widetilde{U}_n\widetilde{U}_{n-1}\dots\widetilde{U}_1|s_0\rangle \otimes |w\rangle \otimes |0\rangle^n\right|^2 .$$

It is worth noting that, although when you apply $\widetilde{U}_k$ you formally act on the space $\left(\bigotimes_{i=0}^n I_i \otimes SG_i\right) \otimes H_{\text{in}}$, actually: 1. A local operation is performed, and 2. The states of $I_i$ and $SG_i$ with $i > k$ do not modify. Therefore, when $\widetilde{U}_k$ with $k < i$ is applied, you do not have to dispose the cells $I_i$ or $SG_i$. This further implies that at the beginning of the computation the tapes length has not to be specified and that more cells can be added as the computation moves on. This is exactly what happens in the classical case.

## 4 Computational Power

From [1] we can deduce that every 1-way classical finite automaton can be effectively transformed into a 1-way classical reversible finite automaton. Our model of quantum automaton can clearly simulate this classical reversible automaton, and then it has at least the same computational power of classical automata.

## 5 Conclusion and Open Questions

The main result of this paper is to clarify the relationship between quantum computing and reversible computing. It is argue that quantum computing is reversible because of unitary evolution and entanglement.

Stressing the role of reversibility, a new model of $1-way$ quantum automaton, at least as powerful as 1-way classical finite automata, is proposed. This is a relevant result since the computational power of the currently accepted model of 1-way quantum finite automata is smaller than that of 1-way classical finite automata.

This paper rises the question of space consumption of quantum computing and that of the computational power of the proposed model.

## References


[1] C.H. Bennett. Logical reversibility of computation. *IBM J. Res. Dev.*, 17:525-532, 1973.

[2] A. Brodosky and N. Pippenger. Characterization of 1-way quantum finite automata, Preprint quant-ph\990301.

[3] E. Fredkin T. Toffoli. Conservative Logic. *Int. J. Theor. Phys.* 21:219-253, 1982.

[4] A. Kondacs and J. Watrous. On the power of quantum finite state automata. In *Proc. 38th FOCS*, pages 66–75, 1997.

# Space-Efficient 1.5-Way Quantum Turing Machine

Andrej Dubrovsky*

Institute of Mathematics and Computer Science, University of Latvia,
Raina bulv. 29, Riga, Latvia,
Andrejs.Dubrovskis@fortech.lv

**Abstract.** 1.5QTM is a sort of QTM (Quantum Turing Machine) where the head cannot move left (it can stay where it is and move right). For computations is used other - work tape. In this paper will be studied possibilities to economize work tape space more than the same deterministic Turing Machine can do (for some of the languages). As an example language $(0^i 1^i | i \geq 0)$ is chosen, and is proved that this language could be recognized by deterministic Turing machine using log(i) cells on work tape , and 1.5QTM can recognize it using constant cells quantity.

## 1 Introduction

Quantum Turing Machine(QTM) is the quantum counterpart of the ordinary Turing machine. As an ordinary Deterministic Turing Machine (DTM) it consists of head and tape with transition function $\delta : Q \times \Sigma \times \Sigma \times Q \times \{\leftarrow, \downarrow, \rightarrow\}$ , where Q is states of QTM, S-tape alphabet and $\{\leftarrow, \downarrow, \rightarrow\}$ represents one of the three available head movement directions. Evolutions of QTM required to be unitary. For arbitrary Turing Machine to be QTM there exists well-formedness conditions (when they are met, machine is QTM).

These well-formedness conditions for QTM's could be found in [G]

1.5 way Quantum Turing Machine (1.5QTM) [AI 99] is a kind of Turing machine with two tapes: one contains input word and the other is for work purposes. The input tape's head cannot move left - only right and remains stationary, however work tape's head can move both directions. All evolutions of this kind of Quantum Turing Machine must, like in ordinary QTM be unitary.

Quantum Fourier Transform (QFT) is used in algorithm to make final accept or reject decision. QFT is a quantum version of ordinary Fourier transform. This transform maps function from time domain to frequency domain. The function obtained after Fourier transform of time function has nonzero values only at a multiples of 1/r where r is a period of original function.

As any other quantum operator Quantum Fourier Transform has its unitary matrix. When QFT matrix is applied to quantum state $|a\rangle$ its maps it as follows:

* Research supported by contract IST–1999–11234 (QAIP) from the European Commision, and grant no. 01.0354 from the Latvian Council of Science. This paper was written with financial support from Dati ltd.

R. Freivalds (Ed.): FCT 2001, LNCS 2138, pp. 380–383, 2001.

$$QFT|a\rangle = \frac{1}{\sqrt{q}} \sum_{l=1}^{n} e^{\frac{2\pi i}{n} jl} |c\rangle \tag{1.1}$$

$$\frac{1}{\sqrt{q}} \begin{bmatrix} 1 & 1 & 1 & \dots & 1 \\ 1 & w & w^2 & \dots & w^3 \\ 1 & w^2 & w^4 & \dots & w^8 \\ \dots & \dots & \dots & \dots & \dots \\ 1 & w^{q-1} & w^{2(q-1)} & \dots & w^{(q-1)^2} \end{bmatrix} \text{Where } w = e^{2\pi/q} \ q\text{-th root of unity.} \tag{1.2}$$

For example, when applied to $|0\rangle$ QFT maps it to the all other states with equal amplitude, namely $1/q$ so the impact of QFT is similar to Hadamart transform. In the case when all states initially has equal amplitudes the impact of QFT is just opposite. Single state gains amplitude 1 and all the other 0.

To further explain use of QFT in language recognition another QTM property should be discussed. That is computation paths interference. When states of QTM are measured, and two computational paths interfere then output probability is computed by using formula:

$$P_a = (A_{1,a} + A_{2,a})^2 \tag{1.3}$$

Where Pa is the probability of the state $|a\rangle$ to be measured and $A_1$,a and $A_2$,a are amplitudes of two interfering computational paths. When two paths do not interfere then the probability to measure state $|a\rangle$ computed by formula:

$$P_a = (A_{1,a})^2 + (A_{2,a})^2 \tag{1.4}$$

Interference between computational paths take place only when classical information both paths operate with is equal. That means that both paths has their head position equal as well as symbol on the tape and the moment of time. If these conditions are violated then interference between computational paths is lost and probability of state $|a\rangle$ changes.

Further in this paper will be discussed space-efficient language recognition problem, using deterministic 1.5way Turing machine and then 1.5way Quantum Turing Machine.

## 2 Example

To prove that 1.5QTM can economize space on work tape better than deterministic TM can, language L is used, containing words in the form $(0^i 1^i | i \geq 0)$. This language can be recognized by probabilistic 2-way finite automata [F 81]. problem is then solved using deterministic TM and then 1.5QTM.

## 3 Using DTM

Using deterministic TM this problem could be solved relatively easy, but it requires at least log(i) cells on work tape [LSH 65] to write quantity of zeros on input tape. There can't be more efficient solution because of limitation on input tape head movement (cannot move left). So when comparing ones and zeros count TM should know exactly how many zeros there was, and most efficient way to do that is to write that number in binary (or with other base) code. If there exists the real necessity to move head not only to the right, but also to the left whole word can be copied to work tape and then all computation performed exactly like 2DTM works. However this technique requires linear space on the work tape with the respect to the input word length.

## 4 Using 1.5QTM

Tape space could be economized if we consider using 1.5QTM instead of DTM. There exists method, how to solve this problem, using only constant count of cells on work tape. 1.5QTM, solving this problem, accepting words $x \in L$ with probability 1 and rejecting those $x \in L$ with probability at least $1 - \varepsilon$, where $\varepsilon$ could be arbitrary small. Algorithm of this QTM is similar to that described in [G] p.160.

At starting symbol QTM splits into superposition of working states, and starts to read from input tape. This moment QTM branches its computation in n parallel paths, and each moves head according to this rule: for each new 0 QTM reads from input tape head stays where it is for i cycles and then moves 1 step to the right. If QTM reads 1 from input tape its head remains stationary for $n - i + 1$ cycles and then moves 1 step right. This warrants that no two computation paths can reach right endmarker simultaneously if word is not in language L.

Because j-th path needs $u * j + v * (n - j + 1)$ cycles to reach right endmarker, and $j^1 th \neq j$ path $u * j1 + v * (n - j1 + 1)$, and for this two numbers to be equal u must be equal to v.

On its way from left to right endmarker all paths checking format of the word. If word is not in the form 0i1j then all the paths sooner or later will come to rejecting state, and the word will be rejected. If the format of the word is not violated then Quantum Fourier Transformation is applied to the superposition of QTM states when each computation path reaches right endmarker. If they reached it simultaneously then QFT results in the single (accepting) state, otherwise new superposition of states is formed with probability of accepting the word no more than 1/n, where n is paths quantity. This result is formed because of computation paths interference. If they reached endmarker simultaneously then they all have equal classical information and so interfere. Otherwise there is no interference between them and probability to accept is at most $1/n$.

To control format of the input word work tape is used. For example, when path for the first time encounters change from zeros to ones it writes on the work tape "1" symbol. When next zero is read from input tape the computational path jumps to the rejecting state.

When each path reaches right endmarker Quantum Fourier Transformation (QFT) is applied to superposition of states of QTM. If all paths reached endmarker simultaneously then result of QFT is single accepting state with probability 1, else accepting state's probability is at most $1/n$.

$$\begin{array}{ll}
V_{\#\Lambda}|q\rangle = \frac{1}{\sqrt{n}}\sum_{j=1}^{n}|r_{j,0}\rangle & \\
D|r_{j,k}\rangle = \downarrow\downarrow n \geq k > 0, 1 < j < n & \\
D|r_{j,0}\rangle = \rightarrow\downarrow 1 < j < n & \\
D|q_{jr}\rangle = \rightarrow\downarrow 1 < j < n & \\
D|q_a\rangle = \rightarrow\downarrow & \\
 & \\
V_{0\Lambda}|r_{j,0}\rangle = |r_{j,j}\rangle & V_{0,1}|r_{j,0}\rangle = |q_{jr}\rangle \\
V_{0\Lambda}|r_{j,k}\rangle = |r_{j,k-1}\rangle & V_{0,1}|r_{j,k}\rangle = |q_{j,k-1}\rangle \\
V_{0\Lambda}|q_a\rangle = |q_a\rangle & V_{0,1}|q_a\rangle = |q_a\rangle \\
V_{0\Lambda}|q_{jr}\rangle = |q_{jr}\rangle & V_{0,1}|q_{jr}\rangle = |q_{jr}\rangle \\
 & \\
V_{1\Lambda}|r_{j,0}\rangle = |r_{j,n-j+1}\rangle(1) & V_{0,1}|r_{j,0}\rangle = |q_{j,n-j+1}\rangle \\
V_{1\Lambda}|r_{j,k}\rangle = |r_{j,k-1}\rangle & V_{0,1}|r_{j,k}\rangle = |q_{j,k-1}\rangle \\
V_{1\Lambda}|q_a\rangle = |q_a\rangle & V_{0,1}|q_a\rangle = |q_a\rangle \\
V_{1\Lambda}|q_{jr}\rangle = |q_{jr}\rangle & V_{0,1}|q_{jr}\rangle = |q_{jr}\rangle \\
 & \\
V_{\$\Lambda}|r_{j,0}\rangle = |q_{jr}\rangle & V_{\$,1}|r_{j,0}\rangle = \frac{1}{\sqrt{n}}\sum_{l=1}^{n} e^{\frac{2\pi i}{n}jl}|q_a\rangle \\
V_{\$\Lambda}|r_{j,k}\rangle = |q_{j,k-1}\rangle & V_{\$,1}|r_{j,k}\rangle = |r_{j,k-1}\rangle \\
V_{\$\Lambda}|q_a\rangle = |q_a\rangle & V_{\$,1}|q_a\rangle = |r_{j,n-j+1}\rangle \\
V_{\$\Lambda}|q_{jr}\rangle = |r_{j,n-j+1}\rangle & V_{\$,1}|q_{jr}\rangle = |q_{jr}\rangle
\end{array} \tag{4.5}$$

$V_{\#\Lambda}$ - QTM initialization matrix, splits initial state of the QTM into superposition of working states

$V_{0\Lambda}$ - Zeroes reading matrix, reads zeroes from input tape

$V_{01}$ - Matrix changes state of computational path to rejecting (this matrix will work if format of the input word is violated and word like $0^i1^j0^k$ is encountered.

$V_{1\Lambda}$ - Matrix for the first "1" read from input tape, it also writes flag to work tape

$V_{11}$ - Matrix that read "1"-es from input tape.

## References


[AI 99] Masami Amano, Kazuo Iwama. Undecidability on quantum finite automata. Proc. STOC, p. 368-375,1999.

[G] Jozef Gruska. Quantum computing. McGraw-Hill, London et al, 1999.

[LSH 65] P. M. Lewis II, R. E. Stearns, and J. Hartmanis. Memory bounds for recognition of context-free and context-sensitive languages. Proc. FOCS, p. 191-202, 1965.

[F 81] Rūsiņš Freivalds. Probabilistic two-way machines. LNCS, v.118, p.33-45, 1981.

# A Combinatorial Aggregation Algorithm for Stationary Distribution of a Large Markov Chain
## (Extended Abstract)

Anna Gambin[1]* and Piotr Pokarowski[2]

[1] Institute of Informatics, email: aniag@mimuw.edu.pl
[2] Institute of Applied Mathematics, email: pokar@mimuw.edu.pl
Warsaw University, Banacha 2, 02-097 Warsaw, Poland
fax. +48 22 55 444 00

**Abstract.** A new aggregation algorithm for computing the stationary distribution of a large Markov chain is proposed. This algorithm is attractive when the state space of Markov chain is large enough so that the direct and iterative methods are inefficient. It is based on grouping the states of a Markov chain in such a way that the probability of changing the state inside the group is of greater order of magnitude than interactions between groups. The correctness of the combinatorial aggregation is justified by the method of *forest expansions* developed recently in [5,6]. In contrast to existing methods our approach is based on combinatorial and graph-theoretic framework and can be seen as an algorithmization of famous Markov Chain Tree Theorem. The general method is illustrated by an example of computing the stationary distribution. We establish also some preliminary results on the complexity of our algorithm. Numerical experiments on several benchmark examples show the potential applicability of the algorithm in real life problems.

## 1 Introduction

Our attention is restricted to finite discrete-time Markov chains (although the presented approach is valid also for continuous time). Such a Markov chain over a state space $\mathcal{S}$ is usually represented by a **transition probability matrix P** of order $n$, where $n$ is the number of states in $\mathcal{S}$. For a transition probability matrix $\mathbf{P}$, any vector $\boldsymbol{\pi}$ satisfying $\boldsymbol{\pi}^T = \boldsymbol{\pi}^T\mathbf{P}$, $\sum_{i\in\mathcal{S}} \pi_i = ||\boldsymbol{\pi}||_1 = 1$ is called a **stationary probability distribution** cf. [4]. The most elegant way to calculate it is to find the analytical formulas for the solution of the system. However, this is usually impossible and the only way is to solve the problem numerically [7]. Problems arise from the computational point of view because of the large number of states which system may occupy. It is not uncommon for thousands of states to be generated even for simple applications. On the other hand these Markov chains are often sparse and possess specific structure.

* This work was partially supported by the KBN grant 8 T11C 039 15

R. Freivalds (Ed.): FCT 2001, LNCS 2138, pp. 384–387, 2001.

**Related research.** A lot of research has been done concerning the numerical solutions of some linear equations that occur when one studies Markov chains (see for example [2,7]). Almost all methods for solving a system of linear equations are adapted into this context. In this paper we focus on *nearly completely decomposable* Markov chains (see [1,7]). Such chains often arise in queueing network analysis, large scale economic modeling and computer systems performance evaluation. The state space of these chains can be naturally divided into groups of states such that transitions between states belonging to different groups are significantly less likely than transitions between states within the same group. For solving nearly uncoupled Markov chains, a family of methods has been proposed. They are jointly classified as *iterative aggregation/disaggregation* [3] methods, and based on a decompositional approach. Our combinatorial aggregation approach can be seen as a generalization of existing aggregation algorithms. There are several important advantages over previous methods. The presented algorithm uses combinatorial properties of *directed forests* in the underlying graph of a Markov chain. Combinatorial and graph-theoretic approach simplifies the description of algorithm and proof of correctness which relies on certain facts about forest expansions of solutions of linear equation systems [5].

**Directed forests method.** A real square matrix $A$ of size $s$ induces a graph $G(A)$ with states $\{1, 2, \ldots, s\}$ and edges between all pairs $(i, j)$ with $a_{ij} \neq 0$. In $G(A)$ we define the **(multiplicative) weight** of a forest $f = (S, E_f)$ and the weight of a set $\mathcal{F}$ of forests by:

$$w(f) = \prod_{(i,j) \in E_f} (-a_{ij}), \qquad w(\mathcal{F}) = \sum_{f \in \mathcal{F}} w(f).$$

It was observed that many facts are valid simultaneously for both discrete and continuous time Markov chains. To deal with them at the same time we use, following [5], a **laplacian matrix**, i.e. matrix $\mathbf{L} = (l_{ij})_{i,j=1}^{s}$, $l_{ij} \in \mathbb{R}$ satisfying $l_{ii} = -\sum_{j:\, j \neq i} l_{ij}$ for $i = 1, \ldots, s$. Denote by $\mathbf{I}$ the identity matrix of size $s$. It is easy to verify that matrix $\mathbf{L} = \mathbf{I} - \mathbf{P}$ is a laplacian matrix. For $U, W \subseteq S$ denote by $\mathbf{A}(U|W)$ the submatrix resulting from deletion of rows and columns indexed by $U$ and $W$ respectively. We express the solution of a system of linear equations as a rational function of directed forest weights (called the **forest expansion**, cf. [5,6]). For stationary distribution this is formulated in the well known theorem:

**Theorem 1 (Markov chain tree theorem).** *If the underlying graph of a Markov chain has exactly one absorbing strong component, then the stationary distribution is given by:*

$$\pi_i = \frac{w(\mathcal{F}(i))}{\sum_{j \in S} w(\mathcal{F}(j))}, \quad \textit{for } i = 1, \ldots s.$$

For given functions $A, B : \mathbb{R} \to \mathbb{R}$, the notation $A(\varepsilon) \sim B(\varepsilon)$ means that: $\lim_{\varepsilon \to 0} \frac{A(\varepsilon)}{B(\varepsilon)} = 1$. A family $\{\mathbf{L}(\varepsilon) = (l_{ij}(\varepsilon))_{i,j=1}^{s},\ \varepsilon \in (0, \varepsilon_1)\}$ of laplacian matrices of size $s \times s$ is a **powerly perturbed** Markov chain, if there exist matrices

$\boldsymbol{\Delta} = (\delta_{ij})_{i,j \in S}$, and $\mathbf{D} = (d_{ij})_{i,j \in S}$, $\delta_{ij} \geq 0$ and $d_{ij} \in \mathbb{R}$, for $i, j \in S$, such that the asymptotic behavior of laplacians $\mathbf{L}(\varepsilon)$ is determined by $\boldsymbol{\Delta}$ and $\mathbf{D}$ as follows:

$$-l_{ij}(\varepsilon) \sim \delta_{ij}\varepsilon^{d_{ij}}. \tag{1.1}$$

We also use the concept of **powerly perturbed** nonnegative vector which is defined analogously. Consider the following graph induced by a matrix $\mathbf{D}$ (we take into account asymptotically nonzero entries): $G^*(\mathbf{D}) = (S, \{(i,j) \in S \times S : \delta_{ij} \neq 0\})$. For an arbitrary forest $f$ and a nonempty set $\mathcal{F}$ of forests in $G^*(\mathbf{D})$ we study parameters $d(f)$ defined as the sum of $d_{ij}$ over all edges $(i,j)$ of forest $f$ and $d(\mathcal{F})$ being the minimal value of $d(f)$ for all forests $f \in \mathcal{F}$. Analogously $\delta(f)$ denotes the product of all $\delta_{ij}$ and $\delta(\mathcal{F})$ the sum of $\delta(f)$ over all $f \in \mathcal{F}$ having minimal $d(f)$. We describe the asymptotic behavior of solutions of system $\mathbf{L}^T(R|R)\mathbf{x} = \mathbf{b}$, related to a powerly perturbed Markov chain, in terms of directed forests expansions. It turns out that a solution of a system of linear equations, for a perturbed chain, can be treated as a perturbed vector.

**Theorem 2 ([6]).** *Let matrices $\boldsymbol{\Delta}$ and $\mathbf{D}$ be such that (1.1) above holds, for a powerly perturbed Markov chain $\{\mathbf{L}(\varepsilon), \varepsilon < \varepsilon_1\}$; let $R \subseteq S$, where $S$ is a set of states. Moreover let vector $\mathbf{b} = (\boldsymbol{\zeta}, \mathbf{z})$ be powerly perturbed vector. Suppose that there exist a forest with the root $R$ in $G^*(\mathbf{D})$. Then the solution $\mathbf{x}(\varepsilon) = (x_i(\varepsilon))_{i \in S \setminus R}$ of the system $\mathbf{L}^T(R|R)(\varepsilon)\mathbf{x}(\varepsilon) = \mathbf{b}(\varepsilon)$ satisfies, for $i \in S \setminus R$, the relation $x_i(\varepsilon) \sim \eta_i \varepsilon^{h_i}$, where the coefficients $\eta_i$, $h_i$ are some constants, $i = 1, \ldots, u$.*

## 2 Combinatorial Aggregation

Before describing the algorithm for computing asymptotic coefficients $\mathbf{h}$ and $\boldsymbol{\eta}$, we explain how it can be used to obtain the approximation of stationary distribution vector. The algorithm takes as an input laplacian $\mathbf{L} = (l_{ij})$ defining Markov chain and parameter $\varepsilon$ and consists of three steps: 1. construct matrices $\boldsymbol{\Delta}$ and $\mathbf{D}$ such that: $-l_{ij} = \delta_{ij}\varepsilon^{d_{ij}}$, where $\varepsilon < \delta_{ij} \leq 1$; 2. run Algorithm 1 to compute vectors $\boldsymbol{\eta}$ and $\mathbf{h}$; 3. set $\pi_i(\varepsilon) := \eta_i \varepsilon^{h_i}$.

**Fast computation of forest expansions.** The algorithm reduces the size of state-space of a Markov chain by lumping together closely related states. This process is repeated in the consecutive phases of aggregation; during each phase graphs induced by matrices $\mathbf{D}$ and $\boldsymbol{\Delta}$ are considered. The algorithm groups states in each closed class of the graph and solves the system of linear equations restricted to this class. Smaller size, hence tractable, systems of equations can be solved by a direct method. The solutions of these systems are used to upgrade the asymptotic coefficients computed for each state of the original Markov chain. Before passing to a next phase, an aggregation procedure is performed, lumping all states in each closed class into a new, aggregated state.

The task of computing exponents $h_i$ is of quite different nature than the task of computing the coefficients $\eta_i$. While the former can be performed using purely

**Algorithm 1** Calculate asymptotic coefficient $\eta$ and $h$.

construct $G^0 = (S^0, E^0)$<br>
$k := 0$<br>
**repeat**<br>
  $k := k + 1$<br>
  find partition of $G^{k-1}$ into closed classes<br>
  construct $S^k$<br>
  **for** each closed class in $S^k$, say $I^k$ **do**<br>
    construct laplacian $L_k$<br>
    compute stationary distribution i. e., solve the system $\mathbf{L}_k^T\mathbf{x} = \mathbf{b}$<br>
    compute $m(I^k)$<br>
    **for** each aggregated state $I^{k-1}$ in $I^k$ **do**<br>
      compute $h^k(I^{k-1}|I^k)$ and $\eta^k(I^{k-1}|I^k)$<br>
      **for** each state $i$ aggregated into state $I^{k-1}$ **do**<br>
        upgrade $\eta_i = \eta(i|I^k)$ and $h_i = h(i|I^k)$<br>
      **end for**<br>
    **end for**<br>
    **for** all neighbors of class $I^k$ **do**<br>
      determine shortest edges<br>
    **end for**<br>
  **end for**<br>
  construct new set of aggregated edges $E^k$<br>
  $G^k := (S^k, E^k)$<br>
**until** $G^k$ has only one closed class

combinatorial methods (hence precisely), the latter uses a procedure of solving a system of linear equations, exposed to numerical errors.

## References


1. Courtois, P. J.: *Decomposability: Queueing and Computer System Applications*, Academic Press, New York, 1977.
2. Dayar, T. and Stewart, W.J.: On the effects of using the Grassman-Taksar-Heyman method in iterative aggregation-disaggregation, *SIAM Journal on Scientific Computing*, **vol. 17**, 1996, pp. 287-303.
3. Kafeety, D.D., Meyer, C.D. and Stewart, W.J.: A General Framework for Iterative Aggregation/Disaggregation Methods, *Proceedings of the Fourth Copper Mountain Conference on Iterative Methods*, 1992.
4. Kemeny, J.G. and Snell, J.L.: *Finite Markov Chains.* Van Nostrand, Princeton, 1960.
5. Pokarowski, P. Directed forests and algorithms related to Markov chains, *PhD thesis* Institute of Mathematics, Polish Academy of Sciences, 1998.
6. Pokarowski, P. Directed forests with applications to algorithms related to Markov chains, *Applicationes Mathematicae*, **vol. 26**, **no. 4**, 1999, pp. 395-414.
7. Stewart, W. J.: *Introduction to the numerical solution of Markov chains*, Princeton University Press, 1994.

# A Primitive for Proving the Security of Every Bit and about Universal Hash Functions & Hard Core Bits

Eike Kiltz

Lehrstuhl Mathematik & Informatik, Fakultät für Mathematik,
Ruhr-Universität Bochum, 44780 Bochum, Germany. Fax:+49-234-3214465
kiltz@lmi.ruhr-uni-bochum.de

**Abstract.** We present a useful primitive, the hidden number problem, which can be exploited to prove that every bit is a hard core of specific cryptographic functions. Applications are RSA, ElGamal, Rabin and others. We give an efficient construction of a hard core predicate of any one-way function providing an alternative to the famous Goldreich-Levin Bit [3]. Furthermore, a conjectured connection between universal hash functions and hard core predicates is disproven.

## 1 Introduction

Due to space restraints we assume that the reader is familiar with basic notations such as one-way functions and hard core predicates. For a detailed and more formal discussion see the full version of this paper [5]. A survey of hard core predicates can be found in [8].

## 2 Main Results and Motivation

In [4] it was shown that every single bit is a hard core of the RSA function. The same proof techniques were applied to show that all (but the first least significant) bits of the discrete exponentiation function are hard. It was already noted in [4] that the multiplicative structure of RSA was crucial to apply these techniques. For instance, by the equation $\mathrm{RSA}(cx) = \mathrm{RSA}(c) \cdot \mathrm{RSA}(x)$ one can compute $\mathrm{RSA}(cx)$, given $\mathrm{RSA}(x)$ and $c$. In this paper we present a useful primitive, the *hidden number problem*, and study under which circumstances it is solvable. As a corollary to our result we conclude the bitsecurity of many known cryptographic functions such as RSA, Rabin and ElGamal.

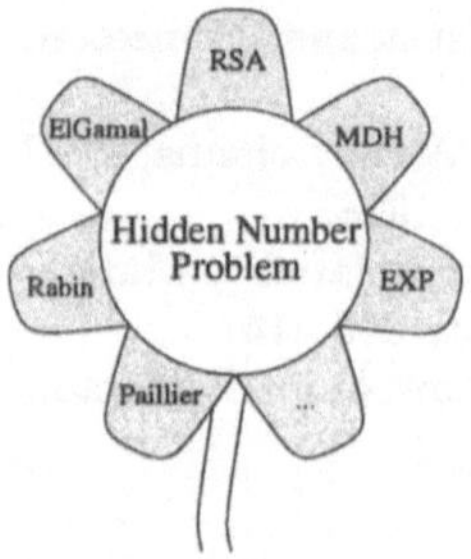


Although the original proofs of bitsecurity of the RSA and the discrete exponentiation (EXP) function are similar there is no straightforward way to conclude the result from each other, i.e. to deduce the bitsecurity of EXP *directly* from the bitsecurity of RSA. The figure on the left illustrates this connection. The hidden number problem was introduced by Boneh and Venkatesan [1] and used to show the security of the collection of $\sqrt{\log n}$ unbiased most significant bits of the Diffie-Hellman function.

R. Freivalds (Ed.): FCT 2001, LNCS 2138, pp. 388–391, 2001.

MAIN RESULTS. Under some reasonable combinatorial assumptions, every bit is a hard core of the following functions:

1. The RSA encryption function.
2. The ElGamal encryption function.
3. A Modified Diffie-Hellman function.
4. The Discrete Exponentiation function (all but the first least significant bits).
5. The Rabin encryption function.
6. Paillier's Encryption function.

Note that 1, 4 and 5 are known results whereas 2, 3 and 6 are new contributions of this paper. Due to space restrictions we only consider the RSA and ElGamal case here. The other proofs exploit the multiplicative properties of the functions in a straight forward way. See [5].
As a second corollary we give as an alternative to the famous Goldreich-Levin Bit [3] a new and very simple construction of hard core predicates for any one-way function. Näslund [7] showed that the predicate $b(x, r, s) := \text{bit}_i(rx + s \bmod p)$ is a hard core of any one-way function. We improve this by showing that the addition "$+s$" is not necessary:

**Theorem 1.** *Let $f$ be an arbitrary length-regular one-way function and let $g$ be defined by $g(x, r) := (f(x), r)$, where $n = |x|$, $p$ is an $n$-bit prime and $r \in \mathbb{Z}_p^*$. Let $b_i(x, r) := \text{bit}_i(rx \bmod p)$. Then for every $i = i(n) \in \{0, \dots, n-1\}$ the predicate $b_i$ is a hard core of the function $g$.*

## 3 The Hidden Number Problem

**Definition 1 (Hidden Number Problem HNP).** *Let $I \subset \mathbb{N}$ be an infinite set of integers and $P$ a polynomial. For all $N \in I$ and all hidden numbers $x \in \mathbb{Z}_N^*$, let $(\mathcal{O}_{N,x})_{N,x}$ be a family of hidden number oracles for the i-th bit with*

$$\Pr[\mathcal{O}_{N,x}(c) = \text{bit}_i(cx \bmod N)] \geq 1/2 + 1/P(n),$$

*where the probability is taken over all $c \in \mathbb{Z}_N^*$, uniformly distributed and over all coin tosses of the oracle. $n$ is the bitlength of $N$.*
*We say that HNP is* efficiently solvable *for bit $i$ if there is a polynomial $Q$ and an oracle pptm $\mathcal{D}^{(\mathcal{O}_{N,x})}$ allowed to make queries to $\mathcal{O}_{N,x}$ such that that for every $N \in I$ and $x \in \mathbb{Z}_N^*$, $\mathcal{D}^{\mathcal{O}_{N,x}}$ outputs $x$ with probability at least $1/Q(n)$.*

**Theorem 2 (Main theorem).**

1. *If $I$ is the set of all odd primes, then HNP is efficiently solvable for all bits.*
2. *If $I$ is the set of all odd integers $N$, then HNP is efficiently solvable for all bits or one gets a non-trivial factor of the integer $N$.*
3. *If for a fixed integer $k$, $I$ is the set of all integers of the form $N = 2^k \cdot q$,* $q$ odd, *then HNP is efficiently solvable for the bits $k < i < n$ or one gets a non-trivial factor of the integer $q$.*

As mentioned before, the proof of this theorem is analogous to the proof of the security of every RSA bit [4]. See the full version [5] for a proof of the special case of the least significant bit. Note that Theorem 1 is a corollary to Theorem 2 (1).

## 4 Sample Applications of the Hidden Number Problem

Due to space restrictions, we only show the bitsecurity of RSA and ElGamal here.

RSA Bits. Let $I_{\text{RSA}} = \{(N,e) : N = p \cdot q, |p| = |q|, p, q \text{ prime}, \gcd(e, \phi(N)) = 1\}$ be the set of all possible RSA instances, where $\phi(x)$ denotes the Euler Totient Function. Given $(N,e) \in I_{\text{RSA}}$ and $x \in \mathbb{Z}_N^*$, the RSA function is defined as $\text{RSA}_{N,e}(x) := x^e \bmod N$. The RSA function is believed to be one-way, which is called the *strong RSA assumption.*

**Theorem 3.** *Under the strong RSA assumption, every bit is a hard core of the RSA function.*

As usual, the proof is by reducio ad absurdum. Assume that the predicate $\text{bit}_i$ is not hard, i.e. that there exists an oracle $\mathcal{O}_{\text{RSA}}$ that non-trivially predicts the $i$-th bit of $x$ given $\text{RSA}_{N,e}(x)$ as input. Then this oracle can be used to construct an oracle pptm $\mathcal{D}^{\mathcal{O}_{\text{RSA}}}$ that inverts the RSA function.
The inversion is done by simulating the hidden number oracle $\mathcal{O}_{N,x}$ for the hidden number $x$, given an instance of the RSA function $\text{RSA}_{N,e}(x) = x^e \bmod N$. For the simulation we set

$$\mathcal{O}_{N,x}(c) := \mathcal{O}_{\text{RSA}}(c^e \cdot \text{RSA}_{N,e}(x)) = \mathcal{O}_{\text{RSA}}(\text{RSA}_{N,e}(c \cdot x)), \tag{4.1}$$

which is $\text{bit}_i(cx)$ in case the RSA oracle did not lie. Now we can apply Theorem 2 (2) which shows that we can compute $x$ or get a factor of $N$. In both cases we can compute $x$. This is a contradiction to the strong RSA assumption.

ElGamal Bits. The ElGamal public key cryptosystem encrypts a message $x \in \mathbb{Z}_p$ given a public key $g^a$ by computing the pair $(g^b, xg^{ab})$. Here $b$ is chosen uniformly at random from the set $\mathbb{Z}_p^*$. Decryption using the private key $a$ is done by computing $(g^b)^a = g^{ab}$ and then dividing to obtain the plaintext $x$.
In order to break this cryptosystem one has to "invert" the ElGamal function

$$\text{El}_{p,g,a,b}(x) := (g^a, g^b, xg^{ab}),$$

in a sense that given $(g^a, g^b, xg^{ab})$ one has to compute $x$. The ElGamal function is believed to be one-way, what follows from the Computational Diffie-Hellman (CDH) assumption.

**Theorem 4.** *Under the CDH assumption, every bit is a hard core of the ElGamal function.*

Assume again there is an ElGamal oracle $\mathcal{O}_{\text{El}}$ that non-trivially predicts the $i$-th bit of $x$ given $\text{El}_{p,g,a,b}(x) := (g^a, g^b, xg^{ab})$. The central equation (corresponding to equation (4.1) in the RSA case) to simulate the hidden number oracle is:

$$\mathcal{O}_{N,x}(c) := \mathcal{O}_{\text{El}}(g^{a+r}, g^{b+s}, c \cdot xg^{(a+r)(b+s)}) = \mathcal{O}_{\text{El}}(\text{El}_{p,g,a+r,b+s}(cx)),$$

which is $bit_i(cx)$ in case the ElGamal oracle did not lie. The integers $s$ and $r$ are due to technical reasons. They are chosen at random from the uniform distribution on $\mathbb{Z}_p^*$ in order to randomize the input.

## 5 Universal Hash Functions & Hard Core Bits

All in the literature known *general constructions* of hard core predicates for any one-way function, for example the Goldreich-Levin Bit [3], are based on some set of universal hash functions (UHF). The natural question, first asked by Näslund [6] in his paper "Universal Hash Functions & Hard Core Bits" and later in [2,7], was whether there is a "nice connection" between universal hash functions and hard core functions. We sketch a simple counterexample to this conjecture.

For a prime $p$ consider the set of UHF $S_p = \{s(x) = (ux + v \bmod p) \bmod 2 : u \in \mathbb{Z}_p^*, v \in \mathbb{Z}_p\}$. It follows from [7] that $S_p$ gives a hard core predicate for any one-way function. Applying the one-way permutation $f(x) = g^x \bmod p$, where $g$ denotes a primitive element of $\mathbb{Z}_p^*$, we construct a new set of UHF $H_p = \{h(x) = (ug^x + v \bmod p) \bmod 2\}$. But the derived predicate $b(x, u, v) := (ug^x + v \bmod p) \bmod 2$ is *not* a hard core for the (special) one-way function $g(x, u, v) := (g^x \bmod p, u, v)$. Theorem 1 gives us a set $T_p = \{t(x) = (ux \bmod p) \bmod 2\}$ giving hard core predicates. In the full paper we show that $T_p$ is only "2/3-universal" which means it is almost universal. Together with the above result this shows that the concepts of UHF and hard core predicates seem to be less related than it was assumed previously. For a more detailed analysis of the relation between universal hash functions & hard core bits see [5].

**Acknowledgment.** This paper greatly benefited from the helpful insight of Hans Ulrich Simon. Furthermore I send handshakes to Jürgen Forster and Mats Näslund for interesting discussions and fruitful comments.

## References

1. D. Boneh and R. Venkatesan. Hardness of computing the most significant bits of secret keys in Diffie-Hellman and related schemes. *Proc. of CRYPTO 1996*, pages 129–142, 1996.
2. Goldmann and Russell. Spectral bounds on general hard core predicates. In *Proc. of STACS*, pages 614–625, 2000.
3. O. Goldreich and L. Levin. A hard-core predicate for all one-way functions. *Proc. of STOC*, pages 25–32, 1989.
4. Johan Håstad and Mats Näslund. The security of all RSA and discrete log bits. *ECCC Report TR99-037*, pages 1–48, 1999.
5. E. Kiltz. A useful primitive to prove security of every bit and about hard core predicates and universal hash functions (full version). *Manuscript*, 2001.
6. M. Näslund. Universal hash functions & hard core bits. *Lecture Notes in Computer Science*, 921:356–366, 1995.
7. Mats Näslund. All bits in $ax + b \bmod p$ are hard (extended abstract). In *Proc. of CRYPTO '96*, pages 114–128, 1996.
8. M. I. González Vasco and M. Näslund. A survey of hard core functions. *Preprint*, 2000 (to appear).

# Pythagorean Triples in Unification Theory of Nilpotent Rings

Ruvim Lipyanski

Department of Mathematics, Ben-Gurion University of the Negev
Beer-Sheva, 84105 Israel
lipyansk@cs.bgu.ac.il

**Abstract.** All solutions of Pythagorean equation (P-equation) $x_1^2 + x_2^2 = x_3^2$ in relatively free rings of varieties of n-nilpotent associative or associative-commutative rings (n=3,4) are described. In particular, it is shown that Pythagorean equation has no minimal and complete set of solutions in free rings of such varieties, so unification type of these varieties is nullary. This is also valid for the variety of associative-commutative 3 (or 4)-nilpotent rings of characteristic two.

Unification theory is concerned with solving equations in a relatively free algebras of varieties. Equational theories which are of unification type unitary or finitary play an important role in automated theorem proving, term rewriting, in logic programming with equality [1]. Investigating the unification hierarchy and determining unification type of equational theories is thus interesting for unification theory and its applications.

We investigate unification theory in the varieties of associative rings without unit and in their subvarieties n-nilpotent rings ($n = 3, 4$). For $n = 2$, i.e., for associative rings with zero multiplication, any equation in free ring of this variety is linear over **Z**. Therefore, unification type of this variety is finitary. We will show that unification in the varieties of n-nilpotent associative or associative-commutative rings ($n = 3, 4$) is nullary. Below, "rings" will always mean a ring without unit, unless otherwise is stipulated.

Unification theory of the varieties of associative and associative-commutative rings with unit have been considered by several authors. Franzen [3] proved that Hilbert's Tenth Problem is of the unification type zero, i.e., variety of associative-commutative rings with 1 is of nullary type. Martin and Nipkov [4] proved that unification in varieties of the Boolean rings and primal algebras is finitary. See survey [1] for unification in other equational theories.

The basic concepts of unification theory in the case of rings are as follows [1]. Let $\mathcal{V}$ be a variety of associative rings and $V = Id\mathcal{V}$ an ideal of identities of the variety $\mathcal{V}$. Denote by $F_{\mathcal{V}}(X)$ and $F_{\mathcal{V}}(A)$ relatively free rings of the variety $\mathcal{V}$ with a countable set of generators $X = \{x_n \mid n < \omega\}$ and $A = \{a_n \mid n < \omega\}$, respectively. We will consider equations in the first ring and look for their solutions in the second one. A solution to equation $w = 0$, $w \in F_{\mathcal{V}}(X)$, in $F_{\mathcal{V}}(A)$ (or in the variety $\mathcal{V}$) is a homomorphism $\xi : F_{\mathcal{V}}(X) \longrightarrow F_{\mathcal{V}}(A)$ such that $\xi(w) = 0$.

R. Freivalds (Ed.): FCT 2001, LNCS 2138, pp. 392–395, 2001.

Let $\Sigma$ be a system of equations in the variables $x_i \in X$. Given two solutions $\tau$ and $\sigma$ of $\Sigma$ we say that $\tau$ is at least as general as $\sigma$ and write $\tau \leq \sigma$ if there exists an endomorphism $\alpha$ of $F_V(A)$ such that $\alpha\tau = \sigma$. There is a naturally associated equivalence relation $\sim$ defined by $\sigma \sim \tau \iff \sigma \leq \tau$ and $\tau \leq \sigma$. A partial order on the equivalence classes of this relation is induced by $\leq$. A solution of the system $\Sigma$ minimal in respect to this ordering, is called minimal (or the most general solution). We say that $\Sigma$ is unitary if this partial order has the smallest element; finitary (infinitary) if the set of the minimal solutions is finite (infinite) and every its element lies above some minimal element. It is nullary if there is a solution which does not lie above any minimal one.

Variety $\mathcal{V}$ is called finitary (infinitary or nullary) if there exists a system of equations having the corresponding type in a free ring of this variety.

**Proposition 1.** *Unification type of P-equation in variety of associative-commutative rings is not finitary.*

*Proof.* Let $F_{Com}(A)$ be a free ring of the variety of associative-commutative rings. Let us prove first that all non-trivial linear solutions to P-equation in $F_{Com}(A)$ are triples $(pf(\overline{a}), qf(\overline{a}), rf(\overline{a}))$, where $(p, q, r)$ are P-triples of integers and $f(\overline{a})$ are linear $\mathbf{Z}$-forms in the variables $a_i \in A$. Let $(\varphi_1(\overline{a}), \varphi_2(\overline{a}), \varphi_3(\overline{a}))$ be a linear solution of P-equation, $\varphi_i(\overline{a}) \in F_{Com}(A)$. Assume that $\varphi_1(\overline{a})$ and $\varphi_2(\overline{a})$ are not proportional and $\varphi_1^2(\overline{a}) + \varphi_2^2(\overline{a}) = \varphi_3^2(\overline{a})$. Then the rank of the form $\varphi_1^2(\overline{a}) + \varphi_2^2(\overline{a})$ over $\mathbf{Q}$ is equal to 2, while the rank of $\varphi_3^2(\overline{a})$ is equal to 1, which is a contradiction. In a similar way one can show that $\varphi_1(\overline{a})$ and $\varphi_3(\overline{a})$ are also proportional.

Obviously, any such linear solution of P-equation can be obtained from solutions $(pa_1, qa_1, ra_1)$. Since $F_{Com}(A)$ is the ring without 1, P-triples $(pa_1, qa_1, ra_1)$ are minimal elements in the set of solutions of P-equation in this ring. Since these solutions are not comparable for different P-triples $(p, q, r)$, the Proposition is proved.

*Remark 1.* This Proposition is valid if the equation is an arbitrary quadratic $\mathbf{Z}$-form.

**Corollary 1.** *Unification type of the variety of associative rings is not finitary.*

Let us now consider the unification type of nilpotent rings. Denoted by $\mathcal{AN}_n$ $(\mathcal{N}_n)$ the varieties of n-nilpotent associative-commutative (associative) rings. Let $V_1$ be the ideal of identities of the variety $\mathcal{AN}_3$ and $F_{V_1}(A)$ a free ring of the variety $\mathcal{AN}_3$ over a countable set of generators $A$. It is easy to prove

**Lemma 1.** *The general solution of P-equation in the variety $\mathcal{AN}_3$ can be written as $(pa_1 + R_1(\overline{a}), qa_1 + R_2(\overline{a}), ra_1 + R_3(a))$, where $(p, q, r)$ are P-triples over $\mathbf{Z}$ and $R_1(\overline{a})$, $R_2(\overline{a})$, $R_3(\overline{a})$ are arbitrary $\mathbf{Z}$-quadratic forms in variables from $A$.*

To investigate the unification type of the variety $\mathcal{AN}_3$ we will use Baader's sufficient condition [2] for the unification type zero. For variety of associative rings, the condition can be formulated as follows.

**Baader's condition:** Let $\Gamma$ be a finite system of equations in $F_{\mathcal{V}}(X)$. By $U_{\mathcal{V}}(\Gamma)$ we denote the set of all solutions of $\Gamma$ in the ring $F_{\mathcal{V}}(A)$. This set satisfies Baader's condition if in $U_{\mathcal{V}}(\Gamma)$ there is a decreasing chain $\theta_1 \geq \theta_2 \geq ... \geq \theta_n \geq ..$, such that: (i) it has no lower bound in $U_{\mathcal{V}}(\Gamma)$; (ii) for all $n \geq 1$ and all $\theta \in U_{\mathcal{V}}(\Gamma)$ with $\theta_n \geq \theta$ there exists $\widehat{\theta} \in U_{\mathcal{V}}(\Gamma)$ such that $\theta \geq \widehat{\theta}$ and $\theta_{n+1} \geq \widehat{\theta}$.

The following proposition is proved in [2]:

**Proposition 2.** *The system of equations $\Gamma$ is of unification type zero in a variety $\mathcal{V}$ if $U_{\mathcal{V}}(\Gamma)$ satisfies Baader's condition.*

**Theorem 1.** *P-equation is nullary in the variety $\mathcal{AN}_3$.*

*Proof.* Let us construct a satisfying Baader's condition chain of solutions to P-equation in the variety $\mathcal{AN}_3$. We choose $(p, q, r) = (3, 4, 5)$ and consider a decreasing chain (S$_1$) of solutions of P-equation in the ring $F_{\mathcal{V}_1}(A)$, $\theta_1 \geq \theta_2 \geq ... \geq \theta_n \geq ...$, where $\theta_n = (3a_1 + \sum_{i=2}^{n+1} a_i^2, 4a_1 + \sum_{i=2}^{n+1} a_i^2, 5a_1 + \sum_{i=2}^{n+1} a_i^2)$. Let us show that this chain has no lower bound in $U_1 = U_{\mathcal{V}_1}(\Gamma)$, where $\Gamma$ is P-equation. Indeed, suppose that there exists a lower bound $\gamma$ of the chain (S$_1$) in $U_1$. According to Lemma 1 we can represent the element $\gamma$ in the following form: $\gamma = (3a_1 + R_1(\overline{a})$, $4a_1 + R_2(\overline{a})$, $5a_1 + R_3(\overline{a})$ . Now, let $F_1 = \overline{F_{\mathcal{V}_1}(A)}$ be the $\mathbf{Z}_3$-algebra of reduced polynomials modulo 3 of the ring $F_{\mathcal{V}_1}(A)$. Denote by $\overline{f(\overline{a})}$ (or simply by $\overline{f}$ ) the image modulo 3 of element $f(\overline{a}) \in F_{\mathcal{V}_1}(A)$ in algebra $F_1$. Consider the decreasing chain (S$_2$), $\overline{\theta}_1 \geq \overline{\theta}_2 \geq ... \geq \overline{\theta}_n \geq ..$ of solutions of P-equation in $F_1$, where $\theta_n \in F_{\mathcal{V}_1}(A)$ are elements of the chain (S$_1$). Clearly, the element $\overline{\gamma} = (\overline{R}_1(\overline{a}),\ a_1 + \overline{R}_2(\overline{a}),\ 2a_1 + \overline{R}_3(\overline{a}))$ is a lower bound in $\overline{U}_1 = U_1(\text{mod}\, 3)$. of the chain (S$_2$). Let us now consider a sequence (S$_3$) of the first coordinates of the chain (S$_2$), $\overline{\theta}_{11}, \overline{\theta}_{21}, ..., \overline{\theta}_{m1}$, where $\overline{\theta}_{m1} = \sum_{k=2}^{m+1} a_k^2$. Obviously, the sequence (S$_3$) is nondegenerate. We can regard $\overline{\theta}_{mi}$ as $Z_3$-quadratic forms in variables $a_k$. Clearly, $rank(\overline{\theta}_{m1}) = m$. Let $r = rank(\overline{R}_1(\overline{a})) + 1$, where $\overline{R}_1(\overline{a})$ is the first coordinate of the lower bound $\overline{\gamma}$. Consider the element $\overline{\theta}_r$ of the chain (S$_2$). Since $\overline{\theta}_r \geq \gamma$, there exists a homomorphism $\psi : F_1 \longrightarrow F_1$ such that $\psi(\overline{R}_1) = \overline{\theta}_{r1}$. However, since $F_1$ is a 3-nilpotent ring homomorphism $\psi$ determines linear transformation $\psi'$ of the variables $a_k \in A$. Comparing the ranks of the elements $\overline{\theta}_{r1}$ and $\psi'(\overline{R}_1)$ we have get contradiction. Condition (i) is proved.

Let $\theta$ be a solution of P-equation satisfying $\theta \leq \theta_n$ for some $n \in \mathbf{N}$. By applying the Lemma 1 we obtain $\theta = (3f(\overline{a}) + L_1(\overline{a}),\ 4f(\overline{a}) + L_2(\overline{a}), 5f(\overline{a}) + L_3(\overline{a}))$, where $f(\overline{a})$ is a linear $\mathbf{Z}$-form and $L_1$, $L_2$, $L_3$ are quadratic $\mathbf{Z}$-forms in variables $a_i \in A$. Let $a_m$ be an element from $A$ that does not occur in representations of elements $\theta$ and $\theta_n$ via of the generators $a_i \in A$. We set $\widehat{\theta} = \theta + (a_m^2, a_m^2, a_m^2)$. Clearly, the element $\widehat{\theta}$ is a solution of P-equation and we can show that the condition (ii) is satisfied for this element. Indeed, since $\theta \leq \theta_n$, there exists a homomorphism $\zeta_1 : F_{\mathcal{V}_1}(A) \longrightarrow F_{\mathcal{V}_1}(A)$ such that $\zeta_1(\theta) = \theta_n$. Define homomorphisms $\zeta_2$ and $\zeta_3 \in Hom(F_{\mathcal{V}_1}(A), F_{\mathcal{V}_1}(A))$ in the following way: $\zeta_2(a_i) = a_i$, if $i \neq m$, and $\zeta_2(a_m) = 0$, $\zeta_3(a_i) = \zeta_1(a_i)$, if $i \neq m$, and $\zeta_3(a_m) = a_{n+1}$, where $a_i \in A$. It is easy to see that $\zeta_2(\widehat{\theta}) = \theta$ and $\zeta_3(\widehat{\theta}) = \theta_{n+1}$. The Theorem is proved.

**Corollary 2.** *Unification in the variety $\mathcal{AN}_3$ is nullary.*

In a similar way one can prove that the varieties $\mathcal{N}_3$, $\mathcal{AN}_4$ and $\mathcal{N}_4$ have nullary unification type.

Denote by $\mathcal{AN}_{n,2}$ ($\mathcal{N}_{n,2}$) the subvariety of the variety $\mathcal{AN}_n$ ($\mathcal{N}_n$) rings of characteristic 2. Variety $\mathcal{AN}_{n,2}$ ($\mathcal{N}_{n,2}$) is a minimal subvariety of variety $\mathcal{AN}_n$ ($\mathcal{N}_n$). We will show now that the variety $\mathcal{AN}_{3,2}$ also has nullary unification type. Note that the rank is not invariant of quadratic form in free associative-commutative rings of characteristic 2. For such rings the proofs nullarity have to be modified

Denote by $V_4$ the ideal of identities of the variety $\mathcal{N}_{3,2}$, and $F_{V_4}(A)$ a free ring of the variety $AN_{3,2}$ over a countable set of generators $A$. The following statement be proved.

**Lemma 2.** *Let $B = a_1a_2 + a_3a_4 + ... + a_{2k-1}a_{2k}$, $0 < k < n$, and $D = a_1a_2 + a_3a_4 + ... + a_{2k-1}a_{2k} + ... + a_{2n-1}a_{2n}$ be elements of the ring $F_{V_4}(A)$. There exists no homomorphism $\varphi \in Hom(F_{V_4}(A), F_{V_4}(A))$ such that $\varphi(B) = D$.*

It is easy to describe the solutions of P-equation in the variety $\mathcal{AN}_{3,2}$.

**Lemma 3.** *The general solution of P-equation in the variety $\mathcal{AN}_{3,2}$ consists of two types of solutions:*

$$(a_1 + \sum_{i=1}^{l_1} a_{2i-1}a_{2i},\ a_2 + \sum_{r=1}^{l_2} a_{2r-1}a_{2r},\ (a_1 + a_2 + \sum_{k=1}^{l_3} a_{2k-1}a_{2k}))\ or$$

$$(\sum_{i=1}^{l_1} a_{2i-1}a_{2i},\ \sum_{k=1}^{l_3} a_{2r-1}a_{2r},\ \sum_{k=1}^{l_3} a_{2k-1}a_{2k}),\ where\ a_i \in A\ and\ l_i \in \mathbf{N}\ (i = 1, 2, 3).$$

Using the Lemma 2 and Lemma 3 one can prove, as in the Theorem 1, the following

**Theorem 2.** *P-equation is nullary in the variety $\mathcal{AN}_{3,2}$.*

Unification type of varieties of n-nilpotent associative-commutative rings for $n \geq 5$ can be investigated in a similar manner. However in this case one should use $k$-forms in variables $a_i \in A$, for $k \geq 3$. This case will be considered elsewhere.

**Acknowledgment.** The author would like to thank G. Belitski, G. Mashevitzky and B.I. Plotkin for many helpful discussions.

## References

1. Baader, F., Siekmann, J.: Unification theory. In: Gabbay, Dov M., Hogger, C., Robinson, J.,(eds.): Handbook of Logic in Artificial Intelligence and Logic Programming, Vol. 2. Clanderon Press, Oxford (1994) 41-124
2. Baader, F.: Unification in varieties of completely regular semigroup. In: Word equation and related topics. Lecture Notes in Computer Science, Vol. 572. Springer-Verlag, Berlin (1992) 210-230
3. Franzen, M.: Hilbert's tenth problem is of unification type zero. J. Automated Reasoning **9** (1992) 169-178
4. Martin, U., Nipkov, T.: Boolean unification – The story so far. J. Symbolic Computation **7** (1989) 275-293

# Two-States Bilinear Intrinsically Universal Cellular Automata*

Nicolas Ollinger

LIP, École Normale Supérieure de Lyon, 46, allée d'Italie
69 364 Lyon Cedex 07, France
Nicolas.Ollinger@ens-lyon.fr

**Abstract.** Linear cellular automata have been studied in details using algebraic techniques [3]. The generalization to families of polynomial cellular automata seems natural. The following step of complexity consists of bilinear cellular automata which study has begun with the work of Bartlett and Garzon [2]. Thanks to bulking techniques [5], two-states bilinear intrinsically universal cellular automata are constructed. This result answers a question from Bartlett and Garzon [2] of 1995.

A cellular automaton consists of a regular network, for example a line of cells, carrying finite values that are updated synchronously on discrete time steps by applying uniformly a local rule. Despite their apparent simplicity, cellular automata exhibit varied, sometimes complex, behaviors.

The properties of linear algebraic objects are easier to describe than the properties of general objects. In the case of cellular automata, the study of linear cellular automata has begun with the work of Martin *et al.* [3]. They showed that linear cellular automata are really simple and they completely described their behavior. In 1995, Bartlett and Garzon [2] studied bilinear cellular automata. They proved that a particular sub-family of bilinear cellular automata, cellular automata over $\mathbb{Z}_p^p$ with $p$ prime, is as complex as the whole family of cellular automata. The question remained open whether bilinear cellular automata over $\mathbb{Z}_m$ were as complex as the whole family of cellular automata for small values of $m$. Moreover, the result from Bartlett and Garzon [2] was given thanks to a notion of simulation and $\pi$-universality that were not formally defined.

In the spirit of Mazoyer and Rapaport [4], we have introduced [5] a tool, called geometrical bulking, to classify and prove properties on cellular automata. This tool is based on a notion of simulation and a notion of space-time diagrams rescaling. Within this scope, we formalized the notion of intrinsic universality implicitly introduced by Albert and Čulik II [1], which corresponds to the notion of $\pi$-universality in the paper of Bartlett and Garzon [2].

In the present paper, we close an open question from Bartlett and Garzon [2] by constructing a two-states bilinear intrinsically universal cellular automaton.

* a longer version of this paper is available from the author, see [6]

R. Freivalds (Ed.): FCT 2001, LNCS 2138, pp. 396–399, 2001.

# 1 Cellular Automata and Geometrical Bulking

In the following, we only consider one-dimensional cellular automata, that is straight lines of cells. We briefly recall some necessary definitions and theorems about cellular automata and geometrical bulking. The interested reader is invited to consult the longer version of this paper [6].

**Definition 1.** *A* cellular automaton $\mathcal{A}$ *is a triple* $(S, \{n_1, \ldots, n_d\}, \delta)$ *such that* $S$ *is a finite set of states,* $N$ *is a finite ordered set of* $d$ *integers called the neighborhood of* $\mathcal{A}$ *and* $\delta$ *is the local transition function of* $\mathcal{A}$ *which maps* $S^d$ *to* $S$.

A configuration $C$ of a cellular automaton $\mathcal{A}$ maps $\mathbb{Z}$ to the states set of $\mathcal{A}$. The state of the $i$-th cell of $C$ is denoted as $C_i$. The local transition function $\delta$ of $\mathcal{A}$ is naturally extended to a global transition function $G_{\mathcal{A}}$ which maps a configuration $C$ of $\mathcal{A}$ to a configuration $C'$ of $\mathcal{A}$ satisfying, for each cell $i$, the equation $C'_i = \delta\left(C_{i+n_1}, \ldots, C_{i+n_d}\right)$.

A sub-automaton of a cellular automaton corresponds to a stable restriction on the states set. A cellular automaton is a sub-automaton of another cellular automaton if (up to a renaming of states) the space-time diagrams of the first one are space-time diagrams of the second one. To compare cellular automata, we introduce a notion of space-time diagrams rescaling. To formalize this idea, we introduce the following notations:

$\sigma^k$. Let $S$ be a finite state set and $k$ be an integer. The shift $\sigma^k$ is the bijective map from $S^{\mathbb{Z}}$ onto $S^{\mathbb{Z}}$ which maps a configuration $C$ to the configuration $C'$ such that, for each cell $i$, the equation $C'_{i+k} = C_i$ is satisfied.

$o^m$. Let $S$ be a finite state set and $m$ be a strictly positive integer. The packing map $o^m$ is the bijective map from $S^{\mathbb{Z}}$ onto $(S^m)^{\mathbb{Z}}$ which maps a configuration $C$ to the configuration $C'$ such that, for each cell $i$, the equation $C'_i = (C_{mi}, \ldots, C_{mi+m-1})$ is satisfied.

**Definition 2.** *Let* $\mathcal{A}$ *be a cellular automaton with states set* $S$. *A* $\langle m, n, k\rangle$-rescaling *of* $\mathcal{A}$ *is a cellular automaton* $\mathcal{A}^{\langle m,n,k\rangle}$ *with states set* $S^m$ *and global transition function* $G_{\mathcal{A}}^{\langle m,n,k\rangle} = \sigma^k \circ o^m \circ G_{\mathcal{A}}^n \circ o^{-m}$.

**Definition 3.** *Let* $\mathcal{A}$ *and* $\mathcal{B}$ *be two cellular automata. Then* $\mathcal{B}$ simulates $\mathcal{A}$ *if there exists a rescaling of* $\mathcal{A}$ *which is a sub-automaton of a rescaling of* $\mathcal{B}$.

This relation of simulation has good properties. In particular, in [5], we proved that the relation of simulation is a quasi-order with a maximal induced equivalence class exactly corresponding to the set of intrinsically universal cellular automata in the sense of Albert and Čulik II [1]. As any cellular automaton can be simulated by a one-way cellular automaton, that is a cellular automaton with neighborhood $\{-1, 0\}$, there exist intrinsically universal one-way cellular automata. Therefore, to prove that a particular family of cellular automata contains an intrinsically universal cellular automaton, it is sufficient to prove that any one-way cellular automaton can be simulated by a cellular automaton from the family. The details and the formal definitions of intrinsically universal cellular automata are presented in the longer version [6].

## 2 Two-States Bilinear Cellular Automata

Bilinear cellular automata are polynomial cellular automata which polynomial is a bilinear functional. Bartlett and Garzon [2] proved the universality of this family of cellular automata in the special case where the states set is of the kind $\mathbb{Z}_p^p$ with $p$ prime. We prove that the family of bilinear cellular automata with states set $\mathbb{Z}_2$ is universal, answering their question concerning bilinear cellular automata with states set $\mathbb{Z}_m$ for small values of $m$.

**Definition 4.** *A* bilinear cellular automaton *is a polynomial cellular automaton of degree* 2*, that is, a cellular automaton which states set is a finite commutative ring and which local transition function can be represented as a polynomial only consisting of quadratic monomials:* $\delta(s_1, \ldots, s_d) = \sum_{i=1}^{d} \sum_{j=1}^{d} b_{i,j} s_i s_j$.

**Theorem 1.** *Each one-way cellular automaton can be simulated by a two-states bilinear cellular automaton.*

*Proof.* Let $\mathcal{A}$ be a one-way cellular automaton $(S, \{-1, 0\}, \delta)$. Let $n$ be the cardinal of $S$. Up to a renaming of states, we can assume that $S = \{0, 1, \ldots, n-1\}$. We construct a two-states bilinear cellular automaton $(\mathbb{Z}_2, \{-r, \ldots, r\}, P)$ which simulates $\mathcal{A}$. The basic idea of the construction is to represent a cell of a configuration of $\mathcal{A}$ by a block of cells all but one in the state 0. The position of the cell with value 1 determines the state for the cell of the configuration of $\mathcal{A}$. To encode the transition $\delta(i, j) = k$, we build a monomial $s_p s_q$ where $p$ is the distance from the position of $k$ to the position of $i$ and $q$ the distance from the position of $k$ to the position of $j$ as represented on Fig. 1. To avoid multiplying the monomial by $(1 - s_l)$ for every $l$ between $p$ and $q$, we must be sure that all these cells can only be 0. Eventually the mapping from $(i, j, k)$ to $(p, q)$ must be injective to avoid any "misinterpretation" of a monomial.

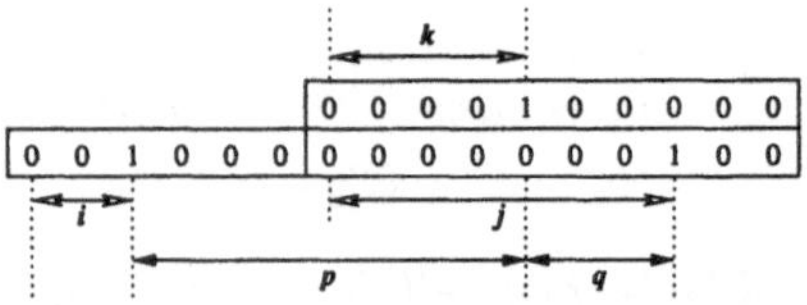


**Fig. 1.** The idea of a cell encoding

A complete and motivated construction can be found in the longer version of this paper [6]. Here, we only provide the technical part of the proof. We choose to discriminate between the encoding of cells of a configuration of $\mathcal{A}$ thanks to the parity of its position into the configuration. An even cell with value $i$ is encoded as a block of cells of size $18n^2$ with value 1 at cell $(6n + 2)i$. An odd cell with value $j$ is encoded as a block of cells of size $18n^2 + 1$ with value 1 at cell $6nj$.

First, we show that the distance between two cells with value 1 permits to know whether it correspond to two next encoded cells. The maximal distance between two cells with value 1 corresponding to two next encoded cells is

$18n^2 + 1 + (6n + 2)n = 24n^2 + 2n + 1$. The minimal distance between two cells with value 1 corresponding to two encoded cells at distance three or more is $18n^2 - (6n + 2)n + 18n^2 + 1 = 30n^2 - 2n + 1$. As $n \geqslant 1$, it is clear that two cells with value 1 correspond to two next encoded cells if and only if their distance is less or equal to $24n^2 + 2n + 1$.

Second, we show that, when building a monomial $s_p s_q$ encoding the transition $\delta(i, j) = k$, the mapping from $(i, j, k)$ to $(p, q)$ is injective. As it is straightforward to compute, if the position of $k$ is odd, $p = 18n^2 - (6n + 2)i + 6nk$ and $q = 6nj - 6nk$; if the position of $k$ is even, $p = 18n^2 + 1 - 6ni + (6n + 2)k$ and $q = (6n + 2)j - (6n + 2)k$. Being given $p$ and $q$, computing $p$ modulo 2 gives the parity of the position of $k$. Then, depending of this parity, $p$ modulo $6n$ permits to obtain $i$ or $k$. From $p$, we then deduce both $i$ and $k$. Finally, we compute $j$ from $q$. The mapping is injective.

From the above computations, we obtain the following polynomial.

$$P(s_{-r}, \ldots, s_r) = \sum_{i=0}^{n-1} \sum_{j=0}^{n-1} \begin{array}{l} s_{18n^2-(6n+2)i+6n\delta(i,j)} s_{6nj-6n\delta(i,j)} \\ + s_{18n^2+1-6ni+(6n+2)\delta(i,j)} s_{(6n+2)j-(6n+2)\delta(i,j)} \end{array}$$

The parameter $r$ can be chosen as $36n^2 + 1$. ■

## 3 Conclusion and Open Problems

In this paper, we have proven, thanks to geometrical bulking, the existence of two-states bilinear intrinsically universal cellular automata, drastically decreasing the previous known number of states (using 2 states instead of $211^{211}$ states in the paper of Bartlett and Garzon [2]). Our result naturally extends to higher dimensions. The difference between linear and non-linear cellular automata is worth studying. To continue the study of bilinear cellular automata, one has to find a bound on the neighborhood size for intrinsical universality (our best today estimation is a radius of 1297 cells).

## References


1. J. Albert and K. Čulik II. A simple universal cellular automaton and its one-way and totalistic version. *Complex Systems*, 1(1):1–16, 1987.
2. R. Bartlett and M. Garzon. Bilinear cellular automata. *Complex Systems*, 9(6):455–476, 1995.
3. O. Martin, A. M. Odyzko, and S. Wolfram. Algebraic properties of cellular automata. *Commun. Math. Phys.*, 93:219–258, 1993.
4. J. Mazoyer and I. Rapaport. Inducing an order on cellular automata by a grouping operation. *Discrete Appl. Math.*, 218:177–196, 1999.
5. N. Ollinger. Toward an algorithmic classification of cellular automata dynamics. LIP RR2001-10, `http://www.ens-lyon.fr/LIP`, 2001.
6. N. Ollinger. Two-states bilinear intrinsically universal cellular automata. LIP RR2001-11, `http://www.ens-lyon.fr/LIP`, 2001.

# Linear Time Recognizer for Subsets of $\mathbb{Z}^2$

Christophe Papazian and Eric Rémila

Laboratoire de l'Informatique du Parallélisme CNRS UMR 5668
Ecole Normale Supérieure de Lyon
46 Allée d'Italie, 69364 Cedex 07 Lyon, France
{Christophe.Papazian,Eric.Remila}@ens-lyon.fr

Graph automata were first introduced by P. Rosenstiehl [5], under the name of *intelligent graphs*, surely because a network of finite automata is able to know some properties about its own structure. Hence P. Rosenstiehl created some algorithms that find Eulerian paths or Hamiltonian cycles in those graphs, with the condition that every vertex has a fixed degree [6]. Those algorithms are called "myopic" since each automaton has only the knowledge of the state of its immediate neighborhood. A. Wu and A. Rosenfeld ([7] [8]) developed ideas of P. Rosenstiehl, using a simpler and more general formalism : the $d$-graphs. Hence, a graph automata is formed from synchronous finite automata exchanging information according to an adjacency graph. A. Wu and A. Rosenfeld gave a linear algorithm allowing a graph automata to know if its graph is a rectangle or not, then, E. Rémila [3] extended this result to other geometrical structures.

We give here *a new and very general method* that allows to recognize a large class of finite subgraphs of $\mathbb{Z}^2$ (and a lot of subclasses) by putting orientation on edges and computing coordinates for each vertex. Depending on the class of graphs we want to recognize, we could use different processes on the border of the detected geometrical structure. The difficulty of this task is due to the finite nature of the automaton. As it has a finite memory, an arbitrarily large number (coordinates) can not be stored in such a memory. Thus we have to use several techniques : we use time differences to compute coordinates, and we will define signal flows to do comparisons between coordinates.

Proposed algorithms have a very satisfying linear or quasi-linear time complexity. Details can be found in [1].

**Definitions.** Let $d$ be a fixed integer such that $d \geq 2$. A $d$-graph is a 3-tuple $(G, v_0, g)$, where $G = (V, E)$ is a symmetric connected graph with only two kinds of vertices : vertices of degree 1 (which are called #-vertices) and vertices of degree $d$; $v_0$ is a $d$-vertex of G which is called the leader, or the general; $g$ is a mapping from $E$ to $\{1, 2, ..., d\}$ such that, for each $d$-vertex $v$ of $V$, the partial mapping $g(v, .)$ is injective. The subgraph $G'$ of $G$ induced by the set of $d$-vertices is called the underlying graph of $G$.

From any graph $G'$ of degree at most $d$, we can construct a $d$-graph $(G, v_0, g)$ whose underlying graph is $G'$. For each vertex, we call an up-edge, an edge that links this vertex to another vertex that is closer from the leader than itself.

**Graph Automata.** A graph automaton is a set $M = (G_d, A)$ with $G_d$ a $d$-graph, and $A$ a finite $d$-automaton $(Q, \delta : Q \times (\mathbb{Z}_d)^d \times Q^d \mapsto Q)$. A configuration

R. Freivalds (Ed.): FCT 2001, LNCS 2138, pp. 400–403, 2001.

$C$ of $M$ is a mapping from the set of vertices of $G_d$ to the set of states $Q$, such that $C(v) = \#$ iff $v$ is a #-vertex.

We define, for each vertex $v$, the neighborhood vector $H(v)$ as in [4]. We compute a new configuration from a previous one by applying the transition function $\delta$ simultaneously to each vertex of $G_d$, by reading its state and the states of its neighbor : $C_{new}(v) = \delta(C(v), H(v), C(\nu_1), ...C(\nu_d))$.

Hence, we have a synchronous model, with local finite memory. There is a *quiescent* state $q_0$ in $Q$ : a vertex $v$ and all its (non-#) neighbors are $q_0$, $v$ will be $q_0$ in the next configuration. The *initial* configuration is a configuration where all vertices are $q_0$, except the leader, which is $q_{init}$.

To simplify our explanations, we will consider that each automaton sends and receives signals to/from its neighbors at each step of computation.To allow simultaneous exchanges, we consider a message as *a set of signals*.

**Recognition of 4-Graphs.** Now, we will only use automata with two particular states : the *accepting* state and the *rejecting* state.

*The class of accepted graphs for one d-automaton A is the class of d-graphs $G_d$ such there is a configuration, with the leader is in the accepting state, that can be reached in $(G_d, A)$.*

*A recognizer is an automaton that rejects all d-graphs that it does not accept.*

So the aim of the recognition of d-graphs is to build a recognizer for a given class of d-graphs. We will study the case $d = 4$ (since many automata are already known on this particular topic). Before this paper, the main recognized classes were the finite classes and some special classes with geometrical properties : grids [7], tori, cylinders, spheres or Moebius's ribbons [3].

The planar grid $\Lambda$ is the infinite symmetric graph isomorphic to $\mathbb{Z}^2$. We want to recognize classes of 4-graphs whose underlying graphs are isomorphic to subgraphs of $\Lambda$. A finite subgraph $G = (V, E)$ of $\Lambda$ is said square compatible if $E$ is a union of elementary squares of $\Lambda$. If there is no vertex of $V$ that is owned by exactly two non-adjacent squares, we say that $G$ is locally square connected.

*The 2-neighborhood of a vertex $\nu$ of a 4-graph $G = (V, E)$ of $\Lambda$ is the subgraph composed by the square containing the vertex $\nu$.*

Notice that two isomorphic locally square connected subgraphs of $\Lambda$ also are isometric (in an Euclidean point of view). The main tool which will be used is the notion of local orientation.

*An orientation $O$ of $G$ is a mapping from $E$ to* {North, East, South, West} *with good obvious local properties.* Each subgraph of $\Lambda$ obviously admits an orientation, but some other graphs also do.

Moreover, an orientation of a locally square connected subgraph of $\Lambda$ is completely determined by the orientations of the edges outgoing from a fixed vertex. This is not true for connected square compatible subgraphs of $\Lambda$. This fact is important for the determination of a possible isomorphism from a given graph to a subgraph of $\Lambda$. It is the reason why we first limit ourselves to the class of locally square connected graphs.

**The Algorithm.** Now, we build a recognizer. The algorithm of recognition is divided into three steps : Orientation, Coordinates and Verification.

**Orientation.** To be able to put an orientation on each edge, 4-automata put indexes $(x, y) \in \mathbb{Z}_6^2$ on the state of each 4-vertex of the 4-graph given. Those indexes will be used as coordinates in $\mathbb{Z}^2$ modulo 6 and canonically induce an orientation of edges.

The process of orientation of edges consists in exploring the potential 2-neighborhood of each 4-vertex of the underlying graph and giving indexes to its neighbors (new indexes have to be compatible, in the sense of coordinates in $\mathbb{Z}^2$ modulo 6, with the previously given indexes).

The process is done by successive five time steps stages. For initialization, the leader takes the $(0,0)$ index. During the first stage, indexes are given to neighbors of the leader vertex. At the $n^{th}$ stage, indexes are given to vertices at distance $n$ from the leader.

Each stage is computed using signals exploring the 2-neighborhoods of vertices. Those signals are indexed by the index of the center of the 2-neighborhood explored, in order to avoid interferences between signals issued from different vertices. They also have an edge index, which indicates the number of the edge from which they leave the center.

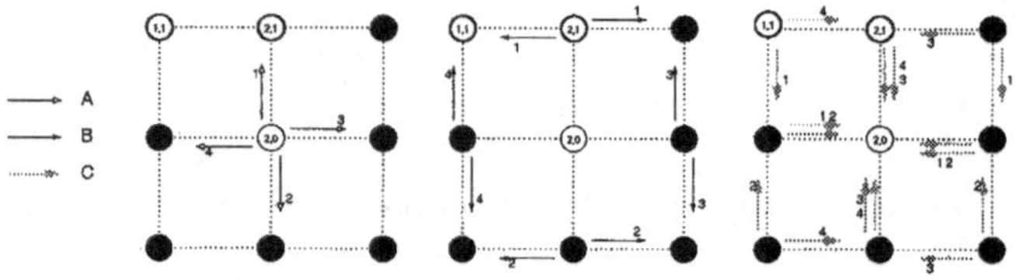


**Fig. 1.** Exploration of a 2-neighborhood

**Coordinates of Vertices.** We would like to place coordinates from $\mathbb{Z}^2$ on each vertex. As finite automata have a finite memory, we can not put coordinates from $\mathbb{Z}^2$ into it, as an arbitrarily number can be as great as we want. So we will encode those coordinates into the time-space diagram of the automata, using a classical process ([2]) as follows :

First, the leader sends two different signals to all its neighbors : A signal `Vertical` and a signal `Horizontal`.

Those signals will spread into the graph, by being sent by each vertex through its down-edges. Each time a vertex receives a signal from its up-edges, it waits one step time and sends the same signal through its down-edges (we say that signals have a speed of $1/2$), except for the `Vertical` signal that has a speed of 1 through the North edges and $1/3$ through the South edges, and for the `Horizontal` signal that have a speed of 1 through the East edges and $1/3$ through the West edges.

**Finalization.** Let $G = (V, E)$ denote the underlying graph of the 4-graph given. If the processes above succeed, one can define a mapping $f$ from $V$ to $Z^2$ such that, for each vertex $v$, $f(v) = (n_h - 2d_l, n_v - 2d_l)$ where $n_h$, $n_v$ represents the time where the vertex receives respectively the `Horizontal` signal or the `Vertical` signal and $d_l$ is the distance to the leader.

We now have to see if $f$ is *injective* or not. As we have a 4-graph, with every edge being oriented and every vertex having coordinates. This property allows

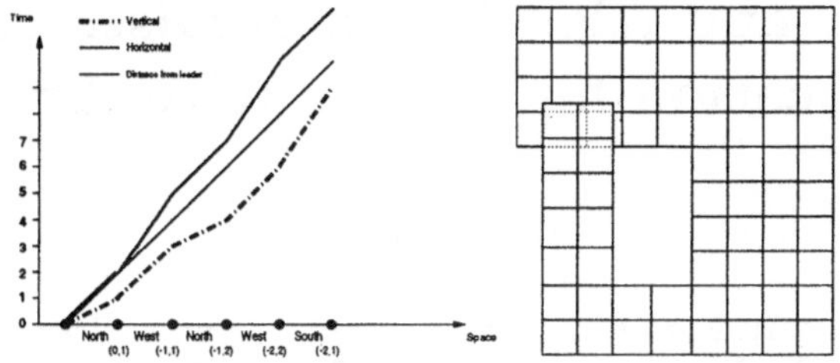


**Fig. 2.** (Left) Space time of the coordinates process, (Right) A graph with 8 vertices covering

us to say that the graph is a subset of the infinite grid $\mathbb{Z}^2$ if and only if there are no two vertices with the same coordinates. This is the problem of the covering.

We give some linear time solution for specific classes, like convex figures, and a $n\log(n)$ optimal solution for the general case using binary signal streams.

**Extensions.** First, it can be extended to other dimensions, like the infinite grid $\mathbb{Z}^3$, or $\mathbb{Z}^n$. The extension to $\mathbb{Z}^n$ just needs to consider more possible local configurations,. We can also see that we do not need any property of planarity in our algorithm. It can be extended to any regular Euclidean network. In fact, we just need a notion of direction (cardinal points), and the "commutativity of edges" : To go from a vertex to another one, we can exchange parts of a path to find another valid path. This property induces a coordinates system as the canonical system we use on $\mathbb{Z}^2$.

The locally square connected property is not necessary for linear time complexity : we can use a global square connected property, with more state in the automaton. We must finally note that there is a trivial algorithm for non-square connected property in exponential time, testing all possible orientations.

## References


1. C. Papazian, E. Rémila, *Graph Automata Recognition*, Research report, LIP (1999)
2. J. Mazoyer, C. Nichitiu, E. Rémila, *Compass permits leader election*, Proceeding of SODA, 948-949, (1999)
3. E. Rémila, *Recognition of graphs by automata*, Theoretical Computer Science 136, 291-332, (1994)
4. E. Rémila, *An introduction to automata on graphs*, Cellular Automata, M. Delorme and J. Mazoyer (eds.), Kluwer Academic Publishers, Mathematics and Its Applications 460, 345-352, (1999).
5. P. Rosensthiel, *Existence d'automates finis capables de s'accorder bien qu'arbitrairement connectés et nombreux*, Internat. Comp. Centre 5, 245-261 (1966).
6. P. Rosensthiel, J.R Fiksel and A. Holliger, *Intelligent graphs: Networks of finite automata capable of solving graph problems*, R. C. Reed, Graph Theory and computing, Academic Press, New-York, 210-265 (1973).
7. A. Wu, A. Rosenfeld, *Cellular graph automata I*, Information and Control 42, 305-329, (1979).
8. A. Wu, A. Rosenfeld, *Cellular graph automata II*, Information and Control 42, 330-353, (1979).

# Fuzzy Sets and Algorithms of Distributed Task Allocation for Cooperative Agents

Tanya Plotkin

Department of Mathematics and Computer Science
Bar-Ilan University, 52-900 Ramat-Gan, Israel
plot@macs.biu.ac.il

**Abstract.** This paper considers the problem of distributed dynamic task allocation by a set of cooperative agents. There are different types of tasks that are dynamically arriving to a system. Each of the agents can satisfy the tasks with some quality (which may be zero). Every task is augmented by the needed qualitative level of task's execution. Thus, relation between agents and task types is fuzzy. The main goal of the agents is to maximize the overall performance of the system and to fulfill the tasks as soon as possible. This problem belongs to the Distributed Problem Solving class of Distributed Artificial Intelligence research. The results differ from that for task allocation in multi-agent environments where each agent tries to maximize its own performance.
The principal result of the paper is a distributed polynomial algorithm for determining probabilistic optimal policy for task allocation in fuzzy environment.

## 1 Introduction

Efficient task allocation is very important when a group of agents try to satisfy a set of tasks. The main problem in the assignment of the tasks is that the agents have different capabilities. We propose to optimize the performance of a set of agents that need to satisfy a set of tasks by modeling these agents with a stochastic closed queueing network [2].The problem is divided into two subproblems: to determine a distributed policy of optimal task allocation and to find the optimal effort levels of the agents subject to certain constraints. A policy for task allocation is a set of probabilities $p_{ij}$ that a task of type $t_j$ is allocated to agent $a_i$. For the first subproblem an algorithm for determining optimal policy is proposed. For the second subproblem an analytical solution on the base of the symmetries of initial objects [5] is given in [3]. When all the variables of the performance function are free, the obtained maximum is global. This provides a way to estimate the quality of different methods.

## 2 Environment

We model the system by a bipartite graph with the agents as left nodes and task types as right nodes. The edges are weighted with the value of agent's ability (or quality) to fulfill a task.

R. Freivalds (Ed.): FCT 2001, LNCS 2138, pp. 404–407, 2001.

We use here the following notations: $T$ - set of task types, $|T| = \tau$, $t$ - a task type, $t \in T$, $A$ - set of agents, $|A| = k$, $a$ - an agent, $a \in A$, $\nu : A \times T \to [0,1]$; $\nu(a,t)$ is interpreted as a level of ability of an agent $a$ to execute a task $t$. It is more convenient to write $\nu(i,j)$, where $i$ is the number of an agent $a_i$, and $j$ is the number of a task type $t_j$. The function $\nu$ distinguishes a fuzzy set $\rho \subset A \times T$. The value $\nu(a,t)$ is a measure of belonging of the pair $(a,t)$ to the subset $\rho$.

Consider a fuzzy subset $A_t \subset A$ for every task type $t$. Measure of belonging of an element $a \in A$ to the subset $A_t$ is the function $\nu_t$ defined by the rule: $\nu_t(a) = \nu(a,t)$. Correspondingly, for fuzzy subset $T_a \subset T$ we have measure $\nu_a(t) = \nu(a,t)$.

In order to make $\delta$ discrete, let us divide the interval $[0,1]$ into 10 parts. Every $\delta \in [0,1]$ belongs to one and only one of these disjoint intervals. We denote by $\delta^*$ the right bound of this interval. Assume that $f(\delta)$ is the distribution function of the variable $\delta$. Probability that $\delta \in [\delta^* - 0.1, \delta^*]$ is $\int_{\delta^*-0.1}^{\delta^*} f(\delta)\, d\delta$.

Consider the Cartesian product $T \times [0,1]$. Take a finite subset of pairs $s = (t, \delta^*)$ in this infinite set. Such $s$ are called *generalized task types*. We also write $t(s) = t$, $\delta^*(s) = \delta^*$. Besides the fuzzy sets $A_t$ and $T_a$ let us treat also ordinary sets $A_s$ and $S_a$. Denote: $A_t^0$ - set of all $a \in A$ such that $\nu_t(a) > 0$, $|A_t^0| = k_t = k_j$, $T_a^0$ - set of all $t \in T$ such that $\nu_a(t) > 0$, $|T_a^0| = \tau_a = \tau_i$.

Define ordinary sets: $A_s$ for every generalized type $s = (t, \delta^*)$ and $S_a$ for every agent $a$. Let $A_s = \{a|\nu(a,t(s)) \geq \delta^*(s) \vee \nu(a,s) = max_a(\nu(a,t(s)))\}$. If for every $a$ we have $\nu(a,t(s)) < \delta^*(s)$ then $A_s$ consists of only those $a$ for which $\nu(a,s)$ is maximal. If $\nu(a,t(s)) \geq \delta^*(s)$ holds true for some $a$, then disjunction is true independently from the second condition. According to this definition, $A_s$ is never empty and if the task of the type $s$ is on the input, it will be served anyway. Let us pass to the set $S_a = \{s|\nu(a,t(s)) \geq \delta^*(s) \vee \nu(a,s) = max_s(\nu(a,t(s)))\}$. The cardinality of this set is $|S_a| = \sigma_a$. $S_a$ is a set of all generalized task types $s$, which an agent $a$ can fulfill with needed level, and if there are no such agents, then this set is the set of $s$ with maximal $\nu(a,t(s))$ for the fixed $a$.

## 3 Methods

We need an algorithm which calculates a probability that the arrived task will be allocated to an agent $a$. Denote this probability by $p_a$. The collection of such probabilities for all of the agents allows to solve the problem of optimization of performance of the system of cooperative agents and to find optimal intensities of the agents. Each arriving task has its type $t$ and also a numerical characteristic $\delta$, i.e., a task is a pair $(t,\delta)$. A task $(t,\delta)$ is allocated to an agent from the set $A_s$, $s = (t,\delta^*)$. Thus, in order to compute the probability $p_a$, we need first the probability $p_{t,\delta}$ that the task has characteristic $(t,\delta)$ and then conditional probability $p_{s,a}$ that if the task has characteristic $(t,\delta)$, then it is allocated to the agent $a$. The following formula determines probabilities $p_a$: $p_{t,\delta} = p_t \int_{\delta^*-0.1}^{\delta^*} f(\delta) d\delta = p_s$ and $p_a = \sum_s p_s p_{s,a}$.

We propose several algorithms to determine probabilities $p_{s,a}$.

**Method 1.** We introduce equivalence $\beta_s$ on the set $A_s$. It is defined by the rule: $a_1\beta_s a_2 \leftrightarrow \nu(a_1,t) = \nu(a_2,t)$, where $t = t(s)$. This equivalence partitions the set $A_s$ into the set of classes of equivalent agents. All the agents of a class have the same abilities from the point of view of the client which issued the task of the generalized type $s$. But these agents are different over other parameters.

The classes are sorted by the value of the function $\nu(a,t)$ constituting several layers: the lowest layer is the class of equivalent agents from $A_s$ with the minimal value of $\nu(a,t)$. Denote a layer containing an agent $a$ by $\beta_s(a)$, its number by $n_{\beta_s}(a)$ and its cardinality by $|\beta_s(a)|$. If $a \notin A_s$, then $p_{s,a} = 0$. Otherwise this agent $a$ belongs to some layer $\beta_s(a)$. All the agents in this layer are equivalent and thus probability to allocate the task to an agent is in inverse proportion to the cardinality of the layer and to the number of the layer, because we wish to save higher layers to the tasks with more strong conditions. The appropriate formula is $p_{s,a} = c_{s,a}(n_{\beta_s}(a)|\beta_s(a)|)^{-1}$. In order to find weight coefficients $c_{s,a}$, we introduced the set $S_a$ of generalized task types which can be fulfilled by an agent $a$, with the cardinality of this set $\sigma_a$. It is evident that the more is $\sigma_a$, the less is probability to send the task to this agent, since this agent can be involved also in other tasks. Hence, weight coefficients can be represented as $c_{s,a} = \frac{\alpha_s}{\sigma_a}$ and then $p_{s,a} = \alpha_s(\sigma_a n_{\beta_s}(a)|\beta_s(a)|)^{-1}$. The set $A_s$ is defined in such a way that it is never empty. This definition gives us opportunity to calculate normalizing coefficients $\alpha_s$, since every task will be allocated to one of the agents and thus all probabilities sum to one: $1 = \sum_{a\in A_s} p_{s,a} = \alpha_s \sum_{a\in A_s} \frac{1}{\sigma_a n_{\beta_s}(a)|\beta_s(a)|}$. Denote $\epsilon^1 = \sum_{a\in A_s} \frac{1}{\sigma_a n_{\beta_s}(a)|\beta_s(a)|}$. Then $\alpha_s = \frac{1}{\epsilon^1}$.

$$p^1_{s,a} = \begin{cases} \frac{1}{\epsilon^1}\frac{1}{\sigma_a n_{\beta_s}(a)|\beta_s(a)|}, & a \in A_s, \\ 0, & a \notin A_s. \end{cases} \tag{1}$$

**Method 2.** Let us introduce an equivalence $\gamma$ on the set $A$ of all agents: $a_1\gamma a_2 \leftrightarrow \sigma_{a_1} = \sigma_{a_2}$ where $\sigma_a = |S_a|$. Thus, we get partition of the set $A$, which induces partition of every $A_s$, and also partition of every layer of $A_s$.

Denote by $\gamma\beta_s$ partition of the layer $\beta_s$ by equivalence $\gamma$. For every $a \in A_s$ we have $\gamma\beta_s(a)$, which is $\gamma\beta_s$ layer, containing $a$. Denote probability $p_s^{\gamma\beta_s(a)}$ that the task of type $t$ will be allocated to the layer $\gamma\beta_s(a)$. This probability is: $p_s^{\gamma\beta_s(a)} = \alpha_s(\sigma_a n_{\beta_s}(a))^{-1}$. The probability to allocate a task to the specific agent $a$ within the layer is $p_{s,a} = \alpha_s(\sigma_a n_{\beta_s}(a)|\beta_s(a)|)^{-1}$.

Take sum over $a \in A_s$ in order to compute $\alpha_s$. The sum is double: first (inner) sum by $\gamma$ in the layer $\gamma\beta_s$ ($\beta_s$ is fixed); external sum is by layers $\beta_s$. The second sum is due to double partitioning.

Denote $\epsilon^2 = \sum_{\beta_s}\sum_\gamma \frac{1}{\sigma_a n_{\beta_s}(a)|\beta_s(a)|}$. Then $\alpha_s = \frac{1}{\epsilon^2}$. Finally,

$$p^2_{s,a} = \begin{cases} \frac{1}{\epsilon^2}\frac{1}{\sigma_a n_{\beta_s}(a)|\beta_s(a)|}, & a \in A_s, \\ 0, & a \notin A_s. \end{cases} \tag{2}$$

**Method 3.** For every agent $a$ we have denoted by $S_a$ a set of generalized task types which this agent can fulfill. Let us consider an event that generalized task type $s$ belongs to $S_a$. Probability of this event $p^{S_a}$ is the sum of all probabilities

$p_s$ that the task is of generalized type $s$ over all $s \in S_a$: $p^{S_a} = \sum_{s \in S_a} p_s$. The idea of the third method is to use this probability $p^{S_a}$ instead of cardinality of the set $S_a$, which is quite natural:

$$p_{s,a} = \alpha_s \frac{1}{p^{S_a} n_{\beta_s}(a)|\beta_s(a)|}, \qquad \epsilon^3 = \sum_{a \in A_s} \frac{1}{p^{S_a} n_{\beta_s}(a)|\beta_s(a)|}, \quad \alpha_s = \frac{1}{\epsilon^3}.$$

$$p^3_{s,a} = \begin{cases} \frac{1}{\epsilon^3} \frac{1}{p^{S_a} n_{\beta_s}(a)|\beta_s(a)|}, & a \in A_s, \\ 0, & a \notin A_s. \end{cases} \tag{3}$$

**Method 4.** In this method we do not substitute $\sigma_a$ in the formula for the probability $p_{s,a}$ by $p^{S_a}$ but use both multipliers:

$$p_{s,a} = \alpha_s \frac{1}{\sigma_a p^{S_a} n_{\beta_s}(a)|\beta_s(a)|}, \qquad \epsilon^4 = \sum_{a \in A_s} \frac{1}{\sigma_a p^{S_a} n_{\beta_s}(a)|\beta_s(a)|}, \quad \alpha_s = \frac{1}{\epsilon^4}.$$

$$p^4_{s,a} = \begin{cases} \frac{1}{\epsilon^4} \frac{1}{p^{S_a} n_{\beta_s}(a)|\beta_s(a)|\sigma_a}, & a \in A_s, \\ 0, & a \notin A_s. \end{cases} \tag{4}$$

**Method 5.** This method combines Method 2 and Method 3.

$$p_{s,a} = \alpha_s \frac{1}{\sigma_a p^{S_a} n_{\beta_s}(a)|\gamma\beta_s(a)|}, \qquad \epsilon^5 = \sum_{\gamma} \sum_{\beta_s} \frac{1}{\sigma_a p^{S_a} n_{\beta_s}(a)|\gamma\beta_s(a)|}; \quad \alpha_s = \frac{1}{\epsilon^5}.$$

$$p^5_{s,a} = \begin{cases} \frac{1}{\epsilon^5} \frac{1}{p^{S_a} n_{\beta_s}(a)|\gamma\beta_s(a)|\sigma_a}, & a \in A_s, \\ 0, & a \notin A_s. \end{cases} \tag{5}$$

## 4 Algorithm

We have proposed five empirical methods of $p_{s,a}$ computation. None of the methods is preferable since in different conditions any of them could be better than others. Thus, we formulate the following algorithm to find the policy of task allocation: (1) Compute $p_{s,a}$ by all methods → (2) Compute $p_a$ using $p_{s,a}$ → (3) Compute performance of the system → (4) Choose the method with maximal performance to be our policy → (5) Allocate arriving tasks according to the optimal probabilities.

## References


1. Billionnet, A., Costa, M.C., Sutter A.: An efficient algorithm for a task allocation problem. Journal of the ACM, **39** (3) (1992) 502–518
2. Bruell, S., Balbo, G.: Computational algorithms for closed queueing networks. North Holland, New York, (1982)
3. Kraus, S., Plotkin, T.: Algorithms of distributed task allocation for cooperative agents. Theoretical Computer Science, **242** (2000) 1–27
4. Li, H.X., Yen, V.C.: Fuzzy sets and fuzzy decision making. CRS Press (1995)
5. Plotkin, T., Peterson, E.: Symmetry and entropy in the problem of optimization of files distribution. Automatic Control and Computer Science, **17** (5) (1983) 5–11

# On Recursively Enumerable Subsets of N and Rees Matrix Semigroups over ($Z_3$ ; + )

Bella V. Rozenblat

Department of Mathematics, Ben-Gurion University of the Negev
Beer-Sheva, 84105 Israel
bella@cs.bgu.ac.il

**Abstract.** Let $H_3 \simeq (\ \mathbf{Z}_3\ ;\ +\ )$ be the three-element group $\{a, a^2, e\}$ with $a^3 = e$; $\mathbf{N}_0 = \mathbf{N} \cup \{0\}$ ; $L_{<\cdot>}$ - the class of all first-order formulas of the signature $< \cdot >$ . For any recursively enumerable (r.e.) set $K \subseteq \mathbf{N}$ we effectively define an $\mathbf{N}_0 \times \mathbf{N}_0$-matrix $P_K$ over $H_3$ and consider the Rees matrix semigroup $C_K = M(H_3,\ \mathbf{N}_0,\ \mathbf{N}_0, P_K)$. The following theorem presents the main result of the paper.

**Theorem.** *There exists a recursive mapping* $\mathbf{N} \to L_{<\cdot>}$, *giving for every* $m \in \mathbf{N}$ *a corresponding closed formula* $\varphi_m \in L_{<\cdot>}$, *in such a way that, for every r.e.* $K \subseteq \mathbf{N}$*:*
$m \in K$ *iff* $\varphi_m$ *is valid on* $C_K$.

Such an interpretation of the membership problem for $K$ in the elementary theory $T(C_K)$ enables us to estimate the complexity of $T(C_K)$; in particular, if $K$ is a non-recursive set then $T(C_K)$ is undecidable.

Throughout this paper we use the following notation: $\rightleftharpoons$ - "equals by definition"; $L_\sigma$ - the class of all first-order formulas of a signature $\sigma$ (the signature may contain constant symbols, symbols for operations and for predicates); $T_\sigma(A)$ - the elementary theory of the algebraic system $A$ of the signature $\sigma$ (this means the class of all closed formulas from $L_\sigma$ that are valid on $A$); $A \models \varphi$ - the formula $\varphi$ is valid on $A$. In the terminology concerning first-order formulas and theories we follow [2]; in particular, the term **algebraic system** is equivalent to **algebraic structure,** and the term **decidability** is equivalent for $T_\sigma(A)$ to **solvability** or **recursivity** and means the existence of an algorithm answering for any closed formula $\varphi \in L_\sigma$, whether $\varphi \in T_\sigma(A)$ or not.

In the terminology concerning completely simple semigroups we follow [1]. Let $C \simeq M(H, I, J, P)$ be a representation of a completely simple semigroup $C$ by a Rees matrix semigroup, where $H$ is the structure group of $C$, $I$ and $J$ are index sets, and $P \rightleftharpoons (p_{ji} \mid j \in J, i \in I)$ is the sandwich-matrix. Then $C$ is isomorphic to the set of all triples $\{(h, i, j) \mid h \in H, i \in I, j \in J\}$ with binary operation $\cdot$ , defined by

$$(h_1, i_1, j_1) \cdot (h_2, i_2, j_2) = (h_1 \cdot p_{j_1 i_2} \cdot h_2, i_1, j_2),$$

where $h_1 \cdot p_{j_1 i_2} \cdot h_2$ denotes the usual product in the group $H$.

R. Freivalds (Ed.): FCT 2001, LNCS 2138, pp. 408–411, 2001.

Now let

$$H_3 \rightleftharpoons \{a, a^2, e\} \text{ with } a^3 = e, \quad \mathbf{N} \rightleftharpoons \{1, 2, ...\}, \quad \mathbf{N}_0 \rightleftharpoons \mathbf{N} \cup \{0\},$$

and let $K \rightleftharpoons \{m(1), \dots, m(i), \dots\}$ be a recursively enumerable (r.e.) subset of $\mathbf{N}$. Let

$$P_K \rightleftharpoons (p_{ji} \mid j, i \in \mathbf{N}_0), \quad \text{where } p_{ji} = \begin{cases} e, & \text{if } j = 0 \text{ or } i = 0, \\ a, & \text{if } i > 0 \text{ and } 0 < j \leq m(i), \\ a^2, & \text{if } i > 0 \text{ and } j > m(i). \end{cases}$$

Let

$$C_K \rightleftharpoons M(H_3,\ \mathbf{N}_0,\ \mathbf{N}_0,\ P_K).$$

The aim of this paper is to interpret the membership problem for $K$ in the elementary theory of $C_K$. The interpretation will be done in two steps, via two-sorted algebraic systems $D(i_0, j_0)$ defined below . Let us note that using two-sorted systems of another kind helped earlier to prove the undecidability of the diophantine theory of a free inverse semigroup with more than one generator [4].

**Definition 1.** *Let $M(H, I, J, P)$ be a Rees representation of a completely simple semigroup $C$. For every $i_0 \in I$, $j_0 \in J$ let $D(i_0, j_0)$ be the two-sorted algebraic system with basic sets $H$ and $I \times J$ of the signature $< \cdot, \circ, \pi >$, where $\cdot$ denotes multiplication on $H$; $\circ$ denotes multiplication on $I \times J$, defined by $(i_1, j_1) \circ (i_2, j_2) = (i_1, j_2)$; $\pi$ is the symbol of the unary function that maps the set $I \times J$ into $H$ according to the rule*

$$\pi((i,j)) = (p_{ji_0})^{-1} \cdot p_{ji} \cdot (p_{j_0 i})^{-1} \cdot p_{j_0 i_0}.$$

*For formulas of the signature $< \cdot, \circ, \pi >$ we will use variables of two kinds: $y_1, y_2, \dots$ with the domain $H$ and $Y_1, Y_2, \dots$ with the domain $I \times J$. Let*

$$\Delta \rightleftharpoons \{D(i_0, j_0) \mid i_0 \in I, j_0 \in J\}.$$

*Remark 1.* The description of isomorphisms between Rees matrix semigroups [3] allows us to show that the class $\Delta$ does not depend on a particular Rees representation of a completely simple semigroup $C$. It depends only on the semigroup $C$, and we can denote it by $\Delta(C)$.

The following proposition gives an exact interpretation of the membership problem for $K$ in the elementary theory of the class $\Delta(C_K)$, for every r.e. $K \subseteq \mathbf{N}$.

**Proposition 1.** *There exists a recursive mapping $\mathbf{N} \rightarrow L_{<\cdot,\circ,\pi>}$, giving for every $m \in \mathbf{N}$ a corresponding closed formula $\delta_m \in L_{<\cdot,\circ,\pi>}$, in such a way that, for every r.e. $K \subseteq \mathbf{N}$:*
*$m \in K$ iff $\Delta(C_K) \models \delta_m$.*

*Proof.* Let us fix an **arbitrary** r.e. set $K \rightleftharpoons \{m(1), \ldots, m(i), \ldots\} \subseteq \mathbf{N}$. Let $P \rightleftharpoons P_K$ , and let $\Delta \rightleftharpoons \Delta(C_K)$. Consider the two-sorted system $D(0,0) \in \Delta$. The function $\pi$ on $D(0,0)$ turns out to be as follows:

$$\pi((i,j)) = (p_{j0})^{-1} \cdot p_{ji} \cdot (p_{0i})^{-1} \cdot p_{00} = p_{ji},$$

because $p_{j0} = p_{0i} = e$ for all $i, j \in \mathbf{N}_0$. Now let

$$neq(Y_1, \ldots, Y_r) \rightleftharpoons \bigwedge_{1 \leq j_1 < j_2 \leq r} (Y_{j_1} \neq Y_{j_2}),$$

$$col(Y_1, \ldots, Y_r, y) \rightleftharpoons \bigwedge_{1 \leq j \leq r} ((Y_j \circ Y_1 = Y_1) \wedge (\pi(Y_j) = y)).$$

**Lemma 1.** *For any $m \geq 1$ let*

$$\gamma_m \rightleftharpoons \exists y (y \neq e \wedge (\exists Y_1, \ldots, Y_m)(neq(Y_1, \ldots, Y_m) \wedge col(Y_1, \ldots, Y_m, y) \wedge$$
$$(\forall Y_{m+1})(col(Y_1, \ldots, Y_{m+1}, y) \to \neg neq(Y_1, \ldots, Y_{m+1})))).$$

*Then $D(0,0) \models \gamma_m$ iff $m \in K$.*

The next lemma gives a property that specifies the system $D(0,0)$ in the class $\Delta$. More precisely, this lemma establishes the negation of such a property.

**Lemma 2.** *For every $i_0, j_0 \in \mathbf{N}_0$, where $i_0 \neq 0$ or $j_0 \neq 0$, there exist $i_1 \in \mathbf{N}_0 \setminus i_0$, $j_1 \in \mathbf{N}_0 \setminus j_0$ such that in the matrix*

$$P(i_0, j_0) \rightleftharpoons ((p_{ji_0})^{-1} \cdot p_{ji} \cdot (p_{j_0 i})^{-1} \cdot p_{j_0 i_0} \mid j,\ i \in \mathbf{N}_0)$$

*the element of the $j_1$-th row and $i_1$-th column equals $e$.*

Note that all the elements of the $i_0$-th column and of the $j_0$-th row of $P(i_0, j_0)$ equal $e$ too.

**Lemma 3.** *Let $\zeta$ be the following formula:*

$$(\exists Y_1, \ldots, Y_4)(neq(Y_1, \ldots, Y_4) \wedge col(Y_1, Y_2, e) \wedge col(Y_3, Y_4, e) \wedge \neg col(Y_1, Y_3, e)).$$

*Then $D(0,0) \models \neg\zeta$ and $D(i_0, j_0) \models \zeta$ for any $i_0$, $j_0 \in \mathbf{N}_0$ such that $i_0 \neq 0$ or $j_0 \neq 0$.*

Now for every $m \in \mathbf{N}$ let $\delta_m{}^\sharp \rightleftharpoons ((\neg\zeta) \to \gamma_m.)$ Then from Lemmas 1 and 3 it follows that, for **every** r.e. $K \subseteq \mathbf{N}$:
$m \in K$ iff $\Delta(C_K) \models \delta_m{}^\sharp$.
To obtain $\delta_m$ it remains to delete the symbol $e$ from $\delta_m{}^\sharp$, i.e. to replace all the expressions of the kind $y = e$ by $y^2 = y$. Proposition 1 is proved.

The following proposition gives an exact interpretation of $T_{<\cdot,\circ,\pi>}(\Delta(C))$ in $T_{<\cdot>}(C)$, for **every** completely simple semigroup $C$.

**Proposition 2.** *There exists a recursive mapping* $L_{<\cdot,\circ,\pi>} \to L_{<\cdot>}$ *, giving for every closed formula* $\varphi \in L_{<\cdot,\circ,\pi>}$ *a corresponding closed formula* $\varphi\prime \in L_{<\cdot>}$*, in such a way that, for every completely simple semigroup* $C$ *:*
$\Delta(C) \models \varphi$ *iff* $C \models \varphi\prime$*.*

The composition of the two mappings given by Propositions 1 and 2 allows us to prove the main result of this paper.

**Theorem.** *There exists a recursive mapping* $\mathbf{N} \to L_{<\cdot>}$*, giving for every* $m \in \mathbf{N}$ *a corresponding closed formula* $\varphi_m \in L_{<\cdot>}$*, in such a way that, for every recursively enumerable* $K \subseteq \mathbf{N}$*:*
$m \in K$ *iff* $\varphi_m$ *is valid on* $C_K$*.*

**Corollary 1.** *The complexity of* $T_{<\cdot>}(C_K)$ *is greater than or equal to the complexity of the membership problem for* $K$*.*

The following corollary gives an example of a completely simple semigroup with the three-element structure group and with undecidable elementary theory.

**Corollary 2.** *If* $K$ *is a recursively enumerable non-recursive subset of* $\mathbf{N}$ *then* $T_{<\cdot>}(C_K)$ *is undecidable.*

## References

1. Clifford, A., Preston G.: The Algebraic Theory of Semigroups, Vol. 1. American Mathematical Society, Providence, R.I. (1964)
2. A.I.Mal'cev, A.: Algebraic Systems. Berlin (1973)
3. Petrich, M., Reilly, N.: Completely Regular Semigroups. Canadian Mathematical Society, Series of Monographs and Advanced Texts **23**, A Willey - Interscience Publication, New York (1999)
4. Rozenblat, B.: Diophantine theories of free inverse semigroups. Sibirsk. Math. Zh.**26** (1985) 101-107. English transl.: Siberian Math. J., Consultants Bureau, New-York - London (1985)

# Quantum Real - Time Turing Machine

Oksana Scegulnaja*

Institute of Mathematics and Computer Science,
University of Latvia, Raina bulv. 29, Riga, Latvia,
sd60032@lanet.lv

**Abstract.** The principles of quantum computation differ from the principles of classical computation very much. Quantum analogues to the basic constructions of the classical computation theory, such as Turing machine or finite 1-way and 2-ways automata, do not generalize deterministic ones. Their capabilities are incomparable. The aim of this paper is to introduce a quantum counterpart for real - time Turing machine. The recognition of a special kind of language, that can't be recognized by a deterministic real - time Turing machine, is shown.

## 1 Introduction

The quantum mechanism gives us a certain kind of power, which cannot be achieved by the deterministic or probabilistic approach. Richard Feynman [1] supposed that it might require exponential time to simulate quantum mechanical processes on classical computers. It was in 1985, when D. Deutsch introduced the notion of quantum Turing machine [2] and proved that quantum Turing machines compute the same recursive functions as classical deterministic Turing machines do. But it will be proved, that it is possible to find quantum Turing machine advantages over deterministic, that have some limitations, such as time or tape space. This paper shows, that there is a language that is accepted by a quantum real - time Turing machine, but can't be accepted by a deterministic real - time Turing machine.

## 2 Preliminaries

The model of the quantum computing will be described here to introduce the notation used further. To get more information on the specific topic please refer to [3]. The unit of quantum information is the quantum bit or qubit. For a qubit the possibility to be 1 or 0 is stated as $\|a\|^2 + \|b\|^2 = 1$, where a and b are the arbitrary complex numbers. If we observe qubit, we get true with probability $\|a\|^2$ and false with probability $\|b\|^2$.

* Research supported by contract IST–1999–11234 (QAIP) from the European Commision, and grant no. 01.0354 from the Latvian Council of Science.

R. Freivalds (Ed.): FCT 2001, LNCS 2138, pp. 412–415, 2001.

We consider quantum systems with m basis states $|q_1\rangle$, $|q_2\rangle$,..., $|q_m\rangle$. Let y be a linear combination of them with complex coefficients

$$\psi = a_1 |q_1\rangle + a_2 |q_2\rangle + ... + a_m |q_2\rangle .$$

The norm of $\psi$ is

$$\|\psi\| = \sqrt{|a_1|^2 + |a_2|^2 + ... + |a_m|^2}.$$

The state of quantum system can be any $\psi$ with $\|\psi\| = 1$. $\psi$ is called a superposition of $|q_1\rangle$, $|q_2\rangle$,..., $|q_m\rangle$. $a_1, a_2, ..., a_m$ are called amplitudes of $|q_1\rangle$, $|q_2\rangle$,..., $|q_m\rangle$.

There are two types of transformations that can be performed on a quantum system. First, there are unitary transformations. A unitary transformation is a linear transformation U that preserves norm (any $\psi$ with $\|\psi\| = 1$ is mapped to $\psi'$ with $\|\psi'\| = 1$).

Second, there are measurements. The simplest measurement is observing $\psi = a_1 |q_1\rangle + a_2 |q_2\rangle + ... + a_m |q_2\rangle$ in the basis $|q_1\rangle$, $|q_2\rangle$,..., $|q_m\rangle$. It gives $|q_i\rangle$ with probability $a_i^2$. After the measurement, the state of the system changes to $|q_i\rangle$.

## 3 Definitions

**Definition 1.** *Real - time deterministic Turing machine (TM) is a set* $M = \langle \Sigma, \Sigma_w, Q, q_0, q_f, I \rangle$, *where* $\Sigma$*- finite alphabet (of input symbols), including symbols # and \$,* $\Sigma_w$ *- finite alphabet (work tape symbols), including symbol* $\lambda$, $Q$ *- set of states,* $q_0$ *- initial state,* $q_f$ *- final state,* $\{\longrightarrow, \longleftarrow, \uparrow\}$ *- movements of the head (left, right, stop), I - set of instructions. Instruction is a row* $\Sigma * \Sigma_w * Q \longrightarrow Q * \Sigma_w * \{\longrightarrow, \longleftarrow, \uparrow\}$.

Such a machine has one endless input tape and one endless work tape with one head moving on each tape. At the beginning machine is in the state $q_0$, the input tape head is on the first symbol of the word from the left. Work tape is empty and TM reads the first symbol of the word from the input tape. As a second step, it reads the second symbol, etc. After the last symbol it reads symbols \$. Let it be the instruction of I: $xyq_k \longrightarrow q_j z \longrightarrow$, where current state is $q_k \in Q$, the machine is reading symbol $x \in \Sigma$ and the work tape head is observing symbol $y \in \Sigma_w$. Then the machine moves to the state $q_j$, replacing the symbol y with z, and moves to the right.

Real - time TM every moment reads a new symbol. When the symbol \$ has been read, the work is finished. Real - time TM accepts the word, if the work is finished, the working tape contains one symbol "1", the rest of the tape is filled with "$\lambda$" and the head observes the symbol "1". It rejects the word, if the work is finished, the working tape contains one symbol "0", the rest of the tape is filled with "$\lambda$" and the head observes the symbol "0". Real - time TM recognizes the language L in time t(x), if for every word $x \in L$ exists a set of instructions from I, that needs not more than t(x) steps to obtain the result 1, and there isn't any word $x \in L$ that a set of instructions from I for x leads to the result 1.

**Definition 2.** *Real - time quantum Turing machine (QTM) is a set* $M = \langle \Sigma, \Sigma_w, Q, q_0, q_f, \delta \rangle$, *where* $\Sigma$ *- finite alphabet (of input symbols), including symbols* # *and* \$, $\Sigma_w$ *- finite alphabet (work tape symbols), including symbol* $\lambda$, $Q$ *- set of states,* $q_0$ *- initial state,* $q_f$ *- final state, transition amplitude mapping* $\delta : Q * \Sigma * \Sigma_w * \Sigma_w * Q * \{\longrightarrow, \longleftarrow, \uparrow\} \longrightarrow C[0,1]$ *is required to be such, that quantum evolution of M is unitary. That means that quantum evolutions of M can be defined as unitary matrices U, where* $UU^* = I$ *and* $U^*$ *is a conjugate transpose of U, i.e. the transposition of U and conjugation of its elements, and I is the unit matrix.*

To be quantum Turing machine, it has to meet so-called well-formedness conditions (see more about unitarity conditions in [3]).

After each step the measurement is performed.

Let it be $\delta : q_k xyz q_j \longrightarrow\!\!\longrightarrow \frac{1}{\sqrt{2}}$, where current state is $q_k \in Q$, the machine is reading symbol $x \in \Sigma$ and the head is observing symbol $y \in \Sigma w$. Then the machine moves to the state $q_j$, replacing the symbol y with z, and moves to the right. Real - time QTM every moment reads a new symbol. The moment, when the symbol \$ has been read, the work is finished. Real - time QTM recognizes the language L with amplitude $\Delta (\Delta \rangle \frac{1}{2})$, if M working on any word x with amplitude not less than $\Delta$ accepts x, if $x \in L$, and rejects x, if $x \notin L$.

**Theorem 1.** *There is a language L, that can be recognized by a real - time QTM, but can't be recognized by a real - time deterministic TM.*

*Proof.* Let L = $\{x \& y \& x^{rev} \& y^{rev}\}$, where x, y = {0,1}*.

First, we'll prove, that L can be recognized by a real - time QTM and second, we'll prove, that L can't be recognized by real - time deterministic TM.

The first step is to split the process into three states, one of which is rejecting state $q_{rr}$, and $q_1$ and $q_2$ compare x and $x^{rev}$ and y and $y^{rev}$ respectively.

Than the word belongs to the language L, if both the branches $q_1$ and $q_2$ say "yes", and doesn't, if any of the branches says "no".

$q_0$ - initial state, $\{q_a, q_{aa}\}$ - a set of accepting states, $\{q_r, q_{rr}\}$ - a set of rejecting states.

Here is a transition function of the QTM. Each vector describes a transition, where the first symbol is that one that is read from the input tape, and the second one is read from the work tape. Symbol "$\varepsilon$" means, that it can be any symbol. Transitions, that don't change the state of QTM, are not shown.

$$V_{\#\varepsilon}\,|q_0\rangle = \frac{1}{\sqrt{3}}\,|q_1\rangle$$
$$V_{\#\varepsilon}\,|q_0\rangle = \frac{1}{\sqrt{3}}\,|q_2\rangle$$
$$V_{\#\varepsilon}\,|q_0\rangle = \frac{1}{\sqrt{3}}\,|q_{rr}\rangle$$

$$\begin{array}{llll} V_{01}\,|q_5\rangle = |q_r\rangle & V_{01}\,|q_8\rangle = |q_{rr}\rangle \\ V_{10}\,|q_5\rangle = |q_r\rangle & V_{10}\,|q_8\rangle = |q_{rr}\rangle \\ V_{\&\varepsilon}\,|q_1\rangle = |q_3\rangle & V_{\&\varepsilon}\,|q_2\rangle = |q_4\rangle \\ V_{\&\varepsilon}\,|q_3\rangle = |q_5\rangle & V_{\&\varepsilon}\,|q_4\rangle = |q_6\rangle \\ V_{\&\varepsilon}\,|q_5\rangle = |q_7\rangle & V_{\&\varepsilon}\,|q_6\rangle = |q_8\rangle \\ V_{\$\varepsilon}\,|q_7\rangle = |q_a\rangle & V_{\$\varepsilon}\,|q_8\rangle = |q_{aa}\rangle \end{array}$$

All the other transitions are arbitrary such that the transformations are unitary (see more in [3]).

Then the first branch moves like that:

$q_1$ - reads x and writes it down to the work tape, moving to the right; $q_3$ - waits while y is read; $q_5$ - reads $x^{rev}$ and goes to the left the work tape, comparing x and $x^{rev}$; $q_7$ - waits while $y^{rev}$ is read.

The second branch:

$q_2$ - waits while x is read; $q_4$ - reads y and writes it down to the work tape, moving to the right; $q_6$ - waits while $x^{rev}$ is read; $q_7$ - reads $y^{rev}$ and goes to the left the work tape, comparing y and $y^{rev}$.

If the branch finds the difference between x and $x^{rev}$ or y and $y^{rev}$, then it goes to one of the rejecting states. Otherwise after the symbol $ is read it goes to one of the accepting states.

If going backward the work tape the symbol read from the work tape doesn't match the symbol read from the input tape, QTM goes to the rejecting states.

When the symbol & is read from the input tape, the QTM changes its state. When the symbol $ is read from the input tape, the QTM finishes work. Then the working states go to the accepting states.

So if the word is from L, then both of the branches say "yes" with probability 2/3; If the word is not from L, then it is rejected by at least one branch, and in total the word is rejected with probability >= 2/3.

Language L can't be recognized by a deterministic TM in time $|w|$, that is the length of the word $w \in L$ (see the standard proves [4], [5], [6]).

## 4 Conclusion

We have proved the existence of the language class, that can be recognized by real - time QTM and can't be recognized by real - time TM. That means that QTM with limitations can be more powerful than deterministic one.

## References


1. Feynman, R.: Simulating physics with computers. Int. J. Of Theor. Phys. Vol. 21 No. 6/7 (1982) 467–488
2. Deutsch, D.: Quantum theory, the Church - Turing principle and the universal quantum computer. Proc. Royal Society London, A400, (1989) 96–117
3. Gruska, J.: Quantum Computing, McGraw Hill (1999)
4. Hennie, F.: On - line Turing machine computation. IEEE Trans. Electr. Comp., EC-15 (1966) 35–44
5. Hartmanis, J.: Computational complexity of one - tape Turing machine computations. J. Assoc. Comput. Mach. 15 (1968) 325–339
6. Freivalds, R.:Complexity of palindromes recognition by Turing machines with an input. "Algebra i Logika", , v.4, No. 1 (1965) 47–58 (in Russian)

# Mathematical Models and Optimal Algorithms of Dynamic Data Structure Control

Andrew V. Sokolov

Karelian Research Center of the Russian Academy of Sciences,
Institute of Applied Mathematical Research,
IAMR KRC RAS, 11, Pushkinskaya St., Petrozavodsk, Karelia, 185610, Russia
avs@krc.karelia.ru

**Abstract.** This paper concerns issues related to building mathematical models and optimal algorithms of stacks and queues [1] control in single- and two-level memory. These models were constructed as 1, 2 and 3-dimensional random walks. In our opinion the algorithms, constructed for concrete data structure, will work better, than universal replacement algorithms in paging virtual and cash-memory. It was confirmed by the practice of construction of stack computers [2]. This research work was supported by the Russian Foundation for Fundamental Research, grant 01-01-00113.

## 1 Introduction

In the case of single-level memory, several methods of stacks and queues [1] presentation in memory may be used. The connected presentation is the first method. In this case any number of lists can coexist inside a shared memory area until the free memory list is exhausted. But on the other hand, this approach requires an additional link field for each element. The second method (Garvic's algorithm) uses the consecutive allocation of one list after another.

It is also possible to allocate stacks consecutively and divide them into pairs of stacks growing towards each other [3]. In the case of queues Knuth determined that operating two queues in common memory is impossible [1](ex. 2.2.2, N 17), however, he does not seem to consider the possibility of the travel of two queues one after the other around a circle. This is the case we analyze here, as in [3], it has been shown that this method of stacks control is optimal.

## 2 On the Problem of Optimal Stack Control

### 2.1 The Optimal Allocation of n Stacks in Single-Level Memory

Let we have a memory of $m \geq 0$ conditional units and there are $n$ stacks divided into pairs of stacks growing towards each other. Let $q_i, p_i$ denote the probabilities of deletion and insertion information into the i-th stack. Deletion from empty stack with probability $q_i$ means that process remain on the same state. The

R. Freivalds (Ed.): FCT 2001, LNCS 2138, pp. 416–419, 2001.

process starts from the state, when stacks are empty. Our task is to determine the optimal initial memory distribution and optimal memory redistribution in case one of the stacks overflows, when optimality is understood in the sense of maximizing the average functioning time until stack overflow. More exactly the problem will be stated for n=3.

## 2.2 The Optimal Allocation of Three Stacks in Single-Level Memory

Suppose there are three stacks located in a memory area of volume $m$ units. The pair of stacks growing towards each other occupies $s$ memory units and $m - s$ memory units are left for the third stack. Let $x_1$, $x_2$, $x_3$ denote the current stack heights. In this case the mathematical model is the three-dimensional random walk inside a prism with three reflecting barriers $x_1 = -1$, $x_2 = -1$, $x_3 = -1$ and two absorbing barriers $x_1 + x_2 = s + 1$, $x_3 = m - s + 1$. The problem of finding optimal initial memory distribution consists in determining the value of $s$ and numbering of the stacks (i.e. determining the number of the stack to be placed separately from the others), to maximize the average time of walk inside the prism until the absorption in its border, provided the process begins from the origin. In other words this task is reduced to choosing an optimal prism.

**The case of three stacks, when only insertions are assumed.** In this case we have the probability of moving out of the position $(x_1, x_2, x_3)$ to the position $(x_1 + 1, x_2, x_3)$ — $p_1$, to the position $(x_1, x_2 + 1, x_3)$ — $p_2$, and to the position $(x_1, x_2, x_3 + 1)$ — $p_3$ where $p_1 + p_2 + p_3 = 1$. *Let* $x = x_1 + x_2,\ y = x_3,\ p = p_1 + p_2,\ q = p_3$.

Then the 2-dimensional random walk in the integer lattice space, where $0 \le x \le s$ , $0 \le y \le m - s$ is used as a mathematical model. The probability of moving out of the position $(x, y)$ to the position $(x+1, y)$ — is $p$, to the position $(x, y + 1)$ is $q = 1 - p$. The process starts from the state $(0, 0)$ and is absorbed at the lines $x = s + 1$ and $y = m - s + 1$. The objective of our study is to find the value $s$, where the mean time of walk to the absorption would be maximal.

## 2.3 The Optimal Allocation of Two Stacks in Two-Level Memory

Let two stacks grow and collide inside a shared memory of volume $m$.

D. Knuth [1] posed the problem to construct the mathematical model of this process. In [4]–[9] the mathematical model of the process has been constructed as the two-dimensional random walk in a triangle with two reflecting boundaries and one absorbing boundary.

In [4] order to solve the problem, the Markov chain theory was used.

In [5]–[9] the asymptotic behavior of stack sizes at the instant of the overflow, as well as the time till the memory overflow were investigated.

In the present paper we consider a generalization of Knuth's problem. In the case of two-level memory the problem is reduced to choosing optimal initial state of the 2-dimensional random walk inside the triangle until the absorption in its border.

### 2.4 The Optimal Management of Three Stacks in Two-Level Memory

In the case of two-level memory the problem is reduced to choosing optimal initial state of the 3-dimensional random walk inside the prism until the absorption in its border[4].

## 3 On the Problem of Optimal Queue Control

### 3.1 The Optimal Allocation of Single Queue in Two-Level Memory

Suppose there is cyclical consecutive queue [1] in a memory area of volume $n$ units. We assume, that in the case of memory overflow the process does not terminate. Instead, swapping with the second level memory occurs, and beginning of queue in fast memory transfer into state $y_0$, and $(n - y_0)$ last elements swap to second-level memory.

Let $y$-denote the current height of beginning of queue in fast memory, $x$-denote current height of new last elements in fast memory, $p$- denote the probability of insertion information, $q = 1 - p$- denote the probability of deletion information from queue, $m = n - 1$- denote the maximal number of elements in the queue. Then the 2- dimensional random walk in the integer lattice space, where $x \geq 0, y \geq 0, x + y \leq m$ is used as mathematical model. The probability of moving out of the position $(x, y)$ to the position $(x+1, y)$ is $p$, to the position $(x, y-1)$ is $q = 1 - p$. The process starts from the state $(0, y_0)$ and is absorbed at the lines $x + y = m + 1$ and $y = -1$.

The objective of our study is to find the state $y_0$, where the mean time of walk to the absorption would be maximal.

### 3.2 The Optimal Allocation of Two Queues in Single-Level Memory

Here we consider the problem of control over several queues in the memory of the same level. Assume that we want to work with k cyclic queues in the memory of the size n. We can arrange the operation of the queues as follows: to separate an individual area in the memory for each queue or to separate a common area for some (probably, for all ) queues and to operate inside the shared pieces so that the queues should travel one after the other around a circle. In any arrangement the following problem emerges: how much memory should be separated to each queue depending on its probabilistic properties? And, of course, it is necessary to answer the main question : which of the arrangements would have greater mean time to overload?

The model of the process is made up for the case k=2. Let us denote the probabilities of insertion and deletion of the elements in the queues by $p_1, q_1, p_2, q_2$.

When the queues are stored individually, let us denote current lengths of queues by $x$ and $y$, the length of memory separated to the first queue by $s$. Then, we'll have, as a model, two-dimensional walk over integer lattice in the region $0 \leq x \leq s, 0 \leq y \leq n - s$ with the corresponding probabilities of transitions. The walk begins in the point $x = y = 0$, here the lines $x = -1$ and $y = -1$

are the reflecting barriers, as well as the lines $x = s$ and $y = n - s$ - absorbing barriers. It is proposed to choose s so that the expectation value of the time to absorption would be maximum. It is the optimal value that must be used for the comparison with the case of shared memory.

In the case of shared storage of queues let us denote current lengths of queues by $x$ and $y$, and the distance from the end of the first queue to the beginning of the second one by $z$. Then we'll have, as a model, 3-dimensional walk over the integer lattice in the region $0 \leq x, 0 \leq y, 0 \leq z, x+y+z \leq n$. Being in the state $(x, y, z)$ where $0 < x, 0 < y$ , the process transfers into the state $(x+1, y, z-1)$ with the probability $p_1$, into the state $(x-1, y, z)$ with the probability $q_1$, into the state $(x, y+1, z)$ with the probability $p_2$, into the state $(x, y-1, z+1)$ with the probability $q_2$. In the state $(0, y, z)$ and $(x, 0, z)$ the walk remains on the spot with the probabilities $q_1$ and $q_2$, respectively. The planes $z = -1$ and $x + y + z = n + 1$ are the absorbing barriers. It is proposed to find the values $0 < z_0 < n$, so that at the exit from the state $(0, 0, z_0)$ the expectation value of the time to absorption would be maximum.

The tasks are solved with the help of the apparatus of absorbing Markov chains as well as the construction and solution of difference equations. The algorithms as well as computational programs in C++ for this problems were developed. In the report the results of numerical experiments have been analysed.

## References

1. D. E. Knuth. *The art of computer programming.* Vol. Addison-Wesley, Reading, MA, 1976.
2. Philip J.Koopman,Jr. Stack Computers. Ellis Horwood, 1989. URL: `http://www.cs.cmu.edu/ koopman/stack_computers/`
3. S. Avierri, FRANKEL. *Paired sequential lists in a memory interval.* Inform. Process Lett, (1979)8,9–10.
4. A. V. Sokolov, A. A.Lemetti.*On the problem of optimal stack control.* In: *Probabilistic methods in discrete mathematics. Proceedings of the Fifth International Petrozavodsk Conference* VSP, Utrecht, The Netnerlands,(2001). To appear.
5. A. V.Sokolov. *About storage allocation for implementing two stacks.* In: *Automation of experiment and data processing.* Petrozavodsk. 1980. P.65–71. (in Russian).
6. A. C. Yao. *An analysis of a memory allocation scheme for implementating stacks.* SIAM J. Computing. (1981)10,398–403.
7. P. Flajolet. *The evolution of two stacks in bounded spase and random walks in a triangle.* In: *Lec. Notes Computer Sci.* (1986)223,325–340.
8. G. Louchard and R. Schott. *Probabilistic analysis of some distributed algorithms.* In: *Lect. Notes Computer Sci.* (1990)431,239–253.
9. G. Louchard, R. Schott, M. Tolley, P. Zimmermann. *Random walks, heat equation and distributed algorithms.* J. Comput. Appl. Math. (1994)53,243–274.
10. R. S. Maier. *Colliding Stacks: A Large Deviations Analysis.* Random Structures and Algorithms. (1991)2,379–421.

# Linear Automata and Recognizable Subsets in Free Semirings

Olga Sokratova

Institute of Computer Science,
University of Tartu J. Liivi 2, 50409 Tartu, Estonia
tel.: +372 7 375 445, fax: +37 27 375 468
olga@cs.ut.ee,
WWW home page: http://www.cs.ut.ee/people/sokratova/

**Abstract.** The recognizable subsets of free monoid semirings are investigated. They are defined using linear automata as recognizers. For a subset of a free monoid semiring, we define the Myhill and Nerode congruences and prove a generalization of the well-known Myhill-Nerode Theorem. We consider recognizable subsets of the semiring of natural numbers. It is shown that every finite subset of and every ideal of $\mathbb{N}_0$ are recognizable. Examples of recognizable subsets of free semirings are also given.

**Keywords:** dynamical (linear) system, recognizable set, semiring.

In 1967 Elinberg considered reconizable subsets in arbitrary monoids. Note that in this case recognizable and rational subsets do not necessarily coinside. By analogy with monoids various concepts of recognizability have been proposed for other algebraic structures. Recognizable subsets were defined in general algebra by Mezei and Wright in terms of finite congruences (see [4]). An equivalent definition suggesting the idea of finite algebras as recognizers was given by Steinby [5]. On the other hand, dynamical (or linear) systems over semirings have been actively investigated for years (we refer to [2] and [3]). Therefore it is of interest to study languages that can be recognized by input semimodules of such systems, which are called linear automata.

In this paper we consider recognizable subsets of free monoid semirings and show that they can be defined using linear automata as recognizers. For a subset of a free monoid semiring, we define the Myhill and Nerode congruences and prove a generalization of the well-known Myhill-Nerode Theorem. It follows that in case of free monoid semirings our definition of recognizability is equivalent to the definition by Mezei and Wright and to the definition by Steinby. Finally we consider recognizable subsets of the semiring of natural numbers. In particular, we show that every finite subset of and every ideal of $\mathbb{N}_0$ are recognizable. We also give examples of recognizable subsets of free semirings.

We refer to [2] for background concepts on semirings. Throughout, we consider semirings with neutral element 0 and identity 1. A *right semimodule* over a semiring $S$ (or right $S$-semimodule) is defined as an additive semigroup $(A, +)$

R. Freivalds (Ed.): FCT 2001, LNCS 2138, pp. 420–423, 2001.

in which for all $a \in A, s \in S$ an action $as \in A$ is given so that the following conditions hold: $a(rs) = (ar)s$, $a1 = a, a0 = 0s = 0$, $(a+b)s = as + bs$, $a(r+s) = ar + as$ for all $a, b \in A$ and $r, s \in S$. Left $S$-semimodules are defined dually. A semiring $R$ which has also a structure of an $S$-semimodule is called an *S-semialgebra.*

Let $S$ be a semiring, and let $\mathrm{Mod}_S$ be a category of right semimodules over $S$. Every system $(A, X, \circ) = (A, X)$ is called a *linear automaton* (in the variety $\mathrm{Mod}_S$), where

- $A \in \mathrm{Mod}_S$ is a semimodule of *states*;
- $X$ is an alphabet of *input signals;*
- $\circ\colon A \times X \to A$ is the *transition function*; for every $x \in X$, the mapping $a \mapsto a \circ x$ is an $S$-homomorphism.

For a monoid $M$, the definition of the *monoid semiring* $S[M]$ is similar to that of a monoid ring. In particular, given a set $X$, the free monoid semiring $S[X^*]$ consists of all polynomials over $S$ in non-commuting variables of $X$.

Given a linear automaton $(A, X, \circ)$, where $A \in \mathrm{Mod}_S$, one can extend it to a linear automaton $(A, SX^*, \circ)$ over the monoid semiring $SX^*$ by extending the transition and output functions as follows:

$$a \circ (s_1u_1 + s_2u_2) = as_1 \circ u_1 + as_2 \circ u_2.$$

We shall investigate recognizable subsets in the monoid semiring $S[X^*]$ motivated by the following

**Proposition 1.** *The monoid semiring $S[X^*]$ is a free $S$-semialgebra over $X$, or, in other words, it is a free semiring over $X$ in the subvariety of all semirings in $\mathrm{Mod}_S$. In particular, the monoid semiring $\mathbb{N}_0[X^*]$ is a free semiring over $X$ in the variety of all semirings.* □

A *linear recognizer* $(A, a_0, F)$ in the variety $\mathrm{Mod}_S$ consists of a linear automaton $(A, X^*)$ in $\mathrm{Mod}_S$, an initial state $a_0 \in A$ and a set $F \subseteq A$ of final states. An linear recognizer $(A, a_0, F)$ is *finite* if $A$ is finite. The *set recognized* by a linear recognizer $(A, a_0, F)$ is

$$L(A) = \{u \in S[X^*] \mid a_0 \cdot u \in F\}.$$

Further, we present some algebraic characterizations of recognizable subsets in $S[X^*]$.

For arbitrary subset $L \subseteq S[X^*]$, define the following equivalence relations on $S[X^*]$:

$$\begin{aligned} u\ \theta_L\ v \text{ if and only if } & (\forall a \in S[X^*], \forall w, w' \in X^*, \forall s \in S) \\ & [wusw' + a \in L \Leftrightarrow wvsw' + a \in L] \\ u\ \rho_L\ v \text{ if and only if } & (\forall a \in S[X^*], \forall w \in X^*, \forall s \in S) \\ & [usw + a \in L \Leftrightarrow vsw + a \in L]. \end{aligned}$$

**Proposition 2.** *$\theta_L$ is the greatest congruence on $S[X^*]$ which saturates $L$.*

*Proof.* Let us prove, for example, that $\theta_L$ is stable with respect to multiplication. Consider an arbitrary nonzero element $c = r_1c_1 + \cdots + r_nc_n \in S[X^*]$, where $r_i \in S, c_i \in X_*$. We are going to show that $\langle u, v\rangle \in \theta_L$ implies $\langle uc, vc\rangle \in \theta_L$. Take arbitrary elements $s \in S, a \in S[X^*]$ and $w, w' \in X^*$. Then

$$\begin{aligned}
&w(uc)sw' + a = wur_1sc_1w' + (wur_2sc_2w' + \cdots + wur_nsc_nw' + a) \in L\\
&\Leftrightarrow wvr_1sc_1w' + (wur_2sc_2w' + \cdots + wur_nsc_nw' + a)\\
&= wur_2sc_2w' + (wvr_1sc_1w' + \cdots + wur_nsc_nw' + a) \in L\\
&\Leftrightarrow wvr_2sc_2w' + (wvr_1sc_1w' + \cdots + wur_nsc_nw' + a) \in L\\
&\Leftrightarrow \dots\\
&\Leftrightarrow wvr_nsc_nw' + (wvr_{n-1}sc_{n-1}w' + \cdots + wvr_1sc_1w' + a) = w(vc)w' \in L.
\end{aligned}$$

Similarly, $\langle uc, vc\rangle, \langle u + c, v + c\rangle \in \theta_L$. Thus $\theta_L$ is a congruence. It is clear that every congruence that saturates $L$ is contained in $\theta_L$. □

The following proposition can be proved similarly.

**Proposition 3.** *$\rho_L$ is the greatest right congruence on $S[X^*]$ which saturates $L$.* □

**Proposition 4.** *$(S[X^*]/\rho_L, X^*)$ is a minimal linear recognizer of $L$.* □

Given a linear automaton $(A, X)$ in $\mathcal{A}$, we have a natural homomorphism $\mu$ from the semirings $S[X^*]$ to the semiring of all $S$-homomorphisms of $A$ defined by

$$a\mu(u) = au, \qquad \text{for } u \in S\Gamma, a \in A.$$

The semiring $S[X^*]/\ker\mu \cong \mu(S[X^*])$ is called the *semiring of transitions* of $(A, X)$.

**Proposition 5.** *$S[X^*]/\theta_L$ is isomorphic to the semiring of all transitions of the linear automaton $(S[X^*]/\rho_L, X^*)$.* □

The following theorem is a generalization of the Myhill-Nerode Theorem and gives a few characterizations of recognizable sets.

**Theorem 1.** *For arbitrary subset $L \subseteq S[X^*]$, the following conditions are equivalent:*

(1) *$L$ is recognized by a finite linear recognizer $(A, a_0, F)$ in the variety $\mathcal{A}$;*
(2) *$L$ is saturated by a congruence of $S[X^*]$ of a finite index;*
(3) *$\theta_L$ is of a finite index;*
(4) *$L$ is saturated by a right congruence of $S[X^*]$ of a finite index;*
(5) *$\rho_L$ is of a finite index;*
(6) *there exist a finite semiring $A$, a homomorphism $\phi\colon S[X^*] \to A$ and a subset $F \subseteq A$ such that $L = F\phi^{-1}$.* □

Theorem 1 allows us to use facts about recognizable subsets in the sense of the definition mentioned in condition (6). Namely, let $A$ be any algebra of signature $\Sigma$. The set Rec($A$) of recognizable subsets of $A$ is defined as follows (see [5]). A subset $L$ of $A$ belongs to Rec($A$) if and only if there exist a finite $\Sigma$-algebra $B$, a homomorphism of $\Sigma$-algebras $\phi$: $A \to B$ and a subset $F \subseteq B$ such that $L = F\phi^{-1}$.

In the case of the semiring $\mathbb{N}_0$,

$$\theta_L = \rho_L = \{\langle u, v\rangle \in \mathbb{N}_0 \times \mathbb{N}_0 \mid u + b \in L \Leftrightarrow v + b \in L, \forall b \in \mathbb{N}_0\}.$$

**Proposition 6.** *Every finite subset of the semiring* $\mathbb{N}_0$ *is recognizable.*

*Proof.* Let $L$ be a finite subset of $\mathbb{N}_0$, and let $a$ be the greatest element of $L$. Then all elements of $\mathbb{N}_0$ greater than $a$ are in the same class of $\theta_L$. Therefore $\theta_L$ is of a finite index, and so $L$ is recognizable. □

**Theorem 2.** *Every ideal of the semiring* $\mathbb{N}_0$ *is a recognizable subset.*

*Proof.* First, we claim that very principal ideal of the semiring $\mathbb{N}_0$ is recognizable. Indeed, consider an arbitrary principal ideal $a\mathbb{N}_0$. We are going to show that every two elements of $\mathbb{N}_0$ that have the same residue modulo $c$ are in the same class of $\theta_{a\mathbb{N}_0}$. Take any two elements $u = au_1 + p$ and $v = av_1 + p$. Assume that $u+b \in a\mathbb{N}_0$, for some $b \in \mathbb{N}_0$. We have $u+b = au_1+p+b = ak$, for some $k$. Hence $ak - au_1 = p + b \geq 0$, and therefore $v + b = av_1 + p + b = a(v_1 + k - u_1) \in a\mathbb{N}_0$. We get $\langle u, v\rangle \in \theta_{a\mathbb{N}_0}$. Thus $\theta_{a\mathbb{N}_0}$ has at most $a$ classes, and so the ideal $a\mathbb{N}_0$ is recognizable.

Further, take an arbitrary ideal $I$ of $\mathbb{N}_0$. It was proved in [1] that for every ideal $I$ of $\mathbb{N}_0$ there exists a finite subset $A$ of $\mathbb{N}_0$ such that $I \cup A$ is a principal ideal of $\mathbb{N}_0$. Obviously, we can choose a set $A$ of this kind so that $I \cap A = \emptyset$. Since the set $I \cup A$ is a principal ideal, it is recognizable in view of the preceding claim. By Proposition 6, the set $A$ is recognizable, too. Since both the sets $I \cup A$ and $A$ are recognizable and $I \cap A = \emptyset$, it follows from the results of [5] that the set $I = (I \cup A) \setminus A$ is recognizable. □

**Corollary 1.** *Let* $L_1 = \{x \in \mathbb{N}_0 \mid x \leq a\}$, *for some* $a \in \mathbb{N}$, *and let* $L_2$ *be a recognizable language in* $X^*$. *Then the subsemigroup* $L$ *of* $(\mathbb{N}_0[X^*], +)$ *generated by* $L_1L_2$ *is a recognizable set.* □

## References

1. P.J. Allen and L. Dale, *Ideal theory in the seniring* $\mathbb{Z}^+$, Publ. Math. Debrecen **22** (1975), 219–224.
2. J.S. Golan, "Semirings and their applications", Kluwer Academic Publishers, Dordrecht, 1999.
3. R.E. Kalman, P.L. Falb and M.A. Arbib, "Topics in Mathematical System Theory ", McGraw-Hill, New York, 1969
4. J. Mezei and J.B. Wright, Algebraic automata and context-free sets, *Information and Control* **11** (1967), 3–29.
5. M. Steinby, *Some algebraic aspects of recognizability and rationality*, Lect. Notes Comput. Sci. **117** (1981), 372–377.

# On Logical Method for Counting Dedekind Numbers*

Mati Tombak, Ain Isotamm, and Tõnu Tamme

Institute of Computer Science, University of Tartu
J. Liivi Str. 2, 50409 Tartu, Estonia

**Abstract.** A description of the property of monotonicity of Boolean functions using propositional calculus is presented, which allows to use #SAT algorithms for computing Dedekind numbers. Using an obvious modification of Davis-Putnam satisfiability algorithm, Dedekind numbers until the seventh have been calculated. Standard arithmetization of propositional logic allows to deduce Kisielewicz's formula in more transparent way.

## 1 Dedekind Numbers

Function $f\colon \{0,1\}^n \to \{0,1\}$ is a Boolean function of $n$ variables. Let $\alpha, \beta \in \{0,1\}^n$. Let $\alpha \prec \beta \equiv \exists i\,[\alpha_i < \beta_i \;\&\; \forall j\,((j \neq i) \to (\alpha_j = \beta_j))]$. By $\prec^+$ we denote the transitive closure of the relation $\prec$. Function $f\colon \{0,1\}^n \to \{0,1\}$ is monotone, if $f(\alpha_1, \dots, \alpha_n) \leq f(\beta_1, \dots, \beta_n)$ whenever $(\alpha_1, \dots, \alpha_n) \prec^+ (\beta_1, \dots, \beta_n)$

**Problem:** How many different monotone $n$-variable Boolean functions there exist?

The problem of finding the number, $D(n)$, was suggested by Dedekind ([2]). Within more then 100 years Dedekind numbers up to 8 were calculated. Although A. Kisielewicz at 1988 ([3]) found a closed formula for $D(n)$:

$$D(n) = \sum_{k=1}^{2^{2^n}} \prod_{j=1}^{2^n-1} \prod_{i=0}^{j-1} \left(1 - b_i^k b_j^k \prod_{m=0}^{\log_2 i} \left(1 - b_m^i + b_m^i b_m^j\right)\right) , \tag{1.1}$$

where $b_i^k = \left[k/2^i\right] - 2\left[k/2^{i+1}\right]$, it does not help very much in computing $D(n)$. For $n = 6$ we must sum $2^{64}$ values which is out of limits of the fastest computers.

## 2 Logical Description of Boolean Function Classes

Our goal is to describe the notion of monotonicity using family of propositional formulae. Every Boolean function of $n$ variables can be represented by its truth-table, so we use $2^n$ propositional variables $x_0, \dots, x_{2^n-1}$; one variable for each entry of the truth-table. For convenience we suppose that indexes of

* Supported in part by Estonian Science Foundation grant no. 3056

R. Freivalds (Ed.): FCT 2001, LNCS 2138, pp. 424–427, 2001.

the variables are binary numbers. The correspondence of the Boolean function $f\colon \{0,1\}^n \to \{0,1\}$ to the bit-string $f_0, \dots, f_{2^n-1}$ is defined by $f(\alpha) = f_\alpha$ for every $\alpha \in \{0,1\}^n$. Using this encoding, we can consider propositional formulae with variables $x_0, \dots, x_{2^n-1}$ as descriptions of the properties of $n$-variable Boolean functions.

**Theorem 1.** *Function $f\colon \{0,1\}^n \to \{0,1\}$ with truth-table $f_0, \dots, f_{2^n-1}$ is monotone if and only if truth assignment $f_0, \dots, f_{2^n-1}$ satisfies propositional formula*

$$\mathcal{M}_n(x_0, \dots, x_{2^n-1}) \equiv \bigwedge_{\alpha,\beta \in \{0,1\}^n;\alpha \prec \beta} (\overline{x}_\alpha \vee x_\beta) \ . \tag{2.2}$$

We omit the proof, which is similar to the proof of Theorem 2. Another possibility to get Dedekind numbers is by counting anti-chains. Function $f\colon \{0,1\}^n \to \{0,1\}$ is anti-chain, if $f(\alpha_1, \dots, \alpha_n) = 0$ or $f(\beta_1, \dots, \beta_n) = 0$, whenever $(\alpha_1, \dots, \alpha_n) \prec^+ (\beta_1, \dots, \beta_n)$. One can establish a bijection between anti-chains and monotone functions by considering anti-chain as a collection of "minimal ones" (or alternatively as a collection of "maximal zeros") of a monotone function.

**Theorem 2.** *Function $f\colon \{0,1\}^n \to \{0,1\}$ with truth-table $f_0, \dots, f_{2^n-1}$ is anti-chain if and only if truth assignment $f_0, \dots, f_{2^n-1}$ satisfies propositional formula*

$$\mathcal{A}_n(x_0, \dots, x_{2^n-1}) \equiv \bigwedge_{\alpha,\beta \in \{0,1\}^n;\alpha \prec^+ \beta} (\overline{x}_\alpha \vee \overline{x}_\beta) \ . \tag{2.3}$$

*Proof.* 1. Let $f$ be anti-chain. By definition of anti-chain for every $\alpha, \beta \in \{0,1\}^n$, $\alpha \prec^+ \beta$ implies $f(\alpha) = 0$ or $f(\beta) = 0$. Suppose $\mathcal{A}_n(f_0, \dots, f_{2^n-1}) =$ **false**. Then at least one of the clauses of $\mathcal{A}_n$, say $\overline{x}_\alpha \vee \overline{x}_\beta$, must be **false** for assignment $f_0, \dots, f_{2^n-1}$. It is possible only if $f_\alpha = 1$ and $f_\beta = 1$, which means that $f(\alpha) = 1$ and $f(\beta) = 1$. From the definition of $\mathcal{A}_n$ we know that $\alpha \prec^+ \beta$ and $f$ is not anti-chain. Contradiction.

2. Let $\mathcal{A}_n(f_0, \dots, f_{2^n-1}) =$ **true**. Suppose $f$ is not anti-chain, then there exist $\alpha, \beta \in \{0,1\}^n$ such that $\alpha \prec^+ \beta$, but $f(\alpha) = 1$ and $f(\beta) = 1$. Then the clause $\overline{x}_\alpha \vee \overline{x}_\beta$ is **false** and the assignment $(f_0, \dots, f_{2^n-1})$ violates $\mathcal{A}_n$. Contradiction.

## 3 Arithmetization

Standard method for representing propositional formula $\mathcal{A}(x_1, \dots, x_n)$ as a polynomial $[\mathcal{A}(x_1, \dots, x_n)]$ consists of two steps:

Step 1. Transform propositional formula into equivalent formula, which contains Boolean operators $\wedge$, $\to$, $\neg$ only.

Step 2. Change Boolean operators into arithmetical ones:

$[\mathcal{B} \wedge \mathcal{C}] \Rightarrow [\mathcal{B}] \cdot [\mathcal{C}]$, $[\mathcal{B} \rightarrow \mathcal{C}] \Rightarrow 1 - [\mathcal{B}] + [\mathcal{B}] \cdot [\mathcal{C}]$, $[\neg \mathcal{B}] \Rightarrow 1 - [\mathcal{B}]$, where $\mathcal{B}$ and $\mathcal{C}$ are propositional formulae. $\mathcal{A}(x_1, \ldots, x_n) = [\mathcal{A}(x_1, \ldots, x_n)]$ for $x_1, \ldots, x_n \in \{0,1\}$.

**Theorem 3 ((A. Kisielewicz, 1988)).** *For any $n \geq 1$*

$$D(n) = \sum_{k=1}^{2^{2^n}} \prod_{j=1}^{2^n-1} \prod_{i=0}^{j-1} \left( 1 - b_i^k b_j^k \prod_{m=0}^{\log_2 i} (1 - b_m^i + b_m^i b_m^j) \right) ,$$

*where $b_i^k = [k/2^i] - 2\,[k/2^{i+1}]$.*

*Proof.* We present here an alternative proof, which consists of transformation and arithmetization of the formula, defining anti-chain from theorem 2:

$$\mathcal{A}_n(x_0, \ldots, x_{2^n-1}) \equiv \bigwedge_{\alpha,\beta \in \{0,1\}^n; \alpha \prec^+ \beta} (\overline{x}_\alpha \vee \overline{x}_\beta) .$$

The condition $\alpha \prec^+ \beta$ can be removed inside as the antecedent of the implication.

$$\mathcal{A}_n(x_0, \ldots, x_{2^n-1}) \equiv \bigwedge_{\alpha \in \{0,1\}^n} \bigwedge_{\beta \in \{0,1\}^n} (\alpha \prec^+ \beta) \rightarrow (\overline{x}_\alpha \vee \overline{x}_\beta) .$$

Using the fact, that $\alpha \prec^+ \beta \equiv \bigwedge_{m=1}^n (\alpha_m \leq \beta_m)$ and that for every $x, y \in \{0,1\}$, $x \leq y \equiv x \rightarrow y$, we can rewrite the formula as

$$\mathcal{A}_n(x_0, \ldots, x_{2^n-1}) \equiv \bigwedge_{\alpha \in \{0,1\}^n} \bigwedge_{\beta \in \{0,1\}^n} \left( \bigwedge_{m=1}^n (\alpha_m \rightarrow \beta_m) \right) \rightarrow (\overline{x}_\alpha \vee \overline{x}_\beta) .$$

Using the equivalence from propositional logic $x \rightarrow (\overline{y} \vee \overline{z}) \equiv \neg(x \wedge y \wedge z)$ and commutativity of conjunction we receive

$$\mathcal{A}_n(x_0, \ldots, x_{2^n-1}) \equiv \bigwedge_{\alpha \in \{0,1\}^n} \bigwedge_{\beta \in \{0,1\}^n} \neg \left( x_\alpha \wedge x_\beta \wedge \left( \bigwedge_{m=1}^n (\alpha_m \rightarrow \beta_m) \right) \right) .$$

After arithmetization we receive

$$[\mathcal{A}_n(x_0, \ldots, x_{2^n-1})] = \prod_{\beta \in \{0,1\}^n} \prod_{\alpha \in \{0,1\}^n} \left( 1 - x_\alpha x_\beta \prod_{m=1}^n (1 - \alpha_m + \alpha_m \beta_m) \right) .$$

Let $b_l^k b_{l-1}^k \ldots b_1^k b_0^k$ be the binary representation of the integer $k$. Then $b_i^k = [k/2^i] - 2\,[n/2^{i+1}]$ and we can use integers instead of bit-strings.

$$[\mathcal{A}_n(x_0, \ldots, x_{2^n-1})] = \prod_{j=0}^{2^n-1} \prod_{i=0}^{2^n-1} \left( 1 - x_i x_j \prod_{m=0}^n (1 - b_m^i + b_m^i b_m^j) \right) .$$

For every $i, j$ $(0 \le i, j \le 2^n)$, $b^i_n \ldots b^i_1 b^i_0 \prec^+ b^j_n \ldots b^j_1 b^j_0$ implies $i \le j$, so we must consider only cases $i \le j$ and compute product $\prod_{m=0}^{n} \left(1 - b^i_m + b^i_m b^j_m\right)$ for $m \le \log_2 i$.

$$[\mathcal{A}_n (x_0, \ldots, x_{2^n - 1})] = \prod_{j=1}^{2^n-1} \prod_{i=0}^{j-1} \left(1 - x_i x_j \prod_{m=0}^{\log_2 i} (1 - b^i_m + b^i_m b^j_m)\right) .$$

Bit-string $f = f_0 \ldots f_{2^n - 1}$ is truth-table of some monotone function if and only if $[\mathcal{A}_n (f_0, \ldots, f_{2^n-1})] = 1$. For computing $D(n)$ we have to add these values for all bit-strings from $\{0,1\}^{2^n}$ or, otherwise, for binary representations of all natural numbers $k$ from 0 to $2^{2^n} - 1$, i.e.

$$D(n) = \sum_{k=0}^{2^{2^n}-1} \prod_{j=1}^{2^n-1} \prod_{i=0}^{j-1} \left(1 - b^k_i b^k_j \prod_{m=0}^{\log_2 i} (1 - b^i_m + b^i_m b^j_m)\right) .$$

The value $D(n)$ does not change, if we change limits of the outer sum to $\sum_{k=1}^{2^{2^n}}$ because the formula does not use the most significant bit of $2^{2^n}$:

$$D(n) = \sum_{k=1}^{2^{2^n}} \prod_{j=1}^{2^n-1} \prod_{i=0}^{j-1} \left(1 - b^k_i b^k_j \prod_{m=0}^{\log_2 i} (1 - b^i_m + b^i_m b^j_m)\right) .$$

## 4 Concluding Remarks

We have already mentioned above, that Kisielewicz's formula does not help us in computing $D(n)$ for $n > 5$. Better idea might be computing the number of satisfying assignments of $\mathcal{M}_n$ or $\mathcal{A}_n$ using some method for counting solutions of propositional formulae. An obvious modification of Davis-Putnam algorithm ([1]) for counting satisfying assignments calculated $D(7)$ but could not cope with calculating $D(8)$. We see at least two directions for future work. Firstly, it would be interesting to try to reduce other combinatorial counting problems to #SAT. Secondly, Dedekind numbers can be considered as a benchmark for #SAT algorithms and this gives a good reason to develop better methods for counting solutions. Counting methods for restricted classes of CNF are also interesting because the formula $\mathcal{A}_n$ is anti-monotone, 2CNF and Horn formula.

## References


1. Davis, M., Putnam, H.: A computing procedure for quantification theory. J. Assoc. Comput. Mach. **7** (1960) 201-215
2. R. Dedekind, R.: Über Zerlegungen von Zahlen durch ihre grôssten gemeinsamen Teiler. Festschrift der Technischen Hochschule zu Braunschweig bei Gelegenheit **der 69** Versammlung Deutscher Naturforscher und Ärzte (1897) 1-40
3. Kisielewicz,A.: A solution of Dedekind's problem on the number of isotone Boolean functions. J. reine angew. Math. **386** (1988) 139-144

# A General Method for Graph Isomorphism*

Gabriel Valiente

Department of Software, Technical University of Catalonia, E-08034 Barcelona

**Abstract.** A general method is presented for testing graph isomorphism, which exploits those sufficient conditions that define linear orderings on the vertices of the graphs. The method yields simple and constructive, low-order polynomial graph isomorphism algorithms for classes of graphs which have a unique ordering, or a small (not necessarily bounded) number of different orderings. The general method is instantiated to several graph classes, including: interval graphs, outerplanar graphs, biconnected outerplanar graphs, and triconnected planar graphs. Although more efficient algorithms are known for isomorphism on some of these classes of graphs, the method can be applied to any class of graphs having a polynomial number of different orderings and an efficient algorithm for enumerating all these orderings.

Considerable effort has been devoted over the last three decades to graph isomorphism and related problems, motivated by the many practical applications but also by the failure of all attempts to determine the complexity of the graph isomorphism problem. A comprehensive survey of the so-called *graph isomorphism disease* can be found in [3,9], while complexity aspects of the graph isomorphism problem are treated in much detail in [2,6,10].

The concept of *graph isomorphism* lies (explicitly or implicitly) behind almost any discussion of graphs, to the extent that it can be regarded as *the* fundamental concept of graph theory. Two graphs are isomorphic if there is a bijective correspondence between their vertex sets which preserves and reflects adjacencies—that is, such that two vertices of a graph are adjacent if and only if the corresponding vertices of the other graph are adjacent.

**Definition 1.** *Two graphs* $G_1 = (V_1, E_1)$ *and* $G_2 = (V_2, E_2)$ *are isomorphic, denoted by* $G_1 \cong G_2$*, if there is a bijection* $h : V_1 \to V_2$ *such that* $\{u, v\} \in E_1$ *if, and only if,* $\{h(u), h(v)\} \in E_2$*, for all* $u, v \in V_1$*. Such a bijection h is called a graph isomorphism between* $G_1$ *and* $G_2$*.*

Algorithms for testing isomorphism of general graphs are usually based either on invariants or on certificates [7]. An *invariant* is a necessary condition for isomorphism, a property that does not depend on the presentation (labeling) of a graph. A *certificate* is a necessary and sufficient condition for isomorphism, a description of a unique representative of a graph in a given isomorphism class.

* Partially supported by the Spanish CICYT project TIC98-0949-C02-01 HEMOSS.

R. Freivalds (Ed.): FCT 2001, LNCS 2138, pp. 428–431, 2001.

Unfortunately, no certificates have been found for general graphs which are not either equivalent to the straight definition of isomorphism, or at least as difficult to compute. Invariants, on the other hand, are useful for demonstrating non-isomorphism, but nothing can be concluded about two graphs which share an invariant.

In some classes of graphs, though, a sufficient condition for graph isomorphism can be stated which defines a unique ordering or numbering of the vertices—or a unique numbering of the edges that induces a unique numbering of the vertices. For a graph $G = (V, E)$, where $E \subseteq V \times V$, $n$ and $m$ will be used to denote the number of vertices and edges in $G$, respectively.

**Definition 2.** *A numbering of a graph $G = (V, E)$ is a bijection $f : V \to \{1, \ldots, n\}$.*

When a sufficient condition for isomorphism in a given class of graphs produces a unique numbering of the vertices of a graph, it can be easily turned into a necessary and sufficient condition. As a matter of fact, since such numberings are one-to-one functions, they define a bijection between the vertices of any two given graphs. Then, since the test for graph isomorphism given a vertex mapping takes linear time, if the sufficient condition for isomorphism in a special class of graphs can be tested in low-order polynomial time this yields a simple low-order polynomial-time method for testing isomorphism in the given class of graphs.

**Definition 3.** *A numbering $f$ of a graph $G_1 = (V_1, E_1)$ together with a numbering $g$ of a graph $G_2 = (V_2, E_2)$ induce a one-to-one mapping $h : V_1 \to V_2$, called the vertex mapping induced by $f$ and $g$ and defined by $h(u) = v$ if, and only if, $f(u) = g(v)$, for all $u \in V_1$ and $v \in V_2$. A vertex mapping $h : V_1 \to V_2$ is adjacency-preserving if $\{h(u), h(v)\} \in E_2$ for all $\{u, v\} \in E_1$, and it it adjacency-reflecting if $\{u, v\} \in E_1$ for all $\{h(u), h(v)\} \in E_2$.*

**Lemma 1.** *Two graphs $G_1 = (V_1, E_1)$ and $G_2 = (V_2, E_2)$ are isomorphic if, and only if, there is a vertex mapping $h : V_1 \to V_2$ which preserves and reflects adjacencies.*

*Proof.* Follows directly from Def. 1 and Def. 3. □

**Proposition 1.** *Two graphs $G_1$ and $G_2$ are isomorphic if, and only if, there is a numbering $f$ of $G_1$ and a numbering $g$ of $G_2$ such that the vertex mapping induced by $f$ and $g$ is adjacency-preserving and adjacency-reflecting.*

*Proof.* (if) Immediate. (only if) Let $G_1 = (V_1, E_1)$ and $G_2 = (V_2, E_2)$ be two isomorphic graphs, let $h : V_1 \to V_2$ be an adjacency-preserving and adjacency-reflecting vertex mapping, let $(v_1, \ldots, v_n)$ be an arbitrary permutation of $V_1$, and let $f : V_1 \to \{1, \ldots, n\}$ be the bijection defined by $f(v_i) = i$ for all $v_i \in V_1$. Let also $g : V_2 \to \{1, \ldots, n\}$ be the bijection defined by $g(v) = f(h^{-1}(v))$ for all $v \in V_2$. Then both $f$ and $g$ are numberings. Moreover, since for all $u \in V_1$ and $v \in V_2$, $h(u) = v$ if, and only if, $f(u) = f(h^{-1}(v)) = g(v)$, it follows that $h$ is the vertex mapping induced by $f$ and $g$, which by hypothesis preserves and reflects adjacencies. □

The previous formulation of graph isomorphism suggests a simple, general method for testing whether two graphs $G_1$ and $G_2$ are isomorphic. Given an arbitrary numbering $f$ of $G_1$, if for some numbering $g$ of $G_2$, the vertex mapping induced by $f$ and $g$ preserves and reflects adjacencies, then $G_1$ and $G_2$ are isomorphic; otherwise (if for all numberings $g$ of $G_2$, the vertex mapping induced by $f$ and $g$ is not adjacency-preserving or it is not adjacency-reflecting) then $G_1$ and $G_2$ are not isomorphic.

Actually, in order to systematically explore the vertex mappings induced by the numberings of the two graphs, cyclic rotations of the numberings need to be taken into account. The following algorithmic scheme encodes the general method for testing graph isomorphism. Let $G_1$ and $G_2$ be two graphs with $n_1 = n_2$. Upon completion, if $G_1 \cong G_2$, the vertex mapping $h$ found is a graph isomorphism between $G_1$ and $G_2$.

```
function isomorphic (G1, G2, h)
  let p be a numbering of graph G1
  for all numberings q of graph G2 do
    for all cyclic rotations q' of q do
      let h be the vertex mapping induced by p and q'
      if h preserves and reflects adjacencies then
        return true {G1 and G2 are isomorphic}
      end if
    end for
  end for
  return false {G1 and G2 are not isomorphic}
end function
```

Given a numbering $f$ of a graph $G_1$ and a numbering $g$ of a graph $G_2$, the vertex mapping $h$ induced by $f$ and $g$ can be computed in time linear in the number of nodes, $h$ can be tested for preserving and reflecting adjacencies in time linear in the number of nodes, and the number of cyclic rotations of $g$ is also linear in the number of nodes. Therefore, the worst-case complexity of the general method is $O(a+bcn^2)$, where $O(a)$ is the cost of finding some numbering $f$ of $G_1$ and $O(b)$ is the cost of finding each of the $O(c)$ numberings of $G_2$. In particular, when the number of different numberings is bounded by a constant and each numbering can be found in linear time, the method gives a simple $O(n^3)$ graph isomorphism algorithm.

Interesting instances of the graph isomorphism problem arise when dealing with restricted classes of graphs, because the graph isomorphism problem can be solved in polynomial time for some classes of graphs. It is the structure of those graphs what makes them polynomially solvable, which is often reflected in a sufficient condition for graph isomorphism, which induces a numbering. As a matter of fact, the general method is efficient for testing graph isomorphism when restricted to classes of graphs that have a unique or a small number of different numberings, which can be enumerated in low-order polynomial time. Notice that general graphs admit $O(n!)$ different numberings.

Interval graphs have an interval representation that defines a unique ordering of the vertices according to interval precedence, and since the interval representation can be found in linear time [1], the general method gives a simple algorithm for isomorphism of interval graphs in $O(n^3)$ time.

Outerplanar graphs have a unique planar embedding such that all vertices lie on a single face, and since the unique planar embedding, which can be found in linear time [8], defines a unique numbering of the graph, the general method gives a simple algorithm for isomorphism of outerplanar graphs in $O(n^3)$ time.

Biconnected outerplanar graphs have a unique Hamiltonian circuit, and since the unique Hamiltonian circuit, which can be found in linear time [8], defines a unique numbering of the graph, the general method gives a simple algorithm for isomorphism of biconnected outerplanar graphs in $O(n^3)$ time.

Triconnected planar graphs (polyhedral graphs) have a unique Eulerian circuit, because they have a unique combinatorial embedding in the plane, and since the unique Eulerian circuit, which can be found in linear time [5,11], defines a unique numbering of the graph, given by an enumeration of the vertices in the order in which they are visited for the first time in a traversal of the Eulerian circuit, the general method gives a simple algorithm for isomorphism of triconnected planar graphs in $O(n^3)$ time, whereas previous methods [5,11] take $O(m^2) = O(n^4)$ time, although more complex algorithms have been proposed [4] which take $O(n \log n)$ time.

## References


1. K. S. Booth and G. S. Lueker. Testing for the consecutive ones property, interval graphs and graph planarity using *PQ*-tree algorithms. *J. Comp. Syst. Sci.*, 13(3):335–379, 1976.
2. D. G. Corneil and D. G. Kirkpatrick. A theoretical analysis of various heuristics for the graph isomorphism problem. *SIAM J. Comput.*, 9(2):281–297, 1980.
3. G. Gati. Further annotated bibliography on the isomorphism disease. *J. Graph Theory*, 3(1):95–109, 1979.
4. J. E. Hopcroft and R. E. Tarjan. An $O(n \log n)$ algorithm for isomorphism of triconnected planar graphs. *J. Comp. Syst. Sci.*, 7(3):323–331, 1973.
5. X. Y. Jiang and H. Bunke. Optimal quadratic-time isomorphism of ordered graphs. *Pattern Recogn.*, 32(7):1273–1283, 1999.
6. J. Köbler, U. Schöning, and J. Turán. *The Graph Isomorphism Problem: its Structural Complexity.* Progress in Theoretical Computer Science. Birkhäuser, 1993.
7. D. L. Kreher and D. R. Stinson. *Combinatorial Algorithms: Generation, Enumeration, and Search.* CRC Press, 1999.
8. S. L. Mitchell. Linear algorithms to recognize outerplanar and maximal outerplanar graphs. *Inform. Process. Lett.*, 9(5):229–232, 1979.
9. R. C. Read and D. G. Corneil. The graph isomorphism disease. *J. Graph Theory*, 1(4):339–363, 1977.
10. U. Schöning. Graph isomorphism is in the low hierarchy. *J. Comp. Syst. Sci.*, 37(3):312–323, 1988.
11. L. Weinberg. A simple and efficient algorithm for determining isomorphism of planar triply connected graphs. *IEEE Trans. Circuit Theory*, 13(2):142–148, 1966.

# Designing PTASs for MIN-SUM Scheduling Problems*
## (Short Version)

F. Afrati[1] and I. Milis[2]

[1] NTU Athens, Department of Electrical and Computer Engineering,
9, Heroon Polytechniou str., 15773, Athens, Greece
[2] Athens University of Economics and Business, Department of Informatics,
76, Patission str., 10434 Athens, Greece

**Abstract.** We review approximability and inapproximability results for MIN-SUM scheduling problems and we focus on two main techniques for designing polynomial time approximation schemes for this class of problems: *ratio partitioning* and *time partitioning*. For both techniques we present examples which illustrate their efficient use.

## 1 Introduction

In the context of scheduling problems, we are given, in general, a set of $n$ jobs, and a number $m$ of machines. Each job has a processing time $p_{ij}$ on machine $i$, a release date $r_j$, a deadline $d_j$ and a positive weight $w_j$. A partial order, $\prec$, describes a *precedence relation* among jobs; we say that jobs are *independent* if $\prec$ is empty. Two different scheduling models can be considered: the preemptive one, where the interruption of a job execution is allowed, and the non-preemptive, where once a job starts executed it should be completed. A schedule $\Sigma$ is an assignment of jobs to machines and an associated starting time $S_j$ for each job $j$. A schedule is feasible if at any time a machine processes at most one job and if $i \prec j$, then job $j$ starts its execution after the completion of job $i$. By $C_j$ is denoted the time at which job $j$ completes its execution and by $D_i$ is denoted the time by which machine $i$ complete the execution of all jobs assigned to it. OPT denotes the objective value of the optimum schedule.

To refer to the several variants of scheduling problems, that can be obtained from the above general description, the standard three-field, $\alpha|\beta|\gamma$, notation scheme of Graham et al. [13] is used. The first field describes the machine environment. A single machine environment is denoted by $\alpha \equiv 1$, (identical) parallel machines by $\alpha \equiv P(m)$ and unrelated (parallel) machines by $\alpha \equiv R(m)$; the optional $m$ denoting a constant number of machines. The second field of the notation describes any special conditions and constraints on the problem parameters (release dates, deadlines, precedence relation, processing times, multiprocessor

* This work has been partially supported by European Commission, Project APPOL-IST-1999-14084

R. Freivalds (Ed.): FCT 2001, LNCS 2138, pp. 432–444, 2001.

jobs, preemption). The third field of the notation describes the optimization criterion. According to optimization criteria, scheduling problems can be classified into two classes: MIN-MAX criteria and MIN-SUM criteria. The most common MIN-MAX criterion is the completion time (makespan) of the schedule, $\min_{\Sigma} \max_j C_j$, and also the maximum lateness, $\min_{\Sigma} \max_j (C_j - d_j)$. The most common MIN-SUM criterion is the total (weighted) completion time, $\min_{\Sigma} \sum_j w_j C_j$, and also the total (weighted) flow time, $\min_{\Sigma} \sum_j w_j F_j$, where $F_j = C_j - r_j$.

It is well known that only some of the simplest variants of scheduling problems can be solved in polynomial time. For a thorough listing of polynomial solved variants as well as complexity results on scheduling problems the reader is referred to the book and a web page of Brucker [5]. Hence, most of the recent research is directed towards designing approximation algorithms for the NP-hard variants of scheduling problems. A *$\rho$-approximation algorithm* computes polynomially a solution within $\rho$ factor of the optimum one. In this setting we are interested in designing $\rho$-approximation algorithms with $\rho$ as small as possible as well as on finding lower bounds for $\rho$. When $\rho$ is a constant, then we say that the approximation algorithm is a *constant factor* one. We say, however, that we have a *Polynomial Time Approximation Scheme* (PTAS) if we give an algorithm which, for any value of $\epsilon$, can construct an $(1+\epsilon)$-approximation solution. If the time complexity of a PTAS is also polynomial in $1/\epsilon$, then it is called a *Fully* PTAS (FPTAS). For lower bounds or inapproximability results, the notion of NP-completeness is used to disprove the existence of good approximation algorithms, unless P=NP. It is also well known that, unless P=NP, there is no a FPATS for *strongly* NP-hard problems.

Historically, MIN-MAX scheduling problems were the first investigated in the approximation algorithm framework and a lot of results have been proposed after Graham's seminal paper [12]. On the other hand, much less was known about the approximability of MIN-SUM scheduling problems until 1996. However, during the last five years, there was an explosive progress on the approximality of MIN-SUM problems, that recently led to PTASs for many of them.

In this paper we present a brief survey of this research on MIN-SUM scheduling focusing on PTASs design techniques. In Section 2 we present the history of known results for constant approximation algorithms and we comment on the techniques used and their limitations. Next, we present two main techniques for designing polynomial time approximation schemes for this class of problems. In Section 3 we present the *ratio partitioning* technique and in Section 4 the *time partitioning* technique. For both cases we give examples which illustrate hoe these techniques may be used to derive PTASs for such problems. Examples are taken from [3,1,2].

## 2 History of Approximation Results and Techniques

Although Shani [27], in 1976, gave a FPTAS for $Pm \mid \mid \sum w_j C_j$, no other approximation result was known until 1991, when Ravi, Agrawal and Klein [26] gave an $O(\log n \log \sum_j w_j)$-approximation algorithm for $1|prec|\sum w_jC_j$. Moreover, much less was also known about the approximability of MIN-SUM scheduling problems even until 1995, despite the fact that there was an extensive literature on the polyhedral structure of these problems (especially of single machine problems). This fact, however, was only exploited for characterizations of polynomial solvable variants and for computing optimum solutions (see Queyranne and Schulz [25] for a thorough survey of this research area).

Philips, Stein and Wein [22], in 1995, gave the first constant approximation algorithms: an $(8+\epsilon)$ for both $1|r_j,pmtn|\sum w_jC_j$ and $P|r_j,pmtn|\sum w_jC_j$), a $(16+\epsilon)$ for $1|r_j|\sum w_jC_j$ and a $(24+\epsilon)$ for $P|r_j|\sum w_jC_j$. Hall, Shmoys and Wein in [15] and its journal version by Hall, Schulz, Shmoys and Wein [14], in 1996 and 1997, improved dramatically the known approximation factors and gave algorithms for many new variants. Their results, some of which are the best known even today (see Table 1 below), were motivated by the successful work done on polyhedral structure of scheduling problems and build on earlier research on computing near-optimum solutions for MIN-MAX scheduling problems, by rounding optimum solutions to linear relaxations. In view of future results, the most important point of their work was the introduction of an *time-interval indexed* LP formulation, since it was proven later very fruitful for designing PTASs for many MIN-SUM problems. The general idea of *time indexed* LP formulation was used in the past in several forms. Potts [23] used decision variables $\delta_{ij}$, where $\delta_{ij}$ implies that job $J_i$ precedes job $J_j$ in the schedule. Dyer and Wosley [9] used variables $x_{jt}$, where $x_{jt}=1$ means that job $J_i$ completes its execution at time $t$. Wosley [42] and Queyranne [24] used as decision variables the completion times $C_j$ of jobs themselves. Hall et al. [15] adopted this last formulation to obtain their results for single machine problems and proposed a different, more compact linear *time-interval indexed* LP formulation: subdivide the time horizon into the intervals $[1,1],(1,1+\epsilon],(1+\epsilon,(1+\epsilon)^2],\ldots,,$ where $\epsilon$ is an arbitrary small positive constant. Then, the linear program only specifies the interval in which the job is completed and since all completion times within an interval are within a $(1+\epsilon)$ factor of each other, the relative schedule within an interval will be of little consequence. This was the first use of *time partitioning*.

After Hall et al. [15,14] there has been an explosion of research in this area with successively smaller constant factor algorithms as well as algorithms for new variants of MIN-SUM scheduling problems. Due to space limitations, here we present, in Table 1, only the best known constant approximation factors and summarize briefly all this research. Except a few combinatorial methods, these algorithms follow the general and successful relaxation method: first an optimum solution to a relaxation of the original problem is polynomially obtained, then this solution is rounded, either to order the jobs in time or to assign the jobs to machines, to obtain a near-optimum optimum solution of the original problem. The large body of algorithms within this method can be classified according two factors: the type of relaxation and the rounding technique used. Types of relaxations include preemptive schedule relaxations and linear and convex programming relaxations, while rounding techniques include scheduling by completion times, scheduling by $\alpha$-points and randomized rounding (see [34] for a elegant survey on LP relaxation algorithms).

Although there is practical evidence [28,43] that LP relaxations can provide very good approximate solutions, all relaxation based algorithms suffer from a major drawback: their solution is not compared directly to the solution of the original problem but to the solution of the relaxed one. However, there are gaps between the solutions of the relaxed and the original problem and any algorithm obtaining such a rounded solution inherits these gaps. Hall et al. [14], Schulz and Skutella [29] and Chekuri and Motwani [7] argue on the fact that several relaxation methods for $1|prec|\sum w_j C_j$ can not improve on the best known 2-approximation algorithm. Moreover, Torng and Uthaisombut [39] have shown that any preemptive relaxation for $1|r_j|\sum C_j$, that uses the SRPT algorithm to solve the relaxed problem, can not led to an approximation factor better than $\epsilon/(\epsilon-1)$, that matches the best known factor of 1.58 [8]. It seems therefore, that such approaches methods can never yield a PTAS for MIN-SUM scheduling problems.

Indeed, until 1998 only FPTASs, based on dynamic programming, for *weakly* NP-hard MIN-SUM problems were known (see Shani's [27] for a FPATS for $Pm \mid \mid \sum w_j C_j$ and [41]). Alon, Azar, Woeginger and Yadid [4], in 1998, obtained a PTAS for $P \mid \mid \sum D_i^2$. Skutella and Woeginger [37] realized that last results implies also a PTAS for $P \mid \frac{w_j}{p_j} = q \mid \sum w_j C_j$ and then in a first step they generalized this to a PTAS for $\frac{w_j}{p_j}$ ratios within a constant range. In a second step they obtained the first PTAS for a *strongly* NP-hard MIN-SUM problem $(P \mid \mid \sum w_j C_j)$. Their main idea was *ratio partitioning*, i.e. the partitioning of the jobs into subsets according to their $\frac{w_j}{p_j}$ ratios and such that the ratios of all jobs in one subset are within a constant range. Then, using the first step, near optimum solutions are computed for all subsets. Finally, these schedules are concatenated in order of nonincreasing ratios in each machine. Subsequently, Afrati, Bampis, Kenyon and Milis [3] based also on ratio partitioning provided a PTAS for $Rm \mid \mid \sum w_j C_j$. However, the concatenation of schedules obtained following the ratio partition technique can not be applied in the presence of release dates. For this case the *time partitioning* technique was recalled by several researchers [1] and it was proven powerful enough to yield PTASs in the presence of release dates. Based also on time partitioning Afrati et al. [2] presented recently PTASs for $P2|fix_j|\sum C_j$ and $Pm|fix_j, pmtn|\sum C_j$ and Fishkin et al. [10] presented PTASs for $Pm|fix_j, r_j|\sum w_j C_j$ and $Pm|size_j, r_j|\sum w_j C_j$.

The important point with all existing PTASs is that they rely either on *time partitioning* or on *ratio partitioning* technique. It seems more important in view of the fact that they succeeded where older techniques had failed and it is most likely that these techniques can be used to obtain PTASs for more involved scheduling variants. Moreover, all known PTASs use a combination of elementary and well understood combinatorial ingredients: partitioning, grouping, geometric rounding, enumeration and dynamic programming. The approach taken, in these PTASs, is to sequence several transformations of the input problem. Some transformations are actual changes to simplify the input, while others are applied as thought experiments to the optimum solution to prove there is a near-optimum solution with nice structure. Each transformation potentially increases the objective value by only $1 + O(\epsilon)$, that is, it produces $1 + O(\epsilon)$ *loss*. Besides problem-variant-specific transformations, some general transformations are used in these techniques. Such transformations are *geometric rounding* and *time stretching*.

**Table 1.** Summary of results (see also [32] for a discussion on open problems).

| Problem | Best known $\rho$ | (F)PTAS or Lower bound |
|---|---|---|
| $1\|r_j\|\sum C_j$ | 1.58 [8] | PTAS [1] |
| $1\|r_j\|\sum w_j C_j$ | 1.69 [11] | PTAS [1] |
| $1\|r_j, pmtn\|\sum w_j C_j$ | 4/3 [31] | PTAS [1] |
| $1\|prec\|\sum w_j C_j$ | 2 [14] [7] | |
| $1\|r_j, prec\|\sum w_j C_j$ | $e + \epsilon$ [29] | |
| $1\|r_j, prec, pmtn\|\sum w_j C_j$ | 2 [14] | |
| $1\|r_j\|\sum F_j$ | $O(n^{1/2})$ [18] | $O(n^{1/2})$ [18] |
| $Pm\| \|\sum w_j C_j$ | | FPTAS [27] |
| $P\| \|\sum D_i^2$ | 1.04 [20] | PTAS [4] |
| $P\|prec, p_j = 1\|\sum C_j$ | | 8/7 [16] |
| $P\|prec\|\sum C_j$ | | 4/3 [16] |
| $P\| \|\sum w_j C_j$ | 1.21 [17] | PTAS [37] |
| $P\|r_j\|\sum w_j C_j$ | 2 [30] | PTAS [1] |
| $P\|r_j, pmtn\|\sum w_j C_j$ | 2 [30] | PTAS [1] |
| $P\|r_j, prec\|\sum w_j C_j$ | 4 [21] | |
| $P\|r_j, prec, pmtn\|\sum w_j C_j$ | 3 [14] | |
| $P\|r_j\|\sum F_j$ | $O(n^{1/2})$ [19] | $\Omega(n^{1/3})$ [19] |
| $P\|r_j, pmtn\|\sum F_j$ | $\Theta(\log n)$ [19] | |
| $P2\|fix_j\|\sum C_j$ | 2 [6] | PTAS [2] |
| $Pm\|fix_j, pmtn\|\sum C_j$ | | PTAS [2] |
| $Pm\|r_j, fix_j\|\sum w_j C_j$ | | PTAS [10] |
| $Pm\|r_j, size_j\|\sum w_j C_j$ | | PTAS [10] |
| $P\|fix_j, p_j = 1\|\sum C_j$ | | $m^{1/2}$ [10] |
| $P\|size_j\|\sum C_j$ | 32 [40] | |
| $Rm\|r_j\|\sum w_j C_j$ | 2 [36] | PTAS [1] |
| $Rm\|r_j, pmtn\|\sum w_j C_j$ | 3 [36] | PTAS [1] |
| $Rm\| \|\sum w_j C_j$ | 3/2 [35] | PTAS [1] |
| $R\| \|\sum w_j C_j$ | 3/2 [35] [33] | NO PTAS [16] |
| $R\|pmtn\|\sum w_j C_j$ | 2 [36] | |
| $R\|r_j\|\sum C_j$ | | NO PTAS [16] |
| $R\|pmtn\|\sum w_j C_j$ | 2 [36] | |
| $R\|r_j, pmtn\|\sum w_j C_j$ | 3 [36] | |

### 2.1 Geometric Rounding and Time Stretching

The first simplification creates a well-structured set of possible processing times and release dates: With $1+\epsilon$ loss, we can assume that all processing times and release dates are rounded to integer powers of $1+\epsilon$. To prove, we change the values in two steps. First multiply every release date and processing time by $1+\epsilon$; this increases the objective by $1+\epsilon$. Then *decrease* each date and time to the next *lower* integer power of $1+\epsilon$ (which is still greater than the original value). This can only improve things.

The second transformation *time stretching* creates idle time *gaps* evenly spread along the schedule. These gaps will be used conveniently in later transformations to accommodate jobs that we are moving around in order to prove that there is a near-optimum schedule with nice structure. Often, we will use time stretching to add an idle amount of $\epsilon p_j$ time units before every job $j$. This will increase each completion time (and hence their sum) by a factor of $1+\epsilon$. According to this last transformation, we may also assume that the starting time of each job $j$ is $S_j \geq \epsilon p_j$: If job $j$ completed at time $t > p_j$ then it now completes at time $(1+\epsilon)t$ and therefore does not start until time $\epsilon t \geq \epsilon p_j$.

## 3 Ratio Partitioning

For the basic $1||\sum w_j C_j$ variant W. Smith, in 1956, designed a very easy greedy algorithm: sequencing in order of non-increasing $w_j/p_j$ ratios produces an optimum schedule [38]. We consider here the case of unrelated machines with no release dates. In this section, by $p_j^{(i)}$ we denote in this section the execution time of job $j$ on machine $i$ and for simplicity of notation we think in terms of two machines; however, it should be clear that it can be generalized for any constant number of machines. If we consider the restriction of the optimum schedule to each one of the machines, then Smith's ratio rule also applies: the jobs executed on machine $M_i$ are processed in order of non-increasing ratios $R_j^{(i)} = w_j/p_j^{(i)}$. It is therefore clear that the only difficulty is to decide, for each job, on which machine to execute it. To this end, we define a *ratio partitioning*, i.e. a partition of the range of ratios into disjoint windows such that the $i^{th}$ window consists of ratios in the range $F_i = (a^i R_{max}, a^{i-1} R_{max}]$, where $R_{max} = \max_{i,j}\{w_j/p_j^{(i)}\}$ and $a = \epsilon^4$.

A first observation is that we can think of each job having its two ratios either in the same window or in adjacent windows. If the processing times of a job are very different on the two machines, then we can directly decide to schedule it on the machine on which it has the shorter processing time. In quantitative terms: We can assume that all jobs such that $p_j^{(1)} < \epsilon p_j^{(2)}$ are scheduled on $M_1$ (we say that this job is $M_1$-*decided*), and that all jobs such that $p_j^{(2)} < \epsilon p_j^{(1)}$ are scheduled on $M_2$ (we say that this job is $M_2$-*decided*). To prove, we show that by moving all such jobs to the machine with the small processing time, the cost does not increase much: we move each such job in the other machine in the place so that it starts before or at time $C_j$ (its completion time in the old schedule). Thus the new completion time of this job is at most $C_j + p_j^{(1)} < C_j + \epsilon p_j^{(2)} < C_j(1+\epsilon)$ The other jobs affected are the jobs in machine $M_1$ (suppose we moved the job to $M_1$) which are delayed. Each such job $k$ is delayed by at most $\epsilon$ times the sum of $M_2$-processing times of moved jobs which completed before time $C_k$ in $M_2$; but this is $\epsilon$ times $C_k$. Thus, in this case, we can put $p_j^{(2)} = \infty$ or $p_j^{(1)} = \infty$ accordingly. Moreover, for each undecided job $p_j^{(1)} < \epsilon p_j^{(2)}$ and $p_j^{(2)} < \epsilon p_j^{(1)}$, that is $\epsilon < R_j^{(1)}/R_j^{(2)} < 1/\epsilon$. Hence, each job is either decided or it has its two ratios either in the same window or in adjacent windows.

Towards to a further problem simplification we define a **job-type** $T_{R,R'}$ as the set of jobs having the same pair of ratios, i.e. $T_{R,R'} = \{j \mid R_j^{(1)} = R \text{ and } R_j^{(2)} = R'\}$. Using this definition, a second observation is that "very different" job types do not affect each other. To state formally, we rewrite the cost function as: $\sum_{j,k \text{ on } M_1} \mathcal{M}_1[j,k] + \sum_{j,k \text{ on } M_2} \mathcal{M}_2[j,k]$, where

$$\forall j,k \in J, \qquad \mathcal{M}_i[j,k] = \begin{cases} p_k^{(i)} w_j & \text{if } j = k \\ \frac{1}{2} p_k^{(i)} w_j & \text{if } j \neq k \text{ and } \frac{w_k}{p_k^{(i)}} = \frac{w_j}{p_j^{(i)}} \\ p_k^{(i)} w_j & \text{if } \frac{w_k}{p_k^{(i)}} > \frac{w_j}{p_j^{(i)}} \\ 0 & \text{otherwise} \end{cases}$$

Notice that an entry $\mathcal{M}_i[j,k]$ represents the contribution to the cost function of job $j$, due to job $k$. Thus, if job $j$ is scheduled on machine $M_1$, and the jobs on $M_1$ with ratio equal to $R_j^{(1)}$ are ordered randomly, then the expected weighted completion time of $j$ satisfies: $w_j C_j = \sum_{k \text{ on } M_1} \mathcal{M}_1[j,k]$. Using this formulation of the cost function, we can prove that if the ratios of two jobs are very different, then we can neglect their interaction:

1. For every pair of jobs $\{j,k\}$ such that $R_j^{(i)} < \epsilon^2 R_k^{(i)}$, we can replace $\mathcal{M}_i[j,k]$ by 0.
2. For $i = 1,2$, and for every pair of jobs $\{j,k\}$ such that $j$ and $k$ are either $M_i$-decided or undecided, and such that $R_j^{(i)} < \epsilon^4 R_k^{(i)}$, we can replace both $\mathcal{M}_1[j,k]$ and $\mathcal{M}_2[j,k]$ by 0.

We prove the first in two steps: First for each $k$ on $M_1$, we look at the jobs $j$ on $M_1$ such that $R_j^{(1)} < \epsilon^2 R_k^{(1)}$, and whose completion times satisfy $C_k < \epsilon C_j$. The presence of $k$ before such a $j$ has only a marginal effect on $j$'s completion time (easy to prove). Second, we look at the pairs $\{j,k\}$ which are scheduled by on $M_1$, such that $R_j^{(1)} < \epsilon^2 R_k^{(1)}$, but whose completion times satisfy $C_j \leq C_k/\epsilon$. The contribution to the cost function of those pairs is very little.

To prove the second: Consider the case $i = 1$. From item (1) above we can replace $\mathcal{M}_1[j,k]$ by 0. If either job is $M_1$-decided, then it will never be placed on $M_2$ and so we can replace $\mathcal{M}_2[j,k]$ by 0. If both are undecided, then we have: $p_j^{(2)} > \epsilon p_j^{(1)}$ and $p_k^{(2)} < p_k^{(1)}/\epsilon$. Thus: $\frac{w_j}{p_j^{(2)}} < \frac{1}{\epsilon}\frac{w_j}{p_j^{(1)}} < \frac{\epsilon^4}{\epsilon}\frac{w_k}{p_k^{(1)}} < \frac{\epsilon^4}{\epsilon}\frac{1}{\epsilon}\frac{w_k}{p_k^{(2)}} = \epsilon^2 \frac{w_k}{p_k^{(2)}}$. By item 1 above, again, we can replace $\mathcal{M}_2[j,k]$ by 0.

Finally, we can bound the number of jobs within each job-type by a constant number. Consider a job-type $T_{R,R'}$ and the sum of the weights of jobs in $T_{R,R'}$,

$W_{R,R'}$. We group small jobs together to build larger compound jobs. Thus, we can assume that every job of a job-type has weight at least $\epsilon^2 W_{R,R'}$, and hence each job-type has at most $1/\epsilon^2 = O(1)$ elements. More specifically, we group greedily so that the sum of weights of the tiny jobs in each group (which now represents the weight of the compound job) is between $\epsilon^2 W_{R,r'}$ and $2\epsilon^2 W_{R,R'}$. Clearly a schedule that uses the compound jobs results in a cruder fractioning of the jobs in the job type among the machines. To take care of that we stretch time by $1+\epsilon$ and this stretching is enough to accommodate the compound jobs. This is because, with $1+O(\epsilon)$ loss, we can discard schedules that put a fraction of a job type smaller than $\epsilon W_{R,R'}$ on one of the machines.

### 3.1 Example: $R2||\sum w_j C_j$

We first simplify the input of the problem by applying geometric rounding on the parameters defining the jobs. Then, we identify the jobs which are $M_1$-decided or $M_2$-decided. We replace all irrelevant processing times (i.e. $p_j^{(2)}$ if $j$ is $M_1$-decided and $p_j^{(1)}$ if $j$ is $M_2$-decided) by $\infty$, which means that the corresponding ratio becomes equal to 0. Then we do all the simplifications of the previous subsection, namely calculating first the $\mathcal{M}_i[j,k]$ and then putting accordingly some of them equal to 0.

Note that, the set of undecided jobs having at least one ratio in a specific window has size $O(\log^2(1/\epsilon)/\epsilon^2)$: Roughly, because of geometric rounding, we have only a constant number of different ratios within a window and, because undecided jobs have their ratios either in the same window or in adjacent windows, there are only a constant number of job types that may contain a job of a particular ratio in one of the machines. Moreover, there is a constant number of jobs within each job type.

Summing up the above analysis: a) Each job type has the two ratios either in the same window or in adjacent windows and b) Job types affect each other only in the stretch of two windows and c) there is a constant number of undecided jobs with at least one ratio in a specific window. An immediate consequence of that is dynamic programming with respect to the windows of ratios. In each stage $i$ of the dynamic programming, we have fixed the schedule for jobs with both ratios in windows $F_1, \ldots F_i$ and keep all possible schedules of jobs with at least one ratio in window $F_i$. Thus, each stage runs in $O(1)$ time.

## 4 Time Partitioning

For an arbitrary integer $x$, we define $R_x = (1+\epsilon)^x$. We partition the time interval $(0, \infty)$ into disjoint intervals of the form $I_x = [R_x, R_{x+1})$. We will use $I_x$ to refer to both the interval and the size $(R_{x+1} - R_x)$ of the interval. We will often use the fact that $I_x = \epsilon R_x$, i.e., the length of an interval is $\epsilon$ times its start time. We consider an optimum schedule and focus on the schedule of one machine. Moving a job $j$ inside the interval in which it runs produces a $1 + O(\epsilon)$ loss because it will only increase its completion time by at most $I_x$ which is less than $\epsilon R_{x+1}$

or less than $\epsilon C_j$. Another useful observation is that a job can not be arbitrarily large: In the worst case, a job starts at time $\epsilon p_j$ and completes at time $\epsilon p_j + p_j$, hence, it crosses at most $s = \lceil \log_{1+\epsilon} \frac{\epsilon p_j + p_j}{\epsilon p_j} \rceil = \lceil \log_{1+\epsilon}(1 + \frac{1}{\epsilon}) \rceil$ intervals.

If a job $j$ crosses several intervals, we know that it crosses at most $s$ intervals, and then we can accumulate idle time for all $s$ intervals in the beginning of job $j$, and we know that the relative size of the 1st and $s$th interval is $\frac{I_x}{I_{x+s}} = \frac{1}{(1+\epsilon)^{s-1}} = \epsilon$. Also know that by time stretching we can create, in each interval an extra idle gap of size $\epsilon I_x$. In what follows in this section, we assume unit weights.

### 4.1 Large and Small Jobs

In many cases, jobs that are much smaller than the interval in which they run are essentially negligible and easy to deal with. The difficulty comes from jobs that are *large*—taking up a substantial portion of the interval. *Small* jobs are a lot like fractional jobs in linear relaxation methods, and fractional solutions are usually easier to find. We assume, in this section, that small jobs are defined to be those with $p_j < \epsilon I_x$, where $I_x$ is the interval where job $j$ runs.

We restrict attention to schedules in which no small job crosses an interval: By time stretching, add in each interval a gap of $\epsilon I_x$ and finish the single small job that may be crossing an interval. Also, note that there is a constant number of large jobs in an interval, namely at most $\frac{1}{\epsilon}$.

Interestingly, we can almost get rid altogether of large jobs (except a constant number of them). We can do that by moving most large jobs in larger intervals without much degrading the quality of the schedule. Thus, we end up with an overall constant number of large jobs:

**Lemma 1.** *With a $1 + O(\epsilon)$ loss, we assume:*
*1. For each job $j$, $S_j \geq \min\{\frac{p_j}{\epsilon^2}, \epsilon^7 OPT\}$.*
*2. All jobs are small in the intervals they run except at most $1/\epsilon^7$.*

*Proof.* The proof of (2) follows from (1): Note that $S_j \geq p_j/\epsilon^2$ means that job $j$ is small when it runs. Also, all jobs starting after time $\epsilon^7 OPT$ are at most $1/\epsilon^7$. The small jobs trivially satisfy this condition in (1). We move around large jobs in larger intervals so that they are now small in the interval that they run. We do that only for large jobs that complete before $\epsilon^7 OPT$.

We move a task that completes before time $(1 + \frac{1}{\epsilon^2})p_j$ in the first gap after time $t = C_j/\epsilon^4$. We have to worry about three considerations:

1. There is space large enough to accommodate all jobs that are landed on a particular gap. This is so because the gap at time $t$ is equal to $\epsilon^2 t$, hence, at least equal to $C_j$, thus can hold all jobs which complete before time $C_j$.

2. There is not some hugely long crossing job in this interval. This is guaranteed by the fact that any crossing job may cross at most $s$ intervals. Thus, we put the moved job in the beginning of the crossing job and still it is in an interval where it is considered small. This is so because the intervals along which a job stretches differ in size by a factor at most $\epsilon$.

3. The added cost is not too much: We need to bound the added cost of the large jobs we moved forward. The last interval from which we advance jobs ends at time $t = \epsilon^7 OPT$. Thus the total completion time of the advanced jobs is $\sum_{R_x < t} \frac{1}{\epsilon} \frac{(1+\epsilon)R_x}{\epsilon^4} \leq \frac{t}{\epsilon^5} \sum_{i \geq 0} 1/(1+\epsilon)^i = \frac{t}{\epsilon^5} \frac{(1+\epsilon)^2}{\epsilon} = \epsilon \cdot \text{OPT}(1+\epsilon)^2 \leq 2\epsilon\text{OPT}$ as desired.

### 4.2 Example: $1| r_j | \sum C_j$

We apply geometrical rounding to all variables of the input of the problem. Thus, jobs are released only in the end of intervals. The preemptive variant of $1| r_j | \sum C_j$ can be solved optimally by SPRT rule. Supposing that, in the optimum schedule of the non preemptive problem all jobs are small, we can set release dates equal to $\max\{r_j, \frac{p_j}{\epsilon^2}\}$. According to Lemma 1, this does not change the feasibility of a nearly optimum schedule. We can now use SPRT rule to obtain an optimum preemptive schedule and then use the gaps in each interval to finish up the preempted jobs. These are small, so they need no more than $\epsilon I_x$ to finish up. Running SPRT followed by finishing up preempted jobs corresponds to running SPT rule.

Our only problem, now, is that the optimum schedule may require some jobs to run when they are large. By Lemma 1, there is still a nearly optimum solution with only a constant number of large jobs. We can schedule these large jobs by complete enumeration and schedule the rest using SPT rule with the new release dates as above. Again, using SPT rule for the small jobs, essentially we use SPRT rule (which still remains optimum in the presence of the fixed large jobs) to obtain a preemptive solution and then finish up the jobs.

### 4.3 Example: $P2|fix_j| \sum C_j$

For this problem, we have two kinds of monoprocessor jobs, the 1-jobs and the 2-jobs dedicated to run on machine $M_1$ and $M_2$ respectively. Biprocessor 12-jobs are dedicated to both machines.

In what follows, we use the following proved in [6]: In any optimum schedule, 1) All jobs of the same type are scheduled according to the shortest processing time rule (SPT). 2) If a biprocessor job is not the first job of the schedule, then its starting time must be equal to the completion time of some other job.

Besides geometric rounding, we need some more transformations. We begin with the following lemma which states that jobs scheduled to run in parallel have comparable processing times.

**Lemma 2.** *With a $1+\epsilon$ loss, we never have two jobs scheduled in parallel whose processing times differ by a factor greater than $\frac{1}{\epsilon^5}$.*

*Proof.* Let $j$ be a job executed w.l.o.g. on processor $M_1$, and let $A$ be the set of jobs scheduled in parallel with $j$ on processor $M_2$ with processing times $< \frac{1}{\epsilon^5} p_j$. Recall that, since the single-machine-jobs on each processor are scheduled in the order of increasing processing times, the jobs in $A$ form an interval. We consider the following two cases:

a) $\sum_{i \in A} p_i < \epsilon p_j$. We use time stretching to move starting time of $j$ to $S_j + \epsilon p_j$, thus jobs in $A$ and job $j$ do not run in parallel any more. b)$\sum_{i \in A} p_i \geq \epsilon p_j$. Put the job $j$ in the *gap* so that it completes at time $\frac{C_j}{\epsilon^2}$. Let $S_j$ be the starting time of job $j$ in the initial schedule. Since for every $i \in A$, $p_i < \epsilon^5 p_j$, we get that at least $\frac{1}{2\epsilon^4}$ jobs in $A$ complete in the time-interval $[S_j + \frac{\epsilon p_j}{2}, S_j + \epsilon p_j]$. Then $\sum_{i \in A} C_i > (S_j + \frac{\epsilon p_j}{2})\frac{1}{2\epsilon^4} > \frac{\epsilon}{2}\frac{1}{2\epsilon^4}(S_j + p_j) = \frac{1}{4\epsilon^3} C_j$. Thus, $\frac{C_j}{\epsilon^2} < 4\epsilon \sum_{i \in A} C_i$. Summing over all jobs $j$, we get an increase of at most $4\epsilon OPT$.

Moreover, it can be easily proven that if the set of jobs $\mathcal{T}$ can be partitioned into subsets $L$ and $S$ such that $\max_{j \in S} p_j < \epsilon^5 \min_{j \in L} p_j$, then, all jobs in $S$ are scheduled before any job in $L$ is scheduled. A separation result allows for partitioning the jobs into "long" jobs and "short" jobs with a few (negligible) "medium" jobs in between. Its proof is a simple algebraic manipulation.

**Lemma 3.** *Let* $L_0 = \{j \in \mathcal{T} | p_j > \epsilon^7 OPT\}$, *and* $L_i = \{j \in \mathcal{T} | \epsilon^{5i}\epsilon^7 OPT < p_j < \epsilon^{5(i-1)}\epsilon^7 OPT\}$. *If* $L_0 \neq \emptyset$, *then there is some* $i < \lceil \log_{1+\epsilon} \frac{1}{\epsilon^7} \rceil$ *such that*

$$OPT(L_0 \cup L_1 \cup \ldots \cup L_i) < (1 + \epsilon^2) OPT(L_0 \cup L_1 \cup \ldots \cup L_{i-1}).$$

$L_i$ is the negligible set of "medium" jobs, $L_0 \cup \ldots \cup L_{i-1}$ are the "long" jobs and the rest are the "short" jobs. It is not hard to prove that, with a $1 + O(\epsilon)$ loss, we can schedule all short jobs before any long or medium job is scheduled. Clearly, we can find such a partition in polynomial time.

The above transformations together with a polynomial algorithm for the preemptive variant [2] yield a PTAS for this problem. For the short jobs, according to the results in the beginning of this section, we can rearrange biprocessor jobs within an interval, so that to obtain only one preemption per interval. Then, we move large monoprocessor jobs forward in intervals where they are small and finish up preempted (monoprocessor) jobs to derive a non-preempted schedule. For the long jobs we find a schedule by complete enumeration and then concatenate the two schedules.

## References


1. F. Afrati, E. Bampis, C. Chekuri, D. Karger, C. Kenyon, S. Khanna, I. Milis, M. Queyranne, M. Skutella, C. Stein, M. Sviridenko: Approximation schemes for minimizing average weighted completion time with release dates. In Proceedings of 40th FOCS (1999) 32–43.
2. F. Afrati, E. Bampis, A. V. Fishkin, K. Jansen, C. Kenyon: Scheduling to minimize the average completion time of dedicated tasks. In Proceedings of 20th FSTTCS (2000) 454-464.
3. F. Afrati, E. Bampis, C. Kenyon, I. Milis: Scheduling to minimize the weighted sum of completion times. Journal of Scheduling **3** (2000) 323–332.
4. N. Alon, Y. Azar, G. J. Woeginger, T. Yadid: Approximation schemes for scheduling on parallel machines. Journal of Scheduling **1** (1998) 55–66.

5. P. Bruker: Scheduling Algorithms. Springer, 1998. See also http://www.mathematik.uni-osnabrueck.de/research/OR/class/
6. X. Cai, C. Y. Lee, C. L. Li: Minimizing total completion time in two-processor task systems with prespecified processor allocations. Naval Research Logistics, **45** (1998) 231–242.
7. C. Chekuri, R. Motwani: Minimizing weigthed completion time on a single machine. In Proceedings of 10th SODA (1999) 873–874.
8. C. Chekuri, R. Motwani, B. Natarajan, C. Stein: Approximation techniques for average completion time scheduling. In Proceedings of 8th SODA (1997) 609–618.
9. M. E. Dyer, L. A. Wosley: Formulating the single machine sequencing problem with release dates as a mixed integer program. Discrete Applied Math. **26** (1990) 255–270.
10. A. V. Fishkin, K. Jansen, L. Porkolab: On minimizing average weigthed time completion time of multiprocessor tasks with release dates. Submitted, 2001.
11. M. X. Goemans, M. Queyranne, A. S. Shulz, M. Skutella, Y. Wang: Single machine scheduling with release dates. Submitted, 1999 (see http://www.math.tu-berlin.de/~skutella/publications.html).
12. R.L. Graham: Bounds on certain multiprocessor anomalies. Bell Systems Tech. J. **45** (1996) 1563–1581.
13. R.L. Graham, E.L. Lawler, J.K. Lenstra, A.H.G. Rinnooy Kan: Optimization and approximation in deterministic sequencing and scheduling. Ann. Discrete Math. **5** (1979) 287–326.
14. L. A. Hall, A. S. Schulz, D. B. Shmoys, J. Wein: Scheduling to minimize average completion time: on-line and off-line approximation algorithms. Mathematics of Operations Research **22** (1997) 513–544.
15. L.A. Hall, D.B. Shmoys, J. Wein: Scheduling to minimize average completion time: on-line and off-line algorithms. In Proceedings of 7th SODA (1996) 142–151.
16. H. Hoogeveen, P. Schuurman, G.J. Woeginger: Non-approximability results for scheduling problems with minsum criteria. In Proceedings of 6th IPCO, LNCS 1412 (1998) 353–366.
17. T. Kawaguchi, S. Kyan: Worst case bound of an LRF schedule for the mean weighted flow-time problem. SIAM J. on Computing **15** (1986) 1119–1129.
18. H. Kellerer, T. Tautenhahnm, G. J. Woeginger: Approximability and nonappproximability results for minimizing total flow time on a single machine. In Proceedings of 28th STOC (1996) 418–426.
19. Leonardi, D. Raz: Approximating total flow time on parallel machines. In Proceedings of 29th STOC (1997) 110-119.
20. J. Y. T. Leung, W. D. Wei: Tighter bounds on a heuristic for a partition problem. Information Processing Letters **56** (1995) 51–57.
21. A. Munier, M. Queyranne, A. S. Schulz: Approximation bounds for a general class of precedence-constrained parallel machine scheduling problems. In Proceedings of 6th IPCO, LNCS 1412 (1998) 367–382.
22. C. Philips, C. Stein, J. Wein: Scheduling job that arrive over time. In Proceedings of 4th WADS, LNCS 955 (1995) 290–301.
23. C.N. Potts: An algorithm for the single machine sequencing problem with precedence constraints. Math. Programming Stud. **13** (1980) 78–87.
24. M. Queyranne: Structure of a simple scheduling polyhedron. Math. Programming **58** (1993) 263–285.
25. M. Queyranne, A. S. Shulz: Polyhedral approaches to machine scheduling. Preprint No. 408/1994, Department of Mathematics, Technical University Berlin, 1994.

26. R. Ravi, A. Agrawal, P. Klein: Ordering problems approximated: single processor scheduling and interval graph completion. In Proceedings of 18th ICALP, LNCS 510 (1991) 751–762.
27. S. Sahni: Algorithms for scheduling independent tasks. J. ACM **23** (1976) 116–127.
28. M. W. P. Savelsbergh, R. N. Uma, J. M. Wein: An experimental study of LP-based approximation algorithms for scheduling problems. In Proceedings of 9th SODA (1998) 453–462.
29. A.S. Schulz, M. Skutella: Random-based scheduling: New approximations and LP lower bounds. In Proceedings of RANDOM'97, LNCS 1269 (1997) 119-133.
30. A.S. Schulz, M. Skutella: Scheduling-LPs bear probabilities: Randomized approximations for min-sum criteria. In Proceedings of 5th ESA, LNCS 1284 (1997) 416-429.
31. A.S.Schulz, M. Skutella: The power of alpha-points in preemptive single machine scheduling. Submitted, 1999 (see http://www.math.tu-berlin.de/~skutella/publications.html).
32. P. Schuurman, G.J. Woeginger: Polynomial time algorithms for machine scheduling: Ten open problems. Manuscript, 1999.
33. J. Sethuraman, M. S. Squillante: Optimal scheduling of multiclass parallel machines. In Proceedings of 10th SODA (1999) 963–964.
34. D. B. Shmoys: Using linear programming in the design and analysis of approximation algorithms: Two illustrative problems. In Proceedings of APPROX'98, LNCS 1444 (1998) 15-32.
35. M. Skutella: Semidefinite relaxations for parallel machine scheduling. In Proceedings of 39th FOCS (1998) 472–481.
36. M. Skutella: Convex quadratic programming relaxations for network scheduling problems. In Proceedings of 7th ESA, LNCS 1643 (1999) 127–138.
37. M. Skutella, G.J. Woeginger: A PTAS for minimizing the weigthed sum of job completion times on parallel machines. In Proceedings of 31th STOC (1999) 400–407.
38. W. Smith: Various optimizers for single-stage production. Naval Res. Logist. Quart. **3**(1956) 59-66.
39. E. Torng and P. Uthaisombut: Lower bounds for srpt-subsequence algorithms for nonpreemptive scheduling. In Proceedings of the 10th SODA (1999) 973–974.
40. J. Turek, W. Ludwing, J. Wolf, P. Yu: Scheduling parallel tasks to minimize average responce times. In Proceedings of 5th SODA (1994) 112-121.
41. G.J. Woeginger: When does a dynamic programming formulation guarantee the existence of an FPTAS? In Proceedings of 10th SODA (1999) 820-829.
42. L. A. Wosley: Mixed integer programming formulations for production planning and scheduling problems. Invited talk at 12th International Symposium on Mathematical Programming, MIT, Cambriddge, 1985.
43. R. N. Uma and J. Wein: On the relationship between combinatorial and lp-based approaches to NP-hard scheduling problems. In Proceedings of the 7th IPCO (1999) 394–408.

# On Robust Algorithms for the Maximum Weight Stable Set Problem

Andreas Brandstädt

Fachbereich Informatik, Universität Rostock, A.-Einstein-Str. 21,
18051 Rostock, Germany.
ab@informatik.uni-rostock.de

**Abstract.** The Maximum Weight Stable Set (MWS) Problem is one of the fundamental algorithmic problems in graphs. It is NP-complete in general, and it has polynomial time solutions on many particular graph classes, some of them defined by forbidden subgraphs. A classical example is the result of Minty that the MWS problem is polynomially solvable for the class of claw-free graphs. The complexity of the MWS problem is unknown for the class of $P_5$-free graphs.
We give a survey on recently obtained efficient algorithms for the MWS problem for several graph classes defined by forbidden subgraphs where the algorithm avoids to recognize whether the (arbitrary) input graph is in the class i.e. the output is either a correct solution of the MWS problem or the fact that the input graph is not in the class. Such algorithms were called *robust* by Spinrad. The algorithms use the concepts of modular decomposition and of clique width of graphs.

**Keywords**: Maximum Weight Stable Set Problem on graphs; robust algorithms; modules and homogeneous sets in graphs; prime graphs; graph structure; clique width.

## 1 Introduction

A vertex set in a finite undirected graph $G = (V, E)$ is *stable* if its elements are pairwise nonadjacent. For a vertex weight function $w$ on $V$, let $\alpha_w(G)$ denote the maximum weight sum of a stable set in $G$. The *Maximum (Weight) Stable Set (M(W)S)* Problem asks for a maximum (weight) stable set in the input graph $G$.

The M(W)S problem is a basic algorithmic graph problem occuring in many models in Computer Science and Operations Research. It is NP-complete even for triangle-free graphs [46] (see [33]) which led to the investigation of a variety of graph classes defined by forbidding small graphs such as claw-free graphs for which a polynomial time algorithm for the MWS problem was given by Minty [43] (and independently for the MS problem by Sbihi [47]). Note that for ($K_{1,4}$,diamond)-free graphs [16] the MS problem is NP-complete.

Minty's algorithm for claw-free graphs has been extended to a polynomial time algorithm for the MWS problem on chair-free graphs by Alekseev in [1].

The complexity of the MWS problem for $P_5$-free graphs is still unknown which recently led to the investigation of some subclasses of $P_5$-free graphs where

R. Freivalds (Ed.): FCT 2001, LNCS 2138, pp. 445–458, 2001.

polynomial time algorithms for the MWS problem were given - see e.g. [2,4,6,7, 11,14,15,29,31].

Summarizing the known complexity results for $P_4$ extensions (see Figure 1) gives: The MWS problem for $F$-free graphs

1. can be solved in polynomial time if $F \in \{$co-gem, chair$\}$
2. is NP-complete if $F \in \{$ co-P, bull, co-chair, house, gem$\}$, and
3. and its complexity is open for $F \in \{P_5, C_5, P\}$

The aim of this note is to give a survey on an approach combining the concepts of

($i$) modular decomposition,
($ii$) clique width and
($iii$) robust algorithms

which recently attracted much attention.

*To (i):* The modular decomposition tree of a finite undirected graph $G$ gives a tree description of $G$ where the leaves are the vertices of $G$ and there are three kinds of internal nodes: *join* (denoted by (1)), *co-join* (denoted by (0)) and *prime* nodes. The papers [41,42,23,24] describe this approach and give linear time algorithms for computing the modular decomposition tree.

It is a simple observation that the MWS problem is solvable in polynomial time for a graph class whenever it is solvable in polynomial time for the prime graphs belonging to this class since $\alpha_w(G_1(1)G_2) = \max(\alpha_w(G_1), \alpha_w(G_2))$, and $\alpha_w(G_1(0)G_2) = \alpha_w(G_1) + \alpha_w(G_2)$.

This immediately leads to polynomial time solutions for the MWS problem using the modular decomposition tree in a bottom-up way for computing $\alpha_w(G)$.

*To (ii):* Bounded clique width allows to efficiently solve all algorithmic problems expressible in a certain kind of Monadic Second Order Logic in linear time [21], among them the MWS Problem. The notion of clique width has been introduced in [20] and is intimately related to modular decomposition of a graph. We give a list of graph classes having bounded clique width.

*To (iii):* In [48], Spinrad defined the concept of a *robust algorithm* for a graph class $\mathcal{C}$ and an algorithmic problem as follows:

– If $G \in \mathcal{C}$ then the algorithm solves the problem correctly.
– If $G \notin \mathcal{C}$ then the algorithm either solves the problem correctly or finds out that $G \notin \mathcal{C}$ (sometimes with a corresponding witness for this fact).

Thus, a robust algorithm delivers a correct answer in any case, solves the problem for every graph in $\mathcal{C}$ and avoids to recognize $\mathcal{C}$. This is of crucial importance whenever the recognition time bound for $\mathcal{C}$ is worse than solving the algorithmic problem on the graph class (in extreme cases, the recognition problem can be NP-complete and the algorithmic problem can have a linear time solution).

We give examples of efficient robust algorithms for the MWS problem on some graph classes such as (bull,chair)-free graphs and ($P_5$,co-chair)-free graphs.

Our results improve previous ones on particular graph classes in several ways:

1. for some classes, the structure investigations imply bounded clique width for the whole class or bounded clique width under suitable assumptions which are useful for solving the MWS problem;
2. for some examples, previous time bounds can be improved due to the fact that robust algorithms avoid to recognize whether the input graph is in the class;
3. for bounded clique width, not only the MWS problem but also many other problems such as Minimum Dominating Set, Steiner Tree, Maximum Weight Clique can be solved efficiently.

## 2 Notions and Preliminary Results

Throughout this paper, let $G = (V, E)$ be a finite undirected graph without self-loops and multiple edges and let $|V| = n$, $|E| = m$. Let $\overline{G} = (V, \overline{E})$ with $xy \in \overline{E}$ if and only if $xy \notin E$ for $x, y \in V$ denote the *complement graph* of $G$.

The edges between two disjoint vertex sets $X, Y$ form a *join* (*co-join*) if for all pairs $x \in X$, $y \in Y$, $xy \in E$ ($xy \notin E$) holds. Let $A(1)B$ ($A(0)B$) denote the corresponding join (co-join) operation between $A$ and $B$.

A vertex $z \in V$ *distinguishes* vertices $x, y \in V$ if $zx \in E$ and $zy \notin E$. A vertex set $M \subseteq V$ is a *module* if no vertex from $V \setminus M$ distinguishes two vertices from $M$ i.e. every vertex $v \in V \setminus M$ has either a join or a co-join to $M$. A module is *trivial* if it is either the empty set, a one-vertex set or the entire vertex set $V$. Nontrivial modules are called *homogeneous sets.* A graph is *prime* if it contains only trivial modules. The notion of modules plays a crucial role in the *modular* (or *substitution*) *decomposition* of graphs (and other discrete structures) which is of basic importance for the design of efficient algorithms - see e.g. [44] for modular decomposition of discrete structures and its algorithmic use.

A homogeneous set $M$ is *maximal* if no other homogeneous set properly contains $M$. It is well-known that in a connected graph $G$ with connected complement $\overline{G}$, the maximal homogeneous sets are pairwise disjoint which means that every vertex is contained in at most one maximal homogeneous set. The existence and uniqueness of the *modular decomposition tree* is based on this property, and recently, linear time algorithms were designed to determine this tree - see [41,42,23,24]. The tree contains the vertices of the graph as its leaves, and the internal nodes are of three types: they represent a join or co-join operation, or a prime subgraph. The graph $G^*$ obtained from $G$ by contracting every maximal homogeneous set to a single vertex is called the *characteristic graph* of $G$. It is not hard to see that $G^*$ is connected and prime.

Let $N(v) := \{u : u \in V, u \neq v, uv \in E\}$ denote the *open neighborhood* of $v$ and $N[v] := N(v) \cup \{v\}$ the *closed neighborhood* of $v$. For $U \subseteq V$ let $G(U)$

denote the subgraph of $G$ induced by $U$. As already mentioned, a vertex set $U \subseteq V$ is *stable* (sometimes called *independent*) in $G$ if the vertices in $U$ are pairwise nonadjacent. A vertex set $U \subseteq V$ is a *clique* in $G$ if $U$ is a stable set in $\overline{G}$.

For a vertex weight function $w$ on $V$, let $\alpha_w(G)$ denote the maximum weight sum of a stable set in $G$ and let $\omega_w(G) := \alpha_w(\overline{G})$ denote the maximum weight of a clique in $G$. If $w(v) = 1$ for all vertices $v$ then we omit the index $w$. Note that for all classes on which the MWS problem can be efficiently solved, the Maximum Weight Clique Problem can be efficiently solved on the complement class.

For $k \geq 1$, let $P_k$ denote an induced chordless path with $k$ vertices and $k-1$ edges, and for $k \geq 3$, let $C_k$ denote an induced chordless cycle with $k$ vertices and $k$ edges. A *hole* is a $C_k$, $k \geq 5$. For a $P_4$ with vertices $a, b, c, d$ and edges $ab, bc, cd$, the vertices $a$ and $d$ ($b$ and $c$) are called the *endpoints* (*midpoints*) of the $P_4$. Note that the $P_4$ is the smallest nontrivial prime graph and the complement of a $P_4$ is a $P_4$ itself (where midpoints and endpoints change their roles).

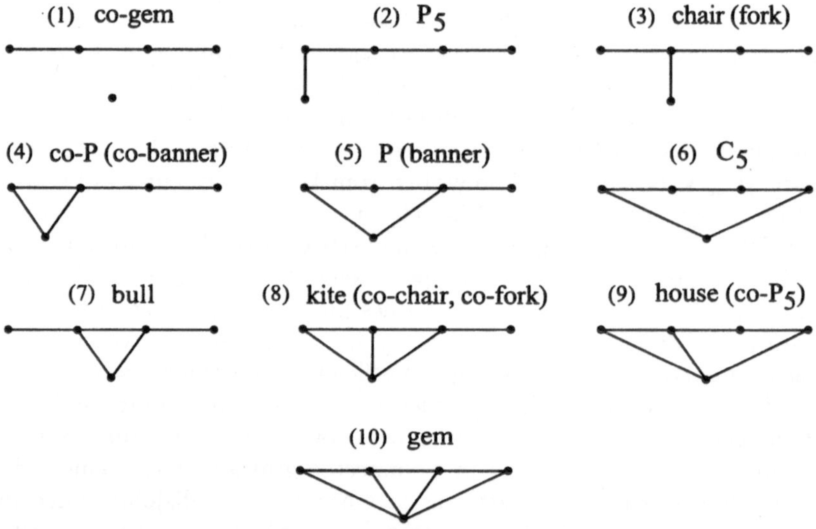


**Fig. 1.** All one-vertex extensions of a $P_4$

See Figure 1 for the definition of the bull, chair, $P$, gem and their complements, the bull, co-chair, co-$P$ and co-gem.

The *diamond* is the $K_4 - e$ i.e. a four vertex clique minus one edge. The *claw* is the graph consisting of four vertices $a, b, c, d$ such that $a$ (the *center* of the claw) is adjacent to the pairwise nonadjacent vertices $b, c, d$. The *domino* is a graph consisting of a $P_5$ plus a vertex adjacent to the central vertex and to the end-vertices of the $P_5$. An $A$ is the graph resulting from a domino by deleting one of its edges between two vertices of degree two.

Let $\mathcal{F}$ denote a set of graphs. A graph $G$ is *$\mathcal{F}$-free* if none of its induced subgraphs is in $\mathcal{F}$. There are many papers on the structure and algorithmic use of prime $\mathcal{F}$-free graphs for $\mathcal{F}$ being a set of $P_4$ extensions; see e.g. [35,36,28,29, 30,31,38,4,6,11].

A graph $G$ is a

- *thin spider* if $G$ is partitionable into a clique $C$ and a stable set $S$ with $|C| = |S|$ or $|C| = |S| + 1$ such that the edges between $C$ and $S$ are a matching and at most one vertex in $C$ is not covered by the matching (an unmatched vertex is called the *head of the spider*);
- *thick spider* if it is the complement of a thin spider;
- *matched co-bipartite* graph if $G$ is partitionable into two cliques $C_1, C_2$ with $|C_1| = |C_2|$ or $|C_1| = |C_2| + 1$ such that the edges between $C_1$ and $C_2$ are a matching and at most one vertex in $C_1$ and $C_2$ is not covered by the matching;
- *co-matched bipartite* graph if it is the complement of a matched co-bipartite graph;
- *bipartite chain graph* if it is a bipartite graph $B = (X, Y, E)$ and for all vertices from $X$ ($Y$), their neighborhoods in $Y$ ($X$) are linearly ordered (bipartite chain graphs appear in [50]; in [40] they are called *difference* graphs);
- *co-bipartite chain graph* if it is the complement of a bipartite chain graph.
- *enhanced co-bipartite chain graph* if it is partitionable into a co-bipartite chain graph with cliques $C_1$, $C_2$ and three additional vertices $a, b, c$ ($a$ and $c$ optional) such that $N(a) = C_1 \cup C_2$, $N(b) = C_1$, and $N(c) = C_2$.
- *enhanced bipartite chain graph* if it is the complement of an enhanced co-bipartite chain graph.

There are some basic tools extending small subgraphs in prime graphs which are of great use in many cases when investigating small classes of prime graphs.

**Lemma 1 ([37]).** *If a prime graph contains an induced $C_4$ then it contains an induced house or $A$ or domino.*

The graph complement version of Lemma 1 is

**Corollary 1.** *If a prime graph contains an induced $2K_2$ then it contains an induced $P_5$ or $\overline{A}$ or co-domino.*

**Lemma 2 ([45]).** *If a prime graph contains a triangle $C_3$ then it contains an induced house or bull or double-gem.*

The graph complement version of Lemma 2 is

**Corollary 2.** *If a prime graph contains a set of three pairwise nonadjacent vertices then it contains an induced $P_5$ or bull or $A$.*

Note that unlike the case of three pairwise nonadjacent vertices, the case of four pairwise nonadjacent vertices leads to infinitely many prime extensions as shown in [10]. Based on the reducing copath method of [51], [9] describes also the extensions of a claw, a diamond and a $P_3 + K_1$ which lead to finitely many extension graphs.

Hoàng defined in [35] that a graph is $P_4$-*sparse* if no set of five vertices in $G$ induces at least two distinct $P_4$'s. From the definition of $P_4$-sparse graphs, it is obvious that a graph is $P_4$-sparse if and only if it contains no $C_5$, $P_5$, $\overline{P_5}$, $P$, $\overline{P}$, chair, co-chair (see Figure 1). The motivation for $P_4$-sparse graphs and variants was given by

- applications in areas such as scheduling, clustering and computational semantics;
- natural generalizations of cographs.

**Theorem 1 ([35]).** *The prime $P_4$-sparse graphs are the spiders.*

Spiders were called *turtles* in [35].

The class of $P_4$-sparse graphs was extended in several ways leading to simple prime graphs - see e.g. [3,29,32].

## 3 Cographs, Clique Width, and Algorithmic Problems

The $P_4$-free graphs (also called *cographs*) play a fundamental role for graph decomposition; see [13] for a survey on this graph class and related ones. For a cograph $G$, either $G$ or its complement is disconnected, and the *cotree* of $G$ expresses how the graph can be recursively generated from single vertices by repeatedly applying join and co-join operations. Thus, the modular decomposition tree of cographs contains no prime nodes. See [19] for linear time recognition of cographs and [17,18,19,13] for more informations on $P_4$-free graphs.

In [20], the join and co-join operations were generalized to the following operations in labeled graphs:

- creation of single vertices with integer label $i$,
- disjoint union (i.e. co-join),
- join between all vertices with label $i$ and all vertices with label $j$ for $i \neq j$, and
- relabeling vertices of label $i$ by label $j$,

[20] then defines the *clique width* $cwd(G)$ of a graph $G$ as the minimum number of labels which are necessary to generate a given graph by using the three operations. Obviously, the clique width of cographs is at most two. A *$k$-expression* for a graph $G$ of clique width $k$ describes the recursive generation of $G$ by repeatedly applying the three operations using only a set at most $k$ different labels.

**Proposition 1** ([21,22]). *The clique width of a graph G is the maximum of the clique width of its prime graphs, and the clique width of its complement graph $\overline{G}$ is at most twice the clique width of G.*

Recently, the concept of clique width of a graph attracted much attention since it gives a unified approach to the efficient solution of many algorithmic graph problems on graph classes of bounded clique width via the expressibility of the problems in terms of logical expressions; in [21], it is shown that every algorithmic problem expressible in a certain kind of Monadic Second Order Logic called *LinEMSOL($\tau_{1,L}$)* in [21], is linear-time solvable on any graph class with bounded clique width for which a $k$-expression can be constructed in linear time.

Hereby, in [21] it is mentioned that, roughly speaking, MSOL($\tau_1$) is Monadic Second Order Logic with quantification over subsets of vertices but not of edges; MSOL($\tau_{1,L}$) is the extension of MSOL($\tau_1$) with the addition of labels added to the vertices. LinEMSOL($\tau_{1,L}$) is the extension of MSOL($\tau_{1,L}$) which allows to search for sets of vertices which are optimal with respect to some linear evaluation functions. The Maximum Weight Stable Set Problem is an example of a LinEMSOL($\tau_{1,L}$) problem.

**Theorem 2** ([21]). *Let $C$ be a class of graphs of clique width at most $k$ such that there is an $\mathcal{O}(f(|E|), |V|)$ time algorithm, which for each graph $G$ in $C$, constructs a $k$-expression defining it. Then for every LinEMSOL($\tau_{1,L}$) problem on $C$, there is an algorithm solving this problem in time $\mathcal{O}(f(|E|), |V|)$.*

Note that the clique width of distance hereditary graphs (which are exactly the (house, hole, domino, gem)-free graphs; see [13] for different characterizations of these graphs) is at most 3 as shown in [34], and thin spiders and bipartite chain graphs are (house, hole, domino, gem)-free. Thus, their clique width is at most 3. Moreover, for thick spiders, co-bipartite chain graphs, matched co-bipartite graphs, co-matched bipartite graphs, enhanced bipartite and co-bipartite chain graphs, induced paths and cycles of arbitrary length as well as for graphs having a fixed number of vertices, it can be seen by using Proposition 1 or in a straightforward way by giving a $k$-expression that their clique width is bounded by a constant.

Recall that Theorem 1 says that the prime $P_4$-sparse graphs are the spiders, and according to Proposition 1 and the fact that the clique width of spiders is bounded by 3, it follows that $P_4$-sparse graphs have bounded clique width. In a similar way, other examples lead to bounded clique width - see the next section.

## 4 Some Classes of Bounded Clique Width

We first mention complete descriptions of prime ($P_5$,$\overline{P_5}$,bull)-free, ($P_5$,$\overline{P_5}$,co-chair)-free and of (bull,chair,co-chair)-free graphs:

**Theorem 3 ([28]).** *If $G$ is a prime ($P_5$,$\overline{P_5}$,bull)-free graph then $G$ or $\overline{G}$ is a $C_5$ or a bipartite chain graph.*

**Theorem 4 ([29]).** *If $G$ is a prime ($P_5$,$\overline{P_5}$,co-chair)-free graph then $G$ is either a bipartite chain graph or a spider or $C_5$.*

Theorem 4 has a slightly simpler proof in [15].

**Theorem 5 ([8]).** *If $G$ is a prime (bull, chair, co-chair)-free graph then $G$ or $\overline{G}$ is co-matched bipartite, a path, or a cycle.*

Our next example gives a complete description of ($P_5$,diamond)-free graphs:

**Theorem 6 ([4]).** *If a connected and co-connected graph $G$ is ($P_5$,diamond)-free then the following two conditions hold:*

(1) *The homogeneous sets of $G$ are $P_3$-free;*
(2) *For the characteristic graph $G^*$ of $G$, one of the following conditions hold:*
 (2.1) *$G^*$ is a matched co-bipartite graph;*
 (2.2) *$G^*$ is a thin spider;*
 (2.3) *$G^*$ is an enhanced bipartite chain graph;*
 (2.4) *$G^*$ has at most 9 vertices.*

Theorem 6 turns out to be useful in some other cases since other classes of prime graphs are contained in the class of ($P_5$,diamond)-free graphs as the subsequent theorems show.

**Theorem 7 ([15,8]).** *Let $G$ be a prime graph.*

*(i) If $G$ is ($P_5$,co-chair,gem)-free then $G$ is ($P_5$,diamond)-free.*
*(ii) If $G$ is ($P_5$,bull,co-chair)-free then $G$ is either the complement of an induced path or cycle or ($P_5$,diamond)-free.*

**Theorem 8 ([5]).** *Let $G$ be a prime graph.*

*(i) If $G$ is ($P_5$,$\overline{P_5}$,gem)-free then $G$ is a distance-hereditary graph or a $C_5$.*
*(ii) If $G$ is ($P_5$,gem,co-gem)-free (($P_5$,bull,gem)-free, ($P_5$,chair,gem)-free) then $G$ is ($P_5$,diamond)-free.*
*(iii) If $G$ is ($P_5$,$P$,gem)-free then $G$ is a matched co-bipartite graph or a gem-free split graph (being distance hereditary) or $C_5$.*

Now, Proposition 1 and the fact that all particular graph occuring in the theorems such as bipartite chain graphs, spiders etc. have bounded clique width, implies:

**Corollary 3.** *The graph classes described in Theorems 3 - 8 have bounded clique width.*

Meanwhile, it was shown in [12] that the class of (chair,co-P,gem)-free graphs has bounded clique width.

It is interesting to study other combinations of forbidden $P_4$ extensions. In some of the cases, it turns out that the class has unbounded clique width since it contains the class of bipartite graphs, split graphs or unit interval graphs or their complement class which classes have unbounded clique width as shown in [34]. In many cases, however, the question whether the clique width is bounded remains open - see [5] for a list of such problems.

## 5 Robust MWS Algorithms

Recall that for all classes of constant-bounded clique width for which $k$-expressions can be found in linear time, the MWS problem can be solved in linear time. This holds true for all examples in the previous section but does not automatically mean a linear time robust algorithm since the recognition time bounds are not necessarily linear.

For ($P_5$,diamond)-free graphs however, there is a slightly larger class $\mathcal{C}$ having linear time recognition and the same clique width which implies that there is a robust linear time MWS algorithm for class $\mathcal{C}$ and thus for ($P_5$,diamond)-free graphs [4]: take $\mathcal{C}$ = the class of graphs whose homogeneous sets are cographs and whose characteristic graph is either matched co-bipartite or a thin spider or an enhanced bipartite chain graph or have at most 9 vertices.

This is also applicable for some subclasses of ($P_5$,diamond)-free graphs mentioned in Theorem 8.

Thus we get the following principle (without using the clique width approach) which solves the MWS problem in linear time on ($P_5$,diamond)-free graphs in a robust way:

**Algorithm $\alpha_w(G)$ for ($P_5$,diamond)-free graphs**

**Input:** A connected and co-connected graph $G$.
**Output:** The maximum weight $\alpha_w(G)$ of a stable set in $G$ or a proof that $G$ is not ($P_5$,diamond)-free ($G$ is not in $\mathcal{C}$).

(1.1) Determine the maximal homogeneous sets $H_1, \ldots, H_k$ of $G$ and check whether they all induce cographs. If not, then STOP - $G$ is not ($P_5$,diamond)-free (is not in $\mathcal{C}$).
(1.2) Otherwise, for all $i \in \{1, \ldots, k\}$ determine $\alpha_w(H_i)$ using the cotree representations of $H_1, \ldots, H_k$.

(1.3) Construct the weighted characteristic graph $G^*$ by shrinking $H_i$ to one vertex $h_i$ and giving $h_i$ the weight $\alpha_w(H_i)$ for all $i \in \{1, \dots, k\}$.

(2) If $G^*$ is a matched co-bipartite graph, a thin spider, an enhanced bipartite chain graph or a graph with at most 9 vertices then solve the problem in a straightforward way;

(3) If $G^*$ is none of these graphs then $G$ is not ($P_5$,diamond)-free ($G$ is not in $\mathcal{C}$).

Note that the Maximum Weight Clique Problem can be solved in a completely analogous way.

**Theorem 9 ([4]).** *Algorithm $\alpha_w(G)$ for ($P_5$,diamond)-free graphs is correct and works in linear time $\mathcal{O}(n+m)$.*

In [12] it is shown that the simple structure of (chair,co-P,gem)-free graphs (leading to bounded clique width) enables a similar approach as for ($P_5$,diamond)-free graphs. In this way, [12] improves the time bound $\mathcal{O}(n^4)$ for the MWS problem given in [39,52] to a robust linear time algorithm.

Now to other examples where we do not get linear time bounds but use some structural results showing that under additional conditions which help to solve the MWS problem, the clique width of some classes is bounded.

**Theorem 10 ([6]).** *Let $G$ be a prime graph with stability number $\alpha(G) \geq 3$.*

*(i) If $G$ is ($P_5$,claw)-free then $G$ is either a thin spider or a 3-sun.*

*(ii) If $G$ is ($P_5$,bull)-free then $G$ is a bipartite chain graph.*

*(iii) If $G$ is (bull,claw)-free then $G$ is an induced $P_k$, $k \geq 5$, or an induced $C_k$, $k \geq 6$.*

Theorem 10, *(i)* improves a result of [7]. Moreover, Theorem 3 is a corollary of Theorem 10, *(ii)*.

Theorem 10 leads to an obvious robust algorithm for the MWS problem on ($P_5$,claw)-free, ($P_5$,bull)-free and (bull,claw)-free graphs with time bound $\mathcal{O}(MM)$ by using the structural result given in Theorem 10 in the case that $\alpha(G) \geq 3$ and computing $\alpha_w(G)$ in a direct way if $\alpha(G) \leq 2$.

In [26], De Simone and Sassano solved the MS problem for bull- and chair-free graphs in time $\mathcal{O}(n^3)$. Moreover, De Simone showed

**Lemma 3 ([25]).** *If a prime (bull,chair)-free graph contains an induced co-diamond then it is bipartite or an induced odd cycle $C_{2k+1}$, $k \geq 2$.*

The subsequent result improves the results by De Simone and Sassano [26, 25] in several ways:

**Theorem 11 ([8]).** *If $G$ is a prime (bull, chair)-free graph with $\alpha(G) \geq 4$ or containing a co-diamond then $G$ is co-matched bipartite or an induced path or cycle.*

This leads to an $\mathcal{O}(nm)$ time bounded robust algorithm for the MWS problem in [8] for (bull,chair)-free graphs: If $G$ is co-gem-free then the problem can be solved in a straightforward way in time $\mathcal{O}(nm)$, and if $G$ contains a co-gem i.e. $G$ contains a co-diamond, Theorem 11 is applicable.

Note that the clique width of (bull,chair)-free graphs is unbounded since every bipartite graph is (co-P,$C_5$,bull,co-chair,house,gem)-free, and in [34] it was shown that an $n \times n$ square grid has clique width $n+1$ which means that bipartite graphs and thus also co-bipartite graphs have unbounded clique width. Thus, the class of (P,$C_5$,bull,chair,$P_5$,co-gem)-free graphs (being a subclass of the (bull,chair)-free graphs) has unbounded clique width.

Our last examples are based on the fact that for $2K_2$-free graphs, the MWS problem can be solved in polynomial time due to a result of Farber [27] showing that $2K_2$-free graphs have $\mathcal{O}(n^2)$ maximal stable sets, and by enumerating these maximal stable sets using the algorithm given in [49], an $\mathcal{O}(n^5)$ time bounded algorithm for the MWS problem is obtained. By using some additional tricks, the time bounds can be improved.

**Theorem 12 ([15]).** *If $G$ is a prime ($P_5$,co-chair)-free graph containing an induced $2K_2$ then $G$ is matched co-bipartite.*

The class of ($P_5$,co-chair)-free graphs has unbounded clique width due to a result of [34] showing that unit interval graphs (which are the claw-free interval graphs) have unbounded clique width.

Note that prime ($P_5$,co-$P$)-free graphs are even $2K_2$-free which implies that the MWS problem is solvable in time $\mathcal{O}(n^5)$ on these graphs.

**Theorem 13 ([11]).** *If $G$ is a prime ($P_5$,gem)-free graph containing an induced $2K_2$ then $G$ is matched co-bipartite.*

We do not know whether the class of ($P_5$,gem)-free graphs has unbounded clique width.

Robust algorithms for the MWS problem have the following time bounds:

1. ($P_5$,co-chair)-free graphs: $\mathcal{O}(nm)$ time [15];
2. ($P_5$,gem)-free graphs: $\mathcal{O}(n^2)$ time [11];

Note that in [14], a robust $\mathcal{O}(nm)$ time algorithm for the (unweighted) MS problem on ($P_5$,$P$)-free graphs is given.

## References


1. V.E. Alekseev, A polynomial algorithm for finding maximum independent sets in fork-free graphs, *Discr. Analysis and Oper. Research* Vol. 6 No. 4 (1999) 3-19

2. C. Arbib, R. Mosca, On the stable set problem in ($P_5$, diamond)-free graphs, *Manuscript* 1995
3. L. Babel, S. Olariu, On the $p$-connectedness of graphs: A survey, *Discrete Applied Math.* 95 (1999) 11-33
4. A. Brandstädt, ($P_5$,diamond)-Free Graphs Revisited: Structure and Linear Time Optimization, *Manuscript* 2000
5. A. Brandstädt, F.F. Dragan, On the clique width of graph classes defined by three forbidden $P_4$ extensions, *Manuscript* 2001
6. A. Brandstädt, V. Giakoumakis, J.-M. Vanherpe, On Prime ($P_5$,Claw)-Free, ($P_5$,Bull)-Free, and (Bull,Claw)-Free Graphs and the Maximum Stable Set Problem, *Manuscript* 2001
7. A. Brandstädt, P.L. Hammer, On the stability number of claw-free $P_5$-free and more general graphs, *Discrete Applied Math.* 95 (1999) 163-167
8. A. Brandstädt, C.T. Hoàng, V.B. Le, Stability number of bull- and chair-free graphs revisited, *Manuscript* 2001
9. A. Brandstädt, C.T. Hoàng, I. Zverovich, Extension of claw-free graphs and $(K_1 \cup P_4)$-free graphs with substitutions, RUTCOR Research Report, Rutgers University, New Brunswick NJ, 28-2001 (2001)
10. A. Brandstädt, C.T. Hoàng, I. Zverovich, All extensions of a four-vertex graph in a prime graph, *Manuscript in preparation*, 2001
11. A. Brandstädt, D. Kratsch, On ($P_5$,Gem)-Free Graphs and Related Graph Classes: Structure and Algorithmic Applications, *Manuscript* 2001
12. A. Brandstädt, H.-O. Le, J.-M. Vanherpe, Structure and Stability Number of (Chair,Co-P,Gem)-Free Graphs Revisited, *Manuscript* 2001
13. A. Brandstädt, V.B. Le, J. Spinrad, Graph Classes: A Survey, *SIAM Monographs on Discrete Math. Appl., Vol.* 3, SIAM, Philadelphia (1999)
14. A. Brandstädt, V.V. Lozin, A note on $\alpha$-redundant vertices in graphs, *Discrete Applied Math.* 108 (2001) 301-308
15. A. Brandstädt, R. Mosca, On the Structure and Stability Number of $P_5$- and Co-Chair-Free Graphs, *Manuscript* 2001
16. D.G. Corneil The complexity of generalized clique packing, *Discrete Applied Math.* 12 (1985) 233-239
17. D.G. Corneil, H. Lerchs, L. Stewart-Burlingham, Complement reducible graphs, *Discrete Applied Math.* 3 (1981) 163-174
18. D.G. Corneil, Y. Perl, L.K. Stewart, Cographs: recognition, applications, and algorithms, *Congressus Numer.* 43 (1984) 249-258
19. D.G. Corneil, Y. Perl, L.K. Stewart, A linear recognition algorithm for cographs, *SIAM J. Computing* 14 (1985) 926-934
20. B. Courcelle, J. Engelfriet, G. Rozenberg, Handle-rewriting hypergraph grammars, *J. Comput. Syst. Sciences*, 46 (1993) 218-270
21. B. Courcelle, J.A. Makowsky, U. Rotics, Linear time solvable optimization problems on graphs of bounded clique width, extended abstract in: *Conf. Proc. WG'98*, LNCS 1517 (1998) 1-16
22. B. Courcelle, S. Olariu, Upper bounds to the clique width of graphs, *Discrete Appl. Math.* 101 (2000) 77-114
23. A. Cournier, M. Habib, A new linear algorithm for modular decomposition, *LIRMM, University Montpellier* (1995), Preliminary version in: *Trees in Algebra and Programming – CAAP '94*, LNCS 787 (1994) 68-84
24. E. Dahlhaus, J. Gustedt, R.M. McConnell, Efficient and practical modular decomposition, Tech. Report TU Berlin FB Mathematik, 524/1996 (1996), in: *Conference Proceedings* 8th SODA (1997), 26-35

25. C. De Simone, On the vertex packing problem, *Graphs and Combinatorics* 9 (1993) 19-30
26. C. De Simone, A. Sassano, Stability number of bull- and chair-free graphs, *Discrete Applied Math.* 41 (1993) 121-129
27. M. Farber, On diameters and radii of bridged graphs, *Discrete Math.* 73 (1989) 249-260
28. J.-L. Fouquet, A decomposition for a class of $(P_5, \overline{P_5})$-free graphs, *Discrete Math.* 121 (1993) 75-83
29. J.-L. Fouquet, V. Giakoumakis On semi-$P_4$-sparse graphs, *Discrete Math.* 165-166 (1997) 267-290
30. J.-L. Fouquet, V. Giakoumakis, H. Thuillier, F. Maire, On graphs without $P_5$ and $\overline{P_5}$, *Discrete Math.* 146 (1995) 33-44
31. V. Giakoumakis, I. Rusu, Weighted parameters in $(P_5, \overline{P_5})$-free graphs, *Discrete Appl. Math.* 80 (1997) 255-261
32. V. Giakoumakis, J.-M. Vanherpe, On Extended $P_4$-Reducible and Extended $P_4$-Sparse Graphs, *Theoretical Computer Science* 180 (1997) 269-286
33. M.C. Golumbic, Algorithmic Graph Theory and Perfect Graphs, *Academic Press*, New York 1980
34. M.C. Golumbic, U. Rotics, On the Clique-Width of Perfect Graph Classes, Intern. Workshop on Graph–Theoretic Concepts in Comp. Sci. WG'98, *Lecture Notes in Comp. Sci.* 1665 (1999) 135-147
35. C.T. Hoàng, *A Class of Perfect Graphs, Ms. Sc. Thesis*, School of Computer Science, McGill University, Montreal (1983)
36. C.T. Hoàng, *Perfect Graphs, Ph. D. Thesis*, School of Computer Science, McGill University Montreal (1985)
37. C.T. Hoàng, B. Reed, Some classes of perfectly orderable graphs, *J. Graph Theory* 13 (1989) 445-463
38. B. Jamison, S. Olariu, A unique tree representation for $P_4$-sparse graphs, *Discrete Appl. Math.* 35 (1992), 115-129
39. V.V. Lozin, Conic reduction of graphs for the stable set problem, *Discrete Math.* 222 (2000) 199-211
40. N.V.R. Mahadev, U.N. Peled, Threshold Graphs and Related Topics, *Annals of Discrete Mathematics* 56 (1995)
41. R.M. McConnell, J. Spinrad, Linear-time modular decomposition and efficient transitive orientation of comparability graphs, 5th. Ann. ACM–SIAM Symp. on Discrete Algorithms, Arlington, Virginia, 1994, 536-543
42. R.M. McConnell, J. Spinrad, Modular decomposition and transitive orientation, *Discrete Math.* 201 (1999) 189-241
43. G.J. Minty, On maximal independent sets of vertices in claw-free graphs, *J. Combin. Theory (B)* 28 (1980) 284-304
44. R.H. Möhring, F.J. Radermacher, Substitution decomposition for discrete structures and connections with combinatorial optimization, *Annals of Discrete Math.* 19 (1984) 257-356
45. S. Olariu, On the closure of triangle-free graphs under substitution, *Information Processing Letters* 34 (1990) 97-101
46. S. Poljak, A note on stable sets and colorings of graphs, *Commun. Math. Univ. Carolinae* 15 (1974) 307-309
47. N. Sbihi, Algorithme de recherche d'un stable de cardinalité maximum dans un graphe sans étoile, *Discrete Math.* 29 (1980) 53-76
48. J.P. Spinrad, Representations of graphs, Book Manuscript, Vanderbilt University, Nashville (TN) 1998

49. S. Tsukiyama, M. Ide, H. Ariyoshi, I. Shirakawa, A new algorithm for generating all the maximal independent sets, *SIAM J. Computing* 6 (1977) 505-517
50. M. Yannakakis, The complexity of the partial order dimension problem, *SIAM J. Algebraic and Discrete Methods* 3 (1982) 351-358;
51. I. Zverovich, Extension of hereditary classes with substitutions, *Rutcor Research Report* RRR 14-2001 (2001)
**http://rutcor.rutgers.edu/~rrr**
52. I.E. Zverovich, I.I. Zverovich, Extended ($P_5$,$\overline{P_5}$)-free graphs, *Rutcor Research Report* RRR 22-2001 (2001)
**http://rutcor.rutgers.edu/~rrr**

# Multicasting in Optical Networks*

Luisa Gargano

Dipartimento di Informatica, Università di Salerno, 84081 Baronissi (SA), Italy

Optics is a key technology in communication networks to enable bandwidth intensive applications, such as video conferencing, real-time medical imaging, broadcasting services to home [5]. Readers interested in the relevant aspects of fiber optic technology are referred to [11,15,17].

In WDM (Wavelength Division Multiplexing) optical networks, the available optical fiber bandwidth is utilised by partitioning it into several channels, each at a different wavelength. Each wavelength can carry a separate stream of data. In general, a WDM network consists of routing nodes (equipped with switches operating directly in the optical domain), interconnected by point–to–point optic fiber links. Each fiber–link can support a given number of wavelengths.

A basic mechanism of communication in a wavelength routed network is a lightpath. A lightpath is an all–optical communication channel between two nodes in the network and it may span more that one fiber link. The intermediate nodes in the fiber path route the lightpath directly in the optical domain using their switches. Data transmission through a lightpath does not require electronic processing at the intermediate nodes, thus reducing delay and improving reliability. In the absence of any wavelength conversion device, the lightpath is required to be on the same wavelength channel through its path in the network. A fundamental requirement in a wavelength routed WDM network is that two or more lightpaths traversing the same fiber link must be on different wavelength channels so that they do not interfere with one another.

Given a communication request from node $x$ to node $y$, one sets up a lightpath for it by choosing a path from $x$ to $y$ in the network and assigning a wavelength to this path. Similarly, given a set of communication requests, one has to set up a corresponding set of lightpaths under the basic constrain recalled above that two lightpaths traversing the same fiber link must be assigned different wavelengths. There is a vast literature dealing with the problem of minimizing the number of wavelengths to set up lightpaths for (classes of) communication requests (see e.g., [1,2,4,7,13,9,14,16]). A summary of graph theoretical problems associated with routing in optical networks can be found in [3,10].

*Multicasting* is the simultaneous transmission of data from a source to a subset of all possible destinations in the network. Multicast service is becoming a key service in computer networks. Many applications such as shared witheboards, distributed interactive simulation, and teleconferencing require efficient multicast, where a sender transmits data to a group of receivers in an efficient way [6,8,12].

* Research partially supported by the European Community under the RTN project: "APPROXIMATION AND RANDOMIZED ALGORITHMS IN COMMUNICATION NETWORKS (ARACNE)"

R. Freivalds (Ed.): FCT 2001, LNCS 2138, pp. 459–460, 2001.

In this talk, we will present several algorithmic problems and results connected to the problem of multicasting in all–optical networks.

## References

1. A. Aggarwal, A. Bar-Noy, D. Coppersmith, R. Ramaswami, B. Schieber, M. Sudan, "Efficient Routing in Optical Networks", *J. of the ACM*, 46 (1996), 973–1001.
2. Y. Aumann and Y. Rabani, "Improved Bounds for All Optical Routing", in: *Proceedings of the 6th Annual ACM-SIAM Symposium on Discrete Algorithms (SODA'95)*, (1995), 567–576.
3. B. Beauquier, J-C. Bermond, L. Gargano, P. Hell, S. Perennes, and U. Vaccaro, "Graph Problems arising from Wavelength-Routing in All-Optical Networks", *Proceedings of WOCS*, Geneve, Switzerland, April 1997.
4. J-C. Bermond, L. Gargano, S. Perennes, A. Rescigno and U. Vaccaro, "Efficient Collective Communications in Optical Networks", *Theoretical Computer Science*, 233, no. 1-2, 2000, 165–189.
5. S. Chattergee, S. Pawlowski, "All–Optical Networks", *Communications of ACM*, 42 (1999), 75–83.
6. C. Diot, W. Dabbous, J. Crowcroft, "Multipoint Communications: a survey of protocols, functions and mechanisms" *IEEE J. Selected Areas in Comm.*, 15, (1990), 277–290.
7. T. Erlebach and K. Jansen, "Scheduling of virtual connections in fast networks", in: *Proc. of Parallel Systems and Algorithms (PASA)*, (1996) 13–32.
8. A. Frank, L. Wittie, and A. Bernstein, "Multicast Communication in Network Computers," *IEEE Software*, 2:49–61, 1985.
9. L. Gargano, P. Hell, S. Perennes, "Colouring All Directed Paths in a Symmetric Tree with Applications to WDM Routing", Proceedings of *24th International Colloquium on Automata, Languages, and Programming (ICALP 97)*, Bologna, Italy, July 1997.
10. L. Gargano, U. Vaccaro, "Routing in All–Optical Networks: Algorithmic and Graph–Theoretic Problems", Numbers, Information and Complexity, I. Althofer et al. (Eds.), Kluwer Academic Publisher, pp. 555-578, Feb. 2000.
11. P. E. Green. *Fiber–Optic Communication Networks*, Prentice–Hall, 1992.
12. V. P. Kompella, J. C. Pasquale, and G. C. Polyzos, "Multicast Routing for Multimedia Communication", *IEEE/ACM Transactions on Networking*, 3: 286–292, 1993.
13. E. Kumar, E. Schwabe, "Improved Access to Optical Bandwidth", *Proceedings of Eighth Annual ACM-SIAM SYpmposium on Discrete Algorithms (SODA'97)*, 437–444, 1997.
14. M. Mihail, K. Kaklamanis, S. Rao, "Efficient Access to Optical Bandwidth", in: *Proceedings of 36th Annual IEEE Symposium on Foundations of Computer Science (FOCS'95)*, (1995), 548–557.
15. B. Mukhergee, *Optical Communication Networks*, McGrow–Hill, New York, 1997.
16. P. Raghavan and E. Upfal, "Efficient Routing in All–Optical Networks", in: *Proceedings of the 26th Annual ACM Symposium on Theory of Computing (STOC'94)*, (1994), 133-143.
17. T.E. Sterne, K. Bala, *MultiWavelength Optical Networks*, Addison–Wesley, 1999.

# Structured Randomized Rounding and Coloring
## Extended Abstract

Benjamin Doerr*

Mathematisches Seminar II, Christian–Albrechts–Universität zu Kiel,
Ludewig–Meyn–Str. 4, D–24098 Kiel, Germany,
bed@numerik.uni-kiel.de,
WWW home page: http://www.numerik.uni-kiel.de/~bed

**Abstract.** In this paper we propose an advanced randomized coloring algorithm for the problem of balanced colorings of hypergraphs (discrepancy problem). It allows to use structural information about the hypergraph in the design of the random experiment. This yields colorings having smaller discrepancy than those independently coloring the vertices. We also obtain more information about the coloring, or, conversely, we may enforce the random coloring to have special properties. Due to the dependencies, these random colorings need fewer random bits to be constructed, and computing their discrepancy can be done faster. We apply our method to hypergraphs of $d$–dimensional boxes. Among others, we observe a factor $2^{d/2}$ decrease in discrepancy and a reduction of the number of random bits needed by a factor of $2^d$.
Since the discrepancy problem is a particular rounding problem, our approach is a randomized rounding strategy for the corresponding ILP-relaxation that beats the usual randomized rounding.

**Keywords:** randomized algorithms, hypergraph coloring, discrepancy, randomized rounding, integer linear programming.

## 1 Introduction and Results

### 1.1 The Discrepancy Problem and Integer Linear Programs

In this paper we deal with a special kind of integer linear programs, namely those that model discrepancy problems. Roughly speaking, the *combinatorial discrepancy problem* is to partition the vertex set of a given hypergraph into two classes in a balanced manner, i.e., such that each hyperedge contains the same number of vertices in each of the two partition classes. To be precise:

We call a pair $\mathcal{H} = (X, \mathcal{E})$, where $X$ is finite set and $\mathcal{E} \subseteq 2^X$, a *hypergraph*. The elements of $X$ are called *vertices*, those of $\mathcal{E}$ *hyperedges*. A partition of $X$ into two classes is usually represented by a coloring $\chi : X \to C$ for some two-element set $C$. The partition then is formed by the color classes $\chi^{-1}(i), i \in C$. It turns

* supported by the graduate school 'Effiziente Algorithmen und Multiskalenmethoden', Deutsche Forschungsgemeinschaft

R. Freivalds (Ed.): FCT 2001, LNCS 2138, pp. 461–471, 2001.

out to be useful to select $-1$ and $+1$ as colors. For a coloring $\chi : X \to \{-1, 1\}$ and a hyperedge $E \in \mathcal{E}$ then the expression

$$\chi(E) := \sum_{x \in E} \chi(x)$$

counts how many of the $+1$–vertices of $E$ cannot be matched by $-1$–vertices. $|\chi(E)|$ is therefore a measure of how balanced the hyperedge $E$ is colored by $\chi$. As it is our aim to color all hyperedges simultaneously in a balanced manner, we define the discrepancy of $\chi$ with respect to $\mathcal{H}$ by

$$\operatorname{disc}(\mathcal{H}, \chi) := \max_{E \in \mathcal{E}} |\chi(E)|.$$

The discrepancy problem originated from number theoretical problems (e. g. van der Waerden [vdW27] or Roth [Rot64]), but due to a wide range of applications and connections it has received an increased attention by computer scientists and applied mathematicians during the last twenty years.

Most notably is the connection to uniformly distributed sets and sequences which play a crucial role in *numerical integration* in higher dimensions (quasi-Monte Carlo methods). This area is also called geometric discrepancy theory. Via the so-called "transference principle", geometric and combinatorial discrepancies are connected with each other. An excellent reference on geometric discrepancies, their connection to combinatorial ones and applications is the book of Matoušek [Mat99].

The notion of linear discrepancy of matrices describes how well a solution of a linear program can be rounded to an integer solution (*lattice approximation problem*). Due to work of Beck and Spencer [BS84] and Lovász et al. [LSV86], the linear discrepancy can be bounded (in a constructive manner) by combinatorial discrepancies.

Further applications are found in *computational geometry* and the theory of *communication complexity*. For these and other applications of discrepancies in theoretical computer science we refer to the new book of Chazelle [Cha00].

Discrepancy problems can be formulated as integer linear programs. Since we believe that our methods can be extended to this more general context, let us briefly sketch the connection: Let $X = \{1, \dots, n\} =: [n]$ and $\mathcal{E} = \{E_1, \dots, E_m\}$. Then the following integer linear program (here given as a $0,1$ ILP) solves the discrepancy problem for $\mathcal{H}$:

**minimize** $2\lambda$

**subject to**

$$\sum_{i \in E_j} x_i - \tfrac{1}{2}|E_j| \le \lambda, \quad j = 1, \dots, m$$

$$-\sum_{i \in E_j} x_i + \tfrac{1}{2}|E_j| \le \lambda, \quad j = 1, \dots, m$$

$$x_i \in \{0, 1\}, \quad i = 1, \dots, n$$

$$\lambda \ge 0.$$

The problem in using the linear relaxation of this ILP is that there always exists the trivial solution $\mathbf{x} = (x_1, \dots, x_n) = \frac{1}{2}\mathbf{1}_n$. Therefore, a fruitful connection between solutions of the $[0,1]$–relaxation and the original problem is not to be expected.

On the other hand, randomized rounding strategies for this trivial solution yield random colorings and, vice versa, generators of random colorings can be interpreted as randomized rounding strategies. Thus both problems are strongly connected. It also turns out that the tools used and the difficulties occurring in both problems are very similar. Thus we think that the methods of this paper might have a broader application and are not restricted to the discrepancy problem.

Note that when applying a randomized rounding strategy to the above ILP, we do not need to care about feasibility (as for most randomized rounding problems). The reason is that any infeasibility inflicted by the rounding, i.e., any violation of the constraints, simply is a discrepancy.

## 1.2 Algorithmic Aspects of Randomized Coloring and Randomized Rounding

Discrepancy is an $NP$–hard problem. It is even $NP$–hard to decide whether a zero discrepancy coloring exists or not. Efficient algorithms finding an optimal coloring therefore are not to be expected. Indeed, very little is known about the algorithmic aspect of discrepancy. For some restrictions of the problem a nice solution exist, e. g. for hypergraphs having vertex degree at most $t$. Beck and Fiala [BF81] gave a polynomial time algorithm leading to a coloring having discrepancy less than $2t$.

A common algorithmic approach for the general case (and in fact the only one known to us) are random colorings obtained by independently choosing a random color for each vertex. Via a Chernoff-bound analysis (see e.g. Alon and Spencer [AS00]) this yields colorings having discrepancy $O(\sqrt{n \log m})$, where as above $n$ shall always denote the number of vertices and $m$ the number of hyperedges. More precisely, they show

**Theorem 1.** *A random coloring obtained by independently choosing a random color for each vertex has discrepancy*

$$\operatorname{disc}(\mathcal{H}, \chi) \le \sqrt{2n \ln(4m)}$$

*with probability at least $\frac{1}{2}$.*

Note that this yields a randomized algorithm computing a coloring of the claimed discrepancy by repeatedly generating and testing a random coloring until the discrepancy guarantee of the theorem is satisfied. This algorithm has expected run-time $O(n(R+m))$, where $R$ is the complexity of generating a random bit. To get rid of the random aspect, several so-called derandomization techniques have been developed. We refer to [Sri01] for a survey. Random constructions show that (at least for suitable values of $n$ and $m$) there are hypergraphs having discrepancy $\Omega(\sqrt{n \log \frac{m}{n}})$. Thus this approach cannot be improved significantly in the general case.

Via the transfer sketched in the previous subsection, all of the above holds for general rounding problems as well. In particular, no randomized rounding strategy for a linear problem of $n$ variables and $m$ constraints can guarantee a violation in the constraints of less than $\Omega(\sqrt{n \log \frac{m}{n}})$.

A central problem with random colorings (random rounding) is therefore how to take into account the special structure of the hypergraph (the ILP). One way to deal with this is to use random colorings as above, but to tighten the analysis using the structural information. Limited dependencies of 'bad' events play a crucial role here. Two papers in this context are Schmidt et al. [SSS95] and Srinivasan [Sri96].

A second approach is to use a different kind of random colorings, i.e., to design the random experiment in a way that it exploits the structure of the hypergraph. This is what we do in this paper.

### 1.3 Our Results

We analyze a way of generating random colorings not by independently coloring the vertices, but by enforcing some dependencies. Thus we are able to exploit structural information about the hypergraph.

This proves to be effective in several ways. Firstly, it allows to generate random colorings having smaller discrepancy. Being a fairly general class of hypergraphs that have some common structure, we analyze hypergraphs of $d$–dimensional boxes. Our randomized colorings beat the ordinary random colorings in terms of discrepancy by a factor roughly $2^{d/2}$.

A second advantage is that we also obtain some more information about the random coloring. For example, we may prescribe that our colorings should be *fair*, that is, have equal-sized color classes. This can be useful in some applications, e. g. the recursive method to construct balanced multi-colorings of [DS01] uses fair colorings. A nice thing from the technical point of view is that we get these fair colorings without extra technical difficulties. Usually, working with fair colorings is more difficult, since the hypergeometric distribution is harder to analyze than the binomial one (cf. Chvátal [Chv79] and Uhlmann [Uhl66]).

A third point concerns the complexity of generating the colorings. Due to the dependencies the number of random bits needed to generate our random colorings is smaller than for ordinary random colorings. For the hypergraphs of $d$–dimensional boxes we reduce the number of random bits needed by a factor of $2^d$. This is important, if generating random bits is costly.

Finally, computing the discrepancy of our random colorings can be done faster compared to ordinary random colorings. The reason is that (depending on the hypergraph, of course) the number of relevant hyperedges, i.e., those for which $\chi(E)$ has to be computed, is reduced. Since a typical randomized algorithm computes a low-discrepancy coloring by repeatedly generating a random coloring and then computing its discrepancy until a satisfactory solution is found, this fact also speeds up computing low-discrepancy colorings.

## 2 Structured Randomized Coloring

As mentioned in the introduction, our aim is to generate random colorings that do not independently color the vertices, but on the contrary use suitable dependencies that reflect the structure of the hypergraph. To do so, we partition the vertex set into classes. Within such a class, we will have perfect dependence, that is, each vertex determines the color of all other vertices in the class. For two vertices lying in different classes, their colors shall be chosen independently. The problem of this very general approach is of course to catch the structure of the hypergraph through the partition and the dependencies in the partition classes. We show an example of how to do so in the next section and proceed by fixing the general framework.

Let $\mathcal{P} = \{P_1, \ldots, P_r\}$ be a partition of the vertex set. Let $\chi_{P_i} : P_i \to \{-1, +1\}$ be colorings such that $|\chi_{P_i}(E \cap P_i)| \leq 1$ holds for all edges $E \in \mathcal{E}$. For a hyperedge $E \in \mathcal{E}$ set

$$I(\mathcal{P}, E) := \{i \in [r] | \chi_{P_i}(E \cap P_i) \neq 0\},$$

hence $\chi_{P_i}(E \cap P_i) \in \{-1, +1\}$ for all $i \in I(\mathcal{P}, E)$. We generate a random coloring like this: For each $i \in [r] := \{1, \ldots, r\}$ we 'flip a coin', i.e., independently and uniformly choose a random sign $\varepsilon_i \in \{-1, +1\}$. Let $\chi : X \to \{-1, +1\}$ denote the union of the $\varepsilon_i \chi_{P_i}$, that is, we have $\chi(x) = \varepsilon_i \chi_{P_i}(x)$ for all $x \in P_i$. We call $\chi$ a *structured random coloring* with respect to $\mathcal{P}$ and the $\chi_{P_i}, i \in [r]$. Here is a discrepancy estimate for such a coloring.

**Lemma 1.** *Let $\chi$ be a structured random coloring with respect to $\mathcal{P}$ and the $\chi_{P_i}, i \in [r]$. For any hyperedge $E \in \mathcal{E}$ we have*

$$P(|\chi(E)| > \lambda) < 2e^{-\frac{\lambda^2}{2|I(\mathcal{P},E)|}}.$$

The proof is not very difficult. We still state it here, as it reveals why our structured random colorings are superior to the ordinary ones.

*Proof.* For each $i \in I(\mathcal{P}, E)$ define a random variable $Z_i = \chi_{P_i}(E \cap P_i) = \sum_{x \in E \cap P_i} \chi_{P_i}(x)$. Set $Z = \sum_{i \in I(\mathcal{P},E)} Z_i$. Note that $Z = \chi(E)$. Since the $Z_i$ are mutually independent $-1, 1$ random variables, we may apply the Chernoff bound (cf. [AS00], Corollary A.1.2) and get

$$P(|Z| > \lambda) < 2e^{-\frac{\lambda^2}{2|I(\mathcal{P},E)|}}.$$

□

Comparing Lemma 1 with the analogous estimate for ordinary random colorings

$$P(|\chi(E)| > \lambda) < 2e^{-\frac{\lambda^2}{2|E|}},$$

we see that in our version we replaced the cardinality $|E|$ of the hyperedge by the possibly smaller number of $P_i$ such that $\chi_{P_i}(E \cap P_i) \neq 0$. We thus reduced the relevant size of the hyperedges.

There is a second way structured random colorings can improve discrepancy bounds, namely by reducing the number of relevant hyperedges. Set

$$E_{\mathcal{P}} := \bigcup\{(E \cap P_i) \,|\, \chi_{P_i}(E \cap P_i) \neq 0\}$$

for all $E \in \mathcal{E}$ and $\mathcal{E}_{\mathcal{P}} := \{E_{\mathcal{P}} | E \in \mathcal{E}\}$. From the definition of structured random colorings it is clear that any structured random coloring $\chi$ with respect to $\mathcal{P}$ and the $\chi_P, P \in \mathcal{P}$ fulfills $\chi(E) = \chi(E_{\mathcal{P}})$. In particular, we have

$$\operatorname{disc}(\mathcal{H}, \chi) = \operatorname{disc}((X, \mathcal{E}_{\mathcal{P}}), \chi).$$

Depending on the partition $\mathcal{P}$ and the colorings $\chi_{P_i}$, the mapping $E \mapsto E_{\mathcal{P}}$ is not injective, and hence $|\mathcal{E}_{\mathcal{P}}| < |\mathcal{E}|$. In this case we only need to consider the smaller number $|\mathcal{E}_{\mathcal{P}}|$ of hyperedges. Since the discrepancy bound depends on the number of hyperedges just logarithmically, this effect is less important compared to the reduction of the relevant sizes of the hyperedges. It can however be useful, as it makes the computation of $\operatorname{disc}(\mathcal{H}, \chi)$ easier.

This observation together with Lemma 1 yields

**Theorem 2.** *Let $s_0 := \max_{E \in \mathcal{E}} |I(\mathcal{P}, E)|$ and $m_0 := |\mathcal{E}_{\mathcal{P}}|$. Then a structured random coloring with respect to $\mathcal{P}$ and the $\chi_P, P \in \mathcal{P}$ has discrepancy at most*

$$\operatorname{disc}(\mathcal{H}, \chi) \leq \sqrt{2 s_0 \ln(4 m_0)}$$

*with probability at least $\frac{1}{2}$.*

*Proof.* Omitted. □

There are two more points to add concerning structured random colorings. One is that we may get information about $\chi$ through properties of the colorings $\chi_P, P \in \mathcal{P}$. For example, if each $\chi_P, P \in \mathcal{P}$ has equal-sized color classes, then this also holds for $\chi$. Conversely of course, we may enforce certain properties on $\chi$ by choosing suitable colorings $\chi_P, P \in \mathcal{P}$.

Secondly, from the definition of structured random colorings it is clear that to generate a structured random coloring with respect to $\mathcal{P}$ and $\chi_P, P \in \mathcal{P}$, we need only $|\mathcal{P}|$ random bits instead of $n$ random bits needed for ordinary random colorings.

## 3 Higher-Dimensional Boxes

In this section we show how the method described above can be applied to an actual example, namely hypergraphs of higher-dimensional boxes. They display some regularity that can be exploited. On the other hand, this is still a fairly general class of hypergraphs. For similarly geometrically defined hypergraphs, so-called cylinder intersections, a discrepancy result was used to prove bounds on multi-party communication complexities by Babai et al. [BHK98].

We say that a hypergraph $\mathcal{H} = (X, \mathcal{E})$ is a *hypergraph of d-dimensional boxes* for some $d \in \mathbb{N}$, if there is a decomposition $X = X_1 \times \cdots \times X_d$ such that each hyperedge $E \in \mathcal{E}$ has a representation $E = E_1 \times \cdots \times E_d$ respecting the decomposition of $X$, i.e., such that $E_i \subseteq X_i$ holds for all $i \in [d]$. Let us agree to call any set $E_1 \times \cdots \times E_d$ such that $E_i \subseteq X_i$ for all $i \in [d]$ a *box*.

For an arbitrary number $r$ we denote by $\lceil r \rceil_2$ the smallest even integer not being smaller than $r$. We show

**Theorem 3.** *Let $\mathcal{H} = (X, \mathcal{E})$ be a hypergraph of d-dimensional boxes. Let $X = X_1 \times \cdots \times X_d$ be a corresponding decomposition. Set $n := |X|$, $n_i := |X_i|$ for $i \in [d]$ and $m := |\mathcal{E}|$. Then there are structured random colorings $\chi : X \to \{-1, 1\}$ having discrepancy at most*

$$\operatorname{disc}(\mathcal{H}, \chi) \leq 2^{-\frac{d-1}{2}} \sqrt{\lceil n_1 \rceil_2 \cdots \lceil n_d \rceil_2 \ln(4m)}$$

*with probability at least $\frac{1}{2}$. Generating these structured random colorings needs $2^{-d} n$ random bits.*

Note that Theorem 1 using ordinary random colorings only proves a bound of $\sqrt{2n_1 \cdots n_d \ln(4m)} = \sqrt{2n \ln(4m)}$. This is worse by a factor of $2^{d/2}$ (in the case of even $n_i$).

*Proof.* Without loss of generality we may assume that $X_i = [n_i]$. We first consider the case that all $n_i, i = 1, \ldots, d$, are even.

Set $\mathcal{P} := \{\{2x_1 - 1, 2x_1\} \times \cdots \times \{2x_d - 1, 2x_d\} \mid \forall i \in [d] : x_i \in [\frac{n_i}{2}]\}$, that is, we partition the vertex set into small cubes of size $2^d$ in a rather canonical way.

The coloring corresponding to each small cube shall be such that adjacent (in the Hamming distance sense) corners always receive opposite colors. More formally, for a given cube $P \in \mathcal{P}$ we define a coloring $\chi_P : P \to \{-1, 1\}$ by

$$\chi_P(x) = 1 \iff \sum_{i \in [d]} x_i \text{ is even}$$

for all $x = (x_1, \ldots, x_d)$.

Let $E \in \mathcal{E}$ and $P \in \mathcal{P}$. As both $E$ and $P$ are boxes, so is $E \cap P$. From the definition of $\chi_P$ we see that any subbox $S$ of $P$ such that $|S| \neq 1$ fulfills $\chi(S) = 0$. Hence $|\chi_P(E \cap P)| \leq 1$ for all $E \in \mathcal{E}$ and $P \in \mathcal{P}$. We may therefore define random structured colorings with respect to $\mathcal{P}$ and the $\chi_P, P \in \mathcal{P}$ as introduced in Section 2. Let $\chi$ be such a coloring.

We have $|I(\mathcal{P},E)| \leq |\mathcal{P}| = 2^{-d}n$. Applying Theorem 2 with $s_0 = 2^{-d}n$, we get the bound

$$\mathrm{disc}(\mathcal{H},\chi) \leq 2^{-\frac{d-1}{2}} \sqrt{n \ln(4m)},$$

which finishes the proof in the case that all $n_i, i = 1, \ldots, d$, are even.

For the general case we consider the hypergraph $\mathcal{H}_1 = ([\lceil n_1 \rceil_2] \times \cdots \times [\lceil n_d \rceil_2], \mathcal{E})$. Since $\mathcal{H}$ is a subhypergraph of $\mathcal{H}_1$, any coloring $\chi_1$ for $\mathcal{H}_1$ by restriction yields a coloring $\chi = (\chi_1)_{|X}$ for $\mathcal{H}$. The claim follows from $\mathrm{disc}(\mathcal{H},\chi) \leq \mathrm{disc}(\mathcal{H}_1,\chi_1)$ and applying the case of even cardinality sets to $\mathcal{H}_1$. □

Apart from this improved discrepancy bound, we also gained some information about the coloring itself. For example, all geometric boxes are colored very nicely. We call a box $B \subseteq X$ a *geometric box*, if it can be represented in the form $B = I_1 \times \cdots \times I_d$ for some intervals $I_i \subseteq [n_i], i \in [d]$. As can be seen easily, these boxes fulfill $|\chi(B)| \leq 2^d$ for any structured random coloring $\chi$ with respect to $\mathcal{P}$ and $\chi_P, P \in \mathcal{P}$.

Furthermore, our colorings are fair, that is, they are perfectly balanced on the whole vertex set. We have $\chi(X) = 0$, if $|X|$ is even, and $\chi(X) \in \{-1, 1\}$, if $|X|$ is odd (note that any odd cardinality set $S$ cannot have discrepancy $\chi(S) = 0$, no matter what the coloring $\chi$ is like).

Fair colorings are important in recursive algorithms and divide-and-conquer procedures. The relation between combinatorial discrepancies and $\varepsilon$–approximations (and thus also the "transfer principle" connecting geometric and combinatorial discrepancies) rely on the concept of fair colorings. We refer to the first chapter of Matoušek [Mat99] for the details. Another example is the recursive method to construct balanced multi-colorings from 2–color discrepancy information (cf. [DS01]).

If $X \in \mathcal{E}$, then fairness can be obtained by recoloring some vertices in the larger color class. This increases the discrepancy by a factor of at most 2. With our structured random colorings, we can get fairness "for free".

To show how such structural knowledge about the random coloring can be used to reduce the number of relevant hyperedges, we examine a special class of box hypergraphs: The hypergraph of *all* $d$–dimensional boxes in $[n_0]^d$ for some $n_0 \in \mathbb{N}$ is $\mathcal{H}^d_{n_0} := ([n_0]^d, \{S_1 \times \cdots \times S_d | S_i \subseteq [n_0]\})$. The usual random colorings (Theorem 1) fulfill

$$\begin{aligned}\mathrm{disc}(\mathcal{H}^d_{n_0}) &\leq \sqrt{2 n_0^d \ln(4\, 2^{n_0 d})} \\ &= \sqrt{2 \ln 2}\, n_0^{\frac{d+1}{2}} \sqrt{d}\, (1 + o(1)) \\ &\approx 1.18\, n_0^{\frac{d+1}{2}} \sqrt{d}\, (1 + o(1))\end{aligned}$$

with probability at least $\frac{1}{2}$. In the following theorem we improve this bound and also show that less than $3^{n_0 d/2}$ of the $2^{n_0 d}$ hyperedges are relevant. For convenience let us concentrate on the case that $n_0$ is even. The general result can be obtained from similar reasoning as in the proof of Theorem 3.

**Theorem 4.** *Let $n_0, d \in \mathbb{N}$, $n_0$ even, $d \geq 2$ and set $n := n_0^d$. There are structured random colorings $\chi$ for $\mathcal{H}_{n_0}^d$ that have*

$$\mathrm{disc}(\mathcal{H}_{n_0}^d, \chi) \leq 1.05\ 2^{-d/2} n_0^{\frac{d+1}{2}} \sqrt{d}$$

*with probability at least $\frac{1}{2}$. Generating these colorings needs $2^{-d}n$ random bits. To compute their discrepancy, only $2^{-d}3^{n_0 d/2}$ hyperedges have to be regarded.*

*Proof.* Set $\mathcal{P} := \{\{2x_1 - 1, 2x_1\} \times \cdots \times \{2x_d - 1, 2x_d\} \mid x_1, \cdots, x_d \in [\frac{n_0}{2}]\}$ and define $\chi_P, P \in \mathcal{P}$ as in the proof of Theorem 3. Let $\chi$ be a random coloring with respect to $\mathcal{P}$ and $\chi_P, P \in \mathcal{P}$. As above we have $|I(\mathcal{P}, E)| \leq 2^{-d} n_0^d$.

Now let us bound the number of hyperedges that are relevant for the discrepancy of $\chi$ with respect to $\mathcal{H}$. We first compute $|\mathcal{E}_\mathcal{P}|$. Let $E = S_1 \times \cdots \times S_d$. Assume that for some $i \in [d]$ and $x \in [\frac{n_0}{2}]$ we have $\{2x-1, 2x\} \subseteq S_i$. Then no box $P = \{2x_1 - 1, 2x_1\} \times \cdots \times \{2x_d - 1, 2x_d\}$ such that $x_i = x$ intersects $E$ in exactly one vertex. From some elementary properties of boxes and the definition of $\chi_P$ we derive $\chi_P(E \cap P) = 0$. Thus $E_\mathcal{P} = (S_1 \times \cdots \times (S_i \setminus \{2x-1, 2x\}) \times \cdots \times S_d)_\mathcal{P}$. By induction we see that $\pi : E \mapsto E_\mathcal{P}$ is a projection of $\mathcal{E}$ onto $\mathcal{E}$. Therefore we need to count its fixed points only to get $|\mathcal{E}_\mathcal{P}|$. We just exhibited that a necessary (and sufficient) condition for a hyperedge $E = S_1 \times \cdots \times S_d$ to be a fixed point is

$$\forall i \in [d] \, \forall x \in [\tfrac{n_0}{2}] : |S_i \cap \{2x - 1, 2x\}| \leq 1.$$

For each $i \in [d], x \in [\frac{n_0}{2}]$ we therefore have exactly three possibilities: $S_i \cap \{2x - 1, 2x\}$ is empty or $\{2x - 1\}$ or $\{2x\}$. This makes $|\mathcal{E}_\mathcal{P}| = 3^{n_0 d/2}$ fixed points.

Still, not all hyperedges in $\mathcal{E}_\mathcal{P}$ are relevant. From the structure of $\chi$ we derive a further reduction: Note that for all $i \in [d]$,

$$\gamma_i : \mathcal{E} \to \mathcal{E}; S_1 \times \cdots \times S_i \times \cdots \times S_d \mapsto S_1 \times \cdots \times ([n_0] \setminus S_i) \times \cdots \times S_d$$

is a fixed-point-free bijection of $\mathcal{E}$ that leaves the set $\mathcal{E}_\mathcal{P}$ of reduced hyperedges invariant and preserves discrepancy: We have

$$\chi(E) = -\chi(\gamma_i(E))$$

for all hyperedges $E \in \mathcal{E}$. In particular, the group $\langle \gamma_1, \ldots, \gamma_d \rangle \simeq \mathbb{Z}_2^d$ acts on $\mathcal{E}$ and $\mathcal{E}_\mathcal{P}$ in such a way that all orbits have length $2^d$. As all elements of an orbit have the same discrepancy with respect to $\chi$, it is enough to consider just one representative from each orbit. Let $\mathcal{E}_0 \subseteq \mathcal{E}$ be system of representatives of the orbits in $\mathcal{E}_\mathcal{P}$, that is, $\mathcal{E}_0$ contains exactly one element of each orbit in $\mathcal{E}_\mathcal{P}$. Since $|\mathcal{E}_0| = 2^{-d}|\mathcal{E}_\mathcal{P}|$, we reduced the number of relevant hyperedges by another factor of $2^d$. From Theorem 2 we finally get (with probability at least $\frac{1}{2}$)

$$\begin{aligned}
\mathrm{disc}(\mathcal{H}, \chi) &= \mathrm{disc}((X, \mathcal{E}_0), \chi) \\
&\leq \sqrt{2\, 2^{-d} n_0^d \ln(4\, 2^{-d} 3^{n_0 d/2})} \\
&\leq \sqrt{\ln 3}\, 2^{-d/2} n_0^{\frac{d+1}{2}} \sqrt{d} \\
&\leq 1.05\ 2^{-d/2} n_0^{\frac{d+1}{2}} \sqrt{d}.
\end{aligned}$$

□

We should remark that the size reduction yields a change in the order of magnitude in terms of $d$, namely the additional $2^{-d/2}$ factor, whereas counting the relevant edges (less than $(7/8)^n$ of the total number of edges) only improves the constant by about 11%. Recall however, that reducing the number of relevant hyperedges does reduce the complexity of checking whether a structured random coloring fulfills the discrepancy bound of the theorem or not.

## 4 Summary and Conclusion

In this paper we presented a new way of generating random colorings for the discrepancy problem of hypergraphs. This allows to use structural information about the hypergraph and thus

- improves discrepancy guarantees,
- allows to prescribe additional properties regarding the coloring, e.g. fairness,
- reduces the number of random bits needed to generate the coloring,
- reduces the number of relevant hyperedges, and thus reduces the complexity of computing the discrepancy of the random coloring and the expected complexity of computing a low-discrepancy random coloring.

Since generating random colorings for a discrepancy problem is equivalent to generating random roundings for the trivial solution of the corresponding ILP-relaxation, we believe that these methods can be applied to a broader range of ILPs as well.

## References

[AS00] N. Alon and J. Spencer. *The Probabilistic Method.* John Wiley & Sons, Inc., 2nd edition, 2000.

[BF81] J. Beck and T. Fiala. "Integer making" theorems. *Discrete Applied Mathematics*, 3:1–8, 1981.

[BHK98] L. Babai, T. P. Hayes, and P. G. Kimmel. The cost of the missing bit: Communication complexity with help. In *Proceedings of the 30th STOC*, pages 673–682, 1998.

[BS84] J. Beck and J. Spencer. Integral approximation sequences. *Math. Programming*, 30:88–98, 1984.

[Cha00] B. Chazelle. *The Discrepancy Method.* Princeton University, 2000.

[Chv79] V. Chvátal. The tail of the hypergeometric distribution. *Discrete Math.*, 25:285–287, 1979.

[DS01] B. Doerr and A. Srivastav. Recursive randomized coloring beats fair dice random colorings. In A. Ferreira and H. Reichel, editors, *Proceedings of the 18th Annual Symposium on Theoretical Aspects of Computer Science (STACS) 2001*, volume 2010 of *Lecture Notes in Computer Science*, pages 183–194, Berlin–Heidelberg, 2001. Springer Verlag.

[LSV86] L. Lovász, J. Spencer, and K. Vesztergombi. Discrepancies of set-systems and matrices. *Europ. J. Combin.*, 7:151–160, 1986.

[Mat99] J. Matoušek. *Geometric Discrepancy.* Springer-Verlag, Berlin, 1999.

[Rot64] K. F. Roth. Remark concerning integer sequences. *Acta Arithmetica*, 9:257–260, 1964.

[Sri96] A. Srinivasan. An extension of the Lovász local lemma, and its applications to integer programming. In *Proceedings of the Seventh Annual ACM-SIAM Symposium on Discrete Algorithms (Atlanta, GA, 1996)*, pages 6–15, New York, 1996. ACM.

[Sri01] A. Srivastav. Derandomization in combinatorial optimization. In P. Pardalos, S. Rajasekaran, J. Reif, and J. D. P. Rolim, editors, *Handbook of Randomization*. Kluver, to appear in 2001.

[SSS95] J. P. Schmidt, A. Siegel, and A. Srinivasan. Chernoff-Hoeffding bounds for applications with limited independence. *SIAM J. Discrete Math.*, 8:223–250, 1995.

[Uhl66] W. Uhlmann. Vergleich der hypergeometrischen mit der Binomial-Verteilung. *Metrika*, 10:145–158, 1966.

[vdW27] B. L. van der Waerden. Beweis einer Baudetschen Vermutung. *Nieuw Arch. Wsk.*, 15:212–216, 1927.

# Optimal Online Flow Time with Resource Augmentation

Leah Epstein[1]* and Rob van Stee[2]**

[1] School of Computer and Media Sciences, The Interdisciplinary Center, Herzliya, Israel. Epstein.Leah@idc.ac.il.

[2] Centre for Mathematics and Computer Science (CWI), Amsterdam, The Netherlands. Rob.van.Stee@cwi.nl.

**Abstract.** We study the problem of scheduling $n$ jobs that arrive over time. We consider a non-preemptive setting on a single machine. The goal is to minimize the total flow time. We use extra resource competitive analysis: an optimal off-line algorithm which schedules jobs on a single machine is compared to a more powerful on-line algorithm that has $\ell$ machines. We design an algorithm of competitive ratio $O(\min(\Delta^{1/\ell}, n^{1/\ell}))$, where $\Delta$ is the maximum ratio between two job sizes, and provide a lower bound which shows that the algorithm is optimal up to a constant factor for any constant $\ell$. The algorithm works for a hard version of the problem where the sizes of the smallest and the largest jobs are not known in advance, only $\Delta$ is known. This gives a trade-off between the resource augmentation and the competitive ratio.
We also consider scheduling on parallel identical machines. In this case the optimal off-line algorithm has $m$ machines and the on-line algorithm has $\ell m$ machines. We give a lower bound for this case. Next, we give lower bounds for algorithms using resource augmentation on the speed. Finally, we consider scheduling with hard deadlines.

## 1 Introduction

Minimizing the total flow time is a well-known and hard problem, which has been studied widely both in on-line and in off-line environments [1,7,8]. The flow time $f(J)$ of a job $J$ is defined as its completion time, $C(J)$, minus the time at which it arrived, $r(J)$ (the release time of $J$). This measure is applicable to systems where the load is proportional to the total number of bits that exist in the system over time (both of running jobs and of waiting jobs). In this paper, we consider on-line algorithms using resource augmentation, and we examine the effects on the performance of an algorithm if it has more or faster machines than the off-line algorithm (see [6,9]).

We consider the following on-line scheduling problem. The algorithm has parallel identical machines, on which it must schedule jobs with different processing

---

* Work carried out while the author was at Tel-Aviv University.

** Research supported by the Netherlands Organization for Scientific Research (NWO), project number SION 612-30-002.

R. Freivalds (Ed.): FCT 2001, LNCS 2138, pp. 472–482, 2001.

requirements that arrive over time. A job $J$ (which arrives at time $r(J)$) with processing requirement $P(J)$ (also called running time or size) that becomes known upon arrival, has to be assigned to one of the machines and run there continuously for $P(J)$ units of time. The objective is to minimize the sum of flow times of all jobs. The total number of jobs is $n$.

We compare on-line algorithms that are running on $\ell m$ machines ($\ell \geq 1$) to an optimal off-line algorithm, denoted by $OPT$, that is running on $m$ machines but knows all the jobs in advance. Such on-line algorithms are also called $\ell$-machine algorithms, since they use $\ell$ times as much machines as the optimal off-line algorithm. An algorithm that uses the same number of machines as the off-line algorithm, but uses machines which are $s > 1$ times faster, is called a $s$-speed algorithm.

For a job sequence $\sigma$ and an on-line algorithm $A$, we denote the total flow time of $\sigma$ in the schedule of $A$ on $\ell m$ machines by $A_{\ell m}(\sigma)$. We denote the optimal total flow time for $\sigma$ on $m$ machines by $OPT_m(\sigma)$. The competitive ratio using resource augmentation is defined by

$$r_{m,\ell m}(A) = \sup_{\sigma} \frac{A_{\ell m}(\sigma)}{OPT_m(\sigma)} ,$$

where the supremum is taken over all possible job sequences $\sigma$. The goal of an on-line algorithm is to minimize this ratio.

Approximating the flow time is hard even in an off-line environment (see [7, 8]). In an on-line environment it is well known that the best competitive ratio of any algorithm that uses a single machine is $n$ (easily achieved by a greedy algorithm). The problem has been studied introducing resource augmentation by Phillips, Stein, Torng and Wein [9]. They give algorithms with augmentation on the number of machines. These are an $O(\log n)$-machine algorithm (which has a competitive ratio $1 + o(1)$) and an $O(\log \Delta)$-machine algorithm (which achieves the competitive ratio 1), where $\Delta$ is the maximum ratio between running times of jobs. Both algorithms are valid for every $m$.

We give an algorithm `Levels` and show $r_{1,\ell}(\texttt{Levels}) = O(\min(n^{1/\ell}, \Delta^{1/\ell}))$, where $n$ is the number of jobs that arrive. This algorithm works for a hard version of this problem where the sizes of the smallest and the largest jobs are not known in advance; only $\Delta$ is known in advance. The algorithm in [9] works only if the job size limits are known in advance.

Furthermore, we show that for all on-line algorithms $A$ and number $m_1$ of off-line machines we have $r_{m_1,\ell}(A) = \Omega\left(\frac{\min(n^{1/\ell}, \Delta^{1/\ell})}{(12\ell)^{\ell}}\right)$. This shows that `Levels` is optimal up to a constant factor for any constant $l$ against an adversary on one machine.

In [4], a related problem on a network of links is considered. It immediately follows from our lower bounds, that any constant competitive algorithm has a polylogarithmic number of machines. More precisely, if $A$ has a constant competitive ratio and $\ell m$ machines, $\ell \geq \Omega\left(\frac{\sqrt{\log(\min(n,\Delta))}}{m\sqrt{\log\log(\min(n,\Delta))}}\right)$. This result can also be deduced from Theorem 10 in [4]. However, using their proof for the general lower bound would give only an exponent of $\frac{1}{2\ell}$. Improving the exponent to be the tight exponent $\frac{1}{\ell}$ is non-trivial. Our results imply that by choosing a given amount of resource augmentation, the competitive ratio is fixed. We adapt the lower bound for the case where the on-line algorithm has faster machines than the off-line algorithm. This results in a lower bound of $\Omega(n^{1/2m^2})$ on the speed of on-line machines, if $\ell = 1$.

We also consider the following scheduling problem studied in [3,9]. Each job $J$ has a deadline $d(J)$. Instead of minimizing the flow time, we require that each job is finished by its deadline, effectively limiting the flow time of job $J$ to $d(J) - r(J)$. The goal is to complete all jobs on time. For this problem, we give lower bounds on the speed and the number of machines required for a non-preemptive on-line algorithm to succeed on any sequence.

Throughout the paper, for a specific schedule $\zeta$ for the jobs, we denote the starting time of job $J$ by $S_\zeta(J)$, and its flow time by $f_\zeta(J) = C_\zeta(J) - r(J)$. We omit the subscripts if the schedule is clear from the context.

## 2 Algorithms with Resource Augmentation

We have the following results for the case where $n$ is not known and the case where OPT has the same number of machines as the on-line algorithm.

**Lemma 1.** *Any on-line algorithm for minimizing the total flow time on parallel machines has a competitive ratio of $\Omega(n)$ if it does not know $n$ in advance, even if it is compared to an off-line algorithm on one machine.*

*Proof.* We use a number $N >> 1$.

One job of size 1 arrives at time 0. When it is started, $N$ jobs of size $1/N$ arrive with intervals of $1/N$ during the next 1 time. If they are all delayed until time 1, no more jobs arrive and we are done. The optimal flow time on one machine is 3 and the online flow time is $O(N)$.

On the other hand, if one of those jobs is started while the first job is running, $N$ jobs of size $1/N^2$ arrive with intervals of $1/N^2$ during the next $1/N$ time. Depending on the decision by the online algorithm, we continue in this way or stop as soon as it delays $N$ jobs (or reaches the last machine).

When all machines are in use, the online algorithm cannot prevent a flow time of $O(N)$. □

**Lemma 2.** $r_{\ell,\ell}(A) = \Omega(n/\ell^2)$ *for all algorithms $A$.*

*Proof.* A single unit job arrives at time 0. Let $t$ be the time at which $A$ starts this job. Let $\mu = \frac{\ell}{2(n-1)}$. For $j = 0, \ldots, \frac{n-1}{\ell}$, $\ell$ jobs of length $\mu$ are released at time $t + j\mu$. It is easy to see that the optimal total flow time is $\Theta(\ell)$ whereas the flow time of $A$ will be $\Omega(n/\ell)$. Consequently, $r_{\ell,\ell}(A) = \Omega(n/\ell^2)$. □

We define an algorithm `Levels` that knows $n$. `Levels` uses $\ell$ priority queues $Q_1, \ldots, Q_\ell$ (one for each machine) and $\ell$ variables $D_1 \geq \ldots \geq D_\ell$. We initialize $Q_i = \emptyset$ and $D_i = 0$. An *event* is either an arrival of a new job or a completion of a job by a machine. Let $\gamma = n^{1/\ell}$, where $n$ is the number of jobs.

*Algorithm* `Levels`

- If a few events occur at the same time, the algorithm first deals with all arrivals before it deals with job completions.
- On completion of a job on machine $i$, if $Q_i \neq \emptyset$, a job of minimum release time among jobs with minimum processing time in $Q_i$ is scheduled immediately on machine $i$. (The job is dequeued from $Q_i$.)
- On arrival of a job $J$, let $i$ be a minimum index of a machine for which $D_i \leq \gamma P(J)$. If there is no such index, take $i = m$. If machine $i$ is idle, $J$ is immediately scheduled on machine $i$, and otherwise, $J$ is enqueued into $Q_i$. If $P(J) > D_i, D_i$ is modified by $D_i \leftarrow P(J)$.

We analyze the performance of `Levels` compared to a preemptive $OPT$ on a single machine. Denote the schedule of `Levels` by $\pi$. Partition the schedule of each machine into blocks. A block is a maximal sub-sequence of jobs of non-decreasing sizes, that run on one machine consecutively, without any idle time.

- Let $N_i$ be the number of blocks in the schedule of `Levels` on machine $i$.
- Let $B_{i,k}$ be the $k^{th}$ block on machine $i$.
- Let $b_{i,k,j}$ be the $j^{th}$ job in block $B_{i,k}$.
- Let $N_{i,k}$ be the number of jobs in $B_{i,k}$.
- Let $P_{i,k}$ be the size of the largest job in blocks $B_{i,1}, \ldots, B_{i,k}$ i.e.

$$P_{i,k} = \max_{1 \leq r \leq k} \max_{1 \leq j \leq N_{i,r}} P(b_{i,r,j})$$
$$P_{i,0} = 0 \quad \text{for all } 1 \leq i \leq \ell.$$

- Let $I = \bigcup_{1 \leq i \leq \ell, 1 \leq k \leq N_i} B_{i,k}$, i.e. $I$ is the set of all jobs.

Similar to the proof in [5], we define a pseudo-schedule $\psi$ on $\ell$ machines, in which job $b_{i,k,j}$ is scheduled on machine $i$ at time $S_\pi(b_{i,k,j}) - P_{i,k-1}$. Note that $\psi$ is not necessarily a valid schedule, since some jobs might be assigned in parallel, and some jobs may start before their arrival times.

The amount that jobs are shifted backwards increases with time. Therefore, if there is no idle time between jobs in $\pi$, there is no idle time between them in $\psi$ either. Note that in $\psi$, the flow time of a job $J$ can be smaller than $P(J)$, and even negative.

We introduce an extended flow problem. Each job $J$ has two parameters $r(J)$ and $r'(J)$, where $r'(J) \leq r(J)$. $r'(J)$ is the pre-release time of job $J$. Job $J$ may be assigned starting from time $r'(J)$. The flow time is still defined by the completion time minus the release time, i.e. $f(J) = C(J) - r(J)$. Going from an input $\sigma$ for the original problem to an input $\sigma'$ of the extended problem, requires definition of the values of $r'$ for all jobs. Clearly, the optimal total flow time for an input $\sigma'$ of the extended problem is no larger than the flow time of $\sigma$ in the original problem.

Let $I_i$ be the set of jobs that run on machine $i$ in $\pi$. We define an instance $I'_i$ for the extended problem. $I'_i$ contains the same jobs as $I_i$. For each $J \in I_i$, $r(J)$ remains the same, Define $r'(J) = \min\{r(J), S_\psi(J)\}$. Clearly

$OPT(I) \geq \sum_{i=1}^{\ell} OPT(I_i) \geq \sum_{i=1}^{\ell} OPT(I_i')$, where $OPT(I_i)$ is the preemptive optimal off-line cost for the jobs that Levels scheduled on machine $i$. We consider a preemptive optimal off-line schedule $\phi_i$ for $I_i'$ on a single machine. In $\phi_i$, jobs of equal size are completed in the order of arrival. Ties are broken as in $\pi$. The following lemma is similar to [5].

**Lemma 3.** *For each job $J \in I_i'$, $f_{\phi_i}(J) \geq f_\psi(J)$.*

*Proof.* Since $r_{\phi_i}(J) = r_\psi(J)$ for each job $J$, we only have to show that in $\phi_i$, $J$ does not start earlier than it does in $\psi$. Assume to the contrary this is not always the case. Let $J_1$ be the first job in $\phi_i$ for which $S_{\phi_i}(J_1) < S_\psi(J_1)$. Note that in this case $r'(J_1) < S_\psi(J_1)$ and hence $r(J_1) < S_\psi(J_1)$. Let $t$ be the end of the last idle time before $S_\psi(J_1)$, and let $B_{i,k}$ be the block that contains $J_1$.

Suppose $P_{i,k-1} \leq P(J_1)$. Then all jobs that run on machine $i$ from time $t$ until time $S_\psi(J_1)$ in $\psi$ are either smaller than $P(J_1)$ or have the same size, but are released earlier. Moreover, these jobs do not arrive earlier than time $t$, hence in $\phi_i$ they do not run before time $t$. They do run before $S_{\phi_i}(J_1)$ because they have higher priority, hence $S_{\phi_i}(J_1) \geq S_\psi(J_1)$, a contradiction.

Suppose $P_{i,k-1} > P(J_1)$. $J_1$ was available to be run in $\psi$ during the interval $[r(J_1), S_\psi(J_1)]$ since $r(J_1) < S_\psi(J_1)$. In $\pi$, all jobs running in the interval $[r(J_1), S_\pi(J_1)]$ are smaller than $J_1$ (or arrived before, and have the same size), except for the first one, say $J_2$. Since in $\psi$, all these jobs are shifted backwards by at least the size of $J_2$, during $[r(J_1), S_\psi(J_1)]$ only jobs with higher priority than $J_1$ are run in $\psi$. $J_1$ is the first job which starts later in $\psi$ than it does in $\phi_i$, so these jobs occupy the machine until time $S_\psi(J_1)$, hence $S_\psi(J_1) \leq S_{\phi_i}(J_1)$. □

**Theorem 1.** $r_{1,\ell}(\texttt{Levels}) = O(n^{1/\ell})$.

*Proof.* Using Lemma 3 we can bound the difference between $\psi$ and $\pi$. Since $\texttt{Levels}(b_{i,k,j}) = C_\psi(b_{i,k,j}) + P_{i,k-1} - r(b_{i,k,j})$, we have

$$\begin{aligned}\texttt{Levels}(I) &= \sum_{1\leq i\leq \ell}\ \sum_{1\leq k\leq N_i}\ \sum_{1\leq j\leq N_{i,k}} (C_\psi(b_{i,k,j}) + P_{i,k-1} - r(b_{i,k,j})) \\ &\leq \sum_{b_{i,k,j}\in I} (C_\psi(b_{i,k,j}) - r(b_{i,k,j})) + \sum_{b_{i,k,j}\in I} P_{i,k-1} \\ &\leq OPT(I) + \sum_{b_{i,k,j}\in I} P_{i,k-1}.\end{aligned}$$

Let $P$ the maximum job size. We show the following properties:

$$P_{i,k-1} \leq \gamma P(b_{i,k,j}) \quad \text{for each job } b_{i,k,j}, 1 \leq i \leq \ell - 1 \tag{2.1}$$

$$P_{\ell,k-1} \leq \frac{P}{\gamma^{\ell-1}} \quad \text{for each job } b_{\ell,k,j} \tag{2.2}$$

Adding both properties together we get

$$\texttt{Levels}(I) \leq OPT(I) + \sum_{\substack{b_{i,k,j}\in I\\ i\neq\ell}} P_{i,k-1} + \sum_{b_{\ell,k,j}\in I} P_{\ell,k-1}$$

$$\leq OPT(I) + \gamma \sum_{b_{i,k,j} \in I} P(b_{i,k,j}) + \sum_{b_{\ell,k,j} \in I} \frac{P}{\gamma^{\ell-1}}$$

$$\leq OPT(I) + \gamma OPT(I) + n \cdot \frac{OPT(I)}{n^{(\ell-1)/\ell}} = (2\gamma + 1) \cdot OPT(I)$$

This holds since $OPT(I) \geq P$ and $OPT(I)$ is at least the sum of all job sizes, and since $|I| = n$.

To prove (2.1) we recall that $b_{i,k,j}$ was assigned to machine $i$ because it satisfied $D_i \leq \gamma P(b_{i,k,j})$. If $P_{i,k-1} \leq P(b_{i,k,j})$ we are done. Otherwise the job of size $P_{i,k-1}$ arrived before $b_{i,k,j}$ and hence when $b_{i,k,j}$ arrived, $D_i$ satisfied $D_i \geq P_{i,k-1}$, hence $P_{i,k-1} \leq D_i \leq \gamma P(b_{i,k,j})$.

To prove (2.2) we show by induction that every job $J$ on machine $i$ in `Levels` satisfies $P(J) \leq P/\gamma^{i-1}$. This is trivial for $i = 1$. Assume it is true for some machine $i \geq 1$, then at all times $D_i \leq P/\gamma^{i-1}$ holds. Hence, a job $J'$ that was too small for machine $i$ satisfied $P(J') \leq D_i/\gamma \leq P/\gamma^i$. This completes the proof. □

We give a variant of `Levels` with a competitive ratio which depends on $\Delta$, the ratio between the size of the largest job and the size of the smallest job.
*Algorithm* `Revised Levels`: Run `Levels` with $\gamma = \Delta^{1/\ell}$.

**Theorem 2.** $r_{1,\ell}(\texttt{Revised Levels}) = O(\Delta^{1/\ell})$.

*Proof.* The proof is very similar to the proof of Theorem 1. The only difference in the proof is that property (2.1) also holds for machine $\ell$ (this follows from property (2.2) and the definition of $\Delta$), hence the competitive ratio is now $\gamma + 1$. □

Taking $\gamma = \min(n^{1/\ell}, \Delta^{1/\ell})$ we can get a competitive ratio of $O(\min(n^{1/\ell}, \Delta^{1/\ell}))$.

## 3 Lower Bounds for Resource Augmentation

**Theorem 3.** *Let $A$ be an on-line scheduling algorithm to minimize the total flow time on $\ell$ machines. Then for any $1 \leq m_1 \leq \ell$ and sequences consisting of $O(n)$ jobs, $r_{m_1,\ell}(A) = \Omega\left(\frac{n^{1/\ell}}{(12\ell)^{\ell-1}}\right)$.*

We first describe a job sequence $\sigma$ and then show that it implies the theorem. Let $n$ be an integer. There will be at most $\sum_{i=0}^{\ell} n^{i/\ell}$ jobs in $\sigma$ (note $\sum_{i=0}^{\ell} n^{i/\ell} = \Theta(n)$). We build $\sigma$ recursively, defining the jobs according to the behavior of the on-line algorithm $A$.

*Definition* A job $j$ of size $\alpha$ is considered *active*, if the previous active job of size $\alpha$ is completed by $A$ at least $\alpha$ units of time before $j$ is assigned, and $j$ finishes before or when the job that caused its arrival finishes.

The first job in $\sigma$ has size $n$ and arrives at time 0. We consider it to be an active job. On an assignment of a job $j$ of size $\alpha$ by $A$, do the following:

- If $j$ is active, and all other machines are running larger jobs (all machines are consequently busy for at least $\alpha$ units of time), $n$ jobs of size 0 arrive immediately. No more jobs will arrive.
- Otherwise, if $j$ is active, then $j$ causes the arrival of $n^{1/\ell}$ jobs of size $\frac{1}{3} \cdot \frac{\alpha}{n^{1/\ell}}$. These jobs arrive starting the time that $j$ is assigned, every $\frac{\alpha}{n^{1/\ell}}$ units of time, until they all have arrived.
- In all other cases ($j$ is not active), no jobs arrive till the next job that $A$ starts.

**Lemma 4.** $OPT_1(\sigma) \leq 6n$.

*Proof.* We show that all jobs can be assigned on a single machine, during an interval of length $2n$, so that a job of length $\alpha$ has a flow time of at most $3\alpha$. The total flow time then follows.

We show how to assign all jobs of a certain size $\alpha$ so that no active jobs of size $\alpha$ are running at the same time on on-line machines, i. e. the intervals used by $A$ to run active jobs of size $\alpha$, and the intervals that are used by $OPT$ to run jobs of size $\alpha$, are disjoint. Smaller jobs are assigned by $OPT$ during the intervals in which $A$ assigned active jobs of size $\alpha$. Hence, the time slots given by the optimal off-line for different jobs are disjoint.

Finally, we show how to define those time slots. A job $j$ of size $\alpha$, that arrives at time $t$, is not followed by other jobs of size $\alpha$ until time $t+3\alpha$. Since an active on-line job starts at least $\alpha$ units of time after the previous active job of this size ($\alpha$) is completed, there is a time slot of size at least $\alpha$ during the interval $[t, t+3\alpha]$ where no active job of size $\alpha$ is running on any of the on-line machines. The optimal off-line algorithm can assign $j$ during that time. This is true also for the first job. Finally, the optimal algorithm can also manage the jobs of size 0 easily by running them immediately when they arrive. Hence, the total time that the optimal off-line machine is not idle is at most $2n$. □

We partition jobs into three types, according to the on-line assignment. A job that arrived during the processing of a job of size $\alpha$, and has size $\frac{1}{3}\frac{\alpha}{n^{1/\ell}}$ is either active or *passive* (if it is not active, but completed before the job of size $\alpha$ is completed). Otherwise, the job is called *late*. Let $P(\alpha), T(\alpha)$ and $L(\alpha)$ denote the number of passive, active and late jobs of size $\alpha$ (respectively). Let $N(\alpha) = P(\alpha) + T(\alpha) + L(\alpha)$.

*Claim.* $T(\alpha) \geq \lceil \frac{1}{2\ell}(P(\alpha) + T(\alpha)) \rceil$

*Proof.* The number of jobs of size $\alpha$ that the on line algorithm can complete during $2\alpha$ units of time (until a job can be active again) is at most $2n$. □

Now we are ready to prove Theorem 3.

*Proof.* (Of Theorem 3.) According to the definition of the sequence, $N(\alpha) = n^{1/\ell} \cdot T(3\alpha n^{1/\ell})$. We distinguish two cases.

**Case 1.** In all phases $L(\alpha) \leq \frac{1}{2}N(\alpha)$. Hence $T(\alpha) \geq \frac{1}{4\ell}N(\alpha)$ for all $\alpha$. This is true for $\alpha = (\frac{1}{3})^{\ell-1}n^{1/\ell}$ (the smallest non-zero jobs) and hence there at least

$n^{\ell-1/\ell} \cdot (\frac{1}{4\ell})^{\ell-1} > 0$ such jobs. Therefore the zero jobs arrive and are delayed by at least $(\frac{1}{3})^{\ell-1} \cdot n^{1/\ell}$ units of time. Since their flow time is at least $n \cdot n^{1/\ell} \cdot (\frac{1}{3})^{\ell-1}$, and the optimal flow time is at most $6n$, the competitive ratio follows.

**Case 2.** There is a phase where $L(\alpha) > \frac{1}{2}N(\alpha)$. Consider the phase with largest $\alpha$ in which this happens. Since for larger sizes $\alpha'$ we have $L(\alpha') \leq \frac{1}{2}N(\alpha')$, we can bound the number of jobs of size $\alpha$ (for $\alpha = (\frac{1}{3})^i n^{1-i/\ell}$) by $N(\alpha) \geq n^{i/\ell}(\frac{1}{4\ell})^i$. The late jobs are delayed by at least $\frac{1}{4} \cdot 3\alpha n^{1/\ell}$ on average. (This is the delay if for each job of size $3\alpha n^{1/\ell}$ the *last* $\frac{1}{2}n^{1/\ell}$ jobs of size $\alpha$ that arrive are the ones that are late; in all other cases, the delay is bigger.)

The total flow time is at least

$$
\begin{aligned}
A_l(\sigma) &\geq L(\alpha) \cdot \frac{1}{4} \cdot 3\alpha n^{1/\ell} \geq \frac{1}{2} n^{i/\ell} \left(\frac{1}{4\ell}\right)^i \frac{1}{4} \left(\frac{1}{3}\right)^{i-1} n^{1-i/\ell+1/\ell} \\
&= \frac{1}{(4\ell)^i} \cdot \frac{1}{8} \left(\frac{1}{3}\right)^{i-1} \cdot n^{1+1/\ell} = \left(\frac{1}{12\ell}\right)^i \frac{3}{8} n^{1+1/\ell} \\
&\geq \frac{1}{(12\ell)^{\ell-1}} \cdot \frac{3}{8} \cdot n^{1+1/\ell} = \Omega\left(\frac{n^{1/\ell}}{(12\ell)^{\ell-1}}\right) \cdot \Theta(n)
\end{aligned}
$$

Since the optimal flow is $\Theta(n)$, the competitive ratio follows. □

**Theorem 4.** *Let $A$ be an on-line scheduling algorithm to minimize the total flow time on $\ell$ machines. Then $r_{m_1,\ell}(A) = \Omega\left(\frac{\Delta^{1/\ell}}{(12\ell)^\ell}\right)$ for any $1 \leq m_1 \leq \ell$ if the maximum ratio between jobs is $\Delta$.*

*Proof.* We adjust $\sigma$ by starting with a job of size $\Delta$ and fixing $n = \Delta/3^\ell$. We assume $\Delta \geq 6^\ell$ so that $n \geq 2^\ell$ and $n^{1/\ell} \geq 2$, which is needed for the construction of the sequence.

Starting from here, we build a sequence $\sigma'$ in exactly the same way as $\sigma$, except that we do not let jobs of size 0 arrive. Clearly, $OPT_1(\sigma') \leq 6\Delta$. We can follow the proof of Theorem 3. However, we now know that all the smallest jobs will be late. If they arrive we are in the second case of the proof; but if they do not, then for an earlier $\alpha$ we must have $L(\alpha) > \frac{1}{2}N(\alpha)$. So only Case 2 remains of that proof.

The total flow is at least $\frac{3}{8}\frac{n^{1/\ell}}{(12\ell)^\ell}\Delta = \frac{1}{8}\frac{\Delta^{1/\ell}}{(12\ell)^\ell}\Delta$ (because now $i \leq \ell$ in stead of $i \leq \ell - 1$), giving the desired competitive ratio. □

A direct consequence of Theorems 3 and 4 is the following bound on the number of machines needed to maintain a constant competitive ratio. This corollary can be also proved using a simple adaptation of Theorem 10 in [4].

**Corollary 1.** *Any on-line algorithm for minimizing total flow time on $m$ machines that uses resource augmentation and has a constant competitive ratio, is an $\Omega\left(\frac{\sqrt{\log(\min(n,\Delta))}}{m\sqrt{\log\log(\min(n,\Delta))}}\right)$-machine algorithm (on sequences of $\Theta(n)$ jobs).*

Next we consider resource augmentation on the speed as well as on the number of machines. We consider an on-line algorithm which uses machines of speed $s > 1$. The optimal off-line algorithm uses machines of speed 1.

**Theorem 5.** *Let $A$ be an on-line scheduling algorithm to minimize the total flow time on $\ell$ machines. Let $s > 1$ be the speed of the on-line machines. Then $r_{m_1,\ell}(A) = \Omega\left(\frac{n^{1/\ell}}{s(12\ell s^2)^{\ell-1}}\right)$ for any $1 \le m_1 \le \ell$ and sequences consisting of $O(n)$ jobs. Furthermore, $r_{m_1,\ell}(A) = \Omega\left(\frac{\Delta^{1/\ell}}{s(12\ell s^2)^{\ell}}\right)$ for any $1 \le m_1 \le \ell$.*

*Proof.* Again, we use a job sequence similar to $\sigma$. The jobs of phase $i$ now have size $1/(3s^2 n^{1/\ell})^i$. For the $\Delta$-part of the proof, we fix $n = \Delta/(3s^2)^\ell$. Similar calculations as in the previous proofs result in the stated lower bounds. □

**Corollary 2.** *Any on-line algorithm for minimizing total flow time on $m$ machines that uses resource augmentation on the speed and has a constant competitive ratio, is an $\Omega(n^{1/(2\ell^2)})$-speed algorithm (on sequences of $\Theta(n)$ jobs) and an $\Omega(\Delta^{1/(2\ell^2)})$-speed algorithm.*

## 4 Hard Deadlines

We consider the problem of non-preemptive scheduling jobs with hard deadlines. Each arriving job $J$ has a deadline $d(J)$ by which it must be completed. The goal is to produce a schedule, in which all jobs are scheduled such that all of them are completed on time (i.e. by their deadlines). We give a lower bound on the resource augmentation required so that all jobs finish on time. We use a similar lower bounding method to the method we used Section 3. We allow the on-line algorithm resource augmentation in both the number of machines and their speed. We compare an on-line algorithm that schedules on $\ell$ machines of speed $s$ to an optimal off-line algorithm that uses a single machine of speed 1.

Let $\Delta$ denote the ratio between the largest job in the sequence and the smallest job. The lower bound sequence consists of $\ell + 1$ jobs $J_0, \ldots, J_\ell$ where $P(J_i) = 1/(2s+1)^i$. We define release times and deadlines recursively; $r(J_0) = 0$ and $d(J_0) = 2 + 1/s$. Let $\pi$ be the on-line schedule, then $r(J_{i+1}) = S_\pi(J_i)$ and $d(J_{i+1}) = C_\pi(J_i)$. Hence $J_{i+1}$ runs in parallel to all jobs $J_0, \ldots, J_i$ in any feasible schedule $\pi$.

**Lemma 5.** *An optimal off-line algorithm on a single machine of speed 1 can complete all jobs on time.*

*Proof.* For each $i > 0$, $P(J_i) = 1/(2s+1)^i$, hence $d(J_i) - r(J_i) = P(J_{i-1})/s = \frac{2s+1}{s} P(J_i)$. This holds also for $J_0$, since $P(J_0) = 1$ and $d(J_0) - r(J_0) = \frac{2s+1}{s}$. All jobs arriving after $J_i$ have release times and deadlines in the interval $[S_\pi(J_i), C_\pi(J_i)]$. The optimal off-line algorithm can schedule $J_i$ outside this time interval, and avoid conflict with future jobs. By induction, previous jobs are scheduled before $r(J_i)$ or after $d(J_i)$, so there is no conflict with them either. If $S_\pi(J_i) -$

$r(J_i) \geq P(J_i)$, schedule $J_i$ at time $r(J_i)$. Otherwise $C_\pi(J_i) = S_\pi(J_i) + P(J_i)/s < r(J_i) + P(J_i)(1 + 1/s)$, hence $J_i$ is scheduled at time $C_\pi(J_i)$ and completed at $C_\pi(J_i) + P(J_i) < r(J_i) + P(J_i)(2 + 1/s) = d(J_i)$.

It is easy to see that the on-line algorithm cannot finish all jobs on time. If the first $\ell$ jobs finish on time, then all $\ell$ machines are busy during the time interval $[r(J_\ell), d(J_\ell)]$ and it is impossible to start $J_\ell$ before time $d(J_\ell)$. We omit the proof of the following theorem:

**Theorem 6.** *The on-line algorithm fails, if* $\Delta \geq (2s+1)^\ell$.

We show some corollaries from the lower bound on $\Delta$. These are necessary conditions for an on-line algorithm to succeed on any sequence. Given machines of constant speed $s$, the number of machines $\ell$ must satisfy $\ell \geq \frac{\log \Delta}{\log(2s+1)}$ i.e. $\ell = \Omega(\log \Delta)$. On the other hand, for a constant number $\ell$ of machines, $s$ has to satisfy $2s + 1 \geq \Delta^{1/\ell}$, i.e. $s = \Omega(\Delta^{1/\ell})$.

The lower bound on $\Delta$ clearly holds also for the case where the optimal off-line algorithm is allowed to use $m_1 > 1$ machines. Consider a $k$-machine algorithm that always succeeds in building a feasible schedule ($k = \ell/m_1$), then $k$ satisfies $k = \Omega(\log \Delta/m)$ for constant $s$. Finally, $s$ satisfies $s = \Omega(\Delta^{1/mk})$ for constant $k$.

## 5 Conclusions and Open Problems

We have presented an algorithm for minimizing the flow time on $\ell$ identical machines with competitive ratio $O(\min(\Delta^{1/\ell}, n^{1/\ell}))$ against an optimal off-line algorithm on a single machine, and we have shown a lower bound of $\Omega\left(\frac{\min(n^{1/\ell}, \Delta^{1/\ell})}{(12\ell)^\ell}\right)$ on the competitive ratio of any algorithm, even against an adversary on one machine. For every constant $\ell$, this gives an exact trade-off between the amount of resource augmentation and the number of on-line machines.

An interesting remaining open problem is to find an algorithm which is optimally competitive against an off-line algorithm on a single machine for any $\ell$.

**Acknowledgements.** We thank Kirk Pruhs for helpful discussions.

## References

1. B. Awerbuch, Y. Azar, S. Leonardi, and O. Regev. Minimizing the flow time without migration. In *Proceedings of the 31st Annual ACM Symposium on Theory of Computing*, pages 198–205, 1999.
2. A. Borodin and R. El-Yaniv. *Online Computation and Competitive Analysis*. Cambridge University Press, 1998.
3. M. L. Dertouzos and A. K.-L. Mok. Multiprocessor on-line scheduling of hard-real-time tasks. *IEEE Transactions on Software Engineering*, 15:1497–1506, 1989.

4. A. Goel, M. R. Henzinger, S. Plotkin and E. Tardos. Scheduling Data Transfers in a Network and the Set Scheduling Problem. In *Proceedings of the 31st Annual ACM Symposium on Theory of Computing*, 1999.
5. J.A. Hoogeveen and A.P.A. Vestjens. Optimal on-line algorithms for single-machine scheduling. In *Proc. 5th Int. Conf. Integer Programming and Combinatorial Optimization*, LNCS, pages 404–414. Springer, 1996.
6. B. Kalyanasundaram and K. Pruhs. Speed is as powerful as clairvoyance. In *Proceedings of 36th IEEE Symposium on Foundations of Computer Science*, pages 214–221, 1995.
7. H. Kellerer, T. Tautenhahn, and G.J.Woeginger. Approximability and nonapproximability results for minimizing total flow time on a single machine. In *Proc. 28th ACM Symposium on the Theory of Computing*, pages 418–426, 1996.
8. S. Leonardi and D. Raz. Approximating total flow time on parallel machines. In *Proc. 29th ACM Symposium on the Theory of Computing*, pages 110–119, 1997.
9. Cynthia A. Philips, Cliff Stein, Eric Torng, and Joel Wein. Optimal time-critical scheduling via resource augmentation. In *Proceedings of the 29th ACM Symposium on Theory of Computing*, pages 140–149, 1997.
10. A.P.A. Vestjens. *On-line Machine Scheduling.* PhD thesis, Technical University Eindhoven, 1997.
11. A. C. Yao. Probabilistic computations: Towards a unified measure of complexity. In *Proc. 12th ACM Symposium on Theory of Computing*, 1980.

# New Results for Path Problems in Generalized Stars, Complete Graphs, and Brick Wall Graphs*

Thomas Erlebach and Danica Vukadinović

Computer Engineering and Networks Laboratory (TIK)
ETH Zürich, CH-8092 Zürich, Switzerland
{erlebach,vukadin}@tik.ee.ethz.ch

**Abstract.** Path problems such as the maximum edge-disjoint paths problem, the path coloring problem, and the maximum path coloring problem are relevant for resource allocation in communication networks, in particular all-optical networks. In this paper, it is shown that maximum path coloring can be solved optimally in polynomial time for bidirected generalized stars, even in the weighted case. Furthermore, the maximum edge-disjoint paths problem is proved *NP*-hard for complete graphs (undirected or bidirected), and a constant-factor approximation algorithm is presented. Finally, an open problem concerning the existence of routings that simultaneously minimize the maximum load and the number of colors is solved: an example for a graph and a set of requests is given such that any routing that minimizes the maximum load requires strictly more colors for path coloring than a routing that minimizes the number of colors.

## 1 Introduction

Resource allocation in communication networks leads to challenging optimization problems concerning paths in graphs. We refer to such problems as *path problems*. For example, if a network is to support bandwidth reservation or guaranteed quality of service, resources must be allocated to a connection on all links along some path between its endpoints. If the resource requirements of individual connections are so large that no two connections can share a link, connections must be routed along edge-disjoint paths. Maximizing the number of accepted connection requests then leads naturally to the *maximum edge-disjoint paths problem*.

In all-optical networks with wavelength-division multiplexing, different connections can use the same fiber link simultaneously if their signals are transmitted on different wavelengths. Establishing a connection requires reserving a certain wavelength on all links along a path from the sender to the receiver (assuming that wavelength conversion is not available). Two connections that are routed through the same link (edge) must be assigned different wavelengths.

* Research partially supported by the Swiss National Science Foundation.

R. Freivalds (Ed.): FCT 2001, LNCS 2138, pp. 483–494, 2001.

Wavelengths are conveniently viewed as colors, and the problem of minimizing the number of wavelengths required to establish a given set of connection requests is called the *path coloring problem.* If the number of wavelengths is a hard constraint and the goal is to maximize the number of accepted connections using only the available wavelengths, the *maximum path coloring problem* is obtained.

For path problems of this type, no approximation algorithms with good approximation ratio are known for general network topologies. Therefore, investigating these problems for specific classes of graphs (where better ratios can often be obtained) is an interesting field of research. In this paper, we present various new results concerning path problems in specific classes of graphs.

**Preliminaries.** The communication network is modeled as a graph $G = (V, E)$. $G$ can be an undirected graph or a directed graph. An important subclass of directed graphs are the *bidirected graphs.* These are directed graphs for which $(u, v) \in E$ implies $(v, u) \in E$. All of the path problems defined in the following can be studied for undirected paths in undirected graphs and for directed paths in directed graphs or bidirected graphs. We consider only undirected graphs and bidirected graphs.

A *request* is given by a pair $(u, v)$ of vertices in $G$. In the directed case, the request $(u, v)$ asks for a directed path from $u$ to $v$ in $G$. In the undirected case, the order of $u$ and $v$ does not matter, and the request $(u, v)$ just asks for an undirected path with endpoints $u$ and $v$ in $G$. Now we can define the following path problems.

**Path coloring (PC):** Given a graph $G = (V, E)$ and a list $R$ of requests in $G$, assign paths and colors to the requests in $R$ such that paths receive different colors if they share an edge. Minimize the number of colors used.

**Maximum path coloring (MaxPC):** Given a graph $G = (V, E)$, a list $R$ of requests in $G$, and a number $k$ of available colors, compute a subset $R'$ of $R$ and assign paths and colors to the requests in $R'$ such that paths sharing an edge receive different colors and at most $k$ colors are used. Maximize $|R'|$.

**Maximum edge-disjoint paths (MEDP):** Given a graph $G = (V, E)$ and a list $R$ of requests in $G$, compute a subset $R'$ of $R$ and assign edge-disjoint paths to the requests in $R'$. Maximize $|R'|$.

Note that MEDP is the special case of MaxPC for $k = 1$. For MEDP and MaxPC, it is also meaningful to consider a weighted version of the problem: each request $r$ has a certain weight $w_r$, and the goal is to maximize the sum of the weights of the requests in $R'$.

For PC, an algorithm is a $\rho$-approximation algorithm if it runs in polynomial time and uses at most $\rho \cdot OPT$ colors, where $OPT$ is the number of colors used in an optimal solution. For MEDP and MaxPC, an algorithm is a $\rho$-approximation algorithm if it runs in polynomial time and accepts at least $OPT/\rho$ requests, where $OPT$ is the number of requests accepted in an optimal solution. For the weighted version, the definition is analogous. If an algorithm is a $\rho$-approximation algorithm, we say that it achieves *approximation ratio* $\rho$.

For a given list $R$ of requests in a graph $G = (V, E)$, we call any assignment of valid paths to the requests in $R$ a *routing*. For each routing $\phi$, the *maximum load* $L(G, \phi)$ is the maximum number of paths going through the same edge. By $L^*(G, R)$ we denote the maximum load of that routing for $R$ in $G$ that minimizes the maximum load. For a routing $\phi$, we denote by $\chi(G, \phi)$ the minimum number of colors required to color the paths in $\phi$. By $\chi(G, R)$ we denote the minimum of $\chi(G, \phi)$ over all routings $\phi$ for $R$ in $G$.

A *star* with $n$ nodes is a graph consisting of one node $c$ in the center and $n-1$ nodes adjacent to $c$ but not adjacent to each other. A *generalized star* is the graph obtained from a star by replacing each edge by a path of arbitrary length. These paths are called *legs*, and generalized stars are also called *spiders*. A *complete graph* is a graph in which every pair of vertices is joined by an edge. The bidirected versions of these graphs are obtained by replacing each undirected edge by two directed edges with opposite directions.

**Previous Work.** The path problems defined above have been studied intensively during the past few years, both for arbitrary directed and undirected graphs as well as for specific classes of graphs. A comprehensive introduction to edge-disjoint paths problems along with several approximation results can be found in [12]. For arbitrary directed graphs, it is known that unless $P = NP$ no approximation algorithm for MEDP with ratio $O(m^{\frac{1}{2}-\varepsilon})$ can exist for any $\varepsilon > 0$, where $m$ is the number of edges of the graph [10].

The MaxPC problem can be solved optimally in polynomial time for undirected or bidirected chains, because there it is equivalent to the maximum $k$-colorable induced subgraph problem for interval graphs [4].

Path coloring has been studied for chains, trees, rings, meshes, and complete graphs, for example. Surveys of known results can be found in [3,11,8]. For bidirected generalized stars, it was shown that PC can be solved optimally in polynomial time and that the optimal number of colors is equal to the maximum load [7]. For complete graphs, an $O(1)$-approximation algorithm for call scheduling, a generalization of path coloring, is given in [5].

**Our Results.** In Section 2, we prove that the weighted version of MaxPC can be solved optimally in polynomial time for bidirected generalized stars. Bidirected generalized stars are the first class of graphs besides chains and bidirected stars for which MaxPC is proved to be solvable in polynomial time. In Section 3, we show that MEDP is $NP$-hard for complete graphs, and we give a constant-factor approximation algorithm for this problem. In Section 4, we solve an open problem that was stated in [3] and [8] by constructing a list $R$ of requests in a bidirected graph $G$ such that $L^*(G, R) = 2$ and any routing with maximum load 2 requires strictly more colors for path coloring than the routing that minimizes the number of colors (for which the maximum load is 3).

## 2 Weighted MaxPC in Generalized Stars

Let $G = (V, E)$ be a bidirected generalized star with $\ell$ legs and let $c$ denote the center of $G$. Since the path for a request in $G$ is uniquely determined by its endpoints, we assume that the input consists of $G$, a list $P$ of weighted paths in $G$, and a number $k$ of available colors. The weight of path $p \in P$ is denoted by $w_p$. We give an efficient algorithm that computes a subset $P' \subseteq P$ satisfying $L(G, P') \leq k$ and maximizing the total weight $w(P') = \sum_{p \in P'} w_p$. Since any set of paths with maximum load at most $k$ can be colored with $k$ colors in a generalized star (see [7]), this set $P'$ gives an optimal solution to the weighted version of MaxPC.

Our algorithm works as follows. We transform the weighted MaxPC problem to a minimum cost network flow problem (see [2] for a definition of this problem) in a directed network $G' = (V', E')$. Intuitively, $G'$ is obtained by replacing each leg of $G$ by an in-leg and an out-leg, connecting a new source $s$ to the beginnings of all in-legs, and connecting the endings of all out-legs to a new target $t$. An additional *path edge* is added for each path in $P$. The costs are assigned to the edges in such a way that the path edges used by a min-cost flow of value $\ell k$ from $s$ to $t$ correspond to the paths in an optimal solution to weighted MaxPC. This is a generalization of the technique used to solve the maximum weight $k$-colorable subgraph problem for interval graphs in [4].

A more formal description of the construction follows. An example is shown in Fig. 1 (where $G$ is drawn as an undirected graph for the sake of simplicity). Define $V' = V^{\text{in}} \cup V^{\text{out}} \cup \{c, s, t\}$, where $V^{\text{in}}$ (resp. $V^{\text{out}}$) contains one copy $v^{\text{in}}$ (resp. one copy $v^{\text{out}}$) of every vertex $v \in V \setminus \{c\}$, and $s$ and $t$ are two new vertices. Edges of $G$ that are directed towards the center are called *inward-edges*, edges directed away from the center *outward-edges*. A leg of $G$ with vertices $v_1, v_2, \ldots, v_j, c$ (listed from the leaf towards the center) creates an in-leg and an out-leg in $G'$. The in-leg consists of the edges $(v_1^{\text{in}}, v_2^{\text{in}})$, $(v_2^{\text{in}}, v_3^{\text{in}})$, $\ldots$, $(v_j^{\text{in}}, c)$. The out-leg has the edges $(c, v_j^{\text{out}})$, $(v_j^{\text{out}}, v_{j-1}^{\text{out}})$, $\ldots$, $(v_2^{\text{out}}, v_1^{\text{out}})$. In addition, we have edges $(s, v^{\text{in}})$ and $(v^{\text{out}}, t)$ in $G'$ for all leaves $v$ of $G$. All edges of $G'$ introduced so far are called *regular edges* and have capacity $k$ and cost 0.

Finally, we add a *path edge* $e_p$ to $G'$ for every path $p \in P$. Assume that $p$ starts at $u$ and ends at $v$. If the first edge of $p$ is an inward-edge, the tail of $e_p$ is $u^{\text{in}}$. If $p$ starts at $c$, the tail of $e_p$ is $c$. If $p$ does not start at $c$ and the first edge of $p$ is an outward-edge, the tail of $e_p$ is $u^{\text{out}}$. The head of $e_p$ is defined in an analogous way. Intuitively, this definition ensures that the path in $G'$ from the tail of $e_p$ to the head of $e_p$ using only regular edges corresponds to the path $p$ in $G$. The path edge $e_p$ corresponding to path $p \in P$ has capacity 1 and cost $-w_p$.

**Lemma 1.** *The minimum cost of a flow of value $\ell k$ from $s$ to $t$ in $G'$ is equal to the negative of the weight of an optimal solution to weighted MaxPC in $G$.*

*Proof.* Note that there is always a minimum cost flow for which the flow on all edges is integral. We prove that a solution $P'$ to weighted MaxPC with total weight $w(P')$ can be transformed into an integral flow of value $\ell k$ and cost $-w(P')$ in $G'$, and vice versa. Assume that a solution $P'$ to weighted MaxPC is given. Assign flow 1 to all path edges $e_p$ for $p \in P'$ and flow 0 to all path edges $e_q$ for $q \in P \setminus P'$. It is easy to see that the flow on the regular edges can

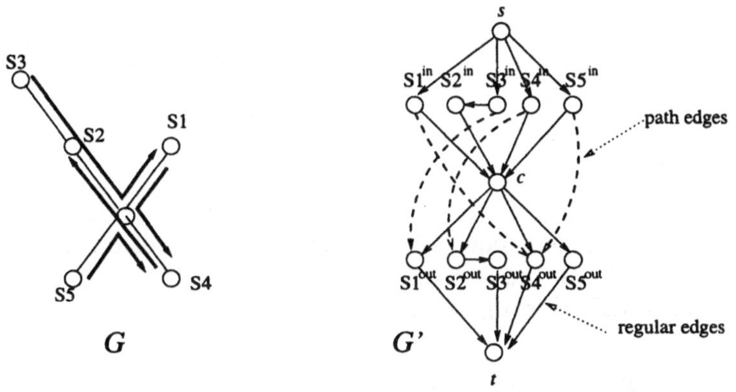


**Fig. 1.** The generalized star $G$ and the corresponding flow network $G'$.

be adjusted so that a valid flow from $s$ to $t$ of value $\ell k$ is obtained: the flow on edges incident to $s$ or $t$ is set to $k$, and the flow on one of the other regular edges $e$ is set to $k - L_e(G, P')$, where $L_e(G, P')$ is the number of paths in $P'$ that contain $e$.

Now assume that an integral flow $f$ of value $\ell k$ and cost $C$ in $G'$ is given. Since $s$ and $t$ have $\ell$ outgoing resp. incoming edges of capacity $k$, the flow on each of these edges must be equal to $k$. Intuitively, we have a flow of value exactly $k$ flowing into each in-leg and out of each out-leg. Let $P'$ be the set of paths corresponding to the path edges with flow 1. Obviously, we have $w(P') = -C$. We claim that $L(G, P') \leq k$, implying that $P'$ is a feasible solution to weighted MaxPC. Assume for a contradiction that $L_e(G, P') > k$ for some edge $e$ of $G$. Assume that $e$ is an outward-edge. (The case for inward-edges is analogous.) Then a total amount of flow larger than $k$ reaches the part of the out-leg containing $e$ that lies between $e$ and the ending of that out-leg. Since only flow at most $k$ can flow out of the out-leg, this contradicts the assumption that we had a valid flow. Therefore, $L_e(G, P') > k$ cannot occur, and $P'$ must be a feasible solution. □

From Lemma 1 and its proof it is clear that weighted MaxPC in bidirected generalized stars can be reduced (in linear time) to the min-cost network flow problem in acyclic directed graphs with integer capacities. Since the latter problem can be solved efficiently (see, e.g., [14]), we obtain the following theorem.

**Theorem 1.** *There exists an efficient optimal algorithm for weighted MaxPC in bidirected generalized stars.*

## 3 MEDP in Complete Graphs

We consider MEDP in complete graphs. For a given list $R$ of requests, the goal is to select a largest subset of $R$ and connect the pairs in the subset along edge-disjoint paths. Multiple occurrence of the same pair in $R$ is allowed; otherwise, the problem is trivial since each request in $R$ can be routed along its direct edge. We prove that this problem is $NP$-hard, and we propose a simple constant-factor approximation algorithm.

### 3.1 NP-Completeness

The problem of deciding for a given list of requests in a graph whether *all* requests can be established along edge-disjoint paths is called the *edge-disjoint paths problem* (EDP). In this section we prove that EDP in complete graphs is $NP$-complete. As MEDP is a generalization of EDP, this implies that MEDP is $NP$-hard.

**Theorem 2.** *EDP in complete graphs is NP-complete, both in the undirected case and in the bidirected case.*

*Proof.* First, we give the proof for the undirected case. We present a reduction from EDP in arbitrary graphs, which is known to be $NP$-complete [6], to EDP in complete graphs. Let an instance $I$ of EDP in arbitrary graphs be given by an undirected graph $H = (V, E)$ and a list $R$ of requests. Take $G$ to be the complete graph with vertex set $V$. Let $F$ denote the edge set of $G$. Let $R'$ be the list of requests consisting of one request $(u, v)$ for every edge $\{u, v\}$ in $F \setminus E$. Thus, $R'$ contains $|F| - |E|$ requests. By $R \circ R'$ we denote the concatenation of the lists $R$ and $R'$. Let $I'$ be the instance of EDP in complete graphs given by the graph $G$ and the list of requests $R \circ R'$. Obviously, $I'$ can be constructed from $I$ in polynomial time. We claim that $I'$ is a yes-instance if and only if $I$ is a yes-instance. This is proved as follows.

Assume that $I$ is a yes-instance, i.e., all requests in $R$ can be routed in $H$ along edge-disjoint paths. Then a solution to $I'$ is obtained by routing the requests in $R$ in the graph $G$ in the same way as in $H$ and routing each request in $R'$ using the direct edge connecting the endpoints of that request. Thus, $I'$ is also a yes-instance in this case.

For the other direction, assume that $I'$ is a yes-instance. Let $\phi$ be a routing of the requests in $R \circ R'$ along edge-disjoint paths in $G$. If each request in $R'$ is routed using the direct edge connecting the endpoints of that request, the paths assigned to the requests in $R$ must be contained in $H$ and, therefore, provide a solution to $I$. Now assume that some request $(u, v)$ in $R'$ is not routed along the edge $\{u, v\}$ by the routing $\phi$. If the edge $\{u, v\}$ is not used by $\phi$ at all, we can simply reroute the request $(u, v)$ to use the edge $\{u, v\}$. If some other request $r$ is routed through edge $\{u, v\}$ by $\phi$, we can replace the edge $\{u, v\}$ on the path assigned to $r$ by the path from $u$ to $v$ assigned to $(u, v)$ by $\phi$ (if the resulting path is not a simple path, discard all loops). Then the request $(u, v)$ can be rerouted using the edge $\{u, v\}$, and the resulting set of paths is still edge-disjoint. This operation can be repeated until all requests in $R'$ are routed along the direct connections. Then the argument above can be applied, showing again that $I$ is a yes-instance.

Therefore, the above construction constitutes a polynomial-time reduction from EDP in arbitrary graphs to EDP in complete graphs, showing that EDP in complete graphs is *NP*-complete. (It is easy to see that the problem EDP is contained in *NP*.)

For the bidirected case, a reduction from EDP in arbitrary directed graphs (which is also known to be *NP*-complete, even if only two requests are given) can be obtained in the same way: the requests in $R'$ are used to ensure that the requests in $R$ must be routed along edges of the given directed graph. □

### 3.2 A Constant-Factor Approximation Algorithm

Let $G = (V, E)$ be an undirected complete graph with $n$ nodes. Split $V$ into three parts, $A, B$ and $C$ of roughly equal size. For the sake of simplicity, we assume in the following that $n$ is a multiple of 6. Then we have $|A| = |B| = |C| = \frac{n}{3}$.

We partition the given list $R$ of requests into three disjoint lists $S_1 = \{(s_i, t_i) \mid s_i, t_i \in B \vee s_i \in A, t_i \in B \vee s_i \in B, t_i \in A\}$, $S_2 = \{(s_i, t_i) \mid s_i, t_i \in C \vee s_i \in B, t_i \in C \vee s_i \in C, t_i \in B\}$ and $S_3 = \{(s_i, t_i) \mid s_i, t_i \in A \vee s_i \in A, t_i \in C \vee s_i \in C, t_i \in A\}$. Note that $S_1$ contains no request with an endpoint in $C$, $S_2$ contains no request with an endpoint in $A$, and $S_3$ contains no request with an endpoint in $B$. We will run an algorithm for each list independently and then choose the largest of the three solutions. In this way we lose at most a factor of 3, i.e., we get a $3c$-approximation for MEDP in complete graphs provided that the algorithm for each list is a $c$-approximation algorithm. This is because at least one third of the paths in the optimal solution must connect requests in the same list.

In the following, we focus on the algorithm for one list, say $S_1$, and its analysis. Denote with $OPT(S_1, H)$ the number of paths in an optimal solution for $S_1$ in graph $H$ and with $ALG(S_1, H)$ the number of paths in the solution computed by an algorithm $ALG$.

Now transform $G$ into $G' = (V', E')$ in the following way: merge all nodes from $C$ into one node $c_m$, and let $V' = A \cup B \cup \{c_m\}$. For all $v \in A \cup B$ there is an edge $\{v, c_m\}$ in $E'$ with capacity $n$. View $S_1$ as a list of requests in the star $G'$, and consider the problem of determining a largest subset $S'$ of $S_1$ such that no edge of $G'$ is used by more than $n$ paths. We claim that an optimal solution for this problem is at least as large as an optimal solution for $S_1$ in $G$.

**Lemma 2.** $OPT(S_1, G') \geq OPT(S_1, G)$

*Proof.* We show that any solution in $G$ can be transformed into a solution in $G'$ of the same cardinality. Let $\phi_G(S_1)$ be a feasible routing for a subset of $S_1$ in $G$. For each path $p_i \in \phi_G(S_1)$ that connects some $s_i$ and $t_i$, we take the path in $G'$ of length 2 from $s_i$ to $t_i$ with intermediate node $c_m$. All these paths constitute a routing $\phi_{G'}(S_1)$ in $G'$. Every node in $G$ has degree $n-1$, thus there can be at most $n-1$ paths in $\phi_G(S_1)$ with the same endpoint. On the other hand, the edge capacities in $G'$ are set to $n$, so we can realize all requests in $\phi_G(S_1)$ in $G'$ without exceeding an edge capacity. Thus $|\phi_G(S_1)| = |\phi_{G'}(S_1)|$. □

Now transform $G'$ into $G''$ by reducing the edge capacities to $\frac{n}{6}$. We claim that an optimal solution for $S_1$ in $G''$ is at least a constant fraction of the optimal solution for $S_1$ in $G'$.

**Lemma 3.** $OPT(S_1, G'') \geq \frac{OPT(S_1,G')}{9}$

*Proof.* The paths in the optimal solution $S^*$ for $S_1$ in $G'$ can be partitioned into $\frac{3n}{2}$ classes of edge-disjoint paths in $G'$. This can be done by edge-coloring the corresponding multigraph containing a vertex for every node in $A \cup B$ and an edge $\{u, v\}$ for every path with endpoints $u$ and $v$ in $S^*$. This multigraph has degree at most $n$. We apply the following classical result due to Shannon [13] on the edge-coloring of multigraphs: Any multigraph can be edge-colored with $\frac{3}{2}\delta_{max}$ colors, where $\delta_{max}$ is the maximum degree of a node in the multigraph. By taking the $\frac{n}{6}$ of these $\frac{3n}{2}$ color classes containing the most paths, we obtain a solution in $G''$ with cardinality at least $OPT(S_1, G')\frac{\frac{n}{6}}{\frac{3n}{2}} = OPT(S_1, G')/9$. □

Furthermore, we can show that a simple greedy algorithm achieves approximation ratio 2 for $S_1$ in $G''$. This greedy algorithm, called *GR*, considers the requests from $S_1$ in arbitrary order and accepts each path if its acceptance does not exceed the edge capacities.

**Lemma 4.** $GR(S_1, G'') \geq \frac{OPT(S_1,G'')}{2}$

*Proof.* Since each path uses only two edges of $G''$, each path accepted by the greedy algorithm can block at most two paths from the optimal solution. □

**Lemma 5.** *There exists an algorithm computing a solution for $S_1$ in $G$ containing at least $\frac{OPT(S_1,G)}{18}$ paths.*

*Proof.* The proof follows from Lemmas 2–4 and the fact that the output of the greedy algorithm for $S_1$ in $G''$ can be transformed into a solution in $G$ of the same cardinality as follows. Let *Greedy*$(S_1, G'')$ be the output of the greedy algorithm. Consider the requests $(s, t)$ in *Greedy*$(S_1, G'')$ in arbitrary order. For request $(s, t)$, find a vertex $v \in C$ such that the edges $\{s, v\}$ and $\{v, t\}$ are not yet used by any other path, and add $(s, t)$ with assigned path $s$–$v$–$t$ to the solution. Such a vertex $v$ can always be found, because $\{s, v\}$ and $\{v, t\}$ are only used by requests with endpoints $s$ or $t$, and *Greedy*$(S_1, G'')$ contains at most $2(\frac{n}{6} - 1) < \frac{n}{3}$ such requests besides $(s, t)$. Note that $C$ contains $\frac{n}{3}$ vertices. □

Since we have an 18-approximation algorithm for each of the lists $S_1$, $S_2$, $S_3$ by Lemma 5, we obtain a 54-approximation algorithm for MEDP in undirected complete graphs by running the algorithm for the individual lists and taking the largest of the three solutions.

In fact, the problem for $S_1$ in $G''$ can be solved optimally in polynomial time: if the list $S_1$ of requests is transformed into a multigraph $M$ similar to the proof of Lemma 3, then the optimal solution in $G''$ corresponds to a subgraph of $M$ with maximum degree $\frac{n}{6}$ such that the number of edges in $M$ is maximized. This problem is a special case of the capacitated $b$-matching problem, which can be solved optimally in polynomial time (see [9, pp. 257–259]), even in the weighted case. If we apply this algorithm instead of the greedy algorithm, we get an optimal solution for each list $S_i$ in the corresponding graph $G''$. So we avoid losing a factor of 2 (Lemma 4) in the approximation ratio and obtain approximation ratio 27 instead of 54. This works also in the weighted case.

Furthermore, our algorithm can be adapted to the bidirected case without any difficulties. In fact, the approximation ratio gets better, since the edges of a bipartite multigraph can always be colored with $\delta_{max}$ colors. Thus, the factor in Lemma 3 becomes 6 instead of 9, giving approximation ratio 18 in this case.

**Theorem 3.** *There is a 27-approximation algorithm for the weighted version of MEDP in undirected complete graphs and an 18-approximation algorithm for bidirected complete graphs.*

Finally, we remark that our analysis can be used to show that the natural *shortest-path-first greedy algorithm* also gives approximation ratio $O(1)$ for MEDP in complete graphs. This algorithm works as follows: As long as one of the given requests can still be routed without intersecting a previously accepted path, select a request that can be routed along a path using the smallest possible number of edges and accept it. Repeat this until all remaining requests are blocked by the accepted paths. In a complete graph, this algorithm will first accept requests that it can route using only one edge, then requests that it can route using two edges, and so on. The proof of Lemma 5 shows that there always exists a solution $S$ that uses only paths of length at most two and whose cardinality is a constant fraction of the cardinality of the optimal solution. We can compare the solution computed by the shortest-path-first greedy algorithm with this solution $S$. Each time the algorithm adds a path of length at most two to the solution, this blocks at most two paths from $S$. By the time the algorithm starts to consider paths of length longer than two, all paths from $S$ must be blocked. Therefore, the solution computed by the algorithm has cardinality at least $|S|/2$.

## 4 Minimizing the Load versus the Number of Colors

The following question is stated as Question 4 in [3] and as Open Problem 3.1 in [8].

> *Does there always exist, for every set $R$ of requests in a bidirected graph $G$, a routing $\phi$ with $L(G,\phi) = L^*(G,R)$ and $\chi(G,\phi) = \chi(G,R)$?*

We solve this open question by giving a negative answer: we give a list of requests $R$ in a bidirected graph $G$ such that the optimal routing with respect to the maximum load differs from the optimal routing with respect to the number of colors. The construction makes use of a variant of the *brick wall graph*, which is a graph similar to the two-dimensional mesh, but with internal vertices of degree 3 instead of 4. Brick wall graphs have been used in [1] to prove extremal results concerning path coloring problems.

More precisely, the graph $G$ consists of a brick wall part with vertices $s_1$, $s_2, \ldots, s_k$ on the left boundary (numbered from top to bottom) and with vertices

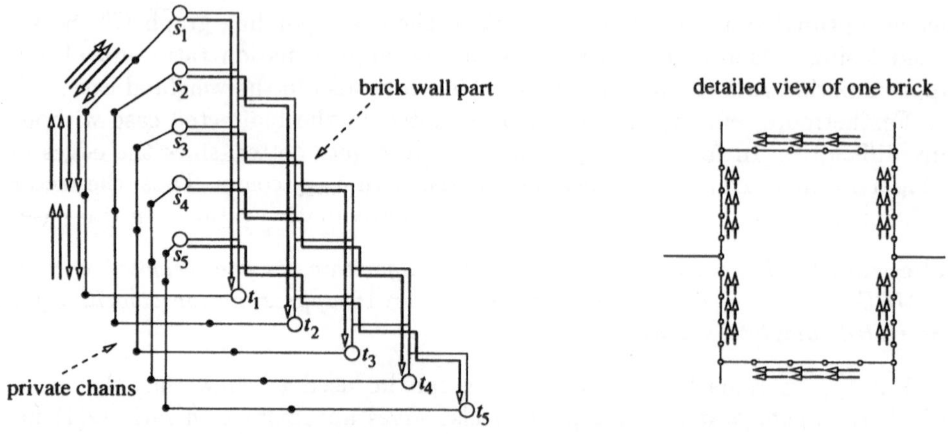


**Fig. 2.** The graph consisting of brick wall part and private chains. The canonical paths for the short requests are shown only on the private chain from $s_1$ to $t_1$. The right-hand side shows an enlarged view of one "brick" and its short requests.

$t_1, t_2, \ldots, t_k$ on the bottom boundary (numbered from left to right), as well as separate chains from $s_i$ to $t_i$ for $i = 1, \ldots, k$, which we call *private chains.* The list $R$ of requests contains the requests $(s_i, t_i)$ for $i = 1, \ldots, k$ as well as additional *short requests* that we will specify below. For $k = 5$, the construction is illustrated in Fig. 2, where $G$ is shown as an undirected graph for the sake of simplicity. The construction can be generalized to arbitrary values of $k$.

The idea of the construction is that the requests $(s_i, t_i)$ can either be routed in the brick wall part of $G$, giving the smallest possible maximum load 2 but requiring $k$ colors for path coloring, or along the private chains, giving a higher load (because of the short requests that we will add) but requiring the smallest possible number of colors.

For $i = 1, \ldots, k$, the private chain from $s_i$ to $t_i$ has the four vertices $r_{i1}$, $r_{i2}$, $r_{i3}$, and $r_{i4}$ between $s_i$ and $t_i$. We add to $R$ two copies of each of the three short requests $(r_{i1}, r_{i2})$, $(r_{i2}, r_{i3})$, and $(r_{i3}, r_{i4})$. These are six short requests in total. We also add the reverse short requests for these six requests. The short requests are illustrated for the private chain from $s_1$ to $t_1$ in Fig. 2.

Each "edge" between two nodes of degree 3 in the brick wall part of the graph is in fact a chain with 4 internal nodes. On each chain corresponding to a horizontal "edge" of the brick wall, we add six short requests from right to left in the same way as for the private chains. On each chain corresponding to a vertical "edge", we add six short requests directed upward. See the right-hand side of Fig. 2.

In total, $R$ contains the $k$ requests from $s_i$ to $t_i$, $i = 1, \ldots, k$, as well as 12 short requests on each of the $k$ private chains and 6 short requests on each "edge" of the brick wall part.

We refer to the routing of a short request along the direct edge connecting its endpoints as the *canonical routing* for that request. If three or more of the six short requests with the same direction on a chain, say on the private chain from $s_i$ to $t_i$, are *not* routed in the canonical way, the load on the edge $(r_{i1}, s_i)$ will be at least 3. If at most two of the short requests are *not* routed in the canonical way, one of the edges $(r_{ij}, r_{i(j+1)})$ must have load 2 already because of the two short requests corresponding to the edge. Therefore, we can state the following fact.

**Fact 1.** *Let $\phi$ be an arbitrary routing of $R$ in $G$ with maximum load 2. Consider a chain from $x$ to $y$ on which six short requests are contained in $R$ in the direction from $x$ to $y$. Then no other request can be routed along this chain in the direction from $x$ to $y$.*

**Theorem 4.** *For the instance constructed as described above, we have:*

*(i) For any routing with maximum load $L^*(G, R) = 2$, at least $k$ colors are required to color the paths.*
*(ii) There exists a routing with maximum load 3 such that the paths can be colored with $\chi(G, R) = 3$ colors.*

*Proof.* First, we convince ourselves that $L^*(G, R) = 2$. Obviously, even the short requests on one private chain cannot be routed with maximum load smaller than two. Therefore, $L^*(G, R) \geq 2$. A routing with maximum load 2 is obtained by routing all short requests in the canonical way and routing the requests $(s_i, t_i)$ in the brick wall part of the graph as sketched in Fig. 2.

(i) Let a routing with maximum load 2 be given. By Fact 1, no path for a request $(s_i, t_i)$ can be routed along a private chain (in either direction), nor can it be routed upward or leftward anywhere in the brick wall part of the graph. Therefore, the path for $(s_i, t_i)$ must run from $s_i$ to $t_i$ traveling only to the right and downward. Furthermore, any two of the paths for the requests $(s_i, t_i)$, $i = 1, \ldots, k$, must meet at some vertex of the brick wall and, by construction, this implies that they intersect in an edge. Therefore, the paths for the $k$ requests $(s_i, t_i)$ must receive different colors.

(ii) The routing is obtained as follows. Route all short requests in the canonical way, and route the $k$ requests $(s_i, t_i)$ along the private chain from $s_i$ to $t_i$. The load of the resulting routing is 3. The paths for the requests $(s_i, t_i)$ can all be assigned the same color, and each path for a short request can be assigned one of two other colors in a greedy way. Therefore, three colors suffice. Since no routing exists for which two colors suffice (see (i)), this implies $\chi(G, R) = 3$. □

We remark that the construction can be modified such that no two requests in $R$ are between the same pair of nodes.

Furthermore, note that the construction can be adapted to undirected graphs as follows. Take the undirected graph underlying the bidirected graph used above. For the list of requests, take the $k$ requests $(s_i, t_i)$ as well as six short requests with the same direction on every private chain. The short requests in the other direction and in the brick wall part are no longer required, because two undirected paths crossing in the brick wall part must always share an edge in the undirected case, since all vertices in the brick wall part have degree at most 3. Again, any routing that minimizes the maximum load requires strictly more colors than the routing that optimizes the number of colors.

## References


[1] A. Aggarwal, A. Bar-Noy, D. Coppersmith, R. Ramaswami, B. Schieber, and M. Sudan. Efficient routing in optical networks. *Journal of the ACM*, 46(6):973–1001, November 1996.

[2] R. K. Ahuja, T. L. Magnanti, and J. B. Orlin. *Network Flows: Theory, Algorithms, and Applications.* Prentice Hall, 1993.

[3] B. Beauquier, J.-C. Bermond, L. Gargano, P. Hell, S. Perennes, and U. Vaccaro. Graph problems arising from wavelength-routing in all-optical networks. In *Proceedings of IPPS'97, Second Workshop on Optics and Computer Science (WOCS)*, 1997.

[4] M. C. Carlisle and E. L. Lloyd. On the *k*-coloring of intervals. *Discrete Appl. Math.*, 59:225–235, 1995.

[5] A. Feldmann. On-line call admission for high-speed networks (Ph.D. Thesis). Technical Report CMU-CS-95-201, School of Computer Science, Carnegie Mellon University, Pittsburgh, PA, October 1995.

[6] M. R. Garey and D. S. Johnson. *Computers and Intractability. A Guide to the Theory of NP-Completeness.* W. H. Freeman and Company, New York, 1979.

[7] L. Gargano, P. Hell, and S. Perennes. Colouring paths in directed symmetric trees with applications to WDM routing. In *Proceedings of the 24th International Colloquium on Automata, Languages and Programming ICALP'97*, LNCS 1256, pages 505–515, 1997.

[8] L. Gargano and U. Vaccaro. Routing in all-optical networks: Algorithmic and graph-theoretic problems. In I. Althöfer et al., editors, *Numbers, Information and Complexity*, pages 555–578. Kluwer Academic Publishers, 2000.

[9] M. Grötschel, L. Lovász, and A. Schrijver. *Geometric Algorithms and Combinatorial Optimization.* Springer-Verlag, Berlin, 1988.

[10] V. Guruswami, S. Khanna, R. Rajaraman, B. Shepherd, and M. Yannakakis. Near-optimal hardness results and approximation algorithms for edge-disjoint paths and related problems. In *Proceedings of the 31st Annual ACM Symposium on Theory of Computing STOC'99*, pages 19–28, 1999.

[11] R. Klasing. Methods and problems of wavelength-routing in all-optical networks. Technical Report CS-RR-348, Department of Computer Science, University of Warwick, September 1998. Presented as invited talk at the MFCS'98 Workshop on Communications.

[12] J. Kleinberg. *Approximation algorithms for disjoint paths problems.* PhD thesis, MIT, 1996.

[13] C. E. Shannon. A theorem on coloring lines of a network. *J. Math. Phys.*, 28:148–151, 1949.

[14] R. E. Tarjan. *Data structures and network algorithms.* SIAM, Philadelphia, PA, 1983.

# On Minimizing Average Weighted Completion Time: A PTAS for Scheduling General Multiprocessor Tasks*

Aleksei V. Fishkin, Klaus Jansen[1], and Lorant Porkolab[2]

[1] Institut für Informatik und Praktische Mathematik,
Christian-Albrechts-Universität zu Kiel, Olshausenstrasse 40, 24 098 Kiel, Germany,
{avf,kj}@informatik.uni-kiel.de

[2] Applied Decision Analysis, PricewaterhouseCoopers, 1 Embankment Place, London WC2N 6RH, United Kingdom, lorant.porkolab@uk.pwcglobal.com

**Abstract.** We study the problem of scheduling $n$ independent general multiprocessor tasks on a fixed number of processors, where the objective is to compute a non-preemptive schedule minimizing the average weighted completion time. For each task, its execution time is given as a function of the subset of processors assigned to the task. We propose here a polynomial-time approximation scheme for the problem that computes a $(1+\epsilon)$-approximate solution in $O(n \log n)$ time for any fixed $\epsilon > 0$ accuracy. This provides a generalization and integration of some recent polynomial-time approximation schemes for scheduling jobs on unrelated machines [1,18] and multiprocessor tasks on dedicated processors [2], respectively, with the average weighted completion time objective, since the latter models are included as special cases in our problem.

**Keywords:** Parallel processing, scheduling, multiprocessor tasks.

## 1 Introduction

In this paper we address multiprocessor scheduling problems, where a set of $n$ tasks has to be executed by a set of $m$ processors such that each processor can work on at most one task at a time and a task can (or may need to be) processed simultaneously by several processors. Here we assume that $m$ is fixed and the objective is to minimize the average weighted completion time $\sum w_j C_j$, where $C_j$ denotes the completion time of task $j$. In the *dedicated* variant of this model, denoted by $Pm|fix_j|\sum w_j C_j$, each task requires the simultaneous use of a prespecified set of processors. In the *parallel* variant, denoted by $Pm|size_j|\sum w_j C_j$, the multiprocessor architecture is disregarded and for each task there is given a prespecified number which indicates that the task can be processed by any subset of processors of the cardinality equal to this number. In the *general* model

* Supported in part by DFG - Graduiertenkolleg "Effiziente Algorithmen und Mehrskalenmethoden" and by EU project APPOL "Approximation and On-line Algorithms", IST-1999-14084

R. Freivalds (Ed.): FCT 2001, LNCS 2138, pp. 495–507, 2001.

$Pm|set_j|\sum w_j C_j$, each task can have a number of *alternative modes*, where each processing mode is specified by a subset of processors and the execution time of the task on that particular processor set.

**Previous results:** Variants of these problems have been studied, but the previous research has mainly focused on the objective of minimizing the makespan $C_{\max} = \max_{j=0}^{n-1} C_j$. Regarding the worst-case time complexity, it is known that $P5|size_j|C_{max}$ [11], $P3|fix_j|C_{max}$ [16] and $P3|set_j|C_{max}$ [16] are strongly NP-hard. However, there is a polynomial-time approximation scheme (PTAS) for $Pm|fix_j|C_{\max}$ [3], and there is a PTAS for $Pm|set_j|C_{\max}$ [10,17].

The first PTAS for a strongly NP-hard scheduling problem minimizing the average weighted completion time was given for scheduling jobs on identical parallel machines $P||\sum w_j C_j$ [18]. Then recently it was proved in [1] that there are PTASs for many different variants of classical scheduling problems. These results include scheduling on unrelated parallel machines $Rm||\sum w_j C_j$ [4]. In the multiprocessor setting, in contrast to the makespan objective, only few approximation results are known. Furthermore, they concern only minimizing the sum of completion times: There are a 2-approximation algorithm for $P2|fix_j|\sum C_j$ [8], a 32-approximation algorithm for $P|size_j|\sum C_j$ [20], and - as it was shown recently - a PTAS for $Pm|fix_j|\sum C_j$ [2].

**New results:** The problem of scheduling general multiprocessor tasks $Pm|set_j|\sum w_j C_j$ can be also viewed as a generalization of two well (but mainly independently) studied scheduling problems: scheduling tasks on unrelated parallel machines $Rm||\sum w_j C_j$ and multiprocessor task scheduling with dedicated processors $Pm|fix_j|\sum w_j\, C_j$. In the case of unrelated machines, for each task (job) there are $m$ processing modes, each with a single processor (machine). In the case of dedicated processor sets, each task has only a single processing mode but including (typically) several processors. Since both of the above special cases are strongly NP-hard [7,8] for general weights and $m \geq 2$, even if there are only a constant number of processors, it is natural to study how closely the optimum can be approximated by efficient algorithms.

In this paper, focusing on the case where $m$ is fixed, we integrate many of the above mentioned recent results that have shown the existence of PTASs for the two special cases, by providing the following generalization:

**Theorem 1.** *There is a PTAS for $Pm|set_j|\sum w_j C_j$ that computes, for any fixed $m$ and $\epsilon > 0$ accuracy, a $(1+\varepsilon)$-approximate solution in $O(n \log n)$ time.*

The actual running time of the proposed algorithm depends exponentially on both $m$ and $1/\varepsilon$. However, the above result is, in some sense, the strongest possible one someone can expect. First, it shows the existence of a PTAS for a problem with fixed parameter $m$ that cannot have a fully PTAS [14]. Second, following the ideas in [16] and by using the results [5,6,12] one can prove that both $P|set_j, p_j = 1|C_{max}$ and $P|set_j, p_j = 1|\sum C_j$ cannot be approximated within a factor of $m^{\frac{1}{2}-\varepsilon}$, neither for some $\varepsilon > 0$, unless P=NP; nor for any $\varepsilon > 0$, unless NP=ZPP. Hence, not only the above results cannot be extended or generalized for the general variant where $m$ is not fixed, but even substantially weaker approximation results cannot be expected.

**Our approach:** In this paper we employ a well known idea of *transformations* – simplify instances and schedules with some loss in the objective. We refine some recent approximation techniques developed in [1,9,15]. In order to be able to cope with general multiprocessor tasks, we make adjustments of processing times defining the task profiles and classifying the tasks as huge and tiny. This requires the creation of a sequence of gaps in the schedule, where all processors are idle for a certain period of time. In our approach, we also apply some recent makespan minimization tools from [17] to schedule tasks within single intervals. For handling tiny tasks, we use a linear programming formulation along with some rounding, and observe that in some near optimal schedule tiny tasks of the same profile can be scheduled by Smith's rule [19]. Then, by using the task delaying technique presented in [1], we introduce special *compact instances* in which there is only a constant number of tasks can be potentially scheduled in an interval. The final idea is to use dynamic programming which integrates all the previous components. The obtained PTAS is a combination of the instance transformations and the dynamic programming algorithm.

The paper is organized as follows: In Section 2, we give the definitions and discribe some techniques. In Section 3, we consider the subproblem of scheduling in one subinterval, adopt the PTAS for $Pm|set_j|C_{\max}$ [17], and and discuss some consequences. In Section 4, we present a dynamic programming framework which can be used to integrate all the previous components.

**Remarks:** This work was motivated by [1], where it was also announced that there is a PTAS for scheduling on unrelated parallel machines with release dates $Rm|r_j|\sum w_j C_j$ (to our best knowledge, the full proof of this result has not yet appeared in literature), and our very recent work [13], where we have shown the existence of a PTAS for $Pm|fix_j, r_j|\sum w_j C_j$. Our original goal was to provide a generalization for all previous results on scheduling problems involving a fixed number of processors (machines), release dates and the average weighted completion time objective. In this paper we don't achieve this goal completely, but provide hopefully a major step towards it by presenting a few novel ideas and techniques that might be also of interest for people working on approximation algorithms for other scheduling problems.

## 2 Preliminaries

Formally, for each instance $I$ of our problem we are given sets $\mathcal{T} = \{0, 1, \ldots, n-1\}$ of $n$ tasks and $M = \{1, \ldots, m\}$ of $m$ processors. (Let $2^M$ denote the set of all subsets of $M$.) Each task $j$ has a positive weight $w_j$ and an associated function $p_{\cdot j} : 2^M \longrightarrow \mathbb{R}^+ \cup \{+\infty\}$ that gives the execution time $p_{\mu j}$ of task $j$ in terms of the set of processors $\mu \subseteq M$ which is assigned to $j$. Given the set $\mu(j) \subseteq M$ allotted to task $j$, the processors of $\mu(j)$ are required to execute task $j$

in union and without preemption, i.e. they all have to start processing of task $j$ at some *starting time* $S_j$, and finish at the *completion time* $C_j := S_j + p_{\mu(j)j}$. A feasible schedule $\sigma$ consists of an *allotment* $\mu(j)$ and a starting time $S_j$ for each task $j \in \mathcal{T}$ such that no processor executes more than one task at each time step. Then, the value $C_w(\sigma) := \sum_{j=0}^{n-1} w_j C_j(\sigma)$ is called the *average weighted completion time* of $\sigma$. Here, the number of processors $m$ is considered to be a fixed constant, and the objective is to find a feasible schedule that minimizes the average weighted completion time.

Further, we write $\sigma(I)$ to denote a schedule $\sigma$ with respect to an instance $I$. Accordingly, a schedule $\sigma_{opt}(I)$ is called *optimal* if $C_w(\sigma_{opt}(I)) = OPT(I)$, where $OPT(I)$ is the minimal average weighted completion time for $I$. Given a schedule $\sigma$, a schedule $\sigma'$ is called an *ε-schedule* of $\sigma$ if $C_w(\sigma')/C_w(\sigma) \leq 1 + K\varepsilon$, where $K$ is some constant. We say that one can transform *with* $1 + O(\varepsilon)$ *loss the objective and in polynomial time* an instance $I$ into instance $\tilde{I}$ if the following holds: $\tilde{I}$ is obtained form $I$ in $p(|I|)$ elementary operations for some polynomial $p(\cdot)$, any feasible schedule of $\tilde{I}$ is also feasible of $I$ and, $OPT(\tilde{I})/OPT(I) \leq 1 + K\varepsilon$, where $K$ is some constant.

We will show below that with $1 + O(\varepsilon)$ loss, any instance $I$ of our problem can be transformed in $O(n \log n)$ time into a special *compact* instance $\tilde{I}$ such that one can find in $O(n)$ time an $\epsilon$-schedule of $\sigma_{opt}(\tilde{I})$. Clearly, this suffices to obtain a PTAS for our original problem.

### 2.1 Basic Techniques

For any fixed accuracy $\varepsilon > 0$, we assume w.l.o.g. that $\log_{1+\varepsilon}(1 + \frac{1}{\varepsilon})$ and $\frac{1}{\varepsilon}$ are integral. We partition the time interval $(0, \infty)$ into disjoint intervals $I_x$ of the form $[R_x, R_{x+1})$, where $R_x = (1 + \varepsilon)^x$ and $x \in \mathbb{Z}$. Notation $I_x$ will also be used to refer to the length $\varepsilon R_x$ of the interval, thus $I_x = R_{x+1} - R_x = \varepsilon R_x$ and $I_{x+1} = (1 + \varepsilon) I_x$. For a schedule $\sigma$, let $y(j) \leq z(j)$ be those indices for which $S_j \in I_{y(j)}$ and $C_j \in I_{z(j)}$, respectively.

In this paper, for a given schedule $\sigma$, we always use the constructive method to find $\epsilon$-schedules, i.e. we show directly how tasks can be rescheduled in $\sigma$ without dramatically increasing the value of the objective function. Next, we describe some techniques that will be applied later. Knowing $\sigma$, we construct a new schedule $\sigma'$ as follows:

**Stretching**: Set $\mu'(j) = \mu(j)$ and $S'_j = (1 + \varepsilon) C_j - p_{\mu(j)j}$ for each task $j \in \mathcal{T}$. This generates $\varepsilon p_{\mu(j)j}$ idle time on $\mu(j)$.

**Rearranging**: Set $\mu'(j)$ and $S'_j$ for each task $j \in \mathcal{T}$ such that a new schedule $\sigma'$ is feasible and $z'(j) = z(j)$, i.e. tasks are rescheduled preserving $C'_j \in I_{z(j)}$. This gives us the ability to rearrange tasks inside intervals. Note that at any time then we use this technique we have to specify the way of rearranging.

**Shifting***: Set $\mu'(j) = \mu(j)$ and $S'_j = S_j - R_{y(j)} + R_{y(j)+1}$ for each task $j \in \mathcal{T}$, i.e. in $\sigma'$ we have $y'(j) = y(j) + 1$, and hence the distance between $S_j$ and the beginning of interval $I_{y(j)}$ is preserved. This generates $\varepsilon(R_{z(j)} - R_{y(j)})$ additional idle time on $\mu'(j)$ after the completion time $C'_j$.

**Shifting****: Set $\mu'(j) = \mu(j)$ and $S'_j = S_j - R_{z(j)} + R_{z(j)+1}$ for each task $j \in \mathcal{T}$, i.e. $z'(j) = z(j) + 1$, and hence the distance between $C_j$ and the end of interval $I_{z(j)}$ is preserved. This generates $\varepsilon(R_{z(j)} - R_{y(j)})$ additional idle time on $\mu(j)$ before the start time $S'_j$.

**Proposition 1.** *If a schedule $\sigma'$ is obtained from a schedule $\sigma$ by stretching, rearranging, or both types of shifting then $\sigma'$ is an $\varepsilon$-schedule of $\sigma$.*

The following lemma that will be used throughout the paper.

**Lemma 1.** *For any schedule $\sigma$ there is an $\epsilon$-schedule $\sigma'$ of $\sigma$ such that the following holds in $\sigma'$: each task $j$ starts not earlier than $\varepsilon p_{\mu'(j)j}$; each task $j$ crosses at most a constant number $s^*(\varepsilon) := \log_{1+\varepsilon}(1+\frac{1}{\varepsilon})$ of intervals; each task $j$ with $p_{\mu'(j)j} \leq \varepsilon^2 I_{y'(j)}$ is non-crossing; each crossing task $j$ starts at one of points $R_{y'(j)} + i\varepsilon^2 I_{y'(j)}$ of $I_{y'(j)}$, where $i \in \{0, 1, \ldots, \frac{1}{\varepsilon^2} - 1\}$.*

## 2.2 Blocks, Gaps, and Profiles

A *block* $\mathcal{B}_i$ is a set $\{I_{b(i)}, \ldots, I_{b'(i)}\}$ of consecutive intervals. A *block structure* $\mathcal{B}_1, \mathcal{B}_2, \ldots$ is a sequence of blocks such that any block $\mathcal{B}_i$ is of the length $\delta_i := b'(i) - b(i) + 1$ which is is at least $2s^*(\varepsilon)$ and at most $2\delta(\varepsilon)$, any pair $\mathcal{B}_i$, $\mathcal{B}_{i+1}$ of consecutive blocks shares exactly one interval $I_{b'(i)} = I_{b(i)}$ (i.e. $b'(i) = b(i+1)$) and the total length of these two blocks $\delta_i + \delta_{i+1} \geq \delta(\varepsilon)$, where $\delta(\varepsilon) := \frac{2s(\varepsilon)}{\varepsilon}$. For a schedule $\sigma$, a *gap* is an interval in time where all the processors of $M$ are idle in $\sigma$. The following Lemma shows that with any schedule one can associate a block structure such that there is a gap in the beginning and the end of each block.

**Lemma 2.** *For a schedule $\sigma$ there is an $\epsilon$-schedule $\sigma'$ of $\sigma$ such that there exists a block structure $\mathcal{B}_1, \mathcal{B}_2, \ldots$ for the schedule $\sigma'$ with the property that for each dynamic block $\mathcal{B}_i$ there is a gap in the first interval $I_{b(i)}$. This gap starts at one of the points $R_{b(i)} + \ell\epsilon^2 I_{b(i)}$, $\ell = 1 \ldots, \frac{1}{\epsilon^2} - 1$, and has a length which is at least $\epsilon^2 I_{b(i)}$.*

For an instance $I$ and task $j \in \mathcal{T}$, let $p_j^{\min} := \min_{\mu \in 2^M} p_{\mu j}$ be the minimal processing time needed to execute task $j$. The value $p_j^{\min}$ is called the *length* of $j$. Then, the following holds.

**Lemma 3.** *With $1 + O(\varepsilon)$ loss one can transform in $O(n)$ time an instance $I$ into instance $\tilde{I}$ such that for each task $j \in \mathcal{T}$ and $\mu \in 2^M$ the following holds in $\tilde{I}$: the processing time $\tilde{p}_{\mu j} = (1+\varepsilon)^{\omega_{\mu j}}$, where $\omega_{\mu j} \in \mathbb{N} \cup +\infty$; if $\tilde{p}_{\mu j} \neq \infty$ then $\tilde{p}_{\mu j} \leq h(m, \epsilon)\tilde{p}_j^{\min}$, where $h(m, \varepsilon)$ is a constant that depends on $m$ and $\varepsilon$. Furthermore, in $\tilde{I}$ the quotients $\tilde{p}_j^{\min}/\tilde{w}_j$ are different for all tasks in $\mathcal{T}$.*

For simplicity, we will use the following notations throughout the paper. By using the above Lemma, for a task $j \in \mathcal{T}$, the corresponding $2^m$-tuple $\omega(j) =< \omega_{\mu j} >_{\mu \in 2^M}$ is called the *execution profile* of $j$. Accordingly, the set of all distinct possible execution profiles is denoted by $\Omega := \{\omega(j) \mid j \in \mathcal{T}\}$. Then, it is not hard to prove that the number of profiles in $\Omega$ is bounded by

$$\nu(m,\epsilon) := \lceil 2 + \log_{1+\epsilon} h(m,\epsilon) \rceil^{2^m}.$$

In addition, for a given instance $I$, we introduce an index $x(j)$ for each task $j \in \mathcal{T}$ that corresponds to the interval $I_{x(j)}$ earlier which processing of $j$ can not be started. (By using Lemma 1, we assume that $R_{x(j)} \leq \epsilon p_j^{\min} \leq R_{x(j)+1}$ for each task $j \in \mathcal{T}$. However, we revise this property in Lemma 10.) Accordingly, a task $j$ is called *huge* if $p_j^{\min} \geq \varepsilon^2 I_{x(j)}/q^*$, and *tiny* if $p_j^{\min} < \varepsilon^2 I_{x(j)}/q^*$, where the parameter $q^* = q^*(m,\varepsilon) \gg 2^m h(m,\varepsilon)$ is specified later in Section 3.2. To distinguish sets of huge and tiny tasks we write $\mathcal{HT}$ and $\mathcal{TT}$, respectively.

For a task set $\mathcal{X} \subseteq \mathcal{T}$, we will use $p^{\min}(\mathcal{X}) := \sum_{j\in\mathcal{X}} p_j^{\min}$ to denote the total length of the tasks in $\mathcal{X}$, use $\mathcal{X}^\omega$ to denote the tasks of $\mathcal{X}$ of profile $\omega \in \Omega$, and $\mathcal{X}_x$ to denote the set of tasks $j \in \mathcal{X}$ with $x(j) = x$. To indicate that $\mathcal{X}$ is associated with particular instance $I$, we will write $\mathcal{X}(I)$. Finally, regarding the objective function we use the following.

**Proposition 2.** *For any instance $I$, with at most $1+\epsilon$ loss one can consider the objective function $\sum w_j R_{z(j)}$ instead of the original function $\sum w_j C_j$.*

## 3 Scheduling Inside Interval

In the first part of this section, we consider the problem of scheduling in a single interval $I_x$. More precisely, we present an algorithm that schedules non-crossing tasks with respect to a known schedule of crossing tasks. In order to achieve this, we generalize the PTAS for $Pm|set_j|C_{\max}$ [17]. Basing on some features of the algorithm, we define the value of parameter $q^* = q^*(m,\varepsilon)$ for tiny tasks, and consider the algorithm as a subroutine of the rearranging technique. After that, we show that tiny tasks are all small corresponding to intervals and can be scheduled by Smith's rule [19]. In the last part of this section, we show how an instance of our problem can be transformed into a *compact* instance in which there is only a a constant number of tasks that can be potentially scheduled in an interval.

### 3.1 Long and Short Tasks, Relative Schedules and LP Formulation

Let $\sigma(I)$ be a feasible schedule for instance $I$. For an interval $I_x$ of $\sigma$, the following sets of tasks (running in $I_x$) are defined: set $\mathcal{W}_x$ of non-crossing tasks and set $\mathcal{K}_x = K_x^1 \cup K_x^2 \cup K_x^3$ of crossing tasks, where $K_x^1$ is the set of *incoming* crossing tasks (that complete in $I_x$), $K_x^2$ is the set of *outgoing* tasks (that start in $I_x$), and $K_x^3$ is the set of *throughgoing* tasks (that go through $I_x$). Suppose that we have applied shifting** to $\sigma(I)$ and obtained $\sigma'(I)$. W.l.o.g. assume that in the schedule $\sigma'(I)$ the tasks of $\mathcal{W}_x$ and $\mathcal{K}_x$ run in interval $I_{x+1}$. Then, there is at least $\varepsilon I_x$ idle time on the processors, between the tasks of $\mathcal{W}_x$ and the outgoing tasks of $K_x^2$ or between the tasks of $\mathcal{W}_x$ and the end of interval $R_{x+2}$.

Assume for simplicity that $\mathcal{W}_x = \{0, \ldots, n'\}$ with $p_0^{\min} \geq p_1^{\min} \geq \ldots \geq p_{n'}^{\min}$ and $K_x^3 = \emptyset$. Then, it holds that $p^{\min}(\mathcal{W}_x) \leq mI_x$. Furthermore, we fix allotment $\mu(j)$ for each crossing task $j \in \mathcal{K}_x$ and define $p_{\mu(j)j} := C_j - R_x$ for each task $j \in K_x^1$ and $p_{\mu(j)j} := R_{x+1} - S_j$ for each task $j \in K_x^2$.

Partition $\mathcal{W}_x$ into two subsets $\mathcal{L}_x = \{0, \ldots, k_x - 1\}$ and $\mathcal{S}_x = \mathcal{W}_x \setminus \mathcal{L}_x$, where the appropriate value for $k_x = k_x(m, \varepsilon) \gg 1$ will be specified later in Lemma 6. Tasks in $\mathcal{L}_x$ and $\mathcal{S}_x$ are called *long* and *short*, respectively. Let $\mathcal{J}_x = \mathcal{L}_x \cup \mathcal{K}_x$ be the set of long and crossing tasks.

A *processor assignment* of $\mathcal{J}_x$ is a mapping $\mu_x : \mathcal{J}_x \longrightarrow 2^M$ such that $\mu_x(j) = \mu(j)$ for each task $j \in K_x^1 \cup K_x^2$. Two tasks $T_k$ and $T_\ell$ are called *compatible*, if $\mu_x(k) \cap \mu_x(\ell) = \emptyset$. A *snapshot* of $\mathcal{J}_x$ is a set of compatible tasks of $\mathcal{J}_x$. A *relative schedule* of $\mathcal{J}_x$ is a pair $\mathcal{R}_x$ of a processor assignment $\mu_x$ of $\mathcal{J}_x$ and a sequence of snapshots $\mathcal{M}_1, \ldots, \mathcal{M}_g$ of $\mathcal{J}_x$ with respect to $\mu_x$, such that each task $j \in \mathcal{J}_x$ occurs in a subsequence of consecutive snapshots $\mathcal{M}_{u_j}, \ldots, \mathcal{M}_{v_j}$, $1 \leq u_j \leq v_j \leq g$, where any two consecutive snapshots $\mathcal{M}_\ell$ and $\mathcal{M}_{\ell+1}$ are different and it holds that $u_j = 1$ if $j \in K_x^1$, $v_j = g$ if $j \in K_x^2$ (see Figure 1). Then, it is not hard to see that the number of snapshots $g$ is bounded by $2(k_x+m)$ and the number of different (appropriate) relative schedules of $\mathcal{J}_x$ is bounded by a constant depending only on $m$ and the number $k_x$ of long tasks in $\mathcal{L}_x$.

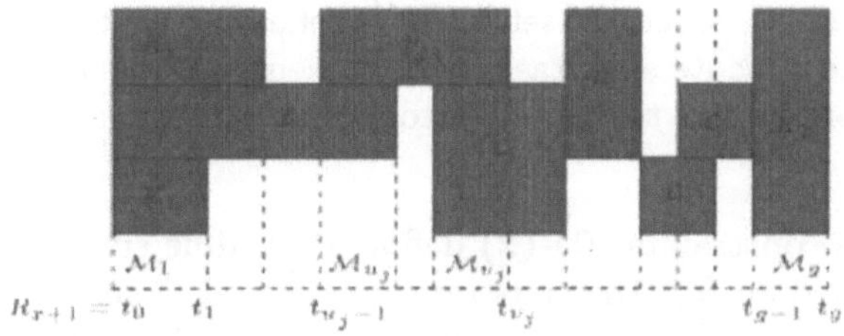


**Fig. 1.** A relative schedule $\mathcal{R}_x$

Given a set $\mu \subseteq M$, a *$\mu$-configuration* $C_\mu$ is a partition of $\mu$ into non-empty sets. Let $N_\mu$ be the total number of $\mu$-configurations and let $C_{1,\mu}, \ldots, C_{N_\mu,\mu}$ be all $\mu$-configurations. Note that $N_M = B(m)$, where $B(m) \leq m!$ is the $m$th Bell number.

Consider a relative schedule $\mathcal{R}_x$, where the processor assignment $\mu_x$ such that no task $j$ in $\mathcal{J}_x$ has the assigned processing time $p_{\mu_x(j)j} = \infty$. Then, let $F_\ell := M \setminus \bigcup_{j \in \mathcal{M}_\ell} \mu_x(j)$ denotes the set of free processors in snapshot $\mathcal{M}_\ell$, $1 \leq \ell \leq g$. For a $\nu(m, \epsilon)$-vector $D := (D^\omega)_{\omega \in \Omega}$, a relative schedule $\mathcal{R}_x$ is called feasible for $D$ if for any $D^\omega \neq 0$ there exists a snapshot $\mathcal{M}_\ell$ in $\mathcal{R}_x$ such that $\mu \subseteq F_\ell$ and $\omega_\mu \neq +\infty$.

Now assume there is a set of tasks $\mathcal{X} \subseteq \mathcal{T}$ such that $p^{\min}(\mathcal{X}^\omega) = D^\omega$ for each profile $\omega \in \Omega$. (Recall that if a task $j \in \mathcal{X}^\omega$ is assigned to a processor set $\mu$, then the processing time of $j$ on $\mu$ is equal to $p_j^{\min}(1+\varepsilon)^{\omega_\mu}$. Thus, if all tasks of $\mathcal{X}^\omega$ are assigned to $\mu$, the total processing time needed to execute them is equal to $D^{\omega}(1+\varepsilon)^{\omega_\mu}$.) Then, in order to find a preemptive schedule of $\mathcal{X}$ with respect to the relative schedule $\mathcal{R}_x$, one can formulate the following linear program $LP(\mathcal{R}_x, D)$ in terms of variables associated with $F_\ell$-configurations:

$$
\begin{array}{lll}
\textbf{Minimize} & t_g - t_0 & \\
\textbf{s.t.} & \textbf{(0)} & t_0 = R_{x+1}, \\
& \textbf{(1)} & t_\ell \geq t_{\ell-1}, \ \ell = 1, \ldots, g, \\
& \textbf{(2)} & t_{v_j} - t_{u_j - 1} = p_{\mu_x(j) j}, \ \forall\, j \in \mathcal{J}_x, \\
& \textbf{(3)} & \sum_{i=1}^{N_{F_\ell}} x_{i,F_\ell} = t_\ell - t_{\ell-1}, \ \ell = 1, \ldots, g, \\
& \textbf{(4)} & \sum_{\ell=1}^{g} \sum_{i\,:\mu \in C_{i,F_\ell}} x_{i,F_\ell} \geq D(\mu) := \sum_\omega D^\omega (1+\varepsilon)^{\omega_\mu} y_{\mu,\omega}, \ \forall\, \mu, \\
& \textbf{(5)} & \sum_\mu y_{\mu,\omega} = 1, \ \forall\, \omega, \\
& \textbf{(6)} & x_{i,F_\ell} \geq 0, \ \ell = 1, \ldots, g, \ i = 1, \ldots, N_{F_l}, \\
& \textbf{(7)} & y_{\mu,\omega} \geq 0, \ \forall\, \omega, \mu,
\end{array}
$$

where the variables have the following interpretation:

$t_\ell$: the time when snapshot $\mathcal{M}_\ell$ ends and $\mathcal{M}_{\ell+1}$ starts. The starting time of the schedule is denoted by $t_0 = R_{x+1}$ and the finishing time by $t_g$ (see Figure 1).

$x_{i,F_\ell}$: the length of the configuration $C_{i,F_\ell}$ in snapshot $\mathcal{M}_\ell$. During an interval of length $x_{i,F_\ell}$ the tasks of $\mathcal{X}$ can be executed on processor subsets $\mu \in C_{i,F_\ell}$,

$y_{\mu,\omega}$: the assignment variable indicating which part of the tasks of $\mathcal{X}^\omega$ is assigned to be executed on a processor set $\mu \in 2^M$, reflecting that the total processing time needed to execute such tasks of $\mathcal{X}^\omega$ is equal to $D^\omega(1+\varepsilon)^{\omega_\mu} y_{\mu,\omega}$,

$D(\mu)$: the total processing time needed to execute the tasks of $\mathcal{X}$ assigned to a processor set $\mu \in 2^M$.

Less formally, the constraints **(0)-(2)** define a schedule structure with respects to the relative schedule $\mathcal{R}_x$, the constraint **(3)** defines a substructure of configurations inside the snapshots of $\mathcal{R}_x$, the constraints **(4)-(5)** define the balance between the free time available in the configurations and the allotment of work that have to be executed in order to complete all tasks. (One can also associate each set $\mathcal{X}^\omega$ with one task of the length $D^\omega$ and think in terms of preemptive scheduling of these $\nu(m,\varepsilon)$ tasks of different profiles such that execution of parts of the same task on different sets in parallel is allowed.)

Let $(t^*, x^*, y^*)$ be an optimum solution of $LP(\mathcal{R}_x, D)$. Then, the following holds [17].

**Lemma 4.** *For any two non-negative $\nu(m,\varepsilon)$-vectors $a$ and $b$ such that a relative schedule $\mathcal{R}_x$ is feasible for $a$ and $a+b$, the following inequality holds*

$$t_g^*(LP(\mathcal{R}_x, a)) \leq t_g^*(LP(\mathcal{R}_x, a+b)) \leq t_g^*(LP(\mathcal{R}_x, a)) + \max_{\omega_\mu \neq \infty, \omega \in \Omega} (1+\varepsilon)^{\omega_\mu} \sum_{\omega \in \Omega} b_\omega .$$

**Lemma 5.** *If a relative schedule $\mathcal{R}_x$ is feasible for the $\nu(m,\varepsilon)$-vector $D = (p^{\min}(S_x^\omega))_{\omega \in \Omega}$, then the optimal value $t_g^* - t_0^*$ of $LP(\mathcal{R}_x, D)$ is not larger than the makespan of any schedule of $\mathcal{J}_x \cup S_x$ that respects the relative schedule $\mathcal{R}_x$.*

### 3.2 Generating a Schedule, Tiny versus Short

Let $(t^*, x^*, y^*)$ be an optimum solution of $LP(\mathcal{R}_x, D)$. We construct a schedule for the tasks in $\mathcal{J}_x$ and $\mathcal{S}_x$ as follows. For each profile $\omega$ and $y^*_{\mu,\omega} > 0$ we select the tasks of $\mathcal{S}_x$ in a greedy manner until the total length does not exceed $y^*_{\mu,\omega} > 0$ (if the total length plus the length of the last selected task exceeds $y^*_{\mu,\omega} > 0$ we mark this task as unbalanced, there can be at most $2^m$ such ones for one profile) and assign them to be executed on the subset $\mu$. After that, starting from the first snapshot, by using the values $x^*_{i,F\ell} > 0$ and accordingly with the subsets $\mu \in C_{i,F_\ell}$, we select the tasks that are assigned to $\mu$ in a greedy manner until their total processing time does not exceed $x^*_{i,F\ell} > 0$. If it happens that for a configuration $C_{i,F_\ell}$ the selected tasks do not fit inside the interval of the length $x^*_{i,F_\ell} > 0$, we increase $x^*_{i,F_\ell} > 0$ by a small amount $\varepsilon_{i,\ell}$, and accordingly, we also adjust the value $t^*_\ell$ by the total increase $\varepsilon_{F_\ell}$ (see Figure 2).

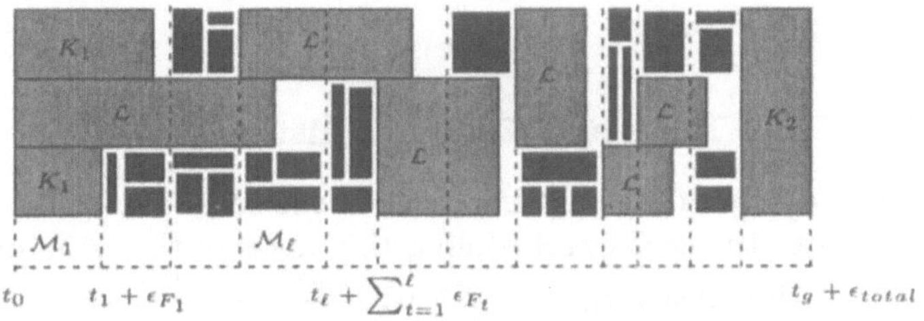


**Fig. 2.** Generating a schedule

Since there are at most $\nu(m,\varepsilon)$ profiles the total number of unbalanced tasks is at most $\nu(m,\varepsilon)2^m$. Furthermore, since the number of snapshots $g \le 2(k_x + m)$ and the number of configurations is bounded by the $m$th Bell number $B(m)$, the total enlargement $\varepsilon_{total}$ is at most

$$h(m,\varepsilon)(p^{\min}_{k_x} + p^{\min}_{k_x+1} + \dots p^{\min}_{k_x+2(k_x+m)B(m)+\nu(m,\varepsilon)2^m-1}),$$

i.e. the maximum processing tasks of the $k_x + 2(k_x+m)B(m) + \nu(m,\varepsilon)2^m$ longest tasks of $\mathcal{S}_x$. The following lemma is a useful tool to select $k_x$ such that $\varepsilon_{total}$ is kept small enough [17]:

**Lemma 6.** *For any interval $I_x$ there is a number $k_x$ with $1 \le k_x \le (q+1)^{\frac{mh(m,\varepsilon)}{\varepsilon^2}-1} + d[1 + (q+1) + \ldots + (q+1)^{\frac{mh(m,\varepsilon)}{\varepsilon^2}-2}]$ such that $h(m,\varepsilon)(p^{\min}_{k_x} + \dots + p^{\min}_{(q+1)k_x+d-1}) \le \varepsilon^2 I_x$, where $q := 3mB(m)$ and $d := \nu(m,\varepsilon)2^m$.*

The final algorithm works as follows: select an appropriate $k_x$, enumerate all relative schedules together with solving LPs and deducing the corresponding schedules, output the schedule with the smallest makespan.

Now, we define $q^*(m,\varepsilon) := \frac{mh(m,\varepsilon)^2 2^m \nu(m,\varepsilon)}{\varepsilon^2}\left((m+1)^{m+2}+1\right)^{\frac{mh(m,\varepsilon)}{\varepsilon^2}}$. By Lemma 1 we may assume that tiny tasks are non-crossing in $\sigma(I)$. Accordingly, let $\mathcal{Y}_x \subseteq \mathcal{W}_x$ be the set of tiny tasks that are non-crossing in $I_x$. Then, the following holds:

**Lemma 7.** *The number $k_x$ of long tasks in $\mathcal{L}_x$ is not larger than the number of non-crossing huge tasks in $I_x$ with $p_j \geq \frac{\varepsilon^2 I_x}{q^*}$. Hence, all tiny tasks are short, i.e. $\mathcal{Y}_x \subseteq \mathcal{S}_x$.*

**Lemma 8.** *Let $\tilde{\mathcal{Y}}_x$ be another set of tiny tasks such that for each profile $\omega \in \Omega$, $p^{\min}(\mathcal{Y}_x^\omega) = 0$ implies $p^{\min}(\tilde{\mathcal{Y}}_x^\omega) = 0$, and $p^{\min}(\mathcal{Y}_x^\omega) \neq 0$ implies either $|p^{\min}(\mathcal{Y}_x^\omega) - p^{\min}(\tilde{\mathcal{Y}}_x^\omega)| \leq \frac{\varepsilon I_x}{2h(m,\varepsilon)\nu(m,\varepsilon)}$ or $p^{\min}(\tilde{\mathcal{Y}}_x^\omega) = 0$. Then algorithm outputs a feasible schedule of $\tilde{W}_x := (\mathcal{W}_x \setminus \mathcal{Y}_x) \cup \tilde{\mathcal{Y}}_x$ inside $I_{x+1}$ with respect to the schedule of $\mathcal{K}_x$ in $\sigma'(I)$.*

*Proof.* The proof follows from Lemmas 4,6,7 and the fact that the interval $I_{x+1}$ contains at least $\varepsilon I_x > \varepsilon^2 I_x + h(m,\varepsilon) \sum_{\omega \in \Omega} \frac{\varepsilon I_x}{2h(m,\varepsilon)\nu(m,\varepsilon)}$ idle time. (Recall that $\max_{\mu \neq \infty, \omega \in \Omega} p_{\mu j} \leq p_j^{\min} h(m,\varepsilon)$.) □

### 3.3 Scheduling Tiny Tasks and Compact Instances

Now consider the problem of placing tiny tasks in the schedule. In the following we restrict ourselves to the case of scheduling tiny tasks of the same profile, say $\omega$. We say that two tiny tasks $k, \ell \in \mathcal{TT}^\omega$ with $\frac{p_k^{\min}}{w_k} < \frac{p_\ell^{\min}}{w_\ell}$ are *scheduled by Smith's rule* in a schedule $\sigma$ if it holds either $z(k) \leq z(\ell)$, or $z(\ell) < x(k)$. In other words, if the two tasks are available at the same interval (that means $\ell$ is not completed before the earliest interval where $k$ can be scheduled), then the task $k$ of smaller value $p_k/w_k$ is scheduled first with respect to intervals. Note that the tasks of $\mathcal{TT}_x^\omega$ have to be scheduled in the order of increasing values $p_j^{\min}/w_j$ [19].

**Lemma 9.** *For a feasible schedule $\sigma(I)$ there is an $\varepsilon$-schedule $\sigma'(I)$ of $\sigma(I)$ such that for any profile $\omega \in \Omega$, the tiny tasks of $\mathcal{TT}^\omega$ are scheduled by Smith's rule in $\sigma'(I)$.*

*Proof.* W.l.o.g. let $I_1$, $I_L$ be the first and the last interval in a feasible schedule $\sigma$. By Lemma 1, assume that all tiny tasks are non-crossing in $\sigma$ and by Lemma 3 all quotients $p_j/w_j$ are different. Let $\mathcal{Y}_x^\omega$ be the set of tiny tasks of profile $\omega$ that are scheduled in interval $I_x$ and let $D^\omega := p^{\min}(\mathcal{Y}_x^\omega)$ be the total length of these tasks in $I_x$. Consider the following $LP(\omega)$:

$$\begin{array}{rl} \textbf{Minimize} & \sum_{j\,:\,j \in \mathcal{TT}^\omega} w_j \sum_{x=x(j)}^{L} y_{j,x} R_x \\ \textbf{s.t.}\ \textbf{(1)} & \sum_{x=x(j)}^{L} y_{j,x} = 1, \quad \forall j \in \mathcal{TT}^\omega, \\ \textbf{(2)} & \sum_{j\,:\,j \in \mathcal{TT}^\omega,\ x(j) \leq x} y_{j,x}\, p_j^{\min} \leq D^\omega, \quad \forall\, I_x, \\ \textbf{(3)} & y_{j,x} \geq 0, \quad \forall j \in \mathcal{TT}^\omega,\ x = x(j), \ldots, L. \end{array}$$

First, one can find a feasible solution of $LP(\omega)$ by assigning the values $y$ with respect to the schedule $\sigma$, i.e. for each task $j \in \mathcal{TT}^\omega$ set $y_{j,x} = 1$ if $z(j) = x$ and

$y_{j,x} = 0$ otherwise. Hence, the objective value of the linear program $LP(\omega)$ is not larger than the weighted average completion time for the tiny tasks of $\mathcal{TT}^{\omega}$ in $\sigma$. In other words, the value of an optimal fractional solution is a lower bound of the weighted completion time $\sum_{j \in \mathcal{TT}^{\omega}} w_j R_{z(j)}$. Consider an optimal solution $(y^*_{j,x})$ of the linear program. Suppose that there are two tasks $\ell$ and $k$ that are not scheduled by Smith's rule. W.l.o.g. we can consider the case when $y^*_{\ell,x_\ell} > 0$, $y^*_{k,x_k} > 0$, $x(k) \le x(\ell) \le x_\ell < x_k$ and $\frac{p_k^{\min}}{w_k} < \frac{p_\ell^{\min}}{w_\ell}$.

Then, there exist values $z_\ell$ and $z_k$ such that $0 < z_\ell \le y^*_{\ell,x_\ell}$ and $0 < z_k \le y^*_{k,x_k}$ and $z_\ell p_\ell^{\min} = z_k p_k^{\min}$. Now we exchange parts of the variables:

$$\begin{array}{ll} y'_{\ell,x_\ell} = y^*_{\ell,x_\ell} - z_\ell & y'_{\ell,x_k} = y^*_{\ell,x_k} + z_\ell \\ y'_{k,x_k} = y^*_{k,x_k} - z_k & y'_{k,x_\ell} = y^*_{k,x_\ell} + z_k \end{array}$$

and $y'_{j,x} = y^*_{j,x}$ for the remaining variables.

The new solution $(y'_{j,x})$ is feasible and the objective value $\sum_{j \in \mathcal{TT}^{\tau}} w_j \sum_{x=x(j)}^{L} y'_{j,x} R_x$ is equal to $\sum_{j \in \mathcal{TT}^{\tau}} w_j \sum_{x=x(j)}^{L} y^*_{j,x} R_x + R_{\ell,k}$, where $R_{\ell,k} = (R_{x_\ell} - R_{x_k})(w_k z_k - z_\ell w_\ell)$. By $z_k = z_\ell \frac{p_\ell^{\min}}{p_k^{\min}}$, the second factor $(w_k z_k - z_\ell w_\ell) = z_\ell (w_k \frac{p_\ell^{\min}}{p_k^{\min}} - w_\ell)$. Since $\frac{p_k^{\min}}{w_k} < \frac{p_\ell^{\min}}{w_\ell}$ and $z_\ell > 0$, the second factor is larger than 0. The inequality $x_\ell < x_k$ implies $R_{x_\ell} < R_{x_k}$ and $R_{\ell,k} < 0$. In other words, the new solution $(y'_{j,x})$ has a lower objective value and gives us a contradiction. This means that the two tasks $\ell$ and $k$ are scheduled by Smith's rule.

Now we use some properties of the above linear program. There is an optimal solution such that for each interval $I_x$ we have at most one task $j_x \in \mathcal{TT}^{\omega}$ with $x_{j,x} \in (0,1)$ and that is assigned for the first time. Otherwise we can use the same argument as above (and the fact that the quotients $p_j^{\min}/w_j$ are different) to improve the objective value. Furthermore, such an optimal solution can be obtained by applying Smith's rule in a greedy manner. To turn such a fractional solution into an integral assignment of tiny tasks to intervals, we need only to increase the values $D^{\omega} = p^{\min}(\mathcal{Y}_x^{\omega})$ by $\frac{\varepsilon^2 I_x}{q^*}$. Then, $j_x$ fits completely into $I_x$. Let $\tilde{\mathcal{Y}}_x^{\omega}$ be the set of tiny tasks of profile $\omega$ that is assigned to an interval $I_x$ with respect to the integral assignment of $LP(\omega)$ (including the task $j_x$). For each interval $I_x$ of schedule $\sigma$ we consider the set $\tilde{\mathcal{Y}}_x = \cup_{\omega \in \Omega} \tilde{\mathcal{Y}}_x^{\omega}$ of all tiny tasks that corresponds to $LP(\omega)$, $\omega \in \Omega$. It is not hard to check that the conditions of Lemma 8 hold. Thus, we apply the shifting* to $\sigma$, replace the sets $\mathcal{Y}_x$ by $\tilde{\mathcal{Y}}_x$ and apply the rearranging technique to each interval $I_{x+1}$. The final schedule is constructed.

To finish the proof, there are two facts. First, the total weighted average completion time of the schedule of tiny tasks which is given by the optimal fractional solutions of $LP(\omega)$, $\omega \in \Omega$ is less than their corresponding total weighted average completion time in $\sigma$. Second, we have used only the shifting and rearranging techniques. □

Furthermore, we can prove the following result:

**Lemma 10.** *With $1 + O(\varepsilon)$ loss and in $O(n \log n)$ time, one can transform an instance $I$ into instance $\tilde{I}$ such that for each profile $\omega \in \Omega$ the following holds: $|\mathcal{T}(I)_x| \leq N^*(m,\varepsilon)$ and $p^{\min}(\mathcal{T}(I)_x) \leq \frac{N^*(m,\varepsilon)}{\varepsilon^3} I_x$, where $N^*(m,\varepsilon)$ is a constant that depends on $m$ and $\varepsilon$.*

## 4 The Dynamic Programming Algorithm

As we mentioned it above, we will use a dynamic program to compute approximate solutions for our scheduling problem. To be able to formulate this dynamic program and show that the algorithm solving it has the desired running time, we need only the following result:

**Lemma 11.** *For a feasible schedule $\sigma(I)$ there is an $\varepsilon$-schedule $\sigma'(I)$ such that in $\sigma'(I)$ the tasks in $\mathcal{T}(I)_x$ are scheduled within a constant number $d^*(m,\varepsilon)$ of intervals that follow $I_x$, i.e. for each task $j \in \mathcal{T}$ it holds that $z'(j) - x(j) \leq d^*(m,\varepsilon)$.*

The last step is to use dynamic programming with blocks as units. By using Lemmas 1,10,11 there is at most a constant number of tasks in $\mathcal{T}_x$ for each interval $I_x$, all of these tasks have to be scheduled within a constant number of intervals that follow $I_x$, hence one can efficiently enumerate all possible schedules of the tasks of $\mathcal{T}_x$. Here (due to space limitation) we omit the formal description, leaving it to the full version of the paper.

## References


1. F. Afrati, E. Bampis, C. Chekuri, D. Karger, C. Kenyon, S. Khanna, I. Millis, M. Queyranne, M. Skutella, C. Stein, and M. Sviridenko, Approximation schemes for minimizing average weighted completion time with release dates, *Proceedings 40th IEEE Symposium on Foundations of Computer Science* (1999), 32-43.
2. F. Afrati, E. Bampis, A. V. Fishkin, K. Jansen, C. Kenyon, Scheduling to minimize the average completion time of dedicated tasks, *Proceedings 20th Conference on Foundations of Software Technology and Theoretical Computer Science*, LNCS 1974, Springer Verlag (2000), 454-464.
3. A. K. Amoura, E. Bampis, C. Kenyon, and Y. Manoussakis, Scheduling independent multiprocessor tasks, *Proceedings 5th European Symposium on Algorithms*, LNCS 1284, Springer Verlag (1997), 1-12.
4. F. Afrati, E. Bampis, C. Kenyon and I. Milis, A PTAS for the average weighted completion time problem on unrelated machines, *Journal of Scheduling* 3 (2000), 323-332.
5. A. Bar-Noy, M. Bellare, M. M. Halldórsson, H. Shachnai, and T. Tamir, On chromatic sums and distributed resource allocation, *Information and Computation* 140 (1998), 183-202.
6. A. Bar-Noy and M. M. Halldórsson and G. Kortsarz and R. Salman and H. Shachnai, Sum multicoloring of graphs, *Proceedings 7th European Symposium on Algorithms*, LNCS 1643, Springer Verlag (1999), 390-401.

7. J. L. Bruno, E. G. Coffman, Jr., R. Sethi, Algorithms for minimizing mean flow time, *Proceedings of the IFIP Congress*, North-Holland, Amsterdam, (1974), 504-510.
8. X. Cai, C.-Y. Lee, and C.-L. Li, Minimizing total completion time in two-processor task systems with prespecified processor allocation, *Naval Research Logistics* 45 (1998), 231-242.
9. S. Chakrabarti, C. A. Philips, A. S. Schulz, D. B. Shmoys, C. Stein, and J. Wein, Improved scheduling algorithms for minsum criteria, *Proceedings 23rd International Colloquium on Automata, Languages and Programming*, LNCS 1099, Springer Verlag (1996), 646-657.
10. J. Chen and A. Miranda, A polynomial time approximation scheme for general multiprocessor job scheduling, *Proceedings 31st ACM Symposium on the Theory of Computing* (1999), 418-427.
11. J. Du and J. Leung, Complexity of scheduling parallel task systems, *SIAM Journal on Discrete Mathematics* 2 (1989), 473-487.
12. U. Feige and J. Kilian, Zero-knowledge and the chromatic number, in *Journal of Computer and System Science* 57(2) (1998), 187-199.
13. A. V. Fishkin, K. Jansen, L. Porkolab, On minimizing average weighted completion time of multiprocessor tasks with release dates, to appear on *ICALP01.*
14. M. R. Garey and D. S. Johnson, Computers and intractability: A guide to the theory of NP-completeness, Freeman, San Francisco, CA, 1979.
15. L. A. Hall, A. S. Schulz, D. B. Shmoys, and J. Wein, Scheduling to minimize average time: Offline and online algorithm, *Mathematics of Operation Research* 22 (1997), 513-544.
16. J. A. Hoogeveen, S. L. Van de Velde, and B. Veltman, Complexity of scheduling multiprocessor tasks with prespecified processor allocations, *Discrete Applied Mathematics* 55 (1994), 259-272.
17. K. Jansen and L. Porkolab, General multiprocessor task scheduling: approximate solution in linear time, *Proceedings 6th International Workshop on Algorithms and Data Structures*, LNCS 1663, Springer Verlag (1999), 110-121.
18. M. Skutella and G. J. Woeginger, A PTAS for minimizing the weighted sum of job completion times on parallel machines, *Proceedings 31st ACM Symposium on Theory of Computing* (1999), 400-407.
19. W. E. Smith, Various optimizers for single-stage production, *Naval Research Logistic Quarterly* 3 (1956), 59-66.
20. J. Turek, W. Ludwig, J. Wolf, and P. Yu, Scheduling parallel tasks to minimize average response times, *Proceedings 5th ACM-SIAM Symposium on Discrete Algorithms* (1994), 112-121.

# Approximation Algorithms for Time-Dependent Orienteering

Fedor V. Fomin*[1] and Andrzej Lingas[2]

[1] Faculty of Mathematics and Mechanics, St. Petersburg State University, Bibliotechnaya sq. 2, St. Petersburg, 198904, Russia. fomin@gamma.math.spbu.ru
[2] Department of Computer Science, Lund University, Box 118, S-221 00, Lund, Sweden. Andrzej.Lingas@cs.lth.se

**Abstract.** The time-dependent orienteering problem is dual to the time-dependent traveling salesman problem. It consists in visiting a maximum number of sites within a given deadline. The traveling time between two sites is in general dependent on the starting time.
We provide a $(2 + \epsilon)$-approximation algorithm for the time-dependent orienteering problem which runs in polynomial time if the ratio between the maximum and minimum traveling time between any two sites is constant. No prior upper approximation bounds were known for this time-dependent problem.

## 1 Introduction

In the well known *orienteering* problem (see, e.g. [1,9]) a traveler wishes to visit the maximum number of sites (nodes) subject to given restrictions on the length of the tour. This problem can be regarded as the problem of traveling salesperson with restricted amount of resources (time, gasoline *etc.*) wishing to maximize the number of visited sites. For this reason, the orienteering problem has been also called "the generalized traveling salesperson problem" or even originally as "the bank robber problem" [3,9]. Even if the ratio between the maximum and minimum amount of resources required for traveling between two sites is constantly bounded, the orienteering problem is MAX-SNP-hard simply because the correspondingly restricted traveling salesman problem is MAX-SNP-hard [5,14] (cf. [4,8,13]).

In this paper we consider a generalization of the orienteering problem which we term *time-dependent orienteering* (TDO for short). In our generalization, the cost of traveling (time cost in our terminology) from any site to any other site in general depends on the start moment.

* The work of the first author was done while he was at the Centro de Modelamiento Matemático, Universidad de Chile and UMR 2071-CNRS, supported by FONDAP and while he was a visiting postdoc at DIMATIA-ITI partially supported by GAČR 201/99/0242 and by the Ministry of Education of the Czech Republic as project LN00A056. Also this work was supported by the RFBR grant N01-01-00235.

R. Freivalds (Ed.): FCT 2001, LNCS 2138, pp. 508–515, 2001.

The orienteering problems considered in [1] are classified as the *path-orienteering*, *cycle-orienteering*, and even *tree-orienteering* problems depending on whether the network to be induced by the set of pairs of consecutive sites visited is supposed to have a form of a path, a cycle, or even a tree, respectively. Additionally, one can wish to have one or more *roots*, which are 'essential' sites required to be visited. Following this classification we will refer to the cases of TDO problems without roots as *path (cycle, tree)*-TDO and to the cases with roots as *rooted-path (cycle, tree)*-TDO.

For illustration, consider the two following examples of possible applications of TDO.

**Kinetic TSP [5,10].** There is given a set of targets and one robot (intercepter) with restricted amount of resources (e.g., fuel). The dynamic of targets is known, i.e., for each target one can specify its location at any discrete time moment. The problem is to find a program for the robot which allows it to hit as many targets as possible within a given time. This problem is an example of path-TDO. If there is a target specified to be intercepted then we have an example of rooted-path-TDO.

**Time-dependent maximum scheduling problem (TDMS).** There is given a set of tasks for a single machine. The execution of any task can start at any discrete moment and its execution time depends on the starting moment. The problem is to find a schedule for the machine maximizing the number of tasks completed within a given time period. It can be interpreted as a special case of TDO where the time of traveling from a site $a$ to a site $b$ does not depend on the site $b$ and is interpreted as the execution time of the task corresponding to $a$. The Web Searching problem studied by Czumaj et al. [7] yields the following appealing motivation for TDMS. Assume that there is a central computer which is being used to collect all the information stored in a number of web documents, located in various sites. The information is gathered by scheduling a number of consecutive client/server connections with the required web sites, to collect the information page by page. The loading time of any particular page from any site can vary at different times, e.g., the access to the page is much slower in peak hours than in off-peak hours. We wish to download the maximum number of pages within a given period of time.

## 1.1 Main Results

An algorithm is said to be *c-approximation* algorithm for a maximization problem $P$ if for any instance of $P$ it yields a solution whose value is at least $1/c$ times the optimum.

Let $n$ be the number of input sites and let $k$ be the ratio between the maximum and minimum time required for traveling between two sites.

We present $(2+\varepsilon)$-approximation algorithms for path-TDOs and cycle-TDOs running in time $O((2k^2(\frac{2+\varepsilon}{\varepsilon}))!\frac{2k^2}{\varepsilon}n^{2k^2(\frac{2+\varepsilon}{\varepsilon})+1})$. In the corresponding rooted cases the time complexity increases by the multiplicative factor $O(\frac{kn}{\varepsilon})$. These bounds immediately carry over to the corresponding time-independent special cases, i.e., the unrooted and rooted, path-orienteering problems and cycle-orienteering problems. Our algorithm is the first constant-factor approximation algorithm for TDO with $k = O(1)$ running in polynomial time. Although for large $k$, our algorithm can be hardly claimed to be practical because of its fairly high running time, it suggests that practical and efficient algorithms might be possible.

### 1.2 Related Results

The authors are not familiar with any explicit prior approximation algorithms for time-dependent orienteering (TDO). Of course, if the ratio between the maximum and minimum distance is $k$ then any approximation algorithm is a $k$-approximation one.

For the time-dependent maximum scheduling problem (TDMS) which can be interpreted as a special case of TDO, a simple greedy 2-approximation algorithm running in time $O(mt)$, where $m$ is the number of available tasks and $t$ is the deadline, can be essentially deduced from Spieksma's algorithm [15] for Job Interval Selection Problem. Also, it follows from the same work [15] that TDMS is MAX-SNP-hard.

As for the classical, i.e., time-independent, orienteering problem, Awerbuch et al. proved that a $c$-approximation algorithm to the so called k-traveling salesperson problem, asking for a shortest cycle visiting $k$ sites (k-TSP), yields a $2c$-approximation algorithm for the orienteering problem [2]. This result combined with known approximation results for k-TSP yields a 6-approximation algorithm for the orienteering problem in metric spaces and a $(2+\epsilon)$-approximation algorithm in the Euclidean plane. The latter result has been subsumed by Arkin et al. who presented 2-approximation algorithms for several variants of the orienteering problem in the plane [1]. More recently, Broden has designed an 4/3-approximation algorithm for the very special case of the orienteering problem where the pairwise distances are constrained to $\{1, 2\}$ [5]. Note here that the recent lower bounds on the constant approximation factor for the analogously restricted traveling salesperson problem [4] easily carry over to the aforementioned special case of the orienteering problem.

For an interesting review of results related to the orienteering problem, including several variants of the traveling salesperson problem, the reader is referred to [1].

The recent works by Hammar et al. [10] and Broden [5] contain a number of inapproximability and approximability results on various restrictions of the problem dual to TDO, i.e., the time-dependent traveling salesperson problem.

## 2 Formal Definition of TDO

For a given set $S$ of sites, a time-travel function $l : S \times S \times \mathbb{N} \cup \{0\} \to \mathbb{R}^+$ and a deadline $t$, the salesperson's tour visiting a subset $T$ of $m$ sites is a sequence of triples

$$(s_1, t_1^+, t_1^-), (s_2, t_2^+, t_2^-), \ldots, (s_k, t_k^+, t_k^-)$$

such that

1. For $i \in \{1, 2, \ldots, m\}$, $t_i^+, t_i^- \in \mathbb{N} \cup \{0\}$;
2. $\bigcup_{i=1}^{m} \{s_i\} = T$;
3. $0 = t_1^+ \le t_1^- \le t_2^+ \le \cdots \le t_m^+ \le t_m^- = t$;
4. For each $i \in \{1, 2, \ldots, m-1\}$, $t_{i+1}^+ - t_i^- = l(s_i, s_{i+1}, t_i^-)$.

It is useful to interpret the moment $t_i^-$ as the moment when salesperson leaves the site $s_i$ and $t_i^+$ as the moment when salesperson enter $s_i$. So $t_{i+1}^+ - t_i^-$ is the time spend in travel from $s_i$ to $s_{i+1}$ and $t_i^- - t_i^+$ is the time the salesperson stays in $s_i$ (importantly, the traveler is allowed to stay at any site any time). The path (or cycle) time-dependent orienteering problem is to find an open (closed, respectively) tour visiting maximum number of sites within the time $t$.

Note that the classical orienteering problem [1] is a special case of TDO where for any sites $a$, $b$, the travel time from $a$ to $b$ is time-independent, i.e., $l(s_a, s_b, t') = l(s_a, s_b, t'')$ for any $t', t'' \in [0, t]$.

## 3 Main Procedure and Algorithms

We may assume w.l.o.g that the minimum travel time between two sites, $\min_{s,s' \in S, t' \in [0,t]} l(s, s', t')$, is 1. For a nonnegative integer $q$ and positive integer $m \le \lceil t/q \rceil$, we shall denote by $s_m(q)$ the subinterval $[q(m-1), \min\{qm, t\}]$ of $[0, t]$.

The following simple procedure is the heart of our algorithms for TDO.

Procedure *Greedy*$(S, q, t)$

1. $T \leftarrow S$;
2. **for** $i = 1, 2, \ldots, \lceil t/q \rceil$ **do**
   let $T_i$ be a maximum cardinality subset of $T$ that can be visited within $s_i(q)$ by a path-tour;
   visit $T_i$ within $s_i(q)$;
   $T \leftarrow T \setminus T_i$

Note that procedure *Greedy*$(S, q, t)$ outputs for each $i \in \{1, 2, \ldots, \lceil t/q \rceil\}$ a salesperson's path-tour for interval $s_i(q)$ but in general the output $T$ of *Greedy*$(S, q, t)$ is not a tour. Obviously, the set $T_i$ can be found in $O(q!|S|^q)$ time by considering all possible choices of a subset of $T$ containing at most $q$ elements and then applying the straightforward $O(n!)$-time brute force method for the time-dependent traveling salesperson problem on the subset. Hence the overall time complexity of *Greedy*$(S, q, t)$ is $O(q!\lceil t/q \rceil |S|^q)$.

Let $k$ be the maximum time needed to travel between two sites, i.e., $k = \max_{s,s' \in S, t' \in [0,t]} l(s, s', t')$. Note that by our initial assumption $k$ is also the ratio between the maximum and minimum time required for traveling between two sites.

Algorithm *GreedyPath*$(S, q, t)$

1. Run procedure *Greedy*$(S, q, t)$;
2. **for** $i = 1, \ldots, \lceil t/q \rceil$ **do**
   Remove from the set of visited sites all sites visited during $[qi - k/2, qi + k/2]$;
   Glue the obtained subtours by forcing the salesperson to go from the last visited site in $[q(i-1) + k/2, qi - k/2]$ to the first visited site in $[q(i) + k/2, q(i+1) - k/2]$

Algorithm *GreedyCycle*$(S, q, t)$ is obtained from *GreedyPath*$(S, q, t)$ by closing the path-route near its endpoints, i.e., by forcing the salesperson to go from the last visited site in $s_{\lceil t/q \rceil - 1}$ to the first visited site from $[k, q - k/2]$.

## 4 Approximation Analysis

**Lemma 1.** *Let $n$ be the maximum number of different sites that can be visited by $\lceil t/q \rceil$ travelers in such a way that for each $i \in \{1, 2, \ldots, \lceil t/q \rceil\}$, the $i$-th traveler operates only within the time interval $s_i(q)$. Then the number of sites participating in subtours produced by Greedy$(S, q, t)$ is at least $\lceil n/2 \rceil$.*

*Proof.* Let $\hat{W}$ be the set of sites returned by *Greedy*$(S, q, t)$, and let $W$ be a set of $n$ sites that can be visited by the $\lceil t/q \rceil$ travelers. We denote by $\hat{W}_i$ the set of sites visited by *Greedy*$(S, q, t)$ during $[0, iq]$ and by $W_i$ the set

$$\{s \in W \setminus \hat{W}_i \text{ and } s \text{ is not visited during } [0, qi] \text{ by the } \lceil t/q \rceil \text{ travellers}\}.$$

In other words, $W_i$ consists of the sites in $W$ that have not been visited either by *Greedy*$(S, q, t)$ or by the first $i$ of the $\lceil t/q \rceil$ travelers during $[0, qi]$.

We claim that for each $i \in \{1, 2, \ldots, \lceil t/q \rceil\}$

$$|W_i| \geq n - 2|\hat{W}_i|$$

Since $W_{\lceil t/q \rceil} = \emptyset$ this claim implies the lemma. We prove it by induction on $i$.

For $i = 1$ this inequality directly follows from the optimality of the solution within $[0, q]$ picked by *Greedy*$(S, q, t)$.

The set $W_{i-1} \setminus W_i$ (the sites in $W$ that are eliminated during $s_i(q)$) is the union of $W_A \cup W_B$ (the case $W_A \cap W_B \neq \varnothing$ is possible) where:

— $W_A$ is the set of sites from $W$ chosen by *Greedy*$(S, q, t)$ during $s_i(q)$
— $W_B$ is the set of sites in $W_{i-1}$ that are visited by the $i$-th traveler during $s_i(q)$.

By the definition, $W_A \subseteq \hat{W}_i \setminus \hat{W}_{i-1}$ and $|W_B| \leq |\hat{W}_i \setminus \hat{W}_{i-1}|$ because of the optimality of the solution on $s_i(q)$. Therefore,

$$|W_{i-1} \setminus W_i| \leq 2|\hat{W}_i \setminus \hat{W}_{i-1}|.$$

Notice that by definition

$$|W_i| = |W_{i-1}| - |W_{i-1} \setminus W_i|,$$
$$|\hat{W}_i| = |\hat{W}_{i-1}| + |\hat{W}_i \setminus \hat{W}_{i-1}|.$$

By induction assumption,

$$|W_{i-1}| \geq n - 2|\hat{W}_{i-1}|.$$

Hence,

$$|W_i| = |W_{i-1}| - |W_{i-1} \setminus W_{i-1}| \geq n - 2|\hat{W}_{i-1}| - 2|\hat{W}_i \setminus \hat{W}_{i-1}| \geq n - 2|\hat{W}_i|$$

and the claim follows.

**Lemma 2.** *For any $\varepsilon > 0$ and $q = 2k(\frac{2+\varepsilon}{\varepsilon})$, GreedyPath$(S, q, t)$ and GreedyCycle$(S, q, t)$ are $(2+\varepsilon)$-approximation algorithms for path- and cycle-TDO running in time $O((2k^2(\frac{2+\varepsilon}{\varepsilon}))!\frac{2k^2t}{\varepsilon}|S|^{2k^2(\frac{2+\varepsilon}{\varepsilon})})$.*

*Proof.* Suppose that an optimal solution to the path- (cycle-) TDO visits $n$ sites. We may assume w.l.o.g. that $n \geq t/k$. The solution trivially yields $\lceil t/q \rceil$-traveler solution satisfying the requirements of Lemma 1. By Lemma 1, the procedure *Greedy*$(S, q, t)$ outputs at least $\frac{n}{2}$ sites. Consequently, each of the procedures *GreedyPath*$(S, q, t)$, *GreedyCycle*$(S, q, t)$ outputs a tour visiting at least $\frac{n}{2} - \frac{kt}{q} = \frac{1}{2}(n - \frac{2kt}{q}) \geq \frac{n}{2}(1 - \frac{2k^2}{q})$ sites. Hence, *GreedyPath*$(S, q, t)$ and *GreedyCycle*$(S, q, t)$) are $(2+\varepsilon)$-approximation algorithms.

By the remark on the time complexity of procedure *Greedy*$(S, q, t)$, we obtain the complexity bound in the lemma thesis.

Lemma 2 and the possibility of assuming $t/k \leq n$ w.l.o.g immediately yield our main result.

**Theorem 1.** *For any $\varepsilon > 0$, the path- and cycle-TDO for $n$ sites admit $(2+\varepsilon)$-approximation algorithms running in time $O((2k^2(\frac{2+\varepsilon}{\varepsilon}))!\frac{2k^2}{\varepsilon}n^{2k^2(\frac{2+\varepsilon}{\varepsilon})+1})$.*

We can trivially model the classical path- and cycle-orienteering problems as special cases of TDO by setting the traveling time between two sites to the distance between them.

**Corollary 1.** *For any $\varepsilon > 0$, the classical path- and cycle-orienteering problems for $n$ sites admit $(2+\varepsilon)$-approximation algorithms running in time $O((2k^2(\frac{2+\varepsilon}{\varepsilon}))!\frac{2k^2n}{\varepsilon}n^{2k^2(\frac{2+\varepsilon}{\varepsilon})})$, where the distance between the furthest site pair is at most $k$ times greater than that between the closest pair.*

## 5 Rooted Case

We can easily extend our technique to include the rooted case of the path- and cycle-TDO. Given a root $s$, we simply run the following modified version of $Greedy(S, q, t)$.

Procedure $GreedyRoot(S, q, t, s)$

1. **for** $j = 1, 2, \ldots, \lceil t/q \rceil$ **do**
   a) $T^j \leftarrow S$;
   b) **for** $i = 1, 2, \ldots, \lceil t/q \rceil$ **do**
      If $i \neq j$ then let $T_i$ be a maximum cardinality subset of $T$ that can be visited within $s_i(q)$ by a path-tour;
      If $i = j$ then let $T_i$ be a maximum cardinality subset of $T$ containing $s$ that can be visited within $s_i(q)$ by a path-tour;
      Visit $T_i$ within $s_i(q)$;
      $T^j \leftarrow T^j \setminus T_i^j$;
2. Choose the set $T^j$ with the maximum number of sites, $T \leftarrow T^j$.

By arguing analogously as in the unrooted case we can derive a rooted version of Lemma 2. The only essential difference is the time complexity which increases by the multiplicative factor of $O(t/q)$, i.e., $O(kn)$. Furthermore, the implementation of $GreedyPath(S, q, t)$ and $GreedyCycle(S, q, t)$ in the rooted case requires special care in order to avoid removing the root $s$ if it happened to be visited in the $k/2$ vicinity of an $s_i(q)$-interval border. For this purpose, it is sufficient to remove $k$ sites before or after $s$, respectively.

Summarizing, we obtain the following rooted version of Theorem 1.

**Theorem 2.** *For any $\varepsilon > 0$, the rooted path- and cycle-TDO for $n$ sites admit $(2+\varepsilon)$-approximation algorithms running in time $O((2k^2(\frac{2+\varepsilon}{\varepsilon}))!\frac{2k^3}{\varepsilon}n^{2k^2(\frac{2+\varepsilon}{\varepsilon})+2})$.*

## 6 Final Remarks

We have used a simple but powerful divide-and-conquer approximation technique: "split" a problem in a number of "small" subproblems, then find exact solutions for each of the subproblems and "glue" these solutions to obtain an approximate solution of the problem.

Our technique can be extended to include orienteering variants of many other optimizations problems (e.g., tree-orienteering) as well variants with parallel travelers. It can be also used in the design of efficient approximation algorithms for time-dependent bicriteria network optimization problems (see [12] and the last chapter in [6]). Finally, it can be applied to derive approximative solutions to the Budget Prize Collecting Steiner Tree problem (see [11]) and its time dependent variant.

## References

1. E. M. ARKIN, J. S. B. MITCHELL, AND G. NARASIMHAN, *Resource-constrained geometric network optimization*, in Proceedings Fourteenth ACM Symposium on Computational Geometry, June 6-10, 1998, pp. 307–316.
2. B. AWERBUCH, Y. AZAR, A. BLUM, AND S. VEMPALA, *Improved approximation guarantees for minimum-weight k-trees and prize-collecting salesman*, in Proceedings 27th Annual ACM Sympos. Theory Comput. (STOC 95), pp. 277-283, 1995.
3. E. BALAS, *The prize collecting traveling salesperson problem*, Networks, 19, pp. 621-636, 1989.
4. H.J. BOCKENHAUER, J. HROMKOVIC, R. KLASING, S. SEIBERT, AND W. UNGER, *An improved lower bound on the approximability of metric TSP and approximation algorithms for the TSP with sharpened triangle inequality*, in Proceedings 17th Annual Symposium on Theoretical Aspects of Computer Science, Lecture Notes in Computer Science, Springer Verlag, pp. 111-112, 2000.
5. B. BRODEN, *Time Dependent Traveling Salesman Problem*, M.Sc. thesis, Department of Computer Science, Lund University, Sweden, 2000.
6. J. CHERIYAN and R. Ravi, Approximation algorithms for network problems, manuscript, 1998. (http://www.gsia.cmu.edu/andrew/ravi/home.html)
7. A. CZUMAJ, I. FINCH, L. GASIENIEC, A. GIBBONS, P. LENG, W. RYTTER, AND M. ZITO, *Efficient Web Searching Using Temporal Factors*, in Proceedings of the 6th Workshop on Algorithms and Data Structures (WADS), F. Dehne, A. Gupta, J.-R. Sack, and R. Tamassia, eds., Springer Verlag, Lecture Notes in Computer Science, vol. 1663, 1999, pp. 294–305.
8. L. ENGEBRETSEN, *An explicit lower bound for TSP with distances one and two*, in Proceedings 16th Annual Symposium on Theoretical Aspects of Computer Science, Lecture Notes in Computer Science, Springer Verlag, pp. 373-382, 1999.
9. B. G. GOLDEN, L. LEVY, AND R. VOHRA, *The orienteering problem*, Naval Res. Logistics, 34 (1991), pp. 307–318.
10. M. HAMMAR AND B. NILSSON, *Approximation results for kinetic variants of TSP*, in Proceedings of the 26th International Colloquium on Automata, Languages, and Programming (ICALP'99), Springer Verlag, Lecture Notes in Computer Science, vol. 1644, 1999, pp. 392–401.
11. D. S. JOHNSON, M. MINKOFF, AND S. PHILLIPS, *The Prize Collecting Steiner Tree Problem: Theory and Practice*, Proc. 11th Ann. ACM-SIAM Symp. on Discrete Algorithms, (2000), pp. 760-769.
12. M. V. MARATHE, R. RAVI, R. SUNDARAM, S. S. RAVI, D. J. ROSENKRANTZ, H. B. HUNT III, *Bicriteria network design problems*, J. Algorithms 28 (1998), pp. 142–171.
13. C.H. PAPADIMITRIOU AND S. VEMPALA, *On the approximability of the traveling salesman problem*, in Proceedings of the the thirty second ACM STOC, pp. 126-133, 2000.
14. C.H. PAPADIMITRIOU AND M. YANNAKAKIS, *The traveling salesman problem with distances one and two*, in Mathematics of Operations Research 18(1), pp. 1-11, 1993.
15. F. C. R. SPIEKSMA, *On the approximability of an interval scheduling problem*, Journal of Scheduling 2 (1999), pp. 215-227.

# On Complexity of Colouring Mixed Hypertrees

Daniel Král'*

Department of Applied Mathematics and
Institute for Theoretical Computer Science**,
Charles University, Malostranské nám. 25,
118 00 Prague, Czech Republic
kral@kam.ms.mff.cuni.cz

**Abstract.** A mixed hypergraph is a triple $(V, \mathcal{C}, \mathcal{D})$ where $V$ is its vertex set and $\mathcal{C}$ and $\mathcal{D}$ are families of subsets of $V$, $\mathcal{C}$–edges and $\mathcal{D}$–edges. We demand in a proper colouring that each $\mathcal{C}$–edge contains two vertices with the same colour and each $\mathcal{D}$–edge contains two vertices with different colours. A hypergraph is a hypertree if there exists a tree such that the edges of the hypergraph induce connected subgraphs of that tree.
We prove that it is NP–complete to decide existence of a proper $k$–colouring even for mixed hypertrees with $\mathcal{C} = \mathcal{D}$ when $k$ is given as part of input. We present a polynomial–time algorithm for colouring mixed hypertrees on trees of bounded degree with fixed number of colours.

## 1 Introduction

Hypergraphs are well established combinatorial objects, see [1]. A hypergraph is a pair $(V, \mathcal{E})$ where $\mathcal{E}$ is a family of subsets of $V$ of size at least 2; the members of $V$ are called vertices and the members of $\mathcal{E}$ are called edges. A hypergraph is a hypertree if there exists a tree with its vertex set equal to $V$ such that the edges $\mathcal{E}$ induce connected subgraphs of $T$. Mixed hypergraphs were introduced in [7] and mixed hypertrees were investigated in [6].

A mixed hypergraph $G$ is a triple $(V, \mathcal{C}, \mathcal{D})$ where $\mathcal{C}$ and $\mathcal{D}$ are families of subsets of $V$; the members of $\mathcal{C}$ are called $\mathcal{C}$–edges and the members of $\mathcal{D}$ are called $\mathcal{D}$–edges. A mixed hypergraph is a mixed hypertree if $(V, \mathcal{C} \cup \mathcal{D})$ is a hypertree. A mixed hypergraph/tree is a mixed bihypergraph/tree if $\mathcal{C}=\mathcal{D}$. A *proper $k$–colouring* $c$ of $G$ is a mapping $c : V \to \{1, \ldots, k\}$ such that there are two vertices with $\mathcal{D}$ifferent colours in each $\mathcal{D}$–edge and there are two vertices with a $\mathcal{C}$ommon colour in each $\mathcal{C}$–edge. A proper colouring $c$ is a *strict $k$–colouring* if it uses all $k$ colours. The mixed hypergraph is colourable iff $G$ has a proper colouring. Mixed hypergraphs can find their application in different areas: colouring block designs (see [2,3]), list–colouring of graphs and others.

The *feasible set* $\mathcal{F}(G)$ of a mixed hypergraph $G$ is the set of all $k$'s such that there exists a strict $k$–colouring of $G$. The *(lower) chromatic number* $\chi(G)$ of $G$

* Supported in part by GAČR 201/1999/0242, GAUK 158/1999 and KONTAKT 338/99.

** Supported by Ministry of Education of Czech Republic as project LN00A056

R. Freivalds (Ed.): FCT 2001, LNCS 2138, pp. 516–524, 2001.

is the minimum number in $\mathcal{F}(G)$ and the *upper chromatic number* $\bar{\chi}(G)$ of $G$ is the maximum number in $\mathcal{F}(G)$. The feasible set of $G$ is *gap–free* (unbroken) iff $\mathcal{F}(G) = [\chi(G), \bar{\chi}(G)]$; we use $[a, b]$ for the set of all the integers between $a$ and $b$ (inclusively). If the feasible set of $G$ contains a gap, we say it is broken. An example of a mixed hypergraph with a broken feasible set was firstly given in [5]. On the other hand, it was proved in [6] that feasible sets of mixed hypertrees are gap–free.

We address several complexity issues concerning mixed hypertrees in this paper. Since a feasible set of any mixed hypertree is gap–free and the chromatic number of a colourable mixed hypertree is at most two (it is one iff the mixed hypertree does not contain any $\mathcal{D}$–edges), it is possible to restrict the complexity issues involving colouring mixed hypertrees to decision problems whether their upper chromatic numbers is at least a given number.

The complexity problems concerning mixed hypertrees are addressed in Section 3. We strengthen the result of Flocos from [4] that it is NP–complete to determine the existence of a strict colouring with a given number of colours for mixed hypertrees to the case of mixed bihypertrees (Theorem 2). We describe a polynomial–time algorithm for finding a strict $k$–colouring (for bounded $k$) of mixed hypertrees with underlying trees of bounded degree (Theorem 3). This extends the previous result of Voloshin (see [8]) for interval mixed hypergraphs, i.e. mixed hypertrees with underlying trees of degree at most two. Our polynomial–time algorithm is based on a new concept of $k$–colourable witnesses (established in Section 2) which is of its own theoretical interest. In particular, we get immediately as a collorary (Corollary 1) that a feasible set of a mixed hypertree is gap–free giving a new proof completely different to the original one in [6].

## 2 Concept of Colourability Witnesses

We introduce the concept of $k$–colourability witnesses in this section.

Let $H = (V, \mathcal{C}, \mathcal{D})$ be a mixed hypertree with underlying tree $T = (V, E)$. Let us consider $T$ as a rooted tree and let level$(v)$ be a level of its vertex $v$, i.e. the distance of $v$ from the root. We call any sequence $w_1, \ldots, w_k$ of vertices $V$ a *witness sequence*. We assume w.l.o.g. in the following that $0 = \text{level}(w_1) < \text{level}(w_2) \leq \text{level}(w_3) \leq \ldots \leq \text{level}(w_k)$; this means in particular that $w_1$ is the root.

Once we have a $k$–colourability witness, we want to find some strict $k$–colouring $c$ of $H$ (if it exists) such that the colours of the vertices $w_1, \ldots, w_k$ are mutually different. In order to do this, we extend the following simple proof from [6] of two–colourability of a colourable mixed hypertree $H$: We colour the root of $T$ arbitrary and then we colour the vertices from root to the leaves — if a vertex form with its father a $\mathcal{C}$–edge, we colour it with the colour of its father; if it does not form a $\mathcal{C}$–edge with its father, we colour it with the colour different from the colour of its father. It is easy to check that this colouring is proper iff $H$ is colourable.

In the following, we divide the vertices of $H$ into three sets: $L$ is the set of the vertices introducing new colours and their siblings, $R$ is the set of the neighbours of the vertices of $L$ and $O$ is the set of other vertices of $H$. Later, we will colour the vertices of $O$ as described in the two–colourability proof above. Next, we construct a mapping $\lambda : V \to \{\mathrm{F}, \mathrm{G}, 1, \ldots, k\}$ which assigns the number $i$ to the vertex/ices introducing the colour $i$, to a vertex which should be coloured with the same colour as its father the value F and to a vertex which should be coloured with the colour different from the colour of its father the value G. Then, we describe a construction of a colouring $\tilde{c}$ which is proper for some choice of $\lambda$ if there is a proper colouring of $H$ assigning to $w_1, \ldots, w_k$ mutually different colours.

Let us define the set of vertices $L$, $R$ and $O$:

$$L = \{v | \exists i, \mathrm{father}(v) = \mathrm{father}(w_i) \vee v = w_i\}$$

$$R = \{v | v \notin L \wedge \exists u \in L, uv \in E\}$$

$$O = V \setminus (L \cup R)$$

We define a special set $\mathcal{L}(v)$ for each vertex as follows:

$$\mathcal{L}(v) = \{\mathrm{F}, \mathrm{G}\} \cup \{i | \mathrm{father}(v) = \mathrm{father}(w_i) \vee v = w_i\} \text{ if } v \in L$$

$$\mathcal{L}(v) = \{\mathrm{F}, \mathrm{G}\} \text{ if } v \in R$$

$$\mathcal{L}(v) = \{\mathrm{F}\} \text{ if } v \in O \text{ and } \{v, \mathrm{father}(v)\} \in \mathcal{C}$$

$$\mathcal{L}(v) = \{\mathrm{G}\} \text{ if } v \in O \text{ and } \{v, \mathrm{father}(v)\} \notin \mathcal{C}$$

We consider a mapping $\lambda : V \to \{\mathrm{F}, \mathrm{G}, 1, \ldots, k\}$; we demand that $\lambda(v) \in \mathcal{L}(v)$ for each vertex $v$.

We define a colouring $\tilde{c}$ of $H$ based on a witness sequence $w_1, \ldots, w_k$ and a mapping $\lambda$:

- $\tilde{c}(v) = 1$ if $w_2$ is an successor of $v$
- $\tilde{c}(v) = \lambda(v)$ if $\lambda(v) \in \{1, \ldots, k\}$
- $\tilde{c}(v) = \tilde{c}(\mathrm{father}(v))$ if $\lambda(v) = \mathrm{F}$
- $\tilde{c}(v) = \tilde{c}^\star(\mathrm{father}(v))$ if $\lambda(v) = \mathrm{G}$

where $\tilde{c}^\star(u)$ is following:

- $\tilde{c}^\star(u) = 2$ if $u$ is the root (note that $\tilde{c}(u) = 1$ in this case)
- $\tilde{c}^\star(u) = \tilde{c}(\mathrm{father}(u))$ if $\tilde{c}(u) \neq \tilde{c}(\mathrm{father}(u))$
- $\tilde{c}^\star(u) = \tilde{c}^\star(\mathrm{father}(u))$ if $\tilde{c}(u) = \tilde{c}(\mathrm{father}(u))$

We introduce notion relating witness sequences to colourings of $H$: The sequence $w_1, \ldots, w_k$ of vertices $V$ is a witness sequence of $k$–colourability *with respect to a strict $k'$–colouring* $c : V \to \{1, \ldots, k'\}$ if $c(w_i) = i$. A witness sequence is *minimal* if $\sum_i \mathrm{level}(w_i)$ is minimal.

We say that the mapping $\lambda$ is *consistent* with a strict $k'$–colouring $c$ and a minimal $k$–colourability witness sequence $w_1, \ldots, w_k$ ($k \leq k'$) with respect to $c$ if it satisfies:

- $\lambda(v) = c(v)$ if $c(v) \in \mathcal{L}(v)$
- $\lambda(v) = \mathrm{F}$ if $c(v) = c(\mathrm{father}(v))$ and $\mathrm{F} \in \mathcal{L}(v)$
  (This holds in particular when $\{v, \mathrm{father}(v)\}$ is a C–edge.)
- $\lambda(v) = \mathrm{G}$ otherwise

If father($v$) does not exist, the second condition does not apply.

The following theorem actually gives the sense to the previous definitions which introduced colourability witnesses:

**Theorem 1.** *If $w_1, \ldots, w_k$ is a minimal $k$-colourability witness sequence (where $k$ is at least 2) with respect to a strict $k'$–colouring $c$ ($k \le k'$) of a mixed hypertree $H$ and if $\lambda$ is consistent with $c$, then $\tilde{c}$ corresponding to $w_1, \ldots, w_k$ and $\lambda$ is a strict $k$–colouring.*

*Proof.* The colouring $\tilde{c}$ clearly uses exactly $k$ colours. It remains to prove that $\tilde{c}$ is proper. Thus it is enough to prove that each edge of $\mathcal{D}$ contains two vertices coloured by $\tilde{c}$ with different colours and each edge of $\mathcal{C}$ contains two vertices coloured by $\tilde{c}$ with the same colours.

Let $E$ be any edge of $\mathcal{D}$ and let $u$ and $v$ be two vertices coloured by $c$ with different colours. We can assume w.l.o.g. that $u$ and $v$ are neighbours and that e.g. $u = \mathrm{father}(v)$. Note that $w_2$ is not an successor of $v$, since otherwise it would hold that $c(u) = c(v) = 1$ due to the minimality of the witness sequence and our assumption that $0 = \mathrm{level}(w_1) < \mathrm{level}(w_2) \le \ldots \le \mathrm{level}(w_k)$. We claim that $\tilde{c}(u) \ne \tilde{c}(v)$. We distinguish several cases:

- $\lambda(v) = \mathrm{F}$
  This case is impossible due to consistency of $\lambda$ with $c$.
- $\lambda(v) = \mathrm{G}$
  It holds that $\tilde{c}(v) = \tilde{c}^\star(\mathrm{father}(v)) \ne \tilde{c}(\mathrm{father}(v))$ — note that $w_2$ is not an successor of $v$ since otherwise $c(u) = c(v) = 1$ due to the minimality of the witness sequence.
- $\lambda(v) \in \{1, \ldots, k\}$
  There is no predecessor of $v$ coloured by $\tilde{c}$ with the colour $\lambda(v) = c(v)$ due to the minimality of the witness sequence; it especially holds that $\tilde{c}(u) \ne \tilde{c}(v)$, in this case.

We have just proved that all the $\mathcal{D}$–edges contain two vertices coloured by different colours. So, we focus our attention on the $\mathcal{C}$–edges.

Let $E$ be any edge of $\mathcal{C}$. If $E$ contains two vertices whose successor is $w_2$, then these two vertices of $E$ are coloured by $\tilde{c}$ with colour 1. We assume further that there is at most one vertex whose successor is $w_2$; clearly this vertex, if it exists, is the vertex of $E$ which is the nearest one in $E$ to the root. Let $u$ and $v$ be two nearest vertices of $E$ coloured by $c$ with the same colour. It is not necessary that $\tilde{c}(u) = \tilde{c}(v)$. We first state a useful observation which is going to be used several times in the proof:

**Observation 1.** If $E$ contains a vertex $u$ such that the both following conditions hold:

- $\lambda(u) \in \{\mathrm{F}, \mathrm{G}\}$
- $\{u, \text{father}(u), \text{father}(\text{father}(u))\} \subseteq E$ **or** $\{u, \text{father}(u)\} = E$

Then $E$ contains two vertices coloured by $\tilde{c}$ with the same colour.

The case that $\lambda(u) = \mathrm{F}$ is trivial. If $\lambda(u) = \mathrm{G}$, then $E$ cannot be $\{u, \text{father}(u)\}$ due to the definition of $\lambda(u)$ and it holds that $\{u, \text{father}(u), \text{father}(\text{father}(u))\} \subseteq E$. Let $u' = \text{father}(u)$ and $u'' = \text{father}(u') = \text{father}(\text{father}(u))$. If $\tilde{c}(u') = \tilde{c}(u'')$ the claim is clear. If $\tilde{c}(u') \neq \tilde{c}(u'')$, then $\tilde{c}(u) = \tilde{c}^\star(u') = \tilde{c}(u'')$ and the claim also holds.

We continue the proof of the theorem. We distinguish several cases to prove that $E$ contains two vertices coloured by $\tilde{c}$ with the same colour:

- **The vertex $v$ is a predecessor of $u$ (in particular** $\text{level}(u) > \text{level}(v)$**); the case that $u$ is a predecessor of $v$ is symmetric.**
  In this case $E$ contains all the vertices between $u$ and $v$, i.e. it contains father($u$) in particular. We distuinguish several cases:
  - $\lambda(u) = \mathrm{F}$
    Then $u$ and father($u$) are coloured with the same colour in this case.
  - $\lambda(u) = \mathrm{G}$
    If $v$ is not a father of $u$, then $E$ contains two vertices coloured by $\tilde{c}$ with the same colour due to the observation. Let us consider the remaining case that $v$ is the father of $u$ (and thus $\tilde{c}(u) \neq \tilde{c}(v)$). Due to consistency of $\lambda$ with $c$, it must hold that $\mathrm{F} \notin \mathcal{L}(u)$ and thus $u \in O$. Then, $E$ must contain at least three vertices, in particular it contains either a son of $u$, a brother of $u$ or a grand–father of $u$:
    * **$E$ contains a son of $u$.** Call it $w$.
      Clearly $w \in R \cup O$ (if $w \in L$, then $u \in R$ and $\lambda(u) = \mathrm{F}$) and $E$ contains two vertices coloured by $\tilde{c}$ with the same colour due to the observation used for $w$.
    * **$E$ contains a brother of $u$.** Call it $w$.
      Clearly $w \in R \cup O$ (if $w \in L$, then also $u \in L$) and thus $\lambda(w)$ is either F or G. If $\lambda(w) = \mathrm{F}$, then $\tilde{c}(w) = \tilde{c}(v)$ and these $v$ and $w$ are two vertices of $E$ coloured by $\tilde{c}$ with the same colour. If $\lambda(w) = \mathrm{G}$, then $\tilde{c}(u) = \tilde{c}(w) = \tilde{c}^\star(v)$ and thus $u$ and $w$ are two vertices of $E$ coloured by $\tilde{c}$ with the same colour.
    * **$E$ contains a grand–father of $u$.**
      In this case $E$ contains two vertices coloured by $\tilde{c}$ with the same colour due to the observation.
  - $\lambda(u) \in \{1, \ldots, k\}$
    If it held that $\lambda(u) = i$, then we could get by substituting $w_i$ (a member of the witness sequence with $\text{level}(w_i) = \text{level}(u) > \text{level}(v)$) with $v$ a $k$–colourability witness sequence with a smaller level sum, contradicting the minimality of the witness sequence.
- **Neither $u$ is a predecessor of $v$ or $v$ is a predecessor of $u$.**
  Let $w$ be the nearest common predecessor of $u$ and $v$. We distinguish several cases to prove that $E$ contains two vertices coloured by $\tilde{c}$ with the same colour:

- $\lambda(u) = \mathrm{F}$ **or** $\lambda(v) = \mathrm{F}$
  The appropriate vertex and its father are coloured by $\tilde{c}$ with the same colour and thus $E$ contains two vertices coloured by $\tilde{c}$ with the same colour.
- $\lambda(u) = \mathrm{G}$ and $\lambda(v) = \mathrm{G}$
  If father$(u) \neq w$ or father$(v) \neq w$, then $E$ contains two vertices of the same colour due to the observation; otherwise it holds that $w =$ father$(u) =$ father$(v)$. Then, it holds that $\tilde{c}(u) = \tilde{c}(v) = \tilde{c}^\star(w)$ and thus $u$ and $v$ are two vertices of $E$ coloured by $\tilde{c}$ with the same colour.
- $\lambda(u) \in \{1, \ldots, k\}$ and $\lambda(v) = \mathrm{G}$ (the case that $\lambda(u) = \mathrm{G}$ and $\lambda(v) \in \{1, \ldots, k\}$ is symmetric)
  If $u$ and $v$ are brothers, then due to the consistency of $\lambda$ with $c$, it has to hold that $\lambda(u) = \lambda(v)$. Thus $u$ and $v$ are not brothers. If father$(v) \neq w$, then $E$ contains two vertices of the same colour due to the observation. Otherwise since $u$ and $v$ are not brothers, $w =$ father$(v)$ and $w$ is the nearest common predecessor of $u$ and $v$, the level of $u$ is greater than the level of $v$, i.e. level$(u) =$ level$(w_i) >$ level$(v)$. But this means that we can get by substituting $w_i$ with $v$ ($c(u) = c(w_i) = c(v)$) a $k$–colourability witness sequence with a smaller level sum, contradicting the minimality of the witness sequence.
- $\lambda(u) \in \{1, \ldots, k\}$ and $\lambda(v) \in \{1, \ldots, k\}$
  If $u$ and $v$ are brothers, then due to the consistency of $\lambda$ with $c$, it holds that $\lambda(u) = \lambda(v)$ and thus $\tilde{c}(u) = \tilde{c}(v)$ and thus $u$ and $v$ are two vertices of $E$ coloured by $\tilde{c}$ with the same colour.
  If $u$ and $v$ are not brothers, then $\mathcal{L}(u) \neq \mathcal{L}(v)$. But due to the consistency of $\lambda$ with $c$ and the fact that $\lambda(u) \in \{1, \ldots, k\}$ and $\lambda(v) \in \{1, \ldots, k\}$, it has to be $c(u) \neq c(v)$. But this contradicts our choice of $u$ and $v$, since we have chosen them to hold that $c(u) = c(v)$.

**Corollary 1.** *If a hypertree $H$ has a strict $k'$–colouring, then it has also a strict $k$–colouring for all $2 \leq k \leq k'$. In particular, the feasible set of any mixed hypertree is gap–free.*

*Proof.* Let $c$ be a strict $k'$–colouring of $H$ and let $w_1, \ldots, w_k$ be any minimal $k$–colourability witness sequence of $H$ with repsect to $c$. Let $\lambda$ be consistent with $c$. Then the colouring $\tilde{c}$ corresponding to the witness sequence $w_1, \ldots, w_k$ and mapping $\lambda$ is a strict $k$–colouring.

It is enough to apply this corollary for $k' = \overline{\chi}(H)$ to get that its feasible set is gap–free.

## 3 Complexity Problems Dealing with Mixed Hypertrees

We first state our negative result concerning the colouring of mixed hypertrees:

**Theorem 2.** *It is NP–complete to decide whether a given mixed bihypertree is strictly $k$–colourable for a given $k$.*

*Proof.* The reduction from the decision problem on independence number of cubic graphs is presented: Let $G$ be any cubic graph with $n$ vertices $w_1, \ldots, w_n$. Let $T$ be a tree with the vertex set equal to $V = \{\star, u_1, \ldots, u_n, v_1, \ldots, v_n\}$ and the edge set equal to $\{\star u_i, u_i v_i | 1 \le i \le n\}$. We define a mixed bihypertree $H$ on the vertex set $V$ as follows: The edges of $H$ are precisely the sets $\{\star, u_i, v_i, u_j\}$ for all $i$ and $j$ such that $w_i w_j$ is an edge of $G$ (since $H$ is a mixed bihypertree, all its edges are both $\mathcal{C}$ and $\mathcal{D}$–edges). We claim that $\overline{\chi}(H) = n + \alpha + 1$ where $\alpha$ is the size of the independent set of $G$. This claim implies the stated NP–completeness of the problem. Note that each edge of the tree $T$ is contained either in 6 or 12 edges of $H$ (the edges incident to the root are contained in 12, the other edges in 6 edges of $H$).

We prove the claim, now. Let $w_{i_1}, \ldots, w_{i_\alpha}$ be an independent set of $G$. We can construct the colouring $c$ of the vertices of $H$ using exactly $n + \alpha + 1$ colours as follows: $c(v_j) = j$, $c(u_{i_j}) = n + j$, $c(\star) = 0$ and $c(u_j) = 0$ for $j \ne i_1, \ldots, i_\alpha$. Let $\{\star, u_i, v_i, u_j\}$ be an edge of $H$. Either $c(u_i) = 0$ or $c(u_j) = 0$, since both $w_i$ and $w_j$ cannot be in the considered independent set and $c(\star) = 0 \ne c(v_i)$. This assures that the constructed colouring $c$ is proper.

On the other hand, let $c$ be a colouring using $n + \alpha + 1$ colours. We construct an independent set of $G$ of size $\alpha$. Let $R_0 = \star, \ldots, R_{n+\alpha}$ (we can assume w.l.o.g. that $c(\star) = 0$) be the minimal $(n + \alpha + 1)$–colourability witness sequence with respect to $T$ rooted at $\star$. We first define a new strict colouring $\tilde{c}$ using $n + \alpha + 1$ colours:

- We set $\tilde{c}(\star) = 0$.
- If both $u_i$ and $v_i$ are among $R_1, \ldots, R_{n+\alpha}$ (a ray of Type 1), we set $\tilde{c}(u_i) = c(u_i)$ and $\tilde{c}(v_i) = c(v_i)$.
- If only $u_i$ is among $R_1, \ldots, R_{n+\alpha}$ (a ray of Type 2), we set $\tilde{c}(u_i) = 0$ and $\tilde{c}(v_i) = c(u_i)$.
- If only $v_i$ is among $R_1, \ldots, R_{n+\alpha}$ (a ray of Type 3), we set $\tilde{c}(u_i) = 0$ and $\tilde{c}(v_i) = c(v_i)$.
- If neither $u_i$ nor $v_i$ is among $R_1, \ldots, R_{n+\alpha}$ (a ray of Type 4), we set $\tilde{c}(u_i) = 0$ and $\tilde{c}(v_i)$ to a completely new colour.

Note that if $c$ uses $\overline{\chi}(H)$ colours, the last case cannot occur. Let $\{\star, u_i, v_i, u_j\}$ be an edge of $H$; $\tilde{c}(\star) \ne \tilde{c}(v_i)$ due to the definition of $\tilde{c}$. If $u_i$ and $u_j$ belong both to rays of Type 1, then the original colouring $c$ cannot be proper. Thus at least one of them belongs to a ray of Type 2, 3 or 4 and is coloured by 0, the same colour as the vertex $\star$. We have just proven that $\tilde{c}$ is a proper colouring. Let $A = \{w_i | \tilde{c}(u_i) \ne c(\star)\}$. The set $A$ is an independent set of $G$, since $\tilde{c}$ is a proper colouring, and its size is exactly $\alpha$, since vertices $\star, v_1, \ldots, v_n$ are coloured by mutually different $n + 1$ colours. This finishes the proof of the claim.

We describe the promised algorithm for colouring mixed hypertrees in the next theorem:

**Theorem 3.** *If $k$ is bounded and the maximum degree of tree $T$ is bounded, it can be decided in polynomial time whether a given mixed hypertree $H$ on $T$ is strict $k$–colourable.*

*Proof.* Consider the following algorithm:

```
for all sequences w_1, ..., w_k of vertices of H such
        that 0 = level(w_1) < level(w_2) ≤ ... ≤ level(w_k)
    do
        construct sets L, R and O for w_1, ..., w_k
        construct sets 𝓛(v) for all vertices v
        for all mappings λ : V → {F, G, 1, ..., k} such that λ(v) ∈ 𝓛(v)
            do
                construct c̃ for w_1, ..., w_k and λ
                if c̃ is a proper colouring then
                    output YES
                    halt
            done
    done
output NO
halt
```

It is clear that if the algorithm outputs YES, then $H$ has a strict $k$–colouring. Suppose that the algorithm outputs NO and $H$ has a strict $k$–colouring — call this colouring $c$. But there certainly exists a minimal witness sequence $w_1, \ldots, w_k$ corresponding to $c$ and the mapping $\lambda$ consistent with $c$. But in the loop when the algorithm considered this witness sequence $w_1, \ldots, w_k$ and this mapping $\lambda$, the constructed colouring $\tilde{c}$ would be strict and thus the algorithm would output YES. But since this did not happen, the strict $k$–colouring $c$ of $H$ cannot exist. We have just proven that the algorithm outputs YES iff $H$ has a strict $k$–colouring.

We give an estimate for running time of the algorithm now. Let $d$ be a maximal degree of $T$. There are $O(n^{k-1})$ choices of the witness sequence in the first step. The sets $L$, $R$, $O$ and $\mathcal{L}(v)$ can be constructed in polynomial time $t_1(n,k)$ given $w_1, \ldots, w_k$ where $n$ is the number of vertices of $H$. We write $m$ for the number of edges of $H$ in the next. It is clear that $|L| \leq k(d-1) \leq kd$ and $|R| \leq k(d-1)^2 + k \leq kd^2$. There are exactly $|\mathcal{L}(v)| \leq k+2$ choices of $\lambda(v)$ for each $v \in L$, two choices of $\lambda(v)$ for each $v \in R$ and one choice of $\lambda(v)$ for each $v \in O$. Thus it holds that $\Pi_{v \in L} |\mathcal{L}(v)| \leq (k+2)^{kd}$ and $2^{|R|} \leq 2^{kd^2}$. The colouring $\tilde{c}$ can be constructed and it can be checked whether $\tilde{c}$ is proper in polynomial time $t_2(n,m,k)$. The running time of the whole algorithm is $O(n^{k-1} t_1(n,k) + n^{k-1}(k+2)^{kd} 2^{kd^2} t_2(n,m,k))$ — this can be clearly majorized by a polynomial in $n$ and $m$ if $k$ and $d$ are bounded.

## Open Problems

The most interesting still open problem is the decision problem of the existence of a strict $k$–colouring of a given mixed hypertree for fixed $k$: Is it NP–complete to decide whether there exists a strict $k$–colouring of a given mixed hypertree even for fixed $k$? There are several other open algorithmic problems concerning colouring mixed hypertrees raised in [6].

**Acknowledgement.** The author is indebted to Jan Kratochvíl for attracting his attention to mixed hypergraphs, fruitful discussions on the topic and suggestions for improving clarity of the statements.

## References

1. C. Berge: Graphs and Hypergrapgs, North Holland, 1973.
2. C. Colbourn, J. Dinitz, A. Rosa: Bicoloring Triple Systems, Electronic J. Combin. 6# 1, paper 25, 16 pages.
3. Ch. J. Colbourn, A. Rosa: Triple Systems, Clarendon Press, Oxford, 1999, sect. 18.6. Strict colouring and the upper chromatic number, 340–341.
4. E. Flocos: The Upper Chromatic Number of Simple Co-Monostars, Anale stiintifice ale Universitatii de Stat din Moldova, Seria Stiinte Reale, Chisinau, 1997, 22–27.
5. T. Jiang, D. Mubayi, Zs. Tuza, V. Voloshin and D. B. West: Chromatic spectrum is broken, 6th Twente Workshop on Graphs and Combinatorial Optimization, 26–28, May, 1999, H. J. Broersma, U. Faigle and J. L. Hurink (eds.), University of Twente, May, 1999, 231–234.
6. D. Král', J. Kratochvíl, A. Proskurowski, H.-J. Voss: Coloring mixed hypertrees, Proceedings 26th Workshop on Graph-Theoretic Concepts in Computer Science, LNCS vol. 1928, 2000, p. 279–289.
7. V. Voloshin: The mixed hypergraphs, Computer Science Journal of Moldova 1, 1993, 45–52.
8. V. Voloshin: On the upper chromatic number of a hypergraph, Australasian Journal of Combinatorics 11, 1995, 25–45.

# Combining Arithmetic and Geometric Rounding Techniques for Knapsack Problems*

Monaldo Mastrolilli

IDSIA, Galleria 2, 6928 Manno, Switzerland, monaldo@idsia.ch

**Abstract.** We address the classical knapsack problem and a variant in which an upper bound is imposed on the number of items that can be selected. We show that appropriate combinations of rounding techniques yield novel and powerful ways of rounding. As an application of these techniques, we present a faster polynomial time approximation scheme requiring only linear storage, that computes an approximate solution of any fixed accuracy in linear time. This linear complexity bound gives a substantial improvement of the best previously known polynomial bound [2].

## 1 Introduction

In the classical *Knapsack Problem* (KP) we have a set $N := \{1, \dots, n\}$ of items and a knapsack of limited capacity. To each item we associate a positive profit $p_j$ and a positive weight $w_j$. The problem calls for selecting the set of items with maximum overall profit among those whose overall weight does not exceed the knapsack capacity $c > 0$. KP has the following Integer Linear Programming (ILP) formulation:

$$\text{maximize} \quad \sum_{j \in N} p_j x_j \tag{1.1}$$

$$\text{subject to} \quad \sum_{j \in N} w_j x_j \leq c \tag{1.2}$$

$$x_j \in \{0, 1\}, \quad j \in N, \tag{1.3}$$

where each binary variable $x_j$, $j \in N$, is equal to 1 if and only if item $j$ is selected. In general, we cannot take all items because the total occupancy of the chosen items cannot exceed the knapsack capacity $c$. In the sequel, without loss of generality, we assume that $\sum_{j \in N} w_j > c$ and $w_j \leq c$ for every $j \in N$.

The *k-item Knapsack Problem* (kKP), is a KP in which an upper bound of $k$ is imposed on the number of items that can be selected in a solution. The

* Supported by the "Metaheuristics Network", grant HPRN-CT-1999-00106, and by Swiss National Science Foundation project 21-55778.98, "Resource Allocation and Scheduling in Flexible Manufacturing Systems".

R. Freivalds (Ed.): FCT 2001, LNCS 2138, pp. 525–534, 2001.

problem can be formulated as (1.1)-(1.3) with the additional constraint

$$\sum_{j \in N} x_j \leq k, \tag{1.4}$$

with $1 \leq k \leq n$.

KP has widely been studied in the literature, see the book of Martello and Toth [8] for a comprehensive illustration of the problem. kKP is the subproblem to be solved when instances of the Cutting Stock Problem with cardinality constraints are tackled by column generation techniques. kKP also appears in processor scheduling problems on computers with $k$ processors and shared memory. Furthermore, kKP could replace KP in the separation of cover inequalities, as outlined in [2].

Throughout our paper let $OPT$ denote the optimal solution value to the given instance and $w(F) = \sum_{j \in F} w_j$ and $p(F) = \sum_{j \in F} p_j$, where $F \subseteq N$. An algorithm $A$ with solution value $z^A$ is called an *ε-approximation algorithm*, $\varepsilon \in (0, 1)$, if $z^A \geq (1 - \varepsilon)OPT$ holds for all problem instances. We will also call $\varepsilon$ the *performance ratio* of $A$.

*Known Results.* It is well known that KP is NP-hard but pseudopolynomially solvable through dynamic programming, and the same properties hold for kKP [2]. Basically, the developed approximation approaches for KP and kKP can be divided into three groups:

1. *Approximation algorithms.* For KP the classical $\frac{1}{2}$-approximation algorithm (see e.g. [7]) needs only $O(n)$ running time. A performance ratio of $\frac{1}{2}$ can be obtained also for kKP by rounding the solution of the linear programming relaxation of the problem (see [2]); this algorithm can be implemented to run in linear time when the LP relaxation of kKP is solved by using the method by Megiddo and Tamir [9].
2. *Polynomial time approximation schemes* (PTAS) reach any given performance ratio and have a running time polynomial in the length of the encoded input. The best schemes currently known requiring linear space are given in Caprara et al. [2]: they yield a performance ratio of $\varepsilon$ within $O(n^{\lceil 1/\varepsilon \rceil - 2})$ and $O(n^{\lceil 1/\varepsilon \rceil - 1})$ running time, for KP and kKP respectively.
3. *Fully polynomial time approximation schemes* (FPTAS) also reach any given performance ratio and have a running time polynomial in the length of the encoded input and in the reciprocal of the performance ratio. This improvement compared to 2. is usually paid for by much larger space requirements, which increases rapidly with the accuracy $\varepsilon$. The first FPTAS for KP was proposed by Ibarra and Kim [5], later on improved by Lawler [7] and Kellerer and Pferschy [6]. In Caprara et al. [2] it is shown that kKP admits an FPTAS.

*New Results.* Rounding the input is a widely used technique to obtain polynomial time approximation schemes [4]. Among the developed rounding techniques, arithmetic or geometric rounding are the most successfully and broadly used ways of rounding to obtain a simpler instance that may be solved in polynomial time (see Sections 2.1 and 2.2 for an application of these techniques to kKP). Our paper contains a new technical idea. We show that appropriate combinations of arithmetic and geometric rounding techniques yields to novel and powerful rounding methods. To the best of our knowledge, these techniques have never been combined together. By using the described rounding technique, we present an improved PTAS for kKP requiring linear space and running time $O(n + k \cdot (1/\varepsilon)^{O(1/\varepsilon)})$. Our algorithm is clearly superior to the one in [2], and it is worth noting that the running time contains no exponent on $n$ dependent on $\varepsilon$. Since KP is a special case of kKP, we also improve the previous result for KP.

## 2 Rounding Techniques for kKP

The aim of this section is to transform any input into one with a smaller size and a simpler structure without dramatically decreasing the objective value. The main idea is to turn a difficult instance into a more primitive instance that is easier to tackle. This will help for efficient enumeration.

In the following we discuss some general techniques that are applied throughout our paper. We discuss several transformations of the input problem. Some transformations may potentially increase the objective function value by a factor of $1 - O(\varepsilon)$, so we can perform a constant number of them while still staying within $1-O(\varepsilon)$ of the original optimum. Others are transformations which do not increase the objective function value. When we describe the first type of transformation, we shall say it produces $1 - O(\varepsilon)$ *loss*, while the second produces *no loss*.

Let $P^H$ denote the solution value obtained in $O(n)$ time by employing the 1/2-approximation algorithm $H^{\frac{1}{2}}$ for kKP described in [2]. In [2], it is shown that

$$OPT \leq P^H + p_{\max} \leq 2P^H, \tag{2.5}$$

where $p_{\max} = \max_j p_j$.

Throughout this section we restrict our considerations to feasible solutions with at most $\gamma$ items, where $\gamma$ is any positive integer not greater than $k$. The first observation is that at most an $\varepsilon$-fraction of the optimal profit $OPT$ is lost by discarding all items $j$ where $p_j \leq \varepsilon P^H/\gamma$, since at most $\gamma$ items can be selected and $P^H \leq OPT$. From now on, consider the reduced set of items with profit values greater than $\varepsilon P^H/\gamma$.

In order to reduce further the set of items, the useful insight is that when profits are identical we pick them in order of their weights. Since the optimal profit is $\leq 2P^H$, among all items with profit value $\bar{p} \in \{p_1, ..., p_n\}$, we can keep the first $\bar{n} = \min\left\{\gamma, \left\lfloor \frac{2P^H}{\bar{p}} \right\rfloor\right\}$ items with the smallest weights, and discard the others with no loss. Of course, we cannot hope to obtain a smaller instance if all profits are different. In the following, we show how the number of different profits can be reduced by rounding the original profits. We revise two rounding techniques and show that an appropriate combination of both leads to a better result. We will call a profit value $\bar{p}$ *large* if $\bar{p} > \frac{2P^H}{\gamma}$, and *small* otherwise.

### 2.1 Arithmetic Rounding

A sequence $a_1, a_2, ...$ is called an *arithmetic sequence* if, and only if, there is a constant $d$ such that $a_i = a_1 + d \cdot (i-1)$, for all integers $i \geq 1$. Let us consider the arithmetic sequence $S_a(\gamma)$ obtained by setting $a_1 = d = \varepsilon P^H/\gamma$. We transform the given instance into a more structured by rounding each profit down to the nearest value among those of $S_a(\gamma)$. Since in the rounded instance the profit of each item is decreased by at most $\varepsilon P^H/\gamma$, and at most $\gamma$ items can be selected, the solution value of the transformed instance potentially decreases by $\varepsilon P^H$. Of course, by restoring the original profits we cannot decrease the objective function value, and therefore, with $1-\varepsilon$ loss, we can assume that every possible profit is equal to $a_i = \frac{\varepsilon P^H}{\gamma} \cdot i$ for some $i \geq 1$. Furthermore, since $p_{\max} = \max_{j \in N} p_j \leq P^H$, the number of different profits is now bounded by $\lfloor \frac{\gamma p_{\max}}{\varepsilon P^H} \rfloor \leq \lfloor \frac{\gamma}{\varepsilon} \rfloor$.

The largest number $n_i$ of items with profit $a_i$, for $i = 1, ..., \lfloor \frac{\gamma}{\varepsilon} \rfloor$, that can be involved in any feasible solution is bounded by

$$n_i \leq \min\{\gamma, \left\lfloor \frac{OPT}{\frac{\varepsilon P^H}{\gamma} i} \right\rfloor\} \leq \min\{\gamma, \left\lfloor \frac{2\gamma}{\varepsilon i} \right\rfloor\},$$

and we can keep the first $n_i$ items with the smallest weights, and discard the others with no loss. Now, the number of items with profit $a_i$ is at most $\gamma$, if $a_i$ is a small profit (i.e. when $i = 1, ..., \lfloor \frac{2}{\varepsilon} \rfloor$), and at most $\lfloor \frac{2\gamma}{\varepsilon i} \rfloor$ otherwise ($i = \lfloor \frac{2}{\varepsilon} \rfloor + 1, ..., \lfloor \frac{\gamma}{\varepsilon} \rfloor$). Thus, by applying the described arithmetic rounding we have at most $\lfloor 2/\varepsilon \rfloor \gamma$ items with small profits and $\sum_{i=\lfloor \frac{2}{\varepsilon} \rfloor + 1}^{\lfloor \frac{\gamma}{\varepsilon} \rfloor} \lfloor \frac{2\gamma}{\varepsilon i} \rfloor$ with large profits. Recall that when a summation can be expressed as $\sum_{k=x}^{y} f(k)$, where $f(k)$ is a monotonically decreasing function, we can approximate it by integral (see, e.g. [3] p. 50): $\sum_{k=x}^{y} f(k) \leq \int_{x-1}^{y} f(k)dk$. Furthermore, we are assuming that $0 < \varepsilon < 1$, and recall that $\ln(1+x) \geq x/(1+x)$, for $x > -1$. Therefore, the total number of items in the transformed instance is bounded by

$$\begin{aligned}
\left\lfloor \frac{2}{\varepsilon} \right\rfloor \gamma + \sum_{i=\lfloor \frac{2}{\varepsilon} \rfloor + 1}^{\lfloor \frac{\gamma}{\varepsilon} \rfloor} \left\lfloor \frac{2\gamma}{\varepsilon i} \right\rfloor &\leq \frac{2}{\varepsilon}\gamma + \frac{2}{\varepsilon}\gamma \sum_{i=\lfloor \frac{2}{\varepsilon} \rfloor + 1}^{\lfloor \frac{\gamma}{\varepsilon} \rfloor} \frac{1}{i} \\
&\leq \frac{2\gamma}{\varepsilon}(1 + \int_{\frac{2}{\varepsilon}-1}^{\frac{\gamma}{\varepsilon}} \frac{di}{i}) = \frac{2\gamma}{\varepsilon}(1 + \ln\gamma - \ln(2-\varepsilon)) \\
&\leq \frac{2\gamma}{\varepsilon}(1 + \ln\gamma - \frac{1-\varepsilon}{2-\varepsilon}) \leq \frac{2\gamma}{\varepsilon}(1 + \ln\gamma) \\
&= O(\frac{\gamma}{\varepsilon}\ln\gamma).
\end{aligned}$$

We see that by applying the described arithmetic rounding we have at most $2\gamma/\varepsilon$ items with small profits and $\frac{2\gamma}{\varepsilon}\ln\gamma$ with large profits.

## 2.2 Geometric Rounding

A sequence $a_1, a_2, ...$ is called a *geometric sequence* if, and only if, there is a constant $r$ such that $a_i = a_1 \cdot r^{i-1}$, for all integers $i \geq 1$. Let us consider the geometric sequence $S_g(\gamma)$ obtained by setting $a_1 = \varepsilon P^H/\gamma$ and $r = \frac{1}{1-\varepsilon}$. We round each profit down to the nearest value among those of $S_g(\gamma)$. Since $a_i = (1-\varepsilon)a_{i+1}$, for $i \geq 1$, each item profit is at most decreased by a factor of $1-\varepsilon$, and consequently, the solution value of the transformed instance potentially decreases by the same factor of $1-\varepsilon$. Therefore, with $1-\varepsilon$ loss, we can assume that every possible profit is equal to $a_i = \frac{\varepsilon P^H}{\gamma} \cdot (\frac{1}{1-\varepsilon})^{i-1}$ for some $i \geq 1$. Furthermore, since $p_{\max} \leq P^H$, the number of different profits is bounded by the biggest integer $\beta$ such that

$$\frac{\varepsilon P^H}{\gamma} \cdot (\frac{1}{1-\varepsilon})^{\beta-1} \leq P^H.$$

Since $\ln(\frac{1}{1-\varepsilon}) \geq \varepsilon$, we have $\beta - 1 \leq \frac{\ln(\gamma/\varepsilon)}{\ln(\frac{1}{1-\varepsilon})} \leq \frac{1}{\varepsilon} \ln \frac{\gamma}{\varepsilon}$. In any feasible solution, the largest number $n_i$ of items with profit $a_i$, for $i = 1, ..., \beta$, is bounded by

$$n_i \leq \min\{\gamma, \left\lfloor \frac{OPT}{\frac{\varepsilon P^H}{\gamma} \cdot (\frac{1}{1-\varepsilon})^{i-1}} \right\rfloor\} \leq \min\{\gamma, \left\lfloor \frac{2\gamma}{\varepsilon}(1-\varepsilon)^{i-1} \right\rfloor\},$$

and we can keep the first $n_i$ items with the smallest weights, and discard the others with no loss. Let $\alpha = \left\lfloor \frac{\ln(\varepsilon/2)}{\ln(1-\varepsilon)} \right\rfloor + 1$. Again, the number of items with profit $a_i$ is at most $\gamma$, if $a_i$ is a small profit (i.e. when $i = 1, ..., \alpha$), and at most $\lfloor \frac{2\gamma}{\varepsilon}(1-\varepsilon)^{i-1} \rfloor$ otherwise ($i = \alpha+1, ..., \beta$). Therefore, the total number of items in the transformed instance is bounded by

$$\alpha\gamma + \sum_{i=\alpha+1}^{\beta} \left\lfloor \frac{2\gamma}{\varepsilon}(1-\varepsilon)^{i-1} \right\rfloor \leq (\frac{1}{\varepsilon}\ln(2/\varepsilon) + 1)\gamma + \frac{\gamma + 2\varepsilon - 2}{\varepsilon} = O(\frac{\gamma}{\varepsilon} \ln \frac{1}{\varepsilon}).$$

We see that by applying the geometric rounding we have at most $\gamma/\varepsilon$ items with large profit, while $O(\frac{\gamma}{\varepsilon} \ln \frac{1}{\varepsilon})$ items with small profits. Contrary to arithmetic rounding, the set of items that has been reduced most is the set with large profits. This suggests us to combine the described rounding techniques.

## 2.3 Arithmetic & Geometric Rounding

We use arithmetic rounding for the set of items with small profits and geometric rounding for large items. More formally, let us consider the *Arithmetic & Geometric* sequence $S_{ag}(\gamma) = (a_1, a_2, ...)$ defined by setting

$$a_i = \frac{\varepsilon P^H}{\gamma} \cdot \begin{cases} i & \text{for } i = 1, ..., \lfloor 2/\varepsilon \rfloor, \\ (\frac{1}{1-\varepsilon})^{\alpha+i-\lfloor 2/\varepsilon \rfloor - 1} & \text{otherwise.} \end{cases}$$

We round each profit down to the nearest value among those of $S_{ag}(\gamma)$. Now, consider every set $N_i$ of items with the same rounded profit value $a_i$, and take the first

$$n_i = \begin{cases} \gamma & \text{for } i = 1, ..., \lfloor 2/\varepsilon \rfloor, \\ \lfloor \frac{2\gamma}{\varepsilon}(1-\varepsilon)^{\alpha+i-\lfloor 2/\varepsilon \rfloor -1} \rfloor & \text{otherwise,} \end{cases}$$

items with the smallest weights. Selecting the first $n_i$ items with the smallest weights can be done in $O(|N_i|)$ time. That is, $O(|N_i|)$ time is sufficient to select the $n_i$-th item with the smallest weight (see [1]) and only $O(|N_i|)$ comparisons are needed to extract the $n_i - 1$ items with smaller weight. Therefore the amortized time is linear.

By using the arithmetic rounding technique for small items, we have at most $2\gamma/\varepsilon$ small items with $1-\varepsilon$ loss (see Section 2.1). While, by using the geometric rounding technique described in Section 2.2 for large items, we have at most $\gamma/\varepsilon$ large items with $1-\varepsilon$ loss. The resulting transformed instance has at most $3\gamma/\varepsilon$ items with $1-2\varepsilon$ loss. Furthermore, let $\psi = \beta - \alpha + \lfloor 2/\varepsilon \rfloor + 1$. Observe that the $\psi$-th element of $S_{ag}(\gamma)$ is not smaller than $P^H$, i.e., $a_\psi \geq P^H$. Consider any subset $S \subseteq N$ of items with at most $\gamma$ items, and let $x_i$ denote the total number of items from $S$ with profit in interval $[a_i, a_{i+1})$, $i = 1, 2, ...\psi$. Let us call vector $(x_1, x_2, ..., x_\psi)$ an $S$-*configuration.* It is easy to see that by using the reduced set of items it is always possible to compute a solution having the same $S$-configuration, for any $S \subseteq N$ with $\gamma$ items. Summarizing:

**Lemma 1.** *For any positive integer $\gamma \leq k$, it is possible to compute in linear time a reduced set $N_\gamma \subseteq N$ of items with at most $3\gamma/\varepsilon$ items, such that, for any subset $S \subseteq N$ with at most $\gamma$ items, there exists a subset $S_\gamma \subseteq N_\gamma$ such that $S_\gamma$ is the subset of $N$ having the same configuration as $S$ and with the least weights.*

**Corollary 1.** *For any subset $S \subseteq N$ with at most $\gamma$ items, there exists a subset $S_\gamma \subseteq N_\gamma$ with $w(S_\gamma) \leq w(S)$, $|S_\gamma| = |S|$ and $p(S_\gamma) \geq p(S) - 2\varepsilon \cdot OPT$.*

## 3 A Faster Linear-Storage PTAS for kKP

Our PTAS for kKP improves the scheme of Caprara et al. [2], and in fact it strongly builds on their ideas. However, there are several differences where a major one is the use of two reduced sets of items instead of the entire set $N$: let $\ell := \min\{\lceil 1/\varepsilon \rceil - 2, k\}$, where $\varepsilon \leq 1/2$ is an arbitrary small rational number; our algorithm uses sets $N_k$ and $N_\ell$ computed by using the Arithmetic & Geometric rounding technique (see Lemma 1) when $\gamma := k$ and $\gamma := \ell$, respectively. We will show that sets $N_k$ and $N_\ell$ help for efficient enumeration.

For any given instance of $kKP$, the approximation scheme performs the following five steps (S-1)-(S-5).

(S-1) Initialize the solution $A$ to be the empty set and set the corresponding value $P^A$ to 0.

(S-2) Compute the reduced sets $N_k$ and $N_\ell$.
(S-3) Consider each $L \subset N_\ell$ such that $|L| \leq \ell - 1$. If $w(L) \leq c$ and $p(L) > P^A$ let $A := L$, $P^A := p(A)$.
(S-4) Consider each $L \subseteq N_\ell$ such that $|L| = \ell$. If $w(L) \leq c$, consider sequence $S_{ag}(\ell) = (a_1, a_2, ...)$ and let $h$ be an integer such that $a_h \leq \min_{j \in L} p_j < a_{h+1}$. Apply algorithm $H^{\frac{1}{2}}$ to the subinstance $S$ defined by item set $\{i \in N_k \backslash L : p_i < a_{h+1}\}$, by capacity $c - w(L)$ and by cardinality upper bound $k - \ell$. Let $T$ and $P^H(S)$ denote the solution and the solution value returned by $H^{\frac{1}{2}}$ when applied to $S$. If $p(L) + P^H(S) > P^A$ let $A := L \cup T$ and $P^A := p(L) + P^H(S)$.
(S-5) Return solution $A$ of value $P^A$.

Observe that in steps (S-3) and (S-4), subsets $L$ are computed by considering just the items from $N_\ell$. On the other hand, in step (S-4), we remark that the subinstances $S$ are defined by using items from $N_k$.

### 3.1 Analysis of the Algorithm

Step (S-2) can be performed in $O(n)$ time by Lemma 1. In step (S-3) the algorithm considers $O(|N_\ell|^{\ell-1})$ subsets, for each one performing operations that clearly require $O(\ell)$ time. In step (S-4) the algorithm considers $O(|N_\ell|^\ell)$ subsets $L$. For each $L$ the definition of subinstance $S$ requires $O(|N_k| \cdot \ell)$ time. Algorithm $H^{\frac{1}{2}}$ applied to subinstance $S$ runs in $O(|S|) = O(|N_k|)$ time [2]. By Lemma 1, $|N_k| = O(k/\varepsilon)$ and $|N_\ell| = O(\ell/\varepsilon)$. Therefore, step (S-4) is performed in $O(|N_\ell|^\ell \cdot |N_k| \cdot \ell) = O(k \cdot (\frac{\ell}{\varepsilon})^{\ell+1}) = k \cdot (1/\varepsilon)^{O(1/\varepsilon)}$. It follows that the overall running time of the algorithm is $O(n + k \cdot (1/\varepsilon)^{O(1/\varepsilon)})$, and it is not difficult to check that steps (S-1)-(S-5) require linear space.

What remains to be shown is that steps (S-1)-(S-5) return a $(1 - O(\varepsilon))$-approximate solution.

If an optimal solution contains at most $\ell$ items, the solution returned is $(1 - 2\varepsilon)$-approximate solution. Indeed, by Corollary 1 the reduction of $N$ to $N_\ell$ results in at most $(1-2\varepsilon)$ loss of profit, and steps (S-3)-(S-4) consider all subsets of $N_\ell$ having at most $\ell$ items.

Otherwise, let $\{j_1, ..., j_\ell, ...\}$ be the set of items in an optimal solution ordered so that $p_{j_1} \geq ... \geq p_{j_\ell} \geq ...$, and let $L^* = \{j_1, ..., j_\ell\}$ be the subset obtained by picking the first $\ell$ items with the largest profit. Consider subinstance $S^*$ defined by item set $\{i \in N \backslash L^* : p_i \leq \min_{j \in L^*} p_j\}$, by capacity $c - w(L^*)$ and by cardinality upper bound $k - \ell$. Clearly,

$$p(L^*) + OPT_{S^*} = OPT, \tag{3.6}$$

where $OPT_{S^*}$ denotes the optimal value of instance $S^*$. Now, consider the reduced set $N_k$ and subinstance $S_k^*$ defined by item set $\{i \in N_k \backslash L^* : p_i \leq \min_{j \in L^*} p_j\}$, by capacity $c - w(L^*)$ and by cardinality upper bound $k - \ell$. By Corollary 1, we have

$$OPT_{S_k^*} \geq OPT_{S^*} - 2\varepsilon OPT, \tag{3.7}$$

where $OPT_{S_k^*}$ denotes the optimal value of instance $S^*$.

Let us use $L$ to denote the set of items having the same configuration as $L^*$ and the least weights. By Lemma 1, in one of the iterations of step (S-4), set $L$ is considered. In the remainder, let us focus on this set $L$, and consider the corresponding subinstance $S$ defined in step (S-4). By Corollary 1, we have

$$p(L) \geq p(L^*) - 2\varepsilon OPT. \tag{3.8}$$

We need to show that the optimal solution value $OPT_S$ of instance $S$ cannot be smaller than $OPT_{S_k^*}$.

**Lemma 2.** $OPT_S \geq OPT_{S_k^*}$.

*Proof.* Recall that the subinstance $S$ is defined by item set $I_S = \{i \in N_k \backslash L : p_i < a_{h+1}\}$, where $a_{h+1}$ is a term of sequence $S_{ag}(\ell) = (a_1, a_2, ...)$ such that $a_h \leq \min_{j \in L} p_j < a_{h+1}$ (see step (S-4)). On the other hand, the subinstance $S_k^*$ is defined by item set $I_{S_k^*} = \{i \in N_k \backslash L^* : p_i \leq \min_{j \in L^*} p_j\}$. Since we are assuming that $L$ has the same configuration as $L^*$, there are no items from $L^*$ with profit in intervals $[a_i, a_{i+1})$, for $i < h$. Therefore, we have $\min_{j \in L^*} p_j \geq a_h$ and $\{i \in N_k \backslash L : p_i < a_h\} = \{i \in N_k \backslash L^* : p_i < a_h\} = \{i \in N_k : p_i < a_h\}$. Furthermore, since there is an item from $L$ with profit in interval $[a_h, a_{h+1})$, and since $L^*$ has the same configuration as $L$, there exists an item from $L^*$ with profit $p_j < a_{h+1}$ and, therefore, $\min_{j \in L^*} p_j < a_{h+1}$. It follows that $I_{S_k^*} \subseteq \{i \in N_k \backslash L^* : p_i < a_{h+1}\}$.

By the previous arguments, the items of $S_k^*$, except for those belonging to $A_h = \{i \in N_k \cap L : a_h \leq p_i < a_{h+1}\}$, are also items of $S$, i.e.,

$$I_{S_k^*} \subseteq I_S \cup A_h.$$

If there exists an optimal solution for $S_k^*$ such that no one of the items from $A_h$ is selected, then $OPT_S \geq OPT_{S_k^*}$, since the knapsack capacity of $S_k^*$ is not greater than the one of $S$, i.e. $c - w(L) \geq c - w(L^*)$ (recall that $L$ is the subset having the same configuration as $L^*$ with the least weights).

Otherwise, let $G_1$ be the subset of items from $A_h$ in an optimal solution for $S_k^*$, and let $g := |G_1|$. Let $G_2$ be any subset of set $\{i \in L^* \backslash L : a_h \leq p_i < a_{h+1}\}$ of exactly $g$ items. It is easy to see that $G_2$ exists. Furthermore, since $G_2 \subseteq L^*$ and $G_1 \subseteq I_{S_k^*}$, we have

$$\min_{j \in G_2} p_j \geq \max_{j \in G_1} p_j. \tag{3.9}$$

Observe that $w(L^*) - w(L) \geq w(G_2) - w(G_1)$. Therefore, the knapsack capacity $c - w(L)$ of $S$ cannot be smaller than $c - w(L^*) + w(G_2) - w(G_1)$. The solution $G_{12}$ obtained from the optimal solution for $S_k^*$ by replacing the items from $G_1$ with those from $G_2$, requires a knapsack of capacity bounded by $c - w(L^*) + w(G_2) - w(G_1)$. Therefore, $G_{12}$ is a feasible solution for $S$ since the capacity of $S$ is greater than the capacity of $S_k^*$ by at least $w(G_2) - w(G_1)$. Finally, from inequality (3.9), the solution value of $G_{12}$ is not smaller than $OPT_{S_k^*}$ and the claim follows.

Let $P^H(S)$ denote the solution value returned by $H^{\frac{1}{2}}$ when applied to $S$. Then we have the following

**Lemma 3.** $p(L) + P^H(S) \geq (1 - 4\varepsilon)OPT$.

*Proof.* Observe that by Lemma 2 and inequality (3.7), we have

$$OPT_S \geq OPT_{S^*} - 2\varepsilon OPT. \tag{3.10}$$

We distinguish between two cases.

1. If $p(L^*) \geq (1 - \varepsilon)OPT$ then by inequalities (3.6), (3.8) and (3.10), we have

$$\begin{aligned} p(L) + P^H(S) &\geq p(L^*) - 2\varepsilon OPT + \frac{1}{2}OPT_S \\ &\geq \frac{1}{2}(2p(L^*) + OPT_{S^*}) - 3\varepsilon \cdot OPT \\ &\geq \frac{1}{2}(p(L^*) + OPT) - 3\varepsilon \cdot OPT \\ &\geq (1 - \varepsilon/2)OPT - 3\varepsilon \cdot OPT \\ &\geq (1 - 7/2\varepsilon) \cdot OPT. \end{aligned}$$

2. If $p(L^*) < (1 - \varepsilon)OPT$ then the smallest item profit in $L^*$, and hence every item profit in $S^*$, is smaller than $\frac{(1-\varepsilon)}{\ell}OPT$. The biggest profit of $S$ is at most $\frac{(1-\varepsilon)}{\ell}OPT + \frac{\varepsilon P^H}{\ell}$. Indeed, since $a_h \leq \frac{(1-\varepsilon)}{\ell}OPT \leq 2(1-\varepsilon)\frac{P^H}{\ell} \leq (\lfloor \frac{2}{\varepsilon} \rfloor - 1)\frac{\varepsilon P^H}{\ell}$, it turns out that $h \leq \lfloor \frac{2}{\varepsilon} \rfloor - 1$, and by definition of $S_{ag}(\ell)$, we have that $a_{h+1} = a_h + \frac{\varepsilon P^H}{\ell}$. Therefore, for each item $j$ belonging to $S$, profit $p_j$ is bounded by

$$p_j \leq \frac{OPT}{\ell}.$$

Since $OPT_S - P^H(S) \leq \max_{j \in S} p_j$ (see inequality (2.5)), we have

$$\begin{aligned} p(L) + P^H(S) + \frac{OPT}{\ell} &\geq p(L) + OPT_S \\ &\geq p(L^*) + OPT_{S^*} - 4\varepsilon \cdot OPT = (1 - 4\varepsilon)OPT. \end{aligned}$$

By the previous lemma, steps (S-1)-(S-5) return a solution that cannot be worse than $(1 - 4\varepsilon)OPT$. Thus, we have proved the following

**Theorem 1.** *There is a PTAS for the k-item knapsack problem requiring linear space and* $O(n + k \cdot (1/\varepsilon)^{O(1/\varepsilon)})$ *time.*

To compare our algorithm with the one provided in [2] notice that the running time complexity of the latter is $O(n^{\lceil 1/\varepsilon \rceil - 1})$, whereas our scheme is linear. As in [2], our algorithm can be easily modified to deal with the *Exact k-item Knapsack Problem*, that is a kKP in which the number of items in a feasible solution must be exactly equal to $k$. The time and space complexity and analysis of the resulting algorithm are essentially the same.

**Acknowledgments.** I would like to thank Klaus Jansen for introducing me to the k-item Knapsack Problem. Thanks are due to referees for many helpful comments.

## References

1. M. Blum, R. W. Floyd, V. Pratt, R.L. Rivest, and R.E. Tarjan, *Time bounds for selection*, Journal of Computer and System Sciences **7** (1973), 448–461.
2. A. Caprara, H. Kellerer, U. Pferschy, and D. Pisinger, *Approximation algorithms for knapsack problems with cardinality constraints*, European Journal of Operations Research **123** (2000), 333–345.
3. T. H. Cormen, C. E. Leiserson, and R. L. Rivest, *Introduction to algorithms*, 6th ed., MIT Press and McGraw-Hill Book Company, 1992.
4. D.S. Hochbaum (ed.), *Approximation algorithms for NP-hard problems*, ITP, 1995.
5. O. H. Ibarra and C. E. Kim, *Fast approximation algorithms for the knapsack and sum of subset problems*, J. Assoc. Comput. Mach. **22** (1975), 463–468.
6. H. Kellerer and U. Pferschy, *A new fully polynomial approximation scheme for the knapsack problem*, APPROX'98 **LNCS 1444** (1998), 123–134.
7. E. L. Lawler, *Fast approximation algorithms for knapsack problems*, Proc. 18th Ann. Symp. on Foundations of Computer Science (1977), 206–218.
8. S. Martello and P. Toth, *Knapsack problems*, Wiley, 1990.
9. N. Megiddo and A. Tamir, *Linear time algorithms for some separable quadratic programming problems*, Operations Research Letters **13** (1993), 203–211.

# The Complexity of Maximum Matroid-Greedoid Intersection*

Taneli Mielikäinen and Esko Ukkonen

Department of Computer Science, P.O. Box 26
FIN-00014 University of Helsinki, Finland

**Abstract.** The maximum intersection problem for a matroid and a greedoid, given by polynomial-time oracles, is shown $NP$-hard by expressing the satisfiability of boolean formulas in 3-conjunctive normal form as such an intersection. Also the corresponding approximation problem is shown $NP$-hard for certain approximation performance bounds. This is in contrast with the maximum matroid-matroid intersection which is solvable in polynomial time by an old result of Edmonds.

## 1 Introduction

A set system $(S, F)$ where $S$ is a finite set (the *domain* of the system) and $F$ is a collection of subsets of $S$ is a *matroid* if

(M1) $\emptyset \in F$;
(M2) If $Y \subseteq X \in F$ then $Y \in F$;
(M3) If $X, Y \in F$ and $|X| > |Y|$ then there is an $x \in X \setminus Y$ such that $Y \cup \{x\} \in F$.

A *greedoid* is a set system $(S, F)$ that satisfies (M1) and (M3).

In applications a matroid or a greedoid is given by an oracle, i.e., by a deterministic algorithm that answers the question whether $X$ belongs to $F$ for any $X \subseteq S$.

Many combinatorial problems can be formulated using matroids or greedoids (see e.g. [5,6]). The seminal example is the maximum matching problem in bipartite graphs. Each instance of the problem can be represented as the intersection of two matroids. The maximum matching corresponds to the largest set in the intersection.

To be able to consider in the matroid-greedoid framework general combinatorial problems which have infinitely many instances we introduce families of matroids and greedoids that have uniform polynomial-time representation. More formally, let $\mathcal{F} = \{(S_h, F_h)_{h \in H}\}$ be a possibly infinite set of matroids or greedoids. Then $\mathcal{F}$ is said to be given by a *uniform polynomial-time oracle* if there is an algorithm $O$, that when given $h$ and some $X \subseteq S_h$ answers whether or not $X \in F_h$. The algorithm $O$ runs in polynomial time in $|h|$ and $|X|$.

* A work supported by the Academy of Finland.

R. Freivalds (Ed.): FCT 2001, LNCS 2138, pp. 535–539, 2001.

Let $\mathcal{F} = \{(S_h, F_h)_{h \in H}\}$ and $\mathcal{G} = \{(S_h, G_h)_{h \in H}\}$ be two such families given by uniform polynomial-time oracles. Note that the index set $H$ is the same for both and for given $h$, both have the same domain $S_h$.

The *maximum intersection problem* for $\mathcal{F}$ and $\mathcal{G}$ is to find, given an index $h \in H$, a set $X \in F_h \cap G_h$ such that $|X|$ is maximum.

Edmonds [3] gave the first polynomial-time solution for the intersection problem in the case that both $\mathcal{F}$ and $\mathcal{G}$ are families of matroids. In this paper we consider the obvious next step, namely the intersection of families of matroids and greedoids.

In Section 2 we show, by reduction from the 3SAT, that the maximum intersection problem for a matroid family and a greedoid family, given by uniform polynomial-time oracles, is $NP$-hard. In Section 3 we modify the above construction to show that the maximum matroid-greedoid intersection is not approximable within a factor $|S_h|^{1-\epsilon}$ for any fixed $\epsilon > 0$ and its weighted version, the maximum weight matroid-greedoid intersection, is not approximable within $2^{|S_h|^k}$ for any fixed $k > 0$, unless $P = NP$.

## 2 $NP$-Hardness

Recall that the $NP$-complete problem 3-*satisfiability* (3SAT) is, given a boolean formula $h$ in 3-conjunctive normal form (3CNF), to decide whether or not there is a truth assignment $Z$ for the variables of $h$ such that $h(Z) = true$.

We construct the instance $(S_h, F_h), (S_h, G_h)$ of matroid-greedoid intersection that corresponds to $h$ as follows. Let $h$ contain $n$ different boolean variables. Then $S_h$ contains symbols $t_1, f_1, \ldots, t_n, f_n$. The symbols $t_1, f_1, \ldots, t_n, f_n$ will be used to encode truth assignments: $t_i$ encodes that the $i$th variable is *true* and $f_i$ that it is *false*.

The subset collection $F_h$ consists of all subsets of $S_h$ that contain at most one of symbols $t_i, f_i$ for $i = 1, \ldots, n$. It is immediate, that $(S_h, F_h)$ satisfies the matroid properties (M1), (M2) and (M3).

The subset collection $G_h$ consists of two groups. The first group A consists of all subsets $X$ of $S_h$ such that $|X| \le n$ and $X \cap \{t_n, f_n\} = \emptyset$. The second group B consists of the sets that represent a truth assignment that satisfies $h$. Such a set is of size $n$ and contains one element from each $t_i, f_i$.

To verify that $(S_h, G_h)$ is a greedoid, first note that (M1) is obviously true. To verify (M3), let $X, Y \in G_h$ such that $|X| > |Y|$.

1. If $|X| < n$ then $X$ and $Y$ must belong to group A. Hence for any element $x \in X \setminus Y$, set $Y \cup \{x\}$ belongs to group A and hence to $G_h$.
2. If $|X| = n$ and $|X \setminus Y| = 1$ then $Y \cup (X \setminus Y) = X$, i.e., property (M3) holds.
3. In the remaining case $|X| = n$ and $|X \setminus Y| > 1$. As $X \setminus Y$ contains at least two elements and no set of $G_h$ contains both $t_n$ and $f_n$, at least one element $x \in X \setminus Y$ must be different from $t_n, f_n$. Then $Y \cup \{x\}$ belongs to group A.

The matroid-greedoid intersection $F_h \cap G_h$ contains a set $X$ such that $|X| = n$ if and only if the group B in the definition of $G_h$ is non-empty, that is, if and only if $h$ is satisfiable. As such a set $X$ is also the largest in $F_h \cap G_h$, we have shown:

**Lemma 1.** *Boolean formula $h$ is satisfiable if and only if the maximum element in $F_h \cap G_h$ for matroid $(S_h, F_h)$ and greedoid $(S_h, G_h)$ is of size $n$ where $n$ is the number of variables of $h$.*

The above construction yields a matroid family $\mathcal{F} = \{(S_h, F_h)_{h \in 3\mathrm{CNF}}\}$ and a greedoid family $\mathcal{G} = \{(S_h, G_h)_{h \in 3\mathrm{CNF}}\}$. Both have a uniform polynomial-time oracle for checking membership in $F_h$ and $G_h$: The only nontrivial task of the oracle is to verify when a truth assignment satisfies a given formula $h$, but this is doable in polynomial time in $|h|$ using well-known techniques. As $|h| = O(n^3)$ for a 3CNF formula $h$ and $|S_h| = 2n$, the running time of the oracle is in fact polynomial in $|S_h|$, as required.

It follows from Lemma 1 that our construction is a polynomial-time reduction of 3SAT to the maximum matroid-greedoid intersection problem. Therefore we have the following.

**Theorem 1.** *The maximum intersection problem for a matroid family and a greedoid family that are given by uniform polynomial-time oracles is $NP$-hard.*

Also the *maximum weight* matroid-greedoid intersection is $NP$-hard since maximum matroid-greedoid intersection is its special case. In this problem one should find, given integer weights $w(x)$ for $x \in S_h$, a set $X \in F_h \cap G_h$ such that $\sum_{x \in X} w(x)$ is maximum.

## 3 Inapproximability

As the maximum matroid-greedoid intersection problem is a maximization problem whose exact solution turned out to be $NP$-hard, it is of interest to see whether or not an *approximation algorithm* with a performance guarantee is possible. An approximation algorithm would find an element in the intersection of the matroid and the greedoid which is not necessarily the largest one.

Following the standard approach (see e.g. [1,2]), we say that maximization problem is *polynomial-time approximable within* $r$ where $r$ is a function from $\mathbb{N}$ to $\mathbb{N}$ if there is a polynomial-time algorithm that finds for each instance $x$ of the problem a feasible solution with value $c(x)$ such that

$$\frac{c_{Max}(x)}{c(x)} \leq r(|x|)$$

where $c_{Max}(x)$ is the largest possible value (the optimal value) of a feasible solution of $x$. The performance ratio of such an approximation algorithm is bounded by the performance guarantee $r$.

**Theorem 2.** *The maximum intersection problem for a matroid family and a greedoid family with domains $\{S_h : h \in H\}$, given by uniform polynomial-time oracles, is not polynomial-time approximable within $|S_h|^{1-\epsilon}$ for any fixed $\epsilon > 0$, unless $P = NP$.*

*Proof.* Assume that for some $\epsilon > 0$, the maximum matroid-greedoid intersection is polynomial-time approximable within $|S_h|^{1-\epsilon}$. We show that then we can solve 3SAT in polynomial time.

As in the proof of Lemma 1, let $h$ again be a boolean formula with $n$ variables in 3-conjunctive normal form. Now set $S_h$ contains in addition to the truth assignment symbols $t_1, f_1, \ldots, t_n, f_n$ also some indicator elements $p_i, 1 \leq i \leq I(\epsilon)$. Here the number of indicators, $I(\epsilon)$, depends on $\epsilon$ as will be shown below. The indicators are needed for padding the elements of the matroid and the greedoid such that the maximum intersection becomes for a satisfiable $h$ sufficiently larger than for a non-satisfiable $h$.

We again construct a matroid $(S_h, F_h)$ and $(S_h, G_h)$ as follows.

The subset collection $F_h$ contains all subsets of $S_h$ that do not contain both $t_i$ and $f_i$ for any $1 \leq i \leq n$. It is again clear, that $(S_h, F_h)$ satisfies properties (M1) and (M2). As regards (M3), let $X, Y \in F_h$ such that $|X| > |Y|$. If there is some indicator $x$ in $X \setminus Y$, then $Y \cup \{x\} \in F_h$. Otherwise $X$ must contain more truth assignment symbols that $Y$. Then there must be index $i$ such that either $t_i$ or $f_i$, call it $x$, belongs to $X$ but neither of $t_i$ and $f_i$ belongs to $Y$. Then $Y \cup \{x\} \in F_h$. Thus $(S_h, F_h)$ is a matroid.

The subset collection $G_h$ consists of three groups. Group A and B are exactly same as in the construction of Lemma 1. Hence the sets in groups A and B do not contain any indicator elements. Group C consists of the sets of size $n$ in groups A and B, padded with indicators in all possible ways. That is, if $X \in A$ or $X \in B$ such that $|X| = n$ and $Q$ is a non-empty subset of $\{p_1, \ldots, p_{I(\epsilon)}\}$, then $X \cup Q$ belongs to group C.

To verify that $(S_h, G_h)$ is a greedoid, property (M1) clearly holds. To verify (M3), let $X, Y \in G_h, |X| > |Y|$ and consider the following cases.

1. If $|Y| < n$ then there is a truth assignment symbol $x \in X \setminus Y$ such that $Y \cup \{x\}$ belongs to group A or to group B as shown in the proof of Lemma 1.
2. If $|Y| \geq n$ then there is there is an indicator $x \in X \setminus Y$ and thus $Y \cup \{x\}$ belongs to group C.

By our construction, the boolean formula $h$ is satisfiable if and only if the largest element in $F_h \cap G_h$ is of size $|S_h| - n = I(\epsilon) + n$. Otherwise the size of the largest element is at most $n - 1$.

Let now $I(\epsilon) = (2n)^{1/\epsilon} - 2n$. Thus $|S_h| = (2n)^{1/\epsilon}$. To test the satisfiability of $h$ we use the approximation algorithm to find a approximately largest element of $F_h \cap G_h$. Let $c$ be the size of this element. If $h$ is not satisfiable then certainly $c < n$. On the other hand, if $h$ is satisfiable, then the largest element of $F_h \cap G_h$ is of size $|S_h| - n$. Therefore

$$\frac{|S_h| - n}{c} \leq |S_h|^{1-\epsilon}.$$

But then

$$c \geq \frac{|S_h| - n}{|S_h|^{1-\epsilon}} \geq \frac{|S_h|}{2|S_h|^{1-\epsilon}} = \frac{|S_h|^{\epsilon}}{2} = n$$

where the second inequality follows from that $|S_h| \geq 2n$. Hence $c \geq n$ if $h$ is satisfiable and $c < n$ if it is not. We have a polynomial-time satisfiability test because $I(\epsilon)$ is a polynomial in $n$ and hence in $|h|$ when $\epsilon$ is fixed, and therefore the matroid family $\{(S_h, F_h)_{h \in 3\text{CNF}}\}$ and the greedoid family $\{(S_h, G_h)_{h \in 3\text{CNF}}\}$ can be represented by uniform oracles whose run times are polynomial in $|S_h|$, hence in $|h|$. □

**Theorem 3.** *The maximum weight intersection problem for a matroid family and a greedoid family with domains $\{S_h : h \in H\}$, given by uniform polynomial-time oracles, is not polynomial-time approximable within $2^{|S_h|^k}$ for any fixed $k > 0$, unless $P = NP$.*

*Proof.* The construction is similar to the proof of Theorem 2.

Domain $S_h$ consists of the truth assignment symbols and only one indicator element. The indicator has weight $n2^{|S_h|^k} - n$ while all the truth assignment symbols have weight equal to 1. Then the formula $h$ is satisfiable if and only if the heaviest element in $F_h \cap G_h$ has weight $n2^{|S_h|^k}$. Otherwise the heaviest element weights less than $n$.

Let $c$ be the weight obtained by an approximation algorithm that is assumed to approximate the optimal solution within $2^{|S_h|^k}$. If $h$ is not satisfiable then $c < n$. Otherwise

$$\frac{n2^{|S_h|^k}}{c} \leq 2^{|S_h|^k}$$

which means that $c \geq n$.

We again have a polynomial-time satisfiability test because $|S_h| = 2n + 1$ and therefore the weights have polynomial-size (binary) representations in $|h|$ and hence the weighted set $S_h$ can be constructed in polynomial time in $|h|$. Moreover, the uniform oracles for the families of $(S_h, F_h)$ and $(S_h, G_h)$ can be made to run in polynomial time in $|h|$ as before. □

## References


1. G. Ausiello, P. Crescenzi, G. Gambosi, V. Kann, A. Marchetti-Spaccamela, and M. Protasi. *Complexity and Approximation: Combinatorial Optimization Problems and Their Approximability Properties.* Springer-Verlag, 1999.
2. P. Crescenzi, V. Kann, R. Silvestri, and L. Trevisan. Structure in approximation classes. *SIAM Journal on Computing* 28 (1999) 1759–1782.
3. J. Edmonds. Minimum partition of a matroid into independent subsets. *Journal of Research of the National Bureau of Standards* 69B (1965) 67–72.
4. M. R. Garey, and D. S. Johnson. *Computers and Intractability: A Guide to the Theory of NP-Completeness.* W. H. Freeman and Company, 1979.
5. B. Korte, and J. Vygen. *Combinatorial Optimization: Theory and Algorithms.* Springer-Verlag, 2000.
6. C. H. Papadimitriou, and K. Steiglitz. *Combinatorial Optimization: Algorithms and Complexity.* Dover Publications, 1998.

# Author Index

# Lecture Notes in Computer Science

For information about Vols. 1–2039
please contact your bookseller or Springer-Verlag

Vol. 2040: W. Kou, Y. Yesha, C.J. Tan (Eds.), Electronic Commerce Technologies. Proceedings, 2001. X, 187 pages. 2001.

Vol. 2041: I. Attali, T. Jensen (Eds.), Java on Smart Cards: Programming and Security. Proceedings, 2000. X, 163 pages. 2001.

Vol. 2042: K.-K. Lau (Ed.), Logic Based Program Synthesis and Transformation. Proceedings, 2000. VIII, 183 pages. 2001.

Vol. 2043: D. Craeynest, A. Strohmeier (Eds.), Reliable Software Technologies – Ada-Europe 2001. Proceedings, 2001. XV, 405 pages. 2001.

Vol. 2044: S. Abramsky (Ed.), Typed Lambda Calculi and Applications. Proceedings, 2001. XI, 431 pages. 2001.

Vol. 2045: B. Pfitzmann (Ed.), Advances in Cryptology – EUROCRYPT 2001. Proceedings, 2001. XII, 545 pages. 2001.

Vol. 2046: H. Daduna, Queueing Networks with Discrete Time Scale. X, 138 pages. 2001.

Vol. 2047: R. Dumke, C. Rautenstrauch, A. Schmietendorf, A. Scholz (Eds.), Performance Engineering. XIV, 349 pages. 2001.

Vol. 2048: J. Pauli, Learning Based Robot Vision. IX, 288 pages. 2001.

Vol. 2049: G. Paliouras, V. Karkaletsis, C.D. Spyropoulos (Eds.), Machine Learning and Its Applications. VIII, 325 pages. 2001. (Subseries LNAI).

Vol. 2050: J.-Y. Le Boudec, P. Thiran, Network Calculus. XIX, 274 pages. 2001.

Vol. 2051: A. Middeldorp (Ed.), Rewriting Techniques and Applications. Proceedings, 2001. XII, 363 pages. 2001.

Vol. 2052: V.I. Gorodetski, V.A. Skormin, L.J. Popyack (Eds.), Information Assurance in Computer Networks. Proceedings, 2001. XIII, 313 pages. 2001.

Vol. 2053: O. Danvy, A. Filinski (Eds.), Programs as Data Objects. Proceedings, 2001. VIII, 279 pages. 2001.

Vol. 2054: A. Condon, G. Rozenberg (Eds.), DNA Computing. Proceedings, 2000. X, 271 pages. 2001.

Vol. 2055: M. Margenstern, Y. Rogozhin (Eds.), Machines, Computations, and Universality. Proceedings, 2001. VIII, 321 pages. 2001.

Vol. 2056: E. Stroulia, S. Matwin (Eds.), Advances in Artificial Intelligence. Proceedings, 2001. XII, 366 pages. 2001. (Subseries LNAI).

Vol. 2057: M. Dwyer (Ed.), Model Checking Software. Proceedings, 2001. X, 313 pages. 2001.

Vol. 2058: S. Brewster, R. Murray-Smith (Eds.), Haptic Human-Computer Interaction. Proceedings, 2000. XIII, 219 pages. 2001.

Vol. 2059: C. Arcelli, L.P. Cordella, G. Sanniti di Baja (Eds.), Visual Form 2001. Proceedings, 2001. XIV, 799 pages. 2001.

Vol. 2060: T. Böhme, H. Unger (Eds.), Innovative Internet Computing Systems. Proceedings, 2001. VIII, 183 pages. 2001.

Vol. 2062: A. Nareyek, Constraint-Based Agents. XIV, 178 pages. 2001. (Subseries LNAI).

Vol. 2064: J. Blanck, V. Brattka, P. Hertling (Eds.), Computability and Complexity in Analysis. Proceedings, 2000. VIII, 395 pages. 2001.

Vol. 2065: H. Balster, B. de Brock, S. Conrad (Eds.), Database Schema Evolution and Meta-Modeling. Proceedings, 2000. X, 245 pages. 2001.

Vol. 2066: O. Gascuel, M.-F. Sagot (Eds.), Computational Biology. Proceedings, 2000. X, 165 pages. 2001.

Vol. 2068: K.R. Dittrich, A. Geppert, M.C. Norrie (Eds.), Advanced Information Systems Engineering. Proceedings, 2001. XII, 484 pages. 2001.

Vol. 2070: L. Monostori, J. Váncza, M. Ali (Eds.), Engineering of Intelligent Systems. Proceedings, 2001. XVIII, 951 pages. 2001. (Subseries LNAI).

Vol. 2071: R. Harper (Ed.), Types in Compilation. Proceedings, 2000. IX, 207 pages. 2001.

Vol. 2072: J. Lindskov Knudsen (Ed.), ECOOP 2001 – Object-Oriented Programming. Proceedings, 2001. XIII, 429 pages. 2001.

Vol. 2073: V.N. Alexandrov, J.J. Dongarra, B.A. Juliano, R.S. Renner, C.J.K. Tan (Eds.), Computational Science – ICCS 2001. Part I. Proceedings, 2001. XXVIII, 1306 pages. 2001.

Vol. 2074: V.N. Alexandrov, J.J. Dongarra, B.A. Juliano, R.S. Renner, C.J.K. Tan (Eds.), Computational Science – ICCS 2001. Part II. Proceedings, 2001. XXVIII, 1076 pages. 2001.

Vol. 2075: J.-M. Colom, M. Koutny (Eds.), Application and Theory of Petri Nets 2001. Proceedings, 2001. XII 403 pages. 2001.

Vol. 2076: F. Orejas, P.G. Spirakis, J. van Leeuwen (Eds.) Automata, Languages and Programming. Proceedings 2001. XIV, 1083 pages. 2001.

Vol. 2077: V. Ambriola (Ed.), Software Process Technology. Proceedings, 2001. VIII, 247 pages. 2001.

Vol. 2078: R. Reed, J. Reed (Eds.), SDL 2001: Meetin UML. Proceedings, 2001. XI, 439 pages. 2001.

Vol. 2079: E. Burke, W. Erben (Eds.), Practice and Theor of Automated Timetabling III. Proceedings, 2001. XII 359 pages. 2001.

Vol. 2080: D.W. Aha, I. Watson (Eds.), Case-Based Reasoning Research and Development. Proceedings, 2001 XII, 758 pages. 2001. (Subseries LNAI).

Vol. 2081: K. Aardal, B. Gerards (Eds.), Integer Programming and Combinatorial Optimization. Proceedings, 2001. XI, 423 pages. 2001.

Vol. 2082: M.F. Insana, R.M. Leahy (Eds.), Information Processing in Medical Imaging. Proceedings, 2001. XVI, 537 pages. 2001.

Vol. 2083: R. Goré, A. Leitsch, T. Nipkow (Eds.), Automated Reasoning. Proceedings, 2001. XV, 708 pages. 2001. (Subseries LNAI).

Vol. 2084: J. Mira, A. Prieto (Eds.), Connectionist Models of Neurons, Learning Processes, and Artificial Intelligence. Proceedings, 2001. Part I. XXVII, 836 pages. 2001.

Vol. 2085: J. Mira, A. Prieto (Eds.), Bio-Inspired Applications of Connectionism. Proceedings, 2001. Part II. XXVII, 848 pages. 2001.

Vol. 2086: M. Luck, V. Mařík, O. Stěpánková, R. Trappl (Eds.), Multi-Agent Systems and Applications. Proceedings, 2001. X, 437 pages. 2001. (Subseries LNAI).

Vol. 2087: G. Kern-Isberner, Conditionals in Nonmonotonic Reasoning and Belief Revision. X, 190 pages. 2001. (Subseries LNAI).

Vol. 2089: A. Amir, G.M. Landau (Eds.), Combinatorial Pattern Matching. Proceedings, 2001. VIII, 273 pages. 2001.

Vol. 2091: J. Bigun, F. Smeraldi (Eds.), Audio- and Video-Based Biometric Person Authentication. Proceedings, 2001. XIII, 374 pages. 2001.

Vol. 2092: L. Wolf, D. Hutchison, R. Steinmetz (Eds.), Quality of Service – IWQoS 2001. Proceedings, 2001. XII, 435 pages. 2001.

Vol. 2093: P. Lorenz (Ed.), Networking – ICN 2001. Proceedings, 2001. Part I. XXV, 843 pages. 2001.

Vol. 2094: P. Lorenz (Ed.), Networking – ICN 2001. Proceedings, 2001. Part II. XXV, 899 pages. 2001.

Vol. 2095: B. Schiele, G. Sagerer (Eds.), Computer Vision Systems. Proceedings, 2001. X, 313 pages. 2001.

Vol. 2096: J. Kittler, F. Roli (Eds.), Multiple Classifier Systems. Proceedings, 2001. XII, 456 pages. 2001.

Vol. 2097: B. Read (Ed.), Advances in Databases. Proceedings, 2001. X, 219 pages. 2001.

Vol. 2098: J. Akiyama, M. Kano, M. Urabe (Eds.), Discrete and Computational Geometry. Proceedings, 2000. XI, 381 pages. 2001.

Vol. 2099: P. de Groote, G. Morrill, C. Retoré (Eds.), Logical Aspects of Computational Linguistics. Proceedings, 2001. VIII, 311 pages. 2001. (Subseries LNAI).

Vol. 2100: R. Küsters, Non-Standard Inferences in Description Logocs. X, 250 pages. 2001. (Subseries LNAI).

Vol. 2101: S. Quaglini, P. Barahona, S. Andreassen (Eds.), Artificial Intelligence in Medicine. Proceedings, 2001. XIV, 469 pages. 2001. (Subseries LNAI).

Vol. 2102: G. Berry, H. Comon, A. Finkel (Eds.), Computer-Aided Verification. Proceedings, 2001. XIII, 520 pages. 2001.

Vol. 2103: M. Hannebauer, J. Wendler, E. Pagello (Eds.), Balancing Reactivity and Social Deliberation in Multi-Agent Systems. VIII, 237 pages. 2001. (Subseries LNAI).

Vol. 2104: R. Eigenmann, M.J. Voss (Eds.), OpenMI Shared Memory Parallel Programming. Proceedings 2001. X, 185 pages. 2001.

Vol. 2105: W. Kim, T.-W. Ling, Y-J. Lee, S.-S. Parl (Eds.), The Human Society and the Internet. Proceedings 2001. XVI, 470 pages. 2001.

Vol. 2106: M. Kerckhove (Ed.), Scale-Space and Mor phology in Computer Vision. Proceedings, 2001. XI, 43! pages. 2001.

Vol. 2108: J. Wang (Ed.), Computing and Combinatorics Proceedings, 2001. XIII, 602 pages. 2001.

Vol. 2109: M. Bauer, P.J. Gymtrasiewicz, J. Vassilev (Eds.), User Modelind 2001. Proceedings, 2001. XIII, 31 pages. 2001. (Subseries LNAI).

Vol. 2110: B. Hertzberger, A. Hoekstra, R. William (Eds.), High-Performance Computing and Networking Proceedings, 2001. XVII, 733 pages. 2001.

Vol. 2111: D. Helmbold, B. Williamson (Eds.), Computational Learning Theory. Proceedings, 2001. IX, 631 pages. 2001. (Subseries LNAI).

Vol. 2116: V. Akman, P. Bouquet, R. Thomason, R.A Young (Eds.), Modeling and Using Context. Proceedings 2001. XII, 472 pages. 2001. (Subseries LNAI).

Vol. 2117: M. Beynon, C.L. Nehaniv, K. Dautenhahr (Eds.), Cognitive Technology: Instruments of Mind. Proceedings, 2001. XV, 522 pages. 2001. (Subseries LNAI)

Vol. 2118: X.S. Wang, G. Yu, H. Lu (Eds.), Advances in Web-Age Information Management. Proceedings, 2001 XV, 418 pages. 2001.

Vol. 2119: V. Varadharajan, Y. Mu (Eds.), Information Security and Privacy. Proceedings, 2001. XI, 522 pages. 2001.

Vol. 2120: H.S. Delugach, G. Stumme (Eds.), Conceptual Structures: Broadening the Base. Proceedings, 2001. X, 377 pages. 2001. (Subseries LNAI).

Vol. 2121: C.S. Jensen, M. Schneider, B. Seeger, V.J. Tsotras (Eds.), Advances in Spatial and Temporal Databases. Proceedings, 2001. XI, 543 pages. 2001.

Vol. 2123: P. Perner (Ed.), Machine Learning and Data Mining in Pattern Recognition. Proceedings, 2001. XI, 363 pages. 2001. (Subseries LNAI).

Vol. 2125: F. Dehne, J.-R. Sack, R. Tamassia (Eds.), Algorithms and Data Structures. Proceedings, 2001. XII, 484 pages. 2001.

Vol. 2126: P. Cousot (Ed.), Static Analysis. Proceedings, 2001. XI, 439 pages. 2001.

Vol. 2129: M. Goemans, K. Jansen, J.D.P. Rolim, L. Trevisan (Eds.), Approximation, Randomization, and Combinatorial Optimization. Proceedings, 2001. IX, 297 pages. 2001.

Vol. 2132: S.-T. Yuan, M. Yokoo (Eds.), Intelligent Agents. Specification. Modeling, and Application. Proceedings, 2001. X, 237 pages. 2001. (Subseries LNAI).

Vol. 2138: R. Freivalds (Ed.), Fundamentals of Computation Theory. Proceedings, 2001. XIII, 542 pages. 2001.

Vol. 2139: J. Kilian (Ed.), Advances in Cryptology – CRYPTO 2001. Proceedings, 2001. XI, 599 pages. 2001.

Vol. 2164: S. Pierre, R. Glitho (Eds.), Mobile Agents for Telecommunication Applications. Proceedings, 2001. XI, 292 pages. 2001.